COMPUTER and INTERNET ESSENTIALS
Preparing for IC³

Audrey Roggenkamp

Nita Rutkosky

Ian Rutkosky

Faithe Wempen

The data files used in this text can be downloaded from
www.emcschool.net/IC3 (hardcover)
www.paradigmcollege.net/IC3 (softcover)

Senior Editor:	Carley Fruzzetti
Production Editor:	Sarah Kearin
Senior Graphic Designer (cover and interior):	Leslie Anderson
Senior Design and Production Specialists:	Jaana Bykonich, Ryan Hamner, Petrina Nyhan
Design and Production Specialist:	Julie Johnston
Copy Editor:	Laura M. Nelson
Proofreader:	Susan Capecchi
Indexer:	Terry Casey

Care has been taken to verify the accuracy of information presented in this book. However, the authors, editors, and publisher cannot accept responsibility for Web, e-mail, newsgroup, or chat room subject matter or content, or for consequences from application of the information in this book, and make no warranty, expressed or implied, with respect to its content.

Trademarks: Some of the product names and company names included in this book have been used for identification purposes only and may be trademarks or registered trade names of their respective manufacturers and sellers. The authors, editors, and publisher disclaim any affiliation, association, or connection with, or sponsorship or endorsement by, such owners.

We have made every effort to trace the ownership of all copyrighted material and to secure permission from copyright holders. In the event of any question arising as to the use of any material, we will be pleased to make the necessary corrections in future printings. Thanks are due to the aforementioned authors, publishers, and agents for permission to use the materials indicated.

CERTIPORT and IC[3] Approved Courseware are trademarks or registered marks of Certiport, Inc.

EMC Publishing is independent from Certiport, Inc. and not affiliated with Certiport in any manner. This textbook may be used in assisting students to prepare for the Internet & Computing Core Certification (IC[3]) Exam. Neither Certiport, Inc., its agents, nor EMC Publishing warrant that use of this material will ensure success in connection with any exam.

ProCert Labs Exam Ready logo is a registered trademark or trademark of ProCert Communications LLC in the United States and/or other countries.

ISBN 978-0-82196-317-3 (Hardcover)
ISBN 978-0-82196-321-0 (Softcover)

© 2013 by EMC Publishing, LLC
875 Montreal Way
St. Paul, MN 55102
Email: educate@emcp.com
Website: www.emcp.com

Printed in the United States of America

21 20 19 18 17 16 15 14 13 12   1 2 3 4 5 6 7 8 9 10

Computer and Internet Essentials: Preparing for IC³ is designed to prepare you with the computer concepts, knowledge of Microsoft applications, and Internet information you need to succeed in a personal or business environment where computer skills are required.

In this textbook, you will learn how to use computer hardware and software; how to use Word 2010 to deliver relevant information to personal and professional audiences; how to solve numeric and mathematical problems using Excel 2010; how to write and produce presentations using PowerPoint 2010; and how to be a responsible and effective network and Internet user. After successfully completing a course using this textbook, you will be able to:

- Select, set up, update, and troubleshoot personal computers and peripherals

- Select the right application software for any business or personal task

- Analyze, synthesize, and evaluate school, work, or home information-processing needs and use application software to meet those needs efficiently and effectively

- Create, design, and produce professional documents using word processing software

- Process, manipulate, and represent numeric data using spreadsheet software

- Use presentation software to design and create informational and motivational slide shows that contain design themes, graphic images, transitions, animations, tables, and audio and video files

- Integrate source data from different applications

- Set up and use a basic computer network

- Perform efficient and productive Internet searches for personal, business, or academic data

- Select the best electronic communication method for various communication situations

- Minimize the privacy and security risks involved with network and Internet use

Elements of the *Computer and Internet Essentials: Preparing for IC³* textbook function individually and collectively to create an inviting, comprehensive learning environment that produces successful computer and Internet users.

Internet & Computer Core Certification (IC³)

Along with providing you with necessary computer and Internet skills, this textbook prepares you for the three exams that comprise Internet and Computing Core Certification (IC³). This certification is an internationally recognized standard for digital literacy and includes exams that focus on computing fundamentals, key applications, and using the Internet. The first exam, Computing Fundamentals, includes questions about selecting and using computers; selecting, protecting, and setting up a computer; using an operating system; and installing, removing, and updating applications. The second exam, Key Applications, includes questions on three Microsoft Office applications—Word, Excel, and PowerPoint. The third exam, Living Online, includes questions regarding understanding and using networks, web browsers, and electronic communications; securing data and safeguarding privacy; identifying legal and ethical computer practices; and being a polite and professional online citizen.

Though the IC³ objectives do not refer to specific operating systems or applications, the questions in the IC³ exams contain specific references to Windows 7 and Office 2010. Those applications are covered in this textbook. Although this text can be used with alternative applications, to achieve the highest success you should complete the exercises and assessments on a personal computer using the Windows 7 operating system; Word 2010, Excel 2010, and PowerPoint 2010; Internet Explorer 9; and Windows Live Mail.

By passing the IC³ exams, you demonstrate your proficiency in using a computer, computer applications, and the Internet. Proof of this proficiency will not only help you to utilize computers for personal and educational purposes—it will also give you a competitive edge in the business world. To learn more about taking the IC³ exams, visit the Certiport website at www.certiport.com.

Topic Organization

Computer and Internet Essentials: Preparing for IC³ is divided into three units. Each unit contains a variety of topics and lessons that teach the skills required to successfully pass the IC³ exam.

Unit 1: Computing Fundamentals

Topic 1 covers computer technology basics and explains how to evaluate and set up a computer system. Subjects include CPUs, memory, storage, and input/output devices and how they work together to create a working computer system. This topic also covers basic measurements of computer performance and explains how to protect, maintain, and troubleshoot computers.

Topic 2 covers available operating systems and their usage. Windows 7 is used to explore how to start up and shut down a PC, how to run programs, how to manage files, how to customize the interface, how to troubleshoot common problems, and how to obtain help and support.

Topic 3 discusses software applications and explains the basic principles behind popular types of software such as word processing, spreadsheet, database, utility, and graphics programs. Topic 3 also identifies which type of application is most appropriate for different business and academic tasks.

Unit 2: Key Applications

Topic 4 discusses the three main applications covered in the text: Microsoft Office Word, Excel, and PowerPoint. The topic describes how to open the applications; identify common screen features; and create, save, open, and close files. This topic also explains how to create files using Office templates and how to utilize the Help resources available within each application.

Topic 5 contains information on the different uses for Microsoft Word. The topic provides practice in navigating within a document, changing document views, and using a variety of document formatting features such as selecting, deleting, moving, and copying text. Topic 5 also introduces proofing tools such as spelling checker, grammar checker, and the Thesaurus.

Word's character and paragraph formatting capabilities are introduced in Topic 6. You will learn how to apply font effects; change the typeface, type size and typestyle of a document; change paragraph alignment, indent text, and change line spacing; and insert bullets and numbers in a document.

Topic 7 presents information on how to organize data such as text, numbers, and formulas into a table in Word. You will learn how to create, format and edit a table; draw a table; and insert a Quick Table. This topic also explains how to sort text in a table and convert text to a table.

Topic 8 introduces formatting features that can be applied to a Word document to enhance the visual display of text. Skills such as inserting page numbers, headers, and footers; changing margins and page orientation; and applying a theme are taught. This topic provides the opportunity to practice adding visual appeal to documents using pictures, clip art images, shapes, WordArt, and SmartArt, and by setting text into columns. You will also learn how to track changes in a document, insert comments, and protect a document.

Topic 9 discusses a variety of uses for Microsoft Excel, including creating and organizing financial statements and budgets as well as using the application as a planning tool to evaluate different scenarios. This topic explains how to enter and edit data in a worksheet, insert formulas, sort and filter data, and apply predesigned formatting to cells in a workbook.

In Topic 10, you will learn how to enhance the visual appearance of data in an Excel worksheet by applying formatting such as bold, italics, and underlining; changing column width and row height; inserting and deleting rows and columns; applying borders, shading, and patterns to cells; and applying a theme to a worksheet. Topic 10 also explains how to use Excel to create charts that provide a visual representation of data.

The Office suite's presentation application, Microsoft PowerPoint, is taught in Topic 11. You will learn how to create, organize, and edit informative and visually appealing slides. You will also practice saving, running, previewing, printing, and closing a presentation along with applying transitions and sounds to enhance a presentation.

Topic 12 discusses adding visual elements to a PowerPoint presentation. You will learn how to insert pictures, clip art images, SmartArt graphics, and shapes in slides. This topic also includes exercises in which you will practice exporting and linking a file from one Office application to another.

Unit 3: Living Online

Topic 13 examines networks and the Internet. After studying this topic, you will be able to identify how networks are used in society, the types of networks available, and their risks and benefits. Read this topic to learn the basic components that comprise the Internet, including the Web and various types of electronic communication. Topic 13 also covers how content is created and maintained on the Internet.

Using a web browser is the subject of Topic 14. You will use Internet Explorer to learn how to browse and search the Web, how to recall sites using the history and favorites features, and how to save content for offline use. This topic invites you to evaluate search results and consider potential legal problems, including plagiarism, that are associated with online information usage.

Topic 15 discusses email. Using Microsoft's free mail client, Windows Live Mail, you will send and receive messages, create and store contacts, send attachments, and manage and organize email. This topic will also help you to discover ways to minimize junk mail and troubleshoot common email problems.

In Topic 16, you will learn about safe and responsible computer usage. This topic covers many types of Internet security and privacy threats and how to safeguard against them. This topic also covers legal and ethical issues in computing, online etiquette, health and safety hazards involved in PC usage, and how to make computers more accessible to people with disabilities.

Design and Features

Computer Concepts This text emphasizes the fundamentals of computer and Internet usage, allowing you to gain the basic computer literacy skills required to succeed in school and business.

Performance Objectives and IC³ Correlations Each topic begins with a list of performance objectives that the topic text will address. Correlations are also included within each topic to identify when a lesson or feature aligns with the IC³ exam objectives.

Lessons Each topic is divided into lessons to provide information on specific concepts or features. Lessons include applicable margin material (quick steps, key terms, shortcuts), figures, charts, and exercises.

Exercises   Each lesson includes an exercise to practice the introduced concepts. Step-by-step instructions guide you to the desired outcome for each exercise. Screen captures illustrate what the computer screen should look like at key points in the exercise.

Drilling Down and Delving Deeper Features   The Drilling Down features provide additional information on key features and sub-features within a lesson. The Delving Deeper features appear at the end of the last lesson in each topic and provide information on IC³ concepts or objectives related to the topic content.

Topic Summaries   The summary at the end of each topic captures the purpose and execution of key features.

Features Summaries   The Features Summary tables provide a visual outline of the major features introduced within the topic, along with the alternative methods you can use to access them.

Key Points Reviews   Key Points Reviews at the end of each topic provide an opportunity to assess your understanding through screen features identification, completion exercises, multiple choice questions, and matching terms with definitions.

Skills Reviews   End-of-topic Skills Reviews require you to complete hands-on computer exercises to reinforce key features and techniques. These activities include some guidance, but less than you receive in the in-topic exercises.

Skills Assessments   End-of-topic Skills Assessments are framed within a workplace project perspective and evaluate your ability to apply topic skills and concepts in solving realistic problems. These assessments require you to demonstrate program skills as well as decision-making skills and include a Help assessment, Internet-based assessment, and an IC³ Challenge assessment that tests your problem-solving skills and mastery of program features.

Critical Thinking and Team Projects   The Critical Thinking projects at the end of each topic require you to analyze a personal or workplace scenario and then plan and execute a multipart project. The Team Projects require you to collaborate to make decisions on specific scenarios and are followed by questions to help encourage classroom discussion.

Index and Glossary   A standard index and glossary are included at the end of the textbook to make it easier for you to find the information you need, when you need it.

Internet Resource Center   You can download all the files needed to complete the exercises, reviews, and assessments from the Internet Resource Center: www.emcschool.net/IC3 (hardcover) and www.paradigmcollege.net/IC3 (softcover). The Internet Resource Center also contains additional materials and helpful resources for both students and instructors.

IC³ objective correlations provided

Figures illustrate the text

Margin materials contain hints, key terms, or shortcuts

Explanatory text included within exercise steps

Lesson number and title

Exercise topic presented clearly

Screen captures illustrate key steps within the exercise

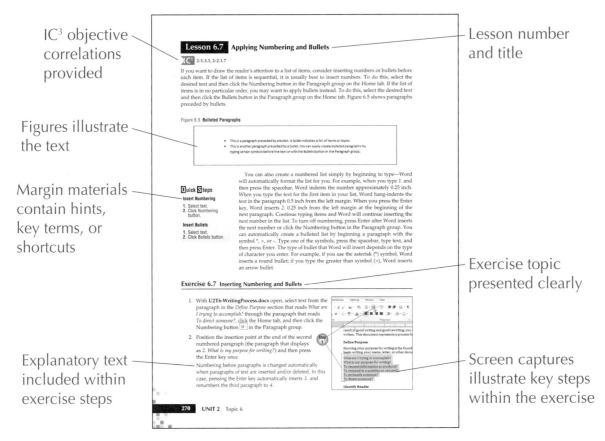

Within each topic, you will find:

Performance Objectives – Topic objectives are clearly identified at the start of each topic.

Margin Material – Quick Steps, Keyboard Shortcuts, and Key Term definitions are available throughout each topic.

Figures, Tables, and Screen Captures – Visual aids help to illustrate important concepts throughout each topic.

Exercises – Each lesson contains exercises to review and reinforce lesson concepts. Nearly all exercises include step-by-step instructions that guide you to the desired outcome. Screen captures illustrate what the computer screen should look like at key points in the activity.

Drilling Down and Delving Deeper Features – IC³ exam topics are identified and explained throughout each topic within the Drilling Down and Delving Deeper features.

The end of each topic contains:

Topic Summaries, Key Terms, and Features Summaries – Concepts, key terms, and features covered in the topic are reviewed and summarized.

Key Points and Skills Reviews – Identification, matching, multiple choice and completion questions, as well as skills review exercises, are presented to review your understanding of the topic.

Skills Assessments – Skills assessment exercises will test your comprehension of the concepts presented in the topic.

Critical Thinking and Team Projects – Projects based on critical thinking scenarios and group work will let you review and deepen your understanding of the concepts covered in the topic.

Screen Resolution and File Extensions

Exercises, reviews, and assessments within this textbook assume that the display of file extensions is turned on and that the monitor display resolution is set at 1280 x 800 pixels. Before beginning the exercises and assessments in this textbook, you may need to change your monitor's resolution settings and turn on the display of file extensions. Your monitor's resolution settings are important because the ribbon in the Microsoft Office suite adjusts according to these settings. A computer monitor set at a higher resolution will have the ability to show more buttons in the ribbon than will a monitor set to a lower resolution. The screen captures in this textbook were created with a screen resolution of 1280 x 800 pixels. Complete the following steps to adjust your monitor display resolution and display file extensions:

Changing Monitor Display Resolution

1. At the Windows 7 desktop, click the Start button and then click *Control Panel*.
2. At the Control Panel dialog box, click the *Adjust screen resolution* option in the Appearance and Personalization category.
3. At the Control Panel Screen Resolution window, click the Resolution option button.
4. Drag the button on the slider bar until 1280 x 800 displays to the right of the slider button.
5. Click in the Control Panel Screen Resolution window to remove the slider bar.
6. Click the Apply button.
7. Click the Keep Changes button.
8. Click OK.
9. Close the Control Panel window.

Displaying File Extensions

1. At the Windows 7 desktop, click the Start button and then click *Computer*.
2. At the Computer window, click the Organize button on the toolbar and then click *Folder and search options* at the drop-down list.
3. At the Folder Options dialog box, click the View tab.
4. Click the *Hide extensions for known file types* check box to remove the check mark.
5. Click the Apply button.
6. Click OK.
7. Close the Computer window.

Instructor Resources

The Instructor Resources for *Computer and Internet Essentials: Preparing for IC*³ correlate directly to the textbook and provide all additional materials required to offer students an excellent computer and Internet literacy course. The Instructor Resources disc features:

Course Planning Resources   The Course Planning material contains course expectations and class schedules as well as information on exercises, skills reviews and assessments, data files, and answer files.

Course Delivery Materials   The Course Delivery material contains lesson plans, vocabulary, visual aids, and much more.

Data Files   The data files include all the files students need to complete the exercises, reviews, and assessments in the text.

- **Student Data Files** (contains the starter files)
- **Student Model Answers** (contains the model answers)

ExamView® Assessment Suite   The **ExamView®** Assessment Suite includes editable question banks keyed to the text as well as the popular **ExamView®** software to make creating tests, quizzes, and additional assessment materials quick and easy.

Answer Files   The Instructor Resources disc includes answers to the exercises, reviews, and assessments as well as rubrics and grading checklists for specific exercises within the student text.

About the Authors

Nita Rutkosky, M.S., began teaching business education courses at Pierce College in Puyallup, Washington, in 1978. Since then she has taught a variety of software applications to students in business technology certificate and degree programs. In addition to *Computer and Internet Essentials: Preparing for IC³*, she has co-authored several series of textbooks for Paradigm Publishing, Inc., including *Benchmark Series Microsoft Office 2010, 2007, 2003*, and prior editions; *Marquee Series Office 2010, 2007, 2003*, and prior editions; *Signature Series Microsoft Word 2010, 2007, 2003*, and prior editions; and *Using Computers in the Medical Office 2010, 2007*, and *2003*. She has also authored textbooks on keyboarding, WordPerfect®, desktop publishing, and voice recognition for Paradigm Publishing, Inc.

Audrey Roggenkamp, M.A., teaches keyboarding, skill building, office procedures, and Microsoft Office programs in the Business Technology department at Pierce College in Puyallup, Washington. In addition to *Computer and Internet Essentials: Preparing for IC³*, she has co-authored *Benchmark Series Microsoft Office 2010* and *2007*; *Marquee Series Office 2010* and *2007*; *Signature Series Microsoft Word 2010* and *2007*; and *Using Computers in the Medical Office 2010, 2007*, and *2003* for Paradigm Publishing, Inc.

Ian Rutkosky, M.B.A., teaches Business Technology courses at Pierce College in Puyallup, Washington. In addition to co-authoring *Computer and Internet Essentials: Preparing for IC³*, he is a co-author of *Using Computers in the Medical Office 2010* and a consultant for the Paradigm SNAP 2010 training and assessment software.

Faithe Wempen, M.A., is a Microsoft Office Master Instructor and an A+ certified PC technician, and the author of over 120 books on computer hardware and software including *Office 2010 for Dummies eLearning Kit*, *Word 2010 In Depth, Strata Study Guide, HTML 5 Step by Step, Windows 7*, and *PC Maintenance: Preparing for A+ Certification*. Her online courses in PC literacy and Microsoft Office have educated over a quarter of a million students for corporate clients including CNET, Sony, and HP. She currently teaches in the Computer Information Technology department of Indiana University/Purdue University at Indianapolis.

Table of Contents

Unit 1 – Computing Fundamentals

Topic 1: Understanding and Selecting a Computer

Lesson 1.1 – Understanding How a Computer Works 4
Lesson 1.2 – Differentiating Between Types of Computers 9
Lesson 1.3 – Understanding CPUs and Memory 13
Lesson 1.4 – Understanding Data Storage 17
Lesson 1.5 – Understanding Input Devices 23
Lesson 1.6 – Understanding Output Devices 29
Lesson 1.7 – Selecting a Computer 33
Lesson 1.8 – Setting Up a Computer 35
Lesson 1.9 – Protecting a Computer 38
Lesson 1.10 – Performing Routine Maintenance Tasks 42
Lesson 1.11 – Troubleshooting Common Hardware Problems 44
Delving Deeper 48
Review and Assessment 49

Topic 2: Using an Operating System

Lesson 2.1 – Understanding Operating Systems 58
Lesson 2.2 – Understanding Microsoft Windows 7 61
Lesson 2.3 – Starting Up and Shutting Down a Windows PC 66
Lesson 2.4 – Running Applications 68
Lesson 2.5 – Working with the Desktop and Icons 73
Lesson 2.6 – Managing Files and Folders 75
Lesson 2.7 – Using the Help System 87
Lesson 2.8 – Customizing Windows Settings 89
Lesson 2.9 – Working with Printers 94
Lesson 2.10 – Troubleshooting Operating System Problems 97
Delving Deeper 100
Review and Assessment 102

Topic 3: Choosing and Using Application Software

Lesson 3.1 – Installing and Removing Applications 113
Lesson 3.2 – Updating and Upgrading Applications 120
Lesson 3.3 – Understanding Types of Application Software 123
Lesson 3.4 – Understanding Word Processing Applications 124
Lesson 3.5 – Understanding Spreadsheet Applications 130
Lesson 3.6 – Understanding Presentation Software 136
Lesson 3.7 – Understanding Database Software 140

Lesson 3.8 – Understanding Graphics and Multimedia Software...143
Lesson 3.9 – Using Utility Programs...148
Lesson 3.10 – Understanding Other Application Types...151
Lesson 3.11 – Sharing Data between Applications...154
Delving Deeper 158
Review and Assessment 159

Unit 2 – Key Applications

Topic 4: Working with Microsoft Office 2010 Applications

Lesson 4.1 – Understanding Microsoft 2010 Applications 174
Lesson 4.2 – Using, Customizing, and Moving Ribbon Commands 178
Lesson 4.3 – Creating and Naming Files 180
Lesson 4.4 – Opening and Saving Files with Save As 182
Lesson 4.5 – Printing a File 185
Lesson 4.6 – Managing Print Jobs..187
Lesson 4.7 – Closing Files and Exiting Applications..191
Lesson 4.8 – Creating Files Using Templates 192
Lesson 4.9 – Saving Files in a Different Format..195
Lesson 4.10 – Customizing Office Application Defaults 198
Lesson 4.11 – Using Help Resources...200
Delving Deeper 204
Review and Assessment 205

Topic 5: Editing a Document in Word

Lesson 5.1 – Scrolling and Navigating in a Document 217
Lesson 5.2 – Inserting and Deleting Text 220
Lesson 5.3 – Selecting Text and Using Undo and Redo 222
Lesson 5.4 – Cutting, Copying, and Pasting Text and Using the Clipboard Task pane 224
Lesson 5.5 – Finding and Replacing Text...228
Lesson 5.6 – Changing Document Views..232
Lesson 5.7 – Previewing and Printing a Document...234
Lesson 5.8 – Using Thesaurus and Displaying Document Statistics...237
Lesson 5.9 – Checking the Spelling and Grammar in a Document 239
Delving Deeper 242
Review and Assessment 245

Topic 6: Formatting Characters and Paragraphs in Word

Lesson 6.1 – Applying Formatting with the Font Group..257
Lesson 6.2 – Applying Formatting and Displaying Nonprinting Characters 261
Lesson 6.3 – Applying Formatting with Format Painter 264
Lesson 6.4 – Aligning Text in Paragraphs...266
Lesson 6.5 – Changing Line Spacing..268
Lesson 6.6 – Changing Paragraph Spacing..270
Lesson 6.7 – Applying Numbering and Bullets 272
Lesson 6.8 – Indenting Text..274
Lesson 6.9 – Applying Borders and Shading...276
Lesson 6.10 – Applying Styles 279
Lesson 6.11 – Setting Tabs 283
Lesson 6.12 – Setting Tabs with Leaders...285
Delving Deeper 287
Review and Assessment 288

Topic 7: Creating and Enhancing Tables in Word

Lesson 7.1 – Creating a Table, Entering Text in Cells, and Navigating within a Table 301
Lesson 7.2 – Selecting Cells in a Table 303
Lesson 7.3 – Applying Table Styles and Shading and Borders 306
Lesson 7.4 – Managing Rows, Columns, and Cells 308
Lesson 7.5 – Changing Column Width and Row Height 310
Lesson 7.6 – Changing Cell Alignment 311
Lesson 7.7 – Changing Cell Margin Measurements 312
Lesson 7.8 – Changing Table Alignment and Resizing and Moving a Table 314
Lesson 7.9 – Inserting a Quick Table 316
Lesson 7.10 – Converting Text to a Table 317
Lesson 7.11 – Drawing a Table 318
Lesson 7.12 – Sorting in a Table 320
Delving Deeper 322
Review and Assessment 323

Topic 8: Formatting a Document in Word with Special Features

Lesson 8.1 – Changing Page Margins, Orientation, and Size 336
Lesson 8.2 – Applying a Theme 339
Lesson 8.3 – Inserting Symbols, Special Characters, and Other Items in a Document 341
Lesson 8.4 – Inserting Page Numbering, Headers and Footers, and a Cover Page 344
Lesson 8.5 – Inserting Page and Section Breaks 347
Lesson 8.6 – Creating and Formatting Text in Columns 350
Lesson 8.7 – Inserting, Sizing, and Moving an Image 351
Lesson 8.8 – Drawing and Formatting Objects 355
Lesson 8.9 – Creating and Modifying WordArt Text 357
Lesson 8.10 – Creating SmartArt Graphics and Organizational Charts 359
Lesson 8.11 – Tracking Changes 363
Lesson 8.12 – Inserting Comments 366
Lesson 8.13 – Protecting a Document 369
Lesson 8.14 – Creating Footnotes and Endnotes 372
Delving Deeper 373
Review and Assessment 376

Topic 9: Analyzing Data Using Excel

Lesson 9.1 – Creating and Saving an Excel Workbook 394
Lesson 9.2 – Editing Data in a Cell and Printing and Closing a Workbook 398
Lesson 9.3 – Entering Data Using the Fill Handle 400
Lesson 9.4 – Inserting Formulas and Selecting Cells 402
Lesson 9.5 – Sorting and Filtering Data 405
Lesson 9.6 – Applying Formatting with Cell Styles and Table Styles 407
Lesson 9.7 – Writing Formulas with Mathematical Operators 409
Lesson 9.8 – Inserting Formulas with Functions 410
Lesson 9.9 – Writing a Formula with the IF Logical Function 414
Lesson 9.10 – Using Absolute and Mixed Cell References in Formulas 417
Lesson 9.11 – Managing Worksheets 417
Lesson 9.12 – Cutting, Copying, and Pasting Cells 419
Delving Deeper 421
Review and Assessment 423

Topic 10: Formatting an Excel Workbook

Lesson 10.1 – Changing Column Width and Row Height 435
Lesson 10.2 – Inserting and Deleting Cells, Rows, and Columns 437

Lesson 10.3 – Applying Font and Alignment Formatting 440
Lesson 10.4 – Applying a Theme and Previewing a Worksheet 443
Lesson 10.5 – Inserting, Sizing, and Moving Clip Art and an Image... 445
Lesson 10.6 – Formatting Numbers 447
Lesson 10.7 – Changing Worksheet Margins and Centering a Worksheet 451
Lesson 10.8 – Inserting Headers and Footers 455
Lesson 10.9 – Creating a Chart 457
Lesson 10.10 – Changing the Chart Design 460
Lesson 10.11 – Changing the Chart Layout 463
Lesson 10.12 – Formatting the Chart Layout 465
Delving Deeper 467
Review and Assessment 469

Topic 11: Preparing a Presentation

Lesson 11.1 – Preparing a Presentation 482
Lesson 11.2 – Choosing a Theme and Creating Slides 484
Lesson 11.3 – Navigating in a Presentation 489
Lesson 11.4 – Printing a Presentation and Changing the Zoom Display 490
Lesson 11.5 – Running a Presentation 494
Lesson 11.6 – Adding Transitions and Transition Sounds to a Presentation 496
Lesson 11.7 – Checking Spelling in a Presentation 499
Lesson 11.8 – Rearranging and Deleting Slides 500
Lesson 11.9 – Applying Fonts and Font Effects.. 502
Lesson 11.10 – Applying Paragraph Formatting 506
Lesson 11.11 – Inserting Headers and Footers 509
Delving Deeper 511
Review and Assessment 512

Topic 12: Inserting Graphic Elements in a Presentation and Integrating Word, Excel, and PowerPoint

Lesson 12.1 – Inserting, Sizing, and Moving a Picture or a Clip Art Image 530
Lesson 12.2 – Inserting and Formatting a SmartArt Graphic... 534
Lesson 12.3 – Drawing and Customizing Shapes in PowerPoint... 539
Lesson 12.4 – Inserting and Navigating with Hyperlinks 543
Lesson 12.5 – Creating a Table in a Slide.. 545
Lesson 12.6 – Formatting with a Slide Master 548
Lesson 12.7 – Applying Animation Effects to Items in a Slide 551
Lesson 12.8 – Inserting Audio and Video Files 553
Lesson 12.9 – Exporting a PowerPoint Presentation to Word.. 555
Lesson 12.10 – Linking an Excel Chart with a Word Document and a PowerPoint Presentation..... 557
Lesson 12.11 – Editing a Linked Object.. 559
Lesson 12.12 – Embedding a Word Table in a PowerPoint Slide 561
Delving Deeper 563
Review and Assessment 564

Unit 3 – Living Online

Topic 13: Understanding Networks and the Internet

Lesson 13.1 – Understanding Computer Networking 585
Lesson 13.2 – Understanding How Networks Operate 588
Lesson 13.3 – Using a Windows Network 597
Lesson 13.4 – Protecting a Network and Its Data 602

Lesson 13.5 – Understanding the Internet 608
Lesson 13.6 – Understanding the World Wide Web 614
Lesson 13.7 – Understanding Electronic Communication Types.. 620
Delving Deeper 624
Review and Assessment 625

Topic 14 – Using a Web Browser

Lesson 14.1 – Browsing the Web 634
Lesson 14.2 – Reviewing Web Browsing History 639
Lesson 14.3 – Using and Managing Favorites 642
Lesson 14.4 – Saving Web Content for Offline Use 648
Lesson 14.5 – Understanding Search Engines 653
Lesson 14.6 – Conducting Searches... 655
Lesson 14.7 – Evaluating Search Results 659
Lesson 14.8 – Using Online Information Properly.. 661
Lesson 14.9 – Configuring a Web Browser 663
Lesson 14.10 – Troubleshooting Web Browsing Problems... 668
Delving Deeper 673
Review and Assessment 674

Topic 15 – Using Email

Lesson 15.1 – Understanding Email Technology 683
Lesson 15.2 – Configuring Windows Live Mail 686
Lesson 15.3 – Sending Email 689
Lesson 15.4 – Managing Addresses 692
Lesson 15.5 – Receiving and Replying to Messages 697
Lesson 15.6 – Sending Attachments.. 700
Lesson 15.7 – Using Email Options 703
Lesson 15.8 – Managing and Organizing Email... 704
Lesson 15.9 – Managing Junk Mail and Solving Email Problems 707
Delving Deeper 712
Review and Assessment 714

Topic 16 – Using PCs and the Internet Safely and Responsibly

Lesson 16.1 – Understanding Secure Data Access... 722
Lesson 16.2 – Avoiding Malware Infection.. 725
Lesson 16.3 – Safeguarding Your Privacy and Identity Online 731
Lesson 16.4 – Protecting Minors Online... 737
Lesson 16.5 – Making Computing More Accessible 740
Lesson 16.6 – Identifying Legal and Ethical Personal Computer and Internet Use 745
Lesson 16.7 – Being a Polite and Professional Online Citizen 748
Lesson 16.8 – Understanding Health and Safety Issues in Computer Use 753
Lesson 16.9 – Understanding Environmentally Responsible Computing 756
Delving Deeper 761
Review and Assessment 762

IC³ Objectives and Correlation 769

Glossary... 777

Index.. 785

UNIT 1

Computing Fundamentals

Topic 1: Understanding and Selecting a Computer

Topic 2: Using an Operating System

Topic 3: Choosing and Using Application Software

Topic 1

Understanding and Selecting a Computer

Performance Objectives

Upon successful completion of Topic 1, you will be able to:

- Understand how a computer works
- Differentiate between types of computers
- Understand the roles and measurements of CPU and memory
- Identify the features and benefits of different storage media
- Identify the types and purposes of input and output devices
- Identify how hardware devices are connected and installed
- Identify factors that affect computer performance
- Protect a computer from theft and hazards
- Perform routine PC maintenance
- Troubleshoot common hardware problems

STUDENT RESOURCES

Before beginning this topic, copy to your storage medium the **Unit1Topic01** subfolder from the *Computer and Internet Essentials: Preparing for IC³* Internet Resource Center. Make this the active folder.

Although this topic does not contain any data files needed to complete topic work, the Internet Resource Center does contain model answers in PDF format for each of the applicable exercises in this topic. Use these files to check your work. The preface of your textbook provides instructions for accessing these files.

Topic Overview

Computer technology has changed the world, and will continue to change it in the future. To function productively in today's society and to prepare for the jobs of tomorrow, you will need a fundamental understanding of computers, software applications, and the Internet. More and more employers expect that new employees will come to the company knowing how to use a computer, as well as other electronic devices like smartphones and digital cameras. By taking this course, you will not only prepare yourself for future employment, you will also become familiar with technologies and applications that can enrich your daily life, making both your work and leisure time more enjoyable and productive.

In this topic, you will begin your journey by learning about computer hardware. You will find out about the key components of a PC and how they work together. You will also learn how to set up a computer, how to perform basic preventive maintenance, and how to troubleshoot common problems.

)(C³ 1-1.1.1, 1-1.1.5, 1-1.1.8

Every computer you will work with has the same key components: a processor, memory, data storage, and input/output devices. These components work together to help users perform tasks such as writing letters, balancing budgets, and accessing the Internet. It used to be easy to say which devices were computers and which were not, but today hundreds of types of computers exist, ranging from a traditional personal computer to a computer inside a refrigerator that orders groceries for itself over the Internet. In this book, when we talk about computers, we are primarily referring to **personal computers (PCs)** with which humans interact directly for business or personal tasks.

personal computer (PC) A computer designed for use by one individual

All computers have certain things in common:

- **Digital operation:** Computers work with digits—usually binary digits—rather than with analog data such as sound.

- **User input:** All computers have some way of accepting user input. On a PC this might be the keyboard or mouse.

- **Processing:** Each computer has a central processing unit (CPU) that performs mathematical operations on the user input.

- **Output:** Each computer has a way of delivering the calculated data back to the user. On a PC this might be the monitor or the printer.

- **Hardware and software:** Each computer consists of some basic physical parts (the hardware) and some sets of instructions that specify how those physical parts should interact with one another (the software).

The following sections describe each of these in more detail.

Distinguishing between Digital and Analog

analog A type of data that is continuously variable and has no precise numeric equivalent

An **analog** device is one that can read and work with a continuously varying stream of data with no precise values, as represented in Figure 1.1. Sound waves are analog, and devices that work with sound, such as radios and telephones, are analog devices. For many decades, analog devices were the dominant form of technology in our society.

Figure 1.1 Representation of Analog Data Note the smooth transition from one value to the next.

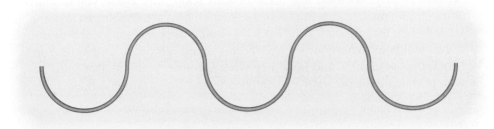

Digital devices base their operation on exact numeric data. A pocket calculator is digital; it takes in numbers, processes numbers, and produces numbers. With digital data, there is no approximation, no room for even the tiniest variation or error. This is important in computing because computers bring numeric certainty to activities and decision-making. There is no "maybe" in computing, only "yes" or "no". The power is on or off; a formula is true or false. Because digital operation precisely defines values, operations and processes are repeatable. If you enter the same input every time, you will get the same output every time. In Figure 1.2, for example, only two possible values exist: up or down.

digital A type of data that is precisely defined using numeric digits

Figure 1.2 Representation of Digital Data   Digital data relies on precise transitions between values.

Understanding Numbering Systems

We humans use a **decimal** numbering system for most math calculations. Decimal numbering is base 10 numbering. Only 10 unique digits are used in our system, 0 through 9. However, other numbering systems also exist, as you may already know from math classes. Computers use the **binary** numbering system to work with data at the most basic level. In a binary numbering system, only two digits are required: 0 and 1. Binary numbering is ideal for a computer because it fits a computer's digital nature. Recall that everything that goes on inside a computer is based on yes or no decisions. In binary numbering, these either-or conditions can easily be described as 1 or 0. A single binary digit is called a **bit** (which is an abbreviation of the two words *BInary* and *digiT*).

decimal A numbering system based on 10 digits; can also refer to a period that separates digits, as in *1.2*

binary A numbering system based on two digits: 0 and 1

bit A single binary digit

byte A string of eight binary digits (bits)

Computers combine strings of bits into eight-bit chunks. A string of eight bits is called a **byte**. In binary numbering, 256 unique combinations are available with a string of eight bits: 00000000 through 11111111. Each of these combinations is assigned a meaning. Furthermore, multiple bytes are often combined to create even more unique combinations. This is how computers turn binary data into programming.

Computers also use hexadecimal numbering for some tasks, such as defining memory addresses. **Hexadecimal** is a numbering system based on sixteen digits, 0 through 9 plus A through F. Hexadecimal is base 16. (*Hex* means 6 and *decimal* means 10.) With hexadecimal numbering, not only do you have digits 0 through 9, but also six letters of the alphabet that function as digits. If you were to count from 1 to 17 in hexadecimal, the order would be 0, 1, 2, 3, 4, 5, 6, 7, 8, 9, A, B, C, D, E, F, 10. Understanding hexadecimal numbering is important because you might see a number like 2EF8 in a device's properties or in an error message. 2EF8 in hexadecimal is the same as 12024 in decimal or 10111011111000 in binary. You can easily convert between numbering systems using the Calculator utility in Windows, as you will see in the following exercise. Sometimes a hexadecimal number has an *h* on the end to help identify it as a hexadecimal, but this letter is not part of the number.

hexadecimal A numbering system based on sixteen digits, 0 through 9 plus A through F

Exercise 1.1 Converting between Numbering Systems Using the Windows Calculator

1. Click Start, click *All Programs*, click *Accessories*, and then click *Calculator*.

   This opens the Calculator application.

2. Click the View menu and then click *Programmer*.

   This switches the calculator to Programmer mode.

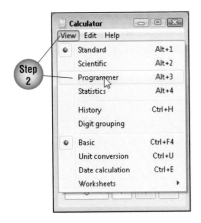

3. Make sure that the *Dec* option is selected, indicating you are in Decimal mode.

4. Enter the number 77. You can either type 77 on your keyboard or click the number buttons on the Calculator application.

5. Click the *Bin* option to switch to Binary mode.

   This changes the number to *1001101*.

6. Click the *Hex* option to switch to Hexadecimal mode.

   This changes the number to *4D*.

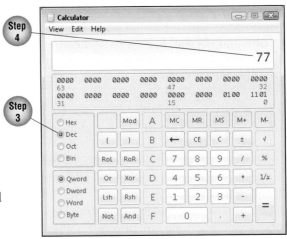

7. Close the Calculator application by clicking the Close button in the upper right corner of the Calculator window.

Understanding Input, Processing, and Output

input Data coming into a computer

output Data going out of a computer

At their core, all computers are calculators. They accept numeric **input** (the data coming in), perform the requested math operation on it, and produce **output** (the data going out). A pocket calculator is a simple computer. You press the buttons for the numbers you want, press a button (such as a plus or minus) for a mathematical operator, and then press the equals button to get the answer.

Personal computers operate under the same basic principle. They accept input from the keyboard or mouse, process it, and send it out to the monitor or another output device. Of course, the data being moved through a PC is much more sophisticated than the data moving through a pocket calculator. Suppose, for example, that you press the letter *k* on the keyboard. Each character on the keyboard is represented by a numeric code. The keyboard sends that code to the PC. The PC's operating system reviews the incoming code and determines what to do with it. Let us say that *k* is part of a sentence you are typing in an application. The PC's operating system tells the monitor to light up certain spots on the screen to form a shape that your eye will recognize as a *k*. You then see a *k* on the screen. This entire process takes only a few milliseconds, so it appears instantaneous.

Some parts of the computer serve in only a single capacity. A keyboard, for example, is an input-only device, and a monitor is an output-only device. Other parts are dual-purpose. For example, a network interface card serves as a two-way communicator between your PC and a network, and a hard disk can both read existing data (that is, deliver output to the user) and write new data (that is, accept new input).

Identifying Components on the Outside of a Computer

Whether you are working at your own computer or someone else's (as in a computer lab or a library), you should be able to identify the key parts of the computer and understand the function of each part. On a typical computer, you will see some or all of the following parts (see also Figure 1.3):

- **Buttons:** At the minimum, every computer has a Power button that turns the computer on and off. The computer may also have additional buttons that mute the sound, adjust the screen, or eject a disc.

- **Indicator lights:** Most computers have at least one light that illuminates while the computer is on, to let you know it is running. Some computers have other indicator lights as well, such as a light that flashes when the hard disk is reading or writing.

- **Externally accessible drives**: Most computers have at least one drive that you can use to insert and remove CDs or DVDs. Older computers also had floppy disk drives, but those have become obsolete.

- **Fan vents**: Computers generate heat as they operate, so most computers contain at least one fan and at least one vent that lets the hot air out of the computer.

- **Ports**: Computers have **ports**, which are sockets into which you can plug various types of cables and expansion devices. The types of ports a computer has depend on the type and age of the computer. Ports are typically located on the back of a desktop PC and along the side and back edges of a notebook PC.

port A socket into which you can connect a cable or device

Figure 1.3 Exterior of a Personal Computer

DVD drive

Power button

indicator light

fan vent

Image courtesy of Dell, Inc.

Identifying Components on the Inside of a Computer

Inside a computer, you will find a complex system of circuit boards and cables. Both desktop and notebook PCs have the same basic components, but components are larger and have more space between them in a desktop PC (see Figure 1.4).

Figure 1.4 Interior of a Personal Computer

power supply

power connector

fan vents

ports

DVD drive (back)

CPU (under plastic hood)

expansion boards

motherboard The large, central circuit board inside a computer

central processing unit (CPU) The part of a computer that performs the mathematical calculations that are the basis of all computing

expansion board A circuit board that is inserted in a slot in the motherboard to add additional capabilities to a computer

hard disk drive A metal box containing metal platters on which data is written in patterns of magnetic polarity

power supply The component that converts the incoming electrical power to a form the device can use

alternating current (AC) Electrical current whose flow reverses (alternates)

direct current (DC) Electrical current that does not change direction; electronics usually require DC power

The inside of a PC contains the following components: motherboard, CPU, hard disk drive(s), expansion boards, and power supply. There may be other components as well, depending on the computer. The **motherboard** is the large, central circuit board that covers most of the bottom of the case. Everything else plugs into the motherboard. On the motherboard is a large chip called the **central processing unit**, or **CPU**, which is the part of the computer that performs mathematical calculations. The chip looks ceramic from the outside, but the ceramic part is just a protective container. The actual CPU is a thin silicon wafer. The motherboard may also have one or more small circuit boards plugged into it at a 90 degree angle. These are **expansion boards** (or expansion cards), and they add additional capabilities to the system. For example, you might have a sound board that enables you to connect speakers and a microphone to the PC, a network board that enables you to connect to a network, or a modem board that enables you to use your telephone to connect to a remote computer system.

Also within the computer is the hard disk drive. The **hard disk drive** is a rectangular metal box containing metal platters that hold data written in patterns of magnetic polarity. The hard disk drive is connected by cable to the motherboard. From the inside of the PC, you can also see the backsides of the externally accessible drives.

The big metal box with all the colored wires coming out of it is the power supply. The **power supply** takes in **alternating current (AC)** from the wall outlet and converts it to the low-voltage **direct current (DC)** that the PC's components need to operate. See Lesson 1.8 for more information.

Drilling Down

Converting between Numbering Systems Manually

Converting between numbering systems (binary to decimal and decimal to binary) is possible without the use of a calculator. For an activity that explains how to do this, visit the Internet Resource Center for this text and access the Numbering Systems Conversion Activity.

Lesson 1.2   Differentiating between Types of Computers

 1-1.1.1, 1-1.2.9

Computers are no longer just big, heavy boxes on a desk. Many types of computers are available, each one designed to meet a specific user need. In this lesson, you will learn about some of the many personal computers available.

Desktop Computers

A **desktop computer** is one that is meant to reside full-time in one location, so it is not designed to be portable. Originally all personal computers were desktop models; portable computers came later. You *can* move a desktop computer, but not without some effort. A desktop computer consists of a rectangular case that contains the parts of the computer and sits on the desk (or sometimes under it), a monitor that connects to the case through a cable, and separate keyboard and mouse devices that also connect through cables or a wireless interface.

> **desktop computer** A nonportable computer with a separate monitor, keyboard, and mouse

Not all desktop PC cases have the same size and shape. Today most cases are towers, which sit upright on their shortest side and have drive bays that are oriented perpendicular to their longest side (see Figure 1.5). The original, mostly obsolete type of desktop case rested flat on its longest side and had drive bays that were oriented parallel to its longest side (see Figure 1.6).

Figure 1.5 Desktop PC in a Tower Case

Figure 1.6 **Desktop PC in a Desktop Case**

Image courtesy of Lenovo

Desktop PCs are designed to be sturdy and to protect the inner components. Desktop PCs are also designed to dissipate heat effectively through the use of multiple cooling fans, to offer many different ports for plugging in devices, to offer room for expansion, and to be easily maintained and upgraded. Since portability is not a factor, a desktop PC can offer these features at a low price. Making components smaller and lighter in weight also makes them more expensive, which is why a portable computer costs more than a desktop model with the same specifications.

Notebooks and Netbooks

notebook computer A portable computer with built-in monitor, keyboard, and pointing device

A **notebook computer**, also called a *laptop*, is designed for portability. The name comes from the fact that the computer is approximately the same size and shape as a large paper notebook. A notebook computer offers the same basic features as a desktop PC, but in a much smaller package. On a notebook computer, the monitor, keyboard, and pointing device (such as a touchpad) are all built in (see Figure 1.7). A notebook computer may have ports for attaching external devices, but they are not required. The computer folds up for storage, with the monitor, keyboard, and pointing device stored safely on the inside.

Figure 1.7 **Notebook Computer**

Image courtesy of Dell, Inc.

netbook computer A small notebook computer

A **netbook computer**, also called a *subnotebook*, is a smaller version of a notebook. It typically has a smaller screen and keyboard, and may have less processing power, too. This device is called a netbook because most people who own them use them primarily for accessing the Internet. Because of a netbook's smaller screen and keyboard, it is not ideal for extended use; your eyes may get tired looking at the small screen and your hands and wrists may get cramped using the small keyboard.

Tablets

A **tablet PC** is a small computer, about the size of a thin paper notebook, that has a touch-sensitive screen that you can use with either your finger or a stylus. Two types of tablet PCs are available—slates and convertibles. A slate-style tablet does not have a keyboard (although it might have an on-screen keyboard that displays at certain times). The Apple iPad and the Motorola Xoom, shown in Figure 1.8, are examples of this type of tablet. A convertible tablet, shown in Figure 1.9, is like a regular notebook computer except that the screen is touch-sensitive and can be rotated and folded down to convert the device into a slate-style tablet.

tablet PC A small computer with a touch-sensitive screen; types of tablets include slates and convertibles

Figure 1.8 Slate-Style Tablet PC

Image courtesy of Motorola

Figure 1.9 Convertible Tablet PC

Image courtesy of Janto Dreijer

Tablet PCs are ideal for active people because they are lightweight and easy to transport. The slate-style screen makes it possible to use the computer as you are walking because you can hold it in one arm as you write or touch with the other hand. However, one drawback of a tablet PC is that it may not have the drives and ports you want. For example, slate-style tablets may not have an optical drive (CD or DVD) and may not have a suitable port for connecting one. Slate-style tablet PCs also do not have a real keyboard (although a virtual keyboard displays on the screen when needed). On convertible tablet PCs, the keyboard only works when the PC is in notebook mode, with the screen rotated to make the keyboard accessible.

Smartphones

Many people use their mobile phones for Internet connectivity. Phones that are designed not only to make calls but also to provide Internet and computing capabilities are known as **smartphones**. Smartphones enable you to browse the Web, send and receive email, and run many third-party applications. Smartphones also allow you to access the Internet in places where there is no wireless network, because they use the cell phone network rather than ordinary Internet access points. Figure 1.10 shows a Motorola Photon 4G smartphone.

smartphone A mobile phone that can also be used to access the Internet

A smartphone can be a great addition to a busy person's life, but it cannot take the place of a personal computer. Most smartphones do not run business applications like Word or Excel, and even if they did, it would be difficult to use them on a phone.

Figure 1.10 Smartphone

Image courtesy of Motorola

Gaming Consoles

Gaming consoles, such as the Xbox, PlayStation, and Wii, are surprisingly sophisticated computers. They have fast, powerful processors; lots of memory; Internet connectivity; high-end graphics; and many of the other features you would expect from a regular PC. However, they usually do not have a keyboard or mouse (although some models allow you to attach them) and they usually use a television as a monitor.

Like a smartphone, a gaming console cannot take the place of a PC. Its processing power is focused narrowly on gaming. All it can do is run games and perhaps some simple Internet activities like downloading new games or sending messages to other players.

Determining Which Type of Computer Is Right for You

Depending on your lifestyle and computing needs, one type of computer might be better for you than another. You should consider portability, processing needs, data needs, and screen size.

Portability A computer's size and weight affect how easily you can transport it. If you need a computer at school and at home and you cannot afford two PCs, or you prefer to always use the same computer wherever you are, you will want a small and lightweight model.

Processing Power If you run graphics editing programs or play games that require a powerful computer, you will need to spend more to get the power you need. Remember that the larger the computer, the less you will pay for the same capabilities. If affordability and performance are equally important to you, you should consider purchasing a desktop PC.

Data Input If you need to input a lot of data into your computer, like typing long research papers or entering numbers in a spreadsheet, you will want a model with a large, comfortable, easy-to-use keyboard. Typing a long document on a tiny keyboard (or worse yet, a phone) can waste time and lead to frustration.

Screen Size The more you plan on looking at a screen, the more you may appreciate one that is large enough to see easily. On a desktop PC you can have a huge monitor, whereas a notebook PC's screen is usually limited to between 13 inches and 17 inches in diameter. Netbooks are even smaller (9 inches to 11 inches), and smartphone screens, at only a few inches, are tiny.

Exercise 1.2 Comparing Types of Computers

1. Using the Internet and a web browser, go to www.dell.com.

2. Find a desktop PC, and examine its specifications to research the following information:

   - How much does it weigh?
   - What are its physical dimensions (height, width, and depth)?
   - How much power does it consume, in watts?
   - Does it come with a monitor, or is that separate?
   - How much does it cost?

3. On the Dell website, find a notebook computer and note the following:

   - How much does it weigh?
   - What are its physical dimensions (height, width, and depth)?
   - How long will it run on battery power?
   - What is the screen size?
   - How much does it cost?

4. On the Dell website, find a tablet computer and answer the same questions you answered in Step 3.

5. Make a list of the top three to five activities for which you would most likely use a computer. Which of these computers would best fit your needs, given your current lifestyle?

6. Write a paragraph explaining which computer you would choose and why.

Lesson 1.3 Understanding CPUs and Memory

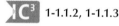 1-1.1.2, 1-1.1.3

Recall that every computer has a central processing unit, or CPU, that performs mathematical calculations. Every computer also has some type of memory, which is used for temporary data storage as data moves into and out of the CPU. In this lesson you will learn the basics of CPU and memory technology.

Understanding CPUs

The CPU is the calculating part of a computer. It takes in data and instructions, performs the instructions on the data, and spits out a result. Inside, a CPU is a complex web of integrated circuits, with millions of electronic components called transistors. **Transistors** are electrical gates that either block power or allow it to pass, depending on their current state. Transistors are the basis of **binary processing**, which is processing based on things being in one of two states: on or off, 1 or 0.

transistor An electrical gate that either blocks power or allows it to pass, depending on the transistor's current state

binary processing Computer data processing based on binary data and instructions

A CPU looks physically like a ceramic block about 2 inches square and a few millimeters thick, but most of that is just packaging. The ceramic material is a heat conductor that helps pull the heat away from the CPU as it operates. The actual CPU is a thin wafer of silicon embedded in the ceramic shell (see Figure 1.11). When you open up a computer to look inside, you might not be able to see the CPU at all because it is often covered by a large cooling fan.

Figure 1.11 **CPU**

Image courtesy of Konstantin Lanzet

As you learned in Lesson 1.1, a CPU's job is to do math. It accepts numbers as input, performs calculations on them, and delivers other numbers as output. The CPU is mostly oblivious to the significance of those numbers; it just runs the instructions it has been given. A common misconception is that the CPU is the brain of the computer, but a processor is not nearly as sophisticated as a human brain. It just does as it is told, like a hand-held calculator, but at a high speed. The operating system is the real brain of the operation, since it feeds the numbers to the processor and uses the results it receives. You will learn about operating systems in Topic 2.

The two most popular brands of CPUs are Intel and Advanced Micro Devices (AMD). Almost all personal computers that run the Windows, Mac OS, or Linux operating systems use one of these two processors. Some people have strong opinions about one brand or the other, but the two companies produce roughly the same types of products.

hertz (Hz) A measurement of CPU speed; the amount of time it takes for a CPU's internal clock to complete a full cycle

megahertz (MHz) One million hertz

gigahertz (GHz) One billion hertz

millions of instructions per second (MIPS) A measurement of the amount of data a CPU can process

multicore A CPU that contains multiple processors that can all operate simultaneously

A CPU's speed is described by the number of cycles it processes per second, measured in **hertz (Hz)**. Each time the CPU's internal clock completes a full cycle, a single Hz has passed. Modern CPUs operate at millions (**megahertz, MHz**) or billions (**gigahertz, GHz**) of cycles per second. The original IBM PC, released in 1981, operated at 4.77 MHz. Processor speeds have increased exponentially since then because of new technological advances, with some of today's fastest CPUs running at more than 3 GHz.

A CPU's raw speed does not always tell the whole story of its performance. Another measurement of processing, called **millions of instructions per second (MIPS)**, describes the number of instructions that a CPU can execute per second. This measurement is different from the speed because many instructions that a CPU carries out take multiple internal cycles to complete. For example, the Intel Core i7 Extreme Edition runs at 3.3 GHz and processes 147,600 MIPS. The Apple iPad 2's CPU runs at 1 GHz and processes 4,000 MIPS. The iPad's CPU is a much simpler CPU, designed for basic tasks like Internet browsing and magazine reading. Even though it has 30% of the processing speed of the Core i7 Extreme Edition CPU, it has only about 2% of its processing power.

Modern CPUs are almost all **multicore**. Cores are separate processors inside the CPU chip that can complete operations simultaneously and separately from one another. CPUs can be dual-core or quad-core, for example. Multiple cores speed up processing not just because they increase the raw number of instructions per second that can be processed, but they also open up more options for task scheduling. If one of the cores is working on a particularly tough calculation, other operations waiting to be processed can go to one of the other cores, so there is no delay. This function is similar to a highway, where more lanes means that there is less chance of a slowdown if one of the lanes becomes congested.

Sometimes a CPU sits idle through one or more cycles because it has not received any data to process. This happens for a variety of reasons. One is that some data has to travel all the way from the memory or hard disk to the CPU, and even though the pathway is fast, it is not fast enough to keep up with the CPU's capability. To avoid this slowdown, CPU makers have looked for ways to keep frequently used data closer at hand, so that it has to travel a shorter distance when the CPU needs it. That is the purpose of a cache. A **cache** is a temporary storage area located near the CPU and connected to it by a high-speed pathway. A cache holds recently used data so the data does not have to be re-retrieved from memory every time.

Modern CPUs have multiple cache levels. The Level 1 (L1) cache is the smallest and is located on the CPU itself. The L1 cache is an integrated part of the die, which is the manufacturing pattern that is used to stamp the CPU pathways into the silicon chip. You cannot get any closer to the CPU than that. The Level 2 (L2) cache is larger and almost as close; it is in the processor chip but not usually part of the die. Some CPUs also have a Level 3 (L3) cache. When the CPU needs data, it first checks the L1 cache and pulls the data from there if it is available. If not, it checks the L2 cache and then the L3 cache. If the data is in none of those places, the CPU retrieves the data from storage.

It is useful to know about caches because when you shop for a computer, you will compare both CPU speeds and cache sizes. When CPU manufacturers list cache sizes in their marketing materials, they typically list only the largest cache (that is, only the highest numbered one). On a multicore CPU, the largest cache is shared among all the cores. For example, the Intel Core i7 processor can have up to 12 MB of L3 cache, shared among four cores.

Understanding Memory

Memory is data storage that uses on/off states on a chip to record patterns of binary data. An *on* value represents 1, and an *off* value represents 0. Memory can be either static or dynamic. **Static memory** (also known as nonvolatile memory) does not require any electricity to maintain its contents. **Dynamic memory** (or volatile memory) has to be constantly powered on to retain its contents.

Broadly speaking, all memory can be divided into one of two types: ROM or RAM. **Read-only memory (ROM)** stores data permanently—you cannot make any changes to its content. It takes a special ROM-writing machine to write to a ROM chip. ROM is always static. The basic startup instructions stored on a PC are typically provided on a ROM chip. The programming on a simple electronic device that will never need to be updated by the user is also provided on a ROM chip. The advantage of ROM is its reliability—you can never accidentally change or delete it. The disadvantages are that it is slow compared to RAM and that you cannot update it without replacing the chip. Because of these drawbacks, ROM is not used as a PC's primary memory source; a PC has only a small amount of ROM.

Random access memory (RAM) can be written and rewritten on the device in which it is installed. Random access memory derives its name from the fact that the data is stored in whatever locations are available, and reading data back from it does not require that the data be in a certain storage location.

RAM can be either static or dynamic. **Static RAM (SRAM)**, also called *flash RAM*, is the type you use when you store files on a USB flash drive. **USB** stands for **universal serial bus** and describes a type of connector used to attach an external device to a computer. SRAM is nonvolatile; you can

cache A temporary storage area for data that the CPU has recently needed or may need soon

memory Data storage that uses on/off states on a chip to record patterns of binary data

static memory Memory that holds its data without being powered; also called nonvolatile memory

dynamic memory Memory that requires constant electrical stimulation to retain its data

read-only memory (ROM) Memory that cannot be erased or changed by the device in which it is used

random access memory (RAM) Memory that can be written and changed by the device in which it is used

static RAM (SRAM) RAM that holds its content until it is erased or changed; does not require electricity

universal serial bus (USB) An interface used to connect many types of external devices to a computer

dynamic RAM (DRAM) RAM that requires constant electrical refreshing to hold its content

disconnect a flash RAM device and carry it around with you and the next time you connect it to a computer, the data will still be there. Most of the memory on a PC's motherboard is **dynamic RAM (DRAM)**, so when someone refers to a computer's memory, or its RAM, you can generally assume they mean the DRAM. DRAM is volatile, which means that when you turn off your computer, the content stored in its DRAM is erased.

The RAM in a computer functions as a work area when the computer is on. The operating system is loaded into it, as are any applications you have open and any data associated with those applications. The more free RAM in the computer, the larger the available workspace, which means you can have more applications and data files open at once.

megabyte (MB) One million bytes; a measurement of storage capacity

gigabyte (GB) One billion bytes; a measurement of storage capacity

Memory is measured in **megabytes (MB)** or **gigabytes (GB)**. A megabyte is a million bytes and a gigabyte is a billion bytes. As you learned in Lesson 1.1, a byte is 8 bits, and a bit is either a 0 or a 1. So if a memory chip holds 1 gigabyte, it holds 8 billion bits.

The DRAM in a PC is mounted on a small circuit board called a Dual Inline Memory Module (DIMM), and that DIMM fits into a slot in the motherboard. On notebook computers, a smaller version of a DIMM is used, called a small-outline DIMM (SO-DIMM). Figure 1.12 shows a DIMM and a SO-DIMM. Because they are easy to insert and remove from the slots, DIMMs and SO-DIMMs make it easy for people to upgrade and replace the RAM in their computers.

Figure 1.12 **DIMM (left) and SO-DIMM (right)**

Images courtesy of Martyn M. and Matthieu Riegler, Wikipedia Commons

Exercise 1.3 Evaluating a Computer's CPU and RAM

1. Click Start and then click *Control Panel*.

2. Click *System and Security*.

3. Under the System heading, click *View amount of RAM and processor speed*.

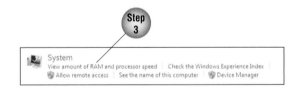

Step 3

4. In the *System* section of the information that displays, review *Processor* to see what CPU you have in your computer.

5. Next, review *Installed memory (RAM)* to see how much RAM you have in your computer.

6. Compare the amount of RAM your PC has to the RAM on your classmates' computers. Are they the same? If not, whose computer has the most?

7. Close the Control Panel window.

Drilling Down

Understanding Virtual Memory

Many operating systems, including Microsoft Windows, use a lot of RAM as they operate, to the point that even a well-equipped PC might not have enough RAM to do everything you want it to do. To avoid being unable to complete an activity due to lack of memory, these operating systems employ virtual memory to create a larger memory pool in which to operate.

With virtual memory, a portion of the hard disk is set aside as a holding area for the contents of RAM. When there is not enough space in RAM to hold new data, the operating system's virtual memory utility temporarily moves some of the least-recently used data in RAM onto the hard disk, making room for the incoming data. If an application calls for the data that was moved out of RAM, the virtual memory utility removes something else and swaps the needed data back in again. Due to all this changeover, the reserved area on the hard disk for virtual memory is sometimes called a *swap file*.

The main drawback of virtual memory is its speed, which is limited to the rate at which the hard drive can store and retrieve data. Compared to the speed of the processor and memory, the hard disk is slow. Therefore, the less physical RAM available in a system, and the more the system has to rely on virtual memory, the more slowly applications will run on that system. This is why adding more RAM to a system is often a worthwhile upgrade.

Lesson 1.4 Understanding Data Storage

 1-1.1.3, 1-1.1.4

Data entering a computer is temporarily stored in RAM, but if the data is to be preserved, it eventually must be saved to a storage device. A variety of storage devices are available for personal computers, each with its own unique set of pros and cons in terms of speed, cost, portability, and convenience. In this lesson, you will learn about some of the most popular storage devices.

Measuring Storage Space

Like RAM, storage space is measured in bytes. Depending on the size of the file and the medium on which you are storing it, that measurement could be in kilobytes (KB, thousands of bytes), megabytes, or gigabytes. The original storage device for the personal computer, the floppy disk, held between 360 KB and 1.44 MB, which seems laughably small today. But at the time, entire applications could be stored on a single disk.

Table 1.1 provides a summary of the various units used to measure storage capacity, along with examples of each. Notice that the units are not exact thousands, but multiples of 1,024. For example, a kilobyte is 1,024 bytes, not exactly 1,000. This is due to the binary nature of number storage in computers. The decimal value 1,024 is 10000000000 when converted to binary numbering (as you did in Exercise 1.1).

Table 1.1 **Units of Measurement for Storage Capacity**

Size	Equivalent	Example
Byte	8 bits	One character of text
Kilobyte (KB)	1,024 bytes	A 1,000-character plain text file, or a tiny graphic (18 × 18 pixels) such as an icon
Megabyte (MB)	1,024 KB	A 600 × 600 pixel photograph, or one minute of a music clip
Gigabyte (GB)	1,024 MB	A full-length audio CD is about 0.8 GB; a two-hour DVD movie is about 4 GB.
Terabyte (TB)	1,024 GB	A large business database containing records of all financial transactions
Petabyte (PB)	1,024 TB	All the data stored by the taxing authority of a large country, such as the U.S. Internal Revenue Service

All of the various storage media you will learn about in this lesson have their own capacity limitations. Table 1.2 summarizes these limitations as of 2011.

Table 1.2 **Capacities of Common Storage Media**

Storage Medium	Maximum Capacity
Hard drive (mechanical)	3 TB
Solid state drive	2 TB
USB flash drive	256 GB
Compact flash card	128 GB
CD	900 MB
Blu-Ray disc	50 GB
Double-sided, dual-layer DVD	17.08 GB

Hard Drives

Two types of storage devices are popularly referred to as hard drives. One is the traditional mechanical hard disk drive, which is the subject of this section. The other is a solid state hard drive, which is not really a disk drive at all but rather a type of flash storage. Solid state hard drives are covered in the next section.

A hard disk drive is a sealed stack of metal platters, each with a read-write head on a retractable arm. The read-write head writes data on the platters by magnetizing bits of iron in patterns of positive and negative magnetic polarity. As the hard disk drive operates, the platters rotate at a high speed, and the read-write heads hover just over the disk surfaces on a cushion of air generated by the spinning. Figure 1.13 shows the inside of a hard disk drive. You would not normally be able to see a hard disk drive this way, because the metal box encasing the platters is permanently sealed; if you take the case apart, you ruin the hard disk drive. The platters are typically 3.5 inches in diameter for full-size hard disk drives (in desktop PCs) and 2.5 inches for the smaller hard disk drives used in notebook PCs.

Figure 1.13 **Interior of a Hard Disk Drive**

Image courtesy of Matthew Field

Both the terms *hard disk* and *hard drive* are correct. The original disks in computers—floppy disks—were removable. A floppy drive was permanently mounted in the computer, and the floppy disks popped in and out of it. The drive and the disk were two separate things. Then came hard disks, which are permanently integrated with their drives. Because they cannot be separated, the hard disk (the platter stack) and the hard drive (the casing and read-write heads) are collectively referred to as the *hard disk drive*. That term can be shortened either to *hard disk* or *hard drive*—both are equally appropriate.

Hard disks are popular for use as a PC's main storage device because they are less expensive per megabyte than most other devices, they hold more data than other devices, and they read and write data quickly. The operating system and most applications on a PC are almost always stored on a hard disk drive. Hard disks vary based on the following factors:

- **Internal or external:** Internal hard disks are faster because they use a faster type of connection to the motherboard. External models are slower, but more portable; you can easily move them between computers.

- **Storage capacity:** Older hard disks may hold only a few gigabytes; newer ones can hold a terabyte or more.

- **Revolutions per minute (RPM):** The faster the platters spin, the faster they can be read.

- **Cache size:** Like the CPU, some hard disks have caches (see Lesson 1.3). The larger the drive's cache, the more it can anticipate the operating system's requests, which leads to faster performance.

revolutions per minute (RPM) A measurement of the rotational speed of the platters in a hard disk drive

Flash Drives and Cards

Devices that store data in **flash RAM** (static RAM) are not technically disk drives, but the term *drive* is widely used to describe them because consumers are accustomed to using that term for any device that holds data. As you learned in Lesson 1.3, static RAM is nonvolatile, meaning it continues to hold whatever you put in it until you make a change. Flash RAM is an example of this type of RAM. Flash RAM gets its name from the way it is written and erased—by a strong pulse (or flash) of electricity.

flash RAM Static RAM that can be written and erased by a strong pulse of electricity

Various sizes and types of flash RAM devices are available, but what they all have in common is that they are **solid state**; that is, they have no moving parts. As a result, they do not wear out from mechanical use, they are not as susceptible to data loss from physical trauma, they are silent when operating, and they use much less electricity than their mechanical counterparts. Some of the devices in this category include USB flash drives, memory cards, and solid state hard drives.

solid state An electronic device that operates only through circuit boards and other non-moving components

A **flash drive**, also called a *thumb drive* or *jump drive*, is a thumb-sized USB device that stores data on nonvolatile memory chips (see Figure 1.14). These devices can hold up to 256 GB of data, and they are useful for transferring files between PCs and between computers and other electronic devices. You might use one of these to store your data files for some of your classes.

flash drive A thumb-sized USB device that stores data on nonvolatile memory chips

Figure 1.14 USB Flash Drive

Image courtesy of Jeem/Stock Xchng

flash memory card
A small plastic wafer that encloses flash RAM, and that is written and read using a card reader device

A **flash memory card**, or *flash RAM card*, is a small plastic wafer that encloses flash RAM and is written and read using a card reader device. Instead of being on a stick-like USB device, the flash memory is embedded in a thin plastic cartridge with metal contacts that fit up against metal contacts in a card reader (see Figure 1.15). Many noncomputer devices use flash memory cards to store data for eventual transfer to a computer. For example, digital cameras, digital video recorders, and some medical devices store their output on flash memory cards.

Figure 1.15 Flash Memory Card

Photo by Dave Kennard

card reader A drive that reads and writes from one or more types of flash RAM cards

Because a flash memory card does not have a connector that fits into any of a computer's standard ports, it must be placed in a **card reader**, which is like a disk drive except it reads memory cards instead of disks. Some computers have built-in card readers, and you can also buy external card readers that connect to a PC's USB port. Several different sizes and shapes of flash RAM cards are available, each with their own specifications and features. Some card readers accept only one type of card; others can read and write multiple card types. Some of the common card types include CompactFlash (CF), SmartMedia (SM), MultiMedia Card (MMC), Secure Digital (SD), Memory Stick, and xD.

Another type of RAM-based storage device is a solid state hard drive. A solid state hard drive is not really a hard drive in that it does not contain any of the hard metal platters that a mechanical hard drive does, but it is called that to maintain consistency with mechanical hard drive terminology. Its central storage component is flash RAM. Solid state hard drives use the same fast internal interfaces in a PC that mechanical hard drives do, and they have similar caches and controllers. Solid state hard drives offer many benefits over mechanical ones and have few drawbacks. For example, a solid state hard drive has a faster startup time, faster access time, silent operation, low heat output, low power consumption, and high reliability and durability ratings.

Until recently, memory costs were so high that it was not feasible to make a flash device that could hold as much data as a mechanical hard disk drive. Now, however, memory manufacturing techniques have become streamlined enough to make this possible. Solid state hard drives are still more expensive than their mechanical counterparts though, making cost one of their few drawbacks. Solid state hard drives are also limited in the number of times a particular area can be rewritten. The limit is so high that most users will never come close to it, but it is still a theoretical drawback.

Optical Discs

optical disc A disc that stores data by using patterns of more or less reflectivity on the disc surface

Each type of storage technology has its own unique way of recording the 1s and 0s that make up a binary storage system. Recall from previous sections that on a mechanical hard disk, 1s and 0s are represented by changes in magnetic polarity, and in flash RAM the 1s and 0s are represented by on/off states of transistors. In contrast to these, an **optical disc** stores data in patterns of more or less reflectivity on the surface of the disc. A laser shines its light on the disc as the disc spins past it, and a sensor measures the amount of light that bounces back. If it detects a change in the amount of reflectivity between two spots, it interprets that as a 1. If it does not detect a change, it interprets that as a 0. The areas of less reflectivity are called **pits**; the areas of more reflectivity are called **lands**.

pit An area of less reflectivity on an optical disc

land An area of greater reflectivity on an optical disc

CDs, DVDs, and Blu-Ray discs are all examples of optical discs. CDs and DVDs use a red laser, and Blu-Ray discs use a blue laser (which is where the name comes from), but other than that, they are all technologically similar. Each disc type comes in both read-only and writeable formats. The names of the ones that are read-only end in ROM, as in CD-ROM or DVD-ROM. The commercial music and movie discs you buy in stores are read-only.

The writeable versions may end in either R (for those that can be written to only once) or RW (for those that can be repeatedly rewritten). For example, CD-R discs are write-once; CD-RW discs are multi-writeable. The same goes for DVD-R and DVD-RW. With writeable DVDs, two different standards for the way they are written exist. One standard is indicated with a plus sign and the other with a minus sign. For example, DVD+R and DVD-R are two separate types of discs. Most writeable DVD drives can read and write both types; however, some older home theater DVD players accept only one or the other type for movie playback.

CDs can hold between 650 and 900 MB of data, depending on the disc type. (The 900 MB type is uncommon; most writeable CD blanks are limited to 800 MB.) DVD discs come in both single-sided and double-sided versions. A DVD can hold 4.7 GB per side. In addition, some DVD discs are double-layer, which enables you to store almost twice as much per side (8.54 GB per side). Blu-Ray discs (BD) are physically similar to DVDs but hold more data, so they are suitable for high-definition movies and high-volume data storage. A BD can hold up to 25 GB per layer and can have up to two layers.

Table 1.3 summarizes the capacities of the various types of optical discs.

Table 1.3 Storage Capacities of Optical Discs

Disc Type	Storage Capacity
CD	650 MB, 800 MB, or 900 MB
Single-Sided, Single-Layer DVD	4.7 GB
Single-Sided, Double-Layer DVD	8.54 GB
Double-Sided, Single-Layer DVD	9.4 GB
Double-Sided, Double-Layer DVD	17.08 GB
8 cm Single-Layer Blu-Ray	7.8 GB
8 cm Double-Layer Blu-Ray	15.7 GB
12 cm Single-Layer Blu-Ray	25 GB
13 cm Double-Layer Blu-Ray	50 GB

Understanding Data Storage and Useful Life

Data storage is not always reliable. With removable-disc drives such as CD and DVD drives, a mechanical failure of the drive is not a problem because you can replace the drive independently of the data and your data will remain safe on the removed disc. However, with drives where the disk and the drive are inseparable, such as a mechanical hard disk drive, a mechanical failure of the drive can mean the data on the platters is inaccessible, even though the data itself may be fine. Certain data recovery companies specialize in the recovery of such data, but they are expensive to use.

Mechanical hard disk reliability is measured in two ways. The **mean time between failures (MTBF)** is the predicted amount of time between expected failures. For a typical hard disk, this is somewhere around 600,000 hours. The **annualized failure rate (AFR)** is the percentage of likelihood that a device will fail in a certain year. A typical AFR rating for hard disks is somewhere between 0.7% and 1%. These are overall averages for all hard disks everywhere, without factoring in their actual ages; as a drive ages, its likelihood of failure increases. When you are shopping for a hard disk drive, you can find out its MTBF or AFR score in the specifications on the box. A higher MTBF number is better and a lower AFR number is better.

Another reason stored data is not reliable indefinitely is that the storage medium may begin to lose its strength. For example, on a magnetic disk, the polarity of the opposing magnetic fields may weaken, making the disk harder to read. On an optical disc like a CD or DVD, the coating or dye on the disc may degrade over time, or the disc may crack or become scratched.

Because optical storage technology is so new, nobody is sure of the exact statistics concerning data reliability over time. However, there is some evidence that home-recorded CDs and DVDs may have a short useful life because of how they write data. They use a photosensitive dye to create the illusion of pits in the disc surface, and over time the dye's physical characteristics may change, making the disc unreadable. The expected life of a writeable CD or DVD based on manufacturer estimates is between 20 and 100 years, depending on the quality of the discs, the quality of the writing drive, and the storage conditions. However, some discs start to degrade in as little as 18 months.

Flash RAM is also so newly developed that there has not been enough time to determine how many years the data stored on it will last. In general, however, flash-based memory is good for around 100,000 writes/rewrites, and a USB connector, in general, can tolerate about 1,500 connects/disconnects from a PC before it wears out.

Because you cannot count on a storage device holding its data forever, you should make sure to back up important data using other storage media. For example, if you store your important word processing files on your hard disk, you should also store backup copies of them on a CD, DVD, flash drive, or online data backup location.

Exercise 1.4 Evaluating a Computer's Storage Devices

1. Click Start and then click *Computer*.

2. A list of disk drives displays. Click the C: drive in the content pane to select it.

3. In the Status bar at the bottom of the window, review the information about the disk drive.

   This information may include the total size, free space, and file system.

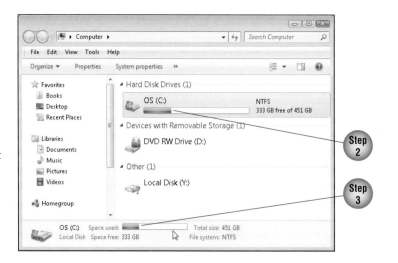

4. Right-click the C: drive and then click *Properties*.

   This opens a properties dialog box.

5. On the General tab, review the information about the disk drive.

   This information includes used space, free space, and capacity (including a chart).

6. Click Cancel to close the dialog box without making any changes.

7. If you have a CD or DVD drive listed in the Computer window, make sure a disc is inserted in it. Repeat Steps 2 through 6 and examine the properties of the inserted disc.

8. Close the Computer window.

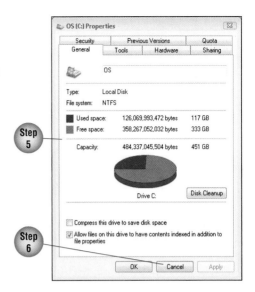

Drilling Down

Understanding Remote Storage and Network Drives

Storage can be either *local* (that is, attached directly to the computer you are working with) or *remote* (stored in a different location, such as on the internet, or attached to a different computer). One type of remote storage is a *network drive*, which is a drive that you access via a network. A network drive may be a disk drive in a file server, a shared drive on another computer, or a *network attached storage (NAS)* device. Network-attached storage devices are intelligent storage devices that contain not only storage space but also a very basic processor and a small amount of memory, plus a network interface that enables them to connect directly to a network without being associated with any particular computer.

Lesson 1.5   Understanding Input Devices

 1-1.1.5, 1-1.1.6, 1-1.18

input device A device designed to help enter data or commands into a computer

As you learned in Lesson 1.1, an **input device** is one that helps you get data or commands into a computer. Input devices are essential to computers because they allow users to tell the computer what to do. In this lesson, you will learn about several types of basic input devices, such as keyboards and mice, as well as some more uncommon input devices like scanners and digital cameras.

Keyboards

Keyboards help you enter text and numeric input for documents and other data files. Figure 1.16 shows a typical keyboard. Electronically, a keyboard is a grid of uncompleted circuits. When you press a key, you lower a contact that completes the circuit and sends a code for that character to the computer. Some keys are modifiers; they trigger a circuit that changes any other values. The Shift key is the most common example. When you press Shift by itself, nothing happens, but when you press Shift along with a letter, an uppercase letter is sent, which is a different value than the regular lowercase letter. Other keys send function codes rather than letters or numbers. For example, the F1 key sends a code that

Figure 1.16 Computer Keyboard

Image courtesy of Microsoft Corporation

represents Function 1. What that entails depends on the operating system and the active application. For example, pressing F1 in Windows opens the Help system.

Keyboards are available in different sizes and layouts. Some keyboards are designed to reduce wrist and hand strain, while others are designed to be compact or to offer additional keys to be used as shortcuts for common activities.

Pointing Devices

pointing device A device designed to move an on-screen arrow pointer; contains buttons you click to issue commands

mouse A device that you can roll across a flat surface to move an on-screen pointer

trackball A stationary device with a ball on top; you roll the ball to move an on-screen pointer

touchpad A touch-sensitive pad, usually found on a notebook computer; you move your finger across the pad to move an on-screen pointer

A **pointing device** is an input device that moves the pointer around on the screen and allows you to click and double-click to issue commands. You move the device, or a part of the device, with your hand or fingers, and sensors measure the direction and distance of the movement and move an on-screen pointer a corresponding amount.

The most common type of pointing device is a **mouse**, which is typically the size and shape of a bar of soap with two buttons on the top (see Figure 1.17). You move the mouse across a table, mouse pad, or other flat surface, and a sensor on the bottom of the mouse measures the direction and distance you move. Press a button to click. Other types of pointing devices include a trackball and a touchpad. A **trackball** is a stationary base with a ball positioned on top that the user rotates (see Figure 1.18). Sensors under the ball measure the direction and distance of the movement. Press a button next to the ball to click. A **touchpad** is a touch-sensitive rectangular pad, usually about 2 inches by 3 inches and built into a notebook computer. See an example in Figure 1.19. You can either press a button under the touchpad or tap the touchpad to click.

Figure 1.17 Mouse

Image courtesy of Microsoft Corporation

Figure 1.18 Trackball

Image courtesy of Kensington Computer Products Group

Figure 1.19 Touchpad

Photo by Erik Araujo

A mouse or trackball can be either mechanical or optical. A **mechanical device** has moving parts; when the ball rolls, it moves internal rollers in the device, whose movement is then translated to the pointer on the screen. An **optical device** works by shining a light and measuring the amount of light that bounces back. With an optical model, when the ball rolls, lights (laser or LED) shine on the desktop (for a mouse) or the ball (for a trackball), and sensors measure the light bouncing back to determine the direction and amount of movement. Most pointing devices are optical; mechanical ones are nearly obsolete.

A mouse or trackball can either be wired or wireless. A **wired device** has a cord that attaches to the PC, usually using the USB port. A **wireless device** may use the computer's Bluetooth interface (a type of wireless port) or it may have a transceiver that connects to a USB port and then communicates wirelessly with the device itself. Wireless devices typically have batteries that power them, whereas wired models use USB port to pull power from the computer.

mechanical device A device with moving parts

optical device A device that works by shining a light and measuring the amount of light that bounces back

wired device A device that connects to a computer with a cord or cable

wireless device A device that connects to a computer using a wireless signal

Exercise 1.5A Experimenting with Pointing Device Settings

1. Click Start, click *Control Panel*, then click *Hardware and Sound*.

2. Under the *Devices and Printers* heading, click *Mouse*.

   This opens the Mouse Properties dialog box.

3. On the Buttons tab, click the *Switch primary and secondary buttons* check box to insert a check mark and then click Apply.

4. Click away from the dialog box and try clicking on some icons on your desktop or the Start menu. Notice that now the right mouse button, rather than the left, is the primary button.

5. At the Mouse Properties dialog box with the Buttons tab selected, click the *Switch primary and secondary buttons* check box to remove the check mark. Click Apply to return the buttons to their regular settings.

6. Click the Pointer Options tab, drag the slider in the *Motion* area all the way to the *Slow* setting and then try moving the mouse.

7. Drag the slider all the way to the *Fast* setting and try moving the mouse again.

8. Drag the slider to a medium setting of your choice.

9. Click OK to close the Mouse Properties dialog box.

10. Close the Control Panel window.

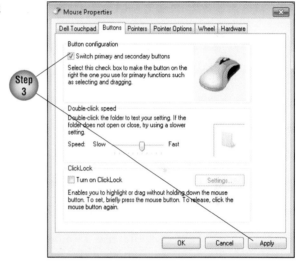

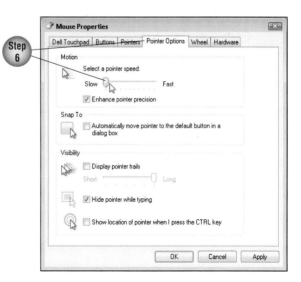

Understanding and Selecting a Computer   25

Game Controllers

game controller An input device designed to be used with one or more types of games on a computer

Game controllers are specialized input devices designed to make it easier to play a certain type of game. Many different types of controllers are available. One of the most common controllers is a joystick, which is used for flight simulator games. Other types include steering wheels (for driving games), dance pads (for dancing games), and hand-held controllers like those that come with popular gaming consoles such as the Xbox or PlayStation.

Scanners

scanner An input device that converts a hard-copy picture to a digital image by measuring the amount of light that bounces back to a sensor as the light hits different parts of the original material

A **scanner** digitizes a hard-copy image, converting it into a graphic file on the PC by measuring the amount of light that bounces back to a sensor as the light hits different parts of the source material. Most scanners are flatbed, like a copier, while others feed documents one page at a time past a stationary scanning unit, like a fax machine. Scanners can be purchased as standalone units, or as part of a multi-function printer-scanner-copier combo device. Most scanners use the USB interface. Figure 1.20 shows an example of a flatbed scanner, the Epson GT-20000 Document Scanner.

Figure 1.20 Flatbed Scanner

Image courtesy of Epson America, Inc.

charge-coupled device (CCD) The photosensitive part of a scanner or digital camera that records the amount of light bouncing off an image and converts that value to an electrical charge

To use a flatbed scanner, you place the original face down on the glass and close the lid. You then either press a button on the scanner or issue a command in a scanning program to start the scan. Inside a scanner is a fixed linear array called a **charge-coupled device (CCD)**. A CCD is a line of photosensitive cells, similar to the eye of an insect, which converts light into an electrical charge. A light bar moves across the page being scanned, and a system of mirrors reflects light to a lens and then onto the CCD. Each of the photosensitive cells produces an electrical signal proportional to the strength of the light that hits it, and that signal is converted to a binary number and sent to the computer. Dark areas have lower numbers and light areas have higher numbers. See Figure 1.21 for an example.

In a color scanner, three separate evaluations of each pixel in the image are performed: amount of red, amount of blue, and amount of green. The original scanners were 1-bit systems: they were black-and-white only and transmitted a single bit of data for each cell in the CCD. The number of bits in a scan is the number of binary digits required to represent each pixel's value. In a 1-bit system, each pixel is 0 or 1, off or on. The next generation scanners were 4-bit (16 unique shades of gray) and 8-bit (256 shades of gray). Today all scanners support at least 24-bit scanning (8 bits each for red, green, and blue). This is known as *true color*, and it uses a 24-digit binary code to represent each pixel.

Figure 1.21 Typical Scanner Process

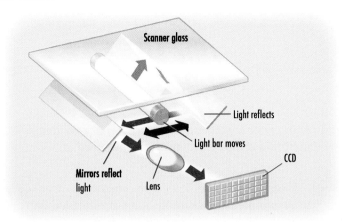

Digital Cameras

A **digital camera** is an input device that captures a picture, digitizes the picture, and saves it until it can be transferred to a computer. A digital camera is like a scanner except it is portable. Rather than scan a flat, two-dimensional image, it projects its vision out to the 3D world and creates an image based on what it "sees."

Technologically, a digital camera has a lot in common with a traditional camera. They both have a focusable lens that sees the image and, usually, a built-in flash. The main difference is that a traditional camera's lens sends its data to film, whereas a digital camera sends its data to a digital storage medium such as a flash memory card. A digital camera can also send data directly to a computer if it is connected to one (as with a webcam).

Like a scanner, the camera lens in a digital camera sends its data to a CCD, which measures the amount of light received in each cell and conveys an electrical charge to the camera's processor in proportion to the amount of light in a particular spot. As with a scanner, a color filter is applied to the CCD to enable color photography. The data passes through an analog-to-digital converter, which turns those electrical charges into binary computer data. Figure 1.22 illustrates how a digital camera captures and transfers an image.

> **digital camera** An input device that captures a picture, digitizes it, and saves it until it can be transferred to a computer

Figure 1.22 Image Digitizing Process

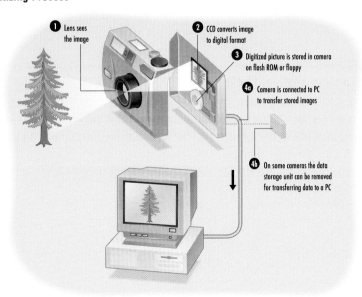

Other Input Devices

Besides the standard input devices common on personal computers, there are many specialty input devices. These include:

- **Remote controls:** The remote control you use to change the channel on your television is an input device, and so are similar-looking remotes used to control a wide variety of digital devices, from radios to security systems.

- **Environmental/scientific probes and sensors:** These devices are used in laboratories and in the field to input data for experiments and monitoring. For example, a digital thermometer or barometer can connect to a computer to automatically feed data into a database at regular intervals.

- **Biomedical sensors:** Like environmental devices, biomedical sensors collect data about living beings and feed it into a computer. For example, a heart rate and blood pressure monitoring machine in a hospital inputs data into a digital system that can then send the data wirelessly to a computer at a nurse's station, allowing nurses to monitor patients remotely.

- **Bar code readers:** Like the bar code scanners found at supermarket cash registers, bar code readers can easily import coded data into an application. They are used not only in retail stores, but also in warehouses and shipping companies to track inventory.

- **Biometric security devices:** Biometric security devices authenticate users based on scans of human body characteristics such as fingerprints, facial features, or retinas.

- **Point of sales systems:** Payment machines can accept and process electronic payments at retail stores, safely and securely inputting the customer's payment information.

Exercise 1.5B Shopping for Digital Cameras

1. Open a web browser and go to https://reviews.cnet.com or another site selected by your instructor.

2. Browse the reviews of digital cameras. Select two cameras: one large and full-featured, the other compact and lightweight.

3. Compare the prices, specifications, and features of the two cameras.

4. Suppose you were looking for a camera for yourself. Which of these two cameras would be better for you and why? Write a paragraph explaining your opinion. Label your work **U1T1-Cameras**.

Drilling Down

Understanding Keyboard Layouts

The keys on almost all keyboards today are arranged in the QWERTY layout. The name QWERTY comes from the first six letters in the top row of letter keys. The QWERTY arrangement was originally conceived for typewriters, with the intention of slowing down the pace of typing enough to prevent the metal arms from jamming. Today, most people still use the same key arrangement, even though other layouts exist that, once mastered, would allow them to type much faster. One such layout is called Dvorak, named for its inventor.

IC³ 1-1.1.5, 1-1.1.7, 1-1.1.9

An **output device** is one that helps you get data out of a computer. Common output devices include printers and monitors. In this lesson, you will learn about the types of monitors, projectors, and printers you may encounter and how they differ from one another.

output device A device designed to display or share data output from a computer

Monitors and Projectors

A **monitor** is a video display screen. On a notebook computer, the monitor is built in; on a desktop computer, it is a separate component attached to the computer with a cable. Most monitors are output-only, but touchscreen monitors are both input and output devices. Most monitors sold today are **liquid crystal display (LCD)**, the same type of flat panel display found in modern TVs.

An LCD screen has two polarized filters, between which are liquid crystals. In order for light to appear on the display screen, the light must pass through both filters and the crystals. The second filter, however, is at an angle to the first, so by default nothing passes through. However, applying electrical current to the crystal causes it to twist, which also twists the light passing through it. If the light twists so that it matches the angle of the second filter, it can pass through and light up an area of the display (see Figure 1.23). On a color LCD, an additional filter splits the light into separate cells for red, green, and blue.

monitor An output device that displays text and/or images to the computer on a display screen

liquid crystal display (LCD) A thin, flat panel monitor that passes electricity through liquid crystals to create an image

Figure 1.23 Liquid Crystal Process In an LCD monitor, liquid crystals twist when electricity is applied to them, enabling light to pass through.

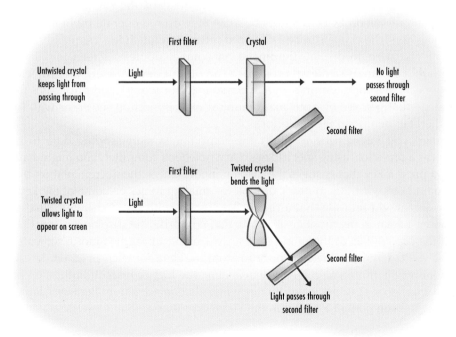

You may also occasionally see an older type of monitor, the cathode ray tube. The **cathode ray tube (CRT)** is a boxy monitor, like an old-style television. A CRT uses electron guns to light up phosphors on glass, which creates an image.

cathode ray tube (CRT) A large, boxy type of monitor that uses electron guns to light up phosphors on glass and create an image

A CRT is essentially a large vacuum tube. At the back is a long, narrow neck containing a cathode, and at the front is a large rectangular piece of glass with colored phosphors on it. When the cathode is heated, it emits negatively charged electrons. Those electrons are attracted to the positively charged front of the CRT, where they strike the phosphors and cause them to light up. A color CRT contains three electron guns, one for each color: red, green, and blue. The actual colors are created by the phosphors on the screen. For each pixel (colored dot) on the screen, there are three phosphors—red, green, and blue—arranged in a triangle formation called a triad. Each electron gun targets only dots of a certain color. So, for example, if a certain pixel is supposed to be purple, the red and blue guns fire at it, but not the green gun (see Figure 1.24). CRT monitors vary in their refresh rate, which is the number of times per second the electron guns refresh the charge on each phosphor. A higher refresh rate makes a monitor image flicker less, for less eye strain.

Figure 1.24 Electron Gun Process within a CRT   A color CRT has three electron guns; one for each phosphor color.

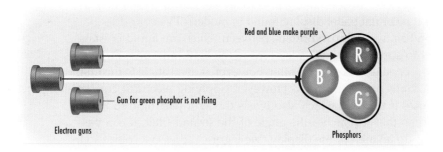

LCD monitors are the modern standard because they are brighter, thinner, and lighter. They take up less space on a desk, consume less electricity, and run cooler. Until the early 2000s, LCD monitors were much more expensive than CRTs, but now the prices are roughly equivalent. Refresh rate (or speed) is not an issue on LCD monitors because they do not operate by lighting up phosphors; the crystals in an LCD need refreshing much less frequently.

digital projector A projector that accepts video input from a computer and uses a projection system to display an enlarged version of that image on a projection screen

If you need to display the image on your computer's screen to a large group, you can use a digital projector as an output device. A **digital projector** connects to a computer like an additional monitor would, and duplicates the image that you see on your main monitor on a projection screen or wall (or wherever you point the projector).

Depending on the computer, you might need to direct the computer to start sending data to an additional video source, such as a projector, using special keys. On a notebook computer, you might have to hold down the Fn key and press a key that changes the display mode. Check the documentation that came with your computer to find out what key to press, or look for small graphics on some of the keys, perhaps in a different color, that might indicate that a certain key works with Fn to change a display setting. A monitor's resolution, which is the number of pixels that comprise the display horizontally and vertically, depends on the capabilities of the monitor's hardware and upon the amount of video memory installed in the PC. A PC requires video memory to store the data for each pixel while it is waiting to be sent to the monitor; the more video memory available, the higher resolution the PC can display. Depending on the computer, it may use video memory installed on a separate display adapter circuit board, or it may share the main pool of RAM with the video display.

Exercise 1.6 Experimenting with Monitor Settings

On a desktop PC's monitor, locate the buttons that control the on-screen image. Look up your monitor online by brand and model to determine what those buttons do, or experiment with them to see what menus and settings are available. For example, you might be able to shift the screen image vertically or horizontally, or enlarge or compress it.

OR

On a notebook PC, look up your computer model online to determine how to control the display, or experiment by holding down the Fn key and pressing some of the keys that have pictures on them. For example, you might hold down Fn and press a key that has a sun with an up arrow on it to increase the display brightness.

Printers

A **printer** is an output device that produces hard-copy printouts of the work you create on the computer. All printers perform the same basic task: they place an image on a piece of paper. To do this, they all have certain subsystems that perform standard tasks, more or less in the following order:

printer An output device that produces hard-copy printouts of the work you create on the computer

- **Receive data from the PC.** Each printer has at least one input interface. This is usually a USB or network connection (wired or wireless). Older printers may use a parallel printer port.

- **Store the data in printer RAM.** A printer contains a small amount of RAM that holds the incoming data before the printer's physical print mechanism outputs it.

- **Convert the data into print instructions.** Each printer contains a motherboard and CPU that accept the data and convert it into instructions for the mechanical parts that transfer the image to paper.

- **Feed the paper in and out.** Inside each printer is a series of gears, rollers, grabbers, and so on, which feed the paper through the printer.

- **Store and dispense ink or toner.** A printer needs some sort of colored material to create the image. This can be either liquid ink (on an inkjet printer) or dry toner (on a laser printer).

- **Transfer the image to the paper.** Liquid ink is squirted out of nozzles onto the page. The force that drives the jets can be either heat or electricity. With dry toner, the magnetic particles in the toner are attracted to a charged drum and then to the paper. The materials then pass through a head unit that melts the plastic particles so they stick to the paper.

Printers vary in terms of cost, quality, printing speed, paper tray size, interfaces, ability to print photos, and additional functions (like scanning and copying). Most printers sold today are either inkjet or laser. An **inkjet printer** (like the Epson Stylus Photo 1400 Ink Jet printer, shown in Figure 1.25) works by squirting liquid ink onto paper. Inkjet printers have between 21 and 256 nozzles for each of the four colors (cyan, yellow, magenta, and black) in the print head, depending on the brand and model. The print engine tells the jets to squirt out ink in different combinations and proportions to create whatever colors are needed. Some photo printers have six or eight cartridges, rather than the usual four, because different types of ink are used in some print jobs.

inkjet printer A printer that creates an image on a page by squirting liquid ink onto the paper

Figure 1.25 Inkjet Printer

Image courtesy of Epson America, Inc.

laser printer A printer that creates an image by writing with a laser on a metal drum, transferring toner to the drum, and then transferring the toner to paper

Total Cost of Ownership (TCO) The amount of money you spend over the lifetime of a device you own

dots per inch (dpi) A measure of the resolution of printer output; higher DPI means a sharper image on the printout

A **laser printer** works much like a photocopier. The main difference is that a photocopier scans a document to produce an image, whereas a laser printer receives digitized data from a computer. A laser printer contains a large cylinder called a drum, which carries a highly negative electrical charge. The printer directs a laser beam to partially neutralize the charge in certain areas of the drum. When the drum rotates past a toner reservoir, the toner clings to the areas of lesser charge, and the page is formed on the drum. Then the drum rotates past positively charged paper, and the toner jumps onto the paper. The paper then passes through a fuser that melts the plastic particles of the toner so that it sticks to the paper. Laser printers are available in color or monochrome models. A color laser printer has four separate toner cartridges: cyan, magenta, yellow, and black. To accurately print a color document, a laser printer must make four passes, laying down a different color each time.

Inkjet printers are less expensive to buy than laser printers, but they have a higher cost per page because of the high cost of the ink cartridges. Laser printers cost more up front and their toner cartridges cost more than ink cartridges, but the toner cartridges print many more pages per cartridge, so the cost per page is lower. The cost involved in owning a printer (or any other device), including both the up-front costs and the costs of consumable supplies, is called the **Total Cost of Ownership (TCO)**.

Printer output resolution is measured in **dots per inch (dpi)**. The greater the number of dots per inch, the smaller the individual dots of color, so the sharper the edges of the image appear. Refer to Figure 1.26, which contrasts the resolution of a character at 300 dpi versus 600 dpi. Notice that at 600 dpi, the edge of the letter, when magnified, is cleaner and smoother. Most laser printers print at 600 to 1200 dpi; an average inkjet printer prints at around 720 dpi in its standard mode and 1440 in its high-quality photo mode (which takes longer and uses more ink).

Figure 1.26 Printer Resolution Higher resolution means more, smaller dots per inch on the paper.

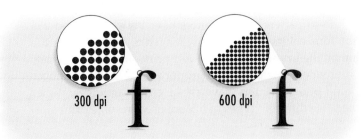

300 dpi   600 dpi

Drilling Down

Exploring Specialty Printers

A variety of specialty printers are available for home, business, and industrial uses. For example, photo printers specialize in printing high-quality images on glossy photo paper. Large document printers are like regular printers except they accept very large sheets of paper; they are used in commercial printing operations to print items such as posters, banners, and billboards. Plotters are printers that create images using pencils or markers rather than dots of ink. Plotters are most commonly used to create precision mechanical drawings for engineering and architecture.

Lesson 1.7 Selecting a Computer

 1-1.1.9, 1-1.2.9

At some point, you may be responsible for making a computer purchase decision. Perhaps you will be a manager at a company that needs new computers, or you will need a computer for your own personal use at home or at work. In this lesson, you will learn about some of the factors involved in purchasing computers and computer-related equipment (**peripherals**).

> **peripherals**
> Computer-related devices that are not part of the computer system itself; examples include printers and scanners

Factors to Consider When Purchasing a Computer

You can purchase computers and peripherals in retail stores or online. Each store type has its benefits and drawbacks. When deciding where to purchase, you should consider the cost (discounts, taxes, shipping), the available brands, the store's return policy, available warranties, the expertise of the sales people, and shipping methods.

Cost Cost is often the driving factor in selecting a particular computer. Brick-and-mortar stores (that is, stores that have a real building, not just a website) have higher operating costs, so their prices might be higher than an online store. Most stores, both online and brick-and-mortar, have sales or offer discounts for volume (or bulk) purchases.

Organizational standards If you are purchasing computers on behalf of an organization or institution, check to see what standards or guidelines you may need to follow. For example, the company's IT policy may prescribe a certain type of input device, or a minimum warranty length.

Useful life A computer's useful life is the length of time before it is considered out of date. Consider how long the computer needs to last. The more cutting-edge the technology, the longer it will take for it to become obsolete. You may choose to pay more upfront to buy an extra year or two of useful life.

Brand If you want a particular brand or model of computer, you may be limited in where you can buy it. Some brands, like HP and Dell, allow you to buy in a variety of places, including local stores, online stores, and the manufacturer's website. Other brands may be sold in only one place.

Return Policy Knowing the return policy of the store is important. If you need to return an item, it is important to know if you can take it back to a local store or if you are required to mail it back. If you do not want to bother with mailing back a return, stick to shopping at local stores.

Warranty A standard warranty for a personal computer is one year on parts and labor. Some computers come with longer warranties that are either included in the base price or available for an extra fee. Some stores also offer their own extended warranties on products they sell.

Factors Affecting Computer Performance and Cost

Besides deciding where to shop, you also must decide what brand and model to purchase. Earlier in this topic you learned about the basic components of a computer, including the CPU, memory, storage devices, and monitor. When shopping for a computer, you should look for the best balance of quality for all these features at the price you can afford. The following factors will affect a computer's performance and can also affect the price of the systems you may be comparing.

Desktop or Portable Your first decision is what type of PC you want to purchase, as you learned in Lesson 1.2. A desktop PC is cheaper for the same performance, but a notebook PC is more convenient to transport.

CPU The faster the CPU speed (measured in GHz), the better the computer will perform. Raw speed is not the only factor in choosing a CPU, though. Other issues include the number of cores (dual core, quad core) and the number of instructions per second (MIPS) that the CPU can process.

RAM The more RAM a computer has, the better its ability to handle running multiple applications at once without slowing down. However, if you are running a 32-bit operating system, such as the 32-bit version of Windows 7, it will not be able to use more than 4 GB of RAM.

Hard Disk Hard disks vary in capacity, in rotational speed (for mechanical drives), and in access time (lower is better). Most hard drives now use the serial ATA interface (SATA), but parallel ATA (PATA), the older, slower technology, is still available. You will pay significantly more for a solid state hard drive than a mechanical one, but it will be quieter, faster, and more reliable.

Optical Drive Almost all computers have at least one optical drive. A DVD drive is more versatile than a plain CD drive because it can read both CDs and DVDs. And a writeable drive is more versatile than one that reads only. Some systems come with a Blu-Ray optical drive, which can accept BD, DVD, and CD discs.

Monitor A larger monitor makes the screen easier to see. This is important if you spend many hours of the day at the computer. However, in a notebook PC, a larger screen will also be bulkier and heavier and you may find it cumbersome to carry around.

Quick Steps

Determine a Computer's Windows Experience Index Score

1. Click Start and then click *Control Panel.*
2. Click *System and Security* heading.
3. Click *Check the Windows Experience Index.*

One way to assess a computer's performance is with the Windows Experience Index. This is a numeric score that describes a computer's performance in five key areas: processor, memory, graphics, gaming graphics, and primary hard disk. The lowest score of these is the base score, which is the overall determinant of how well Windows runs on that PC. For a more detailed explanation of the Windows Experience Index, click the <u>What do these numbers mean?</u> hyperlink below the scores to open a page in the Windows Help system. You cannot usually get the Windows Experience Index for a computer you order online or over the phone, but you can check the score of a display model in a store before you purchase.

Choosing an Operating System

One of the most basic decisions you will make when selecting a computer is which operating system (OS) you want. Microsoft Windows 7 and Mac OS X (where *X* is the Roman numeral for 10, which is the verson number) are the two most common operating systems you will encounter when shopping.

Windows has the advantage of popularity. According to a May 2011 article posted by xbitlabs.com, Microsoft operating systems have over 78% of the operating system market share. Since so many computer users have Windows operating systems, nearly all applications are made to run on Windows. Windows systems may also be a little bit less expensive, since there is more competition in the Windows PC market, whereas computers that run the Mac OS X operating system are made mainly by one manufacturer: Apple. The Mac OS has the reputation of being the preferred operating system for people who work professionally with graphics, page layout, video, and music, and there is a great deal of powerful creative media software available for Macintosh users.

Choosing between Mac and Windows typically comes down to personal preference. Both Mac and Windows do the same basic things, but in slightly different ways. The best way to decide is to try out both operating systems and see which one you most enjoy using.

Exercise 1.7   Shopping for a Computer

1. Open a web browser and go to http://ic3.emcp.net/compshop or another site selected by your instructor.

2. Find a notebook computer and make a note of its specifications, including the brand, model number, price, CPU, RAM, screen size, hard disk size and type, and optical drive type.

3. Find a desktop computer and make a note of its specifications (use the list provided in Step 2).

4. Analyze the two systems and write a paragraph that explains which you would select and why.

Lesson 1.8   Setting Up a Computer

 1-1.1.8

As a computer-literate person, you should be able to take a new computer out of its boxes and set it up. Doing so mainly consists of plugging the cables for the various components into the right sockets on the computer. In this lesson, you will learn about selecting an appropriate location for your computer and how to connect the keyboard, mouse, and monitor.

Unpacking a New Computer

When unpacking a computer, open the box carefully. If you are using a sharp knife to open the packaging, make sure you do not cut too deeply into the box and damage the components. When removing components from the box, be aware that you may have to repack them if the computer turns out to be defective. Save all the packing materials, instructions, and discs. Store the instructions and discs in a safe place because you might need them tomorrow, next week, or next year. Some components, such as the monitor screen or the corners or logos on a case, may be covered by pieces of protective plastic film. Pull off the pieces of film and discard them.

Set the computer either on a solid desk or on the floor, so there is no danger of it falling or being knocked off. If you plan to place the case in a cubbyhole, drawer, or cabinet where there is limited airflow, consider what you can do to increase ventilation to that area so the computer does not overheat.

As you position the desk and the computer, think about where the cords will run. Set the keyboard, mouse, and monitor (if they are separate) where you think you will want them, and note whether the cables will reach to the case, and whether those cables will be draped across any areas where they may be in danger of getting yanked or dragged accidentally. Do not plug in the computer's power until you have plugged in all the other components; power should be the last cable you connect.

Connecting Input Devices

On a notebook computer, the keyboard and mouse are built in. On a desktop computer, however, you will need to connect the keyboard and the mouse.

Most input devices on modern systems (including the keyboard and mouse) connect to a PC using a USB connector like the one shown in Figure 1.27. However, some specialized or older input devices may use other interfaces. For example, some older keyboards and mice use a **PS/2** connector, also called a **mini-DIN** connector (see Figure 1.28).

PS/2 (mini-DIN) A small round connector used to connect keyboards and mice on some older computer systems

Figure 1.27 USB Connector

Image courtesy of Michael Faes

Figure 1.28 PS/2 (mini-DIN) Connector

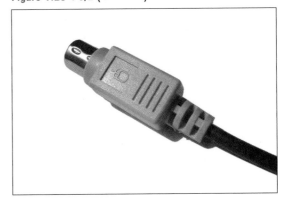

Photo by José Antonio López

Connecting a Monitor

Video Graphics Array (VGA) An analog connection for a monitor that uses a 15-pin D-shaped connector

Digital Video Interface (DVI) A digital connection for a monitor that uses a rectangular block connector

On a notebook computer, the monitor is built in; on a desktop it is separate and must be connected to the computer via a monitor cable. Monitors can use either a VGA or a DVI connector (see Figures 1.29 and 1.30). Some monitors support only one or the other; some have both connector types for maximum flexibility. **VGA** stands for **Video Graphics Array**. This D-shaped, 15-pin analog monitor connection has been the standard for over 20 years and, until recently, was used by almost all monitors. **DVI**, which stands for **Digital Video Interface**, is a newer, rectangular digital connector. The difference between analog and digital video is that with an analog connection, the computer's display adapter must convert the digital instructions from the computer to an analog signal before sending them to the monitor. With a digital connector, the display adapter can pass on the digital data without making that conversion. If available, the DVI connector is preferable because it delivers data more quickly. However, not all monitors and not all computers have DVI connectors.

Figure 1.29 VGA Connector

Image courtesy of Evan Amos

Figure 1.30 DVI Connector

Image courtesy of Evan Amos

Connecting the Power

Desktop PCs typically have a three-prong power cord that attaches the power supply at the back of the computer to the wall outlet. The computer's power supply serves two purposes: it steps down the voltage coming in from the wall outlet to the much lower voltage levels the computer requires, and it converts the power from alternating current (AC) to direct current (DC), which the computer also requires.

A notebook computer's power cord usually contains a **transformer** block. The transformer block has the same purpose as the power supply on a desktop computer: it steps down the voltage and converts the power to DC. That way, the notebook computer does not need to have a large, bulky power supply built into it.

transformer A block built into a device's power cord that converts the power from the wall outlet into a form the device can use

Connecting a Printer

Most printers connect via USB interface. However, if you are hooking up a new printer, do not connect it to the computer until you have run the printer's Setup software. Some printers do not install correctly if you allow the operating system to automatically detect them, which is what will happen if you connect the printer without running the Setup. See Topic 2 for more detailed information about setting up a printer.

Turning On a PC and Peripherals

Once all the components have been connected, it is time to turn on the computer and its peripherals. On each device, look for a button with a power symbol on it, like the symbol shown in Figure 1.31. This is the standard symbol you will find on most of the Power buttons on various peripherals, as well as on the PC itself.

Start by turning on the monitor, if it is separate, so that you will be able to see any startup messages that may appear. Next, turn on the PC. Depending on the model, there may be a Power button on the front of the case (most likely) or a rocker switch on the back. The keyboard and mouse draw their power from the PC, so you do not need to turn them on. (If your mouse is wireless, it may have an on-off switch to save its battery.) Finally, turn on any peripheral devices, such as external hard drives.

If this is the first time anyone has started up this PC, you may be guided through a one-time setup process where you are prompted to create a user name, register the operating system, and/or connect to a network. Follow the prompts as they appear.

Figure 1.31 Power Symbol

Exercise 1.8A Examining a Desktop Computer's Connections

1. On a desktop PC, look on the back to see where the keyboard and mouse are connected.

2. Trace the power cord from the wall outlet to the back of the desktop PC to see where it plugs in. Notice the fan vents near the plug on the power supply.

   A fan inside the power supply helps prevent it and the rest of the PC from overheating.

3. Trace the cord from the monitor to the back of the PC to see where it plugs in.

4. Turn off the computer if it is on.

5. Disconnect the connectors for the keyboard, mouse, monitor, and power, and examine each connector. What type of connector does the monitor use: DVI or VGA? What connectors do the keyboard and mouse use: USB or PS/2?

6. Reconnect all the connectors you disconnected, making sure to get them plugged back into the right ports.

7. Turn the computer on again.

Exercise 1.8B   Evaluating Your Computer

1. Click Start and then type **System Information**.

2. Click *System Information* when it displays at the top of the Start menu.

3. View the system summary information that displays.

   The System Information window contains a lot of information, including the OS version, the amount of RAM, and the processor type.

4. Complete the following steps to export system information to a text file:

   a. Click File on the menu bar and then click *Export* at the drop-down list.

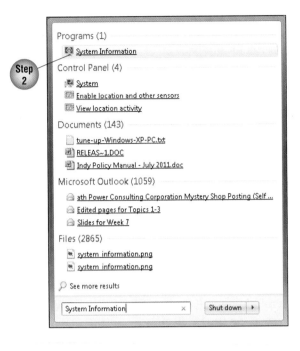

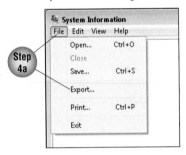

   b. At the Export As dialog box, navigate to the **Unit1Topic01** folder on your storage medium.

   c. Click in the File name text box and then type **U1T1-System**.

   d. Click Save.

5. At the System Information window, click File on the menu bar and then click *Exit* at the drop-down list.

Drilling Down

Accessing New Devices Automatically or Manually

Plug and Play is a software feature in Windows that detects new devices and installs required drivers automatically. A user may want to install devices manually instead of using the Plug and Play or other configuring software to make sure all the helper files that the device needs for its full functionality are installed. To prevent Plug and Play from automatically setting up the device, do not plug the device into the computer right away; instead, run the Setup utility for the device, and connect the device only when prompted to do so.

Lesson 1.9   Protecting a Computer

 1-1.2.1, 1-1.2.2, 1-1.2.3

A computer is a significant investment. It costs a great deal of money and is often used to store private information, so you should do what you can to keep it safe and secure. This means keeping it safe from thieves, accidents, and environmental damage. In Topic 16 you will learn more about protecting your system from online threats such as viruses and other malware. In this lesson, you will learn ways to safeguard your investment by protecting your computer from harm in its own environment.

Protecting a Computer from Theft

Companies lose millions of dollars every year because of computer theft, and millions more due to the data that gets stolen along with the computers. Individual computer owners lose their computers to theft, too, and all must consider the value of the equipment and the value of the data to determine how to best protect themselves from physical theft and loss of data (which may be lost permanently if not backed up on a separate system).

When using or transporting a notebook PC or other portable device in a public place, you should focus on keeping the individual device secured. Make sure you know exactly where your computer is at all times, and do not leave it unattended, even for a minute.

When you are in an environment where you trust the people around you, it is important to keep that environment closed to anyone else. In most business offices, for example, employees routinely leave their computers in their offices while they go to lunch or to meetings, because the office area itself is secure. Companies secure their offices by requiring their employees to use security keycards or traditional keys to access buildings and office areas, hiring professional security guards to monitor entrances, and installing alarm systems.

When you cannot be near your computer at all times and you do not trust your environment, you might want to physically secure the computer with a lock. Various types of locks, cages, and racks are available that are designed to make it difficult for someone to remove a computer from its location.

Many notebook computers have a **K-slot**, or Kensington security slot, which holds a special type of lock made by a company called Kensington. One end of the lock is inserted in the K-slot, while the other end is attached to a security cable that is bolted to the wall or a piece of heavy furniture. The locks are secured either with a key or a combination. Figure 1.32 shows an example of a security cable attached to a K-slot on a notebook PC.

K-slot A slot on a notebook computer for a security lock

Figure 1.32 Computer Lock

Protecting a Computer from Accidents and Breakage

Keeping a computer safe includes not only preventing unauthorized access to it, but also keeping it from becoming physically damaged. Computers are susceptible to several types of damage, including: trauma, short-circuiting, electrical surges, electrical sags or outages, static discharge, and crosstalk.

Trauma When a computer falls off a table, gets kicked, or is stepped on, physical damage can result. The case or screen can crack or separate, and connectors or transistors can come loose inside the computer. To guard against these accidents, make sure you set your computer on a sturdy table or in an out-of-the-way location on the floor where nobody is likely to kick it or step on it. When you travel with a computer, store it in a protective case with padding.

Short-circuiting Water is an excellent conductor of electricity, so if a computer gets wet while it is on, the electricity in the device will run through the water, short-circuiting the device by taking unexpected paths through the circuit board, and usually damaging the circuits in the process. To guard against short-circuiting, keep any liquids far away from the computer. If you are drinking a beverage as you work, place the beverage so that it will not spill on the computer or keyboard if it gets knocked over. If you are using a computer outside and it starts to rain, turn the computer off and put it away immediately.

Electrical Surges The AC power from a wall outlet does not always deliver exactly the same level of voltage. When the voltage increases suddenly for a brief period, it is called a **power surge** (or *power spike*). Power surges can damage sensitive components such as circuit boards and can weaken or even destroy a computer. A power surge can be caused by poor electrical service to your building, or by a storm or lightning strike that affects an electrical transformer near your location. To guard against power surges, connect your computer to a **surge suppressor** power strip (see Figure 1.33) rather than directly to an AC outlet. A surge suppressor contains a component called a **varistor** (variable resistor) that absorbs the excess voltage, preventing it from being passed on to the devices plugged into it.

power surge A brief period of higher than normal AC voltage; also called a *power spike*

surge suppressor A power strip that is able to absorb excess voltage so that devices plugged into it will be protected during a power surge

varistor A variable resistor; the component inside a surge suppressor that absorbs excess voltage

Figure 1.33 Surge Suppressor

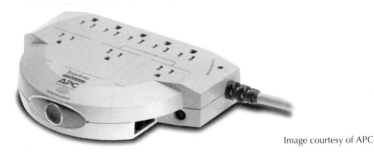

Image courtesy of APC

Electrical Sags or Outages A **power sag**, also called a *brownout*, is the opposite of a power surge—it occurs when the AC outlet does not deliver enough voltage. A sag may occur during times of high electrical usage, especially in an area where the electrical service is poor. A sag does not usually damage a computer physically, but it may cause the computer to reboot or shut down, which can lead to the loss of any unsaved data. To guard against power sags and outages, connect your computer to a battery backup unit such as an **uninterruptible power supply (UPS)**, as shown in Figure 1.34.

power sag A brief period of lower-than-normal AC voltage; also called a *brownout*

uninterruptible power supply (UPS) A battery backup unit for a computer; contains a large battery that is charged from the AC outlet and is used to power its extension outlets when AC power becomes unavailable or inadequate

electrostatic discharge (ESD) A shock that occurs when two objects of unequal electrical potential meet; also called *static electricity*

Static Discharge Computers are extremely sensitive to **electrostatic discharge**, or **ESD** (also called *static electricity*), and even a small static shock can weaken or destroy a circuit board inside a PC. To guard against this, take care not to touch the chips and transistors on the circuit boards inside your computer's case. If you must handle a circuit board, handle it only by its edges. (See the Drilling Down feature at the end of Exercise 1.9 for more information.)

Crosstalk When electricity passes through a cable, such as when it is carrying data, it generates a weak magnetic field around the cable. The opposite is true, too: magnetic fields generate electricity. Therefore, when two side-by-side cables are both carrying data, they can interfere with one another. This is

Figure 1.34 Uninterruptible Power Supply Unit (back view)

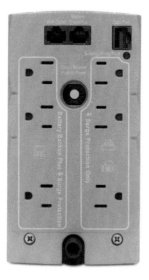

Image courtesy of APC

called **electromagnetic interference (EMI)**, or *crosstalk*. EMI does not usually harm the device, but it may corrupt the data being sent. To avoid this problem, physically separate the cables in a device when possible. For example, if your printer's cable and your monitor's cable are located next to each other, make sure they always stay a few inches apart.

Additional Damaging Factors Other factors can damage computer hardware and media and should be avoided. These include extreme temperatures; electric or magnetic fields; poorly maintained or dirty equipment, including cables, input devices, and printers; and high humidity.

electromagnetic interference (EMI) Data corruption that occurs because of the magnetic fields in two adjacent cables carrying data; also called *crosstalk*

Exercise 1.9   Evaluating Your Work Environment for Safety

Evaluate the PC that you work on most often by answering the following questions and recording your responses in an informative paragraph.

• Is the PC plugged into a surge suppressor or UPS, or directly into a wall outlet?

• Are the cords out of the way so people will not easily trip over them?

• Is the computer sitting on a sturdy table in a spot where it is not likely to be knocked off?

• Are all liquids positioned so that they will not harm the computer if spilled?

Drilling Down

Utilizing LoJack Protection

LoJack is a service that can track computer hardware through a small radio installed inside the device and, in the event that the computer is stolen, disable the computer remotely so that the data on it cannot be viewed. LoJack functionality comes pre-installed in many major brand name notebook computers, including Dell, Lenovo, HP, Toshiba, and Fujitsu. The radio-tracking unit comes free with the computer, but you must pay to install and use the software that enables it. You can learn more about this software at http://ic3.emcp.net/lojack.

continued

Surge Suppression

Recall that a surge suppressor contains a component called a varistor (variable resistor) that absorbs the excess voltage, preventing it from being passed on to the devices plugged into it. The varistor can take only a limited amount of damage before it becomes ineffective. Some surge suppressors have indicator lights that show that they are either working (green) or defective or spent (red). Others do not have lights, so you cannot tell when they are no longer able to protect. For that reason, some experts recommend replacing inexpensive surge suppressors every few years or after each major electrical storm that may have caused your power to fluctuate.

ESD Protection

Computer technicians who work inside computers ground themselves by wearing antistatic wrist straps or standing on antistatic mats. If you do not have any such equipment but have to work inside a PC for some reason, make sure to touch the metal frame of the computer case before touching any of its circuit boards. This equalizes the electrical potential between you and the computer and will prevent you from accidentally shocking the computer. You can also minimize the danger of damaging the computer with ESD by working in a high-humidity room, wearing leather or rubber-soled shoes, and wearing natural-fabric clothing.

Lesson 1.10 Performing Routine Maintenance Tasks

IC³ 1-1.2.5, 1-1.2.6, 1-1.2.7, 1-1.2.9

You can improve your PC's performance by completing some simple maintenance tasks on a regular basis. The word *maintenance* can mean several things in relation to PCs. From an end-user perspective, maintenance may include cleaning a PC's hardware, checking the cable connections to make sure they are snug, and running various utility programs in your operating system. Maintenance tasks that involve opening up the PC and working inside the case are best performed by professionals or with professional help.

Cleaning a Personal Computer

Cleaning a PC not only makes it more enjoyable to use, but it also can extend the PC's life since dirty mechanical parts wear down faster. For example, a dirty keyboard may cause certain keys to become sticky or stop functioning, while dust and hair clumps can clog up a fan vent, causing a computer to run hot and eventually overheat.

Expensive cleaning supplies are not required to clean a PC, but you should be aware of what you are using because not all chemicals are safe for use on computers. The following are some basic supplies you will need to clean your PC:

- A spray cleaning product designed for plastics, preferably one designed for computers. Products designed for computers often contain antistatic properties that regular cleaners lack. You can spray this cleaner on a cloth or paper towel and wipe down the plastic parts on the outside of the computer.

- A monitor cleaner, either in spray or towelette form, designed specifically for cleaning monitors or other electronics screens (like TVs). Do not use a glass-cleaning product that contains ammonia because that chemical can destroy the antiglare coating on some monitors.

- A can of compressed air, for blowing dust out of crevices such as those underneath keyboard keys.

- Cotton swabs and denatured isopropyl alcohol (do not use rubbing alcohol because it contains too much water). Use these for cleaning crevices such as those on the underside of the mouse.

You may also want to have a small hand-held vacuum cleaner designed for electronics. Do not use a regular vacuum cleaner. The filters in regular vacuum cleaners are not fine enough to trap the toner particles inside the vacuum, and regular vacuum cleaners can generate static electricity that can harm your computer equipment.

Cleaning a Monitor Always turn the monitor off before cleaning. That way, if any liquid gets inside a vent, the monitor can air dry without the potential for short-circuiting. Dirt and spots also show up more clearly on a dark screen. First, clean the outer casing of the monitor with a computer-cleaning solution. Spray the cleaner on the cloth, not directly on the PC, to avoid spraying into vent holes. Next, clean the glass (or the viewable area, if not glass) with a cleaner designed specifically for monitors. Do not spray the screen directly, because the liquid may drip down below the bottom edge. Instead, spray a cloth and wipe the screen.

Cleaning External Surfaces Clean the outside casing of PCs, printers, scanners, and similar equipment with a computer-cleaning spray product. Mild general purpose spray cleaner will also work. You can also use mild soapy water and a damp cloth (not soaking wet) to clean the external surfaces only—make sure to avoid any area with a vent or crack that leads inside the computer.

Cleaning Vents Dirt and hair can accumulate around air vents on a PC's case, interfering with the air flow for cooling. You can pick bits of debris out of fan vents with your fingers or with an alcohol-soaked cotton swab, or you can vacuum out the vents with a vacuum designed for electronics.

Cleaning a Keyboard Since it is always at the forefront of computer activity, the keyboard can get very dirty. Although instruction manuals and PC technicians may remind people to keep their computing areas clean, more often than not people neglect to do this. They may type with unwashed hands, eat, drink, or allow their pets near their computers. All this activity leaves dirt, oil, and other residue on the keyboard. Debris can accumulate under the keys, causing them to stop functioning, and the oils and acids from people's fingers can wear away the letters on the keys until they are no longer readable.

To clean the keyboard, first turn off the PC. The keyboard does not need to be unplugged from the PC. Turn the keyboard upside down and shake it to remove any loose debris, or hold it over a trash can and spray beneath the keys with compressed air. What falls out—and the amount of it—is often surprising!

Use a cloth dampened with a spray computer-cleaning solution or a special computer-cleaning towelette to clean all visible surfaces. Get down between the cracks with a cotton swab or a bit of folded paper towel. Removing the keys is not recommended because it can be difficult to get them back on again. If you have access to one, a small handheld vacuum designed for electronics can be useful in removing debris from under the keys.

Cleaning a Mouse The mouse, like the keyboard, gets very dirty because it is constantly being handled. In addition, the ball on a mechanical mouse picks up dirt and lint and moves it inside the mouse as it rolls. As a result, the rollers and sensors on a mechanical mouse can become encrusted with dirt rather quickly, causing the mouse to malfunction. Dirt is less likely to get inside an optical mouse, but dust and hair can still accumulate at the opening where the light shines through. When a mouse is dirty, it may become more difficult to roll, the on-screen pointer may jump or stutter, or it may become unresponsive altogether.

To clean a mouse, first wipe the outside with mild soapy water or a computer-cleaning product. Once the outside is clean, turn the mouse upside down. If it is an optical mouse, use a cotton swab dipped in denatured alcohol to clean out the hollow area where the light shines through. (Alcohol dries more quickly than water, so it is better to use when cleaning the internal areas of electronics.)

If it is a mechanical mouse, rotate the plastic plate that holds the ball in place. Turn the mouse over again, and the ball and plate should fall into your hand. Clean inside the ball's chamber with alcohol on a cotton swab. Clean the ball itself with mild soapy water and dry it thoroughly. Do not use alcohol on a rubber ball because it dries the rubber and makes it brittle.

Exercise 1.10   Cleaning a Keyboard

1. Gather the following cleaning supplies:

   - A mild spray cleaner, preferably one designed for electronics

   - Paper towels

2. Turn off your computer.

3. Pick up your keyboard, hold it upside-down over a trash can, and gently shake it from side to side to remove any loose debris.

4. Put the keyboard back on your desk. Spray a small amount of the cleaner on a paper towel.

5. Thoroughly clean the tops of each key on the keyboard.

6. Fold a clean paper towel several times, and spray a small amount of cleaner on the folded edge.

7. Using the folded edge, clean between the keys on the keyboard.

 Drilling Down

Removing Liquids from a Keyboard

If you spill liquid on a keyboard, immediately unplug the keyboard from the PC (or turn off the PC if the keyboard is built in) and turn the keyboard upside down. Shake the keyboard to release as much of the liquid as possible, and let it dry for at least 48 hours. If the liquid was plain water, the keyboard will probably be fine after it dries. But if the liquid contained sugar, the keyboard may never be completely clean again.

Fixing Common Printer Problems

If an inkjet printer goes unused for an extended period of time, the ink can dry inside the jets and clog them. To fix this, you can run a software-based cleaning utility by pressing certain buttons on the printer (refer to the printer's manual). You can also start the cleaning utility from your operating system, at the printer's Properties dialog box. The exact steps depend on the printer and the software that came with it.

Lesson 1.11   Troubleshooting Common Hardware Problems

 1-1.1.8, 1-1.2.4, 1-1.2.6, 1-1.2.8, 1-1.2.9

When your computer is not working properly, you might be able to fix it without calling a professional. Many common hardware-related problems can be fixed by using a few simple troubleshooting methods. In this lesson, you will learn some basic guidelines for troubleshooting a computer problem. You will also be introduced to some of the more common problems and their solutions.

Troubleshooting a Computer Problem

In most modern computer systems, hardware and software are so closely related that it can be difficult to determine the root cause of an issue: the hardware, the operating system, or an application. Even when a piece of hardware stops working, the root problem could still be with the software. An effective troubleshooting plan is to first check the hardware, then check the operating system, and, finally, check the applications. The following is a general process for troubleshooting a problem with a piece of hardware:

1. **Is there power?** If the device is plugged into a wall outlet or surge suppressor, make certain it is receiving power from that outlet. If it runs on batteries, check that the batteries are charged.

2. **Is it powered on?** If the device has an on/off switch, make sure it is turned on.

3. **Is there damage?** Look for any physical damage to the hardware that might be causing it to malfunction. For example, check to see if the screen or case is cracked.

4. **Is it connected?** Make sure the device is properly connected to the computer. A loose cable connector can make a device seem like it is not working, when it is actually not receiving commands.

5. **Are any lights on?** Some devices have lights that indicate that they are powered on and working properly. Check for lights, codes, or messages on the device that may indicate the problem.

6. **Do any error messages display?** Check for error messages in the operating system that relate to the device.

7. **Is the driver installed?** A device driver is a file that tells Windows how to interact with a particular piece of hardware. Plug and Play can detect some devices and install drivers for them automatically, but it does not work for all devices. Windows requires drivers for most hardware. If you have not yet installed a driver for the device, run the Setup program that came with the device.

8. **Does windows recognize the device?** Look in Device Manager to find out if Windows recognizes the device. To run Device Manager, click Start and type the word *Device*. When you see Device Manager at the top of the Start menu, click it to run it. Locate the device on the list of installed hardware and check its status using the following key:

    - A yellow circle and exclamation point means a problem, such as a bad driver.

    - A down-pointing arrow means the device is disabled.

    - A question mark means Windows cannot identify the device.

Quick Steps

Check a Device in Device Manager

1. Click Start.
2. Type *Device*.
3. Click *Device Manager*.
4. Scan for problems.
5. Double-click problems to review details.

9. **Does the device work in other applications?** If the device works in other applications on your computer, the problem is likely the application and not the device. For example, a scanner might be able to scan pictures in one graphics program but not another.

10. **What does the manufacturer have to say?** Check the tech support forums for the device manufacturer's website for ideas. If you come up with no solution, look into returning or replacing the device because it may be defective. After you find the solution, make sure you document the problem, letting everyone else who uses the computer know the problem you had and the solution you found. You should also make a plan for avoiding similar problems in the future if possible.

Identifying Common Hardware Problems

Table 1.4 lists some common hardware problems and their solutions.

Table 1.4 Common Hardware Problems

Problem	Possible Solution
Wireless device does not work	Most wireless keyboards and mice have to be synched with the wireless transponder that comes with them. This usually involves pressing a button on the device. Check the documentation for the device to find out what to do. Wireless devices also usually require batteries.

continued

Problem	Possible Solution
Wireless network adapter on notebook does not work	Some notebook computers have an on/off button or switch for the built-in wireless adapter somewhere along one side. If you accidentally hit that, the adapter may turn off. Press it again to turn the adapter back on.
No image on monitor	Make sure the PC has power (look for a power light on it) and make sure the monitor is connected firmly to the PC and an AC outlet. Press the Power button on the monitor if no lights appear on the monitor. If there is an amber light, it means the monitor is on but is not receiving a signal from the computer. If there is a green light, the signal from the computer is coming through; the computer is perhaps not sending an image (for example, if it is locked up).
Mouse pointer is erratic	The pointing device (mouse, trackball, etc.) is dirty, or the driver for the mouse or the display adapter is defective or conflicting with something.
Hard disk error / Failed or "crashed" hard drive	If an error message indicates the hard disk cannot be read or the hard drive has crashed, it may have failed physically, or it may be infected with a virus or the software may be malfunctioning. Consult a computer professional to help troubleshoot and to find out if any data can be recovered.
Stripes on inkjet printout	If an inkjet printer goes unused for an extended period of time, the ink can dry inside the jets and clog them. To fix this, you can run a software-based cleaning utility by pressing certain buttons on the printer (refer to the printer's manual). You can also start the cleaning utility from your operating system, at the printer's properties dialog box.
Paper jams in printer	When paper jams in the printer, you may need to open up the printer and remove the jammed paper. If paper continually jams, the paper may be damp due to high humidity or you may need to remove paper debris from inside the printer.
Ink or toner low or out	Printers will usually let you know when ink or toner is low by displaying an error message in the printer's display or in Windows; have spare cartridges ready, and change them following the printer manual's instructions.
Smeared ink or toner	Smeared ink on an inkjet printer may mean roller problems inside or a defective ink cartridge; smeared ink on a laser printer usually results from a bad fuser or a dirty corona wire; consult the printer's manual for detailed troubleshooting help.
Keyboard or mouse non-functional	Check all connecting wires and then try restarting the PC. Try to re-run the Setup program if possible. If the keyboard or mouse still does not work, buy a replacement and swap the old one for the new.

Exercise 1.11   Checking a Computer's Status

1. With your computer running, look for indicators that show it is on. For example, a Power light may be visible, the Power button may be glowing, or you may hear fans spinning.

2. If you have a monitor that is separate from your computer, look for a light on the monitor that indicates it is on. Shut down your computer (click Start, then click *Shut down*) and notice that the light on the monitor changes to amber. Restart the computer.

3. Check to make sure the keyboard is working. One way to do this is to press the F1 key; this opens the Help system in Windows.

4. Check to make sure the mouse is working by moving the mouse and looking for the on-screen pointer.

Running System Maintenance Utilities

Your computer's operating system will likely contain several built-in utilities that you can use to maintain your computer and ensure that it runs efficiently (see Table 1.5). You can access all of these utilities from the properties dialog box for the disk drive, as shown in Figure 1.35.

Experts vary in their opinions of how often these utilities should be run. If your computer is part of a work or school system, a system administrator may tell you how often you should run these utilities and may even schedule them to automatically run at certain intervals without your interaction.

Quick Steps

Open the Properties Dialog Box for a Drive

1. Click Start.
2. Click *Computer*.
3. Right-click hard disk drive.
4. Click *Properties*.

Figure 1.35 **Disk Drive Properties Dialog Box**

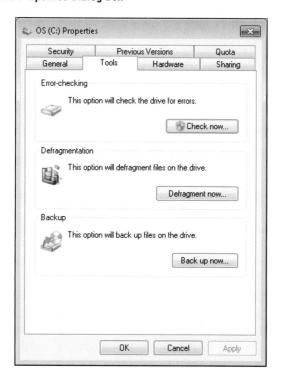

Table 1.5 **Main Windows Utilities and Their Functions**

Utility	Description	When to Run	How to Run
Check Disk	Checks the hard disk's file system for storage errors that could cause file corruption or inability to read or write files	When you suspect a disk error (for example, if you received an error message about reading or writing to the disk)	At the drive's Properties dialog box, click the Tools tab, click the Check now button, click Start and then allow the disk check to complete. You may need to schedule a disk check, which requires the computer to restart.

continued

Utility	Description	When to Run	How to Run
Disk Defragmenter	Relocates the parts of fragmented files to a single physical location, improving the hard disk's access time	When the disk fragmentation is over 10% or according to the schedule recommended by your school or workplace; this utility includes an automatic self-scheduler	At the drive's Properties dialog box, click the Tools tab, click the Defragment now button, select the hard drive from the list, and then click *Analyze Disk*. Based on the analysis, click Defragment disk or click Close.
Windows Backup	Backs up the files you specify to another location	Every day if you have critical files to protect; otherwise weekly or according to the schedule recommended by your school or workplace	At the drive's Properties dialog box, click the Tools tab and then click the Back up now button. Click Back up now to run an existing backup specification, or click Change settings to choose what, when, and how to back up.
Disk Cleanup	Identifies files that may be unneeded, such as temporary files, and helps you delete them to save disk space	When your hard disk is nearly full and you need to free up space. A nearly full hard disk can result in performance slowdown.	At the drive's Properties dialog box, click the General tab, click Disk Cleanup, click check boxes to include or exclude categories, click OK, and then click Delete Files.

Delving Deeper

 1-1.1.7, 1-1.2.6, 1-1.2.7

Maintenance Requiring Professional Help

Some maintenance you can perform on your own, such as defragmenting hard drives, clearing cookies, deleting temporary files, replacing printer cartridges, swapping broken keyboards and mice with working devices, switching monitors or other peripherals, and even upgrading memory. However, other types of computer maintenance are beyond the scope of an ordinary end user's skills. For example, special training is required to upgrade or replace an internal hard drive or circuit board, add memory, or upgrade the CPU. If you need to perform maintenance or repair inside a computer, consult someone who is trained to work inside a computer, such as an A+ certified repair technician. Technicians are available at local repair shops and service centers; if your computer is owned by your school or business, there may be a technician on staff who can help you.

Identifying Additional Computer Devices

Not every computing task requires a PC. Many other computer devices are also available for specialized tasks. For example, scientific calculators perform complex math operations, portable music and media players like the iPod and Walkman store and transport media files, and eBook readers such as the Kindle and Nook enable you to read books and magazines on-the-go. There are also many other small computers built into devices that you might not normally associate with computers, such as vehicles, weather prediction and reporting systems, medical equipment, kitchen and bathroom appliances, and point-of-sale systems in stores and restaurants. Businesses and manufacturing centers also employ specialty computer devices extensively. In factories, computer-controlled industrial robots are used in assembly lines to do a variety of repetitive tasks such as soldering, welding, and assembling parts, significantly increasing production efficiency.

TOPIC SUMMARY

- Computers process information digitally, using the binary digits of 0 and 1. When a computer works with an analog device, it converts the analog data to digital format.

- All computing consists of input, processing, and output. A user inputs data with an input device, such as a keyboard or a mouse, and the data is output to an output device, such as a monitor or a printer.

- Specialized input devices such as scanners, game controllers, and digital cameras enable users to input data in alternate ways.

- Outside a computer are buttons, indicator lights, externally accessible drives, fan vents, and ports for connecting external devices.

- Inside a PC are a motherboard, memory, a CPU, one or more hard disk drives, a power supply, and expansion boards.

- Many different types of computers are available, including desktop PCs, notebook PCs, netbooks, tablets, gaming consoles, and smartphones.

- A CPU takes in data and instructions, performs calculations, and produces the result of those calculations. The outside of a CPU is a ceramic shell. Inside the shell is a thin wafer of silicon containing millions of transistors.

- CPU speed is measured in gigahertz (billions of hertz). Another way of evaluating CPU performance is the number of operations per second it can perform (MIPS, or millions of operations per second).

- Some CPUs have multiple CPU cores in a single chip. For example, dual-core or quad-core CPUs are available.

- A cache is a temporary storage area that holds data that may be needed soon; caches in CPUs increase their performance.

- Memory is data storage that uses on/off states on a chip to record patterns of binary data. Memory is used in computers in several ways. For example, read-only memory (ROM) is used to store startup instructions on the motherboard.

- Dynamic random access memory (DRAM) or Dynamic RAM is used as the primary memory on the motherboard. DRAM loses its contents if it is not constantly refreshed. Static RAM (SRAM) holds its contents without constant refreshing.

- RAM and storage are both measured in bytes. A byte is 8 bits of data. A thousand bytes is a kilobyte. A thousand kilobytes is a megabyte. A thousand megabytes is a gigabyte. A thousand gigabytes is a terabyte. A thousand terabytes is a petabyte.

- Hard drives can be either mechanical (with spinning platters) or solid state (based on flash RAM).

- Flash RAM is static RAM that can be written and erased electrically. You can store data using flash RAM on USB flash drives, flash memory cards, or solid state hard disks.

- An optical disc (such as a CD, DVD, or Blu-Ray) stores data in patterns of more or less reflectivity.

- Input devices include keyboards, mice, trackballs, touchpads, cameras, digital cameras, and gaming controllers. An input device can be mechanical (with moving parts) or optical (using a light sensor) or a combination of the two. Input devices can connect to a PC using a cable or a wireless signal.

- Output devices include monitors, projectors, and printers. An LCD monitor is a flat screen, lightweight monitor that uses liquid crystals to create an image. A CRT monitor is a large boxy monitor that uses phosphors and electron guns to create an image.

- The most common printer types are inkjet (liquid ink) and laser (powdered toner). When considering printers, look at not only the initial cost, but the total cost of ownership, including the cost per page of the toner or ink.

- When deciding how to purchase a computer, consider cost, brands, discounts, taxes, shipping, and return policies.

- When considering which computer to buy, consider whether you want a desktop or portable, what CPU you want, how much RAM, what type and capacity of hard drive, what monitor, and what optical drive.

- When setting up a computer, most devices connect through a USB port, including modern keyboards and mice. A monitor connects with a VGA or DVI connector.

- To reduce the risk of computer theft, make sure you always know where your computer is when in public. In your home or office, either keep the area secure or secure the computer to the desk or other heavy item.

- To prevent electrical damage to a PC, use a surge suppressor. A UPS combines surge suppression and battery backup.

- Electrostatic discharge (ESD) is static electricity; you can accidentally shock sensitive components inside a PC if you do not ground yourself before touching circuit boards. Electromagnetic interference (EMI) is data corruption between adjacent cables carrying data.

- To clean the outside of a PC, use a cleaner designed for electronics, or mild soap and water with a barely-damp cloth. To clean a monitor, use monitor cleaner, not regular glass cleaner.

- Mice and keyboards can get dirty, and may not work right if they get encrusted with debris. Clean them with compressed air, or use alcohol-dipped swabs or dampened paper towels to clean keyboard keys.

- Maintenance utilities in Windows 7 include Check Disk, Disk Defragmenter, Windows Backup, and Disk Cleanup. All of these can be accessed from a disk drive's properties dialog box.

- To troubleshoot computer problems, first check that the device is receiving power and is snugly connected. Then check for error messages, make sure a driver is installed, and check Device Manager in Windows for the device's status.

Key Terms

alternating current (AC), p. 8

analog, p. 4

annualized failure rate (AFR), p. 22

binary, p. 5

binary processing, p. 13

bit, p. 5

byte, p. 5

cache, p. 15

card reader, p. 20

cathode ray tube (CRT), p. 29

central processing unit (CPU), p. 8

charge-coupled device (CCD), p. 26

decimal, p. 5

desktop computer, p. 9

digital, p. 5

digital camera, p. 27

digital projector, p. 30

Digital Video Interface (DVI), p. 36

direct current (DC), p. 8

dots per inch (DPI), p. 32

dynamic memory, p. 15

dynamic RAM (DRAM), p. 16

electromagnetic interference (EMI), p. 41

electrostatic discharge (ESD), p. 40

expansion board, p. 8

flash drive, p. 19

flash memory card, p. 20

flash RAM, p. 19

game controller, p. 26

gaming console, p. 12

gigabyte (GB), p. 16

gigahertz (GHz), p. 14

hard disk drive, p. 8

hertz, p. 14

hexadecimal, p. 5

inkjet printer, p. 31

input, p. 6

input device, p. 23

K-slot, p. 39

land, p. 21

laser printer, p. 32

liquid crystal display (LCD), p. 29

mean time between failures (MTBF), p. 22

mechanical device, p. 25

megabyte (MB), p. 16

megahertz (MHz), p. 14

memory, p. 15

millions of instructions per second (MIPS), p. 14

monitor, p. 29

motherboard, p. 8

mouse, p. 24

multicore, p. 14

netbook computer, p. 10

notebook computer, p. 10

optical device, p. 25

optical disc, p. 20

output, p. 6

output device, p. 29

peripherals, p. 33

personal computer (PC), p. 4

continued

pit, p. 21

pointing device, p. 24

port, p. 7

power sag, p. 40

power supply, p. 8

power surge, p. 40

printer, p. 31

PS/2 (mini-DIN), p. 35

random access memory
    (RAM), p. 15

read-only memory (ROM), p. 15

revolutions per minute
    (RPM), p. 19

scanner, p. 26

smartphone, p. 11

solid state, p. 19

static memory, p. 15

static RAM (SRAM), p. 15

surge suppressor, p. 40

tablet PC, p. 11

Total Cost of Ownership
    (TCO), p. 32

touchpad, p. 24

trackball, p. 24

transformer, p. 37

transistor, p. 13

uninterruptible power supply
    (UPS), p. 40

universal serial bus (USB), p. 15

varistor, p. 40

Video Graphics Array (VGA), p. 36

wired device, p. 25

wireless device, p. 25

KEY POINTS REVIEW

Identification

Part 1 Match the terms to the callouts in Figure 1.36.

1. _____ case

2. _____ DVD drive

3. _____ keyboard

4. _____ monitor

5. _____ mouse

Figure 1.36 Identification Figure

Image courtesy of Lenovo

Part 2 Match the terms to the callouts in Figure 1.37.

1. _____ ports

2. _____ keyboard

3. _____ monitor

4. _____ touchpad

Figure 1.37 Identification Figure

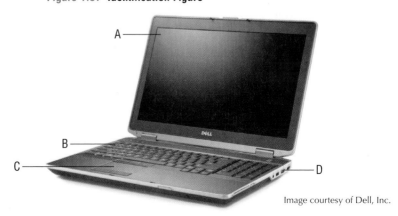

Image courtesy of Dell, Inc.

Completion

In the space provided at the left, indicate the correct term, command, or option.

1. _____ What is a CPU?

2. _____ What term describes billions of bytes?

3. _____ What device in a PC consists of a stack of metal platters for storing data?

4. _____ How is CPU speed measured?

5. _____ What does DRAM stand for?

6. _____ What does a solid state drive use to hold data?

7. _____ What kind of discs store data in patterns of greater or lesser reflectivity?

8. _____ What type of device is either LCD or CRT?

9. _____ What type of connector do most keyboards and mice use?

10. _____ List two types of monitor connectors.

11. _____ What does a UPS provide to a computer system?

12. _____ What is ESD?

13. _____ What does it mean if the status light on a monitor is amber?

14. _____ What type of memory keeps its data without being powered?

15. _____ What component may have multiple cores?

16. _____ List three input devices.

17. _____ List two types of printers.

Multiple Choice

For each of the following items, choose the option that best completes the sentence or answers the question.

1. What activity does a CPU perform?
   A. input
   B. processing
   C. output
   D. storage

2. What numbering system has 10 digits?
   A. binary
   B. octal
   C. decimal
   D. hexadecimal

3. Where do you plug in a keyboard or mouse on a PC?
   A. port
   B. slot
   C. socket
   D. bay

4. What type of computer has a separate monitor, keyboard, and mouse?
   A. notebook
   B. desktop
   C. tablet
   D. smartphone

5. What component has a speed measured in GHz?
   A. hard disk
   B. mouse
   C. monitor
   D. CPU

6. What component has a capacity measured in GB?
   A. hard disk
   B. mouse
   C. monitor
   D. keyboard

7. What type of memory can be written and rewritten on the device in which it is installed?
   A. RAM
   B. CPU
   C. ROM
   D. BIOS

8. How does a solid state hard drive store data?
   A. spinning metal platters
   B. flash RAM
   C. a laser
   D. ROM

9. Which of these would *not* affect a computer's performance?
   A. CPU speed
   B. amount of RAM
   C. hard disk access time
   D. monitor size

10. What does a surge suppressor protect against?
    A. EMI
    B. data corruption
    C. electrical spikes
    D. brownouts

Matching

Match each of the following definitions with the correct term, command, or option.

1. _____ Drive that reads and writes data on reflective discs with a laser
2. _____ Utility in Windows that lists the status of each piece of hardware
3. _____ Utility in Windows that recommends files for deletion
4. _____ Magnetic interference from adjacent cables carrying data
5. _____ Static electricity
6. _____ Condition where the AC outlet does not deliver enough voltage
7. _____ A battery backup and surge suppressor
8. _____ The type of power that comes from a wall outlet
9. _____ A digital connection between a monitor and a computer
10. _____ A device that is not a part of the main computer, such as a printer or projector

A. EMI
B. Disk Cleanup
C. UPS
D. Peripheral
E. Device Manager
F. ESD
G. Sag
H. AC
I. DVI
J. Optical

SKILLS REVIEW

Review 1.1 Performing Number Conversions

1. Open the Calculator application and convert the following numbers from decimal to binary:
   a. 10
   b. 20
   c. 30
   d. 50

2. Convert the following numbers from binary to decimal:
   a. 1011
   b. 111
   c. 10101

3. Close the Calculator window.

Review 1.2 Shopping for a Computer

Suppose you are shopping for a notebook computer for a relative. Your relative wants a screen between 15 inches and 16 inches (diagonal), at least 4GB of RAM, Windows 7, and a Blu-Ray drive.

1. Go to www.hp.com (or some other site if directed by your instructor) and find three computers that meet the criteria. Or, if you do not have Internet access, go to a library or bookstore and look at the ads in a computer magazine.
2. Print or copy information on two computers you think are the best value, analyze both options, and then write a paragraph explaining which you would choose and why.

Review 1.3 Checking a PC for Safety Issues

On a blank piece of paper, write the answers to the following questions.

1. Is your PC protected against power surges? If so, what type of device is in use? If not, what type of device needs to be installed?
2. Is your PC protected against theft? If so, what type of method or device is in use? If not, what would you suggest?
3. Is your PC likely to be damaged in its current location? Why or why not?

SKILLS ASSESSMENT

Assessment 1.1 Getting Hardware Information

1. Click Start and then type **System Information**.
2. When *System Information* displays at the top of the Start menu, click *System Information*.
3. In the System Information dialog box, gather the following information and record the information on a blank sheet of paper:
   - OS name
   - Version
   - System name
   - System manufacturer
   - System model
   - System type
   - Processor
   - BIOS version/date
   - User name
   - Installed physical memory
4. Write your name at the top of the page and submit it to your instructor.

Assessment 1.2 Choosing a Storage Device

Suppose you have a job where you need to back up 1 GB of data every day. You need to choose the best storage device for this job.

1. Make a list of the possible external storage devices that are available for your PC. For example:
   - Writeable CD drive
   - Writeable DVD drive
   - Flash memory drive
   - Memory card reader and memory card
   - External hard disk drive
2. Of the available storage devices, narrow down the list to the two best choices.
3. On a blank piece of paper, write down the two best choices of storage devices.
4. Write a paragraph explaining which one you would choose to back up your work and why.
5. Write your name at the top of the page and submit it to your instructor.

Assessment 1.3 Assessing PC Performance

1. Click Start, and then type **Windows Experience**. When you see *Check the Windows Experience Index* at the top of the Start menu, click it to open that section of the Control Panel.
2. Click the <u>Re-run the assessment</u> hyperlink located in the lower right corner of the window and wait for the Windows Experience Index to be recalculated to ensure it is current.
3. Click the <u>View and print detailed performance and system information</u> hyperlink.
4. In the Performance Information and Tools window, click *Print this page*.
5. In the Print dialog box, click the desired printer if the printer is not already selected, and then click the Print button.
6. Write your name at the top of the printout and submit it to your instructor.
7. Close all open windows.

Assessment 1.4 Finding Support Information Online

1. Open a web browser, and use the Internet to locate the manufacturer's website for your computer. For tips on searching for information online, refer to Topic 14 "Using a Web Browser."
2. At that site, navigate to the Support section.
3. Locate a manual for your computer. *Hint: The manual may be called User Guide, Setup Guide, Service Manual, or some other name.*
4. Print the first page of the manual on your default printer. Write your name on the printout and submit it to your instructor.
5. Close the web browser.

Assessment 1.5 Learning More about Input Devices

1. Open a web browser, and use the Internet to find an input device that was not mentioned in this chapter. For example, it could be an input device used in a certain profession, or a device that helps people with disabilities use a computer. If you need help using a web browser or searching for information online, refer to Topic 14.
2. Write an explanation of the device, including who would use it and for what purpose.
3. Write your name at the top of the paper and submit it to your instructor.

Assessment 1.6 Identifying the Ports on Your Computer

1. Examine the outside of computer to find out what ports (connectors) it has on it.
2. On a blank sheet of paper, make a list of the connectors you find, and give an example of a device that would connect to each one. Some ports you learned about in this chapter; others were not covered. If you do not know what a certain port is, look it up in your computer's user manual (found in Assessment 1.4) or ask a classmate to help you identify it.
3. Write your name on the paper and submit it to your instructor.

CRITICAL THINKING

Selecting a Device

Suppose an elderly relative, who has never owned a computer before, is interested in buying a device that will enable her to read online magazines and get email. She has poor vision, and has difficulty using devices that have small buttons. She is not interested in running complex games or applications, and would like something that she could move between rooms in her house without asking anyone for help.

Evaluate your relative's situation and write a one-page paper recommending the type of computing device that is best suited for the situation. In your paper, explain why you chose that device and why the other types of devices you learned about in this chapter would not be a good fit.

TEAM PROJECT

Troubleshooting Common Computer Problems

1. In teams of two or three students, sabotage one of the computer workstations in your classroom by doing two of the following actions:
   - Unplug the power cord from the computer
   - Turn off the power to the surge suppressor
   - Turn off the monitor
   - Unplug the monitor from the computer
   - Unplug the mouse from the computer
   - Unplug the keyboard from the computer
   - Turn the brightness all the way down on the monitor
   - Take the batteries out of a wireless keyboard or mouse
2. As a team, write a one-paragraph summary of what you did to sabotage the computer.
3. Switch computers with another team, and troubleshoot and fix the problem.
4. As a team, write a one-paragraph summary of what you found to be wrong and how you fixed it.
5. Submit both paragraphs to your instructor.

Discussion Questions

1. How might components become unplugged from a computer?
2. If you were trying to help someone troubleshoot over the phone, what would you tell them to check first? Why?

Topic 2

Using an Operating System

Performance Objectives

Upon successful completion of Topic 2, you will be able to:

- Differentiate between available operating systems
- Identify key elements of Windows 7
- Start up and shut down a Windows 7 PC
- Run programs
- Manage files and folders
- Troubleshoot common problems
- Customize the Windows environment
- Print documents and manage printers
- Use the Windows help system

STUDENT RESOURCES

Before beginning this topic, copy to your storage medium the **Unit1Topic02** subfolder from the *Computer and Internet Essentials: Preparing for IC³* Internet Resource Center. Make this the active folder.

Although this topic does not contain any data files needed to complete topic work, the Internet Resource Center contains model answers in PDF format for each of the applicable exercises in this topic. Use these files to check your work. The preface of your textbook provides instructions for accessing these files.

Topic Overview

In Topic 1, you learned about computer hardware, but hardware is only half of the computing story. Software provides the instructions to the computer by applying algorithms (rules) to process data.

The **operating system (OS)** is the software that performs housekeeping tasks that keep the computer running and provides an interface between the user and the hardware. It also starts a computer and keeps it running while you work, manages applications and files, handles input and output requests, and keeps track of memory and CPU operations.

> **operating system (OS)** Software that performs housekeeping tasks that keep the computer running; provides an interface between the user and the hardware

You probably interact with multiple operating systems every day without realizing it. For example, the Automatic Teller Machine (ATM) at your local bank branch has its own operating system, as do the computerized map kiosks at the mall, cell phones, cars, and the pumps at your local gas station. Those devices are not personal computers, but they are computers, and every computer has an operating system.

The operating system and its settings determine what you, as a user, can do with your personal computer (PC). For example, in a business, a system administrator might configure the operating system on all computers so that employees cannot install software on their company PCs, download files, or change system settings. While this might seem extreme, it does prevent a lot of problems that the system administrator would otherwise have to fix, sometimes on hundreds of PCs.

In this topic, you will learn the basics of using the Microsoft Windows 7 operating system. You will learn how Windows works, how to use the Windows interface, how to run programs and manage files, and how to troubleshoot common Windows problems.

Lesson 2.1 Understanding Operating Systems

IC³ 1-2.1.1, 1-2.1.2, 1-3.1.1, 1-3.1.2, 1-3.1.3, 1-3.1.4

In this lesson, you will learn the purpose of an operating system, the types of operating systems available, and the capabilities and limitations that operating systems possess.

What Is an Operating System?

Recall that an operating system (OS) is software that performs housekeeping tasks that keep the PC running and provides an interface between the user and the hardware. Microsoft Windows is the most popular operating system, but many other operating systems are available such as UNIX, Linux, and Mac OS X.

Operating systems provide the following four functions:

User Interface The OS provides a way for the user to communicate with the computer, including entering commands, inputting data, and receiving output or feedback.

File Management The OS reads and maintains the file systems on the disk drives, and can create, retrieve, store, move, and delete files and folders.

Application Management The OS enables users to install, run, and uninstall applications.

Hardware Management The OS keeps track of what hardware is installed and makes the hardware available to applications.

application Software that enables the user to perform a useful task such as creating a document or playing a game

An operating system does not produce documents or check email or perform research. All those things and more are accomplished using applications. An **application** is a software program that performs specific tasks for the user by providing a customized user interface. The customized interface allows for related tasks to be completed by the user, such as writing a letter, playing a game, or surfing the Web. Examples of applications include Microsoft Word, Solitaire, and Internet Explorer.

Types of Operating Systems

Operating systems can be distinguished from one another in several ways: by the type of user interface, by the number of simultaneous users the OS can support, and by the number of simultaneous tasks the OS can perform.

shell A user interface for an operating system

command prompt A user interface based on typing text commands

graphical user interface (GUI) An operating system interface that relies on pictures and a pointing device for user interaction

Type of User Interface The user interface is also called the **shell**. A shell can be a graphical or a command-line interface. With a command-line interface, users type text commands at a **command prompt** (a user interface based on typing commands). Figure 2.1 shows Bash, a type of UNIX interface. Mouse usage is not supported in a command-line interface, although some applications run from that interface might use a mouse. No menus or pictures display to help you choose commands; users must remember the names and syntax of the commands and manually type them.

Most operating systems, including Windows and the Macintosh OS, provide a graphical user interface (GUI). A **graphical user interface (GUI)** is a picture-based interface that enables the user to issue commands, run programs, and manage files by using a combination of keyboard and mouse input. Users can select commands from menus and click buttons to issue commands. Figure 2.2 shows the Windows desktop, which is a GUI.

Figure 2.1 **Command-line Interface** This user interface requires commands to be typed.

```
mars@marsmain ~ $ pwd
/home/mars
mars@marsmain ~ $ cd /usr/portage/app-shells/bash
mars@marsmain /usr/portage/app-shells/bash $ ls -al
total 130
drwxr-xr-x   3 portage portage  1024 Jul 25 10:06 .
drwxr-xr-x  33 portage portage  1024 Aug  7 22:39 ..
-rw-r--r--   1 root    root    35808 Jul 25 10:06 ChangeLog
-rw-r--r--   1 root    root    27002 Jul 25 10:06 Manifest
-rw-r--r--   1 portage portage  4645 Mar 23 21:37 bash-3.1_p17.ebuild
-rw-r--r--   1 portage portage  5977 Mar 23 21:37 bash-3.2_p39.ebuild
-rw-r--r--   1 portage portage  6151 Apr  5 14:37 bash-3.2_p48-r1.ebuild
-rw-r--r--   1 portage portage  5988 Mar 23 21:37 bash-3.2_p48.ebuild
-rw-r--r--   1 portage portage  5643 Apr  5 14:37 bash-4.0_p10-r1.ebuild
-rw-r--r--   1 portage portage  6230 Apr  5 14:37 bash-4.0_p10.ebuild
-rw-r--r--   1 portage portage  5648 Apr 14 05:52 bash-4.0_p17-r1.ebuild
-rw-r--r--   1 portage portage  5532 Apr  8 10:21 bash-4.0_p17.ebuild
-rw-r--r--   1 portage portage  5660 May 30 03:35 bash-4.0_p24.ebuild
-rw-r--r--   1 root    root     5660 Jul 25 09:43 bash-4.0_p28.ebuild
drwxr-xr-x   2 portage portage  2048 May 30 03:35 files
-rw-r--r--   1 portage portage   468 Feb  9 04:35 metadata.xml
mars@marsmain /usr/portage/app-shells/bash $ cat metadata.xml
<?xml version="1.0" encoding="UTF-8"?>
<!DOCTYPE pkgmetadata SYSTEM "http://www.gentoo.org/dtd/metadata.dtd">
<pkgmetadata>
<herd>base-system</herd>
<use>
  <flag name='bashlogger'>Log ALL commands typed into bash; should ONLY be
    used in restricted environments such as honeypots</flag>
  <flag name='net'>Enable /dev/tcp/host/port redirection</flag>
  <flag name='plugins'>Add support for loading builtins at runtime via
    'enable'</flag>
```

Figure 2.2 **Windows Desktop** The Windows desktop is an example of a graphical user interface (GUI).

Number of Users Operating systems designed for individual personal computers, such as Windows, typically support only one user at a time. Since the computer has only one keyboard, mouse, and monitor, only one person can use the computer at a time, so allowing several people to control it at once is not necessary.

Operating systems designed for servers and multiuser workstations, on the other hand, can support several users at once. The extra users log in through the network and share the PC's processing capabilities remotely. Operating systems that allow for multiple users include UNIX and Windows Server.

Number of Tasks Early operating systems like MS-DOS could run only one program at a time. All operating systems available today can multitask, enabling users to run multiple programs simultaneously.

Some systems with multiple CPUs (central processing units) or multicore CPUs can literally run two processes simultaneously. In addition, operating systems can also multitask by time-slicing; first one application runs for a few milliseconds, then another runs, with the applications switching off so quickly that it appears to the user that they are running simultaneously.

Common Operating Systems

The operating system you choose helps determine the system's capabilities and limitations. Some types of PCs support only one operating system. For example, older Macintosh computers could run only the Macintosh OS. Other types of PCs enable you to install a choice of operating systems. For example, a PC that runs Microsoft Windows could also run Linux.

For desktop PCs, Microsoft Windows is the overwhelming best seller. An example of Microsoft Windows appeared in Figure 2.2. The current version is Microsoft Windows 7, but the previous versions, Microsoft Windows XP and Windows Vista, remain popular as well. Windows 7 is a GUI with a multitasking, single-user environment in which users can easily manage files and run programs through a point-and-click interface.

server A computer that manages and runs network services

A **server**—that is, a computer that manages and runs network services—typically uses a multi-user operating system. Microsoft Windows Server and UNIX are the two most popular operating systems for servers; Linux also can be used to run a server. Although IT professionals manage servers, ordinary users may also need to interact with a server. For example, people who create websites may need to work with a Windows, UNIX, or Linux server to transfer web pages to a publicly accessible location. You will learn more about servers in Unit 3.

Microsoft Windows Server is nearly identical to the desktop version of Windows, except that it is a multi-user OS with extra utilities and tools that allow the OS to function as a server, providing user authentication services, file and print sharing, and other network administration services.

UNIX and Linux are both multi-tasking, multi-user operating systems that use a command-line interface by default. Several different command-prompt shells are available for UNIX, such as bash and korn, and several GUI interfaces are available in commercial distributions for Linux, such as Ubuntu, Red Hat, and Fedora. Linux and UNIX can be used to run both servers and individual-user PCs.

In the professional graphics and publishing industries, Macintosh computers are popular. Whether the Macintosh OS is better suited than the Windows OS for graphics applications is debatable, but because these industries have traditionally used Macs, the Mac versions of graphics and publishing applications are well established and robust.

Table 2.1 summarizes the popular operating systems and their classifications in each of the areas discussed in this topic.

Table 2.1 **Popular Operating Systems**

Operating System	User Interface	Multitasking	Multiuser
MS-DOS	Command line	No	No
Microsoft Windows 7	GUI	Yes	No
Macintosh OS X	GUI	Yes	No
Microsoft Windows Server	GUI	Yes	Yes
Linux	Various available	Yes	Yes
UNIX	Various available	Yes	Yes

Every few years, a new version of an operating system is released. This book is based on the Windows 7 version. Within a version, several editions of Windows 7 are available, including Home Premium, Business, and Ultimate. All these editions operate the same way at a basic level; the differences are mostly in the applications included to work with networks and multimedia. To determine which version and edition you have, click Start and then right-click Computer and choose Properties.

Exercise 2.1 Comparing Windows 7 Editions

1. Open a web browser, and navigate to http://ic3.emcp.net/ComWin7Prod.

2. On a blank sheet of paper, answer the following questions:

    a. Which editions allow the computer to join a network domain?

    b. Which editions include the Bitlocker feature?

    c. Which editions enable you to switch between multiple languages?

    d. Which editions allow you to use a Homegroup network?

3. On your PC, click Start, and then right-click Computer and click Properties. Use the information that appears to determine which version and edition of Windows you have, and write that on the paper.

4. Close the web browser.

Drilling Down

Exploring Additional Devices that use Operating Systems

Handheld devices such as phones, personal organizers, and music players have their own proprietary operating systems, customized by the device maker for the specific needs of the devices. For example, the interface you use on an iPod to select which songs you want to play is generated by the device's operating system.

Non-computer devices like cars and machinery typically contain embedded operating systems. For example, if your car has a digital display that reports your gas mileage or tire pressure, that display has an operating system behind it. And in factories, the computer-aided manufacturing tools that build automobiles and solder steel have operating systems that enable the worker to program them to do the required task. The use of robotics and other automated systems has dramatically increased the efficiency of production.

Lesson 2.2 Understanding Microsoft Windows 7

 1-3.2.2, 1-3.2.3, 1-3.2.4

Windows 7 loads automatically when you start your PC. Depending on how it is configured, the Windows desktop may appear immediately, or you may be prompted to log in by clicking a user name and typing a password. You will learn more about logging in, starting up, and shutting down in Lesson 2.3.

Using the Windows Desktop

All the work you do in Windows (working with files, using programs, and so on) begins at the **desktop**. The desktop is the background (the blue area in Figure 2.3) on which everything else sits. Figure 2.3 shows the Windows desktop and the most important elements that appear there by default. Your desktop might look slightly different than the one pictured. For example, your system might have a different image displayed on the desktop.

desktop The work area of the graphical interface in Windows

Figure 2.3 Windows Desktop

Recycle Bin icon

desktop

Taskbar

Start button

icon A small clickable picture representing an application, folder, document, or other file or location

shortcut A path that leads to a file, folder, or drive

Taskbar The bar at the bottom of the Windows desktop where currently running applications and open windows appear

Start button The button that opens the Start menu

Start menu The main navigation menu in Windows, from which you can start up applications and browse file locations

Quick Steps

Open the Start Menu
Click the Start button.

The Recycle Bin is an example of an icon. An **icon** is a small clickable picture that represents an application, folder, document, or other file or location. In the case of the Recycle Bin, the icon is a shortcut to a hidden storage area where recently deleted files and folders are temporarily stored until they are permanently deleted. A **shortcut** is a path to a file, folder, or drive.

The **Taskbar** is where the names of the currently running applications and open windows appear so you can switch between them easily. (There are no running applications in Figure 2.3.) You will learn more about the Taskbar in Lesson 2.4, when you learn about running programs.

Using the Start Menu

The **Start button** is the round button in the bottom left corner of the Windows desktop. Clicking the Start button opens the Start menu. As the name implies, the **Start menu** enables you to start up or launch programs (applications) installed in Windows. In addition, the Start menu allows you to access system settings, get help, open folders to view files, and shut down the system.

Figure 2.4 shows the Start menu, which can be opened by clicking the Start button or by pressing the Windows logo key on your computer's keyboard. The menu contains the following features: pinned shortcuts, recently used shortcuts, the All Programs menu, the Search box, shortcuts to personal folders, links to Windows features, the Shut down button, and the Shut down button arrow.

Pinned Shortcuts In the top left corner of the menu are shortcuts to your default web browser and email program, plus any other shortcuts you have placed there. These shortcuts remain attached (pinned) to this area regardless of usage or lack of usage.

Recently Used Shortcuts In the bottom left portion of the menu are shortcuts to recently run applications. This list is constantly in flux; as you run applications, the ones you run most often replace others on the list that you have not run recently or frequently.

All Programs Menu Clicking here opens the main part of the menu system, which consists of a hierarchical list of all the installed programs. You will learn more about the All Programs menu in Lesson 2.4.

Search Box In this box you can type the first few letters of an application you want to run to narrow down the list of applications and files, making it easier to find the one you are seeking. You can also type text commands here, as you would from a command prompt.

Shortcuts to Personal Folders Shortcuts to the personal folders for the logged-in user appear in the Start menu as well. These change for each user so that users can maintain their own separate and private documents, pictures, music, and games.

Links to Windows Features Near the bottom right corner of the menu are links to some common system tools, such as Control Panel, Devices and Printers, Default Programs, and Help and Support.

Shut Down Button This button opens a menu from which you can turn the system off or put it in a low-power standby mode.

Shut Down Button Arrow This button opens a submenu of options for logging off, shutting down, and switching users.

Figure 2.4 Windows 7 Start Menu

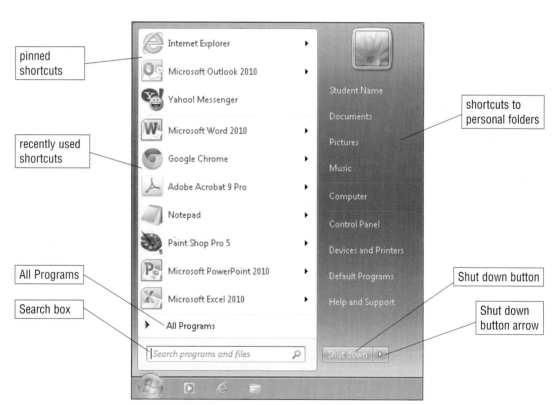

Minimizing, Maximizing, and Restoring a Window

Most of the options on the Start menu open some type of window. A **window** is a rectangular frame in which a file listing, program, message, or utility displays. For example, in Figure 2.5, the Notepad application is open in a window. Each window has three buttons in the top right corner: Minimize, Maximize (or Restore), and Close.

Minimize This button shrinks the window so that it is still open, but hidden. The Taskbar continues to show the window's name, and you can unhide the window by clicking it there.

Maximize or Restore The Maximize button enlarges the window to fill the entire screen. When a window is maximized, a Restore button appears in place of the Maximize button. Click this button to return the window to its original un-maximized size. You can also press F11 to toggle between a maximized and a restored window size (when working with a file listing).

Close This button closes the window and, if an application was running in that window, shuts down that application.

Figure 2.5 **Window Controls in Notepad**

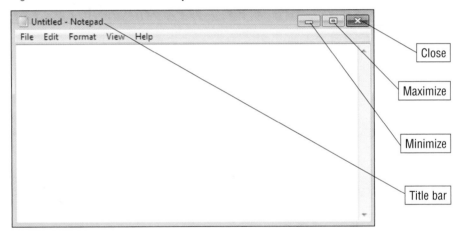

Moving and Resizing a Window

A window also can be moved and resized, provided it is not maximized. To move a window, drag its **title bar** (the bar across the top of the window, where the window's name appears). To resize a window, position the mouse pointer over one of the borders of the window so that the pointer turns into a double-headed arrow, and then drag the border with the mouse until its window is the desired size.

Switching between Windows

Windows is a multitasking operating system, which means you can have multiple applications and windows open at once. Whatever commands you issue take effect in the active window, which is the window on the top of the stack of windows on your desktop. You can tell which window is active because it generally has a different title bar color than the others.

Several methods are available for switching between open windows. Perhaps the easiest is to click the button on the Taskbar for the open window. Each open window has its own rectangular button in the Taskbar, as seen in Figure 2.6.

Figure 2.6 Windows 7 Taskbar The Taskbar contains buttons for each open window.

Another way to switch between windows is to press Alt + Tab. Each time you do, Windows cycles through the open windows, making a different one active. You can also use Alt + Tab in a different way: hold down Alt and press and release Tab while continuing to hold down Alt. Each time you press Tab, a different window's icon appears selected in a selector pane in the middle of the screen. When the icon for the desired window is selected, release the Alt key. Figure 2.7 shows this screen. Notice that there are three Word icons displayed in Figure 2.7 because there are three Word documents open.

Figure 2.7 Alt + Tab Example Hold down Alt and press Tab to cycle through the available windows.

Quick Steps

Move a Window
1. Make sure window is not maximized.
2. Click and drag title bar.
OR
1. Press Alt + spacebar.
2. Click *Move* or press M.
3. Use arrow keys to move window.
4. Click to stop moving.

Resize a Window
1. Point at window border until mouse pointer becomes double-headed arrow.
2. Drag to resize window.
3. Release mouse button.
OR
1. Press Alt + spacebar.
2. Click *Size* or press S.
3. Use arrow keys to size window.
4. Click to stop sizing.

Switch between Open Windows

Click desired window's button on Taskbar.
OR
Press Alt + Tab.
OR
1. Hold down Alt.
2. Press Tab until desired window is selected.
3. Release Alt.

Exercise 2.2 Minimizing, Maximizing, Restoring, and Closing a Window

1. Click Start.

2. Click *Computer* in the Start menu.
   This opens the Computer window.

3. Click the Minimize button 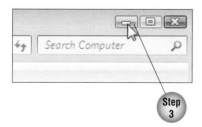 in top right corner of the Computer window.
   This hides the window, but its name continues to appear in the Taskbar.

4. Click the button on Taskbar representing the Computer window.

This redisplays the Computer window.

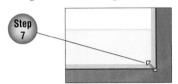

5. Click the Maximize ⬜ button in the window's top right corner.

This enlarges the window to fill the screen.

6. Click the Restore button ⧉ that replaced the Maximize button when you maximized the window in Step 5.

This returns the window to its original size.

7. Drag the bottom right corner of the window inward to shrink the window's size by about 1 inch.

8. Drag the window's title bar to move the window slightly to the left.

9. Click the Close button ✖.

This closes the window.

10. Open the Recycle Bin by double-clicking the Recycle Bin icon on the desktop.

11. Close the Recycle Bin by clicking the Close button.

Lesson 2.3   Starting Up and Shutting Down a Windows PC

)[C³ 1-3.2.1

When you turn on a PC that has Windows 7 as its operating system, one of two things will happen:

- The desktop will appear automatically, without the need to log in. This happens if only one user account is configured for the PC, and if that account is not protected by a password.

- A welcome screen will appear, with icons for the user names set up on the computer. Click one of the icons to indicate which user account you wish to use. If the user account you choose is a password-protected account, you will be prompted to type the correct password before you are allowed access to the system. If you do not know the password or are denied access, contact a system administrator to find out what password to use, or try logging in with the guest account.

Quick Steps

Log Off Windows

1. Click Start.
2. Click Shut down button arrow.
3. Click *Log off.*

When you step away from your desk, you can choose to leave Windows running or you can choose one of the alternatives listed here and illustrated in Figure 2.8 (Sleep and Hibernate options are discussed in Topic 16):

- You can click the Shut down button arrow on the Start menu to open a submenu from which you can choose the *Log off* option. This logs you out of your user account but leaves the computer running so that someone else can log in using his or her own account.

- You can click the Shut down button arrow on the Start menu and choose the *Lock* option to lock the computer. (This is effective only if you have a password-protected user account.) This prevents others from using the computer unless they know the password.

- You can click the Shut down button on the Start menu to shut down the computer completely; this includes logging you out of your account and turning off the power. When you return to your computer, you will need to restart the entire machine. You can also shut down Windows by pressing Alt + F4 when no open windows are active. (If you press Alt + F4 when a window is active, only that window will close.)

Quick Steps

Lock Windows

1. Click Start.
2. Click Shut down button arrow.
3. Click *Lock*.

Shut Down Windows

1. Click Start.
2. Click Shut down button.

Figure 2.8 System Shut Down and Log Off Controls

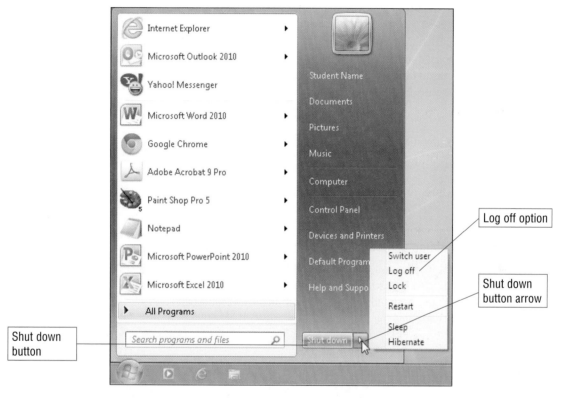

Exercise 2.3 Shutting Down, Logging Off, and Locking Windows

1. If you are logged in to Windows with a user account that is not password-protected, log out and back in again with a password-protected account. Ask your instructor for help if you need to create a password-protected account for this exercise.

2. Click Start, click the Shut down button arrow, and then click *Lock*.

Using an Operating System **67**

3. If more than one user account is configured on the PC, icons appear for all the available users. The term *Locked* appears under your user name. Click your user name to display a password prompt. If only one user is set up on the computer, a password prompt appears for that user automatically.

4. Enter the password and press Enter to return to Windows.

5. Save any existing work and close any applications that you have open.

6. Click Start, click the Shut down button arrow, and then click *Log off*.

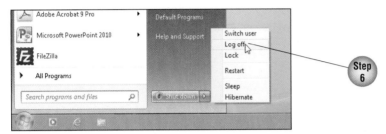

7. If more than one user account is configured on the PC, icons appear for all the available users. Click your user name to display a password prompt. As before, if only one user is set up on the computer, a passwordprompt appears for that user automatically.

8. Enter the password and press Enter to log in again.

9. Click Start and then click the Shut down button.

   This shuts down the computer.

10. Restart the computer and log back in, if prompted.

Drilling Down

Understanding Case-Sensitivity in Passwords

Passwords in Windows are case-sensitive, meaning you must type the password exactly as it was typed when it was originally created, including uppercase or lowercase letters. If you leave the Caps Lock on, an indicator will appear on the Welcome screen to alert you so that you do not accidentally mistype the password.

Lesson 2.4 **Running Applications**

 1-3.2.4, 1-3.2.8

Quick Steps

Start an Application
1. Click Start.
2. Click *All Programs*.
3. Locate application.
4. Click application name.

Windows provides the background platform on which to run applications. Without applications, a person would have no reason to use a computer, and no data files would need managing or manipulating.

Windows comes with many simple applications that you can use to perform everyday tasks, such as WordPad for word processing, Paint for creating and editing drawings and photos, and Calculator for doing simple math. It also comes with Internet Explorer (a web browser).

Starting a program loads the program's instructions into the computer's RAM (random access memory) and makes its window appear on the desktop. The user interfaces with the program through this window. Exiting or shutting down a program closes its window and removes it from RAM, freeing up the RAM for use by other programs.

The Start menu shows a few shortcuts for recently used programs on its top level, as you saw in the previous lesson. If the application you want to run does not appear at that top level, you must locate it within the All Programs menu structure. On the Start menu, click *All Programs*, and then click additional folders if needed to work through the hierarchy until you find the application you want to run (see Figure 2.9).

If you use a particular application frequently, you may want to create a shortcut for it. You can create a shortcut on the desktop by dragging the application to the desktop from the Start menu. To run the application, simply double-click that shortcut.

You can also pin a shortcut either to the Taskbar or to the Start menu. Pinned shortcuts on the Taskbar appear as small icons to the right of the Start button. Pinned shortcuts on the Start menu appear in the upper left section of the Start menu. Figure 2.10 shows some pinned shortcuts.

Figure 2.9 Starting an Application with the All Programs Menu

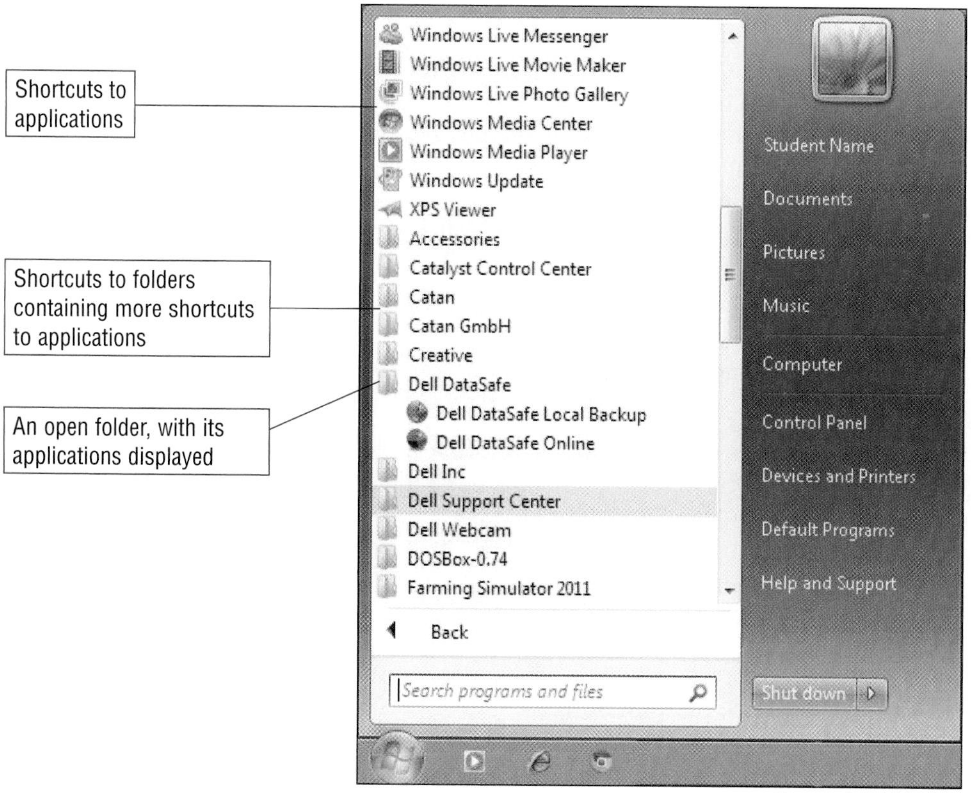

Shortcuts to applications

Shortcuts to folders containing more shortcuts to applications

An open folder, with its applications displayed

Figure 2.10 **Shortcuts on the Desktop, Taskbar, and Start Menu**

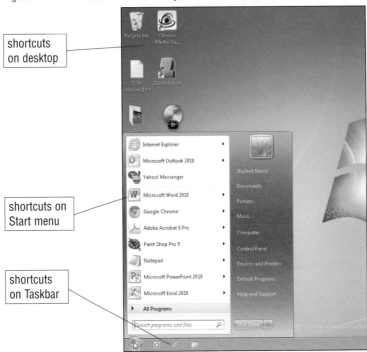

shortcuts on desktop

shortcuts on Start menu

shortcuts on Taskbar

Once an application has been started, you can control it using its menu system. Some applications have a **menu bar** across the top of the window, consisting of one or more words that each represent a drop-down list. Click a word (such as File or Edit) to open a drop-down list, and then click a command within that list. For example, in Figure 2.11, the File drop-down list is open in Notepad.

Some applications also provide toolbars. A **toolbar** is a set of small icons, each representing a command or function in the application. For example, a toolbar may contain a Save button, and clicking it might open a dialog box in which you can save your work. Figure 2.12 shows an application window with both a menu bar and a toolbar.

menu bar A bar across the top of a window containing the names of drop-down lists; clicking a menu name opens that drop-down list

toolbar A bar across the top of a window that contains icons for commonly used features

Quick Steps

Issue a Command from a Drop-down List

1. Click name on menu bar.
2. Click command.

Issue a Command from a Toolbar

Click command button on toolbar.

Figure 2.11 **File Drop-down List** The menu bar in the Notepad application provides access to drop-down lists.

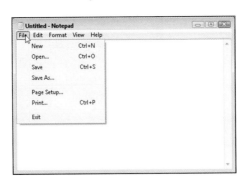

Figure 2.12 Menu Bar and Toolbar in Windows Journal

Not all applications have menus and toolbars; the versions of WordPad and Paint that come with Windows 7 do not, for example, nor do the Office 2007 or 2010 applications. Instead, they have a tabbed ribbon. The **ribbon** is a tabbed toolbar that takes the place of both the menu bar and the toolbar in some applications, providing tabbed pages of buttons you can click to issue commands. Figure 2.13 shows the ribbon interface in WordPad. The versions of WordPad and Paint that come with earlier versions of Windows, such as Windows Vista and Windows XP, use a menu and toolbar system of navigation instead of a ribbon. Some programs, such as Internet Explorer and Windows Media Player, do have menu systems, but they do not display by default. To display the menu bar in these programs, press the Alt key.

ribbon A tabbed toolbar interface that replaces the menu bar and toolbar in some applications

Quick Steps

Issue a Command from a Ribbon

1. Click appropriate ribbon tab.
2. Click desired command.

Figure 2.13 Ribbon Interface in WordPad

Exercise 2.4 Working with the Calculator and WordPad Applications

1. Click Start and then click *All Programs*.

2. Click *Accessories* and then click *Calculator*.

   This opens the Calculator application.

3. Click View on the menu bar in the Calculator window and then click *Programmer* at the drop-down menu.

   The buttons change to a computer programmer's calculator.

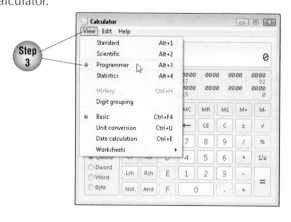

4. Click the 1 button and then click the 3 button twice.

5. Click the *Bin* option (the round button to the left of "Bin") to show the number in binary numbering.

   The number changes to 10000101.

6. Click the Close button in the Calculator window to close the application.

7. Click Start and then click *All Programs*.

8. Click *Accessories* and then click *WordPad*.

   This opens the WordPad application.

9. Type your name in the WordPad window.

10. In the upper left corner of the window, click the Save button (second button from the left), which looks like a floppy disk.

    If you cannot locate the button, press Ctrl + S. Either way, the Save As dialog box opens.

11. At the Save As dialog box, type **U1T2-WordPad** in the *File name* text box.

    When you begin typing the file name, the existing text in the *File name* text box is deleted.

12. Navigate to the **Unit1Topic02** folder on your storage medium..

13. Click the Save button or press Enter.

    You have just created a document file.

14. Click the Close button in the upper right corner of the WordPad window to close the application.

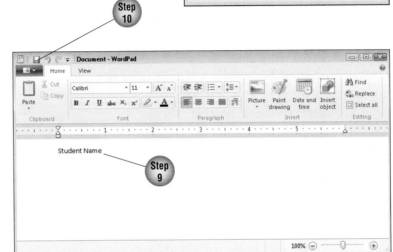

Drilling Down

Finding the Application

If you are not sure where a particular application resides within the All Programs hierarchy, you can search for it using the search box near the bottom of the Start menu. To do this, click Start and then type the first few letters of the application's name. At the list of matching applications that appears at the top of the Start menu, click the shortcut for the one you want.

Setting Up Compatibility Mode

Applications designed for earlier versions of Windows might not install or run correctly under Windows 7. If that is the case, right-click the shortcut to the file (on the Start menu) and then click *Properties* to open its properties dialog box. On the Compatibility tab, set up Compatibility mode for the version of Windows with which the program is designed to work. Experiment with different settings until you find a combination of settings that allow the program to run, or until you have run out of settings to try.

continued

> ### Distinguishing between Bundled Applications and Operating Systems
>
> The distinction between operating system and application may be blurred by the fact that operating systems come with many simple applications preinstalled. For example, Microsoft Windows comes with a simple word processing program called WordPad. WordPad is not an integral part of the Windows OS; it is simply a bonus application included with the operating system.

Lesson 2.5 Working with the Desktop and Icons

 1-3.2.5

The desktop, in addition to serving as a backdrop for all activity in Windows, can also function as a storage area. You can place shortcuts there for quick access to applications, documents, and storage locations that you use frequently. Recall that a shortcut is a path to a file, folder, or drive. You can click a shortcut icon to access quickly the object to which it refers.

Many times when you install new software, it places a shortcut for itself on the desktop. You can leave the shortcut where it is, drag it to a different spot on the desktop, or delete it entirely by selecting it and pressing the Delete key or dragging it to the Recycle Bin. Deleting the shortcut does not do anything to the application itself; you can still run it from the Start menu.

You can create your own shortcuts on the desktop (or anywhere). To do so, click a file or folder to select it and then hold down the right mouse button as you drag it to the desktop or to the desired location. When you release the mouse button, a menu appears. On that menu, choose *Create shortcut(s) here*.

You can also store actual files and folders on the desktop, not just shortcuts to them. For example, you might create a folder on the desktop and use the folder to store shortcuts that you seldom use, or you might direct an Internet download to be stored on the desktop so you can locate it quickly.

Keyboards contain a Print Screen button that you can use to capture the contents of the screen in an image file. That file can then be inserted in a document in an application such as WordPad or Word. To take a screen capture using the Print Screen key, display the desired information on the screen and then press the Print Screen key on your keyboard (generally located in the top row). When you press the Print Screen key, nothing seems to happen, but in fact, the screen image is captured in a file that is inserted in a location called the Clipboard. To insert this file in a document, press the keyboard shortcut Ctrl + V or right-click in a blank location in a document and then click the *Paste* option at the shortcut menu.

Exercise 2.5 Working with Shortcuts

1. Click Start and then click *Computer*.

2. Right-drag (that is, drag with the right mouse button) the icon for the C: drive to the desktop. When you release the mouse button, click *Create shortcuts here* at the shortcut menu.

   This creates a shortcut for the C: drive on the desktop.

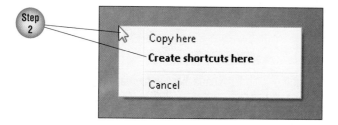

3. Close the Computer window.

4. Verify that the shortcut has an arrow on the bottom left corner of the icon.

5. Right-click the shortcut and then click *Properties* at the shortcut menu.

   This displays a properties dialog box with the Shortcut tab displayed for the drive.

6. In the *Target* box, notice the path C:\.

   The target is the location of the original file to which the shortcut refers.

7. Click the Cancel button to close the properties dialog box.

8. Drag the shortcut to a different location on the desktop.

9. Double-click the C: drive shortcut.

   A window appears showing the drive's content.

10. Close the C: drive window.

11. Capture the contents of the desktop as an image file by pressing the Print Screen key on your keyboard (generally located in the top row).

12. Open the WordPad application by clicking Start, clicking *All Programs*, clicking *Accessories*, and then clicking *WordPad*.

13. Press Ctrl + V to insert the print screen file into the WordPad document.

14. Print the WordPad document by pressing Ctrl + P and then clicking the Print button at the Print dialog box.

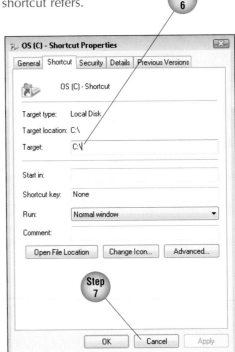

15. Click the Close button located in the upper right corner of the WordPad window to exit WordPad and then click the Don't Save button at the message asking if you want to save the changes.

16. Click the C: drive shortcut once to select it and then press the Delete key on the keyboard.

Drilling Down

Distinguishing between Shortcuts and Files

Being able to distinguish between a shortcut and a file is important because while deleting a shortcut is harmless, deleting a file might cause a problem. This is because a shortcut is not the original file; the original file is stored elsewhere. Most—but not all—shortcuts have an arrow on the bottom left corner of the icon, as shown at the right. A more reliable way to tell if an icon is a shortcut is to right-click the icon and then click *Properties*. If the dialog box that appears contains a Shortcut tab, the icon is a shortcut and can be deleted without causing problems.

Turning Off AutoArrange

If you try to move an icon by dragging it and it snaps back into place, Auto Arrange may be turned on. Right-click the desktop, point to *View*, and then click *Auto arrange icons* to turn off the feature.

Managing Files and Folders

IC³ 1-3.2.5, 1-3.2.6, 1-3.2.7, 1-3.2.8

Windows provides a file management interface called **Windows Explorer** through which you can create, organize, rename, move, copy, and delete files and folders. Whenever you view the content of a drive or folder or browse the Computer window, you are using Windows Explorer. In this lesson you will learn how to navigate Windows Explorer windows and perform some basic file management tasks.

> **Windows Explorer** The file management interface in Microsoft Windows

Understanding the Windows Explorer Interface

Figure 2.14 shows a Windows Explorer window and points out the following key features: Address bar, search box, Command bar, Favorites, Navigation pane, Details pane, menu bar, *Libraries* list, Homegroup, *Computer* list, and Network.

Address Bar The Address bar shows the name of the folder whose contents appear in the window, as well as the folder(s) holding that folder. This list is called the folder's path. A **path** is the full address of a file, including the drive and the folder. You can use this bar, as well as the Back and Forward arrow buttons to the left of it, to navigate to other folders.

> **path** The full address of a file, including the drive and folder

Search Box The search box enables you to enter a file or folder name to tell Windows Explorer to find that file or folder. It also searches in your Outlook data files for email messages and other objects that contain the search text.

Command Bar The Command bar contains buttons for performing common tasks on the displayed content. Its buttons change depending on the type of content displayed. Some of the buttons on the Command bar open menus with additional choices.

Favorites Favorites provide shortcuts for jumping to commonly used folders. You can place your own shortcuts there, too.

Navigation Pane The Navigation pane enables you to move between locations such as different disks and folders.

Details Pane The Details pane displays basic information about the currently selected disk, folder, or file.

Menu Bar The menu bar provides access to a drop-down list system. If the menu bar does not appear automatically, press Alt.

Libraries List The *Libraries* list provides shortcuts to the libraries for documents, music, pictures, and videos belonging to the current user.

Homegroup If present, the Homegroup feature provides a shortcut from which you can browse the local Homegroup network. A **homegroup** is a Windows 7 home or small office network.

> **homegroup** A Windows 7 home or small office network

Computer List The *Computer* list shows a hierarchical tree structure of the drives and folders on your system, starting with the drive letters. You can jump to any location by clicking it in the *Computer* list.

Network If present, the Network feature provides a shortcut from which you can browse the entire network to which the computer is connected. This can include computers within the Homegroup as well as other computers (such as those running earlier versions of Windows).

Figure 2.14 Windows Explorer Window

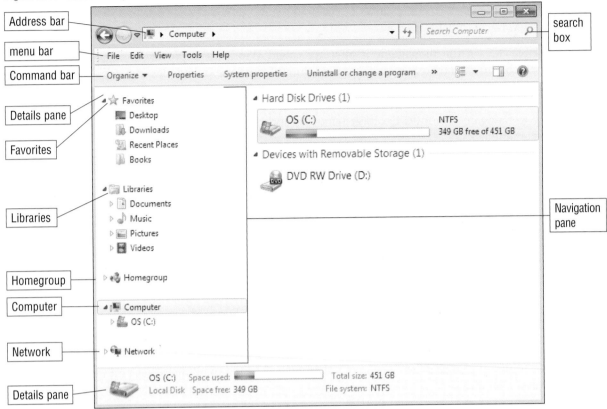

Address bar
menu bar
Command bar
Details pane
Favorites
Libraries
Homegroup
Computer
Network
Details pane

search box
Navigation pane

Browsing Locations

To display the content of a location, you can do any of the following:

- Click the location's name on the *Favorites* list, if it appears there.

- Click the location's name under Computer in the Navigation pane (the left side of the window). Click a drive or folder there to display the subfolders within it, and then click the desired subfolder, and so on until the desired location appears.

- In the Address bar, click and then type the full path to the desired location, starting with the drive letter and separating each folder level with a backslash. For example, to open the Project folder stored in the Personal folder on the C: drive, type *C:\Personal\Project*.

- To go down one level in the folder structure, double-click a folder in the current location's listing.

- To move back to a higher level in the folder structure, click the folder name in the Address bar. If the path is so long that the entire path does not appear in the Address bar, click the << arrow at the left end and select from the menu that appears, as shown in Figure 2.15.

- To go to a previously viewed location, click the Back button (the blue left-pointing arrow). After using the Back button, the Forward button becomes available (the blue right-pointing arrow); it takes you forward to the location you were viewing before you clicked the Back button.

Figure 2.15 Address Bar Example

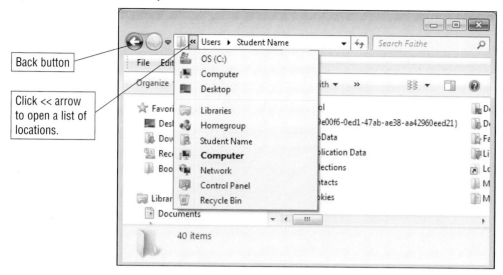

Back button

Click << arrow to open a list of locations.

Exercise 2.6A Browsing Folder Listings

1. Click Start and then click *Computer*.

2. Under Computer in the Navigation pane, click the C: drive icon to display the contents of the C: drive.

3. Double-click the Windows folder to display its contents.

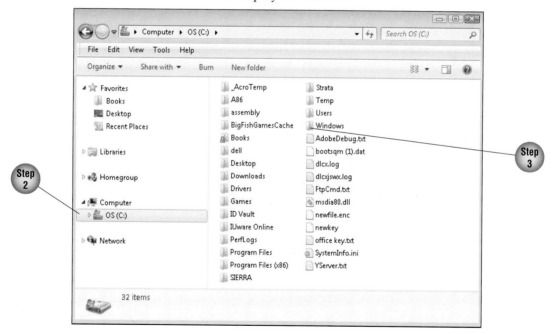

4. Double-click the Help folder within the Windows folder.

5. In the Navigation pane, look under *Computer*. If the C: drive does not appear there, click the small triangle to the left of Computer to expand the listing.

6. If the folders from the C: drive are not already shown in the Navigation pane, click the small triangle to the left of the C: drive to expand the listing.

7. In the Navigation pane, under the C: drive, click the Program Files folder to display its contents.

The folders on your computer will be different from the ones shown here.

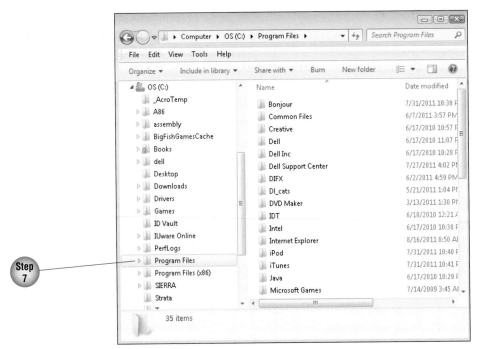

8. In the Address bar, click *Computer*.

The top level view of the file system appears again, including all disk drives.

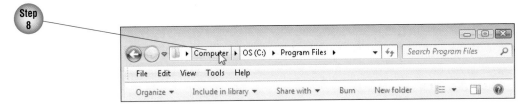

9. Click in the Address bar, type **C:\Users\Public**, replacing the text that was there previously, and then press Enter.

The contents of that folder display.

10. In the Libraries list, click *Documents*.

The contents of that folder display.

11. Close all open windows.

Selecting Multiple Files and Folders

Before you can perform an action on a folder or file, such as deleting or copying, you must select it. Any commands you then issue affect the selected items. Some commands can be performed on multiple items at once, such as moving or copying; other commands work only on individual items.

A selected file or folder appears with a blue or gray selection highlight over it, and information about it appears in the Preview pane. When multiple items are selected, they all appear with the same selection highlight, and the Preview pane reports summary information for them, such as the total aggregate amount of disk space they occupy.

A group of selected files can be either contiguous (meaning they appear next to each other) or noncontiguous (meaning they do not appear next to each other). It makes no difference except in the technique you use to select them. To select a contiguous block of files, hold down Shift as you click on the first and last file in the group. To select a noncontiguous block, hold down Ctrl as you click each file you want. Figure 2.16 shows a noncontiguous group of selected files.

You can change the order in which files appear in the listing (thereby making different files contiguous) by right-clicking an empty area and choosing Sort By, and then clicking what you want to sort by. For example, you can sort by Name, Date Modified, Type, or Size.

Quick Steps

Select Multiple Contiguous Files

1. Select first file.
2. Hold down Shift and select last file.
3. Release Shift.

Select Multiple Noncontiguous Files

1. Select first file.
2. Hold down Ctrl and click each file.
3. Release Ctrl.

Figure 2.16 Noncontiguous Selected Files Select noncontiguous items by holding down Ctrl as you click each one.

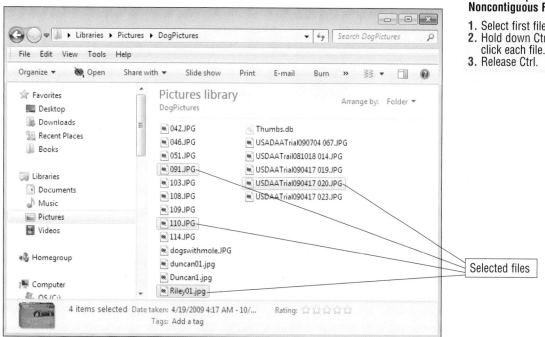

Moving and Copying Files and Folders

Copying a file or folder makes a duplicate of the item and places that duplicate in a new destination. For example, you might have some pictures you have taken on your digital camera. When you connect the camera to the computer, Windows sees the camera as a disk drive, and you can copy the image files to a folder on the hard disk. The original image files remain on the camera until you actively remove them. You can copy files or folders in two ways: with the Windows Clipboard (using the **Cut**, **Copy**, and **Paste** commands) or by using drag-and-drop.

cut To remove selected text from the document and place it on the Clipboard

copy To place a copy of selected text on the Clipboard

paste To insert cut or copied text in the document

Copying or Moving with the Clipboard The Clipboard is a temporary internal storage area in Windows. You can place material onto it by selecting the material and issuing either the Cut or the Copy command. Cut removes the material from its original location and posts it on the Clipboard; Copy leaves the original in place and also posts a copy on the Clipboard. You can then navigate to the new location and issue the Paste command to insert the Clipboard's content.

One advantage of the Clipboard method of moving and copying is that multiple pastes are possible. After you have cut or copied something, you can then paste it into multiple locations without having to re-cut or re-copy it. Another advantage is that you do not have to be able to see both the original and the destination locations at the same time. You can perform the cut or copy operation and then open up the destination location at your leisure.

The Windows Clipboard holds only one item at a time. When you cut or copy something else, whatever was stored there before is removed. Office applications, however, have a more robust Clipboard that is capable of storing multiple items at a time. You will learn more about the Clipboard for the Office applications in Unit 2.

Several methods for issuing the Cut, Copy, and Paste commands are available, as summarized in Table 2.2.

Table 2.2 Cut, Copy, and Paste Commands

	Cut	**Copy**	**Paste**
Keyboard shortcut	Ctrl + X	Ctrl + C	Ctrl + V
Organize button	Organize, Cut	Organize, Copy	Organize, Paste
Menu system (press Alt to access menus)	Edit, Cut	Edit, Copy	Edit, Paste

Copying and Moving to a Folder When a file is selected, two extra commands are available on the Edit menu: *Copy to folder* and *Move to folder*. Each of these combines a multi-part operation into a single activity. If you choose *Copy to folder*, Windows prompts you for a destination location, and then performs a copy-and-paste operation in a single pass. If you choose *Move to folder*, Windows prompts for a destination and then performs a cut-and-paste operation.

Copying or Moving with Drag-and-Drop This method requires having both the source and the destination locations visible at the same time. The locations can be in two separate Windows Explorer windows, or the destination location can be the desktop, or a folder icon on the *Favorites* list or in some other location.

Whether the drag-and-drop operation moves or copies the item depends on the relationship of the source and destination locations to one another. If the source and destination are on the same disk, drag-and-drop moves. If the source and destination are on different disks, drag-and-drop copies. To override the default behavior, you can hold down Ctrl to force a copy or Shift to force a move. You can also right-drag and then choose an action from the shortcut menu that appears.

Creating and Renaming Folders

You might want to create your own folders in which to organize your files. For example, if you are going to copy digital camera image files to your computer, you might want to create a subfolder within the Pictures folder and name it using today's date and a keyword that clearly identifies the image contents. To create a new folder, click the New folder button on the Command bar, type a name for the folder, and then press Enter.

If you change your mind about a folder name later, you can rename the folder. To do so, right-click the folder and then click *Rename* at the shortcut menu. Type a new name for the folder and then press Enter. You can also select the folder, press F2, type the new name, and then press Enter. You can use these same techniques to rename files as well.

Exercise 2.6B Organizing, Moving, and Copying Files and Folders

1. Click Start and then click *Documents*.

   This displays the contents of the Documents folder.

2. Click the New folder button on the Command bar.

3. Type your first name as the folder name and then press Enter.

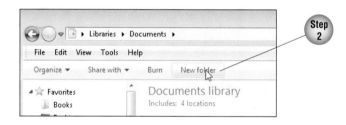

4. Click the new folder, press F2, type your last name, and then press Enter.

5. Navigate to the C:\Windows\Help\Help\en-US folder.

6. Hold down Ctrl and then click each of the following files: *Help.h1c*, *Help.H1T*, and *Resources.H1S*.

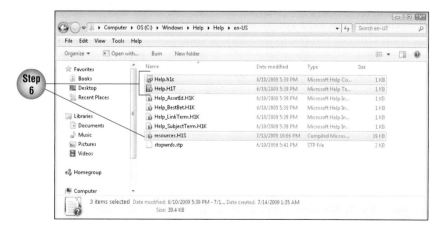

Quick Steps

Copy a File Using Drag-and-Drop

1. Open original location and destination location.
2. Select file.
3. If copying within same drive, hold down Ctrl to force a copy.
4. Drag file to new location.

OR

1. Open original location and destination location.
2. Select file.
3. Right-drag to new location.
4. Release mouse button.
5. At shortcut menu, click *Copy here*.

Move a File Using Drag-and-Drop

1. Open original location and destination location.
2. Select file.
3. If moving to different drive, hold down Shift to force a move.
4. Drag file to new location.

OR

1. Open original location and destination location.
2. Select file.
3. Right-drag to new location.
4. Release mouse button.
5. At shortcut menu, click *Move here*.

Create a New Folder

1. Open location of new folder.
2. Click *New folder*.
3. Type new folder name.
4. Press Enter.

Rename a Folder

1. Select folder.
2. Press F2.
3. Type new name.
4. Press Enter.

OR

1. Right-click folder.
2. Click *Rename*.
3. Type new name.
4. Press Enter.

7. Press Ctrl + C to copy the files to the Clipboard.

8. Click the Back button until the Documents folder appears.

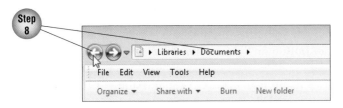

9. Double-click the folder you created.

10. Click the Organize button on the Command bar and then click *Paste* at the drop-down list.

    This pastes the files into the folder.

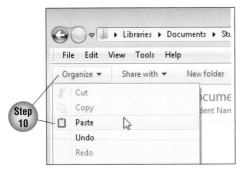

11. Click the **Help.h1c** file in the folder you created, hold down the Ctrl key, and then drag it to the desktop.

    This creates a copy of the file on the desktop.

12. Close all open windows.

Deleting and Restoring Files from the Recycle Bin

When you delete files and folders in Windows, they are not destroyed right away; instead they are moved to a hidden folder. The Recycle Bin icon on the desktop is a shortcut to that folder. From it you can retrieve deleted files and folders or purge the Recycle Bin contents so that others cannot access any deleted personal files. Be aware that only local hard disks are protected by the Recycle Bin. Any files you delete from a removable disk or from a network location will not be sent to the Recycle Bin.

You can delete individual files and folders or groups of files and folders. Deleting a folder deletes everything within the folder, too. To delete, select the item(s) and then press the Delete key on the keyboard, or right-click the selection and then click *Delete* at the shortcut menu. You can also click the Organize button on the Command bar and then click the *Delete* option. If a confirmation box appears, click OK.

To retrieve a deleted file, double-click the Recycle Bin icon on the desktop. Locate the file you want to retrieve and then click the Restore this item button on the Command bar, as seen in Figure 2.17. You can clear the entire Recycle Bin at once by clicking the Empty the Recycle Bin button on the Command bar in the Recycle Bin window. To empty the Recycle Bin without opening the window, right-click the Recycle Bin icon on the desktop and then click *Empty Recycle Bin* at the shortcut menu.

Quick Steps

Delete a File or Folder

1. Select file or folder.
2. Press Delete.

Retrieve a Deleted File or Folder

1. Double-click Recycle Bin icon.
2. Select file or folder.
3. Click Restore this item button.

Empty the Recycle Bin

1. Right-click Recycle Bin icon.
2. Click *Empty Recycle Bin.*

Figure 2.17 Recycle Bin Window

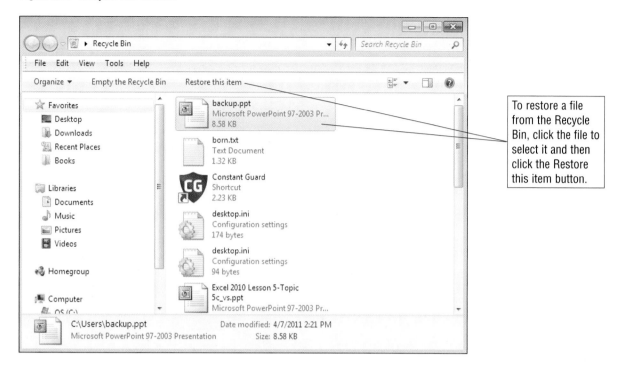

To restore a file from the Recycle Bin, click the file to select it and then click the Restore this item button.

Exercise 2.6C Working with the Recycle Bin

1. Right-click the Recycle Bin icon on the desktop and then click *Empty Recycle Bin*. Click Yes at the confirmation prompt.

2. Click Start and then click *Documents*.

3. Locate the folder you created in the previous exercise and delete it by selecting the folder and then pressing the Delete key. Click Yes to confirm.

4. Open the Recycle Bin.

   Notice that the individual files that were in that folder do not appear in the Recycle Bin. Instead, the whole folder appears.

5. In the Recycle Bin window, select the deleted folder and then click the Restore this item button on the Command bar.

6. In the Documents folder, locate the restored folder and double-click it to open it.

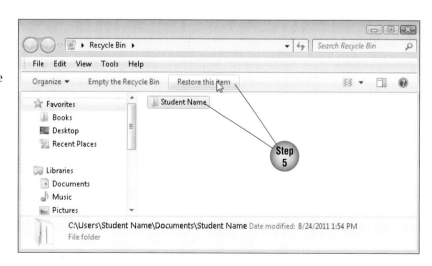

7. Select the three files in the folder. Right-click the selection and then click *Delete* at the shortcut menu.

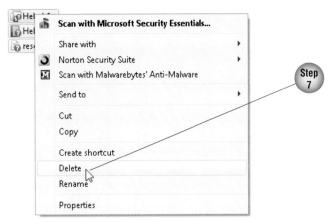

Step 7

8. Click Yes to confirm.

9. Close the Recycle Bin window. Right-click the Recycle Bin icon and then click *Empty Recycle Bin*.

10. Click Yes to confirm.

11. Close all open windows.

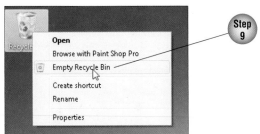

Step 9

Guidelines for Naming and Renaming Files

Program and system files have names that you should not change, but you can assign your own names to the data files you create. You can also rename files using the same process you used to rename folders earlier.

File names can be up to 255 characters in length, but in practice, it is best to keep file names as short as possible while still making them meaningful enough to remember what they contain. File names can use any numbers or letters and any symbols except for the following: \ / * ? " | < >.

extension A code at the end of a file name that tells the operating system what kind of file it is

A period in a file name separates the main part of the name from the file extension. The **extension** is a code (usually three characters) that tells Windows what type of file it is. For example, *study.docx* is a document file that opens in Microsoft Word, and *study.xlsx* is a spreadsheet that opens in Microsoft Excel. If more than one period appears in the file name, only the characters following the final period make up the extension. For example, the file *testing.my.system.exe* has an .exe extension.

By default, Windows hides the extensions for known file types. You might want to change this setting so you can keep a closer eye on what extensions are being used. To view the file extensions, click Start and then click *Computer*. At the Computer window, click the Tools button on the menu bar, and then click *Folder options* at the drop-down list. At the Folder Options dialog box, click the View tab and then click the *Hide extensions for known file types* check box to remove the check mark.

Make sure you keep the same file extension when you rename a file. Changing the extension does not change the type of data stored in the file; it just feeds Windows erroneous information about the file type.

Quick Steps

Change Display of Extensions in Windows
1. Click Start and then click *Computer*.
2. Click Tools and then click *Folder options*.
3. Click View tab.
4. Click *Hide extensions for known file types* check box to remove check mark.
5. Click OK.

Exercise 2.6D Setting File Management Options

1. Right-click the desktop, point to *New* at the shortcut menu, and then click *Text Document* at the side menu.

2. Type **Plane** and then press Enter.

3. Right-click the file you just created and then click *Rename* at the shortcut menu.

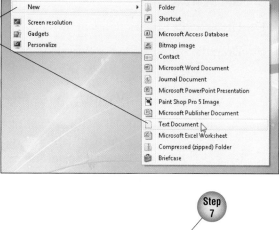

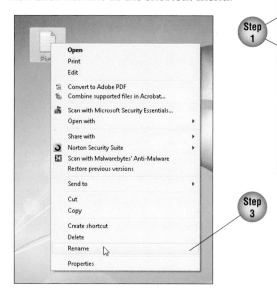

4. Type **Train** and then press Enter.

5. Click Start and then click *Documents*.

6. If necessary, press the Alt key to display the menu bar.

7. Click Tools on the menu bar and then click *Folder options*.

8. Click the View tab.

9. Make sure the *Hide extensions for known file types* check box is cleared. If it is not, click the check box to clear it and then click OK.

   Look at the Train icon on the desktop; notice that it now has a .txt extension displayed.

10. Click the Train icon and then press F2.

    Notice that only the file's name (not its extension) is highlighted for editing.

11. Type **Auto** and then press Enter.

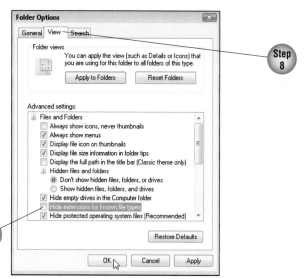

12. Press the Print Screen key on your keyboard to capture the contents of the desktop as an image file.

13. Open the WordPad application.

14. Press Ctrl + V to insert the print screen file into the WordPad document.

15. Print the WordPad document by pressing Ctrl + P and then clicking the Print button at the Print dialog box.

16. Click the Close button located in the upper right corner of the WordPad window to exit WordPad and then click the Don't Save button at the message asking if you want to save the changes.

17. Hide the file extensions again by repeating Steps 5–9 and inserting a check mark in the check box.

18. Drag the Auto icon to the Recycle Bin.

Working with File Properties

file properties
Information about a file, such as its size and type

status flag An on/off switch for a particular property

Each file has a set of **file properties**, including its size, creation date, last-modified date, file type, and status flags. A **status flag** is an on/off switch for a particular file property, such as whether the file is read-only or hidden. You can view some of these properties by selecting a file and looking in the Status bar at the bottom of the window. You can view even more details about a file's properties by right-clicking the file and then clicking *Properties* to open its properties dialog box (see Figure 2.18).

Quick Steps

View a File's Properties

1. Right-click file.
2. Click *Properties*.

Figure 2.18 **File Properties**

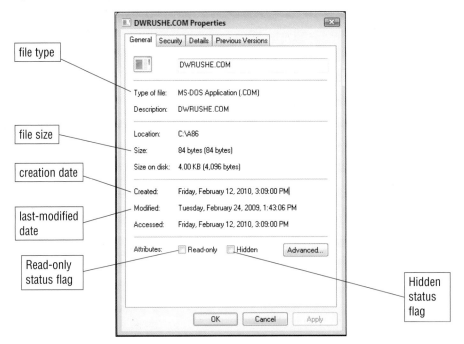

Drilling Down

Troubleshooting Common File Management Problems

Here are some tips for solving problems when working with files (additional troubleshooting methods are listed in the Delving Deeper section):

Problem: A message appears that the file cannot be deleted when you try to delete it.

Solution: Right-click the file and then click *Properties*. At the properties dialog box, make sure the *Read-only* check box is cleared, and then click OK.

Problem: When you double-click a data file to open it, a message appears that Windows cannot open the file but will search online for a program to use to open the file.

Solution: If you do not have a program to open that file type, you might need to download and install one. For example, you might get this message if you do not have Adobe Reader or Adobe Acrobat and you try to open a file with a .pdf extension. If you renamed the file, you might have accidentally changed its extension; check the file name, and change the extension if needed to accurately reflect the file type.

Problem: When you double-click a shortcut, a Problem with Shortcut dialog box appears telling you that the file the shortcut refers to has been deleted.

Solution: Check the Recycle Bin to see if the file can be restored. If the file is gone, delete the shortcut.

Lesson 2.7   Using the Help System

Instead of a paper manual, Windows 7 includes an onscreen Help and Support system, which you can open by clicking *Help and Support* at the Start menu. Figure 2.19 shows the Help and Support window. The Help and Support system combines help information stored in files on your hard disk with additional help information retrieved from the Internet. The combination of hard disk files and data from the Internet ensures that the information you receive is the most current, but also that help is always available, even if you are offline.

Figure 2.19 Windows Help and Support Window

After opening the Windows Help and Support window, you can look for help information in any of the following ways:

Quick Steps

Open the Help System in Windows

Click Start and then click *Help and Support.*

Keyboard Shortcut

Help

F1

- In the *Search Help* box, type a keyword and then press Enter. A list of articles that match your keyword appears; click the article you want to read. Click the Home button to go back to the home page at any time, or click the Back button to go back to a previously viewed page.

- Click the Browse Help button and then, in the list that appears, click a topic area. Keep clicking and narrowing down the topic until you find the article you want.

- Click the Ask button to display a page listing ways of getting more help, such as Windows Remote Assistance (for help from a friend), Microsoft Answers (for help from public newsgroups), and Microsoft Customer Support.

Exercise 2.7 Using the Help System

1. Click Start and then click *Help and Support.*

   This opens the Windows Help and Support window.

2. Click the Browse Help button.

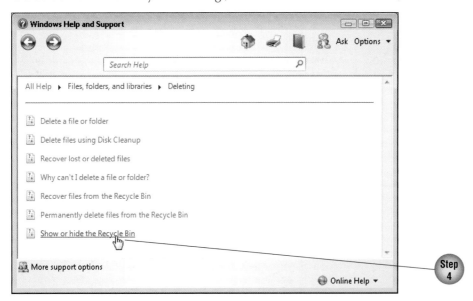

3. Click the *Files, folders, and libraries* option and then click *Deleting.*

   A list of articles appears pertaining to deleting files.

4. Click <u>Show or hide the Recycle Bin</u>.

   If <u>Show or hide the Recycle Bin</u> does not appear, click <u>Using the Recycle Bin</u> and then click <u>Show or hide the Recycle Bin</u>. (The hierarchy of topics within the Help and Support system depends on the edition of Windows you are using.)

5. Read the article that appears explaining how to show or hide the Recycle Bin on the desktop.

6. Use the instructions in the article to hide the Recycle Bin on the desktop.

7. Use the same procedure to redisplay the Recycle Bin.

8. In the Windows Help and Support window, click the Home button to return to the Windows Help and Support home page.

9. Under the *More on the Windows website* heading, click one of the hyperlinks and then read the web page that appears.

10. On the web page, click Help & How To, and then on the menu that appears, click *Windows 7*.

11. Browse the hyperlinks that appear on the web page, and then close the web browser window.

12. Close the Windows Help and Support window.

Lesson 2.8 Customizing Windows Settings

)(C³ 1-3.3.1, 1-3.3.2, 1-3.3.3, 1-3.3.5

You can use the Control Panel to customize Windows in a variety of ways, including changing the display settings, the desktop appearance (wallpaper/background), the keyboard and mouse settings, and much more.

The Control Panel is organized into categories such as System and Maintenance, Security, Network and Internet, and so on. Figure 2.20 shows the top level of categories. You can click a category to view its complete list of options, or click one of the hyperlinks beneath the category name to jump quickly to one of the most common areas within that category.

Quick Steps

Open the Control Panel

1. Click Start.
2. Click *Control Panel.*

Figure 2.20 **Control Panel**

Table 2.3 lists each Control Panel category and its contents. Additional options may be available if you have installed third-party applications. For example, some versions of Symantec Norton Antivirus install a Symantec LiveUpdate option in the Security category. Some items appear in more than one category to make it easier to find them, but the shortcuts all point to the same location.

Table 2.3 **Control Panel Categories**

Category	Contents
System and Security	Action Center Windows Firewall System Windows Update Power Options Backup and Restore Windows Anytime Upgrade Administrative Tools
Network and Internet	Network and Sharing Center Homegroup Internet Options
Hardware and Sound	Devices and Printers AutoPlay Sound Power Options Display Windows Mobility Center
Programs	Programs and Features Default Programs Desktop Gadgets
User Accounts and Family Safety	User Accounts Parental Controls Window CardSpace Credential Manager Mail
Appearance and Personalization	Personalization Display Desktop Gadgets Taskbar and Start Menu Ease of Access Center Folder Options Fonts
Clock, Language, and Region	Date and Time Regional and Language Windows Live Language Setting
Ease of Access	Ease of Access Center Speech Recognition

Exploring Alternate Methods for Accessing the Control Panel

You do not always have to open the Control Panel window to access its settings. For example, to access some of the display settings you can right-click the desktop and then click *Personalize*. To change the screen resolution you can right-click the desktop and then click *Screen resolution*. To change the date and time, click the clock that displays at the right side of the Taskbar. Depending on your computer's settings, it may show the current time in digital form, or both the date and the time. Click *Change date and time settings*. All these tasks can also be completed using the Control Panel, as indicated in Table 2.3.

Using Caution When Changing System Settings

Windows will let you change a wide variety of settings, but before you make changes, verify that the changes you are going to make will improve the system and not harm it in some way. Here are some things to watch out for:

- User accounts: Do not delete anyone else's user account without his or her permission, or without the permission of the computer owner.

- Screen resolution: If you set this to anything other than the monitor's native resolution the display may appear fuzzy or too large.

- Desktop background: If you set this to a very busy pattern or picture, you may have trouble reading the text under the desktop icons.

- Date and time: If you change the date and time by more than an hour or so, some programs that rely on the system date and time may malfunction.

Quick Steps

Change the Screen Resolution

1. Right-click desktop.
2. Click *Screen resolution*.
3. Click *Resolution* option box.
4. Drag slider to change resolution.
5. Click OK.
6. Click Yes if confirmation message displays.

Change the Date and Time

1. Click clock on Taskbar.
2. Click *Change date and time settings*.
3. Click Date and Time tab.
4. Click Change date and time button.
5. Modify date or time as needed.
6. Click OK.
7. Click OK.

Exercise 2.8 Changing Settings with the Control Panel

1. Click Start and then click *Control Panel*.

2. Click <u>Hardware and Sound</u>.

3. Under the Devices and Printers heading, click *Mouse*.

   The Mouse Properties dialog box opens. (Your tabs may differ from those in the figure.)

4. With the Buttons tab active, drag the *Double-click speed* slider all the way to *Fast*.

5. Double-click the folder icon to the right of the slider to test the setting.

6. Drag the *Double-click speed* slider all the way to *Slow*.

7. Double-click the folder icon to test the setting.

8. Drag the *Double-click speed* slider back to the center.

9. Click OK to close the Mouse Properties dialog box.

10. In the Control Panel window, click *Appearance and Personalization* in the left pane.

11. Click <u>Personalization</u>.

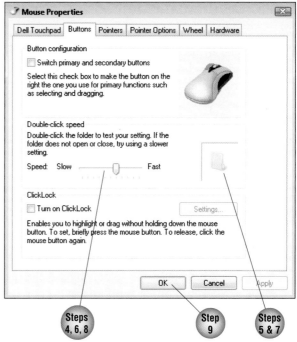

Steps 4, 6, 8

Step 9

Steps 5 & 7

Step 11

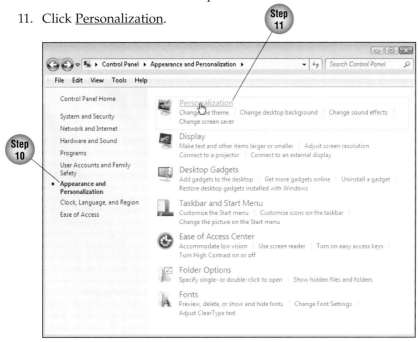

Step 10

12. Under the *Aero Themes* heading, click *Architecture* and then notice how the desktop and settings change.

    You may need to scroll down the list box to display the *Architecture* option.

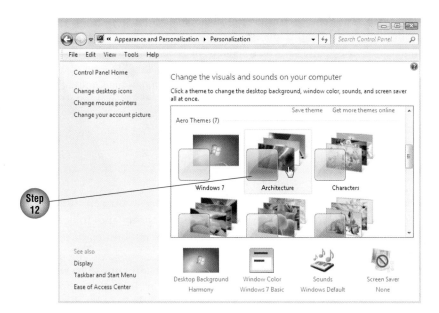

13. Click the *Desktop Background* option that displays toward the bottom of the window.

    Another name for the desktop background is wallpaper.

14. Scroll through the backgrounds, click one that appeals to you, and then click the Save changes button.

15. Click the *Windows 7* option below the *Aero Themes* heading.

    This redisplays the Windows 7 default theme.

16. Click the Back button to return to the Appearance and Personalization window and then click *Hardware and Sound* in the left pane.

17. Click the *Change system sounds* option located below the *Sound* heading.

18. At the Sound dialog box with the Sounds tab selected, click the *Sound Scheme* option down-pointing arrow (displays with *Windows Default*) and then click *Calligraphy* at the drop-down list.

19. Scroll down the *Program Events* list box and then click *Critical Stop*.

20. Click the Test button.

21. Click the Cancel button to cancel the sound scheme changes.

22. Close all open windows.

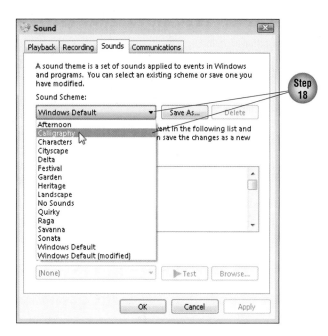

Drilling Down

Accessing Items in the Control Panel

Items in the Control Panel with a multi-colored shield next to them can be changed only by a user whose account includes administrative privileges. When you attempt to open one of those items, a User Access Control dialog box appears to verify that the logged-in account has the appropriate privileges. If you are logged in as an administrator, you can click Yes or OK to move past this warning. If you are logged in as a standard user, you will not be allowed to make the change. Log out and then log in as a user with administrator privileges. You can change the level of a user account in the *User Accounts and Family Safety* (or *User Accounts*) section of the Control Panel.

Lesson 2.9   Working with Printers

 1-1.1.5, 1-3.3.4

default printer The printer that is set to be used automatically if another printer is not specified

Quick Steps

View the Installed Printers

1. Click Start.
2. Click *Devices and Printers*.

View a Printer's Queue from the Devices and Printers Window

1. Double-click printer.
2. If queue does not appear, double-click *See what's printing*.

Pause/Resume a Printer from the Print Queue Window

1. Click Printer on menu bar.
2. Click *Pause Printing* or *Resume Printing*.

Pause/Resume/Cancel an Individual Print Job from the Print Queue Window

1. Click Document on menu bar.
2. Click *Pause, Resume,* or *Cancel*.

Print in an Application

1. Click File and then click *Print*.
2. Set print options as needed.
3. Click Print (or OK).

A printer is one of the most common types of devices you can attach to a computer. They come in many varieties, including laser and inkjet. Some printers are multifunctional devices, combining the capabilities of a printer with those of a scanner, copier, and/or fax machine.

When you print your work in an application, you can choose to which of the installed printers the work should be sent. If you do not specify which printer to use, the print job is sent to the printer designated as the default printer. The **default printer** is the printer that is used automatically if a particular printer is not specified by an application or print job. You can view the list of installed printers in Windows, choose which one will be the default, and even add a new printer to the list. You can also look at the properties for each printer, and make changes to them.

To view the installed printers, click Start and then click *Devices and Printers*. At the Devices and Printers window (see Figure 2.22), you can double-click a printer and then click *See what's printing* to view its queue (that is, the list of files in line to be printed), or right-click the printer's icon and then select from its shortcut menu to view its properties, make it the default printer, and so on. (Two separate commands are available: *Properties* and *Printer properties*; each of these displays separate options.) Manage print jobs using the printer's queue. Options include pausing or resuming the print job. For example, if you have an urgent file at the end of a printer queue, you can pause the jobs that precede it and then resume those files when the urgent file has been printed.

To use a printer, open the application from which you want to print and then issue the Print command. The exact location of the command varies, but the most common place for it is on the File menu or File tab. Clicking *File* and then clicking *Print* typically opens a Print dialog box (or the Print tab Backstage view in Office applications), from which you can change any printer settings as needed before clicking the Print button to print the file.

Figure 2.21 Devices and Printers Window

Right-click printer to display shortcut menu

« Hardware and Sound ▸ Devices and Printers ▸   ▾ | ↻ | Search Devices and Print... 🔎

File   Edit   View   Tools   Help

Add a device   Add a printer   See what's printing   Print server properties   Remove device   ▾ ❓

Dell Photo AIO Printer 926 on FAITHELAPTOP-PC

Fax

HP Deskjet F2400 series on CUTLER-PC

HP P C47

See what's printing
✓ Set as default printer
Printing preferences
Printer properties

Create shortcut

Troubleshoot
Remove device

Properties

HPInkjet (HP Photosmart C4700 series)

Journal Note Writer

Lexmark C510 PS (MS) on E510

Microsoft XPS Document Writer

Send To OneNote 2010

HP Photosmart C4700 series   State: ✅ Default   Status: 0 document(s) in queue
Model: HP Photosmart C4700 s...
Category: Printer

Exercise 2.9 Working with Printers

1. Click Start and then click *Devices and Printers*.

2. Locate the printer icon that has the green circle with a check mark on it.

   This is the default printer.

3. If more than one printer icon displays, right-click one of the others and then click *Set as Default Printer*. Repeat the steps to reset the original printer as the default.

4. Right-click the default printer and then click *Printer properties*.

5. At the properties dialog box with the General tab selected, click the Print Test Page button.

6. Examine the properties on several of the tabs in the properties dialog box and then click Cancel.

7. Double-click the icon for the default printer to open its queue. If the print queue does not open, double-click the *See what's printing* option.

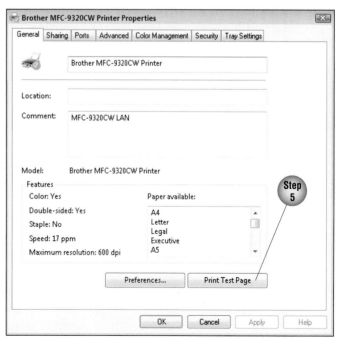

Brother MFC-9320CW Printer Properties

General | Sharing | Ports | Advanced | Color Management | Security | Tray Settings

Brother MFC-9320CW Printer

Location:

Comment: MFC-9320CW LAN

Model: Brother MFC-9320CW Printer

Features
Color: Yes   Paper available:
Double-sided: Yes   A4
Staple: No   Letter
Speed: 17 ppm   Legal
                              Executive
Maximum resolution: 600 dpi   A5

Preferences...   Print Test Page

OK   Cancel   Apply   Help

Step 5

8. In the queue window, click Printer on the menu bar, and then click *Pause Printing* at the drop-down list.

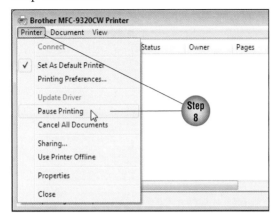

9. Open Notepad by clicking Start, clicking *All Programs*, clicking *Accessories*, and then clicking *Notepad*.

10. Type your full name.

11. Click File on the menu bar and then click *Print* at the drop-down list.

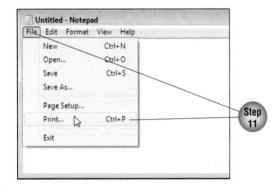

12. At the Print dialog box, click the Print button.

This sends the print job to the printer. Notice that the print job does not print because the queue is paused.

13. Exit Notepad without saving your changes.

14. In the print queue window, click Printer on the menu bar, and then click *Pause Printing*.

This resumes printing and sends the document to the printer.

15. Close all open windows.

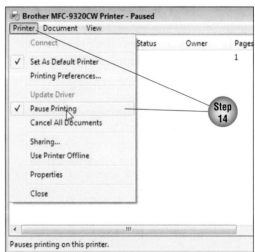

Drilling Down

Installing Printers

You can work through an Add Printer Wizard to set up a new printer, but this is often unnecessary because Windows automatically detects any new printer you have attached to the system and prompts you to insert a disk containing the driver for it. If it is a multifunction printer (one that also has a fax, copier, or scanner), this can be a problem, because the drivers for those extra functions might not install properly with Plug and Play. To get around this, do not connect the new printer to the PC immediately; instead, run the Setup software that came with it and connect it only when the Setup program prompts you to do so.

Lesson 2.10 Troubleshooting Operating System Problems

 1-3.1.5, 1-3.3.7

Knowledgeable users can solve many of the most common problems that occur in Windows on their own, without professional help. The following are a few of the most common problems and their solutions.

Problem System performance is suddenly sluggish.

Solution This can sometimes be caused by an application that has made changes to system settings. If you just installed a new application, uninstall it (from the *Programs* section of the Control Panel) and then use **System Restore** to roll back the system to a time before you installed that application. If you did not recently install any applications, use System Restore to roll back to a time before the system performance started suffering. If desired, you can reinstall the application, but you may need to investigate why the application is slowing down the system. Consider checking the support section of the software manufacturer's website for help.

Windows creates System Restore points automatically every day. You can also create an extra restore point whenever you like, for example, right before you make a change to the system or install an application that you are not sure about.

Problem The application crashes (or does not respond).

Solution If an application locks up ("crashes") as it is running, first use the Task Manager to shut down the application (if it does not shut down automatically). The **Task Manager** is an interface that allows you to view running tasks and shut down any that malfunction. Then restart the computer. If the problem continues to occur, repair the application (if possible), or uninstall and reinstall the application. You might also visit the manufacturer's website to see if any updates are available and to find out if others are experiencing the same problem.

Problem Windows crashes when starting up.

Solution This problem is often a result of unwanted or corrupted background applications that automatically load at startup. To solve this issue, try starting Windows in Safe mode, a special mode in which only the essential drivers and applications load. Then you can take a look at what is loading at startup and disable the item causing the problem.

System Restore A utility for restoring system settings to the way they were at an earlier time

Task Manager An interface for viewing running tasks and shutting down any that malfunction

Quick Steps

Display Task Manager
1. Right-click empty area on Taskbar.
2. Click *Start Task Manager.*

OR
1. Press Ctrl + Alt + Delete.
2. Click *Start Task Manager.*

Start a PC in Safe Mode
1. Restart computer. At startup beep, press F8.
2. At Advanced Boot Options menu, use arrow keys to highlight *Safe mode.*
3. Press Enter.

Exercise 2.10A Using Task Manager and Repairing an Application

1. Open the Paint application by clicking Start, clicking *All Programs,* clicking *Accessories,* and then clicking *Paint.*

2. Right-click an empty area of the Taskbar and then click *Start Task Manager.*

3. At the Windows Task Manager window with the Applications tab active, click *Untitled – Paint* and then click the End Task button.

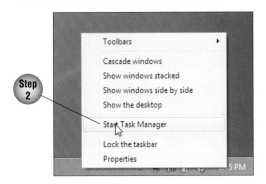

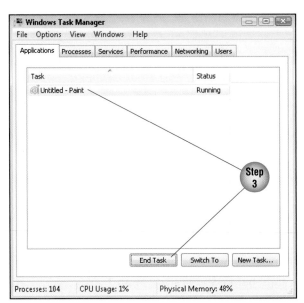

4. Close the Windows Task Manager window.

5. Click Start and then click *Control Panel.*

6. Click the *Uninstall a program* option below the *Programs* heading.

7. Click each application listed and note what buttons appear in the light blue bar above the list.

   Some applications have Uninstall/Change as a single option; others have separate Uninstall and Change buttons; still others have those buttons plus a Repair button.

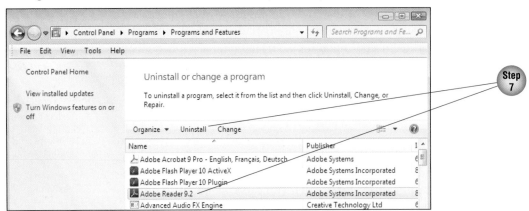

8. Close all open windows.

Exercise 2.10B Using Safe Mode and Viewing Startup Programs

1. Restart the PC and, as it is starting up, press the F8 key.

   The Advanced Boot Options menu appears.

2. Use the arrow keys to highlight *Safe mode* and then press Enter.

   Windows starts up in Safe mode.

3. Click Start, type **MSCONFIG**, and then press Enter.

   The System Configuration utility runs.

4. At the System Configuration dialog box, click the Startup tab.

   A list of all applications that load at startup appears. Your list will contain different applications than the ones shown.

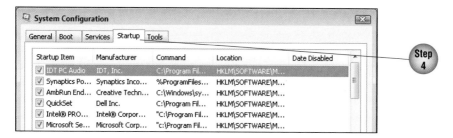

5. Browse through the list of startup programs and pick one that is not essential to system operation. (Your instructor will guide you as needed.)

6. Click the program's check box to remove the check mark.

7. Click the General tab.

   Notice that *Selective startup* has been selected.

8. Click the Tools tab.

   With the Tools tab active, a list of troubleshooting and information-gathering utilities displays.

9. At the System Configuration dialog box, click *Action Center* in the list box and then click the Launch button.

   The Action Center window opens, containing suggestions for solving possible system problems.

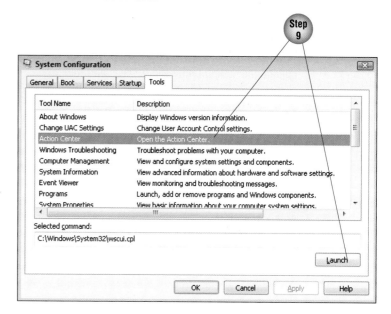

10. Close the Action Center window without making any changes.

11. At the System Configuration dialog box, click OK.

    A message appears that you must restart your computer to apply the changes.

12. Click Restart.

    The PC restarts and does not load the application you disabled.

13. Click Start, type **MSCONFIG**, and then press Enter.

    The System Configuration utility restarts.

14. At the Systems Configuration dialog box with the General tab selected, click *Normal startup*.

15. Click the Startup tab and notice that the check box for the item you previously disabled is marked again.

16. Click OK.

17. When prompted, click Restart to restart the computer again.

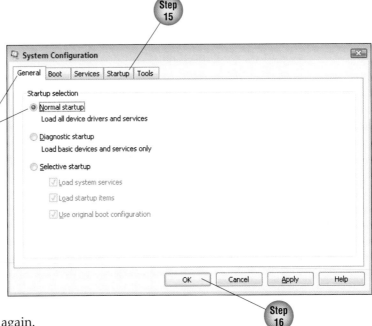

More Information for IC³

Delving Deeper

IC³ 1-1.1.8, 1-3.2.3, 1-3.2.6, 1-3.2.8

Understanding File Properties

A file's properties dialog box contains on/off status flags that assign certain attributes to the file. The General tab of the properties dialog box contains check boxes for two basic properties: Read-only and Hidden. If the *Read-only* check box is marked, the file cannot be edited. If the *Hidden* check box is marked, the file does not appear in file listings (unless you have configured Windows to show hidden files). To control the display of hidden files from Windows Explorer, open the Tools drop-down list and click *Folder Options*. On the View tab of the Folder Options dialog box, change the setting under Hidden files and folders.

Understanding the Purpose of a Device Driver

Each piece of hardware speaks its own language, and cannot communicate with the operating system without a translator. Device drivers are software that provide the needed translation services that allow devices to interact with the operating system. When you buy a new device, it will usually come with a driver installation program on a CD. You can run that program to install the needed driver on your PC. Not all devices require you to install a driver, however; Windows comes with a large library of drivers preinstalled for the most common devices, and in many cases Windows can identify the device and install a usable driver for it automatically, through a process called Plug and Play. The driver that Windows provides for a device may not be the most current, so you may still want to install the driver that came with the device, or better yet, to check the device's website to see if an even more up-to-date driver is available.

continued

Additional Troubleshooting Tips for File Management

Problem: You cannot find a certain file or folder.

Solution: In the Folder Options dialog box (as in Exercise 2.6D), on the View tab, select Show hidden files, folders, and drives. You can also search for a file by its content by typing a keyword in the Search box in the upper right corner of Windows Explorer.

Problem: Error message reports hard drive is becoming full.

Solution: Use the Disk Cleanup utility, as described in Topic 1, to help identify and delete unneeded files.

Problem: A file cannot be opened, shared, or modified.

Solution: Check that the file is not a read-only file and that you have access to the file.

Problem: File access is denied.

Solution: The file may belong to some other user who has set security settings for it. Consult the file's owner to obtain access.

Problem: File is damaged or corrupted.

Solution: Run the Check Disk utility for the drive.

Problem: No application is available to open data files of a certain type.

Solution: Allow Windows to use the Web to find an appropriate application, or look up that file's extension in a Web search (see Topic 14) to determine what program it requires.

Manipulating Open Windows

To show all open windows at once (excluding minimized or closed ones), right-click a blank area of the taskbar and click one of the following options:

- Cascade Windows: Arranges all open windows in an overlapping pattern
- Tile Windows Horizontally: Arranges all open windows in horizontal rows, with no overlap
- Tile Windows Vertically: Arranges all open windows in vertical rows, with no overlap

The Show the Desktop option, also on that same menu, closes all open windows at once.

There are also several ways to browse the open windows and select the one you want to make active. One way is to hold down the Alt key and tap the Tab key. A display appears in the middle of the screen with thumbnail images of each open window. Keep tapping the Tab key until the window you want is selected, and then release the Alt key to bring it to the forefront. You can also select an application from the Windows Task Manager. To do this, right-click the taskbar and choose Start Task Manager. Then in the Windows Task Manager dialog box, on the Applications tab, select the desired application and click Switch To.

TOPIC SUMMARY

- The operating system is the software that starts a PC and keeps it running while you work. It provides a user interface and manages files, applications, and hardware.
- The user interface is called the shell. A shell can either be a command prompt or a graphical user interface (GUI). UNIX is an example of an operating system that uses a command prompt; Windows and the Mac OS use a GUI.
- You can start applications and manage files from the Start menu, which opens when you click the Start button.
- Icons are small clickable pictures representing applications, folders, documents, or other files or locations.
- The bar along the bottom of the Windows desktop is the Taskbar; open windows and programs appear here for easy switching between them.
- To minimize, maximize, or restore a window as well as close a window, use the buttons in the upper right corner of the window.
- To move a window, drag its title bar. To resize a window, drag its border.
- To run an application, select the application from the Start menu. Click *All Programs* on the Start menu to see a full menu of applications available.
- Some applications have a ribbon, which is a tabbed toolbar across the top.
- To manage files, click Start and then click *Computer*. Double-click the desired drive and then double-click the folder in which you want to work.
- To rename a file, select it, press F2, and type the new name.
- To move or copy files, drag-and-drop them. If simple dragging does not produce the desired result, hold down Ctrl to force a copy, or hold down Shift to force a move. You can also move or copy files using the Clipboard to cut (Ctrl + X), copy (Ctrl + C), and paste (Ctrl + V).
- To delete a file, select it and press Delete. The file moves to the Recycle Bin. You can retrieve deleted files by opening the Recycle Bin from its icon on the desktop.
- As you are working with files, you can hold down Shift to select a contiguous group of files or Ctrl to select a noncontiguous group of files.
- To browse the Help system in Windows, press F1, or choose Start and then click *Help and Support*.
- Customize how Windows operates with options at the Control Panel.
- To manage the printers on your system, click Start and then click *Devices and Printers*. You can double-click a printer to open its print queue, and pause or restart a print queue from the queue window.

Key Terms

application, p. 58	icon, p. 62	Start menu, p. 62
command prompt, p. 58	menu bar, p. 70	status flag, p. 86
copy, p. 79	operating system, p. 57	System Restore, p. 97
cut, p. 79	paste, p. 79	Taskbar, p. 62
default printer, p. 94	path, p. 75	Task Manager, p. 97
desktop, p. 61	ribbon, p. 71	title bar, p. 64
extension, p. 84	server, p. 60	toolbar, p. 70
file properties, p. 86	shell, p. 58	window, p. 64
graphical user interface (GUI), p. 58	shortcut, p. 62	Windows Explorer, p. 75
homegroup, p. 75	Start button, p. 62	

Features Summary

Feature	Button, Option	Keyboard Shortcut
Close window	[x]	Alt + F4
Create new folder		Alt, click *File*, *New*, *Folder*
Display Task Manager		Ctrl + Alt + Delete, click *Start Task Manager*
Exit application	[⊠]	Alt + F4
Lock Windows	, Shut down arrow, *Lock*	
Log off Windows	, Shut down arrow, *Log off*	
Maximize window	[□]	
Minimize window	[▬]	
Move window		Alt + Spacebar, M
Open Control Panel	, *Control Panel*	
Open Help	, *Help and Support*	F1
Rename folder		F2
Resize window		Alt + Spacebar, S
Restore window	[⧉]	
Shut down Windows	, Shut down	Alt + F4 (when no open windows are active)
Start application	, *Programs*	
Switch between windows		Alt + Tab
View installed printers	, *Devices and Printers*	

KEY POINTS REVIEW

Completion

In the space provided at the left, indicate the correct term, command, or option.

1. _____ List two of the four functions of an operating system.

2. _____ Windows is an example of what type of user interface?

3. _____ List three operating systems that could be used to run a server.

4. _____ This bar at the bottom of the Windows screen lists all running applications and open windows.

5. _____ To shut down Windows 7, open this menu and click the Shut Down button.

6. _____ Drag this part of a window to move it.

7. _____ This is a pathway to a file, folder, or drive, and typically has an arrow in the bottom left corner of its icon.

8. _____ To select multiple noncontiguous files, hold down this key as you click each one.

9. _____ As you drag-and-drop a file, hold down this key to create a copy of it.

10. _____ List four of the symbols that you cannot use in file names in Windows.

11. _____ This is the suffix following the period in a file's name that tells Windows what type of file it is.

12. _____ This area of Windows enables you to customize its settings.

13. _____ What does a green circle with a check mark indicate when it appears on a printer's icon?

14. _____ If the system starts running sluggishly, you might try using this utility to return to an earlier configuration.

Multiple Choice

For each of the following items, choose the option that best completes the sentence or answers the question.

1. Which of these is not an operating system?
   A. Linux
   B. WordPad
   C. Mac OS
   D. UNIX

2. Which operating system uses only a command-line interface?
   A. Windows 7
   B. Windows Server
   C. MS-DOS
   D. Mac OS X

3. Which of the following would you likely find on the Windows desktop?
   A. icons
   B. a ribbon
   C. a Minimize button
   D. the Shut down command

4. Where is the Taskbar usually found?
   A. at the bottom of the desktop
   B. along the right side
   C. along the left side
   D. at the top of the desktop

5. What does it mean to minimize a window?
   A. to close it
   B. to restore it to its previous size
   C. to make it fill the screen
   D. to shrink it to a button on the Taskbar

6. What keyboard shortcut allows you to switch between windows?
   A. Alt + F4
   B. Ctrl + Tab
   C. Alt + Tab
   D. Alt + spacebar

7. Which of the following is not a command on the Shut Down menu?
   A. Lock
   B. Switch user
   C. Log off
   D. Snooze

8. After clicking the Start button, what should you click to see the installed applications?
   A. *All Programs*
   B. *Folders*
   C. *Computer*
   D. *Default Programs*

9. What does it mean if an icon has a small arrow in one corner?
   A. It is marked for deletion.
   B. It is a shortcut.
   C. Multiple versions are available.
   D. It has no association for its extension.

10. To select multiple noncontiguous files, what key should you hold down as you click each file?
    A. Ctrl
    B. Alt
    C. Shift
    D. Caps Lock

Matching

Match each of the following definitions with the correct term, command, or option.

1. _____ Get Windows troubleshooting and usage assistance here.
2. _____ Use this utility to recover from bad system changes.
3. _____ This is a temporary holding area for data that you cut or copy.
4. _____ In some applications, this menu holds commands for saving files.
5. _____ Click this to open the Start menu.
6. _____ Deleted files go here before they are permanently erased.
7. _____ This is a computer that manages and runs network services.
8. _____ This utility shows you what programs and services are running.
9. _____ Open this from the Start menu to configure Windows settings.
10. _____ Use this utility to control what programs load automatically at startup.

A. Clipboard
B. Server
C. Recycle Bin
D. Help and Support
E. Start button
F. Control Panel
G. File
H. System Restore
I. Task Manager
J. System Configuration

SKILLS REVIEW

Review 2.1 Using an Application to Save and Print Data

1. Start the Notepad application.
2. Click Format on the menu bar and make sure there is a check mark next to *Word Wrap* in the drop-down list. If no check mark appears, click Word Wrap to enable the option.
3. Type the following text:
   NOTICE
   Our company picnic will be held on Saturday, June 25, at Summerland Park. Please make a note of the date; additional details about the event will be announced next week.
4. Save the Notepad file in the **Unit1Topic02** folder on your storage medium and name it **U1T2-R1-Picnic**.
5. Print this document using the default printer.
6. Close the file and exit Notepad.

Review 2.2 Finding and Using a Utility

Note: Do not complete this activity on a solid state hard drive.

1. Find the Disk Defragmenter application and open it.
2. In the Disk Defragmenter dialog box, click Defragment Now to begin the defragmenting process.
3. As the defragmentation is taking place, press the Print Screen key on your keyboard to capture an image of the Windows desktop.
4. Open the Paint application and then paste the image into Paint from the Clipboard.
5. Save the image as a PNG file in the **Unit1Topic02** folder on your storage medium and name it **U1T2-R2-Defrag**.
6. Print the file and then exit Paint.
7. Allow the defragmentation to finish, or cancel it, as desired.
8. Close all open windows.

Review 2.3 Creating a Shortcut

1. Open the Computer window and then browse to the C:\Windows folder.
2. Locate the file **notepad.exe** and then create a shortcut to it on the desktop.
3. Rename the shortcut **Notepad Shortcut**.
4. Press the Print Screen key to capture a an image of the Windows desktop.
5. Open the Paint application and then paste the image into Paint from the Clipboard.
6. Save the image as a PNG file in the **Unit1Topic02** folder on your storage medium and name it **U1T2-R3-Notepad**.
7. Print the file and then exit Paint.
8. Delete the Notepad shortcut.

SKILLS ASSESSMENT

Assessment 2.1 Finding and Using Windows Applications

1. Open the WordPad and Paint applications and then arrange and size their windows so that both are visible at once.
2. In the Paint program, click a color in the Colors section of the Home tab and then drag the mouse in the Paint screen to write your name.
3. In Paint, press Ctrl + A to select the entire file, and then press Ctrl + C to copy.
4. Switch to the WordPad window and then press Ctrl + V to paste.
5. In WordPad, save your work as an RTF file in the **Unit1Topic02** folder on your storage medium and name it **U1T2-A1-WordPad**.
6. Print the file and then exit WordPad.
7. In Paint, save your work as a PNG file in the **Unit1Topic02** folder on your storage medium and name it **U1T2-A1-Paint**.
8. Print the file and then exit Paint.

Assessment 2.2 Setting Windows Display Properties

1. Using the *Appearance and Personalization* section of the Control Panel, make your display resemble the image below as closely as possible. You will need to use the Windows Classic theme, an 800 x 600 display resolution, and a background picture from the Windows Desktop Backgrounds collection.

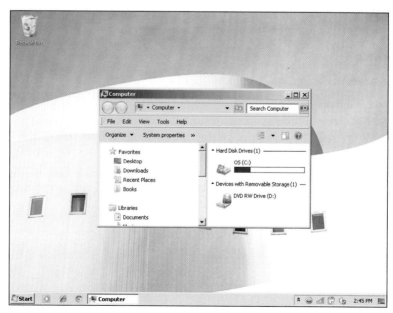

2. Open the Computer window and then size and position it to match the Computer window in the image below Step 1.
3. Press the Print Screen key to capture an image of your desktop.
4. Paste the image into the Paint application.
5. Save the image as a PNG file in the **Unit1Topic02** folder on your storage medium and name it **U1T2-A2-Display**.
6. Print the file and then exit Paint.
7. Apply the Windows 7 theme to return the desktop to the default configuration.
8. Return the display resolution to its previous setting.
9. Close any open windows.

Assessment 2.3 **Creating Shortcuts**

1. Create a shortcut icon on the desktop for the Documents library (accessible from the *Favorites* list in the Computer window).
2. Rename the Documents shortcut **Private Files** and drag it to the upper right corner of the desktop.
3. Create a shortcut to the Windows Help and Support window and place it to the left of the Private Files shortcut.
4. Press the Print Screen key to capture an image of your desktop.
5. Paste the image into the Paint application.
6. Save the image as a PNG file in the **Unit1Topic02** folder on your storage medium and name it **U1T2-A3-Icons**.
7. Print the file and then exit Paint.
8. Drag the two shortcuts you created to the Recycle Bin.
9. Empty the Recycle Bin.

Assessment 2.4 **Finding Information in a Help File**

1. Open the Windows Help and Support window.
2. Find and view an article that explains how to cancel a print job.
3. Print the article on the default printer. Write your name on the paper and submit it to your instructor.
4. Click the Ask button in the Windows Help and Support window and then find another article on the Web about canceling print jobs. Use any of the available help options. For example, you could click the hyperlink for the Windows website.
5. Print the information you find. Write your name on the paper and submit it to your instructor.
6. Close all open windows.

Assessment 2.5 **Getting Windows Troubleshooting Help Online**

1. Suppose you are getting an "Error found: Code 0x80240029" message when trying to update Windows Defender, one of the utilities in Windows 7. Use the Internet to find out how to fix this error.
2. Using Notepad, write an explanation of the information you found and then save the file in the **Unit1Topic02** folder on your storage medium and name it **U1T2-A5-Error**.
3. Print the file and then exit Notepad.

}C³ Assessment 2.6 Browsing Hidden Folders

1. Click Start and then click your user name in the upper right corner of the Start menu. A set of folders that are unique to your user account appears.
2. If an AppData folder is visible, hidden folders are already displayed. Skip to Step 7. If not, continue with Step 3.
3. Click Tools on the menu bar and then click *Folder options.*
4. At the Folder Options dialog box, click the View tab.
5. Click the *Show hidden files, folders, and drives* option that displays in the Advanced settings list box.
6. Click OK.
7. Navigate to the AppData\Roaming\Microsoft\Templates folder.
8. Press the Print Screen key to capture an image of the folder.
9. Open Paint and then paste the image.
10. Save the file in the **Unit1Topic02** folder on your storage medium and name it **U1T2-A6-Hidden**.
11. Print the file and then exit Paint.
12. Close any open windows.

CRITICAL THINKING

Comparing File Properties and Identifying Differences in File Types

1. From the Start menu, open the Documents folder and then navigate to the **Unit1Topic02** folder on your storage medium.
2. Select the **U1T2-A1-Paint.png** file you created in Assessment 2.1 and view its properties in the Details pane at the bottom of the window. Make a note of its file size.
3. Select the **U1T2-A1-Wordpad.rtf** file you created in Assessment 2.1 and view its properties. Make a note of its file size.
4. Given that those two files contain identical data, how do you account for the radical difference in their sizes? If needed, research RTF and PNG file types using the Internet.
5. Open WordPad and then write a one-paragraph summary of your research and conclusions.
6. Save the file in the **Unit1Topic02** folder on your storage medium and name it **U1T2-CT-Sizes**.
7. Print the file and then exit WordPad.

TEAM PROJECT

Comparing Mac and Linux

Suppose your school is thinking of changing the operating system on all the computers to either Ubuntu Linux or Mac OS X. Your class has been asked to research the two operating systems and provide a recommendation.

1. Divide into four teams for research gathering.

   - **Team 1: Ubuntu Linux Fans.** This team will collect data on the benefits of Ubuntu Linux.
   - **Team 2: Mac OS X Fans.** This team will collect data on the benefits of Mac OS X.
   - **Team 3: Linux Skeptics.** This team will collect data on the drawbacks of Ubuntu Linux.
   - **Team 4: Mac Skeptics.** This team will collect data on the drawbacks of Mac OS X.

2. Research your assigned topic and, as a team, prepare a short oral presentation summarizing your findings.
3. Present your findings to the class. Take notes on other teams' findings.
4. After hearing all the information presented, write a paragraph stating which operating system *you* think would be the best choice for the school and why. Use any text editing program you like (Notepad, WordPad, or Microsoft Word). Save the file in the **Unit1Topic02** folder on your storage medium and name it **U1T2-TeamOS.**
5. Print the file and then exit the program.

Discussion Questions

1. Would the school have to buy all new computers if they changed to Mac OS X? What about Ubuntu Linux?
2. Should the fact that Ubuntu Linux is an open-source operating system affect the school's decision? Why or why not?
3. Ubuntu is not the only Linux distribution; others exist such as Fedora and Red Hat. Did you or your classmates encounter any of these other Linux types? If so, how do they compare to Ubuntu? If not, review these Linux types to determine how they differ.

Topic 3

Choosing and Using Application Software

Performance Objectives

Upon successful completion of Topic 3, you will be able to:

- Install and remove applications
- Update and upgrade software
- Identify types of application software
- Understand word processing concepts
- Understand spreadsheet concepts
- Understand presentation software concepts
- Understand database concepts
- Understand graphics and multimedia concepts
- Use utility programs

STUDENT RESOURCES

Before beginning this topic, copy to your storage medium the **Unit1Topic03** subfolder from the *Computer and Internet Essentials: Preparing for IC³* Internet Resource Center. Make this the active folder.

In addition to containing the data files needed to complete topic work, the Internet Resource Center disc contains model answers in PDF format for each of the applicable exercises in this topic. Use these files to check your work. The preface of your textbook provides instructions for accessing these files.

Necessary Data Files

To complete the exercises and assessments, you will need the following data files:

Exercises 3.1–3.3	N/A
Exercises 3.4–3.11	New file
Reviews 3.1–3.3	New file
Review 3.4	ACMESales.xlsx
Review 3.5	New file
Assessment 3.1–3.6	New file

Visual Preview

Exercise 3.6 U1T3–PCPresentation.pptx

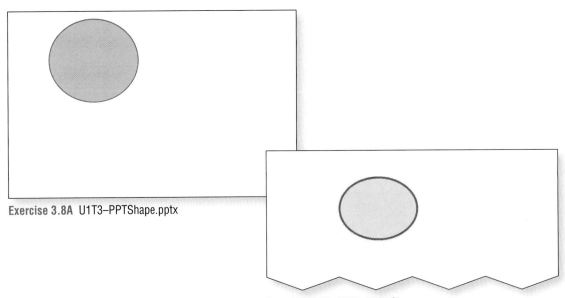

Exercise 3.7 U1T3–ExcelCosts.txt

Exercise 3.8A U1T3–PPTShape.pptx

Exercise 3.8B U1T3–PaintShape.png

Topic Overview

In Topic 2 you learned about operating systems, which keep the computer up and running. However, a computer is not useful unless it can help you *do something*, which is where application software becomes important. Application software is software that enables you to use a computer to create useful output, such as writing a letter, drawing a picture, or completing a spreadsheet.

In this topic you will learn how to select, install, navigate, and remove the user interface of a variety of applications. The applications you use on any particular computer may vary; however, once you are familiar with how application interfaces work and how different applications handle their data, you should be able to figure out new applications you encounter with minimal training.

Lesson 3.1 Installing and Removing Applications

)**C³** 1-2.1.3, 1-3.3.6, 1-3.3.7

In this lesson you will learn what differentiates an application from an operating system and how applications interface with Windows. You will also learn how to install and remove an application.

Recall from Topic 2 that an application is a software program that runs on top of an operating system and performs specific tasks for the user by providing a customized user interface. Generally speaking, applications are sold separately from operating systems. For example, you would buy Microsoft Word, a word processing program, separately from Microsoft Windows, an operating system. However, there are a few exceptions to this rule:

- Several basic applications are included with nearly all versions of Windows, such as WordPad (a simple word processor), Paint (a simple drawing program), Calculator, and Sound Recorder.

- Some computer manufacturers include applications for free with their systems that would normally be sold separately. For example, you might get an application for creating your own DVDs with a new computer that contains a DVD drive.

- Some applications are integrated into a web browser interface, so that when you visit a certain website, an application runs on your computer that is not actually installed on your computer. Examples of these include Java and ActiveX components.

Understanding Program Installation

When an application is installed, three actions typically occur:

- The files needed to run the application are copied to the hard disk. A new folder might be created to hold them, such as a subfolder within the Program Files folder.

- The Windows **Registry** is modified to indicate that the application has been installed. The Registry is a database of settings that tells Windows what hardware and software is present, among other things.

Registry A database of Windows settings that tells Windows what is installed and how to operate

- A shortcut for the program is placed on the Start menu.

Some simple programs do not require all of these actions to occur, but the majority of programs do. For a human user to perform all these steps manually would be tricky—especially the editing of the Registry—so Setup programs typically automatically complete these actions during the installation process.

Most applications cannot run unless the Registry is updated to include their settings. That is why you cannot simply copy an application's files from one computer to another to transfer the application. Running a Setup program for the application ensures that the correct changes are made to the Registry.

Determining What Applications Are Installed in Windows 7

You can determine what applications are installed on your computer in several ways. The simplest method is to browse the Start menu's system of folders. To do this, click the Start button and then click *All Programs*. A list of folders appears on the Start menu; each folder represents an application manufacturer or an individual application; below the folders are shortcuts for applications that are not in any particular folder. To see the contents of a folder, click the folder to expand it. The Accessories folder, for example, contains many of the applications that come free with Windows; this folder is shown expanded in Figure 3.1.

Figure 3.1 Accessories Folder in the Start Menu Browse the Start menu's folder system to see what applications are installed.

Quick Steps

Determine If an Application Is Installed

1. Click Start.
2. Type application name.
3. Look at top of Start menu for application's shortcut.

So many folders exist that locating a particular application on the Start menu may be difficult. If you are not sure where to look for a program, click the Start button and then begin typing its name in the search box at the bottom of the Start menu. A list of applications that match what you typed appears at the top of the Start menu, regardless of the folder in which the applications are stored. Suppose, for example, you are not sure if you have Microsoft Word on your system. Click the Start button and then type *Word* to see all the applications that contain "Word" in their names, as shown in Figure 3.2.

Figure 3.2 Start Menu Search Feature   To search for a certain program, begin typing its name.

Programs matching the typed text

Type part of the name here.

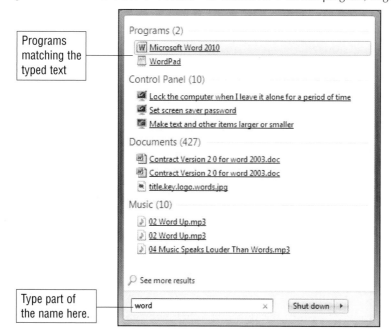

Although almost all installed programs have shortcuts somewhere in the Start menu's folder system, occasionally an installed application might not appear there. This could be because its shortcut has been accidentally or intentionally deleted from the Start menu.

Another way to determine what applications are installed is to consult the listing in the Control Panel. (The Control Panel is also where you go if you want to uninstall an application.) From the Control Panel, click the *Programs* heading, and then click *Programs and Features*. This opens a list of all the installed applications on your computer, as illustrated in Figure 3.3.

Quick Steps

Display a List of Installed Applications

1. Click Start.
2. Click *Control Panel.*
3. Click *Programs.*
4. Click *Programs and Features.*

Figure 3.3 Installed Applications Listed in the Programs and Features Window

List of installed applications

Installing a New Application

You can acquire and install new applications either by purchasing a CD or DVD containing the application's Setup program, or by downloading a Setup file online. The following sections explain each method.

Installing an Application from a CD or DVD The process of installing an application from a CD or DVD is not complicated. You simply insert the disc into your computer. Most discs contain an Autorun.inf file that instructs the computer to run the Setup program on the disc automatically whenever the disc is inserted. Depending on how Windows is configured, the Setup program might load right away, or you might see an AutoPlay dialog box, as in Figure 3.4, asking you what you want the program to do. If you see such a dialog box, click the selection under *Install or run program.* In Figure 3.4, that selection is *Run SetupAsssistant.exe.* From that point on, just follow the prompts to install.

Figure 3.4   AutoPlay Dialog Box

If nothing happens when you insert the CD or DVD into your computer's disk drive, you can manually browse the disc for the Setup program. To do so, double-click the CD/DVD drive icon in the Computer window (click the Start button, then click *Computer*), look for a file that has an *.exe* extension and the word *Setup* somewhere in its name, and then double-click that file. If you want to prevent Autorun.inf from executing when you insert a certain disc, hold down the Shift key as you insert the disc into the drive.

Downloading and Installing an Application You may encounter any of the following types of application downloads online:

- A download might consist of a single **executable file** (*.exe* extension) that contains the Setup utility and all the files needed for the application in a single package. When you double-click the downloaded file, the Setup utility runs and extracts all the files to your hard disk, creating new folders as needed and setting up the application.

- A download might consist of a single file, either with an *.exe* or *.zip* extension, that contains all the files needed for running Setup in a compressed archive package. If it is an .exe file, double-click it to extract those files to a temporary folder on your hard disk, and then locate and run the Setup.exe (or similarly named) file in that location. If it is a .zip file, when you double-click the file, it opens like a folder in Windows. You can then copy all those files to the Clipboard (press Ctrl + A to select all files and then Ctrl + C to copy them), create a new folder, and paste those files into that new folder. From there, you can locate and run the Setup file.

- A download might consist of a single application file with no supporting files. Only simple programs, like a calculator or converter utility, come in this form. You can store such a file anywhere on your hard disk and run the application by double-clicking the file. This type of application does not require Registry edits, so no Setup utility is needed. For more convenient access to the application, you can manually create a shortcut on the Start menu.

Many sources of downloadable applications are available. One good place to look for programs with which to practice is www.download.com, a division of the popular CNET site.

If you download an application that does not have a Setup program, it will not appear on your Start menu. If you want to place a shortcut there, right-click the file and choose *Pin to Start Menu*.

Understanding Software Licensing

Although the majority of the applications you acquire will probably be commercial products, a number of alternatives to commercial software sales exist. The following are some of the license types you might encounter.

Freeware **Freeware** is a type of software license that is completely free. On the small scale, you can get freeware from sites such as www.download.com or from the program creator's personal website. Large companies like Microsoft also sometimes offer products for free because it helps the company to have lots of people using that software. Even though it costs the company money to give the software away for free, they get side benefits that are worth the expense. Examples of such freeware include Google Chrome and Microsoft Internet Explorer. Freeware does not include source code, and users are not allowed to modify the applications.

Open Source **Open source** software exists in the public domain. Not only are the applications free, but the source code (code used by programmers) is also shared to encourage others to contribute to the future development and improvement of the application. Operating systems such as Linux and applications like OpenOffice.org fit in this category. Open source software cannot be sold, although it can be bundled with commercial products.

Shareware A **shareware** license is software that provides a free trial, with the expectation that users will pay for the software if they like it and decide to keep it. In some cases, a shareware version is not the full product; in other cases, it expires after a certain amount of time. Some shareware provides a full and unlimited version to all, with payment requested on the honor system. Much of the software available online is shareware.

Multiuser A multiuser license permits you to install the software on more than one computer. For example, some versions of Microsoft Office allow the user to install the same copy on two or three PCs.

Single User A single-user license allows the software to be installed on only one computer. A common misconception is that a single-user license gives you permission to install software on more than one computer as long as the software is only being used by one person at a time, but that is not accurate. Commercial products sometimes have activation systems that lock the software to a specific PC once installed so you cannot install it elsewhere.

Subscription Rather than buying a copy of an application to be installed on the local PC, users can buy a subscription to an application. The application can then be accessed online at any time. Subscription-based software is a service that is often cheaper for both the end user and the vendor, and users always have the latest version available.

Quick Steps

Install from a Compressed Archive

1. Locate and select downloaded file.
2. Select all files in window.
3. Copy all files to Clipboard.
4. Navigate to location to create new folder for installation files.
5. Click Organize. Click *New folder*.
6. Type folder name and press Enter.
7. Double-click new folder.
8. Paste copied files into new folder.
9. Locate and double-click Setup executable file.

freeware Software that is completely free to use

open source Software that is free, and for which the source code is made available to the public so anyone may modify it

shareware Software that you can try before you buy; if you decide to keep the program you must send payment to the owner

Concurrent License A **concurrent license** allows the software to be installed on many PCs but used concurrently by a smaller number. For example, the application might be installed on 1,000 computers, but only 100 users can use it simultaneously. This is useful in situations where an application needs to be available but is not often used.

Corporate, Campus, or Site License A corporate, campus, or **site license** permits an organization to install an application on an agreed-upon number of PCs. For example, a school might buy a site license of an antivirus program, and allow all students to download and install it freely, to ensure that the school's network remains free of viruses.

Registering and Activating Software

Registering software by providing your contact information to the software maker is not usually required to use software, but many software makers try to make you believe it is in your best interest to register. A software producer benefits by using your personal information for marketing purposes and may sell the information to a third party. A user that registers software may benefit by becoming eligible for discounts on new versions, free updates, or other bonuses.

Some products, especially expensive ones that are frequently pirated, include activation features that lock the installed copy (by installation key code) to a particular PC so it cannot be used on multiple PCs.

The software company does this by maintaining an online database of all the installation key codes. When you install the software, you are prompted to activate the key code. (Usually you have 30 days to do so, or a certain number of uses, before it stops working.) The activation program examines the hardware on your system (processor, motherboard model, and so on) and generates a code that describes the general state of the hardware. It then sends that code to the activation server online.

Removing an Installed Application

You may want to remove an installed application for several reasons. You may want to free up space on your computer for other applications or simply remove applications that you no longer use for the sake of organization and speed. You may also want to remove malfunctioning applications. When an application malfunctions, you can uninstall and then reinstall the application and its files. (Some programs can be repaired without uninstalling; check the options available in the Uninstall utility on your computer.)

To remove an application, open the Control Panel, click the *Programs* heading, and then click *Programs and Features*. At the list of all installed applications that displays, click the program you want to uninstall. Depending on the program, different buttons will display in the toolbar above the listing:

Quick **S**teps

Uninstall an Application

1. Click Start.
2. Click *Control Panel.*
3. Click *Programs.*
4. Click *Programs and Features.*
5. Click application.
6. Click Uninstall or Uninstall/Change.
7. Follow prompts to uninstall.

- **Single Uninstall/Change button:** This button appears for applications that have a single "maintenance" type of utility that enables the user to choose to uninstall, repair, or modify the installation options from a single interface.

- **Separate Uninstall and Change buttons:** These buttons appear for applications that have different utilities for uninstalling and repairing or changing.

- **Uninstall button only:** This button appears for applications that can only be uninstalled, not repaired or changed. The application selected in Figure 3.5 has only an Uninstall button.

Click the button that best represents what you want to do, and follow the prompts to uninstall the application. The exact steps will differ, depending on the application.

Figure 3.5 Uninstall or Change a Program Uninstall an application from the Programs and Features section of the Control Panel.

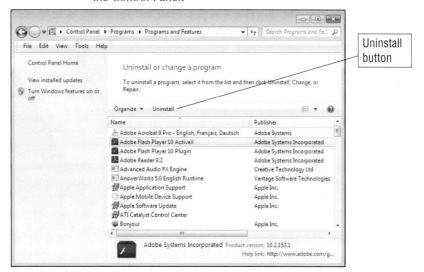

Troubleshooting Application Installation Problems

The following tips will help you troubleshoot application installation problems.

Problem: The installation stops before completion.
Solution: Make sure you are installing from a user account with sufficient permission. Check the website of the application vendor for a FAQ or support file with troubleshooting advice.
Problem: The installed application does not appear on the Start menu or desktop.
Solution: Check other folders on Start menu; the application may have been placed in a different location than you expect, or with a different name.
Problem: Other programs fail to work after the new application is installed.
Solution: Re-run Setup program for application that no longer works and choose Repair option if available. Remove and reinstall application that no longer works.
Problem: Files cannot be read by the new application.
Solution: Check to make sure the file associations are set correctly for the application's file type. To do this, go to the Control Panel and choose Programs, Default Programs, and then Set Associations.
Problem: Access to the online application is denied.
Solution: Make sure you are logged into the online site where the application is hosted with the same account you used when you paid for the application. Contact account support for the site if needed.
Problem: The online application is not available.
Solution: Wait a few hours and try again. Sometimes online applications may be taken offline temporarily for maintenance or repair.
Problem: Your school- or employer-provided computer cannot install or remove applications.
Solution: If using a computer provided by your school or employer, your user account may be blocked from installing or removing applications. Contact a system administrator to get the necessary permissions.

Exercise 3.1   Installing and Removing Applications

1. Using your web browser, navigate to www.download.com.

2. Locate a card game that looks interesting, and download a free, trial, or demo version of it.

Tips for downloading:

- If your browser is set to block pop-ups and is preventing a pop-up from appearing that will download the file, hold down the Shift key as you click the download link; this will override the pop-up blocker.

- If a File Download – Security Warning box appears asking if you want to run, save, or cancel the download, click the Save button. (Depending on the browser settings, the Save As dialog box might appear automatically.) In the Save As dialog box, select a temporary location to which to download. You might want to create a new folder on your C: drive called *Temp* for this purpose.

- After the download is complete, a dialog box might prompt you to run (or open) the file, open the download folder, or close (cancel). Click the Open button or the Run button to run the Setup for the application, or click the Open Folder button to browse for the Setup file in the folder that contains the download.

3. Install the card game program.

The exact steps for doing so will vary; follow the prompts.

4. Play the game for a few minutes.

5. Uninstall the game. Click Start, click *Control Panel*, click the *Programs* heading, and then click *Programs and Features*.

6. At the list of installed applications, click the application you installed and then click the Uninstall button or the Change/Uninstall button.

7. Follow the prompts to complete the uninstall.

8. Close all open windows.

Drilling Down

Accessing Different User Accounts

In Windows, different user account types have different permissions for installing software. You may need to log in with an administrator account in order to install an application. Some application Setup programs prompt you to decide whether the application should be available to the current user only or to all users of the PC. If you are installing software via an administrator account but you plan on using it with other accounts, make sure you make the software available to all users.

Lesson 3.2   Updating and Upgrading Applications

 1-2.1.3

Application makers periodically release updates to their programs to fix or improve them. These updates can be patches and bug fixes, completely new versions of the application, or just general updates.

updates Additional or replacement files for an application that fix or slightly enhance the application; they are usually free of charge

- **Patches and bug fixes:** Patches and bug fixes are updates that are released primarily to fix problems that have been identified in the existing application. These patches add no new features (or minor new features) and are almost always free.

- **Updates:** General **updates** can be a combination of bug fixes and new feature additions to the existing version of the software. They do not upgrade you to a newer version of the software per se, but the version number you have might increment slightly. For example, suppose you have version 1.0 of the program; installing an update might change your version number to 1.1. This type of update is almost always free.

- **Upgrades:** An **upgrade** replaces your version of the application with a totally new, redesigned version with new features. For example, you might go from version 1.0 to version 2.0 of the software. Such upgrades are not typically free; the best you might hope for is a discount offered to users of previous versions.

Understanding the difference between an update and an upgrade is important. An *update* is one or more additional or replacement files for an application that fix and in some cases slightly enhance what you already have and is usually free. An *upgrade* adds significant new features and capabilities and is usually not free.

Getting Application Updates and Patches

To find out if updates or patches are available for an existing application, visit the manufacturer's website. An update could possibly fix a problem you are having with the application, or could add a new feature you might find useful. A link to the website may be available from the Help menu in the application or from the application's folder in the Start menu. For example, in Figure 3.6 the application has a *Check for Updates* option on the Help menu.

Figure 3.6 Check for Updates Option in Paint Shop Pro

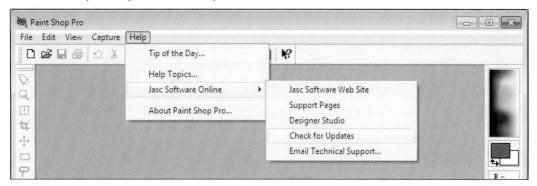

If you do not know the manufacturer's web address or the name of the company that makes the application, look for an *About* option on the Help menu. This typically opens an About dialog box which contains information about your registration and the company. For example, in Figure 3.7, the company's web address appears below the version information.

At the company's website, search for a Support hyperlink that will take you to a section where you can download new versions and updates for your application. You can find out what version you currently have at the About dialog box. If a more recent version is available, you may be able to download an update that will make your version current.

Windows 7 has an automatic update feature that enables you to acquire patches and updates for Microsoft products. To use it, click the Start button, click *All Programs*, and then click *Windows Update*. At the Windows Update window, click the *Check for updates* option (located in the left pane of the window) and if any updates are available, install them. These updates apply mainly to Windows 7 itself, but when updates for Microsoft Office programs are available, you can install them from this utility as well.

Figure 3.7 About Dialog Box

Upgrading to a New Version of an Application

New versions of applications can add exciting new features, but choosing to upgrade a program can also lead to problems. Before upgrading to a new version of an application, consider the following issues you might encounter:

- **Incompatibility:** A new version of an application may not be designed to work with your current operating system. For example, perhaps the version you have works on Windows 2000, but the newest version of the application only works on Windows 7. Check version requirements before upgrading any software.

- **Lack of familiarity:** A new version of an application might have a different interface that will take time to learn, and you might not like the new interface as much as the old interface.

- **Higher costs:** A new version of an application might require that you pay more money to the software publisher. For example, the old version might have been free or shareware, but the new version might be a commercial product.

- **New policies:** A new version of an application might come with strings attached, such as requiring you to agree to accept advertising on your PC or limiting certain features until you pay a fee.

If, after weighing the benefits and drawbacks, you decide to pursue the upgrade, several methods of acquiring upgrades are available. You may be able to download a new version from the manufacturer's website, or you may opt for a retail-boxed version of the program. Depending on the application, you might be able to get an upgrade from within your current version's interface. For example, some applications periodically generate a message telling you that newer or more feature-rich versions are available.

Exercise 3.2   Researching and Installing Software Updates

1. Click Start, click *All Programs*, and then click *Windows Update*.

2. Click the <u>Check for updates</u> hyperlink located in the left pane of the Windows Update window and then wait for the check to complete.

3. If updates are available for Microsoft Office or any other applications, click Install Updates to install them.

   If you are prompted to restart your computer after installing an update, do so.

4. Identify a non-Microsoft application on your hard disk.

   Your instructor may specify which application to use; if not, choose one on your own.

5. Determine the application's manufacturer. This information can usually be found by opening the Help menu and then clicking *About*.

6. Find the company's website.

   You may be able to figure out the correct web address for certain companies. For example, Adobe's web address is www.adobe.com. If that does not work, do a Google search for the company's name.

7. Using Internet Explorer, browse the company's website and find the *Support* section.

8. Check to see whether any updates are available for your version of that application.

9. If any updates are available, download and install them.

Lesson 3.3 Understanding Types of Application Software

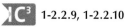 1-2.2.9, 1-2.2.10

To save yourself time and effort, it is important to select the right type of application software for the job you need to do. Most applications are designed to create one specific type of content. Some of them may also be able to create other content, but not as quickly or easily. For example, you can create a web page in any program that saves in web format, including Excel or PowerPoint, but the page would be difficult to maintain using those programs. Web pages are much better when created with a web design program such as Dreamweaver or FrontPage.

Upcoming lessons will explain several of the most popular types of applications in more detail, including conceptual information about how the data in these programs is stored and organized. Table 3.1 provides a quick overview of common applications and their uses.

Table 3.1 **Common Applications and Their Uses**

Application Type	Examples	Used For
Word processing	Microsoft Word, Corel WordPerfect, WordPad	Text-based documents such as reports, letters, and memos
Desktop publishing	Microsoft Publisher, Adobe InDesign, Quark XPress	Documents that combine text and graphics in a page layout, such as newsletters, business cards, and greeting cards
Spreadsheet	Microsoft Excel, Quattro Pro, Lotus 1-2-3	Financial data in row-and-column format, such as budgets, amortization tables, and sales results; graphical charts that represent numeric data
Database	Microsoft Access, SQL, FileMaker	Data records such as addresses, customer order information, and student academic records
Presentation	Microsoft PowerPoint	Slides that serve as visual aids for speeches and presentations delivered live, on disc, or online
Photo-editing and paint	Microsoft Paint, Adobe Photoshop, Corel Paint Shop Pro	Bitmap (raster)-based artwork, digital photo editing, and retouching
Drawing	Adobe Illustrator, Microsoft Visio, AutoCAD	Vector-based artwork, 3-D modeling
Media players	Microsoft Media Player, RealPlayer, iTunes	Playback of digital music and video clips; some programs can also create clips from A/V input
Web design	Adobe Dreamweaver, Microsoft Expression Web	Web pages, websites

To find the best program for a project, you must learn enough about each of the available applications that you can identify their strengths and primary functions. You will learn about several types of applications in the upcoming lessons.

Exercise 3.3   Choosing an Application

Choose the most appropriate type of application for each of the following activities.

A. Word processing
B. Spreadsheet
C. Database
D. Presentation
E. Desktop publishing

F. Media player
G. Web design
H. Drawing
I. Photo-editing

1. _____ Listening to MP3s
2. _____ Designing a newsletter layout
3. _____ Writing a business report
4. _____ Creating a customer order-entry system
5. _____ Creating visual aids for a business meeting
6. _____ Editing a scanned picture
7. _____ Creating a 3-D model of a machine part
8. _____ Tracking sales data and creating a chart

Lesson 3.4   Understanding Word Processing Applications

 1-2.2.1

A word processing program, also known as a word processor, "processes" text by formatting it and enabling you to type, edit, and arrange it on a document page. Word processing programs can also incorporate graphics and other types of data, but their primary purpose remains text-based.

   Microsoft Word is the most popular word processing application. If you are working on a PC that does not have Microsoft Word installed, you can use a free word processor called WordPad that comes with all versions of Windows.

Understanding a Word Processor Interface

Different word processors may have different interfaces, but they usually have certain features in common. Figure 3.8 shows a WordPad window and points out the following features: I-beam pointer, insertion point, Quick Access toolbar, ribbon, Ruler, and File tab.

Figure 3.8 WordPad Window Note that many of these features are also included with other word processing programs.

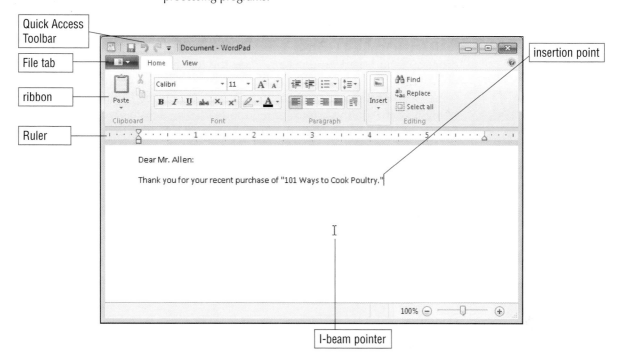

Quick Access Toolbar

File tab

ribbon

Ruler

insertion point

I-beam pointer

Dear Mr. Allen:

Thank you for your recent purchase of "101 Ways to Cook Poultry."

- When the mouse pointer is placed over the text entry area, it turns into an **I-beam pointer**, which looks like a curly capital I.

- The **insertion point** is a flashing vertical line that identifies where your text will be inserted in the document. It is like a cursor. Whatever you type will appear at the insertion point location. You can move the insertion point by clicking where you want it to go. Pressing Backspace deletes the character to the left of the insertion point. Pressing Delete deletes the character to the right of the insertion point.

- Recall that the ribbon is a tabbed toolbar from which you can select commands.

- The Ruler shows how the typed text will correspond to a printout. For example, in Figure 3.8 you can see that the text typed in the second line will occupy approximately four and a half inches on a printout (without the margins).

- The **Quick Access Toolbar** is a customizable toolbar located above the ribbon that provides convenient access to a few frequently used commands.

- The File tab opens a menu for saving, closing, opening, and printing files. In Office 2010 applications, this menu occupies the whole application window and is called **Backstage view**.

I-beam pointer The mouse pointer when it is placed over a text entry area

insertion point The flashing vertical cursor indicating where text will appear when you type

Quick Access toolbar A customizable toolbar containing commonly used commands

Backstage view In Office 2010 applications, the view that appears when you click the File tab; the location from which you can save, close, open, and print files

Insert mode A typing mode where text to the right of the insertion point is moved over to make room for new text

Overtype mode A typing mode where text to the right of the insertion point is replaced by new text

Quick Steps

Toggle between Insert and Overtype Modes in WordPad

Press Insert key.

Toggle between Insert and Overtype Modes in Word

1. Right-click Status bar.
2. Click *Overtype*.

Save Your Work

1. Click Save button on Quick Access toolbar or click File tab and then click Save.
2. Type file name.
3. Change save location (optional).
4. Click Save.

Keyboard Shortcut

Save

Ctrl + S

In a word processor, the large white background in the center of the application window is considered the "page." Whatever you type in a word processor is placed directly on the page. When you place the insertion point in the middle of existing text and start typing, the text to the right of the insertion point moves over to make room. This happens because the program is in **Insert mode**. To replace the text to the right of the insertion point with the new text you type, you can change to **Overtype mode**. In some word processing programs, the Insert key on the keyboard can be set to toggle between these two typing modes. To switch to Overtype mode in Microsoft Word, right-click the Status bar at the bottom of the application window and click *Overtype* at the shortcut menu. Repeat the steps to switch back to Insert mode.

When documents were composed on typewriters, the user was required to press Enter every time a sentence approached the margin. Today's word processors do not require that action because word processors automatically wrap text onto the next line of the page. This feature allows the programs to re-break text if the formatting or content within the document changes.

Saving Your Work

Saving your work is necessary if you want to pick up where you left off in a previous session. If you do not save your work, it will be lost when you close the application. The process for saving your work is the same in most applications, so once you have learned to save in one program you will be able to save in other programs. You saved your work in several applications in Topic 2, so you may already be familiar with this process.

When you are ready to save your work, click the File tab (or File on the menu bar) and then click the Save option. You can also press Ctrl + S. At the Save As dialog box that displays, type the desired file name and then press Enter or click the Save button. You also have the option of changing the location where your document will be saved. Browse for a different location just as you learned to do in Windows Explorer in the previous topic. Figure 3.9 shows the Save As dialog box in WordPad, but it is nearly identical in Word.

If the file has been saved previously, the Save command resaves it with the same name and location as before. This effectively replaces the previous file with the updated one. If you want to save it as a new file by either changing the file location, file name, or file type, use the Save As command instead of the Save command.

Most applications have a Save button on the toolbar or the ribbon that you can use instead of selecting the Save command. The Save button looks like a floppy disk. In Figure 3.9 it is the second icon from the left on the Quick Access toolbar, which is the small toolbar above the ribbon that contains commonly used commands.

Figure 3.9 Save As Dialog Box in WordPad

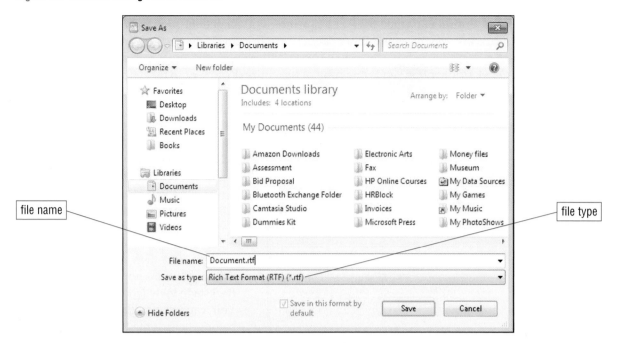

file name

file type

Opening Your Saved Work

To resume work on a saved file, you must first open it. Some applications allow you to have more than one file open at once; other applications close any open files when you open a new file. To open a file, click File on the menu bar (or click the File tab) and then click Open. You can also press Ctrl + O. At the Open dialog box that displays (see Figure 3.10), click the file you want to open. If you changed the save location when you saved the file, you may need to navigate to the new location in the Open dialog box to locate the file. After selecting the file, click Open.

Keyboard Shortcut

Open
Ctrl + O

Figure 3.10 Open Dialog Box in WordPad

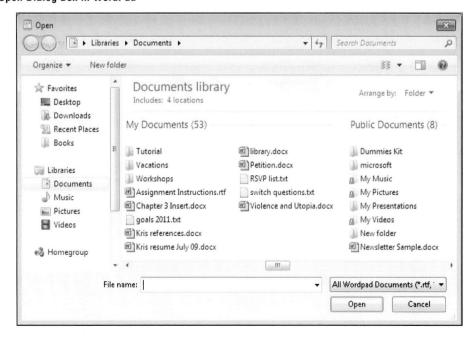

Choosing and Using Application Software

Printing Your Work

If your computer has a printer attached to it (or if a printer is available through your network), you can use it to create a hard copy of your work. WordPad has two printing options: Print and Quick print. The Print option opens a Print dialog box where you can specify the printer, the number of copies, and the page range. The Quick print option sends one copy of the entire document to the default printer without opening a dialog box. To complete a Quick print in WordPad, click the File tab, point to Print, and then click the Quick print command (see Figure 3.11). To complete a print with the Print dialog box, click the File tab and then click the Print command or press Ctrl + P. At the Print dialog box, click the Print button.

To print in Word 2010, click the File tab and then click the Print tab. Printing options appear in the Print tab Backstage view (shown in Figure 3.12). You can change any of the settings before clicking the Print button.

Figure 3.11 Quick Print Command in WordPad

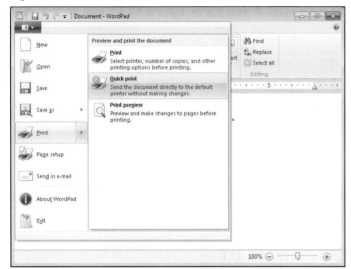

Figure 3.12 Print Tab Backstage View in Word

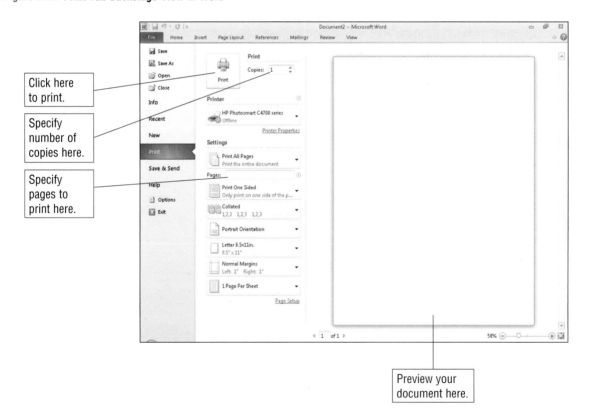

Click here to print.

Specify number of copies here.

Specify pages to print here.

Preview your document here.

Exploring Other Word Processing Capabilities

Word processing programs are designed to make creating documents that consist primarily of text easy for you. In Unit 2 of this book you will learn about Microsoft Word in detail, including how to use some of the following word processing capabilities:

- **Editing:** Word processing programs make it easy to move sections of a document around, as well as edit individual words and sentences.

- **Formatting:** With a word processing program, you can change fonts, font sizes, and font colors, and apply formatting like bold and italics to text. You can also format paragraphs, making them align differently in relation to the margins. You can set and use tabs and make text appear in multiple columns.

- **Error checking:** A built-in spelling and grammar checker points out possible errors and allows you to correct them.

- **Tables:** The Tables feature provides a systematic way to organize and display data such as text, numbers, or formulas in columns and rows.

- **Inserting objects:** Add visual appeal to a document by inserting an object such as a picture, clip art image, shape, or WordArt. Use the SmartArt feature to create visual representations of data such as organizational charts and graphics.

Exercise 3.4 Using a Word Processor

1. Start WordPad by clicking Start, clicking *All Programs*, clicking *Accessories*, and then clicking *WordPad*.

2. Type your last name and then press Enter.

3. Press the left arrow key on your keyboard until the insertion point is positioned to the left of your last name, type your first name, and then press the spacebar.

4. Print your work using the Quick print command by clicking the File tab, pointing to *Print*, and then clicking the Quick print command.

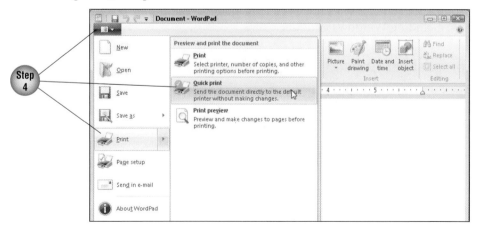

5. Display the Save As dialog box by clicking the Save button on the Quick Access toolbar.

6. At the Save As dialog box, change the save location to the **Unit1Topic03** folder on your storage medium and/or to the location specified by your instructor.

7. Click in the *File name* text box and then type **U1T3-Wordpad**.

   When you start typing *U1T3-Wordpad*, the default text is automatically removed.

8. Click the Save button.

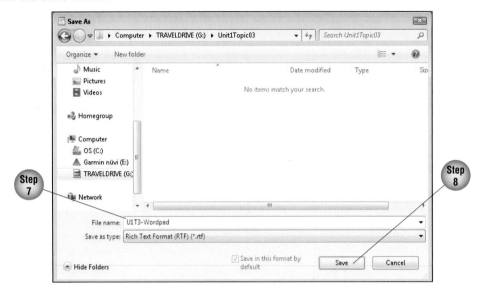

9. Close WordPad.

Lesson 3.5 Understanding Spreadsheet Applications

 1-2.2.2

Spreadsheets are useful for organizing data into orderly rows and columns and for calculating and recalculating numeric data. Spreadsheet programs typically have built-in chart creation tools that allow users to turn numeric data into charts and graphs. Windows does not come with a free spreadsheet program. Microsoft Excel is the most widely used spreadsheet application and is available for multiple operating systems, including Windows and Mac OS X.

Examining Spreadsheet Concepts and Terminology

cell The intersection of a row and a column in a spreadsheet

A spreadsheet is a document comprised of rows and columns. Rows run horizontally and are identified by numbers, while columns run vertically and are identified by letters. A **cell** is the area where a column and a row intersect and is the location where values or text may be entered. Each cell has a unique name consisting of its column number and row letter. For example, the first cell in a spreadsheet (located in the upper left corner) is A1 (column A, row 1), as shown in Figure 3.13.

Figure 3.13 Excel Spreadsheet

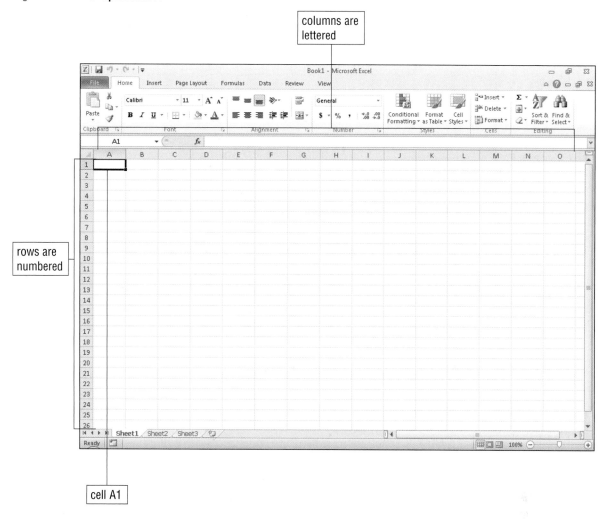

columns are lettered

rows are numbered

cell A1

You can apply formulas to the cells within a spreadsheet. A **formula** is a type of mathematical instruction that can be applied to a cell (or cells) in a spreadsheet and that can reference the value of other cells. For example, in cell C1, you could type the formula *=A1+B1*. This would apply a formula to cell C1 so C1 would display the sum of whatever amounts were entered into cells A1 and B1. If A1 contained 3 and B1 contained 4, C1 would display 7. The formula itself appears in the **Formula bar**, an area above the worksheet that displays information about the active cell and is used to enter and edit formulas (see Figure 3.14). The **active cell** is the cell that is currently selected within the spreadsheet; it is identified with a dark border. Formulas can use any standard math operator, such as minus (-), plus (+), multiply (*), divide (/), and exponent (^), and can use a mixture of cell references and digits.

formula A mathematical instruction that can be applied to a cell and that can reference the values of other cells

Formula bar The area above the worksheet that displays information about the active cell; used to enter and edit formulas

active cell The cell that is currently selected; identified by a dark border

Choosing and Using Application Software   131

Figure 3.14 Formula Bar in Excel

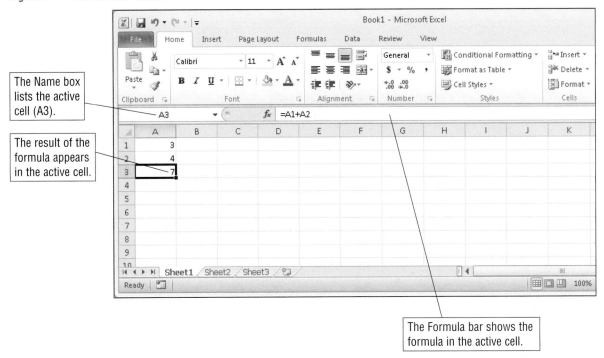

The Name box lists the active cell (A3).

The result of the formula appears in the active cell.

The Formula bar shows the formula in the active cell.

function A predesigned formula that performs calculations

Some mathematical operations, such as averaging, can be tricky to express in a formula, so spreadsheet applications also provide functions. A **function** is a predesigned formula that performs calculations. SUM and AVERAGE are examples of mathematical functions; a logical command such as IF can also be used. When using a function, you put the parameters in parentheses after the function name. For example, to average the values in cells A1 through A6, you would enter =AVERAGE(A1:A6).

Exploring the Excel 2010 Interface

This book uses Excel 2010 to create spreadsheets. Excel is the most popular spreadsheet program in the world and is used almost everywhere.

workbook An Excel data file that contains one or more worksheets

worksheet A single page of a workbook

Excel 2010's interface looks similar to Word 2010, which you saw in Lesson 3.4. The main differences are the different commands and tabs on the ribbon and the composition of the data area (a grid vs. a plain white space). Excel calls its data files **workbooks**. Each workbook has multiple tabbed sheets; these individual spreadsheets are called **worksheets**. You can switch between worksheets by clicking the tabs at the bottom of the window. Figure 3.15 shows a workbook with three tabs, with cell E8 on the Current Data tab as the active cell. Notice in the Formula bar that the active cell contains a function: =AVERAGE(E2:E6).

Navigating in a Spreadsheet

A spreadsheet can have thousands of cells in it, and not all of them can be visible at once in the application window. You can move around in a spreadsheet using the scroll bars, just as you do in other program windows. You can also zoom in and out using the Zoom controls, or by using the keyboard shortcuts described in Table 3.2. Refer to the callouts in Figure 3.15 to locate the scroll bars and Zoom controls.

Figure 3.15 Excel Workbook

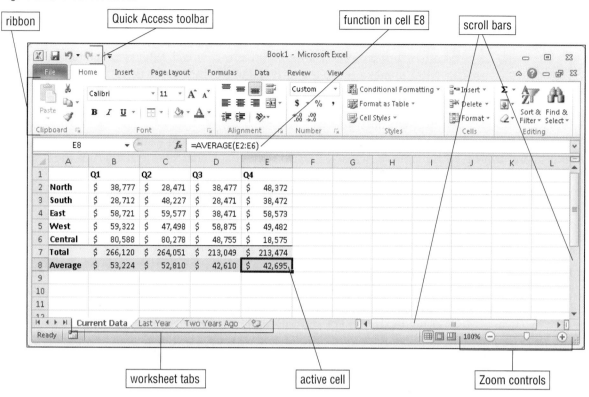

Table 3.2 Keyboard Shortcuts in Excel

To move	Press
One cell in the arrow direction	Arrow keys
To the edge of the current data region	Ctrl + arrow key
To extend the selection by one cell	Shift + arrow key
To the first cell in the current row	Home
To cell A1	Ctrl + Home
To the last cell visible in the window	End
To the last cell that contains data in the current worksheet	Ctrl + End
Down one screen length	Page Down
Up one screen length	Page Up
To the right one screen width	Alt + Page Down
To the left one screen width	Alt + Page Up
To the next sheet in the workbook	Ctrl + Page Down
To the previous sheet in the workbook	Ctrl + Page Up

Entering and Editing Data in Cells

To enter text or numbers in a cell, make the desired cell active by positioning the **cell pointer** (white plus sign) in the desired cell and then clicking the left mouse button. Type your entry in the active cell. When you are finished, press Enter to make active the next cell in the column or press Tab to make active the next cell in the row. To replace an entry in a cell, click in the cell to make it the active cell and then type the new entry. The previous entry is replaced automatically.

To edit an entry in a cell, double-click the cell to place the insertion point inside it and then edit as you would in any text-based program. (Use Backspace to remove the character to the left of the insertion point, and Delete to remove the character to the right.)

You can also edit entries in the Formula bar. The active cell's content always appears in the Formula bar; simply click in the Formula bar to place the insertion point and then make your edit.

Selecting Ranges

Microsoft Excel allows the user to perform an action on multiple cells at once, such as applying a certain formatting or font style. A group of one or more cells on which you perform an action is called a **range**. Ranges are defined using the upper left and lower right cell names. For example, the range that includes A1, A2, A3, B1, B2, and B3 would be called A1:B3.

An easy way to select a range is to drag across it. Click the first cell in the range (for example, A1) and then hold down the left mouse button as you drag to the last cell (for example, B3).

You can also select ranges with the keyboard. Select the first cell in the range and then hold down the Shift key as you press the arrow keys to extend the selection. Release the Shift key when you are finished.

As you drag to select a range, make sure you are dragging from the center of the first cell and not from its bottom right corner. In the bottom right corner of the active cell is a small black square called the fill handle. Dragging the fill handle copies the content of the cell into adjacent cells, which is different from selecting. You will learn about copying cell content when you study Excel in Topic 9.

Quick Steps

Select a Range with the Mouse

1. Click first cell in range.
2. Hold down left mouse button and drag to last cell in range.
3. Release mouse button.

Select a Range with the Keyboard

1. Click first cell in range.
2. Hold down Shift and use arrow keys to select other cells.
3. Release Shift.

Discovering Other Spreadsheet Capabilities

In Unit 2 you will learn much more about Microsoft Excel, as well as about spreadsheets in general. Some of the capabilities of a spreadsheet program such as Excel include the following:

- **Data sorting:** You can reorder the data in a spreadsheet easily, sorting by any column. For example, if you have a list of parts, you could sort that list alphabetically by name or numerically by cost.

- **Formatting:** You can dress up the text and numbers in the cells with different font, size, and color choices; change the background colors of cells; and make certain cells wider or taller.

- **Charts and diagrams:** You can create graphical charts or visual aids from the data in a worksheet, such as pie charts, line graphs, or bar graphs.

Exercise 3.5   Using a Spreadsheet Application

1. Start Microsoft Excel by clicking Start, clicking *All Programs*, clicking *Microsoft Office*, and then clicking *Microsoft Excel 2010*.

   These steps may vary; you may need to check with your instructor on specific steps to start Excel.

2. In cell A1, type **Maria**.

3. Press Enter to make cell A2 active and then type **John**.

4. Click cell B1 to make it active and then type **150**.

5. Press Enter to make cell B2 active and then type **100**.

6. Click cell A3 to make it active and then type **Total**.

7. Press Tab to make cell B3 active, type **=B1+B2**, and then press Enter.

8. Select the range A1:A3 by positioning the cell pointer in cell A1, holding down the left mouse button, dragging down to cell A3, and then releasing the mouse button.

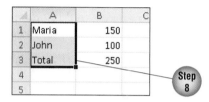

9. Press Ctrl + B to make the text in the selected cells bold.

10. Click the Save button on the Quick Access toolbar.

11. At the Save As dialog box, change the save location to the **Unit1Topic03** folder on your storage medium or to the location specified by your instructor.

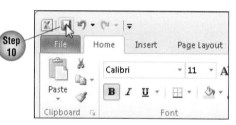

12. Click in the *File name* text box and then type **U1T3-ExcelTotal**. Click Save to save the file.

13. Press Ctrl + P to display the Print tab Backstage view.

14. Click the Print button to print the worksheet.

15. Exit Excel by clicking the Close button ⊠ in the upper right corner of the Excel window.

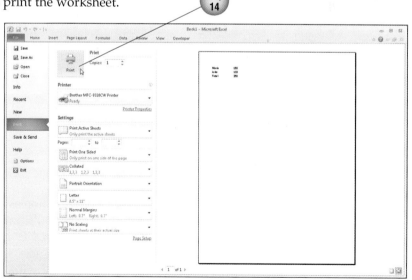

1-2.2.3

Presentation software creates a special type of graphic that is useful as a visual aid when giving a presentation either live, online, or as a handout. Presentation software differs from simple graphics programs because it not only can create each individual graphic to display, but it can organize the graphics in a single file and set them up to play automatically, one after another. Presentation software can also be used to add object animation, transition effects, music, narration, and other special effects.

slide A single "page" of a presentation, designed to be displayed on a projector, computer monitor, or as a printout

A presentation contains one or more slides. A **slide** is an individual presentation page, designed to be displayed on a projector, on a computer monitor, or as a printout. The slides in a presentation usually have a common theme that brings them together visually, such as a common background color and similar fonts. In PowerPoint's Normal view, shown in Figure 3.16, each slide displays as a thumbnail image (a small image) at the left. The slide that is currently selected, the active slide, appears in the center of the work area.

Figure 3.16 **Normal View in PowerPoint**

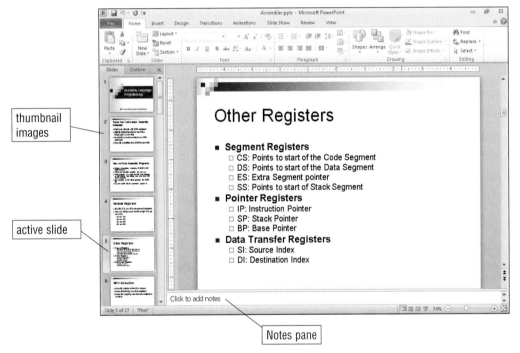

Working with Views

Sometimes you want to see a presentation as a whole, with thumbnail images of all the slides at once; other times you want to look closely at one particular slide. PowerPoint offers several different views, so you can see your work in whatever way is most helpful. Figure 3.16 shows Normal view, which displays thumbnail images at the left while the active slide appears larger on the right. In the Notes pane, located below the slide, you can type private notes to yourself or your collaborators that will not be visible to the audience. In contrast, Figure 3.17 shows Slide Sorter view, which displays thumbnails of all the slides at once. In this view you can drag the slides around to rearrange their order in the presentation.

You can switch views by clicking one of the View buttons at the bottom of the application window, as illustrated in Figure 3.17. Notice that PowerPoint has many of the same features as Excel and Word, such as the Zoom controls and the ribbon.

Figure 3.17 Slide Sorter View in PowerPoint

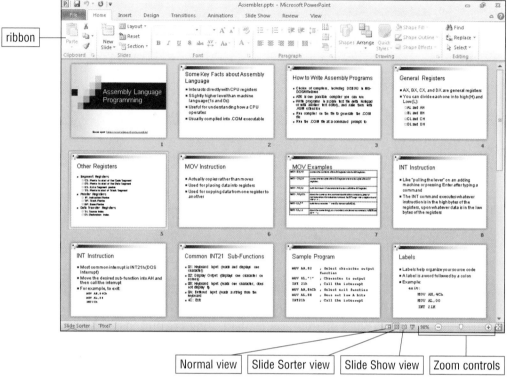

Normal view | Slide Sorter view | Slide Show view | Zoom controls

Inserting Slide Content

To create a new slide, click the New Slide button on the Home tab. By default, each new slide in PowerPoint contains two placeholders—one for the title and one for the content. A **placeholder** is a box that holds title or body text or an object such as a picture, chart, or table. Placeholders are used most often in PowerPoint, but you may also encounter them when working with template documents in Word. To enter text in a placeholder, click the default text that displays inside it. For example, to enter a title in the slide in Figure 3.18, you would click the text *Click to add title*. The default text automatically disappears and the insertion point is placed inside the placeholder. You can now begin typing the title. To add body content to the slide in Figure 3.18, you would either click the text *Click to add text* and begin typing, or click one of the content icons in the center of the placeholder to insert graphical content.

Quick Steps

Create a New Slide

1. Click Home tab.
2. Click New Slide button.

placeholder A box that holds title or body text or an object such as a picture, chart, or table

Figure 3.18 Title and Content Placeholders Fill in the placeholders on a new slide to create slide content.

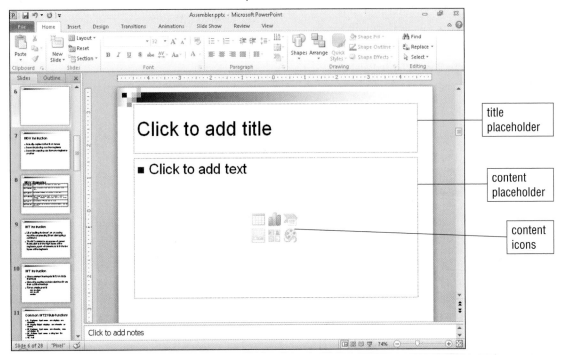

Each placeholder on the slide can hold only one type of content. Therefore, if you type text in the content placeholder, the content icons disappear, and vice versa. The six content icons are shown in Figure 3.19. You can also insert other types of graphical content using the buttons on the Insert tab.

Figure 3.19 Content Icons

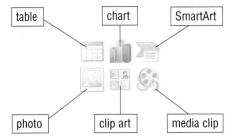

Displaying a Slide Show

Displaying your presentation as a slide show allows you to view your presentation in its final format. Switch to Slide Show view to display a slide show. Do this by clicking the Slide Show view button at the bottom of the application window or by clicking the View tab and then clicking the Slide Show button. Click the left mouse button to advance through the slides in the slide show. Press the Esc key to exit the slide show and return to the previous view.

Exercise 3.6   Creating a Presentation in PowerPoint

1. Start PowerPoint by clicking Start, clicking *All Programs*, clicking *Microsoft Office*, and then clicking *Microsoft PowerPoint 2010*.

   When you open PowerPoint, a new blank presentation opens with a single title slide.

2. Click the placeholder text *Click to add title* and then type **Computer Literacy Basics**.

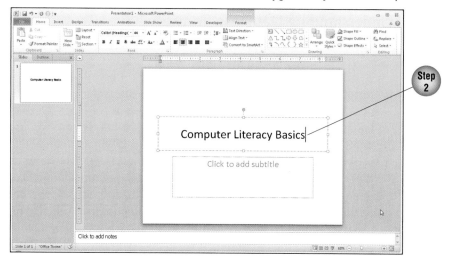

3. Click the placeholder text *Click to add subtitle* and then type the name of your school.

4. Click the New Slide button on the Home tab.

5. In the new slide, click the placeholder text *Click to add title* and then type **Parts of a PC**.

6. Click the content placeholder text *Click to add text* and then type the list as shown below, pressing Enter after each item except the last one.

7. Click the Save button on the Quick Access toolbar.

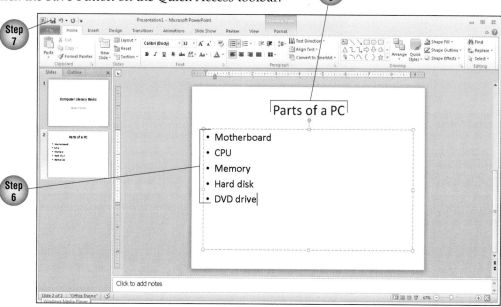

8. At the Save As dialog box, change the save location to the **Unit1Topic03** folder on your storage medium, type **U1T3-PCPresentation** in the *File name* text box, and then press Enter.

9. Press Ctrl + P to display the Print tab Backstage view.

10. Click the Print button to print the presentation.

11. Exit PowerPoint by clicking the Close button in the upper right corner of the screen.

Lesson 3.7 — Understanding Database Software

 1-2.2.4

database A collection of data records

flat file database A single two-dimensional table containing database records

A **database** is a collection of data records. Everyday examples of databases include address books, lists of customers and their contact information, lists of orders placed by customers, and library card catalogs. Databases also work behind the scenes to power websites and data-driven applications such as retail sales software in stores.

Several types of databases are available. A **flat file database** is a simple type of database that consists of a single table of information. You could create this type of database in Excel or in Word. You could even create a flat file database in a plain text editor such as Notepad, using or commas to separate the columns and paragraph breaks to separate the rows. Figures 3.20 and 3.21 show flat file databases in Excel and Notepad, respectively. Note that in Figure 3.21, the columns are separated by tabs.

Figure 3.20 Flat-File Database in Excel

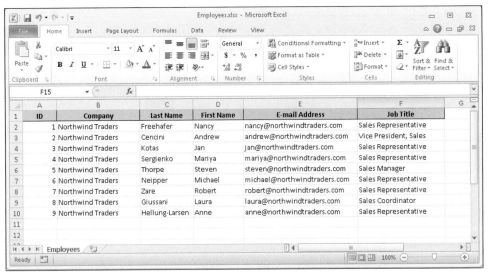

Figure 3.21 Flat-File Database in Notepad

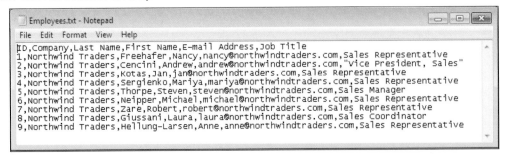

In a database, the information on one particular instance (a person, a company, a transaction, etc.) is called a **record**. Each row is a different record in Figures 3.20 and 3.21. The column headings, which list the types of data collected, are called **fields**. In Figures 3.20 and 3.21, the field names include *ID, Company, Last Name*, and so on.

Sometimes a database needs multiple tables to avoid repetition or duplication of information. For example, suppose your company needs to keep track of customers and their orders. If you repeated the customer's name, address, and phone number in every order record, you would have to do a lot of retyping and the potential for making typos and other errors in the document would increase. Having two separate tables, one for customer information and one for order information, is much more efficient. These two tables can be linked together by a unique customer ID number that is present in both tables. A database that contains multiple related tables is called a **relational database**. Microsoft Access is a relational database program.

In addition to storing multiple tables, an Access file can also contain helper objects. These can include:

- **Queries:** A **query** is a set of saved sort-and-filter criteria used to access selected groups of records.

- **Forms:** A **form** is a formatted data entry template that simplifies creating new records.

- **Reports:** A **report** is a formatted layout of a table or query that is optimized for printing.

Figure 3.22 shows a relational database open in Access; notice that the Navigation pane at the left includes tables, queries, and forms.

record A single row in a database table, listing the information for one instance

field A single column in a database table, listing one type of information

relational database A database consisting of multiple related tables

query A set of saved sort-and-filter criteria that can be used to access a selected group of records

form A formatted data entry template that helps to simplify data entry

report A formatted layout of a table or query that is optimized for printing

Figure 3.22 Relational Database in Access

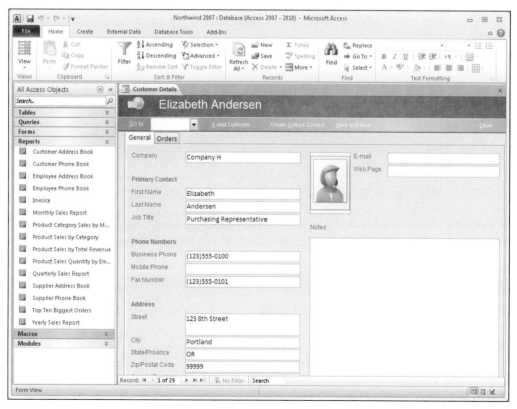

Exercise 3.7 Creating a Single-Table Database Using Excel

1. Start Microsoft Excel.

2. Enter the data shown below.

   As you type text, remember that pressing Tab makes the cell to the right active and pressing Enter makes the cell below active.

	A	B	C
1	Part #	Name	Price
2	1	Flange	$2.00
3	2	Widget	$5.00
4	3	Bolt	$1.00
5	4	Ratchet	$10.00

3. Click the File tab and then click the Save & Send tab.

4. At the Save & Send tab Backstage view, click the *Change File Type* option.

5. Click the *Text (Tab delimited) (*.txt)* option located below the Other File Types heading in the Change File Type section.

   Saving the flat-file database in plain-text format will make it easy to import into any database application.

6. Click the Save As button located below the list of file types.

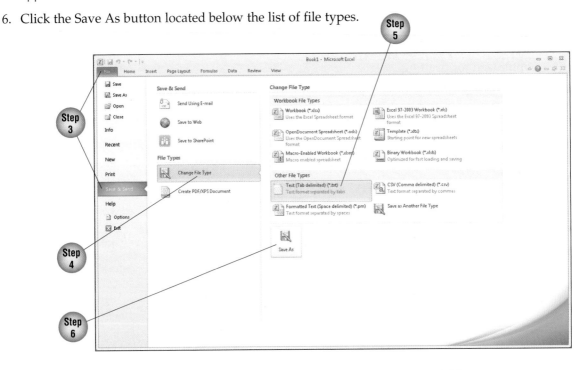

7. At the Save As dialog box, change the save location to the **Unit1Topic03** folder on your storage medium, type **U1T3-ExcelCosts** in the *File name* text box, and then press Enter.

8. At the warning that displays telling you that the selected file type does not support multiple sheets, click OK.

9. At the warning that displays telling you that certain features are not compatible with Text format, click Yes.

10. Close Excel. If prompted to save your changes, click Don't Save.

11. Open Windows Explorer, navigate to the **Unit1Topic03** folder on your storage medium, and then double-click the file.

    The file should open in Notepad.

12. Print the file by clicking File on the menu bar, clicking *Print* at the drop-down list, and then clicking the Print button at the Print dialog box.

13. Close Notepad.

Drilling Down

Understanding Database Normalization

Database normalization is the process of deciding which data goes into which tables. The purpose of this process is to avoid redundancy and prevent the creation of structural problems. Read some well-recognized rules for normalizing a database system at http://ic3.emcp.net/datanorm.

Lesson 3.8   Understanding Graphics and Multimedia Software

 1-2.2.5, 1-2.2.6

Graphics software helps you create your own graphic images, such as original artwork, and also enables you to edit existing graphics, such as retouching photos, rearranging the contents of diagrams, or redesigning items illustrated on blueprints. Two main types of programs are available for creating graphics: vector and bitmap (raster). Each is designed for a different type of graphics work.

Understanding Vector Images

A **vector image**, also called a drawing, is a picture created with a series of mathematical formulas. If you have studied geometry, you know that you can describe a line or a shape by creating a formula and then plotting it on a grid. That is how a drawing program creates each line and shape. It defines where the shape starts and ends (its size) and its overall outline mathematically. Each line or shape also has some properties, like line color, line weight, and fill color, that further define how it appears. To create complex drawings, numerous lines and shapes are overlaid.

vector image A picture consisting of one or more drawn lines or shapes created by math formulas

Vector drawings are small in file size and can be changed to virtually any display or print size. When you resize a vector image, all lines stay as smooth and sharp as in the original. This is because resizing the image alters its formulas and the program immediately redraws a new copy using the updated formulas. Most of the clip art that comes with Microsoft Office is vector. Figure 3.23 shows a simple piece of clip art with one of the lines selected. Even this simple drawing is composed of dozens of lines and shapes. The image can easily be modified by dragging one of the lines or shapes to a different location or applying a different color or fill to the drawing. You can create vector images using the drawing tools in Microsoft Office applications and in flow chart programs such as Microsoft Visio. Adobe Illustrator is a popular drawing program that also creates vector images. Computer Aided Design (CAD) software is a type of vector-based 3-D modeling. Rather than working on a flat image, CAD enables the designer to use vector graphics to create 3-D blueprints and models from which products can be manufactured.

Figure 3.23 Vector Clip Art Image

This drawn line is only one of many in this image

Understanding Bitmap Images

The alternative to a vector image is a **raster image**, also called a *bitmap image*. The photos you take with a digital camera or digitize with a scanner are this type of image. A raster image consists of a grid of colored dots, or pixels. A **pixel** is an individual colored dot in an image or on a display monitor. Each pixel has a numeric value assigned to it that represents its color. This type of image is of a higher quality than vector graphics, but its drawback is the file size. Since each pixel must be individually referenced, file sizes of bitmap images can be large. For example, suppose an image is 800 x 600 pixels in size. If it is a 24-bit color image, each pixel requires 24 bits (3 bytes) of storage space, so this file would occupy at least 600 x 600 x 3 bytes, or 1,440,000 bytes (1.44 megabytes). Certain file formats can compress the image storage requirements, but raster images are always larger than their vector counterparts. Adobe Photoshop is a popular program for creating and editing raster images; lower-budget versions of this program include Paint Shop Pro and Windows 7's own free Paint program. Common file extensions for bitmap images include .bmp, .gif, .jpg, and .png.

Figure 3.24 Resized Raster Image

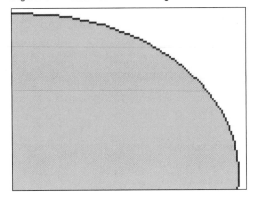

The main advantage of a raster image over a vector image is realism. A raster image can be as clear and realistic as a high-quality photograph. The main disadvantage of a raster image, other than the larger file size, is that it cannot be resized without losing quality. Resizing a raster image, especially an increase in size, makes the lines in the program appear jagged, or *bitmapped*. Figure 3.24 shows an enlarged portion of a "smooth" curve in a raster image that has been resized; notice that resizing has created distortion that would not be present in a resized vector image.

Exercise 3.8A   Drawing in PowerPoint

1. Start PowerPoint.

2. Change the slide layout by clicking the Layout button ⊞ on the Home tab and then clicking the *Blank* option at the drop-down list.

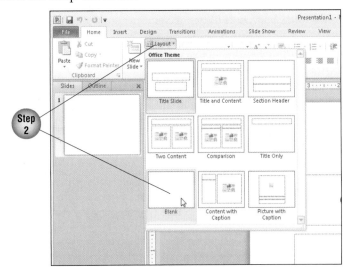

3. Click the Insert tab, click the Shapes button 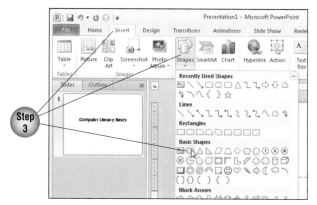, and then click the oval shape (the second option from the left in the Basic Shapes section).

4. Click and drag on the slide to create an oval of any size.

5. Click the Drawing Tools Format tab, click the Shape Fill button arrow 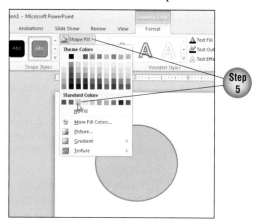, and then click the orange color in the Standard Colors section of the drop-down list.

6. Click the Shape Outline button arrow 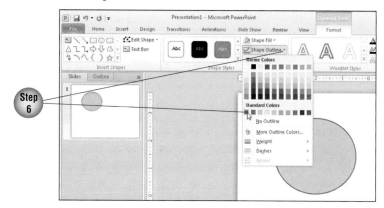 and then click the dark red color in the Standard Colors section of the drop-down list.

7. Click the Shape Effects button, point to *Preset*, and then click the *Preset 2* option (second option from the left in the top row of the *Presets* section).

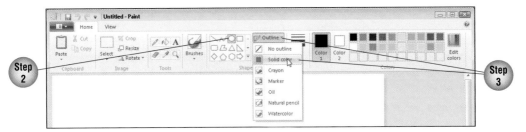

8. Click the Save button on the Quick Access toolbar.

9. At the Save As dialog box, change the save location to the **Unit1Topic03** folder on your storage medium, type **U1T3-PPTShape** in the *File name* text box, and then press Enter.

10. Press Ctrl + P to display the Print tab Backstage view and then click the Print button to print the presentation.

11. Exit PowerPoint.

Exercise 3.8B   Drawing in Microsoft Paint

1. Start Paint by clicking Start, clicking *All Programs*, clicking *Accessories*, and then clicking *Paint*.

2. Click the oval shape in the Shapes group.

3. Click the Outline button and then click *Solid color* at the drop-down list.

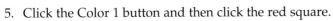

4. Click the Fill button and then click *Solid color* at the drop-down list.

5. Click the Color 1 button and then click the red square.

6. Click the Color 2 button and then click the yellow square.

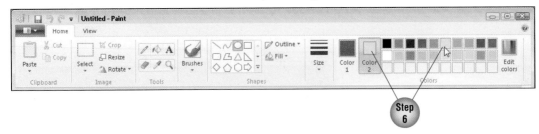

7. Drag on the canvas to create an oval of any size.

8. Click the Save button on the Quick Access toolbar.

9. At the Save As dialog box, change the save location to the **Unit1Topic03** folder on your storage medium, type **U1T3-PaintShape** in the *File name* text box, and then press Enter.

   This saves the file with the default file type (.png).

10. Print the file by pressing Ctrl + P and then clicking the Print button at the Print dialog box.

11. Exit Paint.

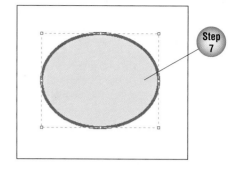

Multimedia Software

In addition to graphics software, a variety of multimedia applications are available. Multimedia literally means multiple media, but in popular usage it has come to mean applications that help you play, record, and/or modify sound, video, or animation. Some of the types of multimedia software available include the following.

Animation Creation Programs Animation creation programs help you create your own moving drawings and diagrams. For example, many educational content developers use Adobe Flash Professional to create animation sequences that can be used to illustrate complex ideas. People developing blueprints and designs for new product patents might also use an animation creation program to illustrate how a product will work before the product has been physically made. Common file extensions for animation files include .qt (Quicktime), .swf (Shockwave Flash), and .flv.

Media Players Media players enable you to play back movie and music clips. Some popular media players include Windows Media Player (see Figure 3.25), RealPlayer, and iTunes. You can transfer music and movies to portable players, **burn** (write) them to CDs or DVDs, and **rip** (copy) them from audio CDs to your hard disk.

burn To write files to a CD or DVD

rip To copy files from a CD or DVD to a computer hard drive

Figure 3.25 Windows Media Player

Sound and Music Editors Sound editors help you manipulate music and sound files. For example, you can convert a music clip from one format to another, decrease its size by cutting its quality level, or cut out sections of the file. Common sound file formats include .mp3 and .wma for music and .wav for sounds.

Video Editors Video editing applications help you create your own videos. You can take raw footage from a home movie you have recorded, for example, and add a music soundtrack and text captions to it. Common movie file formats include .mov, .mp4, and .mpg.

CD and DVD Burning Applications Burning applications specialize in writing content to blank, writeable CDs and DVDs. You can use this type of program to make copies of CDs and DVDs (if you are legally entitled to do so), as well as to make your own original CD and DVD compilations containing music, video, or other data.

Virtual reality Applications Virtual reality is an environment created using software that you interact with as if it were real. To interact with a virtual environment, a person might wear goggles, headphones, wired gloves, and body sensors to help make the experience more realistic. Console devices such as the Wii and the XBox Kinnect also bring a basic type of virtual reality to gaming, without requiring any special gear.

Drilling Down

Understanding Vector Drawings

Simulation games, such as EA Games' The Sims, use 3-D vector drawings to create the characters and scenery. Each character and object is, at its core, a **wireframe**, which is a 3-D image that consists of only the outlines of each piece that makes up the whole. That wireframe is then covered with a color or texture. The costumes you can apply to your characters in these games are nothing more than overlay textures that cover the character's wireframe. Below are a wireframe image (left) and the same image covered with a solid color fill (right).

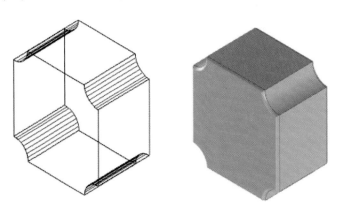

Lesson 3.9   Using Utility Programs

 1-2.2.7

Utilities perform a variety of system maintenance tasks for your PC. Utilities can protect your system against external threats such as viruses, correct file system errors, make disk access faster, and delete unwanted files, among other things.

Some utility programs are included with Windows; others are sold separately. Table 3.3 lists some of the utilities that come with Windows 7, their purposes, and how you can run them. You learned about some of these utilities in Topic 1.

Table 3.3 Utility Programs Included in Windows

Application	Purpose	How to Run
Disk Defragmenter	Relocates separated parts of files to contiguous areas, improving disk access speed	Start > *All Programs > Accessories > System Tools > Disk Defragmenter* OR Start > *Computer*, then right-click a drive and click *Properties*, then click the Tools tab, then click *Defragment Now*
Disk Cleanup	Identifies unnecessary files and gives you the option to delete them to free up hard disk space	Start > *All Programs > Accessories > System Tools > Disk Cleanup* OR Start > *Computer*, then right-click a drive and click *Properties*, then click the General tab, then click *Disk Cleanup*
Check Disk	Finds and fixes file system errors and errors caused by bad spots on the disk	Start > *Computer*, then right-click a drive and click *Properties*, then click the Tools tab, then click *Check now*
Backup	Backs up copies of files you specify to an external source such as a removable hard disk, writeable CD/DVD, or network location	Start > *Control Panel > System and Security > Backup and Restore* OR Start > *Computer*, then right-click a drive and click *Properties*, then click the Tools tab, then click *Backup now*
System Information	Displays detailed information about the installed hardware and software	Start > *All Programs > Accessories > System Tools > System Information*
System Restore	Creates restore points, which are snapshots of the Registry settings, and uses them to restore settings	To create a restore point: Start > *Control Panel > System and Security > System > System Protection*, then click *Create* To restore from a restore point: Start > *All Programs > Accessories > System Tools > System Restore*
Windows Defender	Checks the system for harmful software and helps you remove it	Start, type *Defender*, click *Windows Defender*
Windows Firewall	Protects the system from outside access via network ports	Runs by default; to configure: Start > *Control Panel > System and Security > Windows Firewall*

Before using a utility program, shut down any other applications that may be running. Utilities that access the files on your hard disk may not be able to access files that are in use by applications.

Guidelines vary widely about when to run each utility program. Some people never run any utility programs and their systems work just fine. Other people choose to run multiple utilities every day, or set the utilities to run automatically. Programs like Disk Defragmenter, which increase disk performance a small amount, are entirely optional. Programs like Backup should be run at whatever interval makes the user the most comfortable; some people have critically important data that needs to be backed up every day, and other people do not have anything important enough to back up with any frequency. Programs such as Check Disk, which look for disk errors, are usually run when a problem occurs, such as frequent lockups that might indicate file system errors. Other programs, like Windows Defender and Windows Firewall, are typically always running while the computer is on.

malware Programs that seek to harm your computer and its data; short for *malicious software*

adware Applications that display unwanted advertisements on your computer

spyware Software that records your computer usage

cookie A plain text file that a Web page stores on your hard disk for tracking purposes

antivirus program A program that defends against viruses, worms, and Trojan horses by analyzing and identifying suspicious files; also known as *antivirus software*

virus Computer code that inserts itself into an executable file and executes along with the file to cause harm to a computer or its data

worm A self-transporting application that carries a harmful program with it

Trojan horse An application that appears to do something useful but also performs malicious actions within a computer

Windows Defender is an example of a utility that protects a computer against external threats, mainly from the Internet, but also potentially from other computers on your local network. Windows Defender guards against **malware**, which is a general term referring to programs that seek to harm your computer or its data or invade your privacy. Malware can include the following:

- **Adware: Adware** is software that displays ads without your consent.

- **Spyware: Spyware** is software that tracks your usage habits or obtains your private information and transfers that information to its developer.

- **Cookies:** A **cookie** is a plain text file containing your personal information that web pages place on your hard disk and then access later when you re-visit that same web page; most are harmless, but some can be used to compromise your privacy online.

Another important protection utility is an antivirus program. Since Windows Defender does not look for viruses, you need a separate antivirus program to protect your computer. An **antivirus program** analyzes files on your computer and identifies any that appear to be harmful. Antivirus programs find threats such as the following:

- **Viruses:** A **virus** is a computer code that attaches to an executable file, so when that file runs, the code runs too, usually doing something harmful to the computer system.

- **Worms:** A **worm** is a self-transporting container that spreads a virus or other malware items on a network.

- **Trojan Horses:** A **Trojan horse** is a program that appears to do something useful but is actually malware, causing harm to your computer or invading your privacy.

Windows does not come with an antivirus program, but Microsoft provides a free one called Windows Security Essentials that anyone can download. To download this program, go to http://ic3.emcp.net/SecEss. You will learn much more about malware and viruses in Topic 16.

Exercise 3.9   Checking Your Antivirus Software

1. Click Start and then click *All Programs*.

2. Look for an antivirus program on the menu system.

   Some popular antivirus programs include Norton, Symantec, McAfee, Panda, or AVG in their names. Ask your instructor for help identifying your antivirus software if needed. If you have antivirus software installed, it will appear on the Start menu. If you do not have antivirus software, stop here, and have a discussion in class about why no antivirus software is installed and whether it should be added.

3. In the notification area (the icons immediately to the left of the clock in the lower right corner of the screen), point to each icon and read the name that pops up in a ScreenTip. Continue until you find your antivirus software.

   If antivirus software appears in the notification area, you can assume it is running.

4. Double-click the antivirus program's icon in the notification area to open the program.

   If nothing happens, try right-clicking the icon and looking for an *Open* or *Configure* command on the shortcut menu that appears. The goal is to open a configuration and status window for the antivirus program.

5. View the available options for your antivirus program.

6. Close the antivirus program's window without making any changes.

Lesson 3.10   Understanding Other Application Types

 1-2.2.7, 1-2.2.8

Besides the software types you have learned about so far in this topic, you should be aware of the many other types of software available. Although this course does not cover them in detail, you should know how they work—in a general way—for the IC³ Computer Fundamentals test. This lesson summarizes some of the most significant additional software categories.

Educational Software

Educational software comprises a huge segment of the overall software market. An educational application is one that teaches someone to do something. Educational programs are available for adults, as well as for children of all ages. Many educational programs take the form of games, or sets of games, that teach as they entertain. For example, a spelling program might make a competition out of spelling the most words correctly, and a typing program might award points for typing fast without making any errors.

Entertainment Software

Entertainment software includes games, puzzles, and other pastimes whose main purpose is to amuse the user. Windows 7 comes with a number of games, including Solitaire and Minesweeper (shown in Figure 3.26). Entertainment software may be simple in purpose, but games are some of the most complex applications, with the highest levels of hardware requirements.

Accounting and Personal Finance Software

Figure 3.26 Minesweeper

Accounting software helps businesses and individuals keep track of their finances. For example, a small business might use an application like QuickBooks or Peachtree Accounting to store records of each financial transaction, including check writing, payroll processing, and customer receipts. At the individual level, applications like Quicken (shown in Figure 3.27) help people manage their checkbooks, investments, and budgets.

Figure 3.27 **Quicken**

Messaging and Conferencing Software

A wide variety of software uses the Internet to help people communicate with one another. For simple person-to-person and small-group chatting, instant message programs such as Yahoo! Messenger and AOL Instant Messenger enable users to type back and forth with friends and even use video and audio features. These services can also send messages to mobile phones or email accounts. For more sophisticated business communication, conference programs are available that allow large groups of people to participate in the same conversation. Users can also share applications and data files within the conference. Business conferencing software can be installed on individual PCs or it can be accessed through a Web-based conferencing tool such as Megameeting.

Web Browsing Software

Web browsing software is important to many people's daily lives because it enables them to access Web-based content. Some of the most popular web browsers include Internet Explorer, Google Chrome (shown in Figure 3.28), Mozilla Firefox, and Opera. Almost all web browser software is free, so you can download and install multiple browsers and decide through experience which one you like the best. Topic 14 covers web browsers in detail.

Email Software

An email application (sometimes called an email client) provides features for sorting and organizing your incoming and outgoing mail, as well as filtering out junk mail and managing email address books. Some people send and receive email using a web interface, while others choose to use a full-featured email application such as Windows Live Mail (discussed further in Topic 15) or Microsoft Outlook. Windows Live Mail is free from Microsoft for Windows 7 users; Microsoft Outlook comes with Microsoft Office. Topic 15 helps you get started with using an email application.

Figure 3.28 **Google Chrome**

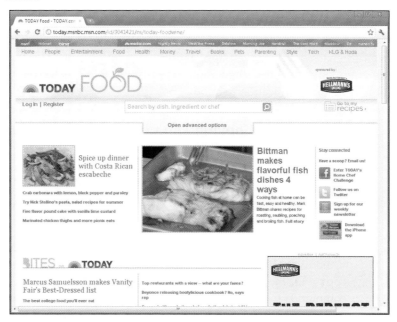

Internet and Desktop Gadgets

Single-purpose tools and accessories called gadgets (or "widgets") are available to add to the desktop. These simple utilities typically access services and information over the Internet to provide useful and timely information such as the local weather forecast, stock prices, and online auction bid statuses.

Web Page Authoring Software

Programs such as Dreamweaver and Microsoft Expression Web enable users to create websites in a point-and-click graphical interface.

Application Suites

Suites (or integrated software packages) combine multiple applications by the same manufacturer into a single package. Microsoft Office is an example of a popular application suite.

Specialized or Industry-Specific Software

Although you do not see it sold in retail stores, custom software is created for businesses. Software packages are available for every type of industry and include software packages for project management, managing dental practices, managing schools, and making air traffic control decisions.

Exercise 3.10   Finding Educational Software

1. Open Internet Explorer and go to www.download.com.

2. Type **typing tutor** in the search box and then press Enter.
   A list of programs appears.

3. Download one of the typing tutor applications you find and install it, as you learned in Lesson 3.1.

4. Try out the software for 5 to 10 minutes.

5. Uninstall the software.

1-2.2.10

Windows enables you to share data between applications, so you do not have to retype or recreate content if you decide you would rather work in another application. In this lesson, you will learn how to move and copy data from one application to another.

Quick Steps

Copy Content between Applications with the Clipboard

1. Select content.
2. Press Ctrl + C or click Copy button.
3. Switch to target application.
4. Click to place insertion point.
5. Press Ctrl + V or click Paste button.

Move Content between Applications with the Clipboard

1. Select content.
2. Press Ctrl + X or click Cut button.
3. Switch to target application.
4. Click to place the insertion point.
5. Press Ctrl + V or click Paste button.

Copy Content with Drag-and-Drop

1. Open windows for both locations.
2. Select content to copy.
3. Hold down Ctrl and drag content to new location.

Move Content with Drag-and-Drop

1. Open windows for both locations.
2. Select content to move.
3. Drag content to new location.

Moving and Copying Data between Applications

In Windows, you can move or copy data between applications in two ways:

- Drag and drop content from one application to another.

- Use the Windows Clipboard to cut or copy and paste data between applications.

In Topic 2, you learned how to move and copy files and folders within Windows. The process for moving and copying data is nearly identical. To copy with the Clipboard method, use the Copy command and then the Paste command; to move, use the Cut command and then the Paste command. These commands are typically found on the Home tab in an application that uses a ribbon (as in Figure 3.29) or on the Edit drop-down list in an application that uses a menu system. The same shortcuts you learned in Topic 2 also work here: Ctrl + C for copy, Ctrl + X for cut, and Ctrl + V for paste. To copy with the drag-and-drop method, hold down Ctrl and drag the content. To move, drag without holding down Ctrl.

Figure 3.29 **Cut, Copy, and Paste Commands on the Ribbon in Word**

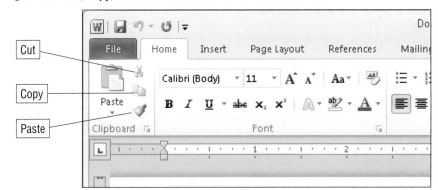

Depending on the applications involved, the content you insert may become a seamless part of the destination file, or it may be reformatted (or have its formatting stripped away). It all depends on how the receiving application is equipped to handle that type of content. For example, if you copy text from Notepad to Word, the text becomes a paragraph using Word's default style. If you copy from Word to Notepad, however, you lose all the formatting on the text because Notepad does not support text formatting.

Linking and Embedding Content

When you copy or move non-text content into an application that does not know how to treat the content, the application might reject it. For example, if you try to drag-and-drop a picture into Notepad, or paste it there from the Clipboard, nothing happens.

Some applications, however, enable you to insert content from other applications as **OLE** objects. OLE stands for **Object Linking and Embedding**. An object is a container for content; the application does not need to know the details of the content, because the content is not being fully integrated into it. Applications that permit objects can support a wide range of content types that the application cannot generate on its own. For example, you could insert a diagram from Microsoft Visio (a diagram-creation program) into a Word document, even though Word does not use or create Visio content.

Applications that support OLE usually have an Insert Object command somewhere in their menu system. In WordPad, it is on the Home tab; in Microsoft Word, Excel, and PowerPoint, it is on the Insert tab.

When you insert an object, you can either **link** it or **embed** it. Linking to an object inserts a shortcut to it in the document, and every time you open the document or update the link, a fresh copy is retrieved from the original file. Therefore, a linked copy is always current. Embedding an object retains a memory of which application it came from, but not which data file. You can double-click the object to open it for editing in its original application, but it does not automatically update.

Linking and embedding both greatly increase file size, so most people use them only when a regular copy-and-paste will not work, or when a project requires the extra features involved in linking or embedding.

When linking or embedding an object, you can do any of the following:

- Insert a portion of an existing saved data file from another application. To do this, use the Copy command to copy it from the original location, and then use the Paste Special command and dialog box (see Figure 3.30) to paste it in the new location.

- Insert an entire existing saved data file from another application. To do this, use the Insert Object command, and then click *Create from File*.

- Create a new data file in another application and insert that new file. To do this, use the Insert Object command, and then in the Insert Object dialog box (see Figure 3.31), click *Create New*. This method only embeds; it does not link the object.

Figure 3.30 Paste Special Dialog Box

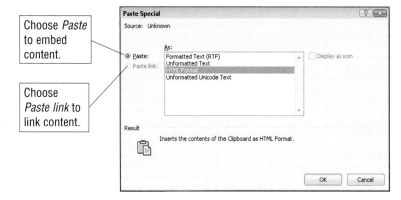

Choose *Paste* to embed content.

Choose *Paste link* to link content.

Object Linking and Embedding (OLE) A technology for including outside content in a data file so that the content retains its original source application or data file information

link To insert a shortcut to external content into a data file so that the copy updates when the source changes

embed To insert a data object into a data file so that the object retains its memory of its original source application and can be edited in that application

Quick Steps

Embed or Link Part of an Existing File

1. Select and copy content.
2. Position insertion point in destination file.
3. Click Paste button arrow.
4. Click *Paste Special*.
5. At Paste Special dialog box, click *Paste* to embed or *Paste Link* to link.
6. Click OK.

Embed or Link an Entire Existing File

1. Position insertion point in destination file.
2. Click Insert Object.
3. At Insert Object dialog box, click Create from File option.
4. Click Browse button, select file to be inserted, and click Open.
5. To link, click *Link* (or *Link to File*) check box. To embed, leave check box empty.
6. Click OK.

Embed a New File

1. Position insertion point in destination file.
2. Click Insert Object.
3. Click Create New option.
4. Select object type.
5. Click OK.
6. Create new file in application that opens.
7. Save file and exit application.

Choosing and Using Application Software   **155**

Figure 3.31 Insert Object Dialog Box

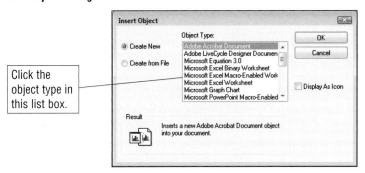

Click the object type in this list box.

Exercise 3.11   Linking Content in Word

1. Open Paint and then create a simple picture of your choosing.

2. Save the file in the 24-bit Bitmap file format. Begin by clicking the Save button on the Quick Access toolbar to display the Save As dialog box.

3. At the Save As dialog box, change the save location to the **Unit1Topic03** folder on your storage medium and then type **U1T3-Paint** in the *File name* text box.

4. Click the Save as type option and then click *24-bit Bitmap (*.bmp;*.dib)* at the drop-down list.

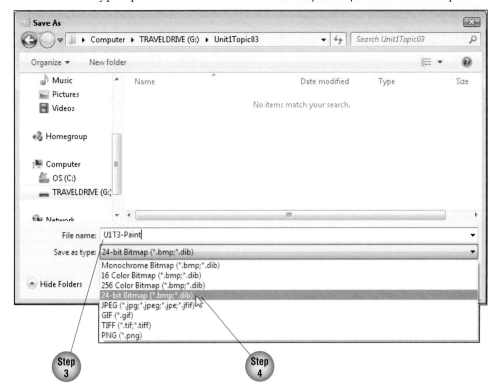

5. Click the Save button.

6. Open Microsoft Word.

7. Click the Insert tab.

8. Click the Object button arrow and then click *Object* at the drop-down list.

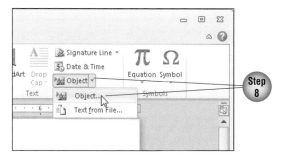

9. At the Object dialog box, click the Create from File tab.

10. Click the Browse button.

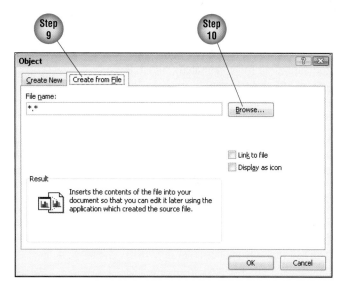

11 At the Browse dialog box, navigate to the **Unit1Topic03** folder on your storage medium and then double-click **U1T3-Paint.bmp**.

12. At the Object dialog box, click the *Link to file* check box to insert a check mark and then click OK.

    This inserts the picture into your Word document.

13. Save the Word document and name it **U1T3-Linked**. Leave Word open.

14. Switch back to Paint and then make a change to your drawing.

15. Save your file and then close Paint.

16. In Word, right-click the picture and then click *Update Link* at the shortcut menu.

    This displays the object with the change you made in Paint.

17. Save the document and then close Word.

Delving Deeper

IC³ 1-2.2.5

Defining Pixel Colors

Pixel colors can be defined using several color models. The most popular model is RGB (red-green-blue). Each pixel has a set of three numbers assigned to it (from 0 to 255) representing the colors red, green, and blue. The numbers indicate how much of that particular color exists within the pixel. The higher the number of a color, the brighter and more intensely that color is represented. For example, a "pure green" pixel would have 255 parts of green and 0 parts of red or blue (0/255/0). A pixel that is "pure red" would be 255/0/0. A dark blue pixel may be listed as 0/0/140; a dark purple would be 140/0/140.

Two other popular color models are CMYK (cyan-magenta-yellow-black), which is popular in commercial printing, and HSL (hue-saturation-luminosity). In each of those models, a color is defined by the numeric values assigned for each of the colors or aspects. The CMYK model's numbers range from 0 to 100, so 100 represents 100% of a value. A pure green pixel (0/255/0 in RGB) would be would be 63/0/100/0 in the CYMK color model, because green is 63% cyan, 0% yellow, 100% magenta, and 0% black. The HSL model uses 0 to 255 as the range, just like RGB does. In the HSL color model, that same green color would be 85/255/128: 85 hue (the tint of green), 255 saturation (fully saturated), and 128 luminosity (about 50% brightness).

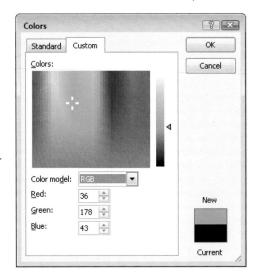

In Office applications you can experiment with color models using the Colors dialog box, which you can access whenever a color is available for an object. For example, in Word, Excel, or PowerPoint, select some text, click the Font Color button arrow, and then click *More Colors* at the drop-down gallery. At the Colors dialog box, click the Custom tab, click the down-pointing arrow at the right of the *Color model* option, and then select a color model from the drop-down list. In some applications, only RGB and HSL color models are available. In others, like Microsoft Publisher (included with some versions of Office), all three color models are available.

Exploring the Autorun.inf File

Lesson 3.1 explained that most discs contain an Autorun.inf file that instructs the computer to run the setup program. If you are curious about what this Autorun.inf file contains, browse the content of the disc and open Autorun.inf in Notepad. To do this, click the Start button and then click *Computer*. At the Computer window, right-click the CD or DVD drive containing the disc and then click *Open* at the shortcut menu. Locate the Autorun.inf file, right-click the file, and then click *Open With*. Click *Notepad* and then click OK. Notepad opens, displaying the programming code. For example, the AutoRun.inf file in the image below opens the Setup program called *SetupAssistant.exe.*

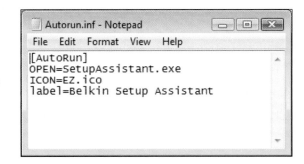

TOPIC SUMMARY

- Windows comes with many applications, and you can install others as needed.
- To install an application means to copy its files to the hard disk, update the Registry, and add a shortcut to the application on the Start menu.
- To install a new application, run the Setup utility for the application. It may run automatically from an inserted CD or DVD.
- To remove an application, open the Control Panel and then click *Uninstall a program* under the *Programs* heading.
- Software can be freeware, open source, shareware, or commercial in its distribution.
- Software can be licensed to a single user or can have a concurrent license or a site license.
- An update applies a fix to an existing version of a program. An upgrade installs a newer version.
- Word processing software such as Microsoft Word is used for text documents. The software allows you to edit and format text, perform error checks, create tables, insert graphics, and more.
- Spreadsheet software such as Excel is used to create spreadsheets with rows and columns of data and to perform calculations.
- Spreadsheets are divided into row-and-column grids; the intersection of a row and a column is called a cell.
- You can insert formulas and functions into a spreadsheet. A formula is a math operation. A function is a word that represents a math calculation, such as AVERAGE.
- Database software such as Access stores data in a structured format, such as an address book or a list of orders. Each person or item is a record; each type of information stored is a field.
- In a relational database program you can create data tables, queries, forms, and reports to help interpret the data.
- Presentation software such as PowerPoint creates slides that serve as visual aids for presentations. You can insert many types of graphics and video clips in the slides, and set up animations and sound effects to add interest.
- Photo-editing software modifies photos and creates new raster-based artwork; drawing software creates vector-based artwork.
- A raster (bitmap) image stores data by describing the color of each dot individually. It is used for photos and other realistic artwork.
- A vector image stores data by describing the color, size, and shape of mathematically drawn lines. It is used for blueprints and technical schematics, and to create moving objects in video games.
- Media players play back digital music and video clips.
- Utility programs perform maintenance and troubleshooting on the computer, or keep it safe from privacy and security threats.
- You can share data between applications by using the Clipboard or by dragging and dropping.
- To link or embed content between applications, use the Paste Special command (for parts of files) or the Insert Object command (for whole files).

Key Terms

active cell, p. 131

adware, p. 150

antivirus program, 150

Backstage view, p. 125

burn, p. 147

cell, p. 130

cell pointer, p. 134

concurrent license, p. 118

cookie, p. 150

database, p. 140

embed, p. 155

executable file, p. 116

field, p. 141

flat file database, p. 140

form, p. 141

formula, p. 131

Formula bar, p. 131

freeware, p. 117

function, p. 132

I-beam pointer, p. 125

insertion point, p. 125

Insert mode, p. 126

link, p. 155

malware, p. 150

Object Linking and Embedding
    (OLE), p. 155

open source, p. 117

Overtype mode, p. 126

pixel, p. 144

placeholder, p. 137

query, p. 141

Quick Access toolbar, p. 125

range, p. 134

raster image, p. 144

record, p. 141

Registry, p. 113

relational database, p. 141

report, p. 141

rip, p. 147

shareware, p. 117

site license, p. 118

slide, p. 136

spyware, p. 150

Trojan horse, p. 150

updates, p. 120

upgrade, p. 121

vector image, p. 143

virus, p. 150

workbook, p. 132

worksheet, p. 132

worm, p. 150

KEY POINTS REVIEW

Completion

In the space provided at the left, indicate the correct term, command, or option.

1. _____ Which of the following is NOT an application: Microsoft Word, Notepad, or Windows 7?

2. _____ Where are settings automatically changed in Windows when an application is installed?

3. _____ What file on a CD causes a program to launch automatically, such as a Setup program, when you insert the CD?

4. _____ How can you determine if updates are available for an application?

5. _____ What type of program would be most appropriate for creating your own business cards?

6. _____ What type of program would be most appropriate for writing business letters?

continued

7. _____ What type of program would be most appropriate for creating an amortization table for a loan?

8. _____ What type of program would be most appropriate for storing business information for a veterinary clinic, including tables of medications, owners, pets, appointments, and treatments?

9. _____ What is the flashing vertical line in a word processing program?

10. _____ In Microsoft Office 2010 applications, how do you enter Backstage view?

11. _____ What is at the intersection of a row and a column in a spreadsheet?

12. _____ In a spreadsheet program, =SUM is an example of what type of element?

13. _____ In PowerPoint, how do you exit Slide Show view?

14. _____ What kind of database consists of a single row-and-column table of information?

15. _____ What kind of database consists of multiple tables with relationships between them?

16. _____ What kind of picture is drawn with mathematically created lines and shapes?

17. _____ In a bitmap image, what is each individual dot called?

18. _____ Which Windows utility identifies unnecessary files and optionally deletes them?

Multiple Choice

For each of the following items, choose the option that best completes the sentence or answers the question.

1. Installing an application does all of these things except:
   A. copying files to the hard drive
   B. modifying the Registry
   C. converting data files from other programs
   D. creating a shortcut on the Start menu

2. To remove an application, go to the *Programs and Features* section of the
   A. hard drive
   B. Control Panel
   C. Computer window
   D. *User Accounts* list

continued

3. Which of these is an executable file?
   A. Word document
   B. spreadsheet
   C. graphic
   D. Setup utility

4. What kind of license would you get to permit a company to install a specified number of copies of an application on employee computers, without regard to how many copies would be running simultaneously?
   A. shareware
   B. site license
   C. concurrent license
   D. open source

5. What software would be most appropriate for managing the finances of a small business?
   A. QuickBooks
   B. Word
   C. Excel
   D. Chrome

6. What is the flashing vertical cursor called in Word?
   A. end-of-file marker
   B. place marker
   C. insertion point
   D. paragraph break

7. In a spreadsheet, a _____ is the intersection of a row and a column.
   A. cursor
   B. table
   C. block
   D. cell

8. Microsoft Access is a program that creates
   A. relational databases
   B. spreadsheets
   C. desktop publishing projects
   D. web pages

9. To _____ is to copy music from an audio CD to your hard disk.
   A. burn
   B. tug
   C. wax
   D. rip

10. To copy data between applications, you can use the:
    A. Transfer Panel
    B. Clipboard
    C. arrow keys
    D. Control Panel

Matching

Match each of the following definitions with the correct term, command, or option.

1. _____ Feature for linking and embedding content between applications
2. _____ A type of software that enables users to chat in real time
3. _____ The Windows program that checks for malware
4. _____ To write to a blank CD or DVD
5. _____ An individual colored dot in an image or on a display monitor
6. _____ An element of a worksheet that is identified by a letter of the alphabet
7. _____ An element of a worksheet that is identified by a number
8. _____ A math calculation in Excel beginning with an equals sign
9. _____ In Excel, a keyword like AVERAGE or SUM that represents a math operation
10. _____ An editing mode in a word processing program in which existing content is replaced by new text

A. Messaging
B. Pixel
C. Row
D. Function
E. Burn
F. Formula
G. Overtype
H. Column
I. OLE
J. Defender

SKILLS REVIEW

Review 3.1 **Installing and Removing an Application**

Your instructor will provide an application for you to install and remove. If you are not working with an instructor, you can use any application that has an executable Setup file, such as one you might download from www.download.com.

1. Install the application from its Setup file.
2. Press the Print Screen key to capture the *Programs and Features* list in the Control Panel that shows the application installed.
3. Open Paint and then paste the captured image in the open file.
4. Save the file in the **Unit1Topic03** folder on your storage medium and name it **U1T3-R1-Apps**.
5. Print the file.
6. Close the file and the exit Paint.
7. Run the application to confirm that it works.
8. Uninstall the application from the *Programs and Features* list. (Use the Uninstall or Uninstall/ Change button.)

Review 3.2 **Downloading and Installing an Application Update**

1. Identify at least four non-Microsoft applications installed on your PC.

   _____

   _____

   _____

   _____

2. Choose one of the applications you identified and visit the manufacturer's website. Find the *Support* section and determine whether an update is available for the application. Check the version number of the update against the version number of your installed application to see if the update is newer than what you have.
3. If you cannot find an update, or if the update is not newer than what you have, try another application from your list until you find one that will benefit from updating.
4. Use the Print Screen key to capture an image of of the web page that shows the update you plan to download and install.
5. Open Paint, paste the captured image in the file, and then save the file in the **Unit1Topic03** folder on your storage medium and name it **U1T3-R2-Download**.
6. Print and then close the file and then exit Paint.
7. Download and install the update.
8. Run the application to confirm that it works.

Review 3.3 **Comparing Word Processing and Text Editing Applications**

1. Open Notepad and WordPad in side-by-side windows.
2. In WordPad, type the following paragraph (as you type, do not press Enter; WordPad will wrap each line automatically as it reaches the edge of the window):

This is a test to compare the formatting capabilities of WordPad versus Notepad. WordPad has some formatting features, whereas Notepad does not. However, they are both good text editing applications, suitable for a range of tasks.

3. In WordPad, select the text by pressing Ctrl + A and then copy the text to the Clipboard by pressing Ctrl + C.
4. Click inside the Notepad window and then press Ctrl + V to paste the copied text. (Notepad might not wrap each line automatically. You can use the horizontal scroll bar to scroll to the right and see the end of the paragraph, or click Format on the menu bar and then click *Word Wrap* at the drop-down list.)
5. Make WordPad active and then click the Italic button to apply italic formatting to the selected text. (Notice that Notepad does not have a toolbar or any way to italicize text.)
6. Make Notepad active and then save your work as a .txt file in the **Unit1Topic03** folder on your storage medium with the name **U1T3-R3-Notepad**.
7. Print and then close the file and then exit Notepad.
8. With WordPad active, save your work as an .rtf file in the **Unit1Topic03** folder on your storage medium with the name **U1T3-R3-WordPad**.
9. Print and then close the file and then exit WordPad.

Review 3.4 **Working with a Spreadsheet**

1. Start Microsoft Excel 2010 and then open the file named **ACMESales.xlsx** from the **Unit1Topic03** folder on your storage medium.
2. In cell D4, type **=AVERAGE(B4:C4)**.
3. In cell D5, type **=AVERAGE(B5:C5)**, or copy the content of D4 to D5.
4. In cell D6, type **=AVERAGE(B6:C6)**, or copy the content of D4 to D6.
5. In cell B7, type **=SUM(B4:B6)**.
6. In cell C7, type **=SUM(C4:C6)**, or copy the content of B7 to C7.
7. Use Save As to save the file in the **Unit1Topic03** folder on your storage medium and name it **U1T3-R4-ACMESales**.
8. Print one copy of the file.
9. Close the file and then exit Excel.

SKILLS ASSESSMENT

Assessment 3.1 **Determining Installed Applications and Their Types**

1. Open the *Programs and Features* section of the Control Panel.
2. Using the list of common application types in Table 3.1, categorize as many of the installed applications as possible. Not all installed applications will fit in one of the categories from Table 3.1; if the category is not obvious, run the application (from the Start menu) to see if that helps you determine its type. Write your answers in the chart on the next page or write them on a separate sheet of paper to submit to your instructor. An example has been completed for you.

Application	Type
Microsoft Word (example)	Word processor (example)

Assessment 3.2 Creating a PowerPoint Presentation

1. Start PowerPoint.
2. On the title slide, type your name as the title and the name of this class as the subtitle.
3. Click the New Slide button.
4. On the new slide, in the title placeholder, type **Types of Content in Presentations**.
5. In the content placeholder, type the following bulleted list:

   - **Photos**
   - **Clip Art**
   - **SmartArt**
   - **Charts**
   - **Sounds**
   - **Videos**
   - **Tables**

6. Click the New Slide button again.
7. On the new slide, in the title placeholder, type **Photos**.
8. In the content placeholder, click the Insert Picture from File placeholder icon (the first icon in the second row).
9. In the Insert Picture dialog box, double-click any picture. (The pictures available will depend on your PC's content. If you have no pictures available, ask your instructor what picture to use.)
10. Save the presentation in the **Unit1Topic03** folder on your storage medium and name it **U1T3-A2-Slides**.
11. Print and then close the presentation and then exit PowerPoint.

Assessment 3.3 Drawing a Logo with Vector Drawing Tools

1. Start Word.
2. Create the logo shown at the right. Begin by clicking the Insert tab.
3. Click the Shapes button and then click the Rectangle shape (first shape from the left in the *Rectangles* section of the drop-down list).
4. Drag in the document to draw a rectangle that is approximately 2.5 inches square. (Use the Ruler to gauge the size.)
5. On the Drawing Tools Format tab, use the Shape Fill button to apply a dark blue fill to the rectangle.
6. On the Drawing Tools Format tab, click the 5-Point Star shape (located in the Insert Shapes group).
7. Draw a star that is as large as possible while still fitting inside the rectangle.
8. On the Drawing Tools Format tab, use the Shape Fill button to apply a white fill to the star.
9. On the Drawing Tools Format tab, click the Oval shape (located in the Insert Shapes group).
10. Draw an oval inside the center of the star so that the edges of the oval touch the inner points of the star.
11. On the Drawing Tools Format tab, use the Shape Fill button to apply a yellow fill to the oval.
12. Hold down the Ctrl key and click the rectangle, the star, and the oval to select them all.
13. On the Drawing Tools Format tab, click the arrow on the Outline Fill button, point to *Weight*, and click *1/4 point*.
14. Save the document in the **Unit1Topic03** folder on your storage medium and name it **U1T3-A3-WordLogo**.
15. Print and close the document and then exit Word.

Assessment 3.4 Using Paint

1. Open Paint.
2. As closely as possible, duplicate the logo shown in Assessment 3.3.
3. Save the file in the **Unit1Topic03** folder on your storage medium and name it **U1T3-A4-PaintLogo**.
4. Print and close the file and then exit Paint.

Assessment 3.5 Discovering Other Utilities in Windows

1. Open the Windows Help and Support window and search for information on administrative tools. Find and then read the article "What are Administrative Tools?"
2. From the information in the article, identify the purpose of the following utilities. Write your answers in the space provided, or on a separate sheet of paper to submit to your instructor.

Utility	Purpose
Data Sources (ODBC)	
Event Viewer	
Performance Monitor	
Services	
Task Scheduler	

Assessment 3.6 Finding Low-Cost Applications

1. OpenOffice is a free alternative to Microsoft Office that contains many of the same features. Go to http://ic3.emcp.net/OpenOffice and read about this software suite.
2. Find at least two additional websites that provide information about the pros and cons of using OpenOffice. List the websites below:

_____

_____

continued

3. Do a Google search for *freeware*. Find free alternative applications that might substitute for at least three of the applications installed on your PC. Write the information you find in the space provided or on a separate sheet of paper.

Application	Website	Substitutes for

Assessment 3.7 **Troubleshooting Application Problems**

Suppose you just bought a new game and are trying to install it on your PC. Using the Web to research as needed, indicate what you would do in the following situations:

1. Nothing happens when you insert the disc to install the game.
2. The Setup program crashes when you try to run it, or the Setup program completes successfully but the game crashes when you try to run it.
3. The game's video looks choppy and the sound cuts in and out.

CRITICAL THINKING

Producing an Electronic Game

Imagine you have designed an electronic game that you want to produce and sell to the public. Consider how you will manage this process. Will you try to do everything yourself so you can keep all the profits from your game, or will you hire others to help you with certain parts of the work? For example, will you:

- program the game yourself or hire a programmer?

- duplicate the discs yourself or use an outside vendor?

- design the product packaging yourself or hire a designer?

- contract with a large company to distribute your game or sell it on your own website?

In a Word document, write a business plan that explains your management choices. Support your choices with logical reasoning. Save the document as **U1T3-CT-Software**. Print and then close the document and exit Word.

TEAM PROJECT

Comparing Microsoft Office and Free Software

Microsoft Office is the most popular application suite on the market, and millions of people use it for their daily computing needs. However, other application suites are available that do almost exactly the same things but are cheaper or even free. OpenOffice is one such suite (www.openoffice.org). Another is Google Docs (docs.google.com). Yet another is Zoho (www.zoho.com).

Working as a team, choose one of the competitors to Microsoft Office, research the features in that suite's three key applications (word processing, spreadsheet, and presentation creation), and then create a spreadsheet in Excel that compares features to show what, if anything, users would miss out on by using the chosen alternative instead of Microsoft Office. Save the file in the **Unit1Topic03** folder on your storage medium and name it **U1T3-TeamProject**. Print and then close the file and exit Excel.

Discussion Questions

1. What overall impression do you have of the application suite you researched compared to Microsoft Office? What features in the suite do you prefer over Microsoft Office?
2. What might be the downside(s) to using a free application suite?
3. Would Web-only products (such as Google docs) pose problems that other products would not?
4. Based on the information you and your classmates gathered in during your research, which type of program would you want for your home computer? Support your choice by identifying the specific features that appeal to you and which application suite best suits your needs.

UNIT 2 Key Applications

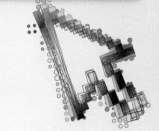

Topic 4: Working with Microsoft Office 2010 Applications

Topic 5: Editing a Document in Word

Topic 6: Formatting Characters and Paragraphs in Word

Topic 7: Creating and Enhancing Tables in Word

Topic 8: Formatting a Document in Word with Special Features

Topic 9: Analyzing Data Using Excel

Topic 10: Formatting an Excel Workbook

Topic 11: Preparing a Presentation

Topic 12: Inserting Graphic Elements in a Presentation and Integrating Word, Excel, and PowerPoint

Topic 4

Working With Microsoft Office 2010 Applications

Performance Objectives

Upon successful completion of Topic 4, you will be able to:

- Open an Office application
- Identify common screen features in Office applications
- Switch between Office applications
- Use ribbon commands
- Customize and change locations of commands
- Create and name files

- Open and save files with Save As
- Print files and manage print jobs
- Close files and exit Office applications
- Create files using templates
- Save as different file format
- Change Office application defaults
- Use Help resources

STUDENT RESOURCES

Before beginning this topic, copy to your storage medium the **Unit2Topic04** subfolder from the *Computer and Internet Essentials: Preparing for IC³* Internet Resource Center. Make this the active folder.

In addition to containing the data files needed to complete topic work, the Internet Resource Center contains model answers in PDF format for each of the applicable exercises in this topic. Use these files to check your work. The preface of your textbook provides instructions for accessing these files.

Necessary Data Files

To complete the exercises and assessments, you will need the following data files:

Exercises 4.1 & 4.2	N/A
Exercise 4.3	New file
Exercises 4.4–4.7	SoftwareApps.docx DISalesAnalysis.xlsx CFJobSearch.pptx
Exercise 4.8	New file
Exercise 4.9	Previously created file (Ex. 4.4–4.7)
Exercise 4.10	CFJobSearch.pptx CFPotential.pptx GMDeptMeeting.pptx SGCMeeting.pptx

continued

Exercise 4.11	N/A
Review 4.1	CompKeyboards.docx EPSales.xlsx
Review 4.2	New file
Review 4.3	CFPotential.pptx
Review 4.4	Previously created file (Review 1)
Assessments 4.1–4.4	New file
Team Project	New file

Visual Preview

Exercises 4.3–4.4, 4.7, 4.10
U2T4-ProdSoftware.docx

Exercises 4.8 **U2T4-Letter.docx**

Topic Overview

In Topic 4, you will learn how to open Microsoft Office Word, Excel, and PowerPoint, and how to identify common screen features among the three applications. You will also learn how to create, save, open, and close Word documents, Excel spreadsheets, and PowerPoint presentations. You will practice creating a document from an Office template and customizing Office defaults. In this topic, you will also learn about the Help feature, which is an on-screen reference manual providing information on features and commands for each application in the Office suite.

Lesson 4.1 Understanding Microsoft 2010 Applications

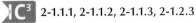 2-1.1.1, 2-1.1.2, 2-1.1.3, 2-1.2.3

Microsoft Office 2010 contains several different programs, including Word, a word-processing program used to create letters, reports, and research papers; Excel, a spreadsheet program used to analyze and evaluate numerical and financial information; and PowerPoint, a presentation graphics program used to organize and present information. In each of these applications, you can create, save, edit, and print files. The steps to open Word, Excel, and PowerPoint may vary depending on your system setup. Generally, to open Word, Excel, or PowerPoint, click the Start button on the Taskbar at the Windows desktop, point to *All Programs*, click *Microsoft Office*, and then click *Microsoft Word 2010*, *Microsoft Excel*

2010, or *Microsoft PowerPoint 2010*. Figure 4.1 identifies the features of the Word screen, Figure 4.2 identifies the features of the Excel screen, and Figure 4.3 identifies the features of the PowerPoint screen. Some common screen features among applications are described in Table 4.1.

Figure 4.1 Blank Document Screen in Word

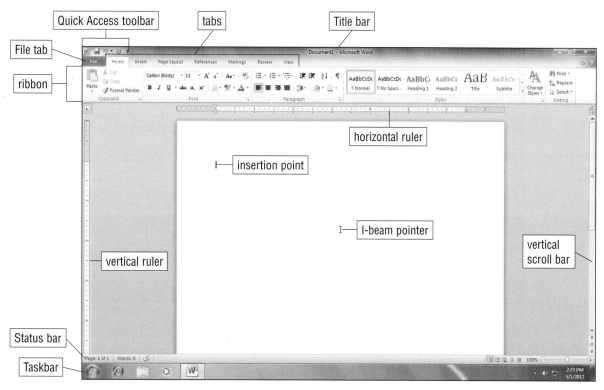

Figure 4.2 Blank Worksheet Screen in Excel

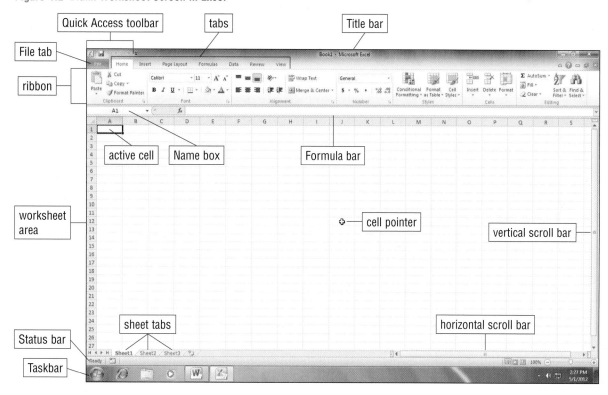

Figure 4.3 Blank Presentation Screen in PowerPoint

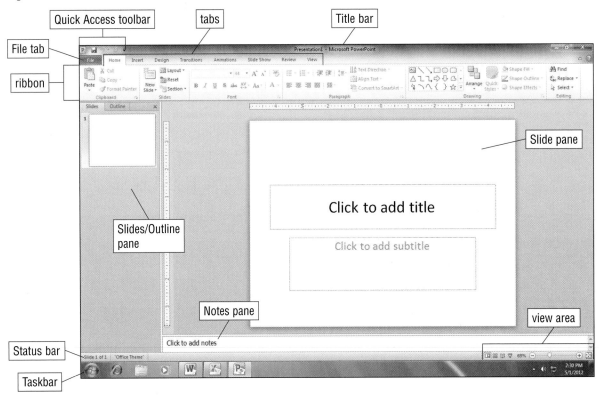

Table 4.1 Microsoft Office Screen Features

Feature	Description
File tab	When clicked, displays Backstage view containing buttons and tabs for working with and managing files
horizontal ruler	Used to set left and right margins, indents, and tabs
I-beam pointer	Used to move the insertion point or to select text
insertion point	Indicates the location of the next character entered at the keyboard
Quick Access toolbar	Contains buttons for commonly used commands
ribbon	Contains tabs and commands divided into groups
Status bar	Displays number of pages and words, view buttons, and Zoom slider bar
tabs	Contain commands and features organized into groups
Taskbar	Divided into three sections: the Start button, the task buttons area, and the notification area
Title bar	Displays the file name followed by the program name
vertical ruler	Used to set top and bottom margins
vertical scroll bar	Used to view various parts of the file

Use the Minimize, Restore Down, and Maximize buttons in the active file window to change the size of the active window. In an active file that is expanded to fill the screen, the Restore Down button is located immediately left of the Close button. (The Close button is marked with an X.) The Minimize button is located immediately to the left of the Restore Down button. When you minimize a file, the Restore Down button becomes the Maximize button. If you click the Minimize button in the active file, the file is reduced and displays as the application button on the Taskbar. To maximize a file that has been minimized, click the application button on the Taskbar.

Windows allows you to have many applications open simultaneously, with multiple files open within each application. Switch between applications and files by clicking the desired application button on the Taskbar and then clicking the file thumbnail.

Exercise 4.1 Exploring Office Applications

1. At the Windows desktop, click Start, point to *All Programs* at the pop-up menu, click *Microsoft Office*, and then click *Microsoft Word 2010*.

   Depending on your system configuration, these steps may vary.

2. At the Word blank document, identify the various features by comparing your screen with the one shown in Figure 4.1.

3. Click the Minimize button located in the upper right corner of the window.

4. At the Windows desktop, click the Start button on the Taskbar, point to *All Programs* at the pop-up menu, click *Microsoft Office*, and then click *Microsoft Excel 2010*.

5. At the Excel blank worksheet, identify the various features by comparing your screen with the one shown in Figure 4.2.

6. Click the Minimize button located in the upper right corner of the window.

7. At the Windows desktop, click the Start button on the Taskbar, point to *All Programs* at the pop-up menu, click *Microsoft Office*, and then click *Microsoft PowerPoint 2010*.

8. At the blank PowerPoint presentation, identify the various features by comparing your screen with the one shown in Figure 4.3.

9. On the Taskbar, notice the Word button, the Excel button, and the PowerPoint button.

10. Switch to the Excel file by clicking the Excel button on the Taskbar.

11. Switch to the Word file by clicking the Word button on the Taskbar.

12. Leave the three applications open.

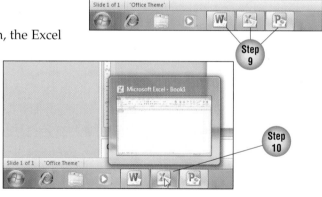

Drilling Down

Pinning an Application to the Taskbar

If you consistently use an application, you can pin the application icon to the Taskbar so the icon always appears when you are working in Windows. To pin an application to the Taskbar, open the desired application, right-click the icon that displays on the Taskbar, and then click *Pin this program to taskbar* at the pop-up list that displays. Another method for pinning an application icon to the Taskbar is to click the Start button located at the left side of the Taskbar, display the application in the Start menu, right-click the application, and then click *Pin to Taskbar* at the pop-up list that displays. You can remove the application icon from the Taskbar by right-clicking the icon and then clicking *Unpin this program from taskbar* at the pop-up menu.

Lesson 4.2 Using, Customizing, and Moving Ribbon Commands

2-1.1.4

ScreenTip A small window that displays descriptive text when the mouse pointer is positioned on a button or command

dialog box launcher A button that displays the dialog box of options associated with the group

Keyboard Shortcut

Minimize/Maximize Ribbon

Ctrl + F1

Quick Steps

Customize the Quick Access Toolbar

1. Click Customize Quick Access Toolbar button.
2. Insert check mark before desired command(s).
3. Remove check mark before desired command(s).

Recall that the ribbon displays toward the top of each of the application screens and displays tabs and common commands divided into groups. A ScreenTip will display whenever you hover the mouse pointer for a few seconds over any button or thumbnail in the ribbon. A **ScreenTip** is a pop-up window that provides information about the button command such as the formatting applied when clicked, whether other options are associated with the command, or what the keyboard shortcut is to execute the command.

Many groups in the ribbon include a dialog box launcher option. Clicking a **dialog box launcher** will display the dialog box associated with the group. For example, if you click the Font group dialog box launcher, the Font dialog box displays.

If you want to free up some room on the screen, you can minimize the ribbon by clicking the Minimize the Ribbon button that displays immediately left of the Microsoft Help button located in the upper right corner of the screen. You can also minimize the ribbon with the keyboard shortcut Ctrl + F1. Click the Minimize the Ribbon button or press Ctrl + F1 and the ribbon is reduced to tabs. To redisplay the ribbon, click the Expand the Ribbon button (previously the Minimize the Ribbon button), press Ctrl + F1, or double-click one of the tabs.

As its name implies, the Quick Access toolbar provides quick access to buttons for some of the most commonly performed tasks. By default, it contains the Save, Undo, and Redo buttons. You can easily add or remove buttons to and from the Quick Access toolbar with options at the Customize Quick Access Toolbar drop-down list, shown in Figure 4.4. Display this list by clicking the Customize Quick Access Toolbar button that displays at the right of the toolbar. Insert a check mark for the commands you want displayed on the toolbar and remove the check mark from those you do not want to appear. You can also remove buttons from the toolbar by right-clicking the desired button and then clicking *Remove from Quick Access Toolbar* at the pop-up list. By default, the Quick Access toolbar is positioned above the ribbon. You can move the toolbar below the ribbon by clicking the *Show Below the Ribbon* option at the Customize Quick Access Toolbar button drop-down list.

Figure 4.4 Customize Quick Access Toolbar Button Drop-down List

Click the Customize Quick Access Toolbar button to display this drop-down list of some of the most commonly used commands.

Exercise 4.2 Using and Moving the Ribbon and Customizing the Quick Access Toolbar

1. With Word the active application, click on each of the tabs located in the ribbon and notice the groups containing common commands for editing a document, inserting special features, changing document layout, referencing information in a document, performing a mail merge, reviewing a document, and viewing a document.

2. Click the Excel button on the Taskbar.

3. Click each of the tabs located in the ribbon and notice the groups containing commands for editing a worksheet, inserting special features, changing worksheet layout, inserting formulas in a worksheet, organizing data in a worksheet, reviewing a worksheet, and viewing a worksheet.

4. Click the PowerPoint button on the Taskbar.

5. Click each of the tabs located in the ribbon and notice the groups containing commands for editing a presentation, inserting special features, applying a design, inserting transitions between slides, adding animations to elements in a presentation, setting up a slide show, reviewing a presentation, and viewing a presentation.

6. With PowerPoint the active application, minimize the ribbon by clicking the Minimize the Ribbon button 🔺 that displays immediately left of the Microsoft PowerPoint Help button located in the upper right corner of the screen.

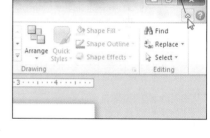

7. Redisplay the ribbon by double-clicking one of the tabs. You can also redisplay the ribbon by clicking the Expand the Ribbon button 🔽 or by pressing Ctrl + F1.

8. Click the Word button on the Taskbar.

9. Display the Font dialog box by clicking the dialog box launcher in the Font group.

   If you hover the mouse pointer over the dialog box launcher, a ScreenTip displays with an image of the dialog box.

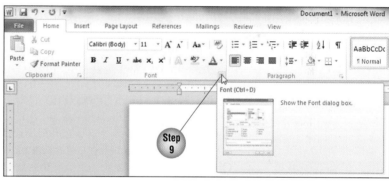

10. Close the Font dialog box by clicking the Close button ❎ that displays in the upper right corner of the dialog box.

11. Add the Open button to the Quick Access toolbar by clicking the Customize Quick Access Toolbar button 🔽 that displays at the right side of the toolbar and then clicking *Open* at the drop-down list.

12. Click the Open button 📂 on the Quick Access toolbar.

   This displays the Open dialog box.

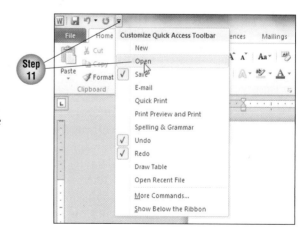

13. Close the Open dialog box by clicking the Close button located in the upper right corner of the dialog box.

14. Remove the Open button from the Quick Access toolbar by right-clicking the Open button and then clicking *Remove from Quick Access Toolbar* at the pop-up list.

15. Leave the three applications open.

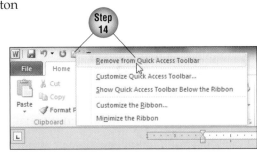

 Drilling Down

Additional Methods for Adding Buttons to the Quick Access Toolbar

The Customize Quick Access Toolbar button drop-down list contains eleven of the most commonly used commands. You can also insert many other commands on the toolbar. To display the available commands, click the Customize Quick Access Toolbar button and then click *More Commands* at the drop-down list. This displays the options dialog box with *Quick Access Toolbar* selected in the left panel. Select a command in the list box and then click the Add button. You can also add buttons or commands from a tab to the Quick Access toolbar. To do this, click the tab, right-click the desired option, and then click *Add to Quick Access Toolbar* at the shortcut menu.

Lesson 4.3   Creating and Naming Files

 2-1.2.1, 2-1.2.4

When you open an application, you can type information to create a letter, report, term paper, table, statement, album, and so on. Word documents, Excel spreadsheets, and PowerPoint presentations are based on templates that apply default formatting. The font type Calibri is the default font in all three applications. Some basic default Word formatting includes 1.15 line spacing and 10 points of spacing after paragraphs. In a Word document, each time you press the Enter key, a new paragraph begins and 10 points of spacing is inserted after the previous paragraph. If you want to move the insertion point down to the next line without including the additional 10 points of spacing, use the New Line command, Shift + Enter.

word wrap The automatic process of wrapping text from one line to the next

As you type text in a file, you do not need to press the Enter key at the end of each line—the application will wrap text from one line to the next. The automatic wrapping of text is called **word wrap**. You need to press the Enter key only to end a paragraph, create a blank line, or end a short line.

Office applications also contain the AutoCorrect feature. With AutoCorrect, Office applications automatically correct certain words as you type them. For example, if you type *adn* instead of *and*, the application automatically corrects your typing when you press the spacebar after the word. To turn off the AutoCorrect feature, click the File tab and then click the Options button at the Backstage view. At the options dialog box, click the Proofing button at the left side of the dialog box and then click the AutoCorrect Options button in the *AutoCorrect options* section. At the AutoCorrect Options dialog box with the AutoCorrect tab selected, click the *Replace text as you type* option to remove the check mark and then click OK to close the dialog box.

Quick Steps

Save a File
1. Click File tab.
2. Click Save button.
3. Type file name.
4. Click Save or press Enter.

OR

1. Click Save button on Quick Access toolbar.
2. Type file name.
3. Click Save or press Enter.

If you want to use a file in the future, make sure to save it. You can save files to the default location on the computer's hard disk; to a portable device such as a USB device, disk, or writable CD/DVD; to a specified directory or folder on the hard disk or a network drive; or to the operating system's desktop. To save a file, click the Save button on the Quick Access toolbar. At the Save As dialog box (shown in Figure 4.5), type the name of the file and then press Enter or click the Save button located in the lower right corner of the dialog box. You can also save a file by clicking the File tab and then clicking the Save button or by using the keyboard shortcut Ctrl + S.

Keyboard Shortcut

Save File

Ctrl + S

Figure 4.5 Save As Dialog Box in Word

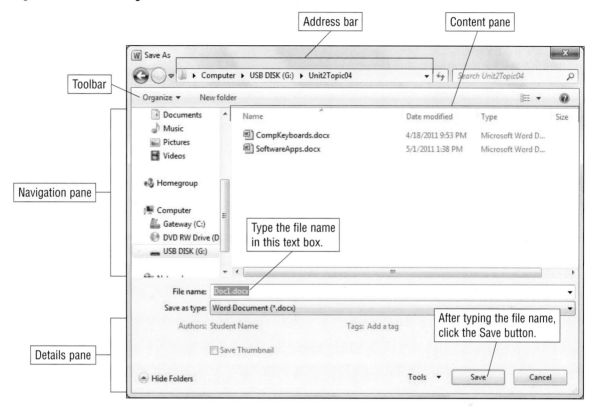

Exercise 4.3 Creating and Saving a Word Document

1. At the blank Word document, type **Productivity Software** as shown in Figure 4.6.

2. Hold down the Shift key, press the Enter key, and then release the Shift key.

   Shift + Enter is the New Line command. Using this command keeps lines of text within the same paragraph, which creates less space between one line and the next.

3. Type **Word Processing** and then press Shift + Enter.

4. Type **Microsoft Office Word** and then press Enter.

5. Type the remainder of the text shown in Figure 4.6.

   Type the text as shown. When you type *teh* and then press the spacebar, AutoCorrect corrects it to *the*. When you type *adn* and then press the spacebar, the AutoCorrect feature will automatically correct it to *and*. Do not press the Enter key to end a line of text within a paragraph. Word automatically wraps text to the next line.

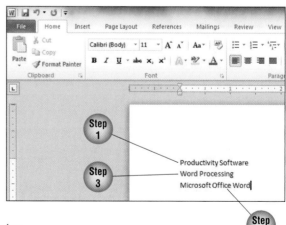

6. Save the document by clicking the Save button 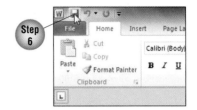 on the Quick Access toolbar.

7. At the Save As dialog box, navigate to the **Unit2Topic04** folder on your storage medium, type **U2T4-ProdSoftware** in the *File name* text box, and then press Enter or click the Save button.

Word automatically adds the file extension .docx to the end of a document name. The Address bar at the Save As dialog box displays the active folder. If you need to make the **Unit2Topic04** folder

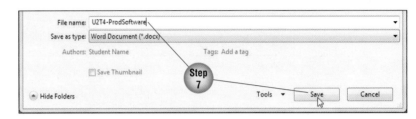

the active folder, click the drive in the *Folders* list box in the Navigation pane that contains your storage medium and then double-click the **Unit2Topic04** folder in the Content pane.

8. Leave **U2T4-ProdSoftware.docx** open.

Figure 4.6 Exercise 4.3 Text

> Productivity Software
> Word Processing
> Microsoft Office Word
>
> Word processing is a type of productivity software that allows users to communicate essential skills and knowledge. Microsoft Office Word is teh most widely used word processing application adn can be used to create documents, organize data, analyze information, and visually display materials. Microsoft Office Word easily allows users to create, edit, and format text with numerous functions and features.

Drilling Down

Naming Files

File names created in Word, Excel, and PowerPoint can be up to 255 characters in length, including drive letter and folder names, and may include spaces. File names cannot include any of the following characters:

forward slash (/)	question mark (?)
backslash (\)	quotation mark (")
greater than sign (>)	colon (:)
less than sign (<)	semicolon (;)
asterisk (*)	pipe symbol (|)

Lesson 4.4 Opening Files and Saving Files with Save As

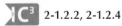 2-1.2.2, 2-1.2.4

Click the File tab in Word and the Backstage view displays as shown in Figure 4.7. Use buttons and tabs at this view to perform tasks such as opening, closing, saving, and printing a file. If you want to exit the Backstage view without completing an action, click the File tab, click any other tab in the ribbon, or press the Esc key on your keyboard.

Figure 4.7 Backstage View in Word

Click the File tab to display the Backstage view.

buttons in Quick Commands area

tabs

buttons

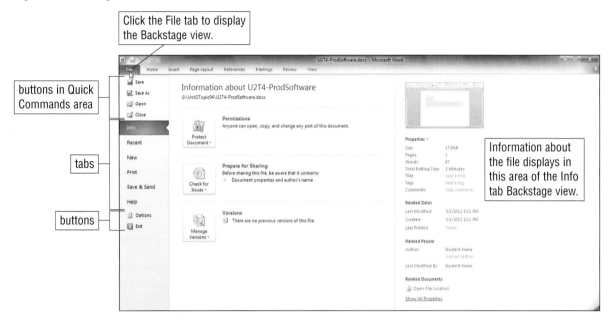

Information about the file displays in this area of the Info tab Backstage view.

If you have previously created, saved, and then closed a file, you can open it at the Open dialog box (shown in Figure 4.8). To display this dialog box, click the File tab and then click the Open button. You can also display the Open dialog box using the keyboard shortcut Ctrl + O. At the Open dialog box, open a file by double-clicking the file name or clicking the file once and then clicking the Open button.

Quick Steps

Open a File

1. Click File tab.
2. Click Open button.
3. Double-click file name.

Keyboard Shortcut

Open Dialog Box

Ctrl + O

Figure 4.8 Open Dialog Box in Word

Address bar

Toolbar

Navigation pane

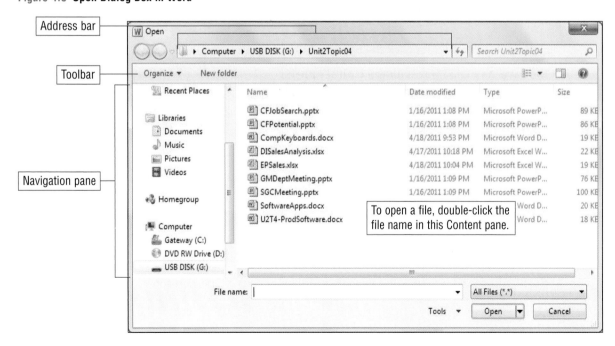

To open a file, double-click the file name in this Content pane.

Save a File with Save As
1. Click File tab.
2. Click Save As button.
3. Navigate to desired folder.
4. Type file name.
5. Click Save or press Enter.

Keyboard **S**hortcut

Save As Dialog Box

F12

If you want to see a list of the most recently opened files in an application, click the File tab and then click the Recent tab. This displays the Recent tab Backstage view containing a list of the most recently opened files. To open a file from the list, scroll down the list and then click the desired file.

If you open a previously saved file and want to save it with a new name, use the Save As button at the File tab Backstage view rather than the Save button. When you click the Save As button, the Save As dialog box displays. At this dialog box, type the new name for the file and then press Enter.

Exercise 4.4 Opening and Saving a File with Save As

1. With Word the active application and **U2T4-ProdSoftware.docx** open, click the File tab and then click the Open button in the Quick Commands area located at the left side of the Backstage view.

2. At the Open dialog box, make sure the **Unit2Topic04** folder on your storage medium is the active folder, and then double-click *SoftwareApps.docx* in the list box.

   Your list of documents may vary from what you see at the right.

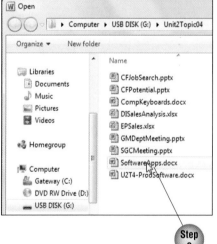

3. Click the File tab and then click the Save As button.

4. At the Save As dialog box with the **Unit2Topic04** folder on your storage medium active, type **U2T4-SoftwareApps** in the *File name* text box and then press Enter.

   If you open an existing document, make changes to it, and then want to save it with the same name, click the Save button on the Quick Access toolbar or click the File tab and then click the Save button. If you want to keep the original document and save the changed document with a new name, click the File tab and then click the Save As button.

5. Click the Excel button on the Taskbar to make Excel the active application.

6. At the blank worksheet, click the File tab and then click the Open button.

7. At the Open dialog box, navigate to the **Unit2Topic04** folder on your storage medium and then double-click *DISalesAnalysis.xlsx* in the list box.

Since you are using the Excel application to access the **Unit2Topic04** folder, only Excel files will display in the Open dialog box.

8. Click the File tab and then click the Save As button.

9. At the Save As dialog box, type **U2T4-DISalesAnalysis** in the *File name* text box and then press Enter.

10. Click the PowerPoint button on the Taskbar to make PowerPoint the active application.

11. At the blank presentation, click the File tab and then click the Open button.

12. At the Open dialog box, navigate to the **Unit2Topic04** folder on your storage medium and then double-click *CFJobSearch.pptx* in the list box.

13. Click the File tab and then click the Save As button.

14. At the Save As dialog box, type **U2T4-CFJobSearch** in the *File name* text box and then press Enter.

15. Leave **U2T4-CFJobSearch.pptx** as the active file.

 Drilling Down | **Pinning a File to the Recent Tab Backstage View**

When you click the File tab and then click the Recent tab, the most recently opened files display in the recent files list box (the name of the list box varies between applications). If you want a file to remain in the list, "pin" the file to the list by clicking the pin button that displays at the right side of the file name. This changes the dimmed gray stickpin to a blue stickpin. The next time you display the Recent tab Backstage view, the file you pinned displays at the top of the recent file list. To "unpin" the file, click the stickpin button to change it from blue back to gray.

Lesson 4.5 Printing a File

 2-1.4.3

Many of the files you create on your PC will need to be printed. A printed, paper file is referred to as **hard copy** and an electronic file displayed on the screen is referred to as **soft copy**. Print a file from the Print tab of the Backstage view. Figure 4.9 displays the Print tab Backstage view in Word. To display this view, click the File tab and then click the Print tab. You can also display the Print tab Backstage view with the keyboard shortcut Ctrl + P.

hard copy A printed copy of a file

soft copy An electronic copy of a file

Keyboard **S**hortcut

Print Tab Backstage View

Ctrl + P

Figure 4.9 **Print Tab Backstage View in Word**

Print Preview

Click the Print button to send the file to the specified printer.

Print tab

Navigation buttons

Zoom slider

The left side of the Print tab Backstage view displays three categories—Print, Printer, and Settings. Click the Print button in the Print category to send the file to the printer; specify the number of copies you want printed in the *Copies* option text box. Use the gallery in the Printer category to specify the desired printer. The Settings category contains a number of galleries, each with different options for printing your file. Use the galleries to specify whether or not you want the pages to be collated when printed; the orientation, page size, and margins of your file; and how many pages of your file you want to print on a page.

Exercise 4.5 Printing Files

1. Click the Word button on the Taskbar and then click the thumbnail representing **U2T4-SoftwareApps.docx**.

2. Print the document by clicking the File tab, clicking the Print tab at the Backstage view, and then clicking the Print button.

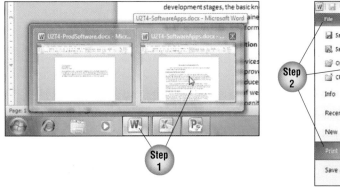

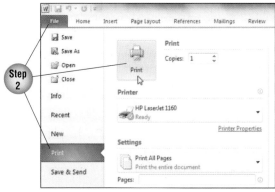

3. Click the Excel button on the Taskbar.

4. Specify that you want three copies of the workbook printed. Begin by clicking the File tab and then clicking the Print tab at the Backstage view.

5. At the Print tab Backstage view, click two times the up-pointing arrow located to the right of the *Copies* text box.

   The number *3* should now display in the *Copies* text box.

6. Check to make sure the desired printer is selected in the Printer category. If not, click the gallery in the Printer category and then click the desired printer at the drop-down list.

7. Click the Print button.

8. Leave **U2T4-DISalesAnalysis.xlsx** the active file.

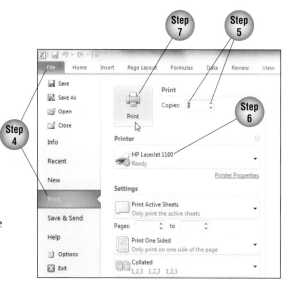

Drilling Down

Adding a Quick Print Button to the Quick Access Toolbar

Another method for printing a document is to insert the Quick Print button on the Quick Access toolbar and then click the button. This sends the document directly to the printer without displaying the Print tab Backstage view. To insert the button on the Quick Access toolbar, click the Customize Quick Access Toolbar button and then click *Quick Print* at the drop-down list.

Lesson 4.6   Managing Print Jobs

IC³ 2-1.4.4, 2-1.4.5

You may have multiple printers available for printing a file. Recall that to set a printer as the default printer for all print jobs, you can select options in the *Devices and Printers* section of the Control Panel in Windows. A list of all devices and printers attached to the computer displays in the *Devices and Printers* section. An icon of a check mark in a green circle displays next to the default printer. You can change the default printer by right-clicking the desired printer and then clicking *Set as default printer*.

Most printers now use a Universal Serial Bus (USB) interface. When a printer is connected to a computer for the first time, the USB printer uses the Plug and Play process in which Windows recognizes the device and either automatically installs a driver or prompts you for a driver location. A print driver is a program within Windows that communicates with the printer.

Once you send a file to the printer, the file displays in the **print queue**, which is a list of all active print jobs and the status of the print jobs. Display the print queue of the default printer by clicking the default printer in the *Devices and Printers* section of the Control Panel in Windows and then clicking the *See what's printing* option on the Command bar located near the top of the panel. This displays a dialog box containing a list of all the print jobs and the status of the print jobs, as shown in Figure 4.10. With options in this dialog box, you can pause, resume, restart, or cancel a print job. You can also display

Quick Steps

Set the Default Printer
1. Click Start button.
2. Click *Devices and Printers*.
3. Right-click desired printer.
4. Click *Set as default printer*.

Display the Print Queue
1. Click Start button.
2. Click *Devices and Printers*.
3. Right-click the default printer.
4. Click *See what's printing*.

OR

Double-click printer icon on Taskbar.

print queue A list of all active print jobs and the status of the print jobs for a particular printer

the print queue by right-clicking the desired printer in the Control Panel and then clicking *See what's printing* at the drop-down list. Another method for viewing the print queue is to double-click the printer icon that displays on the Taskbar when a print job begins.

Figure 4.10 Print Queue Dialog Box

Print jobs in the print queue

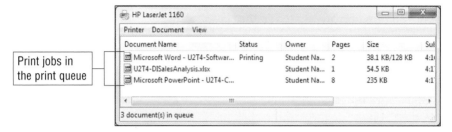

Exercise 4.6 Viewing Print Jobs

1. Click the Word button on the Taskbar and then click **U2T4-SoftwareApps.docx**.

2. Click the File tab, click the Print tab, and then check to make sure the selected printer in the Printer section is the default printer.

    An icon of a check mark inside a green circle will display next to the default printer. If the default printer is not selected, click the Printer gallery and then select the default printer at the drop-down list.

3. Click the Print button to send the document to the printer.

4. View the printer's properties by clicking the Start button on the Taskbar and then clicking *Devices and Printers* at the pop-up menu.

5. At the Control Panel, double-click the default printer.

    Your default printer name may vary from the one shown at the right.

6. Notice the information that displays about the printer, such as the printer's status and how many files are in the print queue.

    Your printer's information may display with no documents in the queue since your document may have already finished printing.

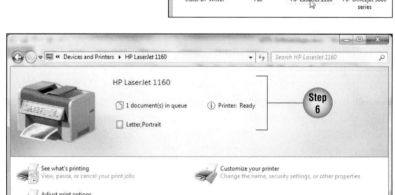

7. Click the Back button on the Command bar to view the *Devices and Printers* section.

8. Right-click the default printer and notice the pop-up menu that displays.

With options at this pop-up menu, you can view the printer's properties, view the print queue, set the printer as the default printer if it is not already the default, and remove the printer from the *Devices and Printers* section.

9. With the default printer still selected (it will display with a blue background), click the *See what's printing* option on the Command bar.

This displays the print queue for the printer.

10. If a document displays in the print queue, click the document once to select it.

11. With a document selected in the print queue, click Document on the Printer menu bar.

With the options that display in the drop-down list, you can pause, resume, restart, or cancel a print job. Refer to the screen capture below to view these options if you do not have any documents in the print queue.

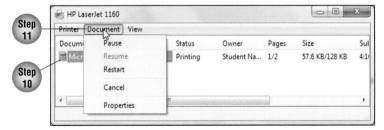

12. Close the print queue and then close the Control Panel.

13. Leave **U2T4-SoftwareApps.docx** the active file.

Drilling Down

Troubleshooting Print Problems

Sometimes a problem occurs that prevents a print job from printing as intended. The problem may be with the printer, the print queue, or with the file you are attempting to print. If the file does not print or does not print as intended, use the information below to determine how to fix the problem.

Problem with the Printer	
Is the printer turned on?	Check to make sure a power light displays indicating the printer is turned on. If not, turn on the printer.
Is the printer online?	Check the printer's panel or display to determine if a light or message displays indicating that the printer is offline. This may occur if paper has jammed in the printer or the ink or toner is low. Most printer displays will indicate the specific problem.
Is the printer connected to the computer?	This connection can be through a cable, Bluetooth, wireless, or Local Area Network (LAN).
Does the printer have paper?	Check to make sure the paper trays in the printer contain paper.
Does the printer have ink or toner?	If the printer is running low on ink or toner, you may get a warning message on your printer or a message may display on your screen.
Does the file fail to print and the application stop responding?	Your computer may not recognize the printer driver. You may need to download an updated printer driver, which you usually can do from the manufacturer's website.

Problem with the File Settings	
When you try to print, does an error message display that states the file does not fit within the margins of the paper?	You need to change the margins of the file.
Does the printed file cut off the headers and/or footers?	You need to increase the distance between the top of the page and the header text and/or the bottom of the page and the footer text. Or, check to make sure the paper size set in the application is the actual size of the paper in the printer.

Problem with the Print Queue	
Is the desired printer set as the default printer?	Check to make sure the appropriate printer is selected at the *Devices and Printers* section of the Control Panel.
Has the print job in the print queue been paused or canceled?	Check the print queue to resume any paused or canceled print jobs.

Lesson 4.7   Closing Files and Exiting Applications

When you save a file it is saved on your storage medium and remains open in the application screen. To remove the file from the screen, click the File tab and then click the Close button or use the keyboard shortcut Ctrl + F4. When you close a file, the file is removed from the application window. At this screen, you can open a previously saved file, create a new file, or exit the application.

When you are finished working with an application and have saved all necessary information, exit the application by clicking the File tab and then clicking the Exit button located below the Help tab. You can also exit the application by clicking the Close button located in the upper right corner of the screen or with the keyboard shortcut Alt + F4.

Quick Steps

Close a File
1. Click File tab.
2. Click Close button.

Exit an Application
1. Click File tab.
2. Click Exit button.

OR

Click Close button in upper right corner of screen.

Keyboard Shortcuts

Close File
Ctrl + F4

Exit Application
Alt + F4

Exercise 4.7 Closing Files and Exiting Applications

1. Click the Excel button on the Taskbar.

2. With **U2T4-DISalesAnalysis.xlsx** open, close the workbook by clicking the File tab and then clicking the Close button in the Quick Commands area.

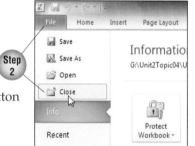

3. Exit Excel by clicking the File tab and then clicking the Exit button located below the Help tab.

4. Click the PowerPoint button on the Taskbar and then close **U2T4-CFJobSearch.pptx** by clicking the File tab and then clicking the Close button in the Quick Commands area.

5. Exit PowerPoint by clicking the Close button located in the upper right corner of the screen.

6. Click the Word button on the Taskbar and then click the **U2T4-ProdSoftware.docx** thumbnail.

   Skip this step if **U2T4-ProdSoftware.docx** is already the active document.

7. Close **U2T4-ProdSoftware.docx** and then close **U2T4-SoftwareApps.docx**.

8. Leave Word open.

   No document should display in Word. If a document does display, close the document.

Drilling Down

Closing Files and Exiting Applications Using KeyTips

Word, PowerPoint, and Excel provide access keys you can press to use a command in a program. Press the Alt key on the keyboard to display KeyTips that identify the access key you need to press to execute a command. For example, to close a worksheet in Excel using KeyTips, press the Alt key on the keyboard, press the F key to access the File tab, and then press the C key to close the worksheet. To exit Excel using KeyTips, press the Alt key, press the F key, and then press the X key.

Lesson 4.8 Creating Files Using Templates

IC³ 2-1.2.4, 2-2.1.16, 2-2.2.3

Microsoft Office includes a number of template files formatted for specific use within each application. Each Word document, Excel worksheet, and PowerPoint presentation is based on a template, with the Normal template the default. With additional Office templates, you can easily create a variety of files such as letters, faxes, awards, budgets, reports, and albums. Display templates by clicking the File tab and then clicking the New tab. This displays the New tab Backstage view. Figure 4.11 shows the New tab Backstage view in Word.

Figure 4.11 New Tab Backstage View in Word

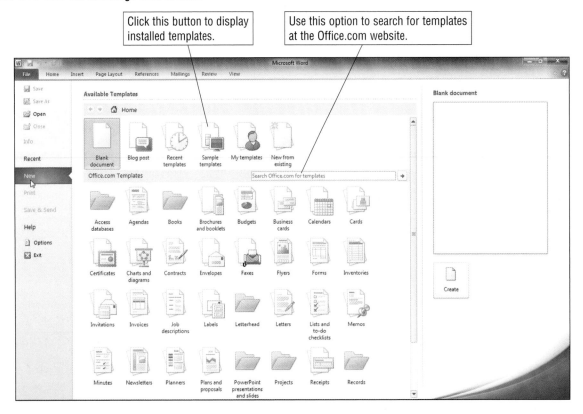

Click this button to display installed templates.

Use this option to search for templates at the Office.com website.

Quick Steps

Create a File Using a Template

1. Click File tab.
2. Click New tab.
3. Click Sample templates button.
4. Double-click desired template.

Click the Sample templates button in the Available Templates category to display the installed templates. Click the desired template in the *Sample templates* list box and a preview of the template displays at the right side of the screen. With options below the template preview, you can choose to open the template as a document or as a template. Click the Create button and the template opens and displays on the screen. Locations for personalized text display in placeholders in the template document. Select the placeholder text and then type the desired text.

Exercise 4.8 Using a Template to Create a Business Letter

1. In Word, click the File tab and then click the New tab.

2. At the New tab Backstage view, click the Sample templates button.

3. Click the *Equity Letter* template (you may need to scroll down the list to display the *Equity Letter* template) and then click the Create button that displays below the letter in the preview section.

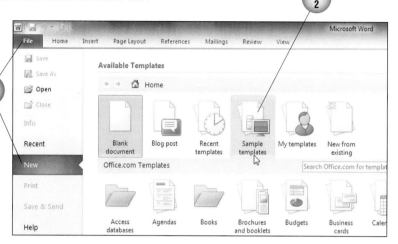

4. Click the placeholder text *[Pick the date]* and then type the current date. (Your date will automatically change to numbers when you click outside the placeholder.)

5. Select the name that displays below the date and then type your first and last names.

6. Click the placeholder text *[Type the sender company name]* and then press the Delete key three times.

   Pressing the Delete key three times deletes the placeholder text, the placeholder, and the blank line.

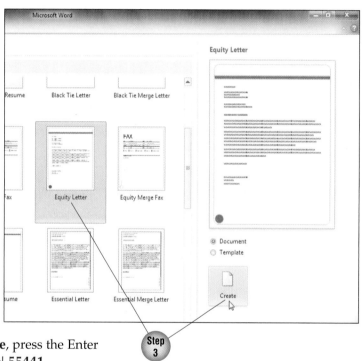

7. Click the placeholder text *[Type the sender company address]*, type **4525 Lakeside Drive**, press the Enter key, and then type **Plymouth, MN 55441**.

8. Click the placeholder text *[Type the recipient name]* and then type **Mr. Juan Quezada**.

9. Click the placeholder text *[Type the recipient address]* and then type **City of Thomasville**.

10. Press the Enter key and then type **1010 East Lane Boulevard**.

11. Press the Enter key and then type **Thomasville, MN 56778**.

12. Click the placeholder text *[Type the salutation]* and then type **Dear Mr. Quezada:**.

13. Click on any character in the three paragraphs of text in the body of the letter and then type the following text:

At our local activity center, I read an announcement requesting volunteers for the after-school recreation program. I am interested in volunteering for the program and can commit to approximately 10 hours a week.

14. Press Enter and then type **Please forward my name and contact information to the coordinator of the program. I can be reached by telephone at (763) 555-5467 or by email at name@emcp.net.**

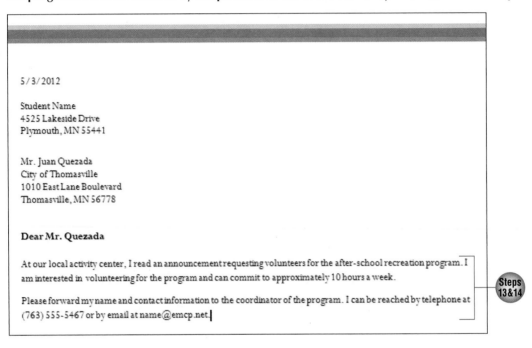

15. Click the placeholder text *[Type the closing]* and then type **Sincerely,**.

16. Make sure your first and last names display below *Sincerely*.

17. Click the placeholder text *[Type the sender title]* and then press the Delete key.

18. Click the placeholder text *[Type the sender company name]* and then press the Delete key two times.

19. Click the Save button on the Quick Access toolbar.

20. At the Save As dialog box, navigate to the **Unit2Topic04** folder on your storage medium, type **U2T4-Letter** in the *File name* text box, and then press Enter.

21. Save the letter document to your desktop by clicking the File tab and then clicking the Save As button.

22. At the Save As dialog box, click *Desktop* in the Navigation pane located at the left side of the dialog box and then click the Save button.

23. Close the document and then exit Word.

24. At your computer desktop, double-click the document named U2T4-Letter.docx.

    Double-clicking the document on your desktop opens Word and opens the document.

25. Print the letter by clicking the File tab, clicking the Print tab, and then clicking the Print button.

26. Close **U2T4-Letter.docx**.

Drilling Down

Using Online Templates

If you are connected to the Internet, Microsoft offers a number of predesigned templates you can download. Templates are grouped into categories and the category names display in the *Office.com Templates* section of the New tab Backstage view. Click the desired template folder to display available templates. Click the desired template and then click the Download button to download a template.

Lesson 4.9   Saving Files in a Different Format

 2-1.2.4

When you save a file, the file is automatically saved within a particular application. Word saves a file as a Word document and adds the file extension *.docx*, Excel saves a file as an Excel spreadsheet and adds the file extension *.xlsx*, and PowerPoint saves a file as a PowerPoint presentation and adds the file extension *.pptx*. If you need to share a document with someone who is using a different word processing program, a different spreadsheet program, a different presentation program, or a different version of the applications, you may want to save the document in another format. You can do this with the *Save as type* option at the Save As dialog box or with options at the Save & Send tab Backstage view. Display the Save & Send tab Backstage view by clicking the File tab and then clicking the Save & Send tab. Click the *Change File Type* option in the File Types category and the view displays as shown in Figure 4.12. With options in the *Change File Type* section, you can choose to save a file in the default format, in a previous version of the application, as a template, or in a variety of other formats specific to each application.

Quick Steps

Save a File in a Different Format
1. Click File tab.
2. Click Save & Send tab.
3. Click *Change File Type* option in File Types category.
4. Click desired format in *Change File Type* section.

Figure 4.12 Save & Send Tab Backstage View in Word

> Click the *Change File Type* option to display options for saving a file in a different format.

> Click the desired file type and then click the Save As button.

Exercise 4.9 Saving a File in a Different File Format

1. In Word, open **U2T4-SoftwareApps.docx**.

2. You need to send the **U2T4-SoftwareApps.docx** document to a colleague who uses Word 2003, so you need to save the document in that format. With **U2T4-SoftwareApps.docx** open, click the File tab and then click the Save As button.

3. At the Save As dialog box, type **U2T4-SoftwareAppsWd2003** in the *File name* text box.

4. Click the *Save as type* option button and then click *Word 97-2003 Document (*.doc)* at the drop-down list.

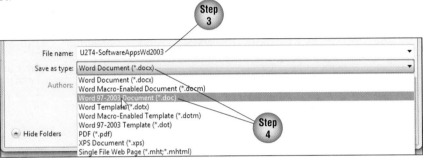

5. Click the Save button located in the lower right corner of the dialog box.

   Notice the file extension in the Title bar now ends with *.doc*.

6. Close **U2T4-SoftwareAppsWd2003.doc**.

7. Capture the screen contents and insert the file in a document. Begin by displaying the Open dialog box in Word.

8. Press the Print Screen key on your keyboard (generally located in the top row).

9. Close the Open dialog box and then press Ctrl + N to display a new, blank document.

10. At the blank document, press Ctrl + V to insert the print screen file into the document.

11. Print the document by clicking the File tab, clicking the Print tab, and then clicking the Print button at the Print tab Backstage view.

12. Close the document without saving it and then exit Word.

13. Open Excel and then display the Open dialog box.

14. Navigate to the **Unit2Topic04** folder on your storage medium and then double-click **U2T4-DISalesAnalysis.xlsx**.

15. Save **U2T4-DISalesAnalysis.xlsx** as a template. Begin by clicking the File tab and then clicking the Save & Send tab.

16. At the Save & Send tab Backstage view, click the *Change File Type* option in the File Types category.

17. Click the *Template (.xltx)* option in the *Workbook File Types* section and then click the Save As button.

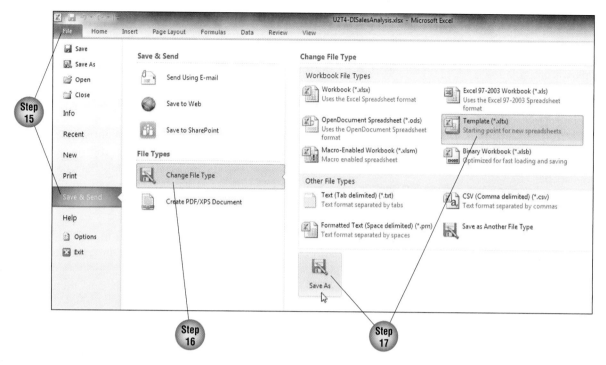

18. At the Save As dialog box with the *Save as type* option set to *Excel Template (.xltx)*, type **U2T4-DISalesAnalysisTemplate** and then press Enter.

Notice the file extension in the Title bar now ends with *.xltx*.

19. Display the Open dialog box in Excel and then press the Print Screen key.

20. Open Word and then press Ctrl + V to insert the print screen file.

21. Print the document, close the document without saving changes, and then exit Word.

22. Close the Open dialog box in Excel, close **U2T4-DISalesAnalysisTemplate.xltx**, and then exit Excel.

 Drilling Down

Saving in PDF and XPS Formats

You can also save a file in the portable document format (PDF) or the XPS format. The PDF file format is used to capture all of the elements of a file as an electronic image, and the XPS file format is used for publishing content in an easily viewable format. You can open a PDF file in Adobe Reader or in your web browser, and you can open an XPS file in your web browser. Both file formats allow you to view a file in a page layout format no matter the operating system on which you view the file. To save a file in PDF or XPS format, click the File tab, click the Save & Send tab, click the Create PDF/XPS button in the File Types category, and then click the Create a PDF/XPS button in the Create a PDF/XPS Document category of the Backstage view. This displays the Publish as PDF or XPS dialog box with the *PDF (*.pdf)* option selected in the *Save as type* option button. If you want to save the document in XPS format, click the *Save as type* option button and then click *XPS Document (*.xps)* at the drop-down list. Type a name for the file in the *File name* text box and then click the Publish button. If you save the document in PDF format, the file opens in Adobe Reader, and if you save the file in XPS format, the file opens in the XPS Viewer window.

IC³ 2-1.1.7

Office applications automatically save your files in the default file format and in a default folder on your computer. Office applications also automatically save a backup of your open files every 10 minutes. You can use the options dialog box in each application to change the default format for saving a file, the default folder in which you save your files, and the frequency with which the application automatically saves your open files.

Recall that Office applications keep a list of the most recently opened files and folders in the Recent tab Backstage view. Generally, the names of the twenty most recently opened files display in the Recent tab Backstage view. You can change the number of files that display in the Recent tab Backstage view with the options available in the application's options dialog box with the Advanced button selected.

The Recent tab Backstage view also contains the option for adding files to the Backstage navigation bar (the panel at the left) below the Close button in the Quick Commands area. In PowerPoint, you can insert a check mark in the *Quickly access this number of Recent Presentations* check box and then change the number of displayed presentation names by increasing or decreasing the number that displays at the right side of the *Quickly access this number of Recent Presentations* option. A maximum of six files can display in the Backstage navigation bar. You can also add files to the Backstage navigation bar in Word and Excel.

Exercise 4.10   Customizing Word and PowerPoint Defaults

1. Open Word.

2. At the blank document, change the default location for saving files and decrease the AutoRecover time to two minutes. Begin by clicking the File tab and then clicking the Options button located below the Help tab.

3. At the Word Options dialog box, click *Save* in the left panel.

4. Notice the default file format in the *Save files in this format* option box.

5. Notice the file path that displays in the *Default file location* option box.

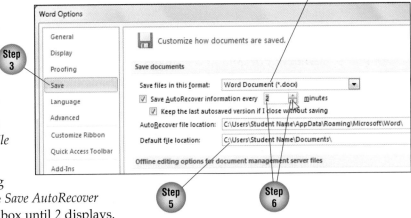

6. Click the down-pointing arrow at the right of the *Save AutoRecover information every* option box until 2 displays.

7. Click OK to close the dialog box.

8. Open **U2T4-ProdSoftware.docx**.

9. Press Ctrl + End to move the insertion point to the end of the document, press the Enter key two times, and then type your first and last names.

10. Leave the document open for over two minutes without making any changes. After a couple of minutes have passed, click the File tab and then notice the AutoRecovered document that displays to the right of the Manage Versions button.

If an AutoRecovered document does not display, click the File tab to return to the document, wait a few more minutes, and then click the File tab again to view the AutoRecovered document.

11. Click the Close button at the Backstage view to close **U2T4-ProdSoftware.docx**.

12. At the message that displays asking if you want to save changes made to the document, click the Don't Save button.

13. Exit Word.

14. Open PowerPoint.

15. Navigate to the **Unit2Topic04** folder on your storage medium. Open and then close **CFJobSearch.pptx**, **CFPotential.pptx**, **GMDeptMeeting.pptx**, and **SGCMeeting.pptx**.

PowerPoint should be open but no presentation should display in the window.

16. Change the number of presentations that display in the *Recent Presentations* section of the Recent tab Backstage view to 3. Begin by clicking the File tab and then click the Options button.

17. At the PowerPoint Options dialog box, click *Advanced* in the left panel.

18. In the *Display* section, click the down-pointing arrow next to the *Show this number of Recent Documents* option until 3 displays.

19. Click OK to close the dialog box.

20. Click the File tab.

Notice that only three of the four presentations you opened in Step 15 display.

21. Click the *Quickly access this number of Recent Presentations* check box to insert a check mark.

22. Click the down-pointing arrow at the right side of the number 3 until the number 2 displays.

23. Notice the two presentation names that now display below the Close button on the Backstage navigation bar.

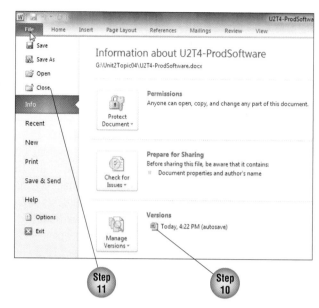

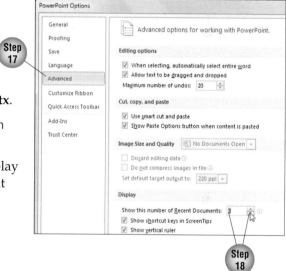

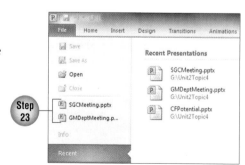

24. Change the *Quickly access this number of Recent Presentations* option back to 3 and then click the check box to remove the check mark.

25. Click the Exit button in the Backstage view to exit PowerPoint.

Drilling Down

Recovering Unsaved Files

When you save a file, Word deletes the AutoRecovered version of the file. However, if you are working in a file that you close without saving (after 10 minutes) or the power is disrupted, the application keeps the backup file in the UnsavedFiles folder on the hard drive. You can access this folder by clicking the Manage Versions button in the Info tab Backstage view and then clicking *Recover Unsaved Documents* in Word, *Recover Unsaved Workbooks* in Excel, or *Recover Unsaved Presentations* in PowerPoint. At the Open dialog box that displays, double-click the desired backup file you want to open. You can also display the UnsavedFiles folder with a button at the Recent tab Backstage view. To do this in Word, click the File tab, click the Recent tab, and then click the Recover Unsaved Documents button that displays toward the bottom of the screen. In Excel, click the Recover Unsaved Workbooks button at the Recent tab Backstage view, and click the Recover Unsaved Presentations button at the PowerPoint Recent tab Backstage view.

Lesson 4.11 Using Help Resources

 2-1.1.8, 2-1.1.9

You can turn to a variety of resources to receive help with an application. Help can come from application textbooks, online blogs or tutorials, instructors, classmates, or coworkers. Many organizations have an online help desk to answer application questions and help troubleshoot issues you may encounter. You can also receive help on an application by calling or emailing customer support. Some online application support provides quick responses through instant messaging. Third party user groups and online forums are another way to get answers to specific questions about an application.

Quick Steps

Use Help
1. Click Microsoft Help button.
2. Type topic or feature.
3. Press Enter.
4. Click desired topic.

Keyboard Shortcut

Help
F1

Microsoft Office 2010 also provides an extensive Help feature. Microsoft's Help feature is an on-screen reference manual containing information about all application features and commands. The Help feature is similar in each application and also similar to the Windows Help feature. In Word, access the Help feature by clicking the Microsoft Word Help button located in the upper right corner of the screen (a question mark in a circle) or by pressing the keyboard shortcut F1. This displays the Word Help window. Click the see all hyperlink located toward the bottom right corner of the Help window and categories display with options you can click to learn how to accomplish specific tasks in an application. In the Help window, you can also type a topic, feature, or question in the *Search* text box and then press Enter. Topics related to the search text display in the Word Help window below the *Search* text box. Click a topic that interests you. If the topic window contains a Show All hyperlink in the upper right corner, click this hyperlink and the information expands to show all help information related to the topic. When you click the Show All hyperlink, it becomes the Hide All hyperlink. Complete similar steps to get help with features in Excel and PowerPoint. You can narrow your search results by using search strategies such as the Boolean operators *AND*, *OR*, and *NOT*. For example, you can search for information on saving and printing by typing *print AND save* in the Help window *Search* text box.

The Help tab Backstage view, shown in Figure 4.13, contains an option for displaying the Word Help window as well as other options. To display the Help tab Backstage view, click the File tab and then click the Help tab. At the Help tab Backstage view, click the Microsoft Office Help button in the *Support* section to display the Help window for the active application and click the Getting Started button to access the Microsoft website that displays information about getting started with the active application. Click the Contact Us button in the *Support* section and the Microsoft Support website displays. Click the Options button in the *Tools for Working With Office* section and the options dialog box for the active application displays. Click the Check for Updates button and the Microsoft Update website displays with information on available updates. The right side of the Help tab Backstage view displays information about Office and the active application.

Figure 4.13 Help Tab Backstage View in Word

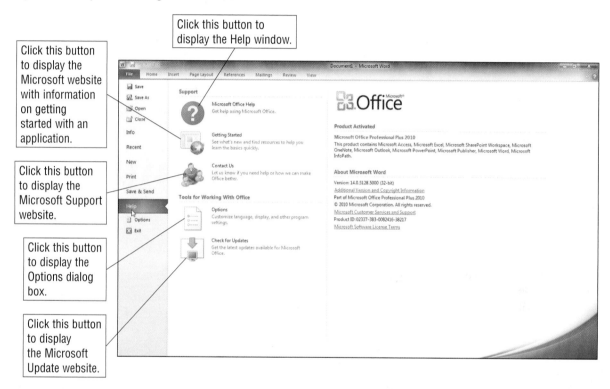

Click this button to display the Help window.

Click this button to display the Microsoft website with information on getting started with an application.

Click this button to display the Microsoft Support website.

Click this button to display the Options dialog box.

Click this button to display the Microsoft Update website.

Exercise 4.11 Using Help to Find Information on Saving a Document

1. Open Word.

2. At the blank document, click the Microsoft Word Help button located in the upper right corner of the screen.

   You can also press the F1 key to display the Word Help window.

Step 2

3. At the Word Help window, click the see all hyperlink that displays toward the bottom of the dialog box.

This displays help categories in the dialog box.

4. Click the Creating documents hyperlink.

5. Look at the help topics that display about creating a document, and then click twice on the Back button located at the left side of the Help toolbar.

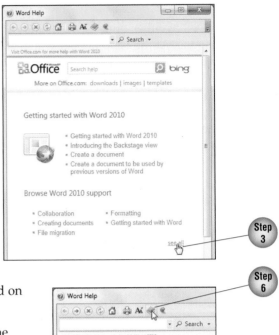

6. Click the Show Table of Contents button located on the Help toolbar.

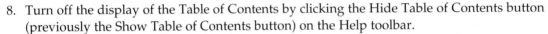

7. Scroll down the Table of Contents pane, click the Saving and printing hyperlink, and then notice the help options available.

8. Turn off the display of the Table of Contents by clicking the Hide Table of Contents button (previously the Show Table of Contents button) on the Help toolbar.

9. Type **save** in the *Search* text box and then press the Enter key.

10. When the list of topics displays, click the Save a document in Word hyperlink.

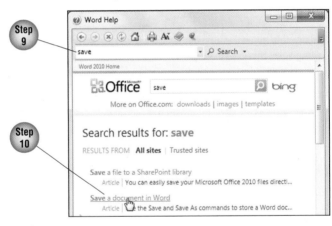

If your Word Help window does not display the online options, check the lower right corner of the window. If the word Offline displays, click Offline and then click the *Show content from Office.com* option at the drop-down list.

11. Click the Show All hyperlink that displays in the upper right corner of the window.

12. Read the information about saving a document and then click the Back button on the Help toolbar.

13. Limit your search to only save topics and not save as topics by typing **save NOT save as** in the *Search* text box and then pressing Enter.

Notice that fewer topics display when you limit your search.

14. Click the Close button to close the Word Help window.

15. Click the File tab and then click the Help tab.

16. At the Help tab Backstage view, click the Getting Started button in the Support section. You must be connected to the Internet to display the web page.

17. Look at the information that displays at the website and then click the Close button located in the upper right corner of the web page.

18. Click the File tab and then click the Help tab.

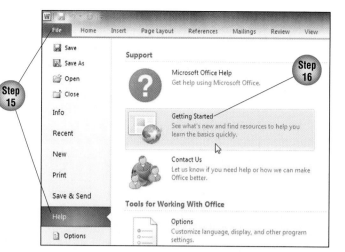

19. At the Help tab Backstage view, click the Contact Us button. At the Microsoft Support website, locate the options for emailing, online chatting, and calling customer support. Close the web page.

20. Close the blank document without saving changes and then exit Word.

Drilling Down

Getting Help in a Dialog Box or Backstage View

Some dialog boxes, as well as the Backstage view, contain a Help button you can click to display a Help window with specific information about the dialog box or Backstage view. After reading and/or printing the information, close the dialog box by clicking the Close button located in the upper right corner of the dialog box or close the Backstage view by clicking the File tab or clicking any other tab in the ribbon.

Delving Deeper

 2-1.2.6

Understanding Common Problems with Opening Files

File Cannot be Located

If you cannot locate a file you created, and you know you saved the file before exiting the application, you can use the search box located near the bottom of the Start menu to search for the file. Refer to Lesson 2.2 to learn more about the search box in the Start menu.

You may not be able to locate a file if you are in the incorrect application. For example, if you are in PowerPoint and searching for a Word document, the Word files will not display in the PowerPoint Open dialog box unless you change the file type option in the dialog box to *All Files*.

If you are unable to access a file located on remote storage, such as a network drive or the Internet, make sure you are connected to the server and that you have permission to access the drive.

continued

Incorrect Application

You cannot open a file type specified for one application in another application. For example, if you attempt to open a PowerPoint presentation in Excel, an error message displays stating that the file format is not valid or there are problems with the contents of the file (as shown below).

Incompatible Versions

A file that is created in an Office 2007 or 2010 application cannot be opened in Office 2003 or earlier versions unless you install a free compatibility pack from Microsoft's website. The compatibility pack will allow you to open the file, make minor edits, and then save the file. If you create a file in Office 2010 and need to send it to a person who uses Office 2003 or an earlier version, save the file with another extension. Change the extension type with the *Save as type* option at the Save As dialog box. If you are using Office 2010 and open a file created in an earlier version of office, you may receive a message indicating that the document was created in an earlier version and some of the contents may be lost.

Corrupted Files

Another reason a file may fail to open is because it has become corrupted. When you attempt to open a corrupted file, you will generally get a warning message indicating why the file will not open. Files may become corrupted for the following reasons: some of the data has been lost, part of the file is missing, the file has a virus, or the storage medium containing the file becomes unreadable or damaged. To help prevent losing data due to file corruption, keep backup copies of all important files. You should also keep your storage mediums (flash drives, compact discs) protected from scratches and dirt.

TOPIC SUMMARY

- Open an Office application by clicking the Start button on the Taskbar, pointing to *All Programs*, clicking *Microsoft Office*, and then clicking the desired application name.
- Navigate to other open applications by clicking the desired application button on the Taskbar.
- The ribbon contains tabs with commands and options divided into groups.
- The Quick Access toolbar is located above the File tab and contains buttons for commonly used commands.
- Click the File tab to display the Backstage view containing tabs and buttons for working with and managing files.
- Minimize the ribbon by clicking the Minimize the Ribbon button that displays immediately left of the Microsoft Help button or with the keyboard shortcut Ctrl + F1. Maximize the ribbon by clicking the Expand the Ribbon button (previously the Minimize the Ribbon button), with the keyboard shortcut Ctrl + F1, or by double-clicking one of the tabs.
- Customize the Quick Access toolbar with options from the Customize Quick Access Toolbar button drop-down list.
- Word, Excel, and PowerPoint include a number of template files you can use to create a variety of documents, worksheets, and presentations. Display the list of template files by clicking the File tab, clicking the New tab, and then clicking the Sample templates button.
- Save a file in a previous version of an application, as a template, or in a variety of other formats with options at the Save & Send tab Backstage view or with the *Save as type* option at the Save As dialog box.
- The names of recently opened files and recently accessed locations display in the Recent tab Backstage view. At this view, you can display below the Close button a maximum of six names of the most recently opened files.
- By default, Office applications automatically save a backup of your open files every 10 minutes. You can change this default setting with the *Save AutoRecover information every* option at the options dialog box with *Save* selected. Display this dialog box by clicking the File tab, clicking the Options button, and then clicking *Save* in the left panel.
- The Help feature in the Office applications is an on-screen reference manual that contains information about all Office application features and commands.
- Click the Microsoft Help button or press F1 to display the Help window. At this window, type a topic and then press the Enter key.

Key Terms
dialog box launcher, p. 178
hard copy, p. 185
print queue, p. 187
ScreenTip, p. 178
soft copy, p. 185
word wrap, p. 180

Features Summary

Feature	File Tab	Button	Keyboard Shortcut
Close	Close	X	Ctrl + F4
Exit application	Exit		Alt + F4
Help		?	F1
Help tab Backstage view	Help		
Open dialog box	Open		Ctrl + O
Print tab Backstage view	Print		Ctrl + P
Save As dialog box	Save As		F12
Save file	Save	💾	Ctrl + S
Save & Send tab Backstage view	Save & Send		

KEY POINTS REVIEW

Identification

Match the terms to the callouts on the Word window in Figure 4.14.

1. _____ vertical scroll bar
2. _____ tabs
3. _____ Quick Access toolbar
4. _____ Status bar
5. _____ ribbon
6. _____ I-beam pointer

7. _____ Title bar
8. _____ Taskbar
9. _____ horizontal ruler
10. _____ File tab
11. _____ insertion point
12. _____ vertical ruler

Figure 4.14 **Identification Figure**

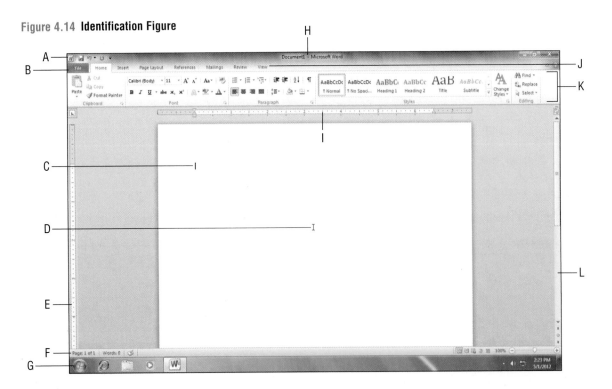

Multiple Choice

For each of the following items, choose the option that best completes the sentence or answers the question.

1. When saving a new spreadsheet, this is the default file extension for Excel 2010.
   A. .xls
   B. .xlsx
   C. .xltx
   D. .xlsm

2. Click this option at the New tab Backstage view to display available templates.
   A. *Recent templates*
   B. *Sample templates*
   C. *My templates*
   D. *New from existing*

3. By default, Office applications automatically save a file after this number of minutes.
   A. 2
   B. 5
   C. 10
   D. 20

4. Click this tab in the Backstage view to display options for saving a file in a different format.
   A. New
   B. Help
   C. Recent
   D. Save & Send

5. This icon displays next to the default printer in the *Devices and Printers* section of the Control Panel.
   A. a check mark in a green circle
   B. a check mark in a red circle
   C. an X in a green circle
   D. an X in a red circle

6. Use this feature to change the location in which you save a file.
   A. Save As dialog box
   B. File tab
   C. Home tab
   D. Quick Access toolbar

7. To open an Office application from the desktop (without using shortcuts), begin by clicking this button.
   A. Recycle Bin
   B. Start
   C. Windows Explorer
   D. Internet Explorer

8. Close a file without exiting the Office application by clicking this button in the Backstage view.
   A. Exit
   B. Close (red X button)
   C. Close
   D. Print

9. Click this tab to display the Backstage view.
   A. File
   B. Insert
   C. View
   D. Home

10. To create a file using a template, start by clicking this tab at the Backstage view.
    A. Open
    B. New
    C. Help
    D. Recent

Matching

Match each of the following definitions with the correct term, command, or option.

1. _____ Use this application to format letters, reports, and research papers.
2. _____ To switch between applications, click application buttons here.
3. _____ This displays the name of the active file, the file extension, and the active application.
4. _____ Use this application to format a presentation.
5. _____ Use this application to create a spreadsheet.
6. _____ This displays a list of all active print jobs.
7. _____ Click this button in the options dialog box to display options for the automatic recovery of files.
8. _____ Click this tab to display the Backstage view.
9. _____ Display this dialog box to save a previously saved file with a different file name.
10. _____ Use this button on the Taskbar to open Office applications.

A. Taskbar
B. PowerPoint
C. File
D. Word
E. Title bar
F. Save
G. Excel
H. Save As
I. Print queue
J. Start

SKILLS REVIEW

Review 4.1 Customizing Office Applications

1. Open Word.
2. Open Excel.
3. Open PowerPoint.
4. Make Word the active application and then open the file named **CompKeyboards.docx** from the **Unit2Topic04** folder on your storage medium.
5. Save the document with Save As and name it **U2T4-R1-CompKeyboards**.
6. Press Ctrl + End, and then type the text as shown in Figure 4.15.
7. Save the document.
8. Make Excel the active application.
9. Add the Print Preview and Print button to the Quick Access toolbar.
10. Open the file named **EPSales.xlsx**.
11. Print the workbook by clicking the Print Preview and Print button on the Quick Access toolbar and then clicking the Print button at the Print tab Backstage view.
12. Remove the Print Preview and Print button from the Quick Access toolbar.
13. Close **EPSales.xlsx** without saving changes.
14. Exit Excel.
15. Make PowerPoint the active application.
16. Minimize the ribbon.
17. Display the ribbon.
18. Click the Insert tab and then hover the mouse pointer over the buttons on the tab, reading the ScreenTips that display.
19. Exit PowerPoint.
20. With Word the active application, print **U2T4-R1-CompKeyboards.docx**, close the document, and then exit Word.

Figure 4.15 **Review 4.1 Text**

DVORAK Keyboard

The DVORAK keyboard is an alternative to the QWERTY keyboard. On the DVORAK keyboard, the most commonly used keys are placed close to the user's fingertips and this increases typing speed. You can install software on a QWERTY keyboard that emulates a DVORAK keyboard. The ability to emulate other keyboards is convenient especially when working with foreign languages. Keyboards have different physical appearances. Many keyboards have a separate numeric keypad, like that of a calculator, containing numbers and mathematical operators. Some keyboards are sloped and "broken" into two pieces to reduce strain. All keyboards have modifier keys that enable the user to change the symbol or character entered when a given key is pressed.

Review 4.2 Preparing a Fax Sheet in Word

1. Open Word.
2. At a blank document, display the New tab Backstage view, click the Sample templates button in the *Available Templates* section, click the *Equity Fax* template, and then click the Create button.
3. Insert the following information in the specified location:
   - To: **Marjorie Stansfield**
   - From: (Type your first and last names)
   - Fax: **(781) 555-8989**
   - Pages: **3**
   - Phone: **(781) 555-8900**
   - Date: (Insert the current date)
   - Re: **Employment Applications**
   - cc: (Delete this placeholder)
   - Insert a capital **X** in the *Please Reply* check box.
   - Type the following comment: **Please review the applications for employment delivered to your office today and then call me so we can schedule interviews.**
4. Save the document and name it **U2T4-R2-Fax**.
5. Print and then close **U2T4-R2-Fax.docx** and then exit Word.

Review 4.3 Saving a File in a Different Format

1. Open PowerPoint and then open the presentation named **CFPotential.pptx**.
2. Save the presentation in the PowerPoint 97-2003 format and name the presentation **U2T4-R3-CFPotential97-2003**.
3. Close **U2T4-R3-CFPotential97-2003.ppt**.
4. Open **CFPotential.pptx**.
5. Save the presentation as a PowerPoint show and name the presentation **U2T4-R3-CFPotentialShow**.
6. Close **U2T4-R3-CFPotentialShow.ppsx**.
7. At the Windows desktop, click the Start button and then click Computer at the side menu.
8. Navigate to the **Unit2Topic04** folder on your storage medium and then double-click the file **U2T4-R3-CFPotentialShow.ppsx**.
9. Read through the slides and click the left mouse button until a black screen displays, indicating the end of the slide show.
10. Click the left mouse button one more time to exit the slide show.
11. Display the Open dialog box in PowerPoint and then press the Print Screen key.
12. Open Word and then press Ctrl + V to insert the print screen file.

13. Print the document, close the document without saving changes, and then exit Word.
14. Close the Open dialog box in PowerPoint and then exit the application.

Review 4.4 Changing the AutoRecover Time in Word

1. Open Word and then open the document named **U2T4-R1-CompKeyboards.docx**.
2. Display the Word Options dialog box and then click *Save* in the left panel.
3. Change the *Save AutoRecover information every* option to 1 minute and then close the dialog box.
4. Press Ctrl + End to move the insertion point to the end of the document.
5. Type the current date.
6. Wait a few minutes and then click the File tab to view the AutoRecovered document that displays to the right of the Manage Versions button.
7. Display the Word Options dialog box, click *Save* in the left panel, and then change the *Save AutoRecover information every* option to the default of 10 minutes.
8. Close the Word Options dialog box.
9. Close **U2T4-R1-CompKeyboards.docx** without saving changes and then exit Word.

SKILLS ASSESSMENT

Assessment 4.1 Customizing the Quick Access Toolbar in Word

1. In Word, add the New button and the Quick Print button to the Quick Access toolbar.
2. In the Word document, type the steps you followed to add the buttons to the Quick Access toolbar.
3. Press the Print Screen key, click the New button on the Quick Access toolbar, and then press Ctrl + V to insert the print screen file.
4. Click the Quick Print button on the Quick Access toolbar to print the document.
5. Save the document in the Word 97-2003 document format to the **Unit2Topic04** folder on your storage medium and name it **U2T4-A1-QAButtons**.
6. Close **U2T4-A1-QAButtons.doc**.
7. Save the document with the steps you wrote as *Plain Text* and name it **U2T4-A1-QASteps**.
8. Print **U2T4-A1-QASteps.txt**.
9. At the Word document, remove the New and Quick Print buttons from Quick Access toolbar.
10. Close Word.

Assessment 4.2 Using Help to View a Training Video about Excel

1. Open Excel and display the Excel Help window.
2. At the Excel Help window, click the <u>see all</u> hyperlink that displays toward the bottom of the window.
3. Scroll down the window and then click the <u>Training courses</u> hyperlink.
4. At the list of Excel training courses, click a hyperlink that interests you and view the training video. (Check below the hyperlink text to make sure that the word *Training* rather than the word *Article* displays.)
5. After viewing the training video, exit Excel, open Word and then type a short paragraph describing the content of the training video, the length of the video, and which features described in the video interest you most.
6. Save the document and name it **U2T4-A2-Training**.
7. Print and then close **U2T4-A2-Training.docx** and then exit Word.

Assessment 4.3 Downloading an Online Template

1. Open Word.
2. Make sure you are connected to the Internet and then display the New tab Backstage view. Click the *Certificates* option in the *Office.com Templates* list, click the *Academic awards certificates* folder, and then download an award certificate for student of the month.
3. Identify yourself as the student of the month and River High School as the school.
4. Save the certificate document and name it **U2T4-A3-Award**. Print and then close the document.

 ### Assessment 4.4 Creating a Letter Using a Template

1. With Word open, display the New tab Backstage view and then open the *Black Tie Letter* template.
2. Create the letter shown in Figure 4.16. Type your name in the *[Type the sender name]* placeholder and delete placeholders where necessary.
3. Save the document and name it **U2T4-A4-Letter**.
4. Print and then close **U2T4-A4-Letter.docx**.

CRITICAL THINKING

Researching System Requirements and Identifying Helfpul Applications

Part 1 You are a recent hire at a bookstore. Your boss, Mary Harrison, is considering updating her work computer to Microsoft Office 2010. She has asked you to use the Internet to go to the Microsoft home page at www.microsoft.com and then use the search feature to find information on the system requirements for Office Professional Plus 2010. When you find the information, type a document in Microsoft Word that contains the Office Professional Plus 2010 system requirements for the computer and processor, memory, hard disk space, and operating system. Save the document and name it **U2T4-CT01-SystemReq**. Print and then close the document.

Part 2 Mary Harrison has asked you to determine what type of files you could create with Word, Excel, and PowerPoint to help her manage and promote the bookstore. Open Word and create a document listing two to three types of files you can create for each application. Save the document and name it **U2T4-CT02-Apps**. Print and then close the document.

Figure 4.16 Assessment 4.4 Letter

STUDENT NAME

2193 Lafayette Drive
New Orleans, LA 70124

5/1/2012

Mrs. Gloria Beaumont
Willowdale Hotel
1205 Willowdale Avenue
New Orleans, LA 70119

DEAR MRS. BEAUMONT:

I am writing in response to the post at your company website offering summer internship opportunities. As a sophomore at Riverside Community College working towards a management degree, I am very interested in the hotel management field and believe my education and work experience provide me with a valuable understanding of the hotel management field.

In addition to my education, I have held several part-time jobs working as an administrative assistant. I am presently employed as a part-time administrative assistant for Jet-Pro Corporation. This position involves typing and formatting business documents using Microsoft Word and preparing spreadsheets using Microsoft Excel.

I would like to meet with you to discuss the available internship positions. If you wish to arrange an interview, please contact me by telephone at (504) 555-3841 or by email at name@emcp.net. Thank you for your time and consideration.

Sincerely,

Student Name

TEAM PROJECT

Researching Printers

1. As a team, research on the Internet one of the following types of printers:
   - Black and white laser printer
   - Color laser printer
   - Inkjet printer
   - 3-in-1 printer (printer, scanner, fax)
2. As you research the printers, identify three printers in your selected category and type your response to these questions in a Word document:
   - How many pages per minute does each printer print?
   - How much does each printer cost?
   - What was the cheapest price you found for each printer and on what website did you find it?
   - How much do ink refills for each printer cost?
3. Save the document and name it **U2T4-TeamProject**.
4. Print the document and then exit Word.

Discussion Questions

As a class, discuss the printers identified by each team.

1. What are the pros and cons of each type of printer?
2. What are the pros and cons of purchasing printers through a website versus a retail store?
3. Is a printer's pages-per-minute average a useful feature for comparing printers? Why or why not?

Topic 5

Editing a Document in Word

Performance Objectives

Upon successful completion of Topic 5 you will be able to:

- Scroll and navigate in a document
- Insert, replace, and delete text
- Select text
- Use Undo and Redo
- Cut, copy, and paste text
- Use Office Clipboard
- Find and replace text

- Change document views
- Preview and print a document
- Use the Thesaurus
- Display document statistics
- Check the spelling and grammar in a document

STUDENT RESOURCES

Before beginning this topic, copy to your storage medium the **Unit2Topic05** subfolder from the *Computer and Internet Essentials: Preparing for IC³* Internet Resource Center. Make this the active folder.

In addition to containing the data files needed to complete topic work, the Internet Resource Center contains model answers in PDF format for each of the applicable exercises in this topic. Use these files to check your work. The preface of your textbook provides instructions for accessing these files.

Necessary Data Files

To complete the exercises and assessments, you will need the following data files:

Exercises 5.1–5.8	DesQualities.docx
Exercise 5.4	Skills.docx
Exercise 5.9	SGCAnalysis.docx
Review 5.1	OutputStor.docx
Review 5.2	LeaseAgrmt.docx BuildingAgrmt.docx
Review 5.3	New file
Assessment 5.1	OrientMemo.docx
Assessment 5.2	Computers.docx
Assessment 5.3	FCTAdventure.docx
Assessment 5.4	MultimediaAI.docx
Assessment 5.5	New file

continued

Assessment 5.6	New file
Critical Thinking	Agreement.docx
Team Project	TeamDoc01.docx TeamDoc02.docx TeamDoc03.docx

Visual Preview

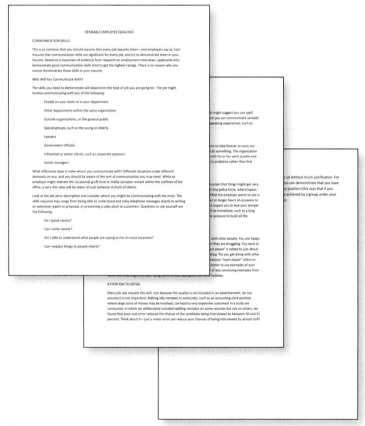

Exercise 5.1–5.8 **U2T5-DesQualities.docx**   Exercise 5.9 **U2T5-SGCAnalysis.docx**

Topic Overview

Microsoft Word is a word-processing program used to create many different types of short documents, including letters, contracts, memos, and brochures; and long documents, including reports, newsletters, and research papers. Microsoft Word also provides options for publishing documents to web pages and blogs. In Topic 5, you will practice navigating in a document and changing document views. You will learn how to edit Microsoft Word documents by selecting and then deleting, moving, or copying text. You will also learn how to display statistics about a document, and how to use proofing tools such as spelling checker, grammar checker, and the Thesaurus.

Lesson 5.1 Scrolling and Navigating in a Document

IC³ 2-1.1.2, 2-1.1.3

You will inevitably need to change or edit documents you create. To edit a document, use the mouse, the keyboard, or the mouse in combination with the keyboard to move the insertion point to specific locations in the document. To move the insertion point using the mouse, position the I-beam pointer where you want to place the insertion point and then click the left mouse button.

In addition to moving the insertion point to a specific location, you can use the mouse to move the display of text in the document screen. Use the mouse in conjunction with the vertical scroll bar to scroll through text in a document. The **vertical scroll bar** is located at the right side of the screen and contains scrolling arrows and a scroll box for moving through a document. Click the up scroll arrow at the top of the vertical scroll bar to scroll up through the document; click the down scroll arrow to scroll down through the document. The **scroll box** on the scroll bar indicates the location of the text on the document screen in relation to the remainder of the document. To scroll up one screen at a time, position the arrow pointer above the scroll box (but below the up scroll arrow) and then click the left mouse button. To scroll down a screen, position the arrow pointer between the scroll box and the down scroll arrow and click the left mouse button. If you hold down the left mouse button, the action becomes continuous. You can also position the arrow pointer on the scroll box, hold down the left mouse button, and then drag the scroll box along the scroll bar to reposition text on the document screen. As you drag the scroll box along the vertical scroll bar in a multi-page document, page numbers display in a box at the right side of the document screen. Scrolling in a document changes the text displayed on the screen but does not move the insertion point.

Along with scrolling options, Word contains navigation buttons for moving the insertion point to specific locations within a document. These buttons display toward the bottom of the vertical scroll bar and include the Previous button, the Select Browse Object button, and the Next button. The names of the Previous and Next buttons and the tasks they complete vary depending on the last navigation selected. The Select Browse Object button allows you to select options for browsing through a document. Click this button to display a palette of browsing choices. Position the arrow pointer on an option in the palette and the option name displays below the options. The options on the palette and their locations vary depending on the last function performed.

Word also includes a *Go To* option you can use to move the insertion point to a specific page within a document. To move the insertion point to a specific page, click the Find button arrow located in the Editing group on the Home tab and then click *Go To* at the drop-down list. At the Find and Replace dialog box with the Go To tab selected, type the page number in the *Enter page number* text box and then press the Enter key. Click the Close button to close the dialog box.

To move the insertion point with the keyboard, use the arrow keys located to the right of the regular keys on the keyboard (if your keyboard contains these keys). You can also use the arrow keys on the numeric keypad. If you use these keys, make sure the Num Lock on your keyboard is off. Use the arrow keys together with other keys to move the insertion point to various locations in the document. Table 5.1 describes these commands. When moving the insertion point, Word considers a word to be any series of characters between spaces. A paragraph is any text followed by a stroke of the Enter key. A page is text separated by a soft or hard page break.

vertical scroll bar The bar located at the right side of the screen; used for scrolling in a document

scroll box A box on the vertical scroll bar that indicates the location of the text on the document screen in relation to the remainder of the document

Keyboard Shortcuts

Select Browse Object
Alt + Ctrl + Home

Go To
Ctrl + G

Table 5.1 Insertion Point Movement Commands

To move insertion point	Press
One character left	Left Arrow
One character right	Right Arrow
One line up	Up Arrow
One line down	Down Arrow
One word to the left	Ctrl + Left Arrow
One word to the right	Ctrl + Right Arrow
To end of a line	End
To beginning of a line	Home
To beginning of current paragraph	Ctrl + Up Arrow
To beginning of next paragraph	Ctrl + Down Arrow
Up one screen	Page Up
Down one screen	Page Down
To top of previous page	Ctrl + Page Up
To top of next page	Ctrl + Page Down
To beginning of document	Ctrl + Home
To end of document	Ctrl + End

Navigation pane When turned on, displays at the left side of the screen and contains options for navigating in a document and searching for specific text

To navigate using the Navigation pane, click the View tab and then click the *Navigation Pane* check box in the Show group. The **Navigation pane** displays at the left side of the screen and includes a search text box and a pane with three tabs. Click the second tab and thumbnails of each page display in the pane. Click a thumbnail to move the insertion point to the specific page. Close the Navigation pane by clicking the *Navigation Pane* check box in the Show group on the View tab or by clicking the Close button located in the upper right corner of the pane.

Exercise 5.1 Scrolling and Navigating in a Document

1. Open Microsoft Word 2010 and then open **DesQualities.docx** from the **Unit2Topic05** folder on your storage medium.

2. Save the document with Save As and name it **U2T5-DesQualities**.

3. Position the mouse pointer on the down scroll arrow on the vertical scroll bar and then click the left mouse button several times.

   This scrolls down through the lines of text in the document. Scrolling changes the text that displays on the page but does not move the insertion point.

Step 3

4. Position the mouse pointer on the vertical scroll bar below the scroll box and then click the left mouse button a couple of times.

The scroll box on the vertical scroll bar indicates the location of the text in the document screen in relation to the remainder of the document. Clicking on the vertical scroll bar below the scroll box scrolls down one screen of text at a time.

Step 5

5. Position the mouse pointer on the scroll box on the vertical scroll bar, hold down the left mouse button, drag the scroll box to the top of the vertical scroll bar, and then release the mouse button.

Dragging the scroll box to the top of the vertical scroll bar displays the text at the beginning of the document.

6. Click the Next Page button located above the Select Browse Object button.

Clicking the Next Page button moves the insertion point to the beginning of the next page. The full names of and the tasks completed by the Previous and Next buttons vary depending on the last navigation completed.

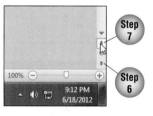

Step 7

Step 6

7. Click the Previous Page button located below the Select Browse Object button.

8. Click the Select Browse Object button located in the lower right corner of the screen and then click the *Go To* option.

The location of the *Go To* option may vary. Position the arrow pointer on an option and the name of the option displays at the top (or bottom) of the palette. Click on other options at the palette to browse document features such as fields, endnotes, footnotes, comments, sections, headings, or graphics.

Step 8

9. At the Find and Replace dialog box with the Go To tab selected, type **2** in the *Enter page number* text box, press the Enter key, and then click the Close button.

With options at the Find and Replace dialog box with the Go To tab selected, you can move the insertion point to various locations in a document such as a specific page, section, line, or bookmark.

Step 9

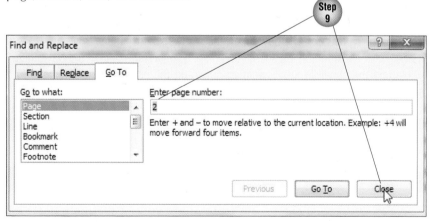

10. Click the Find button arrow 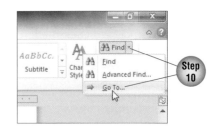 in the Editing group on the Home tab and then click *Go To* at the drop-down list.

11. At the Find and Replace dialog box with the Go To tab selected, type **1** in the *Enter page number* text box, press the Enter key, and then click the Close button.

12. Click the View tab and then click the *Navigation Pane* check box in the Show group.

13. Click the middle tab in the Navigation pane.

   Clicking the middle tab displays thumbnails of each page in the document in the Navigation pane.

14. Click the page 2 thumbnail in the Navigation pane.

   This moves the insertion point to the beginning of page 2.

15. Close the Navigation pane by clicking the Close button that displays in the upper right corner of the pane or by clicking the *Navigation Pane* check box in the Show group on the View tab.

16. Save the document by clicking the Save button on the Quick Access toolbar.

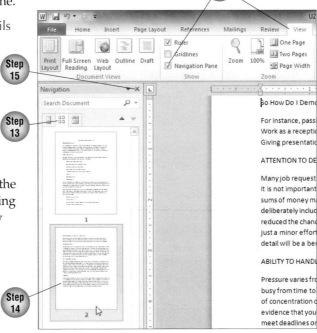

 Drilling Down

Using the Navigation Pane

When you insert a check mark in the *Navigation Pane* check box in the Show group on the Home tab, the Navigation pane displays at the left side of the screen. The Navigation pane includes a search text box and a pane with three tabs. Click the first tab to display a list of titles and headings with styles applied. Click the second tab to display thumbnails of each page, and click the third tab to browse through the document to view current search results. With the third tab selected, type search text in the search text box and any occurrence of the text in the document is highlighted. A fragment of the text surrounding the search text displays in a thumbnail in the Navigation pane as well. Click a text thumbnail in the Navigation pane and the occurrence of the search text is automatically selected in the document.

Lesson 5.2   Inserting and Deleting Text

 2-1.3.1, 2-1.3.2

insert To add text or objects to a document

delete To remove text or objects from a document

Many documents you create will require editing that may include adding text, called **inserting**, and/or removing text, called **deleting**. To insert text, position the insertion point in the desired location and then type the text. To delete text, press the Backspace key or the Delete key.

Exercise 5.2 Inserting and Deleting Text

1. With **U2T5-DesQualities.docx** open, click at the beginning of the first paragraph in the *So How Do I Demonstrate These Skills on My Vitae?* section located at the top of the second page in the document (the paragraph that begins with *For instance, passing a typing test…*), and then type **You could draw on your work history.** Press the spacebar once after typing the period.

   By default, text you type in a document is inserted in the document and existing text is moved to the right.

So How Do I Demonstrate These Skills on My Vitae?

You could draw on your work history. For instance, passing accurately, as would shorthand skills. Work as a receptionis can talk verbally and effectively. Giving presentations to clie experiences, such as Toastmaster, look good.

ATTENTION TO DETAIL

2. Press Ctrl + End to move the insertion point to the end of the document and then move the insertion point to the beginning of the last word in the document (*others*).

3. Press the Delete key until the word *others* and the period following the word have been deleted.

   Pressing the Delete key deletes the character immediately to the right of the insertion point.

4. Press the Backspace key until you have deleted the remainder of the last sentence.

   Pressing the Backspace key deletes the character immediately to the left of the insertion point.

5. Save **U2T5-DesQualities.docx**.

Drilling Down

Using Overtype Mode

By default, text you type in a document is inserted in the document and existing text is moved to the right. If you want to type over something, you need to turn on Overtype mode. In Overtype mode, anything you type will replace existing text. To turn on Overtype mode, click the File tab and then click the Options button located below the Help tab. At the Word Options dialog box, click *Advanced* in the left panel. In the *Editing options* section, insert a check mark in the *Use Overtype mode* check box if you always want to use Overtype mode when working in the document. Alternatively, you can insert a check mark in the *Use the Insert key to control Overtype mode* check box if you want to use the Insert key to turn Overtype mode on and off. After making your selection, click OK to close the dialog box.

Using Option Buttons

As you insert and edit text in a document, you may notice an option button popping up in your text. The name and appearance of this option button varies depending on the action. If a word you type is corrected by AutoCorrect, if you create an automatic list, or if autoformatting is applied to text, the AutoCorrect Options button appears. Click this button to undo the specific automatic action. If you paste text in a document, the Paste Options button appears near the text. Click this button to display options for controlling the formatting of pasted text.

Lesson 5.3 Selecting Text and Using Undo and Redo

IC³ 2-1.3.3

selection bar The space located toward the left side of the document screen between the left edge of the page and the text

You can use the mouse and/or keyboard to select a specific amount of text. Refer to Table 5.2 for a list of ways to select text using the mouse. Some of the steps in Table 5.2 refer to the **selection bar**, which is the space located toward the left side of the document screen between the left edge of the page and the left margin of text. When the mouse pointer is positioned in the selection bar it displays as a white arrow pointing up and to the right.

Table 5.2 **Selecting with the Mouse**

To select	Complete these steps
A word	Double-click the word
A line of text	Click in the selection bar to the left of the line
Multiple lines of text	Drag in the selection bar to the left of the lines
A sentence	Hold down the Ctrl key, then click anywhere in the sentence
A paragraph	Double-click in the selection bar next to the paragraph or triple-click anywhere in the paragraph
Multiple paragraphs	Drag in the selection bar
An entire document	Triple-click in the selection bar

When text is selected, it displays with a blue background (as shown in Figure 5.1) and the Mini toolbar, which contains options for common tasks, displays in a dimmed fashion. Move the mouse pointer over the Mini toolbar to activate it.

Figure 5.1 **Selected Text and Mini Toolbar**

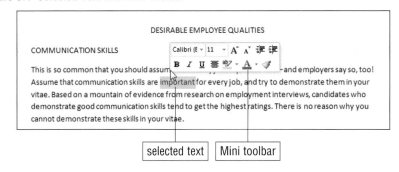

selected text   Mini toolbar

Keyboard Shortcuts

Undo
Ctrl + Z

Redo
Ctrl + Y

If you make a mistake and delete text that you did not intend to delete, or if you change your mind after deleting text and want to retrieve it, you can use the Undo or Redo buttons on the Quick Access toolbar. For example, if you type text and then click the Undo button, the text will be removed. If you change your mind after using the Undo button, click the Redo button and the text will be restored.

Exercise 5.3 Selecting Text and Using the Undo and Redo Buttons

1. With **U2T5-DesQualities.docx** open, press Ctrl + Home to move the insertion point to the beginning of the document.

2. Position the mouse pointer on the word *important* (located in the second sentence of the document) and then double-click the left mouse button.

   Selected text displays with a blue background. You can also drag through text with the mouse to select the text.

DESIRABLE EMPLOYEE QUALITIES

COMMUNICATION SKILLS

This is so common that you should assume that every job requires ther
Assume that communication skills are important for every job, and try
vitae. Based on a mountain of evidence from research on employment

Step 2

3. Type **significant**.

   When you type *significant*, it replaces the word *important*. If you select text and then decide you want to deselect it, click in the document window outside the selected text.

4. Move the insertion point immediately left of the comma located after the word *accurately* in the second sentence of the *So How Do I Demonstrate These Skills on My Vitae?* section on the second page, and then press the F8 function key on the keyboard. Press the right arrow key until the text *as would shorthand skills* is selected. (Do not select the period after the word *skills*.)

   Pressing the F8 function key turns on Extend mode. Use the arrow keys to select text in Extend mode.

So How Do I Demonstrate These Skills on My Vitae?

You could draw on your work history. For instance, pa:
accurately, as would shorthand skills. Work as a recep
can talk verbally and effectively. Giving presentations
experiences, such as Toastmaster, look good.

Step 4

5. Press the Delete key.

   Pressing the Delete key deletes the selected text. If you want to cancel a selection, press the Esc key and then press any arrow key.

6. Position the mouse I-beam pointer over any character in the last sentence in the *Attention to Detail* section (the sentence that begins *Paying attention to detail...*), hold down the Ctrl key, click the mouse button, and then release the Ctrl key.

   Holding down the Ctrl key while clicking the mouse button selects the entire sentence.

7. Press the Delete key to delete the selected sentence.

8. Click the Undo button on the Quick Access toolbar.

   When you click the Undo button, the deleted sentence reappears. Clicking the Undo button reverses the last command or deletes the last entry you typed.

Step 8

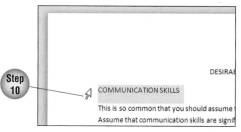

9. Click the Redo button on the Quick Access toolbar.

   Clicking the Redo button deletes the selected sentence. If you click the Undo button and then decide you do not want to reverse the original action, click the Redo button.

10. Press Ctrl + Home to move the insertion point to the beginning of the document. Position the mouse pointer between the left edge of the page and the heading *COMMUNICATION SKILLS* until the pointer turns into an arrow pointing up and to the right (instead of up and to the left) and then click the left mouse button.

Step 10

DESIRA

COMMUNICATION SKILLS

This is so common that you should assume
Assume that communication skills are signi

   The space between the left edge of the page and the text is referred to as the selection bar. Use the selection bar to select specific amounts of text. Refer to Table 5.1 for information on selecting text.

11. Deselect the text by clicking in the document outside the selected area.

12. Save **U2T5-DesQualities.docx**.

Drilling Down

Undoing Multiple Actions

Word maintains actions in temporary memory. If you want to undo an action performed earlier, click the Undo button arrow. This causes a drop-down list to display, containing all changes made to the document since it was opened. The drop-down list displays the most recent change at the top of the list. To make a selection from this drop-down list, click the desired action. The action is undone, along with any actions listed above it in the drop-down list.

Lesson 5.4 — Cutting, Copying, and Pasting Text and Using the Clipboard Task Pane

 2-1.3.2

When editing a document, you may need to delete text, move text to a different location in the document, or copy text to various locations in the document. You can complete these activities using buttons in the Clipboard group on the Home tab.

Word offers different methods for deleting text from a document. To delete a single character, you can use either the Delete key or the Backspace key. To delete more than a single character, select the text and then press the Delete key on the keyboard or click the Cut button in the Clipboard group. When you press the Delete key, the text is removed and can only be restored by clicking the Undo button on the Quick Access toolbar. However, recall that when you click the Cut button, the text is removed and inserted in the Clipboard.

Clipboard A temporary area of memory that holds text while it is being moved or copied to a new location in the document or to a different document

Word's **Clipboard** is a temporary area of memory that holds text the user has cut or copied. The user can then move the text to a new location within the original document or within a different document. The Clipboard can hold up to 24 items at one time. To use the Clipboard, click the Clipboard group dialog box launcher located in the lower right corner of the Clipboard group. This displays the Clipboard task pane at the left side of the screen in a manner similar to that shown in Figure 5.2.

Figure 5.2 **Clipboard Task Pane**

To move text to a different location in the document, select the text and any desired spaces, click the Cut button in the Clipboard group, position the insertion point at the location where you want to insert the text, and then click the Paste button in the Clipboard group. When a selected item is cut from a document and inserted in the Clipboard, it remains the active item in the Clipboard until another item is inserted in the Clipboard. For this reason, you can paste text from the Clipboard more than just once.

The ability to copy selected text can be useful in documents that contain repetitive portions of content because it prevents you from having to retype the text over and over again. After you have selected the text, copy it to all desired locations using the Copy and Paste buttons in the Clipboard group on the Home tab.

Once you have copied text to the Clipboard, you can insert the text in another document by positioning the insertion point in the desired location and then clicking the button representing the item in the Clipboard task pane. If the copied item is text, the first 50 characters display beside the button in the Clipboard task pane. When you have finished inserting all of the desired items from the Clipboard, click the Clear All button to remove any remaining items from the Clipboard task pane. When you turn off your computer, any items remaining in the Clipboard are deleted. To save Clipboard content permanently, paste it into a separate document and save the document.

When you paste selected text, the Paste Options button displays in the lower right corner of the text. Click this button (or press the Ctrl key on the keyboard) and the Paste Options gallery displays as shown in Figure 5.3. Use options from this gallery to specify how you want information pasted in the document. Hover the mouse arrow pointer over a button in the gallery and Live Preview will display the text in the document as it would appear when pasted. **Live Preview** is a feature that provides the user with an opportunity to see how the selected text or document will appear using a selected format. By default, pasted text retains the original formatting. You can choose to change the formatting of the pasted text to match the formatting of the destination or to paste only the text without retaining formatting. To determine the function of a button in the Paste Options gallery, hover the mouse arrow pointer over the button. A ScreenTip will display with an explanation of the button function as well as the keyboard shortcut.

Figure 5.3 Paste Options Gallery

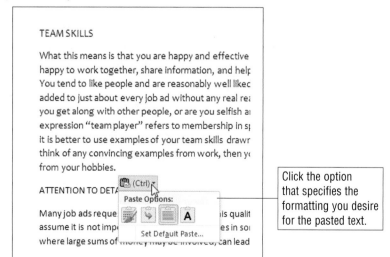

Click the option that specifies the formatting you desire for the pasted text.

Exercise 5.4 Cutting, Copying, and Pasting Text and Using the Clipboard Task Pane

1. With **U2T5-DesQualities.docx** open, move the *ABILITY TO HANDLE PRESSURE* section above the *ATTENTION TO DETAIL* section. Begin by selecting the *ABILITY TO HANDLE PRESSURE* heading, the paragraph of text below it, and the space that follows the paragraph.

2. Click the Cut button in the Clipboard group on the Home tab.

   Clicking the Cut button places the text in the Clipboard. If you click the wrong button, immediately click the Undo button to reverse the action.

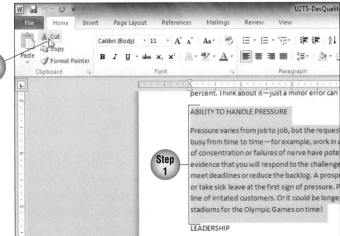

3. Move the insertion point to the beginning of the *ATTENTION TO DETAIL* heading and then click the Paste button in the Clipboard group on the Home tab.

   A Paste Options button (Ctrl) ▾ displays below the pasted text. Clicking this button displays options for formatting the pasted text.

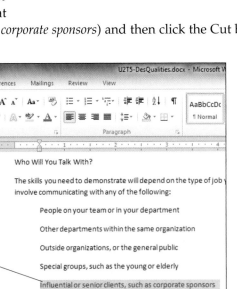

4. Select the fifth indented paragraph and the space after the paragraph in the *Who Will You Talk With?* section (the text that reads *Influential or senior clients, such as corporate sponsors*) and then click the Cut button in the Clipboard group.

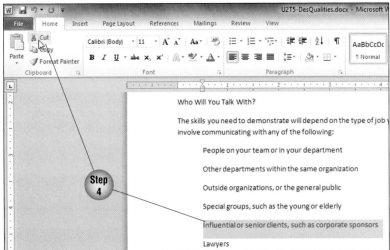

5. Position the insertion point at the beginning of the last indented paragraph in the *Who Will You Talk With?* section (the text that reads *Senior managers*) and then click the Paste button in the Clipboard group.

   If the two sentences run together, press the Enter key to move the sentence to the next line.

6. Copy text from another document and paste it in the Desirable Employee Qualities document using the Clipboard task pane. Begin by opening **Skills.docx** from the **Unit2Topic05** folder on your storage medium.

7. Display the Clipboard task pane by clicking the Clipboard group dialog box launcher ☐. If any items display in the Clipboard task pane, click the Clear All button located in the upper right corner of the task pane.

8. Select the *ENERGY, DYNAMISM, ENTHUSIASM, DRIVE, AND INITIATIVE* heading and the paragraph of text below it and then click the Copy button ☐ in the Clipboard group.

   Notice how the copied item is represented in the Clipboard task pane.

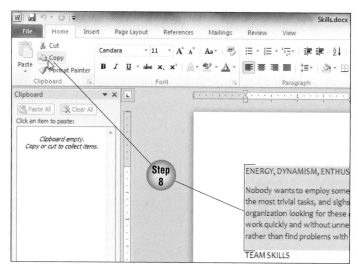

9. Select the *TEAM SKILLS* heading and the paragraph of text below it and then click the Copy button.

10. Click the Word button on the Taskbar and then click the document representing **U2T5-DesQualities.docx**.

11. Click the Clipboard group dialog box launcher to display the Clipboard task pane.

12. Position the insertion point at the beginning of the *ATTENTION TO DETAIL* section heading and then click the *TEAM SKILLS* item in the Clipboard task pane.

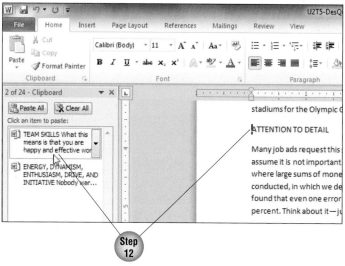

13. Click the Paste Options button ☐ (Ctrl)▾ and then click the Merge Formatting button at the Paste Options gallery.

14. Position the insertion point at the beginning of the *ABILITY TO HANDLE PRESSURE* section heading and then click the item in the Clipboard task pane that begins with *ENERGY*.

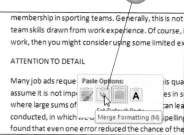

15. Click the Paste Options button and then click the Merge Formatting button at the Paste Options gallery.

16. Click the Clear All button located toward the upper right corner of the Clipboard task pane.

17. Close the Clipboard task pane by clicking the Close button ![X] located in the upper right corner of the task pane.

18. Save **U2T5-DesQualities.docx**.

19. Click the Word button on the Taskbar, click the **Skills.docx** document, and then close the document.

    Closing the Skills.docx document displays the U2T5-DesQualities.docx document.

Step 16   *Step 17*

Drilling Down

Moving and Copying Text with the Mouse

As an alternative to using the buttons in the Clipboard group, you can move selected text using the mouse. To do this, select the text with the mouse and then move the I-beam pointer inside the selected text until the I-beam pointer turns into an arrow pointer. Hold down the left mouse button, drag the arrow pointer (which displays with a gray box attached) to the location where you want to insert the selected text, and then release the button. You can copy and paste selected text by following similar steps. The difference is that to copy you must hold down the Ctrl key while dragging with the mouse. When you hold down the Ctrl key, a box containing a plus symbol displays near the gray box by the arrow pointer.

Lesson 5.5 Finding and Replacing Text

 2-1.3.4

Quick Steps

Find Text

1. Click Home tab.
2. Click Find button.
3. Type search text.

Click the Find button in the Editing group on the Home tab (or press the keyboard shortcut Ctrl + F) and the Navigation pane displays at the left side of the screen with the third tab selected. With this tab selected, type the text you want to find in the search text box. Any occurrence of the text in the document will appear highlighted within the document and a fragment of the text surrounding the search text will also display in a thumbnail in the Navigation pane. For example, search for *job* in the U2T5-DesQualities.docx document and the screen displays as shown in Figure 5.4. Notice that any occurrence of *job* displays highlighted in yellow in the document, while the Navigation pane displays thumbnails of text surrounding the occurrences of *job*. If you hover your mouse pointer over a text thumbnail in the Navigation pane, the page number displays in a small box near the mouse pointer. Click a text thumbnail in the Navigation pane to go to that place in the document. You can move to the next occurrence of the search text by clicking the Next Search Result button located toward the upper right of the Navigation pane. Click the Previous Search Result button to move to the previous occurrence of the search text.

Figure 5.4 Navigation Pane Showing Search Results

Click this down-pointing arrow to display a drop-down list with options for displaying find and replace dialog boxes and options for specifying what you want to find in the document.

Type search text in this text box.

Click this button to move to the next occurrence of search text.

Occurrences of search text are highlighted in the document.

Click this button to move to the previous occurrence of search text.

Text thumbnails display search text in document and text surrounding the search text.

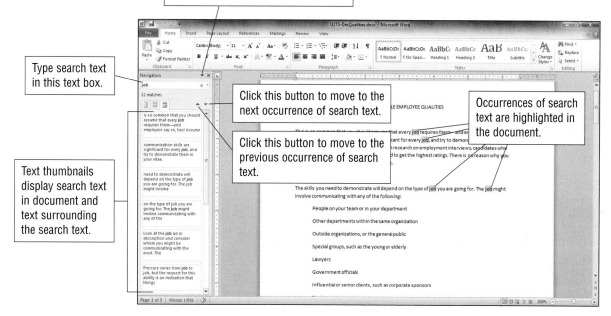

To find and replace text, click the Replace button in the Editing group on the Home tab or use the keyboard shortcut Ctrl + H. Either action displays the Find and Replace dialog box with the Replace tab selected, as shown in Figure 5.5. Type the text you want to find in the *Find what* text box, press the Tab key, and then type the replacement text in the *Replace with* text box.

The Find and Replace dialog box contains several command buttons. Click the Find Next button to tell Word to find the next occurrence of the text. Click the Replace button to replace the text and find the next occurrence. If you know that you want all occurrences of the text in the *Find what* text box replaced with the text in the *Replace with* text box, click the Replace All button. This replaces every occurrence from the location of the insertion point to the beginning or end of the document (depending on the search direction). Click the Cancel button to close the Find and Replace dialog box. If you make a mistake when replacing text, close the Find and Replace dialog box and then click the Undo button on the Quick Access toolbar.

Quick Steps

Find and Replace Text

1. Click Home tab.
2. Click Replace button.
3. Type search text.
4. Press Tab key.
5. Type replace text.
6. Click Replace or Replace All button.

Keyboard Shortcut

Find Text Using Navigation Pane

Ctrl + F

Find and Replace Dialog Box

Ctrl + H

Figure 5.5 Find and Replace Dialog Box with Replace Tab Selected

Type search text in the *Find what* text box.

Type replacement text in the *Replace with* text box.

Exercise 5.5 Finding and Replacing Text

1. With **U2T5-DesQualities.docx** open, press Ctrl + Home to move the insertion point to the beginning of the document.

2. Find all occurrences of the word *job*. Begin by clicking the Find button in the Editing group on the Home tab.

3. In the Navigation pane, with the third tab selected, type **job** in the search text box.

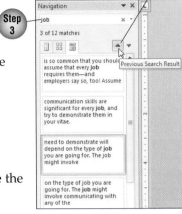

4. After a moment, Word will highlight all occurrences of *job* in the document and display text thumbnails in the Navigation pane. Click a couple of the text thumbnails in the Navigation pane to select the text in the document.

5. Click the Previous Search Result button to select the previous occurrence of *job* in the document.

6. Close the Navigation pane and then press Ctrl + Home to move the insertion point back to the beginning of the document.

7. You decide to change *vitae* to *resume*. Display the Find and Replace dialog box by clicking the Replace button in the Editing group on the Home tab.

8. At the Find and Replace dialog box, with the Replace tab selected, type **vitae** in the *Find what* text box and then press the Tab key.

   Pressing the Tab key moves the insertion point to the *Replace with* text box.

9. Type **resume** in the *Replace with* text box and then click the Replace All button located towards the bottom of the dialog box.

   Clicking the Replace All button replaces all occurrences of the specified text in the document. If you want to control which occurrences you replace, click the Replace button to replace an occurrence or click the Find Next button to move to the next occurrence.

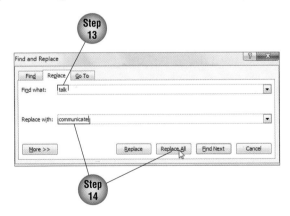

10. At the message telling you that four replacements were made, click OK.

11. Click the Close button to close the Find and Replace dialog box.

12. You decide to replace the word *talk* with the word *communicate*. Click the Replace button in the Editing group on the Home tab.

13. At the Find and Replace dialog box with the Replace tab selected, type **talk**.

14. Press the Tab key, type **communicate** in the *Replace with* text box, and then click the Replace All button.

15. At the message telling you that three replacements were made, click OK.

16. Click the Close button to close the Find and Replace dialog box.

17. Save **U2T5-DesQualities.docx**.

*Drilling
Down*

Exploring Options at the Expanded Find and Replace Dialog Box

The Find and Replace dialog box contains a variety of search option check boxes that you can use to conduct a search. To display these options, click the More button located at the bottom of the dialog box. This causes the Find and Replace dialog box to expand (as shown at the right) and the More button to change to the Less button. Search options within the Find and Replace dialog box are described in the following table.

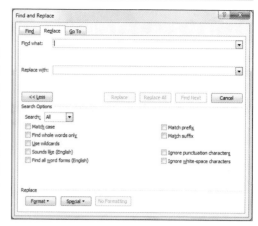

Option	Function
Match case	Finds occurrences of the search text that exactly match the case of the search text. For example, if you search for *Book* and select the *Match case* option, Word will stop at *Book* but not *book* or *BOOK*.
Find whole words only	Finds the search text only when it occurs as a whole word, not a part of a word. For example, if you search for *her* and do not select *Find whole words only*, Word will stop at *there*, *here*, *hers*, etc.
Use wildcards	Searches for wildcard characters (characters that represent strings of text such as the asterisk and the question mark), special characters, or special search operators.
Sounds like	Finds words that sound alike but are spelled differently such as *know* and *no*.
Find all word forms	Finds all forms of the search word. For example, if you enter *hold*, Word will stop at *held* and *holding* as well as *hold*.
Match prefix	Finds only those words that begin with the search text. For example, if you enter *per*, Word will stop at *perform* and *perfect* but skip *super* and *hyperlink*.
Match suffix	Finds only those words that end with the search text. For example, if you enter *ly*, Word will stop at *accurately* and *quietly* but skip over *catalyst* and *lyre*.
Ignore punctuation	Ignores punctuation between characters when searching. For example, if you enter *US*, Word will stop at *U.S.*
Ignore white space	Ignores spaces between letters when searching. For example, if you enter *F B I*, Word will stop at *FBI*.

Lesson 5.6 Changing Document Views

)IC³ 2-1.1.5, 2-1.1.6

By default, a Word document displays in Print Layout view. In this view, the document displays on the screen as it will appear when printed. Other available views include Draft view, which is designed to maximize efficient editing and formatting, and Full Screen Reading view, which promotes easy viewing and reading. Change views with buttons in the view area on the Status bar or with options on the View tab. Figure 5.6 identifies the buttons in the view area on the Status bar. Along with the view buttons, the Status bar also contains a Zoom slider bar. Drag the button on the Zoom slider bar or use the Zoom In and Zoom Out buttons to increase or decrease the display size of the document.

Figure 5.6 View Buttons and Zoom Slider Bar

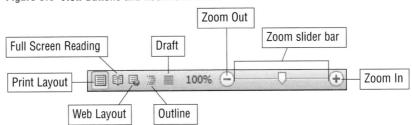

Quick Steps

Display a Document in Full Screen Reading View

Click Full Screen Reading button in view area on Status bar.

OR

1. Click View tab.
2. Click Full Screen Reading button.

You can navigate in Full Screen Reading view using the keys on the keyboard. Table 5.3 explains how to do this. You can also navigate in Full Screen Reading view with options from the View Options button that displays toward the top right of the screen or with the Next Screen and Previous Screen buttons located at the top of the window and at the bottom of each page. You can customize the Full Screen Reading view with options from the View Options drop-down list. Display this list by clicking the View Options button located in the upper right corner of the Full Screen Reading window.

Table 5.3 Navigating in Full Screen Reading View

Press this key...	...to complete this action
Page Down key or spacebar	Move to the next page or section
Page Up key or Backspace key	Move to the previous page or section
Right Arrow key	Move to next page
Left Arrow key	Move to previous page
Home	Move to first page in document
End	Move to last page in document
Esc	Return to previous view

Quick Steps

Hide White Space

1. Position mouse pointer at top of page until pointer displays as Hide White Space icon.
2. Double-click left mouse button.

Show White Space

1. Position mouse pointer on thin line separating pages until pointer displays as Show White Space icon.
2. Double-click left mouse button

To save space on the screen in Print Layout view, you can remove the white space at the top and bottom of pages. Position the mouse pointer at the top or bottom edge of a page, or between pages, until the pointer displays as the Hide White Space icon and then double-click the left mouse button. To redisplay the white space, position the mouse pointer on the thin, gray line that separates the pages until the pointer turns into the Show White Space icon and then double-click the left mouse button.

Exercise 5.6 Changing Document Views

1. With **U2T5-DesQualities.docx** open, press Ctrl + Home to move the insertion point to the beginning of the document and then change to Draft view by clicking the View tab and then clicking the Draft button ⊞ in the Document Views group.

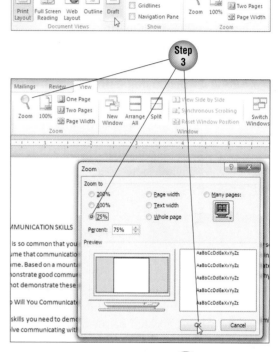

   You can also change to Draft view by clicking the Draft button located in the view area near the right side of the Status bar.

2. Click the Print Layout button ⊞ in the Document Views group.

3. Change the zoom by clicking the Zoom button ◎ in the Zoom group on the View tab. At the Zoom dialog box, click *75%* in the *Zoom to* section and then click OK.

   You can also display the Zoom dialog box by clicking the percentage that displays at the left side of the Zoom slider bar. The Zoom slider bar displays at the right side of the Status bar.

4. Return the zoom to 100% by positioning the mouse pointer on the button on the Zoom slider bar and then dragging the button to the right until *100%* displays at the left side of the bar.

5. To save space on the screen, remove the white and gray space that displays at the top and bottom of each page. To do this, position the mouse pointer on the gray space at the top of the page until the pointer turns into the Hide White Space icon and then double-click the left mouse button.

6. Scroll through the document and then redisplay the white and gray space at the top and bottom of each page. To do this, position the mouse pointer on the gray line at the top of the page until the pointer turns into a Show White Space icon and then double-click the left mouse button.

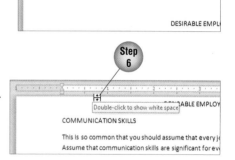

7. Click the Full Screen Reading button ⊞ in the Document Views group and then navigate in the document using the commands shown in Table 5.3.

   Full Screen Reading view displays a document for easy viewing and reading. You can also display the document in Full Screen Reading view by clicking the Full Screen Reading button located in the view area on the Status bar.

8. Return to Print Layout view by clicking the Close button located in the upper right corner of the screen.

9. Click the Two Pages button  in the Zoom group to display two pages on the screen and then click the One Page button in the Zoom group.

10. Click the Page Width button in the Zoom group to display the document so the width of the page matches the width of the window.

11. Drag the button on the Zoom slider bar, or click the Zoom Out button ⊟ or Zoom In button ⊞, until *100%* displays at the left side of the bar.

12. Save **U2T5-DesQualities.docx**.

Drilling Down

Displaying a Document in Web Layout View

Use Web Layout view to see how a document would display as a web page. In Web Layout view, the text wraps to fit the window, backgrounds are visible, and graphics appear just as they would display in a browser. Display a document in Web Layout view by clicking the View tab and then clicking the Web Layout button in the Document Views group or by clicking the Web Layout button in the view area on the Status bar.

Lesson 5.7   Previewing and Printing a Document

 2-1.4.2, 2-1.4.3

When you display the Print tab Backstage view, a preview of the page in which the insertion point is currently positioned displays at the right side (see Figure 5.7). Click the Next Page button (the right-pointing arrow), located below and to the left of the page, to view the next page in the document and click the Previous Page button (the left-pointing arrow) to display the previous page in the document. Use the Zoom slider bar to increase or decrease the size of the page, and click the Zoom to Page button to fit the page in the viewing area in the Print tab Backstage view.

Figure 5.7 **Print Tab Backstage View**

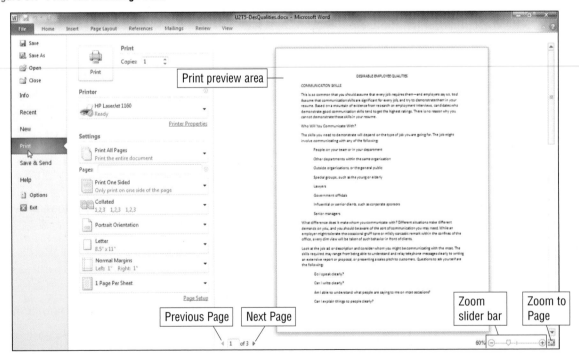

As discussed in Topic 4, the left side of the Print tab Backstage view displays three categories—Print, Printer, and Settings. Click the Print button in the Print category to send the document to the printer and specify the number of copies you want printed with the *Copies* option. Use the gallery in the Printer category to specify the desired printer. Click the first gallery in the Settings category and a drop-down list displays with options for printing all pages in the document, selected text, the current page, or a custom range of pages in the document. If you want to select and then print a portion of the document, choose the *Print Selection* option. With this option, only the text that you have selected in the current document prints. (This option is dimmed unless text is selected in the document.) Click the *Print Current Page* option to print only the page on which the insertion point is currently located. With the *Print Custom Range* option, you can identify a specific page, multiple pages, and/or a range of pages to print. If you want to print multiple non-sequential pages or ranges of pages, use a comma (,) to indicate *and* and use a hyphen (-) to indicate *through*. For example, to print pages 2 and 5, you would type *2,5* in the *Pages* text box. To print pages 6 through 10, you would type *6-10*.

With the other galleries available in the Settings category of the Print tab Backstage view, you can specify the sides of the paper on which you want to print, change the page orientation (portrait or landscape), specify how you want the pages collated, choose a page size, specify margins, and specify how many pages you want to print on each sheet of paper.

Quick Steps

Preview a Document
1. Click File tab.
2. Click Print tab.

Print a Document
1. Click File tab.
2. Click Print tab.
3. Click Print button.

Print a Specific Page
1. Click File tab.
2. Click Print tab.
3. Click in *Pages* text box.
4. Type desired page number.
5. Click Print button.

Keyboard Shortcuts

Print Tab Backstage View

Ctrl + P

Alt + Ctrl + I

Exercise 5.7 **Previewing and Printing a Document**

1. With **U2T5-DesQualities.docx** open, press Ctrl + Home to move the insertion point to the beginning of the document (if necessary).

2. Click the File tab and then click the Print tab.

3. Click the Next Page button located below and to the left of the preview page to display the next page in the document.

4. Click twice on the Zoom Out button (containing a minus symbol) that displays at the left side of the Zoom slider bar to display two pages of the document.

   Click the Zoom Out button to decrease the size of the page or click the Zoom In button (containing a plus symbol) to increase the size of the page.

5. Click the Zoom to Page button located at the right side of the Zoom slider bar.

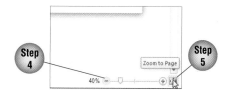

6. Print only page 2 of the document by clicking in the *Pages* text box (located in the Settings category), typing **2**, and then clicking the Print button.

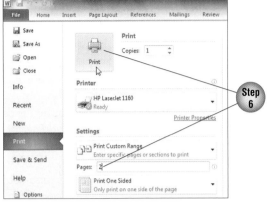

7. Print only pages 1 and 3 of the document. Begin by clicking the File tab and then clicking the Print tab.

8. At the Print tab Backstage view, click in the *Pages* text box (located below the *Print Custom Range* gallery in the Settings category) and then type **1,3**.

9. Click the Print button.

10. Click the File tab and then click the Print tab.

11. At the Print tab Backstage view, click the gallery that displays *1 Page Per Sheet* and then click *2 Pages Per Sheet* at the drop-down gallery.

12. Click the up-pointing arrow to the right of the *Copies* text box.

The number *2* should now display in the text box.

13. Click the Print button.

14. Save **U2T5-DesQualities.docx**.

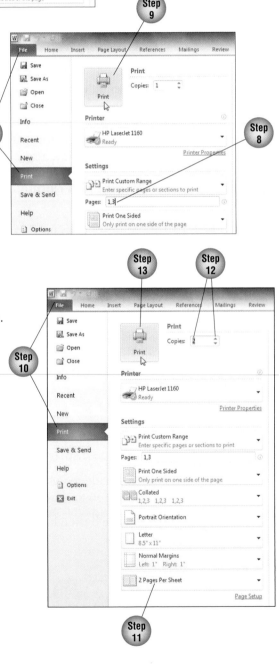

Drilling Down

Printing Collated or Uncollated Pages

To print more than one copy of a document, use the *Copies* text box located to the right of the Print button. When you print several copies of a document that has multiple pages, Word automatically collates the pages as they print. For example, if you print two copies of a three-page document, pages 1, 2, and 3 are printed, and then the pages are printed a second time in the same order. Printing collated pages is helpful for assembly but takes more printing time. To reduce printing time, you can tell Word *not* to print collated pages by clicking the *Collated* gallery in the Settings category and then clicking *Uncollated.*

Lesson 5.8 Using the Thesaurus and Displaying Document Statistics

 2-2.2.1

With the **Thesaurus** feature in Word you can find synonyms, antonyms, and other related terms for a particular word. *Synonyms* are words that have the same or nearly the same meaning; *antonyms* are words that have opposite meanings. To use the Thesaurus, click the Review tab and then click the Thesaurus button in the Proofing group. (You can also use the keyboard shortcut Shift + F7.) At the Research task pane that displays, click in the *Search for* text box located toward the top of the task pane, type the word for which you want to find synonyms or antonyms, and then press the Enter key or click the Start searching button (the button containing a white arrow on a green background). A list of synonyms and antonyms displays in the task pane list box. Figure 5.8 shows the Research task pane with synonyms for the word *candidates* displayed.

> **Thesaurus** A feature that finds synonyms, antonyms, and related terms for a particular word

Quick Steps

Use the Thesaurus
1. Click Review tab.
2. Click Thesaurus button.
3. Type word in *Search for* text box.
4. Press Enter.

Keyboard Shortcut

Thesaurus

Shift + F7

Figure 5.8 Research Task Pane

Type a word in this text box and press Enter. Synonyms and antonyms for the word display in the list box below.

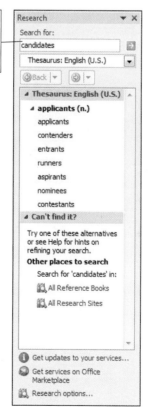

Display Word Count

Click word count section
of Status bar.

OR

1. Click Review tab.
2. Click Word Count
   button.

Depending on the word you look up, the words that display in the Research task pane list box may be followed by *(n.)* for *noun*, *(adj.)* for *adjective*, or *(adv.)* for *adverb*. When antonyms display, they appear at the end of the list of related synonyms and are followed by *(Antonym)*.

Along with the Thesaurus feature, the Proofing group on the Review tab includes the Word Count button. Click the Word Count button and a Word Count dialog box displays (similar to the one shown in Figure 5.9). This dialog box provides information such as the number of pages, paragraphs, and lines in the document. You can also display the Word Count dialog box by clicking the word count located toward the left side of the Status bar. If you want to count the words in a portion of the document, select the desired text first.

Figure 5.9 Word Count Dialog Box

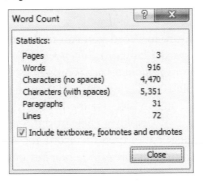

Exercise 5.8 Using Thesaurus and Displaying Document Statistics

1. With **U2T5-DesQualities.docx** open, change the word *candidates* to *applicants* using the Thesaurus. Begin by clicking anywhere in the word *candidates* (located in the third sentence of the *COMMUNICATION SKILLS* section), clicking the Review tab, and then clicking the Thesaurus button 📖 in the Proofing group.

2. At the Research task pane, position the mouse arrow pointer on the word *applicants* in the task pane list box, click the down-pointing arrow, and then click *Insert* at the drop-down list.

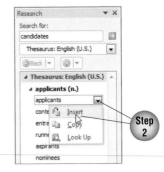

3. Close the Research task pane by clicking the Close button ☒ located in the upper right corner of the task pane.

4. Position the mouse pointer on the word *results* (located in the third sentence in the *ATTENTION TO DETAIL* section) and then click the right mouse button. At the shortcut menu that displays, point to *Synonyms* and then click *outcomes* at the side menu.

   If the shortcut menu does not display, check to make sure you clicked the right mouse button.

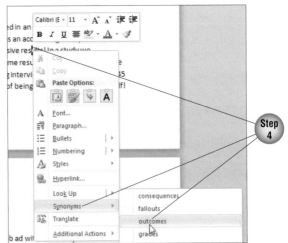

5. Read the document statistics by clicking the word count section of the Status bar.

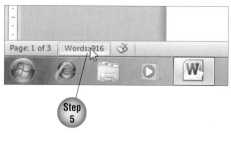

6. After reading the statistics in the Word Count dialog box, click the Close button.

7. Redisplay the Word Count dialog box by clicking the Review tab and then clicking the Word Count button in the Proofing group.

Step 5

8. Click the Close button to close the Word Count dialog box.

9. Save, print, and then close **U2T5-DesQualities.docx**.

Drilling Down

Using the Research Task Pane

The Research task pane offers options that you can use to search for and request specific information from online resources (such as online encyclopedias, atlases, and language translation tools). Determine which resources are available by clicking the down-pointing arrow at the right of the resources option box (the option box located below the *Search for* text box). The drop-down list includes reference books, dictionaries, research sites, business and financial sites, and options for translating text from one language into another.

Lesson 5.9 · Checking the Spelling and Grammar in a Document

 2-1.3.5, 2-2.2.1

Word includes two proofing tools you can use when creating a document—a spelling checker and a grammar checker. Use Word's **spelling checker** to find and correct misspelled words and find duplicated words (such as *and and*). The spelling checker compares words in your document with words in its dictionary. If a match exists in the dictionary, the spelling checker ignores the word. If no match is found, the spelling checker stops, selects the word, and offers replacements. The **grammar checker** searches a document for errors in grammar, punctuation, and word usage.

To complete a spelling and grammar check, click the Review tab and then click the Spelling & Grammar button in the Proofing group. You can also begin checking spelling and grammar by pressing the keyboard shortcut, F7. As the spelling and grammar checker points out potential errors in the document, use the options in the Spelling and Grammar dialog box (shown in Table 5.4) to either correct or ignore them. The spelling and grammar checker can help you create a well-written document but it does not replace the need for proofreading.

The spelling and grammar checkers will not flag all of the mistakes within a written document. If a word is spelled and used correctly, the spelling and grammar checkers will pass over it, even if it does not make logical sense within a sentence. Consider the following sentence: "The sales associate was rude to me, so I asked to see a manger." This sentence would not be flagged in a spelling and grammar check, even though the writer likely meant that he or she asked to see a *manager* (the person in charge) rather than a *manger* (a trough, container, or crib).

spelling checker A proofing tool that identifies misspelled words in a document by comparing them against the words in a dictionary

grammar checker A proofing tool that checks text for grammatical errors

Quick Steps

Check Spelling and Grammar

1. Click Review tab.
2. Click Spelling & Grammar button in Proofing group.
3. Ignore or change as needed.
4. Click OK.

Keyboard Shortcut

Spelling and Grammar Checker

F7

Table 5.4 Spelling and Grammar Dialog Box Buttons

Button	Function
Ignore Once	During spell checking, skips selected occurrence of the word; in grammar checking, leaves selected text as written
Ignore All	During spell checking, skips all occurrences of the word in the document
Ignore Rule	During grammar checking, leaves selected text as written and ignores the current rule for the remainder of the grammar check
Add to Dictionary	Adds selected word to the main spelling check dictionary
Delete	Deletes selected text
Change	Replaces selected text with selected text in the *Suggestions* list box
Change All	Replaces all occurrences of selected text in the document with selected text in the *Suggestions* list box
Explain	During grammar checking, displays information about the grammar rule that applies to selected text
AutoCorrect	Inserts selected word and the correct spelling of the word in the AutoCorrect dialog box so that the change will be made automatically in the future
Undo	Reverses most recent spelling and grammar action
Next Sentence	Accepts manual changes made to sentence and then continues grammar check
Options	Displays a dialog box with options for customizing the spelling and grammar check

Exercise 5.9 Checking the Spelling and Grammar in a Document

1. Open **SGCAnalysis.docx** and then save the document with Save As and name it **U2T5-SGCAnalysis**.

2. Click the Review tab and then click the Spelling & Grammar button ABC in the Proofing group.

3. When the spelling checker selects the word *Schramberg* in the document, click the Ignore All button in the Spelling and Grammar dialog box.

   The word Schramberg is spelled correctly, so clicking the Ignore All button tells Word to leave the word as written whenever the spelling checker encounters it. Refer to Table 5.4 for an explanation of the buttons in the Spelling and Grammar dialog box.

4. When the spelling checker selects the word *Enclosed* in the document, make sure *Enclosed* is selected in the *Suggestions* list box and then click the Change button in the Spelling and Grammar dialog box.

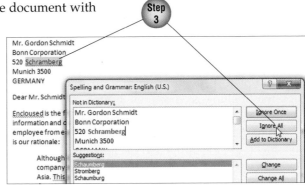

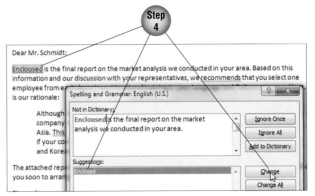

5. When the grammar checker selects the sentence that begins *Based on this information…*, click the Explain button, read the information on Subject-Verb Agreement that displays in the Word Help window, and then click the Close button ☒ to close the window.

6. Make sure *recommend* is selected in the *Suggestions* list box and then click the Change button.

7. When the spelling checker selects *employes*, make sure *employees* is selected in the *Suggestions* list box (if it is not selected, click *employees* to select it) and then click the Change button.

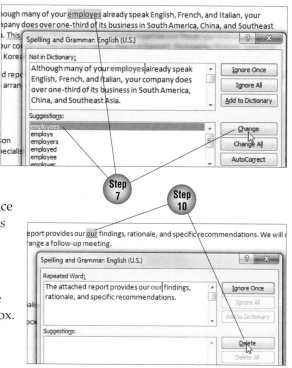

8. When the spelling checker selects the word *Portugese*, click the Change button.

9. When the grammar checker selects the sentence *This suggest that you…*, make sure *This suggests* is selected in the *Suggestions* list box and then click the Change button.

10. When the spelling checker selects the word *our* (this word appears twice), click the Delete button in the Spelling and Grammar dialog box.

11. Click OK at the message box telling you that the spelling and grammar check is complete.

12. Save, print, and then close **U2T5-SGCAnalysis.docx**.

Drilling Down

Editing While Checking Spelling and Grammar

When checking a document, you can temporarily leave the Spelling and Grammar dialog box by clicking in the document. To resume the spelling and grammar check, click the Resume button, which was formerly the Ignore button.

Changing Spelling Options

Control spelling and grammar checking options at the Word Options dialog box with the *Proofing* option selected. Display this dialog box by clicking the File tab and then clicking the Options button located below the Help tab. At the Word Options dialog box, click *Proofing* at the left side of the dialog box. With options in the dialog box, you can tell the spelling checker to ignore certain types of text, create custom dictionaries, show readability statistics, and hide spelling and/or grammar errors in the document.

Delving Deeper

 2-2.1.16

Using Word to Format Correspondence
Formatting a Personal Business Letter

A variety of formatting options are available for formatting a personal business letter (a letter from you as an individual rather than you representing a company), but the block style is one of the most common. In a block style format, all elements of the letter are aligned at the left margin as shown in the following example.

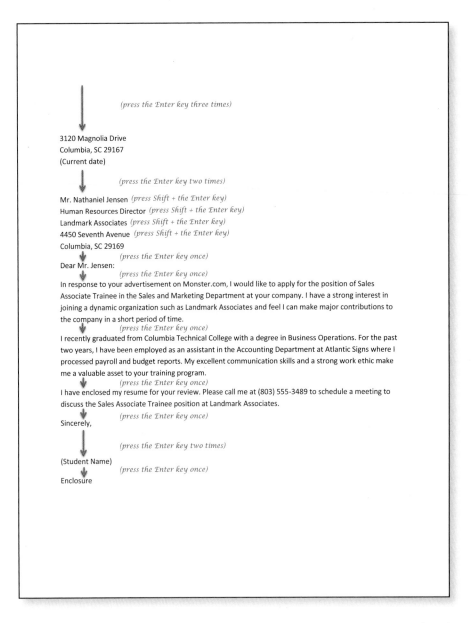

continued

Formatting a Business Letter

When creating a business letter, the block style is again one of the most common formats to use. Make sure to include your reference initials at the end of a business letter, as shown in the following example (where the *XX* indicates your initials). Business letters contains standard punctuation, which includes a colon after the salutation (*Dear Mrs. Cardoza:*) and a comma after the complimentary close (*Sincerely,*).

April 10, 2012

↓ *(press the Enter key two times)*

Mrs. Tina Cardoza *(press Shift + the Enter key)*
2314 Magnolia Drive *(press Shift + the Enter key)*
P.O. Box 231 *(press Shift + the Enter key)*
San Francisco, CA 94336 *(press the Enter key)*

Dear Mrs. Cardoza: *(press the Enter key)*

Now is the time to sign up for a sun-filled and fun-filled family vacation. We are offering three-day, seven-day, and ten-day fun-in-the-sun vacation packages to several southern destinations, including Los Angeles, Orlando, Miami, New Orleans, and Maui. Limited by a budget? No problem. We can find the perfect vacation for you and your family that fits within your budget. *(press the Enter key)*

We know we can create a vacation package that is as exciting and adventurous as your previous vacation. Right now, you can spend seven days and six nights in beautiful and tropical Maui, Hawaii, at the Pacific Beach Cabanas for under $700 per person including airfare! We also have a four-day, three-night vacation package to Orlando, Florida, for less than $400 per person. To find out about these fabulous and affordable vacations, stop by our office and talk to a travel consultant or give us a call and book your next fun-in-the-sun family vacation. *(press the Enter key)*

Sincerely,

↓ *(press the Enter key two times)*

Mandy Takada *(press Shift + the Enter key)*
Travel Consultant *(press the Enter key)*

XX *(press Shift + the Enter key)*
BlockLetter.docx

5530 Bayside Drive ❖ San Francisco CA 94320 ❖ 1-888-555-8890 ❖ www.emcp.net/bayside

continued

Formatting a Memo

The formatting of interoffice correspondence documents, referred to as *memos* (short for *memorandums*), varies from company to company. However, the content of a memo should be brief and to the point, and the format should support quick reading, easy distribution, and efficient filing. You can create a memo with the default Microsoft Word 2010 line and paragraph spacing, or remove the spacing and then create the memo. Include your reference initials at the end of the memo, as shown in the following example (where the *XX* indicates your initials). You can also include the document name below the initials, though this is optional.

DATE: ➝ February 28, 2012 *(press the Enter key)*
(*Tab twice*)
TO: ➝ Nancy Martinez, Resources Coordinator *(press the Enter key)*
(*Tab twice*)
FROM: ➝ Isabelle Carlson, Training Coordinator *(press the Enter key)*
(*Tab twice*)
SUBJECT: ➝ Network and Internet Books *(press the Enter key)*
(*Tab once*)

While attending the Southern Computer Technology Conference earlier this month, I discovered several excellent network and Internet security reference books. Two of these reference books, *Managing Network Security* by Douglas Baker (published by Evergreen Publishing House) and *Network Management* by Geraldine Kingston (published by Bonari & Jenkins), I would like you to order and make available in the business section of the library. Both books retail for approximately $55. If you have enough in your budget, please order two copies of each book. *(press the Enter key)*

Two other reference books, *Internet Security* by Jeong Pak (published by Meridian Publishers) and *Protecting and Securing Data* by Glenn Rowan (published by Canon Beach Publishing), I would like you to order for the technical support team training that will take place in April. I will need 15 copies of *Internet Security* and 20 copies of *Protecting and Securing Data*. *(press the Enter key)*

XX *(press Shift + the Enter key)*
BookMemo.docx

TOPIC SUMMARY

- You can use the mouse, the keyboard, or a combination of the two to move the insertion point throughout a document without interfering with the text.
- The scroll box on the vertical scroll bar indicates the location of the text in the document in relation to the remainder of the document.
- Click the Select Browse Object button located at the bottom of the vertical scroll bar to display options for browsing through a document.
- You can use the keyboard to move the insertion point by character, word, screen, or page, and from the first to the last character in a document. Refer to Table 5.1 for more information.
- Navigate in a document using the Navigation pane. Display the pane by clicking the *Navigation Pane* check box in the Show group on the View tab.
- You can delete text by character, word, line, several lines, or partial page using specific keys or by selecting text using the mouse or keyboard.
- Use the Undo button on the Quick Access toolbar to reverse actions such as typing, deleting, or formatting text. Use the Redo button to redo an action that has been undone.
- Use the Find feature to search for specific characters or formatting. Use the Find and Replace feature to search for specific characters or formatting and replace them with other characters or formatting.
- Cut, copy, and paste text using the buttons in the Clipboard group on the Home tab or with the keyboard shortcuts.
- When you paste text, the Paste Options button displays in the lower right corner of the text. Click the button and the Paste Options gallery displays with buttons for specifying how you want information to be pasted in the document.
- With the Office Clipboard, you can collect up to 24 items and then paste them within a document.
- At the Find and Replace dialog box, click the Find Next button to find the next occurrence of the text. Click the Replace button to replace the text and find the next occurrence, or click the Replace All button to replace all occurrences of the text.
- You can change the document view with buttons in the view section on the Status bar or with options on the View tab.
- Print Layout is the default view in Word. Use the View tab to change to other views such as Draft view or Full Screen Reading view.
- Draft view displays the document in a format conducive to efficient editing and formatting.
- Full Screen Reading view displays a document in a format for easy viewing and reading.
- Use the Zoom slider bar to change the percentage of the display.
- Preview a document at the Print tab Backstage view. Scroll through the pages in the document with the Next Page and the Previous Page buttons that display below the preview page. Use the Zoom slider bar to increase or decrease the display size of the preview page.
- At the Print tab Backstage view you can customize the print job by changing the page orientation, size, and margins; specifying how many pages you want to print on one page; specifying the number of copies and whether or not the pages should be collated; and specifying the printer.
- The Word Count dialog box displays the number of pages, words, characters, paragraphs, and lines in a document. Display this dialog box by clicking the word count section of the Status bar or clicking the Word Count button in the Proofing group on the Review tab.
- Use the Thesaurus to find synonyms and antonyms for words in your document. Display synonyms and antonyms at the Research task pane or display synonyms by right-clicking a word and then pointing to *Synonyms* at the shortcut menu.
- The spelling checker matches the words in your document with the words in its dictionary. If a match does not exist, the spelling checker selects the word and suggests possible replacements.
- The grammar checker searches a document for errors in grammar, style, punctuation, and word usage. When the grammar checker detects an error, you can review information about the error by clicking the Explain button at the Spelling and Grammar dialog box.

Key Terms

Clipboard, p. 224	scroll box, p. 217
delete, p. 220	selection bar, p. 222
grammar checker, p. 239	spelling checker, p. 239
insert, p. 220	Thesaurus, p. 237
Live Preview, p. 225	vertical scroll bar, p. 217
Navigation pane, p. 218	

Features Summary

Feature	Ribbon Tab, Group	Button	Keyboard Shortcut
Clipboard	Home, Clipboard		
Copy selected text	Home, Clipboard		Ctrl + C
Cut selected text	Home, Clipboard		Ctrl + X
Find and Replace dialog box with Replace tab selected	Home, Editing		Ctrl + H
Navigation pane	Home, Editing		Ctrl + F
Paste selected text	Home, Clipboard		Ctrl + V
Print tab Backstage view	File, Print		Ctrl + P
Redo an action			Ctrl + Y
Research task pane for synonyms and antonyms	Review, Proofing		Shift + F7
Spelling & Grammar	Review, Proofing		F7
Undo an action			Ctrl + Z
Word Count dialog box	Review, Proofing		

KEY POINTS REVIEW

Identification

Match the terms to the callouts on the Word window in Figure 5.10.

1. _____ incorrect grammar
2. _____ misspelled word
3. _____ Clipboard task pane
4. _____ Clipboard task pane Options button
5. _____ Find button
6. _____ Clipboard item
7. _____ Paste Options button
8. _____ view buttons on Status bar
9. _____ Paste button
10. _____ dialog box launcher

Figure 5.10 Identification Figure

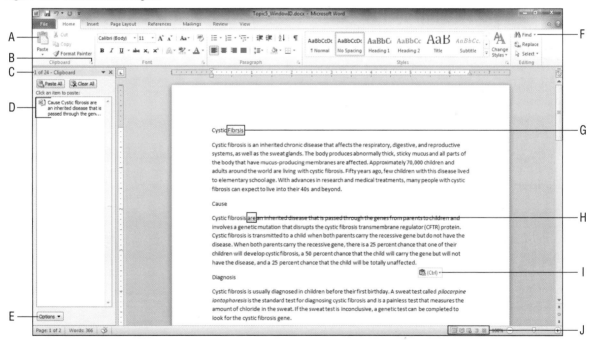

Multiple Choice

For each of the following items, choose the option that best completes the sentence or answers the question.

1. Use this keyboard command to move the insertion point to the beginning of the document.
   A. Ctrl + Page Up
   B. Ctrl + Home
   C. Home
   D. Page Up

2. This button, located towards the bottom of the vertical scroll bar, contains options for browsing through a document.
   A. Previous Page
   B. Next Page
   C. Select Browse Object
   D. Zoom In

3. To select a sentence, hold down this key and then click anywhere in the sentence.
   A. Ctrl key
   B. Shift key
   C. Alt key
   D. Tab key

4. To begin checking the spelling and grammar in a document, click this tab and then click the Spelling & Grammar button in the Proofing group.
   A. View
   B. Review
   C. References
   D. Insert

5. Click this option in the Spelling and Grammar dialog box to display grammar rule information about the selected text.
   A. Options
   B. Next Sentence
   C. Change
   D. Explain

6. This group on the Home tab contains the Cut, Copy, and Paste buttons.
   A. Font
   B. Paragraph
   C. Styles
   D. Clipboard

7. You can collect up to _____ items in the Office Clipboard.
   A. 14
   B. 18
   C. 24
   D. 48

8. This view displays a document in a format for easy viewing and reading.
   A. Print Layout
   B. Full Screen Reading
   C. Draft
   D. Outline

9. If you want to replace every occurrence of a certain word in a document, click this button at the Find and Replace dialog box.
   A. Replace
   B. More
   C. Replace All
   D. Find Next

10. Click the Find button in the Editing group on the Home tab to display the _____ pane.
    A. Navigation
    B. Research
    C. Clipboard
    D. Styles

Matching

Match each of the following definitions with the correct term, command, or option.

1. _____ Click this tab to display the Backstage view.
2. _____ This button displays in the lower right corner of newly pasted text.
3. _____ This key removes the character to the right of the insertion point.
4. _____ This keyboard shortcut copies selected text in a document.
5. _____ To select various amounts of text using the mouse, click in this bar.
6. _____ This key removes the character to the left of the insertion point.
7. _____ This task pane provides a list of alternative words for a selected word.
8. _____ This keyboard shortcut cuts selected text in a document.
9. _____ To display detailed statistics of a document, click this button in the Proofing group on the Review tab.
10. _____ Use this keyboard command to move the insertion point to the end of the document.

A. Ctrl + C
B. Delete
C. Research
D. File
E. Ctrl + X
F. Ctrl + End
G. Selection
H. Backspace
I. Paste Options
J. Word Count

SKILLS REVIEW

Review 5.1 Formatting an Essay

1. Open **OutputStor.docx** and then save the document with Save As and name it **U2T5-R1-OutputStor**.
2. Insert the word *feverishly* between *working* and *to* in the first sentence of the first paragraph.
3. Move the insertion point to the beginning of the first paragraph below the *Increased Optical Disc Storage Capacity* heading and then type the sentence **Computer users needing huge storage capacities may be pleased with a new type of optical disc storage called FMD-ROM.**
4. Select and then delete the sentence *Data is stored in the incoherent light.* located in the second paragraph below the *Increased Optical Disc Storage Capacity* heading.
5. Undo the deletion and then redo the deletion.
6. Select and then delete the third paragraph below the *Increased Optical Disc Storage Capacity* heading (the paragraph that begins *FDM-ROM discs are compatible with…*).
7. Undo the deletion and then deselect the text.
8. Move the insertion point to the beginning of the document and then complete a spelling and grammar check on the document (*Almaden* is spelled correctly).
9. Save, print, and then close **U2T5-R1-OutputStor.docx**.

Review 5.2 Formatting a Lease Agreement

1. Open **LeaseAgrmt.docx** and then save the document with Save As and name it **U2T5-R2-LeaseAgrmt**.
2. Find all occurrences of *Lessee* and replace them with *Terry Hayes*.
3. Find all occurrences of *Lessor* and replace them with *Donna Blaine*.
4. Select the *Rent* heading and the paragraph of text below it and then move the section above the *Damage Deposit* heading.
5. Open **BuildingAgrmt.docx**, copy the last paragraph (the paragraph that begins *IN WITNESS WHEREOF*) as well as the signatures lines and then paste the copied text to the end of **U2T5-R2-LeaseAgrmt.docx**. Make **BuildingAgrmt.docx** the active document and then close it.
6. Replace the word *Builder* (below the signature line) with *Terry Hayes*.
7. Replace the word *Owner* (below the signature line) with *Donna Blaine*.
8. Save, print, and then close **U2T5-R2-LeaseAgrmt.docx**.

Review 5.3 Typing a Memo

1. At a blank document, type the memo shown in Figure 5.11. Type the text exactly as written. To align the information after *DATE:*, *TO:*, and *FROM:*, press the Tab key twice. Press the Tab key once after typing *SUBJECT:*.
2. After typing the memo, complete a spelling check on the document (proper names are spelled correctly).
3. Save the document and name it **U2T5-R3-TrainingMemo**.
4. Print and then close **U2T5-R3-TrainingMemo.docx**.

Figure 5.11 Review 5.3 Memo

DATE: April 26, 2012

TO: All Employees

FROM: Lillian Vaughn

SUBJECT: Microsoft Word Training

As part of the computer training series, the Computer Technology Department is offering a five-hour Microsoft Word training class. The class will be held in the training center on Friday, May 11, 2012, from 9:30 a.m. to 2:30 p.m. If you are interested in registering for this training, plaese contact me at extension 3220 or contact Jack Sullivan at extension 3225.

Over the next few months, the Computer Technology Department will offer training classes on Microsoft Excel, PowerPoint, and Access. I willl send you a memo when specific dates and times are determined for upcoming classes.

XX
U2T5-R3-TrainingMemo.docx

SKILLS ASSESSMENT

Assessment 5.1 Editing a Memo

1. Open **OrientMemo.docx** and then save the document with Save As and name it **U2T5-A1-OrientMemo**.
2. Use the Tab key to align the headings in the same manner as the headings in Figure 5.11.
3. Move the insertion point to the blank line below the paragraph of text in the body of the memo and then add the following information (enter the information in paragraph form—do not use bullets):
   - The orientation will take place in Conference Room 23-C.
   - The orientation is scheduled from 9:00 a.m. to 3:30 p.m. with a half-hour lunch.
   - Employees should bring their new employee handbook and a pencil or pen for taking notes.
   - Each employee must inform his or her supervisor of the orientation date and time.
4. Complete a spelling and grammar check on the memo.
5. Save, print, and then close **U2T5-A1-OrientMemo.docx**.

Assessment 5.2 Formatting a Report

1. Open **Computers.docx** and then save the document with Save As and name it **U2T5-A2-Computers**.
2. At the end of the paragraph in the *Accuracy* section, insert the sentence **The computer user is responsible for entering data correctly and making certain that programs are correct.**
3. Move the *Versatility* section above the *Storage* section.
4. Move the *Communications* section to the end of the document (after the *Storage* section).
5. Use the Thesaurus to replace the word *growing* (located in the first sentence in the *Speed* section) with *increasing*.
6. Save, print, and then close **U2T5-A2-Computers.docx**.

Assessment 5.3 Formatting an Adventure Document

1. Open **FCTAdventure.docx** and then save the document with Save As and name it **U2T5-A3-FCTAdventure**.
2. Insert the words *and regions* between the words *cities* and *in* located in the sentence below the title *AUSTRALIAN STUDY ADVENTURE*.
3. Select and then delete the last sentence in the *Small Groups* section.
4. Select and then delete the heading *Intercontinental Flights* and the paragraph of text that follows the heading.
5. Move the insertion point to the beginning of the document. Search for all occurrences of *fct* and replace them with *First Choice Travel*.
6. Search for all occurrences of *Australia Study Adventure* and replace them with *African Wildlife Journey*.
7. Search for all occurrences of *Australia* and replace them with *Africa*.
8. Complete a spelling and grammar check on the document.
9. Save, print, and then close **U2T5-A3-FCTAdventure.docx**.

Assessment 5.4 Finding Information on Changing Grammar Checking Options

1. Display Help information on checking spelling and grammar by displaying the Word Options dialog box (click File tab, Options), clicking *Proofing*, and then clicking the Help button (contains a question mark) located in the upper right corner of the dialog box. Read the information on checking spelling and grammar. Learn how to change the writing style from *Grammar Only* to *Grammar & Style*.
2. After reading the information, open **MultimediaAI.docx** and then save the document with Save As and name it **U2T5-A4-MultimediaAI**.
3. Change the writing style to *Grammar & Style*.
4. Complete a spelling and grammar check on the document.
5. Change the *Writing style* option back to *Grammar Only*.
6. Save, print, and then close **U2T5-A4-MultimediaAI.docx**.

Assessment 5.5 Locating Information and Writing a Memo

1. Using the Internet, locate information on three colleges in your state. Research a specific degree program that interests you at each college.
2. At a blank document, write a memo to your instructor describing each college, the specific degree program you researched at that college, and any other information you feel is pertinent about the schools.
3. Save the completed memo and name it **U2T5-A5-CollegeMemo**.
4. Print and then close **U2T5-A5-CollegeMemo.docx**.

Assessment 5.6 Typing a Personal Business Letter

1. At a blank document, type the personal business letter shown in Figure 5.12. Refer to the Delving Deeper section on page 240 to determine the spacing in the letter.
2. Save the completed letter and name it **U2T5-A6-Letter**.
3. Search for all occurrences of *Secretarial* and replace them with *Administrative*.
4. Complete a spelling and grammar check.
5. Save, print, and then close **U2T5-A6-Letter.docx**.

Figure 5.12 **Assessment 5.6 Letter**

734 East Alder Road
Milwaukee, WI 53219
July 18, 2012

Ms. Erin Wright
Vice President of Marketing
Fielding Properties
1800 Landmark Way
Milwaukee, WI 53212

Dear Ms. Wright:

In response to your advertisement in the Milwaukee Express, I would like to apply for the position of Secretarial Assistant in the Sales and Marketing Department at your company. My background includes high-level customer and account management experience as well as complex project management responsibilities. My four years of professional experience have taught me that my talents and expertise are best suited to a role that involves sales, customer interaction, multiple task management, and high performance expectations.

Your company's products, reputation, and growth potential are exciting. I believe my skills will be a good fit for your needs as you expand. I have enclosed my resume for your review. Please call me at (414) 555-5600 to schedule a meeting to discuss the Secretarial Assistant position at Fielding Properties.

Sincerely,

Leslie Angelos

Enclosure

CRITICAL THINKING

Exploring the Find and Replace Dialog Box Options

Part 1 1. The Find and Replace dialog box contains a More button that, when clicked, displays additional options for finding and replacing text. Learn more about the options available when you expand the dialog box by reading the Drilling Down section on page 229.

2. Open **Agreement.docx**, save the document with Save As, and name it **U2T5-CT01-Agreement.docx**.

3. Find all occurrences of *BUYER* (matching the case) and replace them with *George Summers*.

4. Find all occurrences of *SELLER* (matching the case) and replace them with *Veronica Schroeder*.

5. Find all word forms of the word *buy* and replace them with *purchase*.

6. Save, print, and then close **U2T5-CT01-Agreement.docx**.

Part 2 Create a memo to your instructor explaining the options you used at the expanded Find and Replace dialog box to complete the find and replace tasks in Part 1. Save the memo with the name **U2T5-CT02-ReplaceMemo**. Print and then close the memo.

TEAM PROJECT

Creating and Formatting an Informational Article

1. As a team, create a document related to robots, online shopping, or Fifth Disease. To complete this task, open the documents **TeamDoc01.docx**, **TeamDoc02.docx**, and **TeamDoc03.docx**, which contain information on all three topics, and use features and functions in Word to create one complete document on your topic. Collect the information from three documents and insert all of the relevant information into a new Word document. Determine a title for the document as a team.

2. Save the completed team document with Save As and name it **U2T5-Team_[document]** (replace *[document]* with the title of your document).

3. Print and then close the document.

Discussion Questions

1. What method(s) did you use to find the information on your topic?
2. How did you decide to organize the information in the document and why?

Topic 6

Formatting Characters and Paragraphs in Word

Performance Objectives

Upon successful completion of Topic 6, you will be able to:

- Apply fonts and font effects
- Apply formatting with Format Painter
- Align text in paragraphs
- Change line spacing
- Change paragraph spacing

- Apply bullets and numbering
- Indent text in paragraphs
- Apply borders and shading to text
- Apply styles
- Set tabs

STUDENT RESOURCES

Before beginning this topic, copy to your storage medium the **Unit2Topic06** subfolder from the *Computer and Internet Essentials: Preparing for IC³* Internet Resource Center. Make this the active folder.

In addition to containing the data files needed to complete topic work, the Internet Resource Center contains model answers in PDF format for each of the applicable exercises in this topic. Use these files to check your work. The preface of your textbook provides instructions for accessing these files.

Necessary Data Files

To complete the exercises and assessments, you will need the following data files:

Exercises 6.1–6.5	ProConcepts.docx
Exercises 6.6–6.10	WritingProcess.docx
Exercise 6.11	New file
Exercise 6.12	Previously created file (Ex. 6.11)
Review 6.1	CompTech.docx
Review 6.2	Qualities.docx
Review 6.3	New file
Review 6.4	New file
Assessment 6.1	ResumeStyles.docx
Assessment 6.2	CoverLetters.docx
Assessment 6.3	New file
Assessment 6.4	CoverLetters.docx
Assessment 6.5	New file

continued

Assessment 6.6	New file
Critical Thinking	New file
Team Project	New file

Visual Preview

themselves are continually improving. This ongoing cycle causes computers to grow in capacity and speed, while shrinking in size and cost every year.

Unfortunately, a similar effect has yet to be seen in the software development area. Software is still written manually, and the entire process is powered by the human mind. Since human minds are not doubling their capabilities every two years, the rate of improvement is slow. However, if science gets to the point of creating artificially intelligent machines that are capable ...we are

...nt Name
.../14/2012

ON THE HORIZON: PROGRAMMING CONCEPTS AND LANGUAGES

As with nearly every area of information technology, the capabilities and opportunities afforded by the Internet are influencing the path of programming and application design. Among the new directions are collaborative online software development, the founding of an open-source organization for developers, and the use of artificial intelligence to develop software.

Development Service Providers

Development service providers (DSPs) are a new class of online software development packages that allow software developers in geographically separate locations to work together on the same software. A development team in Chicago, for example, might work closely with another group in Germany. The tools provided include version control, bug tracking, virtual meeting rooms, and project management software. The main difference between this type of software and previous software development groupware such as CASE tools is the additional element of using the Internet to take the process online. Similar techniques have been used for years by developers of systems that span the world, such as Linux programmers.

DSPs are under development at Borland, Merant Solutions, and Rational Software. This new element of online collaborations is expected to boost software production and reduce travel and communication costs for developers who work on joint projects with widespread teams.

Open-Source Development Toolkit

In November 2001, IBM announced the Eclipse project, which has the goal of developing a universal development tool platform into which various vendors can integrate best-of-breed software development tools. This is a significant step toward establishing an open-source development toolkit that would be governed under the common public license for software. As of May 2003, the consortium of vendors included such prominent names as Borland, Rational Software, Red Hat, SAP, Oracle, and Intel. The group first established a governing board to develop technical standards and the direction of the open-source programming community. The group has now broadened its scope to include research and education.

Software Writing Software

The development of robotics systems for building smaller computer components is the driving force behind the miniaturization of computers. Human beings could never fashion these chips and boards by hand, no matter how skilled they are. Robotics systems improve each year, which in turn allows them to build even better machines. This means that the computers

Exercises 6.1–6.5 U2T6-ProConcepts.docx

Edit and Proofread

Editing and proofreading are essential to good writing. Planning and drafting allow you to get your information on paper; editing and proofreading help you communicate your ideas as clearly as possible to the reader.

REFERENCES

• What information should I not include?

To answer these questions, you may find it helpful to spend a few minutes listing all the information you *could* include in your document. You may also find it helpful to write a rough draft of your document. Write the draft quickly, including any information that comes to you. Once you have it all on paper, you can work with it, deciding what to include and what to leave out.

THE WRITING PROCESS

An effective letter or memo does not simply appear on your paper or computer screen. Instead, it begins to take shape when you think carefully about the situation within which you must write, when you define your purpose for writing. It continues to develop as you consider your reader, the information you must communicate, and the way in which you plan to present that information. Finally, a document that communicates clearly is the result of good writing and good rewriting; you can usually improve anything you have written. This document represents a process for approaching any writing task.

Define Purpose

Knowing your purpose for writing is the foundation of any written project. Before you begin writing your memo, letter, or other document, ask yourself the following questions:

1. What am I trying to accomplish?
2. What is my purpose for writing?
   a. To inform someone?
   b. To request information or products?
   c. To respond to a question or request?
   d. To persuade someone?
   e. To direct someone?

Identify Reader

As you define your purpose, you will need to develop a good picture of the person who will be reading your document. Ask yourself:

1. Who is my reader?
2. What do I know about my reader that will help determine the best approach?
3. Is my reader a coworker, a subordinate, a superior, or a customer?
4. How is the reader likely to feel about my message?

Select and Organize Information

Once you have defined your purpose and identified your reader, decide what information you will include. Ask yourself questions such as:

• What does my reader want or need to know?
• What information must I include?
• What information will help my reader respond positively?

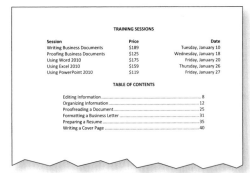

TRAINING SESSIONS		
Session	**Price**	**Date**
Writing Business Documents	$189	Tuesday, January 10
Proofing Business Documents	$125	Wednesday, January 18
Using Word 2010	$175	Friday, January 20
Using Excel 2010	$159	Thursday, January 26
Using PowerPoint 2010	$119	Friday, January 27

TABLE OF CONTENTS

Editing Information 8
Organizing Information 12
Proofreading a Document 25
Formatting a Business Letter 31
Preparing a Resume 35
Writing a Cover Page 40

Exercises 6.11–6.12 U2T6-Training.docx

Exercises 6.6–6.10 U2T6-WritingProcess.docx

Topic Overview

In this topic, you will learn how to apply character formatting in a variety of ways, such as changing the typeface, type size, and typestyle as well as adding font effects such as bolding and italicizing. The Paragraph group on the Home tab includes buttons for applying formatting to a paragraph of text, which is any amount of text followed by a stroke of the Enter key. In this topic, you will learn to apply paragraph formatting by changing text alignment, indenting text, applying formatting with Format Painter, and changing line spacing. You will also learn how to insert numbers and bullets in a document, how to apply borders and shading to paragraphs of text in a document, and how to manipulate tabs on the Ruler and at the Tabs dialog box.

Lesson 6.1   Applying Formatting with the Font Group

 2-1.3.6

The appearance of a document in the document screen and how it looks when printed is called the **format**. The Font group (shown in Figure 6.1) contains a number of buttons you can use to apply character formatting to text in a document. The top row contains buttons for changing the font as well as buttons for increasing and decreasing the size of the font. The bottom row contains buttons for applying typestyles such as bold, italic, underlining, strikethrough, subscript, and superscript. You can remove character or paragraph formatting from text by clicking the Clear Formatting button in the Font group. You can also remove character formatting by using the keyboard shortcut Ctrl + spacebar or remove paragraph formatting by using the keyboard shortcut Ctrl + Q. You can use keyboard shortcuts to *apply* character formatting as well. The keyboard shortcuts, along with their corresponding buttons in the Font group, are described in Table 6.1.

format The appearance of a document in the document screen and how it looks when printed

Figure 6.1 Font Group Buttons

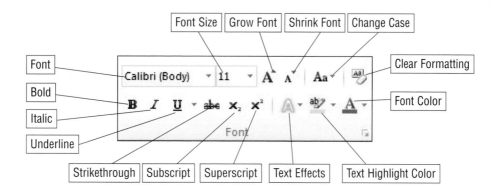

Table 6.1 Font Keyboard Shortcuts

Font Group Button	Keyboard Shortcut	Font Group Button	Keyboard Shortcut
Font	Ctrl + Shift + F	Bold	Ctrl + B
Font Size	Ctrl + Shift + P	Italic	Ctrl + I
Grow Font	Ctrl + >	Underline	Ctrl + U
Shrink Font	Ctrl + <	Subscript	Ctrl + =
Clear Formatting	Ctrl + spacebar (character formatting)	Superscript	Ctrl + +
Clear Formatting	Ctrl + Q (paragraph formatting)	Change Case	Shift + F3

typeface A set of characters with a common design and shape

font The complete set of characters in a particular typeface

monospaced A style of typeface in which each character is allotted the same amount of horizontal space

proportional A style of typeface in which characters are allotted varying amounts of space

serif The small line that finishes off the top and bottom of a character; to describe a typeface as *serif* means that its characters contain these lines

sans serif A term used to describe a typeface whose characters do not contain serifs

By default, new Word documents are created using a template that formats text in 11-point Calibri. You may want to choose a new font for your document for such reasons as changing the tone of the document, enhancing the visual appeal, or increasing the readability of the text. You can preview different fonts by clicking the Font button arrow in the Font group and hovering the mouse arrow pointer over various typefaces in the list. When you do this, the text in your document changes to reflect how the document would look using the selected font. Recall that this feature, referred to as Live Preview, provides you with an opportunity to see how the document will appear with different font formatting before you make a final choice.

A font consists of three elements—typeface, type size, and typestyle. A **typeface** is a set of characters with a common design and shape. Word refers to the complete set of characters in a particular typeface as a **font**. A typeface can be decorative or plain and either monospaced or proportional. A **monospaced** typeface allots the same amount of horizontal space for each character, while a **proportional** typeface allots varying amounts of space for each character. Typefaces are divided into two main categories: serif and sans serif. A **serif** is a small line that finishes off the top or bottom of a character; to refer to a typeface as *serif* means that its characters contain these lines. A **sans serif** typeface is one that does not include serifs on its characters. Serif typefaces are best for text-intensive documents because the serifs help move the reader's eyes across the page. Use sans serif typefaces for headings, headlines, and advertisements. Table 6.2 shows examples of serif and sans serif typefaces.

Table 6.2 Serif, Sans Serif, and Monospace Typefaces

Serif Typefaces	Sans Serif Typefaces	Monospaced Typefaces
Cambria	Calibri	Consolas
Constantia	Candara	Courier
Times New Roman	Corbel	Letter Gothic
Bookman Old Style	Arial	

Type size is a measurement of character height. The size of proportional type is measured vertically in units called points. A point is approximately 1/72 of an inch, and the higher the point size, the larger the character. Within a typeface, various typestyles may be available. **Typestyles** are variations within a typeface and are divided into four main categories: regular, bold, italic, and bold italic. Apply a particular typestyle to text with the Bold or Italic buttons in the bottom row in the Font group. You can apply more than one style to text. For example, you can bold and italicize the same text.

type size A measurement of type height in points

typestyle The variations within a typeface, such as bold or italic

Exercise 6.1 Applying Formatting with Buttons in the Font Group

1. Open **ProConcepts.docx** and then save the document with Save As and name it **U2T6-ProConcepts**.

2. Select *On the Horizon: Programming Concepts and Languages* and then click the Bold button **B** in the Font group on the Home tab.

3. With *On the Horizon: Programming Concepts and Languages* still selected, click the Change Case button **Aa⁻** in the Font group and then click *UPPERCASE* at the drop-down list.

   Use options at the *Change Case* drop-down list to specify the case of selected text.

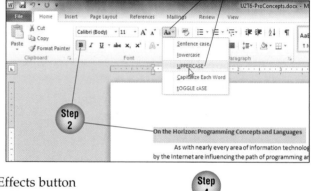

4. With the title still selected, click the Text Effects button in the Font group and then click *Gradient Fill - Blue, Accent 1* at the drop-down gallery.

5. Click anywhere in the document to deselect the title. After viewing the text effect applied to the title, click the Undo button on the Quick Access toolbar to remove the text effect.

6. With the title selected, click the Text Effects button, point to *Shadow*, and then click *Offset Right* in the *Outer* section of the side menu.

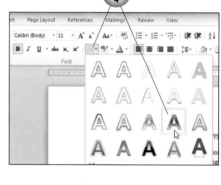

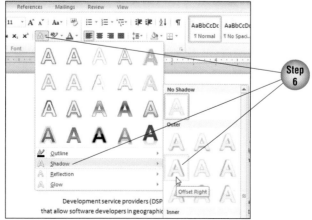

7. Select the heading *Development Service Providers* and then click the Italic button 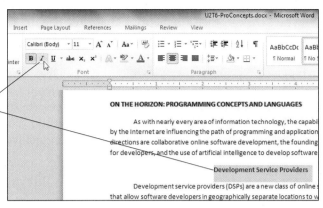 in the Font group.

8. Select and then italicize the two remaining headings, *Open-Source Development Toolkit* and *Software Writing Software.*

9. Select the word *CASE* that displays in the *Development Service Providers* paragraph and then click the Underline button 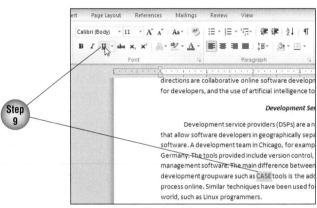 in the Font group.

10. Select the entire document by clicking the Select button in the Editing group on the Home tab and then clicking *Select All* at the drop-down list.

11. Click the Font button arrow in the Font group. Hover the mouse pointer over various fonts in the list and notice how the text in the document reflects the selected font.

12. Scroll down the list and then click *Cambria*.

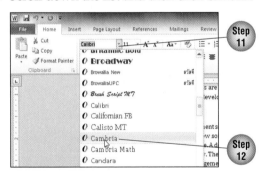

13. Click the Font Size button arrow and then click *12* at the drop-down list.

14. Click the Font Color button arrow 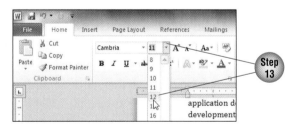 and then click the Dark Blue color at the color palette (second color from the right in the *Standard Colors* row).

15. Click anywhere in the document to deselect the text.

16. Click the Save button on the Quick Access toolbar to save the document.

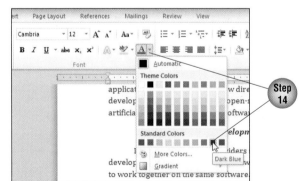

Drilling Down

Using Fonts Introduced in Word 2007

In the previous version of Word, Word 2007, Microsoft introduced six new fonts designed for extended on-screen reading. These typefaces included the default font, Calibri, as well as Cambria, Candara, Consolas, Constantia, and Corbel. Calibri, Candara, and Corbel are sans serif typefaces; Cambria and Constantia are serif typefaces; and Consolas is monospaced.

Lesson 6.2 Applying Formatting and Displaying Nonprinting Characters

 2-2.1.6

To provide users with easy access to some of the most commonly used commands, Word contains the **Mini toolbar**. When you select text, the Mini toolbar displays in a dimmed fashion above the selected text, as shown in Figure 6.2. Hover the mouse arrow pointer over the Mini toolbar to activate it. Click a button on the Mini toolbar to apply formatting to selected text.

Mini toolbar A semitransparent toolbar that displays when you select text and contains buttons for formatting

Figure 6.2 Mini Toolbar

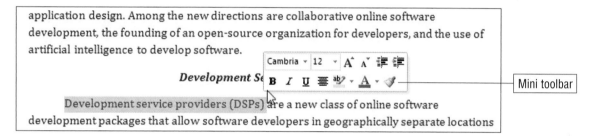

In addition to buttons in the Font group and on the Mini toolbar, you can use options at the Font dialog box (shown in Figure 6.3) to change the typeface, type size, and typestyle of text as well as apply font effects. Display the Font dialog box by clicking the Font group dialog box launcher. The Font group dialog box launcher is a small square containing a down-pointing diagonal arrow that displays in the lower right corner of the Font group.

The Font dialog box contains the *Hidden* option in the *Effects* section of the dialog box. With this option, you can select and then hide text. If you want to view the hidden text, turn on the display of nonprinting characters by clicking the Show/Hide ¶ button in the Paragraph group on the Home tab or by pressing the keyboard shortcut Ctrl + Shift + *. When it is active, the Show/Hide ¶ button displays with an orange background and nonprinting formatting symbols display, such as paragraph symbols, tab symbols, and line, page, and section breaks. Hidden text displays with a dotted underline. To redisplay hidden text, click the Show/Hide ¶ button to make it active, select the text, display the Font dialog box, and then remove the check mark from the *Hidden* option.

Quick Steps

Change the Font at the Font Dialog Box

1. Click Font group dialog box launcher.
2. Choose desired font.
3. Click OK.

Keyboard Shortcut

Font Dialog Box

Ctrl + D

Figure 6.3 Font Dialog Box

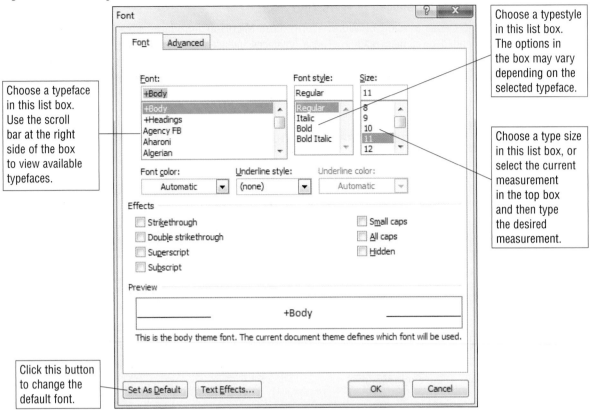

Choose a typeface in this list box. Use the scroll bar at the right side of the box to view available typefaces.

Choose a typestyle in this list box. The options in the box may vary depending on the selected typeface.

Choose a type size in this list box, or select the current measurement in the top box and then type the desired measurement.

Click this button to change the default font.

Exercise 6.2 Applying Formatting Using the Mini Toolbar and the Font Dialog Box

1. With **U2T6-ProConcepts.docx** open, select the words *Development service providers (DSPs)* that display at the beginning of the paragraph in the *Development Service Providers* section, point to the Mini toolbar that displays above the selected text, and then click the Italic button *I* on the Mini toolbar.

The Mini toolbar displays in a dimmed manner until you point to it and activate it. The Mini toolbar disappears when you move the mouse pointer away from it or click one of its buttons.

2. Select the title *ON THE HORIZON: PROGRAMMING CONCEPTS AND LANGUAGES*, point to the Mini toolbar, and then click the Grow Font button A̅ on the Mini toolbar.

This increases the size of the title text to 14 points.

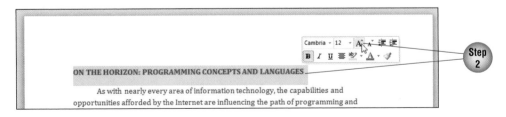

3. Select the second sentence in the first paragraph in the document (the sentence that begins *Among the new directions are…*), point to the Mini toolbar, click the Text Highlight Color button arrow 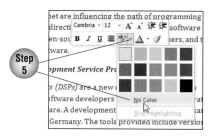 on the Mini toolbar, and then click the yellow color (first option in the top row) at the drop-down list.

You can also highlight text by clicking the Text Highlight Color button in the Font group. When you click the Text Highlight Color button, the mouse pointer displays with a highlighter pen attached. The highlighting tool stays on until you click the Text Highlight Color button again.

4. Select the last sentence in the first paragraph in the *Development Service Providers* section (the sentence that begins, *Similar techniques have been used…*), point to the Mini toolbar, and then click the Text Highlight Color button.

5. Select the highlighted sentence in the first paragraph (the sentence you highlighted in Step 3) and remove the highlighting from the text by clicking the Text Highlight Color button arrow on the Mini toolbar and then clicking the *No Color* option at the drop-down list.

6. Press Ctrl + Home to move the insertion point to the beginning of the document and then select the entire document by pressing Ctrl + A.

Ctrl + A is the keyboard shortcut to select the entire document.

7. Click the Font group dialog box launcher to display the Font dialog box.

The dialog box launcher displays as a small button containing a diagonal arrow.

8. At the Font dialog box, click *Constantia* in the *Font* list box (you will need to scroll down the list box to display this option) and click *11* in the *Size* list box.

9. Click the down-pointing arrow at the right side of the *Font color* option and then click *Black, Text 1* (second choice from the left in the top row).

10. Click OK to close the dialog box.

11. Select the title *ON THE HORIZON: PROGRAMMING CONCEPTS AND LANGUAGES.*

12. Click the Font group dialog box launcher.

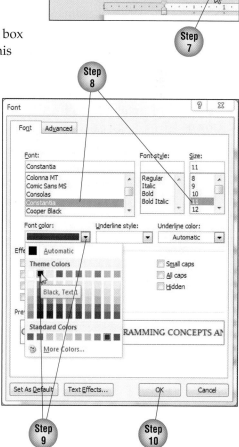

13. Click the *Hidden* option in the *Effects* section to insert a check mark and then click OK to close the dialog box.

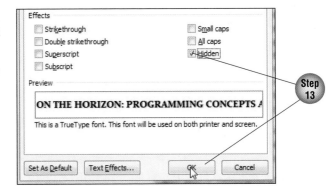

Notice that the title no longer displays in the document since the text is hidden.

14. Click the Show/Hide ¶ button ¶ in the Paragraph group on the Home tab to display nonprinting characters.

The hidden text is now visible and displays with a dotted underline.

15. Redisplay the hidden text by selecting the title *ON THE HORIZON: PROGRAMMING CONCEPTS AND LANGUAGES*, displaying the Font dialog box, clicking the *Hidden* option in the *Effects* section to remove the check mark, and then clicking OK to close the dialog box.

16. With the title still selected, click the Font Size button arrow in the Font group and then click *12* at the drop-down list.

17. Press Ctrl + End to move the insertion point to the end of the document. Press Shift + Enter and notice the New Line command symbol that displays in the document.

18. Press the Backspace key to remove the New Line command symbol and then click the Show/Hide ¶ button to turn off the display of nonprinting characters.

19. Save **U2T6-ProConcepts.docx**.

Drilling Down

Turning Off the Display of the Mini Toolbar

If you do not want the Mini toolbar to display when you select text, you can turn it off. To do this, click the File tab and then click the Options button located below the Help tab. At the Word Options dialog box with the *General* option selected in the left panel, click the *Show Mini Toolbar on selection* check box to remove the check mark.

Lesson 6.3 Applying Formatting with Format Painter

 2-1.3.6

Quick Steps

Apply Formatting with Format Painter

1. Click formatted text.
2. Double-click Format Painter button.
3. Select text to apply formatting.
4. Click Format Painter button.

The Clipboard group on the Home tab contains a button for copying character formatting to different locations in the document. This button, called the Format Painter, contains a paintbrush icon. To use the Format Painter button, position the insertion point on a character containing the desired formatting, click the Format Painter button, and then select the text to which you want to apply the character formatting. When you click the Format Painter button, the mouse I-beam pointer displays with a paintbrush attached. If you want to apply character formatting just one time, click the Format Painter button once. If, however, you want to apply the character formatting in more than one location in the document, double-click the Format Painter button. After selecting all of the text or clicking on all of the words to which you want to apply the formatting, click the Format Painter button to turn it off.

Format Painter

Ctrl + Shift + C

Exercise 6.3 Formatting with Format Painter

1. With **U2T6-ProConcepts.docx** open, select the heading *Development Service Providers* and then click the Font group dialog box launcher.

2. Click *Candara* in the *Font* list box (you may need to scroll through the list box to display this option), click *Bold* in the *Font style* list box, and then click *12* in the *Size* list box.

3. Click OK to close the dialog box and then deselect the heading.

4. Click once on any character in the heading *Development Service Providers* and then double-click the Format Painter button in the Clipboard group on the Home tab.

   When Format Painter is active, the mouse pointer displays with a paintbrush attached.

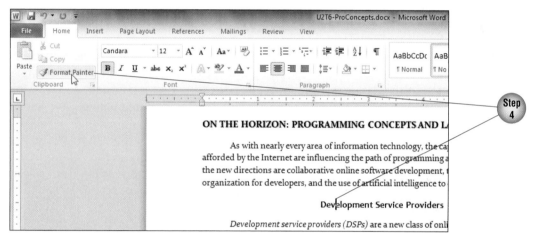

5. Scroll down in the document and then select the heading *Open-Source Development Toolkit*.

   With Format Painter active, selecting text applies formatting.

6. Select the heading *Software Writing Software*.

   This action applies the formatting to the heading.

7. Click once on the Format Painter button in the Clipboard group to turn off Format Painter.

8. Save **U2T6-ProConcepts.docx**.

Drilling Down

Changing the Default Font

When you create a new Word document, it is based by default on the Normal template, whose default font is 11-point Calibri. If you want future documents to automatically use a different font, you can change the default font at the Font dialog box. To do this, click the Font group dialog box launcher. At the Font dialog box, change to the desired font, font style, and font size, and then click the Set As Default button located toward the bottom of the dialog box. At the message that displays asking if you want to change the default, click the Yes button, and then click OK to close the Font dialog box.

Lesson 6.4   Aligning Text in Paragraphs

Alignment refers to the positioning of the lines of text in a document. By default, paragraphs in a Word document are aligned at the left margin and ragged at the right margin. Change this default alignment with the buttons in the Paragraph group on the Home tab or with the keyboard shortcuts shown in Table 6.3.

alignment The positioning of the lines of text in a document

Table 6.3 **Paragraph Alignment Buttons and Keyboard Shortcuts**

Alignment	Paragraph Group Button	Keyboard Shortcut
Left margin	▤	Ctrl + L
Center (between margins)	▤	Ctrl + E
Right margin	▤	Ctrl + R
Justified (left and right margins)	▤	Ctrl + J

You can change the alignment of text in paragraphs before or after you type it. If you change the alignment before you type the text, the alignment formatting is inserted in the paragraph mark. When you press Enter at the end of the paragraph, the paragraph formatting is continued. For example, if you click the Center button in the Paragraph group, type text for the first paragraph, and then press the Enter key, the insertion point for the second paragraph still displays centered between the left and right margins.

To return paragraph alignment to the default left-aligned setting, click the Align Left button in the Paragraph group. Recall that you can also return all paragraph formatting to the default by using the keyboard shortcut Ctrl + Q. This keyboard shortcut removes paragraph formatting from selected text. If you want to remove all formatting from selected text including character and paragraph formatting, click the Clear Formatting button in the Font group.

Quick Steps

Change Paragraph Alignment

Click desired alignment button in Paragraph group.

OR

1. Click Paragraph group dialog box launcher.
2. Click *Alignment* option down-pointing arrow.
3. Click desired alignment.
4. Click OK.

To change the alignment of existing text in a paragraph, position the insertion point anywhere within the paragraph and then apply the desired paragraph alignment. You do not need to select the entire paragraph. To change the alignment of several adjacent paragraphs in a document, select a portion of the first paragraph through a portion of the last paragraph and then apply paragraph alignment. You do not need to select all of the text in the paragraphs.

In addition to using the alignment buttons in the Paragraph group or the keyboard shortcuts to change paragraph alignment, you can also use the *Alignment* option at the Paragraph dialog box (shown in Figure 6.4). Display this dialog box by clicking the Paragraph group dialog box launcher located in the lower right corner of the Paragraph group on the Home tab. To change alignment, click the down-pointing arrow at the right side of the *Alignment* option box, click the desired alignment at the drop-down list, and then click OK to close the dialog box.

Figure 6.4 **Paragraph Dialog Box**

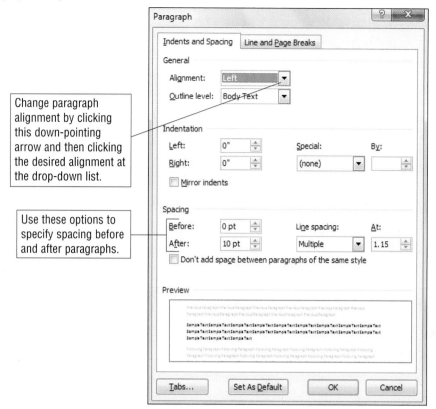

Change paragraph alignment by clicking this down-pointing arrow and then clicking the desired alignment at the drop-down list.

Use these options to specify spacing before and after paragraphs.

Exercise 6.4 Aligning Text in Paragraphs

1. With **U2T6-ProConcepts.docx** open, click any character in the title *ON THE HORIZON: PROGRAMMING CONCEPTS AND LANGUAGES* and then click the Center button ≡ in the Paragraph group on the Home tab.

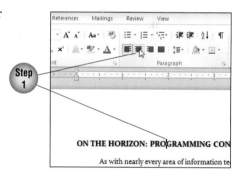

2. Click any character in the *Development Service Providers* heading and then press Ctrl + L to align the heading at the left margin.

3. Click any character in the *Open-Source Development Toolkit* heading and then press Ctrl + L to align the heading at the left margin.

4. Click any character in the *Software Writing Software* heading and then press Ctrl + L.

5. Click any character in the first paragraph of text in the document and then click the Justify button ≡ in the Paragraph group.

6. After looking at the justified paragraph, you decide to return to left alignment. To do this, click the Align Text Left button ≡ in the Paragraph group.

7. Press Ctrl + End to move the insertion point to the end of the document and then press the Enter key.

8. Press Ctrl + R.

   This keyboard shortcut changes the text alignment to right.

9. Type your first and last names and then press Enter.

10. Type **Date:**, press the spacebar once, and then press Alt + Shift + D.

    Alt + Shift + D is the keyboard shortcut to insert the current date.

11. Press the Enter key.

12. Return the alignment to left. To do this, click the Paragraph group dialog box launcher.

13. At the Paragraph dialog box, click the down-pointing arrow at the right side of the *Alignment* option and then click *Left* at the drop-down list.

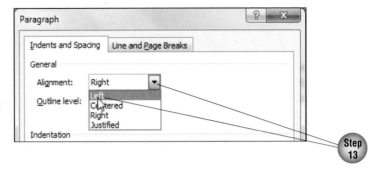

Step 13

14. Click OK to close the Paragraph dialog box.

15. Save **U2T6-ProConcepts.docx**.

Drilling Down | **Justifying Text**

When you apply the *Justify* alignment option to text, Word inserts additional space between the words and characters to expand the lines of text to align at the right margin. When justifying text, use a proportional typeface (rather than a monospaced typeface), edit text to fix lines that contain too much additional space between words, and consider hyphenating words. Use the Hyphenation button in the Page Setup group on the Page Layout tab to manually or automatically hyphenate words in a document.

Lesson 6.5   Changing Line Spacing

 2-2.1.1, 2 2.1.6

line spacing The vertical spacing between lines of text

Quick Steps

Change Line Spacing Using the Line and Paragraph Spacing Button

1. Click Line and Paragraph Spacing button.
2. Click desired option at drop-down list.

The default **line spacing**, or vertical space between lines of text, for Word documents is 1.15. In some documents, you may want to change to different line spacing such as single, 1.5, or double spacing. Change line spacing using the Line and Paragraph Spacing button in the Paragraph group on the Home tab, with keyboard shortcuts, or with options at the Paragraph dialog box. Open the Paragraph dialog box by clicking the Paragraph group dialog box launcher or by clicking the Line and Paragraph Spacing button and then clicking *Line Spacing Options*. Table 6.4 lists the keyboard shortcuts you can use to change line spacing.

Table 6.4 Line Spacing Keyboard Shortcuts

To change line spacing to	Press
single spacing	Ctrl + 1
double spacing	Ctrl + 2
1.5 line spacing	Ctrl + 5

You can also change line spacing at the Paragraph dialog box with the *Line spacing* option or the *At* option. If you click the down-pointing arrow at the right side of the *Line spacing* option, a drop-down list displays with a variety of spacing options. For example, to change the line spacing to double, you would click *Double* at the drop-down list. You can type a specific line spacing measurement in the *At* text box. For example, to change the line spacing to 1.75, type *1.75* in the *At* text box.

Quick Steps

Change Line Spacing Using the Paragraph Dialog Box

1. Open Paragraph dialog box.
2. Click *Line Spacing* option down-pointing arrow.
3. Click desired option.
4. Click OK.

OR

1. Open Paragraph dialog box.
2. Type desired line spacing in *At* text box.
3. Click OK.

Exercise 6.5 Changing Line Spacing

1. With **U2T6-ProConcepts.docx** open, select the entire document by pressing Ctrl + A.

2. Click the Line and Paragraph Spacing button in the Paragraph group on the Home tab and then click *1.5* at the drop-down list.

3. Deselect the text and then scroll through the document. After viewing the document with 1.5 line spacing, you decide to decrease the line spacing to 1.3. To begin, press Ctrl + A to select the entire document, click the Line and Paragraph Spacing button, and then click *Line Spacing Options* at the drop-down list.

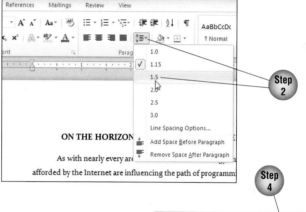

Clicking *Line Spacing Options* causes the Paragraph dialog box to display.

4. At the Paragraph dialog box, click in the *At* text box in the *Spacing* section and then type **1.3**.

The Paragraph dialog box also contains a *Line spacing* option. Click the down-pointing arrow at the right side of the option to display a drop-down list with spacing choices.

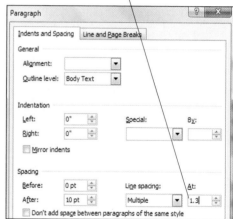

5. Click OK to close the dialog box and then deselect the text.

6. Save, print, and then close **U2T6-ProConcepts.docx**.

Drilling Down

Revealing Formatting

You can use the Reveal Formatting task pane to display the font, paragraph, and section formatting, such as line spacing, that has been applied to specific text in a document. To do this, select or position the insertion point near the text whose formatting you want to reveal. Display the Reveal Formatting task pane by pressing the keyboard shortcut Shift + F1.

Lesson 6.6 Changing Paragraph Spacing

)IC³ 2-2.1.1; 2-2.1.6

By default, Word applies 10 points of spacing after each paragraph, but you can remove, increase, or decrease this spacing. You can also insert spacing above the paragraph. To change spacing before or after a paragraph, use the *Spacing Before* and *Spacing After* measurement boxes located in the Paragraph group on the Page Layout tab, or the *Before* and/or *After* options at the Paragraph dialog box with the Indents and Spacing tab selected.

Spacing before or after a paragraph is part of the paragraph and will be moved, copied, or deleted with the paragraph. If there is spacing before a paragraph and the paragraph falls at the top of a page, such as with a title or heading, Word ignores the spacing.

Spacing, either before or after paragraphs, is measured in points. A vertical inch contains approximately 72 points. To add spacing before or after a paragraph, click the Page Layout tab, select the current measurement in the *Spacing Before* or the *Spacing After* measurement box, and then type the desired number of points. You can also click the up- or down-pointing arrows at the right side of the *Spacing Before* and *Spacing After* measurement boxes to increase or decrease the amount of spacing.

If you apply paragraph or line spacing to text in a document and then want to apply the same formatting in other locations in the document, consider using the Repeat command. The Repeat command, the F4 key, and the keyboard shortcut Ctrl + Y all repeat the last action performed. Note that the Repeat command only works for the action that was most recently performed—you cannot use it to repeat any previous actions.

Exercise 6.6 Changing Paragraph Spacing

1. Open **WritingProcess.docx** and then save the document with Save As and name it **U2T6-WritingProcess**.

2. Press Ctrl + A to select the entire document and then change the font to Cambria and the font size to 12. Click anywhere in the document to deselect the text.

3. Press Ctrl + Home to move the insertion point to the beginning of the document.

4. With the insertion point positioned at the beginning of the title *THE WRITING PROCESS*, click the Line and Paragraph Spacing button and then click *Add Space After Paragraph*.

   This inserts 12 points of space below the heading.

5. Press Ctrl + End, click anywhere in the *REFERENCES* title, click the Line and Paragraph Spacing button, and then click *Add Space After Paragraph*.

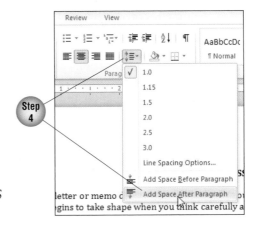

6. Click anywhere in the *Define Purpose* heading and then click the Page Layout tab.

7. Click twice on the up-pointing arrow at the right side of the *Spacing Before* option in the Paragraph group.

    12 pt should now display in the measurement box.

8. Click once on the up-pointing arrow at the right side of the *Spacing After* option in the Paragraph group.

    6 pt should now display in the measurement box.

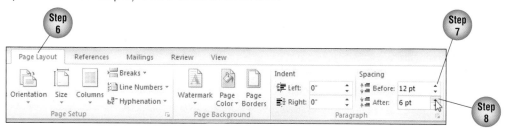

9. Click anywhere in the *Identify Reader* heading and then click the Paragraph group dialog box launcher.

10. At the Paragraph dialog box, click twice on the up-pointing arrow at the right side of the *Before* option.

    Clicking twice on the up-pointing arrow at the right side of the *Before* text box inserts *12 pt* in the text box.

11. Click once on the up-pointing arrow at the right side of the *After* option.

    This action inserts *6 pt* in the text box.

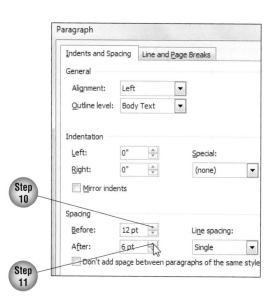

12. Click OK to close the dialog box.

13. Click anywhere in the *Select and Organize Information* heading and then press F4.

    Pressing F4 repeats the paragraph spacing you selected in Steps 10 and 11.

14. Click anywhere in each of the remaining headings (*Write First Draft, Write Strong Paragraphs, Use Active Voice,* and *Edit and Proofread*) and then press F4.

15. Save **U2T6-WritingProcess.docx**.

Drilling Down

Comparing Formatting

Along with displaying formatting applied to text, you can use the Reveal Formatting task pane to compare formatting of two text selections to determine what formatting is different. To compare formatting, press Shift + F1 to display the Reveal Formatting task pane and then select the first instance of formatting to be compared. Click the *Compare to another selection* check box located toward the top of the task pane and then select the second instance of formatting. Any differences between the two selections will display in the *Formatting differences* list box.

Lesson 6.7 Applying Numbering and Bullets

2-1.3.1, 2-2.1.7

If you want to draw the reader's attention to a list of items, consider inserting numbers or bullets before each item. If the list of items is sequential, it is usually best to insert numbers. To do this, select the desired text and then click the Numbering button in the Paragraph group on the Home tab. If the list of items is in no particular order, you may want to apply bullets instead. To do this, select the desired text and then click the Bullets button in the Paragraph group on the Home tab. Figure 6.5 shows paragraphs preceded by bullets.

Figure 6.5 Bulleted Paragraphs

- This is a paragraph preceded by a bullet. A bullet indicates a list of items or topics.
- This is another paragraph preceded by a bullet. You can easily create bulleted paragraphs by typing certain symbols before the text or with the Bullets button in the Paragraph group.

Quick Steps

Insert Numbering

1. Select text.
2. Click Numbering button.

Insert Bullets

1. Select text.
2. Click Bullets button.

You can also create a numbered list simply by beginning to type—Word will automatically format the list for you. For example, when you type *1.* and then press the spacebar, Word indents the number approximately 0.25 inch. When you type the text for the first item in your list, Word hang-indents the text in the paragraph 0.5 inch from the left margin. When you press the Enter key, Word inserts *2.* 0.25 inch from the left margin at the beginning of the next paragraph. Continue typing items and Word will continue inserting the next number in the list. To turn off numbering, press Enter after Word inserts the next number or click the Numbering button in the Paragraph group. You can automatically create a bulleted list by beginning a paragraph with the symbol *, >, or -. Type one of the symbols, press the spacebar, type text, and then press Enter. The type of bullet that Word will insert depends on the type of character you enter. For example, if you use the asterisk (*) symbol, Word inserts a round bullet; if you type the greater than symbol (>), Word inserts an arrow bullet.

Exercise 6.7 Inserting Numbering and Bullets

1. With **U2T6-WritingProcess.docx** open, select text from the paragraph in the *Define Purpose* section that reads *What am I trying to accomplish?* through the paragraph that reads *To direct someone?*, click the Home tab, and then click the Numbering button in the Paragraph group.

2. Position the insertion point at the end of the second numbered paragraph (the paragraph that displays as *2. What is my purpose for writing?*) and then press the Enter key once.

   Numbering before paragraphs is changed automatically when paragraphs of text are inserted and/or deleted. In this case, pressing the Enter key automatically inserts *3.* and renumbers the third paragraph to *4.*

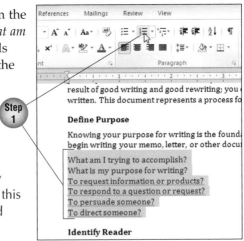

3. Type **To inform someone?**

4. Move the insertion point to the beginning of the sentence *To inform someone?* and then press the Tab key.

    Pressing the Tab key indents the text, inserts the letter *a.*, and automatically renumbers the subsequent text.

5. Indent the remaining four numbered text lines to the same level as the letter *a.*

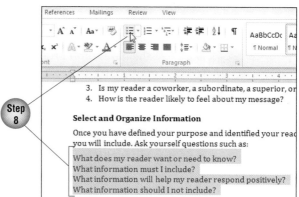

6. Select text from the paragraph in the *Identify Reader* section that reads *Who is my reader?* through the paragraph *How is the reader likely to feel about my message?* and then click the Numbering button in the Paragraph group.

7. Select the sentence *Is the audience one person or a group?* and then press the Delete key.

    This action deletes the paragraph and automatically renumbers the remaining paragraphs.

8. Select text from the paragraph in the *Select and Organize Information* section that reads *What does my reader want or need to know?* through the paragraph *What information should I not include?* and then click the Bullets button ⊞ in the Paragraph group on the Home tab.

    Clicking the Bullets button inserts a round bullet before each paragraph. Other bullet options are available by clicking the Bullets button arrow.

9. Select text from the paragraph in the *Use Active Voice* section that begins *Your writing is formal…* through the paragraph that begins *You wish to deemphasize…* and then click the Bullets button.

10. Save **U2T6-WritingProcess.docx**.

Drilling Down

Turning Off Automatic Numbering and Bulleting

If you do not want automatic numbering or bulleting in a document, turn off the features at the AutoCorrect dialog box with the AutoFormat As You Type tab selected. To display this dialog box, click the File tab and then click the Options button located below the Help tab. At the Word Options dialog box, click the *Proofing* option in the left panel and then click the AutoCorrect Options button. At the AutoCorrect dialog box, click the AutoFormat As You Type tab, and then click the *Automatic numbered lists* check box and/or the *Automatic bulleted lists* check box to remove the check mark.

Inserting Multilevel List Numbering

Use the Multilevel List button in the Paragraph group on the Home tab to specify the type of numbering for paragraphs of text at the left margin, first tab, second tab, and so on. Apply predesigned multilevel numbering to text in a document by clicking the Multilevel List button and then clicking the desired numbering style at the drop-down gallery.

Lesson 6.8   Indenting Text

2-2.1.2, 2-2.1.3

indent A type of formatting that sets lines of text away from the margins

hanging indent Paragraph formatting where every line except the first one is indented

Quick Steps

Indent Text

Drag indent marker(s) on Ruler.

OR

1. Click Paragraph group dialog box launcher.
2. Insert measurement in *Left*, *Right*, and/or *By* text box.
3. Click OK.

By default, text in Word aligns at the left margin. You can change this by changing the text alignment or by applying an **indent** to the text, which is a type of formatting that sets lines of text away from the margins. You can indent the first line of text in a paragraph, indent all lines of text in a paragraph, or indent all lines of a paragraph except the first one (called a **hanging indent**). You can indent text from the left margin, the right margin, or both. Several methods are available for indenting, including using the buttons in the Paragraph group on the Home tab, the markers on the Ruler, the options at the Paragraph dialog box, and the keyboard shortcuts.

Click the Decrease Indent button in the Paragraph group on the Home tab to decrease the indent and click the Increase Indent button to increase the indent. You can also indent text with markers on the Ruler, as shown in Figure 6.6. If the Ruler is not visible, turn it on by clicking the View Ruler button located at the top of the vertical scroll bar. In addition to buttons in the Paragraph group and markers on the Ruler, you can indent text with the keyboard shortcut commands shown in Table 6.5.

Table 6.5 Keyboard Shortcuts for Indenting Text

Indentation	Keyboard Shortcut
Indent text from left margin	Ctrl + M
Decrease indent from left margin	Ctrl + Shift + M
Create hanging indent	Ctrl + T
Remove hanging indent	Ctrl + Shift + T

Figure 6.6 Ruler and Indent Marker

Alignment button | First Line Indent marker

Left Indent marker | Hanging Indent marker | Right Indent marker

Exercise 6.8   Indenting Text

1. With **U2T6-WritingProcess.docx** open, click anywhere in the first paragraph of text (the paragraph that begins *An effective letter or memo…*).

2. Position the mouse pointer on the First Line Indent marker on the Ruler, hold down the left mouse button, drag the marker to the 0.5-inch mark on the Ruler, and then release the button.

Step 2

If the Ruler is not visible, turn it on by clicking the View Ruler button located at the top of the vertical scroll bar. If you want to position a marker at a precise location on the Ruler, hold down the Alt key while dragging the marker.

3. Select the numbered and lettered paragraphs in the *Define Purpose* section and then click the Increase Indent button ⊞ in the Paragraph group on the Home tab.

4. Select the numbered paragraphs in the *Identify Reader* section and then press F4.

5. Select the bulleted paragraphs in the *Select and Organize Information* section and then press F4.

6. Select the bulleted paragraphs in the *Use Active Voice* section and then click the Paragraph group dialog box launcher, located in the lower right corner of the Paragraph group.

7. At the Paragraph dialog box, click the up-pointing arrow at the right side of the *Left* option box in the *Indentation* section until *0.5"* displays in the option box.

8. Click the up-pointing arrow at the right side of the *Right* option box in the *Indentation* section until *0.5"* displays in the option box.

9. Click OK to close the Paragraph dialog box.

10. Press Ctrl + End to move the insertion point to the end of the document and then select the paragraphs of text below the title *REFERENCES*.

11. Press Ctrl + T.

Ctrl + T is the keyboard shortcut to create a hanging indent. In a hanging indent, the text in the first line is aligned at the left margin and second and subsequent lines are indented. The Ctrl + T keyboard shortcut indents the second and subsequent lines of the paragraph one-half inch from the left margin. You can change this measurement with the *By* option in the *Indentation* section of the Paragraph dialog box.

12. Save **U2T6-WritingProcess.docx**.

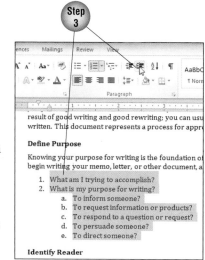

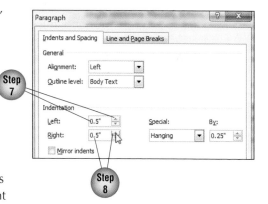

Drilling Down

Creating an Outdent

Another type of indent is a negative indent, referred to as an "outdent," which moves the text out into the left margin. Use an outdent to highlight or call specific attention to a section of writing. To create an outdent, select the text or paragraphs you want to extend into the left margin, and then click the Page Layout tab. Click the down-pointing arrow at the right side of the *Indent Left* measurement box (located in the Paragraph group) until the desired negative measurement displays in the measurement box.

Lesson 6.9 Applying Borders and Shading

IC³ 2-2.1.6

border A frame that surrounds an item in a document, such as a paragraph or an entire page

Every paragraph you create in Word is surrounded by an invisible frame. When you make this frame visible, it is known as applying a **border**. You can apply a border to specific sides of a paragraph or to an entire paragraph, group of paragraphs, or page. You can also customize the border lines and add shading. You may want to apply borders to highlight a specific paragraph of text or to add visual appeal to your document. Add borders and shading to paragraphs in a document using the Borders and Shading buttons in the Paragraph group or options from the Borders and Shading dialog box.

When a border is added to a paragraph, the border expands and contracts as text is inserted or deleted from the paragraph. You can create a border around a single paragraph or around multiple paragraphs. One method for creating a border is to use options from the Borders button in the Paragraph group. Click the Borders button arrow to display a drop-down list with options for creating or removing borders.

shading A formatting technique that applies color behind text and objects

With the Shading button in the Paragraph group, you can add shading to text in a document. **Shading** is a formatting technique that applies color behind text and objects. Select the text or object you want to shade and then click the Shading button. This applies a background color behind the text. Click the Shading button arrow and a Shading drop-down gallery displays with options for applying or removing shading.

Quick Steps

Insert Borders and Shading

1. Select text.
2. Click Borders button arrow.
3. Click *Borders and Shading*.
4. Choose desired border(s).
5. Click Shading tab.
6. Choose desired shading.
7. Click OK.

If you want to further customize paragraph borders and shading, use options at the Borders and Shading dialog box. Display this dialog box by clicking the Borders button arrow and then clicking *Borders and Shading* at the drop-down list. This displays the Borders and Shading dialog box with the Borders tab selected, as shown in Figure 6.7. At this dialog box, specify the desired border, style, color, and width. Click the Shading tab to display shading options, as shown in Figure 6.8.

Figure 6.7 Borders and Shading Dialog Box with the Borders Tab Selected

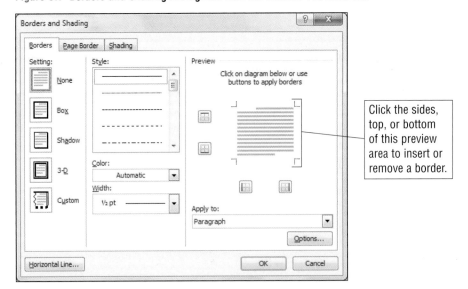

Click the sides, top, or bottom of this preview area to insert or remove a border.

Figure 6.8 Borders and Shading Dialog Box with the Shading Tab Selected

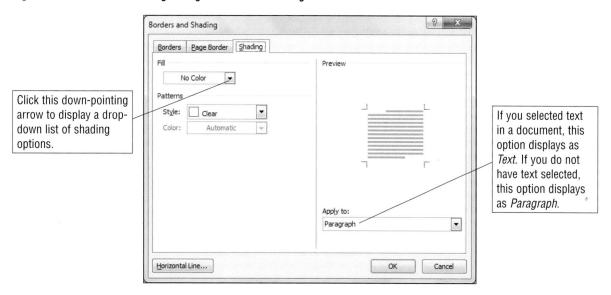

Click this down-pointing arrow to display a drop-down list of shading options.

If you selected text in a document, this option displays as *Text.* If you do not have text selected, this option displays as *Paragraph.*

Exercise 6.9 Applying Borders and Shading

1. With **U2T6-WritingProcess.docx** open, position the insertion point on any character in the title *THE WRITING PROCESS.*

2. Click the Borders button arrow ⊞▾ in the Paragraph group on the Home tab and then click *Bottom Border* at the drop-down list.

3. Click the Shading button arrow ◇▾ in the Paragraph group and then click *Olive Green, Accent 3, Lighter 40%* at the drop-down gallery.

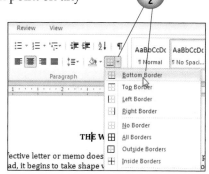

Step 2

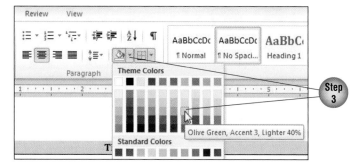

Step 3

4. Click once on the Format Painter button in the Clipboard group on the Home tab.

5. Click on any character in the title *REFERENCES* (located toward the end of the document).

   Since Format Painter is turned on, clicking in the *REFERENCES* title applies the border and shading formatting.

6. Click on any character in the heading *Define Purpose.*

7. Click the Borders button arrow and then click *Borders and Shading* at the drop-down list.

8. At the Borders and Shading dialog box with the Borders tab selected, click the down-pointing arrow at the right side of the *Style* list box until the first double-line option displays and then click the double-line option.

9. Click the *None* option in the *Setting* section located at the left side of the dialog box.

10. Click the down-pointing arrow at the right side of the *Color* option box and then click *Olive Green, Accent 3, Darker 50%*.

11. Click the down-pointing arrow at the right side of the *Width* option box and then click *3/4 pt* at the drop-down list.

12. Click the bottom border of the box in the *Preview* section of the dialog box.

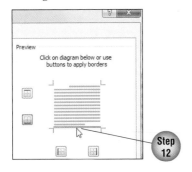

13. Click the Shading tab.

14. Click the down-pointing arrow at the right side of the *Fill* option and then click *Olive Green, Accent 3, Lighter 60%*.

15. Click OK to close the dialog box.

16. Click anywhere in the heading *Identify Reader* and then press F4.

    This repeats the border and shading formatting you applied to the *Define Purpose* heading.

17. Click anywhere in each of the remaining headings (*Select and Organize Information*, *Write First Draft*, *Write Strong Paragraphs*, *Use Active Voice*, and *Edit and Proofread*) and then press F4.

18. Save and then print **U2T6-WritingProcess.docx**.

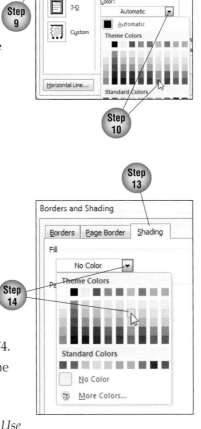

Drilling Down

Inserting Horizontal Lines

Word includes a horizontal line feature that inserts a horizontal line graphic in a document. To display the Horizontal Line dialog box (shown at the right), display the Borders and Shading dialog box with any tab selected and then click the Horizontal Line button located toward the bottom of the dialog box. Click the desired horizontal line in the list box and then click OK to insert the line in the document.

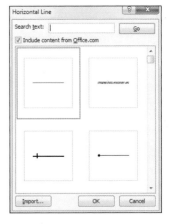

Lesson 6.10 Applying Styles

 2-2.1.11

A Word document contains a number of predesigned paragraph and character formats called **Quick Styles** that work together to help you create a professional-looking document. Some of the styles in the default Quick Styles set display as style thumbnails in the Styles group on the Home tab. Display additional styles by clicking the More button that displays at the right side of the style thumbnails. This displays a drop-down gallery of style choices. To apply a style, position the insertion point in the paragraph of text to which you want to apply the style, click the More button at the right side of the thumbnails in the Styles group, and then click the desired style at the drop-down gallery.

Recall that Word documents contain default formatting that includes 10 points of spacing after paragraphs and line spacing of 1.15. You can remove this default formatting, as well as any character formatting that has been applied to the text in your document, by applying the No Spacing style to your text. This style is located in the Styles group.

Word contains a number of Quick Styles sets that you can use to apply formatting to a document. To change to a different Quick Styles set, click the Change Styles button in the Styles group on the Home tab and then point to *Style Set*. At the side menu that displays, click the desired set to change your document's formatting. Use options at the Change Styles button drop-down list to change the Quick Styles set colors and fonts. Click the Change Styles button and point to *Paragraph Spacing* and a side menu displays predesigned paragraph spacing styles you can apply to the document. Hover the mouse arrow pointer over a style in the side menu to display a ScreenTip describing what formatting the style will apply.

You can also create your own style based on formatting you have applied to a document. To do this, apply the desired formatting, click the More button at the right side of the style thumbnails in the Styles group, and then click *Save Selection as a New Quick Style* at the drop-down gallery. At the Create New Style from Formatting dialog box, type a name for the new style and then click OK. The style is inserted in the Quick Styles gallery and is available for the current document.

You can also modify an existing style. When you do this, Word automatically updates any areas in the document to which the style has already been applied. To modify an existing style, right-click the style thumbnail in the Styles group and then click *Modify* at the shortcut menu. At the Modify Styles dialog box, make the desired changes and then click OK.

Quick Styles
Predesigned paragraph and character formats that work together to help you create professional-looking documents

Quick Steps

Change Quick Styles Set

1. Click Change Styles button.
2. Point to *Style Set*.
3. Click desired set.

Apply a Quick Style

1. Position insertion point in desired paragraph.
2. Click desired style in Styles group.

Create a Style

1. Apply formatting to text.
2. Click More button in Styles group.
3. Click *Save Selection as a New Quick Style*.
4. Type new style name.
5. Click OK.

Modify a Style

1. Right-click desired style in Styles group.
2. Click *Modify*.
3. Make desired changes.
4. Click OK.

Keyboard Shortcuts

Heading 1 Style
Alt + Ctrl + 1

Heading 2 Style
Alt + Ctrl + 2

Heading 3 Style
Alt + Ctrl + 3

Normal Style
Ctrl + Shift + N

Exercise 6.10 Applying, Creating, and Modifying Styles

1. With **U2T6-WritingProcess.docx** open, press Ctrl + Home to move the insertion point to the beginning of the document.

2. Click the Change Styles button in the Styles group on the Home tab, point to *Style Set*, and then click *Formal* at the drop-down gallery.

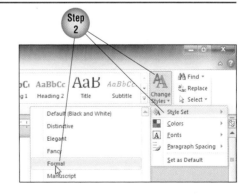

3. Position the insertion point on any character in the title *THE WRITING PROCESS* and then click the Heading 1 style thumbnail in the Styles group on the Home tab.

The Heading 1 style in the Formal Quick Styles set changes the font color, adds spacing before and after the heading, and inserts a bottom border. Applying this heading style also removes the border and shading you inserted in the previous activity.

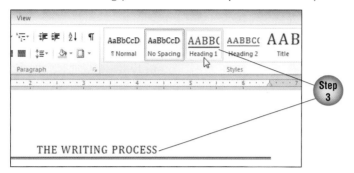

4. Press Ctrl + End, click anywhere in the title *REFERENCES*, and then click the Heading 1 style thumbnail in the Styles group.

5. Click anywhere in the heading *Define Purpose* and then click the Heading 2 style thumbnail in the Styles group.

The most recently selected styles display in the Styles group.

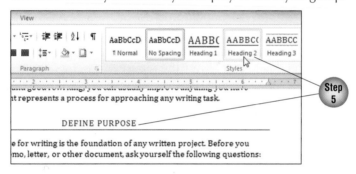

6. Apply the Heading 2 style to the remaining headings in the document (*Identify Reader, Select and Organize Information, Write First Draft, Write Strong Paragraphs, Use Active Voice,* and *Edit and Proofread*).

7. Save and then print **U2T6-WritingProcess.docx**.

8. Click the Change Styles button in the Styles group on the Home tab, point to *Style Set,* and then click *Traditional* at the drop-down gallery.

9. Change the font colors for the *Traditional* Quick Styles set by clicking the Change Styles button, pointing to *Colors,* and then clicking *Austin* at the drop-down gallery.

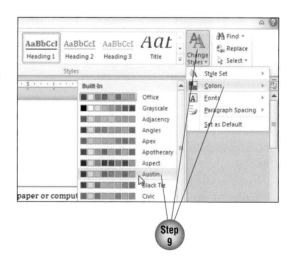

10. Change the fonts applied by the *Traditional* Quick Styles set by clicking the Change Styles button, pointing to *Fonts*, scrolling down the gallery, and then clicking *Civic* at the drop-down gallery.

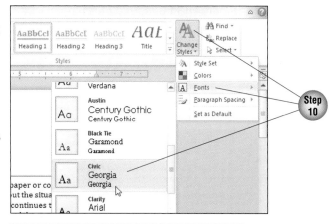

Step 10

11. Change the paragraph spacing applied by the *Traditional* Quick Styles set by clicking the Change Styles button, pointing to *Paragraph Spacing*, and then clicking *Tight* at the drop-down gallery.

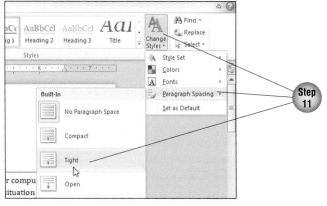

Step 11

12. Position the insertion point on any character in the paragraph of text below the heading THE WRITING PROCESS, click the Justify button in the Paragraph group, click the Line and Paragraph Spacing button in the Paragraph group, and then click *1.0* at the drop-down gallery.

13. Create a style based on the paragraph formatting you applied in the previous step. Begin by clicking the More button at the right side of the thumbnails in the Styles group and then clicking *Save Selection as a New Quick Style* at the drop-down gallery.

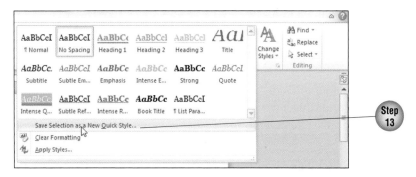

Step 13

14. At the Create New Style from Formatting dialog box, type **ReportPara** and then click OK.

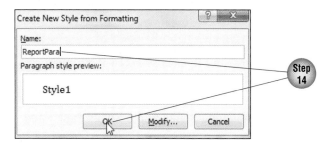

Step 14

15. Position the insertion point on any character in the first paragraph of text below the heading *Define Purpose* and then click the *ReportPara* style in the Styles group.

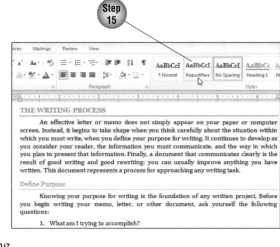

16. Following steps similar to those in Step 15, apply the ReportPara style to the following paragraphs:

    - First paragraph below the *Identify Reader* heading
    - First paragraph below the *Select and Organize Information* heading
    - Paragraph below the bulleted paragraphs in the *Select and Organize Information* section
    - Paragraph below the *Write First Draft* heading
    - Two paragraphs below the *Write Strong Paragraphs* heading
    - First paragraph below the *Use Active Voice* heading
    - Paragraph below the *Edit and Proofread* heading

17. Save the document and then print the first page of the document.

18. Modify the ReportPara style by right-clicking the ReportPara thumbnail in the Styles group and then clicking *Modify* at the drop-down list.

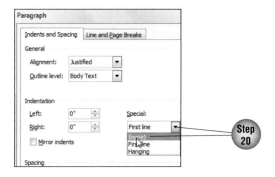

19. At the Modify Style dialog box, click the Format button located toward the bottom of the dialog box and then click *Paragraph* at the drop-down list.

20. At the Paragraph dialog box, click the down-pointing arrow at the right side of the *Special* option box and then click *(none)* at the drop-down list.

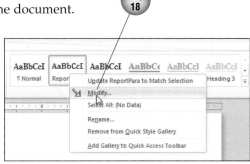

21. Click the up-pointing arrow at the right side of the *Before* option in the *Spacing* section (this inserts *6 pt* in the *Before* option box) and then click OK to close the dialog box.

22. Click OK to close the Modify Style dialog box.

    Scroll through the document and notice that all paragraphs to which the ReportPara style had been applied were automatically updated.

23. Save, print, and then close **U2T6-WritingProcess.docx**.

Drilling Down

Applying Styles at the Styles Task Pane

The Styles task pane provides another method for applying a style. Display the Styles task pane by clicking the Styles group dialog box launcher. The styles in the currently selected Quick Styles set display in the task pane followed by either a paragraph symbol (¶) or a character symbol (a). A paragraph symbol indicates that the style applies paragraph formatting and a character symbol indicates that the style applies character formatting. If both characters display to the right of a style, the style applies both paragraph and character formatting.

Lesson 6.11 Setting Tabs

 2-2.1.4

Another default setting in Word is that each document contains left tabs set every 0.5 inch. However, you have the option to change this setting. You can set your own tabs using the Ruler or the Tabs dialog box. The types of tabs that can be set on the Ruler are left, center, right, decimal, and bar. The small button at the left side of the Ruler is called the Alignment button. Each time you click the Alignment button, a different tab or paragraph alignment symbol displays. To set a tab, display the desired alignment symbol on the Ruler and then click on the Ruler at the desired position. Table 6.6 lists the Alignment button symbols and what type of tab each will set.

Quick Steps

Set a Tab on the Ruler
1. Display desired alignment symbol on Alignment button.
2. Click desired position on Ruler.

Table 6.6 **Tab Alignment Symbols**

Alignment Button Symbol	Type of Tab	Description
L	Left tab	Aligns text at the left
⊥	Center tab	Distributes text equally at each side of tab
⌐	Right tab	Aligns text at the right
⊥	Decimal tab	Aligns text at the decimal point
I	Bar tab	Inserts a vertical bar at the location of the tab

Exercise 6.11 Setting Tabs

1. Open a blank document by pressing Ctrl + N.

   Ctrl + N is the keyboard shortcut for opening a new document.

2. Click the No Spacing style thumbnail in the Styles group on the Home tab.

3. Type **TRAINING SESSIONS** centered and bolded, as shown in Figure 6.9.

4. Press the Enter key twice and then return the paragraph alignment back to left and turn off bold.

5. Make sure the left tab symbol ⌐ displays in the Alignment button at the left side of the Ruler.

6. Position the arrow pointer below the 0.5-inch mark on the Ruler and then click the left mouse button.

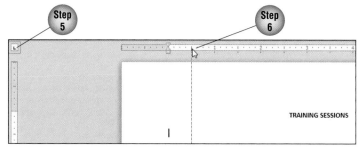

7. Click once on the Alignment button located at the left side of the Ruler to display the center tab symbol ⊥.

8. Position the arrow pointer below the 3.25-inch mark on the Ruler and then click the left mouse button.

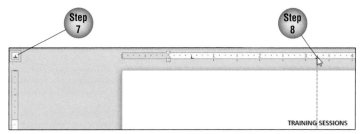

9. Click once on the Alignment button located at the left side of the Ruler to display the right tab symbol ⌐.

10. Position the arrow pointer below the 6-inch mark on the Ruler and then click the left mouse button.

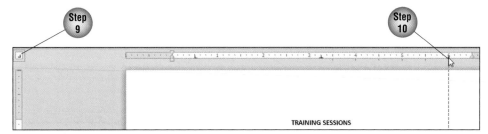

11. Type the text shown in Figure 6.9, pressing the Tab key before typing each tabbed entry. Make sure you press the Tab key before typing the entry in the first column and that you bold the text in the first row.

12. After typing the last entry in the third column, press the Enter key twice and then click the Clear Formatting button 🧹 in the Font group on the Home tab.

    Clicking the Clear Formatting button removes paragraph and character formatting. You can also remove paragraph formatting by pressing the keyboard shortcut Ctrl + Q and remove character formatting by pressing the keyboard shortcut Ctrl + spacebar.

13. Save the document and name it **U2T6-Training**.

Figure 6.9 Exercise 6.11 Text

TRAINING SESSIONS

Session	Price	Date
Writing Business Documents	$189	Tuesday, January 10
Proofing Business Documents	$125	Wednesday, January 18
Using Word 2010	$175	Friday, January 20
Using Excel 2010	$159	Thursday, January 26
Using PowerPoint 2010	$119	Friday, January 27

Drilling Down

Moving a Tab

Move a tab on the Ruler by positioning the mouse pointer over the tab marker you wish to move. Hold down the left mouse button, drag the symbol to the new location on the Ruler, and then release the mouse button.

Deleting a Tab

Delete a tab from the Ruler by positioning the arrow pointer on the tab marker, holding down the left mouse button, dragging the symbol down into the document, and then releasing the mouse button.

Setting a Decimal Tab

Word gives you the option of setting a decimal tab for column entries you want aligned at the decimal point. To set a decimal tab, click the Alignment button located at the left side of the Ruler until the decimal tab symbol displays and then click on the desired position on the Ruler.

Lesson 6.12 Setting Tabs with Leaders

IC³ 2-2.1.4

You can also set tabs with leaders, which are useful for documents in which you want to guide the reader's eyes from one element to another (such as from a chapter title to a page number in a table of contents). **Leaders** are a visual element designed to direct a reader's eye across a page. They can be periods, hyphens, underlines, or a variety of other characters. You can set tabs with leaders using the options at the Tabs dialog box. To display this dialog box (shown in Figure 6.10) click the Paragraph group dialog box launcher and then click the Tabs button at the Paragraph dialog box. At the Tabs dialog box, choose the type of tab, the type of leader, and then enter a tab position measurement.

leaders Visual elements, such as periods or hyphens, designed to direct a reader's eyes across the page

Quick Steps

Set a Tab with Leaders
1. Click Paragraph group dialog box launcher.
2. Click Tabs button.
3. Type tab measurement.
4. Click desired alignment.
5. Click desired leader.
6. Click Set.
7. Click OK.

Figure 6.10 Tabs Dialog Box

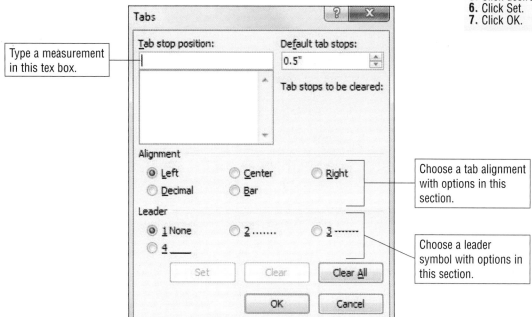

Type a measurement in this tex box.

Choose a tab alignment with options in this section.

Choose a leader symbol with options in this section.

Exercise 6.12 Setting Tabs and Tabs with Leaders

1. With **U2T6-Training.docx** open, press Ctrl + End to move the insertion point to the end of the document.

2. Click the No Spacing style thumbnail in the Styles group on the Home tab.

3. Type **TABLE OF CONTENTS** bolded and centered, as shown in Figure 6.11.

4. Press the Enter key twice and then return the paragraph alignment back to left and turn off bold.

5. Set a left tab and a right tab with leaders at the Tabs dialog box. To begin, click the Paragraph group dialog box launcher and then click the Tabs button located in the lower left corner of the Paragraph dialog box.

6. At the Tabs dialog box, make sure *Left* is selected in the *Alignment* section of the dialog box. (If it is not, click *Left*.) With the insertion point positioned in the *Tab stop position* text box, type **1** and then click the Set button.

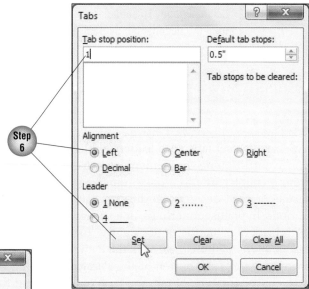

7. Type **5.5** in the *Tab stop position* text box, click *Right* in the *Alignment* section of the dialog box, and then click 2..... in the *Leader* section of the dialog box.

8. Click the Set button and then click OK to close the dialog box.

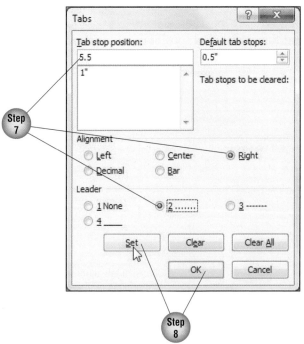

9. Type the remaining text shown in Figure 6.11, making sure you press the Tab key before typing the first text entry.

10. Save, print, and then close **U2T6-Training.docx**.

Figure 6.11 Exercise 6.12 Text

TABLE OF CONTENTS

Editing Information 8
Organizing Information 12
Proofreading a Document... 25
Formatting a Business Letter 31
Preparing a Resume 35
Writing a Cover Page 40

Drilling Down

Clearing Tabs at the Tabs Dialog Box

At the Tabs dialog box, you can clear an individual tab or all tabs in a document. To clear all tabs, click the Clear All button. To clear an individual tab, specify the tab position and then click the Clear button.

Delving Deeper

More Information for IC³

 2-2.1.16

Formatting a Business Report

Business reports are typically multiple-page, informative documents written for a specific purpose: to analyze data, to present a proposal, to report on activities, to discuss various solutions to a problem, and so on. Report formats vary widely among organizations, so whatever formatting options you choose, be certain they are consistent throughout the document. The front matter of a business report typically includes a letter of transmittal, a cover page or title page, a table of contents, a list of tables or figures, and a preface. The body of a business report generally includes a summary of the report; a background section, which describes the circumstances that led to the report; a section for supporting data or findings of the report; a conclusion that relates the findings to the purpose of the report; recommendations based on the conclusion; and a follow-up section that states the ways in which the writer intends to act on the report's recommendations. The end matter of a business report usually includes endnotes, a works cited page, and appendices.

Business reports are generally formatted as single-spaced with 1-inch top, bottom, left, and right margins. A half inch of extra space is added to the top margin for the first page of the report, and if the report is bound, an additional half inch of extra space is applied to the margin on the bound side. When a business report is unbound or left-bound, page numbering is inserted in the top right margin of the page. Arabic numbers (1,2,3) are used for the body of the report and the appendices, while lowercase Roman numerals (i, ii, iii) are used for the preface pages.

TOPIC SUMMARY

- The appearance of a document on the document screen and how it looks when printed is called the document's format.
- In Word, a paragraph is any amount of text followed by a paragraph mark or line break (a stroke of the Enter key).
- The top row in the Font group on the Home tab contains buttons for changing the font and font size. The bottom row contains buttons for applying typestyles and effects.
- With buttons in the Font group, you can apply font effects such as superscript, subscript, and strikethrough.
- Some buttons in the Font group have corresponding keyboard shortcuts. Refer to Table 6.1 for a list of these shortcuts.
- A font consists of three elements: typeface, type size, and typestyle.
- A typeface is a set of characters with a common design and shape. Typefaces are either monospaced or proportional. Proportional typefaces are divided into two main categories: serif and sans serif.
- Type size is measured in points—the higher the point size, the larger the characters.
- A typestyle is a variation of style within a certain typeface. You can apply typestyle formatting with buttons in the Font group.
- The Mini toolbar automatically displays above selected text. Use buttons on this toolbar to apply formatting to selected text.
- With options at the Font dialog box, you can change the font, font size, and font style and apply specific effects.
- Click the Show/Hide ¶ button in the Paragraph group on the Home tab or press Ctrl + Shift + * to turn on the display of nonprinting characters.
- Use the Format Painter button in the Clipboard group on the Home tab to copy character formatting that you have already applied to text to different locations in the document.
- By default, paragraphs in a Word document are aligned at the left margin and ragged at the right margin. Change this default alignment with buttons in the Paragraph group, at the Paragraph dialog box, or by using the keyboard shortcuts for left, center, right, or justify.
- When you create a new paragraph, Word inserts into the paragraph mark any paragraph formatting that is turned on.
- Change line spacing by using the Line and Paragraph Spacing button in the Paragraph group on the Home tab, keyboard shortcuts, or the options at the Paragraph dialog box.
- Increase or decrease spacing before and after paragraphs using the *Spacing Before* and *Spacing After* measurement boxes in the Paragraph group on the Page Layout tab or using the *Before* and/or *After* options at the Paragraph dialog box.
- Repeat the last action by pressing the F4 key or Ctrl + Y.
- Number paragraphs with the Numbering button in the Paragraph group on the Home tab, and insert bullets before paragraphs with the Bullets button.
- Indent text in paragraphs by using the indent buttons in the Paragraph group on the Home tab, the indent buttons in the Paragraph group on the Page Layout tab, keyboard shortcuts, the options at the Paragraph dialog box, the markers on the Ruler, or the Alignment button on the Ruler. Refer to Table 6.5 for a description of the various methods for indenting text.
- Word documents contain a number of predesigned formats grouped into style sets called Quick Styles. Change to a different Quck Styles set by clicking the Change Styles button in the Styles group on the Home tab, pointing to *Style Set*, and then clicking the desired set.
- By default, tabs are set every 0.5 inch but this can be changed on the Ruler or at the Tabs dialog box.
- Use the Alignment button at the left side of the Ruler to specify the type of tab and then click at the desired location on the Ruler to set the tab.
- At the Tabs dialog box, you can set tabs, set tabs with leaders, and clear one or more tabs.

Key Terms

alignment, p. 266	leaders, p. 285	sans serif, p. 258
border, p. 276	line spacing, p. 268	serif, p. 258
font, p. 258	Mini toolbar, p. 261	shading, p. 276
format, p. 257	monospaced, p. 258	typeface, p. 258
hanging indent, p. 274	proportional, p. 258	type size, p. 259
indent, p. 274	Quick Styles, p. 279	typestyle, p. 259

Features Summary

Feature	Ribbon Tab, Group	Button, Option	Keyboard Shortcut
1.5 line spacing	Home, Paragraph	*1.5*	Ctrl + 5
Align left	Home, Paragraph		Ctrl + L
Align right	Home, Paragraph		Ctrl + R
Bold	Home, Font	**B**	Ctrl + B
Border	Home, Paragraph		
Bullets	Home, Paragraph		
Center	Home, Paragraph		Ctrl + E
Change case	Home, Font	Aa	Shift + F3
Change Styles	Home, Styles		
Clear formatting	Home, Font		Ctrl + Q
Decrease indent	Home, Paragraph		Ctrl + Shift + M
Double line spacing	Home, Paragraph	*2.0*	Ctrl + 2
Font	Home, Font	Calibri (Body)	
Font color	Home, Font	A	
Font dialog box	Home, Font		Ctrl + Shift + F
Font size	Home, Font	11	Ctrl + Shift + P
Format Painter	Home, Clipboard		Ctrl + Shift + C
Hanging indent			Ctrl + T
Highlight	Home, Font		
Increase indent	Home, Paragraph		Ctrl + M

continued

Feature	Ribbon Tab, Group	Button, Option	Keyboard Shortcut
Italic	Home, Font	I	Ctrl + I
Justify	Home, Paragraph	▤	Ctrl + J
Line spacing	Home, Paragraph	↕☰▾	
Numbering	Home, Paragraph	☷▾	
Paragraph dialog box	Home, Paragraph	▣	
Remove hanging indent			Ctrl + Shift + T
Shading	Home, Paragraph	◌▾	
Single line spacing	Home, Paragraph	↕☰▾ , *1.0*	Ctrl + 1
Spacing after	Page Layout, Paragraph		
Spacing before	Page Layout, Paragraph		
Styles	Home, Styles		
Tabs dialog box	Home, Paragraph	▣ , Tabs	
Underline	Home, Font	U ▾	Ctrl + U

KEY POINTS REVIEW

Identification

Match the terms on the next page to the callouts on the Word window in Figure 6.12.

Figure 6.12 **Identification Figure**

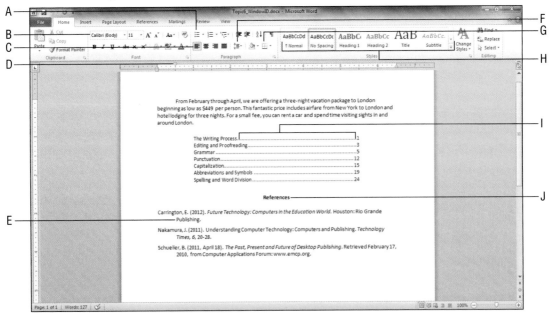

1. _____ hanging indent
2. _____ leaders
3. _____ center aligned text
4. _____ first line indent
5. _____ Bullets button

6. _____ Style thumbnails
7. _____ Borders button
8. _____ Align Text Left button
9. _____ Line and Paragraph Spacing button
10. _____ Font button

Multiple Choice

For each of the following items, choose the option that best completes the sentence or answers the question.

1. Click this button in the Paragraph group to turn on the display of nonprinting characters.
   A. Borders
   B. Justify
   C. Show/Hide ¶
   D. Sort

2. Repeat the last action by pressing F4 or by using this keyboard shortcut.
   A. Ctrl + V
   B. Ctrl + Y
   C. Ctrl + X
   D. Ctrl + Z

3. In this type of paragraph, the first line of text remains aligned at the left margin and the remaining lines of text are indented to the first tab.
   A. hanging indent
   B. first line indent
   C. left indent
   D. right indent

4. Return all paragraph formatting to the default setting by pressing this keyboard shortcut.
   A. Ctrl + Q
   B. Ctrl + E
   C. Ctrl + J
   D. Ctrl + R

5. Bulleted lists with hanging indents are automatically created when you begin a paragraph with the asterisk symbol (*), the hyphen (-), or this symbol.
   A. <
   B. #
   C. ^
   D. >

6. A font consists of three elements:
   A. typeface, type size, and typestyle
   B. typeface, type area, and typestyle
   C. typeset, type size, and typestyle
   D. type set, type size, and type theme

7. By default, paragraphs in a Word document are aligned at this margin.
   A. top
   B. bottom
   C. left
   D. right

8. Use this keyboard shortcut to underline selected text.
   A. Ctrl + D
   B. Shift + D
   C. Ctrl + U
   D. Shift + U

9. You can apply typestyle formatting with the buttons in this group.
   A. Clipboard
   B. Paragraph
   C. Editing
   D. Font

10. A Word document contains a number of predesigned formats grouped into style sets called this.
    A. Quick Styles
    B. Normal Styles
    C. Heading Styles
    D. Themed Styles

Matching

Match each of the following definitions with the correct term, command, or option.

1. _____ This type of typeface assigns the same amount of horizontal space to each character.

2. _____ This automatically displays above selected text.

3. _____ Use this feature to copy character formatting that you have already applied to text to different locations in the document.

4. _____ This term refers to text that is raised slightly above the regular text line.

5. _____ The bold button is located in this group on the Home tab.

6. _____ Click this button in the Font group to display the Font dialog box.

7. _____ This term refers to text that is lowered slightly below the regular text line.

8. _____ This is the name of the button that displays at the left side of the Ruler.

9. _____ This type of typeface allocates varying amounts of space for each character.

10. _____ Set tabs at the Tabs dialog box or by using this feature.

A. Proportional
B. Superscript
C. Dialog box launcher
D. Monospaced
E. Subscript
F. Font
G. Format Painter
H. Ruler
I. Mini toolbar
J. Alignment

SKILLS REVIEW

Review 6.1 Formatting an Essay

1. Open **CompTech.docx** and then save it with Save As and name it **U2T6-R1-CompTech**.
2. Select the entire document, change the font to Cambria, and change the font size to 12 points.
3. Set the title *ON THE HORIZON: COMPUTER TECHNOLOGY* in 16-point Candara (make sure the bold formatting remains).
4. Set the heading *Embedded Computers* in 14-point Candara (make sure the bold formatting remains) and apply small caps to the heading. (The Small Caps option is available in the Effects section of the Font dialog box.) Use Format Painter to apply the same formatting to the remaining headings (*On-Demand Computing, Wireless Devices,* and *Faster Communication*).
5. Apply the *Offset Diagonal Top Right* shadow effect to the title *ON THE HORIZON: COMPUTER TECHNOLOGY.* **Hint: Use options at the Text Effects button drop-down list.**
6. Change the paragraph alignment to Justify for the paragraph below the title *ON THE HORIZON: COMPUTER TECHNOLOGY.*
7. Select the entire document, change the line spacing to 1.5, and then deselect the document.
8. Click anywhere in the heading EMBEDDED COMPUTERS , display the Paragraph dialog box, and then change the paragraph spacing before to 6 points and after to 6 points.
9. Use the Repeat command to insert 6 points of spacing before and after the remaining headings (ON-DEMAND COMPUTING, WIRELESS DEVICES, and FASTER COMMUNICATION).
10. Select the three paragraphs of text in the FASTER COMMUNICATION section (beginning with *Radio took 38 years…* and ending with *The Internet took only…*), and then insert bullets.
11. Save and then print **U2T6-R1-CompTech.docx**.
12. Change the Quick Styles set to *Traditional.*
13. Apply the Heading 1 style to *ON THE HORIZON: COMPUTER TECHNOLOGY.*
14. Apply the Heading 2 style to the headings EMBEDDED COMPUTERS, ON-DEMAND COMPUTING, WIRELESS DEVICES, and FASTER COMMUNICATION.
15. Change the Quick Styles set color to *Foundry.*
16. Save, print, and then close **U2T6-R1-CompTech.docx**.

Review 6.2 Formatting an Employment Document

1. Open **Qualities.docx** and then save the document and name it **U2T6-R2-Qualities**.
2. Select the entire document, change the font to Candara, and then change the paragraph alignment to Justify.
3. Select the title *DESIRABLE EMPLOYEE QUALITIES*, change the font size to 14, and then change the paragraph alignment to Center.
4. Select the nine paragraphs of indented text in the *Who Will You Communicate With?* section (the text that begins with *People on your team or in your department*), click the Decrease Indent button to remove the indent, and then insert bullets.
5. Select the three paragraphs of indented text in the *Who Will You Communicate With?* section (the text that begins with *Do I speak clearly?*), click the Decrease Indent button to remove the indent, and then insert numbers.
6. Insert the text **Can I write clearly?** between the first and second numbered paragraphs. (The text you type should be numbered 2.)
7. Click on any character in the title *DESIRABLE EMPLOYEE QUALITIES* and then insert a single-line top border, a double-line bottom border, and apply *Red, Accent 2, Lighter 40%* paragraph shading.
8. Click on any character in the heading *COMMUNICATION SKILLS*, insert a single-line bottom border with a width of 1 ½ pt, and apply *Red, Accent 2, Lighter 60%* paragraph shading.
9. Apply to the heading *TEAM SKILLS* the same border and shading you applied to *COMMUNICATION SKILLS*.
10. Click on any character in the heading *Who Will You Communicate With?*, insert a single-line bottom border with a width of 1 pt, and apply *Red, Accent 2, Lighter 80%* paragraph shading.
11. Apply to the heading *So How Do I Demonstrate These Skills on My Resume?* the same border and shading you applied to *Who Will You Communicate With?*.
12. Save, print, and then close **U2T6-R2-Qualities.docx**.

Review 6.3 Setting Tabs

1. Starting with a blank document, type the text shown in Figure 6.13 with the following specifications:
   a. Type the title *EMPLOYMENT HISTORY* centered and bolded as shown in Figure 6.13.
   b. Press the Enter key and then change the paragraph alignment to Left and turn off bold.
   c. Set a left tab at the 0.5-inch mark, a center tab at the 3.25-inch mark, and a right tab at the 6-inch mark on the Ruler and then type the tabbed text shown in Figure 6.13.
2. Save the completed document and name it **U2T6-R3-EmpHistory**.
3. Print and then close **U2T6-R3-EmpHistory.docx**.

Figure 6.13 Review 6.3 Text

	EMPLOYMENT HISTORY	
Marketing Director	Research Corporation	2007 to Present
Programs Manager	San Jose Technologies	2004 to 2007
Field Administrator	Analysis Group	2001 to 2004
Activities Coordinator	Medical Systems	1996 to 2001
Marketing Manager	Mercantile Trust	1991 to 1996

Review 6.4 Setting Tabs with Leaders

1. Starting with a blank document, type the text shown in Figure 6.14 with the following specifications:
   a. Type the title *EDUCATION* centered and bolded as shown in Figure 6.14.
   b. Press the Enter key and then change the paragraph alignment to Left.
   c. Set a left tab at 0.5″ and a right tab with leaders at 6″ and then type the tabbed text shown in Figure 6.14.
2. Save the completed document and name it **U2T6-R4-Education**.
3. Print and then close **U2T6-R4-Education.docx**.

Figure 6.14 Review 6.4 Text

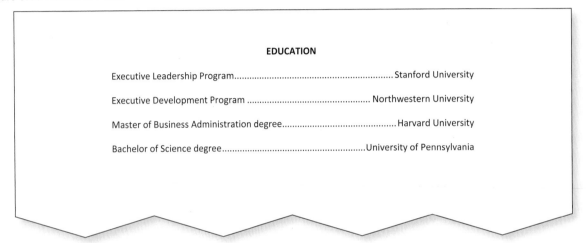

EDUCATION

Executive Leadership Program...Stanford University

Executive Development Program ....Northwestern University

Master of Business Administration degree..Harvard University

Bachelor of Science degree..University of Pennsylvania

SKILLS ASSESSMENT

Assessment 6.1 Formatting a Resume Styles Document

1. Open **ResumeStyles.docx** and then save the document with Save As and name it **U2T6-A1-ResumeStyles**.
2. Select the entire document and then change the font to Constantia.
3. Center-align the title and set the title in 14-point Corbel bold.
4. Select the heading *The Chronological Resume* and then change the font to 12-point Corbel bold.
5. Use Format Painter to apply 12-point Corbel bold to the remaining two headings in the document (*The Functional Resume* and *The Hybrid Resume*).
6. Indent the first line of the first paragraph in the document 0.5 inch from the left margin.
7. Select the paragraphs of text below the heading *The Chronological Resume* and then indent the text 0.5 inch from the left margin and the right margin.
8. Indent the paragraph of text below the heading *The Functional Resume* 0.5 inch from the left margin and the right margin.
9. Indent the paragraph of text below the heading *The Hybrid Resume* 0.5 inch from the left margin and the right margin.
10. Select from the paragraph below the heading *The Chronological Resume* that reads *Personal contact information* through the remaining three paragraphs in the heading section and then apply bullets.
11. Apply a double-line top border and a single-line bottom border to the title *RESUME STYLES* and also apply a paragraph shading color of your choosing.
12. Apply a single-line top and bottom border and paragraph shading color of your choosing to the three headings in the document.
13. Save, print, and then close **U2T6-A1-ResumeStyles.docx**.

Assessment 6.2 Formatting a Cover Letters Document

1. Open **CoverLetters.docx** and then save the document with Save As and name it **U2T6-A2-CoverLetters**.
2. Select the entire document and then make the following changes:
   a. Change the font to Cambria.
   b. Change the line spacing to 1.15.
   c. Apply 6 points of spacing before paragraphs.
3. Select the paragraphs that begin with bolded text and then apply numbering.
4. Change the Quick Styles set to *Formal*.
5. Apply the Heading 1 style to the title of the document, the Heading 2 style to the two headings *Writing Cover Letters to People You Know* and *Writing Cover Letters to People You Do Not Know*, and apply the Heading 3 style to the heading *The Four Types of Cover Letters to People You Know*.
6. Change the spacing after paragraphs to 18 for the title and three headings in the document.
7. Save, print, and then close **U2T6-A2-CoverLetters.docx**.

Assessment 6.3 Setting Tabs

1. At a blank document, click the No Spacing style in the Styles group on the Home tab.
2. Type the first title *WORK EXPERIENCE* and the text in columns below the title as shown in Figure 6.15 with the following specifications:
   a. Center and bold the title as shown.
   b. Set the tabbed text as shown using a left tab for the first column, a center tab for the second column, and a right tab for the third column.
3. After typing the tabbed text, press the Enter key twice, and then click the Clear Formatting button.
4. Click the No Spacing style in the Styles group on the Home tab.
5. Type the second title *COMMUNITY/VOLUNTEER ACTIVITIES* and the text in columns below the title as shown in Figure 6.15 with the following specifications:
   a. Center and bold the title as shown.
   b. Set the tabbed text as shown using a left tab for the first column and a right tab with leaders for the second column. ***Hint: Choose the underline leaders at the Tabs dialog box.***
6. Save the document and name it **U2T6-A3-WorkExp**.
7. Print and then close **U2T6-A3-WorkExp.docx**.

Figure 6.15 Assessment 6.3 Text

WORK EXPERIENCE

Title	Location	Years
Research Assistant	Arizona State University	2009 to Present
Teaching Assistant	Mesa Community College	2008 to Present
Project Manager	P&P International	2006 to 2008
Customer Service Rep.	Bank of Phoenix	2003 to 2006

COMMUNITY/VOLUNTEER ACTIVITIES

Red Cross Blood Drive	2005 to Present
Sunlight Foundation	2002 to 2009
Big Sisters of Phoenix	2001 to 2006
American Heart Association	1998 to 2000

Assessment 6.4 Finding Information on Widow/Orphan Control and Keeping Text Together

1. Use Word's Help feature to learn how to prevent page breaks between paragraphs and how to place at least two lines of a paragraph at the top or bottom of a page to prevent a widow (last line of a paragraph by itself at the top of a page) or orphan (first line of a paragraph by itself at the bottom of a page).
2. Create a document containing the following information:
   a. Create a title for the document.
   b. Write a paragraph that explains how to prevent page breaks between paragraphs and the steps required to complete the task. Make sure to include steps on how to prevent a widow or orphan on a page.
3. Save the completed document and name it **U2T6-A4-PageBreaks**.
4. Print and then close **U2T6-A4-PageBreaks**.
5. Open **CoverLetters.docx**.
6. Save the document with Save As and name it **U2T6-A4-CLBreak**.
7. Select the entire document, change the line spacing to 1.5, and then apply 6 points of spacing after paragraphs.
8. Apply the Heading 1 style to the title *WRITING A COVER PAGE*, the Heading 2 style to the two headings *Writing Cover Letters to People You Know* and *Writing Cover Letters to People You Do Not Know*, and apply the Heading 3 style to the heading *The Four Types of Cover Letters to People You Know*.
9. Change the Quick Styles set to *Fancy*.
10. Select the entire document, change the font to Candara, and then remove italic formatting.
11. Position the insertion point on the heading *Writing Cover Letters to People You Do Not Know* and then insert a command to keep lines of text together with the next line.
12. Save the document and then print only page 2 of **U2T6-A4-CLBreak**.
13. Close **U2T6-A4-CLBreak**.

Assessment 6.5 Researching Fonts

1. Using the Internet, search for information on downloading fonts. Find at least two websites that allow free downloading of fonts.
2. Starting with a blank document, write a memo to your instructor in which you describe the two websites and provide steps on how to download fonts.
3. Save the completed memo document and name it **U2T6-A5-FontMemo**.
4. Print and then close **U2T6-A5_FontMemo.docx**.

Assessment 6.6 Creating and Formatting a Resume

1. Create the resume shown in Figure 6.16. Change the font to Cambria and apply the paragraph, border, shading, and bullet formatting as shown in the figure.
2. Save the completed document and name it **U2T6-A6-Resume**.
3. Print and then close **U2T6-A6-Resume.docx**.

Figure 6.16 Assessment 6.6 Resume

CYNTHIA ROVAN

4405 Georgia Avenue, NW, #412, Silver Springs, MD 20901 (301) 291-8512, crovan@emcp.com

NETWORK ADMINISTRATION PROFESSIONAL
Pursuing **Cisco Certified Network Associate (CCNA)** and **Network+** credentials
Proficient in Microsoft Office applications in Windows XP/NT environment

EDUCATION

Information Systems (IS), Avery College, Arlington, VA 2008
Medical Specialist, Northern Virginia College, Alexandria, VA .... 2005 to 2007
Medical Terminology, Texas Health & Sciences College, Irving TX 2005

APPLIED RESEARCH PROJECTS

Completed **Applied Research Projects (ARPs)**, in conjunction with IS degree requirements, covering all aspects of design and management of organizational technical resources, as follows:

- <u>**Organizational Culture and Leadership**</u> (2006): Evaluated the organizational culture of Belmont Surgery Center's endoscopy unit and operating room (OR) in order to ensure that the mission and vision statements were being appropriately applied at the staff level.
- <u>**Human Resources (HR) Management**</u> (2006): Established a comprehensive orientation package for the Belmont Surgery Center's clinical staff.
- <u>**Strategic Management and Planning**</u> (2005): Conducted internal/external environmental assessments in order to identify an approach for Belmont Surgery Center to expand its OR facilities.
- <u>**Financial Accounting**</u> (2004): Created a quarterly operating budget for the Belmont Surgery Center and implemented an expenditure tracking system.
- <u>**Database Management Systems**</u> (2004): Created an inventory-control system that optimizes inventory maintenance in a cost-effective manner.
- <u>**Statistics and Research Analysis**</u> (2003): Generated graphics to illustrate the Good Sheppard Hospital Center's assisted-reproduction success rate.
- <u>**Management Support Systems**</u> (2003): Identified solutions to resolve inventory-control vulnerabilities at minimal cost for Good Sheppard Hospital Center.

PROFESSIONAL EXPERIENCE

CERTIFIED SURGICAL TECHNOLOGIST

Belmont Surgery Center, Silver Springs, MD .... 2007 to Present
Good Sheppard Hospital Center, Vienna, VA .... 2005 to 2007
Kenmore Ambulatory Surgery Center, Irving, TX .... 2003 to 2005
Swedish Medical Center, Arlington, TX .... 2002 to 2003

CRITICAL THINKING

Identifying and Applying Appropriate Fonts

Part 1 You work for the student newspaper, and the editor, Leah Gardner, would like to maintain consistency in articles submitted for the monthly newspaper. She wants you to explore various decorative and plain fonts. She would like you to choose two handwriting fonts, two decorative fonts, and two plain fonts and then prepare a document containing an illustration of each of these fonts. Save the document and name it **U2T6-C01-Fonts**. Print and then close the document.

Part 2 Leah Gardner has asked you to write a short article for the next issue of the newspaper. In the article, she would like you to describe an upcoming event at your school or in your local community. Make sure to effectively use at least two of the fonts you examined in **U2T6-C01-Fonts.docx** in your article. Save the document and name it **U2T6-C02-Article**. Print and then close the document.

TEAM PROJECT

Designing Menus and Recipes Using Word

Part 1 You are currently working at a Mediterranean restaurant. Your boss has asked you to create separate menus for four different types of Mediterranean cuisine: Italian, Greek, Moroccan, and Turkish. As a team, choose a cuisine and then create breakfast, lunch, and dinner menus. Each menu should consist of at least three types of food and two types of beverages. Include in the menus prices and descriptions of the food, if necessary. When creating the menus, consider the following formatting suggestions:

- Create bulleted or numbered list.

- Change font colors and/or font sizes to help identify different dishes.

- Insert shading in the heading text.

Save the documents and name them **U2T6-TeamMenu[Breakfast, Lunch, or Dinner]**. Print and then close the documents.

Part 2 Your team has been asked by the head chef to research a new recipe for your cuisine. Using the Internet, find a recipe that interests your team and then prepare a Word document containing the recipe and ingredients. Use bullets before each ingredient and use numbering for each step in the recipe preparation. Save the document and name it **U2T6-TeamRecipe**. Print and then close the document.

Discussion Questions

1. What font(s) did you use when creating the menus? Why did you choose those fonts?
2. How did you use formatting to enhance the visual appeal of the menus? What specific formatting choices did you make and why?
3. Compare your menus with the menus created by the other teams. Which menu contains the most appealing formatting? What makes one menu more appealing than another?

Topic 7

Creating and Enhancing Tables in Word

Performance Objectives

Upon successful completion of Topic 7, you will be able to:

- Create a table, enter text in cells, and navigate within a table
- Apply table styles, shading, and borders
- Select cells
- Insert and delete rows and columns
- Merge and split cells and tables
- Change column width and height
- Change cell alignment
- Change cell margin measurements and cell direction
- Change table alignment, change table size, and move a table
- Insert a Quick Table
- Draw a table
- Convert text to a table
- Sort text in a table

STUDENT RESOURCES

Before beginning this topic, copy to your storage medium the **Unit2Topic07** subfolder from the *Computer and Internet Essentials: Preparing for IC³* Internet Resource Center. Make this the active folder.

In addition to containing the data files needed to complete topic work, the Internet Resource Center contains model answers in PDF format for each of the applicable exercises in this topic. Use these files to check your work. The preface of your textbook contains instructions for accessing these files.

Necessary Data Files

To complete the exercises and assessments, you will need the following data files:

Exercise 7.1	New file
Exercises 7.2–7.7	Previously created file (Ex. 7.1)
Exercise 7.8	Previously created file (Ex. 7.1–7.7) EducationTable.docx
Exercise 7.9	New file
Exercises 7.10–7.12	SchedTables.docx
Review 7.1	New file
Review 7.2	New file
Assessment 7.1	New file
Assessment 7.2	New file
Assessment 7.3	ContactInfo.docx

continued

Assessment 7.4	New file
Assessment 7.5	CFExpenses.docx
Assessment 7.6	New file
Assessment 7.7	New file
Critical Thinking	New files
Team Project	New file

Visual Preview

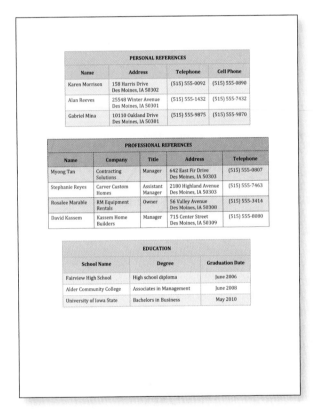

Exercises 7.1–7.8 U2T7-ResumeTables.docx

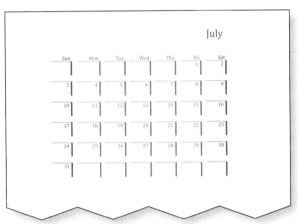

Exercise 7.9 U2T7-Calendar.docx

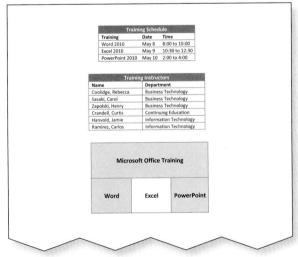

Exercises 7.10–7.12 U2T7-SchedTables.docx

Topic Overview

Tables provide a systematic way to organize and display data in a document. The Tables feature in Word allows you to organize data such as text, numbers, and formulas into columns and rows, which you can then combine with paragraphs of text to form a complete document. In this topic, you will learn to create tables using several different methods, including drawing a table and inserting a Quick Table. You will learn how to format data in a table; apply table styles; insert and delete columns and rows; merge cells; and change cell size, alignment, and margins. You will also learn to sort text in a table and convert text to a table.

Lesson 7.1 Creating a Table, Entering Text in Cells, and Navigating within a Table

IC³ 2-2.1.13

When you create a table in Word, it is made up of boxes of information called cells. Recall that a cell is the intersection between a row and a column. A cell can contain text, characters, numbers, graphics, or formulas. Create a table by clicking the Insert tab, clicking the Table button, dragging down and to the right until the correct number of rows and columns displays, and then releasing the mouse button. You can also create a table with options at the Insert Table dialog box. Display this dialog box by clicking the Table button in the Tables group on the Insert tab and then clicking *Insert Table* at the drop-down list.

Figure 7.1 shows an example of a table with three columns and four rows. Various parts of the table are identified, including the gridlines (the lines that form the cells of the table), move table column marker, end-of-cell marker, end-of-row marker, and resize handle. In a table, nonprinting characters identify the end of a cell and the end of a row. To view these characters, click the Show/Hide ¶ button in the Paragraph group on the Home tab. The end-of-cell marker displays inside each cell and the end-of-row marker displays at the end of each row of cells.

Quick Steps

Create a Table
1. Click Insert tab.
2. Click Table button.
3. Drag to create desired number of columns and rows.
4. Release mouse button.

OR

1. Click Insert tab.
2. Click Table button.
3. Click *Insert Table*.
4. Specify number of columns and rows.
5. Click OK.

Figure 7.1 Table in Word

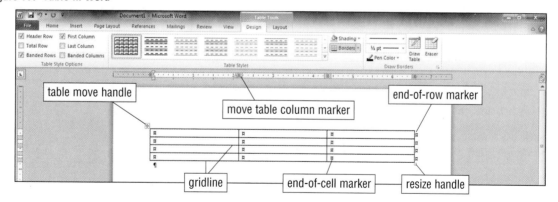

Each cell in a table has a cell designation based on the row and column in which it is located. Although you cannot see the column and row designations in a Word table, the columns are lettered from left to right, beginning with A, and the rows are numbered from top to bottom, beginning with 1. The cell in the upper left corner of the table is cell A1. The cell to the right of A1 is B1, the cell to the right of B1 is C1, and so on. When you create a table, the insertion point automatically displays in cell A1.

With the insertion point positioned in a cell, you can enter new content or edit the cell's existing content. If the text you type does not fit on one line, it wraps to the next line within the same cell. If you press the Enter key within a cell, the insertion point moves to the next line within that cell. The cell lengthens to accommodate the text, along with the rest of the cells in that row.

Exercise 7.1 Creating and Entering Data in a Table

1. At a blank document, click the Insert tab and then click the Table button ⊞ in the Tables group.

2. Drag the mouse arrow pointer down and to the right until the text above the grid displays as *3x5 Table*, and then click the mouse button.

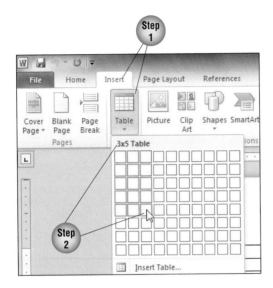

3. Type text in the cells as shown in Figure 7.2.

   Press the Tab key to move the insertion point to the next cell or press Shift + Tab to move the insertion point to the previous cell. When typing text in the cells in the second column, type the street address, press the Enter key, and then type the city, state, and zip code. After typing text in the last cell, do not press the Tab key (this action would insert another row). If you press the Tab key accidentally, immediately click the Undo button. To move the insertion point to different cells within the table using the mouse, click in the desired cell. If you type the incorrect text in a cell and do not realize it until after you have navigated away from the cell, press the Tab key or Shift + Tab until the incorrect text is selected and then type the correct text.

4. Press Ctrl + End to move the insertion point to the end of the document and then press the Enter key once.

5. Click the Insert tab, click the Table button in the Tables group, and then click *Insert Table* at the drop-down list.

6. At the Insert Table dialog box, type **4** in the *Number of columns* text box.

   The insertion point is automatically positioned in this text box.

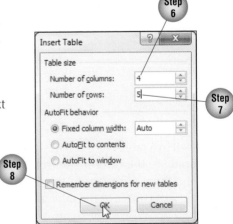

7. Press the Tab key to move the insertion point to the *Number of rows* option and then type **5**.

8. Click OK to close the dialog box.

9. Type the text in the cells as shown in Figure 7.3.

10. Save the document and name it **U2T7-ResumeTables**.

Figure 7.2 Exercise 7.1 Table 1

Name	Address	Telephone
Karen Morrison	158 Harris Drive Des Moines, IA 50302	(515) 555-0092
Alan Reeves	25548 Winter Avenue Des Moines, IA 50301	(515) 555-1432
Sylvia Wickers	798 East Summit Road Des Moines, IA 50307	(515) 555-5450
Gabriel Mina	10110 Oakland Drive Des Moines, IA 50301	(515) 555-9875

Figure 7.3 Exercise 7.1 Table 2

Name	Company	Address	Telephone
Myong Tan	Contracting Solutions	642 East Fir Drive Des Moines, IA 50303	(515) 555-0807
Stephanie Reyes	Carver Custom Homes	2180 Highland Avenue Des Moines, IA 50303	(515) 555-7463
Rosalee Marable	RM Equipment Rentals	56 Valley Avenue Des Moines, IA 50308	(515) 555-3414
David Kassem	Kassem Home Builders	715 Center Street Des Moines, IA 50309	(515) 555-8080

Drilling Down

Displaying the Horizontal Ruler

When the insertion point is positioned in a cell in the table, the move table column markers display on the horizontal ruler. If the horizontal ruler is not visible, you can display it by clicking the View Ruler button located toward the top of the vertical scroll bar. The move table column markers represent the end of a column and can be used to change the width of columns.

Lesson 7.2   Selecting Cells in a Table

 2-2.1.13

You can use the mouse arrow pointer to select a cell, column, row, or an entire table. Table 7.1 provides instructions for doing this. The left edge of each cell, between the left column border and the end-of-cell marker (if the cell is empty) or first character in the cell (if the cell contains text), is called the **cell selection bar**. When you position the mouse pointer in the cell selection bar, the mouse pointer turns into a black arrow pointing up and to the right. Click the left mouse button to select the cell. Each row in a table contains a **row selection bar**, which is the space immediately to the left of the left edge of the table. When you position the mouse pointer in the row selection bar, the mouse pointer turns into a white arrow pointing up and to the right. Click the left mouse button to select the row.

cell selection bar The left edge of each cell, between the left column border and the end-of-cell marker or first character in the cell; clicking here selects the cell

row selection bar The space immediately left of the left edge of each row; clicking here selects the row

Table 7.1 Selecting in a Table with the Mouse

To select	Complete the following actions
A cell	Position the mouse pointer in the cell selection bar at the left edge of the cell until it turns into a black arrow pointing up and to the right and then click the left mouse button.
A row	Position the mouse pointer in the row selection bar at the left edge of the table until it turns into a white arrow pointing up and to the right and then click the left mouse button. To select nonadjacent rows, hold down the Ctrl key while selecting rows.
A column	Position the mouse pointer on the uppermost horizontal gridline of the table in the appropriate column until it turns into a short, down-pointing arrow and then click the left mouse button. To select nonadjacent columns, hold down the Ctrl key while selecting columns.
Adjacent cells	Position the mouse pointer in the first cell to be selected, hold down the left mouse button, drag the mouse pointer to the last cell to be selected, and then release the mouse button.
All cells in a table	Click the table move handle or position the mouse pointer in any cell in the table, hold down the Alt key, and then double-click the left mouse button. You can also position the mouse pointer in the row selection bar for the first row at the left edge of the table until it turns into an arrow pointing up and to the right. Hold down the left mouse button, drag down to select all rows in the table, and then release the left mouse button.
Text within a cell	Position the mouse pointer at the beginning of the text and then hold down the left mouse button as you drag the mouse across the text. (When a cell is selected, the background color of the entire cell changes to blue. When text within a cell is selected, only those lines appear with a blue background.)

Another way to select specific cells within a table is to use the keyboard. Table 7.2 presents the commands for selecting specific portions of a table.

Table 7.2 Selecting in a Table with the Keyboard

To select	Complete the following actions
The next cell's contents	Press Tab.
The previous cell's contents	Press Shift + Tab.
The entire table	Press Alt + 5 (on the numeric keypad with Num Lock off).
Adjacent cells	Hold down the Shift key and then use the arrow keys to select cells.
A column	Position the insertion point in the top cell of the column, hold down the Shift key, and then press the down arrow key until the entire column is selected.

You can also select different parts of a table by using the Select button, located in the Table group on the Table Tools Layout tab. To select with this button, position the insertion point in the desired cell, column, or row and then click the Select button. At the drop-down list that displays, specify what you want to select—a cell, column, row, or the entire table.

Exercise 7.2 Selecting Cells and Applying Formatting

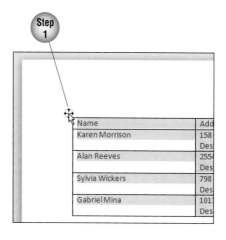

1. With **U2T7-ResumeTables.docx** open, change the font of the text in the top table. Begin by hovering the mouse arrow pointer over any cell in the top table until the table move handle displays near the upper-left corner of the table. Position the mouse arrow pointer over the table move handle until the pointer displays as a four-headed arrow and then click the left mouse button.

   This selects the entire table.

2. Click the Home tab, click the Font button arrow, and then click *Cambria* at the drop-down gallery.

3. Deselect the table by clicking in any cell in the table.

4. Center the text in cells in the third column of the top table. Begin by positioning the mouse arrow pointer in the cell below the *Telephone* heading [the cell containing *(515) 555-0092*], holding down the mouse button, and then dragging down to the bottom cell in the table [the cell containing the telephone number *(515) 555-9875*].

5. Make sure the Home tab is active and then click the Center button in the Paragraph group.

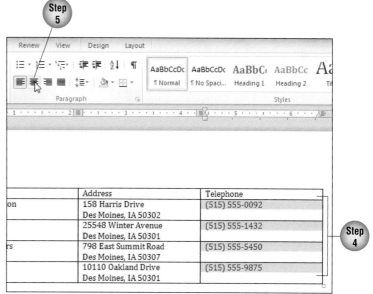

6. Position the mouse arrow pointer in the row selection bar at the left side of the first row in the top table until the pointer turns into an arrow pointing up and to the right and then click the left mouse button.

   This selects the entire first row of the top table.

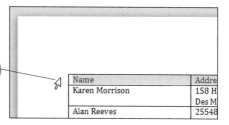

7. Make sure the Home tab is active, click the Bold button in the Font group, and then click the Center button in the Paragraph group.

8. Complete steps similar to those in Steps 1 through 7 to apply the same formatting to the bottom table.

9. Save and then print **U2T7-ResumeTables.docx**.

Drilling Down

Using the Keyboard to Select Text in a Cell

If you want to use the keyboard to select only the text within a cell rather than the entire cell, press F8 to turn on the Extend mode and then use the arrow keys to move the insertion point. When a cell is selected, the background color of the entire cell changes to blue. When text within a cell is selected, only those selected words display with a blue background.

Lesson 7.3 Applying Table Styles and Shading and Borders

 2-2.1.13, 2-2.1.14, 2-2.1.15

Quick Steps

Apply Borders to a Table

1. Click Table Tools Design tab.
2. Click Borders button arrow.
3. Click desired border option at drop-down list.

OR

1. Click Table Tools Design tab.
2. Click Borders button arrow.
3. Click *Borders and Shading* at drop-down list.
4. Select desired border options.
5. Click OK.

Apply Shading to a Table

1. Click Table Tools Design tab.
2. Click Shading button arrow.
3. Click desired shading color.

When you insert a table, the Table Tools Design tab (shown in Figure 7.4) becomes active. This tab contains options for applying and changing table styles as well as buttons for applying shading and borders.

With options in the Table Styles group on the Table Tools Design tab, you can apply a predesigned style to a table. Display additional styles by clicking the More button that displays at the right of the style thumbnails. Hover the mouse arrow pointer over an option in the drop-down gallery and the table in the document displays with the formatting applied. Once you have applied a predesigned style to a table, you can make additional modifications to the columns and rows with the options in the Table Style Options group. For example, if your table contains a total row, you can insert a check mark in the *Total Row* option.

Apply additional design formatting to the cells in a table with the Shading and Borders buttons in the Table Styles group. Click the Shading button arrow and a drop-down gallery displays with options for applying shading. Click the Borders button arrow to display a drop-down gallery of border options. If you want further control over inserting a border in a table, click the *Borders and Shading* option at the Borders button drop-down list. This displays the Borders and Shading dialog box with the Borders tab selected. With options at this dialog box, you can choose the style, color, and width of your border, as well as specify where in the table you wish to apply it. You can also apply shading to a table using options in this dialog box with the Shading tab selected.

Figure 7.4 **Table Tools Design Tab**

Exercise 7.3 Applying Styles and Customizing Shading and Borders

1. With **U2T7-ResumeTables.docx** open, click anywhere in the top table and then click the Table Tools Design tab.

2. Click the More button ⬓ that displays at the right side of the table style thumbnails in the Table Styles group.

   This displays a drop-down gallery of style choices.

3. Scroll down the list of table styles and then click the *Light Grid - Accent 5* option (second option from the right in the third row in the *Built-In* section).

Notice the color and border style formatting that this option applies.

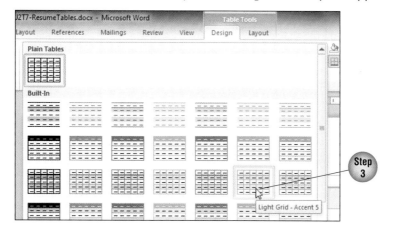

4. Change table formatting by clicking the *First Column* option in the Table Style Options group to remove the check mark and then clicking the *Header Row* option to remove the check mark.

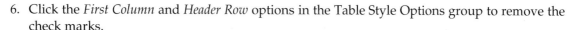

5. Click anywhere in the bottom table and then apply the *Medium Shading 1 - Accent 2* table style to the table.

6. Click the *First Column* and *Header Row* options in the Table Style Options group to remove the check marks.

7. Remove borders in the bottom table. To do this, select the bottom table by clicking the table move handle that displays in the upper-left corner of the table (a square with a four-headed arrow inside), click the Borders button arrow in the Table Styles group on the Table Tools Design tab, and then click *No Border* at the drop-down list.

8. With the bottom table still selected, apply new borders to the table by clicking the Borders button arrow in the Table Styles group on the Table Tools Design tab and then clicking *Inside Borders* at the drop-down list.

9. Change the shading of the first row in the bottom table by selecting the first row (contains the headings *Name*, *Company*, *Address*, and *Telephone*), clicking the Shading button arrow in the Table Styles group on the Table Tools Design tab, and then clicking *Red, Accent 2, Lighter 40%* at the drop-down gallery.

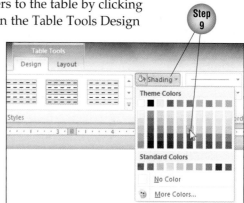

10. Apply *Aqua, Accent 5, Lighter 40%* shading to the first row in the top table.

11. Save **U2T7-ResumeTables.docx**.

Drilling Down

Drawing Borders

Another way to insert borders in a table is to draw them with the pen pointer. To do this, click the Draw Table button in the Draw Borders group on the Table Tools Design tab. This changes the mouse arrow pointer to a pen pointer and causes the Draw Table button to display with an orange background. Draw along the table gridlines to insert a border or to change the color or weight of a border. To choose the line style of the border you wish to draw, click the Line Style button arrow. To choose the line weight, click the Line Weight button arrow, and to choose the color, click the Pen Color button arrow and then click the desired color at the color palette. When you are finished, click the Draw Table button to turn off the feature.

Lesson 7.4 Managing Rows, Columns, and Cells

 2-2.1.13, 2-2.1.14

You can also format a table with options in the Table Tools Layout tab (shown in Figure 7.5). This tab contains options for selecting specific cells within the table, deleting and inserting rows and columns, merging and splitting cells, and specifying the height and width of cells. The Table Tools Layout tab also includes buttons for customizing the table layout such as changing cell size, alignment, direction, and margins; sorting data; and converting a table to text.

Figure 7.5 **Table Tools Layout Tab**

With buttons in the Rows & Columns group on the Table Tools Layout tab, you can insert and delete rows and columns. To do this, click the button that inserts a row or column in the desired location, such as above, below, or to the left or right of the active row or column. To delete a row, a column, or the entire table, click the Delete button and then click the option specifying what you want to delete. To merge selected cells, click the Merge Cells button in the Merge group on the Table Tools Layout tab.

Exercise 7.4 Managing Rows, Columns, and Cells

1. With **U2T7-ResumeTables.docx** open, add cell phone numbers to the top table. To do this, position the insertion point in the *Telephone* cell in the top table, click the Table Tools Layout tab, and then click the Insert Right button ⊞ in the Rows & Columns group.

   Figure 7.5 displays the Table Tools Layout tab.

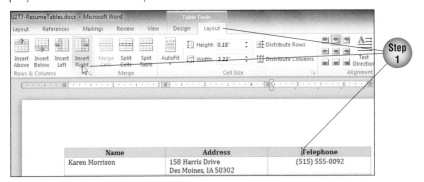

2. Click in the top cell of the new column, type **Cell Phone**, and then press the down arrow key. Type the cell phone numbers in the remaining cells as shown at the right.

Press the down arrow key to move to the next cell.

3. Add a new column to the right of the *Company* column in the bottom table by completing actions similar to those in Steps 1 and 2. Type **Title** in the top cell of the new column and type the titles in the remaining cells as shown at the right.

4. Inserting the new column deleted the vertical borders in the table. Select the bottom table by clicking the table move handle that displays in the upper-left corner of the table. Next, apply vertical and outside borders by clicking the Table Tools Design tab, clicking the Borders button arrow in the Table Styles group, and then clicking *All Borders* at the drop-down list.

5. Delete the *Sylvia Wickers* row in the top table. To do this, click anywhere in the text *Sylvia Wickers*, click the Table Tools Layout tab, click the Delete button ⊠, and then click *Delete Rows* at the drop-down list.

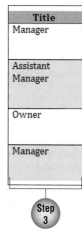

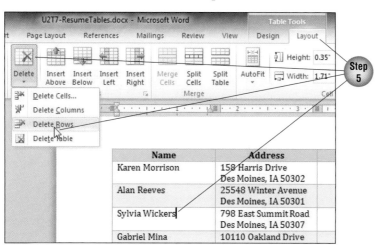

6. Insert a row above *Name* in the top table. To do this, click anywhere in the text *Name* and then click the Insert Above button in the Rows & Columns group.

7. With the new top row selected, merge the cells by clicking the Merge Cells button in the Merge group.

8. Type **PERSONAL REFERENCES** in the top row.

9. Insert a row above *Name* in the bottom table and merge the cells by completing actions similar to those in Steps 6 and 7. Type **PROFESSIONAL REFERENCES** in the new row.

10. Save **U2T7-ResumeTables.docx**.

Splitting Cells or Splitting a Table

To split selected cells, click the Split Cells buttons in the Merge group on the Table Tools Layout tab. When you click the Split Cells button, the Split Cells dialog box displays. At this dialog box, specify the number of columns or rows into which you want to split the active cell. If you want to split one table into two tables, position the insertion point in a cell in the row that you want to become the first row in the new table, and then click the Split Table button in the Merge group on the Table Tools Layout tab.

Lesson 7.5 Changing Column Width and Row Height

 2-2.1.13, 2-2.1.14

When you first create a table, its columns are of equal width and its rows are of equal height. You can customize the width of columns and the height of rows with buttons in the Cell Size group on the Table Tools Layout tab. Use the *Table Row Height* measurement box to increase or decrease the height of rows and use the *Table Column Width* measurement box to increase or decrease the width of columns. The Distribute Rows button and the Distribute Columns button distribute equally the selected rows or columns.

You can also change column width by using the move table column markers on the horizontal ruler or by using the table gridlines. To change column width using the move table column markers, position the mouse arrow pointer on a marker until it turns into a white, double-headed arrow pointing left and right, and then drag the marker to the desired position. To change column width using gridlines, position the arrow pointer on the gridline separating two columns until it turns into a double-headed arrow pointing left and right with a short double line between and then drag the gridline to the desired position. You can adjust row height in a manner similar to that used to adjust column width—drag the adjust table row marker on the vertical ruler or drag the gridline separating rows. Use the AutoFit button in the Cell Size group to make the column widths in a table automatically fit the contents (row heights automatically adjust to fit the contents by default).

Exercise 7.5 Changing Column Width and Row Height

1. With **U2T7-ResumeTables.docx** open, position the mouse arrow pointer on the gridline between the first and second columns in the top table until the pointer turns into a double-headed arrow pointing left and right with a short double line between. Hold down the left mouse button, drag to the left until the table column marker displays at approximately the 1.25-inch mark on the horizontal ruler, and then release the mouse button.

2. Position the mouse arrow pointer on the gridline between the second and third columns until the pointer turns into a double-headed arrow pointing left and right with a short double line between, and then drag to the left until the table column marker displays at the 3-inch mark on the horizontal ruler.

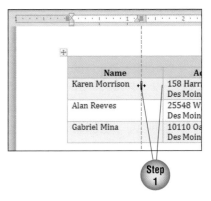

3. Following the same procedure, drag the gridline between the third and fourth columns in the top table to the left until the table column marker displays at the 4.25-inch marker on the horizontal ruler, and drag the gridline at the right border of the fourth column in the top table to the 5.5-inch marker on the horizontal ruler.

4. Drag the gridline between the third and fourth columns in the bottom table to the left until the table column marker displays at the 3.5-inch marker on the horizontal ruler.

5. Click anywhere in the text *PERSONAL REFERENCES* in the top table, click the Table Tools Layout tab, and then click the up-pointing arrow at the right side of the *Table Row Height* option box in the Cell Size group until *0.3"* displays.

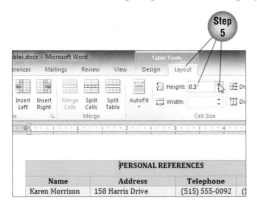

6. Click in any cell in the second row of the top table (the row containing the headings *Name*, *Address*, *Telephone*, and *Cell Phone*) and then click the up-pointing arrow at the right side of the *Table Row Height* option box until *0.2"* displays.

7. Complete steps similar to those in Steps 5 and 6 to increase the height of the row containing the text *PROFESSIONAL REFERENCES* in the bottom table to *0.3"* and increase the height of the row containing the headings *Name*, *Company*, *Title*, *Address*, and *Telephone* to *0.2"*.

8. Save **U2T7-ResumeTables.docx**.

Drilling Down | **Automatically Adjusting Column Widths**

If you do not want to manually adjust the column widths in a table, you can automatically adjust them to fit the longest entry. To do this, position the mouse arrow pointer on the gridline at the right side of the column you want to adjust until the pointer displays as a double-headed arrow pointing left and right with a short double line between, and then double-click the left mouse button.

Lesson 7.6 Changing Cell Alignment

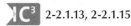 2-2.1.13, 2-2.1.15

The Alignment group on the Table Tools Layout tab includes a number of buttons for specifying the horizontal and vertical alignment of text in cells. The buttons contain a visual representation of the alignment they apply, but you can also hover the mouse arrow pointer over a button to display a ScreenTip containing the name of the alignment.

You can also change the alignment of the text in a cell with options at the Table Properties dialog box with the Cell tab selected. Display this dialog box by clicking the Properties button in the Table group on the Table Tools Layout tab. Click the Cell tab to display the *Vertical alignment* section of the dialog box, which contains options to align text at the top, center, or bottom of cells.

Exercise 7.6 Aligning Text in Cells

1. With **U2T7-ResumeTables.docx** open, click in the cell containing the text *PERSONAL REFERENCES* in the top table and then click the Align Center button in the Alignment group on the Table Tools Layout tab to change the horizontal and vertical alignment of text in the cell to center.

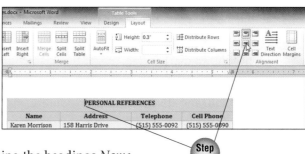

2. Select the four cells in the top table containing the headings *Name*, *Address*, *Telephone*, and *Cell Phone* and then click the Align Bottom Center button in the Alignment group.

3. Select the cell in the bottom table containing the text *PROFESSIONAL REFERENCES* and then click the Align Center button in the Alignment group.

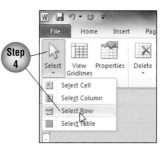

4. Select the five cells in the bottom table containing the headings *Name*, *Company*, *Title*, *Address*, and *Telephone* by clicking anywhere in the *Name* cell, clicking the Select button in the Table group on the Table Tools Layout tab, and then clicking *Select Row* at the drop-down list.

5. With the second row of the bottom table selected, click the Align Bottom Center button in the Alignment group.

6. Save **U2T7-ResumeTables.docx**.

Drilling Down

Viewing Gridlines

When you create a table, the lines that separate the rows and columns in the table are called *gridlines*. By default, gridlines have a thin black border applied to them. You can remove or change the borders. If you remove the borders, the table's gridlines display as dashed blue lines so that you can still see where each cell begins and ends. The dashed gridlines do not print. If you want to turn off the display of gridlines, click the View Gridlines button in the Table group on the Table Tools Layout tab.

Lesson 7.7 Changing Cell Margin Measurements

  2-2.1.13, 2-2.1.15

The cells in a Word table have specific default margin settings. The top and bottom margins in a cell have a default setting of 0 inches and the left and right margins have a default setting of 0.08 inch. You can change these default settings with options at the Table Options dialog box (shown in Figure 7.6). Display this dialog box by clicking the Cell Margins button in the Alignment group on the Table Tools Layout tab. Use the options in the *Default cell margins* section to change the top, bottom, left, or right cell margin measurements.

Changing the cell margins affects all cells in a table. If you want to change the cell margin measurements for one cell or for a group of selected cells, position the insertion point in the cell or select the desired cells and then click the Properties button in the Table group on the Table Tools Layout tab. (You can also click the Cell Size group dialog box launcher.) At the Table Properties dialog box, click the Cell tab and then click the Options button that displays in the lower right corner of the dialog box. This displays the Cell Options dialog box (shown in Figure 7.7).

Figure 7.6 **Table Options Dialog Box**

Use options in this section to increase or decrease margin measurements in cells.

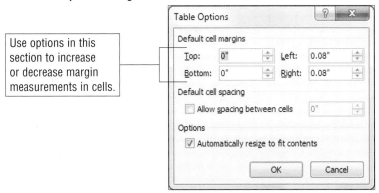

Figure 7.7 **Cell Options Dialog Box**

Remove the check mark from this option and cell margin options become available.

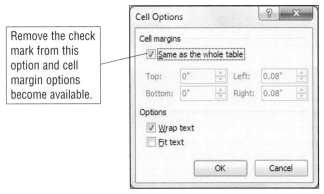

Before you can set new cell margin measurements, you must remove the check mark from the *Same as the whole table* option. After you remove the check mark from this option, the cell margin options become available. Specify the new cell margin measurements and then click OK to close the dialog box.

Exercise 7.7 Changing Cell Margin Measurements

1. With **U2T7-ResumeTables.docx** open, change the top and bottom margins for all cells in the top table. Begin by positioning the insertion point in any cell in the top table. Click the Table Tools Layout tab and then click the Cell Margins button ▤ in the Alignment group.

2. At the Table Options dialog box, change the *Top* and *Bottom* measurements to *0.04"* and then click OK to close the dialog box.

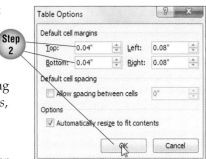

3. Change the top and bottom cell margin measurements for the second row of cells in the top table. Begin by selecting the second row of cells (contains the headings *Name*, *Address*, *Telephone*, and *Cell Phone*) and then clicking the Properties button ▦ in the Table group.

4. At the Table Properties dialog box, click the Cell tab and then click the Options button located at the bottom right side of the dialog box.

5. At the Cell Options dialog box, click the *Same as the whole table* option to remove the check mark.

6. Change the *Top* and *Bottom* measurements to *0.1"* and then click OK to close the Cell Options dialog box.

7. Click OK to close the Table Properties dialog box.

8. Complete actions similar to those in Steps 1 through 7 to change the top and bottom margins of the bottom table to *0.04"* and change the top and bottom cell margins for the second row of the bottom table to *0.1"*.

9. Save **U2T7-ResumeTables.docx**.

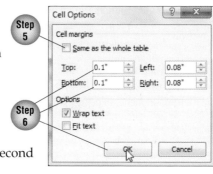

 Drilling Down

Changing Cell Direction

You can change the direction of text in a cell with the Text Direction button in the Alignment group on the Table Tools Layout tab. Each time you click the Text Direction button, the text in the cell rotates 90 degrees.

Lesson 7.8 Changing Table Alignment and Resizing and Moving a Table

 2-2.1.13, 2-2.1.15

Quick Steps

Change Table Alignment
1. Click in table.
2. Click Table Tools Layout tab.
3. Click Properties button.
4. Click Table tab.
5. Click desired alignment option.
6. Click OK.

Change Table Size with the Resize Handle
1. Hover mouse arrow pointer over table.
2. Position mouse on resize handle in lower right corner of table.
3. Drag resize handle to increase or decrease size and proportions of table.

Move a Table
1. Position mouse arrow pointer on table move handle until pointer displays as a four-headed arrow.
2. Drag table to desired position.
3. Release mouse button.

By default, tables in Word align at the left margin. Change the alignment of a table with options at the Table Properties dialog box with the Table tab selected, as shown in Figure 7.8. To change the alignment, click the desired alignment option in the *Alignment* section of the dialog box.

Figure 7.8 **Table Properties Dialog Box with Table Tab Selected**

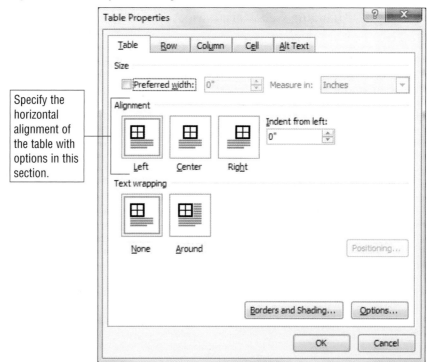

Specify the horizontal alignment of the table with options in this section.

When you hover the mouse arrow pointer over a table, a resize handle displays. The **table resize handle** is a small, white square in the lower right corner of the table that can be used to increase or decrease the size and proportions of the table. A table move handle, located in the upper left corner of a table, also displays when you hover the mouse arrow pointer over a table. The **table move handle** is an icon that can be used to move a table in a document. To move a table, position the mouse arrow pointer on the table move handle until the pointer displays with a four-headed arrow attached, hold down the left mouse button, drag the table to the desired position, and then release the mouse button.

table resize handle
A small, white square that displays in the lower right corner of a table; can be used to change the size and proportions of the table

table move handle
An icon that displays in the upper left corner of a table when you position the mouse arrow pointer in the table; can be used to move a table in a document

Exercise 7.8 Moving and Resizing Tables

1. With **U2T7-ResumeTables.docx** open, press Ctrl + End to move the insertion point to the end of the document and then press the Enter key.

2. Open **EducationTable.docx** from the **Unit2Topic07** folder on your storage medium.

3. Select the entire table by hovering the mouse arrow pointer over any cell in the table until the table move handle displays in the upper left corner of the table. Position the mouse arrow pointer over the table move handle until the pointer displays as a four-headed arrow and then click the left mouse button.

4. Click the Copy button in the Clipboard group on the Home tab.

5. Click the Word button on the Taskbar and then click the document thumbnail representing **U2T7-ResumeTables.docx**.

6. With the insertion point positioned at the end of the document, click the Paste button in the Clipboard group.

7. Click anywhere in the top table and change the table alignment by clicking the Table Tools Layout tab and then clicking the Properties button in the Table group.

8. At the Table Properties dialog box, click the Table tab, click the *Center* option in the *Alignment* section, and then click OK to close the dialog box.

9. Resize the bottom table (the table you pasted into the document in Step 6) by positioning the mouse arrow pointer on the resize handle located in the lower right corner of the bottom table. Hold down the left mouse button, drag down and to the right until the width and height of the table increase by approximately 0.5 inches, and then release the mouse button.

Step 8

EDUCATION		
School Name	**Degree**	**Graduation Date**
Fairview High School	High school diploma	June 2006
Alder Community College	Associates in Management	June 2008
University of Iowa State	Bachelors in Business	May 2010

Step 9

10. Move the bottom table by hovering the mouse arrow pointer over the table and then positioning the mouse arrow pointer on the table move handle until the pointer displays with a four-headed arrow attached. Hold down the left mouse button, drag the table so it is positioned equally between the left and right margins, and then release the mouse button.

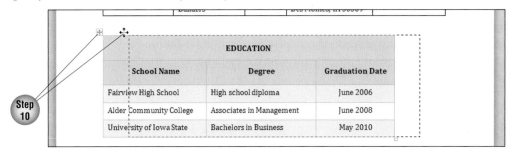

EDUCATION		
School Name	Degree	Graduation Date
Fairview High School	High school diploma	June 2006
Alder Community College	Associates in Management	June 2008
University of Iowa State	Bachelors in Business	May 2010

Step 10

11. Save, print, and then close **U2T7-ResumeTables.docx**.

12. Close **EducationTable.docx**.

Drilling Down

Changing Table Size Proportionally

You can use the table resize handle to increase or decrease the size of a table. If you want to maintain the proportions of the table (height and width ratio), hold down the Shift key while dragging the table resize handle.

Lesson 7.9 Inserting a Quick Table

IC³ 2-2.1.13

Quick Steps

Insert a Quick Table
1. Click Insert tab.
2. Click Table button.
3. Point to *Quick Tables* in drop-down list.
4. Click desired table at side menu.

Word includes a Quick Tables feature you can use to insert predesigned tables in a document. A quick table is a template provided by Microsoft to save you time creating and formatting a table. To insert a quick table, click the Insert tab, click the Table button, point to Quick Tables, and then click the desired table at the side menu. When the quick table is inserted in the document, the Table Tools Design tab becomes active. Use options in this tab to further customize the table.

Exercise 7.9 Inserting a Quick Table

1. At a blank document, click the Insert tab.

2. Click the Table button, point to *Quick Tables*, and then click *Calendar 3* at the side menu.

3. Edit text in each of the cells so the month, year, and days reflect the current date.

4. Save the completed monthly calendar with the name **U2T7-Calendar**.

5. Print and then close **U2T7-Calendar.docx**.

Step 1

Step 2

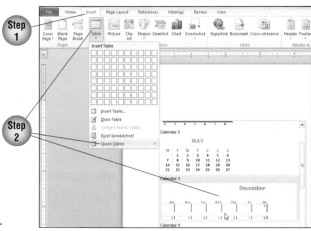

Drilling Down

Using Office.com Templates

In addition to the Quick Table templates available by clicking the Table button on the Insert tab and then pointing to the *Quick Tables* option, you can find additional templates at the New tab Backstage view. Click the File tab and then click the New tab to display the New tab Backstage view. Notice the template options available in the *Office.com Templates* section. Click an option to display specific templates or template folders. Double-click the desired template and the template is downloaded from Office.com and opened in the document screen.

Lesson 7.10 Converting Text to a Table

 2-2.1.13

You can create a table and then enter data in the cells, or you can enter data and then convert the text into a table. To convert text to a table, first type the text, making sure to use characters such as commas or tabs to separate items that will appear in different columns. The separator characters identify where you want text divided into columns. Next, select the text, click the Insert tab, click the Table button in the Tables group, and then click *Convert Text to Table* at the drop-down list. At the Convert Text to Table dialog box (shown in Figure 7.9), insert the numbers of columns and/or rows for the new table; determine how to fit the text in the table; and identify where to separate the text to make the table, such as at the paragraphs, commas, or tabs.

Quick Steps

Convert Text to a Table
1. Select text.
2. Click Insert tab.
3. Click Table button.
4. Click *Convert Text to Table*.
5. Make necessary changes at Convert Text to Table dialog box.
6. Click OK.

Figure 7.9 Convert Text to Table Dialog Box

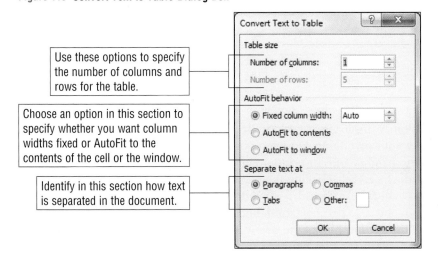

Use these options to specify the number of columns and rows for the table.

Choose an option in this section to specify whether you want column widths fixed or AutoFit to the contents of the cell or the window.

Identify in this section how text is separated in the document.

Exercise 7.10 Converting Text to a Table

1. Open **SchedTables.docx** from the **Unit2Topic07** folder on your storage medium and then save the file with Save As and name it **U2T7-SchedTables**.

2. Select the five lines of text located at the beginning of the document (the text that begins with *Training Schedule*).

3. Click the Insert tab, click the Table button in the Tables group, and then click *Convert Text to Table* at the drop-down list.

4. At the Convert Text to Table dialog box, type **3** in the *Number of columns* text box, click the *AutoFit to contents* option in the *AutoFit behavior* section, click the *Commas* option in the *Separate text at* section, and then click OK to close the dialog box.

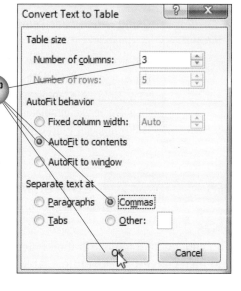

5. Select and then merge the cells in the top row (the row containing the title *Training Schedule*) and then change the alignment to Align Center.

6. With the top row still selected, change the font size to *12*.

7. Apply the *Light List - Accent 4* table style and click to remove the check mark from the *First Column* check box in the Table Style Options group on the Table Tools Design tab.

8. Select the second row of the table and apply bold formatting.

9. Drag the table so it is centered between the left and right margins (centered above the bottom table).

10. Save **U2T7-SchedTables.docx**.

Drilling Down

Converting a Table to Text

You can convert a table to text by positioning the insertion point in any cell of the table, clicking the Table Tools Layout tab, and then clicking the Convert to Text button in the Data group. At the Convert Table to Text dialog box, specify the desired separator and then click OK.

Lesson 7.11   Drawing a Table

IC³ 2-2.1.13

Quick Steps

Draw a Table

1. Click Insert tab.
2. Click Table button.
3. Click *Draw Table* at drop-down list.
4. Drag pen pointer in document to create table.

In addition to inserting a table with predesigned rows and columns, you can draw your own table. Drawing your own table allows you to create cells of varying heights and/or widths within a column or row. Draw a table by clicking the Insert tab, clicking the Table button in the Tables group, and then clicking *Draw Table* at the drop-down list. This turns the mouse arrow pointer into a pen and also displays guidelines on the horizontal and vertical rulers that identify the location of the pen in the document. Using the guidelines as a reference, drag the pen pointer in the document screen to create the table and the cells within it.

The first time you release the mouse button when drawing a table, the Table Tools Design tab becomes active. Use the buttons on this tab to customize the table as well as to apply table styles, shading, and borders. If you make a mistake while drawing a table, click the Eraser button in the Draw Borders group (this changes the mouse arrow pointer to an eraser) and then drag over or click on any border lines you want to erase.

Exercise 7.11 Drawing a Table

1. With **U2T7-SchedTables.docx** open, press Ctrl + End to move the insertion point to the end of the document and then press the Enter key.

2. Draw the table shown in Figure 7.10. Begin by clicking the Insert tab, clicking the Table button in the Tables group, and then clicking *Draw Table* at the drop-down list.

3. Move the pen pointer to approximately the 1.5-inch marker on the horizontal ruler and the 3.5-inch marker on the vertical ruler. Press and hold down the left mouse button, drag down and to the right until the guideline displays at approximately the 5-inch marker on the horizontal ruler and the 5.5-inch marker on the vertical ruler, and then release the mouse button.

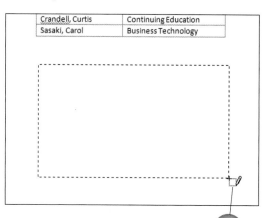

Step 3

4. With the pen still active, draw the horizontal line and two vertical lines within the table as shown in Figure 7.10.

5. After drawing the table, click the Draw Table button in the Draw Borders group on the Table Tools Design tab to deactivate it.

6. Type the text in the table as shown in Figure 7.10.

7. Apply the *Colorful Shading - Accent 4* table style to the table.

8. Select the table, change the font size to *14*, turn on bold, and then center-align the text in the cells.

9. Adjust the border lines so that the text displays on one line in each cell.

10. Drag the table so it is positioned below the middle table and centered between the left and right margins.

11. Save **U2T7-SchedTables.docx**.

Figure 7.10 Exercise 7.11 Example

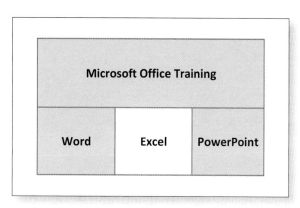

Drilling Down

Using Options in the Draw Borders Group

When drawing a table in a document, you can customize the type of lines you draw using the options in the Draw Borders group on the Table Tools Design tab. Click the Line Style button arrow and a drop-down list displays containing a variety of styles such as single lines, double lines, triple lines, thick and thin double or triple lines, shaded lines, and lines with designs. Click the Line Weight button arrow and a drop-down list displays with various line widths. The higher the width measurement, the wider the line. Use the palette that displays when you click the Pen Color button in the Draw Borders group to change the color of the line you use to create your table. If you want to erase lines in a table, click the Eraser button and then drag over or click on the lines in the table you want to remove. When you are finished drawing the table, click the Draw Table button in the Draw Borders group on the Table Tools Design tab or press the Esc key.

Lesson 7.12 Sorting in a Table

 2-2.1.13, 2-2.1.15

Quick Steps

Sort Text in Tables
1. Select desired rows in table.
2. Click Sort button on Table Tools Layout tab.
3. Specify column containing text to sort.
4. Click OK.

You can sort text in a table alphabetically, numerically, or by date. For example, you can sort text in a table alphabetically by last name, you can sort sales amounts from highest to lowest or lowest to highest, or sort dates from most recent to oldest or oldest to most recent. Sort data in a table with options at the Sort dialog box shown in Figure 7.11. Display this dialog box by positioning the insertion point in a cell in the table and then clicking the Sort button in the Data group on the Table Tools Layout tab. Make sure the column you want to sort is selected in the *Sort by* option and then click OK. If the first row in the table contains data such as headings that you do not want to include in the sort, click the *Header row* option in the *My list has* section of the Sort dialog box. If you want to sort specific cells in a table, select the cells first and then click the Sort button.

Figure 7.11 Sort Dialog Box

In this section, specify the column on which you want to sort, the type of sort, and the sort order.

Use these options to sort on more than one column.

Specify whether or not your table has a header row.

Exercise 7.12 Sorting Text in a Table

1. With **U2T7-SchedTables.docx** open, select all the rows containing names (from *Coolidge, Rebecca* through *Sasaki, Carol*) in the middle table.

2. Click the Table Tools Layout tab and then click the Sort button in the Data group.

3. At the Sort dialog box, click OK.

   This sorts the last names in the first column in alphabetical order.

4. After looking at the table, you decide to sort by department. With rows 3–8 still selected, click the Sort button in the Data group.

5. At the Sort dialog box, click the down-pointing arrow at the right side of the *Sort by* option box and then click *Column 2* at the drop-down list.

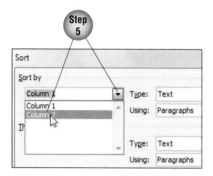

6. Click OK to close the dialog box.

7. Deselect the rows.

8. Save, print, and then close **U2T7-SchedTables.docx**.

Specifying the Sort Type

The *Type* option at the Sort dialog box has a default setting of *Text*. In addition to a text sort, you can sort by numbers and by date. In a text sort, Word arranges text in the following order: text beginning with a special symbol, such as *$* or *#*, first; text preceded by numbers second; and alphabetically by letter third. In a number sort, Word arranges text in numeric order and ignores any alphabetic text. Only the numbers 0 through 9 and symbols pertaining to numbers are recognized. These symbols include *$*, *%*, *( )*, a decimal point, a comma, and the symbols for the four basic operations: + (addition), - (subtraction), * (multiplication), and / (division). Word can sort numbers in ascending or descending order. In a date sort, Word chronologically sorts dates that are expressed in a common date format, such as 06-01-2013; 06/01/2013; June 1, 2013; or 1 June 2013. Word does not sort dates that include abbreviated month names without periods. Word does not sort dates that are expressed as a month, day, or year only. Like number sorts, date sorts can be in ascending or descending order.

Delving Deeper

 2-2.13.13

Performing Calculations in a Table in Word

You can use the Formula button in the Data group on the Table Tools Layout tab to insert formulas that make calculations using the data in a table. Numbers in the cells of a table can be added, subtracted, multiplied, and divided. In addition, you can calculate averages, percentages, and minimum and maximum values.

To perform a calculation on data in a table in Word, position the insertion point in the cell where you want the result of the calculation to display and then click the Formula button in the Data group on the Table Tools Layout tab. This displays the Formula dialog box, shown on the next page. At this dialog box, accept the default formula that displays in the *Formula* text box or type the desired calculation and then click OK.

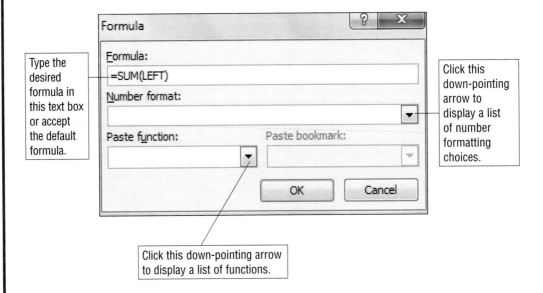

Type the desired formula in this text box or accept the default formula.

Click this down-pointing arrow to display a list of number formatting choices.

Click this down-pointing arrow to display a list of functions.

In the default formula, the SUM part of the formula is called a function. Word provides other functions you can use to write a formula. These functions are available at the *Paste function* drop-down list in the Formula dialog box. For example, you can use the AVERAGE function to average numbers in cells. Specify the numbering format at the *Number format* drop-down list in the Formula dialog box. For example, if you are calculating money amounts, you can specify that the calculated numbers display with no numbers or two numbers following the decimal point. Note that while you can perform a variety of calculations in Word, an Excel worksheet is more suitable when you need to manipulate data in a complex manner.

TOPIC SUMMARY

- Use the Tables feature to create columns and rows in which you can insert data. A cell is the intersection between a column and a row.
- A table can contain text, characters, numbers, graphics, or formulas.
- Create a table by clicking the Insert tab, clicking the Table button in the Tables group, dragging the mouse arrow pointer down and to the right until the desired number of columns and rows display in the grid, and then releasing the mouse button. You can also create a table with options at the Insert Table dialog box.
- Columns in a table are lettered from left to right beginning with A. Rows are numbered from top to bottom beginning with 1.
- The lines that form the cells of the table are called gridlines.
- To use the mouse to move the insertion point to different cells within a table, simply click in the desired cell.
- Position the mouse arrow pointer on the cell selection bar, the row selection bar, or the top gridline of a column to select a cell, row, or column. Click the table move handle to select the entire table.
- Refer to Table 7.2 for a list of keyboard commands for selecting specific cells within a table.
- You can select a cell, row, column, or table using the Select button in the Table group on the Table Tools Layout tab.
- When you insert a table in a document, the Table Tools Design tab becomes active.
- Apply formatting to a table with the table styles available in the Table Styles group on the Table Tools Design tab.
- Further refine predesigned table style formatting applied to columns and rows with options in the Table Style Options group on the Table Tools Design tab.
- Use the Shading button in the Table Styles group on the Table Tools Design tab to apply shading to a cell or selected cells and use the Borders button to apply borders.
- Customize shading and borders with options at the Borders and Shading dialog box. Display this dialog box by clicking the Borders button arrow and then clicking *Borders and Shading* at the drop-down list.
- Change the layout of a table with options and buttons on the Table Tools Layout tab.
- Insert and delete columns and rows with buttons in the Rows & Columns group on the Table Tools Layout tab.
- Merge selected cells with the Merge Cells button and split cells with the Split Cells button, both located in the Merge group on the Table Tools Layout tab.
- Change column width and row height using the height and width measurement boxes in the Cell Size group on the Table Tools Layout tab; by dragging the move table column markers on the horizontal ruler, adjusting table row markers on the vertical ruler, or adjusting gridlines in the table; or with the AutoFit button in the Cell Size group.
- Change the alignment of text in cells with buttons in the Alignment group on the Table Tools Layout tab.
- Change cell margins with options at the Table Options dialog box.
- Change the table alignment at the Table Properties dialog box with the Table tab selected.
- Use the table resize handle to change the size of the table and use the table move handle to move the table.
- Quick tables are predesigned tables you can insert in a document by clicking the Insert tab, clicking the Table button, pointing to Quick Tables, and then clicking the desired option at the side menu.
- Convert text to a table with the Convert Text to Table option at the Table button drop-down list.
- Draw a table in a document by clicking the Insert tab, clicking the Table button, and then clicking *Draw Table* at the drop-down list. Using the mouse, drag within the document to create the table.
- Sort selected rows in a table with the Sort button in the Data group.

Key Terms

cell selection bar, p. 303
row selection bar, p. 303
table move handle, p. 315
table resize handle, p. 315

Features Summary

Feature	Ribbon Tab, Group	Button, Option	Keyboard Shortcut
AutoFit table contents	Table Tools Layout, Cell Size		
Cell alignment	Table Tools Layout, Alignment		
Convert text to table	Insert, Tables	, *Convert Text to Table*	
Create table	Insert, Tables		
Delete column	Table Tools Layout, Rows & Columns	, *Delete Columns*	
Delete row	Table Tools Layout, Rows & Columns	, *Delete Rows*	
Delete table	Table Tools Layout, Rows & Columns	, *Delete Table*	
Draw a table	Insert, Tables	, *Draw Table*	
Insert column left	Table Tools Layout, Rows & Columns		
Insert column right	Table Tools Layout, Rows & Columns		
Insert Quick Table	Insert, Tables	, *Quick Tables*	
Insert row above	Table Tools Layout, Rows & Columns		
Insert row below	Table Tools Layout, Rows & Columns		
Insert Table dialog box	Insert, Tables	, *Insert Table*	
Merge cells	Table Tools Layout, Merge		
Move insertion point to next cell			Tab
Move insertion point to previous cell			Shift + Tab
Move insertion point to tab stop within cell			Ctrl + Tab

continued

Feature	Ribbon Tab, Group	Button, Option	Keyboard Shortcut
Select table	Table Tools Layout, Table	⬚, *Select Table*	
Sort text in table	Table Tools Layout, Data	⬚	
Table Options dialog box	Table Tools Layout, Alignment	⬚	
Table Properties dialog box	Table Tools Layout, Table	⬚	

KEY POINTS REVIEW

Identification

Match the terms to the callouts on the Word window in Figure 7.12.

1. _____ move table column marker
2. _____ Sort button
3. _____ cell height and width options
4. _____ Delete button
5. _____ Insert row buttons

6. _____ Table Properties button
7. _____ end-of-cell marker
8. _____ cell alignment options
9. _____ merged cells
10. _____ end-of-row marker

Figure 7.12 Identification Figure

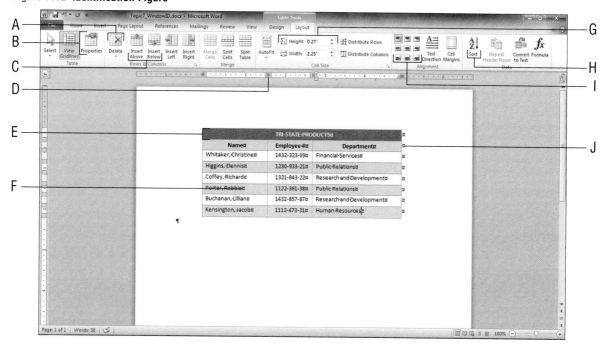

Multiple Choice

For each of the following items, choose the option that best completes the sentence or answers the question.

1. The Table button is located in this tab.
   A. Home
   B. Insert
   C. Page Layout
   D. Review

2. This term refers to the intersection between a row and a column.
   A. crosshair
   B. handle
   C. marker
   D. cell

3. When you hover the mouse arrow pointer over a table, this displays in the upper left corner of the table.
   A. move table column marker
   B. move table row marker
   C. resize handle
   D. table move handle

4. Use this keyboard command to move the insertion point to the previous cell.
   A. Tab
   B. Shift + Tab
   C. Shift + Enter
   D. Enter

5. When you insert a table in a document, this tab is active.
   A. Table Tools Format tab
   B. Table Tools Layout tab
   C. Table Tools Design tab
   D. Insert tab

6. Use this feature to insert predesigned tables in a document.
   A. Quick Tables
   B. Fast Tables
   C. Predesigned Tables
   D. Formatted Tables

7. Insert and delete columns and rows with buttons in this group on the Table Tools Layout tab.
   A. Table
   B. Rows & Columns
   C. Cell Size
   D. Alignment

8. Use this measurement box on the Table Tools Layout tab to increase or decrease the height of rows.
   A. Distribute Rows
   B. Distribute Columns
   C. Table Row Height
   D. Table Column Width

9. This is the default setting for the left and right margins in a cell.
   A. 0.8 inch
   B. 0.6 inch
   C. 0.4 inch
   D. 0.2 inch

10. The Alignment group on the Table Tools Layout tab contains this many cell alignment options.
    A. 4
    B. 6
    C. 9
    D. 10

Matching

Match each of the following definitions with the correct term, command, or option.

1. _____ One way to change column width is to drag this on the horizontal ruler.
2. _____ Hover the mouse arrow pointer over a table and this displays in the lower right corner of the table.
3. _____ Click this button in the Insert tab to display the *Convert Text to Table* option.
4. _____ Change the table alignment at this dialog box with the Table tab selected.
5. _____ The Sort button is located in this group on the Table Tools Layout tab.
6. _____ Click this button to display the end of a cell and the end of a row marker.
7. _____ Modify predesigned table formatting applied to columns and rows with options in this group on the Table Tools Design tab.
8. _____ Combine selected cells with this button on the Table Tools Layout tab.
9. _____ Columns in a table are labeled with this.
10. _____ Rows in a table are labeled with this.

A. Resize handle
B. Data
C. Table
D. Merge Cells
E. Numbers
F. Move table column marker
G. Letters
H. Show/Hide ¶
I. Table Properties
J. Table Style Options

SKILLS REVIEW

Review 7.1 Creating and Modifying a Team Table

1. At a blank Word document, create the table and enter text in the table exactly as shown in Figure 7.13.
2. Insert a new column between the *Title* and *Telephone* columns and then insert the following information in the new column:
   Department
   Executive
   Executive
   Finance
   Finance
   Production
   Production
3. Move the *Telephone* column right border to the 5-inch mark on the horizontal ruler.
4. Move the *Ext.* column right border to the 5.5-inch mark on the horizontal ruler.
5. Insert a new row at the beginning of the table, merge the cells in the first row, change the alignment to *Align Top Center*, and then type the text **ADMINISTRATIVE TEAM**.
6. Apply the *Medium Shading 1 – Accent 4* table style to the table and remove the check mark from the *First Column* check box in the Table Style Options group on the Table Tools Design tab.
7. Select the second row (the row containing *Name*, *Title*, *Department*, *Telephone*, *Ext.*) and then apply bold formatting.
8. Drag the table so it is centered between the left and right margins.
9. Save the document and name it **U2T7-R1-Team**.
10. Print and then close **U2T7-R1-Team.docx**.

Figure 7.13 **Review 7.1 Table**

Name	Title	Telephone	Ext.
Warren Brown	President	(351) 555-8902	110
Gabrielle Lopez	Vice President	(351) 555-8902	125
Nicholas Shane	Director	(351) 555-8945	223
Tina Wallace	Assistant Director	(351) 555-8945	248
Isaac Abrahams	Director	(351) 555-8984	329
Casey Collier	Assistant Director	(351) 555-8984	337

Review 7.2 Creating and Formatting a Tour Package Table

1. At a blank document, type the title and then create the table and enter the text in the table as shown in Figure 7.14.
2. Set the title *Sun Travel Tour Packages* in 16-point bold and then center the title.
3. Apply the *Medium Shading 1 - Accent 5* table style.
4. Remove the check mark from all check boxes in the Table Style Options group on the Table Tools Design tab.
5. Apply the *Orange, Accent 6, Lighter 40%* orange fill to the first row and then apply bold formatting.
6. Apply the *Orange, Accent 6, Lighter 80%* orange fill to the third and fifth rows in the table.
7. Save the document with the name **U2T7-R2-Tours**.
8. Print and then close **U2T7-R2-Tours.docx**.

Figure 7.14 **Review 7.2 Table**

Sun Travel Tour Packages

Name	Duration	Costs	Discount
Jamaican Fun in the Sun	5 days and 4 nights	From $709 to $1049	20% in March
Jamaican Nights	8 days and 7 nights	From $1079 to $1729	10% in March and April
Jamaican Fun Tours	10 days and 9 nights	From $1999 to $2229	15% in April and May
Jamaican Land Tours	14 days and 13 nights	From $2499 to $3099	10% in May and June

SKILLS ASSESSMENT

Assessment 7.1 Creating and Formatting a Training Cost Table

1. At a blank document, create the table shown in Figure 7.15 with the following specifications:
   a. Create a table with two columns and eight rows.
   b. Merge the cells in the top row and then change the alignment to Align Center.
   c. Type the text in the cells as shown in Figure 7.15.
   d. Apply the Align Center Left alignment to the cells in the left column beginning with *Human Resources*.
   e. Apply the Align Center Right alignment to the cells containing the money amounts.
   f. Move the gridline between the first and second columns to the 2-inch mark on the horizontal ruler.
   g. Move the right border of the table to the 3-inch mark on the horizontal ruler.
   h. Apply the *Medium Shading 2 - Accent 4* table style.
   i. Change the font size to 14 and apply the Align Center alignment to the text in cell A1.
   j. Use the resize handle located in the lower right corner of the table to increase the width and height of the table by approximately 1 inch.
2. Save the document with the name **U2T7-A1-TrainCosts**.
3. Print and then close **U2T7-A1-TrainCosts.docx**.

Figure 7.15 **Assessment 7.1 Table**

TRAINING COSTS	
Human Resource	$23,150
Research and Development	$78,455
Public Relations	$10,348
Purchasing	$22,349
Administration	$64,352
Sales and Marketing	$18,450
Total	$217,104

Assessment 7.2 Creating and Modifying a Table

1. At a blank document, create the table shown in Figure 7.16. Modify the table and apply formatting as shown in the figure.
2. Save the document and name it **U2T7-A2-Schedule**.
3. Print and then close **U2T7-A2-Schedule.docx**.

Figure 7.16 **Assessment 7.2 Table**

FALL SCHEDULE				
Course	**Name**	**Days**	**Time**	**Instructor**
BT110	Business Applications	MTWRF	9:00-9:50 a.m.	Gunderson
BT140	Introduction to Business	MWF	10:00-11:20 a.m.	Morgenstern
SO210	Demographics	MTWRF	1:00-1:50 p.m.	Adams
AT101	Introduction to Anthropology	MW	2:00-3:20 p.m.	Tan-Mien

Assessment 7.3 Converting Text to a Table and Sorting Text in the Table

1. Open **ContactInfo.docx** from the **Unit2Topic07** folder on your storage medium, save the document with Save As, and name it **U2T7-A3-ContactInfo**.
2. Select the text and then convert the text to a table.
3. Apply the *Medium Grid 2 - Accent 2* table style.
4. Click the *First Column* option in the Table Style Options group to remove the check mark.
5. Merge the cells in the top row and then center-align the title.
6. Select the second row and apply bold formatting.
7. Change the width of the second column to 3.5".
8. Change the width of the first column to 2".
9. Sort the table by employee number in ascending order.
10. Save, print, and then close **U2T7-A3-ContactInfo.docx**.

Assessment 7.4 Creating a Monthly Calendar with a Quick Table

1. Use the Quick Table feature to create a monthly calendar for next month.
2. Apply additional formatting to enhance the visual appeal of the calendar.
3. Save the document and name it **U2T7-A4-Calendar**.
4. Print and then close **U2T7-A4-Calendar.docx**.

Assessment 7.5 Inserting Formulas in a Table

1. Use Word's Help feature to learn how to perform calculations in a table and specifically how to total numbers in a row or column.
2. Open **CFExpenses.docx** and then save the document and name it **U2T7-A5-CFExpenses**.
3. Using the information you learned about totaling numbers in a row or column, insert a formula in the cell immediately below *Total* that sums the amount in the cell immediately below *First Half* and the amount in the cell immediately below *Second Half*.
4. Insert a formula in each of the remaining cells in the *Total* column that sums the amount in the *First Half* with the amount in the *Second Half*.
5. Save, print, and then close **U2T7-A5-CFExpenses.docx**.

Assessment 7.6 Locating Company Information and Create a Table

1. Using the Internet (or other resources available to you), locate information on three companies for which you would be interested in working.
2. Create a table that includes information about each company such as name, address, telephone number, website address, email address, and so on. You determine the information to include in the table and then apply design and layout features to enhance the visual appeal of the table.
3. Save the document and name it **U2T7-A6-Companies**.
4. Print and then close **U2T7-A6-Companies.docx**.

Assessment 7.7 Creating a Cover Letter Containing a Table

1. At a blank document, create the document shown in Figure 7.17. Create and format the table as shown in the figure. *Hint: Apply the* **Light Grid - Accent 3** *table style*.
2. Save the completed document and name it **U2T7-A7-CoverLtrTable**.
3. Print and then close **U2T7-A7-CoverLtrTable.docx**.

Figure 7.17 **Assessment 7.7 Document**

8448 Rainier Drive
Olympia, WA 98501
July 15, 2012

Ms. Madison Santos
Cascade Hills News
100 Second Avenue
Olympia, WA 98501

Dear Ms. Santos:

Your advertised opening for a corporate communications staff writer describes interesting challenges. As you can see from the table below, my skills and experience are excellent matches for the position.

QUALIFICATIONS AND SKILLS	
Your Requirements	**My Experience, Skills, and Value Offered**
Two years of business writing experience	Four years of experience creating diverse business messages, from corporate communications to feature articles and radio broadcast material.
Ability to complete projects on deadline	Proven project coordination skills and tight deadline focus. My current role as producer of a daily three-hour talk-radio program requires planning, coordination, and execution of many detailed tasks, always in the face of inflexible deadlines.
Oral presentation skills	Unusually broad experience, including high-profile roles as an on-air radio presence and "the voice" for an on-hold telephone message company.
Relevant education (BA or BS)	BA in Mass Communications; one year post-graduate study in Multimedia Communications.

As you will note from the enclosed resume, my experience encompasses corporate, print media, and multimedia environments. I offer a diverse and proven skill set that can help your company create and deliver its message to various audiences to build image, market presence, and revenue. I look forward to meeting with you to discuss the value I can offer your company.

Sincerely,

Matthew Tolliver

Enclosure: Resume

CRITICAL THINKING

Creating an Employment Application Form

Part 1 You work for Summit Fitness Center and have been asked by your supervisor to create an employment application form that a person fills out when applying for a job with the center. Create a form using a table that minimally includes the following information along with space for the applicant to handwrite the information: name, address, telephone number, cell phone number, experience, references, education, and any other information you determine is necessary for an employment application form. Save the completed form and name it **U2T7-C01-AppForm**. Print and then close the document.

Part 2 Create a memo to your instructor that explains how you designed the table and what formatting you applied to the table and why. Describe any advantages to creating the application form using a table rather than typing the text directly into the document. Save the memo document and name it **U2T7-C02-Memo**. Print and then close the document.

TEAM PROJECT

Designing an Informative Table

Part 1 As a team, choose a vacation destination. Using the Internet or other resources, identify three airlines that fly to the destination, three hotels, and three interesting activities at the destination. Create a table with the information you find. Apply formatting to the table to enhance the visual appeal. Save the completed document and name it **U2T7-TeamDest**. Print the document.

Part 2 Add the following information to the table: airline ticket prices, daily hotel rates, and the activity prices per person. Make any necessary formatting changes to accommodate the new columns. Save, print, and then close **U2T7-TeamDest.docx**.

Discussion Questions

1. What resources did each team use to find the information about the destination? Which of the resources provided the most information?
2. Compare your table with the tables created by the other teams. Which table contains the most appealing formatting? What makes one table more appealing than another?

Topic 8

Formatting a Document in Word with Special Features

Performance Objectives

Upon successful completion of Topic 8, you will be able to:

- Change page margins, orientation, and size
- Apply a theme
- Insert symbols, special characters, files, and the date and time in a document
- Insert predesigned page numbering, headers, footers, and a cover page
- Insert page and section breaks
- Create and format text in columns
- Insert, size, and move images

- Draw and format shapes
- Select and align objects
- Create and modify WordArt text
- Use SmartArt to create organizational charts and diagrams
- Track changes
- Insert comments
- Protect a document

STUDENT RESOURCES

Before beginning this topic, copy to your storage medium the **Unit2Topic08** subfolder from the *Computer and Internet Essentials: Preparing for IC³* Internet Resource Center. Make this the active folder.

In addition to containing the data files needed to complete topic work, the Internet Resource Center contains model answers in PDF format for each of the applicable exercises in this topic. Use these files to check your work. The preface of your textbook provides instructions for accessing these files.

Necessary Data Files

To complete the exercises and assessments, you will need the following data files:

Exercises 8.1 & 8.2	PrepResume.docx
Exercise 8.3	PrepResume.docx Information.docx
Exercise 8.4	PrepResume.docx
Exercises 8.5 & 8.6	CompAdv.docx
Exercise 8.7	SGCQualities.docx SGCLogo.jpg
Exercises 8.8 & 8.9	SGCQualities.docx
Exercise 8.10	New file
Exercises 8.11–8.13	CompComm.docx
Exercise 8.14	InterApps.docx

continued

Review 8.1	Computers.docx
Reviews 8.2 & 8.3	WritingSteps.docx
Review 8.4	New file
Review 8.5	NewsltrLayout.docx
Assessment 8.1	CompChapters.docx
Assessment 8.2	New file
Assessment 8.3	New file VALogo.jpg
Assessment 8.4	KLHPlan.docx
Assessment 8.5	FirstAid.docx
Assessment 8.6	Resume.docx
Critical Thinking	RecyclingPolicy.docx
Team Project	CPNewsltr.docx

Visual Preview

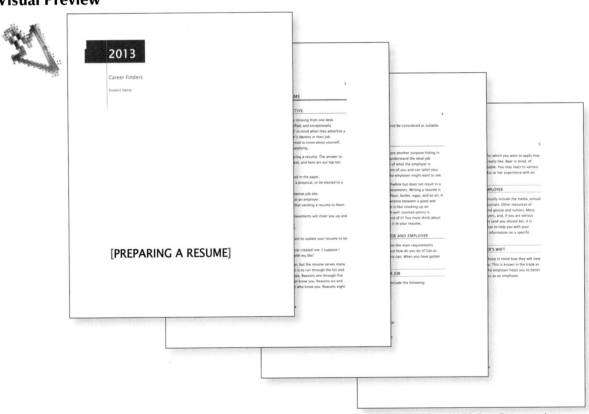

Exercises 8.1–8.4 **U2T8-PrepResume.docx**

Exercises 8.5–8.6 **U2T8-CompAdv.docx**

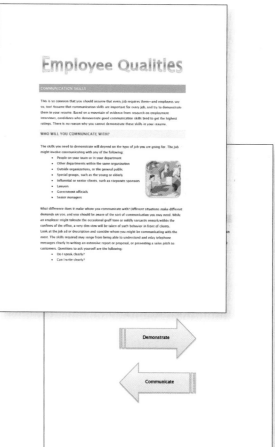

Exercises 8.7–8.9 **SGCQualities.docx**

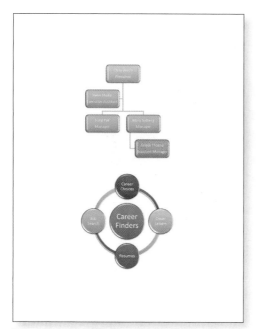

Exercise 8.10 **U2T8-SmartArtGraphics.docx**

Exercises 8.11–8.13 **U2T8-CompComm.docx**

Formatting a Document in Word with Special Features

Exercise 8.14 **U2-T8-InterApps-Footnotes.docx**

Exercise 8.14 **Page 2 of**
U2T8-InterApps-Endnotes.docx

Topic Overview

Word contains special formatting features you can apply in a document to enhance the visual display of text. For example, you can improve the appearance of documents by inserting page numbering, headers, and footers; changing margins and page orientation; and applying a theme. Add visual appeal to a document with pictures, clip art images, shapes, and WordArt. Use the SmartArt feature to create visual representations of data such as organizational charts and graphics. Improve the ease with which a person can read and understand groups of words by setting text in columns. In this topic, you will learn about these features along with information on how to track changes in a document, insert comments, protect a document, and how to insert footnotes and endnotes in a document.

Lesson 8.1 Changing Page Margins, Orientation, and Size

 2-1.4.1

The Page Setup group on the Page Layout tab contains a number of options for formatting pages in a document. With options in this group, you can perform such actions as changing margins, page orientation, and page size, as well as inserting page breaks.

Quick Steps

Change Margins

1. Click Page Layout tab.
2. Click Margins button.
3. Click desired option.

By default, a Word document contains 1-inch top, bottom, left, and right page margins. Change page margins with options at the *Margins* drop-down list (Figure 8.1). To display this list, click the Page Layout tab and then click the Margins button in the Page Setup group. To change margins, click one of the preset margin options that displays in the drop-down list. You can also customize margins by clicking the *Custom Margins* option at the drop-down list. This opens the Page Setup dialog box (Figure 8.2). To change margins, select the current measurement in the *Top*, *Bottom*, *Left*, or *Right* text box and then type the new measurement. Increase a measurement by clicking the up-pointing arrow at the right side of the text box. Click the down-pointing arrow to decrease the measurement. As you make changes to the margin measurements at the Page Setup dialog box, the sample page in the *Preview* section illustrates the effect of the changes.

Figure 8.1 Margins Drop-down List **Figure 8.2 Page Setup Dialog Box with Margins Tab Selected**

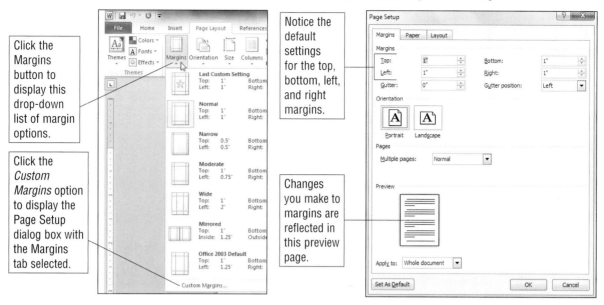

Click the Margins button to display this drop-down list of margin options.

Click the *Custom Margins* option to display the Page Setup dialog box with the Margins tab selected.

Notice the default settings for the top, bottom, left, and right margins.

Changes you make to margins are reflected in this preview page.

By default, Word uses the portrait orientation for a document. **Orientation** refers to the layout position of a page for printing. Click the Orientation button in the Page Setup group on the Page Layout tab and two options display— *Portrait* and *Landscape*. At the portrait orientation the page is 11 inches tall and 8.5 inches wide, and at the landscape orientation the page is 8.5 inches tall and 11 inches wide.

By default, Word uses a page size of 8.5 inches wide and 11 inches tall. You can change this default setting with options at the *Size* drop-down list shown in Figure 8.3. Display this drop-down list by clicking the Size button in the Page Setup group on the Page Layout tab.

orientation The layout position of a page for printing

Quick Steps

Change Orientation
1. Click Page Layout tab.
2. Click Orientation button.
3. Click desired orientation option.

Change Page Size
1. Click Page Layout tab.
2. Click Size button.
3. Click desired size option.

Figure 8.3 Size Drop-down List

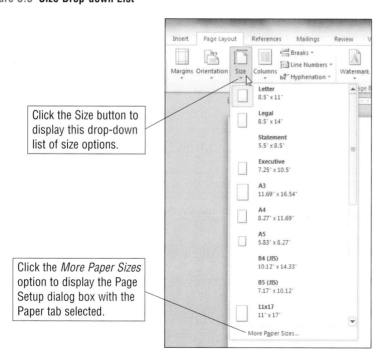

Click the Size button to display this drop-down list of size options.

Click the *More Paper Sizes* option to display the Page Setup dialog box with the Paper tab selected.

Exercise 8.1 Changing Page Margins, Orientation, and Size

1. Open **PrepResume.docx** from the **Unit2Topic08** folder on your storage medium and save the document and name it **U2T8-PrepResume.docx**.

2. Change the margins by clicking the Page Layout tab, clicking the Margins button in the Page Setup group, and then clicking the *Office 2003 Default* option at the drop-down list.

   The *Office 2003 Default* option changes the left and right margins to 1.25, which is the default for Word 2003.

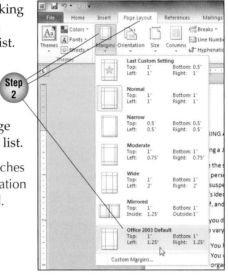

3. Change the page orientation by clicking the Orientation button in the Page Setup group on the Page Layout tab and then clicking *Landscape* at the drop-down list.

   At the landscape orientation, Word considers a page 11 inches wide and 8.5 inches tall. You can also change page orientation at the Page Setup dialog box with the Margins tab selected.

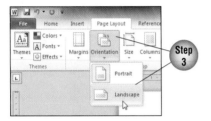

4. With the document in landscape orientation, you decide to make changes to the margins. To begin, click the Margins button in the Page Setup group on the Page Layout tab and then click the *Custom Margins* option that displays at the bottom of the drop-down list.

5. At the Page Setup dialog box with the Margins tab selected, click the down-pointing arrow at the right side of the *Bottom* option until 1″ displays. Click the up-pointing arrow at the right side of the *Left* option until 1.5″ displays.

   You can also change a margin measurement by selecting the current measurement and then typing the new measurement.

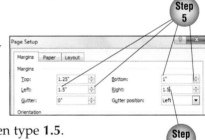

6. Select the current measurement in the *Right* text box and then type **1.5**.

7. Click OK to close the Page Setup dialog box.

8. With the insertion point positioned at the beginning of the document, print page 1.

9. Change to portrait orientation by clicking the Orientation button in the Page Setup group on the Page Layout tab and then clicking *Portrait* at the drop-down list.

10. Return margins to the default measurements by clicking the Margins button in the Page Setup group and then clicking *Normal* at the drop-down list.

11. Experiment with paper size by clicking the Size button in the Page Setup group on the Page Layout tab and then clicking the *Legal* option at the drop-down list.

    Legal paper size is 8.5 inches wide and 14 inches tall.

12. Scroll through the document and notice how the document is affected by the legal page size. After looking at the document, return to the default page size. To do this, click the Size button in the Page Setup group and then click *Letter* at the drop-down list.

13. Save **U2T8-PrepResume.docx**.

Drilling Down

Changing Paper Size at the Page Setup Dialog Box

With options at the Page Setup dialog box with the Paper tab selected as shown at the right, you can choose a paper size, specify width and height measurements, and identify printer paper sources such as the default paper tray or other available trays. Display this dialog box by clicking the Size button in the Page Setup group on the Page Layout tab and then clicking *More Paper Sizes* at the drop-down list.

Lesson 8.2   Applying a Theme

 2-2.1.11

Word provides a number of themes you can use to format text in your document. A **theme** is a set of formatting choices that includes a color theme (a set of colors), a font theme (a set of heading and body text fonts), and an effects theme (a set of line and fill effects). To apply a theme, click the Page Layout tab and then click the Themes button in the Themes group. At the drop-down gallery that displays, click the desired theme. You can hover the mouse pointer over a theme and the Live Preview feature will display your document with the theme formatting applied.

You can change a theme with the buttons that display at the right side of the Themes button. A theme contains specific color formatting, which you can change with options from the Theme Colors button in the Themes group. Click this button and a drop-down gallery displays with named color themes. The names of the color themes correspond to the names of the overall themes. Each theme also applies specific fonts, which you can change with the options from the Theme Fonts button in the Themes group.

theme A set of formatting choices that includes a color theme, a font theme, and an effects theme

Quick Steps

Apply a Theme
1. Click Page Layout tab.
2. Click Themes button.
3. Click desired theme.

Exercise 8.2 Applying a Theme

1. With **U2T8-PrepResume.docx** open, press Ctrl + Home to move the insertion point to the beginning of the document and then click the Home tab.

2. Click the Change Styles button in the Styles group on the Home tab, point to *Style Set*, and then click *Formal* at the drop-down list.

3. Apply the Heading 1 style to the title *PREPARING A RESUME*.

4. Apply the Heading 2 style to the headings *Becoming a Job Detective*, *The Right Mix*, and *Getting Information about the Job and Employer*.

5. Press Ctrl + Home to move the insertion point to the beginning of the document, and apply a theme to the document by clicking the Page Layout tab, clicking the Themes button 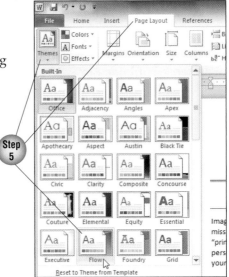 in the Themes group, and then clicking *Flow* at the drop-down gallery.

6. Change the theme colors by clicking the Theme Colors button 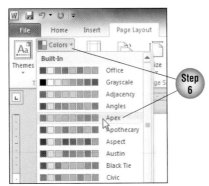 in the Themes group and then clicking *Apex* at the drop-down gallery.

7. Change the theme font by clicking the Theme Fonts button Ⓐ in the Themes group and then clicking *Apothecary* at the drop-down gallery.

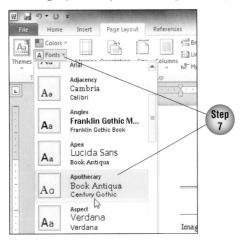

8. Save **U2T8-PrepResume.docx**.

Drilling Down

Changing Theme Effects

The Themes group on the Page Layout tab includes the Theme Effects button. Click this button and a drop-down gallery displays with named effect themes. The names of the effect themes correspond to the names of the overall themes. Click an effect theme at the drop-down gallery and the theme effects are applied to any graphics in your document containing lines and fill.

Lesson 8.3 — Inserting Symbols, Special Characters, and Other Items in a Document

IC³ 2-2.1.8

Word contains a number of features on the Insert tab that you can use to insert items such as symbols, special characters, the current date and time, or text from another document. Click the Symbol button in the Symbols group on the Insert tab and a drop-down list displays with the most recently inserted symbols and a *More Symbols* option. Click one of the symbols that displays in the list to insert it in the document, or click the *More Symbols* option to display the Symbol dialog box, shown in Figure 8.4. At the Symbol dialog box, double-click the symbol you want to insert and then click Close; or, click the symbol you want to insert, click the Insert button, and then click Close. At the Symbol dialog box with the Symbols tab selected, you can change the font by using the *Font* option. When you change the font, different symbols display in the dialog box. Click the Special Characters tab and a list of special characters displays, along with the keyboard shortcuts you can use to create them.

Quick Steps

Insert a Symbol

1. Click Insert tab.
2. Click Symbol button.
3. Click desired symbol at drop-down list.

OR

1. Click Insert tab.
2. Click Symbol button.
3. Click *More Symbols*.
4. Select desired font.
5. Double-click desired symbol.
6. Click Close.

Figure 8.4 Symbol Dialog Box with Symbols Tab Selected

Use the *Font* option to select the desired set of characters.

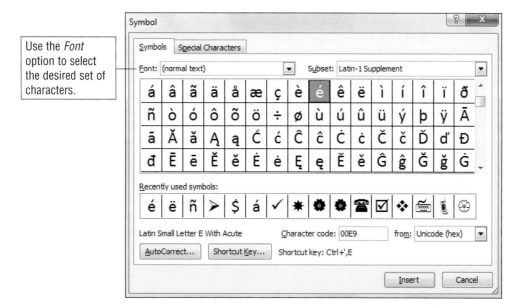

Use the Date & Time button in the Text group on the Insert tab to insert the current date and time into a document. Click this button and the Date and Time dialog box displays, as shown in Figure 8.5. (The date that displays on your screen will vary from the one you see in the figure.) At the Date and Time dialog box, click the desired date and/or time format in the *Available formats* list box. If the *Update automatically* check box at the bottom of the dialog box does not contain a check mark, the date and/or time that you click is inserted in the document as normal text that can be edited in the usual manner.

Quick Steps

Insert the Date and Time

1. Click Insert tab.
2. Click Date & Time button.
3. Click option in list box.
4. Click OK.

Figure 8.5 Date and Time Dialog Box

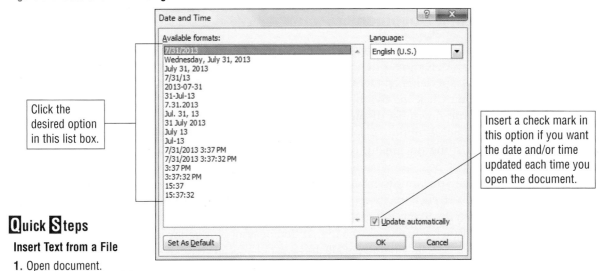

Click the desired option in this list box.

Insert a check mark in this option if you want the date and/or time updated each time you open the document.

Quick Steps

Insert Text from a File

1. Open document.
2. Position insertion point at desired location.
3. Click Insert tab.
4. Click Object button arrow.
5. Click *Text from File*.
6. Locate document.
7. Double-click document name.

If you want to insert the contents of one document into another, use the Object button in the Text group on the Insert tab. Open the document into which you want to insert content, position the insertion point at the desired location, click the Object button arrow, and then click *Text from File* to display the Insert File dialog box. This dialog box is similar to the Open dialog box. Navigate to the desired folder and then double-click the document whose contents you want to insert in the open document.

Exercise 8.3 Inserting a File, a Symbol, and the Date and Time

1. With **U2T8-PrepResume.docx** open, press Ctrl + End to move the insertion point to the end of the document and then press the Enter key.

   The insertion point should be positioned on the line below the last paragraph of text.

2. Insert a file at the end of the existing document. Begin by clicking the Insert tab, clicking the Object button arrow ⊞ in the Text group, and then clicking *Text from File* at the drop-down list.

Step 2

3. At the Insert File dialog box, navigate to the **Unit2Topic08** folder and then double-click **Information.docx**.

   This inserts the **Information.docx** document into the **U2T8-PrepResume.docx** document.

4. Apply the Heading 3 style to the headings *Information about the Job*, *Information about the Employer*, and *Understanding an Employer's WIIFT* in the document.

5. Press Ctrl + End to move the insertion point to the end of the document and then type **Created by: Roberto Cede**.

6. Click the Insert tab, click the Symbol button ⊠ in the Symbols group, and then click *More Symbols* at the drop-down list.

7. At the Symbol dialog box, make sure the *Font* option displays as *(normal text)*, double-click the ñ symbol (located in approximately the tenth, eleventh, or twelfth row), and then click the Close button.

8. Type **o**.

9. Press Shift + Enter and then type **Career Finders**.

10. Insert the registered trademark symbol (®) at the end of the company name. Begin by clicking the Symbol button and then clicking *More Symbols* at the drop-down list.

11. At the Symbol dialog box, click the Special Characters tab, double-click the ® symbol (tenth option from the top), and then click the Close button.

12. Press Shift + Enter to start a new line.

13. Insert the current date below the company name. Begin by clicking the Date & Time button in the Text group.

14. At the Date and Time dialog box, click the third option from the top in the *Available formats* list box and then click OK to close the dialog box.

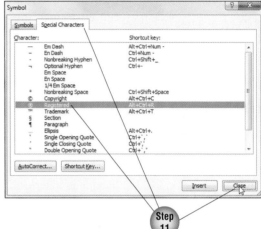

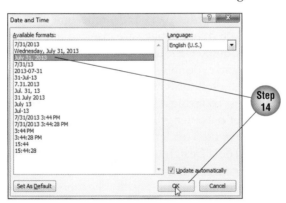

15. Press Shift + Enter.

16. Insert the current time by clicking the Date & Time button, clicking the third option from the bottom in the *Available formats* list box, and then clicking OK to close the dialog box.

17. Save **U2T8-PrepResume.docx**.

Drilling Down

Inserting the Date and/or Time as a Field

The advantage to inserting the date or time as a field is that you can update the field with the keyboard shortcut F9. Insert a check mark in the *Update automatically* check box at the Date and Time dialog box to insert the date and/or time as a field. You can also insert the date as a field using the keyboard shortcut Alt + Shift + D and insert the time as a field with the keyboard shortcut Alt + Shift + T.

Lesson 8.4   Inserting Page Numbering, Headers and Footers, and a Cover Page

IC³ 2-2.1.9, 2-2.1.10

header The text that appears at the top of every page

footer The text that appears at the bottom of every page

cover page A predesigned page containing placeholders that is inserted at the beginning of a document

Word, by default, does not number document pages. If you want to insert page numbers, use the Page Number button in the Header & Footer group on the Insert tab. A drop-down list displays with options for specifying the page number location. Point to an option and a drop-down list of predesigned page formats displays. Scroll through the options in the drop-down list and then click the desired option. You can remove page numbering by clicking the Page Number button and then clicking *Remove Page Numbers* at the drop-down list.

When you insert page numbers, Word inserts Arabic numbers (1, 2, 3, etc.) by default and numbers the pages sequentially beginning with number 1. You can customize these default settings with the options at the Page Number Format dialog box. To display this dialog box, click the Insert tab, click the Page Number button in the Header & Footer group, and then click *Format Page Numbers* at the drop-down list.

Text that appears at the top of every page is called a **header** and text that appears at the bottom of every page is referred to as a **footer**. Headers and footers are common in manuscripts, textbooks, reports, and other publications. Insert a predesigned header in a document by clicking the Insert tab and then clicking the Header button in the Header & Footer group. At the *Header* drop-down list, click the desired predesigned header option and the header is inserted in the document. Insert a predesigned footer in the same manner. A header or footer is visible in Print Layout view but not Draft view. Remove a header or footer by clicking the Header or Footer button in the Header & Footer group and then clicking *Remove Header* or *Remove Footer* at the drop-down list. Predesigned headers and page numbers inserted at the top of the page are inserted in a header pane and predesigned footers and page numbers inserted at the bottom of the page are inserted in a footer pane. To return to your document, double-click in the document. If you want to make a header or footer pane active, double-click in the pane.

If predesigned headers and footers provided by Word do not meet your needs, you can create your own. To create a header, click the Insert tab, click the Header button in the Header & Footer group, and then click *Edit Header* at the drop-down list. This displays the Header pane in the document and also displays the Header & Footer Tools Design tab. With options on this tab you can insert elements such as page numbers, pictures, and clip art; navigate to other headers or footers in the document; and position headers and footers on different pages in a document. Create a footer following similar steps.

If you are preparing a document for distribution to others, or if you simply want to improve a document's visual appeal, consider inserting a cover page. In Word, a **cover page** is a predesigned page containing placeholders that is inserted at the beginning of the document. With the Cover Page button in the Pages group on the Insert tab, you can insert a predesigned, formatted cover page and then type text in specific locations on the page to customize it.

A predesigned header, footer, or cover page may contain placeholders where you can enter specific information. For example, a cover page might contain the placeholder *[Type the document title]*. Click anywhere in the placeholder text and the default placeholder text is selected. With the placeholder text selected, type the desired text. You can delete a placeholder by clicking anywhere in the placeholder text, clicking the placeholder tab, and then pressing the Delete key.

Exercise 8.4 Inserting Page Numbering, Headers and Footers, and a Cover Page

1. With **U2T8-PrepResume.docx** open, move the insertion point to the beginning of the document and then apply the Concourse theme.

2. Number pages at the top of each page by clicking the Insert tab, clicking the Page Number button ⊞ in the Header & Footer group, and then pointing to *Top of Page*.

3. At the gallery of predesigned page numbers, scroll down the list, and then click the *Accent Bar 1* option.

4. Double-click in the body of the document and then scroll through the document and notice how the page numbers display toward the top of each page.

5. Insert a predesigned footer in the document by clicking the Insert tab, clicking the Footer button ⊞ in the Header & Footer group, scrolling down the footer list, and then clicking the *Puzzle (Odd Page)* footer.

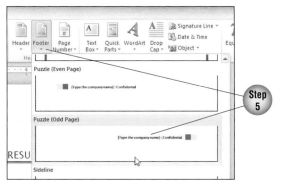

6. Click anywhere in the placeholder text *[Type the company name]* and then type **Career Finders**.

7. Double-click in the body of the document.

8. Save and then print page 1 of the document.

9. Remove page numbering by clicking the Insert tab, clicking the Page Number button in the Header & Footer group, and then clicking *Remove Page Numbers* at the drop-down list.

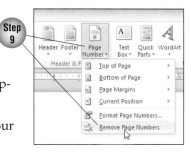

10. Insert a header by clicking the Header button ⊞ in the Header & Footer group and then clicking *Edit Header* at the drop-down list.

11. With the insertion point positioned in the Header pane, type your first and last names.

12. Press the Tab key two times.

    The insertion point should be located at the right margin.

13. Click the Page Number button in the Header & Footer group in the Header & Footer Tools Design tab, point to *Current Position*, and then click *Plain Number* option.

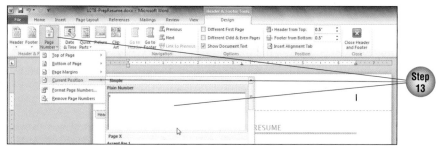

14. Click the Page Number button in the Header & Footer group and then click *Format Page Numbering* at the drop-down list.

15. At the Page Number Format dialog box, click the *Start at* option in the *Page numbering* section, type the number **3**, and then click the OK button.

16. Double-click in the body of the document.

17. Remove the footer by clicking the Insert tab, clicking the Footer button in the Header & Footer group, and then clicking *Remove Footer* at the drop-down list.

18. Insert a footer by clicking the Footer button in the Header & Footer group and then clicking *Edit Footer* at the drop-down list.

19. With the insertion point located in the Footer pane, press the Tab key.

This moves the insertion point so it is centered approximately between the left and right margins.

20. Type **U2T8-PrepResume.docx**.

21. Double-click in the body of the document.

22. Insert a cover page at the beginning of the document by clicking the Insert tab, clicking the Cover Page button in the Pages group, and then clicking *Austere* at the drop-down list.

23. Click anywhere in the placeholder text *[Year]*, click the down-pointing arrow that displays at the right side of the placeholder, and then click the Today button at the bottom of the drop-down calendar.

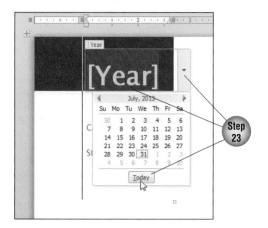

24. Click anywhere in the placeholder text that displays below *Career Finders*, click the Author placeholder tab, and then type your first and last names. (If a name displays in the placeholder, select the name and then type your first and last names.)

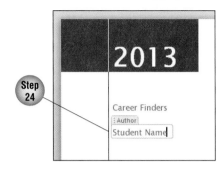

25. Click anywhere in the placeholder text *[TYPE THE DOCUMENT TITLE]* and then type **preparing a resume**.

26. Click anywhere in the placeholder text below the document title, click the Abstract tab, and then press the Delete key.

27. Scroll through the document and notice how the header and footer appear on each page except the cover page.

28. Click anywhere in the company name in the cover page and then click the Company tab.

    Clicking the Company tab selects the company name and placeholder.

29. Change the font size by clicking the Home tab, clicking the Font Size button arrow, and then clicking *16* at the drop-down list.

30. Save, print, and then close **U2T8-PrepResume.docx**.

Drilling Down

Inserting Elements in Headers and Footers

Use buttons in the Insert group on the Header & Footer Tools Design tab to insert elements in the header or footer such as the date and time, pictures, and clip art images. Click the Date & Time button, and the Date and Time dialog box displays with options for inserting the current date as well as the current time. Click the Quick Parts button, and a drop-down list displays with options for inserting predesigned building blocks and fields. Click the Picture button, and the Insert Picture dialog box displays. At this dialog box, navigate to the desired folder and double-click the picture file. Click the Clip Art button, and the Clip Art task pane displays. At this task pane, you can search for and then insert an image into a header or footer.

Lesson 8.5 Inserting Page and Section Breaks

 2-2.1.5

Word assumes that you are using standard-sized paper, which is 8.5 inches wide and 11 inches long. With default top and bottom margins of 1 inch, a Word document contains approximately 9 inches of text on a page. At approximately the 10-inch mark, Word automatically inserts a page break. You can insert your own page break in a document with the keyboard shortcut Ctrl + Enter or with the Page Break button in the Pages group on the Insert tab.

Quick Steps

Insert a Page Break
1. Click Insert tab.
2. Click Page Break button.

A page break automatically inserted by Word is considered a **soft page break**; a page break that you insert is considered a **hard page break**. A soft page break adjusts automatically when you add or delete text from a document. A hard page break does not adjust and is therefore less flexible than a soft page break. If you add or delete text from a document with a hard page break, check the break to determine whether it is still in a desirable location. Turn on the display of nonprinting characters by clicking the Show/Hide ¶ button in the Paragraph group on the Home tab and a hard page break displays as a row of dots with the words *Page Break* in the center. To delete a page break, position the insertion point immediately below the page break and then press the Backspace key or position the insertion point above the page break and then press the Delete key. You can also delete a page break by turning on the display of nonprinting characters, positioning the insertion point on the page break, and then pressing the Delete key.

You can change the layout and formatting of specific portions of a document by inserting section breaks. For example, you can insert section breaks and then change margins for the text between the section breaks or format specific text in a document into columns. Insert section breaks with the Breaks button in the Page Setup group on the Page Layout tab. You can insert a section break that begins a new page or a continuous section break. A **continuous section break** separates the document into sections but does not insert a page break.

A section break inserted in a document is not visible in Print Layout view. Click the Draft button and a section break displays in the document as a double row of dots with the words *Section Break* in the center. You can also display a section break by turning on the display of nonprinting characters. Depending on the type of section break you insert, text follows *Section Break*. For example, if you insert a continuous section break, the words *Section Break (Continuous)* display in the middle of the rows of dots. If you delete a section break, the text that follows the section break takes on the formatting of the text preceding the break. To delete a section break, display the document in Draft view or turn on the display of nonprinting characters, click on the section break (this moves the insertion point to the left margin on the section break), and then press the Delete key.

Exercise 8.5 Inserting a Page Break and a Section Break

1. Open **CompAdv.docx** and then save the document and name it **U2T8-CompAdv**.

2. Position the insertion point at the beginning of the heading *Communications*.

3. Insert a page break by clicking the Insert tab and then clicking the Page Break button in the Pages group.

   You can also insert a hard page break with the keyboard shortcut, Ctrl + Enter.

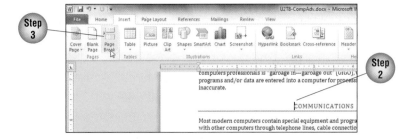

4. Position the insertion point at the beginning of the paragraph below the title *THE COMPUTER ADVANTAGE*.

5. Insert a continuous section break by clicking the Page Layout tab, clicking the Breaks button in the Page Setup group, and then clicking *Continuous* in the *Section Breaks* section of the drop-down list.

    This divides the document into two sections but does not insert a page break.

6. Position the insertion point at the beginning of the heading *Speed* and then insert a continuous section break.

7. Move the insertion point to any character in the first paragraph below the title *THE COMPUTER ADVANTAGE* and then change the left and right margins to 1.5 inches.

    Notice the margins of the text changed only within the continuous section breaks.

8. Click the Draft button in the view area on the Status bar and then scroll through the document and notice the section breaks that display across the screen.

9. Click the Print Layout button in the view area on the Status bar.

10. Save and then print **U2T8-CompAdv.docx**.

11. Delete the first section break by clicking the Draft button in the view area on the Status bar, positioning the insertion point on the section break below the title *THE COMPUTER ADVANTAGE*, and then pressing the Delete key.

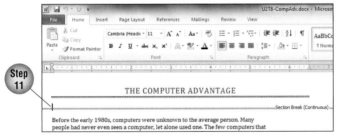

12. Position the insertion point on the section break above the heading *Speed* and then press the Delete key.

13. Click the Print Layout button in the view area on the Status bar.

14. Move the insertion point to the beginning of the *Communication* heading and then click the Show/Hide button in the Paragraph group on the Home tab to turn on the display of nonprinting characters. Delete the page break by positioning the insertion point on the page break that displays above the *Communication* heading and then pressing the Delete key. Click the Show/Hide button to turn off the display of nonprinting characters.

15. Save **U2T8-CompAdv.docx**.

Drilling Down

Inserting Even-Page and Odd-Page Section Breaks

You can insert a section break that automatically starts the new section on the next even-numbered page or the next odd-numbered page. Do this by clicking the Page Layout tab, clicking the Breaks button in the Page Setup group, and then clicking the *Even Page* option at the drop-down list or the *Odd Page* option at the drop-down list.

Lesson 8.6 Creating and Formatting Text in Columns

When you are preparing any document that contains text, the readability of the document is an important consideration. Line length in a document can enhance or detract from the readability of the text. If the length is too long, the reader may lose his or her place on the line. To improve the readability of documents such as newsletters or reports, you may want to set the text in multiple columns.

Quick Steps

Create Columns

1. Click Page Layout tab.
2. Click Columns button.
3. Click desired number of columns.

You can set text in columns with the Columns button in the Page Setup group on the Page Layout tab or with options from the Columns dialog box. The Columns button creates columns of equal width. To create columns with varying widths, use the Columns dialog box. A document can include as many columns as space permits on the page with each column at least 0.5 inch in width. To create columns with the Columns button, click the Columns button in the Page Setup group on the Page Layout tab and then click the desired number of columns at the drop-down list. To create columns with the Columns dialog box, shown in Figure 8.6, click the Columns button in the Page Setup group and then click *More Columns* at the drop-down list.

Figure 8.6 Columns Dialog Box

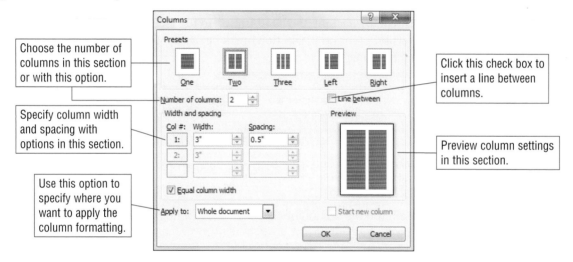

Choose the number of columns in this section or with this option.

Specify column width and spacing with options in this section.

Use this option to specify where you want to apply the column formatting.

Click this check box to insert a line between columns.

Preview column settings in this section.

Quick Steps

Create Columns at the Columns Dialog Box

1. Click Page Layout tab.
2. Click Columns button.
3. Click *More Columns* at drop-down list.
4. Specify column options.
5. Click OK.

Using options at the Columns dialog box, you can specify the style and number of columns, enter your own column measurements, and create unequal columns. You can also insert a line between columns. By default, column formatting is applied to the whole document or the section in which the insertion point is positioned. The *Preview* section of the dialog box displays an example of how the columns will appear in your document.

To remove column formatting using the Columns button, position the insertion point in the section containing columns, click the Page Layout tab, click the Columns button, and then click *One* at the drop-down list. You can also remove column formatting at the Columns dialog box by selecting the *One* option in the *Presets* section.

In documents that contain text formatted into columns, Word automatically lines up (balances) the last line of text at the bottom of each column, except on the last page. Text in the first column of the last page may flow to the end of the page, while the text in the second column may end far short of the end of the page. You can balance columns by inserting a continuous section break at the end of the text.

Exercise 8.6 Formatting Text into Columns

1. With **U2T8-CompAdv.docx** open, move the insertion point to the beginning of the paragraph of text below the title *THE COMPUTER ADVANTAGE* and then insert a continuous section break.

2. Make sure the insertion point is positioned below the section break and then format the text (except the title) into three columns by clicking the Page Layout tab, clicking the Columns button in the Page Setup group, and then clicking *Three* at the drop-down list.

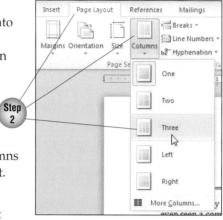

3. Scroll through the document and notice the text set in three columns.

4. You decide to format the document into two columns with a line down the middle. Begin by clicking the Columns button and then click *More Columns* at the drop-down list.

5. At the Columns dialog box, click *Two* in the *Presets* section and then click the *Line between* check box to insert a check mark.

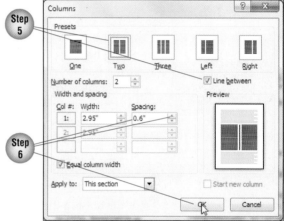

6. Click the up-pointing arrow at the right of the *Spacing* option box to display *0.6"* and then click OK to close the dialog box.

7. Press Ctrl + End to move the insertion point to the end of the document and then balance the columns by clicking the Page Layout tab, clicking the Breaks button, and then clicking *Continuous* at the drop-down list.

8. Save, print, and then close **U2T8-CompAdv.docx**.

Drilling Down

Inserting a Column Break

When Word formats text into columns, it automatically breaks the columns to fit the page. At times, column breaks may appear in an undesirable location. You can insert a column break by positioning the insertion point where you want the column to end, clicking the Page Layout tab, clicking the Breaks button, and then clicking *Column* at the drop-down list. You can also insert a column break with the keyboard shortcut Ctrl + Shift + Enter.

Lesson 8.7 Inserting, Sizing, and Moving an Image

 2-1.3.7

You can insert an image such as a picture or clip art in a Word document with buttons in the Illustrations group on the Insert tab. Click the Picture button to display the Insert Picture dialog box where you can specify the desired picture file or click the Clip Art button and then choose from a variety of images available at the Clip Art task pane. The Clip Art task pane contains clip art images and displays at the right side of the document when the Clip Art button is clicked. When you insert a picture or a clip art image in a document, the Picture Tools Format tab displays (as shown in Figure 8.7).

Insert a Picture
1. Click Insert tab.
2. Click Picture button.
3. Navigate to desired folder.
4. Double-click picture file.

Insert Clip Art Image
1. Click Insert tab.
2. Click Clip Art button.
3. Type category information in *Search for* text box.
4. Click Go button.
5. Click clip art image.

With options in the Adjust group on the Picture Tools Format tab you can change the color of the picture or clip art image, change the brightness and contrast of the image, and apply additional effects to the image. You can also reset the picture or clip art back to its original color or change to a different image. Word provides predesigned styles you can apply to your image. These styles are available in the Picture Styles group along with buttons for changing the image border and applying effects to the image. Use options in the Arrange group to position the image on the page, specify text wrapping in relation to the image, align the image with other objects in the document, and rotate the image. Use the Crop button in the Size group to remove any unnecessary parts of the image and specify the image size with the Shape Height and Shape Width boxes.

Figure 8.7 Picture Tools Format Tab

You can change the size of an image with the Shape Height and Shape Width boxes in the Size group on the Picture Tools Format tab or with the **sizing handles** that display around the selected image. To change size with a sizing handle, position the mouse pointer on a sizing handle until the pointer turns into a double-headed arrow and then hold down the left mouse button. Drag the sizing handle in or out to decrease or increase the size of the image and then release the mouse button. Use the middle sizing handles at the left or right side of the image to make the image wider or thinner. Use the middle sizing handles at the top or bottom of the image to make the image taller or shorter. Use the sizing handles at the corners of the image to change both the width and height at the same time. Hold down the Shift key while increasing or decreasing the size of an image to maintain the proportions of the image.

sizing handles Small circles or squares that appear on the border of a selected image and are used to size the image

Move an image to a specific location on the page with options from the Position button drop-down gallery. The Position button is located in the Arrange group on the Picture Tools Format tab. When you choose an option at the Position button drop-down gallery, the image is moved to the specified location on the page and square text wrapping is applied to the image.

You can also move the image by dragging it to the desired location. Before dragging an image, you must first choose a text wrapping style by clicking the Wrap Text button in the Arrange group and then clicking the desired wrapping style at the drop-down list. After choosing a wrapping style, move the image by positioning the mouse pointer on the image border until the arrow pointer displays with a four-headed arrow attached. Hold down the left mouse button, drag the image to the desired position, and then release the mouse button.

Exercise 8.7 Inserting, Sizing, and Moving an Image

1. Open **SGCQualities.docx** and then save the document and name it **U2T8-SGCQualities**.

2. Insert a clip art image by clicking the Insert tab and then clicking the Clip Art button ⊞ in the Illustrations group.

   This displays the Clip Art task pane at the right side of the screen.

3. Type **business** in the *Search for* text box and then click the Go button or press the Enter key.

4. Scroll down the Clip Art task pane list box and then click the image shown at the right. If this image is not available, choose another image related to business.

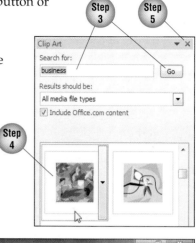

The image is inserted in the document, it is selected (sizing handles display around the image), and the Picture Tools Format tab displays as shown in Figure 8.7.

5. Close the Clip Art task pane by clicking the Close button located in the upper right corner of the task pane.

6. With the image selected, click the Wrap Text button ⊞ in the Arrange group and then click *Tight* at the drop-down list.

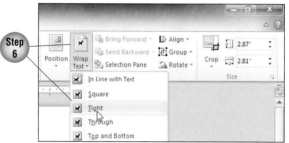

7. Click in the Shape Height measurement box in the Size group, type **1.6**, and then press the Enter key.

When you change the height measurement, the width measurement is automatically changed to maintain the proportions of the image.

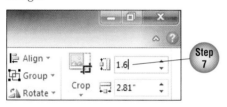

8. With the image selected, move the clip art image by positioning the mouse pointer on the image until the arrow pointer displays with a four-headed arrow attached, hold down the left mouse button, drag the image to the location shown at the right, and then release the mouse button.

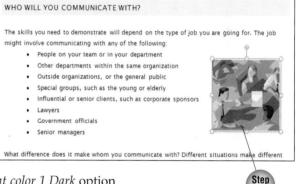

9. Change the color of the clip art image by clicking the Color button 🎨 in the Adjust group, and then clicking the *Turquoise, Accent color 1 Dark* option (second option from the left in the second row).

10. Click the Corrections button ⚙ in the Adjust group and then click the *Brightness: +20% Contrast: +20%* option at the drop-down gallery (fourth option from the left in the fourth row).

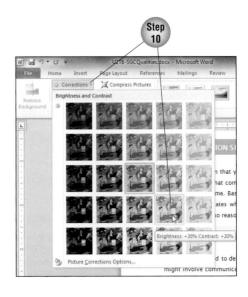

11. Apply a border effect to the clip art image by clicking the More button at the right side of the picture style thumbnails in the Picture Styles group and then clicking the *Bevel Rectangle* option.

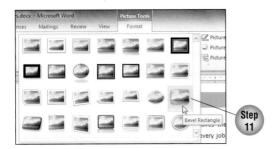

12. Press Ctrl + End to move the insertion point to the end of the document and then press the Enter key twice.

13. Insert the Severson Grisham Communications logo at the end of the document. To begin, click the Insert tab and then click the Picture button ⊞ in the Illustrations group.

14. At the Insert Picture dialog box, display the folder where your data documents are located and then double-click **SGCLogo.jpg**.

15. With the image selected in the document, hold down the Shift key and then drag the bottom right corner sizing handle (small, white circle) to reduce the size of the logo so it displays as shown at the right.

    Holding down the Shift key while increasing or decreasing the size of an image maintains the proportions of the image.

16. Apply a shadow effect to the logo by clicking the More button at the right side of the picture style thumbnails in the Picture Styles group on the Picture Tools Format tab and then clicking the *Reflected Bevel, White* option at the drop-down gallery.

17. Apply a border to the logo by clicking the Picture Border button arrow ⊠ in the Picture Styles group and then clicking *Turquoise, Accent 1, Lighter 60%* at the drop-down gallery.

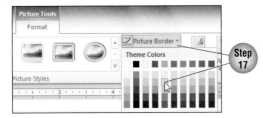

18. With the image still selected, click the Home tab and then click the Center button in the Paragraph group.

19. Save **U2T8-SGCQualities.docx**.

Rotating an Image

You can rotate an image, such as a picture or clip art, by positioning the mouse pointer on the green, round rotation handle that displays above a selected image until the pointer displays with a circular arrow attached. Hold down the left mouse button, drag the image in the desired direction, and then release the mouse button.

Lesson 8.8 Drawing and Formatting Objects

 2-1.3.7

The Illustrations group on the Insert tab contains a Shapes button with a variety of line and shape options you can use to create a graphic element in a Word document. When you click the Shapes button, a drop-down list displays with line options, basic geometric shapes, block arrows, flowchart shapes, callouts, stars, and banners. When you click a shape at the drop-down list, the mouse pointer displays as a crosshairs (plus sign). Click in the document to insert the shape or position the crosshairs where you want the shape to begin, hold down the left mouse button, drag to create the shape, and then release the mouse button. This inserts the shape in the document and also displays the Drawing Tools Format tab, shown in Figure 8.8. Use buttons on this tab to replace the shape with another shape, apply a style to the shape, position or arrange the shape, or change the size of the shape. This tab contains many of the same options and buttons contained on the Picture Tools Format tab.

Quick Steps

Draw a Shape
1. Click Insert tab.
2. Click Shapes button.
3. Click desired shape in drop-down list.
4. Drag in document to create shape.

Figure 8.8 Drawing Tools Format Tab

Once you have drawn a shape, you can copy it to another location in the document. To do this, select the shape and then click the Copy button in the Clipboard group on the Home tab. Position the insertion point at the location where you want to insert the copied image and then click the Paste button. You can also copy a selected shape by holding down the Ctrl key while dragging the shape to the desired location.

You can select multiple shapes by clicking a shape, holding down the Shift key, clicking each additional shape you want selected, and then releasing the Shift key. Any formatting you apply is applied to all selected shapes. In addition to holding down the Shift key and clicking shapes, you can select and then group shapes. To group shapes, select the desired shapes, click the Group button in the Arrange group on the Drawing Tools Format tab and then click the *Group* option at the drop-down list. This makes the selected shapes a single object and any formatting you apply is applied to the object as a whole. You can ungroup an object by clicking the *Ungroup* option at the Group button drop-down list.

Quick Steps

Copy a Shape
1. Select desired shape.
2. Click Copy button.
3. Position insertion point at desired location.
4. Click Paste button.

OR
1. Select desired shape.
2. Hold down Ctrl key.
3. Drag shape to desired location.

Group Objects
1. Select desired objects.
2. Click Drawing Tools Format tab.
3. Click Group button.
4. Click *Group* at drop-down list.

The Align button in the Arrange group on the Drawing Tools Format tab contains options for aligning multiple shapes in a document. To align shapes, select the desired shapes, click the Align button in the Arrange group, and then click the desired alignment option at the drop-down list. For example, if you want to align all of the shapes at the left side of the page, click the *Align Left* option at the Align button drop-down list. If you want to distribute the selected shapes horizontally on the page, click the *Distribute Horizontally* option at the Align button drop-down list.

When you draw a shape in a document, you can type text directly in the shape. Select the text and then use options in the WordArt Styles group on the Drawing Tools Format tab to format the text. You can also apply formatting to text in a shape with options available at other tabs such as the Home tab.

Exercise 8.8 Inserting, Formatting, and Copying a Shape

1. With **U2T8-SGCQualities.docx** open, press Ctrl + End to move the insertion point to the end of the document.

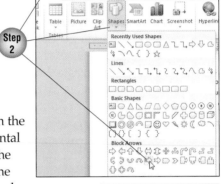

2. Insert an arrow shape into the document by clicking the Insert tab, clicking the Shapes button in the Illustrations group, and then clicking *Striped Right Arrow* in the *Block Arrows* section of the drop-down list.

3. Position the mouse pointer (which displays as a crosshair) in the document at approximately the 1.5-inch mark on the horizontal ruler and the 5-inch mark on the vertical ruler, hold down the Shift key and the left mouse button, drag to the right until the tip of the arrow is positioned at approximately the 5-inch mark on the horizontal ruler, and then release the mouse button and the Shift key.

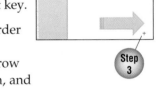

4. With the arrow selected, position the mouse pointer on the arrow border until the mouse pointer displays with a four-headed arrow attached, hold down the Ctrl key, drag down until the outline of the copied arrow displays just below the top (original) arrow, release the mouse button, and then release the Ctrl key.

This inserts a copy of the arrow shape below the original arrow shape.

5. With the bottom arrow selected, click the Drawing Tools Format tab, click the Rotate button in the Arrange group, and then click *Flip Horizontal* at the drop-down list.

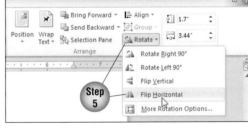

6. Click the top arrow to select it and then type the text **Demonstrate**.

7. Select the word *Demonstrate* and then change the font size to 14 and turn on bold.

8. Click the bottom arrow to select it and then type the text **Communicate**.

9. Select the word *Communicate* and then change the font size to 14 and turn on bold.

10. With the bottom arrow selected, hold down the Shift key, click the top arrow, and then release the Shift key.

Both arrows are now selected.

11. With the two arrows selected, click the Drawing Tools Format tab, click the More button in the Shape Styles group, and then click *Subtle Effect - Turquoise, Accent 1* at the drop-down gallery.

12. Click the Shape Outline button in the Shape Styles group, point to *Weight* in the drop-down gallery, and then click 1½ pt at the side menu.

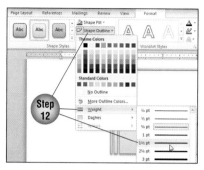

13. Move the arrows up the document by positioning the mouse pointer on the border of one of the selected arrows until the mouse pointer displays with a four-headed arrow attached, holding down the left mouse button, and then dragging the selected arrows up approximately 0.25-inch.

The top arrow should display directly below the logo image.

14. Click once on the top arrow to select it, click the Align button in the Arrange group, and then click *Distribute Horizontally* at the drop-down list.

15. Click once on the bottom arrow, click the Align button, and then click *Distribute Horizontally* at the drop-down list.

16. Save **U2T8-SGCQualities.docx**.

Drilling Down

Editing a Shape

The Drawing Tools Format tab contains an Edit Shape button in the Insert Shapes group. Click this button and a drop-down list displays with options to change the shape. Click the Edit Shape button and then point to the *Change Shape* option and a side menu displays with shape options. Click the desired shape option and the shape in the document changes to the chosen shape.

Lesson 8.9 Creating and Modifying WordArt Text

)C³ 2-1.3.7

You can use the **WordArt** feature to distort or modify text to conform to a variety of shapes. Consider using WordArt to create a company logo, letterhead, flier title, or headings. Insert WordArt in a document by clicking the Insert tab and then clicking the WordArt button in the Text group. This displays the WordArt drop-down list shown in Figure 8.9. Select the desired option at the drop-down list and a *WordArt* text box is inserted in the document containing the words *Your text here* and the Drawing Tools Format tab becomes active. Type the desired WordArt text and then format the WordArt with options on the Drawing Tools Format tab.

With options in the WordArt Styles group on the Drawing Tools Format tab, you can apply formatting to the WordArt text. You can apply a predesigned WordArt style, change the WordArt text color or text outline color, and apply a text effect such as shadow, reflection, glow, bevel, 3-D rotation, and transform. With the *Transform* option, you can conform the WordArt text to a specific shape. To do this, click the Text Effects button, point to *Transform*, and then click the desired shape at the drop-down gallery. Use options in the Arrange group to specify the position, alignment, and rotation of the WordArt text, and specify the size of the WordArt with options in the Size group.

WordArt A feature used to distort or modify text to conform to a variety of shapes

Quick Steps

Insert WordArt
1. Click Insert tab.
2. Click WordArt button.
3. Click desired WordArt option at drop-down list.
4. Type desired WordArt text.

Figure 8.9 WordArt Drop-down List

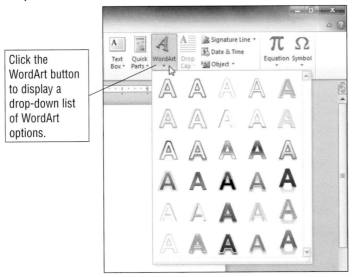

Click the WordArt button to display a drop-down list of WordArt options.

Exercise 8.9 Creating and Modifying WordArt Text

1. With **U2T8-SGCQualities.docx** open, press Ctrl + Home to move the insertion point to the beginning of the document, press the Enter key two times, and then move the insertion point back to the beginning of the document.

2. Insert WordArt by clicking the Insert tab, clicking the WordArt button ⒶⒶ in the Text group, and then clicking the *Gradient Fill - Turquoise, Accent 1* option at the drop-down list (fourth option from the left in the third row).

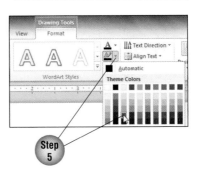

Step 2

3. Type **Employee Qualities**.

4. Click the outside border of the *WordArt* text box so it displays as a solid line instead of a dashed line.

5. Click the Text Outline button arrow ⒶⒶ in the WordArt Styles group on the Drawing Tools Format tab and then click the *Light Turquoise, Background 2, Darker 75%* option.

Step 5

6. Click the Text Effects button ⒶⒶ, point to *Glow*, and then click the *Turquoise, 5 pt glow, Accent color 1* option in the *Glow Variations* section.

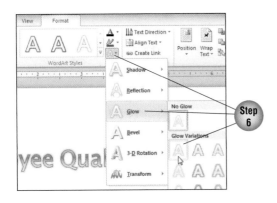

Step 6

7. Click the Text Effects button, point to *Transform,* and then click the *Deflate* option in the *Warp* section (second option from the left in the sixth row in the *Warp* section).

8. Click in the Shape Height measurement box and then type **1**.

9. Click in the Shape Width measurement box and then type **6.5**.

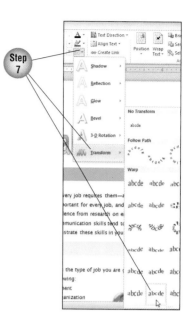

Step 7

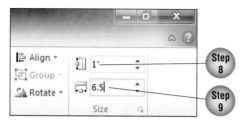

Step 8

Step 9

10. Click outside the WordArt text to deselect it.

11. Save, print, and then close **U2T8-SGCQualities.docx**.

 Drilling Down

Formatting Existing Text as WordArt and Removing WordArt Style Formatting

You can apply WordArt formatting to existing text in a document. To do this, select the text, click the Insert tab, click the WordArt button in the Text group, and then click the desired style at the drop-down gallery. Remove WordArt style formatting from text by selecting the text, clicking the Home tab, and then clicking the Clear Formatting button in the Font group.

Lesson 8.10 — Creating SmartArt Graphics and Organizational Charts

 2-1.3.7, 2-2.2.2

With Word's **SmartArt** feature you can insert graphics in a document that are a visual representation of data such as diagrams and organizational charts. SmartArt graphics are available at the Choose a SmartArt Graphic dialog box, shown in Figure 8.10. At this dialog box, *All* is selected in the left panel and all available predesigned graphics display in the middle panel.

Use the scroll bar at the right side of the middle panel in the dialog box to scroll down the list of graphics. Click a graphic in the middle panel and the name of the graphic displays in the right panel along with a description of the graphic. SmartArt includes graphics for presenting a list of data; showing data processes, cycles, and relationships; and presenting data in a matrix or pyramid. Double-click a graphic in the middle panel of the dialog box and the graphic is inserted in the document.

Apply design formatting to a SmartArt graphic with options on the SmartArt Tools Design tab. With options and buttons on this tab you can add objects, change the graphic layout, apply a style to the graphic, and reset the graphic back to the original formatting. Apply formatting to a SmartArt graphic with options on the SmartArt Tools Format tab. With options and buttons on this tab you can change the size and shape of objects in the graphic; apply shape styles and WordArt styles; change the shape fill, outline, and effects; and arrange and size the graphic. Type text in a SmartArt graphic by selecting the desired graphic shape and then typing the text in the shape.

SmartArt A visual representation of information, such as an organizational chart or diagram

Quick Steps

Create a SmartArt Graphic
1. Click Insert tab.
2. Click SmartArt button.
3. Click desired category in left panel of Choose a SmartArt Graphic dialog box.
4. Double-click desired chart.

Create an Organizational Chart
1. Click Insert tab.
2. Click SmartArt button.
3. Click *Hierarchy* at Choose a SmartArt Graphic dialog box.
4. Double-clicked desired organizational chart.

Figure 8.10 **Choose a SmartArt Graphic Dialog Box**

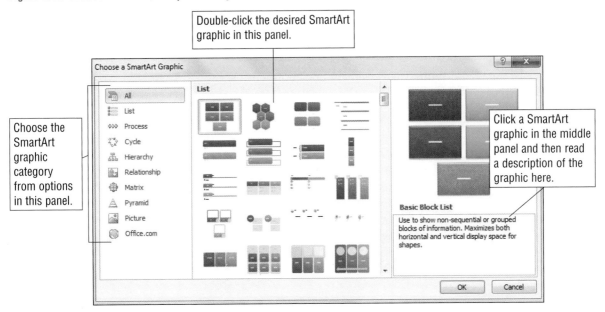

Double-click the desired SmartArt graphic in this panel.

Choose the SmartArt graphic category from options in this panel.

Click a SmartArt graphic in the middle panel and then read a description of the graphic here.

If you need to visually illustrate hierarchical data, consider creating an organizational chart with a SmartArt graphic. To display organizational chart SmartArt options, click *Hierarchy* in the left panel of the Choose a SmartArt Graphic dialog box and organizational chart options display in the middle panel of the dialog box. Double-click the desired organizational chart and the chart is inserted in the document.

Exercise 8.10 Creating a SmartArt Graphic and an Organizational Chart

1. At a blank document, click the Insert tab and then click the SmartArt button ⧉ in the Illustrations group.

2. At the Choose a SmartArt Graphic dialog box, click *Hierarchy* in the left panel of the dialog box and then double-click the *Organization Chart* option in the middle panel (first option in the middle panel).

   This displays the organizational chart in the document with the SmartArt Tools Design tab selected.

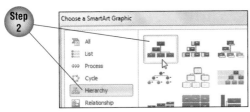

3. If the *Type your text here* window displays, close the window by clicking the Text Pane button ⧉ in the Create Graphic group.

   You can also close the window by clicking the Close button that displays in the upper right corner of the window.

4. Delete one of the boxes in the organizational chart by clicking the border of the box in the lower right corner to select it and then pressing the Delete key.

   Make sure that the selection border that surrounds the box is a solid line and not a dashed line. If a dashed line displays, click the box border again. This should change it to a solid line.

5. With the bottom right box selected, click the Add Shape button arrow 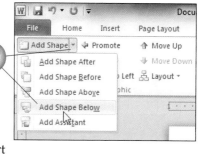 and then click the *Add Shape Below* option.

Your organizational chart should contain the same boxes as shown in Figure 8.11.

6. Click *[Text]* in the top box, type **Chris Vance**, press the Enter key, and then type **President**. Click in each of the remaining boxes and type the text as shown in Figure 8.11.

7. Click the More button located at the right side of the SmartArt Styles group and then click the *Inset* option located in the *3-D* section.

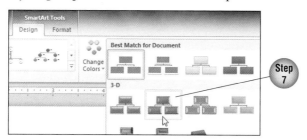

8. Click the Change Colors button 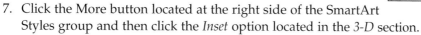 in the SmartArt Styles group and then click the *Colorful Range - Accent Colors 4 to 5* option in the *Colorful* section.

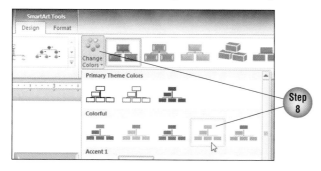

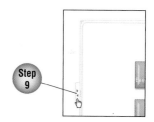

9. Click the tab (displays with a right- and left-pointing triangle) that displays at the left side of the SmartArt graphic border.

10. Using the mouse, select the text that displays in the *Type your text here* window.

11. Click the SmartArt Tools Format tab, click the Change Shape button 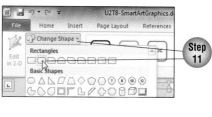 in the Shapes group, and then click the rounded rectangle shape (second shape from the left in the top row).

12. Click the Shape Outline button arrow 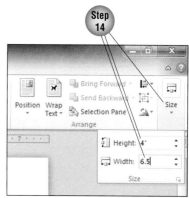 in the Shape Styles group and then click the dark blue color (second color from the right in the *Standard Colors* section).

13. Click inside the organizational chart border but outside any shape.

14. Click the Size button located at the right side of the tab. Click in the *Height* box and then type **4**. Click in the *Width* box, type **6.5**, and then press the Enter key.

15. Save the document and name it **U2T8-SmartArtGraphics**.

16. Press Ctrl + End to move the insertion point to the end of the document and then press the Enter key twice.

17. Click the Insert tab and then click the SmartArt button in the Illustrations group.

18. At the Choose a SmartArt Graphic dialog box, click *Cycle* in the left panel and then double-click the *Radial Cycle* diagram in the middle panel.

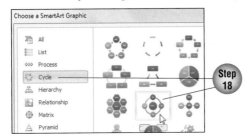

19. With the insertion point positioned after the first bullet in the *Type your text here* window, type **Career Finders**.

20. Click *[Text]* that displays after the first indented bullet and then type **Career Choices**.

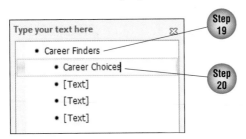

21. Continue clicking *[Text]* and typing text so your graphic contains the same text as the one shown in Figure 8.12.

22. Click the More button located at the right side of the SmartArt Styles group and then click the *Polished* option in the *3-D* section.

23. Click the Change Colors button in the SmartArt Styles group and then click *Colorful - Accent Colors* in the *Colorful* section.

24. Click the SmartArt Tools Format tab.

25. Using the mouse, select the text that displays in the *Type your text here* window.

26. Click the SmartArt Tools Format tab and then click once on the Larger button ⊞ in the Shapes group to slightly increase the size of the graphic circles.

27. Click the Shape Outline button arrow in the Shape Styles group and then click the dark blue color (second color from the right in the *Standard Colors* section).

28. Click inside the graphic border but outside any shape.

29. Click the Size button located at the right side of the tab and then click the up arrow in the *Height* box to change the measurement to 4″. Click the up arrow in the *Width* box to change the measurement to 6.5″.

30. Click outside the SmartArt graphic to deselect it.

31. Save, print, and then close **U2T8-SmartArtGraphics.docx**.

Figure 8.11 Organizational Chart

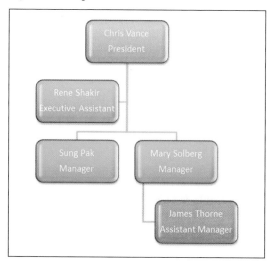

Figure 8.12 Cycle Diagram

Drilling Down

Moving or Sizing a SmartArt Graphic or Organizational Chart

Before moving a SmartArt graphic, you must select a text wrapping style. To do this, select the graphic, click the SmartArt Tools Format tab, click the Arrange button located toward the right side of the tab, click the Wrap Text button, and then click the desired wrapping style at the drop-down list. Move the graphic by positioning the arrow pointer on the graphic border until the pointer displays with a four-headed arrow attached, holding down the left mouse button, and then dragging the graphic to the desired location. You can increase the size of the graphic with the *Height* and *Width* options or by dragging a corner of the graphic border. If you want to maintain the proportions of the graphic, hold down the Shift key while dragging the border to increase or decrease the size.

Lesson 8.11   Tracking Changes

IC³ 2-2.2.2, 2-2.2.3

If more than one person in a work group needs to review and edit a document, consider using the Track Changes feature in Word. When Track Changes is turned on, Word tracks each deletion, insertion, or formatting change made to a document. For example, when you delete text, it is not removed from the document. Instead, it displays in a different color with a line through it. Word uses a different color (up to eight) for each person who makes changes to the document. In this way, anyone looking at the document can identify which user made which changes.

Turn on tracking by clicking the Review tab and then clicking the Track Changes button in the Tracking group. You can also turn on tracking by pressing Ctrl + Shift + E. Turn off tracking by completing the same steps. By default, Word displays tracked changes such as deletions and insertions in the document. Formatting tracked changes, such as changing the font or font size, display in the document along with a vertical line at the left margin to indicate where a formatting change has been made.

You can specify what tracking information displays in a document with options at the Balloons side menu. To show all revisions in balloons at the right margin, click the Show Markup button, point to *Balloons*, and then click *Show Revisions in Balloons* at the side menu. Click the *Show Only Comments and Formatting in Balloons* option at the side menu, and insertions and deletions display in the text while comments and formatting changes display in balloons at the right margin.

Quick Steps

Turn on Track Changes

1. Click Review tab.
2. Click Track Changes button.

Keyboard Shortcut

Turn on Track Changes

Ctrl + Shift + E

Use the Next and Previous buttons in the Changes group on the Review tab to navigate to revisions in a document. Click the Next button, and Word selects the next revision in the document. Click the Previous button to select the preceding revision.

You can accept or reject changes made to a document. Click the Accept button to accept the change and move to the next change. Click the Reject button to reject the change and move to the next change. Click the Reject button arrow, and a drop-down list displays with options to reject the change and move to the next change, reject the change, reject all changes shown, or reject all changes in the document. Similar options are available at the Accept button arrow drop-down list.

Exercise 8.11 Tracking Changes Made to a Document

1. Open **CompComm.docx** and save the document with the name **U2T8-CompComm**.

2. Turn on tracking by clicking the Review tab and then clicking the Track Changes button in the Tracking group.

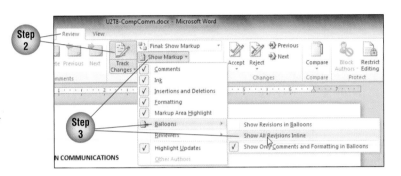

3. Specify that you want revisions to display inline by clicking the Show Markup button, pointing to *Balloons*, and then clicking *Show All Revisions Inline*.

4. Type the word **originally** between *were* and *stand-alone* in the first paragraph of text.

   The text you type displays in the document underlined and in a different color.

5. Delete *innovation* in the last sentence in the *Telecommunications* section.

   The deleted text displays in the document as strikethrough text.

6. Type **modernization**.

7. Move a paragraph of text by selecting the heading *Publishing* and the paragraph of text below the heading and then pressing Ctrl + X to cut the text.

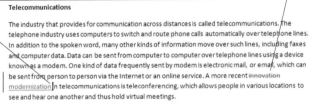

   The text stays in the document and displays in red with strikethrough characters.

8. Position the insertion point at the beginning of the heading *COMPUTERS IN ENTERTAINMENT* and then press Ctrl + V to insert the cut text.

   This inserts the text in green with a double underline in the new location and also changes the text in the original location to green with double-strikethrough characters.

9. Turn off tracking by clicking the Track Changes button in the Tracking group.

10. Display the revisions in balloons by clicking the Show Markup button, pointing to *Balloons*, and then clicking *Show Revisions in Balloons* at the side menu.

364 **UNIT 2** Topic 8

11. After looking at the revisions in balloons, click the Show Markup button, point to *Balloons*, and then click *Show All Revisions Inline* at the side menu.

12. Print the document with the markups by clicking the File tab, clicking the Print tab, clicking the first gallery in the *Settings* category, and then making sure a check mark displays before the *Print Markup* option that displays below the drop-down list.

    If the *Print Markup* option is not preceded by a check mark, click the option.

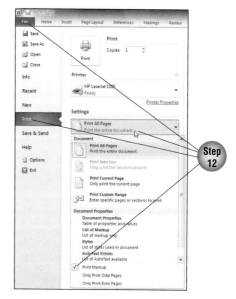

Step 12

13. Click the Print button.

14. Press Ctrl + Home to move the insertion point to the beginning of the document.

15. Navigate to the first tracked change by clicking the Next button in the Changes group.

    The first tracked change is selected.

16. Click the Next button again to select the second change and then click the Previous button to select the first change.

17. With the word *originally* selected, accept the change to insert the word by clicking the Accept button in the Changes group.

Step 17   Step 16

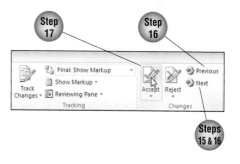

Steps 15 & 16

18. Reject the rest of the changes in the document by clicking the Reject button arrow in the Changes group and then clicking *Reject All Changes in Document* at the drop-down list.

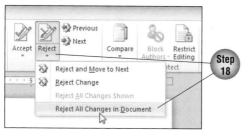

Step 18

19. Save **U2T8-CompComm.docx**.

Drilling Down

Displaying Information about Tracked Changes

You can display information about tracked changes by positioning the mouse pointer on a change. After approximately one second, a box displays above the change listing the author of the change, the date, the time, and the type of change (for example, whether it was a deletion or insertion). You can also display information about tracked changes by displaying the Reviewing pane. Display this pane by clicking the Reviewing Pane button in the Tracking group on the Review tab. Each change is listed separately in the pane. Use the up and down scroll arrows at the right of the Reviewing pane to scroll through and view each change.

Lesson 8.12 Inserting Comments

 2-2.2.2, 2-2.2.3

Quick Steps

Insert a Comment in a Balloon

1. Select text.
2. Click Review tab.
3. Click New Comment button.
4. Type comment in balloon.

You can provide feedback and suggest changes to a document that someone else has written by inserting comments into it. Similarly, you can obtain feedback on a document that you have written by distributing it electronically to work group members and having them insert their comments. To insert a comment in a document, select the text or item you would like to comment on or position the insertion point at the end of that text, click the Review tab, and then click the New Comment button in the Comments group. Generally, clicking the New Comment button displays a comment balloon at the right margin, as shown in Figure 8.13.

Figure 8.13 **Word Document with Comment Balloon**

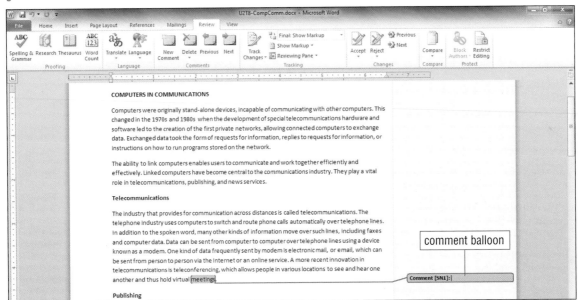

Quick Steps

Insert a Comment in the Reviewing Pane

1. Click Review tab.
2. Click Show Markup button.
3. Point to *Balloons*.
4. Click *Show All Revisions Inline* at side menu.
5. Click the New Comment button.
6. Type comment in Reviewing pane.

If default settings have been changed, clicking the New Comment button may display the Reviewing pane at the left side of the document rather than a comment balloon at the right margin. If this happens, click the Show Markup button in the Tracking group on the Review tab, point to *Balloons*, and then click *Show Only Comments and Formatting in Balloons* at the side menu. An advantage to using comment balloons is that you can easily view and respond to viewer comments.

You can insert comments in the Reviewing pane rather than in comment balloons, if you prefer. The Reviewing pane displays inserted comments as well as changes tracked with the Track Changes feature. To insert a comment in the Reviewing pane, click the Show Markup button in the Tracking group on the Review tab, point to *Balloons*, and then click *Show All Revisions Inline* at the side menu. The Reviewing pane displays at the left side of the screen, as shown in Figure 8.14. Click the New Comment button in the Comments group and then type your comment in the Reviewing pane. If the pane does not display, turn it on by clicking the Reviewing Pane button in the Tracking group. (The Reviewing pane might display along the bottom of the screen rather than at the left side. To specify where you want the pane to display, click the Reviewing Pane button arrow in the Tracking group on the Review tab and then click *Reviewing Pane Vertical* or *Reviewing Pane Horizontal*.)

Figure 8.14 Vertical Reviewing Pane

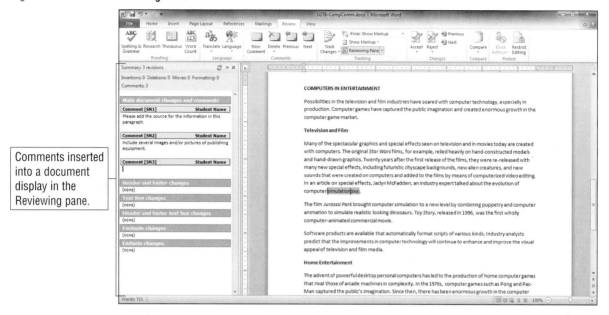

Comments inserted into a document display in the Reviewing pane.

When you are working in a long document with many inserted comments, the Previous and Next buttons in the Comments group on the Review tab can be useful. Click the Next button to move the insertion point to the next comment or click the Previous button to move the insertion point to the preceding comment.

You can edit a comment in the Reviewing pane or in a comment balloon. To edit a comment in the Reviewing pane, click the Reviewing Pane button to turn on the pane and then click in the comment that you want to edit. Make the desired changes to the comment and then close the Reviewing pane. To edit a comment in a comment balloon, turn on the display of comment balloons, click in the comment balloon, and then make the desired changes.

Quick Steps

Edit a Comment

1. Click Review tab.
2. Click Reviewing Pane button.
3. Click in comment in pane.
4. Make desired changes.

OR

1. Click Review tab.
2. Turn on display of comment balloons.
3. Click in comment balloon.
4. Make desired changes.

Exercise 8.12 Inserting Comments

1. With **U2T8-CompComm.docx** open, insert comments in balloons. Begin by clicking the Show Markup button, pointing to *Balloons*, and then clicking *Show Revisions in Balloons* at the side menu.

2. Position the insertion point at the end of the paragraph in the *Telecommunications* section, click the Review tab, and then click the New Comment button in the Comments group.

   If the Reviewing pane displays, turn it off by clicking the Reviewing Pane button in the Tracking group.

3. Type **Please add the source for the information in this paragraph.** in the comment balloon.

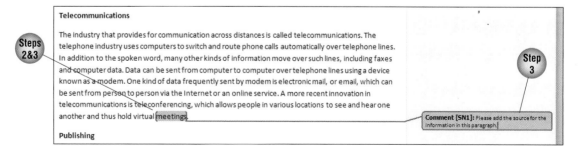

4. Move the insertion point to the end of the paragraph in the *Publishing* section, click the New Comment button in the Comments group, and then type **Include several images and/or pictures of publishing equipment.** in the comment balloon.

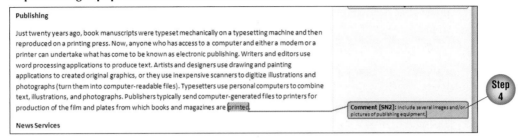
Step 4

Publishing

Just twenty years ago, book manuscripts were typeset mechanically on a typesetting machine and then reproduced on a printing press. Now, anyone who has access to a computer and either a modem or a printer can undertake what has come to be known as electronic publishing. Writers and editors use word processing applications to produce text. Artists and designers use drawing and painting applications to created original graphics, or they use inexpensive scanners to digitize illustrations and photographs (turn them into computer-readable files). Typesetters use personal computers to combine text, illustrations, and photographs. Publishers typically send computer-generated files to printers for production of the film and plates from which books and magazines are printed.

Comment [SN2]: Include several images and/or pictures of publishing equipment.

News Services

5. Display comments in the Reviewing pane by clicking the Show Markup button, pointing to *Balloons*, and then clicking *Show All Revisions Inline* at the side menu.

6. Click the Reviewing Pane button in the Tracking group on the Review tab.

7. Move the insertion point to the end of the first paragraph of text in the *Television and Film* section, click the New Comment button and, with the insertion point positioned in the Reviewing pane, type **Include hyperlinks to websites.**

8. Click in the document, press Ctrl + Home to move the insertion point to the beginning of the document, and then click the Next button in the Comments group.

This moves the insertion point to the first comment reference and places the insertion point in the first pane of the Reviewing pane.

9. Click the Next button again to display the second comment.

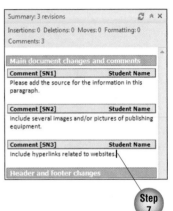
Step 7

Summary: 3 revisions

Insertions: 0 Deletions: 0 Moves: 0 Formatting: 0
Comments: 3

Main document changes and comments

Comment [SN1]   Student Name
Please add the source for the information in this paragraph.

Comment [SN2]   Student Name
Include several images and/or pictures of publishing equipment.

Comment [SN3]   Student Name
Include hyperlinks related to websites.

Header and footer changes

Step 9

10. With the insertion point positioned in the Reviewing pane, edit the second comment to read *Include several clip art images, photos, or other images of publishing equipment.*

11. Click the Reviewing Pane button in the Tracking group to close the pane.

12. Click the Show Markup button, point to *Balloons*, and then click *Show Only Comments and Formatting in Balloons* at the side menu.

13. Move the insertion point to the first paragraph in the *Television and Film* section and then click in the comment balloon that displays at the right.

14. Move the insertion point immediately left of the period at the end of the sentence and then type **and include any pertinent websites**.

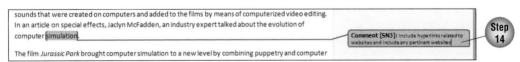
Step 14

sounds that were created on computers and added to the films by means of computerized video editing. In an article on special effects, Jaclyn McFadden, an industry expert talked about the evolution of computer simulation.

Comment [SN3]: Include hyperlinks related to websites and include any pertinent websites

The film *Jurassic Park* brought computer simulation to a new level by combining puppetry and computer

15. Click in the document, click the Show Markup button, point to *Balloons*, and then click *Show All Revisions Inline*.

16. Save **U2T8-CompComm.docx.**

Drilling Down

Deleting a Comment

You can delete a comment by clicking the Next button in the Comments group on the Review tab until the desired comment is selected and then clicking the Delete button. If you want to delete all comments in a document, click the Delete button arrow and then click _Delete All Comments in Document_ at the drop-down list.

Lesson 8.13 Protecting a Document

 2-2.2.4

If you create a document that contains sensitive, restricted, or private information, consider protecting it by saving it as a read-only document or securing it with a password. You can limit users from formatting and editing in a document with options at the Restrict Formatting and Editing task pane. Display this task pane by clicking the Review tab and then clicking the Restrict Editing button in the Protect group.

With options in the _Formatting restrictions_ section of the Restrict Formatting and Editing task pane (shown in Figure 8.15), you can lock specific styles used in a document, thus allowing the use of only those styles and prohibiting a user from making other formatting changes. Use the _Editing restrictions_ option at the task pane to limit the types of changes a user can make to a document. Insert a check mark in the _Allow only this type of editing in the document_ option and the drop-down list below the option becomes active. Click the down-pointing arrow at the right of the option box to specify what type of editing you will allow in the document. With options at the Restrict Formatting and Editing task pane you can protect the integrity of a document.

Quick Steps

Protect a Document
1. Click Review tab.
2. Click Restrict Editing button.
3. Specify formatting and/or editing options.
4. Click Yes, Start Enforcing Protection button.

Figure 8.15 Restrict Formatting and Editing Task Pane

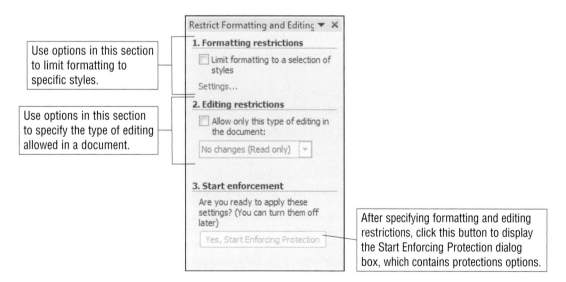

Specifying formatting and editing restrictions and any exceptions to those restrictions is the first step to protecting your document. The next step is to start the enforcement of the restrictions you have specified. Click the Yes, Start Enforcing Protection button in the task pane to display the Start Enforcing Protection dialog box, shown in Figure 8.16.

Formatting a Document in Word with Special Features

369

Figure 8.16 **Start Enforcing Protection Dialog Box**

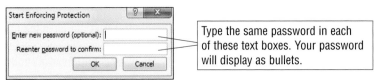

Type the same password in each of these text boxes. Your password will display as bullets.

At the Start Enforcing Protection dialog box, the *Password* option is selected automatically. To add a password, type what you want to use as the password in the *Enter new password (optional)* text box. Click in the *Reenter password to confirm* text box, type the same password again, and then click OK.

In addition to using options at the Start Enforcing Protection dialog box, you can protect a document with a password by clicking the Protect Document button at the Info tab Backstage view and then clicking the *Encrypt with Password* option at the drop-down list. At the Encrypt Document dialog box that displays, type your password in the text box (the text will display as round bullets) and then press the Enter key (or click OK). At the Confirm Password dialog box, type your password again (the text will display as round bullets) and then press the Enter key or click OK. When you apply a password, the message *A password is required to open this document.* displays to the right of the Protect Document button.

Quick Steps

Encrypt a Document
1. Click File tab.
2. Click Protect Document button at Info tab Backstage view.
3. Click *Encrypt with Password*.
4. Type password and press Enter.
5. Type password again and press Enter.

Exercise 8.13 Protecting a Document

1. With **U2T8-CompComm.docx** open, restrict editing to comments only. Begin by clicking the Review tab and then clicking the Restrict Editing button in the Protect group.

2. At the Restrict Formatting and Editing task pane, click the *Allow only this type of editing in the document* check box to insert a check mark.

3. Click the down-pointing arrow at the right side of the option box below *Allow only this type of editing in the document* and then click *Comments* at the drop-down list.

4. Click the Yes, Start Enforcing Protection button located at the bottom of the task pane.

5. At the Start Enforcing Protection dialog box, type **editing** in the *Enter new password (optional)* text box.

    Bullets will display in the text box in place of the letters you type.

6. Press the Tab key (this moves the insertion point to the *Reenter password to confirm* text box) and then type **editing**.

7. Click OK to close the dialog box.

8. Save and then close **U2T8-CompComm.docx**.

9. Open **U2T8-CompComm.docx**.

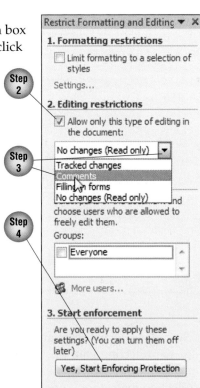

10. Click each of the ribbon tabs and notice the buttons and options that are dimmed and unavailable.

11. Make sure the Restrict Formatting and Editing task pane displays.

    If the task pane does not display, click the Review tab and then click the Restrict Editing button in the Protect group.

12. Read the information that displays in the task pane telling you that the document is protected from unintentional editing and you may only insert comments.

13. Move the insertion point immediately right of the period that ends the first sentence in the last paragraph of the *Home Entertainment* section (the sentence that begins with *Other computer games make use…*).

14. Click the New Comment button in the Comments group and then type the following in the Reviewing pane: **What type of hand-held devices?**

15. Close the Reviewing pane.

16. Click the Stop Protection button located toward the bottom of the Restrict Formatting and Editing task pane.

17. Type **editing** as the password at the Unprotect Document dialog box and then click OK.

18. Close the Restrict Formatting and Editing task pane.

19. Protect the document with a password so that the password is required to open the document. Click the File tab, click the Protect Document button [icon] in the Info tab Backstage view, and then click *Encrypt with Password* at the drop-down list.

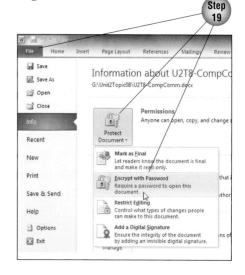

20. At the Encrypt Document dialog box, type **final** as the password and then press the Enter key.

    Your text will display as round bullets.

21. At the Confirm Password dialog box, type **final** again and then press the Enter key.

22. Save and then close U2T8-CompComm.docx.

23. Open **U2T8-CompComm.docx**. At the Password dialog box, type **final** and then press the Enter key.

24. Save, print, and then close **U2T8-CompComm.docx**.

Drilling Down

Identifying a Document as Read-Only

A read-only document can be opened and you can make changes to the document, but you cannot save those changes with the same name. Word protects the original document and does not allow you to save the changed document with the same name. You can, however, open a document as read-only, make changes to it, and then save the document with a different name.

To save a document as read-only, display the Save As dialog box, click the Tools button, and then click *General Options* at the drop-down list. At the General Options dialog box, click *Read-only recommended* to insert a check mark in the check box. When a person opens the document, a message displays asking whether he or she wants to open the file as read-only.

Lesson 8.14   Creating Footnotes and Endnotes

2-2.2.2

footnote An explanatory note or reference printed at the bottom of the page where it is referenced

endnote An explanatory note or reference printed at the end of the document

Quick Steps

Insert a Footnote

1. Click References tab.
2. Click Insert Footnote button.
3. Type footnote text.

Insert an Endnote

1. Click References tab.
2. Click Insert Endnote button.
3. Type endnote text.

Keyboard Shortcut

Insert Footnote

Ctrl + Alt + F

Insert Endnote

Ctrl + Alt + D

A research paper or report usually contains information from a variety of sources. To give credit to those sources, you can insert footnotes or endnotes in the document. A **footnote** is an explanatory note or reference that is printed at the bottom of the page where it is referenced. An **endnote** is also an explanatory note or reference, but it is printed at the end of the document.

Two steps are involved in creating a footnote or endnote. First, the note reference number is inserted in the document at the location where the note is referenced. The second step is to type the note entry text. Footnotes and endnotes are created in a similar manner. To create a footnote, position the insertion point at the location where you want the reference number to appear, click the References tab, and then click the Insert Footnote button in the Footnotes group. This inserts a number in the document and also inserts a two-inch separator line at the bottom left of the page with a superscript number below it. With the insertion point positioned immediately right of the superscript number, type the footnote entry text. Complete similar steps to insert an endnote, except click the Insert Endnote button in the Footnotes group. Word automatically numbers footnotes with superscript Arabic numbers and endnotes with superscript lowercase Roman numerals.

When you print a document containing footnotes, Word automatically reduces the number of text lines on each page by the number of lines in the footnotes on that page plus the separator line. If the page does not contain enough space, the footnote number and footnote entry text are taken to the next page. If a document contains endnotes, Word prints all endnote references at the end of the document, separated from the text by a two-inch separator line.

Lesson 8.14 Inserting and Printing Footnotes and Endnotes

1. Open **InterApps.docx** and then save the document with Save As and name it **U2T8-InterApps-Footnotes**.

2. Position the insertion point at the end of the paragraph in the *Speech Recognition* section.

3. Create a footnote by clicking the References tab and then clicking the Insert Footnote button AB¹ in the Footnotes group.

4. With the insertion point positioned at the bottom of the page immediately following the superscript number, type the following: **Everson, Heather and Nicolas Reyes, "Integrating Speech Recognition,"** *Design Technologies***, January/February 2013, pages 24-26.**

5. Position the insertion point at end of the second paragraph in the *Natural-Language Interface* section, click the Insert Footnote button in the Footnotes group, and then type the following: **Glenovich, James, "Language Interfaces,"** *Corporate Computing*, **November 2012, pages 8-12.**

6. Position the insertion point at end of the last paragraph in the document, click the Insert Footnote button, and then type the following: **Beal, Marilyn, "Challenges of Artificial Intelligence,"** *Interface Designs*, **April 2013, pages 10-18.**

7. Save, print, and then close **U2T8-InterApps-Footnotes.docx**.

8. Open **InterApps.docx** and then save the document with Save As and name it **U2T8-InterApps-Endnotes**.

9. Position the insertion point at the end of the first paragraph in the document, click the References tab, and then click the Insert Endnote button 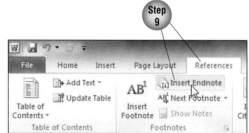 in the Footnotes group.

10. With the insertion point located at the end of the document immediately following the superscript roman numeral, type the following: **Novak, Kevin,** *Artificial Intelligence*, **Home Town Publishing, 2013, pages 45-51.**

11. Position the insertion point at the end of the paragraph in the *Virtual Reality* section, click the Insert Endnote button in the Footnotes group, and then type the following: **Curtis, William,** *Virtual Reality Worlds*, **Lilly-Harris Publishers, 2013, pages 53-68.**

12. Save the document and then print only page 2.

13. Close **U2T8-InterApps-Endnotes.docx**.

 Delving Deeper

More Information for IC³

IC³ 2-1.4.6, 2-1.4.7

Outputting Documents in Electronic Format

With the increase of online technology, saving and distributing documents in an electronic format is becoming more popular, and Word contains a variety of options to help you do this. Click the File tab and then click the Save & Send tab to view options for sending your document as an email attachment or Internet fax, saving your document as a different file type, and posting your document to a special location such as a blog.

Sending a Document Using E-mail

With the *Send Using E-mail* option selected in the Save & Send category, options for sending a document display. You can choose to send a copy of the document as an attachment to an email, create an email that contains a link to the document, attach a PDF or XPS copy of the open document to an email, or send an email as an Internet fax. To send the document as an email attachment, you need to set up an Outlook email account. If you want to create an email that contains a link to the document, you need to save the document to a web server. The *Send as Internet Fax* option allows you to fax your document without using a fax machine, but to do this you must be signed up with a fax service provider.

With the remaining two options in the Send Using E-mail category of the Save & Send tab Backstage view, you can send the document in PDF or XPS format. The letters PDF stand for

continued

portable document format, which is a document format developed by Adobe Systems that captures all of the elements of a document as an electronic image. An XPS document is a Microsoft document format for publishing content in an easily viewable format. The letters XPS stand for *XML paper specification*, and the letters XML stand for *extensible markup language*, which is a set of rules for encoding documents electronically.

Saving to SkyDrive

If you want to share documents with others, consider saving documents to SkyDrive, a file storage and sharing service that allows you to upload files and access them from a web browser. To save a document to SkyDrive, you need a Windows Live ID account. If you have a Hotmail, Messenger, or Xbox LIVE account, you have a Windows Live ID account. To save a document to SkyDrive, open the document, click the File tab, click the Save & Send tab, and then click the *Save to Web* option in the Save & Send category (as shown below). In the *Save to Windows Live* section, click the Sign In button. At the connecting dialog box, type your email address and password, and then press the Enter key. Once you are connected to your Windows Live ID account, specify whether you want the file saved to your personal folder or your shared folder, and then click the Save As button. At the Save As dialog box, click the Save button or type a new name in the *File name* text box and then click the Save button. One method for accessing your file from SkyDrive is to log in to your Windows Live ID account and then look for the SkyDrive hyperlink. Click this hyperlink to display your personal and shared folder contents.

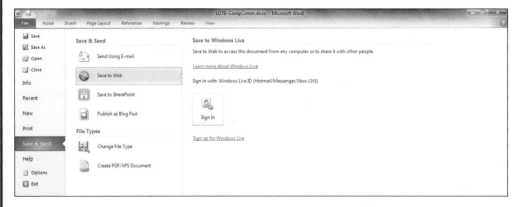

continued

Saving to SharePoint

Microsoft SharePoint is a collection of products and software that includes a number of components. If your company or organization uses SharePoint, you can save a document in a library on your organization's SharePoint site so you and your colleagues have a central location for accessing documents. To save a document to a SharePoint library, open the document, click the File tab, click the Save & Send tab, and then click the *Save to SharePoint* option (as shown below).

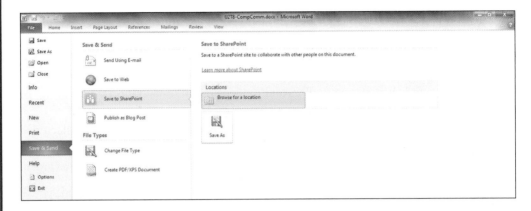

Saving a Document as a Blog Post

You can save a Word document as a blog post with the *Publish as Blog Post* option in the Save & Send tab Backstage view. To save a blog post, you must have a blog site established. Click the *Publish as Blog Post* option and information about supported blog sites displays at the right side of the Save & Send tab Backstage view (as shown below). To publish a document as a blog post, open the document, click the File tab, click the Save & Send tab, click the *Publish as Blog Post* option in the Save & Send category, and then click the Publish as Blog Post button in the Publish as Blog Post section. The document opens in a new window. Type a title for the blog post and then click the Publish button that displays in the Blog group on the Blog Post tab.

Though distributing documents in an electronic format is fast and convenient, problems can occur when viewing and printing an electronic version of a document. You may encounter issues with incompatible file formats, file sizes that are too large for transfer, or formatting features that get lost when converting from one file type to another.

TOPIC SUMMARY

- By default, a Word document contains 1-inch top, bottom, left, and right page margins. Change margins with preset margin settings at the Margins button drop-down list or with options at the Page Setup dialog box with the Margins tab selected.

- The default page orientation is portrait, which you can change to landscape with the Orientation button in the Page Setup group on the Page Layout tab.

- The default page size is 8.5 by 11 inches, which you can change with options at the Size button drop-down list or options at the Page Setup dialog box with the Paper tab selected.

- Apply a theme and change theme colors and fonts using buttons in the Themes group on the Page Layout tab.

- Insert symbols with options at the Symbol dialog box with the Symbols tab selected, and insert special characters with options at the Symbol dialog box with the Special Characters tab selected.

- Click the Date & Time button in the Text group on the Insert tab to display the Date and Time dialog box.

- Insert the contents of another document into an open document with the Object button in the Text group on the Insert tab.

- Insert predesigned and formatted page numbering with the Page Number button in the Header & Footer group on the Insert tab.

- By default, Word inserts Arabic numbers (1, 2, 3, etc.) as page numbers and numbers the pages in a document sequentially beginning with number 1. Change these default settings with options at the Page Number Format dialog box.

- Insert predesigned headers and footers in a document using the Header and Footer buttons in the Header & Footer group on the Insert tab.

- A header or footer displays in Print Layout view but will not display in Draft view.

- Insert a predesigned and formatted cover page using the Cover Page button in the Pages group on the Insert tab.

- Insert a section break in a document to apply formatting to a portion of a document. You can insert a continuous section break or a section break that begins a new page. View and/or delete a section break in Draft view because section breaks are not visible in Print Layout view.

- Set text in columns to improve readability of documents such as newsletters or reports. Format text in columns using the Columns button in the Page Setup group on the Page Layout tab or with options at the Columns dialog box.

- Insert an image such as a picture or clip art with buttons in the Illustrations group on the Insert tab.

- Customize and format an image with options and buttons on the Picture Tools Format tab.

- Size an image with the Shape Height and Shape Width measurement boxes on the Picture Tools Format tab or with the sizing handles that display around a selected image.

- To insert a clip art image, click the Insert tab, click the Clip Art button, and then click the desired image in the Clip Art task pane. To search for specific types of clip art images, type the desired topic in the *Search for* text box in the Clip Art task pane.

- Draw shapes in a document using the Shapes button in the Illustrations group on the Insert tab. Customize a shape with options on the Drawing Tools Format tab.

- Copy a shape by holding down the Ctrl key while dragging the selected shape.

- Select multiple shapes by holding down the Shift key while clicking each desired shape.

- Group objects to apply the same formatting or make the same adjustments to the size or rotation of objects. Group objects by selecting the objects, clicking the Drawing Tools Format tab, clicking the Group button in the Arrange group, and then clicking *Group* at the drop-down list.

continued

- Use the Align button in the Arrange group on the Drawing Tools Format tab to align multiple shapes in a document.
- Insert text in a shape by clicking in the shape and then typing the desired text.
- Use WordArt to distort or modify text to conform to a variety of shapes.
- Customize WordArt with options on the Drawing Tools Format tab.
- Use the SmartArt feature to insert predesigned diagrams and organizational charts in a document.
- Format a SmartArt graphic with options and buttons on the SmartArt Tools Design tab and the SmartArt Tools Format tab.
- Use the Track Changes feature when more than one person is reviewing a document and making changes to it.
- Move to the next change in a document by clicking the Next button in the Changes group on the Review tab. Click the Previous button to move to the previous change.
- Use the Accept and Reject buttons in the Changes group on the Review tab to accept or reject revisions made in a document.
- Insert a comment in a document by clicking the New Comment button in the Comments group on the Review tab.
- You can insert and edit comments in the Reviewing pane or in comment balloons.
- Turn the display of the Reviewing pane on and off with the Reviewing Pane button in the Tracking group on the Review tab.
- Navigate through comments using the Previous and Next buttons in the Comments group on the Review tab.
- Restrict formatting and editing in a document and apply a password with options at the Restrict Formatting and Editing task pane.
- To restrict editing in a document, click the *Allow only this type of editing in the document* option at the Restrict Formatting and Editing task pane, click the down-pointing arrow at the right of the options box, and then click the desired option.
- Enforce editing and formatting restrictions by clicking the Yes, Start Enforcing Protection button in the Restrict Formatting and Editing task pane and make changes to what is allowed at the Start Enforcing Protection dialog box.
- Protect a document with a password by clicking the Protect Document button at the Info tab Backstage view and then clicking *Encrypt with Password*.
- Footnotes and endnotes are explanatory notes or references. Footnotes are inserted and printed at the bottom of the page and endnotes are printed at the end of the document.

Key Terms

continuous section break, p. 348

cover page, p. 344

endnote, p. 372

footer, p. 344

footnote, p. 372

hard page break, p. 348

header, p. 344

orientation, p. 337

sizing handles, p. 352

SmartArt, p. 359

soft page break, p. 348

theme, p. 339

WordArt, p. 357

Features Summary

Feature	Ribbon Tab, Group	Button, Option
Accept changes	Review, Changes	
Balloons	Review, Tracking	, *Balloons*
Clip Art task pane	Insert, Illustrations	
Columns	Page Layout, Page Setup	
Columns dialog box	Page Layout, Page Setup	, *More Columns*
Comment	Review, Comments	
Continuous section break	Page Layout, Page Setup	, *Continuous*
Cover Page	Insert, Pages	
Date and Time dialog box	Insert, Text	
Encrypt Document dialog box	File	, *Encrypt with Password*
Endnote	References, Footnotes	
Footer	Insert, Header & Footer	
Footnote	References, Footnotes	AB^1
Header	Insert, Header & Footer	
Insert file	Insert, Text	, *Text from File*
Insert Picture dialog box	Insert, Illustrations	
Margins	Page Layout, Page Setup	
Next comment	Review, Comments	
Next revision	Review, Changes	
Page break	Insert, Pages	
Page numbering	Insert, Header & Footer	
Page orientation	Page Layout, Page Setup	
Page Setup dialog box	Page Layout, Page Setup	
Page size	Page Layout, Page Setup	

continued

Feature	Ribbon Tab, Group	Button, Option
Previous comment	Review, Comment	
Previous revision	Review, Changes	
Reject changes	Review, Changes	
Restrict Formatting and Editing task pane	Review, Protect	
Reviewing pane	Review, Tracking	
Section break	Page Layout, Page Setup	
Shapes	Insert, Illustrations	
Show markup	Review, Tracking	
SmartArt	Insert, Illustrations	
Symbol dialog box	Insert, Symbols	
Theme Color	Page Layout, Themes	
Theme Fonts	Page Layout, Themes	
Themes	Page Layout, Themes	
Track changes	Review, Tracking	
WordArt	Insert, Text	

KEY POINTS REVIEW

Identification

Match the terms to the callouts on the Word window in Figure 8.17.

1. _____ image height and width
2. _____ tracked change
3. _____ sizing handles
4. _____ comment balloon
5. _____ clip art image
6. _____ header
7. _____ column text
8. _____ Reviewing pane
9. _____ WordArt
10. _____ footer

Figure 8.17 Identification Figure

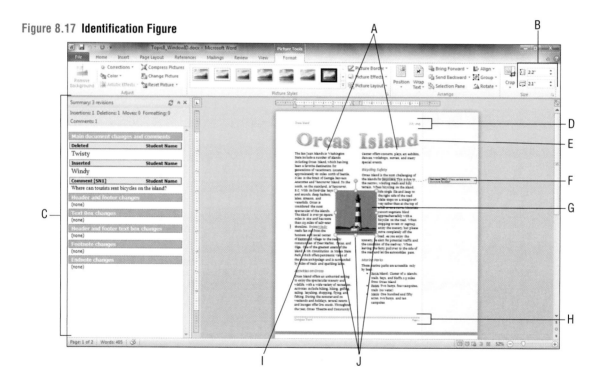

Multiple Choice

For each of the following items, choose the option that best completes the sentence or answers the question.

1. This pane displays inserted comments as well as changes tracked with the Track Changes feature.
   A. Editing
   B. Reviewing
   C. Revisions
   D. Track Changes

2. Use this feature to distort or modify text to conform to a variety of shapes.
   A. WordArt
   B. SmartArt
   C. Clip art
   D. Images

3. This is the default measurement for the top, bottom, left, and right margins.
   A. 0.25 inches
   B. 0.5 inches
   C. 1 inch
   D. 1.5 inches

4. Use options in this section of the Restrict Formatting and Editing task pane to limit the types of editing changes a user can make to a document.
   A. Formatting restrictions
   B. Editing restrictions
   C. Start enforcement
   D. Stop enforcement

5. The Cover Page button is located in the Pages group on this tab.
   A. Home
   B. Insert
   C. Page Layout
   D. Review

6. Click the File tab and then click this tab to display the Protect Document button.
   A. Help
   B. New
   C. Recent
   D. Info

7. The Date & Time button is located in this group on the Insert tab.
   A. Illustrations
   B. Header & Footer
   C. Text
   D. Pages

8. This is the default page size.
   A. 8.5 x 11 inches
   B. 8.5 x 14 inches
   C. 11 x 17 inches
   D. 14 x 17 inches

9. Turn on the tracking feature by clicking the Track Changes button in this group on the Review tab.
   A. Language
   B. Tracking
   C. Changes
   D. Compare

10. If you insert page numbers in a document, by default Word uses this type of numbering.
    A. a, b, c
    B. A, B, C
    C. 1, 2, 3
    D. i, ii, iii

Matching

Match each of the following definitions with the correct term, command, or option.

1. _____ This is the text that appears at the top of every page.
2. _____ This is the default page orientation.
3. _____ A predesigned cover page generally contains these, which are locations where you can enter specific information.
4. _____ When changing the size of an image, maintain the image proportions by holding down this key while dragging a corner sizing handle.
5. _____ This is a page break that Word automatically inserts.
6. _____ The Group button is located in this group on the Drawing Tools Format tab.
7. _____ Copy a selected shape by holding down this key while dragging the shape to the desired location.
8. _____ This is the text that appears at the bottom of every page.
9. _____ This is a page break that you manually insert.
10. _____ This is an explanatory note or reference that prints at the bottom of the page where it is referenced.

A. Portrait
B. Shift
C. Footnote
D. Header
E. Placeholders
F. Footer
G. Hard page break
H. Arrange
I. Ctrl
J. Soft page break

SKILLS REVIEW

Review 8.1 Formatting a Computer Document

1. Open **Computers.docx** and then save the document and name it **U2T8-R1-Computers**.
2. Apply the Heading 1 style to the title THE COMPUTER ADVANTAGE, and the Heading 2 style to the five bolded headings (*Speed, Accuracy, Versatility, Storage,* and *Communications*).
3. Change the Quick Styles set to *Newsprint*.
4. Apply the Foundry theme.
5. Change the theme colors to Civic.
6. Change the top and bottom margins to *0.5*.
7. Insert the *Pinstripes* header and then type **The Computer Advantage** in the *[Type the document title]* placeholder.
8. Insert the *Pinstripes* footer and then type your first and last names in the *[Type text]* placeholder.
9. Insert the *Pinstripes* cover page and then make the following changes to the cover page:
   a. Make sure the title *The Computer Advantage* displays in the top placeholder. If the title does not display, type **The Computer Advantage** in the *[Type the document title]* placeholder.
   b. Select and then delete the *[Type the document subtitle]* placeholder.
   c. Insert the current date in the *[Pick the date]* placeholder.
   d. Type the company name **Computer Connections** in the *[Type the company name]* placeholder.
   e. Type your first and last names in the *[Type the author name]* placeholder. (If a name already displays on the *Author* tab, select and delete the text before typing your first and last names.)
10. Insert a continuous section break at the beginning of the first paragraph of text below the title THE COMPUTER ADVANTAGE on the second page of the document.
11. Format the text below the continuous section break into two columns with a line between columns.
12. Balance the columns on the last page.
13. Center the title.
14. Save, print, and then close **U2T8-R1-Computers.docx**.

Review 8.2 Inserting Graphic Elements in a Document

1. Open **WritingSteps.docx** and then save the document and name it **U2T8-R2-WritingSteps**.
2. With the insertion point positioned at the beginning of the document, insert WordArt with the following specifications:
   a. Use the WordArt style named *Gradient Fill - Green, Accent 1*.
   b. Type **The Writing Process**.
   c. Click the border of the WordArt text to change the border to a solid line and then apply the *Tan, Accent 5, Darker 50%* text outline color.
   d. Apply the *Can Up* transform text effect.
   e. Apply the *Circle* bevel text effect.
   f. Change the WordArt height to 0.9 inches and the width to 6.5 inches.
3. Move the insertion point to the blank line above the heading *Define Purpose* and then insert a SmartArt graphic with the following specifications:
   a. Display the Choose a SmartArt Graphic dialog box, click *Process* in the left panel, and then double-click *Continuous Block Process* (first option in the third row).
   b. Apply the *Cartoon* SmartArt style.
   c. Click inside the graphic border but outside any shape. Click the SmartArt Tools Format tab, click the Size button, and then change the height to 2.2 inches and the width to 6.5 inches.
   d. Add two additional shapes to the SmartArt graphic.
   e. Type the text in the boxes as shown in Figure 8.18.
4. Insert a clip art image with the following specifications:
   a. Insert a clip art image related to *writing*.
   b. Change the text wrap to *Tight*.
   c. Move and size the image so it is positioned at the right side of the bulleted items in the *Define Purpose* section.
   d. Consider making any other changes to enhance the visual appeal of the image.
5. Move the insertion point to the end of the document and then create the shape shown in Figure 8.19 with the following specifications:
   a. Use the *Bevel* shape (located in the *Basic Shapes* section of the drop-down list).
   b. Change the height to 2.0 inches and the width to 3.9 inches.
   c. Apply the *Subtle Effect - Green, Accent 1* shape style.
   d. Apply the *Tan, 18 pt glow, Accent color 5* glow shape effect.
   e. Align the shape between the left and right margins by clicking the Align button in the Arrange group and then clicking *Distribute Horizontally* at the drop-down list.
   f. Type the text inside the shape as shown in Figure 8.19. After typing the text, select the text and then change the font size to *16*, the font color to *Green, Accent 1, Darker 50%*, and apply bold formatting.
6. Save and then print **U2T8-R2-WritingSteps.docx**.

Figure 8.18 Review 8.2 SmartArt Graphic

Figure 8.19 **Review 8.2 Shape**

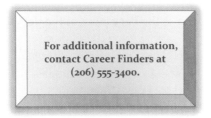

For additional information,
contact Career Finders at
(206) 555-3400.

Review 8.3 Inserting Comments, Tracking Changes, and Protecting a Document

1. With **U2T8-R2-WritingSteps.docx** open, save the document with Save As and name it **U2T8-R3-WritingSteps**.
2. Turn on track changes and then make the following changes:
   a. Delete the word *achieve* in the first bulleted paragraph in the *Define Purpose* section and then type **accomplish**.
   b. Move the insertion point to the beginning of the second bulleted paragraph in the *Select and Organize Information* section, press the Enter key, move the insertion point up to the new bullet, and then type **What information must I include?**
   c. Select and then move the *Write First Draft* section below the *Edit and Proofread* section.
   d. Turn off track changes.
3. Print the document showing markups.
4. Accept all of the changes in the document *except* the change moving the *Write First Draft* section below the *Edit and Proofread* section.
5. Insert the following comments:
   a. Insert the comment **Please provide an example of a first draft.** at the end of the paragraph in the *Write First Draft* section.
   b. Insert the comment **What types of useful tools can you use to edit and proofread a document?** at the end of the paragraph in the *Edit and Proofread* section.
6. Save the document.
7. Encrypt the document with the password *writing*.
8. Close **U2T8-R3-WritingSteps.docx**.
9. Open **U2T8-R3-WritingSteps.docx** and enter the password *writing* when prompted.
10. Print and then close the document.

Review 8.4 Preparing and Formatting an Organizational Chart

1. At a blank document, create the SmartArt organizational chart shown in Figure 8.20 with the following specifications:
   a. Display the Choose a SmartArt Graphic dialog box, click *Hierarchy* in the left panel, and then double-click *Hierarchy* in the middle panel.
   b. Type the text in the boxes as shown in Figure 8.20.
   c. Apply the *Inset* SmartArt style.
   d. Change the color range to *Colorful Range – Accent Colors 2 to 3*.
   e. Click inside the SmartArt organizational chart border but outside any shape, click the SmartArt Tools Format tab, click the Size button, and then change the height to 4 inches and the width to 6.5 inches.
   f. Click the Position button and then click *Position in Middle Center with Square Text Wrapping* at the drop-down list.
   g. Apply the *Fill - Olive Green, Accent 3, Powder Bevel* WordArt style to the organizational chart.
2. Save the document and name it **U2T8-R4-OrgChart**.
3. Print and then close **U2T8-R4-OrgChart.docx**.

Figure 8.20 Review 8.4 SmartArt Organizational Chart

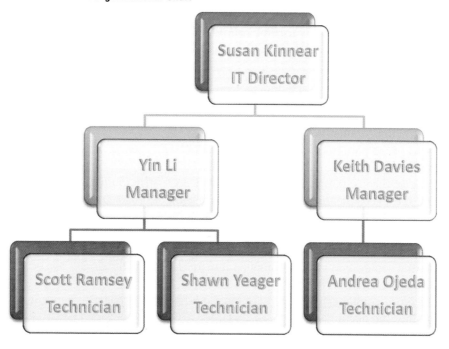

Review 8.5 Inserting Footnotes in a Document

1. Open **NewsltrLayout.docx** and then save the document with Save As and name it **U2T8-R5-NewsltrLayout**.
2. Position the insertion point at the end of the paragraph in the *Choosing Paper Size and Type* section and then insert the following footnote: **Alverso, Monica, "Paper Styles for Newsletters,"** *Design Technologies*, **March 2013, pages 45-51.**
3. Position the insertion point at the end of the paragraph in the *Choosing Paper Weight* section and then insert the following footnote: **Sutton, Keith, "Newsletter Paper Styles and Weight,"** *Graphic Designs and Technologies*, **March/April 2013, pages 8-11.**
4. Position the insertion point at the end of the last paragraph in the document and then insert the following footnote: **Maddock, Arlita G., "Guidelines for Dynamic Newsletters,"** *Business Computing*, **June 2013, pages 9-14.**
5. Save, print, and then close **U2T8-R5-NewsltrLayout.docx**.

SKILLS ASSESSMENT

Assessment 8.1 Formatting a Computer Risks Document

1. Open **CompChapters.docx** and then save the document and name it **U2T8-A1-CompChapters**.
2. Apply the Heading 1 style to the titles *CHAPTER 1: COMPUTER VIRUSES* and *CHAPTER 2: SECURITY RISKS* and apply the Heading 2 style to the headings *Types of Viruses, Methods of Virus Operation, Systems Failure, Employee Theft,* and *Cracking Software for Copying.*
3. Change the Quick Styles set to *Formal.*
4. Apply the Oriel theme.
5. Apply the Slipstream theme colors.
6. Change the top and bottom margins to 0.5 inches.

7. Insert the *Alphabet* footer and then type your first and last names in the *[Type text]* placeholder.
8. Insert the *Puzzle* cover page and then make the following changes to the placeholders:
   a. Insert the current year in the *[Year]* placeholder.
   b. Type **Computer Risks** in the *[Type the document title]* placeholder.
   c. Type **Viruses and Security** in the *[Type the subtitle]* placeholder.
   d. Delete the Abstract placeholder.
   e. Type your first and last names in the Author placeholder.
   f. Type **Northland Computing** in the *[Type the company name]* placeholder.
9. Insert the following comments:
   a. At the end of the paragraph in the *TYPES OF VIRUSES* section, insert the comment *Insert information on the latest virus.*
   b. At the end of the last paragraph in the *METHODS OF VIRUS OPERATION* section, insert the comment *Include information on the latest virus to affect our company.*
   c. At the end of the last paragraph in the document, insert the comment *Include information about laws related to copying software.*
10. Turn on tracking and then make the following changes:
    a. Edit the first sentence in the document so it reads *The computer virus is one of the most familiar forms of risk to computer security.*
    b. Type the word **computer's** between *the* and *motherboard* in the last sentence in the first paragraph of the document.
    c. Delete the word *real* in the second sentence of the *TYPES OF VIRUSES* section and then type **significant**.
    d. Select and then delete the third sentence in the second paragraph of the *Methods of Virus Operation* section (the sentence that begins *Polymorphic viruses alter themselves randomly...*).
    e. Turn off tracking.
11. Print the document showing markups.
12. Accept all of the changes in the document.
13. Save, print, and then close **U2T8-A1-CompChapters.docx**.

Assessment 8.2 Creating an Announcement

1. At a blank document, create an announcement for Career Finders by typing the text shown in Figure 8.21.
2. Change the font for the entire document to a decorative font, size, and color of your choosing.
3. Insert, size, and move a clip art image of your choosing in the document. Choose a clip art image related to the subject of the announcement.
4. Save the document and name it **U2T8-A2-CFAnnounce**.
5. Print and then close **U2T8-A2-CFAnnounce.docx**.

Figure 8.21 Assessment 8.2 Text

CAREER FINDERS
Career Exploration
February 8, 1:30 to 4:30 p.m.
Resume Writing
February 9, 9:30 to 11:30 a.m.
Interviewing Skills
February 10, 2:00 to 5:00 p.m.
Contact Kyle Silvers for additional workshop information.

Assessment 8.3 Inserting a Logo and Creating a SmartArt Organizational Chart and Graphic

1. At a blank document, press the Enter key four times, move the insertion point back to the beginning of the document, and then insert the **VALogo.jpg** image. (Do this with the Picture button in the Illustrations group on the Insert tab.) Make the following modifications to the logo:
   a. Apply the *Reflected Rounded Rectangle* picture style.
   b. Apply the *Black, Text 1* color to the picture border.
   c. Change the height of the logo to 1".
   d. Apply the *Square* text wrapping.
   e. Move the logo so it is centered between the left and right margins.
2. Press Ctrl + End to move the insertion point below the logo and then create an organizational chart with the following information:

Noel Alderton
Owner

Jayden Elroy	Owen Landers	Ella Braun
Personnel Manager	Production Manager	Finance Manager

3. Apply formatting and/or design to enhance the visual display of the organizational chart and to complement the company logo. Apply the *Square* text wrapping and then drag the organizational chart between the left and right margins.
4. Press Ctrl + End, make sure the insertion point is positioned below the organizational chart, and then create a SmartArt graphic with the following text (use the *Converging Radial* diagram in the Relationship group in the Choose a SmartArt Graphic dialog box):

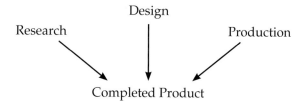

5. Apply formatting and/or design to enhance the visual display of the graphic and to complement the logo and organizational chart. Apply the *Square* text wrapping and then drag the graphic between the left and right margins.
6. Make sure the logo, organizational chart, and graphic fit on one page.
7. Save the document and name it **U2T8-A3-VAImages**.
8. Print and then close **U2T8-A3-VAImages.docx**.

Assessment 8.4 Customizing Theme Colors in a Health Plan Document

1. Use the Help feature to learn how to customize theme colors.
2. Open **KLHPlan.docx** and save it with Save As and name it **U2T8-A4-KLHPlan**.
3. Apply the Heading 1 style to the headings *Plan Highlights*, *Quality Assessment*, *Provider Network*, and *Key Life Health Plan*.
4. Apply the *Thatch* Quick Styles set.
5. Apply the Foundry theme.
6. Display the Create New Theme Colors dialog box and make the following changes:
   a. Change the *Accent 1* color to *Sky Blue, Accent 3, Darker 25%*.
   b. Change the *Accent 2* color to *Green, Accent 1, Darker 50%*.
   c. Change the *Accent 5* color to *Light Green, Accent 2, Lighter 40%*.
   d. Type your first and last names in the *Name* option box and then click Save.
7. Scroll through the document and notice the color changes made to the headings and SmartArt graphic.
8. Click the Theme Colors button in the Themes group and notice the custom heading with your first and last names displayed at the top of the drop-down gallery.
9. Save, print, and then close **U2T8-A4-KLHPlan.docx**.

Assessment 8.5 Downloading and Inserting a Clip Art Image from Office.com

1. Go to the Office.com website (using the Clip Art task pane) and then search for and download a clip art image related to first aid.
2. Open **FirstAid.docx** and save it with Save As and name it **U2T8-A5-FirstAid**.
3. Insert the first aid clip art image you downloaded. Apply formatting to the clip art image to coordinate with the appearance of the document.
4. Save, print, and then close **U2T8-A5-FirstAid.docx**.

Assessment 8.6 Formatting a Document on Preparing a Resume

1. Open **Resume.docx** and then save it with Save As and name it **U2T8-A6-Resume**.
2. Format the report so it appears as shown in Figure 8.22 with the following specifications:
   a. Change the Quick Styles set to *Modern*.
   b. Apply the Heading 3 style to the two headings in the report. ***Hint: You may need to apply the Heading 2 style first to display the Heading 3 style.***
   c. Change the theme to Clarity and change the theme colors to *Equity*.
   d. Insert the WordArt text *Résumé Writing* with the following specifications:
      • Use the *Gradient Fill – Orange, Accent 1* option (fourth option from the left in the third row).
      • Type the text **Résumé Writing** and insert the *é* symbol using the Insert Symbol dialog box.
      • Apply the *Can Up* transform text effect.
      • Change the width of the WordArt to 5.5 inches and the height to 0.9 inch.
      • Change the position to *Position in Top Center with Square Text Wrapping* (middle option in the top row of the *With Text Wrapping* section).
   e. Format the report into two columns, beginning with the first paragraph of text, and balance the columns on the second page.
   f. Insert the cake clip art image with the following specifications:
      • Insert the clip art image shown in the figure. If this image is not available, choose a similar image of a cake.

- Change the image color to *Orange, Accent color 1 Light*, change the width to 1.2 inches, and change the text wrapping to *Tight*.
- Position the cake image as shown in Figure 8.22.
   g. Insert the *Conservative* footer.
3. Save, print, and then close **U2T8-A6-Resume.docx**.

Figure 8.22 Assessment 8.6 Example

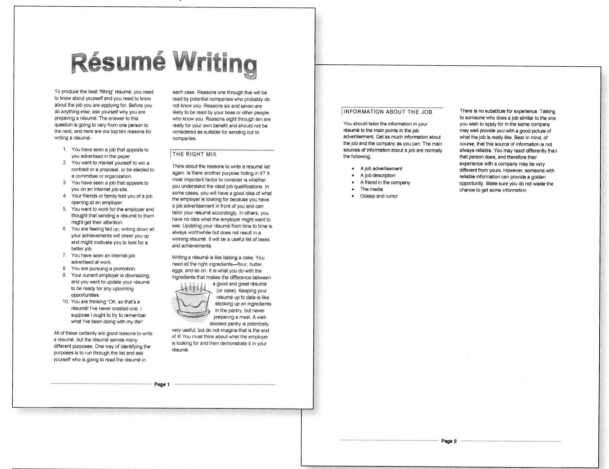

CRITICAL THINKING

Formatting a Company Guidelines Document

Part 1 The Chief Operating Officer of Richardson Engineering has just approved your draft of the company's new recycling policy (see the file named **RecyclingPolicy.docx** in the **Unit2Topic08** folder). Use the concepts and techniques you learned in this topic to format the recycling policy manual, including a cover page, appropriate headers and footers, and page numbers. Add at least one image where appropriate. Format the document using a Quick Styles set and styles. Save the manual and name it **U2T8-C01-Manual**. Restrict editing to only comments and then protect the manual with the password *recycle*. Print the manual.

Part 2 Create a memo to your instructor that lists the formatting you applied to the recycling policy manual. Save the completed memo and name it **U2T8-C02-Memo**. Print and then close **U2T8-C02-Memo.docx**.

TEAM PROJECT

Designing a Newsletter

1. Open **CPNewsltr.docx** and save the document with the name **U2T8-CPNewsltr-Team#** (insert your team number in place of the # symbol).
2. Insert the title *Cascade Pediatrics* as WordArt and format the body of the newsletter into two columns.
3. Insert a clip art image, a header and/or footer, and change the top margin to 1.5 inches.
4. Apply a heading style to the headings in the document, apply a Quick Styles set, and then apply a theme of your choosing. Make sure the text of the newsletter flows onto the second page.
5. Move the insertion point to the end of the document and then balance the columns on the page.
6. Press the Enter key twice, insert a shape of your choosing, and then type the clinic's days and hours of operation in the shape (you determine the days and hours).
7. Save, print, and then close **U2T8-CPNewsltr-Team#.docx**.

Discussion Questions

1. What formatting did you apply and what elements did you insert in the newsletter?
2. How did you use the formatting and elements to enhance the visual appeal of the newsletter?
3. Compare your newsletter with the newsletters created by the other teams. Which newsletter is the most appealing? What makes one newsletter more appealing than another?

Topic 9

Analyzing Data Using Excel

Performance Objectives

Upon successful completion of Topic 9, you will be able to:

- Create and save a workbook
- Edit data in a workbook
- Print and close a workbook
- Enter data in a workbook using AutoFill
- Insert formulas using the AutoSum button
- Select cells
- Sort and filter data
- Apply predesigned formatting to cells in a workbook

- Create formulas using mathematical operators
- Insert functions to be used in formulas
- Insert, delete, move, and rename worksheets, and change worksheet tab colors
- Print all worksheets in a workbook
- Cut, copy, and paste rows and columns of cells

STUDENT RESOURCES

Before beginning this topic, copy to your storage medium the **Unit2Topic09** subfolder from the *Computer and Internet Essentials: Preparing for IC³* Internet Resource Center. Make this the active folder.

In addition to containing the data files needed to complete topic work, the Internet Resource Center contains model answers in PDF format for each of the applicable exercises in this topic. Use these files to check your work. The preface of your textbook provides instructions for accessing these files.

Necessary Data Files

To complete the exercises and assessments, you will need the following data files:

Exercises 9.1 & 9.2	New File
Exercises 9.3 & 9.4	AutoFill.xlsx
Exercises 9.5 & 9.6	SalesData.xlsx
Exercise 9.7	VAComms.xlsx
Exercise 9.8	VARDTests.xlsx
Exercise 9.9	SGSales.xlsx
Exercise 9.10	GMSalesTrain.xlsx
Exercise 9.11	QtrlyExpenses.xlsx
Exercise 9.12	IncomeExpenses.xlsx
Review 9.1	New file
Review 9.2	VASemiSales.xlsx
Review 9.3	GMQuotas.xlsx

continued

Assessment 9.1	SGBudget.xlsx
Assessment 9.2	GMSales.xlsx
Assessment 9.3	GMSalesBonus.xlsx
Assessment 9.4	SGDeptBudgets.xlsx
Assessment 9.5	New File
Assessment 9.6	StatePopulation.xlsx
Assessment 9.7	VARDSalaries.xlsx
Team Project	New File

Visual Preview

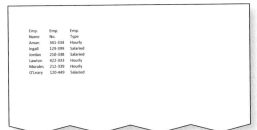

Exercises 9.1–9.2 **U2T9-Employees.xlsx**

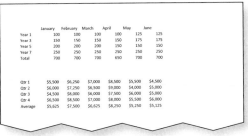

Exercises 9.3–9.4 **U2T9-AutoFill.xlsx**

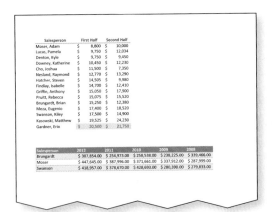

Exercises 9.5–9.6 **U2T9-SalesData.xlsx**

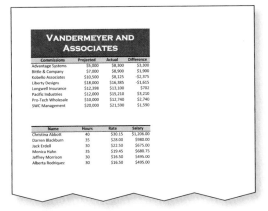

Exercise 9.7 **U2T9-VAComms.xlsx**

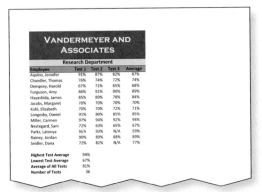

Exercise 9.8 **U2T9-VARDTests.xlsx**

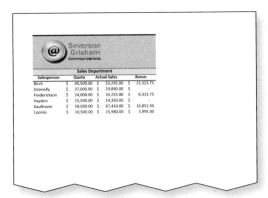

Exercise 9.9 **U2T9-SGSales.xlsx**

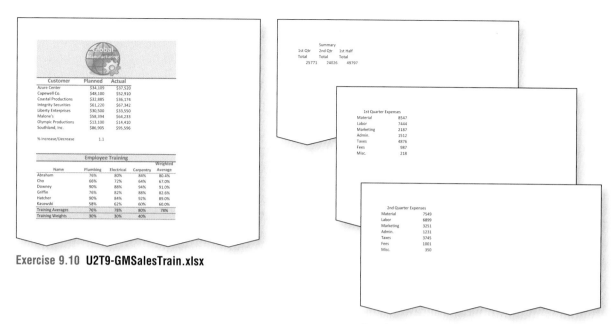

Exercise 9.10 U2T9-GMSalesTrain.xlsx

Exercise 9.11 U2T9-QtrlyExpenses.xlsx

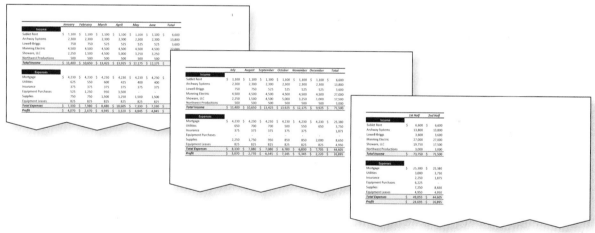

Exercise 9.12 U2T9-IncomeExpenses.xlsx

Topic Overview

IC³ 2-3.1.10

Many companies use spreadsheets to organize numerical and financial data and to analyze and evaluate information. An Excel spreadsheet can be used for such activities as creating financial statements, preparing budgets, managing inventory, and analyzing cash flow. Using Excel, numbers and values in spreadsheets can also be easily manipulated to create "what if" situations. For example, a person in a company can ask a question such as "How would decreasing the value in this category affect the department budget?" and, using the tools available in Excel, see the answer almost immediately. In this way, a spreadsheet can be used not only for creating and organizing financial statements or budgets, but also as a planning tool to evaluate different scenarios.

Lesson 9.1   Creating and Saving an Excel Workbook

 2-3.1.3

Use Excel to create spreadsheets that you can use to analyze and evaluate data. When you open Excel, you are presented with a blank worksheet like the one shown in Figure 9.1. The elements of a blank Excel worksheet are described in Table 9.1.

Figure 9.1 **Blank Worksheet in Excel**

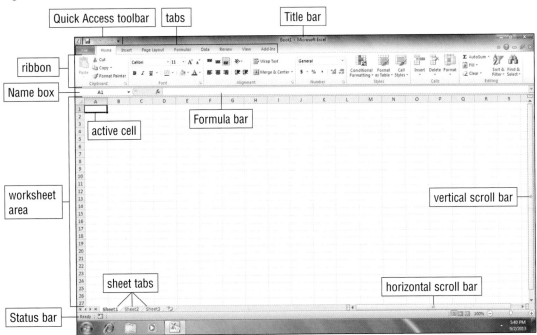

Table 9.1 **Elements of an Excel Worksheet**

Feature	Description
File tab	When clicked, displays Backstage view that contains buttons and tabs for working with and managing documents
Quick Access toolbar	Contains buttons for commonly-used commands
Title bar	Displays workbook name followed by program name
Tab	Contains commands and features organized into groups
Ribbon	Contains tabs and commands divided into groups
Name box	Displays cell address (also called cell reference), which includes column letter and row number
Formula bar	Provides information about active cell; used for entering and editing formulas
Scroll bars	Display on the bottom and the right side of the spreadsheet; used to navigate within a worksheet
Worksheet area	Area of cells that make up the worksheet
Sheet tabs	Display toward bottom of screen and identify current worksheet
Status bar	Displays information about worksheet and active cell, also contains view buttons and Zoom slider bar

Recall from Topic 3 that an Excel file made up of multiple individual worksheets (or *sheets*) is referred to as a workbook. Notice the tabs located toward the bottom of the Excel window that are named *Sheet1, Sheet2,* and so on. The horizontal and vertical lines that define the cells in each worksheet are called **gridlines**. The area containing the gridlines in the Excel window is called the **worksheet area**. Figure 9.2 identifies the elements of the worksheet area. The columns in a worksheet are labeled with letters of the alphabet and the rows are numbered.

gridlines The horizontal and vertical lines defining cells in a worksheet

worksheet area The area in an Excel worksheet that contains the gridlines

Figure 9.2 Elements of the Worksheet Area

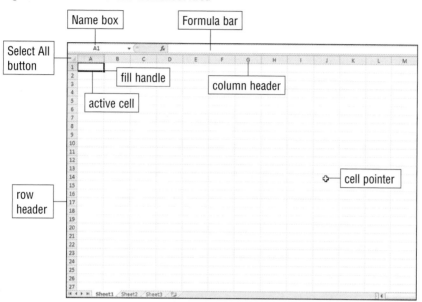

When a cell is active (displays with a black border), the cell address displays in the Name box. The **cell address**, or cell reference, is the unique name given to each cell and includes the column letter and row number. For example, if the first cell of the worksheet is active, the cell reference *A1* displays in the Name box. A thick black border surrounds the active cell.

To enter data such as text, a number, or a value in a cell, make the desired cell active and then type the data. To make the next cell active, press the Tab key. Table 9.2 displays additional commands for making a specific cell active. If you want to insert data on more than one line in a cell, type the data, press Alt + Enter, and then type the next line of text. See Table 3.2 for additional keyboard shortcuts in Excel.

cell address The unique name for each cell, consisting of the column letter and row number in which the cell is located

Table 9.2 Commands for Making a Specific Cell Active

To make this cell active	Press
Cell below current cell	Enter
Cell above current cell	Shift + Enter
Next cell	Tab
Previous cell	Shift + Tab
Cell at beginning of row	Home

continued

To make this cell active	Press
Next cell in the direction of the arrow	Up, Down, Left, or Right Arrow keys
Last cell in worksheet	Ctrl + End
First cell in worksheet	Ctrl + Home
Cell in next screen in worksheet	Page Down
Cell in previous screen in worksheet	Page Up
Cell in screen to right	Alt + Page Down
Cell in screen to left	Alt + Page Up

If the data you enter in a cell consists of text and the text does not fit into the cell, it overlaps the next cell. If, however, you enter a number that does not fit in a cell, and you specify it as a number (rather than text), Excel changes the display of the number to number symbols (###). This automatic adjustment occurs to make certain that numbers that are partially displayed in a cell are not mistaken for the complete contents of the cell.

Along with the keyboard, you can use the mouse to make a specific cell active. To do this, simply position the mouse arrow pointer on the desired cell and then click the left mouse button. When the mouse pointer arrow is positioned in a cell, it displays as a white plus sign and is called the **cell pointer**.

Scroll through a worksheet using the horizontal and/or vertical scroll bars. Scrolling shifts the display of cells in the worksheet area, but does not change the active cell. Scroll through a worksheet until the desired cell is visible and then click the desired cell.

When you are finished working in a workbook, save the workbook to a specific location on your hard drive or a removable storage medium (such as a USB flash drive). To save an Excel workbook in the **Unit2Topic09** folder on your storage medium, display the Save As dialog box, click the drive representing your storage medium in the Navigation pane on the left side, and then double-click the **Unit2Topic09** folder in the Content pane.

cell pointer The mouse pointer that displays when positioned in a cell in a worksheet

Quick Steps

Save a Workbook

1. Click Save button on Quick Access toolbar.
2. Type workbook name.
3. Press Enter.

Keyboard Shortcut

Save

Ctrl + S

Exercise 9.1 Entering Data in a Worksheet and Saving a Workbook

1. Open Excel by clicking Start, pointing to *All Programs*, clicking *Microsoft Office*, and then clicking *Microsoft Excel 2010*.

2. Enter data into the worksheet as shown in Figure 9.3. Begin by making sure cell A1 is active (it should display with a thick black border).

3. Type **Emp.**, press Alt + Enter to move the insertion point to the next line within cell A1, and then type **Name**.

4. Press the Tab key.

   This automatically increases the height of the first row and then makes cell B1 active.

5. Type **Emp.**, press Alt + Enter, and then type **No.**.

6. Press the Tab key.

   This makes cell C1 active.

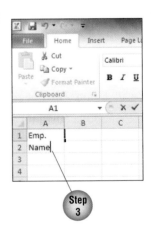

Step 3

7. Type **Emp.**, press Alt + Enter, and then type **Type**.

8. Press the Enter key to move the insertion point to cell A2.

9. With cell A2 active, type the name **Aman**.

10. Continue typing the data shown in Figure 9.3.

    For commands that make specific cells active, refer to Table 9.2.

11. Save the workbook by clicking the Save button 🔲 on the Quick Access toolbar.

12. At the Save As dialog box, make sure the **Unit2Topic09** folder on your storage medium is the active folder, type **U2T9-Employees** in the *File name* text box, and then press Enter or click the Save button.

    Excel automatically adds the file extension .*xlsx* to the end of a workbook name. The Address bar at the Save As dialog box displays the active folder. If you need to make the **Unit2Topic09** folder active, click the drive below *Computer* in the Navigation pane that contains your storage medium and then double-click the **Unit2Topic09** folder in the Content pane.

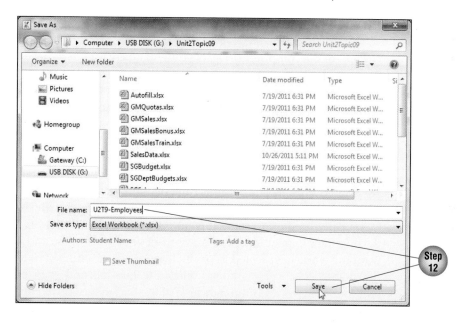

Figure 9.3 Exercise 9.1 Data

	A	B	C	D
1	Emp. Name	Emp. No.	Emp. Type	
2	Aman	341-334	Hourly	
3	Hansen	129-399	Salaried	
4	Jordan	210-338	Salaried	
5	Laton	422-333	Hourly	
6	Morales	212-339	Hourly	
7	O'Leary	120-449	Salaried	
8				
9				

Lesson 9.2 Editing Data in a Cell and Printing and Closing a Workbook

Recall that you can edit data being typed in a cell by pressing the Backspace key to delete the character to the left of the insertion point or by pressing the Delete key to delete the character to the right of the insertion point. To replace the data in a cell, click the cell once to make it active and then type the new data. When a cell containing data is active, anything typed will take the place of the existing data.

If you want to edit only a portion of the data in a cell, double-click the cell. This makes the cell active, moves the insertion point inside the cell, and displays the word *Edit* at the left side of the Status bar. If you are using the keyboard, you can press the Home key to move the insertion point to the first character in the cell or Formula bar, or press the End key to move the insertion point to the last character. Recall that the Formula bar is an area above the worksheet that displays information about the active cell and is used to enter and edit formulas.

Quick Steps

Print a Workbook

1. Click File tab.
2. Click Print tab.
3. Click Print button.

Close a Workbook

1. Click File tab.
2. Click Close button.

OR

Click Close Window button.

Exit Excel

Click Close button.

OR

1. Click File tab.
2. Click Exit button.

Open a Workbook

1. Click File tab.
2. Click Open button.
3. Double-click desired workbook name.

Keyboard Shortcuts

Print
Ctrl + P

Close
Ctrl + F4

Open
Ctrl + O

To print a workbook, click the File tab to display the Backstage view, as shown in Figure 9.4.. Use buttons and tabs at this view to work with and manage workbooks; this may include opening, closing, saving, and printing a workbook. If you want to remove the Backstage view without completing an action, click the File tab, click any other tab in the ribbon, or press the Esc key on your keyboard.

Many of the computer projects you will be creating will need to be printed. Print a workbook from the Print tab of the Backstage view. To display this view, click the File tab and then click the Print tab. You can also display the Print tab Backstage view with the keyboard command Ctrl + P.

The left side of the Print tab Backstage view displays three categories—*Print*, *Printer*, and *Settings*. Click the Print button in the Print category to send the workbook to the printer and specify the number of copies you want printed in the *Copies* text box. Use the gallery in the Printer category to specify the desired printer. The Settings category contains a number of galleries, each with options to specify how you want the workbook printed. Use the galleries to indicate whether or not you want the pages collated when printed; specify the orientation, page size, and margins of your workbook; and indicate if you want the worksheet scaled to print all rows and columns of data on one page.

To close an Excel workbook, click the File tab and then click the Close button in the Quick Commands area of the Backstage view. You can also close a workbook by clicking the Close Window button located toward the upper right corner of the screen (white x). Position the mouse arrow pointer on the button and a ScreenTip displays with the name *Close Window*.

To exit Excel, click the Close button (white x in red rectangle) that displays in the upper right corner of the screen. If you position the mouse arrow pointer on the button, a ScreenTip displays with the name *Close*. You can also exit Excel by clicking the File tab and then clicking the Exit button located below the Help tab at the Backstage view.

Open an existing Excel workbook by displaying the Open dialog box and then double-clicking the desired workbook name. Display the Open dialog box by clicking the File tab and then clicking the Open button in the Quick Commands area of the Backstage view.

Figure 9.4 Print Tab Backstage View

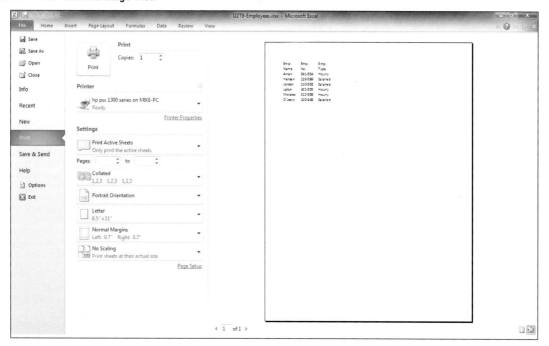

Exercise 9.2 Editing Data in a Cell and Printing and Closing a Workbook

1. With **U2T9-Employees.xlsx** open, double-click cell A5 (contains *Laton*).

2. Move the insertion point immediately left of the *t* and then type a **w**.

   This changes the spelling to *Lawton*.

3. Click once in cell A3 (contains *Hansen*) and then type **Ingall**.

   Clicking only once allows you to type over the existing data.

4. Click the Save button on the Quick Access toolbar to save the workbook again.

5. Print the worksheet by clicking the File tab and then clicking the Print tab at the Backstage view. At the Print tab Backstage view, make sure the correct printer is selected and then click the Print button.

   The gridlines will not print.

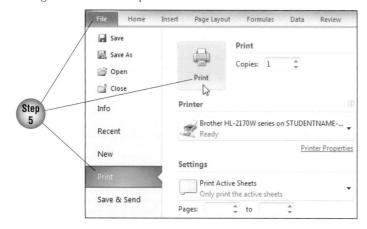

6. Close the workbook by clicking the Close Window button ☒ that displays toward the upper right corner of the screen.

Step 6

Make sure you click the Close Window button and not the Close button.

7. To re-open **U2T9-Employees.xlsx**, click the File tab and then click the Open button in the Quick Commands area of the Backstage view. At the Open dialog box, make sure the **Unit2Topic09** folder on your storage medium is active, and then double-click **U2T9-Employees.xlsx**.

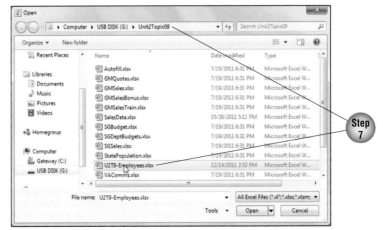

Step 7

8. Close the workbook by clicking the Close Window button located towards the upper right corner of the screen.

Drilling Down

Using the Go To Feature

Another method for making a specific cell active is to use the Go To feature. To use this feature, click the Find & Select button in the Editing group on the Home tab and then click *Go To* at the drop-down list. At the Go To dialog box, type the cell reference in the *Reference* text box and then click OK.

Lesson 9.3 Entering Data Using the Fill Handle

 2-3.1.3

fill handle A small square in the bottom right corner of the active cell used to copy data to adjacent cells

When a cell is active, a thick black border surrounds it and a small black square displays in the bottom right corner of the border. This black square is called the fill handle (see Figure 9.2). The **fill handle** is a small square in the bottom right corner of an active cell used to copy data to adjacent cells. With the fill handle, you can quickly fill a range of cells with the same data or with consecutive data. For example, suppose you need to insert the year 2013 in consecutive cells. To do this quickly, type *2013* in the first cell, position the cell pointer on the fill handle, hold down the left mouse button, drag across the cells in which you want the year inserted, and then release the mouse button.

You can also use the fill handle to insert a series in consecutive cells. For example, suppose you are creating a worksheet with data for all of the months in the year. Type *January* in the first cell, position the cell pointer on the fill handle, hold down the left mouse button, drag down or across to 11 more cells, and then release the mouse button. Excel automatically inserts the other 11 months in the year in the proper order. When using the fill handle, the cells must be adjacent. Table 9.3 identifies the sequence inserted in cells by Excel when specific data is entered.

Table 9.3 Fill Handle Series

If a cell contains this data*	Using the fill handle will insert this sequence in adjacent cells
January	February, March, April, etc.
Jan	Feb, Mar, Apr, etc.
8-Jan, 9-Jan	10-Jan, 11-Jan, 12-Jan, etc.…
Monday	Tuesday, Wednesday, Thursday, etc.
Product 1	Product 2, Product 3, Product 4, etc.
Qtr 1	Qtr 2, Qtr 3, Qtr 4
2, 4	6, 8, 10, etc.

Commas represent data in separate cells.

Certain sequences, such as *2, 4* and *Jan 08, Jan 09*, require that both cells be selected before using the fill handle. If only the cell containing 2 is active, the fill handle will insert 2s in the selected cells. The list in Table 9.3 is only a sampling of what the fill handle can do. You will likely find other sequences that can be inserted in a worksheet using the fill handle.

Exercise 9.3 Inserting Data in Cells with the Fill Handle

1. Open **AutoFill.xlsx**.

   This workbook is located in the **Unit2Topic09** folder on your storage medium.

2. Add data to cells as shown in Figure 9.5. Begin by making cell B1 active and then typing **January**.

3. Position the cell pointer on the fill handle for cell B1, hold down the left mouse button, drag across to cell G1, and then release the mouse button.

4. Make cell B2 active, type **100**, and then use the fill handle to fill cells C2 through E2.

5. Practice creating sequences using the fill handle. Begin by making cell A2 active and then typing **Year 1**.

6. Make cell A3 active, type **Year 3**, and then press the Enter key.

7. Select cells A2 and A3 by positioning the cell pointer in cell A2, holding down the left mouse button, dragging down to cell A3, and then releasing the mouse button.

8. Drag the fill handle for cell A3 to cell A5.

   This inserts *Year 5* in cell A4 and *Year 7* in cell A5.

9. Make cell A10 active, type **Qtr 1**, and then use the fill handle to fill cells A11 through A13.

   Check Figure 9.5 and make sure your worksheet looks like the worksheet in the figure.

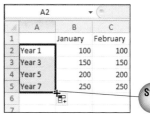

10. Click the File tab and then click the Save As button in the Quick Commands area of the Backstage view.

11. At the Save As dialog box, type **U2T9-AutoFill** in the *File name* text box and then press the Enter key.

Figure 9.5 **Exercise 9.3 Data**

⊿	A	B	C	D	E	F	G	H
1		January	February	March	April	May	June	
2	Year 1	100	100	100	100	125	125	
3	Year 3	150	150	150	150	175	175	
4	Year 5	200	200	200	150	150	150	
5	Year 7	250	250	250	250	250	250	
6								
7								
8								
9								
10	Qtr 1	$5,500	$6,250	$7,000	$8,500	$5,500	$4,500	
11	Qtr 2	$6,000	$7,250	$6,500	$9,000	$4,000	$5,000	
12	Qtr 3	$4,500	$8,000	$6,000	$7,500	$6,000	$5,000	
13	Qtr 4	$6,500	$8,500	$7,000	$8,000	$5,500	$6,000	
14								
15								

Drilling Down

Using the Auto Fill Options button

An Auto Fill Options button displays when you fill cells with the fill handle. Click this button and a list of options displays for filling the cells. By default, data and formatting are filled in each cell. You can choose to fill only the formatting in the cells or fill only the data without the formatting.

Lesson 9.4 Inserting Formulas and Selecting Cells

 2-3.2.6

Quick Steps

Insert a Formula Using the AutoSum Button

1. Click in desired cell.
2. Click AutoSum button.
3. Check range identified; change if necessary.
4. Press Enter.

Insert an Average Formula Using the AutoSum Button

1. Click in desired cell.
2. Click AutoSum button arrow.
3. Click *Average*.
4. Check range identified; change if necessary.
5. Press Enter.

Excel is a powerful planning tool containing data that can be manipulated to answer "what if" questions. Excel allows the user to insert a formula in a worksheet and manipulate the data to make projections. You can use the AutoSum button in the Editing group on the Home tab to insert a formula that adds numbers automatically with the SUM function. When the AutoSum button is used, Excel looks above the active cell for a range of cells containing numbers. If the cells above do not contain numbers, then Excel looks to the left of the active cell. Excel suggests the range of cells to be added. If the suggested range is correct, press the Enter key to accept it. If the selected range is not correct, use the cell pointer to select the desired range and then press Enter. You can also double-click the AutoSum button to insert the SUM function with the range Excel chooses.

The AVERAGE function is often used in Excel formulas. This function adds a range of cells together and then divides the sum by the number of cell entries. The AVERAGE function is available on the AutoSum button. Click the AutoSum button arrow and a drop-down list will display containing a number of common functions.

In a worksheet, you may want to insert the same formula in numerous cells. If you plan on copying a formula to other locations in a worksheet, use relative cell references within the formula. A **relative cell reference** is one that adjusts when copied. Copy a formula containing relative cell references and the cell references adjust to reflect the new location. For example, if you enter the formula =SUM(A2:C2) in cell D2 and then copy it relatively to cell D3, the formula in cell D3 will display as =SUM(A3:C3). Use the fill handle to copy a formula relatively in a worksheet.

You can select cells in a worksheet using the mouse or the keyboard. Methods for selecting cells using the mouse display in Table 9.4 and methods for selecting with the keyboard display in Table 9.5.

relative cell reference A cell reference that adjusts when copied

Quick **S**teps

Copy a Formula Relatively Using the Fill Handle

1. Insert formula in cell.
2. Make cell containing formula active.
3. Use fill handle to drag through cells you want to contain formula.

Table 9.4 Selecting Cells Using the Mouse

To select this	Complete the following actions
Column	Position the cell pointer on the column header (a letter) and then click the left mouse button.
Row	Position the cell pointer on the row header (a number) and then click the left mouse button.
Adjacent cells	Click and drag the mouse to select specific cells.
Nonadjacent cells	Hold down the Ctrl key while clicking column headers, row headers, or specific cells.
All cells in worksheet	Click Select All button (refer to Figure 9.2).

Table 9.5 Selecting Cells Using the Keyboard

To select from active cell to	Press
Cells in direction of arrow key	Shift + arrow key
Cell at the beginning of row	Shift + Home
Cell at the beginning of worksheet	Shift + Ctrl + Home
Last cell in worksheet containing data	Shift + Ctrl + End
Entire column	Ctrl + spacebar
Entire row	Shift + spacebar
Entire worksheet	Ctrl + A or Ctrl + Shift + spacebar

Selected cells, except the active cell, display with a light blue background (this color may vary) rather than a white background. The active cell is the first cell in the selection block and displays with a white background. Selected cells remain selected until you click a cell with the mouse or press an arrow key on the keyboard.

Exercise 9.4 Using the AutoSum Button and Copying a Formula Relatively

1. With **U2T9-AutoFill.xlsx** open, make cell A6 active and then type **Total**.

2. Make cell B6 active and then calculate the sum of cells by clicking the AutoSum button Σ in the Editing group on the Home tab.

3. Excel inserts the formula =SUM(B2:B5) in cell B6. This is the correct range of cells, so press Enter.

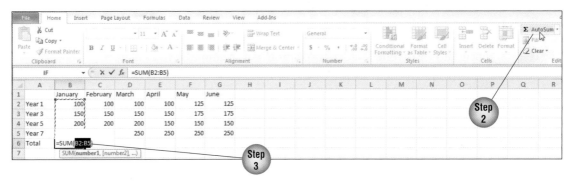

4. Make cell C6 active and then click the AutoSum button in the Editing group.

5. Excel inserts the formula =SUM(C2:C5) in cell C6. This is the correct range of cells, so press Enter.

6. Make cell D6 active and then double-click the AutoSum button.

   This inserts the formula =SUM(D2:D5) in cell D6 and inserts the sum *700*.

7. Insert the sum in multiple cells by selecting cells E6 through G6. To do this, position the cell pointer in cell E6, hold down the left mouse button, drag to cell G6, and then release the mouse button.

8. Click the AutoSum button.

   This inserts a sum amount in cells E6, F6, and G6.

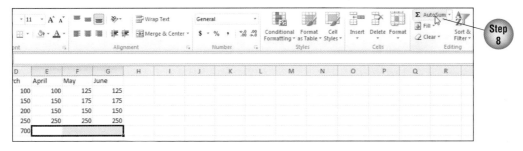

9. Make cell A14 active and then type **Average**.

10. Insert the average of cells B10 through B13. Begin by making cell B14 active.

11. Click the AutoSum button arrow and then click *Average* at the drop-down list.

12. Excel inserts the formula =AVERAGE(B10:B13) in cell B14. This is the correct range of cells, so press Enter.

13. Copy the formula relatively to cells C14 through G14. Begin by making cell B14 active.

14. Position the cell pointer on the fill handle, hold down the left mouse button, drag across to cell G14, and then release the mouse button.

15. Save, print, and then close **U2T9-AutoFill.xlsx**.

Drilling Down

Inserting the SUM Function with a Keyboard Shortcut

Excel contains a number of keyboard shortcuts you can use to apply formatting or perform a function. To insert the SUM function with a keyboard shortcut, make the desired cell active, hold down the Alt key on the keyboard, press the equals (=) key, and then release the Alt key.

Selecting Data within Cells

Using the selection commands presented in Table 9.4 and Table 9.5 will select the entire cell, but you can also select specific characters within a cell. To do this with the mouse, position the cell pointer in the desired cell and then double-click the left mouse button. Drag with the I-beam pointer through the data you want to select. Data selected within a cell displays in white with a black background. If you are using the keyboard to select data in a cell, hold down the Shift key and then use the arrow keys to move the insertion point in the desired direction. As the insertion point passes through data, that data is selected. You can also press F8 to turn on the Extend Selection mode, move the insertion point in the desired direction to select the data, and then press F8 to turn off the Extend Selection mode. When the Extend Selection mode is on, the words *Extend Selection* display toward the left side of the Status bar.

Lesson 9.5 Sorting and Filtering Data

 2-3.2.1, 2-3.2.2, 2-3.2.10

The Editing group on the Home tab contains a Sort & Filter button you can use to alphabetize text in columns or arrange numbers numerically. To sort data, select the cells (within the same column) containing the data you want to sort, click the Sort & Filter button in the Editing group, and then click the option representing the desired sort. The available sort options vary depending on the data in selected cells. For example, sort options for sorting alphabetically display if the first column of selected cells contains text. If the selected cells contain numbers, sort options display for sorting from smallest to largest and largest to smallest; and if the selected cells contain dates, sort options display for sorting oldest to newest and newest to oldest. Sorting can be used to rank data to make it easier to interpret. For example, a list of city populations can be ranked from largest to smallest using the sort options.

You can place a restriction, called a **filter**, on data in a worksheet to temporarily isolate specific data. To turn on filtering, make active a cell containing data, click the Sort & Filter button in the Editing group on the Home tab, and then click *Filter* at the drop-down list. This turns on filtering and filtering arrows display in each column label in the worksheet. You do not need to select cells before turning on filtering because Excel automatically searches for column labels in the worksheet. To filter data, click the filtering arrow in the heading you want to filter. This displays a drop-down list with options for filtering all records, creating a custom filter, or selecting an entry that appears in one or more of the cells in the column. After data has been filtered, the filter icon that once appeared in the column will change to a funnel icon, indicating that a filter has been applied. If you print a worksheet containing filtering arrows, the arrows do not print.

Quick Steps

Sort Data
1. Select cells.
2. Click Sort & Filter button.
3. Click desired sort option.

filter A restriction placed on data to temporarily isolate specific data

Quick Steps

Turn on Filtering Arrows
1. Click Sort & Filter button.
2. Click *Filter* option.

Exercise 9.5 Sorting and Filtering Data

1. Open **SalesData.xlsx** and then save the workbook and name it **U2T9-SalesData**.

2. Sort in reverse alphabetical order (from Z to A) the names in rows 2 through 16. Begin by selecting cells A2 through C16.

   You need to select data in columns B and C to ensure that the sales amounts stay with the correct salesperson after the sort.

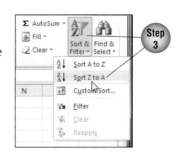

3. Click the Sort & Filter button ![icon] in the Editing group on the Home tab and then click *Sort Z to A* at the drop-down list.

4. Sort the first half sales amounts from smallest to largest. Begin by selecting cells B2 through B16.

5. Click the Sort & Filter button in the Editing group and then click the *Sort Smallest to Largest* option at the drop-down list.

6. At the Sort Warning dialog box that displays, read the information in the dialog box, make sure the *Expand the selection* option is selected, and then click the Sort button.

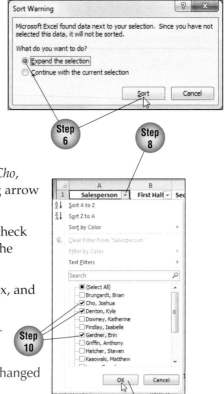

7. Make cell A1 active and then turn on the filtering arrows by clicking the Sort & Filter button in the Editing group and then clicking *Filter* at the drop-down list.

   This inserts filtering arrows at the right side of the cell containing the heading *Salesperson*, the cell containing *First Half*, and the cell containing *Second Half*.

8. Filter the data in rows A2 through A16 so only sales for *Cho*, *Denton*, and *Gardner* display. To do this, click the filtering arrow at the right side of the cell containing *Salesperson*.

9. At the drop-down list that displays, click the *(Select All)* check box to remove the check marks from the names of all of the salespersons.

10. Click the *Cho, Joshua* check box, the *Denton, Kyle* check box, and the *Gardner, Erin* check box.

    This inserts a check mark in each of the three check boxes.

11. Click OK.

    Notice that the filtering arrow in the *Salesperson* cell has changed to a funnel icon.

12. Clear the filter from the *Salesperson* column by clicking the funnel icon that displays at the right side of the *Salesperson* cell and then clicking the *Clear Filter From "Salesperson"* option at the drop-down list.

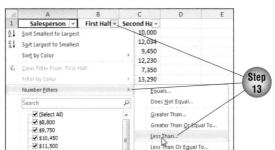

13. Filter first half sales to display amounts less than $15,000 by clicking the filtering arrow at the right side of the *First Half* cell, pointing to *Number Filters* at the drop-down list, and then clicking the *Less Than* option at the side menu.

14. At the Custom AutoFilter dialog box, type **15000** and then click OK.

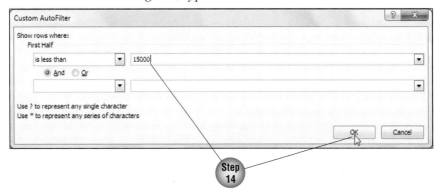

Step
14

15. Remove the filter and filtering arrows by clicking the Sort & Filter button and then clicking *Filter* at the drop-down list.

16. Save and then print **U2T9-SalesData.xlsx**.

Drilling Down

Customizing a Sort

You can sort in more than one column with options at the Sort dialog box. Display this dialog box by selecting the cells you want sorted, clicking the Sort & Filter button, and then clicking *Custom Sort* at the drop-down list. At the Sort dialog box, specify the first column you want sorted in the *Sort by* option box, click the Add Level button, and then specify the second column in the first *Then by* option box. Add additional *Then by* option boxes by clicking the Add Level button.

Lesson 9.6 | Applying Formatting with Cell Styles and Table Styles

 2-3.1.8

An Excel worksheet contains default formatting. For example, letters and words are aligned at the left of a cell, numbers are aligned at the right, and data is set in 11-point Calibri. Excel provides predesigned styles you can use to apply formatting to cells in a worksheet. If you apply a table style to cells, Excel inserts filtering arrows in each cell in the first row of selected cells. Excel automatically inserts these arrows because it assumes that data formatted into a table is filterable.

Use the Cell Styles button in the Styles group on the Home tab to highlight or accentuate certain cells. You can apply formatting to a single cell or a group of selected cells. Click the Cell Styles button in the Styles group on the Home tab and a drop-down gallery of style options displays. Hover your mouse arrow pointer over a style option and the cell or selected cells display a preview of the style. The Cell Styles button drop-down gallery is an example of the Live Preview feature, which allows you to see how the selected formatting affects cells in your worksheet without having to return to the worksheet.

Format a range of cells and convert the cells into a table using options at the Format as Table button drop-down gallery. Click the Format as Table button and a drop-down gallery of style options displays. Hover your mouse over an option and the formatting is applied to the selected cells in the worksheet. Choose a table style by clicking the desired style.

Quick Steps

Apply a Cell Style
1. Select desired cell(s).
2. Click Cell Styles button.
3. Click desired cell style.

Apply Table Formatting
1. Select desired cells.
2. Click Format as Table button.
3. Click desired table style.
4. Click OK at Format As Table dialog box.

Exercise 9.6 Applying Cell and Table Styles

1. With **U2T9-SalesData.xlsx** open, select cells A1 through C1.

2. Apply a cell style to the selected cells by clicking the Cell Styles button in the Styles group on the Home tab and then clicking the Heading 3 style in the *Titles and Headings* section of the drop-down gallery.

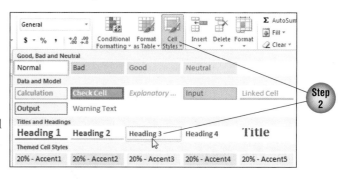

3. Select cells B16 and C16, click the Cell Styles button in the Styles group, and then click the Good style in the *Good, Bad and Neutral* section of the drop-down gallery.

4. Select cells A20 through G25.

5. Apply a table style by clicking the Format as Table button in the Styles group on the Home tab and then clicking the *Table Style Medium 2* option at the drop-down gallery.

   This option is the second style option from the left in the first row in the *Medium* section.

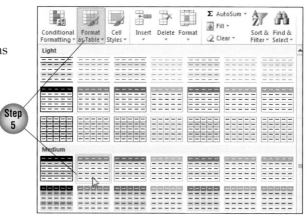

6. At the Format As Table dialog box, click OK.

7. Select cells B21 through G25, click the Home tab, click the Cell Styles button in the Styles group, and then click the *Currency* option in the *Number Format* section of the drop-down gallery.

8. Sort the data by the *Average* column from largest to smallest by clicking the filtering arrow in cell G20 and then clicking the *Sort Largest to Smallest* option at the drop-down list.

9. Sort the data in cells A21 through A25 in ascending alphabetical order by clicking in cell A20, clicking the filtering arrow, and then clicking the *Sort A to Z* option at the drop-down list.

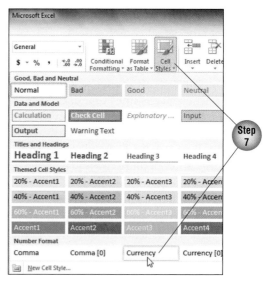

10. Filter the 2012 sales data to display sales greater than $250,000 by clicking the filtering arrow in cell B20, pointing to *Number Filters* in the drop-down list, and then clicking *Greater Than* at the side menu.

11. At the Custom AutoFilter dialog box, type **250000** and then click the OK button.

12. Save, print, and then close **U2T9-SalesData.xlsx**.

Drilling Down

Applying Conditional Formatting

With the Conditional Formatting button in the Styles group on the Home tab you can highlight or accentuate values in cells and provide a visual representation of the data in selected cells. For example, you can select cells containing values and then apply data bars. The length of the data bar in each cell reflects the value in relation to the other values in the selected cells. Click the Conditional Formatting button and a drop-down list displays with options for applying data bars, color scales, or icon sets to selected cells. The drop-down list also contains options for creating, clearing, and managing conditional formatting rules.

Lesson 9.7 Writing Formulas with Mathematical Operators

 2-3.2.4

In addition to the AutoSum button, you can write your own formulas using mathematical operators. Commonly used mathematical formulas and their functions are described in Table 9.6. When writing your own formula, begin the formula with the equals (=) sign. For example, to divide the contents of cell B2 by the contents of cell C2 and insert the result in cell D2, you would make D2 the active cell and then type =B2/C2.

Table 9.6 Mathematical Operators

Function	Operator
Addition	+
Subtraction	-
Multiplication	*
Division	/
Percent	%
Exponentiation	^

Exercise 9.7 Inserting and Copying Formulas

1. Open **VAComms.xlsx** and then save the workbook with Save As and name it **U2T9-VAComms**.

2. Make cell D3 active, type the formula **=C3-B3**, and then press the Enter key.

3. Make cell D3 active and then use the fill handle to copy the formula relatively to cells D4 through D10.

4. Make the following changes to cell contents:

   C4: Change *$4,750* to *8900*
   B8: Change *$10,250* to *12000*
   C8: Change *$14,110* to *15210*

5. Make cell D15 active, type **=B15*C15**, and then press the Enter key.

6. Make cell D15 active and then use the fill handle to copy the formula relatively to cells D16 through D20.

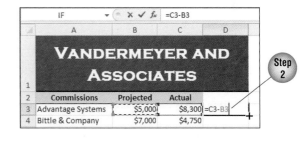

7. Make the following changes to cell contents:

B16: Change *40* to *35*
C17: Change *$21.75* to *22.50*
B19: Change *15* to *30*

8. Save, print, and then close **U2T9-VAComms.xlsx**.

Drilling Down

Changing the Order of Operations

If a formula contains two or more operators, Excel uses the same order of operations used in algebra. From left to right in a formula, this order, called the *order of operations*, begins with negations (a negative number, which is preceded by a minus (-) sign), then percents (%), then exponentiations (^), followed by multiplications (*), divisions (/), additions (+), and finally subtractions (-). If you want to change the order of operations, use parentheses around the part of the formula you want calculated first. For example, say that you want to create a formula using cells A1, B1, and C1, with each cell containing the value 5. If a formula is written as =A1+B1*C1, the results would be 30. However, if you place a parenthesis around the first two cells so the formula displays as =(A1+B1)*C1, the results would be 50.

Writing a Formula by Pointing

You can create a formula by pointing to the cells you wish to include in it. This is a more accurate method than typing the cell references, which leaves more room for human error. To write a formula by pointing, click the cell that will contain the formula, type the equals sign to begin the formula, and then click the cell you want to reference in the formula. Type the desired mathematical operator and then click the next cell reference. Continue in this manner until all cell references are specified, and then press the Enter key. When writing a formula by pointing, you can also select a range of cells you want to include in a formula.

Lesson 9.8   Inserting Formulas with Functions

 2-3.2.5; 2-3.2.7

Recall that functions such as =SUM or =AVERAGE are predesigned formulas that perform calculations. Using a function when creating a formula takes fewer keystrokes. Along with the functions available at the AutoSum button drop-down list, Excel provides other functions that are available in the Function Library group on the Formulas tab. The group contains a number of buttons for inserting functions from a variety of categories such as Financial, Logical, Text, and Date & Time.

To display the Function dialog box (shown in Figure 9.6), click the Insert Function button on the Formula bar or in the Formulas tab. At the Insert Function dialog box, the most recently used functions display in the *Select a function* list box. You can choose a function category by clicking the down-pointing arrow at the right side of the *Or select a category* list box and then clicking the desired category at the drop-down list. Use the *Search for a function* option to locate a specific function.

Figure 9.6 **Insert Function Dialog Box**

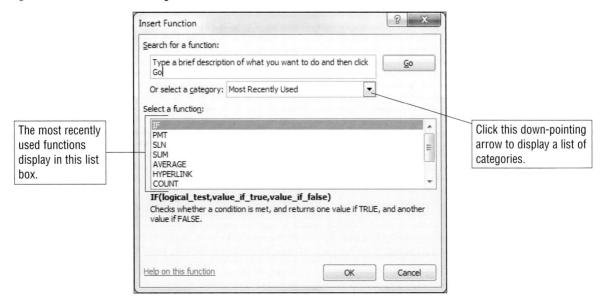

The most recently used functions display in this list box.

Click this down-pointing arrow to display a list of categories.

The MAX function in a formula returns the maximum value in a cell range and the MIN function returns the minimum value in a cell range. As an example, you could use the MAX and MIN functions in a worksheet containing employee hours to determine which employee worked the most number of hours and which worked the least. In a worksheet containing sales commissions, you could use the MAX and MIN functions to determine the salesperson who earned the most commission dollars and the one who earned the least. The COUNT function counts the amount of cells containing numbers within a range. This data can be useful in advanced statistical functions that ask for sample size.

In some situations, you may need to display the formulas in a worksheet rather than the results of the formulas. You may want to turn on formulas for auditing purposes or check formulas for accuracy. Display all formulas in a worksheet rather than the results by clicking the Display Formulas button in the Formula Auditing group on the Formula tab or by pressing Ctrl + ` (this is the grave accent). Press Ctrl + ` to turn off the display of formulas or click the Display Formulas button.

Quick Steps

Display Formulas
1. Click Formula tab.
2. Click Display Formulas button.

Keyboard Shortcut

Display Formulas
Press Ctrl + `.

Exercise 9.8 Inserting Formulas in a Worksheet

1. Open **VARDTests.xlsx** and then save the workbook with Save As and name it **U2T9-VARDTests**.

2. Make cell E4 active and then click the Insert Function button f_x on the Formula bar.

3. At the Insert Function dialog box, click the down-pointing arrow at the right side of the *Or select a category* list box and then click *Statistical* at the drop-down list.

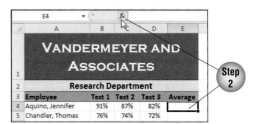

Step 2

4. Click *AVERAGE* in the *Select a function* list box and then click OK.

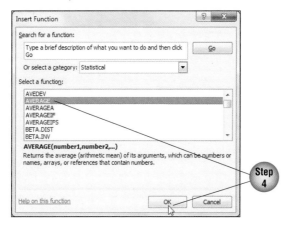

5. At the Function Arguments palette, make sure *B4:D4* displays in the *Number1* text box and then click OK.

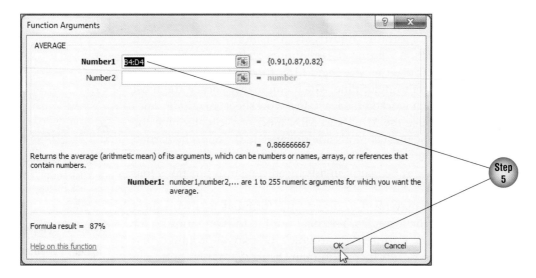

6. With cell E4 active, use the fill handle to copy the formula relatively to cells E5 through E16.

7. Save and then print **U2T9-VARDTests.xlsx**.

8. After viewing the averages of test scores, you notice that a couple of people have a low average. You decide to see what happens to the average score if students make up tests where they scored the lowest. You decide that a student can score a maximum of 70% on a retake of the test. Make the following changes to test scores to see how the changes will affect the test average:

   B9: Change *50* to *70*
   C9: Change *52* to *70*
   D9: Change *60* to *70*
   B10: Change *62* to *70*
   B14: Change *0* to *70*
   D14: Change *0* to *70*
   D16: Change *0* to *70*

9. Save and then print **U2T9-VARDTests.xlsx**. Compare the test averages for Margaret Jacobs, Elizabeth Kohl, Latonya Parks, and Dana Seidler to see what the effect of retaking the tests has on their final test averages.

The AVERAGE function will ignore text in cells and blank cells (not zeros). For example, in the worksheet containing test scores, a couple of cells contained a *0%* entry. This entry was included in the averaging of the test scores. If you did not want that particular test to be included in the average, enter text in the cell such as *N/A* (for *not applicable*) or leave the cell blank.

10. Make cell B18 active, click the AutoSum button arrow in the Editing group on the Home tab, and then click *Max* at the drop-down list.

11. Type **E4:E16** and then press Enter.

12. With cell B19 active, click the Insert Function button on the Formula bar.

13. At the Insert Function dialog box, make sure *Statistical* is selected in the *Or select a category* list box, click *MIN* in the *Select a function* list box (you will need to scroll down the list box), and then click OK.

You may need to scroll down the list to display *MIN*.

14. At the Function Arguments palette, type **E4:E16** in the *Number1* text box and then click OK.

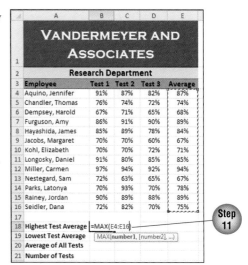

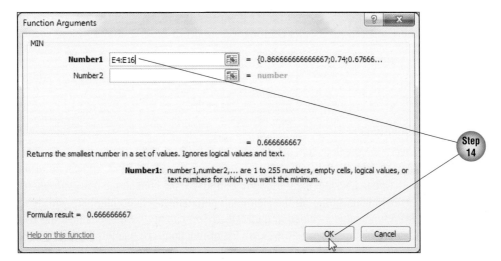

15. Make cell B20 active, click the Formulas tab, and then click the Insert Function button f_x in the Function Library group.

16. At the Insert Function dialog box, make sure *Statistical* is selected in the *Or select a category* list box, click *AVERAGE* in the *Select a function* list box, and then click OK.

17. At the Function Arguments palette, type **E4:E16** in the *Number1* text box, and then click OK.

18. Make cell B21 active, click the Home tab, click the AutoSum button arrow in the Editing group, and then click *Count Numbers* at the drop-down list.

19. Use the mouse to select the range B4:D16, and then press Enter.

20. Make cell A3 active, press Ctrl + ` to turn on the display of formulas, and then print the worksheet with the formulas displayed.

	A	B	C	D	E
1	**VANDERMEYER AND ASSOCIATES**				
2		**Research Department**			
3	**Employee**	**Test 1**	**Test 2**	**Test 3**	**Average**
4	Aquino, Jennifer	0.91	0.87	0.82	=AVERAGE(B4:D4)
5	Chandler, Thomas	0.76	0.74	0.72	=AVERAGE(B5:D5)
6	Dempsey, Harold	0.67	0.71	0.65	=AVERAGE(B6:D6)
7	Furguson, Amy	0.86	0.91	0.9	=AVERAGE(B7:D7)
8	Hayashida, James	0.85	0.89	0.78	=AVERAGE(B8:D8)
9	Jacobs, Margaret	0.7	0.7	0.6	=AVERAGE(B9:D9)
10	Kohl, Elizabeth	0.7	0.7	0.72	=AVERAGE(B10:D10)
11	Longosky, Daniel	0.91	0.8	0.85	=AVERAGE(B11:D11)
12	Miller, Carmen	0.97	0.94	0.92	=AVERAGE(B12:D12)
13	Nestegard, Sam	0.72	0.63	0.65	=AVERAGE(B13:D13)
14	Parks, Latonya	0.7	0.93	0.7	=AVERAGE(B14:D14)
15	Rainey, Jordan	0.9	0.89	0.88	=AVERAGE(B15:D15)
16	Seidler, Dana	0.72	0.82	0.7	=AVERAGE(B16:D16)
17					
18	Highest Test Average	=MAX(E4:E16)			
19	Lowest Test Average	=MIN(E4:E16)			
20	Average of All Tests	=AVERAGE(E4:E1			
21	Number of Tests	=COUNT(B4:D16)			

Step 20

21. Press Ctrl + ` to turn off the display of formulas.

22. Change the *70%* values (which were previously *0%*) in cells B14, D14, and D16 to *N/A*.

This will cause the test scores average for Latonya Parks and Dana Seidler to increase and will change the minimum number and average of all test scores. It will also decrease the total amount of tests from 39 to 36 because those 3 cells no longer contain numbers, changing the result of the COUNT function.

23. Save, print, and then close **U2T9-VARDTests.xlsx**.

Drilling Down

Using Excel Functions

Excel includes over 200 functions that are divided into 11 different categories including Financial, Date & Time, Math & Trig, Statistical, Lookup & Reference, Database, Text, Logical, Information, Engineering, and Cube. Clicking the AutoSum button in the Function Library group on the Formulas tab or the Editing group on the Home tab automatically adds numbers with the SUM function. The SUM function is included in the Math & Trig category. Excel includes the Formula AutoComplete feature that displays a drop-down list of functions. To use this feature, click in the desired cell or click in the *Formula bar* text box, type the equals sign (=), and then type the first letter of the desired function. This displays a drop-down list with functions that begin with the letter. Double-click the desired function, enter the cell references, and then press Enter.

Lesson 9.9   Writing a Formula with the IF Logical Function

 2-3.2.7

conditional function A function that performs logical tests on values and formulas

logical test A question that can be answered with true or false

The IF function is considered a conditional function. A **conditional function** is a function that performs logical tests on values and formulas. With the IF function you can perform logical tests on values and formulas. A question that can be answered with true or false is considered a **logical test**. The IF function performs an action based on the answer to a logical test. If the answer is true, then one action is performed; if the answer is false, then another action is performed.

For example, you can use an IF function to write a formula that calculates a salesperson's bonus as 10% if the quota of $100,000 is met or exceeded, and zero if the quota is less than $100,000. That formula would look like this: *=IF(quota=>100000,quota*0.1,0)*. The formula contains three parts—the condition or logical test *IF(quota=>100000)*, the action taken if the condition or logical test is true *(quota*0.1)*, and the action taken if the condition or logical test is false *(0)*. Commas separate arguments within a function. In this case, the commas separate the logical test and the actions performed if the result is true or false. In the bonus formula, if the quota is equal to or greater than $100,000, then the quota is multiplied by 10%. If the quota is less than $100,000, then the bonus is zero.

Exercise 9.9 Writing a Formula with an IF Function and Editing the Formula

1. Open **SGSales.xlsx** and then save the workbook with Save As and name it **U2T9-SGSales**.

2. Write a formula with the IF function that will insert a bonus of 15% of the actual sales if the quota is exceeded or insert a zero if the quota is not met. Begin by making cell D4 active.

3. Type **=IF(C4>B4,C4*0.15,0)** and then press Enter.

4. Make cell D4 active and then use the fill handle to copy the formula to cells D5 through D9.

5. Print the worksheet.

6. Revise the formula so it will insert a 25% bonus if the quota has been exceeded. Begin by making cell D4 active.

7. Click in the Formula bar, edit the formula so it displays as *=IF(C4>B4,C4*0.25,0)*, and then press the Enter key.

8. Copy the formula down to cells D5 through D9.

9. Save, print, and then close **U2T9-SGSales.xlsx**.

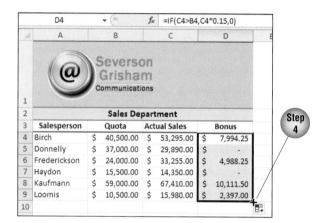

Step 4

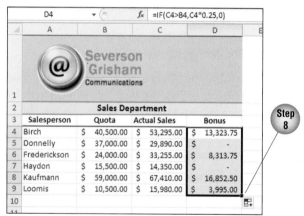

Step 8

Drilling Down

Editing a Formula

Edit a formula by making active the cell containing the formula and then editing the formula in the cell or in the Formula bar text box. After editing the formula, press Enter or click the Enter button on the Formula bar and Excel will recalculate the result of the formula.

Lesson 9.10   Using Absolute and Mixed Cell References in Formulas

IC³ 2-3.2.3; 2-3.2.8

absolute cell reference Refers to a cell in a specific location; will not change within a formula if it is relatively copied

mixed cell reference A reference where either the column remains absolute and the row is relative or the column is relative and the row is absolute

A cell reference can be relative, absolute, or mixed. Relative cell references (the default) refer to the location of cells in relation to the location of the formula in which they appear. Absolute references refer to cells in a specific location, regardless of the location of the formula in which they appear. When a formula is copied and pasted, a relative cell reference adjusts while an **absolute cell reference** remains constant. A **mixed cell reference** contains relative and absolute cell references; so either the column remains absolute and the row is relative or the column is relative and the row is absolute. To designate a cell reference as absolute, type a dollar sign ($) in front of both the column letter and row number within the formula. To create a mixed cell reference, type a dollar sign in front of either the column letter or row number within a formula.

Earlier in this topic you learned to copy a formula with relative references, which is the default in Excel. For example, when the formula =*SUM(A2:C2)* in cell D2 is copied relatively to cell D3, the formula changes to =*SUM(A3:C3)*. In Exercise 9.10, you will add a column for projected job earnings and then practice copying formulas containing absolute cell references.

Exercise 9.10 Inserting and Copying Formulas with Absolute Cell References

1. Open **GMSalesTrain.xlsx** and then save the workbook with Save As and name it **U2T9-GMSalesTrain**.

2. Determine the effect on actual job earnings with a 20% increase. To do this, make cell C3 active, type the formula **=B3*$B$12**, and then press Enter.

3. Make cell C3 active and then use the fill handle to copy the formula to cells C4 through C10.

4. Save and then print **U2T9-GMSalesTrain.xlsx**.

5. Determine the effect on actual job earnings with a 10% decrease by making cell B12 active, typing **0.9**, and then pressing Enter.

6. Save and then print **U2T9-GMSalesTrain.xlsx**.

7. Determine the effects on actual job earnings with a 10% increase by typing **1.1** in cell B12 and then pressing Enter.

8. Save and then print **U2T9-GMSalesTrain.xlsx**.

9. Insert a formula that determines the weighted average of training scores. Begin by making cell E17 active.

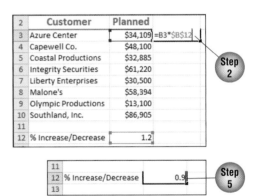

10. Type the following formula: **=$B$24*B17+$C$24*C17+$D$24*D17**

11. Copy the formula in cell E17 down to cells E18 through E22.

12. Insert a formula in cell B23 that averages the percentages in cells B17 through B22.

13. Copy the formula in cell B23 to cells C23 through E23.

14. Save and then print **U2T9-GMSalesTrain.xlsx**.

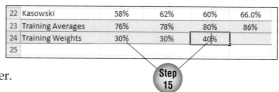

15. With the worksheet still open, determine the effect on weighted training scores if the weighted values change. To do this, make cell B24 active, type **30** and then press Enter. Make cell D24 active, type **40**, and then press Enter.

16. Save, print, and then close **U2T9-GMSalesTrain.xlsx**.

Using F4 to Change Cell Reference Types

Instead of typing a dollar sign next to a cell reference in a formula, you can create an absolute or mixed cell reference by pressing the F4 key. For example, type *=A41* in a cell, press F4, and the cell reference changes to *=$A$41*. Press F4 again and the cell reference changes to *=A$41*. The next time you press F4, the cell reference changes to *=$A41*. Press F4 one more time to change the cell reference back to *=A41*.

Lesson 9.11   Managing Worksheets

 2-3.1.1, 2-3.1.4

Recall from Topic 3 that Excel data files are called workbooks. By default, each Excel workbook contains three worksheets, but you can add or delete worksheets as desired. The advantage of using multiple worksheets within a workbook is that you can break down data into different sheets so that it is easier to interpret and manipulate. Excel has been programmed so that you can refer to cells or groups of cells in different worksheets when creating formulas or using functions. This creates a dynamic, three-dimensional environment within the program.

You can use the worksheet tabs and worksheet tab shortcut menu to manage worksheets within a workbook. Insert a worksheet by clicking the Insert Worksheet tab or by pressing Shift + F11. Delete a worksheet by right-clicking the worksheet tab and then clicking *Delete* at the shortcut menu. You may want to change a worksheet's name to provide a more descriptive name for the contents. To rename a worksheet, right-click the worksheet tab and then click *Rename* at the shortcut menu. This selects the current worksheet name. Type the new name for the worksheet and then press Enter. You can move worksheets within the worksheet tabs area by dragging the worksheet

Quick Steps

Insert a Worksheet

Click Insert Worksheet tab.

Delete a Worksheet

1. Right-click worksheet tab.
2. Click *Delete*.

Rename a Worksheet

1. Right-click worksheet tab.
2. Click *Rename*.
3. Type new worksheet name.
4. Press Enter.

Keyboard Shortcut

Insert Worksheet

Shift + F11

tab to the desired location. Additionally, you can apply color to a worksheet tab by right-clicking the worksheet tab, pointing to the *Tab Color* option at the shortcut menu, and then clicking the desired color. Applying a color to a worksheet tab enhances usability and visual appeal.

By default, Excel prints only the currently displayed worksheet. If you want to print all of the worksheets in a workbook, display the Print tab Backstage view, click the first gallery in the Settings category, click *Print Entire Workbook* at the drop-down list, and then click the Print button.

Exercise 9.11 Inserting, Deleting, Moving, and Renaming Worksheets and Changing Worksheet Tab Color

1. Open **QtrlyExpenses.xlsx** and then save the workbook with Save As and name it **U2T9-QtrlyExpenses**.

2. Insert a new worksheet into the workbook. To do this, click the Insert Worksheet tab in the worksheet tabs area.

   This inserts a new worksheet with the name *Sheet4*.

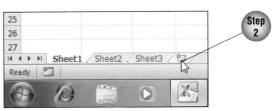

3. Delete a worksheet from the workbook by right-clicking the worksheet tab labeled *Sheet3* and then clicking *Delete* at the shortcut menu.

4. At the dialog box that displays a warning, click the Delete button.

   This dialog box displays if a worksheet you are attempting to delete contains data.

5. Rename Sheet1 by right-clicking the worksheet tab labeled *Sheet1* and then clicking *Rename* at the shortcut menu.

6. Type **1stQtr** and then press Enter.

7. Rename Sheet2 to *2ndQtr* and Sheet4 to *Summary* using the same method you used to rename Sheet1.

8. Move the Summary worksheet to the left of the 1stQtr worksheet by positioning the mouse pointer on the Summary tab, holding down the left mouse button, dragging the Summary tab to the left side of the 1stQtr worksheet tab, and then releasing the mouse button.

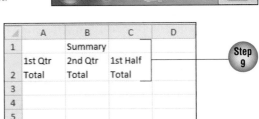

9. Create a worksheet that summarizes first half sales by entering the text in the Summary worksheet as shown at the right.

10. Insert the total of first quarter sales in cell A3. Begin by making cell A3 active and then clicking the AutoSum button.

11. Click the 1stQtr worksheet tab, select cells B2 through B8, and then press Enter.

12. Insert the total of second quarter sales in cell B3 using the same method you used in steps 11 and 12.

13. Insert the first half total in cell C3 by making cell C3 active and then double-clicking the AutoSum button.

14. Change the color of the Summary tab to green by right-clicking the Summary tab, pointing to *Tab Color* on the shortcut menu, and then clicking the green color at the gallery (sixth color from the left in the *Standard Colors* section).

15. Change the color of the 1stQtr tab to blue and the 2ndQtr tab to red using the same method you used in step 14.

16. Print the entire workbook by displaying the Print tab Backstage view, clicking the first gallery in the Settings category, clicking *Print Entire Workbook* at the drop-down list, and then clicking the Print button.

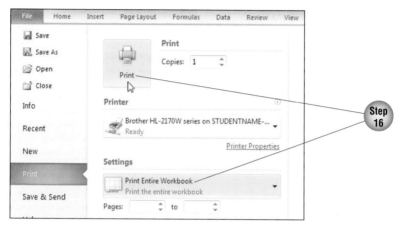

17. Save and then close **U2T9-QtrlyExpenses.xlsx**.

Lesson 9.12 Cutting, Copying, and Pasting Cells

)IC³ 2-3.1.2, 2-3.1.4

Situations may arise where you need to move or copy cells or columns or rows of cells to a different location within a worksheet. You can perform these actions by selecting the desired cells, rows, or columns, and then using the Cut, Copy, and Paste buttons in the Clipboard group on the Home tab. You can also perform these actions with the mouse.

To move selected cells, rows, or columns using the buttons on the Home tab, select the cells and then click the Cut button in the Clipboard group. This causes a moving dashed border to display around the selected cells. Click the cell where you want the first selected cell to be inserted and then click the Paste button in the Clipboard group. If you change your mind about moving the selected cells before you click the Paste button, press the Esc key or double-click in any cell to remove the moving dashed line border. To move selected cells with the mouse, select the cells and then position the mouse pointer on any border of the selected cells until the pointer turns into an arrow pointer with a four-headed arrow attached. Hold down the left mouse button, drag the outline of the selected cells to the desired location, and then release the mouse button.

Copying cells, rows, or columns can be useful in worksheets that contain repetitive data. To copy, select the desired cells and then click the Copy button in the Clipboard group on the Home tab. Click the cell where you want the first selected cell to be inserted and then click the Paste button in the Clipboard group. To use the mouse to copy selected cells, hold down the Ctrl key while dragging the selected cells.

Quick Steps

Move Cells

1. Select cells.
2. Click Cut button.
3. Click destination cell.
4. Click Paste button.

Copy Cells

1. Select cells.
2. Click Copy button.
3. Click destination cell.
4. Click Paste button.

Keyboard Shortcuts

Cut

Ctrl + X

Copy

Ctrl + C

Paste

Ctrl + V

When you paste cells, rows, or columns, the Paste Options button displays in the lower right corner of the pasted material. Display a drop-down list of paste options by clicking the button or by hovering the mouse pointer over the button and pressing the Ctrl key. Hover your mouse pointer over a button in the drop-down list and the descriptive name of the button displays along with the keyboard shortcut. When you copy and then paste a cell containing a value as well as a formula, you can use buttons in the Paste Options button drop-down list to specify what you want to paste. With the buttons in the Paste Values section of the Paste Options button drop-down list, you can choose to insert the value only, the value with numbering formatting, or the value with the source formatting.

Exercise 9.12   Copying and Pasting Columns and Rows

1. Open **IncomeExpenses.xlsx** and then save the workbook with Save As and name it **U2T9-IncomeExpenses**.

2. Select column F by positioning the cell pointer on the column F header (the letter F at the top of the column) and then clicking the left mouse button.

3. With the column selected, click the Copy button in the Clipboard group on the Home tab.

4. Make cell G1 active and then click the Paste button in the Clipboard group.

5. Click in cell G1 and then type **June**.

6. Select row 6 by positioning the cell pointer on the row header (the number 6) and then clicking the left mouse button.

7. Click the Copy button in the Clipboard group.

8. Click the *2ndHalf* worksheet tab, make cell A6 active, and then click the Paste button.

9. Make cell H5 active and then use the fill handle to relatively copy the formula down to cell H6.

10. Select column H (the *Total* column) and then click the Copy button in the Clipboard group.

11. Click the *1stHalf* worksheet tab.

12. Make cell H1 active and then click the Paste button in the Clipboard group.

13. With column H (the *Total* column) still selected, click the Copy button.

14. Click the *Summary* worksheet tab, click in cell B1, and then click the Paste button.

15. Click the Paste Options button that displays at the right side of the pasted cells. At the drop-down list that displays, click the Values & Source Formatting button in the *Paste Values* section.

16. Click the *2ndHalf* worksheet tab, select column H (the *Total* column), and then click the Copy button.

17. Click the *Summary* worksheet tab, click in cell C1, and then click the Paste button.

18. Click the Paste Options button and then click the Values & Source Formatting button in the *Paste Values* section.

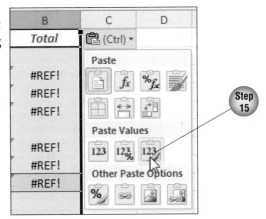

19. Click in cell B1 and then type **1st Half**.

20. Click in cell C1 and then type **2nd Half**.

21. Print the entire workbook (all three worksheets).

22. Save and then close **U2T9-IncomeExpenses.xlsx**.

Delving Deeper

 2-3.2.8

Exploring Common Formula/Function Errors in Excel

Excel is a sophisticated program that requires data input and formula creation to follow strict guidelines in order to function properly. When guidelines that dictate how data or formulas are entered are not followed, Excel will display one of many error codes. When an error is identified with a code, tracking down the issue in order to fix it is easier. The following table lists some common error codes.

Error Code	Meaning
#DIV/0	A formula is attempting to divide a number by zero
#N/A	An argument parameter has been left out of a function
#NAME?	A function name is not entered correctly
#NUM!	An argument parameter does not meet a function's requirements
#REF!	A cell no longer exists within a worksheet
#VALUE	The data entered is the wrong type (i.e., text instead of numbers)

Most errors in Excel are the result of a user incorrectly inputting data into a worksheet. However, most error messages will not display until the data is used in a formula or function. Common mistakes made while inputting data include: placing text in a cell that requires a number, entering data in the wrong location, and entering numbers in an incorrect format. Other errors are the result of entering a formula or function improperly. A formula will often display an error message if it is trying to divide a number by zero or if it contains a circular reference (when a formula within a cell uses the results of that formula in the same cell). Functions tend to display error messages if the arguments of a particular function are not correctly defined or if a function name is typed incorrectly.

 1-2.2.2

Understanding Financial Functions

Excel includes many functions that can be used to manipulate data. Some functions, categorized as financial functions, can provide important information on loans and lending. Most financial functions utilize similar variables. The following concepts are common variables found within most financial functions.

- **Rate:** The rate is the interest rate for a payment period. The rate may need to be modified in order for the function to work properly. For example, most Rate values are given in APR (annual percentage rate), which is the percentage rate for one year, not a payment period. So a percentage rate may be given as 12% APR, but if the payment period is a month then the percentage rate for the function would be 1%, not 12% APR.

continued

- **Nper:** The Nper is the number of payment periods in an investment. The Nper may also need to be modified depending on what information is provided. For example, if a loan duration is expressed in years but the payments are paid each month, the Nper value would need to be adjusted accordingly. A five-year loan would have an Nper of 60 (five years times 12 months in each year).

- **Pmt:** The Pmt is the payment amount for each period. This variable describes the payment amount for a period and is commonly expressed as a negative value because it is an outflow of cash. However, the Pmt value can be entered as a positive value if the present value (PV) or future value (FV) are entered as negative values. Whether the Pmt value is positive or negative depends on who created the workbook. For example, a home owner would list the variable as outflow, while the lending service would list it as inflow.

- **PV:** The PV is the present value of an investment, expressed in a lump sum amount. The PV variable is generally the initial loan amount, or the amount of money invested. For example, if an individual is purchasing a new home, the PV would be the amount of money the buyer borrowed to buy the home. PV can be expressed as a negative value, which denotes it as an investment instead of a loan. For example, if a bank issues a loan to a home buyer, they would enter the PV value as a negative, because it is an outflow of cash for them. (In this example, payment would be expressed as a positive value because it would be an inflow of cash for the bank.)

- **FV:** The FV is the future value of an investment, expressed in a lump sum amount. The FV variable is generally the loan amount plus the amount of interest paid during the loan. In the example of a home buyer, the FV would be the sum of payments, which includes both the principle and interest paid on the loan. In the example of a bank, the FV would be the total amount received after a loan has been paid off. FV can also be expressed as either a positive or negative value depending on which side of the transaction you review.

TOPIC SUMMARY

- A file created in Excel is called a workbook and consists of individual worksheets. The worksheet area contains columns labeled by letters and rows labeled by numbers. The intersection of a column and a row is referred to as a cell.

- An Excel window contains the following elements: Quick Access toolbar, File tab, Title bar, tabs, ribbon, Name box, Formula bar, scroll bars, sheet tabs, and Status bar.

- To replace data in a cell, click the cell once and then type the new data. To edit data within a cell, double-click the cell and make necessary changes.

- Print a workbook by clicking the File tab, clicking the Print tab, and then clicking the Print button.

- Close a workbook by clicking the Close Window button located in the upper right corner of the worksheet area or by clicking the File tab and then clicking the Close button.

- To populate cells with similar or consecutive data, click the fill handle located at the bottom right of the cell containing the first entry in the series. Hold down the mouse button, drag the cell pointer to the desired range of cells, and then release the mouse button.

- Use the AutoSum button in the Editing group on the Home tab to find the total (=SUM), average (=AVERAGE), count of numbers (=COUNT), minimum (=MIN), or maximum (=MAX) of data in columns or rows.

- Select cells using the mouse by clicking a column header to select the entire column, a row header to select the entire row, the Select All button to select all cells in the worksheet, or by dragging with the mouse to select adjacent cells. Select nonadjacent cells by holding down the Ctrl key while clicking a column header, row header, or specific cells. You can also use the keyboard to select cells.

- Sort data in a worksheet with options from the Sort & Filter button in the Editing group on the Home tab.

- Use the filter feature to temporarily isolate specific data. Turn filtering on by clicking the Sort & Filter button in the Editing group on the Home tab and then clicking *Filter* at the drop-down list. Use the filtering arrows that display in each column label to specify the filter data.

- Apply formatting styles to cells with options from the Cell Styles button drop-down gallery and apply a table style to selected cells with options from the Format as Table button drop-down gallery. Both buttons are located in the Styles group on the Home tab.

- After a range of cells has been formatted as a table, sort or filter data by clicking the filtering arrow at the right side of header cells. Data can be sorted by letters or numbers and can be filtered using conditions such as greater than or equal to.

- Create your own formula with commonly used operators such as addition (+), subtraction (-), multiplication (*), division (/), percent (%), and exponentiation (^). When writing formulas, always begin with the equals sign (=).

- Use functions within a formula to perform common tasks such as calculating an average. The AutoSum button and Formulas tab contain functions that can be used in formulas.

- A reference identifies a cell or a range of cells in a worksheet and can be relative, absolute, or mixed. Identify an absolute cell reference by inserting a dollar sign ($) before the column letter and row number.

- Insert a worksheet in a workbook by clicking the Insert Worksheet button.

- Right-click a worksheet tab to display a shortcut menu with options for deleting, renaming, and recoloring the worksheet tab.

- Move a worksheet by dragging the worksheet tab to the desired location.

continued

- Print all worksheets in a workbook with the first gallery in the *Settings* category at the Print tab Backstage view.
- Move selected cells within or between worksheets with the Cut and Paste buttons in the Clipboard group on the Home tab and copy cells with the Copy and Paste buttons.
- When pasting data, use the Paste Options button to specify what you want pasted.

Key Terms

absolute cell reference, p. 416
cell address, p. 395
cell pointer, p. 396
conditional function, p. 414

fill handle, p. 400
filter, p. 405
gridlines, p. 395
logical test, p. 414

mixed cell reference, p. 416
relative cell reference, p. 403
worksheet area, p. 395

Features Summary

Feature	Ribbon Tab, Group	Button	File Tab	Keyboard Shortcut
AutoSum button drop-down list	Home, Editing	Σ		
Cells Styles drop-down gallery	Home, Styles			
Close workbook		X	Close	Ctrl + F4
Copy	Home, Clipboard			Ctrl + C
Cut	Home, Clipboard			Ctrl + X
Display formulas	Formulas, Formula Auditing			Ctrl + `
Exit Excel		X	Exit	
Filter	Home, Editing			
Format as Table drop-down gallery	Home, Styles			
Insert Function dialog box	Formulas, Function Library	fx		Alt + =
Open workbook			Open	Ctrl + O
Paste	Home, Clipboard			Ctrl + V
Print workbook			Print, Print	
Save workbook			Save	Ctrl + S
Sort	Home, Editing			

KEY POINTS REVIEW

Identification

Match the terms to the callouts on the Excel window in Figure 9.7.

1. _____ heading
2. _____ Format as Table button
3. _____ scroll bar
4. _____ File tab
5. _____ Close Workbook button
6. _____ Formula bar
7. _____ Quick Access toolbar
8. _____ Name box
9. _____ selected cells
10. _____ AutoSum button

Figure 9.7 **Identification Figure**

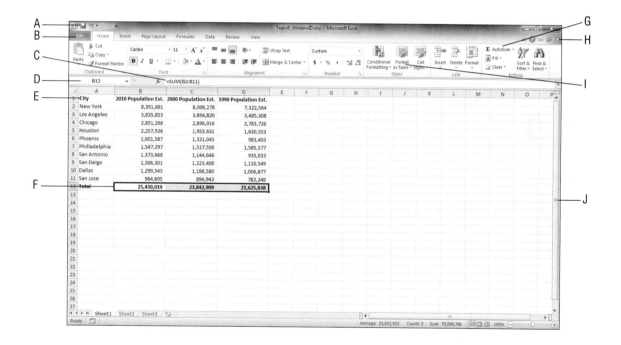

Multiple Choice

For each of the following items, choose the option that best completes the sentence or answers the question.

1. This is an Excel file containing data.
   A. tableset
   B. database
   C. chartbook
   D. workbook

2. When a cell is active, this displays in the Name box.
   A. cell properties
   B. row reference
   C. cell reference
   D. table name

3. Excel can perform calculations on data by using this feature.
   A. formula
   B. calculator
   C. the Internet
   D. Windows

4. The Backstage view contains important features such as these options.
   A. Font, Font size, Font color, and other font options
   B. formulas, functions, and sorting
   C. Save, Save As, Open, Close, and Print
   D. Cut, Copy, Paste, and Format Painter

5. This button inserts common formulas such as Sum, Average, Count Numbers, Min, and Max.
   A. Sort & Filter
   B. AutoSum
   C. Financial
   D. Format

6. This is the purpose of formatting data using the Format as Table button in the Styles group on the Home tab.
   A. to show the formulas contained in the table
   B. to improve the visual appearance of the data and to show the formulas contained in the table
   C. to change how data is displayed (i.e. number, currency, percent, and text)
   D. to improve the visual appearance of the data and to provide sorting and filtering options

7. Every formula begins with this symbol.
   A. a plus sign (+)
   B. an equals sign (=)
   C. a pound symbol (#)
   D. a left parenthesis (()

8. In a formula, the asterisk symbol (*) is used to perform this calculation.
   A. addition
   B. subtraction
   C. multiplication
   D. division

9. This type of cell reference uses a $ before both the column letter and row number.
   A. absolute
   B. mixed
   C. relative
   D. range

10. These are predesigned formulas used in Excel.
    A. tables
    B. cell references
    C. cell styles
    D. functions

Matching

Match each of the following definitions with the correct term, command, or option.

1. _____ Columns in a worksheet are labeled with this.
2. _____ With this function, a range of cells is added together and then divided by the number of cell entries.
3. _____ When typing a formula, begin the formula with this sign.
4. _____ Press this key on the keyboard to move the insertion point to the next cell.
5. _____ Press these keys on the keyboard to move the insertion point to the previous cell.
6. _____ Rows in a worksheet are labeled with this.
7. _____ The horizontal and vertical lines that define the cells in a worksheet area are referred to as this.
8. _____ This is the operator to multiply values in a formula.
9. _____ This function returns the largest value in a set of values.
10. _____ This is the keyboard shortcut to display formulas in a worksheet.

A. Asterisk (*)
B. Ctrl + `
C. AVERAGE
D. Letters
E. Equals (=)
F. MAX
G. Shift + Tab
H. Gridlines
I. Numbers
J. Tab

SKILLS REVIEW

Review 9.1 Creating a Worksheet Using the Fill Handle

1. Create the worksheet shown in Figure 9.8. Type **Monday** in cell B2 and then use the fill handle to fill in the remaining days of the work week. Use the fill handle to enter other repetitive data.
2. Create a Total column and use the Auto Sum button to calculate the Budget and Actual totals.
3. Format the cells B3 to G4 using the Currency cell style.
4. Save the workbook with Save As and name it **U2T9-R1-Months**.
5. Print and then close **U2T9-R1-Months.xlsx**.

Figure 9.8 **Review 9.1 Example**

	A	B	C	D	E	F	G
1	Capital Funds						
2		Monday	Tuesday	Wednesday	Thursday	Friday	Total
3	Budget	350	350	350	350	350	
4	Actual	300	310	320	330	340	
5							

Review 9.2 Inserting AVERAGE, MAX, and MIN Functions

1. Open **VASemiSales.xlsx** and then save the workbook with Save As and name it **U2T9-R2-VASemiSales**.
2. Use the AVERAGE function to determine the average monthly sales (cells H4 through H11).
3. Total each monthly column including the Average column (cells B12 through H12).
4. Use the MAX function to determine the highest monthly total (for cells B4 through G11) and insert the amount in cell B13.
5. Use the MIN function to determine the lowest monthly total (for cells B4 through G11) and insert the amount in cell B14.

6. Select rows 6 and 7, copy the selected cells, click the *Sheet2* tab, make cell A6 active, and then paste the cells.
7. Change the name of the *Sheet1* worksheet tab to *1stHalfSales* and change the tab color to blue.
8. Change the name of the *Sheet2* worksheet tab to *2ndHalfSales* and change the tab color to yellow.
9. Print both worksheets in the workbook.
10. Save and then close **U2T9-R2-VASemiSales.xlsx**.

Review 9.3 Writing Formulas with Absolute Cell References

1. Open **GMQuotas.xlsx** and then save the workbook with Save As and name it **U2T9-R3-GMQuotas**.
2. Insert a formula in cell C4 using an absolute reference to determine the projected quotas with an increase of 5% of the current quotas (105%). Copy the formula in cell C4 down to cells C5 through C14.
3. Save and then print **U2T9-R3-GMQuotas.xlsx**.
4. Determine the projected quotas with an increase of 10% of the current quota by changing the text in cell A15 to *10% Increase* and the number in cell B15 to *1.1*.
5. Save and then print **U2T9-R3-GMQuotas.xlsx**.
6. Determine the projected quotas with an increase of 20% of the current quota.
7. Save, print, and then close **U2T9-R3-GMQuotas.xlsx**.

SKILLS ASSESSMENT

Assessment 9.1 Inserting Data in a Worksheet

1. Open **SGBudget.xlsx** and then save the workbook with Save As and name it **U2T9-A1-SGBudget**.
2. Insert data in the worksheet as shown in Figure 9.9 using the fill handle to insert repetitive data in cells.
3. Insert the word *Average* in cell H3 and then insert a formula in cell H4 that determines the average of cells B4 through G4. Copy the formula down to cells H5 through H8.
4. Insert the word *Total* in cell A9 and then use the AutoSum button to find the total for each month (cells B9 through G9) and the average (cell H9).
5. Save, print, and then close **U2T9-A1-SGBudget.xlsx**.

Figure 9.9 Assessment 9.1 Example

	A	B	C	D	E	F	G	H
1	@ Severson Grisham Communications							
2				Department Budget				
3		January	February	March	April	May	June	
4	Salaries	$ 235,600	$ 235,600	$ 235,600	$ 259,160	$ 259,160	$ 259,160	
5	Benefits	$ 35,250	$ 35,250	$ 35,250	$ 38,775	$ 38,775	$ 38,775	
6	Equipment	$ 4,000	$ 4,000	$ 4,000	$ 2,500	$ 2,500	$ 2,500	
7	Supplies	$ 1,500	$ 1,500	$ 1,500	$ 1,500	$ 1,500	$ 1,500	
8	Misc.	$ 1,000	$ 1,000	$ 1,000	$ 1,000	$ 1,000	$ 1,000	
9								

Assessment 9.2 Formatting Data as a Table and Sorting and Filtering Data in a Table

1. Open **GMSales.xlsx** and then save the workbook with Save As and name it **U2T9-A2-GMSales**.
2. Use the AVERAGE function to determine the yearly average for each salesperson (for cells D4 through D14).
3. Select cells A3 through D14 and then format the selected cells as a table and apply the *Table Style Medium 4* style.
4. Sort the data to display the *Average* column data from largest to smallest.
5. Add a filter to the *Average* column to display only salespersons with a yearly average greater than $15,000.
6. Save, print, and then close **U2T9-A2-GMSales.xlsx**.

Assessment 9.3 Writing an IF Statement Formula and Inserting a COUNT Function

1. Open **GMSalesBonus.xlsx** and then save the workbook with Save As and name it **U2T9-A3-GMSalesBonus**.
2. Insert a formula in cell C4 that contains an IF statement that will insert a bonus of 10% of the actual sales if the quota is met or exceeded and will insert the text *N/A* if the quota is not met. (For assistance in writing the formula, refer to Exercise 9.9. You will need to insert quotation marks around the N/A for the text to display correctly.)
3. Copy the formula in cell C4 to cells C5 through C14.
4. Insert a COUNT function in cell B16 that counts the number of salespeople receiving a bonus (the range is cells D4 through D14).
5. Save and then print **U2T9-A3-GMSalesBonus.xlsx**.
6. Display the formulas in the worksheet.
7. Print **U2T9-A3-GMSalesBonus.xlsx**.
8. Turn off the display of the formulas.
9. Save and then close **U2T9-A3-GMSalesBonus.xlsx**.

Assessment 9.4 Inserting Formulas with Absolute Cell References

1. Open **SGDeptBudgets.xlsx** and then save the workbook with Save As and name it **U2T9-A4-SGDeptBudgets**.
2. Make the following changes to the worksheet:
   - Insert a formula using an absolute reference to determine the projected budget with an increase of 10% of the current budget.
   - Insert formulas to total the budget amounts and the projected budget amounts.
   - Determine the projected budget with an increase of 5% of the current budget by changing the text in cell A3 to *5% Increase* and the number in cell B3 to *1.05*.
3. Save, print, and then close **U2T9-A4-SGDeptBudgets.xlsx**.

Assessment 9.5 Using the Help Feature to Learn about Keyboard Shortcuts

1. Use the Help feature to learn more about keyboard shortcuts in Excel 2010.
2. Read and then print the information provided by Help.
3. Create a worksheet that contains information on keyboard shortcuts. Start with two columns. Type the keyboard shortcut in the first column and a short description of the keyboard shortcut in the second column. Create a title for the worksheet.
4. Select the cells in your worksheet containing data and then apply a table style to the cells.
5. Save the completed workbook with Save As and name it **U2T9-A5-Shortcuts**.
6. Print and then close **U2T9-A5-Shortcuts.xlsx**.

Assessment 9.6 Researching Population Data to Create a Table

1. Using the Internet, select ten states of your choice and research the 2011 population of each state.
2. Open **StatePopulation.xlsx** and then save the workbook with Save As and name it **U2T9-A6-StatePopulation**.
3. Insert the name of the ten states you selected in the first column, starting at cell A3.
4. Insert the population figures of the ten states in the second column, starting at cell B3.
5. Select cells A2 through B12 and then apply a Medium table style of your choice.
6. Use the filtering arrow at the right side of cell B2 to sort the population figures from largest to smallest.
7. Save, print, and then close **U2T9-A6-StatePopulation.xlsx**.

Assessment 9.7 Creating and Formatting a Worksheet

1. Open **VARDSalaries.xlsx** and then save the workbook with Save As and name it **U2T9-A7-VARDSalaries**.
2. Insert the data as shown in Figure 9.10 but instead of typing the payment amounts in cells E4 to E16, insert a relative formula.
3. To apply the formatting, select cells A3 through E16 and then apply the *Table Style Medium 5* table style.
4. After applying the table style, remove the filtering arrows from row 3.
5. Display the formulas in the worksheet.
6. Save, print, and then close **U2T9-A7-VARDSalaries.xlsx**.

Figure 9.10 Assessment 9.7 Example

	A	B	C	D	E
1	VANDERMEYER AND ASSOCIATES				
2	Research Department				
3	*Employee*	*Classification*	*Hours*	*Rate*	*Payment*
4	Aquino, Jennifer	Salaried	40	$35.00	$1,400.00
5	Chandler, Thomas	Salaried	40	$32.50	$1,300.00
6	Dempsey, Harold	Salaried	40	$32.50	$1,300.00
7	Furguson, Amy	Salaried	40	$32.50	$1,300.00
8	Hayashida, James	Salaried	40	$27.25	$1,090.00
9	Jacobs, Margaret	Salaried	40	$27.25	$1,090.00
10	Kohl, Elizabeth	Salaried	40	$27.25	$1,090.00
11	Longosky, Daniel	Hourly	40	$25.00	$1,000.00
12	Miller, Carmen	Hourly	40	$25.00	$1,000.00
13	Nestegard, Sam	Hourly	25	$19.75	$493.75
14	Parks, Latonya	Hourly	25	$19.75	$493.75
15	Rainey, Jordan	Hourly	25	$19.75	$493.75
16	Seidler, Dana	Hourly	25	$19.75	$493.75
17					

CRITICAL THINKING

Understanding Excel Formulas and Functions

Imagine that you are applying for new position that requires you to be proficient in Microsoft Excel. The application process requires you to take a test to show that you understand common Excel formulas. Your interviewer has provided you with a set of problems and an image of an Excel file (shown in Figure 9.11). Using the information provided, determine the result of each problem. Record your results on the lines provided or as directed by your instructor.

1. _____ =SUM(A1:C1)   6. _____ =B1+(A1*C1)

2. _____ =AVERAGE(A1:C1)   7. _____ =C1*(B1-A1)

3. _____ =MAX(A1:C1)   8. _____ =C1/(B1-A1)

4. _____ =MIN(A1:C1)   9. _____ =A1+C1-B1

5. _____ =COUNT(A1:C1)   10. _____ =B1+C1*A1

Figure 9.11 Critical Thinking

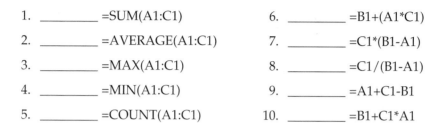

	A	B	C	D
1	5	15	10	
2				

TEAM PROJECT

Creating a Workbook and Analyzing Data

1. As a team, create a new workbook in Excel. You will use this workbook to record and analyze the data obtained by each team member tossing a coin ten times.
2. Type a title for the workbook in cell A1 and then type the heading **Name** in cell A2. Type the heading **Toss #1** in cell B2 and then use the fill handle to fill cells C2 through K2 (Toss #2 to Toss #10). Type the heading **Average** in cell L2.
3. Enter the last name of each team member in the first column, starting in cell A3.
4. Each team member will toss a coin ten times and record the data in the row with their name. When the coin lands tails, enter a 0 (zero) in the proper cell and when it lands heads, enter a 1 (one) in the proper cell.
5. After each team member has completed their ten tosses, use the AutoSum button to insert the AVERAGE function in cell L3 (make sure the correct range is selected in the formula) and then use the fill handle to fill the formula relatively down to each team member's row. The figures in the *Average* column represent the percent chance of heads coming up on ten tosses.
6. Find the average of all tosses by inserting the AVERAGE function in the cell below the last row in column L. (Double-check that the range is the data in column L.)
7. Format the *Average* column to display the data in percentage format. (Format the data as percentages using the Percent option at the Cell Styles button drop-down gallery.)
8. Save the workbook with Save As and name it **U2T9-Team[team name]**.
9. Print and then close the workbook.

Discussion Questions

1. What was the percentage of heads landing for all tosses in the team?
2. What would happen to the percentage of heads landing for the team if one team member's tosses all landed tails? Explain your reasoning.
3. If each team member tossed the coin 100 times, what would the percentage of heads landing likely be?
4. Consider the purpose of the workbook your team created. What formatting would you recommend to improve the workbook's readability or appeal? Support your recommendations with logical reasoning.

Topic 10

Formatting an Excel Workbook

Performance Objectives

Upon successful completion of Topic 10, you will be able to:

- Change column widths and row heights
- Insert and delete cells, rows, and columns in a worksheet
- Clear data in cells
- Apply font and alignment formatting to data in cells
- Apply a theme
- Preview a worksheet

- Format numbers
- Change Page Setup options
- Change Sheet Options
- Insert headers and footers
- Create a chart
- Change chart design, layout, and formatting

STUDENT RESOURCES

Before beginning this topic, copy to your storage medium the **Unit2Topic10** subfolder from the *Computer and Internet Essentials: Preparing for IC³* Internet Resource Center. Make this the active folder.

In addition to containing the data files needed to complete topic work, the Internet Resource Center contains model answers in PDF format for each of the applicable exercises in this topic. Use these files to check your work. The preface of your textbook provides instructions for accessing these files.

Necessary Data Files

To complete the exercises and assessments, you will need the following data files:

Exercises 10.1–10.3	GMPurchases.xlsx
Exercise 10.4	VAPayroll.xlsx
Exercises 10.5 & 10.6	VAInvoices.xlsx
Exercises 10.7 & 10.8	Budget.xlsx
Exercise 10.9	QtrlySales.xlsx
Exercise 10.10	SGBudget.xlsx
Exercise 10.11	Population.xlsx
Exercise 10.12	SGPercents.xlsx
Review 10.1	GMEquipBudget.xlsx
Review 10.2	GMFirstHalfSales.xlsx
Review 10.3	GMTotalSales.xlsx

continued

Assessment 10.1	FFCPlans.xlsx
Assessment 10.2	EMSales.xlsx
Assessment 10.3	New file
Assessment 10.4	FinAnalysis.xlsx GMLogo.jpg
Assessment 10.5	New file
Assessment 10.6	New file
Team Project	TeamProject1.xlsx TeamProject2.xlsx

Visual Preview

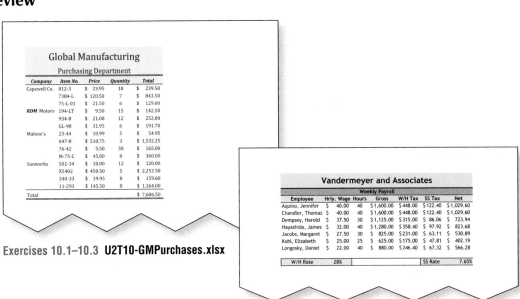

Exercises 10.1–10.3 **U2T10-GMPurchases.xlsx**

Exercise 10.4 **U2T10-VAPayroll.xlsx**

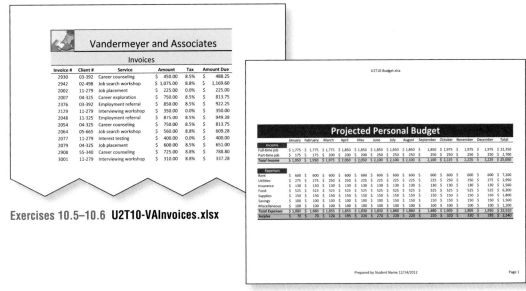

Exercises 10.5–10.6 **U2T10-VAInvoices.xlsx**

Exercises 10.7–10.8 **U2T10-Budget.xlsx**

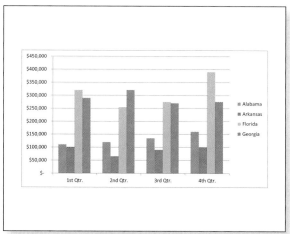

Exercise 10.9 **U2T10-QtrlySales.xlsx**

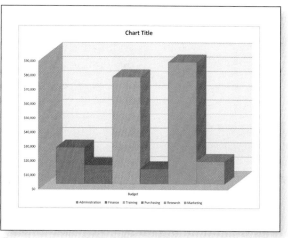

Exercise 10.10 **U2T10-SGBudget.xlsx**

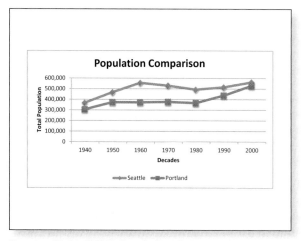

Exercise 10.11 **U2T10-Population.xlsx**

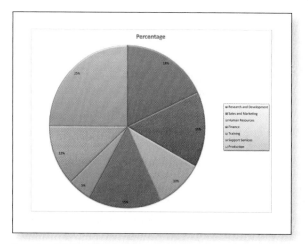

Exercise 10.12 **U2T10-SGPercents.xlsx**

Topic Overview

Although the primary function of Excel is to analyze and evaluate information, it can also be used to present data or information. An Excel spreadsheet can be customized to enhance the visual appearance of data by applying formatting such as bold, italics, and underlining. Additional types of formatting available within Excel include changing column width and row height; specifying number formatting; inserting and deleting rows and columns; and applying borders, shading, and patterns to cells. Excel also includes a feature called themes, which applies predesigned formatting options to data in a worksheet. In addition to formatting options and the use of themes, Excel can create charts, which are a visual representation of selected data in a worksheet.

Lesson 10.1 Changing Column Width and Row Height

 2-3.1.4

By default, all columns in a worksheet are the same width and all rows are the same height. To change column width with the mouse, position the mouse arrow pointer on the boundary line in the column header between the columns until the mouse arrow pointer turns into a double-headed arrow pointing left and right. Drag the boundary to the right to increase the size or to the left to decrease the size. You can change the size of multiple adjacent columns at once by selecting the columns and then dragging one of the column boundaries with the selected columns since the same adjustment will apply to all selected columns. As a column boundary is being dragged, the column width displays in a box above

Change Column Width

Drag column boundary line.

OR

Double-click column boundary.

Change Row Height

Drag row boundary line.

OR

Double-click row boundary.

the mouse arrow pointer. This number represents the average number of standard-font characters that fits in the column. You can adjust a column width in an existing worksheet to fit the longest entry in the column by positioning the mouse pointer on the column boundary at the right side of the column and then double-clicking the left mouse button. You can also adjust a column width to accommodate the longest entry by clicking the Format button in the Cells group on the Home tab and then clicking *AutoFit Column Width* at the drop-down list.

Change row height in much the same manner as column width. As you drag a row boundary, the row height displays in a box above the mouse arrow pointer. The row height number represents a point measurement. A vertical inch contains approximately 72 points. You can change row height to fit the contents by double-clicking the boundary below the row heading or by clicking the Format button in the Cells group on the Home tab and then clicking *AutoFit Row Height* at the drop-down list.

Exercise 10.1 Changing Column Width and Row Height

1. Open **GMPurchases.xlsx** and then save the workbook with Save As and name it **U2T10-GMPurchases**.

2. Insert a formula in cell D2 that multiplies the price in cell B2 by the quantity in cell C2 (the formula is =B2*C2). Copy the formula in cell D2 to cells D3 through D14.

3. Make cell D15 active and then insert a function that calculates the sum of cells D2 through D14.

4. Change the width of column D by positioning the mouse arrow pointer on the column boundary in the column header between columns D and E until it turns into a double-headed arrow pointing left and right. Hold down the left mouse button, drag the column boundary to the right until *Width: 11.00 (82 pixels)* displays in the box, and then release the mouse button.

5. Select columns A and B. To do this, position the mouse pointer on the column A header, hold down the left mouse button, drag to the column B header, and then release the mouse button.

6. Position the mouse pointer on the column boundary between columns A and B until it turns into a double-headed arrow pointing left and right. Hold down the left mouse button, drag the column boundary to the right until *Width: 12.00 (89 pixels)* displays in the box, and then release the mouse button.

7. Click in cell A1 to deselect the columns.

8. Adjust the width of column C to accommodate the longest entry in the column. To do this, position the mouse pointer on the column boundary between columns C and D until the arrow pointer turns into a double-headed arrow pointing left and right and then double-click the left mouse button.

9. Change the height of row 1 by positioning the mouse arrow pointer in the row header on the row boundary between rows 1 and 2 until the pointer turns into a double-headed arrow pointing up and down. Hold down the left mouse button, drag the row boundary down until *Height: 19.50 (26 pixels)* displays in the box, and then release the mouse button.

10. Select rows 2 through 14 by positioning the mouse pointer on the number 2 in the row header, holding down the left mouse button, dragging to the number 14 in the row header, and then releasing the mouse button.

11. Position the mouse pointer on the boundary between rows 2 and 3 until it turns into a double-headed arrow pointing up and down. Hold down the left mouse button, drag the row boundary down until *Height: 16.50 (22 pixels)* displays in the box, and then release the mouse button.

12. Increase the height of row 15 by dragging the row boundary down until *Height: 20.25 (27 pixels)* displays in the box.

13. Save and print **U2T10-GMPurchases.xlsx**.

Changing Column Width and Row Height Using a Dialog Box

At the Column Width dialog box, you can specify a column width number. The number represents the number of characters in the default font and size that can be displayed at that cell width. Increase the column width number to make the column wider or decrease the column width number to make the column narrower. To display the Column Width dialog box, click the Format button in the Cells group on the Home tab and then click *Column Width* at the drop-down list. At the Column Width dialog box, type the number representing the desired width and then press Enter or click OK.

To change row height using a dialog box, click the Format button in the Cells group on the Home tab and then click *Row Height* at the drop-down list. At the Row Height dialog box, enter the desired number and then press Enter or click OK.

Lesson 10.2   Inserting and Deleting Cells, Rows, and Columns

IC³ 2-3.1.4

After you create a worksheet, you can insert and/or delete cells, rows, and columns. To insert a row, select the row below where the row is to be inserted and then click the Insert button in the Cells group on the Home tab. By default, a row is inserted above the row containing the active cell. You can also insert a row by making a cell active in the row below where the row is to be inserted, clicking the Insert button arrow, and then clicking *Insert Sheet Rows*. If you want to insert more than one row, select the same amount of rows that you want to insert and then click the Insert button.

Insert columns in a worksheet in much the same way as rows. To insert a column, select the column to the right of where you want the column inserted and then click the Insert button, or make a cell active in the column immediately to the right of where the new column is to be inserted, click the Insert button arrow and then click *Insert Sheet Columns* at the drop-down list. If you want to insert more than one column, select the amount of columns that you want to insert, click the Insert button arrow, and then click *Insert Sheet Columns*.

You can delete specific cells, rows, or columns in a worksheet. To delete a row or column, select the row or column and then click the Delete button in the Cells group on the Home tab. Delete a cell or group of cells by making the cell(s) active, clicking the Delete button arrow, and then clicking *Delete Cells* at the drop-down list. This displays the Delete dialog box shown in Figure 10.1. At the Delete dialog box, specify what you want deleted, and then click OK.

Quick Steps

Insert Row
1. Select row.
2. Click Insert button.

OR

1. Click Insert button arrow.
2. Click *Insert Sheet Rows* at drop-down list.

Insert Column
1. Select column.
2. Click Insert button.

OR

1. Click Insert button arrow.
2. Click *Insert Sheet Columns* at drop-down list.

Figure 10.1 Delete Dialog Box

Clear Data in Cells

1. Select desired cells.
2. Press Delete key.

OR

1. Select desired cells.
2. Click Clear button.
3. Click *Clear Contents* at drop-down list.

If you want to delete cell contents but not the cell, make the cell active or select desired cells and then press the Delete key. Another method for deleting cell contents is to make the cell active or select desired cells, click the Clear button in the Editing group on the Home tab, and then click *Clear Contents* at the drop-down list. With the options at the Clear button drop-down list you can clear the contents of the cell or selected cells as well as formatting and comments. Click the *Clear Formats* option to remove formatting from cells or selected cells while leaving the data. You can also click the *Clear All* option to clear the contents of the cell or selected cells in addition to the formatting.

Exercise 10.2 Inserting and Deleting Rows and Columns

1. With **U2T10-GMPurchases.xlsx** open, insert a row at the beginning of the worksheet. Begin by making cell A1 active.

2. Click the Insert button arrow in the Cells group on the Home tab and then click *Insert Sheet Rows* at the drop-down list.

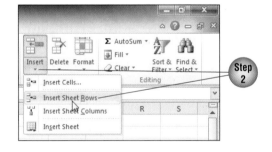

3. Insert another row by clicking the Insert button arrow and then clicking *Insert Sheet Rows* at the drop-down list.

4. Make sure cell A1 is active and then type **Global Manufacturing**.

5. Make cell A2 active, type **Purchasing Department**, and then press Enter.

6. Change the height of row 1 to 42.00 (56 pixels).

7. Change the height of row 2 to 21.00 (28 pixels).

8. Insert two rows by selecting rows 7 and 8 and then clicking the Insert button in the Cells group on the Home tab.

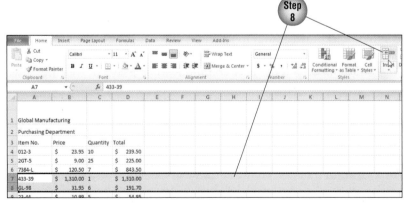

9. Type the following data in the specified cells (you do not need to type the dollar sign in cells containing money amounts):

A7 = 75-L-01
B7 = 21.50
C7 = 6
A8 = 120-30
B8 = 10.99
C8 = 20

10. Make cell D6 active and then use the fill handle to copy the formula down to cells D7 and D8.

11. Click in any cell in column B and then insert a column by clicking the Insert button arrow in the Cells group on the Home tab and then clicking *Insert Sheet Columns* at the drop-down list.

This inserts a new column B.

12. Make cell B3 active, type **Date**, and then press Enter.

13. Click in any cell in column A and then insert a column by clicking the Insert button arrow and then clicking *Insert Sheet Columns* at the drop-down list.

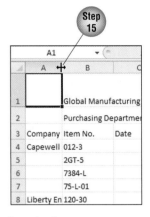

14. Type the following data in the specified cells:
A3 = **Company**
A4 = **Capewell Co.**
A8 = **Liberty Enterprises**
A11 = **Malone's**
A15 = **Sunworks**
A19 = **Total**

15. Make cell A1 active and then adjust the width of column A to accommodate the longest entry.

16. Click in any cell in column C and then delete the column by clicking the Delete button arrow in the Cells group on the Home tab, and then clicking *Delete Sheet Columns* at the drop-down list.

17. Select row 5 and then delete the row by clicking the Delete button in the Cells group.

18. Select rows 7 and 8 and then clear the row contents by clicking the Clear button in the Editing group on the Home tab and then clicking *Clear Contents* at the drop-down list.

19. Type the following data in the specified cells:

A7 = **RDM Motors**
B7 = **194-LT**
C7 = **9.50**
D7 = **15**
B8 = **934-8**
C8 = **21.00**
D8 = **12**

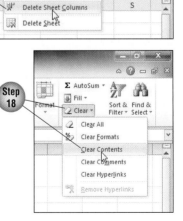

20. Make cell E6 active and then copy the formula down to cells E7 and E8.

21. Save and then print **U2T10-GMPurchases.xlsx**.

Drilling Down

Inserting Rows and Columns at the Insert Dialog Box

Another method for inserting a row is to click the Insert button arrow and then click *Insert Cells*. This displays the Insert dialog box as shown at the right. At the Insert dialog box, click *Entire row*. This inserts a row above the active cell. If you want to insert a column, click the *Entire column* option at the Insert dialog box.

Lesson 10.3   Applying Font and Alignment Formatting

 2-3.1.6, 2-3.1.7

After you have created a worksheet, you may decide that you want to adjust its formatting. You can apply a variety of formatting to cells in a worksheet using options in the Font group on the Home tab. With buttons in the Font group, you can change the font (typeface), font size (type size), and font color; bold, italicize, and underline data in cells (typestyle); change the text color; and apply a border or add fill to cells. With the Borders button in the Font group, you can insert a border on any or all sides of the active cell or any or all sides of selected cells. The name of the button changes depending on the most recent border applied to a cell or selected cells.

Double-click in a cell and then select data within the cell and the Mini toolbar displays in a dimmed fashion above the selected data. Hover the mouse arrow pointer over the Mini toolbar and it becomes active. Recall that the Mini toolbar contains buttons for applying font formatting such as font, font size, and font color as well as bold and italic formatting.

The default alignment of data in cells depends on the type of data entered. Enter words or text combined with numbers in a cell and the text is aligned at the left edge of the cell. Enter numbers in a cell and the numbers are aligned at the right side of the cell. Use options in the Alignment group to align text at the left, center, or right side of the cell; align text at the top, center, or bottom of the cell; increase and/or decrease the indent of text; and change the orientation of text in a cell. **Cell orientation** means the rotation of text in a cell. Click the Merge & Center button to merge selected cells and center data within the merged cells. If you have merged cells and want to split them again, select the cells and then click the Merge & Center button.

cell orientation The rotation of text in a cell

Quick Steps

Repeat Last Action
1. Apply formatting.
2. Press F4 or Ctrl + Y.

Click the Orientation button and a drop-down list displays with options for rotating text in a cell. If data typed in a cell is longer than the cell, it overlaps the next cell to the right. If you want data to remain in a cell and wrap to the next line within the same cell, click the Wrap Text button in the Alignment group. If you want to apply similar formatting, such as number, border, or shading formatting to other cells in a worksheet, use the Repeat command by pressing F4 or Ctrl + Y. The Repeat command repeats the last action performed.

Exercise 10.3 Applying Font and Alignment Formatting

1. With **U2T10-GMPurchases.xlsx** open, make cell B1 active and then click the Wrap Text button in the Alignment group on the Home tab.

   This wraps the company name within the cell.

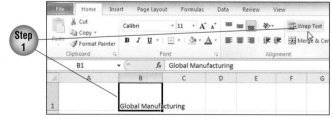

2. Make cell B2 active and then click the Wrap Text button.

3. Instead of wrapping text within cells, you decide to spread out the text over several cells and vertically align text in cells. To do this, select cells A1 through E1, click the Merge & Center button ☒ in the Alignment group on the Home tab, and then click the Middle Align button ☰ in the Alignment group.

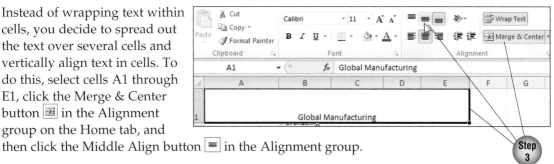

4. Select cells A2 through E2, click the Merge & Center button, and then click the Middle Align button.

5. Select cells A3 through E3 and then rotate text in the cells by clicking the Orientation button ≫ in the Alignment group and then clicking *Angle Counterclockwise* at the drop-down list.

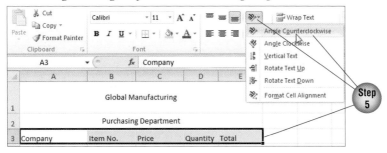

6. Return the orientation back to horizontal by clicking the Undo button on the Quick Access toolbar.

7. Make cell A1 active, click the Font button arrow in the Font group on the Home tab, scroll down the drop-down gallery, and then click *Cambria*.

8. Click the Font Size button arrow in the Font group and then click *22* at the drop-down gallery.

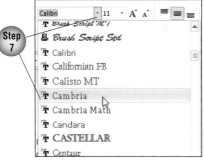

9. Click the Font Color button arrow ☒ and then click the *Dark Blue* color in the *Standard* section of the drop-down color palette.

10. Make cell A2 active and then complete steps similar to those in Steps 7 through 9 to change the font to Cambria, the font size to 16, and the font color to Dark Blue.

11. Select cells A3 through E3, click the Center button ☰ in the Alignment group, click the Bold button B in the Font group, and then click the Italic button I.

12. Select cells A3 through E18 and then change the font to Cambria.

13. Double-click cell A7, select the letters *RDM* (this causes the Mini toolbar to display above the selected letters), click the Bold button and then the Italic button on the Mini toolbar.

Step 13

14. Adjust columns A through E to accommodate the longest entry in each column.

15. Select cells D4 through D17 and then click the Center button in the Alignment group.

16. Make cell A2 active and then add a double-line bottom border by clicking the Borders button arrow in the Font group on the Home tab, and then clicking the *Bottom Double Border* option at the drop-down list.

Step 16

17. Select cells A3 through E3 and then add a single-line bottom border to cells by clicking the Borders button arrow and then clicking the *Bottom Border* option.

18. Select cells A1 through E3 and then apply fill color by clicking the Fill Color button arrow in the Font group and then clicking the *Aqua, Accent 5, Lighter 80%* color option.

Step 18

19. Select cells A18 through E18 and then add a top border and a double-line bottom border to the cells.

20. Save, print, and then close **U2T10-GMPurchases.xlsx**.

Drilling Down

Applying Formatting at the Font Dialog Box

The Format Cells dialog box with the Font tab selected, as shown at the right, provides another method for applying font formatting. Display this dialog box by clicking the Font group dialog box launcher. As you choose options in the dialog box, the *Preview* section displays how the formatting affects text.

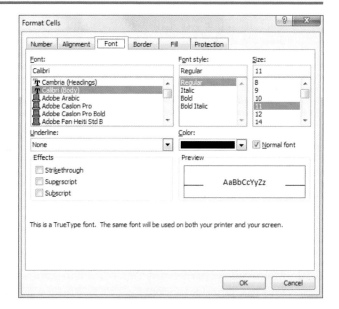

Lesson 10.4 Applying a Theme and Previewing a Worksheet

 2-3.1.8

Excel provides a number of themes you can use to format text and cells in a worksheet. Recall that a theme is a set of formatting choices that includes a color theme (a set of colors), a font theme (a set of heading and body text fonts), and an effects theme (a set of line and fill effects). To apply a theme, click the Page Layout tab and then click the Themes button in the Themes group. At the drop-down gallery that displays, click the desired theme. Position the mouse arrow pointer over a theme and the live preview feature displays the worksheet with the theme formatting applied. With the Live Preview feature you can see how the theme formatting affects your worksheet before you make your final choice.

Before printing a worksheet, consider previewing it to see how it will appear when printed. To preview a worksheet, click the File tab, and then click the Print tab at the left side of the Backstage view. A preview of the worksheet displays in the *Print Preview* area of the Print tab Backstage view.

Quick Steps

Use Print Preview

1. Click File tab.
2. Click Print tab.

Keyboard Shortcut

Print Preview

Ctrl + P

Exercise 10.4 Applying a Theme and Previewing a Worksheet

1. Open **VAPayroll.xlsx** and then save the workbook with Save As and name it **U2T10-VAPayroll**.

2. Make cell A8 active, insert a new row, and then type the following text in the cells in the new row:
   A8 = **Jacobs, Margaret**
   B8 = **27.50**
   C8 = **30**

3. Make D4 the active cell, insert the formula *=B4*C4*, and then copy the formula down to cells D5 through D10.

   The formula multiplies the hourly wage by the hours.

4. Automatically adjust the width of column D.

5. Make E4 the active cell, insert the formula *=D4*B$12*, and then copy the formula down to cells E5 through E10.

   The formula multiplies the gross pay by the withholding rate percentage, which is identified as the mixed cell reference.

6. Make F4 the active cell, insert the formula *=D4*G$12*, and then copy the formula down to cells F5 through F10.

   The formula multiplies the gross pay by the Social Security rate, which is identified as the mixed cell reference.

7. Make G4 the active cell, insert the formula *=D4-E4-F4*, and then copy the formula down to cells G5 through G10.

   The formula subtracts the withholding and Social Security rates from the gross pay.

8. Increase the height of row 1 to 36.00.

9. Make cell A1 active, click the Middle Align button in the Alignment group, click the Font Size button arrow, click *18* at the drop-down list, and then click the Bold button.

10. Type **Vandermeyer and Associates** in cell A1.

11. Select cells A2 through G3 and then click the Bold button.

12. Click the Page Layout tab.

13. Click the Themes button in the Themes group and then click *Verve* at the drop-down gallery.

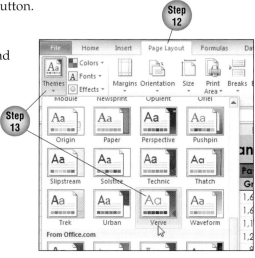

You might want to position the mouse arrow pointer on various themes to see how the theme formatting affects the worksheet.

14. Click the Colors button in the Themes group and then click *Equity* at the drop-down gallery.

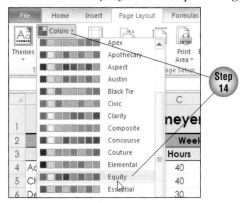

15. Click the Fonts button in the Themes group, scroll down the drop-down gallery, and then click *Opulent*.

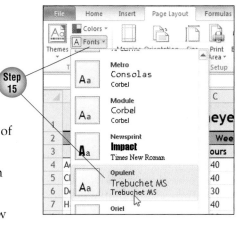

16. Select columns A through G and then adjust the width of the columns to accommodate the longest entries.

17. Preview the worksheet by clicking the File tab and then clicking the Print tab.

18. Notice the display of the worksheet in the Print Preview area of the Print tab Backstage view.

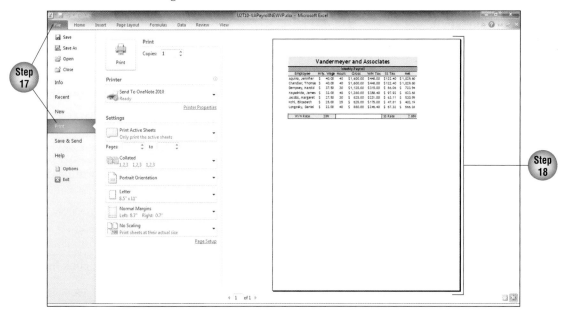

19. Click the Zoom to Page button 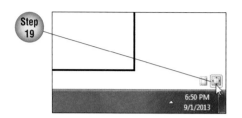 located in the bottom right corner of the Print Preview area.

This zooms the Print Preview area of the Print tab Backstage view to the cells containing data.

20. Click the Print button to print the worksheet.

21. Save and then close **U2T10-VAPayroll.xlsx**.

Drilling Down

Using the Zoom Slider Bar

Change the size of the worksheet display in Normal view using the Zoom slider bar that displays at the right side of the Status bar. To change the percentage display, drag the button on the slider bar to increase or decrease the percentage of display. You can also click the Zoom Out button located at the left side of the slider bar to decrease the percentage of display or click the Zoom In button located at the right side of the slider bar to increase the percentage of display.

Lesson 10.5 Inserting, Sizing, and Moving Clip Art and an Image

Add visual appeal to a workbook by inserting a graphic image such as a logo, picture, or clip art in a worksheet. **Clip art** is a predesigned image, usually created by hand or by using computer graphics programs. Insert a clip art image at the Clip Art task pane. Display this task pane by clicking the Clip Art button in the Illustrations group on the Insert tab. At the Clip Art task pane, type a category in the *Search for* text box and then press Enter. In the list of clip art images that displays, click the desired image. The image is inserted in the worksheet and the Picture Tools Format tab becomes active.

clip art A predesigned image, usually created by hand or using computer-aided graphic programs

Insert an image from a drive or folder with the Picture button in the Illustrations group on the Insert tab. Once the desired image is inserted in the worksheet, you can use buttons on the Picture Tools Format tab (shown in Figure 10.2) to recolor the picture, apply a picture style, arrange the picture in the worksheet, and size the image. You can also size an image using the sizing handles that display around the selected image and move the image using the mouse arrow pointer.

Figure 10.2 Picture Tools Format Tab

Exercise 10.5 Inserting, Sizing, and Moving a Clip Art Image

1. Open **VAInvoices.xlsx** and then save the workbook and name it **U2T10-VAInvoices**.

2. Change the width of column C to 21.00, column D to 10.00, column E to 7.00, and column F to 12.00.

3. Select row 1 and then click the Insert button in the Cells group.

4. Change the height of row 1 to 48.00.

5. Select cells B1 through F1 and then click the Merge & Center button in the Alignment group.

6. With cell B1 active, change the font size to 24 points.

7. Click the Fill Color button arrow in the Font group and then click the *Purple, Accent 4, Lighter 80%* color option.

8. Click the Borders button arrow in the Font group and then click the *Top and Thick Bottom Border* option.

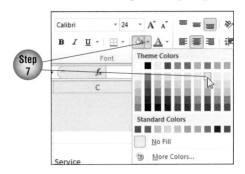

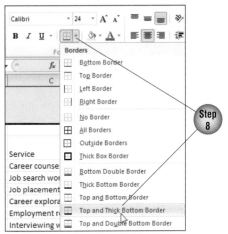

9. With cell B1 still active, type **Vandermeyer and Associates** and then press Enter.

10. Click the Insert tab and then click the Clip Art button in the Illustrations group.

11. At the Clip Art task pane, click the down-pointing arrow at the right of the *Results should be* option box and then click in the *Photographs*, *Videos*, and *Audio* check boxes to remove the check marks. (The *Illustrations* check box should be the only one with a check mark.)

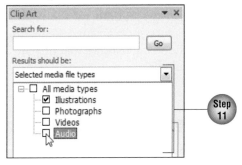

12. At the Clip Art task pane, select any text that displays in the *Search for* text box, type **interview**, and then press Enter.

13. Click the clip art shown at the right. (If this clip art image is not available, choose a similar image.)

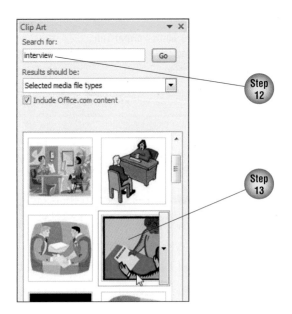

14. With the clip art image selected, click the Color button in the Adjust group and then click the *Purple, Accent color 4 Light* option from the drop-down gallery.

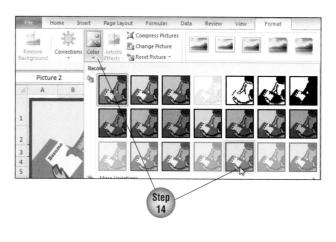

15. Resize the image by typing **0.68** in both the *Height* and *Width* text boxes in the Size group.

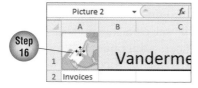

Step 15

Step 14

16. Using the mouse, position the clip art image in cell A1 and then close the Clip Art task pane.

Step 16

17. Save and then print **U2T10-VAInvoices.xlsx**.

Drilling Down

Formatting Images with Buttons in the Adjust Group on the Picture Tools Format Tab

You can format images in a worksheet with buttons and options on the Picture Tools Format tab. Use the buttons in the Adjust group to correct the brightness and contrast of the image; change the image color; reset the image to its original size, position, and color; and compress the picture size. You can also use the buttons in the Adjust group to apply an artistic effect and to remove the background of an image. After you remove an image's background, you can place the image on top of an existing background to give it a more integrated appearance.

Lesson 10.6 Formatting Numbers

 2-3.1.5

Numbers in a cell, by default, are aligned at the right and decimals and commas do not display unless they are typed in the cell manually. If you type numbers in a cell without a symbol such as the dollar sign ($) or percent sign (%), Excel applies the General number formatting. You can change the number formatting to something other than General (such as Currency, Accounting, or Percentage) using the buttons in the Number group on the Home tab or with options at the Format Cells dialog box with the Number tab selected. You can also control the formatting of numbers by typing a specific symbol in a cell.

Symbols you can use to manually format numbers include a percent sign (%), a comma (,), and a dollar sign ($). For example, if you type the number *$45.50* in a cell, Excel automatically applies Currency formatting to the number. If you type *45%*, Excel automatically applies the Percent formatting to the number. The Number group on the Home tab contains five buttons you can use to format numbers in cells, as shown and described in Table 10.1.

Table 10.1 Number Formatting Buttons in the Number Group on the Home Tab

Button	Applies this formatting
Accounting Number Format	Adds a dollar sign, any necessary commas, and a decimal point followed by two decimal digits, if none are typed; right-aligns number in cell
Percent Style	Multiplies cell value by 100 and displays result with a percent symbol; right-aligns number in cell
Comma Style	Adds any necessary commas and a decimal point followed by two decimal digits, if none are typed; right-aligns number in cell
Increase Decimal	Increases number of decimal places displayed after decimal point in selected cells
Decrease Decimal	Decreases number of decimal places displayed after decimal point in selected cells

The Number group on the Home tab also contains the Number Format button. Click the Number Format button arrow and a drop-down list displays containing common number formats. Click the desired format at the drop-down list to apply the formatting to the selected cell or cells.

Along with buttons in the Number group, you can format numbers with options at the Format Cells dialog box with the Number tab selected, as shown in Figure 10.3. Display this dialog box by clicking the Number group dialog box launcher or by clicking the Number Format button arrow and then clicking *More Number Formats* at the drop-down list. The left side of the dialog box displays number categories with the General category selected by default. At this setting no specific formatting is applied to numbers except right-aligning numbers in cells. Table 10.2 describes five of the number categories. (For an explanation of the other categories, refer to the Drilling Down feature in this lesson.)

Figure 10.3 Format Cells Dialog Box with Number Tab Selected

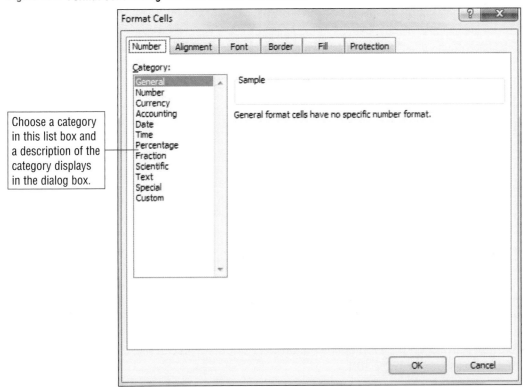

Choose a category in this list box and a description of the category displays in the dialog box.

Table 10.2 Five Number Categories at the Format Cells Dialog Box

Category	Formatting applied by Excel and/or available options
Number	Applies general number display; options allow user to select the number of decimal places, whether to use a thousand separator (,), and how negative numbers should display
Currency	Applies general monetary values; options allow user to select the number of decimal places, what monetary symbol should be included, and how negative numbers should display
Accounting	Lines up currency symbols and decimal points in a column; options allow user to select the number of decimal places and the monetary symbol used
Date	Applies date and time serial numbers as date values; options allow user to designate the type of date display and location
Percentage	Multiplies the cell value by 100 and displays the result with a percentage symbol; options allow user to select the number of decimal places

Exercise 10.6 Formatting Numbers

1. With **U2T10-VAInvoices.xlsx** open, select cells A2 through F2 and then click the Merge & Center button in the Alignment group on the Home tab.

2. With cell A2 active, change the font size to 18 and then click the Fill Color button in the Font group (this will fill the cell with light purple color). Click the Borders button arrow in the Font group and then click the *Bottom Border* option at the drop-down list.

   If light purple fill color does not display in cell A2, click the Fill Color button arrow and then click the *Purple, Accent 4, Lighter 80%* color option.

3. Change the height of row 2 to 30.00.

4. Select cells A3 through F3, click the Bold button in the Font group, and then click the Center button in the Alignment group.

5. With cells A3 through F3 still selected, click the Borders button arrow and then click the *Bottom Border* option.

6. Change the height of row 3 to 18.00.

7. Select cells E4 through E16 and then click the Percent Style button %️ in the Number group.

8. With the cells still selected, click once on the Increase Decimal button ⬆️ in the Number group.

   The percent numbers should contain one decimal place.

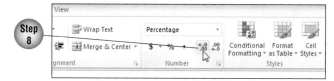 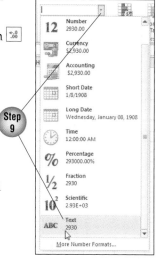

9. Select A4 through B16, click the Number Format button arrow, scroll down the drop-down list, and then click *Text*.

10. With A4 through B16 still selected, click the Center button in the Alignment group.

11. Select cells D4 through D16 and then click the Number group dialog box launcher.

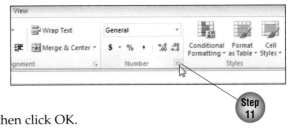

12. At the Format Cells dialog box with the Number tab selected, click *Accounting* in the *Category* list box, make sure a 2 displays in the *Decimal places* option box and a dollar sign *$* displays in the *Symbol* option box, and then click OK.

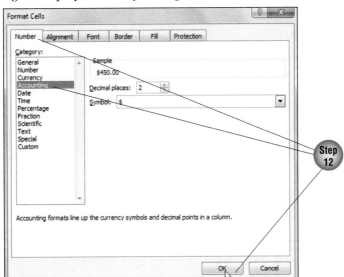

13. Apply Accounting formatting to cells F4 through F16 by completing steps similar to those in Steps 11 and 12.

14. Make cell F4 active, type the formula =(D4*E4)+D4, and then copy the formula down to cells F5 through F16.

15. Save, print, and then close **U2T10-VAInvoices.xlsx**.

Drilling Down

Applying Number Formatting

In addition to the categories described in Table 10.2, the Format Cells dialog box with the Number tab selected includes the following additional categories:

Category	Formatting applied by Excel and/or available options
Time	Displays time as a time value; options allow user to specify the type of time formatting and location as desired
Fraction	Options allow user to specify how fractions display
Scientific	Allows the letter *E* to be used to tell Excel to move the decimal point a specified number of positions
Text	Designates the number as text so that the number is displayed exactly as typed
Special	Options allow user to select a numbering type (such as Zip Code, Phone Number, or Social Security) to apply
Custom	Options allow user to select a numbering type

Lesson 10.7 Changing Page Setup and Sheet Options

IC³ 2-3.1.9

The Page Setup group on the Page Layout tab contains options for specifying a worksheet's margins, orientation, page breaks, and print areas. Use options in the Sheet Options group to print gridlines, column letters, and row numbers.

By default, a worksheet contains default margin settings of 0.75 inches for the top and bottom and 0.7 inches for the left and right. You can change worksheet margins with the Margins button in the Page Setup group on the Page Layout tab. Click the Margins button and a drop-down list of predesigned margin options displays. Click an option to apply it.

To customize margins, click the *Custom Margins* option at the bottom of the Margins drop-down list. This displays the Page Setup dialog box with the Margins tab selected as shown in Figure 10.4. A worksheet page showing the cells and margins displays in the dialog box. As you increase or decrease the margin measurements, the sample worksheet page reflects the changes.

Quick Steps

Change Worksheet Margins
1. Click Page Layout tab.
2. Click Margins button.
3. Click desired predesigned margin option.

OR

1. Click Page Layout tab.
2. Click Margins button.
3. Click *Custom Margins* at drop-down list.
4. Change top, left, right, and/or bottom measurements.
5. Click OK.

Figure 10.4 **Page Setup Dialog Box with Margins Tab Selected**

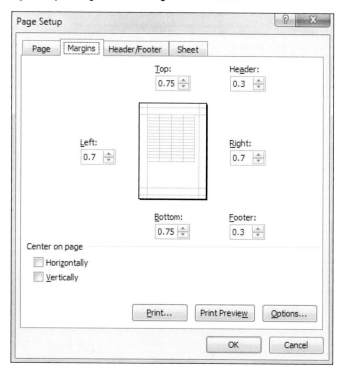

By default, worksheets print in the upper left corner of the page. To center a worksheet, use the *Horizontally* and/or *Vertically* options that display at the bottom of the Page Setup dialog box with the Margins tab selected. If you click one or both of these options, the worksheet page in the *Preview* section displays how the worksheet will print on the page.

Click the Orientation button in the Page Setup group and a drop-down list displays with two choices, *Portrait* and *Landscape*. The two choices are represented by sample pages. A sample page that is taller than it is wide shows how the default orientation (Portrait) prints data on the page. The other choice, Landscape, will rotate the data and print it on a page that is wider than it is tall.

Quick Steps

Center Worksheet Horizontally/Vertically
1. Click Page Layout tab.
2. Click Margins button.
3. Click *Custom Margins* at drop-down list.
4. Click *Horizontally* or *Vertically* option.
5. Click OK.

Change Page Orientation
1. Click Page Layout tab.
2. Click Orientation button.
3. Click desired orientation at drop-down list.

Quick Steps

Insert Page Break

1. Select column or row.
2. Click Page Layout tab.
3. Click Breaks button.
4. Click *Insert Page Break.*

Define Print Area

1. Select desired cells.
2. Click Page Layout tab.
3. Click Print Area button.
4. Click *Set Print Area.*

Print Column and Row Titles

1. Click Page Layout tab.
2. Click Print Titles button.
3. Type row range in *Rows to repeat at top* option.
4. Type column range in *Columns to repeat at left* option.
5. Click OK.

Print Gridlines, Row Numbers, and Column Letters

1. Click Page Layout tab.
2. Click *Print* check boxes in Gridlines and Headings sections of Sheet Options group.

Excel automatically inserts a page break in a worksheet when it contains more than 7 inches of cells horizontally or more than 9.5 inches of cells vertically. You can also insert your own page breaks. To do this, select the column or row, click the Breaks button in the Page Setup group on the Page Layout tab, and then click *Insert Page Break* at the drop-down list. A page break is inserted immediately left of the selected column or immediately above the selected row. The page breaks automatically inserted by Excel may not be visible initially in a worksheet. One way to display the page breaks is to first display the worksheet in the Print tab Backstage view. When you return to the worksheet, the page breaks will be displayed.

With the Print Area button in the Page Setup group, you can select and print specific areas of a worksheet. To do this, select the cells you want to print, click the Print Area button, and then click *Set Print Area* at the drop-down list. This inserts a border around the selected cells. Display the Print tab Backstage view and click the Print button, and the cells within the border are printed. Clear a print area by clicking the Print Area button and then clicking *Clear Print Area* at the drop-down list.

Columns and rows in a worksheet are usually titled. If a worksheet prints on more than one page, printing column and/or row titles on each page can be useful. To do this, click the Print Titles button in the Page Setup group. At the Page Setup dialog box with the Sheet tab selected, specify the range of row and/or column cells you want to print on each page.

By default, gridlines, row numbers, and column letters do not print. To set these features to print, click the *Print* check boxes in the Gridlines and Headings sections of the Sheet Options group on the Page Layout tab to insert check marks.

Exercise 10.7 Changing Page Setup

1. Open **Budget.xlsx** and save the workbook with Save As and name it **U2T10-Budget**.

2. Click the Page Layout tab, click the Margins button in the Page Setup group, and then click *Narrow* at the drop-down list.

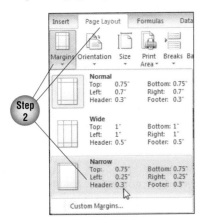

3. Click the Margins button and then click *Custom Margins* at the drop-down list.

4. At the Page Setup dialog box with the Margins tab selected, click the up-pointing arrow at the right side of the *Top* text box until *4.5* displays.

5. Click the up-pointing arrow at the right side of the *Bottom* text box until *1.5* displays.

6. Preview the worksheet by clicking the Print Preview button located toward the bottom of the Page Setup dialog box.

   The worksheet appears to be a little low on the page, so you may decide to horizontally and vertically center the worksheet.

7. Click the Page Layout tab, click the Margins button in the Page Setup group, and then click *Custom Margins* at the drop-down list.

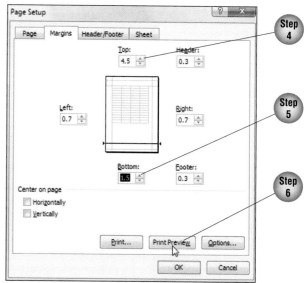

8. At the Page Setup dialog box with the Margins tab selected, change the Top measurement to 1.5.

9. Click the *Horizontally* option.

   This inserts a check mark in the check box.

10. Click the *Vertically* option.

    This inserts a check mark in the check box.

11. Click OK to close the dialog box.

12. Click the Orientation button in the Page Setup group on the Page Layout tab and then click *Landscape* at the drop-down list.

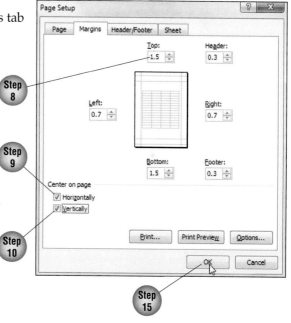

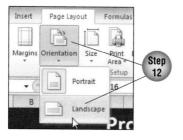

13. Click the File tab and then click the Print tab to display the worksheet in the Print tab Backstage view. Notice how the worksheet will print on the page.

14. Click the Page Layout tab, click the Orientation button, and then click *Portrait* at the drop-down list.

15. Insert a page break between columns G and H by selecting column H, clicking the Breaks button in the Page Setup group, and then clicking *Insert Page Break* at the drop-down list.

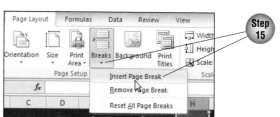

16. Insert a page break between rows 6 and 7 by selecting row 7, clicking the Breaks button in the Page Setup group, and then clicking *Insert Page Break* at the drop-down list.

17. Display the worksheet in Print tab Backstage view and then click the Next Page button a couple of times to display pages of the worksheet.

18. Remove the page breaks you inserted by clicking the Page Layout tab, clicking the Breaks button in the Page Setup group, and then clicking *Reset All Page Breaks* at the drop-down list.

19. Specify that you want to print cells A2 through C17. To do this, select cells A2 through C17, click the Print Area button in the Page Setup group on the Page Layout tab, and then click *Set Print Area* at the drop-down list.

Step 19

20. Print the specified cells by clicking the File tab, clicking the Print tab, and then clicking the Print button at the Print tab Backstage view.

21. Remove the print area by clicking the Print Area button and then clicking *Clear Print Area* at the drop-down list.

22. Select row 11 and then insert a page break.

23. Specify that you want row and column titles to print on each page. Begin by clicking the Print Titles button in the Page Setup group.

24. At the Page Setup dialog box with the Sheet tab selected, click in the *Rows to repeat at top* text box and then type **A2:N2**.

25. Click in the *Columns to repeat at the left* text box, type **A2:A17**, and then click OK.

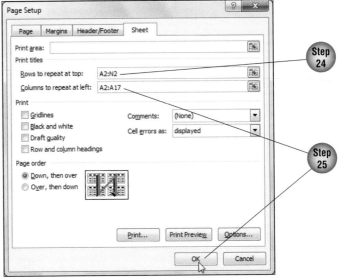

Step 24

Step 25

26. Specify that you want gridlines, row numbers, and column letters to print by clicking both *Print* check boxes in the Sheet Options group to insert check marks.

27. Click the File tab and then the Print tab to display the worksheet in Print tab Backstage view.

28. Click the Next Page button a couple of times to display pages in the worksheet.

29. Print only page 2 of the worksheet. To do this, click in the first text box to the right of the *Pages* option in the *Settings* category and then type **2**. Click in the second text box to the right of the *Pages* option, type **2**, and then click the Print button.

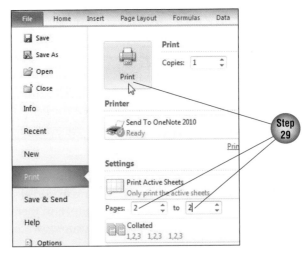

Step 29

30. Click both of the *Print* check boxes in the Sheet Options group to remove the check marks.

31. Change the orientation to *Landscape* and remove all page breaks.

32. Save **U2T10-Budget.xlsx**.

Drilling Down

Changing Page Size

By default, an Excel worksheet page size is set at 8.5 x 11 inches. You can change this default page size by clicking the Size button in the Page Setup group. At the drop-down list that displays, notice that the default setting is *Letter* and the measurements 8.5" x 11" display below *Letter*. This drop-down list also contains a number of page sizes such as *Executive*, *Legal*, and a number of envelope sizes.

Scaling Data

With buttons in the Scale to Fit group on the Page Layout tab, you can adjust the printed output by a percentage to fit the number of pages specified. For example, if a worksheet contains too many columns to print on one page, click the Width button arrow in the Scale to Fit group on the Page Layout tab and then click *1 page*. This causes the data to shrink so all columns display and print on one page.

Lesson 10.8   Inserting Headers and Footers

 2-3.1.9

Similar to other Office Suite programs, Excel contains text that prints at the top of each worksheet page and is called a header and text that prints at the bottom of each worksheet page that is called a footer. You can create a header and/or footer with the Header & Footer button in the Text group on the Insert tab, in Page Layout view, or with options at the Page Setup dialog box with the Header/Footer tab selected.

To create a header with the Header & Footer button, click the Insert tab and then click the Header & Footer button in the Text group. This displays the worksheet in the Page Layout view and displays the Header & Footer Tools Design tab. Use buttons in this tab to insert predesigned headers and/ or footers or insert header and footer elements such as the page number, date, time, path name, and file name. You can also create a different header or footer on the first page of the worksheet or create one header or footer for even pages and another for odd pages.

When you insert a header or footer, the view changes to Page Layout view. To return to the Normal view, which is the default, click the View tab and then click the Normal button in the Workbook Views group.

In addition to options in the Header & Footer Tools Design tab, you can insert a header or footer in a worksheet with options at the Page Setup dialog box with the Header/Footer tab selected. Display this dialog box by clicking the Page Layout tab, clicking the Page Setup group dialog box launcher, and then clicking the Header/Footer tab at the Page Setup dialog box. You can also display the dialog box by displaying the Print tab Backstage view, clicking the <u>Page Setup</u> hyperlink, and then clicking the Header/Footer tab at the Page Setup dialog box. Use options at the dialog box to insert headers and footers and specify header and footer options.

Quick Steps

Insert a Header or Footer

1. Click Insert tab.
2. Click Header & Footer button.
3. Click Header or Footer button.
4. Click predesigned header or footer.

Exercise 10.8 Inserting a Header and Footer in a Worksheet

1. With **U2T10-Budget.xlsx** open, click the Insert tab and then click the Header & Footer button in the Text group.

2. Click the Header button located at the left side of the Header & Footer Tools Design tab and then click *U2T10-Budget.xlsx* at the drop-down list.

   This inserts the workbook name in the middle header box.

3. Click the Insert tab and then click the Header & Footer button in the Text group.

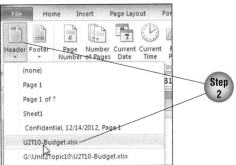

4. Click the Footer button located at the left side of the Header & Footer Tools Design tab and then click the last option at the drop-down list.

   The last option displays the words *Prepared by* in the middle header box. This is followed by your name or another name designated by the school and the current date. The word *Page* followed by the page number displays in the header box at the right.

5. Click in any cell in the worksheet containing data, click the View tab, and then click the Normal button in the Workbook Views group.

6. Preview the worksheet using the Print tab Backstage view to determine how the header and footer will print on each page.

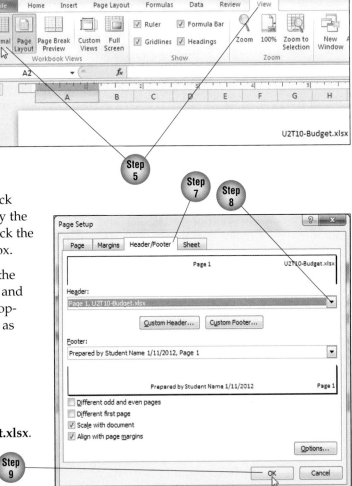

7. In the Print tab Backstage view, click the Page Setup hyperlink to display the Page Setup dialog box and then click the Header/Footer tab in the dialog box.

8. Click the down-pointing arrow at the right side of the *Header* option box and then click the first option in the drop-down list (the option that displays as *Page 1, U2T10-Budget.xlsx*).

9. Click OK to close the dialog box.

10. Click the Print button to print the worksheet.

11. Save and then close **U2T10-Budget.xlsx**.

Drilling Down | **Inserting Headers and Footers in Page Layout View**

You also can insert a header and/or footer by switching to Page Layout view. In Page Layout view, the top of the worksheet page displays with the text *Click to add header*. Click this text and the insertion point is positioned in the middle header box. Type the desired header in this box or click in the left box or the right box and then type the header. Create a footer in a similar manner. Scroll down the worksheet until the bottom of the page displays and then click the text *Click to add footer*. Type the footer in the center footer box or click the left or right box and then type the footer.

Lesson 10.9 Creating a Chart

 2-3.2.9

In the previous Excel activities, you learned to create data in worksheets. While a worksheet does an adequate job of representing data, you can present some data more effectively by charting the data. A **chart** is sometimes referred to as a *graph* and is a visual representation of numeric data.

In Excel, create a chart with buttons in the Charts group on the Insert tab. With buttons in the Charts group you can create a variety of charts such as a column chart, line chart, pie chart, and much more. Excel provides 11 basic chart types as described in Table 10.3. To create a chart, select cells in a worksheet that you want to chart, click the Insert tab, and then click the desired chart button in the Charts group. At the drop-down gallery that displays, click the desired chart style. You can also create a chart by selecting the desired cells and then pressing Alt + F1. This keyboard shortcut, by default, inserts the data in a 2-D column chart (unless the default chart type has been changed).

chart A visual representation of numeric data; sometimes referred to as a *graph*

Quick Steps

Create a Chart
1. Select cells.
2. Click Insert tab.
3. Click desired chart button.
4. Click desired chart style at drop-down list.

Create a Chart Using the Default Chart Type
1. Select cells.
2. Press Alt + F1.

Table 10.3 **Types of Charts**

Chart Type	Description
Area	Emphasizes the magnitude of change, rather than time and the rate of change; also shows the relationship of parts to a whole by displaying the sum of the plotted values
Bar	Shows individual figures at a specific time, or shows variations between components but not in relationship to the whole
Bubble	Compares sets of three values in a manner similar to a scatter chart, with the third value displayed as the size of the bubble marker
Column	Displays data changes over a period of time or displays comparisons among items
Doughnut	Shows the relationship of parts to the whole
Line	Shows trends and change over time at even intervals; emphasizes the rate of change over time rather than the magnitude of change
Pie	Shows proportions and relationships of parts to the whole
Radar	Emphasizes differences and amounts of change over time and variations and trends; each category has its own value axis radiating from the center point and lines connect all values in the same series

continued

Stock	Shows four values for a stock: open, high, low, and close
Surface	Shows trends in values across two dimensions in a continuous curve
XY (Scatter)	Either shows the relationships among numeric values in several data series or plots the interception points between x and y values; shows uneven intervals of data and is commonly used to display scientific data

When you create a chart, the chart is inserted in the same worksheet as the selected cells. The chart is inserted in a floating frame that you can size and/or move in the worksheet. To size the chart, position the mouse arrow pointer on the four small dots located in the middle of the border you want to size until the pointer turns into a two-headed arrow, hold down the left mouse button, and then drag to increase or decrease the size of the chart. To increase or decrease the height and width of the chart at the same time, position the mouse arrow pointer on the three small dots that display in a chart border corner until the pointer displays as a two-headed arrow, hold down the left mouse button, and then drag to the desired size. To increase or decrease the size of the chart and maintain the proportions of the chart, hold down the Shift key while dragging a chart corner border. To move the chart, make sure the chart is selected (light gray border displays around the chart), position the mouse arrow pointer on a border until the pointer displays with a four-headed arrow attached, hold down the left mouse button, and then drag to the desired position.

The cells you select to create the chart are linked to the chart. If you need to change data for a chart, edit the data in the desired cell and the corresponding section of the chart is automatically updated.

In a worksheet containing data in cells as well as a chart, you have the option to print only the chart. To do this, select the desired chart and then display the Print tab Backstage view by clicking the File tab and then clicking the Print tab. At the Print tab Backstage view, make sure *Print Selected Chart* is selected in the *Print what* section and then click the Print button.

Exercise 10.9 Creating a Chart

1. Open **QtrlySales.xlsx** and then save the workbook with Save As and name it **U2T10-QtrlySales**.

2. Select cells A1 through E5.

3. Press Alt + F1.

   This keyboard shortcut inserts the data in a 2-D column chart.

4. Position the mouse arrow pointer on the bottom right corner of the chart border until the pointer turns into a two-headed arrow pointing diagonally.

5. Hold down the Shift key, hold down the left mouse button, drag out approximately one-half inch, and then release the mouse button and then the Shift key.

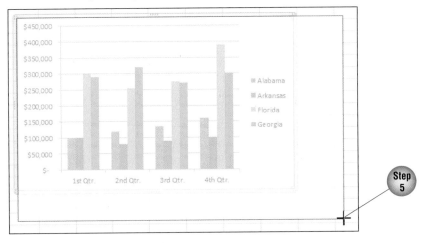

6. Position the mouse arrow pointer on the chart border until the pointer displays with a four-headed arrow attached.

7. Hold down the left mouse button, drag the chart so it is positioned below the cells containing data, and then release the mouse button.

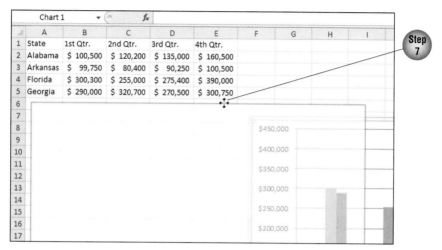

8. With the chart selected, print only the chart by clicking the File tab and then clicking the Print tab. At the Print tab Backstage view, make sure *Print Selected Chart* is selected in the *Print Area* option drop-down list, and then click the Print button.

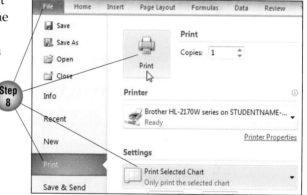

9. Make the following changes to the specified cells:
   B2 = Change *100,500* to *110,750*
   C3 = Change *80,400* to *65,250*
   B4 = Change *300,300* to *320,500*
   E5 = Change *300,750* to *275,800*

   Notice that the chart reflects the changes made to the data in cells.

10. Click just inside the chart to select it (a light gray border surrounds the chart) and then print the chart using steps similar to those in Step 8.

11. Save and then close **U2T10-QtrlySales.xlsx**.

Drilling Down

Previewing a Chart

You can use the Print Preview area of the Print tab Backstage view to see how a chart will look when you print it. Display the Print tab Backstage view by clicking the File tab and then clicking the Print tab. At the Print tab Backstage view you can click the <u>Page Setup</u> hyperlink to display the Page Setup dialog box. With options at this dialog box with various tabs selected, you can change the worksheet page and margins and insert a header or footer. You can also change the chart to draft quality before printing, or print the chart in black and white.

Lesson 10.10   Changing the Chart Design

IC³ 2-3.2.9

When you insert a chart in a worksheet the Chart Tools Design tab displays as shown in Figure 10.5. With options in this tab, you can change the chart type, specify a different layout or style for the chart, and change the location of the chart so it displays in a separate worksheet.

Figure 10.5 Chart Tools Design Tab

Quick Steps

Change Chart Type and Style

1. Make chart active.
2. Click Chart Tools Design tab.
3. Click Change Chart Type button.
4. Click desired chart type and style.
5. Click OK.

The chart feature offers a variety of preformatted custom charts and varying styles for each chart type. You can choose a chart style with buttons in the Charts group by clicking a chart button and then choosing from the styles offered at the drop-down list. You can also choose a chart style with the Change Chart Type button on the Chart Tools Design tab. Click this button and the Change Chart Type dialog box displays as shown in Figure 10.6. Click the desired chart type in the panel at the left side of the dialog box and then click the desired chart style at the right.

Figure 10.6 Change Chart Type Dialog Box

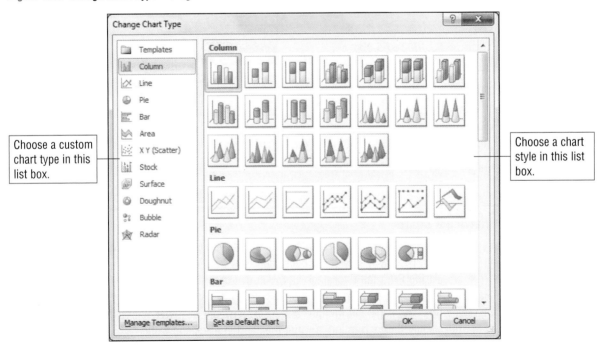

Choose a custom chart type in this list box.

Choose a chart style in this list box.

When you create a chart, the chart is inserted in the currently open worksheet as an embedded object. You can change the location of a chart with the Move Chart button in the Location group. Click this button and the Move Chart dialog box displays as shown in Figure 10.7. Click the *New sheet* option to move the chart to a new sheet within the workbook. Excel automatically names the sheet *Chart1*. Click the down-pointing arrow at the right side of the *Object in* option box and then click the desired location. The drop-down list will generally display the names of the worksheets within the open workbook. You can use the keyboard shortcut F11 to create a chart using the default chart type (usually a column chart). Excel automatically inserts the new chart in a separate sheet.

Quick Steps

Change Chart Data Series

1. Make chart active.
2. Click Chart Tools Design tab.
3. Click Switch Row/Column button.

Change Chart Location

1. Make chart active.
2. Click Chart Tools Design tab.
3. Click Move Chart button.
4. Click *New Sheet* option.
5. Click OK.

Figure 10.7 Move Chart Dialog Box

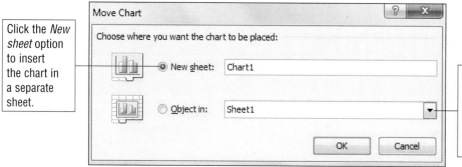

Click the *New sheet* option to insert the chart in a separate sheet.

To move the chart to a different sheet, click this down-pointing arrow and then click the desired sheet.

Exercise 10.10 Creating a Chart and Changing the Chart Design

1. Open **SGBudgets.xlsx** and then save the workbook with Save As and name it **U2T10-SGBudgets**.

2. Select cells A3 through B9, click the Insert tab, and then click the Bar button in the Charts group.

3. Click the first option from the left in the *Cylinder* section (*Clustered Horizontal Cylinder*).

4. With the chart selected and the Chart Tools Design tab active, change the data series by clicking the Switch Row/Column button located in the Data group.

5. Click the Change Chart Type button located in the Type group.

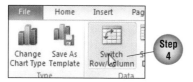

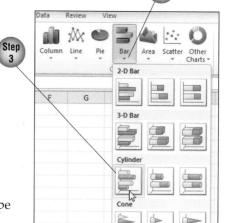

6. At the Change Chart Type dialog box, click the *Column* option in the left panel, click the *3-D Cylinder* option in the *Column* section (fourth chart style from the left in the second row of the *Column* section), and then click OK.

7. Click the Change Chart Type button in the Type group, click *3-D Clustered Column* (fourth column style from the left in the top row), and then click OK.

8. Change the chart layout by clicking the *Layout 3* option in the Chart Layouts group (third option from the left).

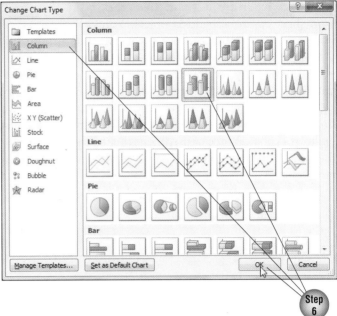

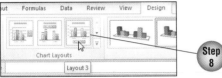

9. Change the chart style by clicking the More button located at the right side of the Chart Styles group and then clicking *Style 34* (second option from the left in the fifth row).

10. Move the chart to a new location. Begin by clicking the Move Chart button in the Location group.

11. At the Move Chart dialog box, click the *New sheet* option and then click OK.

The chart is inserted in a worksheet named Chart1.

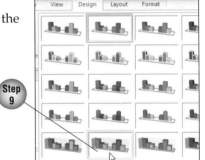

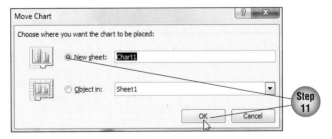

12. Print only the worksheet containing the chart.

13. Save and then close **U2T10-SGBudget.xlsx**.

Drilling Down

Deleting a Chart

You can delete a chart created in Excel by clicking once in the chart to select it and then pressing the Delete key. If you move a chart to a different worksheet in the workbook and then delete the chart, the chart will be deleted but the worksheet will not. To delete the worksheet as well as the chart, position the mouse arrow pointer on the Chart1 tab, click the right mouse button, and then click *Delete* at the shortcut menu. At the message box telling you that selected sheets will be permanently deleted, click OK.

2-3.2.9

Customize the layout of labels in a chart with options on the Chart Tools Layout tab (shown in Figure 10.8). With buttons on this tab, you can change the layout and/or insert additional chart labels. Certain chart labels are automatically inserted in a chart including a chart legend and labels for the x-axis and y-axis. Add chart labels to an existing chart with options in the Labels group on the Chart Tools Layout tab. In addition to chart labels, you can also insert shapes, pictures, and/or clip art and change the layout of 3-D chart labels.

Figure 10.8 Chart Tools Layout Tab

Exercise 10.11   Creating a Chart and Changing the Chart Layout

1. Open **Population.xlsx** and then save the workbook with Save As and name it **U2T10-Population**.

2. Select cells A2 through H4 and then click the Insert tab.

3. Click the Bar button in the Charts group and then click the *Clustered Bar in 3-D* option in the *3-D Bar* section.

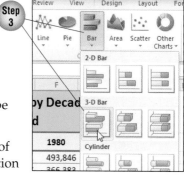

4. Change to a Line chart. Begin by clicking the Change Chart Type button in the Type group.

5. At the Change Chart Type dialog box, click *Line* at the left side of the dialog box, click the *Line with Markers* option in the *Line* section (fourth option from the left), and then click OK.

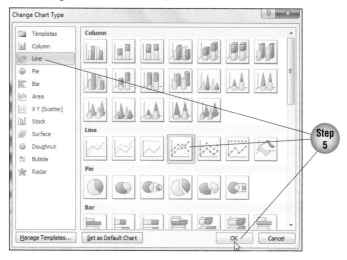

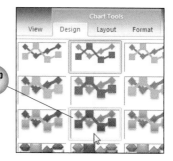

6. Click the More button in the Chart Styles group on the Chart Tools Design tab and then click *Style 18* at the drop-down gallery (second option from left in the third row).

7. Click the Chart Tools Layout tab.

8. Click the Legend button 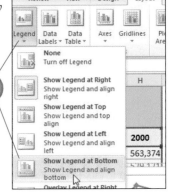 in the Labels group and then click *Show Legend at Bottom* at the drop-down list.

9. Click the Chart Title button in the Labels group and then click *Above Chart* at the drop-down list.

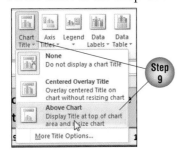

10. Select the text *Chart Title* in the chart title text box and then type **Population Comparison**.

11. Click the Axis Titles button in the Labels group, point to the *Primary Horizontal Axis Title* option at the drop-down list, and then click *Title Below Axis* at the side menu.

12. Select the text *Axis Title* located in the title text box and then type **Decades**.

13. Click the Axis Titles button, point to the *Primary Vertical Axis Title* option at the drop-down list, and then click *Rotated Title* at the side menu.

This inserts a rotated title at the left side of the chart containing the text *Axis Title*.

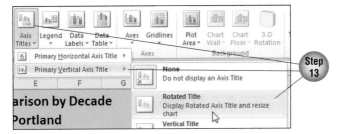

14. Select the text *Axis Title* in the axis title text box and then type **Total Population**.

15. Print only the selected chart.

16. Save and then close **U2T10-Population.xlsx**.

Drilling Down

Inserting Shapes

The Insert group on the Chart Tools Layout tab contains three buttons with options for inserting shapes or images in a chart. Click the Shapes button in the Insert group and a drop-down list displays with a variety of shape options. Click the desired shape at the drop-down list and the mouse arrow pointer turns into a thin, black plus symbol. Drag with this pointer symbol to create the shape in the chart. The shape is inserted in the chart with default formatting. You can change this formatting with options on the Drawing Tools Format tab. This tab contains many of the same options as the Chart Tools Format tab. For example, you can insert a shape, apply a shape or WordArt style, and arrange and size the shape.

Lesson 10.12 **Formatting the Chart Layout**

2-3.2.9

Customize the format of a chart and its elements with options on the Chart Tools Format tab (shown in Figure 10.9). With buttons in the Current Selection group you can identify a specific element in the chart and then apply formatting to that element. You can also click the Reset to Match Style button in the Current Selection group to return the formatting of the chart back to the original layout.

Figure 10.9 **Chart Tools Format Tab**

With options in the Shape Styles group, you can apply formatting styles to specific elements in a chart. Identify the desired element either by clicking the element to select it or by clicking the down-pointing arrow at the right side of the Chart Elements button in the Current Selection group and then clicking the desired element name at the drop-down list. With the chart element specified, apply formatting by clicking a style button in the Shape Styles group. You can access additional shape styles by clicking the More button located at the right side of the shape styles thumbnails. Click the up-pointing or the down-pointing arrow at the right of the drop-down gallery to cycle through the available options.

Exercise 10.12 Creating and Formatting a Pie Chart

1. Open **SGPercents.xlsx** and then save the workbook and name it **U2T10-SGPercents**.

2. Select cells A3 through B10, click the Insert tab, click the Pie button in the Charts group, and then click the first pie option from the left in the *2-D Pie* section.

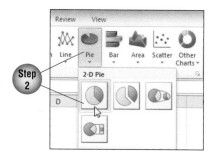

3. Click the More button located at the right side of the Chart Styles group and then click *Style 26* (second option from the left in the fourth row) at the drop-down gallery.

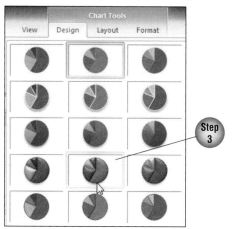

4. Click the Chart Tools Layout tab.

5. Insert data labels by clicking the Data Labels button in the Labels group and then clicking *Inside End* at the drop-down list.

6. Click the Chart Tools Format tab.

7. Click the down-pointing arrow at the right side of the Chart Elements option box in the Current Selection group and then click *Legend* at the drop-down list.

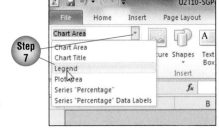

8. Click the More button in the Shape Styles group and then click the *Subtle Effect - Blue, Accent 1* option (second option from the left in the fourth row).

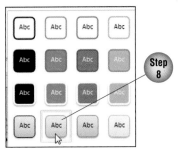

9. Click the down-pointing arrow at the right side of the Chart Elements option box in the Current Selection group and then click *Chart Title*.

10. Click the More button at the right side of the WordArt styles in the WordArt Styles group and then click the *Gradient Fill - Blue, Accent 1* option (fourth option from the left in the third row).

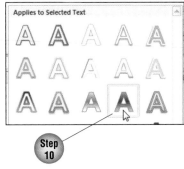

11. With the chart selected, click the Chart Tools Design tab and then click the Move Chart button in the Location group.

12. At the Move Chart dialog box, click the *New sheet* option and then click OK.

13. Print only the worksheet containing the chart.

14. Save and then close **U2T10-SGPercents.xlsx**.

Drilling Down

Changing the Chart Height and Width

You can size a chart by selecting the chart and then dragging a sizing handle. You can also size a chart to specific measurements with the Shape Height and Shape Width buttons in the Size group on the Chart Tools Format tab. Change the height or width by clicking the up- or down-pointing arrows that display at the right side of the button or select the current measurement in the text box and then type a specific measurement.

IC³ 2-3.1.1, 2-3.1.2, 2-3.1.10

Considering Worksheet Purpose and Appeal

A worksheet should be designed to clearly and accurately convey its purpose and to provide factual information. Review the following design considerations:

- **Define Purpose:** Each worksheet serves a purpose, whether it is simply displaying data or using complex formulas and functions to answer a question. Before creating a worksheet, clearly define the exact purpose that the worksheet will address.
- **Specify Data:** In most cases, data entered into Excel is numeric, so collecting data that is both accurate and authentic is important. If a worksheet will be part of a research project, you must cite the data sources. If data is not accurate or authentic, the worksheet will not meet its purpose.
- **Determine Calculations**: Once you have defined the purpose and collected the data, you should outline the method you will use to find the desired results. For example, if a worksheet's purpose is to show how much monthly payments would be on different car loan options, you must determine the proper functions before creating the worksheet. This will increase the likelihood that the calculations will provide accurate, informative information.

Although accuracy, functionality, and purpose are important in creating useful worksheets, you should also consider the worksheet's appearance. Below are some key points of good worksheet design.

Layout

- Start each worksheet in the top left corner. Most English readers naturally look at this area of a document first because English reads from left to right and top to bottom.
- Design a worksheet from top to bottom rather than left to right. In general, the worksheet should be narrow and long instead of wide and short.
- Add titles and labels to identify data in a worksheet, keeping in mind that additional information will likely be added in the future.
- Design a workbook with a number of worksheets instead of trying to include all data in one worksheet.

Formatting

- Format important information (such as titles, headings, and results) so it is easily identified.
- Choose fonts and fill colors that provide contrast to make the data easy to read.
- Bold column headings so that readers can more easily identify the data.
- Keep formatting simple. Do not add too much color or too many images—this makes it more difficult for others to print the worksheet.
- Break down information so that the worksheet can be sorted or selected using smaller bits of information. For example, if the worksheet contains first and last names, put them in separate columns.

continued

Using Excel to Draw Conclusions

As noted in the Topic Overview, Excel is a powerful program that can aid in the decision-making process. Most importantly, Excel allows decision makers to pose "what-if" questions and receive real-time feedback. For example, suppose a car sales manager wants to know how many cars of differing models need to be sold in order for the company to break even for the month. The manager can change the initial conditions in a worksheet, such as car prices and volume, and immediately see the results of these modifications. Additionally, the manager can change values such as the interest or tax rate to see what effects these modifiers have on an initial value. When a value that is used in formulas or functions is changed, Excel automatically updates the entire worksheet with recalculated values, making forecasting both easy and efficient.

Aside from using formulas and functions to answer "what-if" questions, Excel can be used to draw conclusions by using tabulated data or by using charts to find trends within data. If data is entered in a well-formatted, tabulated fashion, decision makers can easily identify changes in data contained in a row or column. Seasonal or cyclical data can be easier to spot when data is displayed in a tabulated manner as well. Charts are a visual representation of a worksheet, so they, too, can be used to draw conclusions on data. For example, if a company's sales history is presented in a line graph, assumptions can be made about future sales. If a company wants to identify where it is spending money in terms of basic cost categories, a pie chart could be created that identifies each category's percentage of the total company expenses.

TOPIC SUMMARY

- Change column width using the mouse on the column boundaries or with options at the Column Width dialog box.
- Change row height using the mouse on the row boundaries or with options at the Row Height dialog box.
- Insert a row in a worksheet with the Insert button in the Cells group on the Home tab or with options at the Insert dialog box.
- Insert a column in a worksheet with the Insert button in the Cells group or with options at the Insert dialog box.
- Delete a specific cell by clicking the Delete button arrow in the Cells group on the Home tab and then clicking *Delete Cells* at the drop-down list. At the Delete dialog box, specify if you want to delete just the cell or an entire row or column.
- Delete a selected row(s) or column(s) by clicking the Delete button in the Cells group.
- Delete cell contents by pressing the Delete key or clicking the Clear button in the Editing group on the Home tab and then clicking *Clear Contents* at the drop-down list.
- Apply font formatting with buttons in the Font group on the Home tab.
- Use the Mini toolbar to apply font formatting to selected data in a cell.
- Apply alignment formatting with buttons in the Alignment group on the Home tab.
- Use the Themes button in the Themes group on the Page Layout tab to apply a theme to cells in a worksheet that applies formatting such as color, font, and effects. Use the other buttons in the Themes group to customize the theme.
- Insert an image in a workbook with options at the Clip Art task pane. Display this task pane by clicking the Insert tab and then clicking the Clip Art button in the Illustrations group.
- With options at the Clip Art task pane, you can narrow the search of images to specific locations and to specific images.
- Format numbers in cells with buttons in the Number group on the Home tab. You can also apply number formatting with options at the Format Cells dialog box with the Number tab selected.
- Use options in the Page Setup group on the Page Layout tab to change worksheet margins and page orientation, insert and remove page breaks, identify specific cells for printing, and specify row and/or column titles that you want printed on each page.
- Use options in the Sheet Options group on the Page Layout tab to specify that you want gridlines, row numbers, and column letters printed.
- Create a header and/or footer with the Header & Footer button in the Text group on the Insert tab, in Page Layout view, or with options at the Page Setup dialog box with the Header/Footer tab selected.
- A chart is a visual presentation of data. Excel provides 11 basic chart types: Area, Bar, Bubble, Column, Doughnut, Line, Pyramid, Radar, Stock, Surface, and XY (Scatter).
- To create a chart, select cells containing data you want to chart, click the Insert tab, and then click the desired chart button in the Charts group.
- Data in cells used to create the chart are linked to the chart. If you change the data in cells, the chart reflects the changes.
- Use options on the Chart Tools Layout tab to change the layout and/or insert additional chart labels, shapes, pictures, or clip art images.
- Use options on the Chart Tools Format tab to customize the format of the chart and chart elements.

Key Terms

cell orientation, p. 440

clip art, p. 445

chart, p. 457

Features Summary

Feature	Ribbon Tab, Group	Button	Keyboard Shortcut
Accounting Number Format	Home, Number	$ ⌄	
Align Text Left	Home, Alignment	≡	
Align Text Right	Home, Alignment	≡	
Bold	Home, Font	**B**	Ctrl + B
Borders	Home, Font	⊞ ⌄	
Bottom Align	Home, Alignment	≡	
Center	Home, Alignment	≡	
Change Chart Type dialog box	Chart Tools Design, Type	▮▮	
Clear cell or cell contents	Home, Editing	⌁	
Decrease Decimal	Home, Number	.00 →.0	
Decrease font size	Home, Font	A⌄	
Delete cells, rows, columns	Home, Cells	▤✕	
Fill Color	Home, Font	⬙ ⌄	
Font	Home, Font	Calibri ⌄	
Font Color	Home, Font	A ⌄	
Font Size	Home, Font	11 ⌄	
Increase Decimal	Home, Number	←.0 .00	

continued

Feature	Ribbon Tab, Group	Button	Keyboard Shortcut
Increase font size	Home, Font	A	
Insert cells, rows, columns	Home, Cells		
Insert default chart in separate sheet			F11
Insert default chart in worksheet			Alt + F1
Italic	Home, Font	*I*	Ctrl + I
Merge & Center	Home, Alignment		
Middle Align	Home, Alignment		
Number Format	Home, Number	General	
Orientation	Home, Alignment		
Percent Style	Home, Number	%	Ctrl + Shift + %
Repeat			F4 or Ctrl + Y
Themes	Page Layout, Themes	Aa	
Top Align	Home, Alignment		
Underline	Home, Font	U	Ctrl + U
Wrap Text	Home, Alignment		

KEY POINTS REVIEW

Identification

Match the terms to the callouts on the Excel window in Figure 10.10.

1. _____ Insert button
2. _____ Font group
3. _____ Zoom slider bar
4. _____ chart data
5. _____ Page Layout tab
6. _____ Number Format button
7. _____ Insert tab
8. _____ pie chart
9. _____ Alignment group
10. _____ active worksheet

Figure 10.10 Identification Figure

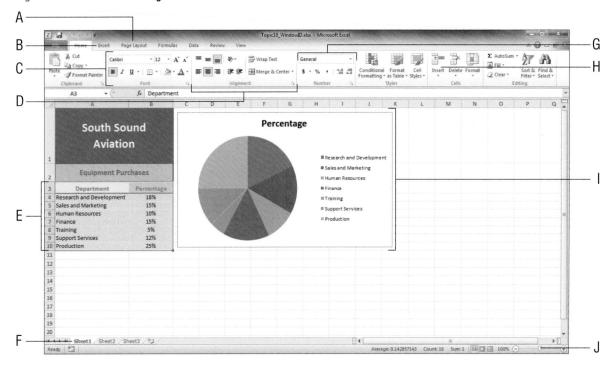

Multiple Choice

For each of the following items, choose the option that best completes the sentence or answers the question.

1. The Clear button drop-down list contains all of the following options *except* this option.
    A. Clear All
    B. Clear Cell
    C. Clear Contents
    D. Clear Hyperlinks

2. To automatically adjust the width of a column, _____ the column boundary.
    A. right-click
    B. click-drag
    C. double-click
    D. delete

3. By default, numbers are aligned at this position within a cell.
    A. right
    B. center
    C. left
    D. middle

4. Repeat the last action performed by using any of the following options *except* this option.
    A. Ctrl + Y
    B. Format Painter
    C. F4
    D. Ctrl + C

5. This is the default left and right margin measurement.
    A. 1"
    B. 200 points
    C. 0.7"
    D. 0.5"

6. This formatting option puts a dollar sign on the left side of a cell and a value on the right side.
    A. Accounting
    B. Currency
    C. Currency(0)
    D. Percent

7. This button will combine cells and place text in the middle of the resulting cell.
    A. Format
    B. Cell Styles
    C. Merge & Center
    D. AutoSum

8. This type of chart shows proportions and relationships of parts to the whole.
    A. Pie
    B. Bar
    C. Line
    D. Histogram

9. Change the direction of text contained within a cell using this button.
    A. Merge & Center
    B. Orientation
    C. Wrap Text
    D. Right Align

10. Excel includes predesigned themes and options, which are located in this group on the Page Layout tab.
    A. Format
    B. Page Setup
    C. Sheet Options
    D. Themes

Matching

Match each of the following definitions with the correct term, command, or option.

1. _____ By default, a column is inserted in this direction from the column containing the active cell.

2. _____ When you create a chart, the chart is inserted in this location by default.

3. _____ To delete a row, select the row and then click the Delete button in this group on the Home tab.

4. _____ Select data in a cell and this item displays in a dimmed fashion above the selected data.

5. _____ Click this button in the Alignment group on the Home tab to rotate data in a cell.

6. _____ This bar displays in the lower right corner of the screen and changes the percentage of display.

7. _____ The Themes button is located in the Themes group on this tab.

8. _____ If you type a number with a percent sign, such as 25%, Excel automatically applies this formatting to the number.

9. _____ This is the keyboard shortcut to create a chart with the default chart type.

10. _____ Click the Header & Footer button in the Text group on the Insert tab and the worksheet displays in this view.

A. Page Layout View
B. Percent
C. Page Layout
D. Zoom slider bar
E. Worksheet containing data
F. Alt + F1
G. Orientation
H. Mini toolbar
I. Cells
J. Left

SKILLS REVIEW

Review 10.1 Formatting a Supplies and Equipment Worksheet

1. Open **GMEquipBudget.xlsx** and then save the workbook with Save As and name it **U2T10-R1-GMEquipBudget**.
2. Select cells A1 through D19 and then change the font to Cambria and the font color to dark blue.
3. Select and then merge and center cells A1 through D1.
4. Select and then merge and center cells A2 through D2.
5. Make cell A1 active and then change the font size to 22 points and turn on bold.
6. Make cell A2 active and then change the font size to 12 points and turn on bold.
7. Change the row height of row 1 to 36.00.
8. Change the row height of row 2 to 21.00.
9. Change the width of column A to 15.00.
10. Select cells A3 through A17, turn on bold, and then click the Wrap Text button in the Alignment group.
11. Select cells A1 and A2 and then click the Middle Align button in the Alignment group.
12. Make cell B3 active and then change the number formatting to Currency with no decimal places.
13. Select cells C6 through C19 and then change the number formatting to Percentage with one decimal place.
14. Automatically adjust the width of columns B and C.
15. Make cell D6 active and then type a formula that multiplies the absolute cell reference $B$3 with the percentage in cell C6. Copy the formula down to cells D7 through D19.
16. With cells D6 through D19 selected, change the number formatting to Currency with no decimal places.

17. Make cell D8 active and then clear the cell contents. (The copied formula inserted $0 in this cell.) Use the Repeat command, F4, to clear the contents from cells D11, D14, and D17.
18. Add light blue fill color to the following cells: A1, A2, A5 through D5, A8 through D8, A11 through D11, A14 through D14, and A17 through D17.
19. Add borders and/or shading of your choosing to enhance the visual appeal of the worksheet.
20. Save, print, and then close **U2T10-GMEquipBudget.xlsx**.

Review 10.2 Creating a Company Sales Column Chart

1. Open **GMFirstHalfSales.xlsx** and then save the workbook with Save As and name it **U2T10-R2-GMFirstHalfSales**.
2. Select cells A3 through C9 and then create a column chart with the following specifications:
   a. Click the *3-D Clustered Column* chart option at the Chart button drop-down list.
   b. At the Chart Tools Design tab, click the *Layout 3* option in the Chart Layouts group.
   c. Change the chart style to *Style 26*.
   d. Select the text *Chart Title*, type **Company Sales**, and then click in the chart but outside any chart elements.
3. Move the location of the chart to a new sheet.
4. Print only the worksheet containing the chart.
5. Save and then close **U2T10-R2-GMFirstHalfSales.xlsx**.

Review 10.3 Creating a Quarterly Domestic and Foreign Sales Bar Chart

1. Open **GMTotalSales.xlsx** and then save the workbook and name it **U2T10-R3-GMTotalSales**.
2. Select cells A3 through E5 and then create a bar chart with the following specifications:
   a. Click the *Clustered Bar in 3-D* option at the Bar button drop-down list.
   b. At the Chart Tools Design tab click the *Layout 2* option in the Chart Layouts group.
   c. Click the *Style 19* option in the Chart Styles group.
   d. Select the text *Chart Title*, type **Quarterly Sales**, and then click in the chart but outside any chart elements.
3. Move the location of the chart to a new sheet.
4. Print only the worksheet containing the chart.
5. Save and then close **U2T10-R3-GMTotalSales.xlsx**.

SKILLS ASSESSMENT

Assessment 10.1 Formatting a Health Club Worksheet

1. Open **FFCPlans.xlsx** and then save the workbook and name it **U2T10-A1-FFCPlans**.
2. Make the following changes to the worksheet:
   a. Insert a new column left of the *Quarterly* column and then type **Monthly** in cell C1.
   b. Insert a new row above the *Deluxe* row and then type **Standard Plus** in cell A4.
   c. Insert a new row 1, merge and center cells A1 through D1, and then type **Ferndale Fitness Center**.
   d. Change the width of column A to 13.00 and the width of columns B, C, and D to 11.00.
   e. Select cells B3 through D8 and then change the number formatting to Accounting with two decimal places and a dollar sign symbol.
   f. Make cell B3 active and then type **500.00**.
   g. Make cell B4 active and then insert a formula that adds the amount in B3 and the product (multiplication) of B3 multiplied by 10%. (The formula should look like this: **=B3+(B3*10%)**. The Economy plan is the base plan and each additional plan costs 10% more than the previous plan.)

h. Copy the formula in cell B4 down to cells B5 through B8.
i. Insert a formula in cell C3 that divides the amount in cell B3 by 12 (the formula should look like this: **=B3/12**) and then copy the formula down to cells C4 through C8.
j. Insert a formula in cell D3 that divides the amount in cell B3 by 4 and then copy the formula down to cells D4 through D8.
3. Apply formatting to enhance the visual appeal of the worksheet.
4. Save and then print **U2T10-A1-FFCPlans.xlsx**.
5. Change the yearly dues in cell B3 from *$500.00* to *$600.00*.
6. If clients are late with their quarterly or monthly dues payments, a late fee is charged. Select column D and then insert a new column. Type **Late Fees** in cell D2 and also in cell F2.
7. Insert a formula in cell D3 that multiplies the amount in C3 by 5%. Copy this formula down to cells D4 through D8.
8. Insert a formula in cell F3 that multiplies the amount in cell E3 by 7%. Copy this formula down to cells F4 through F8. If necessary, change the number formatting for cells F3 through F8 to Accounting with two decimal places and a dollar sign symbol.
9. Make any adjustments to table formatting needed to maintain consistency.
10. Save, print, and then close **U2T10-A1-FFCPlans.xlsx**.

Assessment 10.2 Formatting a Data Analysis Worksheet

1. Open **EMSales.xlsx** and then save the workbook and name it **U2T10-A2-EMSales**.
2. Insert a formula in cell H4 that averages the amounts in cells B4 through G4. Copy the formula in cell H4 down to cells H5 through H11.
3. Insert a formula in cell B12 that adds the amounts in cells B4 through B11. Copy the formula in cell B12 over to cells C12 through H12.
4. Select cells B11 through H11 and then insert a single-line bottom border.
5. Automatically adjust the width of columns A through H.
6. Change the orientation of the worksheet to *Landscape*.
7. Change the top margin to 3 inches and the left margin to 1.2 inches.
8. Save and then print **U2T10-A2-EMSales.xlsx**.
9. Horizontally and vertically center the worksheet on the page and change the top margin to 1 inch.
10. Change the orientation back to *Portrait*.
11. Insert a header that prints the workbook name.
12. Insert a footer that prints your name, the page number, and the current date.
13. Save, print, and then close **U2T10-A2-EMSales.xlsx**.

Assessment 10.3 Creating a Funds Allocation Pie Chart

1. At a clear worksheet window, create a worksheet with the following data:

Budget Allocation

Department	Percentage
Production	47%
Research	23%
Human Resources	18%
Finance	12%

2. Using the data above, create a pie chart as a separate worksheet with the following specifications:
a. Create a title for the pie chart.
b. Add data labels to the chart.
c. Add any other enhancements that will improve the visual presentation of the data.
3. Save the workbook and name it **U2T10-A3-BudgetChart**.
4. Print only the worksheet containing the chart.
5. Close **U2T10-A3-BudgetChart.xlsx**.

Assessment 10.4 Formatting a Financial Analysis Worksheet

1. Use the Help feature to learn how to insert a picture from a file into a worksheet.
2. Open **FinAnalysis.xlsx** and then save the workbook and name it **U2T10-A4-FinAnalysis**.
3. Make cell B9 active and then insert a formula that averages the percentages in cells B3 through B8. Copy the formula to the right to cells C9 and D9.
4. Increase the height of row 1 to 90.00.
5. Insert the file named **GMLogo.jpg** into the worksheet.
6. Move and size the logo so it fits in cell A1.
7. Save, print, and then close **U2T10-A4-FinAnalysis.xlsx**.

Assessment 10.5 Preparing and Formatting an Equipment Worksheet

1. Using the Internet, search for the following fitness center equipment for a local fitness center:
   - Search for elliptical machines for sale. Locate two different models and, if possible, find at least two companies that sell both models. Make a note of the company names, model numbers, and prices.
   - Search for recumbent bikes for sale. Locate two different models and, if possible, find at least two companies that sell both models. Make a note of the company names, model numbers, and prices.
   - Search for upright bikes for sale. Locate two different models and, if possible, find at least two companies that sell both models. Make a note of the company names, model numbers, and prices.
2. Using the information you found on the Internet, prepare an Excel worksheet with the following information:
   - Equipment name
   - Equipment model
   - Price
   - A column that multiplies the price by the number of units required for the fitness center (which is 5).
3. Include the fitness center name, Ferndale Fitness Center, and any other information you determine is necessary to the worksheet.
4. Apply formatting to enhance the appearance of the worksheet.
5. Save the workbook and name it **U2T10-A5-Equipment**.
6. Print and then close **U2T10-A5-Equipment.xlsx**.

Assessment 10.6 Creating a Budget Pie Chart

1. Use the following information to calculate the percentage of the budget for each item and then create a pie chart (in a separate worksheet) with the information. You determine the chart style, layout, and formatting.

   Total Budget: $6,000,000

Building Costs	=	$720,000
Salaries	=	$2,340,000
Benefits	=	$480,000
Advertising	=	$840,000
Marketing	=	$600,000
Client Expenses	=	$480,000
Equipment	=	$420,000
Supplies	=	$120,000

2. Save the workbook and name it **U2T10-A6-DeptChart**.
3. Print the worksheet containing the data and print the worksheet containing the pie chart.
4. Close **U2T10-A6-DeptChart.xlsx**.

CRITICAL THINKING

Selecting the Most Appropriate Chart

Read the following three scenarios and identify what type of chart (bar, column, pie, or scatter chart) would best accomplish the desired effect. Write a sentence explaining which chart you would use for each scenario and why.

1. The VP of Accounting has asked for a chart that will portray the company's different expense categories in percentages.

   _____

   _____

2. The VP of Accounting has asked for a chart that will portray the company's expense categories in relation to the total amount of expenses for each of the last five years.

   _____

   _____

3. A researcher has asked for a chart that will portray the relationship between an individual's IQ and age using a sample of 100 people of all different ages.

   _____

   _____

TEAM PROJECT

Enhancing the Visual Appeal of Data

1. As a team, open the workbook **TeamProject1.xlsx** and then save the workbook and name it **U2T10-TeamProject1**. Also, open the workbook **TeamProject2.xlsx** and then save the workbook and name it **U2T10-TeamProject2**.
2. Apply formatting to each of the workbooks to enhance the visual appeal of the data.
3. As a team, discuss and then choose a chart that best portrays the data visually for each of the data series.
4. Create and insert the charts beneath each data series and apply formatting to improve the visual display of the charts.
5. Save, print, and then close both **U2T10-TeamProject1.xlsx** and **U2T10-TeamProject2.xlsx**.

Discussion Questions

1. Explain why the team chose the formatting it did for the worksheet data.
2. Explain why the team selected the particular chart types to represent the data in each worksheet and explain what formatting the team applied to each chart.
3. Compare your team's worksheets and charts with the ones created by other teams. What are the similarities and differences?
4. As a class, choose the chart that best represents the data in each workbook.

Topic 11

Preparing A Presentation

Performance Objectives

Upon successful completion of Topic 11, you will be able to:

- Prepare a presentation
- Choose a design theme
- Create slides
- Navigate in a presentation
- Print a presentation
- Run a presentation
- Add transitions to a presentation
- Add sound to a presentation
- Check spelling of text in a presentation
- Rearrange and delete slides
- Apply fonts and font effects
- Apply paragraph formatting
- Insert headers and footers

STUDENT RESOURCES

Before beginning this topic, copy to your storage medium the **Unit2Topic11** subfolder from the *Computer and Internet Essentials: Preparing for IC³* Internet Resource Center. Make this the active folder.

In addition to containing the data files needed to complete topic work, the Internet Resource Center contains model answers in PDF format for each of the applicable exercises in this topic. Use these files to check your work. The preface of your textbook provides instructions for accessing these files.

Necessary Data Files

To complete the exercises and assessments, you will need the following data files:

Exercise 11.1	CFJobSearch.pptx
Exercise 11.2	New file
Exercises 11.3–11.6	Previously created file (Ex. 11.2)
Exercises 11.7–11.11	CFResumeStrategies.pptx
Review 11.1	New file
Review 11.2	New file
Assessment 11.1	New file
Assessment 11.2	CTToronto.pptx
Assessment 11.3	CTEnglandTour.pptx
Assessment 11.4	New file
Assessment 11.5	New file
Team Project	CTHawaiiTour.pptx

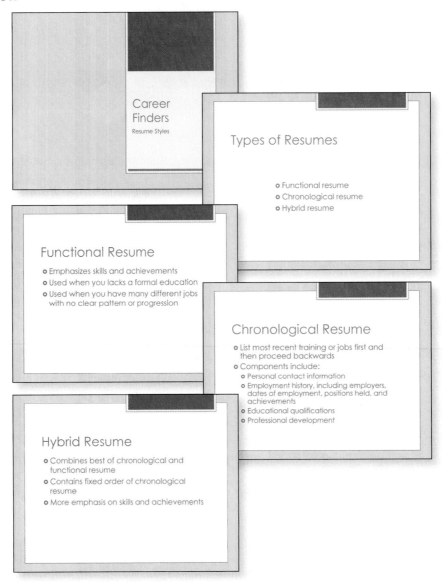

Career Finders
Resume Styles

Types of Resumes

- Functional resume
- Chronological resume
- Hybrid resume

Functional Resume

- Emphasizes skills and achievements
- Used when you lacks a formal education
- Used when you have many different jobs with no clear pattern or progression

Chronological Resume

- List most recent training or jobs first and then proceed backwards
- Components include:
  - Personal contact information
  - Employment history, including employers, dates of employment, positions held, and achievements
  - Educational qualifications
  - Professional development

Hybrid Resume

- Combines best of chronological and functional resume
- Contains fixed order of chronological resume
- More emphasis on skills and achievements

Exercises 11.2–11.6 **U2T11-Resumes.pptx**

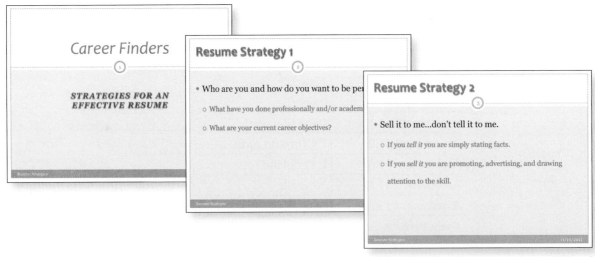

Career Finders
①
STRATEGIES FOR AN EFFECTIVE RESUME

Resume Strategy 1
②

- Who are you and how do you want to be per
  - What have you done professionally and/or academ
  - What are your current career objectives?

Resume Strategy 2
③

- Sell it to me...don't tell it to me.
  - If you *tell it* you are simply stating facts.
  - If you *sell it* you are promoting, advertising, and drawing attention to the skill.

continued

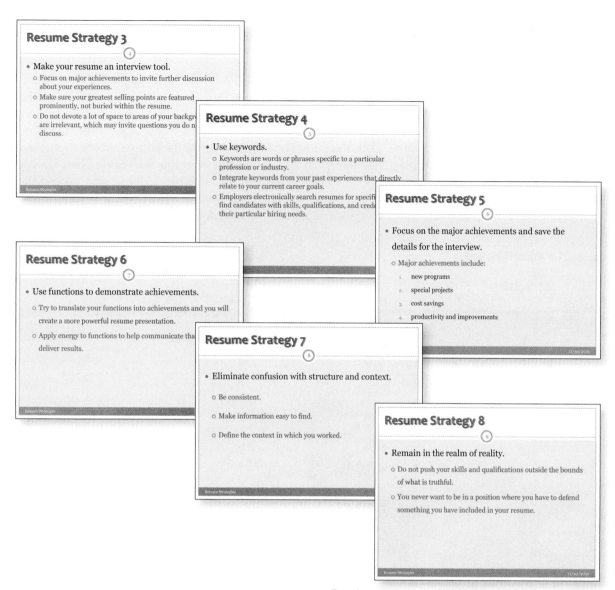

Exercises 11.7–11.11 **U2T11-CFResume Strategies.pptx**

Topic Overview

You can create colorful and powerful presentations using PowerPoint, Microsoft's presentation program. PowerPoint presentations allow you to create informative and visually appealing slides that can be used to facilitate meetings, teach complex concepts, or illustrate a point. PowerPoint presentations are versatile and can be presented in person, delivered over the Internet, or printed to be used as a handout. Prepare a presentation using a template provided by PowerPoint or create your own presentation and apply formatting with a design theme. Preparing a presentation consists of general steps such as creating and editing slides; adding enhancements to slides; and saving, running, previewing, printing, and closing a presentation. In this topic, you will learn how to format text in slides and apply transitions and sound to create visually appealing PowerPoint presentations.

IC³ 2-4.1.1, 2-4.1.3, 2-4.1.11

When working in PowerPoint, you complete a number of steps to prepare a presentation, including opening PowerPoint; creating and editing slides; saving, printing, running, and closing the presentation; and then closing PowerPoint. Follow steps similar to those in Word and Excel to open, save, and close a presentation. To run a presentation, click the Slide Show button in the view area on the Status bar or click the Slide Show tab and then click the From Beginning button in the Start Slide Show group. Navigate through slides in the presentation by clicking the left mouse button. If you want to end the slide show without viewing all of the slides in the presentation, press the Esc key on your keyboard. The elements of the PowerPoint screen are identified in Figure 11.1 and described in Table 11.1.

Figure 11.1 PowerPoint Screen

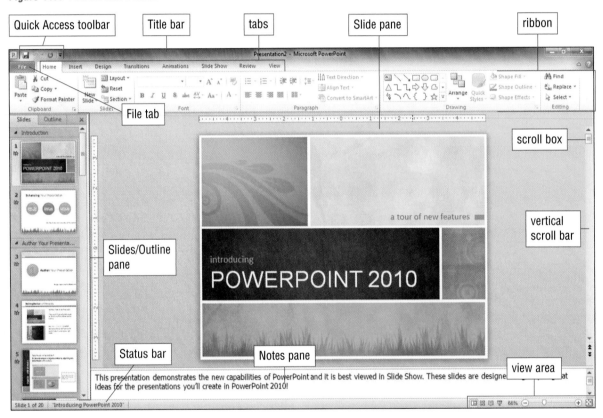

Table 11.1 PowerPoint Screen Elements

Feature	Description
Quick Access toolbar	Contains buttons for commonly-used commands
File tab	When clicked, displays the Backstage view containing tabs and buttons for working with and managing presentations
Title bar	Displays the presentation name followed by the program name
Tabs	Contains commands and features organized into groups
Ribbon	Contains the tabs and commands divided into groups

continued

Feature	Description
Slides/Outline pane	Displays at the left side of the window with two tabs—Slides and Outline; with the Slides tab selected, slide thumbnails display in the pane; with the Outline tab selected, presentation contents display in the pane
Slide pane	Displays the slide and slide contents
Notes pane	Displays notes that have been added to the presentation
Vertical scroll bar	Used to display different slides in a presentation
Horizontal scroll bar	Used to shift text left or right in the Slide pane
I-beam pointer	Used to move the insertion point or to select text
Insertion point	Indicates location of the next character entered at the keyboard
View area	Located toward the right side of the Status bar; contains button for changing the presentation view
Status bar	Displays the slide number and number of slides, name of the applied design theme, view buttons, and the Zoom slider bar

Exercise 11.1 Completing the Presentation Cycle

1. Open PowerPoint by clicking Start, pointing to *All Programs*, clicking *Microsoft Office*, and then clicking *Microsoft PowerPoint 2010*.

   Depending on your operating system, these steps may vary.

2. At the PowerPoint window, click the File tab and then click the Open button.

3. At the Open dialog box, navigate to the **Unit2Topic11** folder on your storage medium and then double-click *CFJobSearch.pptx* in the content pane.

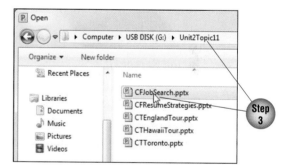

4. Save the presentation by clicking the File tab and then clicking the Save As button.

5. At the Save As dialog box, press the Home key on the keyboard to move the insertion point to the beginning of the file name, type **U2T11-**, and then press Enter.

   Pressing the Home key saves you from having to type the entire file name.

6. Run the presentation by clicking the Slide Show tab and then clicking the From Beginning button in the Start Slide Show group.

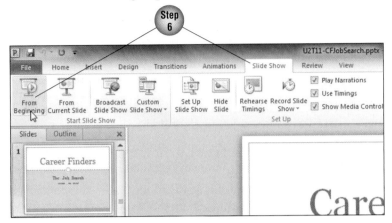

Step 6

7. When the first slide fills the screen, read the information that displays in the slide and then click the left mouse button. Use the left mouse button to advance the slides and continue reading the information in each slide. When a black screen displays, click the left mouse button to end the slide show.

8. Click the From Beginning button in the Start Slide Show group to begin running the presentation and then press the Esc key on your keyboard to end the presentation.

9. Close the presentation by clicking the File tab and then clicking the Close button.

   If a message displays asking if you want to save the presentation, click Yes.

10. Close PowerPoint by clicking the Close button in the upper-right corner of the screen.

    You can also close PowerPoint by clicking the File tab and then clicking the Exit button.

Drilling Down

Using ScreenTips

PowerPoint, like other Microsoft Office programs, provides enhanced ScreenTips for buttons and options. Hover the mouse arrow pointer on a button or option and, after approximately one second, an enhanced ScreenTip displays with the name of the button or option, a shortcut command if one is available, and a description of the button or option.

Lesson 11.2 Choosing a Theme and Creating Slides

 2-4.1.2, 2-4.1.4, 2-4.1.5

Quick Steps

Choose a Design Theme
1. Click File tab.
2. Click More button at right side of design theme thumbnails.
3. Click desired theme at drop-down gallery.

PowerPoint provides a number of predesigned themes you can use when creating slides for a presentation. These themes include formatting such as color, background, and fonts. Display these predesigned themes by clicking the Design tab and then clicking the More button that displays at the right side of the design theme thumbnails in the Themes group. At the drop-gallery that displays, click the desired theme. Hover the mouse arrow pointer over one of the design themes and the slide in the Slide pane displays with the design theme formatting applied. This is an example of the Live Preview feature. Recall that the Live Preview feature allows you to view a design theme before actually applying it to the presentation.

You can also customize a design theme by changing the theme colors and/or fonts. To change the design theme colors, click the Colors button in the Themes group and then click the desired color option at the drop-down gallery. Change the design fonts by clicking the Fonts button and then clicking the desired option. You can further customize a design theme with the buttons in the Background group. Apply a different background with options from the Background Styles button or hide the background by clicking the *Hide Background Graphics* check box.

When you open PowerPoint, a blank presentation displays with one slide in the Title Slide layout. This layout provides two text placeholders for text—title and subtitle. Recall that in PowerPoint a placeholder is a box in a slide layout that holds title and body text or an object such as a picture, chart, or table. You can change the slide layout by using the Layout button in the Slides group on the Home tab. Click the Layout button and a drop-down list of layouts displays. Click the desired layout to apply it to the current slide.

Create a new slide in a presentation by clicking the New Slide button in the Slides group on the Home tab. By default, PowerPoint inserts a new slide with the Title and Content layout. You can choose a different layout for the new slide by clicking the New Slide button arrow and then clicking the desired layout at the drop-down list. When you insert a new slide in a presentation, the slide is inserted immediately after the currently active slide.

To insert text in a placeholder in a slide, click the placeholder text. This selects the placeholder, moves the insertion point inside the placeholder, and removes the default placeholder text. With the insertion point positioned in the placeholder, type the desired text. You can edit text in a placeholder in the same way you would edit text in a Word document. You can use keys on the keyboard to move the insertion point to various locations within the text in a placeholder. Refer to Table 11.2 for a list of placeholder insertion point movement commands.

Quick Steps

Choose a Slide Layout

1. Click Layout button in Slides group on Home tab.
2. Click desired layout option at drop-down list.

Insert a New Slide

Click New Slide button in Slides group on Home tab.

Size a Placeholder

1. Click inside placeholder.
2. Drag sizing handles to increase or decrease size.

Move a Placeholder

1. Click inside placeholder.
2. Position mouse arrow pointer on border until pointer displays as a four-headed arrow.
3. Hold down left mouse button.
4. Drag to desired location.
5. Release mouse button.

Keyboard Shortcut

Insert New Slide

Ctrl + M

Table 11.2 **Placeholder Insertion Point Movement Commands**

To move insertion point within text in placeholder	Press
One character left	Left Arrow
One character right	Right Arrow
One line up	Up Arrow
One line down	Down Arrow
One word to the left	Ctrl + Left Arrow
One word to the right	Ctrl + Right Arrow
To end of a line of text	End
To beginning of a line of text	Home
To beginning of current paragraph	Ctrl + Up Arrow
To beginning of previous paragraph	Ctrl + Up Arrow twice
To beginning of next paragraph	Ctrl + Down Arrow
To beginning of text	Ctrl + Home
To end of text	Ctrl + End

An active placeholder displays surrounded by a dashed border with sizing handles and a green rotation handle. Drag the sizing handles to increase or decrease the size of the placeholder. You can move an active placeholder by positioning the mouse arrow pointer on the border of the placeholder until the pointer displays with a four-headed arrow attached, holding down the left mouse button, dragging to the desired location in the slide, and then releasing the mouse button.

A PowerPoint presentation screen displays in Normal view with three panes available for entering text—the Slides/Outline pane, Slide pane, and Notes pane. Use either the Slide pane or the Slides/Outline pane with the Outline tab selected to enter text in a slide. Use the Notes pane to type a note in a slide.

Exercise 11.2 Choosing a Design Theme and Creating New Slides

1. Open PowerPoint.

2. At the PowerPoint window, click the Design tab.

3. Click the More button at the right side of the design theme thumbnails in the Themes group and then click the *Austin* theme.

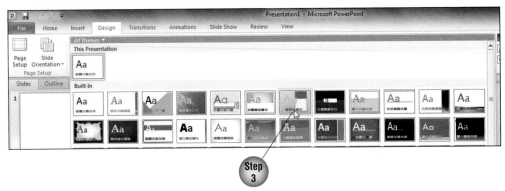

4. Change the theme colors by clicking the Colors button in the Themes group and then clicking *Equity* at the drop-down gallery.

5. Change the theme fonts by clicking the Fonts button in the Themes group, scrolling down the drop-down gallery, and then clicking the *Essential* option.

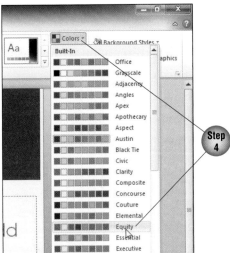

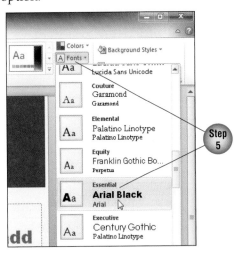

6. Click the Background Styles button in the Background group and then click the *Style 9* option (first option from the left in the third row).

7. Click anywhere in the text *Click to add title* that displays in the slide in the Slide pane and then type **Career Finders**.

   Clicking in the text removes the text and moves the insertion point inside the top placeholder.

8. Click anywhere in the text *Click to add subtitle* that displays in the slide and then type **Resume Styles**.

   Clicking in the subtitle placeholder text removes the text and moves the insertion point inside the bottom placeholder.

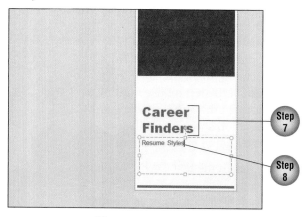

9. Click the Home tab and then click the New Slide button in the Slides group.

   When you click this button, a new slide with the Title and Content layout displays in the Slide pane.

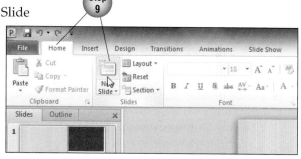

10. Click anywhere in the text *Click to add title* that displays in the slide and then type **Types of Resumes**.

11. Click anywhere in the text *Click to add text* that displays in the slide and then type **Functional resume**.

12. Press the Enter key and then type **Chronological resume**. Press the Enter key again and then type **Hybrid resume**.

    Refer to Table 11.2 for a list of placeholder insertion point movement commands.

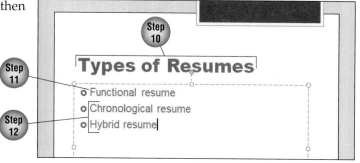

13. With the placeholder selected, decrease the size by positioning the mouse arrow pointer on the bottom sizing handle on the right border until the pointer turns into a double-headed arrow pointing diagonally up and to the left and down and to the right. Hold down the left mouse button, drag up and to the left until the border is near the bulleted text, and then release the mouse button.

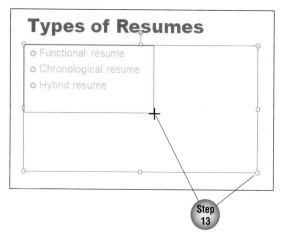

14. Move the placeholder so it is positioned as shown in the image at the right. To do this, position the mouse arrow pointer on the placeholder border until the pointer displays with a four-headed arrow attached, hold down the left mouse button, drag to the approximate location shown, and then release the mouse button.

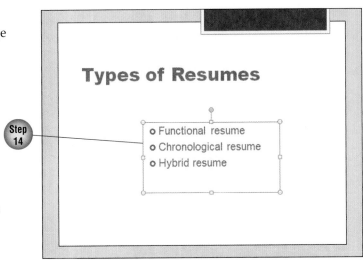

15. Click in the text *Click to add notes* in the Notes pane and then type **Include information on resume types for the Internet.**

16. Click the New Slide button in the Slides group on the Home tab.

17. Click the Outline tab at the top of the Slides/Outline pane.

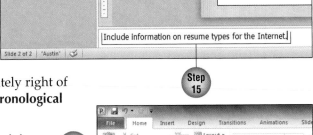

18. Click in the Slides/Outline pane immediately right of the slide icon after the number 3, type **Chronological Resume** and then press Enter.

19. Press the Tab key, type **List most recent training or jobs first and then proceed backwards** and then press the Enter key.

    Pressing the Tab key demotes the insertion point to the next level while pressing Shift + Tab promotes the insertion point to the previous level.

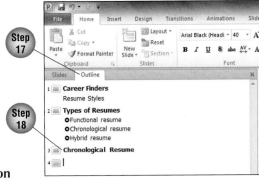

20. Type **Components include:** and then press Enter.

21. Press the Tab key, type **Personal contact information** and then press Enter.

22. Type **Employment history, including employers, dates of employment, positions held, and achievements** and then press Enter.

23. Type **Educational qualifications** and then press Enter.

24. Type **Professional development**.

25. Click the Slides tab located toward the top of the Slides/Outline pane.

26. Click the Save button on the Quick Access toolbar.

27. At the Save As dialog box, make sure the **Unit2Topic11** folder on your storage medium is the active folder, type **U2T11-Resumes** in the *File name* text box, and then press Enter.

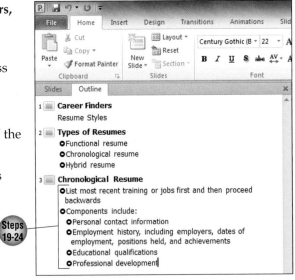

Using Tabs

PowerPoint commands and features are organized into command tabs that display in the ribbon area below the Quick Access toolbar. Commands and features are organized into groups within a tab. For example, the Home tab contains the Clipboard, Slides, Font, Paragraph, Drawing, and Editing groups. Hover the mouse over a button and a ScreenTip displays with the name of the button, a keyboard shortcut (if available), and a description of the purpose of the button.

Lesson 11.3 Navigating in a Presentation

 2-4.1.1

In the Normal view, change the slide that displays in the Slide pane by clicking the Previous Slide or Next Slide buttons located at the bottom of the vertical scroll bar. You can also change to a different slide using the mouse arrow pointer on the vertical scroll bar. To do this, position the mouse arrow pointer on the scroll box on the vertical scroll bar, hold down the left mouse button, drag up or down until a box displays with the desired slide number, and then release the button.

You can use the keyboard to display slides in a presentation. In Normal view, press the Down Arrow or Page Down key to display the next slide or press the Up Arrow or Page Up key to display the previous slide in the presentation. Press the Home key to display the first slide in the presentation and press the End key to display the last slide in the presentation. Navigate in the Slides/Outline pane with the Slides tab selected by clicking the desired slide thumbnail.

Exercise 11.3 Navigating in a Presentation

1. With **U2T11-Resumes.pptx** open, press the Home key to display the first slide in the Slide pane.

2. Navigate in the presentation by clicking the Next Slide button ⬇ located at the bottom of the vertical scroll bar.

   Clicking this button displays the next slide, Slide 2, in the presentation. Notice that *Slide 2 of 3* displays at the left side of the Status bar.

3. Click the Previous Slide button ⬆ located toward the bottom of the vertical scroll bar to display Slide 1.

   When you click the Previous Slide button, *Slide 1 of 3* displays at the left side of the Status bar.

4. Display Slide 2 in the Slide pane by clicking the Next Slide button located at the bottom of the vertical scroll bar.

5. Insert a new slide between Slides 2 and 3 by clicking the New Slide button in the Slides group.

6. Click anywhere in the text *Click to add title* in the slide that displays in the Slide pane and then type **Functional Resume**.

7. Click anywhere in the text *Click to add text* in the slide and then type the bulleted text as shown at the right. Press the Enter key after each item *except* the last item.

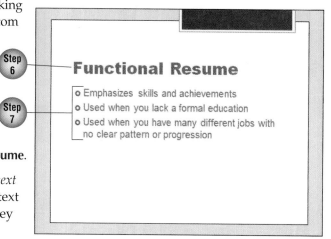

Functional Resume

○ Emphasizes skills and achievements
○ Used when you lack a formal education
○ Used when you have many different jobs with no clear pattern or progression

8. Click the Outline tab located at the top of the Slides/Outline pane.

9. Click immediately right of the text *Professional development* located at the end of the pane, press the Enter key, and then press Shift + Tab two times.

   This moves the insertion point back two levels and inserts the number 5 followed by a slide icon.

10. Type **Hybrid Resume**, press the Enter key, and then press the Tab key. Type the remaining text for Slide 5 as shown. Do not press the Enter key after typing *More emphasis on skills and achievements*.

   When you are finished typing the text, the presentation will contain five slides.

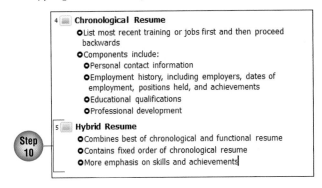

11. Click the Slides tab located toward the top of the Slides/Outline pane.

12. Click the Save button in the Quick Access toolbar to save **U2T11-Resumes.pptx**.

Drilling Down

Using Installed Templates

Microsoft provides a number of predesigned presentation templates you can view and use to prepare your own presentation. To display the installed templates, click the File tab and then click the New tab. This displays the New tab Backstage view. In this view, available templates and themes display as well as online templates. To display available templates, click the *Sample templates* option in the Available Templates and Themes category. To open a template presentation, double-click the desired template.

Lesson 11.4   Printing a Presentation and Changing the Zoom Display

IC³ 2-4.1.3, 2-4.1.8, 2-4.1.9, 2-4.1.10

Keyboard Shortcut

Display Print Tab
Backstage View

Ctrl + P

You can print a PowerPoint presentation in a variety of formats. You can print each slide on a separate piece of paper; print each slide at the top of the page, leaving the bottom of the page for writing comments or notes; print up to nine slides on a single piece of paper; print speaker notes (text located in the Notes pane) with slides; or print the slide titles and topics in outline form. Use options at the Print tab Backstage view, shown in Figure 11.2, to specify what and how you want to print. Display this view by clicking the File tab and then clicking the Print tab.

Figure 11.2 Print Tab Backstage View

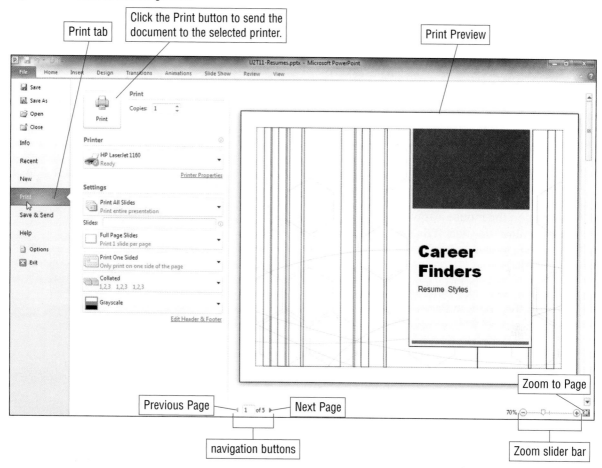

Print tab

Click the Print button to send the document to the selected printer.

Print Preview

Previous Page

Next Page

navigation buttons

Zoom to Page

Zoom slider bar

Quick Steps

Print a Presentation

1. Click File tab.
2. Click Print tab.
3. Click Print button.

Like other Office applications, the left side of the Print tab Backstage view in PowerPoint contains three categories—Print, Printer, and Settings. Click the Print button in the Print category to send the presentation to the printer, and use the *Copies* option to specify the number of copies you want to print. The two other categories contain galleries. For example, use the gallery in the Printer category to specify the desired printer. Click the first gallery in the Settings category and options display for specifying what you want printed, such as all of the presentation or a few specific slides. The Settings category also contains a number of galleries that describe how the slides will print.

In the Settings category, you can use a hyphen to specify a range of slides you want to print and commas to specify a list of slides you want to print. For example, to print Slides 2 through 6, you would type *2-6* in the *Slides* text box. To print Slides 1, 3, and 5, you would type *1,3,5*. You can also combine hyphens and commas. For example, to print Slides 1 through 3 and Slide 7, you would type *1-3,7*.

A preview of how a slide or slides will print displays at the right side of the Print tab Backstage view. Use the Next Page button and Previous Page button to navigate in the presentation, use the Zoom slider bar to increase or decrease the size of the slide(s) in the viewing area, and click the Zoom to Page button to fit the slide in the viewing area.

You can choose to print a presentation as individual slides, handouts, notes pages, or an outline. If you print a presentation as a handout or an outline, PowerPoint will automatically print the current date in the upper right corner of the page and the page number in the lower right corner. If you print the presentation as notes pages, PowerPoint will automatically print the page number in the lower right corner. PowerPoint does not insert the date or page number automatically when you print individual slides.

In addition to the Zoom slider bar on the Print tab Backstage view, the Status bar in the PowerPoint window contains a Zoom slider bar you can use to increase or decrease the size of the slide display in the Slide pane. A Fit slide to current window button displays to the right of the Zoom slider bar on the Status bar. Click this button to change the Zoom percentage so the slide fits in the Slide pane.

Exercise 11.4 Printing a Presentation and Changing Zoom Display

1. With **U2T11-Resumes.pptx** open, press the Home key to display Slide 1 in the Slide pane, click the File tab, and then click the Print tab.

2. At the Print tab Backstage view, click the Next Page button located below and at the left side of the slide in the viewing area to display Slide 2 in the presentation.

3. Position the mouse arrow pointer on the Zoom slider bar button (located at the bottom right of the Print tab Backstage view), drag the button to the right to increase the size of the slide in the viewing area, and then drag the button to the left to decrease the size.

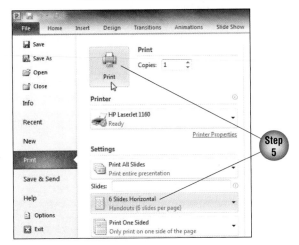

4. Click the Zoom to Page button ⊞ located to the right of the Zoom slider bar.

   This adjusts the size of the slide to fill the viewing area on the Print tab Backstage view.

5. Print the presentation as a handout with six slides horizontally per page by clicking the *Full Page Slides* option (the second gallery) in the Settings category, clicking *6 Slides Horizontal* in the *Handouts* section, and then clicking the Print button.

6. Print Slide 2 as a notes page. To begin, click the File tab and then click the Print tab to display the Print tab Backstage view.

7. Click in the *Slides* text box located in the Settings category and then type **2**.

8. Click the *6 Slides Horizontal* option in the Settings category, click *Notes Pages* in the *Print Layout* section, and then click the Print button.

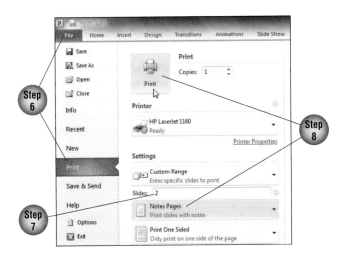

9. Print Slides 1 through 3 and Slide 5. Begin by displaying the Print tab Backstage view.

10. Select the number 2 in the *Slides* text box located in the Settings category and then type **1-3,5**.

11. Click the *Notes Pages* option in the Settings category, click *4 Slides Horizontal* in the *Handouts* section, and then click the Print button.

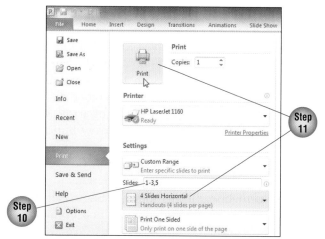

12. Print the presentation as an outline. Begin by displaying the Print tab Backstage view.

13. Select and then delete the numbers *1-3,5* in the *Slides* text box.

14. Click the *4 Slides Horizontal* option in the Settings category, click *Outline* in the *Print Layout* section, and then click the Print button.

15. Increase the display of the slide in the Slide pane by clicking three times on the Zoom In button ⊕ that displays at the right side of the Zoom slider bar on the Status bar.

16. Decrease the size of the slide in the Slide pane by clicking the Fit slide to current window button that displays at the right side of the Zoom slider bar.

17. Save **U2T11-Resumes.pptx**.

Drilling Down

Changing Views

PowerPoint provides a variety of viewing options for a presentation. You can change the view with buttons in the view area on the Status bar or with options in the Presentation Views group on the View tab. The viewing choices include:

- **Normal view:** This is the default view and displays three panes—Slides/Outline, Slide, and Notes. With these three panes, you can work with all features in one place and write and design your presentation.
- **Slide Sorter view:** Clicking the Slide Sorter view displays all slides in the presentation in slide thumbnails. In this view, you can easily add, move, rearrange, and delete slides.
- **Notes Page view:** Change to the Notes Page view and an individual slide displays on a page with any added notes displayed below the slide.
- **Reading view:** Use the Reading view when you deliver your presentation to someone viewing the presentation on his or her own computer. Or, use this to view the presentation in a window with controls that make the presentation easy to view.
- **Slide Show view:** Use the Slide Show view to run a presentation. When you select this view, the slide fills the screen.

2-4.1.3, 2-4.1.11

You can run a presentation by clicking the Slide Show button in the view area on the Status bar or by clicking the Slide Show tab and then clicking the From Beginning button in the Start Slide Show group (or press F5). This group also contains a From Current Slide button. Use this button (or press Shift + F5) to begin running the slide show from the currently active slide rather than the first slide in the presentation.

You can also run a presentation using buttons on the Slide Show toolbar. To display this toolbar, run the presentation and then move the mouse arrow pointer. The Slide Show toolbar displays dimmed in the lower left corner of the screen. Click the right arrow button on the toolbar to display the next slide and click the left arrow button to display the previous slide. Click the slide icon button and a pop-up menu displays with the following options: *Next, Previous, Last Viewed, Go to Slide, Custom Show, Screen, Help, Pause,* and *End Show.* Use these options to navigate to a particular slide in the presentation, display the Slide Show Help window, and pause or end the show. Click the pen button and a pop-up menu displays with the following options: *Arrow, Pen, Highlighter, Ink Color, Eraser, Erase All Ink on Slide,* and *Arrow Options.* Click the *Pen* option and the mouse pointer displays as a small dot. Using the mouse, you can draw lines in a slide to draw attention to a specific item on the slide. Choose the *Highlighter* option and the mouse pointer displays as a small, yellow rectangle. Drag in the slide to highlight content. Return to the mouse arrow pointer by clicking the *Arrow* option at the pop-up menu. Use the *Ink Color* option to choose a specific color for drawing with the pen in a slide. Click the *Eraser* option and the mouse pointer displays as a whiteboard eraser. Erase a line from the slide that you drew with the pen or highlighter by clicking the specific line or highlighting. Erase all lines you drew with the pen or highlighting you inserted in a slide by clicking the *Erase All Ink on Slide* option.

PowerPoint provides keyboard commands for navigating through slides during a presentation. These keyboard commands are identified in the Slide Show Help window shown in Figure 11.3. Display this window by running the presentation, clicking the slide icon button on the Slide Show toolbar, and then clicking *Help* at the pop-up menu. You can also display a specific slide during a presentation by typing the slide number and then pressing the Enter key.

Figure 11.3 Slide Show Help Window

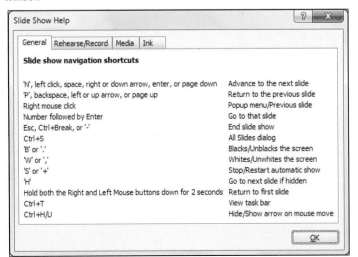

Exercise 11.5 Running a Presentation

1. With **U2T11-Resumes. pptx** open, click the Slide Show tab and then click the From Beginning button in the Start Slide Show group.

    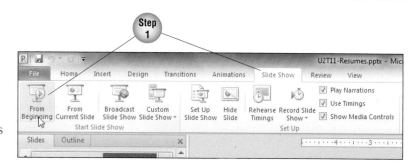

    Clicking this button begins the presentation. Slide 1 fills the entire screen.

2. After viewing Slide 1, click the left mouse button to advance to the next slide.

3. After viewing Slide 2, click the left mouse button to advance to the next slide.

4. At Slide 3, move the mouse arrow pointer until the Slide Show toolbar displays in the lower left corner of the slide, and then click the left arrow button on the toolbar to display the previous slide (Slide 2).

5. Click the right arrow button on the Slide Show toolbar to display the next slide (Slide 3).

6. Display the previous slide (Slide 2) by clicking the right mouse button and then clicking *Previous* at the shortcut menu.

    Clicking the right mouse button causes a shortcut menu to display with a variety of options including options to display the previous or next slide.

7. Display the next slide by clicking the slide icon button on the Slide Show toolbar and then clicking the *Next* option.

8. Display Slide 5 by typing the number **5** on the keyboard and then pressing Enter.

    Move to any slide in a presentation by typing the slide number and pressing Enter.

9. Change to a black screen by typing the letter **B** on the keyboard.

    When you type the letter B, the slide is removed from the screen and the screen displays black. This might be useful in a situation where you want to discuss something with your audience unrelated to the slide.

10. Return to Slide 5 by typing the letter **B** on the keyboard.

    Typing the letter B switches between the slide and a black screen. Type the letter W if you want to switch between the slide and a white screen.

11. Click the left mouse button to display the black screen at the end of the presentation. At the black screen, click the left mouse button again.

    This returns the presentation to the Normal view.

12. Display Slide 2 by clicking the Next Slide button located at the bottom of the vertical scroll bar.

13. Click the From Current Slide button ⬚ in the Start Slide Show group in the Slide Show tab.

    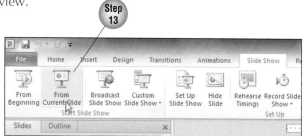

    Clicking this button begins the presentation with the active slide.

14. Run the presentation by clicking the left mouse button at each slide. At the black screen, click the left mouse button again.

15. Press the Home key to display Slide 1 in the Slide pane.

16. Save **U2T11-Resumes.pptx**.

Drilling Down

Hiding and Displaying the Mouse Arrow Pointer During a Presentation

During a presentation, the mouse arrow pointer is set, by default, to disappear after three seconds of inactivity. The mouse arrow pointer will appear again when you move the mouse. You can change this default setting by clicking the pen button on the Slide Show toolbar, pointing to *Arrow Options*, and then clicking *Visible* if you always want the mouse arrow pointer to be visible during the presentation or *Hidden* if you do not want the mouse to display at all during the presentation. The *Automatic* option is the default setting.

Lesson 11.6 Adding Transitions and Transition Sounds to a Presentation

 2-4.1.6

transition The way in which one slide is removed from the screen and the next slide displays when running a presentation

You can apply interesting transitions and transition sounds to a presentation. A **transition** is the way in which one slide is removed from the screen during a presentation and the next slide displays. Interesting and exciting transitions include cuts, fades, pushes, wipes, splits, reveals, and random bars. Transition sound can be added to slides as well. Add a sound to a transition and the sound plays when the slides change. Add transitions and transition sounds with options on the Transitions tab. To apply the transition and transition sound to all sides in the presentation, click the Apply To All button in the Timing group on the Transitions tab. Use the *Duration* option in the Timing group to increase or decrease how long the transition lasts.

When you apply most transitions, the Effect Options button in the Transition to This Slide group becomes active (note that some transitions do not have any effect options associated with them). Click this button and a drop-down gallery displays with effect options for the transition. The options at the drop-down gallery vary depending on the transition you choose.

When you apply a transition to slides in a presentation, an animation icon displays below each slide number in the Slides/Outline pane and below slides in Slide Sorter view. Click an animation icon for a particular slide and the slide displays the transition effect. To remove a transition, click the *None* transition thumbnail in the Transition to This Slide group. To remove transitions from all slides, click *None* transition thumbnail and then click the Apply To All button in the Timing group. To remove transition sound from a slide, click the down-pointing arrow at the right side of the *Sound* option and then click *[No Sound]* at the drop-down gallery. Click the Apply To All button to remove transition sound from all slides.

Quick Steps

Apply a Transition to All Slides in a Presentation

1. Click Transitions tab.
2. Click desired transition in Transition to This Slide group.
3. Click Apply To All button.

Apply a Transition Sound to All Slides in a Presentation

1. Click Transitions tab.
2. Click down-pointing arrow at right of *Sound* option.
3. Click desired sound.
4. Click Apply To All button.

Exercise 11.6 Adding Transitions and Transition Sounds to a Presentation

1. With **U2T11-Resumes.pptx** open, click the Transitions tab.

2. Click the *Push* transition thumbnail in the Transition to This Slide group.

   Notice that a transition icon displays below the slide number in the Slides/Outline pane.

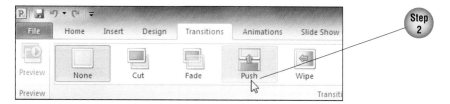

3. Click the animation icon that displays below the slide number in the Slides/Outline pane.

   This plays the animation for the slide in the Slide pane.

4. Click the *None* transition thumbnail in the Transition to This Slide group to remove the transition.

5. Click the More button located at the right side of the transition thumbnails that display in the Transition to This Slide group and then click the *Glitter* option in the *Exciting* section.

6. Click the Effect Options button ⬛ in the Transition to This Slide group and then click the *Hexagons from Top* option at the drop-down gallery.

7. Decrease the duration time of the transition by clicking in the *Duration* option box in the Timing group, typing **2**, and then pressing Enter.

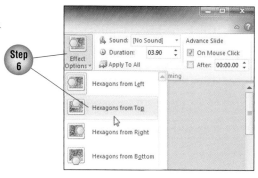

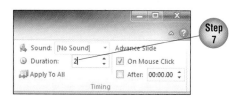

8. Click the down-pointing arrow at the right side of the *Sound* option box in the Timing group and then click *Chime* at the drop-down gallery.

9. Apply the transition and sound to all slides in the presentation by clicking the Apply To All button  in the Timing group.

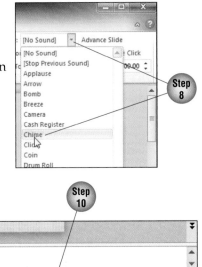

10. Run the presentation by clicking the Slide Show button in the view area on the Status bar.

11. Click the left mouse button to advance each slide.

12. At the black screen that displays after the last slide, click the left mouse button again to return the presentation to the Normal view.

13. Click the More button located at the right side of the transition thumbnails that display in the Transition to This Slide group and then click the *Box* option in the *Exciting* group.

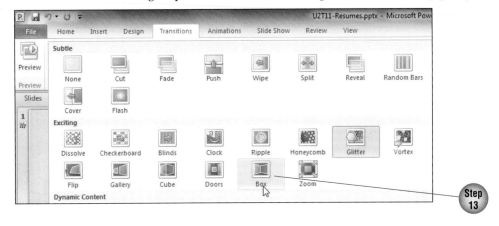

14. Click the Effect Options button and then click *From Bottom* at the drop-down gallery.

15. Click the Apply To All button in the Timing group.

16. Run the presentation.

17. Save **U2T11-Resumes.pptx**.

18. Close the presentation by clicking the File tab and then clicking the Close button.

Drilling Down

Running a Slide Show Automatically

You can set the slides in a slide show to advance automatically after a specific number of seconds with options in the Timing group on the Transitions tab. To advance slides automatically, click in the *After* check box and then insert the desired number of seconds in the text box. Do this by selecting the current time in the text box and then typing the desired time or by clicking the up- or down-pointing arrows to increase or decrease the time. Click the *On Mouse Click* check box to remove the check mark. If you want the transition time to affect all slides in the presentation, click the Apply To All button. In Slide Sorter view, the transition time displays below each affected slide.

Lesson 11.7   Checking Spelling in a Presentation

IC³ 2-4.1.1

Use PowerPoint's spelling checker to find and correct misspelled and duplicated words. Like the spelling checkers in other Microsoft Office programs, the spelling checker in PowerPoint compares words in the slide with words in its dictionary. If a match is found, the word is passed over. If no match is found for the word, the spelling checker stops, selects the word, and offers replacement suggestions in the Spelling dialog box. Table 11.3 describes the options available at the Spelling dialog box. Begin a spelling check by clicking the Review tab and then clicking the Spelling button in the Proofing group. When the spelling checker stops at a word, you can choose to ignore the word, delete the word, add the word to the spelling dictionary, or replace the word with one of the options in the *Suggestions* list box.

Quick Steps

Complete a Spelling Check

1. Click Review tab.
2. Click Spelling button.
3. Make necessary changes.
4. Click OK.

Keyboard Shortcut

Start Spelling Checker

F7

Table 11.3 Spelling Dialog Box Options

Button	Function
Ignore	Skips that occurrence of the word
Ignore All	Skips that occurrence of the word and all other occurrences of the word in slides
Change	Replaces selected word in slide with selected word in *Suggestions* list box
Change All	Replaces selected word in slide and all other occurrences of the word with selected word in *Suggestions* list box
Add	Adds selected word to the main spelling check dictionary
Suggest	Makes active the first suggestion in the *Suggestions* list box
AutoCorrect	Inserts selected word and correct spelling of word in AutoCorrect dialog box
Close	Closes the Spelling dialog box
Options	Displays PowerPoint Options dialog box with *Proofing* selected that contains options for customizing a spelling check

Exercise 11.7   Checking the Spelling in a Presentation

1. Open **CFResumeStrategies.pptx** located in the **Unit2Topic11** folder on your storage medium and then save the presentation and name it **U2T11-CFResumeStrategies**.

2. Begin the spelling check by clicking the Review tab and then clicking the Spelling button 🏴 in the Proofing group.

3. When the spelling checker selects *Strategeis* and displays *Strategies* in the *Change to* text box in the Spelling dialog box, click the Change button.

4. When the spelling checker selects *professionaly* and displays *professionally* in the *Change to* text box in the Spelling dialog box, click the Change button.

5. When the spelling checker selects the second occurrence of *are*, click the Delete button in the Spelling dialog box.

   The spelling checker selects *are* because it is a duplicate of the previous word.

6. When the spelling checker selects *easly*, click *easy* in the *Suggestions* list box in the Spelling dialog box and then click the Change button.

7. When the spelling checker selects *qualfications* and displays *qualifications* in the *Change to* text box in the Spelling dialog box, click the Change button.

8. At the message telling you that the spelling check is complete, click OK.

9. Make Slide 1 active.

10. Save **U2T11-CFResumeStrategies.pptx**.

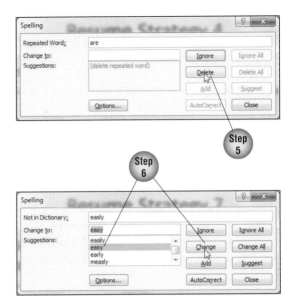

Drilling Down

Changing Spelling Options

You can control spelling options at the PowerPoint Options dialog box with *Proofing* selected in the left panel. Display this dialog box by clicking the File tab and then clicking the Options button below the Help tab. At the PowerPoint Options dialog box, click *Proofing* in the left panel. You can use the options in the dialog box to tell the spelling checker to ignore certain types of text, create custom dictionaries, and hide spelling errors in the presentation.

Lesson 11.8   Rearranging and Deleting Slides

 2-4.1.1, 2-4.1.3, 2-4.1.7

As you edit a presentation, you may need to reorganize slides, insert a new slide, duplicate a slide, or delete an existing slide. You can manage slides in the Slides/Outline pane or in Slide Sorter view. Switch to Slide Sorter view by clicking the Slide Sorter button in the view area on the Status bar or by clicking the View tab and then clicking Slide Sorter in the Presentation Views group.

Quick Steps

Delete a Slide

1. Click slide thumbnail in Slides/Outline pane.
2. Press Delete key.

Move a Slide

1. Click slide thumbnail in Slides/Outline pane.
2. Position mouse on selected slide.
3. Hold down left mouse button.
4. Drag to desired position.
5. Release mouse button.

As you learned in Lesson 11.2, clicking the New Slide button in the Slides group on the Home tab inserts a new slide in the presentation, immediately following the active slide. You can duplicate an existing slide by selecting the slide, clicking the New Slide button arrow, and then clicking *Duplicate Selected Slides* at the drop-down list. Delete a slide in Normal view by clicking the slide thumbnail in the Slides/Outline pane and then pressing the Delete key.

You can move slides in a presentation in Normal view or Slide Sorter view. To move a slide in Normal view, position the mouse arrow pointer over the desired slide in the Slides/Outline pane (with the Slides tab selected), hold down the left mouse button, drag up or down until a thin horizontal line displays in the desired location, and then release the mouse button. In Slide Sorter view, position the mouse arrow pointer on the selected slide, hold down the left mouse button, drag until a thin vertical line displays in the desired location, and then release the mouse button.

Exercise 11.8 Rearranging and Deleting Slides

1. With **U2T11-CFResumeStrategies** open, apply the Civic theme and the Executive theme colors to the presentation.

2. Duplicate the first slide by clicking the Home tab, clicking the New Slide button arrow, and then clicking *Duplicate Selected Slides* at the drop-down list.

3. Click the Slide Sorter button 🔠 in the view area on the Status bar.

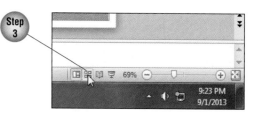

4. Click Slide 11 to select it and then press the Delete key on the keyboard.

   A slide selected in Slide Sorter view displays surrounded by an orange border.

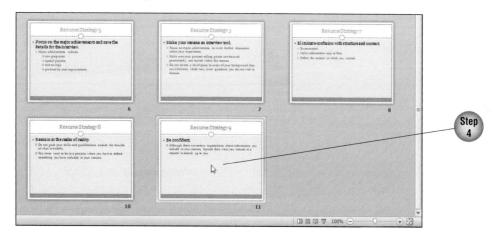

5. Position the mouse arrow pointer on Slide 2, hold down the left mouse button, drag the arrow pointer (with a square attached) to the right of Slide 10, and then release the mouse button.

6. Position the mouse arrow pointer on Slide 6, hold down the left mouse button, drag the arrow pointer (with a square attached) between Slides 3 and 4, and then release the mouse button.

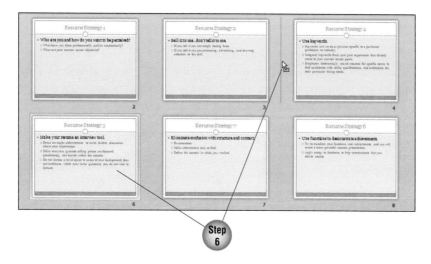

7. Click the Normal button 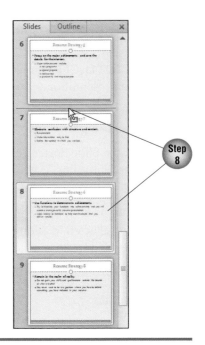 located in the view area on the Status bar.

8. Scroll down the Slides/Outline pane until Slide 8 displays. Position the mouse arrow pointer on the Slide 8 thumbnail, hold down the left mouse button, drag up until a thin, horizontal line displays immediately below the Slide 6 thumbnail, and then release the mouse button.

9. Make Slide 10 active, select the text *STRATEGIES FOR AN EFFECTIVE RESUME*, and then type **1-800-555-8550**.

    This replaces the selected text with the telephone number.

10. Run the presentation by clicking the Slide Show tab and then clicking the From Beginning button in the Start Slide Show group. Click the left mouse button to advance each slide.

11. Save **U2T11-CFResumeStrategies.pptx**.

 Drilling Down

Copying Slides within a Presentation

Copying a slide within a presentation is similar to moving a slide. To copy a slide, position the arrow pointer on the desired slide (in the Slides/Outline pane if you are in Normal view), and hold down the Ctrl key and the left mouse button. Drag to the location where you want the copy of the slide to display, release the left mouse button, and then release the Ctrl key. When you drag the slide using the mouse, a square and a plus symbol appear beside the mouse arrow pointer. You can also copy a slide by making the desired slide active and then clicking the Copy button in the Clipboard group on the Home tab or pressing Ctrl + C. Make active the slide immediately before the location where you want to paste the copy of the slide and then click the Paste button in the Clipboard group or press Ctrl + V.

Lesson 11.9 Applying Fonts and Font Effects

 2-4.1.1

The Font group on the Home tab contains a number of buttons for applying font formatting to text in a slide, such as changing the font, font size, font color, and applying font effects. Table 11.4 describes the buttons in the Font group, along with any available keyboard shortcuts you can use to apply font formatting.

Table 11.4 **PowerPoint Home Tab Font Group Buttons**

Button	Name	Function	Keyboard Shortcut
Calibri ▾	Font	Changes selected text to a different font	
32 ▾	Font Size	Changes selected text to a different font size	
A▴	Increase Font Size	Increases font size of selected text to next available larger size	Ctrl + Shift + >
A▾	Decrease Font Size	Decreases font size of selected text to next available smaller size	Ctrl + Shift + <

continued

Button	Name	Function	Keyboard Shortcut
	Clear All Formatting	Clears all character formatting from selected text	Ctrl + Spacebar
B	Bold	Adds or removes bold formatting to or from selected text	Ctrl + B
I	Italic	Adds or removes italic formatting to or from selected text	Ctrl + I
U ▾	Underline	Adds or removes underline formatting to or from selected text	Ctrl + U
S	Text Shadow	Adds or removes shadow formatting to or from selected text	
abc	Strikethrough	Inserts or removes a line through the middle of selected text	
AV ↔ ▾	Character Spacing	Adjusts spacing between characters	
Aa ▾	Change Case	Changes the case of selected text	Shift + F3
A ▾	Font Color	Changes the font color for selected text	

Design themes automatically apply a font to text in slides. You may want to change this default font for such reasons as changing the mood of a presentation, enhancing the visual appeal of slides, and increasing the readability of the text in slides. Change the font with the Font and Font Size buttons in the Font group in the Home tab. In addition to buttons in the Font group in the Home tab, you can use options at the Font dialog box shown in Figure 11.4 to apply character formatting to text. Display the Font dialog box by clicking the Font group dialog box launcher or by using the keyboard shortcut Ctrl + Shift + F. Recall that a dialog box launcher is the small button containing a diagonal arrow that displays in the lower right corner of a group and that, when clicked, displays a dialog box. Use options at the Font dialog box to choose a font, font style, font size, and to apply special effects such as Superscript, Subscript, and Double Strikethrough.

Keyboard Shortcut

Display Font Dialog Box
Ctrl + Shift + F

Figure 11.4 Font Dialog Box

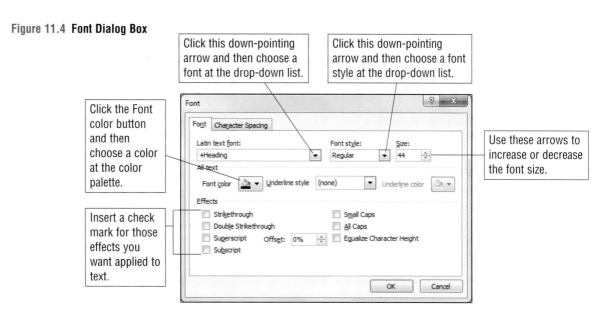

Click this down-pointing arrow and then choose a font at the drop-down list.

Click this down-pointing arrow and then choose a font style at the drop-down list.

Click the Font color button and then choose a color at the color palette.

Use these arrows to increase or decrease the font size.

Insert a check mark for those effects you want applied to text.

When you select text, the Mini toolbar displays in a dimmed fashion above the selected text. Recall that the Mini toolbar contains buttons for formatting the text. Hover the mouse arrow pointer over the Mini toolbar and it becomes active. Click a button on the Mini toolbar to apply formatting to selected text.

Keyboard Shortcut

Repeat Command

F4 or Ctrl + Y

If you apply character formatting to text and then want to apply the same formatting to other text in the presentation, consider using the Repeat command. To use this command, apply the desired formatting, move the insertion point to the next location where you want to apply the formatting, and then press the F4 key or press Ctrl + Y. The Repeat command will repeat only the last action you performed. You can use these shortcuts in Excel and Word documents as well.

Exercise 11.9 Applying Font and Font Effects

1. With **U2T11-CFResumeStrategies.pptx** open, display Slide 1 in the Slide pane.

2. Select the title *Career Finders*, click the Home tab, and then click the Italic button I in the Font group.

3. With the title still selected, click the Font button arrow in the Font group, scroll down the drop-down gallery, and then click *Candara*.

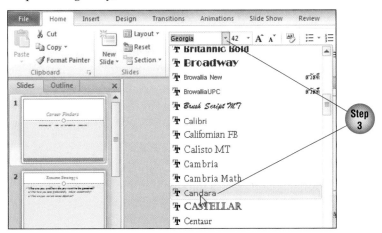

4. Change the font size of the title by clicking the Font Size button arrow and then clicking *54* at the drop-down gallery.

5. Select the subtitle *STRATEGIES FOR AN EFFECTIVE RESUME*, click three times on the Increase Font Size button A^{*} in the Font group, click the Italic button, and then click the Text Shadow button S.

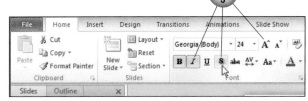

6. Make Slide 2 active in the Slide pane, select the title *Resume Strategy 1*, and then click the Font group dialog box launcher on the Home tab.

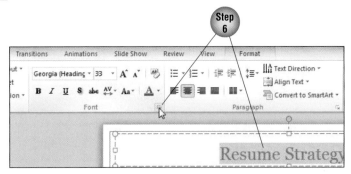

7. At the Font dialog box, click the down-pointing arrow at the right side of the *Latin text font* option box, and then click *Candara* at the drop-down list.

8. Click the down-pointing arrow at the right side of the *Font style* option box, and then click *Bold* at the drop-down list.

9. Select the current measurement in the *Size* text box and then type **40**.

10. Click the Font color button in the *All text* section and then click the *Orange, Accent 3, Darker 25%* option.

11. Click OK to close the Font dialog box.

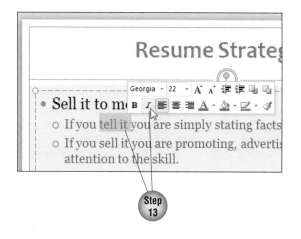

12. Apply the same formatting to the titles in the next seven slides (not the last slide) by selecting each title and then pressing F4.

The F4 key is the Repeat command. The Repeat command repeats only the last action performed.

13. Make Slide 3 active in the Slide pane, select the text *tell it* in the second bulleted item, hover the mouse arrow pointer over the Mini toolbar to make it active, and then click the Italic button in the Mini toolbar.

14. Select the text *sell it* in the third bulleted item in Slide 3 and then apply italic formatting using the Mini toolbar.

15. Delete Slide 10 by scrolling down the Slides/Outline pane, clicking the Slide 10 miniature, and then pressing the Delete key.

16. Save **U2T11-CFResumeStrategies.pptx**.

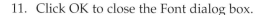

Drilling Down

Choosing Typefaces

Recall that a typeface is a set of characters with a common design and shape. PowerPoint and other Office programs refer to a typeface as a *font*. Typefaces can be decorative or plain and are either monospaced or proportional. A monospaced typeface allots the same amount of horizontal space for each character while a proportional typeface allots a varying amount of space for each character. Proportional typefaces are divided into two main categories: serif and sans serif. A serif is a small line at the top and bottom of a character. Consider using a serif typeface for text-intensive slides because the serifs help move the reader's eyes across the text. Use a sans serif typeface for titles, subtitles, headings, and short text lines.

Lesson 11.10 Applying Paragraph Formatting

IC³ 2-4.1.1

The Paragraph group on the Home tab contains a number of buttons for applying paragraph formatting to text in a slide, such as applying bullets and numbers, increasing and decreasing list levels, changing the horizontal and vertical alignment of text, changing line spacing, and rotating text in a placeholder. Table 11.5 describes the buttons in the Paragraph group along with any available keyboard shortcuts.

Recall from Lesson 6.3 in Topic 6 that the Format Painter button can be used to apply character and paragraph formatting in more than one location in a Word document. The Format Painter button works the same in PowerPoint—you can use it to apply formatting to multiple slides.

If you want to apply formatting in only one other location in a presentation, click the Format Painter button once. The first time you click or select text, the formatting is applied and the Format Painter button is deactivated. If you want to apply formatting in multiple locations, double-click the Format painter button, click or select the desired text, and then click the Format Painter button to deactivate it.

Quick Steps

Use Format Painter to Apply Formatting
1. Position insertion point on formatted text.
2. Double-click Format Painter button.
3. Select text or click word to format.
4. Click Format Painter button.

Table 11.5 **PowerPoint Home Tab Paragraph Group Buttons**

Button	Name	Function	Keyboard Shortcut
	Bullets	Adds or removes bullets to or from selected text	
	Numbering	Adds or removes numbers to or from selected text	
	Decrease List Level	Moves text to the previous tab stop (level)	Shift + Tab
	Increase List Level	Moves text to the next tab stop (level)	Tab
	Line Spacing	Increases or reduces spacing between lines of text	
	Align Text Left	Left-aligns text	Ctrl + L
	Center	Center-aligns text	Ctrl + E
	Align Text Right	Right-aligns text	Ctrl + R
	Justify	Justifies text	
	Columns	Splits text into two or more columns	
	Text Direction	Rotates or stacks text	
	Align Text	Changes the alignment of text within a text box	
	Convert to SmartArt Graphic	Converts selected text to a SmartArt graphic	

Exercise 11.10 Applying Paragraph Formatting

1. With **U2T11-ResumeStrategies.pptx** open, make Slide 1 active.

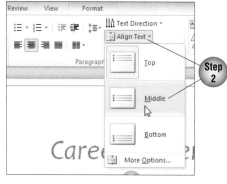

2. Click in the text *STRATEGIES FOR AN EFFECTIVE RESUME*, click the Align Text button 🔲 in the Paragraph group in the Home tab, and then click *Middle* at the drop-down gallery.

3. Make Slide 2 active, click in the bulleted text, and then click the placeholder border to change it to a solid-line border.

4. Click the Line Spacing button 🔲 in the Paragraph group and then click *2.0* at the drop-down gallery.

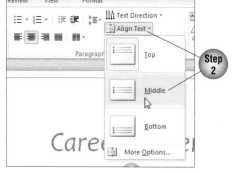

5. Make Slide 3 active, click in the bulleted text, click the placeholder border to change it to a solid-line border, and then press F4.

   Pressing the F4 key repeats the last command.

6. Make Slide 8 active, click in the bulleted text, click the placeholder border to change it to a solid-line border, and then press F4.

7. Make Slide 2 active, select the title *Resume Strategy 1*, click the Text Shadow button in the Font group in the Home tab, and then click the Align Text Left button 🔲 in the Paragraph group.

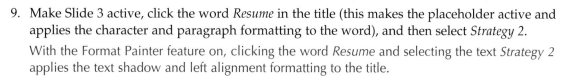

8. With the title still selected, double-click the Format Painter button 🔲 in the Clipboard group.

9. Make Slide 3 active, click the word *Resume* in the title (this makes the placeholder active and applies the character and paragraph formatting to the word), and then select *Strategy 2*.

   With the Format Painter feature on, clicking the word *Resume* and selecting the text *Strategy 2* applies the text shadow and left alignment formatting to the title.

10. Make Slide 4 active, click the word *Resume*, and then select *Strategy 3*.

11. Make each of the remaining slides active, click the word *Resume*, and then select the remaining text in the title.

12. Click the Format Painter button to turn the feature off.

13. Make Slide 6 active, select the last four bulleted items (*new programs* through *productivity and improvements*), click the Numbering button 🔲 in the Paragraph group, and then click the Decrease List Level button 🔲.

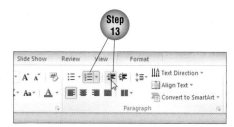

   Clicking the Numbering button changes the bullets to numbers for the selected text.

14. Click the bulleted and numbered text placeholder border to change it to a solid-line border, click the Line Spacing button in the Paragraph group, and then click *1.5* at the drop-down gallery.

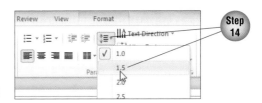

Step 14

15. Make Slide 7 active, click in the bulleted text, click the placeholder border to change it to a solid-line border, and then press F4.

    Pressing F4 repeats the 1.5 line spacing command.

16. Make Slide 9 active, click in the bulleted text, click the placeholder border to change it to a solid-line border, and then press F4.

17. Print all slides as a handout with 9 slides horizontally per page. Begin by pressing Ctrl + P to display the Print tab Backstage view.

18. Click the *Full Page Slides* option (the second gallery) in the Settings category, click *9 Slides Horizontal* in the *Handouts* section, and then click the Print button.

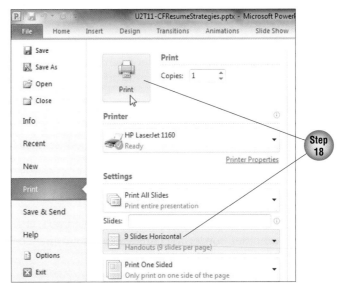

Step 18

19. Save **U2T11-CFResumeStrategies.pptx**.

Drilling Down

Formatting with the Paragraph Dialog Box

Click the Paragraph group dialog box launcher and the Paragraph dialog box displays. With options at this dialog box you can change text alignment, and indent text and specify the amount of indentations. You can also change the line spacing and insert additional spacing before and after paragraphs of text.

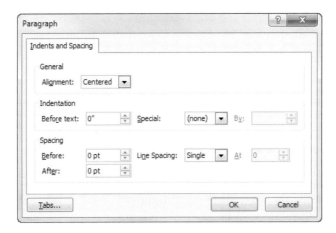

Lesson 11.11 Inserting Headers and Footers

IC³ 2-4.1.2

Remember that if you print a presentation as a handout or an outline, PowerPoint automatically prints the current date in the upper right corner of the page and the page number in the lower right corner. If you print the presentation as notes pages, PowerPoint automatically prints the page number. The date and page numbers are considered header and footer elements. You can modify existing header and footer elements or insert additional elements with options in the Header and Footer dialog box. Display the Header and Footer dialog box shown in Figure 11.5 by clicking the Header & Footer button in the Text group on the Insert tab, clicking the Date & Time button in the Text group, or clicking the Slide Number button in the Text group. You can also display the Header and Footer dialog box by displaying the Print tab Backstage view and then clicking the Edit Header & Footer hyperlink that displays below the galleries in the Settings category.

Figure 11.5 Header and Footer Dialog Box with Notes and Handouts Tab Selected

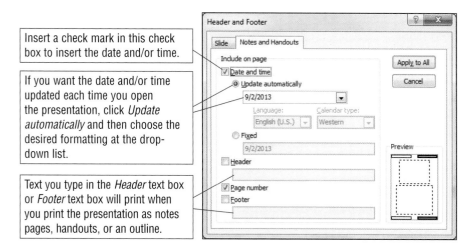

Insert a check mark in this check box to insert the date and/or time.

If you want the date and/or time updated each time you open the presentation, click *Update automatically* and then choose the desired formatting at the drop-down list.

Text you type in the *Header* text box or *Footer* text box will print when you print the presentation as notes pages, handouts, or an outline.

The Header and Footer dialog box has two tabs: the Slide tab and the Notes and Handouts tab. The options in the dialog box are similar with either tab selected. With options at the dialog box, you can insert the date and time, a header, a footer, and page numbers. If you want all changes you make to the Header and Footer dialog box to apply to all slides or all handouts, notes pages, and outline pages, click the Apply to All button located in the upper right corner of the dialog box.

Quick Steps

Display the Header and Footer Dialog Box

1. Click Insert tab.
2. Click Header & Footer button, Date & Time button, or Slide Number button.

Exercise 11.11 Inserting Headers and Footers

1. With **U2T11-ResumeStrategies.pptx** open, insert a footer that prints at the bottom of each slide. To begin, click the Insert tab and then click the Header & Footer button ▤ in the Text group.

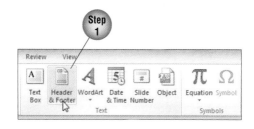

2. At the Header and Footer dialog box with the Slide tab selected, click the *Date and time* check box to insert a check mark. If necessary, click the *Update automatically* option to insert a circle in the option button.

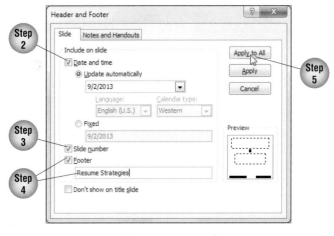

Step 2

Step 5

Step 3

Step 4

3. Click the *Slide number* check box to insert a check mark.

4. Click the *Footer* check box to insert a check mark and then type **Resume Strategies** in the *Footer* text box.

5. Click the Apply to All button.

6. Make Slide 5 active, click in the Notes pane, and then type **Provide a list of effective keywords.**

7. Insert a header in notes and handouts by clicking the Header & Footer button on the Insert tab.

8. At the Header and Footer dialog box, click the Notes and Handouts tab.

9. Click the *Date and time* check box to insert a check mark and then, if necessary, click the *Update automatically* option to insert a circle in the option button.

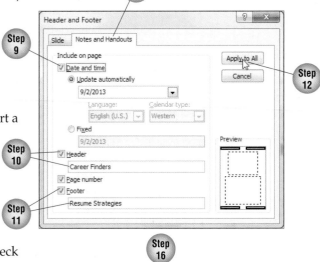

Step 8

Step 9

Step 12

Step 10

Step 11

10. Click the *Header* check box to insert a check mark and then type **Career Finders**.

11. Click the *Footer* check box to insert a check mark and then type **Resume Strategies**.

12. Click the Apply to All button.

13. Print the presentation as handouts with nine slides horizontally per page.

14. Print Slide 5 as a notes page. Begin by clicking the File tab, clicking the Print tab, clicking the second gallery (contains the text *9 Slides Horizontal*) in the Settings category, and then clicking *Notes Pages* in the Print Layout section.

15. Click in the *Slides* text box (located below the first gallery in the Settings category) and then type **5**.

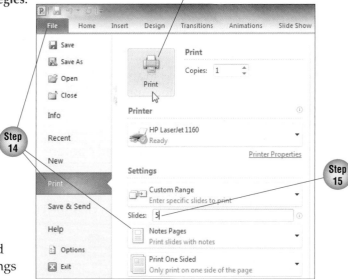

Step 16

Step 14

Step 15

16. Click the Print button.

17. Save and then close **U2T11-CFResumeStrategies.pptx**.

18. Exit PowerPoint.

Resizing and Moving a Header or Footer Placeholder

To resize a header or footer placeholder, click the header or footer. A placeholder border surrounds it, containing sizing handles, which are small, white circles or squares. Position the mouse pointer on one of the sizing handles until the mouse pointer displays as a two-headed arrow, hold down the left mouse button, drag to the desired size, and then release the mouse button. To move a header or footer placeholder, click the header or footer, position the mouse pointer on the placeholder border until the pointer displays with a four-headed arrow attached. Drag the placeholder to the desired position and then release the mouse button.

More Information for IC³

 2-4.1.8, 2-4.1.12

Planning a Presentation

You can plan and design a PowerPoint presentation for a number of situations. For example, you might create a presentation for a company meeting or training session, prepare a presentation for a prospective investor, or organize a classroom presentation on a specific topic. Whatever your subject and whoever your audience, consider these basic guidelines for preparing the content of your presentation:

- **Determine the main purpose of the presentation.** Do not try to cover too many topics. Identifying the main point of the presentation will help you stay focused and convey a clear message to the audience.
- **Determine the output.** To help decide the type of output needed, consider the availability of equipment, the size of the room where you will make the presentation, and the number of people who will be attending the presentation.
- **Show one idea per slide.** Each slide in a presentation should convey only one main idea. Too many ideas on a slide may confuse the audience and cause you to stray from the purpose of the slide.
- **Maintain a consistent design.** A consistent design and color scheme for slides in a presentation will create continuity and cohesiveness. Do not use too much color or too many pictures or other graphic elements.
- **Keep slides easy to read and uncluttered.** Keep slides simple and easy for the audience to read. Keep words and other items such as bullets to a minimum.
- **Determine printing needs.** Will you be providing audience members with handouts? If so, will these handouts consist of a printing of each slide? an outline of the presentation? a printing of each slide with space for taking notes? Consider how many of these handouts you will need and plan accordingly.

TOPIC SUMMARY

■ Creating and presenting a PowerPoint presentation generally includes the following steps: opening PowerPoint; creating and editing slides; saving, printing, running, and closing the presentation; and then closing PowerPoint.

■ Apply a design theme to a presentation by clicking the Design tab, clicking the More button at the right side of the design theme thumbnails, and then clicking the desired theme at the drop-down gallery. Customize a design with the Colors and Fonts buttons in the Themes group and the Background Styles button and *Hide Background Graphics* check box in the Background group.

■ Many slide layouts contain a placeholder. Use the sizing handles to increase or decrease the size of the placeholder. Move a selected placeholder by positioning the mouse arrow pointer on the placeholder border until the pointer displays as a four-headed arrow and then dragging the placeholder to the desired location.

■ The Normal view displays with three panes for entering text: the Slides/Outline pane, the Slide pane, and the Notes pane.

■ In Normal view, navigate through slides by clicking the Previous Slide or Next Slide buttons located at the bottom of the vertical scroll bar or by using the mouse to drag the scroll box on the vertical scroll bar. You can also use the Down Arrow, Page Down, Up Arrow, Page Up, Home, and End keys on the keyboard to navigate through slides.

■ Print a presentation with options at the Print tab Backstage view.

■ The Status bar contains a Zoom slider bar with options for increasing and decreasing the size of the slide display in the Slide pane.

■ Run a slide show by clicking the Slide Show button in the view area on the Status bar or by clicking the Slide Show tab and then clicking the From Beginning button in the Start Slide Show group. Run a slide show beginning with a specific slide by making the slide active, clicking the Slide Show tab, and then clicking the From Current Slide button.

■ You can run a presentation with buttons on the Slide Show toolbar. Display this toolbar by running the presentation and then moving the mouse arrow pointer.

■ You can navigate through slides when running a presentation by using keyboard commands (see Figure 11.3).

■ Add transitions and transition sounds to slides with options on the Transitions tab. The Apply To All button in the Timing group on the Transitions tab applies the transition and transition sound to all slides.

■ When you apply a transition, use the Effect Options button in the Transition to This Slide group on the Transitions tab to customize the transition.

■ When you apply a transition to slides, an animation icon displays below each slide number in the Slides/Outline pane and below slides in the Slide Sorter view.

■ You can move or delete a selected slide in Normal view in the Slides/Outline pane or in Slide Sorter view. To move a slide, use the mouse to drag the slide to the desired location. To delete a selected slide, press the Delete key on the keyboard.

■ Apply font and font effects to text in slides with buttons in the Font group on the Home tab and with options at the Font dialog box.

■ Use the Repeat command, F4 (or Ctrl + Y), to apply the same formatting to other text in the presentation.

■ Apply paragraph formatting to text in slides with buttons in the Paragraph group on the Home tab.

■ Use the Format Painter button in the Clipboard group on the Home tab to apply formatting to more than one location in a slide or presentation.

■ Insert information at the top or bottom of individual slides or the top or bottom of individual printed notes and handout pages with options at the Header and Footer dialog box.

Key Term

transition, p. 496

Features Summary

Feature	Ribbon Tab, Group	Button	File Tab	Keyboard Shortcut
Apply transitions and sounds to all slides	Transitions, Timing			
Close presentation			Close	Ctrl + F4
Design theme	Design, Themes			
Font dialog box	Home, Font			Ctrl + Shift + F
Format Painter	Home, Clipboard			
Header and Footer dialog box	Insert, Text			
Layout	Home, Slides			
New slide	Home, Slides			Ctrl + M
Normal view	View, Presentation Views			
Notes Page view	View, Presentation Views			
Open dialog box			Open	Ctrl + O
Paragraph dialog box	Home, Paragraph			
Print tab Backstage view			Print	Ctrl + P
Run presentation from current slide	Slide Show, Start Slide Show			Shift + F5
Run presentation from Slide 1	Slide Show, Start Slide Show			F5
Save			Save	Ctrl + S
Save As			Save As	F12
Slide Sorter view	View, Presentation Views			
Transition duration	Transitions, Timing			
Transition sound	Transitions, Timing			
Transitions	Transitions, Transition to This Slide			

KEY POINTS REVIEW

Identification

Match the terms to the callouts on the PowerPoint window in Figure 11.6.

1. _____ placeholder
2. _____ Zoom slider bar
3. _____ Slides/Outline pane
4. _____ vertical scroll bar
5. _____ Zoom to Page button
6. _____ sizing handles
7. _____ scroll box
8. _____ dialog box launcher
9. _____ Notes pane
10. _____ Font button

Figure 11.6 Identification Figure

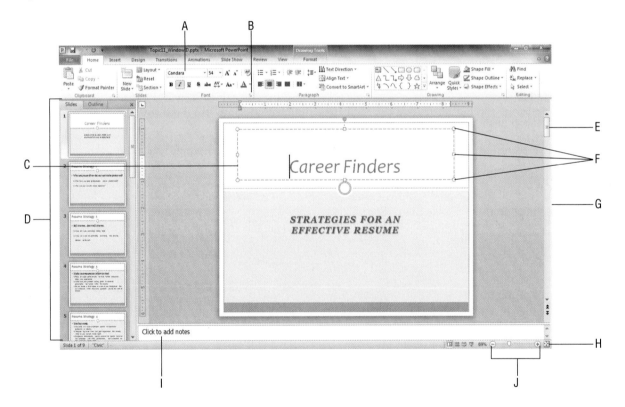

Multiple Choice

For each of the following items, choose the option that best completes the sentence or answers the question.

1. Apply a theme template to a presentation by clicking this tab.
   A. Home
   B. Animations
   C. Slide Show
   D. Design

2. This is the default view; it displays three panes.
   A. Normal
   B. Notes Page
   C. Slide Sorter
   D. Reading

3. Create a slide with this button in the Slides group on the Home tab.
   A. Add Slide
   B. Create Slide
   C. New Slide
   D. Insert Slide

4. This toolbar displays above selected text and contains commonly used formatting options.
   A. Slide toolbar
   B. Mini toolbar
   C. Master toolbar
   D. Formatting toolbar

5. Change the colors of a theme using the Colors button in this group on the Design tab.
   A. Styles
   B. Page Setup
   C. Slide Show
   D. Themes

6. Use these to increase or decrease the size of a selected placeholder.
   A. rotation markers
   B. sizing handles
   C. height and width icons
   D. increase markers

7. Print a presentation with six slides per page by clicking the *6 Slides Horizontal* option in this section of the Print tab Backstage view.
   A. Layout
   B. Notes
   C. Settings
   D. Printer Properties

8. This is the most common way to advance a slide in Slide Show view.
   A. clicking the left mouse button
   B. clicking the right mouse button
   C. pressing the Enter key
   D. pressing the Esc key

9. The Format Painter button is located in this group on the Home tab.
   A. Font
   B. Paragraph
   C. Styles
   D. Clipboard

10. Change the amount of time a transition displays by changing the value in this box in the Timing group on the Transitions tab.
    A. Time
    B. Duration
    C. Transition
    D. After

Matching

Match each of the following definitions with the correct term, command, or option.

1. _____ The New Slide button is located on this tab.

2. _____ Add transitions and transition sounds to a presentation with options in this tab.

3. _____ To run a presentation beginning with Slide 1, click the Slide Show tab and then click this button.

4. _____ Change the design theme colors with the Colors button on this tab.

5. _____ Press this key on the keyboard to change to a black screen while running a presentation.

6. _____ This bar displays in the lower right corner of the screen and changes the percentage of display.

7. _____ Press this key on the keyboard to end a presentation without running all of the slides.

8. _____ The Spelling button is located in the Proofing group on this tab.

9. _____ The Normal view contains the Slides/Outline pane, the Slide pane, and this pane.

10. _____ Move the mouse while running a presentation and this toolbar displays.

A. From Beginning
B. Notes pane
C. Home
D. Design
E. Transitions
F. B
G. Slide Show
H. Review
I. Esc
J. Zoom slider

SKILLS REVIEW

Review 11.1 Creating a Presentation on Interviewing Tips and Strategies

1. Open PowerPoint, click the Design tab, click the More button at the right side of the Themes group, and then click *Perspective* in the drop-down gallery.

2. Click the Colors button in the Themes group and then click *Metro* at the drop-down gallery.

3. Type the title and subtitle for Slide 1 as shown in Figure 11.7.

4. Click the Home tab and then click the New Slide button in the Slides group.

5. Type the text shown for Slide 2 in Figure 11.7.

6. Continue creating the slides for the presentation as shown in Figure 11.7.

7. Apply the *Flip* transition, change the effect options to *Left*, and change the duration to *00.75* for all slides in the presentation.

8. Add the *Whoosh* transition sound to all slides in the presentation.

9. Run the presentation beginning with Slide 1.

10. Save the presentation and name it **U2T11-R1-CFInterview**.

11. Print the presentation with all six slides horizontal on the page.

12. Change the design theme to *Austin*, the theme colors to *Aspect*, and the theme fonts to *Aspect*.

13. Insert a new Slide 4 between the current Slides 3 and 4 with the Title Slide layout. Type **Interviewing for the Job** as the title and **Job Interviewing Strategies** as the subtitle.

14. Make Slide 2 active and then change the bulleted text line spacing to *1.5*.

15. Make Slide 3 active and then change the bulleted text line spacing to *1.5*.

16. Make Slide 4 active, click in the Notes pane, and then type **Provide some sample interview questions.**

17. Display the Header and Footer dialog box with the Notes and Handouts tab selected and then specify that you want the current date and time, the page number, and the footer *Career Finders* inserted on printed pages.

18. Run the presentation.
19. Print the presentation with all six slides horizontally on the page.
20. Print Slide 4 as a notes page.
21. Save and then close the presentation.

Figure 11.7 Review 11.1 Text

| Slide 1 | Title | = | Interviewing for the Job |
| | Subtitle | = | Job Interviewing Tips |

Slide 2   Title   =   Company Research
           Bullets   =
- Gather company background information.
- Review company's website.
- Ask employer for company history.
- Search online for information on company.

Slide 3   Title   =   Practice
           Bullets   =
- Practice interviewing with a friend.
- Record interview responses and listen to determine how well you did.
- Prepare answers to commonly-asked interview questions.

Slide 4   Title   =   Prepare for Interview
           Bullets   =
- Prepare a list of questions for the interviewer.
- Bring extra copies of your resume and list of references.
- Be on time to the interview.
- Know the interviewer's name and use it during the interview.

Slide 5   Title   =   Maintain Composure
           Bullets   =
- Ask for clarification on questions.
- Take a moment or two to frame your responses.
- At the end of the interview:
  - Thank the interviewer.
  - Reiterate your interest in the position.
- Send a thank you note restating your interest.

Review 11.2 Creating a Presentation for the East Shore Restaurant

1. With PowerPoint open, create slides and type text in the slides as shown in Figure 11.8.
2. Apply the Concourse design theme and change the theme fonts to *Austin*.
3. Make Slide 1 active, select the title *East Shore Restaurant*, and then change the font color to *Turquoise, Accent 1, Darker 25%*.
4. Make Slide 5 active, select the title *Resource*, and then use the Repeat command to apply the turquoise font color formatting.
5. Make Slide 2 active and then select the title *Accommodations*. Change the font size to *44*, the font color to *Red, Accent 2, Darker 50%*, and the paragraph alignment to *Center*.
6. Use Format Painter to apply the same formatting you applied to the *Accommodations* title to the titles in Slides 3 and 4. (Make sure the titles are centered.)
7. Make Slide 2 active, select the bulleted text, change the paragraph alignment to *Center*, change the alignment to *Middle*, and change the line spacing to *1.5*.
8. Make Slide 3 active, select the bulleted text, and then change the line spacing to *2.0*. Decrease the size of the placeholder by dragging in the right border so it is positioned near the bulleted text and then move the placeholder so the bulleted text is approximately centered below the title.
9. Make Slide 4 active, click in the bulleted text, and then decrease the size of the placeholder by dragging in the right border so it is positioned near the bulleted text. Move the placeholder so the bulleted text is approximately centered below the title.
10. Apply the *Doors* transition with a duration of *00.75* and the transition sound *Cash Register* to all slides in the presentation.
11. Insert the text *East Shore Restaurant* as a footer at the bottom of each slide in the presentation.
12. Save the presentation and name it **U2T11-R2-ESRInfo**.
13. Run the presentation.
14. Print the presentation with all five slides horizontally on one page.
15. Close **U2T11-R2-ESRInfo.pptx**.

Figure 11.8 Review 11.2 Text

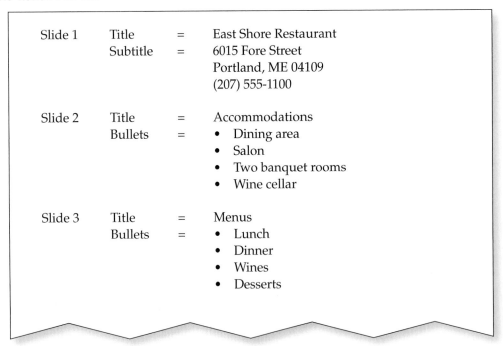

Slide 1	Title	=	East Shore Restaurant
	Subtitle	=	6015 Fore Street
			Portland, ME 04109
			(207) 555-1100
Slide 2	Title	=	Accommodations
	Bullets	=	• Dining area
			• Salon
			• Two banquet rooms
			• Wine cellar
Slide 3	Title	=	Menus
	Bullets	=	• Lunch
			• Dinner
			• Wines
			• Desserts

continued

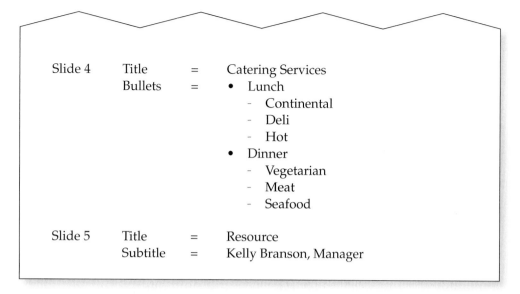

Slide 4   Title   =   Catering Services

Bullets =
- Lunch
  - Continental
  - Deli
  - Hot
- Dinner
  - Vegetarian
  - Meat
  - Seafood

Slide 5   Title   =   Resource

Subtitle = Kelly Branson, Manager

SKILLS ASSESSMENT

Assessment 11.1 Preparing a Presentation for Vandermeyer and Associates

1. Prepare a presentation for Vandermeyer and Associates with the information shown in Figure 11.9. Apply the Concourse design theme and change the design theme colors to *Urban*.
2. After creating the five slides, complete a spelling check on the text in the presentation.
3. Make Slide 2 active and then change the line spacing for the bulleted text to *1.5*.
4. Make Slide 3 active and then change the line spacing for the bulleted text to *2.0*.
5. Make Slide 4 active and then change the line spacing for the bulleted text to *2.0*.
6. Make Slide 5 active and then change the line spacing for the bulleted text to *1.5*.
7. Add a transition and transition sound of your choosing to all slides in the presentation.
8. Display the Header and Footer dialog box with the Notes and Handouts tab selected and then specify that you want the current date and time, the page number, and the footer *Vandermeyer and Associates* inserted on printed pages.
9. Run the presentation.
10. Print the presentation with all five slides horizontally on one page.
11. Save the presentation and name it **U2T11-A1-VAMeeting**.
12. Close **U2T11-A1-VAMeeting.pptx**.

Figure 11.9 Assessment 11.1 Text

| Slide 1 | Title | = | Vandermeyer and Associates |
| | Subtitle | = | Executive Meeting |

Slide 2 Title = Accounting Policies
Bullets =
- Cash Equivalents
- Short-term Investments
- Inventory Valuation
- Property and Equipment
- Foreign Currency Translation

Slide 3 Title = Financial Instruments
Bullets =
- Investments
- Derivative Instruments
- Credit Risks
- Fair Value of Instruments

Slide 4 Title = Inventories
Bullets =
- Products
- Raw Material
- Equipment
- Buildings

Slide 5 Title = Employee Plans
Bullets =
- Stock Options
- Bonus Plan
- Savings and Retirement Plan
- Defined Benefits Plan
- Foreign Subsidiaries

Assessment 11.2 Formatting a Presentation on Toronto

1. Open **CTToronto.pptx** in the **Unit2Topic11** folder on your storage medium and then save the presentation and name it **U2T11-A2-CTToronto.pptx**.
2. Format the presentation so it appears as shown in Figure 11.10 with the following specifications:
   a. Apply the Civic design theme and change the design theme colors to *Origin*.
   b. Apply formatting to the text and arrange the placeholder containing the text so your slides display similar to the slides shown in the figure.
3. Insert the text *Toronto, Canada* as a footer at the bottom of each slide in the presentation.
4. Add a transition and sound of your choosing to all slides in the presentation.
5. Run the presentation.
6. Print the presentation with the six slides horizontally on the same page.
7. Save and then close **U2T11-A2-CTToronto.pptx**.

Figure 11.10 Assessment 11.2 Example

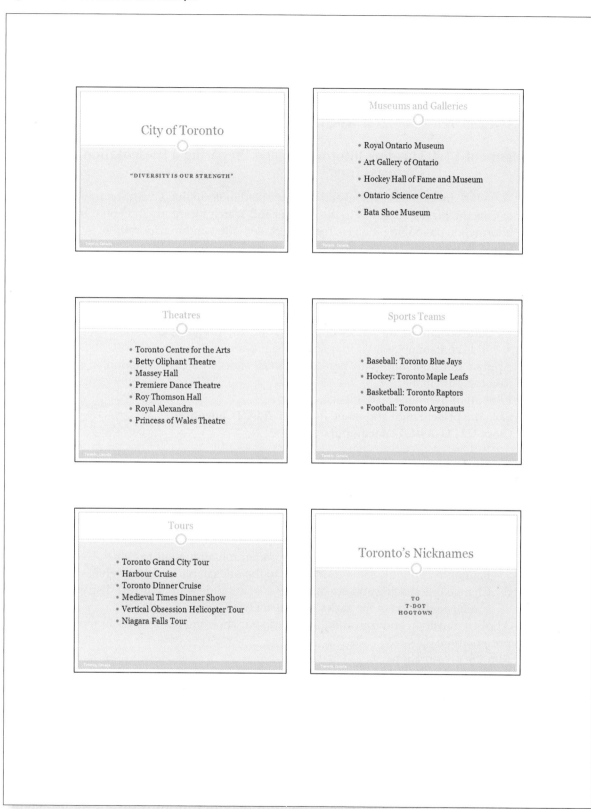

Assessment 11.3 Finding Information on Setting Slide Show Timings

1. Open **CTEnglandTour.pptx**.
2. Save the presentation as **U2T11-A3-CTEnglandTour**.
3. Use the Help feature to learn how to set slide show timings.
4. Set up the presentation so that, when running the presentation, each slide advances after five seconds.
5. Run the presentation.
6. Save and then close **U2T11-A3-CTEnglandTour.pptx**.

Assessment 11.4 Locating Information and Preparing a Presentation for Compass Travel

1. You work for Compass Travel and are interested in arranging a vacation travel package to Cancun, Mexico. Connect to the Internet and search for information on Cancun. Locate information on lodging (hotels), restaurants, activities, and transportation.
2. Using PowerPoint, create a presentation about Cancun that contains the following:
   * Title slide containing the company name *Compass Travel* and the subtitle *Vacationing in Cancun*
   * Slide containing the names of at least three major airlines that travel to Cancun
   * Slide containing the names of at least four hotels or resorts in Cancun
   * Slide containing the names of at least four restaurants in Cancun
   * Slide containing at least four activities in Cancun
3. Apply a transition and transition sound to all slides in the presentation.
4. Run the presentation.
5. Print all of the slides on one page.
6. Save the presentation and name it **U2T11-A4-CTCancun**.
7. Close **U2T11-A4-CTCancun.pptx**.

Assessment 11.5 Creating and Formatting an Online Learning Presentation

1. Create the presentation shown in Figure 11.11 by applying the following specifications:
   a. Apply the Newsprint design theme and change the theme colors to *Elemental*.
   b. Change the background style to *Style 1*.
   c. Select the title in Slide 2, change the font size to *48*, change the font color to *Blue, Accent 1, Darker 25%*, and change the paragraph alignment to *Center*. Use Format Painter to apply the same formatting to the titles in Slides 3 through 6.
   d. Change line spacing and size and move placeholders so your text displays on slides similar to the text in the slides in Figure 11.11.
2. Apply a transition and transition sound of your choosing to all slides in the presentation.
3. Run the presentation.
4. Save the presentation and name it **U2T11-A5-OnlineLearning**.
5. Print the presentation as a handout with all six slides horizontally on the same page.
6. Close the presentation.

Figure 11.11 Assessment 11.5 Example

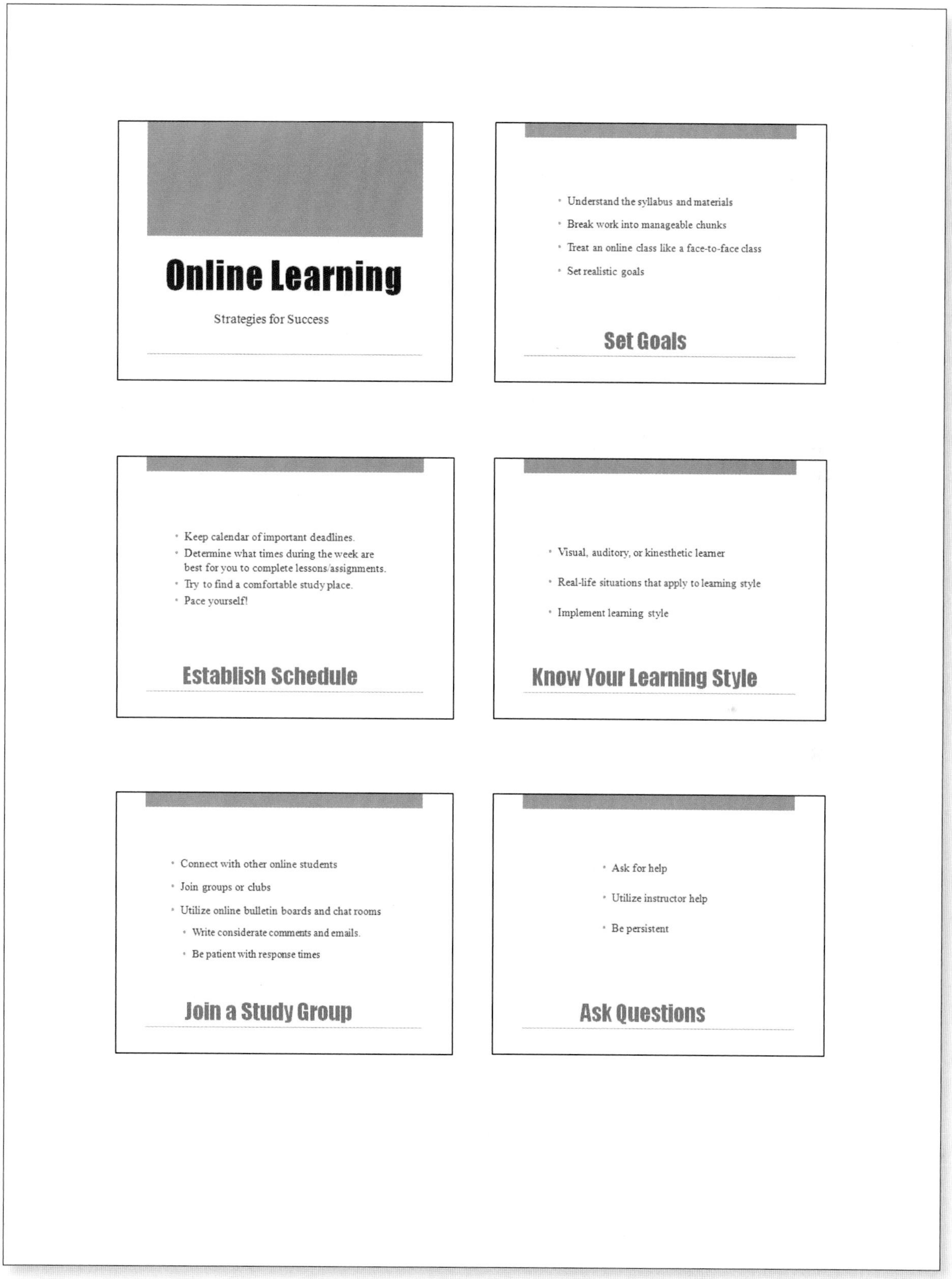

CRITICAL THINKING

Suggesting Improvements to Slide Designs

Look at each slide below and then determine at least two things you would do to improve the slide. Use the information in the Delving Deeper section in this topic as a reference for deciding what you would change in each slide. Create a Word document and type a list of the changes you would make to each slide. Apply formatting to the Word document as needed. Save the completed Word document and name it **U2T11-CT-Slides**. Print and then close **U2T11-CT-Slides.docx**.

Slide 1

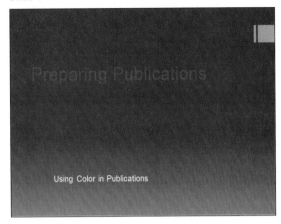

Preparing Publications

Using Color in Publications

Slide 2

Color Terminology

1. Balance: Amount of light and dark in a picture
2. Color wheel: Device used to illustrate color relationships
3. Contrast: Amount of gray in a color
4. Gradient: Gradual varying of color
5. Hue: Variation of a color, such as green–blue
6. Pixel: Each dot in a picture or graphic
7. Resolution: The number of dots that make up an image on a screen or printer
8. Reverse: Black background on white foreground or white type against a colored background
9. Saturation: Purity of a color

Slide 3

Communicating and Printing with Color

- Color in a publication can elicit feelings, emphasize important text, and attract attention
- Choose one or two colors
- Use "spot color" by using color only in specific areas
- Print all copies on a color printer
- Print on a color printer and duplicate with a color photocopier
- Print on colored paper or specialty paper

TEAM PROJECT

Researching and Presenting Design Guidelines

Divide into teams and, as a team, conduct Internet research to find guidelines for designing a PowerPoint presentation. Find at least three design guidelines and then create a presentation with a title and a slide for each guideline. Apply formatting to enhance the visual appeal of the presentation and make sure the text on the slides is easy to read. Save the presentation and name it **U2T11-GuidelinesTeam#** (where you enter a team number in place of the # symbol). Print the presentation with six slides horizontally per page and then close the presentation.

Applying Design Guidelines

As a team, open **CTHawaiiTour.pptx** and then save the presentation with Save As and name it **U2T11-HawaiiTourTeam#** (where you enter a team number in place of the # symbol). Using the information you gathered on design guidelines along with the information in the Delving Deeper section in this topic, apply a design theme and apply formatting to the presentation to make it visually appealing and easy to read. Save the formatted presentation, print the presentation with six slides horizontally per page, and then close the presentation.

Discussion Questions

1. What design theme did you choose for the guidelines presentation? What character and/or paragraph formatting did you apply to text in slides?
2. How did you use the design theme and formatting choices to enhance the visual appeal of the presentation? What specific design and formatting decisions did you make and why?
3. Of the presentations created in class, which is the most appealing? What makes one presentation more appealing than another? Did teams find similar or different guidelines? Which team found the most helpful guidelines for designing a presentation?
4. What design theme did you choose for the Hawaii Tour presentation, what character and/or paragraph formatting did you apply to text in slides, and what changes did you make to placeholders in slides?
5. How did you use the design theme and formatting choices to enhance the visual appeal of the Hawaii Tour presentation? What specific design, formatting, and customizing decisions did you make and why?
6. Compare your Hawaii Tour presentation with the presentations formatted by the other teams. Which presentation is the most appealing? What makes one presentation more appealing than another?

Topic 12

Inserting Graphic Elements in a Presentation and Integrating Word, Excel, and PowerPoint

Performance Objectives

Upon successful completion of Topic 12, you will be able to:

- Insert, size, and move a picture or clip art image
- Insert and format a SmartArt graphic
- Draw and customize shapes
- Insert and navigate with hyperlinks
- Create and format a table
- Create, customize, and format a chart
- Format a presentation with a slide master

- Apply animation and animation effects to items in a slide
- Insert audio and video files
- Export a PowerPoint presentation to Word
- Link an Excel chart with a Word document and PowerPoint presentation
- Edit a linked object
- Embed and edit a Word table in a PowerPoint slide

STUDENT RESOURCES

Before beginning this topic, copy to your storage medium the **Unit2Topic12** subfolder from the *Computer and Internet Essentials: Preparing for IC³* Internet Resource Center. Make this the active folder.

In addition to containing the data files needed to complete topic work, the Internet Resource Center contains model answers in PDF format for each of the applicable exercises in this topic. Use these files to check your work. The preface of your textbook provides instructions for accessing these files.

Necessary Data Files

To complete the exercises and assessments, you will need the following data files:

Exercises 12.1–12.7	VAPresentation.pptx VALogo.jpg VABudget.xlsx
Exercise 12.8	CTEcoTours.pptx EcoTours.wmv CTAudioFile-01.mid
Exercise 12.9	CFJobSearch.docx
Exercises 12.10 & 12.11	GMRevenues.docx GMDeptMeeting.pptx GMRevChart.xlsx

continued

Exercise 12.12	GMPresDates.docx
Review 12.1	CTAdventureTours.pptx CTLogo.jpg
Review 12.2	HMCenter.pptx CTAudioFile-02.mid HMEDEnroll.docx
Review 12.3	CFStrategies.pptx
Review 12.4	SGCMeeting.pptx SGCSales.xlsx
Review 12.5	SGContacts.docx Previously created file (Rev. 12.4)
Assessment 12.1	WEPlanMtg.pptx WELogo.jpg WERevenues.xlsx
Assessment 12.2	CTVacations.pptx
Assessment 12.3	GPACEnroll.pptx GPACEnrollChart.xlsx
Assessment 12.4	GPACContacts.docx Previously created file (Rev. 12.3)
Assessment 12.5	RMFMLogo.pptx RMFMClasses.pptx
Assessment 12.6	New file
Assessment 12.7	New file ESRLogo.jpg
Team Project	New file CTMorocco.pptx

Visual Preview

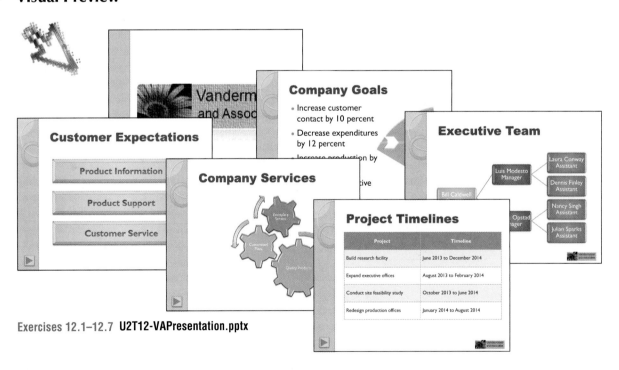

Exercises 12.1–12.7 **U2T12-VAPresentation.pptx**

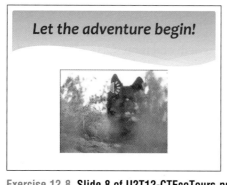

Exercise 12.8 **Slide 8 of U2T12-CTEcoTours.pptx**

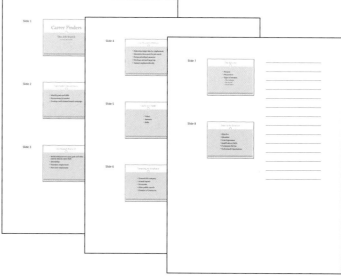

Exercise 12.9 **U2T12-CFJobSearchHandout.docx**

Exercise 12.10 **U2T12-GMRevenues.docx and Slide 4 of U2T12-GMDeptMeeting.pptx**

Exercise 12.11 **U2T12-GMRevChart.xlsx, U2T12-GMRevenues.docx, and Slide 4 of U2T12-GMDeptMeeting.pptx**

Exercise 12.12 **Slide 5 of U2T12-GMDeptMeeting.pptx**

Topic Overview

Presentations that contain only text may make it difficult for the audience to identify the most important information. Adding visual elements where appropriate can help you deliver a more focused message by adding interest and impact to the parts of your presentation you most want your audience to remember.

In this topic, you will learn how to add visual appeal to your presentations by inserting pictures, clip art images, SmartArt graphics, and shapes. You will also learn how to apply animation effects to elements on a slide. For example, you can specify that you want bulleted items to display one at a time, or you can have elements appear on the slide and then disappear.

The Microsoft Office suite allows you to export a file in one application in the suite to a file in another application. For example, you can export a PowerPoint presentation to a Word file. You can also integrate, or combine, data such as text or objects from two or more Office programs into one. For example, you can copy an Excel chart and then paste it in a Word document and/or a PowerPoint presentation. When you copy data from one application to another, you can paste, link, or embed the data. In this topic, you will learn how to export a file from one application in the Office suite to another as well as how to copy and link and copy and embed data between applications.

Lesson 12.1   Inserting, Sizing, and Moving a Picture or a Clip Art Image

 2-1.3.7, 2-4.1.2, 2-4.1.12

Quick Steps

Insert a Picture

1. Click Insert tab.
2. Click Picture button.
3. Navigate to desired folder.
4. Double-click desired picture.

Insert a Clip Art Image

1. Click Insert tab.
2. Click Clip Art button.
3. Type search word(s).
4. Press Enter.
5. Click desired image in Clip Art task pane.

You can increase the visual appeal of your presentation by inserting a graphic image in a slide. Generally, you would insert only one graphic in a slide. The graphic should enhance the slide text and not overwhelm or distract from the slide content. Use a graphic only if it helps to illustrate information in a slide. You can insert a graphic such as a picture or a clip art image into a slide by using buttons in the Images group on the Insert tab. Click the Picture button to display the Insert Picture dialog box and double-click a picture file, or click the Clip Art button and choose from a variety of images available in the Clip Art task pane.

When you insert an image in a slide, the image is selected and the Picture Tools Format tab becomes active. Use buttons on this tab to apply formatting to the image. With options in the Adjust group on the Picture Tools Format tab, you can correct the sharpness, brightness, and contrast of the image or recolor the image. Use the Compress Pictures button to compress the size of the image file. Other buttons on the Picture Tools Format tab allow you to reset the image back to its original color or change to a different image.

PowerPoint provides predesigned styles you can apply to your image. These styles are available in the Picture Styles group, along with buttons for changing the image border, applying effects to the image, and laying out the image.

Use options in the Arrange group to position the image on the page, specify text wrapping in relation to the image, align the image with other objects in the slide, and rotate the image. Use the Crop button in the Size group to remove any unnecessary parts of the image, and use the *Height* and *Width* measurement boxes to specify the image size.

You can also modify an image by using your mouse and keyboard:

- To change the size of an image, start by positioning the mouse arrow pointer on one of the image's sizing handles until the pointer turns into a double-headed arrow. Hold down the left mouse button, drag the image in or out to the desired size, and then release the mouse button.
- To move an image, position the mouse arrow pointer on the image border until the arrow pointer turns into a four-headed arrow. Then you have two options: either hold down the left mouse button, drag the image to the desired position, and release the mouse button; or use the arrow keys on the keyboard to move the image in the desired direction. To move the image in small increments (called *nudging*), hold down the Ctrl key while pressing an arrow key.

- To rotate an image, position the mouse arrow pointer on the green, round rotation handle until the pointer displays as a circular arrow. Hold down the left mouse button, drag the image in the desired direction, and then release the mouse button.

Exercise 12.1 Inserting, Sizing, and Moving a Picture and a Clip Art Image in PowerPoint

1. Open **VAPresentation.pptx** located in the **Unit2Topic12** folder on your storage medium and then save the presentation with Save As and name it **U2T12-VAPresentation**.

2. With Slide 1 active in the Slide pane, change the layout of the slide by clicking the Layout button in the Slides group on the Home tab and then clicking *Blank* at the drop-down list.

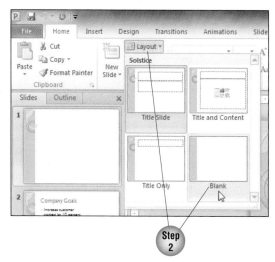

3. Insert the company logo in the blank slide as shown in Figure 12.1. To begin, click the Insert tab and then click the Picture button in the Images group.

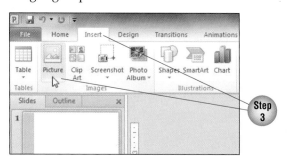

4. At the Insert Picture dialog box, navigate to the **Unit2Topic12** folder on your storage medium and then double-click the file named **VALogo.jpg**.

   The image is inserted in the slide, selection handles display around the image, and the Picture Tools Format tab is active.

5. Increase the size of the logo by clicking in the *Width* measurement box in the Size group, typing **8**, and then pressing Enter.

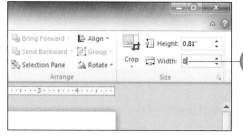

   When you change the width of the logo, the height automatically changes to maintain the proportions of the logo. You can also size an image using the sizing handles that display around the selected image. Use the middle sizing handles to increase or decrease the width of an image. Use the top and bottom handles to increase or decrease the height, and use the corner sizing handles to increase or decrease both the width and height of the image at the same time.

6. Click the Artistic Effects button in the Adjust group and then click the *Texturizer* option (second option from the left in the fourth row).

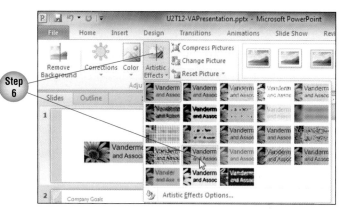

Inserting Graphic Elements in a Presentation and Integrating Word, Excel, and PowerPoint   **531**

7. Click the Reflected Rounded Rectangle style thumbnail in the Picture Styles group on the Picture Tools Format tab.

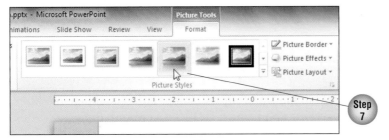

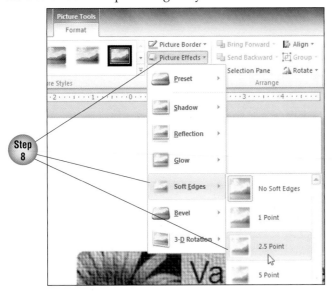

8. Click the Picture Effects button ☐ in the Picture Styles group, point to *Soft Edges*, and then click *2.5 Point* at the drop-down gallery.

9. Move the logo so it is positioned as shown in Figure 12.1. To do this, position the mouse arrow pointer on the image until the pointer displays with a four-headed arrow attached, drag the image to the position shown in the figure, and then release the mouse button.

10. Make Slide 2 active and notice that the clip art image does not pertain to the bulleted text. Delete the clip art image by clicking the image to select it and then pressing the Delete key on the keyboard.

11. Insert a new clip art image related to the bulleted text. Begin by clicking the Insert tab and then clicking the Clip Art button ☐ in the Images group.

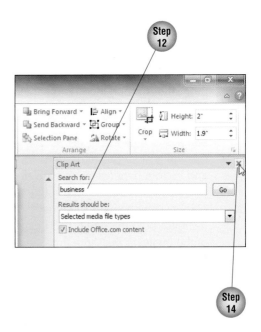

12. At the Clip Art task pane, type **business** in the *Search for* text box and then press Enter.

13. Click the clip art image shown in Figure 12.2.

    If this image is not available, choose another image related to business.

14. Close the Clip Art task pane by clicking the Close button that displays in the upper right corner of the task pane.

15. Change the color of the image by clicking the Color button 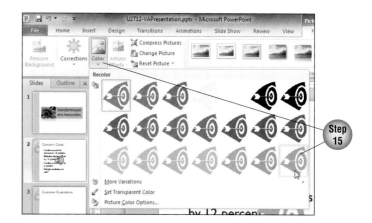 in the Adjust group and then clicking the *Lavender, Accent color 6 Light* option (last option in the third row).

16. Click the Corrections button in the Adjust group and then click the *Brightness: 0% (Normal) Contrast: +20%* option at the drop-down gallery (third option from the left in the fourth row).

17. Click the Picture Effects button in the Picture Styles group, point to *Shadow*, and then click the *Offset Diagonal Top Right* option (first option from the left in the bottom row of the *Outer* section).

18. Click in the *Height* measurement box, type **3.3**, and then press the Enter key.

19. Using the mouse, drag the image so it is positioned as shown in Figure 12.2.

20. Save **U2T12-VAPresentation.pptx**.

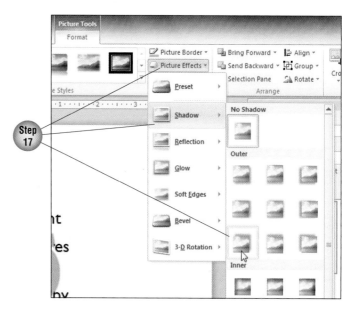

Figure 12.1 **Exercise 12.1 Slide 1**

Figure 12.2 Exercise 12.1 Slide 2

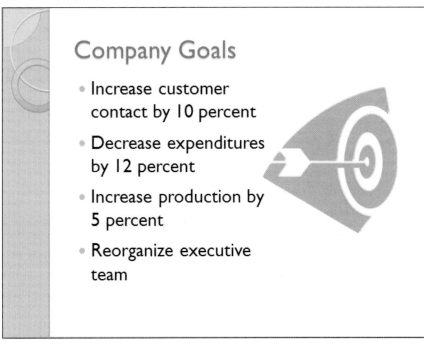

Company Goals

- Increase customer contact by 10 percent
- Decrease expenditures by 12 percent
- Increase production by 5 percent
- Reorganize executive team

Drilling Down

Downloading Clip Art Images

If you are connected to the Internet, you can download clip art images from the Microsoft website. To do this, display the Clip Art task pane and then click the <u>Find more at Office.com</u> hyperlink that displays toward the bottom of the task pane. This displays a page at the Microsoft website containing images you can download. To search for images in a specific category, type the desired category in the search text box and then press Enter. To download an image, hover your mouse arrow pointer over the desired image and then click the <u>download</u> hyperlink. At the File Download dialog box, click the Save button. At the Save As dialog box, navigate to the desired folder and then click the Save button.

Lesson 12.2   Inserting and Formatting a SmartArt Graphic

 2-1.3.7

With the SmartArt feature, you can insert in a slide a graphic such as a diagram or organizational chart. Use a SmartArt graphic to create a visual representation of information in a slide to help you effectively communicate your message.

Insert a SmartArt graphic with options at the Choose a SmartArt Graphic dialog box. Display this dialog box by clicking the Insert tab and then clicking the SmartArt button in the Illustrations group, or by clicking the Insert SmartArt Graphic button in the Content placeholder. At the Choose a SmartArt Graphic dialog box, click the desired graphic category in the list at the left side of the dialog box and then double-click the desired graphic in the middle section of the dialog box. This inserts the SmartArt graphic in the slide and makes the SmartArt Tools Design tab active. Use buttons and options on this tab to add objects, change the graphic layout, apply a style to the graphic, and reset the graphic back to the original formatting.

Quick Steps

Insert a SmartArt Graphic

1. Click Insert tab.
2. Click SmartArt button.
3. Double-click desired SmartArt graphic.

Apply formatting to a SmartArt graphic with options at the SmartArt Tools Format tab. With options and buttons on this tab you can change the size and shape of objects in the graphic; apply shape styles and WordArt styles; change the shape fill, outline, and effects; and arrange and size the graphic. Move a SmartArt graphic by positioning the mouse arrow pointer on the graphic border until the pointer turns into a four-headed arrow, holding down the left mouse button, and then dragging the graphic to the desired location.

Exercise 12.2 Inserting and Formatting a SmartArt Organizational Chart and Diagram

1. With **U2T12-VAPresentation.pptx** open and Slide 2 active, click the Home tab, click the New Slide button arrow in the Slides group, and then click *Title Only* at the drop-down list.

2. Click the text *Click to add title* and then type **Executive Team**.

3. Create the organizational chart shown in Figure 12.3. To begin, click the Insert tab, and then click the SmartArt button in the Illustrations group.

4. At the Choose a SmartArt Graphic dialog box, click *Hierarchy* in the left panel of the dialog box and then double-click *Horizontal Hierarchy* in the middle panel (last option in the third row).

   This displays the organizational chart in the slide with the SmartArt Tools Design tab selected.

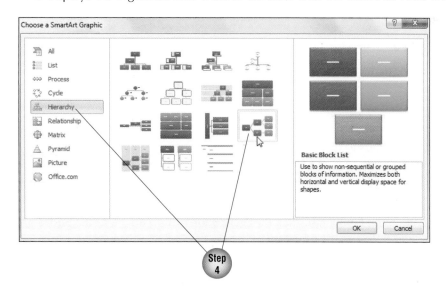

5. If the words *Type your text here* display, close the window by clicking the Text Pane button in the Create Graphic group on the SmartArt Tools Design tab.

   You can also close the window by clicking the Close button that displays in the upper right corner of the window.

6. Insert an additional box in the organizational chart by clicking the border of the bottom box in the second level of the chart, clicking the Add Shape button arrow 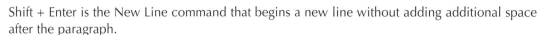, and then clicking *Add Shape Below* at the drop-down list.

Your organizational chart should contain the same boxes as shown in Figure 12.3.

7. Click *[Text]* in the first box at the left, type **Bill Caldwell**, press Shift + Enter, and then type **Director**. Click in each of the remaining boxes and type the text as shown in Figure 12.3.

Shift + Enter is the New Line command that begins a new line without adding additional space after the paragraph.

8. Click outside the box but inside the SmartArt border.

This deselects the box and selects the entire SmartArt graphic.

9. Click the Change Colors button in the SmartArt Styles group and then click the *Colorful Range - Accent Colors 4 to 5* option (fourth color option from the left in the *Colorful* section).

10. Click the More button located at the right side of the SmartArt Styles group and then click the *Inset* option located in the *3-D* section.

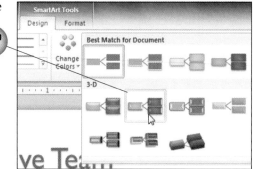

11. Click the SmartArt Tools Format tab.

12. Click in the *Width* measurement box in the Size group, type **8**, and then press Enter.

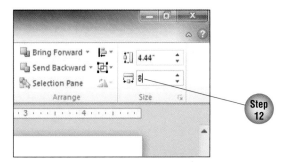

13. Move the organizational chart to the middle of the slide by positioning the mouse arrow pointer anywhere on the chart border until the pointer displays with a four-headed arrow attached, holding down the left mouse button, and then dragging to the left until the chart is positioned as shown in Figure 12.3.

14. Make Slide 4 active, click the Home tab, click the New Slide button arrow in the Slides group, and then click *Title and Content* at the drop-down list.

15. Click the text *Click to add title* and then type **Company Services**.

16. Create the diagram shown in Figure 12.4. To begin, click the Insert SmartArt Graphic button in the content placeholder.

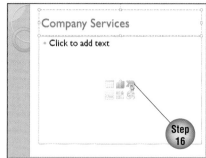

17. At the Choose a SmartArt Graphic dialog box, click *Relationship* in the left panel of the dialog box and then double-click the *Gear* option in the middle panel.

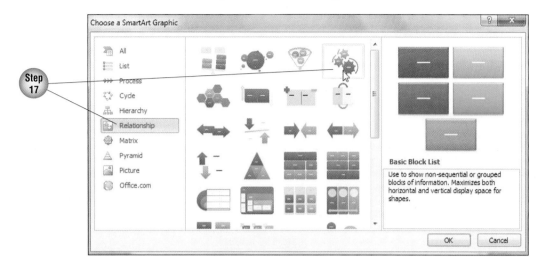

18. Click in the top shape and then type **Exemplary Service**. Click in the middle shape and then type **Customized Plans**. Click in the bottom shape and then type **Quality Products**.

    Refer to Figure 12.4.

19. Click inside the SmartArt border but outside any SmartArt shapes.

20. Click the Change Colors button in the SmartArt Styles group and then click the *Colorful - Accent Colors* option (first option from the left in the *Colorful* section).

21. Click the More button located at the right side of the SmartArt Styles group and then click the *Cartoon* option located in the *3-D* section.

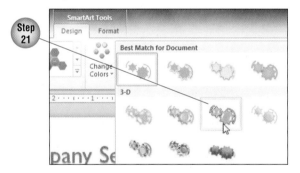

22. Select each gear in the diagram by clicking one of the gears, holding down the Ctrl key and then clicking the remaining two gears.

    The arrows will not be selected.

23. Click the SmartArt Tools Format tab.

24. Click the Shape Outline button arrow ✐ and then click *Purple* at the drop-down gallery (last option in the *Standard Colors* section).

25. Save **U2T12-VAPresentation.pptx**.

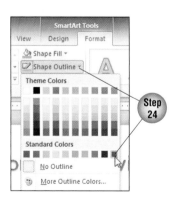

Figure 12.3 **Exercise 12.2 Slide 3**

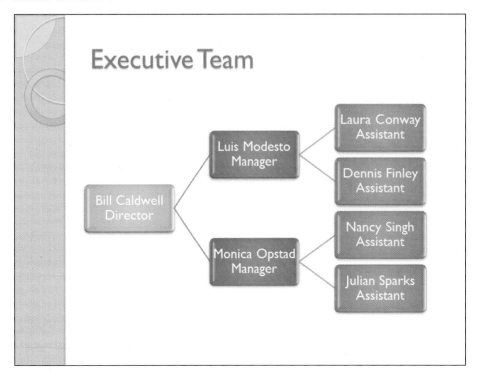

Figure 12.4 **Exercise 12.2 Slide 5**

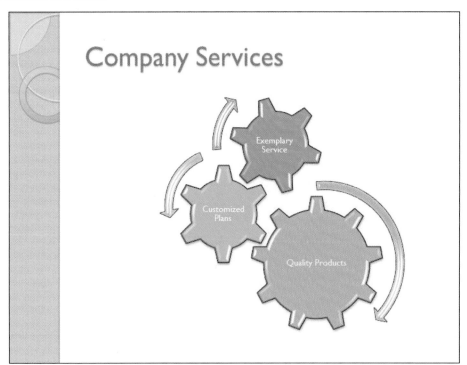

Drilling Down

Creating a SmartArt Graphic with Bulleted Text

To improve the visual appeal of text and to create a professional-looking presentation, consider converting bulleted text into a SmartArt graphic. To do this, select the placeholder containing the text you want to convert and then click the Convert to SmartArt Graphic button in the Paragraph group on the Home tab. Click the desired SmartArt graphic at the drop-down gallery. This displays the Choose a SmartArt Graphic dialog box, where you can choose a SmartArt graphic.

Inserting Text in the Text Pane

You can enter text in a SmartArt shape by clicking in the shape and then typing the text. You can also insert text in the SmartArt shape by typing text in the Text pane. Display the Text pane by clicking the Text Pane button in the Create Graphic group on the SmartArt Tools Design tab.

Lesson 12.3   Drawing and Customizing Shapes in PowerPoint

 2-1.3.7, 2-4.1.2

You can add visual appeal or interest to a slide by drawing lines or shapes. Draw lines to emphasize text, point to specific items, or connect objects. Draw a shape in a slide to emphasize specific data, create an artistic element, or to contain text (such as in a banner or callout). In addition to lines and shapes, you can draw an action button in a slide that, when clicked during a presentation, performs an action such as displaying the next, previous, first, or last slide.

Draw a line, shape, or action button in a slide with the shape options in the Drawing group on the Home tab or with the Shapes button on the Insert tab. You can choose a shape to draw a line, basic shape, block arrow, flow chart shape, callout, star, or banner. Click a shape in the Drawing group or click the Insert tab, click the Shapes button, and then click a shape at the drop-down list and the mouse arrow pointer displays as a crosshairs (plus sign). Drag in the slide to draw a line or click in the slide to insert a shape. You can also position the crosshairs where you want the shape to begin, hold down the left mouse button, drag to create the shape, and then release the mouse button. This displays the Drawing Tools Format tab. Use buttons on this tab to change the line or shape, apply a style, and arrange or change the size of the line or shape.

If you choose a shape in the *Lines* section of the drop-down list, the shape you draw is considered a **line drawing**. If you want to draw a straight line, hold down the Shift key while drawing the line. If you choose an option in the other sections of the drop-down list, the shape you draw is considered an **enclosed object**. You can type text directly into an enclosed object. When drawing an enclosed object, holding down the Shift key will maintain the proportions of the shape.

With options at the Shapes button drop-down list, you can insert an action button in a slide. An **action button** is a drawn object on a slide that has a routine attached to it. This routine is activated when the viewer or speaker clicks the object when running a presentation. For example, you can insert an action button that displays the next slide, previous slide, a file in another program, or a specific web page. To insert an action button, click the Shapes button and then click the desired action button at the drop-down list. Click in the slide to insert the button. Make any desired changes at the Action Settings dialog box that displays and then click OK. Use options on the Drawing Tools Format tab to customize the action button.

Quick Steps

Insert a Shape

1. Click Insert tab.
2. Click Shapes button.
3. Click desired shape at drop-down list.
4. Drag in slide to create shape.

line drawing A shape drawn with an option in the *Lines* section of the Shapes button drop-down list

enclosed object An object drawn with any option in the Shapes button drop-down list except the options in the *Lines* section

action button A drawn object on a slide that has a routine attached to it; the routine is activated when the object is clicked during a presentation

Quick Steps

Insert an Action Button

1. Click Insert tab.
2. Click Shapes button.
3. Click desired action button.
4. Click in slide.
5. Make desired changes at Action Settings dialog box.
6. Click OK.

Exercise 12.3 Drawing and Customizing a Shape and an Action Button

1. With **U2T12-VAPresentation.pptx** open, make Slide 4 active.

2. Create the shapes shown in Figure 12.5. Begin by clicking the Insert tab, clicking the Shapes button ⬚ in the Illustrations group, and then clicking the *Bevel* shape (first shape from the left in the third row in the *Basic Shapes* section of the drop-down list).

3. Click in the slide below the title.

   This inserts a bevel shape in the slide and makes the shape active.

4. Click the Drawing Tools Format tab.

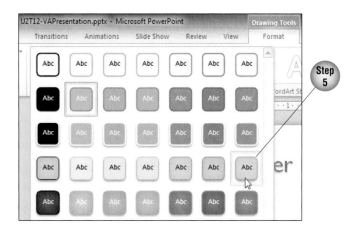

5. Click the More button at the right side of the shape style thumbnails in the Shape Styles group on the Drawing Tools Format tab and then click the *Subtle Effect - Lavender, Accent 6* option.

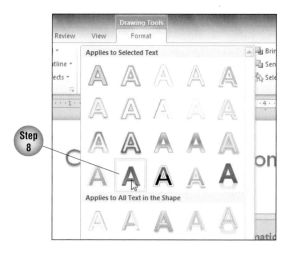

6. Click in the Shape Width measurement box in the Size group on the Drawing Tools Format tab, type **7**, and then press the Enter key.

7. With the shape selected, type **Product Information**.

8. Select *Product Information*, click the More button at the right side of the WordArt style thumbnails in the WordArt Styles group, and then click the *Gradient Fill - Lavender, Accent 6, Inner Shadow* option.

9. Click the Home tab and then click four times on the Increase Font Size button in the Font group.

10. Click the border of the shape to change the border to a solid line and then drag the shape so it is centered approximately one-half inch below the title.

11. Copy the selected shape by positioning the mouse arrow pointer on the shape border until the mouse arrow pointer displays with a four-headed arrow attached. Hold down the Ctrl key and then the left mouse button. Drag the shape down below the first shape, release the left mouse button, and then release the Ctrl key.

12. Copy the shape a third time and position it below the first two shapes using methods similar to those in Step 11.

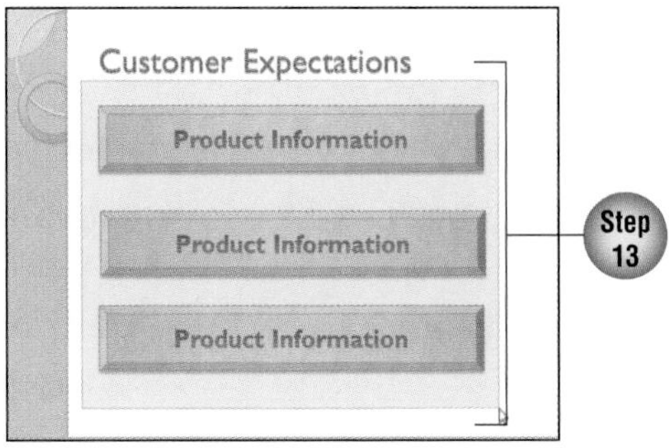

13. Select the three shapes by using the mouse to draw a border around them.

    When you release the mouse button, the three shapes are selected.

14. Align the objects at the left by clicking the Drawing Tools Format tab, clicking the Align button in the Arrange group, and then clicking *Align Left* at the drop-down list.

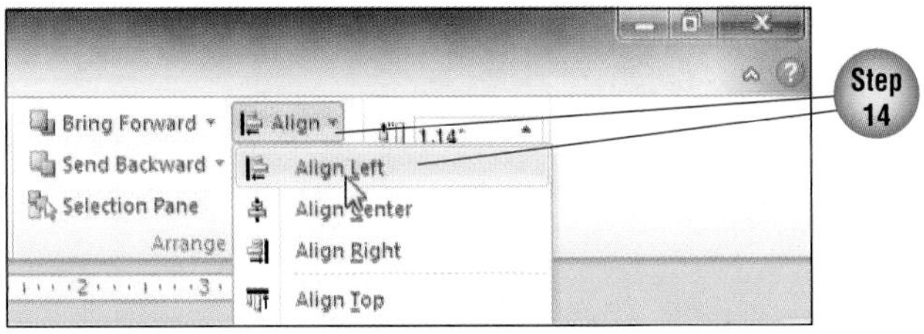

15. Vertically distribute the shapes by clicking the Align button in the Arrange group and then clicking *Distribute Vertically* at the drop-down list.

    Your shapes should now display in a manner similar to the shapes in Figure 12.5.

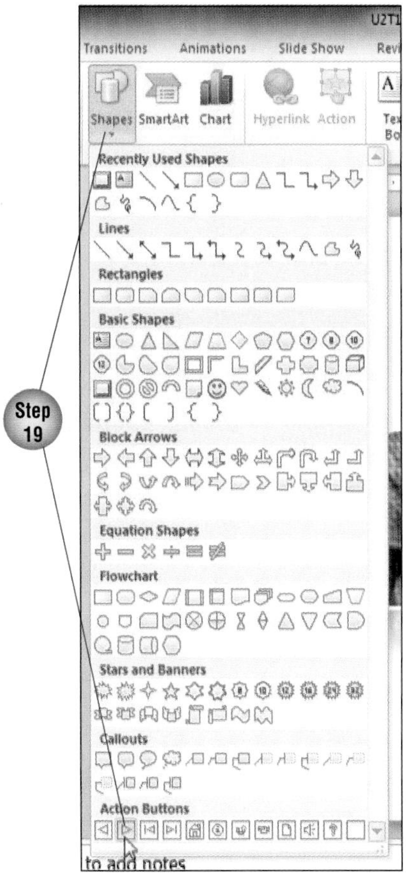

16. Select the text in the middle shape and then type **Product Support**.

17. Select the text in the bottom shape and then type **Customer Service**.

18. Make Slide 1 active.

19. Click the Insert tab, click the Shapes button, and then click the *Action Button: Forward or Next* button located at the bottom of the drop-down list (second option from the left).

20. Move the crosshair pointer to the lower left corner of the purple sidebar in the slide and then click the left mouse button.

    This inserts the action button in the slide.

21. At the Action Settings dialog box, click OK.

    The default setting for the action button is *Hyperlink to Next Slide*.

22. With the button selected, click the Drawing Tools Format tab and then change the shape height and width to *0.5″*.

    The Shape Height and Shape Width buttons are located at the right side of the Drawing Tools Format tab in the Size group.

23. Click the More button at the right side of the shape style thumbnails in the Shape Styles group and then click the *Subtle Effect - Lavender, Accent 6* option (last option in the fourth row).

24. If necessary, drag the action button so it is positioned in the lower left corner of the slide (inside the purple side bar) as shown in Figure 12.5.

25. With the action button selected, click the Home tab and then click the Copy button in the Clipboard group.

26. Make Slide 2 active and then click the Paste button in the Clipboard group on the Home tab.

27. Paste the action button into each of the remaining slides.

28. Save **U2T12-VAPresentation.pptx**.

Figure 12.5 **Exercise 12.3 Slide 4 Shapes**

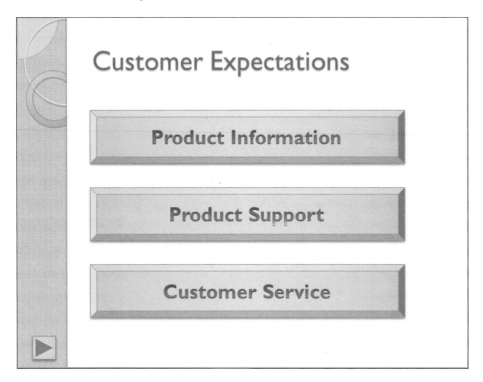

Drilling
Down

Displaying Rulers and Gridlines

To help position objects such as images and shapes, consider displaying the horizontal and vertical rulers and gridlines. You can turn the horizontal and vertical rulers on and off with the *Ruler* check box in the Show group on the View tab. The Show group also contains a *Gridlines* check box. Insert a check mark in this check box and gridlines display in the active slide. Gridlines are intersecting lines that create a grid on the slide and are useful for aligning objects.

Lesson 12.4   Inserting and Navigating with Hyperlinks

IC³ 2-4.1.11

In the previous lesson you inserted action buttons in a slide that linked to other slides in the presentation. Another way to insert a link in a presentation is to create a hyperlink using options at the Insert Hyperlink dialog box, shown in Figure 12.6. To insert a hyperlink, select a key word, phrase, or object in a slide, click the Insert tab, and then click the Hyperlink button in the Links group. You can link to a website, a place in the current presentation, a new or existing presentation, or an email address. Click the desired location in the *Link to* section of the dialog box and then specify the website, file, or presentation. Navigate to a hyperlink's destination by clicking the hyperlink in the slide when running the presentation.

Quick Steps

Insert Hyperlink

1. Click Insert tab.
2. Click Hyperlink button.
3. Make desired changes at Insert Hyperlink dialog box.
4. Click OK.

Keyboard Shortcut

Insert Hyperlink Dialog Box

Ctrl + K

Figure 12.6 **Insert Hyperlink Dialog Box**

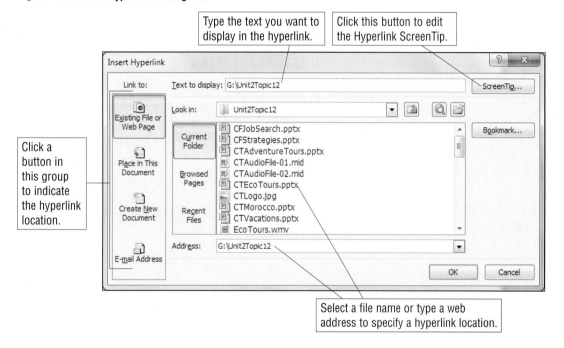

Type the text you want to display in the hyperlink.

Click this button to edit the Hyperlink ScreenTip.

Click a button in this group to indicate the hyperlink location.

Select a file name or type a web address to specify a hyperlink location.

Exercise 12.4 Inserting Hyperlinks in a Presentation

1. With **U2T12-VAPresentation.pptx** open, make Slide 2 active.

2. Insert a hyperlink to an Excel file. Begin by selecting the text *expenditures* that displays in the second bulleted item.

3. Click the Insert tab and then click the Hyperlink button in the Links group.

Inserting Graphic Elements in a Presentation and Integrating Word, Excel, and PowerPoint   **543**

4. At the Insert Hyperlink dialog box, click the Existing File or Web Page option in the *Link to* section.

5. Click the down-pointing arrow at the right side of the *Look in* option and then navigate to the **Unit2Topic12** folder on your storage medium.

6. Double-click *VABudget.xlsx*.

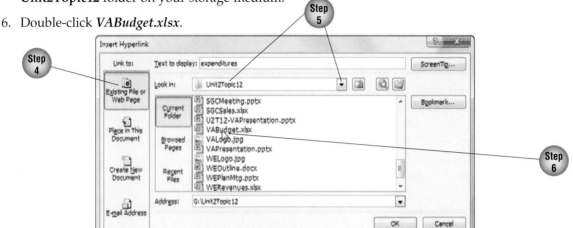

7. Make Slide 1 active and then run the presentation by clicking the Slide Show button in the view area on the Status bar.

8. Click the left mouse button to display Slide 2.

9. Click the expenditures hyperlink.

10. After looking at the Excel file, click the Close button in the upper right corner of the screen to close the file and exit Excel.

11. Press the Esc key on your keyboard to end the presentation.

Company Goals

- Increase customer contact by 10 percent
- Decrease expenditures by 12 percent

12. Make Slide 2 active and then insert a hyperlink to another slide in the presentation. Begin by selecting the text *executive team* that displays in the last bulleted item.

13. Click the Insert tab and then click the Hyperlink button in the Links group.

14. At the Insert Hyperlink dialog box, click the Place in This Document option in the *Link to* section.

15. Click *3. Executive Team* in the *Select a place in this document* list box and then click OK.

16. Make Slide 1 active and then run the presentation. Click the left mouse button once to display Slide 2.

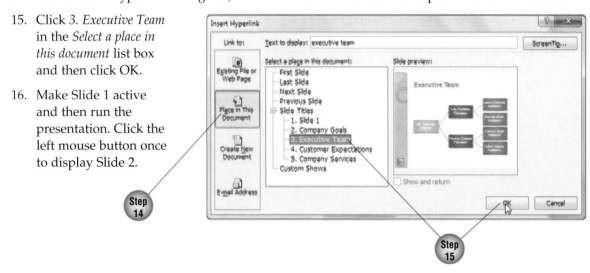

17. Click the <u>executive team</u> hyperlink.

    This displays Slide 3 containing the executive team organizational chart.

18. Press the Esc key to end the presentation.

19. Save **U2T12-VAPresentation.pptx**.

Lesson 12.5 Creating a Table in a Slide

 2-4.1.2

PowerPoint includes a Table feature you can use for displaying columns and rows of data. As in most Microsoft Office applications, a table in PowerPoint is an object containing columns and rows for entering data. This feature is useful in informative presentations to display data. Insert a table in a slide with the Insert Table button in the Content placeholder or with the Table button on the Insert tab. Click the Insert Table button in the Content placeholder and the Insert Table dialog box displays. At this dialog box, type the number of columns, press the Tab key (this moves the insertion point to the *Number of rows* text box), type the number of rows, and then press Enter or click OK. You can also click the *Insert Table* option at the Table button drop-down list to display the Insert Table dialog box. To insert a table with the Table button, click the button, drag the mouse down and to the right to select the desired number of columns and rows, and then click the left mouse button.

> **Quick Steps**
> **Insert a Table**
> 1. Click Insert Table button in Content placeholder.
> 2. Type number of columns.
> 3. Press Tab key.
> 4. Type number of rows.
> 5. Click OK.
> **OR**
> 1. Click Insert tab.
> 2. Click Table button.
> 3. Drag in grid to set desired number of columns and rows.
> 4. Click left mouse button.

When you insert a table in a slide, the Table Tools Design tab is active. Use buttons on this tab to enhance the appearance of the table. For example, with options in the Table Styles group, you can select a predesigned style that applies color and border lines to a table or use options to apply specific shading, border lines, or effects to a table. Maintain further control over the predesigned style formatting applied to columns and rows with options in the Table Style Options group. Apply additional design formatting to cells in a table with the Shading and Borders buttons in the Table Styles group. Draw a table or draw additional rows and/or columns in a table with options in the Draw Borders group. Click the Table Tools Format tab to display options and buttons for inserting and deleting columns and rows; changing cell size, alignment, direction, and margins; changing the table size; and arranging the table in a slide.

Exercise 12.5 Creating a Table in a Slide

1. With **U2T12-VAPresentation.pptx** open, make Slide 5 active and then click the New Slide button in the Slides group on the Home tab.

2. Click the text *Click to add title* and then type **Project Timelines**.

3. Create the table shown in Figure 12.7. Begin by clicking the Insert Table button that displays in the slide Content placeholder.

4. At the Insert Table dialog box, type **2** in the *Number of columns* text box.

5. Press the Tab key and then type **5** in the *Number of rows* text box.

6. Click OK to close the Insert Table dialog box.

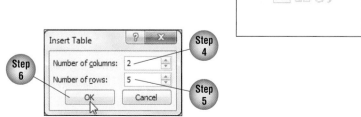

7. Type the following text in the table (refer to Figure 12.7).

Press the Tab key to move the insertion point to the next cell or press Shift + Tab to move the insertion point to the previous cell.

Project	Timeline
Build research facility	June 2013 to December 2014
Expand executive offices	August 2013 to February 2014
Conduct site feasibility study	October 2013 to June 2013
Redesign production offices	January 2014 to August 2014

8. Click the More button at the right side of the table style thumbnails in the Table Styles group on the Table Tools Design tab and then click *Medium Style 1 - Accent 6* at the drop-down gallery (last option in the first row in the *Medium* section).

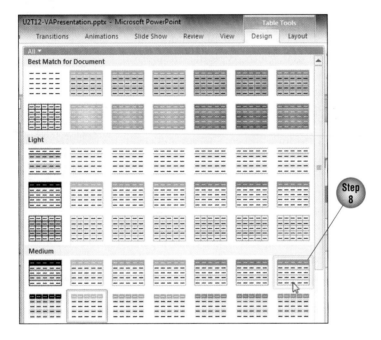

9. Click the Pen Color button 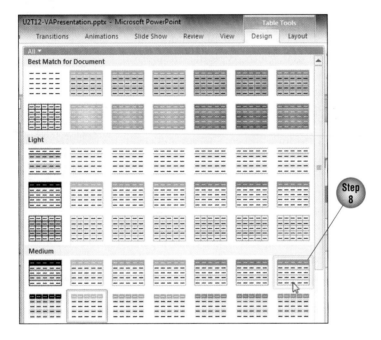 and then click the *Lavender, Accent 6, Lighter 40%* color option (located in the last column).

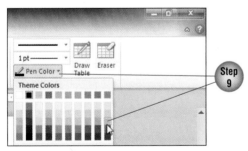

10. Using the mouse, drag down the white column line that displays between the cells in the first row and then continue drawing down the table to the bottom border.

11. Click the Draw Table button ▦ to turn off the feature.

12. Click the Table Tools Layout tab.

13. Click in the *Height* measurement box in the Table Size group, type **4.3**, and then press Enter.

14. Click in the *Width* measurement box in the Cell Size group, type **3.9**, and then press Enter.

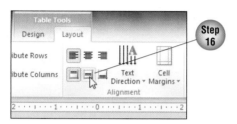

Step 14

15. Select the table by positioning the mouse arrow pointer on the table border until the pointer displays with a four-headed arrow attached and then clicking the left mouse button.

16. Align the text vertically in the cells by clicking the Center Vertically button ▤ in the Alignment group on the Table Tools Layout tab.

Step 16

17. Select the first row by positioning the mouse arrow pointer on the left side of the first row in the table until the pointer turns into a black, right-pointing arrow and then clicking the left mouse button.

18. Click the Center button ▤ in the Alignment group.

   Your table should now display in a manner similar to the table in Figure 12.7.

19. Click outside the table to deselect it.

20. Make Slide 5 active and then copy the action button (located in the lower left corner of the slide). Make Slide 6 active and then paste the action button in the same location.

21. Since this is the last slide in the presentation, edit the action button so that, when clicked, it will display the first slide in the presentation (rather than the next slide). To begin, position the mouse arrow pointer on the action button, click the right mouse button, and then click *Edit Hyperlink* at the shortcut menu.

22. At the Action Settings dialog box, click the down-pointing arrow at the right of the *Next Slide* option, click *First Slide* at the drop-down list, and then click OK.

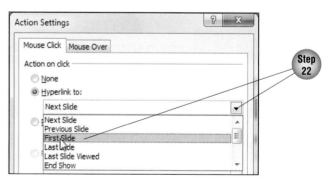

Step 22

23. Make Slide 1 active and then run the presentation using the action buttons in the lower left corner of the slides. After viewing the presentation at least twice, press the Esc key.

24. Save **U2T12-VAPresentation.pptx**.

Figure 12.7 Exercise 12.5 Slide 6 Table

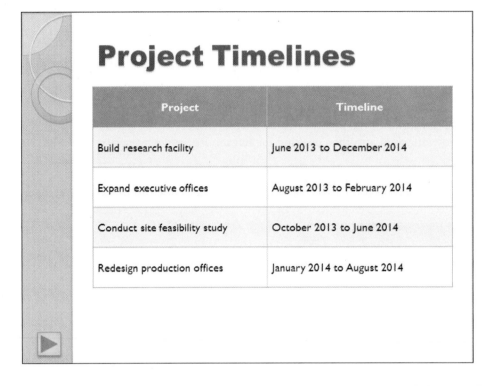

 Drilling Down

Moving and Sizing a Table

To increase or decrease the size of a table, type the desired measurements in the *Height* and *Width* measurement boxes in the Table Size group on the Table Tools Layout tab. You can also drag a table border to increase or decrease the size. When the insertion point is positioned in a table, a border surrounds the table and the border contains sizing handles that display as a series of dots in the middle of the top, bottom, left, and right borders as well as each corner. Position the mouse arrow pointer on one of the sizing handles until the pointer displays as a two-headed arrow, hold down the left mouse button, and then drag to increase or decrease the size. Drag a corner sizing handle to change the size of the table proportionally. To move the table, position the mouse arrow pointer on the table border until the pointer displays with a four-headed arrow attached and then drag the table to the desired position.

Lesson 12.6 Formatting with a Slide Master

 2-4.1.1

A slide master is a formatting and layout template that applies to multiple (or all) slides in a presentation. Each presentation has at least one slide master, and when you change a presentation's design, those design changes are applied to the slide master. If you want to make the same formatting change to all the slides in a presentation, or all slides of a certain layout or design, consider making the change on the slide master.

To display slide masters, click the View tab and then click the Slide Master button in the Master Views group. The available slide masters display in the slide thumbnail pane at the left side of the screen. Beneath the slide master (the top slide) are thumbnails representing each of the layouts associated with the currently chosen design. These are called layout masters. When you apply a formatting change to a layout master in Slide Master view, the formatting change is automatically applied to all slides in the presentation that use that layout. This automatic application reduces the number of steps needed to apply formatting changes to your entire presentation. Once you have applied formatting to the desired slide masters, click the Close Master View button in the Close group to return to Normal view.

If you edit the formatting of text in a slide in Normal view, the link to the slide master is broken. Changes you make to a slide master in Slide Master view will not affect the individually formatted slide. For this reason, make formatting changes in Slide Master view before editing individual slides in a presentation.

Quick Steps

Display Slide Master View
1. Click View tab.
2. Click Slide Master button.

Exercise 12.6 Formatting with a Slide Master

1. With **U2T12-VAPresentation.pptx** open, make Slide 1 active.

2. Click the View tab and then click the Slide Master button ⊞ in the Master Views group.

   Hover your mouse arrow pointer over a slide master in the slide thumbnail pane at the left side of the screen and a ScreenTip displays with information about the slide layout and the number of slides in the presentation that use the layout.

3. Click the first slide master thumbnail in the left pane.

   Hover your mouse over the slide master thumbnail and the ScreenTip *Solstice Slide Master: used by slide(s) 1-6* displays.

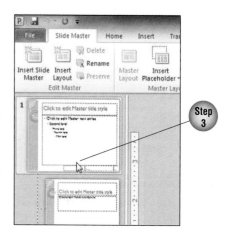

4. Select the text *Click to edit Master title style* and then change the font color by clicking the Home tab, clicking the Font Color button arrow, and then clicking the *Purple* option (last option in the *Standard Colors* section).

5. Click the Font button arrow and then click *Arial Black* at the drop-down gallery.

6. Click in the text *Click to edit Master text styles*.

7. Change the color of the bullet by clicking the Bullets button arrow and then clicking the *Bullets and Numbering* option at the drop-down gallery. At the Bullets and Numbering dialog box, click the Color button, click the *Aqua, Accent 3, Darker 25%* option (located in the seventh column from the left), and then click OK to close the dialog box.

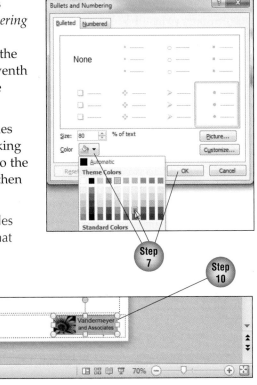

8. Insert a picture in the bottom right corner of the slides (except the first slide) by clicking the Insert tab, clicking the Picture button in the Images group, navigating to the **Unit2Topic12** folder on your storage medium, and then double-clicking the file named **VALogo.jpg**.

   The image is inserted in the slide master, sizing handles display around the image, and the Picture Tools Format tab is active.

9. Decrease the size of the logo by clicking in the *Width* measurement box in the Size group, typing **1.5**, and then pressing Enter.

10. Drag the logo so it is positioned in the lower right corner of the slide master.

11. Click the Slide Master tab and then click the Close Master View button ☒ in the Close group.

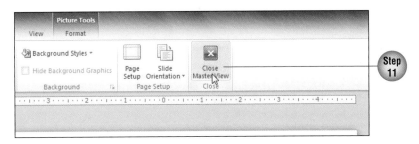

12. Run the presentation and notice the logo in the lower right corner of Slides 2 through 6 and the formatting changes you made to the slide master.

13. Save **U2T12-VAPresentation.pptx**.

Drilling Down

Applying More Than One Design Theme to a Presentation

Each design theme applies specific formatting to slides. You can apply more than one design theme to slides in a presentation. To do this, select the specific slides and then apply the desired theme. The design theme is applied only to the selected slides. If you apply more than one design theme to a presentation, multiple slide masters will display in Slide Master view.

Lesson 12.7 Applying Animation Effects to Items in a Slide

IC³ 2-4.1.2

You can animate an individual object and/or portion of text in a slide by applying an animation effect with options in the Animations tab. An **animation effect** is an entrance, exit, or motion effect applied to an element in a PowerPoint slide. Click the Animations tab and the ribbon displays with a variety of animation styles and options for customizing and applying time durations to animations in a presentation. Click the More button at the right side of the thumbnails in the Animation group and a gallery of animation styles displays that you can apply to items as they enter a slide, exit a slide, and/or follow a path. You can also apply animations to emphasize items in a slide. You can customize an animation effect by clicking the Effect Options button in the Animation group and then clicking the desired option at the drop-down list. The options in the drop-down list vary with each animation.

If you want the same animation applied to other items in a presentation, use the Animation Painter button in the Advanced Animation group on the Animations tab.

You can use animations to create a build for bulleted items. A **build** is an animation that displays paragraphs (such as bulleted text) in a slide one paragraph at a time. A build is useful for keeping the audience's attention focused on the point being presented because it prevents them from reading ahead.

If you want to view the animation effects applied to items in a slide without running the presentation, click the Preview button on the Animations tab. When you apply animation effects to items in a slide, an animation icon displays below the slide number in the Slides/Outline pane. Remove animation effects from an item by clicking the item and then clicking the *None* option in the Animation group on the Animations tab.

animation effect An entrance, exit, or motion effect applied to an element in a slide

Quick Steps

Apply an Animation
1. Click desired item in slide.
2. Click Animations tab.
3. Click More button in Animation group.
4. Click desired animation at drop-down gallery.

build A type of animation that displays paragraphs in a slide one paragraph at a time

Exercise 12.7 Applying Animations to Items in Slides

1. With **U2T12-VAPresentation.pptx** open, make Slide 1 active.

2. Click anywhere in the logo and apply an animation by clicking the Animations tab and then clicking the *Float In* option in the Animation group.

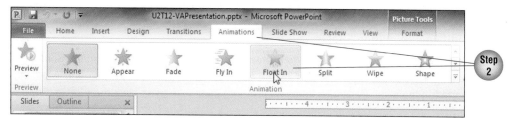

3. Click the Effect Options button ⬆ in the Animation group and then click *Float Down* at the drop-down list.

4. Make Slide 2 active and then click in the bulleted text.

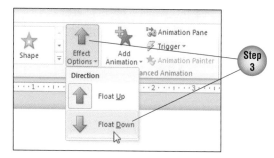

5. Click the *Fly In* option in the Animation group.

   This creates a build for the bulleted text.

6. Click twice on the up-pointing arrow at the right side of the *Duration* option in the Timing group.

   This inserts *01.00* in the option box.

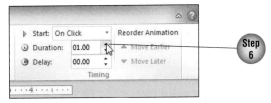

7. Make Slide 3 active and then click the SmartArt organizational chart to select it.

   Do not select any shapes within the chart.

8. Click the *Fade* option in the Animation group.

9. Click the Effect Options button and then click *Level One by One* at the drop-down gallery.

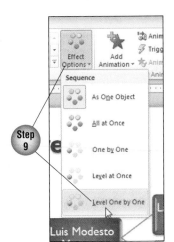

10. Apply the same animation to a SmartArt graphic in another slide. Begin by clicking in the SmartArt organizational chart to select it (do not select any shapes within the chart) and then clicking the Animation Painter button in the Advanced Animation group.

11. Make Slide 5 active and then click anywhere in the SmartArt graphic.

    This applies the *Fade* animation and the *Level One by One* effect option to the SmartArt graphic. Because you clicked the Animation Painter button only once, it was turned off as soon as you clicked in the SmartArt graphic in Slide 5.

12. Make Slide 1 active and then run the presentation using the mouse to advance slides and to display the company logo, bulleted text, and SmartArt graphics. (Do not use the action buttons in the lower left corner of the slides.)

13. Print the presentation as handouts with four slides horizontally per page.

14. Save and then close **U2T12-VAPresentation.pptx**.

Drilling Down

Modifying Animation Effects

When you apply an animation effect to an item, you can use options in the Timing group to modify the animation effect. Use the *Start* option drop-down list to specify when you want the item inserted in the slide. Generally, items display in a slide when you click the mouse button. Click the *Start* option down-pointing arrow and then click *With Previous* or *With Next* at the drop-down list to make the item display on the slide with the previous item or the next item. Use the *Duration* option to specify the length of an animation and use the *Delay* option to specify when to play an animation after a specific amount of time.

Lesson 12.8   Inserting Audio and Video Files

2-4.1.2

Adding audio and/or video files to a presentation turns a slide show into a multimedia experience for your audience. Including a variety of elements in a presentation stimulates interest in your presentation and keeps the audience engaged. To add an audio file to your presentation, click the Insert tab and then click the Audio button in the Media group. At the Insert Audio dialog box, navigate to the desired folder and then double-click the audio file. You can also insert audio by clicking the Audio button arrow and then clicking an option at the drop-down list. With the drop-down list options you can choose to insert an external audio file, insert a clip art audio file, or record an audio file. When you insert an audio file in a presentation, you can customize the file with options on the Audio Tools Format tab and the Audio Tools Playback tab.

Inserting a video file in a presentation is similar to inserting an audio file. Click the Video button in the Media group on the Insert tab to display the Insert Video dialog box. You can also display the Insert Video dialog box by clicking the Video button and then clicking *Video from File* at the drop-down list or by clicking the Insert Media Clip button in the Content placeholder. At the Insert Video dialog box, navigate to the folder containing the video file and then double-click the file. Customize the video file with options on the Video Tools Format tab and the Video Tools Playback tab.

Quick Steps

Insert an Audio File
1. Click Insert tab.
2. Click Audio button.
3. Locate and double-click desired audio file.

Insert a Video File
1. Click Insert tab.
2. Click Video button.
3. Locate and double-click desired video file.

OR

1. Click Insert Media Clip button in Content placeholder.
2. Locate and double-click desired video file.

Exercise 12.8   Inserting a Video and an Audio File in a Presentation

1. Open **CTEcoTours.pptx** and then save the presentation with Save As and name it **U2T12-CTEcoTours**.

2. Make Slide 7 active and then click the New Slide button on the Home tab.

3. Click the text *Click to add title* and then type **Let the adventure begin!**.

4. Click the Insert Media Clip button 🖳 in the Content placeholder (or click the Video button in the Media group on the Insert tab).

5. At the Insert Video dialog box, navigate to the **Unit2Topic12** folder on your storage medium and then double-click *EcoTours.wmv*. (The **EcoTours.wmv** file is a low-resolution video. If you have access to sample videos in Windows 7, use the **Wildlife.wmv** video located in the Videos folder in the *Libraries* section of the hard drive. Double-click the Sample Videos folder and then double-click **Wildlife.wmv**. This video is high resolution.)

   This inserts the video clip in a window in the slide with the Video Tools Format tab selected. Use options and buttons on this tab to preview the video clip; change the brightness, contrast, and color of the video; apply a formatting style to the video window; and arrange and size the video in the slide.

6. Click the Play button ▶ in the Preview group (left side of the Video Tools Format tab) to preview the video clip.

   The video plays for approximately 30 seconds.

7. After viewing the video, click the Video Tools Playback tab.

8. Click the up-pointing arrow at the right side of the *Fade In* text box until *01.00* displays and then click the up-pointing arrow at the right side of the *Fade Out* text box until *01.00* displays.

9. Click the Volume button 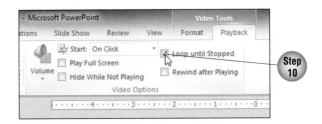 in the Video Options group and then click *Low* at the drop-down list.

10. Click the *Loop until Stopped* check box in the Video Options group to insert a check mark.

11. Make Slide 1 active and then run the presentation. When the slide containing the video clip displays, move the mouse over the video clip window and then click the Play button located at the bottom left side of the video clip window.

12. After viewing the video a couple of times, press the Esc key twice.

13. Make sure Slide 8 is active, click the video clip window, and then click the Video Tools Playback tab.

14. Click the *Play Full Screen* check box in the Video Options group to insert a check mark and click the *Loop until Stopped* check box to remove the check mark.

    With the check mark removed from the *Loop until Stopped* check box, the video will play only once when you run the presentation.

15. Click the down-pointing arrow at the right side of the *Start* option in the Video Options group and then click *Automatically* at the drop-down list.

16. Make Slide 1 active and then run the presentation. When the slide displays containing the video, the video will automatically begin. When the video is finished playing, press the Esc key to return to Normal view.

17. With Slide 8 active, click the Insert tab and then click the Audio button in the Media group.

18. At the Insert Audio dialog box, navigate to the **Unit2Topic12** folder on your storage medium and then double-click the file named **CTAudioFile-01.mid**.

    This inserts the audio clip in the slide with the Audio Tools Format tab active.

19. Click the Audio Tools Playback tab.

20. Click the down-pointing arrow at the right side of the *Start* option in the Audio Options group and then click *Automatically* at the drop-down list.

21. Click the *Hide During Show* check box in the Audio Options group to insert a check mark and then click the *Loop until Stopped* check box to insert a check mark.

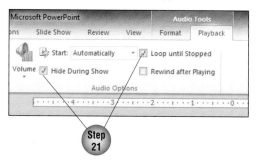

Step 21

22. Make Slide 1 active and then run the presentation. When the last slide displays, watch the video and then listen to the audio clip for about a minute or two and then press the Esc key to return to Normal view.

23. Save the presentation and then print only Slide 8.

24. Close **U2T12-CTEcoTours.pptx**.

Drilling Down

Inserting a Link to a Video File at a Website

You can insert a link in a slide to a video file located at a website. To do this, click the Video button arrow in the Media group on the Insert tab and then click *Video from Web Site* at the drop-down list. This displays the Insert Video From Web Site dialog box. Information in this dialog box tells you that you can insert a link to a video file you have uploaded to a website by copying the embedded code from the website and pasting it into the *Dialog Box* text box.

Lesson 12.9   Exporting a PowerPoint Presentation to Word

In the Microsoft Office suite, you can export a file in one application to create a file in another application. For example, you can export a PowerPoint presentation file to Word to create a document with the presentation information. To export presentation data to Word, click the File tab, click the Save & Send tab, click the *Create Handouts* option, and then click the Create Handouts button. At the Send To Microsoft Word dialog box that displays, specify the layout of the data in the Word document, indicate whether you want to paste or paste link the data, and then click OK. The advantage of sending presentation data to a Word document is that you have greater control over the formatting of the data in Word.

Quick Steps

Export a PowerPoint Presentation to Word
1. Click File tab.
2. Click Save & Send tab.
3. Click *Create Handouts* option.
4. Click Create Handouts button.
5. Click desired options at Send To Microsoft Word dialog box.
6. Click OK.

Exercise 12.9   Exporting a PowerPoint Presentation to Word

1. In PowerPoint, open **CFJobSearch.pptx** and then save the presentation with Save As and name it **U2T12-CFJobSearch**.

2. Click the File tab, click the Save & Send tab, click the *Create Handouts* option, and then click the Create Handouts button.

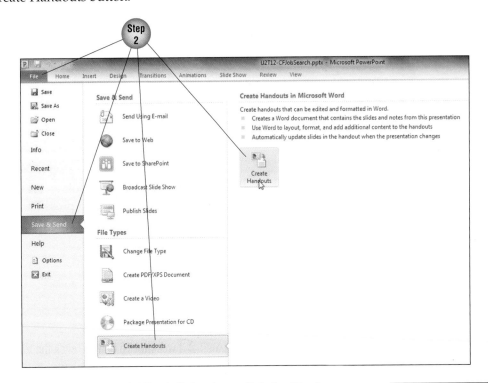

3. At the Send To Microsoft Word dialog box, click the *Blank lines next to slides* option.

4. Click the *Paste link* option located toward the bottom of the dialog box and then click OK.

5. Click the Word button on the Taskbar.

   The slides display in a Word document as thumbnails followed by blank lines.

6. Save the Word document and name it **U2T12-CFJobSearchHandout**.

7. Print and then close **U2T12-CFJobSearchHandout.docx**.

8. Click the PowerPoint button on the Taskbar.

9. Make Slide 6 active, move the insertion point immediately right of the *Other public records* entry, press the Enter key, and then type **Chamber of Commerce**.

10. Make Slide 8 active, move the insertion point immediately right of the *Community Service* entry, press the Enter key, and then type **Professional Organizations**.

11. Save and then close **U2T12-CFJobSearch.pptx**.

12. Make Word the active program and then open **U2T12-CFJobSearchHandout.docx**. At the message asking if you want to update the document with the data from the linked files, click the Yes button.

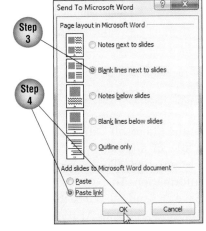

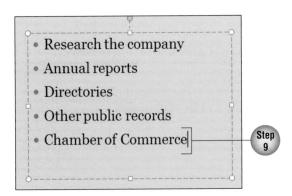

13. Scroll through the Word document and notice that the document reflects the changes you made to Slides 6 and 8 in the PowerPoint file.

   If the changes to Slides 6 and 8 do not display, right-click Slides 6 and 8 in the Word document, and then click *Update Link* at the shortcut menu.

14. Save, print, and then close **U2T12-CFJobSearchHandout.docx**.

Drilling Down

Pasting and Linking Data

The *Paste* option at the Send To Microsoft Word dialog box is selected by default and is available for all of the page layout options. With this option selected, the data inserted in Word is *not* connected or linked to the original data in the PowerPoint presentation. If you plan to update the data in the presentation and want the data updated in the Word document, click the *Paste link* option at the Send To Microsoft Word dialog box. This option is available for all of the page layout options except the *Outline only* option.

Lesson 12.10   Linking an Excel Chart with a Word Document and a PowerPoint Presentation

source program The program containing the data to be copied, linked, or embedded

destination program The program into which the data is pasted, linked, or embedded

Quick Steps

Link Data between Programs

1. Open desired programs and files.
2. Select content in source program.
3. Click Copy button.
4. Switch to destination program.
5. Click Paste button arrow.
6. Click *Paste Special*.
7. Click object in *As* list box.
8. Click *Paste link*.
9. Click OK.

As you learned in Topic 3, with the Microsoft Office suite, you can integrate data, such as text or objects, from two or more programs into one file. You can integrate the data by copying and pasting the data between programs, copying and linking the data, or copying and embedding the data. The program containing the data to be copied is called the **source program** and the program where the data is pasted, linked, or embedded is called the **destination program**. If you plan to update the data in the future, then copying and linking it is the best option. When data is linked, it remains in the source program, although you can view it in the destination program. Since the data is located only in the source program, any changes made to the data in the source program are reflected in the destination program.

To link data or an object, open the desired programs and then open the desired program files. In the source program file, select the text or click the desired object to select it, and then click the Copy button in the Clipboard group on the Home tab. Click the button on the Taskbar representing the destination program file, position the insertion point in the desired location in the file, click the Paste button arrow in the Clipboard group on the Home tab, and then click *Paste Special* at the drop-down list. At the Paste Special dialog box, click the type of object in the *As* list box, click the *Paste link* option located at the left side of the *As* list box, and then click OK.

Exercise 12.10 Linking an Excel Chart with a Word Document and PowerPoint Presentation

1. Make sure Word and PowerPoint are open and then open Excel.

2. Make Word the active program and then open the document named **GMRevenues.docx**.

3. Save the document with Save As and name it **U2T12-GMRevenues**.

4. Make PowerPoint the active program, open the presentation named **GMDeptMeeting.pptx**, and then save the presentation with Save As and name it **U2T12-GMDeptMeeting**.

5. Make Slide 4 the active slide.

6. Make Excel the active program and then open the workbook named **GMRevChart.xlsx**.

7. Save the workbook with Save As and name it **U2T12-GMRevChart**.

8. Copy and link the chart to the Word document and the PowerPoint presentation. Begin by clicking once in the chart to select it.

   Make sure you select the chart and not a specific chart element. Try selecting the chart by clicking just inside the chart border.

9. With the chart selected, click the Copy button in the Clipboard group on the Home tab.

10. Click the Word button on the Taskbar.

11. Press Ctrl + End.

   This moves the insertion point to the end of the document.

12. Click the Paste button arrow and then click *Paste Special* at the drop-down list.

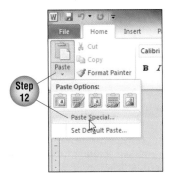

13. At the Paste Special dialog box, click the *Paste link* option, click *Microsoft Excel Chart Object* in the *As* list box, and then click OK.

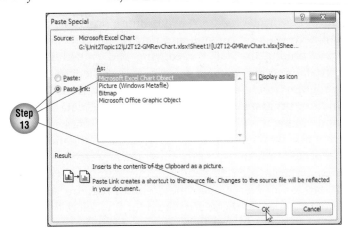

14. Save, print, and then close **U2T12-GMRevenues.docx**.

15. Click the PowerPoint button on the Taskbar.

16. With Slide 4 the active slide, click the Paste button arrow and then click *Paste Special*.

17. At the Paste Special dialog box, click the *Paste link* option, make sure *Microsoft Excel Chart Object* is selected in the *As* list box, and then click OK.

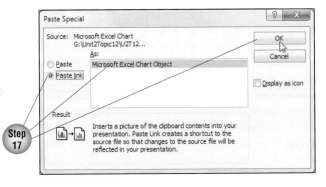

18. Increase the size of the chart so it better fills the slide and then move the chart so it is centered on the slide.

19. Click outside the chart to deselect it.

20. Save the presentation, print only Slide 4, and then close the presentation.

21. Click the Excel button on the Taskbar.

22. Click outside the chart to deselect it.

23. Save and then close **U2T12-GMRevChart.xlsx**.

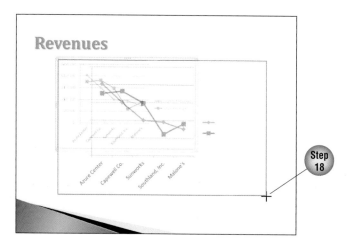

Drilling Down

Linking Data or an Object within a Program

In this lesson, you learned to link content from a file in another program using the Paste Special dialog box. You can also link an object using options at the Object dialog box. Use the Object dialog box when you are linking entire files, and use Paste Special when you are linking only a part of a file. To link with the Object dialog box, click the Insert tab and then click the Object button. At the Object dialog box, click the Create from file tab. At the dialog box, type the desired file name in the *File* text box or click the Browse button and then select the desired file from the appropriate folder. Click the *Link to file* check box to insert a check mark and then click OK.

Lesson 12.11 Editing a Linked Object

The advantage of linking data or an object over copying is that editing the data or object in the source program will automatically update the data or object in the destination program(s). To edit linked data or an object, open in the source program the file containing the data or object, make the desired edits, and then save the file. The next time you open the file in the destination program, the data or object is updated. You can also open the file in the source program for editing by opening the file in the destination program and then double-clicking the linked data or object. You cannot edit linked data or objects in the file in the destination program.

Exercise 12.11 Editing a Linked Chart

1. Make sure the Word, Excel, and PowerPoint programs are open.

2. Make Excel the active program and then open the workbook named **U2T12-GMRevChart.xlsx**.

3. You discover that one customer was not included on the revenues chart. Add a row to the worksheet by clicking once in cell A5 to make it the active cell. Click the Insert button arrow in the Cells group on the Home tab and then click *Insert Sheet Rows*.

4. Insert the following data in the specified cells:

A5 = **Universal Systems**
B5 = **125000**
C5 = **107500**

5. Click in cell A3.

6. Save, print, and then close **U2T12-GMRevChart.xlsx**.

7. Make Word the active program and then open **U2T12-GMRevenues.docx**. At the message asking if you want to update the linked file, click Yes.

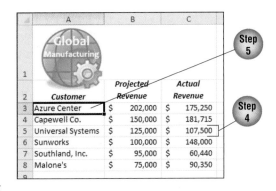

8. Notice how the linked chart is automatically updated to reflect the changes you made to the chart in the Excel file.

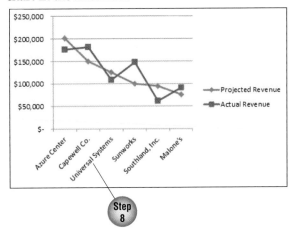

9. Save, print, and then close **U2T12-GMRevenues.docx**.

10. Make PowerPoint the active program and then open **U2T12-GMDeptMeeting.pptx**.

11. At the message telling you that the presentation contains links, click the Update Links button.

12. Make Slide 4 the active slide and then notice how the linked chart is automatically updated to reflect the changes you made to the chart in the Excel file.

13. Save **U2T12-GMDeptMeeting.pptx** and then print only Slide 4.

Drilling Down

Manually Updating a Link

When you open a file containing linked data in the destination program, you will be asked if you want to update the link. At this message, you can specify whether or not you want the linked data updated. If you do not want this message to display and you want control over when you update the linked data, you can specify that you want to update a link manually. To do this in a Word document, open the document containing a linked object, right-click the object, point to *Linked (type of object) Object*, and then click *Links*. At the Links dialog box, click the *Manual update* option and then click OK. With *Manual update* selected, a link is only updated when you right-click a linked object and then click *Update Link*; or display the Links dialog box, click the link in the list box, and then click the Update Now button.

Lesson 12.12 Embedding a Word Table in a PowerPoint Slide

 2-4.1.2

As you learned in Lesson 12.11, linked content retains the memory of both the application and the specific data file from which it came, so that if the original changes, the linked copy changes too. In contrast, embedded content does not retain any connection to the data file from which it came. However, it does remember what application originally created it, so you can edit the content in the destination program using the tools of the source program.

To embed an object, open the desired programs and then open the program files. In the source program file, select the text or click the desired object to select it, and then click the Copy button in the Clipboard group on the Home tab. Click the button on the Taskbar representing the destination program file, position the insertion point in the desired location in the file, click the Paste button arrow in the Clipboard group on the Home tab, and then click *Paste Special* at the drop-down list. At the Paste Special dialog box, click the type of object in the *As* list box and then click OK.

To edit an embedded object in the destination program, double-click the object in the file in the destination program and the tools from the source program display. For example, when you double-click a Word table that is embedded in a PowerPoint slide, the Word tabs and ribbon display.

Quick Steps

Embed Data or an Object

1. Open desired programs and files.
2. Select content in source program.
3. Click Copy button.
4. Click button on Taskbar representing destination program.
5. Click Paste button arrow.
6. Click *Paste Special*.
7. Click object in *As* list box.
8. Click OK.

Exercise 12.12 Embedding a Word Table in a PowerPoint Slide

1. With PowerPoint as the active program, make sure the presentation named **U2T12-GMDeptMeeting.pptx** is open, and then make Slide 5 the active slide.

2. Make Word the active program and then open the document named **GMPresDates.docx**.

3. Click in a cell in the table and then select the table. To do this, click the Table Tools Layout tab, click the Select button in the Table group, and then click *Select Table* at the drop-down list.

4. Click the Home tab and then click the Copy button in the Clipboard group.

5. Click the PowerPoint button on the Taskbar.

6. With Slide 5 the active slide, click the Paste button arrow and then click *Paste Special* at the drop-down list.

7. At the Paste Special dialog box, click *Microsoft Word Document Object* in the *As* list box and then click OK.

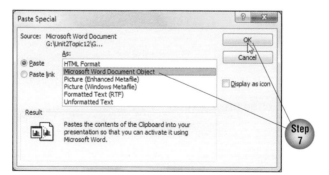

8. Increase the size and position of the table in the slide so it displays as shown below.

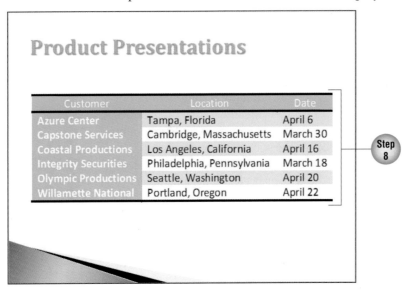

Step 8

9. The presentation date for Integrity Securities has been changed to March 25. Edit the date by double-clicking the table in the slide.

   Double-clicking the table displays the Word tabs and ribbon at the top of the screen. A horizontal and a vertical ruler also display around the table.

10. Using the mouse, select *18* after *March*, and then type **25**.

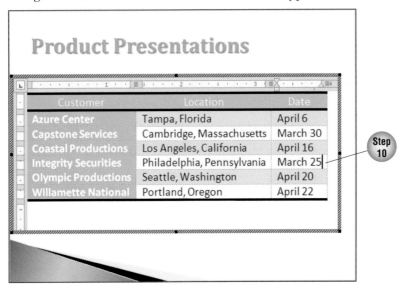

Step 10

11. Click outside the table to deselect it.

    Clicking outside the table deselects it and also removes the Word tabs.

12. Print Slide 5 of the presentation.

13. Apply a transition and sound to each slide in the presentation.

14. Run the presentation.

15. Save and then close **U2T12-GMDeptMeeting.pptx**.

16. Click the Word button on the Taskbar and then close **GMPresDates.docx** without saving the file.

17. Exit Word, PowerPoint, and Excel.

Drilling Down

Displaying an Embedded Object as an Icon

An embedded object displays in the destination program as it displays in the source program. You can embed an object as an icon in the destination program representing the object. You may want to embed an object as an icon to save space in a file or to identify that the object is embedded. To change the embedded object to an icon, right-click the object, point to *Document Object* (this option will vary depending on the type of object), and then click *Convert*. At the Convert dialog box, click the *Display as icon* option, and then click OK. To view the embedded object in the source program, double-click the icon in the destination program.

Delving Deeper

 2-4.1.12

Designing a Presentation

In the Delving Deeper section of Topic 11, you learned some basic guidelines for planning a presentation. Once you have planned the presentation, the next step is to design it. When designing your presentation, consider the following guidelines on formatting text, inserting graphics, and applying animations:

- When formatting text:
  - Use bulleted points or an outline list and avoid paragraphs of text.
  - Add excess information to the Notes pane to avoid overcrowding your slide (do not include too many bulleted points in a single slide).
  - Make sure the font and font size are legible to your audience.
  - Keep text fonts consistent throughout your presentation.
  - Avoid backgrounds that make text hard to read.
- When inserting graphics:
  - Limit your graphics to one per slide (such as a picture, clip art image, or chart).
  - Make sure graphics and charts enhance the slide text and simply illustrate relevant points. Do not use graphics or charts if they distract from the content.
- When applying animations:
  - Use animations sparingly.
  - Be consistent with the animation you apply to slides.
  - Make sure animations execute quickly.

TOPIC SUMMARY

- Insert a picture or clip art in a slide with the Picture button or Clip Art button in the Images group on the Insert tab.
- Format and size pictures and clip art images with buttons on the Picture Tools Format tab.
- Insert a SmartArt graphic with options at the Choose a SmartArt Graphic dialog box. Format and size a SmartArt graphic with buttons on the SmartArt Tools Format tab and the SmartArt Tools Design tab.
- Draw a shape in a slide by clicking the Insert tab, clicking the Shapes button, clicking the desired shape at the drop-down list, and then clicking or dragging in the slide.
- Insert an action button in a slide by clicking the desired action button in the Shapes button drop-down list.
- Format and customize a shape or action button with buttons and options in the Drawing Tools Format tab.
- With options at the Insert Hyperlink dialog box, you can create a hyperlink to a web page, another presentation, a location within a presentation, a new presentation, or to an email address.
- Use the Tables feature to create columns and rows of information. Insert a table in a slide with the Insert Table button in the Content placeholder or with the Table button on the Insert tab.
- Change the table design with options on the Table Tools Design tab and change the table layout with options on the Table Tools Layout tab.
- Reduce formatting steps by making formatting changes in Slide Master view.
- Apply animation effects to items in slides with buttons and options on the Animations tab. Use the Animation Painter button in the Advanced Animation group to apply the same animation to other items in a presentation.
- Insert an audio file in a slide with the Audio button in the Media group on the Insert tab. Customize the audio file with options on the Audio Tools Format tab and the Audio Tools Playback tab.
- Insert a video file in a slide with the Video button in the Media group on the Insert tab or with the Insert Media Clip button in the Content placeholder. Use options on the Video Tools Format tab and the Video Tools Playback tab to format and customize the video file.
- Integrate data in the Office suite by copying and pasting the data between programs, copying and linking the data, or copying and embedding the data.
- Use the *Create Handouts* option to send a PowerPoint presentation to Word.
- Link data by copying the data in the source program and then pasting it in the destination program.
- Edit linked data in the source program and the data in the destination program is automatically updated.
- Copy an object in the source program and then embed it in the destination program. An embedded object can be edited in the destination program using the tools of the source program.

Key Terms

action button, p. 539

animation effect, p. 551

build, p. 551

destination program, p. 557

enclosed object, p. 539

line drawing, p. 539

source program, p. 557

Features Summary

Feature	Ribbon Tab, Group	Button, Option
Animations	Animations, Animation	
Audio	Insert, Media	
Clip art image	Insert, Images	
Insert Hyperlink dialog box	Insert, Links	
Paste Special dialog box	Home, Clipboard	, *Paste Special*
Picture	Insert, Images	
Send To Microsoft Word dialog box	File tab, Save & Send tab	, *Create Handouts*
Shapes	Insert, Illustrations	
Slide Master view	View, Master Views	
SmartArt	Insert, Illustrations	
Table	Insert, Tables	
Video	Insert, Media	

KEY POINTS REVIEW

Identification

Match the terms to the callouts on the PowerPoint window in Figure 12.8.

1. _____ clip art image
2. _____ logo image
3. _____ SmartArt graphic
4. _____ shape
5. _____ Excel chart

6. _____ animation icon
7. _____ Preview button
8. _____ audio file icon
9. _____ SmartArt organizational chart
10. _____ table

Figure 12.8 Identification Figure

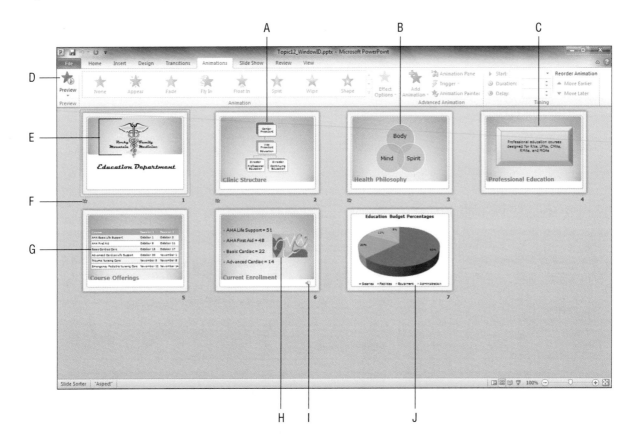

Multiple Choice

For each of the following items, choose the option that best completes the sentence or answers the question.

1. Click the Clip Art button in the Images group on the Insert tab and this item displays.
    A. Insert Picture dialog box
    B. Clip Art task pane
    C. Picture task pane
    D. Insert Clip Art dialog box

2. Use this feature to insert in a slide a visual representation of information such as an organizational chart.
    A. Clip art
    B. Table
    C. Picture
    D. SmartArt

3. This is a drawn object on a slide that has a routine attached to it.
    A. action button
    B. animation button
    C. line drawing
    D. bevel shape

4. Use this feature to display data in columns and rows.
    A. SmartArt
    B. grid
    C. clip art
    D. table

5. To apply formatting to multiple slides at the same time, display the presentation in this view.
    A. Draft
    B. Slide Master
    C. Reading
    D. Slide Sorter

6. Customize animation effects with options at this button drop-down list.
    A. Animate Effects
    B. Transition Effects
    C. Effect Options
    D. Motion Options

7. Display the Insert Video dialog box by clicking this button in the Content placeholder.
    A. Video
    B. Video Clip
    C. Insert Video Clip
    D. Insert Media Clip

8. A PowerPoint presentation can be turned into a Word handout document using what tab within the File tab?
    A. Save & Send
    B. Publish
    C. Save As
    D. Print

9. This is the term used to describe the program to which other files link.
    A. link program
    B. source program
    C. destination program
    D. embedded program

10. An object that allows the use of tools contained in a different Office suite program is called this.
    A. a linked object
    B. a handout
    C. a tool
    D. an embedded object

Matching

Match each of the following definitions with the correct term, command, or option.

1. _____ The Picture button is located in this tab.
2. _____ Use these objects that display around an image to change the size of the image.
3. _____ Move an image in small increments by holding down this key while pressing an arrow key.
4. _____ Choose an action button with options at this button drop-down list.
5. _____ Change to Slide Master view by clicking the Slide Master button in the Master Views group on this tab.
6. _____ This is the program in the Office suite into which data is pasted, linked, or embedded.
7. _____ Apply this to bulleted text to display bulleted points one at a time.
8. _____ The Audio button is located in this group on the Insert tab.
9. _____ This is the program in the Office suite containing the data to be copied, linked, or embedded.
10. _____ Display the Paste Special dialog box by clicking the *Paste Special* option at this button drop-down list.

A. Shapes
B. View
C. Build
D. Media
E. Source
F. Paste
G. Sizing handles
H. Ctrl
I. Insert
J. Destination

SKILLS REVIEW

Review 12.1 Customizing a Travel Presentation

1. Open **CTAdventureTours.pptx**.
2. Save the presentation with Save As and name it **U2T12-R1-CTAdventureTours**.
3. Apply the Apothecary design theme, change the theme colors to *Flow*, and change the theme fonts to *Angles*.
4. Insert a new slide at the beginning of the presentation with the Blank slide layout. Insert the picture image named **CTLogo.jpg** into the slide, change the height of the image to *6"*, and then position the image in the middle of the slide.
5. Make Slide 5 active and then select the clip art image. Change the height of the image to *2.2"*, the color to *Blue, Accent color 1 Light*, and the correction to *Brightness: -20% Contrast: +40%*.
6. Make Slide 4 active and then complete the following steps:
   a. Insert a table with 2 columns and 5 rows. Insert the following data in the cells in the table:

Location	Accommodation
Viti Levu	Southern Resort and Spa
Savusavu	Blue Lagoon Resort
Taveuni Island	Charter Plaza
Yasawa Island	Sea Breeze Resort

   b. Apply the *Medium Style 1 - Accent 1* table style.
   c. Change the table height to *4"*.
   d. Click in a cell in the first column and then change the cell width to *3"*.
   e. Select the entire table and then change the alignment to *Center Vertically*.
   f. Change the font size to *24* for all text in the table.
   g. Drag the table so it is centered on the slide below the title.

7. Make Slide 6 active and complete the following steps:
    a. Insert a horizontal scroll shape in the slide. (The *Horizontal Scroll* option is located in the second row in the *Stars and Banners* section of the Shapes button drop-down list.)
    b. Change the height of the horizontal scroll shape to 5" and the width to 7.5".
    c. Use the Align button in the Arrange group on the Drawing Tools Format tab to distribute the shape horizontally and vertically on the slide.
    d. Apply the *Subtle Effect - Blue, Accent 1* shape style.
    e. Type the following inside the shape: **Compass Travel is offering a 15 percent discount on Fiji tours booked between May 1 and July 31.**
    f. Select the text you just typed, change the font size to *28*, and then change the font color to *Dark Blue*.
8. Apply the *Push* transition and the *Camera* transition sound to all slides in the presentation.
9. Run the presentation.
10. Print the presentation with all six slides horizontally on the page.
11. Save and then close **U2T12-R1-CTAdventureTours.pptx**.

Review 12.2 Customizing a Medical Center Presentation

1. Open **HMCenter.pptx**.
2. Save the presentation with Save As and name it **U2T12-R2-HMCenter**.
3. Display the presentation in Slide Master view, click the top slide thumbnail in the slide thumbnail pane, and then select the text *Click to Edit Master title style* (located towards the bottom of the slide). Change the font size to *36* and the font color to *Dark Red, Accent 5, Darker 25%*.
4. Close the Slide Master view.
5. Make Slide 3 active, select the title *Educational Courses*, and then create a hyperlink to the Word document named **HMEDEnroll.docx**.
6. With Slide 3 active, insert a new slide with the Title and Content layout. Type the title in the slide as shown in Figure 12.9 and then create the SmartArt organizational chart as shown in the slide in the figure (use the *Hierarchy* SmartArt graphic). Select and then delete the bottom left box, type the text in the boxes as shown in the figure, change the colors to *Colorful Range - Accent Colors 5 to 6*, and then change the height of the SmartArt to 5".
7. With Slide 4 active, insert a new slide with the Title and Content layout. Type the title in the slide as shown in Figure 12.10 and then create the SmartArt diagram shown in the slide in the figure (use the *Basic Venn* relationship SmartArt graphic). Type the text in the SmartArt shapes as shown in the figure, change the colors to *Colorful Range - Accent Colors 5 to 6*, and change the height of the SmartArt to 5".
8. Make Slide 3 active and then apply the *Split* animation to the bulleted text.
9. Make Slide 4 active, apply the *Wipe* animation to the SmartArt organizational chart, and then change the effect option to *Level One by One*.
10. Make Slide 5 active, apply the *Wipe* animation to the SmartArt diagram, and then change the effect option to *One by One*.
11. Make Slide 6 active and then insert the audio file **CTAudioFile-02.mid** (located in the **Unit2Topic12** folder on your storage medium) and then make the following changes on the Audio Tools Playback tab:
    a. Change the volume to *Medium*.
    b. Specify that you want the audio file to start automatically.
    c. Specify that you want the audio file to loop until stopped and that you want the audio file icon to hide during the slide show.
12. Make Slide 1 active and then run the presentation. After listening to the audio file in Slide 6 for about a minute, press the Esc key to end the presentation.
13. Print the presentation with all six slides horizontally on the page.
14. Save and then close **U2T12-R2-HMCenter.pptx**.

Figure 12.9 **Review 12.2, New Slide 4 Example**

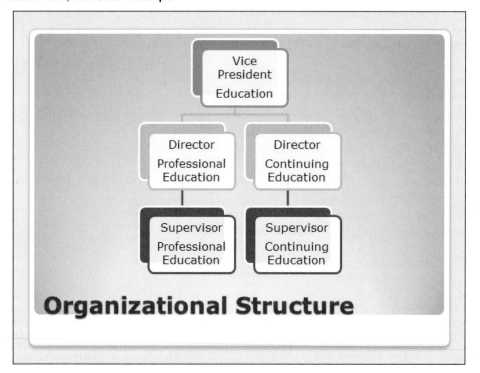

Figure 12.10 **Review 12.2, New Slide 5 Example**

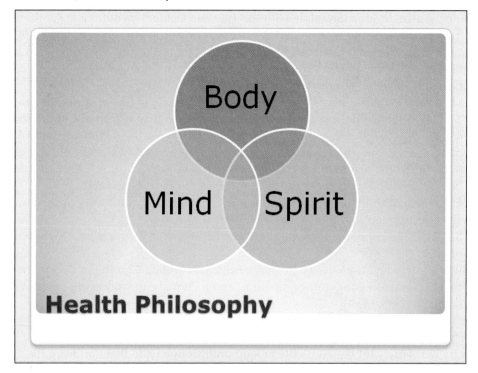

Review 12.3 Exporting and Linking a PowerPoint Presentation to Word

1. Open PowerPoint, open **CFStrategies.pptx**, and then save the presentation with Save As and name it **U2T12-R3-CFStrategies**.
2. Send the PowerPoint data to Word as slides with blank lines next to the slides by clicking the *Blank lines next to slides* option and the *Paste link* option at the Send To Microsoft Word dialog box.
3. Make Word active and then save the document and name it **U2T12-R3-CFStratHandout**.
4. Print and then close **U2T12-R3-CFStratHandout.docx**.
5. Click the button on the Taskbar representing the PowerPoint presentation **U2T12-R3-CFStrategies.pptx**.
6. Make Slide 3 active and then type the word **References** below *Salary requirements*.
7. Make Slide 6 active and then type the words **Bring a list of references** below *Smile*.
8. Save the presentation, print Slides 3 and 6, and then close the presentation.
9. Make Word the active program, open **U2T12-R3-CFStratHandout.docx**, and then click Yes at the question asking if you want to update the link. If the inserted text does not display in Slides 3 and 6, right-click Slides 3 and 6 in the Word document and then click *Update Link* at the shortcut menu.
10. Save, print, and then close **U2T12-R3-CFStratHandout.docx** and then exit Word.

Review 12.4 Linking an Excel Chart in a PowerPoint Slide

1. With PowerPoint open, open Excel.
2. Make PowerPoint the active program, open **SGCMeeting.pptx**, and then save the presentation with Save As and name it **U2T12-R4-SGCMeeting**.
3. Make Slide 4 active.
4. Make Excel the active program, open the workbook named **SGCSales.xlsx**, and then save the workbook with Save As and name it **U2T12-R4-SGCSales**.
5. Click the chart in the Excel file once to select it (make sure you select the entire chart and not a chart element) and then copy and link the chart to Slide 4 in the **U2T12-R4-SGCMeeting.pptx** PowerPoint presentation. (Be sure to use the Paste Special dialog box to link the chart.)
6. Increase the size of the chart so it better fills the slide, move the chart so it is centered on the slide, and then click outside the chart to deselect it.
7. Save the presentation, print only Slide 4, and then close the presentation.
8. Click the button on the Taskbar representing the Excel workbook **U2T12-R4-SGCSales.xlsx**.
9. Click outside the chart to deselect it.
10. Save and then print **U2T12-R4-SGCSales.xlsx**.
11. Insert another salesperson in the worksheet (and chart) by making cell A7 active, clicking the Insert button arrow in the Cells group on the Home tab, and then clicking *Insert Sheet Rows* at the drop-down list. (This creates a new row 7.) Type the following text in the specified cells:
    A7 = **Haydon**
    B7 = **15500**
    C7 = **14350**
12. Click in cell A3.
13. Save, print, and then close **U2T12-R4-SGCSales.xlsx** and then exit Excel.
14. With PowerPoint the active program, open **U2T12-R4-SGCMeeting.pptx**. At the message telling you that the presentation contains links, click the Update Links button. Display Slide 4 and then notice the updates made to the chart.
15. Save **U2T12-R4-SGCMeeting.pptx** and then print only Slide 4.

Review 12.5 Embedding and Editing a Word Table in a PowerPoint Slide

1. With **U2T12-R4-SGCMeeting.pptx** open, make Slide 5 the active slide.
2. Open Word and then open the document named **SGCContacts.docx**.
3. Select the table and then copy and embed it in Slide 5 in the **U2T12-R4-SGCMeeting.pptx** presentation. (Make sure you use the Paste Special dialog box.)
4. With the table selected in the slide, use the sizing handles to increase the size and change the position of the table so it better fills the slide.
5. Click outside the table to deselect it and then save **U2T12-R4-SGCMeeting.pptx**.
6. Double-click the table and then make the following changes:
   a. Edit the telephone number *503-555-7755* so it displays as *503-555-1388*.
   b. Edit the company name *Massey-Lowell, Inc.* so it displays as *Maston-Lowell, Inc.*
7. Click outside the table to deselect it.
8. Print Slide 5 of the presentation.
9. Run the presentation.
10. Save and then close **U2T12-R4-SGCMeeting.pptx** and then exit PowerPoint.
11. Close the Word document **SGCContacts.docx** and then exit Word.

SKILLS ASSESSMENT

Assessment 12.1 Preparing a Presentation for Worldwide Enterprises

1. Open PowerPoint, open **WEPlanMtg.pptx**, and then save the presentation with Save As and name it **U2T12-A1-WEPlanMtg**.
2. Apply the Median design theme, change the design theme colors to *Trek*, and change the design theme fonts to *Module*.
3. With Slide 1 active, insert the **WELogo.jpg** image (use the Picture button). Change the height of the image to *3.5"* and then position the image so it is centered on the slide below the design theme horizontal bar.
4. Make Slide 2 active, select the clip art image, change the height to *3.5"*, and then change the color to *Brown, Accent color 2 Dark*.
5. Make Slide 4 active, create the SmartArt graphic as shown in Figure 12.11 using the process *Continuous Block Process* graphic, and change the colors to *Colorful Range - Accent Colors 5 to 6*.
6. Make Slide 5 active and then create the SmartArt graphic as shown in Figure 12.12 using the *Organization Chart* hierarchy graphic. Delete a shape so your organization chart matches the one in Figure 12.12 and change the colors to *Colorful - Accent Colors*.
7. Make Slide 6 active and then complete the following steps:
   a. Insert a table with 2 columns and 5 rows. Insert the following data in the cells in the table:

Customer	Location
Valley Manufacturing	Portland, Oregon
ABT Systems	Houston, Texas
Integrity Hardware	New York, New York
Lopez-Thompson Company	Miami, Florida

   b. Apply the *Light Style 3 - Accent 1* table style.
   c. Change the table height to *3.5"*.
   d. Change the width of the first column to *4"* and the width of the second column to *3.5"*.
   e. Center the text vertically in all cells in the table.
   f. Change the font size to *20* for all text in the table.
   g. Drag the table so it is centered on the slide below the title.

8. Make Slide 3 active and then insert a star shape with the following specifications:
   a. Use the *5-Point Star* shape at the Shapes button drop-down list and insert the star shape in the lower right corner of the slide.
   b. Change the height and width of the star shape to *3"*. If necessary, reposition the star in the lower right corner of the slide.
   c. Apply the *Light 1 Outline, Colored Fill - Orange, Accent 1* shape style.
9. Make Slide 2 active, apply the *Fly In* animation to the bulleted text, and change the effect options to *From Left*.
10. Make Slide 3 active and then apply the same animation and animation effect option to the bulleted text that you applied to the bulleted text in Slide 2.
11. Make Slide 4 active and then apply the *Fade* animation to the SmartArt graphic and change the effect options to *One by One*.
12. Make Slide 5 active and then apply the *Wipe* animation to the SmartArt organizational chart graphic and change the effect options to *One by One*.
13. Make Slide 3 active, select the text *New customers* in the third bulleted item, and then create a hyperlink to the Excel file named **WERevenues.xlsx**.
14. Run the presentation and click the <u>New customers</u> hyperlink that displays in Slide 3.
15. Print the presentation with all six slides horizontally on the page.
16. Save and then close **U2T12-A1-WEPlanMtg.pptx**.

Figure 12.11 Assessment 12.1, Slide 4 Example

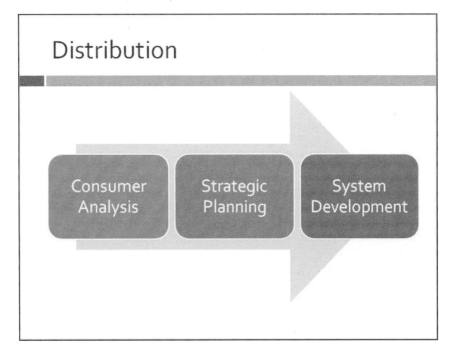

Figure 12.12 **Assessment 12.1, Slide 5 Example**

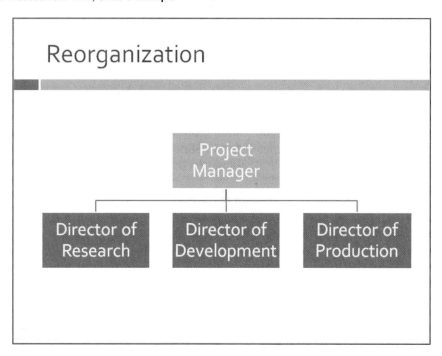

Assessment 12.2 Exporting a PowerPoint Presentation to Word

1. In PowerPoint, open **CTVacations.pptx** and then save the presentation with Save As and name it **U2T12-A2-CTVacations**.
2. Send and link the PowerPoint data to Word as slides with blank lines next to the slides.
3. Click the Word button on the Taskbar and then save the Word document and name it **U2T12-A2-CTVacSpecials**.
4. Print and then close **U2T12-A2-CTVacSpecials.docx**.
5. Click the PowerPoint button on the Taskbar.
6. Make Slide 4 active and then change *$950* to *$1,050*, change *$1,175* to *$1,275*, and change *$1,215* to *$1,315*.
7. Save the presentation, print Slide 4, and then close the presentation.
8. Make Word the active program, open **U2T12-A2-CTVacSpecials.docx**, and then click Yes at the question asking if you want to update the link. If the updated prices do not display in Slide 4, right-click Slide 4 in the Word document and then click *Update Link* at the shortcut menu.
9. Print only page 2 of **U2T12-A2-CTVacSpecials.docx**.
10. Save and close the document and then exit Word.

Assessment 12.3 Linking and Editing an Excel Chart in a PowerPoint Slide

1. With PowerPoint open, open Excel.
2. Make PowerPoint the active program, open **GPACEnroll.pptx** and then save the presentation with Save As and name it **U2T12-A3-GPACEnroll**.
3. Make Slide 3 active.
4. Make Excel the active program, open **GPACEnrollChart.xlsx**, and then save the workbook with Save As and name it **U2T12-A3-GPACEnrollChart**.
5. Click the chart once to select it (make sure you select the entire chart and not a chart element) and then copy and link the chart to Slide 3 in the **U2T12-A3-GPACEnroll.pptx** PowerPoint presentation.
6. Increase the size of the chart to better fill the slide and then center the chart on the slide.
7. Click outside the chart to deselect it.

8. Save the presentation, print only Slide 3, and then close the presentation.
9. Click the Excel button on the Taskbar.
10. Click outside the chart to deselect it.
11. Save and then print **U2T12-A3-GPACEnrollChart.xlsx**.
12. Insert another department in the worksheet (and chart) by making cell A7 active, clicking the Insert button arrow in the Cells group on the Home tab, and then clicking *Insert Sheet Rows* at the drop-down list. (This creates a new row 7.) Type the following text in the specified cells:
    A7 = **Directing**
    B7 = **18**
    C7 = **32**
    D7 = **25**
13. Click in cell A4.
14. Save, print, and then close **U2T12-A3-GPACEnrollChart.xlsx**.
15. Exit Excel.
16. In PowerPoint, open **U2T12-A3-GPACEnroll.pptx**. At the message telling you that the presentation contains links, click the Update Links button.
17. Display Slide 3 and then notice the change to the chart.
18. Save the presentation and then print only Slide 3.

Assessment 12.4 Embedding and Editing a Word Table in a PowerPoint Slide

1. With **U2T12-A3-GPACEnroll.pptx** open, make Slide 4 the active slide.
2. Open Word and then open the document named **GPACContacts.docx**.
3. Select the table and then copy and embed it in Slide 4 in the **U2T12-A3-GPACEnroll.pptx** presentation.
4. With the table selected in the slide, use the sizing handles to increase the size and change the position of the table so it better fills the slide.
5. Click outside the table to deselect it and then save the presentation.
6. Double-click the table, select *Editing* in the name *Emerson Editing*, and then type **Edits**.
7. Click outside the table to deselect it.
8. Print Slide 4 of the presentation.
9. Apply a transition and transition sound of your choosing to all slides in the presentation.
10. Run the presentation.
11. Save and then close **U2T12-A3-GPACEnroll.pptx** and then exit PowerPoint.
12. Close the Word document **GPACContacts.docx** and then exit Word.

Assessment 12.5 Using the Help Feature to Learn How to Save a Slide as a .jpg File

1. Open PowerPoint and then use the Help feature to learn how to save a PowerPoint slide as a .jpg file.
2. Open **RMFMLogo.pptx** and then save the presentation (one slide) with Save As and name it **U2T12-A5-RMFMLogo**.
3. Save the slide as a .jpg file named **U2T12-A5-RMFMLogoImage**.
4. Close the presentation without saving changes.
5. Open **RMFMClasses.pptx** and then save the presentation with Save As and name it **U2T12-A5-RMFMClasses**.
6. With Slide 1 active, insert the **U2T12-A5-RMFMLogoImage.jpg** image you created. (Use the Picture button on the Insert tab.)
7. Change the height of the logo image to *5.5"* and then drag the image so it is centered above the title *Spring Class Schedule*.
8. Print only Slide 1 of the presentation.
9. Save and then close **U2T12-A5-RMFMClasses.pptx**.

Assessment 12.6 Preparing a Presentation about Online Job Websites

1. Using the Internet, locate three online job websites.
2. Create a PowerPoint presentation about the online job websites and, on the first slide, create a title and subtitle for your presentation.
3. On the second slide, complete the following steps:
   a. Create a shape of your choosing and type the web address of the first online job website in the shape. Apply formatting to enhance the visual appeal of the shape.
   b. Copy the shape two times.
   c. Select the text in the second shape and then type the web address of the second online job website.
   d. Select the text in the third shape and then type the web address of the third online job website.
   e. Align and position the shapes attractively on the slide.
4. On the third slide, include information about the services available at the first online job website. Create an appropriate title for the slide.
5. On the fourth slide, include information about the services available at the second online job website. Create an appropriate title for the slide.
6. On the fifth slide, include information about the services available at the third online job website. Create an appropriate title for the slide.
7. Insert a clip art image in at least one of the slides in the presentation.
8. Apply animations and animation effects of your choosing to objects in the slides.
9. Save the presentation and name it **U2T12-A6-OnlineJobSites**.
10. Run the presentation.
11. Print the presentation with six slides horizontally per page.
12. Close **U2T12-A6-OnlineJobSites.pptx**.

Assessment 12.7 Creating and Formatting a Presentation

1. Create the presentation shown in Figure 12.13 with the following specifications:
   a. Apply the Concourse design theme.
   b. Use the *Blank* layout for Slide 1 and insert the **ESRLogo.jpg** picture image in the slide. Change the height of the image to *6.5"* and then move the logo so it is positioned as shown in the first slide in Figure 12.13.
   c. Use the Title and Content layout for Slide 2 and change the line spacing to *2.0* for the bulleted text in the slide.
   d. Use the Title and Content layout for Slide 3 and insert the *Hierarchy* SmartArt organizational chart (in the *Hierarchy* category in the Choose a SmartArt Graphic dialog box). Delete the bottom left box so your organization chart contains the same boxes as the organization chart in Figure 12.13. Type the text in the boxes as shown in the figure and then apply the *Colorful Range - Accent Colors 5 to 6* color option.
   e. Use the Title and Content layout for Slide 4 and insert the *Radial Venn* SmartArt graphic (in the *Cycle* category in the Choose a SmartArt Graphic dialog box). Type the text in the shapes as shown in the figure and then apply the *Colorful Range - Accent Colors 3 to 4* color option.
   f. Use the Title and Content layout for Slide 5.
   g. Use the Title and Content layout for Slide 6 and change the line spacing to *1.5* for the bulleted text in the slide. Insert the clip art image shown in Slide 6 in Figure 12.13, change the color of the image to *Turquoise, Accent color 1 Dark*, change the height of the image to *5"*, and then position the image as shown in Slide 6 in Figure 12.13. (If this clip art image is not available to you, click another image related to food.)

h. Make Slide 1 active and then display the presentation in Slide Master view. Insert the **ESRLogo.jpg** image in the third layout master (*Title and Content Layout: used by slide(s) 2-6*), change the height to *1"*, and then position the image in the lower right corner of the layout master. Close Slide Master view.

2. Save the completed presentation and name it **U2T12-A7-ESRestaurant**.
3. Run the presentation.
4. Print the presentation as a handout with all six slides horizontally on the same page.
5. Close the presentation.

Figure 12.13 Assessment 12.7 Example

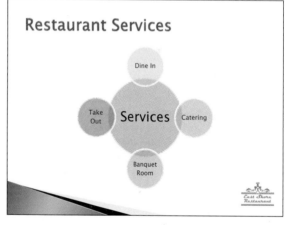

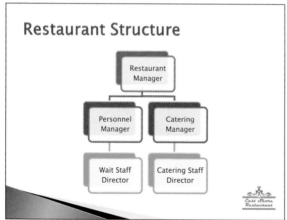

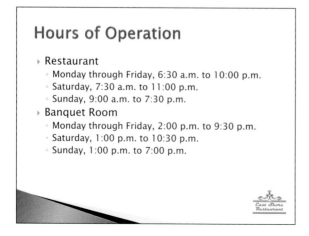

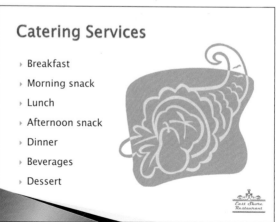

CRITICAL THINKING

Improving the Visual Appeal of Slides

Analyze each slide below and then determine at least two things you would do to improve the visual appeal of the slide or the readability of the text. Use the information in the Delving Deeper section of this topic as a reference for deciding what you would change in each slide. Create a Word document and explain the changes you would make to each slide and support your views. Apply formatting as needed to the Word document. Save the completed document and name it **U2T12-CT-Slides**. Print and then close **U2T12-CT-Slides.docx**.

Slide 1

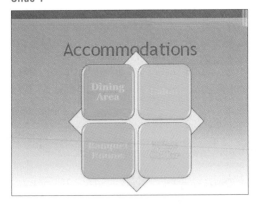

Slide 2

Slide 3

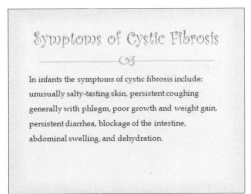

TEAM PROJECT

Researching and Creating a Presentation on the Use of Color in a Presentation

Part 1 Divide into teams and, as a team, research on the Internet guidelines for using color in a PowerPoint presentation. Find at least three suggestions for using color in a presentation (such as color combination suggestions, color combinations to avoid, the purpose of color, color backgrounds, and so on) and then create a presentation with a title and a slide for each color suggestion. Apply formatting and color to enhance the visual appeal of the presentation and make sure the text on each slide is easy to read. Save the presentation and name it **U2T12-ColorsTeam#** (where you enter a team number in place of the # symbol). Print the presentation with six slides horizontally per page and then close the presentation.

Part 2 As a team, open **CTMorocco.pptx** and then save the presentation with Save As and name it **U2T12-CTMoroccoTeam#** (where you enter a team number in place of the # symbol). Using the information you gathered on using color in a presentation in Part 1, make at least the following changes to the presentation:

- Choose an appropriate background style.
- In Slide Master view, click the top slide miniature, click the text *Click to edit Master text styles*, and then apply an appropriate color to the text. Close Slide Master view
- In Slide 2, apply a shape style to the shape that complements the slide background and makes the text easy to read.
- In Slide 3, apply a different color to the clip art image.
- In Slide 6, apply a table style to the table that complements the slide background and makes the text in the table easy to read.

Save the formatted presentation, print the presentation with six slides horizontally per page, and then close the presentation.

Discussion Questions

1. What design theme did you choose for the guidelines presentation in Part 1? Did you make any changes to colors in the presentation? If so, what changes did you make?

2. How did you use the design theme and color choices to enhance the visual appeal of the presentation in Part 1?

3. Compare your color guidelines presentation with the presentations created by the other teams. Which presentation is the most effective at using color? What makes one presentation more appealing than another? Did teams find similar or different color guidelines? Which team found the most helpful color guidelines for creating a presentation?

4. What color changes did you choose for the Morocco presentation in Part 2? What were the specific changes you made to the slides?

5. Compare your Part 2 presentation with the presentations formatted by the other teams. Which presentation uses color the most effectively? What makes one presentation more appealing than another?

UNIT 3 Living Online

Topic 13: **Understanding Networks and the Internet**

Topic 14: **Using a Web Browser**

Topic 15: **Using Email**

Topic 16: **Using PCs and the Internet Safely and Responsibly**

Topic 13

Performance Objectives

Upon successful completion of Topic 13, you will be able to:

- Identify how networks are used in society
- Understand the benefits and risks of networking
- Explain how networks differ from one another
- Identify principles of network security
- Understand the difference between the Internet and the Web
- Understand the types of electronic communication
- Choose the best electronic communication medium for a situation
- Explain how content is created and maintained on the Internet

STUDENT RESOURCES

Before beginning this topic, copy to your storage medium the **Unit3Topic13** subfolder from the *Computer and Internet Essentials: Preparing for IC³* Internet Resource Center. Make this the active folder.

In addition to containing the data files needed to complete topic work, the Internet Resource Center contains model answers in PDF format for each of the applicable exercises in this topic. Use these files to check your work. The preface of your textbook provides instructions for accessing these files.

Necessary Data Files

To complete the exercises and assessments, you will need the following data files:

Exercises (all)	N/A
Reviews (all)	N/A
Assessments 13.1–13.5	N/A
Assessment 13.6	FlowerCompany1.docx FlowerCompany2.xlsx
Critical Thinking	N/A
Team Project	N/A

Visual Preview

Exercise 13.6A **U3T13-Notepad.htm**

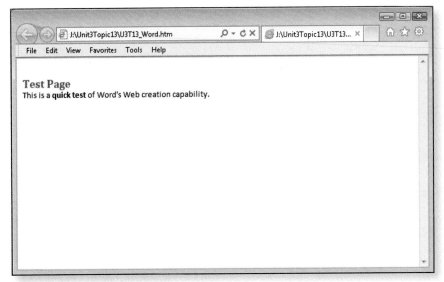

Exercise 13.6B **U3T13-Word.htm**

Topic Overview

In this topic, you will learn the essential concepts and terminology related to networking. You will find out how networks operate and how they safeguard user privacy and security. You will find out how the Internet carries data and how various electronic communication types (such as instant messaging, texting, and email) help people keep in touch with one another. Finally, you will learn about the World Wide Web and discover how people use web pages to share information globally.

A **network** is a group of connected devices that share data or resources. Although many people think first of the Internet when they hear the term *network*, several other types of global network systems exist, such as the networks that carry telephone and satellite data. In addition, many homes, schools, and businesses maintain their own internal computer and telephone networks.

network A group of connected devices that share data or resources

Most people use networks multiple times a day without realizing it. Identify which of the following activities you have engaged in over the last 24 hours:

- Making a phone call
- Watching a TV show
- Using a GPS device to get directions
- Using an ATM to deposit or withdraw money
- Checking email
- Viewing a web page

Each of these activities is made possible by networking. Computer networking creates connections between computers (and devices that contain computers) through a system of cables or wireless signals. As the data moves along the pathways, controller devices direct the data to its intended destination. Each type of networking relies on a complex set of communication rules to route the data where it needs to go.

Not all networks involve computers and the Internet. Telephone networks, which enable people to have one-on-one audio conversations, have been around since the 1900s—long before the invention of computers. Telephone networks were originally analog, carrying sound on copper wires, but modern telephone networks have been upgraded to digital service. This means that the analog sounds sent and received through a phone call are converted to digital, sent across a digital network, and converted back to analog at the other end. Digital telephone service has better call clarity, which makes voices easier to understand and results in less lag time when communicating across long distances, such as internationally.

Television networks were also originally analog, broadcasting data that viewers picked up with antennas, but over the past several years, the United States has moved to all-digital television broadcasts. Cable and satellite TV providers distribute programs digitally as well. Television networking was traditionally a one-way process: the TV station sent out a signal, and viewers received it but could not send anything back. Digital television networking opened up new two-way communication possibilities, allowing users to request content using on-demand and pay-per-view systems.

A global positioning system (GPS) device, like the one shown in Figure 13.1, enables you to find out where you are on a map, and to get directions to some other location, by communicating with a satellite network. These satellites rotate around the earth and send signals to GPS devices, which compute the user's current position based on that data. GPS communication is one-way: the GPS device does not send a signal back to the satellite. It performs its own calculations and uses the results on its own.

Figure 13.1 Global Positioning System (GPS) Device

Photo courtesy of Garmin, LTD.

ATMs help banks process customer transactions by taking in and giving out money when no human tellers are available. An ATM uses a financial services network to access bank account information, which it uses to debit or credit your account. The financial services network shares information not only with your own bank, but with all other banks that participate in the system worldwide. The banking network that supports ATMs is huge, but most consumers do not think about it because they do not interact with the entire global network—they only interact with one individual ATM, and one individual bank account, at a time.

Computer networks (networks that users can connect to using their personal computers) have changed the world in the last few decades. People connect to the Internet to exchange messages with one another, to learn, to share data, to process financial transactions, and much more. Whether you connect with a PC, a tablet, or a smartphone, you access the same Internet as everyone else in the world.

Some of the benefits of networking include: communication, information gathering and sharing, and e-commerce. Computer networks allow you to communicate using email and instant messaging, as well as audio and video conferencing. You can also download shared files or post your own files to share with other users. In addition, computer networks allow you to buy and sell products and services. Buying and selling products over the Internet is called **e-commerce**, which is short for electronic commerce. E-commerce is one of the most popular activities on the Internet. Some popular e-commerce sites include Amazon.com, Overstock.com, and eBay.com.

e-commerce Short for electronic commerce; the practice of using a computer network to buy and sell

Understanding Educational Networks

Schools, colleges, and universities use networks to connect devices located in different buildings and on different campuses. Networking school computers saves time and money by allowing the school's computer support staff to install updates and fixes on all the computers at once, without having to physically walk to each computer. Networking school computers also makes it possible for a single copy of an educational program to be shared with hundreds of students at a time (provided the school has the appropriate distribution license) and helps to ensure that all the school's faculty and staff have access to the most up-to-date student records. If the school network is connected to the Internet, it can also be used to send information, such as emails about school closings or upcoming events, to students' and parents' home computers. Many schools, colleges, and universities offer classes that students can take through the Internet using their own computers; this is called **online learning**, or *e-learning*. See Figure 13.2 for an example of a lesson from an online high school course. E-learning is often the most cost-effective form of education, because it does not require travel to a campus, room-and-board, or printed textbooks, making it an attractive option for people of all income levels.

online learning Education courses available through the Internet that allow students access to instruction without physically attending a school; also called *e-learning*

Figure 13.2 Online Lesson Example Students can use the Internet to take classes such as this class about Shakespearean plays.

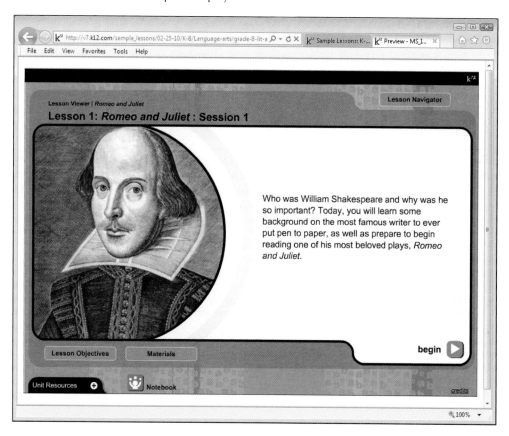

Networking in Business

Businesses benefit from networking because employees can share information with one another without leaving their desks. Networking also allows employees to **telecommute**, meaning that they work from home but are connected to the company using a computer or telephone network. Employees within a company can now work, communicate, and collaborate globally using network applications and resources. A telecommuter's home computer must be connected to the company's network in some manner—usually through the Internet, but sometimes through a separate dedicated phone or networking line. Employees can easily access data about customers, products, orders, and other employees using the network. And, if the network is connected to the Internet, they can get information about competitors' products and communicate with their customers. Employeess can also interact with automated systems for payroll, insurance, and other employee benefits.

Because the Internet is not a secure network environment, companies that need greater security may choose to create a **virtual private network** (**VPN**), which is a secure network tunnel within the larger structure of the Internet. VPNs add an extra layer of security so that employees who connect to the main office remotely can do so without worrying about network security. Companies may also choose to use the Internet for telephone service rather than having a separate telephone network. This is called **Voice over IP** (**VoIP**). IP stands for Internet Protocol, which you will learn more about in Lesson 13.2.

telecommute To work from home while staying connected to the company through a computer or telephone network

virtual private network (VPN) A secure network that operates through a larger unsecure network such as the Internet

Voice over IP (VoIP) A system that uses a computer network such as the Internet to deliver telephone services

Residential Networking

In a residential setting, networks can help users accomplish tasks such as sharing files and printers. For example, a printer might be attached to one person's computer but be available through the network for everyone else in the house to use too. Networks can enable users to play music and movies anywhere in the house, regardless of which computer stores the actual files. If a home network is connected to the Internet, all computers on the network can share a single Internet connection. Users can also play music and movies from the Internet on their computers or on home theater devices hooked up to televisions.

Mobile Networking

Smartphones, tablets, and notebook PCs allow users to connect to the Internet from almost any location. Tablet and notebook PCs typically have wireless networking support built into them, so they can tap into an Internet connection wherever one is available (for example, in a school, restaurant, or library). Cell phones typically connect to the Internet using the phone service provider's network. Depending on the user's rate plan, Internet connectivity may be included or billed by the minute as an extra service. Some portable computing devices also have the ability to create temporary networks with nearby devices to share data.

Exercise 13.1 Identifying Computer Networks in Daily Life

1. Write down any tasks you completed over the last 24 hours that involved an electronic device.

2. Place a check mark next to each activity that involved a network of some kind.

3. Count up your check marks and compare your list and numbers with your classmates' lists and numbers.

Lesson 13.2 Understanding How Networks Operate

IC³ 3-1.1.4, 3-1.1.5, 3-1.1.6

Understanding basic networking concepts will enable you to differentiate between types of networks and how you can connect to them. In this lesson, you will learn some of the ways in which networks differ from one another, as well as the traits that all networks have in common.

packet A container file for sending data over a network; contains the data itself plus a header and footer

frame The header and footer that accompany the data when it is sent in a packet over a network

When you send a letter to a friend using the postal system, you place it in an envelope, include both the recipient's address and your own on the envelope, and place the envelope in a mailbox. The process is roughly the same when you send data using a network. The data is first divided up into chunks and placed in packets. A **packet** is a container file used to send data over a network, much like an envelope is used to send a letter. The packet contains the data as well as an identifying header and footer. The header and footer (without the data) are known as the **frame**. The header is like the address on a mailing label. It specifies the destination and the protocols used in the transmission. The footer contains error-checking information that ensures the data will be delivered accurately. When the receiving PC gets the packet, it strips off the frame and reads the data. All of the packaging and opening of data is performed by the computer, its network adapter, and the operating system; the user is not involved in this process.

Devices in a network use protocols to govern the communication between them. A **protocol** is a format or language for transmitting data between devices. The protocol determines things like the type of error-checking, how the sending and receiving devices signal to each other that they have finished, and what data compression method should be used, if any. The most common protocol in Windows-based networking, as well as on the Internet, is **TCP/IP**, which stands for **Transmission Control Protocol/Internet Protocol**. TCP/IP is actually not a single protocol, but rather a group of related protocols that function together.

Distinguishing between Wired and Wireless Networks

Networks can be either wired or wireless. A **wired network** is a network that uses physical cables and connector boxes to join the computers and devices. Most of the Internet uses wired networking hardware because wired networks can transmit data faster than wireless ones and are also more secure. A **wireless network** uses radio frequency (RF) signals to transmit data, with each device having its own radio transmitter and antenna. Various wireless networking technologies exist, but the most popular one for computers is Wireless Fidelity (**Wi-Fi**) a wireless version of Ethernet. **Ethernet** is a popular networking standard that forms the basis for nearly all home and business networks.

Understanding Networking Hardware

Each computer or device in a network must have a network adapter. A **network adapter** translates instructions from the operating system into data that can be sent over the network. It also manages the incoming and outgoing network requests. A network adapter can either be built into the computer's motherboard or attached as an add-on device such as an expansion board or a USB-connected external device. A network adapter can be either wired or wireless. If a network adapter is wired, it has a connector into which the user can plug a cable. If a network adapter is wireless, it has a transmitter or antenna which may be visible or may be built into the adapter.

A network must have some sort of gathering point to which the individual PCs and other devices can connect. On a wired network, this point is a switch or a router. A **switch** is a simple box that manages traffic on the devices directly plugged into it. A **router** is a more complex version of a switch that is able to intelligently route network requests out of the local network to other networks (like the Internet). On a wireless network, the gathering point is a **wireless access point (WAP)** or a wireless router. Figure 13.3 shows the back of a router with cables plugged into it. Notice that it also has antennae—this router doubles as both a wired and wireless model, allowing computers to use either method to connect to the network.

Figure 13.3 Router A router is a connection box for network adapters to connect to, either with cables or wirelessly.

protocol A format or language for transmitting data between devices

Transmission Control Protocol/Internet Protocol (TCP/IP) A suite of protocols that govern network transmission on the Internet and on most Windows networks

wired network A network that uses physical cables and connector boxes to join the computers and devices

wireless network A network that uses radio frequency (RF) signals to transmit data, with each device having its own radio transmitter and antenna

Wi-Fi Short for Wireless Fidelity; a wireless version of Ethernet

Ethernet A popular networking standard that forms the basis for nearly all home and business networks

network adapter A device that translates instructions from the operating system into data that can be sent over the network

switch A network connection box to which the cables for all the computers in the network connect

router An advanced switch that not only physically connects and routes local network traffic, but also is able to manage incoming and outgoing traffic from an outside network such as the Internet

wireless access point (WAP) A wireless version of a switch

1000BaseT A wired Ethernet standard that transfers data at up to 1 Gbps

10GBaseT A wired Ethernet standard that transfers data at up to 10 Gbps

Wi-Fi 802.11n The current standard for wireless Ethernet, transferring data at up to 160 Mbps

Unshielded Twisted Pair (UTP) A type of cable that carries data on pairs of copper wires that are twisted around each other to minimize the interference between the wires

Category 5e (Cat5e) cable A type of UTP cable that can carry data at up to 1Gbps

Category 6 (Cat6) cable A type of UTP cable that can carry data at up to 10Gbps

RJ-45 connector A connector type that is typically used for wired Ethernet UTP cables; looks like a telephone connector but slightly wider

As mentioned earlier, Ethernet is a popular networking standard—so popular, in fact, that nearly all computer networks use it. The Ethernet standard defines the rules by which devices send data across the network. End-users do not have to worry about these rules; as long as all the devices are Ethernet-compatible, they will know how to communicate with one another. Different types of wired and wireless Ethernet are available, each with its own speed and range limitations, but the different types are typically compatible with one another. The transmission speed adjusts automatically to accommodate the slowest device involved in the communication. Table 13.1, which appears later in this lesson, summarizes the speeds of various types of networks. The current standard for wired Ethernet is **1000BaseT**, which transfers data at up to 1 Gbps, or **10GBaseT**, which transfers data at up to 10 Gbps. The current standard for wireless Ethernet is **Wi-Fi 802.11n**, which transfers data at up to 160 Mbps.

Most wired Ethernet devices use a type of cable called **Unshielded Twisted Pair (UTP)**. UTP cable carries the data on pairs of copper wires that are twisted around each other to minimize the magnetic interference between the wires. UTP cable is unshielded in that it does not have any special coating that would block interference from adjacent outside cables.

Several categories of UTP cable exist, each with a maximum data rate it can reliably support. Modern Ethernet networks use **Category 5e (Cat5e)** or **Category 6 (Cat6)** cable. Cat5e cable is used for 1000BaseT and Cat6 cable is used for 10GBaseT. UTP cable typically has an RJ-45 connector on each end. An **RJ-45 connector** looks like a telephone connector except it is slightly wider and has eight wires rather than the usual two or four (see Figure 13.4).

Figure 13.4 RJ-45 Connector

Identifying Non-Ethernet Networks

Although Ethernet is the predominant type of computer network, many types of specialty network connections are available. For example, a phone can connect to a wireless headset using a Bluetooth connection, and a portable PC can connect to a Bluetooth-enabled printer. **Bluetooth** is a short-range wireless technology used to directly connect devices with peripherals. Bluetooth is a different standard for wireless communications than Wi-Fi, the wireless Ethernet standard. Bluetooth is designed for short-range communications and requires no switch or router. The devices talk directly to one another at up to 2 Mbps.

Mobile phone service is another type of non-Ethernet network. Depending on the phone company and its network type, a wireless phone network may transfer data at anywhere from 2 Mbps to 1 Gbps. Currently, the fastest type of mobile phone network is **4G**, which can transfer data at 1 Gbps when the device is sitting relatively still (for example, in a parked car or in a pedestrian's hand) or 100 Mbps when the device is moving (for example, in a moving car on the highway).

Bluetooth A short-range wireless technology used to directly connect devices with peripherals, such as cell phones with wireless headsets

4G A standard for cellular wireless communications that transfers data at up to 1 Gbps

Infrared is an older wireless networking technology that predates Bluetooth. **Infrared technology** requires a clear line of sight between the two devices, because it sends data using infrared light rather than radio signals. You may encounter infrared ports on some older notebook computers and handheld computing devices.

infrared technology An older wireless technology; moves data between devices using infrared light

Determining Network Types Based on Physical Location

Computers can be networked with other computers in the same home or office, or with computers halfway around the world. One way to describe a network is based on how close all the devices are to each other physically.

- **Personal Area Network (PAN):** A network in which personal devices exist at close range, such as a cell phone and a notebook computer in the same room.

- **Local Area Network (LAN):** A network confined to a small local area, such as a home, office, building, or small group of buildings. LANs can be either wired or wireless.

- **Metropolitan Area Network (MAN):** A network within a large campus of a school or company or within a city. MANs usually have a wired backbone, but may connect individual users using routers.

- **Wide Area Network (WAN):** A network that covers a large geographical area and is made up of many smaller networks. The Internet is a WAN. Like MANs, a WAN typically has a wired backbone, but individual users may connect wirelessly.

Distinguishing between Private and Public Networks

Some networks allow anyone to connect to them. For example, if you go to a local coffee shop that offers Internet access, you may be able to connect to the Internet without providing your identity to anyone or getting any permission. The Internet itself is a public network, and Internet access points are often public as well. In contrast, private networks allow only authorized users to connect to them. For example, a business may have a LAN that connects all their users, and access to that LAN may be restricted to guard business information and employee privacy.

Private networks can be wired or wireless. To connect to a wired network, you must plug into a router or switch with a cable, which makes it hard for anyone who is not physically in the building to gain unauthorized access. On a wireless network, a security access code may be required the first time you try to connect wirelessly to the wireless router or WAP. You will learn more about network security in Lesson 13.3.

When you connect to a public network, you run the risk of others gaining access to your private files and folders. Therefore, you should disable file and folder sharing in Windows whenever you connect to a public network. In Windows Vista and Windows 7, when you connect to a wireless network, you are prompted to choose whether it is a Home, Work, or Public network (as shown in Figure 13.5). If you specify a public network, file and printer sharing is automatically disabled for that network connection.

Figure 13.5 **Network Location**

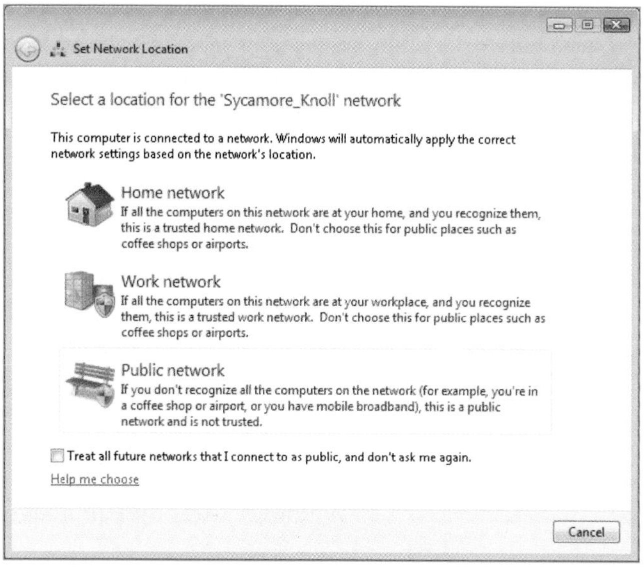

Distinguishing between Network Models

client A PC that an end-user employs

client/server A type of network that includes client PCs and at least one server

Two basic models for networks are available: client/server and peer-to-peer. A **client** is an ordinary PC that an end-user employs. Recall from Topic 2 that a **server** is a PC that exists to route network traffic and provide access to shared files and printers. It manages the connections between the client PCs and serves as a storage repository for files that users want to make available to others. A server can be an ordinary PC with a special server operating system installed (such as Windows Server) that enables it to provide network services. **Client/server** is the network model used for almost all business networks because the presence of the server takes the networking burden off the clients. The main drawback to a client/server network is that at least one PC must be designated to run solely as a server, and not every company or home can spare the extra computer. Server versions of operating systems also cost more than client versions. Figure 13.6 illustrates a client/server network.

Figure 13.6 **Client/Server Network**

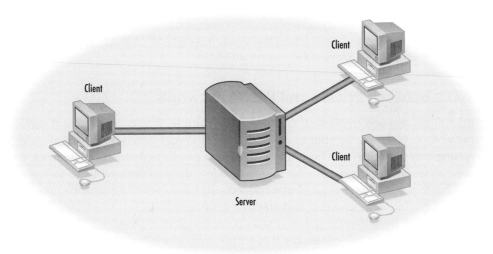

Large networks often have many servers, each with a specific function. For example, one might be a file server, one might be a print server, and one might provide Internet services. In large organizations, a server may be a much more powerful computer than an ordinary desktop PC, and may include many processors and a large amount of RAM.

Having a server does not prevent individual client PCs from sharing their available resources with other clients. For example, even if you have a central file server, users can still share folders stored on their own hard disks.

peer-to-peer (P2P) network A type of network that does not include a server; also called a *workgroup*

In a **peer-to-peer (P2P) network**, or *workgroup*, there is no server; each of the client PCs takes on a portion of the burden of maintaining the network (see Figure 13.7). Instead of a server managing the traffic, all the PCs in the network listen for traffic and grab any messages that are addressed to them. Instead of a server storing shared files, the shared files remain on the individual client hard disks. Small networks, such as those found in a home, are often set up as P2P networks. The homegroup networking feature in Windows 7 sets up P2P networks, for example.

Figure 13.7 **Peer-to-Peer Network**

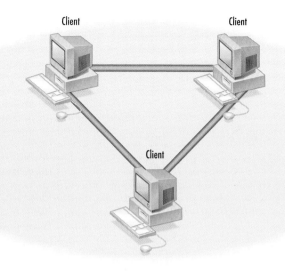

Networking Bandwidth

Networks provide varying amounts of bandwidth. The official definition of bandwidth is the theoretical number of bits that can be transmitted over a network at once, similar to the number of lanes on a highway. In practice, though, the networking industry uses the term **bandwidth** as a measure of the maximum rate of data transmission in bits per second. Bandwidth is a measure of a network's potential speed; **data throughput** is a measure of its actual speed. In practice, the data throughput never approaches the bandwidth rating because of **latency**, which refers to delays in network transmissions (due to various reasons, such as network traffic and data availability).

Ethernet networks may have different bandwidths depending on the networking standard to which the hardware conforms. The slowest type of network is a **dial-up network**, in which a modem is used with a telephone line to manually connect to (dial up) a remote computer that also has a modem. A **modem** is device that converts a computer's digital data to analog sound and transmits it through a telephone to another modem in a different location, which in turn converts the incoming analog data back to digital for the receiving computer to use. Modems were very common for Internet connections in the early days of the Internet, but are infrequently used now because they are so slow compared to other Internet connection methods. Tables 13.1 and 13.2 list various networking technologies and their maximum bandwidths.

bandwidth The maximum theoretical rate of data transmission for a communication medium

data throughput The actual rate of data transmission, or speed, of a communication medium

latency Delays in data transmission on a network

dial-up network A network in which users connect using modems

modem A device that converts between digital and analog data to transmit it over analog telephone lines

Table 13.1 Wired Networking Technologies and Their Speeds

Technology	Bandwidth	Notes
Dial-up modem	56 Kbps	Connects a computer to an Internet provider through a phone line; older and slower method
DSL	640 Kbps to 8 Mbps	A newer, faster method of connecting to an Internet provider through a phone line (compared to the older dial-up modem method)
Cable modem	4 Mbps to 16 Mbps	A method of connecting to an Internet provider through the same cables used for cable TV
Ethernet	10BaseT (Ethernet): 10 Mbps 100BaseT (Fast Ethernet): 100 Mbps 1000BaseT (Gigabit Ethernet): 1 Gbps 10GBaseT: 10 Gbps	Speed is limited by the highest speed that all devices in the local network can collectively agree on. Network adapters, switches, routers, and cables support one of these standards and are backward-compatible with slower ones.
Fiber optic dedicated line	20 Mbps to 50 Mbps	Commonly used to connect major network segments, such as different buildings in a large company

Table 13.2 Wireless Networking Technologies and Their Speeds

Technology	Bandwidth	Notes
Bluetooth	Version 2.0: 2 Mbps Version 3.0: 24 Mbps	Connects devices to peripherals at short range, such as headsets, wireless keyboards and mice, and printers
Mobile phone service	GSM: 3 Mbps CDMA: 3 Mbps 3G: 2.4 Mbps 4G: 1 Gbps	Cellular phone calls and Internet access using phones
Wi-Fi (Wireless Ethernet)	802.11a: 54 Mbps 802.11b: 11 Mbps 802.11g: 54 Mbps 802.11n: 160 Mbps	Speed is limited to the highest speed that a network adapter in a device can negotiate with the wireless router or WAP to which it connects.
WiMAX	75 Mbps	WiMAX is a wireless MAN, blanketing an area of up to 6 miles with network access.

Exercise 13.2 Examining Your Networking Setup

1. Look on the back of your PC and determine if you have an Ethernet cable.

   If an Ethernet cable is plugged into the computer, you have a wired network connection. If not, you either have a wireless connection or no connection at all.

2. Click Start and then type **Device**.

3. Click *Device Manager*.

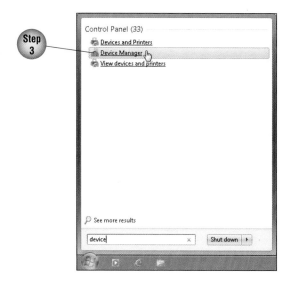

4. Double-click the Network adapters category to expand it.

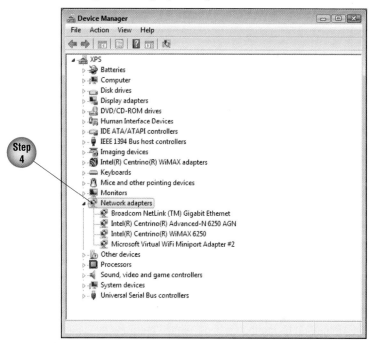

5. Locate the primary wired network adapter on the list if more than one adapter displays.

   In the previous screen capture, the primary adapter is the one that has *Gigabit Ethernet* in its name.

6. Double-click the primary wired network adapter to view its properties.

7. Click through each of the tabs in the dialog box and examine the settings.

8. Click Cancel.

9. Repeat Steps 6–8 for any other network adapters you have in your PC.

10. Close Device Manager.

11. Click Start and then type **Network**.

12. At the Start menu, click *Network and Sharing Center*.

    This opens the Network and Sharing Center utility.

13. Examine the network status that displays.

    The following screen capture shows the house icon, which represents the router in

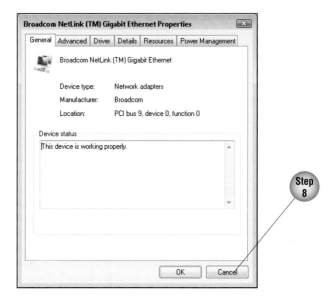

a Home network called Sycamore_Knoll. The globe icon represents connectivity to the Internet. This image shows a wireless network connection; if you have a wired one, your screen may look different.

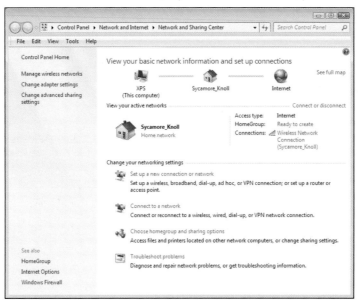

14. Close all open windows.

Drilling Down

Networking Computers Using HomePlug

HomePlug is a technology that allows you to set up an Ethernet network using the power lines in your home or office. You buy a set of small adapter boxes that plug into power outlets; each of the boxes has an RJ-45 jack for connecting a wired Ethernet cable. The power lines act as a conduit so that the computers think they are physically connected to one another through a cable. HomePlug technology was developed before wireless networking became popular and provided a way for people to create networks without running Ethernet cables throughout their homes. However, wireless Ethernet solves the same problem in an even simpler way, so HomePlug is no longer an attractive option for most people.

3-1.1.2

Now that you understand how a network operates, you are ready to examine how networks are used in everyday life. In this lesson, you will learn how to use a network to share a folder, share a printer, and access other people's shared folders and printers.

Two ways to manage file and printer sharing exist in Windows 7—sharing with a homegroup and sharing without a homegroup. A homegroup is a small, tightly controlled workgroup with preset permissions for sharing within that group. This is the ideal solution for most home networks and small offices. The main drawbacks are that all the computers have to be running Windows 7 or higher and each computer must be configured individually. The next few sections assume you want to use the homegroup method of sharing. You will learn how to share without a homegroup later in this lesson. To create a homegroup, or connect to an existing one, follow the steps outlined in the next exercise.

Exercise 13.3A   Create a Windows 7 Homegroup

1. Click Start, click *Control Panel*, click *Network and Internet*, and then click *Network and Sharing Center*.

2. Click *Choose homegroup and sharing options*.

3. Click *Create a homegroup*.

4. Click all the check boxes to insert check marks.

5. Click Next.

6. A password displays on the screen, consisting of randomly generated characters. Record the password for future reference.

7. Click Finish.

8. On another computer on the same network, click Start, click *Control Panel*, click *Network and Internet*, and then click *Network and Sharing Center*.

9. Click *Choose homegroup and sharing options*.

10. Click Join Now.

11. Mark all the check boxes.

12. Click Next.

13. Type the password and click Next.

14. Click Finish.

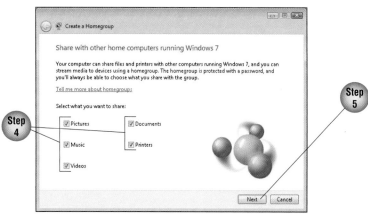

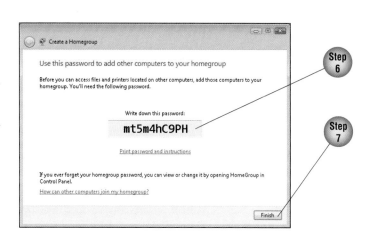

Sharing Other Folders with a Homegroup

Quick Steps

Share a Folder with a Homegroup

1. Right-click folder.
2. Point to *Share with.*
3. Click desired option.

When you initially connect to the homegroup, you are limited to sharing certain folder locations (Documents, Pictures, etc.) because those are the only choices available in the dialog box that sets up the homegroup. However, after you are connected, you can share other files and folders as needed within the homegroup. To share any folder while connected to a homegroup, right-click the folder, point to *Share with*, and then click one of the following options (also shown in Figure 13.8):

- **Nobody:** This option turns off sharing of that folder.

- **Homegroup (Read):** This option allows people in your homegroup to view your files but does not allow them to make changes.

- **Homegroup (Read/Write):** This allows people in your homegroup to read and make changes to your files.

- **Specific people:** This option opens a dialog box in which you can specify individuals or groups with whom you wish to share the folder and assign specific permissions. You can also use this option without a homegroup, as you will see in the following section.

Figure 13.8 **Options for Sharing a Folder**

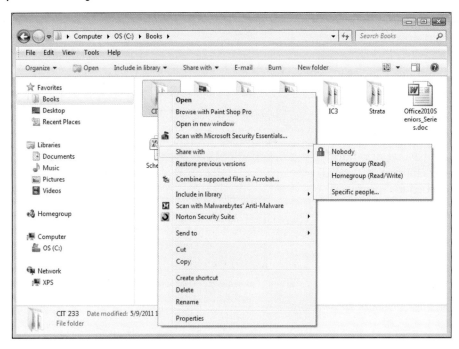

Sharing a Folder without a Homegroup

Quick Steps

Share a Folder

1. Right-click folder.
2. Point to *Share with.*
3. Click *Specific people.*
4. Type *Everyone* or user's name and click Add.
5. Click Share.
6. Click Done.

If you do not have a homegroup or you want to share folders with other network users who are not in your homegroup, you can use the normal Windows sharing procedure. To share without using the homegroup feature, right-click the folder, point to *Share with*, and then click *Specific people*. If you want to share the folder with everyone (all network users), type *Everyone* and then click Add. The Everyone group is predefined in Windows 7 and all users are included in it. You can also click or enter individual user names in the dialog box, as shown in Figure 13.9.

Another way to share a folder is through the folder's properties dialog box. Right-click the desired folder and click *Properties*. Click the Sharing tab and then click the Share button to open the same dialog box shown in Figure 13.9.

Figure 13.9 File Sharing Dialog Box

Accessing Shared Folders

Browse the network to access folders that other users have shared. To do this, open any Windows Explorer window (such as Computer or Documents) and then scroll down and find the *Network* section in the navigation pane at the left. Double-click a computer's name under the *Network* heading to see its shared resources or double-click *Network* to browse the available computers. In Figure 13.10, the computer is sharing three folders: Books, Temp, and Users.

Figure 13.10 Shared Network Resources

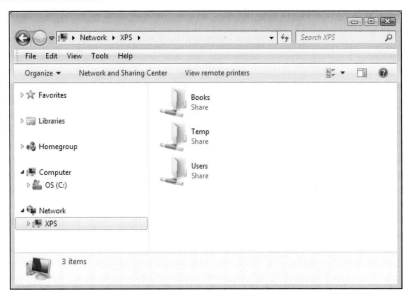

Sharing a Printer

Often a single printer serves multiple computers. Two ways that a printer can be configured so that more than one computer can use it are:

- If the printer has its own network adapter, it can connect directly to the network.

- If the printer is connected directly to one of the computers (using a printer cable, for example), that computer can share the printer on the network.

One drawback of sharing a printer through one of the network computers is that the printer will be available to others only when that PC is running. That is why most users prefer to set up a printer as an independent device on the network rather than running the printer through an individual PC. However, not all printers have network adapters, so sometimes printer sharing may be necessary. To share a printer, open the properties dialog box for that printer and insert a check mark in the *Share this printer* check box on the Sharing tab, as shown in Figure 13.11.

Figure 13.11 Turning on Printer Sharing

Connecting to a Network Printer

To connect to a shared printer, you must first set up the printer on your PC. You can do this by adding a new printer using the Add Printer Wizard in Windows. When prompted, specify that the printer is a network printer. Windows will then check the network and present you with a list of the available printers it finds (see Figure 13.12). The printers on the list will include both those that individual users are sharing and those that are connected directly to the network. Follow the prompts to set up the printer. These prompts may differ depending on the printer.

Quick Steps

Share a Printer on a Network

1. Click Start.
2. Click Devices and Printers.
3. Right-click printer and click *Printer properties*.
4. Click Sharing tab.
5. Click *Share this printer* check box.
6. Click OK.

Quick Steps

Add a Network Printer

1. Click Start.
2. Click *Devices and Printers*.
3. Click *Add a printer*.
4. Click *Add a network, wireless or Bluetooth printer*.
5. Click printer and click Next.
6. Follow prompts.

Figure 13.12 Finding a Network Printer

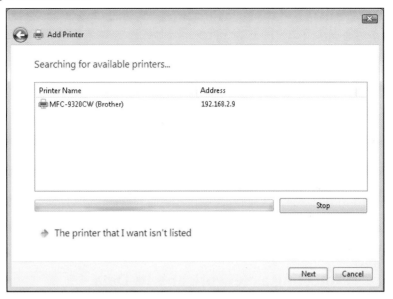

Exercise 13.3B Browsing for Network Resources

1. Click Start and then click *Computer*.

2. Double-click *Network* in the left pane to open a list of network resources.

3. Determine if any computers are listed in the *Computer* section. If so, double-click one of them to browse its shared folders and printers and then click the Back arrow to return to the main Network listing.

4. Determine if any printers are listed in the *Printers* section. If so, double-click one of them.

   If that printer is already set up on your computer, the printer's web page or print queue may display, depending on the printer and its settings. If that printer is not already set up on your computer, Windows may automatically install a driver for it (or attempt to).

5. Close the Network window.

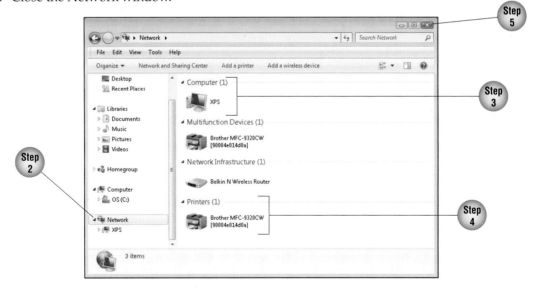

6. Click Start and then click *Devices and Printers*.

7. Click one of the printers listed and look in the Status bar at the bottom of the window to see if it has an indicator that shows it is connected to the network. Do this for each of the printers listed. This will help you identify which printers are accessible through the network.

8. Close all open windows.

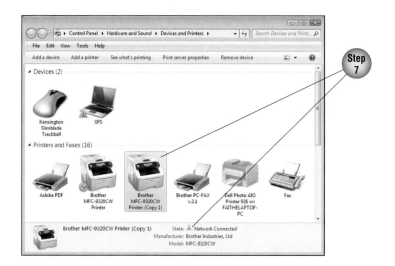

Lesson 13.4 Protecting a Network and Its Data

 3-1.1.3, 3-1.1.7, 3-4.2.3

Ideally, computers would always allow access to the right people and applications and keep out the wrong people and applications. Of course, current computer systems do not always work that way; they make mistakes in both directions. Effective computer security is created by a balance between safety and convenience. In this lesson, you will learn about some of the network-based threats to user security and privacy, and how to guard against threats and attacks without placing unnecessary obstacles in the way of legitimate users.

Identifying Risks of Networked Computing

Connecting your computer to a network enables you to share folders, files, and printers. However, it also opens up your computer to the possibility of harm, including:

- **Information theft:** People may be able to gain access to the data on your computer without your consent. If you work at a company that develops new products, for example, someone might steal the plans for a new invention.

- **Data loss:** People might delete important files accidentally or maliciously.

- **Privacy invasion:** People might obtain information that you would prefer to keep private, like your contact information, financial data, or personal journals and letters.

- **Identity theft:** Armed with personal information that they have collected, people might be able to impersonate you and purchase items using your credit cards or open credit accounts in your name.

- **Virus infection:** Some types of computer viruses spread through networks, so by connecting to a network and performing everyday operations like reading email, you allow viruses access to your computer through the network.

- **Inability to access data:** If you rely on a network connection to access critical data, you are at the mercy of that connection. In the event of a network-wide system failure, anyone who relies on network data will not be able to do their jobs.

Because of these potential threats, making sure that you share information on a network carefully and selectively is important. For example, instead of sharing your entire hard drive, share only one folder that contains all of the necessary files, and instead of giving everyone read/write access, give them only read access; they can save copies to their own hard disk if they want to make changes. Keeping an antivirus program running at all times can also help guard against virus infection; you will learn more about antivirus software in Topic 16.

Understanding Access Control Methods

Access control refers to the technologies and techniques for controlling who has access to a system. Access control can take many forms, including physical security (such as keeping a door locked) and user authentication. **User authentication** refers to the technologies and techniques used to verify a person's identity. The most popular type of user authentication is a user ID and password login system, but other methods are available.

User IDs and Passwords User IDs and passwords are the foundation of most computer access systems. You use an ID and password combination to log in to everything from your operating system to your bank's website. Access control for an operating system (like Windows) on an individual PC is usually local to that computer. In other words, the valid user names and passwords are stored on that computer in encrypted form, so no matter where that PC goes, or what network it connects to, the authorized users remain the same. The security risk in such a system is that someone could break the encryption code on the file where the passwords are stored and gain access to everything on that computer. This type of login system is also not practical in schools and businesses where people do not always use the same computer.

As an alternative, some schools and companies that have client/server networks choose to manage user access through an independent directory service stored on a separate server. For Windows servers, this is called **Active Directory**. When logins are managed using the network, users can potentially sit down at any PC anywhere on the network and log in with their own credentials. The Active Directory service then retrieves the users' preferences, data folders, and other settings.

A strong password is required for good computer security. A strong password is one that would be difficult for someone to guess. Strong passwords are:

- **Long:** The longer the better. At least eight characters is optimal.

- **Varied:** The password should contain at least one capital letter and at least one number or symbol.

- **Unusual:** The password should not appear in a dictionary and should not be a proper noun.

Passwords that are easy to guess are considered weak passwords. Some of the worst passwords are things like *qwerty*, *12345*, the user ID, and the word *password*. Only slightly better are the names of people, pets, or places.

Even though a password should be difficult for others to guess, it should be easy for you to remember. To do this, try combining numbers and letters that make sense to you but will not make sense to other people. For example, suppose you had a cousin Tony who grew up in Atlanta, and his phone number was 555-1122. An effective password might be *Tony-Atlanta#1122*.

access control The technologies and techniques used to control who or what has access to a computer system

user authentication The technologies and techniques used to verify a person's identity

Active Directory A user management service that runs on a Windows server and manages the user logins for all PCs in the network

smart card A
card containing a
microchip that a card
reader can scan to
verify or exchange
information

Smart Cards A **smart card** is a plastic card, similar in dimensions to a credit card, that contains a microchip that a card reader can scan to verify someone's identity or read information. Smart cards can be used as employee badges or student ID cards, enabling their owners to access restricted areas of a building or purchase meals in a cafeteria. Smart cards are also used in some countries, such as France, to store and transfer health care information.

Smart cards can also be used to allow or prevent computer access. For example, to use a PC, a user may be required to swipe a smart card through the PC's card reader, or the PC's card reader may automatically read the chip when the smart card comes into range.

Smart cards are sometimes used as a substitute for user IDs and passwords. In other situations they are combined with PIN numbers or used as an add-on to a standard login system to give an additional layer of security verification. For a person to gain unauthorized access, they would have to not only know a user's ID and password or PIN, but also be in possession of the user's smart card. This makes accessing the computer's information much more difficult.

biometric reader A
security scanner that
identifies users by
scanning for one or
more physical traits

Biometric Readers A **biometric reader** identifies users by scanning for one or more physical traits. Some common types of biometric devices include fingerprint recognition, facial recognition, voice recognition, and retina scanning.

Law enforcement agencies have been using fingerprint recognition for over 100 years, and no two prints have yet been found to be identical, even in people who have identical genes. Recently, computerized fingerprint scanners, like the one shown in Figure 13.13, have taken the place of manual ink prints in areas such as law enforcement and personnel recordkeeping and the technology for reading fingerprints has become so affordable that it is now built into many computer systems, including consumer-level notebook PCs. Some fingerprint scanners use a rapid laser to detect the ridges in a person's fingers, while others have an electrostatically sensitive pad that detects the current formed by the small quantities of water in a person's skin.

Retina scanners are another form of biometric reader. These devices use a camera to look into a person's eye(s). Each person's retina has a unique pattern formed by the capillaries inside it, so a retina is as unique as a fingerprint.

Figure 13.13 Fingerprint Reader

Photo courtesy of DigitalPersona

Facial recognition software works with a camera (such as a built-in webcam) to scan the face of the user. The facial scan is matched with previous pictures taken of that same person, allowing the user access to his or her account. Some notebook PCs now come with an option of logging in to Windows using facial recognition instead of a login password. Figure 13.14 shows the configuration panel for FastAccess, one brand of facial recognition software.

Figure 13.14 Facial Recognition Software Facial recognition software enables you to log in to your computer using your webcam rather than by typing a password.

Understanding Wireless Network Security

Wireless networks pose a special security challenge because they have no physical security. The only way a computer can access a wired network is to physically connect to a router or switch using a cable, so if administrators control access to the routers and switches, they can control network access. In contrast, anyone in relatively close proximity to a wireless router or access point can easily access the network, unless security measures are in place.

To limit access to a wireless network, administrators can set up encryption on the wireless router or access point. If a network is secured in this way, users must type an encryption key, which is similar to a password, when connecting to it for the first time with a particular PC. Typically, the next time they use the same PC with the same wireless network, they will not need to retype the encryption key.

Some wireless networks are open, meaning an encryption key is not required to access them. While anyone might connect to an open network, connecting alone may not allow sufficient access to all of the network's services (such as Internet access). An additional login may be required. For example, if you are a guest at a hotel, you might be able to connect to a wireless router from your room, but to gain Internet access through that router, you might need to log in and agree to pay an additional fee. In such situations, when you open a web browser window, a redirect operation displays a login page on which you may need to accept a user agreement, enter or create a user name and password, and/or provide credit card information to obtain Internet access.

Understanding Wireless Encryption Types

Several types of wireless encryption are available for use on wireless routers and access points. If you ever need to set up the security on a wireless router, such as in your home or for a small business, you will need to understand the choices. You might also need to know what type of encryption a router uses when connecting your PC to one using a wireless network adapter.

Wired Equivalent Privacy (WEP) An older but still commonly used method of network encryption, controlled by entering a 128-bit or 256-bit key

Wi-Fi Protected Access (WPA) A method of wireless network encryption that improves upon the older WEP technology and offers encryption capabilities for large networks using an authentication server

Wi-Fi Protected Access 2 (WPA2) A newer version of WPA, with stronger security capabilities than WPA

Wired Equivalent Privacy (WEP) **Wired Equivalent Privacy (WEP)** is an older, but still commonly used, method of encryption that is controlled by entering a 128-bit or 256-bit key consisting of up to 26 hexadecimal digits. Two authentication methods are used with WEP: Open System authentication and Shared Key authentication.

Wi-Fi Protected Access (WPA) A newer type of encryption that is more flexible and secure than WEP is known as **Wi-Fi Protected Access** or **WPA**. Two types of WPA exist: WPA-Personal, which is similar to WEP in terms of setup, and WPA-Enterprise, which is designed for large networks (and requires an authentication server). Two encryption protocols are used: Temporal Key Integrity Protocol (TKIP) and Computer Mode with Cipher Block Chaining Message Authentication Code Protocol (CCMP), which is sometimes called Advanced Encryption Standard (AES).

Wi-Fi Protected Access 2 (WPA2) **Wi-Fi Protected Access 2 (WPA2)** is an even-newer version of WPA, with even stronger security capability. On a small network, if you have a choice, you should use WPA2-Personal mode with TKIP encryption. This combination offers the best balance of security and ease of setup for a home or small office environment. The following exercises will allow you to explore where these properties are controlled on an individual PC and on a wireless router.

Exercise 13.4A Exploring Wireless Security on a PC

This exercise requires a computer that is already connected wirelessly to the network. If you do not have access to this type of computer, skip this exercise.

1. Click Start, click *Control Panel*, click *Network and Internet*, and then click *Network and Sharing Center*.

2. In the *View your active networks* section, next to *Connections*, find the hyperlink for your wireless network connection.

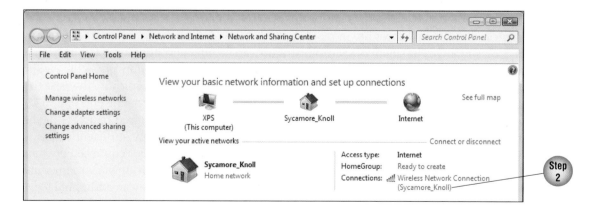

3. Click the wireless connection name.

   This opens a connection status dialog box for the wireless connection.

4. Click the Wireless Properties button.

   This opens a properties dialog box for the wireless connection.

5. Click the Security tab.

6. Note the *Security type* setting.

7. Note the *Encryption* type.

8. Click Cancel.

   This closes the properties dialog box without making any changes.

9. Click Close to close the connection status dialog box.

10. Close the Control Panel window.

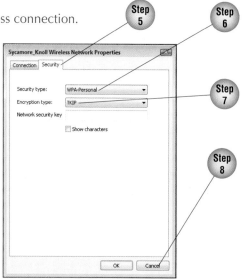

Exercise 13.4B Exploring Wireless Security on a Wireless Router

The process for determining how a wireless router or access point controls security is different for each brand and model of router or access point, so you might need to modify these steps for your situation. Skip this exercise if you do not have access to the configuration settings for a wireless router or access point.

1. Open a web browser window.

2. Type the address of the wireless router or access point in the Address bar. If you do not know it, ask your instructor.

3. Enter the user name and password if prompted. Your instructor may have this information for you.

   This opens a web page showing the router or access point's status and settings.

4. Browse the web page and click the link for security settings.

5. Look for a security mode setting (or an equivalent setting), and note to what specifications the security mode is set.

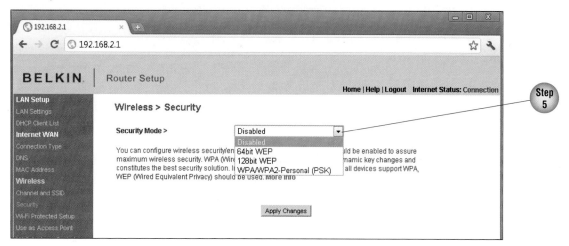

6. Close the web browser window without making any changes.

Lesson 13.5   Understanding the Internet

IC³ 3-3.1.4, 3-4.1.1

Internet A global wide area network (WAN) comprised of many smaller networks linked together under a common set of protocols

The **Internet** is a global WAN (wide area network) comprised of hundreds of thousands of small interconnected networks owned by individuals, schools, governments, and businesses, all working cooperatively under a common set of protocols.

The Internet grew out of a U.S. Department of Defense project in the 1960s called the Advanced Research Project Agency Network (ARPANET). Decentralization and path redundancy were key features of ARPANET, and the same is true of today's Internet. Each server is in charge of only a tiny piece of the whole network, so the failure of a single server or router cannot harm the whole. Many possible paths exist between every point A and every point B, so if one path is not available, the data can simply take another route. The Internet achieves redundancy by connecting each router to several other routers (see Figure 13.15).

The Internet can also be a vital tool for individuals, schools, businesses, and governments in times of natural or man-made disaster. Because of the redundant nature of Internet communication lines, the Internet may be the fastest and most reliable means of communication during disaster recovery.

Figure 13.15 Path Redundancy Data can take any of a variety of paths from one point to another on the Internet.

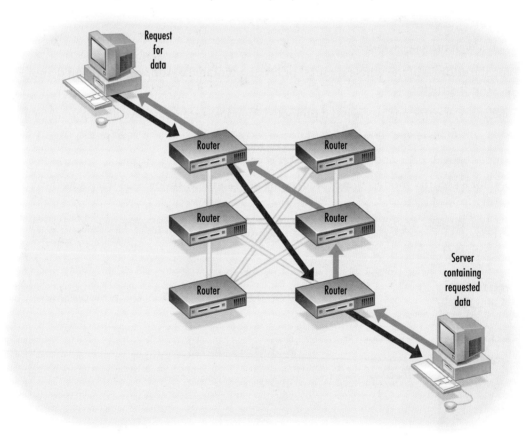

The Internet enables people to communicate and share information, whether it be across the globe or across the classroom. The benefits of the Internet to students, governments, businesses, and individuals are many and varied. The following are just a few examples:

School Students can use the Internet to:
- Take online courses
- Get homework help
- Research topics for reports
- Collaborate with classmates
- Communicate with instructors
- Find information on school closings and other announcements
- Compare and apply to colleges and universities

Government Government agencies and workers can use the Internet to:
- Provide the public with quicker and easier access to elected officials
- Inform the public about new laws and regulations
- Assess and collect taxes
- Provide consumer safety information
- Recruit for government employment opportunities
- Provide printable forms and manuals
- Help people apply for retirement or disability benefits

Business Employees and businesses can use the Internet to:
- Advertise products and services for sale
- Offer specials and discounts to customers
- Educate potential buyers
- Recruit new employees
- Research competitors' products and prices
- Provide training and continuing education to employees
- Communicate and collaborate with coworkers
- Provide payroll and benefits information to employees

Home Home users can use the Internet to:
- Communicate with family and friends
- Play games and pursue hobbies
- Take classes and learn about new subjects
- Read online newspapers and magazines
- Listen to music and watch movies

Understanding Internet Addresses

The Internet's primary protocol is Transmission Control Protocol/Internet Protocol (TCP/IP). TCP/IP is a group of protocols (rules) governing how data is transmitted and received on a network. Under TCP/IP, each computer is uniquely identified by an **IP address**, which is a numeric address that identifies a computer on a network. A governing body known as the Internet Corporation for Assigned Names and Numbers (ICANN) assigns IP addresses on the Internet.

Most networks, including the Internet, use **IP version 4 (IPv4)**, which consists of four numbers (each between 0 and 255) separated by periods (such as 202.51.5.12).

IP address Short for Internet Protocol address; a numeric address that uniquely identifies a computer on a network

IP version 4 (IPv4) A version of Internet protocol in which each computer is uniquely identified by four numbers, each between 0 and 255, separated by periods

Because the Internet has grown so large, available IP addresses are in short supply. This makes large quantities of IP addresses difficult to acquire. To help work around this, various translation systems have been created to enable large groups of computers on an internal network to share one or two IP addresses on the Internet, but this has not been enough. Therefore, a new version of Internet protocol called IP version 6 (IPv6) has been developed, with a much larger number of unique digit combinations, and it will at some point be implemented as the new means of identifying computers on the Internet. An **IP version 6 (IPv6)** number consists of eight 4-digit hexadecimal numbers, separated by colons, like this: 4FFE:190A:4542:0002:0200:F8FF:FA21:67CF.

Since the long strings of numbers in an IP address would be difficult for humans to remember, the Internet allows users to use domain names instead. A **domain name** is a text-based name that uniquely identifies a company or server on the Internet. For example, if you want to visit Microsoft's website, instead of typing the IP address for it into a web browser, you would type www.microsoft.com. Special servers called **DNS (Domain Name Service) servers** translate requests back and forth between IP addresses and domain names, so the process is invisible to most users. The process is sometimes called resolving an address. To **resolve** an address means to translate a domain name into an IP address. Note that all web addresses end in a top-level domain. A **top-level domain** is the domain represented by the characters following the final period in a domain name (such as .com, .gov, or .edu).

Exploring Types of Internet Connections

To use the Internet, you must be connected to a network that is connected to the Internet. Schools, government agencies, and large businesses often maintain their own servers and data communication lines that connect to the Internet, and all computers in their local area network share that Internet connectivity. The equipment and connections required for this type of connection can cost thousands of dollars per month, so most individual consumers cannot afford to connect using this method. Instead, individual consumers contract with **Internet Service Providers (ISPs)**, which are companies that provide access to the Internet for a fee.

A decade or so ago, most people connected to their ISP through a modem. Recall that a modem, short for modulator-demodulator, is an analog-to-digital and digital-to-analog converter that translates computer data into sounds that can be sent over a regular telephone line. Another modem at the other end converts the analog signal back to digital.

Modems are less common now, because most people use broadband connections for Internet access. *Broadband* literally means a wide pathway, capable of carrying data at a high rate of speed. Two major technologies in the broadband Internet service market for homes and small businesses include Digital Subscriber Line (DSL) and cable Internet. **Digital Subscriber Line (DSL)** carries high-speed Internet through telephone lines. Even though DSL uses the same telephone lines as a dial-up modem, the connection speed is much faster because DSL uses a different channel in the phone lines than voice calls do. Data is sent and received digitally, so no conversion back and forth with analog is required. **Cable Internet** carries Internet through the same cables that deliver cable TV service. Several other less common technologies are also available in the broadband Internet market, including satellite Internet and broadband service over cell phones. Figure 13.16 illustrates the various ways companies and individuals connect to the Internet.

IP version 6 (IPv6) A version of Internet protocol in which each computer is uniquely identified by eight 4-digit hexadecimal numbers, separated by colons

domain name A text-based name that uniquely identifies a company or server on the Internet

Domain Name Service (DNS) server A server that translates between IP addresses and domain names on the Internet

resolve To translate a domain name to an IP address

top-level domain The domain represented by the characters following the final decimal point in a domain name, such as .com or .edu

Internet Service Provider (ISP) A company that provides access to the Internet for a fee

Digital Subscriber Line (DSL) A technology for delivering broadband Internet service through telephone lines

cable Internet A technology for delivering broadband Internet through cable TV lines

Figure 13.16 **Types of Internet Connections** Some companies have their own Internet servers; others connect through an ISP.

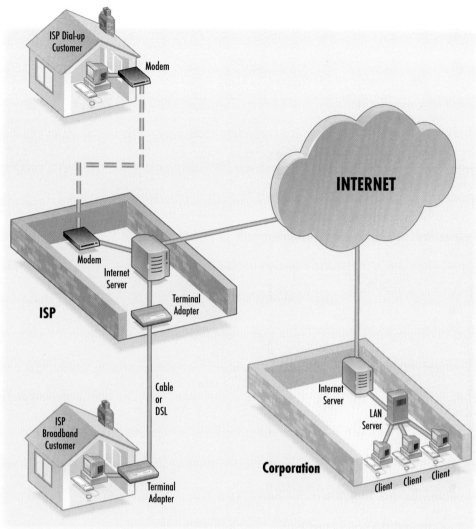

When you sign up for broadband Internet service, you get a broadband modem (sometimes referred to as a cable modem, a DSL modem, or a terminal adapter) that is compatible with the provider's system. A broadband modem has at least two connectors on it: an input jack for phone or TV cable, and an output jack for an Ethernet cable. You can connect that Ethernet cable directly to a computer to have Internet on only one PC, or you can connect that Ethernet cable to a router to share the Internet connection among multiple PCs. The modem has lights that indicate its status (see Figure 13.17).

Figure 13.17 **DSL Modem**

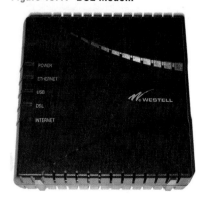

Broadband Internet service can theoretically operate at fast speeds—up to 100 Mbps in some cases. However, the speed at which you experience Internet service typically depends on the service plan you are using (faster plans are more expensive), how many other users in your area are using the connection at the same time, what sites you are accessing, and the overall traffic level on the Internet at the time of access.

network address translation (NAT) A function of a router that enables the router to change the addressing on network packets to allow multiple computers to share a single Internet connection

You can share almost any broadband Internet connection on a LAN by connecting the Internet input to a router and then connecting all the computers in your LAN to that router. A router (either wired or wireless) is able to do **network address translation (NAT)** to allow multiple computers to share a single Internet connection. NAT changes the addressing on each packet of data before it goes out to the Internet so that it appears to be coming from a single computer. Then, when the data comes back, the router delivers the packets back to the individual computers as appropriate.

Exercise 13.5 Discovering IP Addresses

1. Click Start, type **cmd**, and then press Enter.

   This action opens a command prompt.

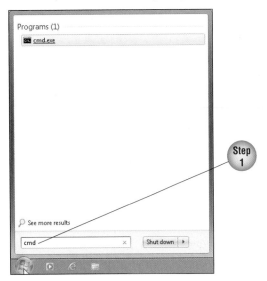

Step 1

2. Type **ipconfig** and then press Enter.

   This displays the IP addresses of each network adapter in your computer.

```
Administrator: C:\Windows\system32\cmd.exe

C:\Users\Student Name>ipconfig

Windows IP Configuration

Ethernet adapter Bluetooth Network Connection 3:

   Media State . . . . . . . . . . . : Media disconnected
   Connection-specific DNS Suffix  . :

Wireless LAN adapter Wireless Network Connection 3:

   Media State . . . . . . . . . . . : Media disconnected
   Connection-specific DNS Suffix  . :

Wireless LAN adapter Wireless Network Connection:

   Connection-specific DNS Suffix  . : Belkin
   Link-local IPv6 Address . . . . . : fe80::dd5f:db8:72bc:4c3f%20
   IPv4 Address. . . . . . . . . . . : 192.168.2.2
   Subnet Mask . . . . . . . . . . . : 255.255.255.0
   Default Gateway . . . . . . . . . : 192.168.2.1

C:\Users\Student Name>
```

Step 2

3. Locate the IP address for your main network connection, if there is more than one. Ask your instructor for help if needed. The information might look like the image below.

The IPv4 address listed for your network adapter is the IP address on your LAN, not necessarily on the Internet, because your router and/or your ISP may employ network address translation to change the address.

```
Wireless LAN adapter Wireless Network Connection:

Connection-specific DNS Suffix . . : Belkin

Link-local IPv6 Address . . . . .: fe80::dd5f:db8:72bc:4c3f%22

IPv4 Address . . . . . . . . . . : 192.168.2.2

Subnet Mask . . . . . . . . . . .: 255.255.255.0

Default Gateway . . . . . . . .: 192.168.2.1
```

4. Type **ping www.facebook.com** and press Enter.

The ping utility checks the availability of an Internet server, and also tells you its IP address. In this case, you are looking up the IP address of Facebook. It may look something like this:

```
Pinging www.facebook.com [66.220.153.15] with 32 bytes of data:

Reply from 66.220.153.15: bytes= 32 time=42ms TTL=244

Reply from 66.220.153.15: bytes= 32 time=41ms TTL=244

Reply from 66.220.153.15: bytes= 32 time=41ms TTL=244

Reply from 66.220.153.15: bytes= 32 time=42ms TTL=244</Text>
```

5. Following the same process as in Step 4, use ping to find the IP address of another website of your choice.

6. Close the open window.

Drilling Down

Understanding IP Addresses

As you learned earlier in the lesson, IPv4 addresses consist of four numbers, each between 0 and 255, separated by periods. The limit is 255 numbers because the largest 8-digit binary number possible is 255 (11111111).

The common convention of writing IP addresses as four numbers separated by periods is actually just a shorthand way of writing them that makes the numbers easier for humans to read. Each of the four numbers, when converted to binary, is an eight-digit binary number between 00000000 and 11111111. String them all together, and you have the single binary number that is the "true" IP address.

Suppose the IP address is 192.168.4.155. Recall from Topic 1 that you can use the Calculator application to convert each of those number sets to binary numbers. Doing so results in the following:

192 = 11000000

168 = 10101000

4 = 00000100

155 = 10011011

The IP address as the computer understands it is 11000000101010000000010010011011. However, humans have a hard time with large binary numbers, often accidentally leaving out, transposing, or adding digits, which is why IP addresses are written with decimal numbers and periods rather than in their raw format.

Understanding the World Wide Web

3-3.1.1, 3-3.1.2, 3-3.1.3, 3-3.2.1

Hypertext Markup Language (HTML) The programming language used to create web pages

Hypertext Transfer Protocol (HTTP) The networking protocol used to distribute web content

web page A single document, usually in HTML format, that contains web content

website A group of related, interconnected web pages

hyperlink A clickable link to a web page or some other content

The World Wide Web (more often referred to as the Web) is one of the most popular parts of the Internet. At its most basic level, the Web is a network of documents written in **Hypertext Markup Language (HTML)**, and distributed using the **Hypertext Transfer Protocol (HTTP)**. Although millions of people use the Web every day, few understand what goes on behind the scenes of a web browser. This lesson explores the technology of the Web and shows you how to create web content.

Information on the Web is stored in documents called **web pages**. These pages are usually written in HTML, and their files have .htm or .html extensions. A **website** is a group of related, interconnected web pages, usually with a common design and navigation system. In Figure 13.18, a web page displays with navigation bars along the top and sides. These navigation bars contain hyperlinks to the other pages in the site. A **hyperlink** is a clickable link to a web page or some other content.

Figure 13.18 Web Page Example

web server A server that is connected to the Internet and that has the appropriate software to be able to process requests for web content

dedicated server A server that is devoted to a single website, company, or activity

web hosting company A business that owns and maintains web servers and rents space on the servers to others

Web pages are stored on **web servers**. Recall that a web server is a server that is connected to the Internet and has the appropriate software to be able to process requests for web content. Schools, government agencies, and large companies typically have their own dedicated web servers. A **dedicated server** is one that is devoted to a single website, company, or activity. Small businesses and individuals either obtain web hosting from their ISP or rent the amount of web server space they need from a **web hosting company**. Web hosting companies own and maintain web servers and rent space on the servers to others. A web portal is a web page created to provide access to other Internet content. A web portal contains organized links and a search engine. Yahoo! and MSN are examples of web portals.

Understanding Web Addresses

Websites have unique addresses, called **Uniform Resource Locators (URLs)**. A web address typically begins with *www* (to indicate that a web server is being referenced, not some other type of Internet server such as mail or file storage) and is followed by the domain name of the company or individual that the site represents. For example, http://www.emcp.com.

The prefix *http://* indicates that the HTTP protocol should be used to request and retrieve the page. Typing *http://* is optional, because the web browser automatically assumes that prefix.

When the web browser sends such a request out to the Internet, the request goes to a DNS server. As you learned in Lesson 13.5, a DNS server translates between domain names and IP addresses. The DNS server looks up the domain name and provides the equivalent IP address. That IP address is then used to locate the web server where that site is hosted, and to convey the request for the page. The hosting website sends the requested page back to the web browser and the web browser displays the requested page for the user.

The URL http://www.emcp.com specifies a domain name but not a specific page. If you do not indicate a page name, you get the home (default) page for that site. Most websites have multiple pages, some of which may be stored in different folders on the server. To display a particular page (if you happen to know its complete URL), type the complete path and filename of the page after the domain name, separated by forward slashes (/), like this: http://www.emcp.com/swf/main.html.

Uniform Resource Locator (URL) The address of an Internet resource; begins with a communications protocol such as *http://*

Understanding HTML and XML

Hypertext Markup Language (HTML) is the basic programming language of websites. The *markup* part of the name refers to the way HTML codes blocks of text to receive certain formatting by marking them with bracketed codes called **tags** at the beginning and end of the blocks. For example, you might have the following code in HTML:

tag An HTML markup code enclosed in angle brackets, for example, *<p>*

```
<p>We had a <i>great</i> time at the party.</p>
<ul>
<li>We played cards.</li>
<li>We ate chips and salsa.</li>
</ul>
```

The <p> code signals the beginning of a paragraph, and the </p> code signals its end. The <i> code signals the beginning of an italicized block of text, and the </i> code signals its end. The <ul> code signals the beginning of an unordered list (that is, a bulleted list), and </ul> signals its end. Within the list, <li> marks the beginning of a bulleted paragraph, and </li> marks its end. On a web page, this line would look something like the text shown in Figure 13.19, although minor font and formatting differences may occur in different web browsers.

Figure 13.19 HTML Example

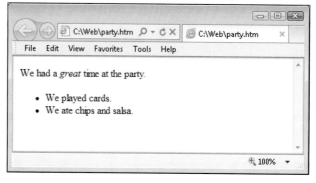

Learning to code documents in HTML is not difficult, but it does require some study and practice. Many schools offer classes in HTML, and you can also learn on your own with books and study materials online.

Extensible Markup Language (XML) is also a markup language, but is is a much more versatile language than HTML because developers can create their own tags. XML is often used in developing web-accessible databases

Extensible Markup Language (XML) A versatile markup language that allows users to create custom tags and document libraries. End-users of the web do not interact directly with XML, but programmers who develop web content do so extensively.

Exercise 13.6A Creating a Web Page in Notepad

1. In Notepad, type the following:

   <DOCTYPE HTML>

   <html>

   <head>

   <title>Daily News</title>

   </head>

   <body>

   <h1>The Daily News</h1>

   <p>This page is under construction.</p>

   </body>

   </html>

3. Click File on the menu bar and then click *Save*.

4. In the Save As dialog box, navigate to the **Unit3Topic13** folder.

5. In the File name text box, type **U3T13-Notepad.htm**.

   Make sure you include the *.htm* extension. If you save the file with the default Notepad extension of *.txt*, you will not be able to open the file as a web page in a web browser.

6. Click Save to finish saving the file.

7. Print **U3T13-Notepad.htm** and then close Notepad.

8. Open Windows Explorer, navigate to the folder where you saved the file in Windows Explorer, and then double-click *U3T13-Notepad.htm*.

   This opens the file in your default web browser.

9. Close the web browser.

Identifying Other Ways to Create Web Pages

Web development can be a huge, complex process involving dozens of programmers, several programming languages, and expensive web design software, or it can be as simple as one person hand-coding each individual HTML file in Notepad, as you learned in Exercise 13.6A.

One way to develop web content inexpensively is to create it in a program you already have and then save the content in a file format that is web-compatible. Many applications enable you to save your work in one or more web formats. For example, as shown in Figure 13.20, Microsoft Word 2010 lets you save documents in the following web-compatible formats:

- **Single File Web Page**: A single file web page stores the document in a file with an *.mht* extension. The advantage of this type of file is that text and all the graphics (if any) are included in a single file, so you do not have to worry about separate files for each graphic. The disadvantage of this file type is that some older web browsers do not display this file type.

- **Web Page:** A web page stores the document in a Word-optimized web file with an *.htm* extension. The advantage of this type of file is that you can reopen the file in Word later and it will retain most of its Word-specific features. A disadvantage is that the file is much larger than a regular .htm file because it includes all the Word formatting codes in addition to the HTML codes.

- **Web Page, Filtered:** A filtered web page stores the file in pure HTML format, with no special codes for display in Word. This method is beneficial because it generates a small, cleanly coded HTML file that can be edited in any HTML editor, but you might lose some of the special Word-specific formatting.

You can also use programs such as Adobe Dreamweaver or Microsoft Expression Web, both of which are designed specifically to create websites. These programs take longer to learn because their interfaces are different from most software you may have worked with before. However, they also provide shortcuts and assistance for developing web content and maintaining links between pages. This is helpful when you are developing a large and complicated site.

Figure 13.20 **Web-Based File Format Options in Word**

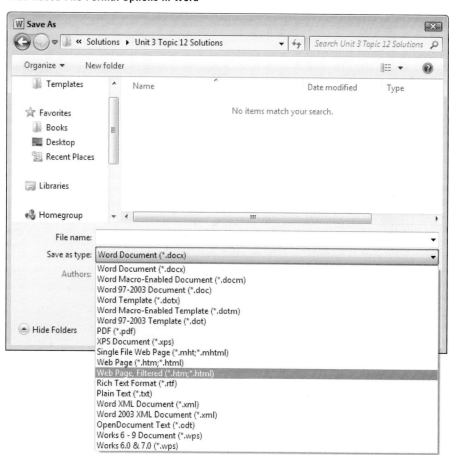

Exercise 13.6B Creating a Web Page in Word

1. Start Microsoft Word and type the following text in a new document:

   Test Page

   This is a quick test of Word's web page creation capability.

2. Select the first line, *Test Page*, and then apply the Heading 1 style (from the Styles group on the Home tab).

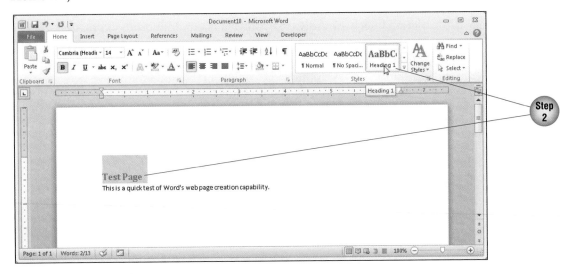

3. Select the words *quick test* and then click the Bold button.

4. Click the Save button on the Quick Access toolbar.

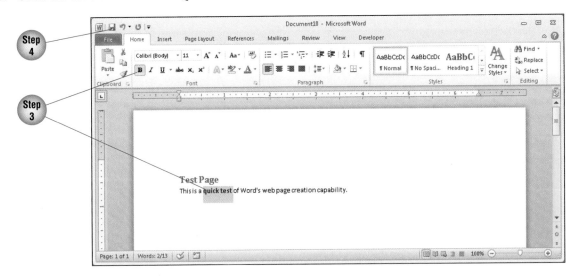

5. At the Save As dialog box, change the *Save as type* option to *Web Page, Filtered (*.htm; *.html)*.

6. In the *File name* text box, type **U3T13-Word**.

7. Click Save.

8. At the confirmation box, click Yes.

9. In Windows Explorer, navigate to the folder where you saved the file and then double-click the file.

   This opens the file in your default web browser.

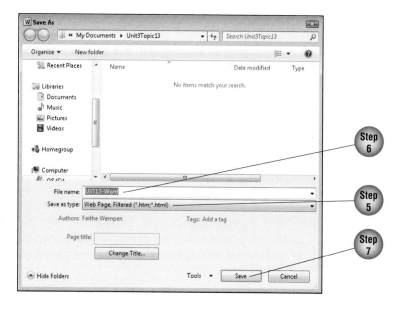

10. Close the web browser window.

11. Open the file **U3T13-Word.htm** in Notepad and browse the HTML code.

    Notice that the majority of the code is in the <head> section, defining the fonts in use. Scroll down to the bottom of the code to see the actual text that displays on the page.

12. Close Notepad without saving changes.

Publishing Content to the Web

Individuals can create websites and publish them to web servers, allowing them to make their ideas available to the entire Internet community. Some social networking sites, like Facebook, enable users to post content without having to own a domain name or maintain a website, but creating a more professional online presence typically requires that users maintain their own sites.

Suppose you want to publish a small website for a business. You might take steps similar to the following:

1. **Register a domain name for the business.** Choose a domain name that fits the business's identity and purpose. For example, if the business's name is Big Purple Shoes, you might try bigpurpleshoes.com. You can use any domain registrar company, such as www.domainspricedright.com. Registering a domain gives you exclusive rights to use that domain name for as long as it is registered to you.

2. **Sign up with a web hosting company for web server space to place the new site.** Configure the hosting accounts so that the domain name points to that server. Some domain registrars also provide hosting services, so you may be able to host at the same site where you registered the domain.

3. **Create the website.** You can use a website creation application, or you can code each individual page in a text editor like Notepad.

4. **Upload the website to the server.** One way is to use a **File Transfer Protocol (FTP)** application, which uses the FTP protocol to transfer files to and from network servers. The web hosting company might provide alternative ways, too, such as uploading from a web interface.

File Transfer Protocol (FTP) A protocol used for efficiently transferring files to and from Internet servers

Drilling Down

Identifying Top-Level Domain Names

Each domain name must end in one of the acceptable top-level domains, such as *.com*, *.org*, .gov, and so on. Recall that a top-level domain is the domain represented by the characters following the final period in a domain name. Top-level domains organize domain names in one of a few dozen broad categories, based on the location or purpose of the site. ICANN manages the top-level domains and the DNS servers that resolve the addresses that use them. When you register a domain name, you usually have your choice of several top-level domains. Businesses typically pick *.com*, which stands for *commercial*. Nonprofits and clubs often pick *.org*, short for *organization*. Companies and organizations that are Internet-based might select *.net*, which is short for *Internet* or *network*. Government organizations in the United States almost always use *.gov*, which is short for *government*, or *.us*, which stands for *United States*.

Many top-level domains exist, but some of them are open only to people and businesses in certain geographical locations or industries. For example, the *.edu* top-level domain is open only to schools, and *.tz* is open only to companies that have a presence in the country of Tanzania.

Lesson 13.7 **Understanding Electronic Communication Types**

 3-2.1.1, 3-2.1.2, 3-2.1.3, 3-2.3.1, 3-2.3.2, 3-2.3.3

The Internet is much bigger and more diverse than just the Web, and it uses many technologies to help people communicate. In this lesson, you will learn about some of the ways that people use the Internet to communicate, including email, instant messaging, blogs, and web conferencing.

Understanding Email

email A system that enables people to send and receive messages electronically

Electronic mail, or **email**, enables people to exchange private messages with one another. It may take anywhere from a few seconds to a few hours for a message to be delivered, so it is not an instant communication method. However, email is extremely fast compared to postal mail. Email is also usually free (or nearly free), so it is a much more economical way of reaching multiple people than sending them all postal mail.

Email is a store-and-forward system. When you send someone an email message, it travels from your PC to your outgoing mail server. From there it goes to the incoming mail server of the recipient, where it is stored, and waits until the recipient connects to the incoming mail server to retrieve it. At that point the message is forwarded (delivered) to the Inbox of the email software on the recipient's computer. The recipient might have the email program configured to automatically check for new messages every few minutes, but if the recipient's computer is turned off, or the email program is not running, the recipient will not get the message until he or she returns to the computer and connects to the mail server. Email is good at preserving records of conversations and file transfers; incoming messages stay in the Inbox until you delete them, and you can move messages to other folders for permanent archiving.

Different types of email servers are available. Some of them are Web-only, and require you to log in to a website to send and receive mail (see Figure 13.21). Others enable you to use an email application such as Outlook or Windows Live Mail to manage your mail. You will learn much more about email in Topic 15, including how mail servers and applications work and what protocols they use.

Understanding Instant Messaging and Web Conferencing

Instant messaging (IM), also called *chatting* or *IMing*, establishes a real-time, person-to-person conversation space using the Internet. You can chat with someone using a web interface (for example, Facebook chat) or a separate application such as Yahoo! Messenger, AOL Instant Messenger, or ICQ.

Figure 13.21 Web-based Email Interface

Conversations are typically between only two people, but some services allow multiple people to chat in a group conference. Instant messaging is usually associated with text communication, but some IM software blurs the line between IMs and other communication media by providing voice chat and/or video chat in the same interface. Instant messaging is called **texting** when it is done using a cell phone rather than a computer. Instant messaging and texting are informal means of communication, used more for casual conversations than for formal business. One of the limitations of the technology is that the number of characters you can send per message is often limited.

instant messaging (IM) A type of real-time, person-to-person communication on the Internet; also called *chatting*

texting Instant message delivery using a cell phone

Instant messaging software designed for business and professional use is also available; this software may include increased audio and video capabilities that enable companies to conduct virtual meetings. Business-oriented IM software is sometimes called **web conferencing software** or video conferencing software. Web conferencing software usually includes capabilities for sharing software and documents in the chat interface, so in addition to seeing and hearing one another, participants can also collaboratively edit documents. Some conferencing software is web-hosted, so participants can simply log in to a website to use it. Other software requires downloading and installing on each of the participating users' PCs.

web conferencing software Multiuser chat software that enables full-featured audio, video, and text conferencing, as well as file sharing and application collaboration

Understanding VoIP

As mentioned in Lesson 13.1, Voice over IP (VoIP) technology uses the Internet for telephone services. It converts the analog voice from a telephone to digital format and sends the data over the Internet to its destination, where it is converted back to analog so the person on the other end of the line can hear it. VoIP is an inexpensive alternative to traditional telephone service, and it can provide the same features, including call waiting, call forwarding, and voicemail.

A whole-house VoIP system consists of a converter box that connects to any unused phone jack and to the Internet connection. The converter box enables all the telephones on that line to make and receive phone calls through the Internet. That way, each PC does not need its own telephone, and vice-versa. Vonage is one popular whole-house VoIP service. Some Internet service providers that bundle services, such as your cable company, may also provide phone service through their own brand of VoIP.

Some VoIP services provide VoIP through a computer or smartphone interface, such as Skype. These services use the processing power of the computer, or other device, to manage the calls. Because they are connected to a computing device, they can incorporate features like video chatting and file sharing into the conversations, something normal phone service cannot do.

Understanding Blogging

blog An ongoing journal that displays on a publicly accessible website

A **blog** is an ongoing journal that displays on a publicly accessible website. The term is an abbreviated form of *web log*. Blogs can be part of a business's or individual's website, or can be hosted on a website designed specifically for blogging, like WordPress, Blogspot, or LiveJournal. Blogs have changed mainstream ideas about journalism and news reporting. No longer is news and creative content distributed only by professional journalists and music and video companies; blogs and other personal websites have enabled individuals to publish their own content, and many news stories that became global headline issues have originated from blogs.

Blog posts are ordered from newest to oldest, so the most recent post displays at the top of the page. Individuals create blogs for many reasons, including to express themselves; to share information about their hobbies, interests, or travels; and to build support for causes. Businesses may create a company blog to add a personal touch to their business's image and to build interest in the company in an informal way. Blogging is an even less immediate technology than email; in some cases people may discover and read a blog post months or even years after it was written.

Because blogs are public, anyone can read them. Although a blog might seem like a private journal or writings shared with just a select few people who happen to read and comment on it, keep in mind that many more people may be reading your material. For security reasons, you should not post identifying information, like your phone number or address, on a personal blog. Companies, on the other hand, typically post this information because the company wants to make their contact information public and prominent so customers can find them.

Understanding Podcasting

Podcasts are audio recordings that are made available online for people to download to. They are similar to radio shows except they are not live and you can access them at your convenience. You can download podcasts from the individual websites of the people who create them, from podcast directory websites, or from content services such as the Apple Store. You can then listen to them on your computer or on a portable media player. You can even create your own podcast and publish it online; all you need is a computer, a microphone, and a server on which to host the podcast.

Understanding Social Networking

social networks Websites or other online services that exist to help people keep in touch with one another

status update A brief message that a user posts publicly using a social networking service

Social networks are websites or other online services that exist to help people communicate with one another. Some social networking sites are available to everyone, like Facebook and MySpace. Others have special purposes or are limited to members of certain clubs or communities. For example, Ancestry.com is an online community that helps people collaborate on genealogy research.

Some social networking services provide only one type of communication. For example, Twitter enables users to post **status updates**, which are like text messages except they are broadcast to anyone who subscribes to that user's feed. A **feed** is all the information a user or organization posts. For example, you might subscribe to the feeds of your family members to find out what they are doing throughout the day. To **subscribe** to someone's feed is to sign up to receive their status updates.

Other social networks provide additional services and capabilities as well. For example, Facebook, in addition to allowing you to post status updates, also enables you to post longer articles and journal entries, play games, recommend links, post videos, share photos, and so on.

Social networking is based on the relationships you create with people you know online. On Facebook, to **friend** someone means to request a connection from your online profile to theirs on a social networking service. (*Friend* is not really a verb, but it has become popular usage to use it that way.) This adds the person to your Friends list, so that you see each other's posts.

As with blogs, be careful what you post on social networking sites and who you allow to access your information. Do not post any information that a potential predator or criminal could use to find you, such as your address, phone number, or schedule. You should also make sure you do not make any comments that you will later regret or that you do not want everyone on your Friends list to see, such as saying unkind things about someone or complaining about an employer or family member. It is not uncommon to hear about the negative effects of poor online communication and posting decisions. Many people have lost jobs and friendships because something they posted on a social networking site was seen by an unintended person.

A more indirect type of social networking is **RSS,** which means either **Really Simple Syndication** or RDF Site Summary (the original meaning, now less commonly used). RSS is a way of subscribing to a frequently updated web page, much like you subscribe to a person's social networking feed, so that if the page's content changes, the new information is delivered to you automatically. RSS blurs the lines between websites, email, and social networking by allowing web content to be automatically distributed in other formats.

Pages that support RSS use a standard file format that enables the content to be viewed in a consistent way by many different programs. RSS feeds can be read using **feed reader** software, which is sometimes called an RSS reader or aggregator. Feed readers can be web based, stand-alone applications, or mobile device applications.

Understanding Public Discussion Forums

There are many opportunities online for you to express your thoughts and opinions in public forums. Public forums can take any of the following forms:

- **Email-based discussion groups:** These groups allow members to communicate with the entire group at once via email. Whenever anyone posts something to the group, the message is automatically sent by email to the other group members. Yahoo! Groups hosts free email-based groups for individuals and organizations, and private servers can also run software that hosts email groups. Email groups are convenient because you do not have to remember to check a particular site to participate, but active groups can create a lot of extra mail in your Inbox.

- **Newsgroups:** These public groups, most of which are hosted by Usenet servers, allow public discussions on a wide variety of topics. There are over 20,000 active Usenet newsgroups all over the world. You can use a newsgroup reading application to access them, or read them on a website that provides access. Some email applications can be configured to read newsgroups.

- **Web-based message boards:** Many websites host message forums, or message boards, in which the public can ask questions and receive peer answers or answers from company representatives. Browsing support-related message boards can be a good way of finding troubleshooting help for a product or posting your comments or questions.

Exercise 13.7 Exploring RSS Feeds

If your instructor wants you to create a Google account or sign in to an existing Google account to complete this exercise, complete the following steps. If not, skip this exercise.

1. Open a web browser and go to www.google.com/reader. Sign into your Google account when prompted, and then click Subscribe.

2. Type **msnbc.com** and click Add.

   Several new stories are added to your feed.

3. Click one of the news stories to read a summary of it and then click its headline to view it at the MSNBC.com website.

4. Close the web browser window.

Drilling Down

The Paper Trail

Some types of electronic communication are better than others for maintaining a written record of what was communicated. Written records are also known as "paper trails" because people can use them to understand or piece together previous discussions or decisions. An email program can be programmed to save a copy of every message you send and received message remain in your inbox until you delete them, so email is considered one of the better methods of maintaining communication records. Instant messaging and video conferencing, on the other hand, do not always store archives of the conversations (although some programs can be configured to do so). Try to determine whether you want a conversation to be retrievable later, and make sure the communication medium you select supports your choice.

More Information for IC³

Delving Deeper

 3-3.1.2

Exploring Types of Web Pages

New technologies have made websites more interactive and dynamic than was possible in the past. As a result, although the Web is still based on HTML, not every web page is a basic HTML document anymore. Other types of content you might encounter on the Web include:

- **Java Server Pages (.jsp):** These pages are generated as needed using the Java programming language on the server. They may be HTML-based, but are generated using separate programming. For example, if you are browsing at a website that sells computers and you do a search for a particular brand, the page that shows the results might be in this format.
- **Active Server Pages (.asp):** These pages are much the same as Java Server Pages except they use a Microsoft technology.
- **Flash (.swf):** Flash is an animated graphics format that can be used to create complex, interactive graphical systems. For example, a Flash-based page might display a a clickable map of the world that displays a different page depending on what country you click.

Many websites provide online applications that users can interact with, such as a symptom checker at a medical website or productivity tools such as Google Docs. These online applications are usually written in web-compatible programming language like Java or Flash, rather than in plain HTML.

TOPIC SUMMARY

- A network is a group of connected devices that share data or resources. Schools, businesses, government agencies, and homes all use networks to work more efficiently.
- Networking sends information in packet, according to transmission rules specified by protocols. The most common network protocol is TCP/IP, which is also used on the Internet.
- To create a network, each device needs a network adapter and a central access point to connect to the devices, such as a router, switch, or wireless access point.
- Ethernet is the dominant network type. Wired Ethernet standards include 1000BaseT and 10GBaseT. Wireless Ethernet (Wi-Fi) standards include 802.11g and 802.11n.
- Ethernet cables are Unshielded Twisted Pair (UTP) conforming to Category 5e or Category 6 standards. They use an RJ-45 connector, which is like a wide telephone plug, on each end.
- Bluetooth is a short-range wireless technology used to directly connect devices with peripherals such as headsets.
- A Local Area Network (LAN) is a network of computers physically near one another. A Wide Area Network (WAN) is a network in which computers are not physically near one another.
- A client/server network is a network that has at least one server. A peer-to-peer network consists only of clients (end-user PCs).
- Bandwidth refers to the maximum rate of data transmission on a network, in bits per second.
- The Homegroup feature in Windows 7 can set up a small peer-to-peer network and easily configure file and printer sharing.
- To share a folder, right-click the folder, click *Share With*, and then click the type of sharing. To share a printer, right-click the printer, click *Printer Properties*, and then click the *Share this printer* check box on the Sharing tab.
- The risks of networking include information theft, data loss, privacy invasion, and virus infection.
- Access control on a network is either controlled locally or using an Active Directory server. Other methods of access control include smart cards and biometric readers that scan fingerprints, faces, or retinas.
- Wireless network encryption types include WEP, WPA, and WPA2.
- The Internet is a global WAN comprised of many smaller networks linked together under a common set of protocols.
- The Internet uses IP addresses; currently it uses IPv4 addresses (such as 211.25.58.26), but at some point will transition to IPv6 addresses.
- DNS servers resolve requests on the Internet between IP addresses and domain names.
- Web pages are stored on web servers. A collection of web pages is a website. Web pages contain hyperlinks that link to other pages. Web addresses are called Uniform Resource Locators (URLs).
- Hypertext Markup Language (HTML) is the language in which web pages are created. HTML uses tags, which are bracketed codes, to define how text should be formatted.
- Email, instant messaging, texting, blogging, VoIP, social networking, and RSS are all electronic communication methods.

Key Terms

1000BaseT, p. 590

10GBaseT, p. 590

4G, p. 590

access control, p. 603

Active Directory, p. 603

bandwidth, p. 593

biometric reader, p. 604

blog, p. 622

Bluetooth, p. 590

cable Internet, p. 610

Category 5e (Cat5e), p. 590

Category 6 (Cat6), p. 590

client, p. 592

client/server, p. 592

data throughput, p. 593

dedicated server, p. 614

dial-up network, p. 593

Digital Subscriber Line (DSL), p. 610

domain name, p. 610

Domain Name Service (DNS) server, p. 610

continued

Understanding Networks and the Internet   625

e-commerce, p. 586

email, p. 620

Ethernet, p. 589

Extensible Markup Language (XML), p. 615

feed, p. 623

feed reader, p. 623

File Transfer Protocol (FTP), p. 619

frame, p. 588

friend, p. 623

hyperlink, p. 614

Hypertext Markup Language (HTML), p. 614

Hypertext Transfer Protocol (HTTP), p. 614

infrared technology, p. 591

instant messaging (IM), p. 621

Internet, p. 608

Internet Service Provider (ISP), p. 610

IP address, p. 609

IP version 4 (IPv4), p. 609

IP version 6 (IPv6), p. 610

latency, p. 593

modem, p. 593

network, p. 585

network adapter, p. 589

network address translation (NAT), p. 614

online learning, p. 586

packet, p. 588

peer-to-peer (P2P) network, p. 592

protocol, p. 589

Really Simple Syndication (RSS), p. 623

resolve, p. 612

RJ-45 connector, p. 590

router, p. 589

smart card, p. 604

social networks, p. 622

status update, p. 623

subscribe, p. 623

switch, p. 589

tag, p. 615

telecommute, p. 587

texting, p. 621

top-level domain, p. 610

Transmission Control Protocol/ Internet Protocol (TCP/IP), p. 589

Uniform Resource Locator (URL), p. 615

Unshielded Twisted Pair (UTP), p. 590

user authentication, p. 603

virtual private network (VPN), p. 587

Voice over IP (VoIP), p. 587

web conferencing software, p. 621

web hosting company, p. 614

web page, p. 614

web server, p.614

website, p. 614

Wi-Fi, p. 589

Wi-Fi 802.11n, p. 590

Wi-Fi Protected Access (WPA), p. 606

Wi-Fi Protected Access 2 (WPA2), p. 606

Wired Equivalent Privacy (WEP), p. 606

wired network, p. 589

wireless access point (WAP), p. 589

wireless network, p. 589

KEY POINTS REVIEW

Completion

In the space provided at the left, indicate the correct term, command, or option.

1. _____ This term is used to refer to telephone service over the Internet.

2. _____ This term describes a secure network that operates through a larger unsecure network.

3. _____ This is a set of rules for data transmission; TCP/IP is one example.

4. _____ This is a more complex version of a switch; it is able to route network requests between networks.

5. _____ Wi-Fi is a wireless version of this.

6. _____ Cat5e and Cat6 are types of networking ____.

continued

7. _____ What does WAN stand for?

8. _____ A ____/server network contains one or more servers.

9. _____ Bandwidth is a measure of this.

10. _____ List two risks involved in networking.

11. _____ List two methods of user authentication.

12. _____ Fingerprint readers and retina scanners are examples of this type of user access control.

Multiple Choice

For each of the following items, choose the option that best completes the sentence or answers the question.

1. Which of these is not a wireless encryption type?
   A. WEP
   B. WPA2
   C. WAP
   D. WPA

2. Which of these is an IPv4 address?
   A. 192.168.0.1
   B. 4FFE:190A:4542:0002:0200:F8FF
   C. 521.55.944.6
   D. 4FFE:190A:4542:0002:0200:F8FF:FA21:67CF.

3. A(n) _____ server resolves IP addresses with domain names.
   A. ISP
   B. DNS
   C. DSL
   D. BIOS

4. A company that provides Internet service to customers is a(n) _____.
   A. ISP
   B. DNS
   C. DSL
   D. IP

5. Which of these is a type of Internet connection that uses a phone line?
   A. NAT
   B. DSL
   C. IPv4
   D. IP

6. A router can use _____ to enable multiple computers to share a single Internet connection.
   A. BIOS
   B. DNS
   C. DSL
   D. NAT

7. This is the protocol used for web pages.
   A. HTTP
   B. FTP
   C. HTML
   D. URL

8. This is the language in which web pages are written.
   A. HTTP
   B. FTP
   C. HTML
   D. URL

9. In the address *http://www.emcp.com*, which part of the address is the top-level domain?
   A. http
   B. emcp
   C. www
   D. com

10. Twitter is an example of what kind of communication?
    A. blog
    B. VoIP
    C. social network
    D. RSS

Matching

Match each of the following definitions with the correct term, command, or option.

1. _____ Employees working from home using the Internet or phone to keep in contact with the office
2. _____ Phone service over the Internet
3. _____ Delays in transmission on the network
4. _____ The protocol suite used on the Internet
5. _____ A Wi-Fi standard
6. _____ An older type of wireless connection where both devices must be in sight of each other
7. _____ A non-Ethernet wireless technology used for short-range connections like headsets
8. _____ A network in which all computers are near each other, such as in the same building
9. _____ A network within a metropolitan area, such as a city
10. _____ A workgroup network with no servers

A. 802.11n
B. Bluetooth
C. Infrared
D. LAN
E. Latency
F. MAN
G. P2P
H. TCP/IP
I. Telecommuting
J. VoIP

SKILLS REVIEW

Review 13.1 **Identifying Networks in Your School**

1. Open a new Word document.
2. Make a list of all the types of networks you and your peers have access to during class. Include both computer and phone networks.
3. For each network, explain how you could use the network for class research.
4. For each network, explain the rules your institution has for using the network during class hours.
5. Print your document.
6. Save the Word document and name it **U3T13-R1-Networks**, close the document, and then exit Word.

Review 13.2 **Finding Website IP Addresses**

1. Open a new Notepad file.
2. Click Start, type **cmd**, and then press Enter.
3. Type **ping www.google.com** and press Enter.
4. In the Notepad file, type the IP address shown.
5. Using the same procedure, check five other websites of your instructor's choice.
6. Type in the Notepad file each site's URL and the IP address reported for the website.
7. Print the document.
8. Save the Notepad document and name it **U3T13-R2-Ping**. Close the document and exit Notepad.

Review 13.3 **Browsing a Network**

1. Start a new document in Word and then type the following:
   Computer:
   Folder:
   File:
2. Open the Computer window and then click *Network* to see which computers have shared resources available to be browsed.

3. Browse the shared content on one of the computers, and find a file you can open in one of your own applications. Check with your instructor as he or she may ask you to obtain a particular file.
4. In Word, type the computer name, folder name, and file name next to the labels you typed in Step 1.
5. Press Enter to start a new paragraph.
6. Switch back to the Computer window and double-click the file to open it.
7. Select one paragraph of the file (if it contains text) or press Ctrl + A to select the entire file if it is a graphic.
8. Press Ctrl + C to copy the selection to the Clipboard.
9. Switch to Word and then paste the selection into the Word document.
10. Save the Word document as **U3T13-R3-Sharing**.
11. Print the document and then close all open windows.

SKILLS ASSESSMENT

Assessment 13.1 **Creating and Using a Windows 7 Homegroup**

In this exercise, you will use two Windows 7 computers to create a homegroup and share files between them. You can work in pairs, with each person running one of the computers, or you can work individually by moving between two PCs.

1. Open the Network and Sharing Center on both computers.
2. If either computer is already a part of a homegroup, leave the homegroup. (To leave the homegroup, click *Choose homegroup and sharing options* and then click *Leave the homegroup*.)
3. Create a new homegroup on computer 1, and click to share pictures and documents. Record the password when it displays onscreen.
4. Join the homegroup on computer 2. Use the password you recorded in Step 3 to connect to it. Click to share pictures and documents.
5. Create a new folder on computer 1 and name it A2.
6. Share the A2 folder with the homegroup with read-only access.
7. In the A2 folder, create a new Notepad file. In the file, type your full name (or the names of both people, if working as a team), followed by **Sharing Test**. Name the file **U3T13-A1-Sharing**.
8. Close Notepad.
9. Browse the network for the shared A2 folder on computer 2. Copy the **U3T13-A1-Sharing.txt** file to that PC's desktop.
10. Print the file and submit it to your instructor.

Assessment 13.2 **Choosing an ISP**

In this exercise, you will do research to determine the best Internet connection method and ISP for someone who lives near your school and wants the best possible Internet service for $40 a month or less.

1. Open a web browser and go to http://ic3.emcp.net/speedtest. Search for Internet service providers in your ZIP code.
2. Find at least one cable Internet provider and at least one DSL provider on the list (or two different types of providers, if both DSL and cable are not available) and note the providers' names and the URLs for their company websites.
3. Visit the websites for these two companies and find out what the price would be for monthly service to a residence near your school. Find the best package that costs $40 a month or less.
4. Compare the two packages, including the cost, bandwidth, and special features.
5. Type a paragraph in a Word document explaining which one is a better value and why.
6. Save the document as **U3T13-A2-Compare**.
7. Print the document and then close all windows.

Assessment 13.3 **Researching Domain Names**

1. Open a web browser and go to www.domainspricedright.com or another similar site that your instructor specifies.
2. Open a new Notepad file and use it to record the results of the following steps.
3. Use the search utility on the website to find out if the following domains are already taken (or use other domain suggestions provided by your instructor). Record the results in the Notepad file.
   - MySummerVacation.com
   - SeasideHolidays4Less.com
   - BusinessLettersAndMore.com
   - SuperiorCleaning.com
4. Imagine you are creating a website for a company called Chad's Computer Cleaners & Maintenance. Find an available domain name that is appropriate for this company. Type the domain name in your Notepad file.
5. Save the Notepad file as **U3T13-A3-Domains**.
6. Print the file and then close all open windows.

Assessment 13.4 **Troubleshooting a Network Connection**

1. If you have a wired Internet connection, disconnect the cable from the back of the PC. Or, if you have a wireless Internet connection, do one of the following:
   - If your computer has a button that enables/disables the wireless adapter, press it to disable the connection.
   - Click Start, type **Device Manager**, and then click *Device Manager* at the top of the menu. Right-click your wireless network adapter, located beneath the Network adapters heading.
2. Click *Disable*. Leave Device Manager open.
3. At the Control Panel, click Network and Internet, open the Network and Sharing Center, and then click *Troubleshoot problems.*
4. Click *Network Adapter*.
5. Use the troubleshooter to see if it can find the problem.
6. Open Notepad and type a paragraph documenting the steps that the troubleshooter took you through and whether the troubleshooter was able to correctly identify the problem. Save the file as **U3T13-A4-Help**. Print the file and then close Notepad.
7. Reconnect the network cable, push the button to re-enable the wireless adapter, or re-enable the wireless adapter in Device Manager (by right-clicking the wireless adapter and clicking *Enable*).

Assessment 13.5 **Testing Your Connection Speed**

The advertised speed of an Internet connection is for ideal conditions; the actual speed you achieve may be much lower. To test the speed of your Internet connection, go to http://ic3.emcp.net/speedtest and try one of the speed tests there. The test results will include both an upload and a download speed. It is normal for the upload speed to be much slower than the download speed. Make a note of the speeds reported. Run the test two more times, recording the speeds each time. (If a button is not available for rerunning the test, press F5 to refresh the web page.) Type the results in a Notepad file and then save the file as **U3T13-A5-Speed**. Print the file and then close Notepad.

)(C³ **Assessment 13.6** **Creating Web Content in Office Applications**

1. Open the file **FlowerCompany1.docx** in Word.
2. Save the file as a Single File Web Page and name it **U3T13-A6-FlowerCompany1**.
3. Open the file **FlowerCompany2.xlsx** in Excel.
4. Save the file as a Web Page and name it **U3T13-A6-FlowerCompany2**.
5. Open each of those files in a web browser, and compare them side-by-side with the original files in their native applications. Type a report in Word explaining how they differ visually.
6. If you have another web browser application available to you, open the files in that web browser and compare their look to what you recorded in Step 5. Note any differences in your report.
7. Save your report and name it **U3T13-A6-Report**.
8. Print **U3T13-A6-Report** and then close Word.

CRITICAL THINKING

Analyzing Communication Methods

Topic 13 discusses numerous communication methods used in today's society. Imagine that you have been asked to explain proper communication methods to a group of young students. In preparation, you decide to come up with three scenarios to describe these methods. In a Word document, type your answers to the following questions:

1. Describe a situation where sending a letter through postal mail would be the most appropriate way to communicate. Explain why email and text messaging would not be as acceptable.
2. Describe a situation where sending an email would be the most appropriate way to communicate. Explain why postal mail and text messaging would not be the best options.
3. Describe a situation where sending a text message or IM would be the most appropriate way to communicate. Explain why postal mail and email would not be the best options. Save the document as **U3T13-CT-Comm**.

TEAM PROJECT

Creating a Shared Document Library

Suppose your instructor decided to make the data files for this class available in a shared location on your school's network. This would allow access to everyone taking the class. Your team has been asked to develop a recommendation for a location for these folders as well as a plan to transfer the files.

1. As a team, make a recommendation to your instructor about where the best location would be for the folders containing the data files. To determine this, research the following questions and record your answers in a Word document.
   - Does your school have a file server where the files could be stored?
   - Where have shared data files been stored for other classes?
   - Do any special restrictions exist regarding where files may be stored?
   - Are any security permissions required to place files in the chosen location?
2. Identify the best location for the folders and record your team's choice in the Word document.
3. Present your choice to your class and confirm that your instructor agrees with your choice of locations.
4. In the **U3T113-CT-Comm.docx** Word document, write instructions about how to access the data files that could be given to someone who is taking the class next semester.

5. At the end of the document, type **Prepared by:**, press the spacebar, and then type the names of the people on your team.
6. Save the Word document and name it **U3T13-TeamFiles**.
7. Print **U3T13-TeamFiles.docx** and close all open windows.

Discussion Questions

1. What is the advantage of putting the files in a network-accessible location?
2. Should the files be posted to the location as read-only files? Why or why not?

Topic 14

Using a Web Browser

Performance Objectives

Upon successful completion of Topic 14, you will be able to:

- Identify features of Internet Explorer
- Browse the Web
- Recall previous websites through History and Favorites lists
- Save content for offline use
- Search the Web using search engines and keywords
- Evaluate search results
- Avoid legal problems associated with the use of online information
- Configure a web browser
- Troubleshoot web browsing problems

STUDENT RESOURCES

Before beginning this topic, copy to your storage medium the **Unit3Topic14** subfolder from the *Computer and Internet Essentials: Preparing for IC³* Internet Resource Center. Make this the active folder.

Although this topic does not contain any data files needed to complete topic work, the Internet Resource Center does contain model answers in PDF format for each of the applicable exercises in this topic. Use these files to check your work. The preface of your textbook provides instructions for accessing these files.

Topic Overview

When you have a web browser and an Internet connection, a nearly unlimited amount of information and content becomes available to you. With Internet access you can read online news, manage your finances, find product reviews, make purchases, look up movie times, send online greeting cards, and much more. This topic explains how to use the World Wide Web to browse websites, find and evaluate information, configure a web browser, and troubleshoot web browsing problems.

Although Internet Explorer 9 is used for all step-by-step procedures in Topic 14, other browsers are also available, including Firefox, Chrome, Safari, and earlier versions of Internet Explorer. If you are using one of these other browsers, the conceptual information in this topic will still apply, but the procedural steps may vary.

Browsing the Web

)IC³ 3-3.1.3, 3-3.1.5, 3-3.1.6

To browse the Web, you need web browsing software such as Internet Explorer. Web browsers enable you to view web pages, download files from websites, watch online videos, listen to streaming music, participate in web-based discussion forums, and much more. The first step in browsing the Web is to open a web browser such as Internet Explorer with one of the following methods:

- Click Start and then click *Internet Explorer*.

- Click Start, click *All Programs*, and then click *Internet Explorer*.

- Click a URL hyperlink in a document or email.

- Double-click the icon for an HTML file.

- Click the Internet Explorer icon on the Quick Launch toolbar.

Recall that a Uniform Resource Locator (URL) is an Internet address. URLs begin with the protocol used to access that address—for example, Web URLs begin with *http://*. Other types of URLs exist, such as *ftp://* and *telnet://*, but they are less commonly used in web browsers.

Understanding the Parts of the Internet Explorer Interface

The Internet Explorer window has a number of features (see Figure 14.1) that can be used to find and display documents and information from the Web. They include an Address bar for typing URLs, various buttons for navigating between pages and controlling their loading, and buttons that open menus from which you can manage the application.

Figure 14.1 Internet Explorer Window

Address Bar The Address bar (see Figure 14.2) is where a website's address displays. You can type URLs into the Address bar to open different web pages, or you can use the Address bar as a search box by typing keywords into it and then clicking the Search button.

To type a URL into the Address bar, click the Address bar's current content to select it, type the new address, and then press Enter. Note that if the insertion point is already located in the Address bar, clicking once in the Address bar simply moves the insertion point within the address; it does not select the entire current address. In that case, press Ctrl + A to select the entire address.

Quick Steps

Display a Web Page
1. Click in Address bar.
2. Type desired URL.
3. Press Enter.

Figure 14.2 Address Bar in Internet Explorer

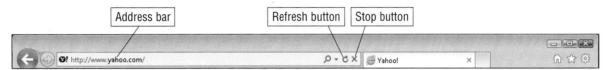

Back and Forward Buttons The Back and Forward buttons become active after you begin browsing in Internet Explorer. These buttons enable you to navigate back and forth between all of the pages you've viewed during your browsing session. For example, after opening a new page, you might want to return to the page you were on before. Do this by clicking the Back button. When you click and hold the Back button, a menu opens, containing a list of your previously viewed pages. Click a page on this menu to go back multiple steps at once.

After you go back, the Forward button becomes available. You can use this button to return to the page(s) you were on before you clicked the Back button. You can also click and hold the Forward button to display a menu that enables you to jump forward multiple steps.

Refresh Button The Refresh button reloads or "refreshes" the current page by re-requesting the web address from the Internet. If you notice that a page is not loading promptly (in comparison to your usual Internet speed), or if the content appears garbled, there may have been a glitch in transferring the page to your PC. You can try the operation again by clicking the Refresh button (shown in Figure 14.2). Clicking the Refresh button is also useful when you are viewing a page whose content is constantly being updated. For example, you might repeatedly press the Refresh button when visiting an online auction site that is counting down the number of seconds until the end of an auction.

Stop Button The Stop button stops the current page from loading or stops a requested action (if the action has not yet been performed). If a page is taking too long or you entered its address in error, you can click the Stop button (shown in Figure 14.2) to stop the page from continuing to load. Any portions of the page that have already loaded will remain on the screen.

Home Button Clicking the Home button brings you back to the default opening page for your browser, known as the **home page**. Your home page may be set to MSN, Yahoo, Google, or some other popular search site, or your school or workplace may have it set to a page specific to your organization. You will learn how to change your home page in Lesson 14.9.

Favorites Button Clicking the Favorites button opens the **Favorites Center,** which is a pane containing a list of web pages you have recently viewed or bookmarked. The Favorites Center has three tabs: Favorites, Feeds, and History. You will learn more about the Favorites Center later in this topic.

home page The page that displays automatically when you open your web browser

Favorites Center A pane containing a list of recently viewed and bookmarked web pages, organized into three tabs: Favorites, Feeds, and History

Tools Button The Tools button opens a menu of tools you can use to configure and control Internet Explorer. You can use these tools to diagnose connection problems, reopen the last browsing session, and manage add-ons. The Tools button's menu contains a different list of items than the Tools menu on the menu bar, so when following instructions in this topic, pay attention to whether the steps call for you to use the Tools button or the Tools menu.

Tabs Tabs enable you to have multiple web pages open at once in the same browser window. To switch between open web pages, click the desired page's tab. Open a new tab by clicking the New Tab button (the blank tab to the right of the other tabs).

Status Bar The Status bar displays messages regarding the status of a web page. For example, if you are waiting for a page to load, the Status bar might display a message that says *Waiting for a response*. The Status bar also displays a hyperlink's URL when you hover the mouse arrow pointer over the hyperlink. The Status bar might not display by default in your browser window. If the Status bar does not display, right-click the window's Title bar and then click *Status bar* at the shortcut menu.

Following Hyperlinks

Most web pages contain various hyperlinks that you can use to access other web pages and online content. A hyperlink is an electronic link that, when clicked, opens a web page, a data file, or an email composition window. Hyperlinks on web pages most often link to other web pages. Hyperlinks can display in the form of either text or graphics. Text hyperlinks sometimes appear underlined or become underlined when you hover over them with the mouse pointer. For example, notice that in Figure 14.3 the headline that the mouse pointer is touching appears underlined and that the mouse arrow pointer has become a hand graphic (called the *Link Select pointer*). Graphic hyperlinks often do not have any obvious indicators that they are hyperlinks, but when the mouse arrow pointer hovers over a graphic hyperlink the pointer becomes a Link Select pointer and the URL displays in the Status bar. Once you click a hyperlink, the new page may replace the existing one on the same tab, open in a separate tab, or open in a separate browser window, depending on the way the web page is coded.

Figure 14.3 Text Hyperlinks and Graphic Hyperlinks

graphic hyperlinks

The mouse pointer becomes a Link Select pointer when hovering over a hyperlink.

text hyperlinks

Displaying the Menu Bar

Internet Explorer has a menu bar, but by default it does not display when you first open your web browser. You can make the menu bar display at any time by pressing the Alt key. Once the menu bar is displayed, you can use it as you would use any other application's menu system.

If you would like the menu bar to display all the time, press Alt + V to open the View menu, point to *Toolbars*, and then click *Menu bar* (see Figure 14.4). Note that when the menu bar is displayed, it takes up extra room in the window, so you may need to scroll more often when viewing web pages. You may want to display the menu bar for the duration of your work using this book—otherwise, every time a step calls for using the menu bar, you will have to press Alt to display it.

Keyboard Shortcut

Display Menu Bar

Alt

Quick Steps

Permanently Display the Menu Bar

1. Press Alt + V.
2. Point to *Toolbars*.
3. Click *Menu bar*.

Figure 14.4 Menu Bar with Open Menu Displayed

Finding Information on a Web Page

When you are looking for specific information on a web page, it may be easier to search for a particular word or phrase than to visually skim for it. To use the Find feature to search for text on a web page, click Edit (remember to press Alt if needed to display the menu bar) and then click *Find on this page*. Another way to select the Find feature is to press Ctrl + F. In the Find bar's text box, type the appropriate word or phrase and press Enter. You can choose to *Match whole word only* or *Match case* by clicking the Options button on the Find bar and then clicking to insert a check mark in those check boxes. Click the Close button at the left side of the Find bar to close it.

Quick Steps

Open the Find Feature

1. Click Edit.
2. Click *Find on this page*.
3. Type the word or phrase.
4. Press Enter.

Keyboard Shortcut

Find Feature

Ctrl + F

Opening Additional Pages

You can open other web pages without closing the one you are viewing. One way is to display a page in another tab. To do this, you can first open the new tab (File, New Tab or Ctrl+T) and then browse to another page, or you can right-click a hyperlink and choose Open in new tab or hold down the Ctrl key as you click the hyperlink. Similarly, you can open additional copies of the web browser window. To open a hyperlink in a new window, right-click the hyperlink and choose Open in new window, or hold down the Shift key as you click the hyperlink.

Figure 14.5 Find Feature in Internet Explorer

Click Next to jump to the next instance.

text to be found

found text

Exercise 14.1   Using Internet Explorer to View Web Pages

1. Click Start and then click *Internet Explorer*.

2. Type **www.microsoft.com** in the Address bar and then press Enter.

3. Click the Stop button ☒ immediately.

    This action stops the page from completing the loading process.

    Step 4   Step 3

4. Click the Refresh button ↻ to reload the page.

5. Click a text hyperlink on the page that displays.

    This action opens a different web page.

6. Click the Back button ⬅.

    This action returns you to www.microsoft.com. Note that the Forward button ➡ becomes available once you use the back button.

7. Type **news.google.com** in the Address bar and press Enter.

8. Click Edit and then click *Find on this page*.

9. In the Find box, type **war** and press Enter to find a news story about a war.

10. Click Next to find the next story. Review all the instances that appear on the web page and then click the hyperlink to display one of the news articles.

11. Click the Back button to return to the main news page.

12. Click the Home button 🏠 to return to the home page.

13. Click the Close button ▇✕▇ to close the Find bar.

Drilling Down

Making Internet Explorer Your Default Browser

Internet Explorer may not be your default web browser. To set Internet Explorer as your default browser, open Internet Explorer, press Alt + T to open the Tools menu, and then click *Internet options*. On the Programs tab, click the Make default button and then click OK.

RSS Feeds

As you learned in Topic 13, RSS stands for Really Simple Syndication. RSS enables you to subscribe to a web page so that you are notified when it is updated. The Feeds tab in the Favorites Center enables you to save and organize bookmarks to feeds, which are web content delivered in RSS format. A page with content that is available as an RSS feed is said to be syndicated. To check out some pre-bookmarked feeds, open the Favorites Center and click a link on the Feeds tab. To add a feed to your Feeds tab, display a page that is syndicated in RSS format and then find and click a <u>Subscribe to RSS Feed</u> hyperlink.

Lesson 14.2 **Reviewing Web Browsing History**

)IC³ 3-3.1.7

Closing your browser window clears the Back button's memory, which means you cannot use the Back button to access websites you visited during previous sessions. However, two other methods of recalling previously visited websites exist. One is through the Address bar and the other is through your History list.

The Address bar has a drop-down list from which you can select recently typed URLs. Click the down arrow at the right end of the Address bar to open this drop-down list (see Figure 14.6). Although it is not a complete record, the Address bar will list URLs that you have recently typed or pasted. The Address bar's ability to recall previous addresses is called Address Bar Autocomplete.

Figure 14.6 Previously Visited URLs Display in the Address Bar

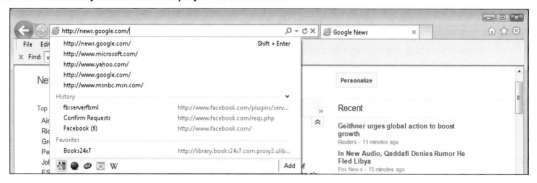

Quick Steps

Open the History List

1. Click Favorites button or press Alt + C.
2. Click History.
3. Click a date interval.

View History Options

1. Click down arrow on View by Date button.
2. Click the desired sort order.

Keyboard Shortcut

History List

Ctrl + H

If you require a more complete record of the websites you have visited, consult your web browser's History list. You can use the History list to examine previously viewed URLs by date, by website, by URL, or by the frequency of visits. These sort options allow you to use the History list more efficiently.

You can access the History list from the Favorites Center. Click the Favorites button or press Alt + C to open the Favorites Center, click the History tab, and then click the time frame you want to browse (see Figure 14.7). The Favorites Center pane is resizable. Drag its border to make it wider (to more easily read long entries) or narrower (to reduce the amount of space it takes up).

Figure 14.7 History List from the Favorites Center

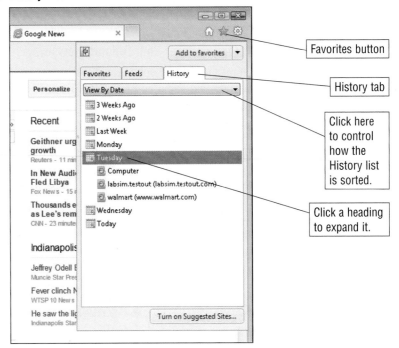

Clearing the History List

To protect your privacy, you may want to clear the History list on your browser. Although this does not prevent sites you visit later from being added to the History list, it will remove sites you have already viewed. You might consider clearing your History list if you are using a public computer or if other people will have access to your personal computer. InPrivate browsing, which is explained in Topic 16, can be used to prevent the recording of your browser history.

To clear the History list, press Ctrl + Shift + Delete or click Tools and then click *Delete browsing history*. In the Delete Browsing History dialog box that displays, click the *History* check box to insert a check mark and then click the Delete button (see Figure 14.8). This clears the History list both in the Favorites Center and the Address bar. See the Drilling Down feature at the end of this lesson for additional information.

Quick Steps

Clear the History List

1. Click Tools on menu bar.
2. Click *Delete browsing history*.
3. Click *History* check box to insert a check mark.
4. Click Delete.

Figure 14.8 Delete Browsing History Dialog Box

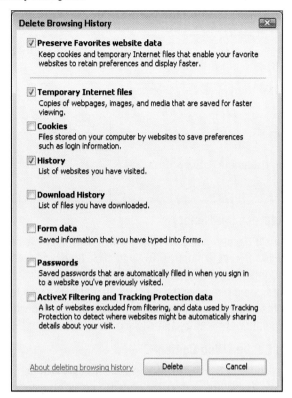

Exercise 14.2   Working with Browser History

1. Open Internet Explorer.

2. Visit a few websites to populate your browser history.

3. Open the drop-down list on the Address bar and click a previously visited site.

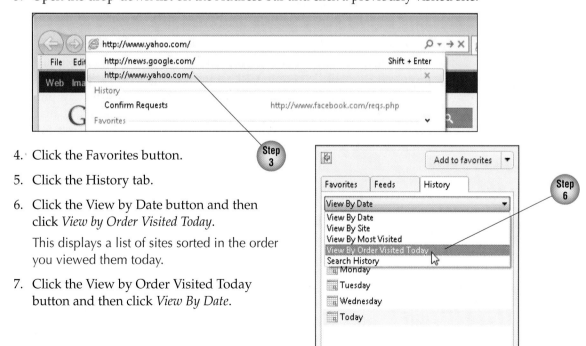

4. Click the Favorites button.

5. Click the History tab.

6. Click the View by Date button and then click *View by Order Visited Today*.

   This displays a list of sites sorted in the order you viewed them today.

7. Click the View by Order Visited Today button and then click *View By Date*.

8. Click *Today*.

   This displays a list of sites visited today.

9. Click one of the hyperlinks on the *Today* list.

10. Click the Favorites button to close the list.

11. Click the Tools menu and then click *Delete browing history*.

12. Click *History* check box.

13. Click Delete.

14. Click Close to close the Internet Options dialog box.

Drilling Down

Clearing the Address Bar History

Clearing the browser history might not clear all the entries from the Address bar's history. This is a known issue with Internet Explorer 9. To fix it, click Tools and then click *Internet options*. Click Settings on the Content tab in the *AutoComplete* section, and click the *Use Windows Search for better results* check box to remove the check mark. Click OK twice to close all open dialog boxes and try clearing the history again. Alternatively, you can clear individual entries from the Address bar's history by pointing to an entry and clicking the Close icon at the far right side of the entry.

Understanding Cached Web Content

As you can see in Figure 14.8, you can also delete temporary Internet files from the Delete Browsing History dialog box. These are cached (or stored) copies of web pages, or parts of web pages (like graphics and mini-applications), that the browser retains to help the pages load more quickly when you revisit them later. It is possible but unlikely that someone would inspect your temporary Internet files to spy on your past usage, but there is another reason to consider deleting them—disk space. Temporary files take up space on your hard disk, and if your hard disk is almost full, that space could make a difference in system performance and storage capability.

Lesson 14.3 Using and Managing Favorites

 3-3.1.9

favorite A shortcut to a URL found in a web browser, also called a *bookmark*

In the context of web browsers, **favorites** (called *bookmarks* in some applications) are stored shortcuts to certain URLs. Internet Explorer maintains a Favorites list from which you can conveniently select and return to any previously stored web address. In this lesson, you will learn to view and manage your Favorites list, including adding, opening, and organizing web addresses within the list.

Saving a URL to the Favorites List

To bookmark the currently displayed page, click the Favorites button and then click *Add to Favorites* to open the Add a Favorite dialog box (shown in Figure 14.9). This dialog box displays the name assigned to the favorite, which is what will display in your Favorites list. By default, the name of the favorite is the title of the web page, but you have the option to change it. You can also use the *Create in* option to add the favorite to any of the available folders in the Favorites list. The Favorites folder is selected by default in the *Create in* option, which means the shortcut will be created at the top level of the Favorites list hierarchy. If you want to place the URL in one of the subfolders, open the *Create in* list and click one of the subfolders, or click New folder to create a new subfolder. When you are finished, click Add to add the URL to the selected folder in the Favorites list.

Some web pages include a copyright or trademark symbol in the title of the page, but Internet Explorer does not allow these non-keyboard symbols to display in the titles on the Favorites list. If a web page title contains a non-keyboard symbol, you might see an error message when you try to save it to the Favorites list. If this happens, rename that favorite to remove the offending symbol.

Quick Steps

Add Current Page to Favorites List

1. Click Favorites button.
2. Click *Add to Favorites.*

OR

1. Press Ctrl + D
2. Change *Name* entry (optional).
3. Open *Create in* list and then click a folder (optional).
4. Click Add.

Figure 14.9 Add a Favorite Dialog Box

Opening a Web Address from the Favorites List

To open a web address from the Favorites list, click the Favorites button (or press Alt + C) and then click the Favorites tab (see Figure 14.10). Click the desired URL's name. Depending on the length of the list and your screen resolution, you might need to scroll through the list to find the desired URL. You can also access the Favorites list by clicking Favorites on the menu bar.

Quick Steps

Open a Favorite

1. Click Favorites button.
2. Locate and click desired URL.

Figure 14.10 Favorites List

Organizing the Favorites List

As you add more and more URLs to your Favorites list, keeping the list organized is important. This will allow you to easily find what you need when you need it. Organize your Favorites list by adding folders and subfolders, deleting unused favorites, and rearranging favorites within the list. All of these actions can be completed at the Organize Favorites dialog box.

To access the Organize Favorites dialog box, click the Favorites button and then click the Add to favorites button arrow to open a drop-down list. From there, click *Organize favorites* (see Figure 14.11) to open the Organize Favorites dialog box (shown in Figure 14.12). Alternatively, you can open the Favorites drop-down list by clicking Favorites on the menu bar and then clicking *Organize favorites*. From the Organize Favorites dialog box you can rename, delete, and move favorites, as well as create new folders in the Favorites list.

Figure 14.11 **Open Organize Favorites Dialog Box**

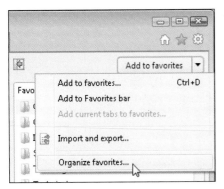

Figure 14.12 **Organize Favorites Dialog Box**

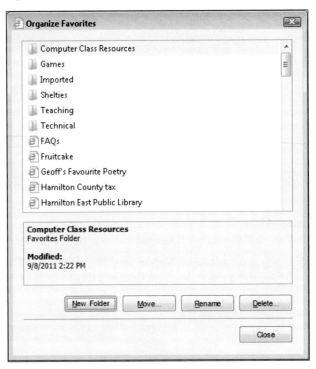

Quick Steps

Create a Folder for Favorites

1. Click Favorites button.
2. Right-click empty area.
3. Click *Create new folder*.
4. Type folder name.
5. Press Enter.

Create a Subfolder for Favorites

1. Open Organize Favorites dialog box.
2. Select existing folder.
3. Click New Folder button.
4. Type folder name.
5. Press Enter.

Creating Folders for Favorites Having multiple folders on the Favorites list enables you to organize and categorize the individual favorites so that you can find them more easily. To create a new folder at the top level of the Favorites hierarchy, open the Favorites list, right-click an empty area, and then click *Create new folder*. Type a name for the new folder and press Enter.

You can add more levels to the folder hierarchy by creating folders within folders. To create a new subfolder of another folder, open the Organize Favorites dialog box, click the folder that will contain the new folder, and then click the New Folder button. Type a name for the new folder and press Enter.

Moving a Favorite You can move items up or down on the Favorites list or you can move them into different folders. If you just want to rearrange the order of the items on the Favorites list, the easiest way is to drag-and-drop the items into the order you prefer. Dragging a favorite up or down on the list repositions it in the new location. For more complex reorganization, such as moving a favorite from one subfolder into another, use the Organize Favorites dialog box. Open the Organize Favorites dialog box, click the favorite you want to move, and then click the Move button. Clicking Move opens a Browse for Folder dialog box, from which you can select one of the existing folders or create a new folder. When a folder has subfolders within it, a triangle displays next to the folder (see Figure 14.13). You can click the triangle to expand the list of subfolders. Once you have selected a folder in the Browse for Folder dialog box, click OK to move the URL to the selected folder.

Renaming a Favorite Giving your favorites clear, descriptive names will help you to use your Favorites list more efficiently. Favorites can be renamed at any time. To rename a favorite, right-click the favorite and then click *Rename* at the shortcut menu. Type the new name and press Enter. If you do not press Enter, the new name will not be saved. You can also rename a favorite at the Organize Favorites dialog box.

Deleting a Web Address from the Favorites List In time, some of the URLs on your Favorites list may become broken or may no longer be useful to you. When this happens, you should remove those favorites from your list. To delete an item from your Favorites list, open the Favorites list, right-click the item, and then click *Delete* at the shortcut menu (see Figure 14.14). At the confirmation dialog box that displays, click Yes.

Quick Steps

Move a Favorite

1. Click Favorites button.
2. Drag favorite to new location.

OR

1. Click Add to favorites button arrow.
2. Click *Organize favorites.*
3. Click favorite.
4. Click Move.
5. Click destination.
6. Click OK.

Rename a Favorite

1. Click Favorites button.
2. Right-click favorite.
3. Click *Rename.*
4. Type new name.
5. Press Enter.

Delete a Favorite

1. Click Favorites button.
2. Right-click item.
3. Click *Delete.*
4. Click Yes.

Figure 14.13 Browse for Folder Dialog Box

Figure 14.14 Delete a Favorite

Using the Favorites Bar

Display or Hide the Favorites Bar

1. Right-click Title bar of Internet Explorer window.
2. Click *Favorites bar.*

Add a URL to the Favorites Bar

1. Display desired page.
2. Click Add to Favorites bar button.

Delete a Button from the Favorites Bar

1. Right-click button.
2. Click *Delete.*

In Internet Explorer, you can also create shortcuts to your favorite websites using a toolbar called the Favorites bar. Placing a favorite on the Favorites bar creates a button that you can use for convenient one-click access to the URL whenever you want to visit it. To view the Favorites bar, right-click the Title bar and click *Favorites bar* at the drop-down list that displays. The Favorites bar already contains a few Microsoft-supplied hyperlinks, which you can choose to keep or delete as you customize the Favorites bar to include your favorite websites. Figure 14.15 shows a Favorites bar that has been updated with a user's own favorite sites.

To add a web address to the Favorites bar, display the web page you wish to add and then click the Add to Favorites bar button at the left end of the Favorites bar. To remove a button from the Favorites bar, right-click the button in the Favorites bar and then click *Delete* from the shortcut menu.

Figure 14.15 Favorites Bar

Add to Favorites bar button

Exercise 14.3   Working with Favorites in Internet Explorer

1. Open Internet Explorer and go to www.emcp.com.

2. Click the Favorites button.

3. Click the Add to favorites button.

4. At the Add a Favorite dialog box, click Add.

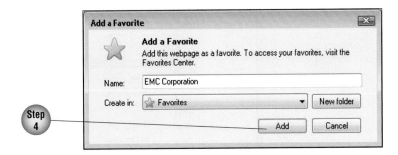

5. Click the Favorites button to display the Favorites list.

6. Find the entry you just created (located at the bottom of the Favorites list). Right-click the entry and then click *Rename.*

7. Type **EMC-Paradigm Home Page** and press Enter.

8. Click the Add to favorites button arrow and then click *Organize favorites*.

9. Click New Folder.

10. Type **Computer Class Resources** and press Enter.

11. Click the EMC-Paradigm Home Page favorite and then click Move.

12. In the Browse for Folder dialog box, click *Computer Class Resources* and then click OK.

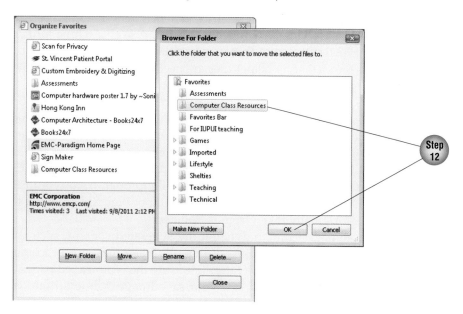

13. Click Close to close the Organize Favorites dialog box.

14. Open the Favorites list again and drag the Computer Class Resources folder to the top of the Favorites list.

15. Close Internet Explorer.

Drilling Down

Organizing Favorites in Windows Explorer

The items on the Favorites list are actually Windows shortcuts, each in its own separate shortcut file. You might find it easier to organize your Favorites list from the Windows Explorer interface than from within Internet Explorer. To browse your favorites as files, click the Start button and then click the user name in the top right corner of the Start menu. Double-click the Favorites folder in the folder that opens. You can then move, copy, or delete your favorites just as you would regular files.

Lesson 14.4 Saving Web Content for Offline Use

)C³ 3-3.1.10, 3-3.1.11, 3-3.1.12

As you explore the information available on the Web, you will likely encounter content that you want to save for later use. Adding a URL to your Favorites list is a great way to identify a web page that you want to remember, but the content of the web page may not always be available. In this lesson you will learn various ways to save web content to your computer so that you do not have to rely on its availability online. Be aware that the content of most websites is protected by copyright and you may be limited in how you use the content. A **copyright** indicates ownership of an original artistic or literary work. See Lesson 14.8 for more information.

copyright Ownership of an original artistic or literary work

Making a Web Page Available Offline

One of the simplest ways of ensuring the continued availability of a web page is to save a copy of it to your hard disk. For greatest storage convenience, pages can be saved in a Web Archive format. A Web Archive format is like a regular HTML file except that it encapsulates all the graphics on the page within the file so that no helper files are needed to view the file. A file saved in Web Archive format has an *.mht* extension.

To save a web page to your hard disk, click File and then click Save As. At the Save Webpage dialog box (shown in Figure 14.16), click a file name and location and set the file type to Web Archive, Single File (.mht). Click Save. To open the page, double-click the saved page to display it in Internet Explorer. Alternatively, you can click File, click Open in Internet Explorer (or press Ctrl + O), and then specify the file to open from within Internet Explorer. Note that the page you saved will not be updated when the web page it was originally taken from is updated.

Some web pages contain dynamically generated content, such as search results. If you save such pages offline, the page may not be complete or up-to-date when you access it later. To ensure that your saved pages contain all of the material you need, test your saved pages while offline. To work offline, click File on the menu bar and then click *Work offline*. To return to working online, click *Work offline* again to turn off the feature.

Quick Steps

Save a Web Page to Your Hard Disk

1. Click File.
2. Click *Save As*.
3. Change file name and location as desired.
4. Open *Save as type* drop-down list.
5. Click *Web Archive, single file (*.mht)*.
6. Click Save.

Open a Saved Web Page

1. Click File.
2. Click *Open*.

OR

1. Press Ctrl + O.
2. Click *Browse*.
3. Click saved page.
4. Click Open.

Figure 14.16 Save Webpage Dialog Box

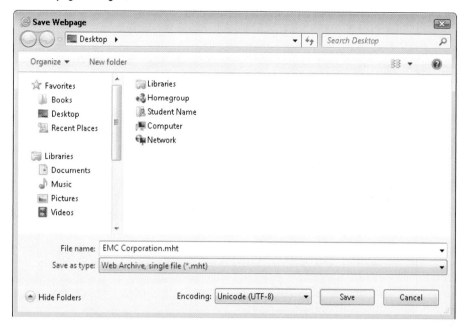

Copying Text from a Website

In addition to saving entire web pages, you can also save individual blocks of text from websites. To do this, you will need another application into which you can copy the text. You can use any of the following applications:

- **Notepad:** Saves plain text only; does not retain formatting

- **WordPad:** Saves text and simple formatting in a format that is compatible with many word processing systems

- **Microsoft Word:** Saves text and most types of text formatting; may not be compatible with other systems that do not have Microsoft Word installed

To copy text from a website, select the text and press Ctrl + C to copy it. Open the application into which you want to place the text and press Ctrl + V to paste.

Quick Steps

Copy Text from a Web Page

1. Select text.
2. Press Ctrl + C.
3. Open destination program.
4. Press Ctrl + V.

Saving an Image from a Website

If you copy a block of text that contains pictures and then paste it into a program that accepts graphics, such as WordPad or Word, the pictures within the selection will also be pasted. However, you can also save a picture to your hard disk as a separate file. The easiest way to do this is to right-click the graphic on the web page and then click *Save picture as*. The Save Picture dialog box opens (see Figure 14.17). Rename the file and specify a different location in which to save it, if desired, and then click Save. The picture is now available for later use in any application that supports graphics.

Quick Steps

Save a Picture as a Separate File

1. Right-click picture.
2. Click *Save picture as*.
3. Rename file and specify location.
4. Click Save.

Figure 14.17 Save Picture Dialog Box

Printing All or Part of a Web Page

Quick Steps

Print a Web Page
1. Select content (optional).
2. Click File.
3. Click *Print*.
4. Select printer.
5. Select *All*, *Selection*, or *Pages*.
6. Enter desired number of copies.
7. Click Print.

Printing a web page is another way of saving content for later use. To open the Print dialog box in Internet Explorer, click File and then click *Print*. From the Print dialog box (shown in Figure 14.18), you can choose to print an entire page, a specific page, a range of pages, or only a selection of text. Note that in this context, *page* refers to a page in the printout, not a full web page. A single web page may actually print on multiple sheets of paper if it contains a lot of content. If you want to print specific content, select the content before you issue the Print command. As in other applications, the Print dialog box in Internet Explorer allows you to choose a printer in the *Select Printer* area and specify the number of copies to print.

Figure 14.18 Print Dialog Box

Downloading a File from a Website

Some websites provide hyperlinks that download files to your computer. For example, you can get the files for the exercises in this book from the publisher's website, and you can download trial versions of games and other applications on other sites. In most cases, all you have to do to download a file is click its hyperlink. Internet Explorer recognizes that the hyperlink points to a file for download, and displays a dialog box asking you what you want to do with the file. Figure 14.19 shows a dialog box with three options: run the file, save the file, or cancel the operation. Click Save to download the file and store it on your hard disk.

Quick **S**teps

Download a File
1. Click hyperlink.
2. Click Save.
3. Change location as desired.
4. Click Save.

Figure 14.19 **File Download - Security Warning Message Box**

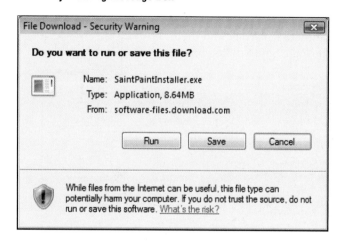

Exercise 14.4 Working with Offline Content

1. Open Internet Explorer and go to http://ic3.emcp.net/prodcatalog.

2. Click File and then click *Save as*.

3. In the Save Webpage dialog box, set the location to the **Unit3Topic14** folder.

4. Save the file as a *Web Archive, single file (*.mht)* and name it **U3T14-WebPage**.

5. Click Save.

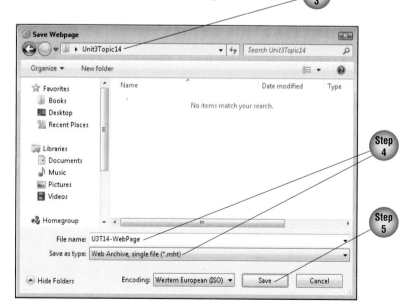

6. Click File and then click *Work offline*.

7. Close Internet Explorer, open the **Unit3Topic14** folder, and double-click **U3T14-WebPage**.

   The file opens in Internet Explorer. Notice that the URL in the Address bar refers to your hard disk, not the Internet.

8. Click one of the hyperlinks on the web page.

   A message at the bottom of the window tells you that Internet Explorer went online to view the content.

9. Click File and then click *Page setup*.

10. Change the orientation to *Landscape* and then click OK to close the Page Setup dialog box.

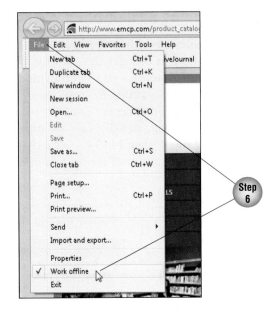

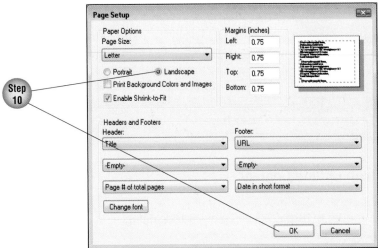

11. Select the copyright information at the bottom of the web page. Select the last paragraph on the page if there is no copyright information.

12. Click File and then click *Print*.

    This opens the Print dialog box.

13. Click *Selection* and then click Print.

    Only the selected copyright information prints.

14. Right-click the EMC Publishing logo and then click *Save picture as*.

15. In the Save As dialog box, change the file name to **U3T14- Logo**.

16. Change the save location to the **Unit3Topic14** folder.

17. Click Save.

Downloading Files: Running vs. Saving

When downloading a file from the Internet, clicking the Run button (see Figure 14.19) downloads the file to your hard disk temporarily. This temporary save allows the file to exist on your hard disk just long enough to run the file. Internet Explorer then deletes the copy it downloaded or leaves it in a temp folder for later cleanup. Note, however, that if you need to re-run the installation (if it fails the first time, for example), you must re-download the original file. Clicking Save and then running the file after it has been downloaded to your hard disk is usually the best method. You can manually delete the file after you are finished with the program.

Lesson 14.5   Understanding Search Engines

)(C³ 3-3.1.8, 3-3.2.2, 3-3.2.3

To locate specific information or websites online, you can enter keywords or terms into a search engine and receive results that relate to your search criteria. A **search engine** is a utility that displays a list of relevant websites from a computer-compiled database in response to a keyword search.

search engine A utility that displays lists of relevant websites from a computer-compiled database in response to a keyword search

Understanding How Search Results are Generated

The term *search engine* is often used generically to refer to any site where you can search for online content, but two different types of search sites exist: crawler-based search engines and human-powered web directories.

Search engine technically describes only the search sites that gather their data by automated means. Search engines gather their data by sending out self-navigating programs on the Web to read, classify, and index each page and send the information back to the database. These programs are known as crawlers, spiders, or bots (which is short for robots). Such sites can maintain enormous databases because the information is continuously and automatically collected and updated. A search engine has three parts. The first is the crawler program. A **crawler** program visits a web page, reads it, and then follows links to other pages within the site. It returns to the site every month or so to look for changes. The second part of a search engine is the database of information, also called the index or catalog. The third part is the search engine software, which is the program used to run queries within the database. Table 14.1 lists some popular search engines.

crawler A program that visits websites and catalogs their content; it then sends the information back to its owner

Table 14.1 **Search Engines**

Search Engine	URL
AltaVista	www.altavista.com
Excite	www.excite.com
HotBot	www.hotbot.com
Go	www.go.com
Google	www.google.com
Bing	www.bing.com
Web Crawler	www.webcrawler.com

A **web directory** is human powered, meaning it relies on people to create and update its listings. Website owners who want their sites to be included in a directory can submit a short description of their website to the directory; however, most directories also have employees who examine websites and write descriptions of them to add to the directory. When a user searches a directory, the search results depend on the content of the descriptions—actual content from the site is not displayed in the results. Web directories can provide information that search engines cannot, such as subjective evaluations of a site's usefulness or its reliability as an information source. However, since web directories are manually updated, some listings might not be current. Table 14.2 lists some examples of web directories.

Table 14.2 Web Directories

Web Directory	URL
Yahoo! Directory	dir.yahoo.com
Open Directory Project	www.dmoz.org
World Wide Web Virtual Library	vlib.org
JoeAnt	www.joeant.com

Understanding How Search Results Rank Pages

Almost any keyword search you perform will return thousands of results. A search engine prioritizes the results of a search using different methods. Although it would be most helpful to users if search engines ranked results strictly based on relevance, the highest positions in the list often go to sites for which advertisers have paid the highest fees. Businesses can sign up for online marketing programs that work with search engine companies to ensure that their clients' pages appear near the top of the results listings. After the paid advertisers' sites, however, the remaining results in the list are based primarily on the search engine's evaluation of how relevant the page is to the specific search criteria.

Search engines use algorithms (sets of rules) to determine a page's relevance in relation to a particular word. One consideration is the frequency and location of the keyword(s) on the page. Pages on which the searched-for word appears more often and higher up on the page are considered more relevant. Another consideration is whether other pages link to the website. A site that thousands of other sites link to is considered more relevant, all other factors being equal, than a site to which only a few other sites link.

Search engine optimization refers to the task of coding a page in a specific way so that it displays higher in search engine rankings. Web designers can use tricks to increase a page's ranking, and entire websites and books are devoted to teaching these techniques. Legitimate methods of search engine optimization exist, as well as deceptive methods. Deceptive measures include creating links on a different site or adding multiple, unrelated keywords to a page; both practices would raise a site's rank within the search engine.

One of the simplest ways of ensuring that a crawler identifies a certain keyword within a page is to place the keyword in a metatag in the page's HTML code. A **metatag** is an HTML code that provides metadata—meaning data about data. For example, if your page is about dogs but the word "dog" does not appear on the opening page, you might add a metatag like this to its code: <meta name="keywords" content="dogs" />. This ensures that the crawler will identify the key word on the web page. Metatags do not display on a web page, but you can see them if you view the source code for a page by opening the View drop-down list and clicking *Source*.

Exercise 14.5 Exploring Search Engine Sites

1. Open Internet Explorer and go to www.bing.com.

2. In the search box, type **rhinoceros** and then click the Search icon (magnifying glass).

3. Create a new Notepad file. Save the document with Save as and name it **U3T14-SearchEngines**.

4. In the Notepad file, type **Bing** and then press Enter. Copy and paste the URLs for the first three sites found by the Bing search.

5. Type **Google** and then press Enter.

6. Switch back to Internet Explorer. Go to www.google.com and repeat the search for *rhinoceros*.

7. Copy and paste the URLs for the first three sites into **U3T14-SearchEngines.txt** under the *Google* heading.

8. Repeat the procedure for any two other sites from Table 14.1, typing the search engine's name in Notepad and then pasting below it the URLs it identifies.

9. Compare the results you collected.

   Different search engines will typically contain some overlap in their results, but they will also rank pages in different order depending on their advertisers and on the way they rank and prioritize pages.

10. Discuss your results with your classmates.

11. Save, print, and then close **U3T14-SearchEngines .txt**.

12. Close Notepad and then close Internet Explorer.

Lesson 14.6 Conducting Searches

IC³ 3-3.1.8, 3-3.2.2, 3-3.2.3

A single-keyword search may not produce useful results, simply because so many pages exist on the Web. You can obtain better results by using multiple keywords (known as a search string). In this lesson, you will learn how to use multiple keywords and other techniques to improve your searches.

If you enter multiple keywords with spaces between them and no other punctuation, the search results will prioritize pages that contain all of the words, but will also show those pages that have only one of the words further down on the list. If you want to search for a multiword phrase in which the words must be adjacent, put the entire phrase in quotation marks. For example, search for "monarch butterflies" to find information about monarch butterflies without including pages that contain non-adjacent occurrences of the keywords.

Most search engines allow you to use **Boolean operators** to combine keywords in your search criteria. These are logical operators such as AND, NOT, and OR that you can use to further define what you are looking for. Some search engines use plus (+), minus (-), and pipe (|) symbols for the AND, NOT, and OR operators, respectively. Table 14.3 identifies these Boolean operators and their variants. Boolean operators are named for George Boole, the inventor of Boolean algebra, which is the basis of all modern computer arithmetic. Many search engines also allow additional special keywords to be included in searches, as listed in Table 14.4.

Boolean operators Words that represent logical yes/no statements, such as AND, OR, and NOT

Table 14.3 Boolean Searches

Search for this	Or this	To get pages that contain this
daisy AND flower	daisy + flower	Both "daisy" and "flower"
daisy NOT flower	daisy –flower (Note that there is no space between – and flower.)	"Daisy" but not "flower"
daisy OR flower	daisy | flower	Either "daisy" or "flower" or both

Table 14.4 Special Keywords

Special Keyword	Use	Example
contains:	Specifies that matching sites must contain links to the specified file type	butterfly contains:jpg
site:	Finds all documents on the specified domain and its subdomains	butterfly site:www.us.gov
intitle: or inbody:	Finds all documents that have the search word in the page title (intitle:) or in the body text (inbody:)	intitle:"Charlie Cutler"
url:	Finds all pages with addresses beginning with the specified URL	url:www.purdue.edu
link:	Finds all pages that contain a hyperlink to the specified URL	link:www.sycamoreknoll.com

Managing Search Providers in Internet Explorer

Internet Explorer 9 has a built-in search feature that enables you to search the Web using your choice of search engines without having to navigate to the search engine's website. You can type your search terms directly into the Address bar of Internet Explorer. By default Internet Explorer uses Bing, the Microsoft search engine, but this can be customized for other search engines. To use this feature, type the keyword(s) of your search. As you type, a menu will open below the Address bar. You can press Enter or click the Search icon (magnifying glass) to search using the default provider, or click one of the search site icons that display (see Figure 14.20). The results will display in the main browser window.

Figure 14.20 Address Bar Search Feature in Internet Explorer Search terms can be typed directly into the Address bar in Internet Explorer.

To add additional search engines to the Address bar's menu, click the down arrow on the Address bar to open the menu, and then click the Add button in the lower right corner (see Figure 14.20). In the Internet Explorer Gallery Add-Ons website that displays, click the search category (see Figure 14.21), and then click the search engine you want to add.

Figure 14.21 Internet Explorer Gallery Add-ons Website

Click the search category to display search engines.

A page displays for the chosen service. Click the Add to Internet Explorer button and the Add Search Provider dialog box opens, as shown in Figure 14.22. Click the Add button in the Add Search Provider dialog box to add the service to Internet Explorer. Reopen the Address bar's menu. The icon for the new provider displays at the bottom.

Figure 14.22 Add Search Provider Dialog Box

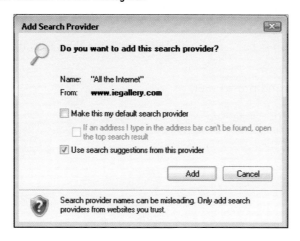

Quick Steps

Add Search Provider

1. Click down arrow on Address bar.
2. Click Add button.
3. Click search category.
4. Click desired search provider.
5. Click Add to Internet Explorer button.
6. Click Add button.

To manage search providers in Internet Explorer, click Tools and then click *Manage add-ons*. Click *Search Providers* in the Add-on Types pane at the left side of the dialog box (see Figure 14.23). From there, click a provider and then click either the Set as default button or the Remove button. You can also reorder the icons (left to right, where 1 represents the leftmost position) by using the Move up and Move down hyperlinks.

Figure 14.23 Manage Add-ons Dialog Box

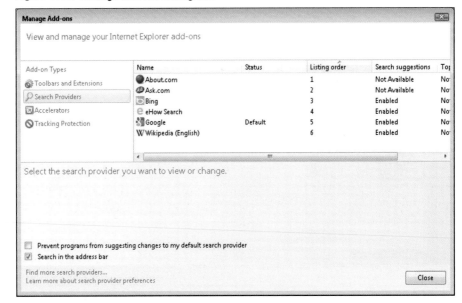

Exercise 14.6   Searching for Information on the Web

1. Open Internet Explorer and go to www.google.com.

2. Type **"rare books"** in the search box on the Google.com page and press Enter.

3. Locate the sponsored links on the results page.

   The sponsored links display down the right side of the page and in the shaded area at the top of the list.

4. In Internet Explorer, open the Address bar's menu and then click the Bing icon if it is not already selected.

5. Type **"rare books" NOT textbooks** and press Enter.

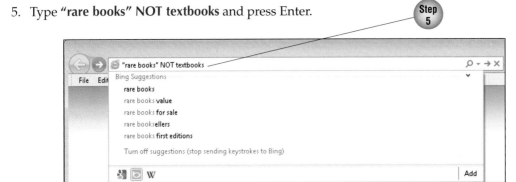

6. Open the Address bar's menu and click the Add button.

7. Add the Ask.com provider to the list by completing the following steps:

   a. Click the search category.

   b. Click *Ask.com*.

   c. Click the Add to Internet Explorer button.

   d. Click the Add button.

Step 7d

8. Open the Address bar's menu and click the Ask.com icon. Repeat your last search using the Ask.com search engine.

9. Open the Address bar's menu and click the Google icon. Repeat your last search using Google.

10. One of the booksellers that may be close to the top of the list in Google results is alibris.com. To find out what other sites link to alibris.com, in the Google search box (either on the web page or in the browser), type **link:alibris.com** and press Enter.

    Only web pages that contain links to alibris.com will display in the results list.

11. Close Internet Explorer.

Lesson 14.7 Evaluating Search Results

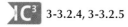 3-3.2.4, 3-3.2.5

To use the Internet effectively, knowing how to distinguish between reliable and unreliable online sources is important. When analyzing a website's reliability, consider the following topics in relation to the website: objectivity, authority, consensus, and current date.

Evaluating a Website's Objectivity

A reliable source is objective and provides impartial information, meaning the site does not promote an agenda or sell a product. While it may not be immediately clear if a website is objective, there are ways to evaluate a website for objectivity:

- Identify what organization, group, or individual created or sponsored the website. You may find this information easily or you may have to do some research. Identifying a sponsor will help you determine a website's objectivity.

- Determine whether the website is selling any products or linking to sites that sell products. If the site is selling a product directly or indirectly (some sites may be partners and share sales profits), it is likely that the information it presents will be overly optimistic. When a website profits from the information it presents, you should consider the information nonobjective.

Determining If a Website Has Authority

The information you find on a website may come from a well-known and highly-regarded expert in the field, or it may come from an unknown and unqualified source such as a student with less experience in the subject than you or your instructor. Complete the following research to identify whether or not a website has authority:

- Conduct a web search on the business or individual who runs the site. Identify what other people have to say about the business or individual and the content of the website.

- Check the sources that the page cites to determine where the content originated. Websites that do not provide external references or citations may contain fabricated information.

Analyzing a Website for Consensus

Consider whether the information on a website agrees or aligns with other websites and other information on the subject. If you have any doubt about the information provided, confirming the facts with other sources is essential to determining a site's reliability.

- Check general information sources such as online dictionaries and encyclopedias.

- If one or more sources disagree with the majority, try to determine whether the difference may be motivated by profit or politics. For example, if the website is selling a dietary supplement, or affiliated with a company that sells one, you might suspect articles on that site about the supplement's active ingredients to be biased. Also check whether there is a valid controversy or disagreement among experts in the field over the disputed point.

Identifying the Age of the Information

Confirm that the information presented on the web page is current or has been recently updated. Pages that were accurate a year ago may now be out-of-date, especially pages that describe new technologies or events.

- Check the date that is displayed on the page. If a date does not exist, you might be able to locate the date of the last update from the page's source code. In Internet Explorer 9, you can display the source code for the page by clicking View on the menu bar and then clicking *Source* at the drop-down list. (Press Alt to display the menu bar.)

- Narrow a search by date. This prevents older information from displaying in the results. This is especially important if you are looking up information on recent technologies or current events. Do this by using the advanced options available through most search engines. For example, in Google's advanced search capabilities, you can restrict a search to pages updated within a specific time frame, such as during the last 6 months or 1 year.

Exercise 14.7   Evaluating Information Sources

1. Open Internet Explorer and use any search provider to search for "Serial Attached SCSI."

2. On the first page of the search results, choose what you believe to be the three best sources in terms of authority and objectivity. Copy and paste the URLs into a Word document.

   Make sure to visit the pages and evaluate the information to make an informed decision.

3. Of the sources you identified as the most authoritative and objective, identify the source that contains the most up-to-date information. Write a paragraph in your Word document in which you identify this website and explain how you evaluated its content. Support your reasoning.

4. Compare the information you found with the information that a classmate found. Perform additional research to resolve any differences in your information.

5. Discuss any points that differ and record the differences in your Word document.

6. Save the file as **U3T14-Reliable**.

7. Print and close **U3T14-Reliable .docx**.

8. Close Word and then close Internet Explorer.

 Drilling Down

Exploring Wikis

Wikis are a rich source of online information. A wiki is an information database that is collaboratively maintained. Any user can make changes to the entries. The largest and most popular wiki is Wikipedia (www.wikipedia.org). Wikis are usually very objective and provide balanced perspectives because multiple authors with different points of view contribute to them. However, wikis are not authoritative sources of information since the people providing the information are not always recognized experts; but just people who care enough to post. While wikis should not be used as an official resource for research, a wiki can be a good place to start your research, because wiki articles typically contain hyperlinks to other content sources that are more authoritative.

Lesson 14.8 Using Online Information Properly

 3-3.2.6

Information from the Internet is easy to acquire and is usually free, but it can come with some hazards. One of these hazards, as you learned in the previous lesson, is questionable accuracy. Another hazard is that you may get into legal or academic trouble by improperly using information you find on the Internet.

The content of a website may be copyright protected. In fact, unless you see a notice that specifically states that a site's content can be freely used by the public, you should assume that you need to get permission from the site owner to use or reproduce the content you find there, especially for commercial ventures. If you use copyrighted information without permission, you could find yourself failing a class, or, worse, involved in a lawsuit. Although referencing online material for academic research is considered fair use, all sources should be acknowledged with proper citations.

Understanding Copyright Restrictions

The majority of the information presented online is copyrighted, meaning that someone owns the information and has the legal right to control how it can be used. For example, if you want to use descriptions or pictures of a product in your own work, you must get permission from the copyright holder first.

Copyright holders can set any terms and conditions they wish for others to use their material. Many sites maintain different policies for different types of usage. For example, a site owner might allow a charitable organization to reprint content for free but require businesses to pay a usage fee. You must consult the fine print of the website to find out what restrictions are in place. For example, you might be able to use certain photographs of products without a fee as long as you credit the company for the photo, or you might be able to use certain text as long as you do not change it or charge money for it. Figure 14.24 shows the policy on one website, as an example.

Finding copyright information on a site may be difficult. Look for a site map that might provide a link to the copyright page or a copyright notice at the bottom of a page that may contain a hyperlink to the site's policy on reprints. If the site is searchable, search for "reprint" or "terms of service."

Figure 14.24 Website Copyright Policy Example

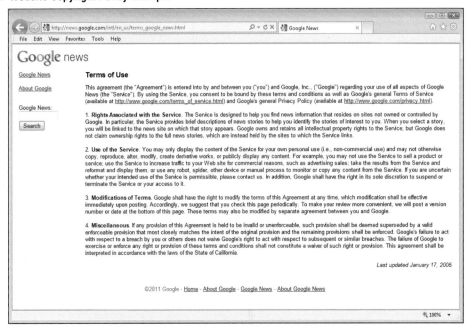

Understanding Plagiarism

Plagiarism refers to the act of using someone else's ideas or content without citation, so that others think the content is your own original work. Copying text word-for-word out of an encyclopedia or from a website for a school paper is plagiarism. Copying another student's paper or copying the marketing materials of a competitor is also plagiarism.

Being unaware of source citation rules can result in unintentional plagiarism. For example, if you quote directly from a source, you should not only cite that source in your paper, but you should also place quotation marks around the directly-quoted material. Failure to use quotation marks around direct quotations is a form of plagiarism, although not as serious a breach as failing to cite the source entirely.

Plagiarism is unethical, and can also be illegal, depending on the copyright on the source from which you are stealing. In most schools, plagiarism can be grounds for a failing grade on an assignment, a failing grade in a class, or even expulsion from school. Suppose you read the following information on www.emcp.com: *The academic world encourages the transfer of knowledge and ideas from individual to individual; however, plagiarism in any form has no place in an educational setting.* You decide the quote would work well in a paper you are writing, so you copy the quote into your own document, deleting some words but basically quoting the source verbatim: *The academic world encourages the transfer of knowledge from individual to individual; however, plagiarism has no place in an educational setting.*

This is an example of plagiarism. To avoid it, always remember to take the following steps:

- Cite the source.

- Place direct quotations in quotation marks.

- Use ellipses (…) to indicate that text has been removed from direct quotations.

A correct use of the cited material might look like this: *According to www.emcp.com, "The academic world encourages the transfer of knowledge and ideas from individual to individual; however, plagiarism . . . has no place in an academic setting."* Purdue University's Online Writing Lab (OWL) offers a guide to safe practices for avoiding plagiarism, available at http://ic3.emcp.net/OWLplagiarism.

Exercise 14.8 Using Web Information Responsibly

1. Open Internet Explorer and navigate to www.wikipedia.org.

2. View the Terms of Use information on Wikipedia.org by clicking the Terms of use hyperlink at the bottom of the main page.

   This opens a page for the Wikimedia Foundation, the parent site of Wikipedia.

3. In the Terms of Use, review the Attribution information in the section *Information for re-users*.

4. Return to Wikipedia.org, type **artificial intelligence** in the website's search feature, and read the article that you find.

5. Using the information from the article, write an explanatory paragraph on artificial intelligence. Quote and cite the article using the guidelines you reviewed in Step 3. Save the document with Save as and name it **U3T14-WebCitation**.

6. Print and close **U3T14-WebCitation .docx**.

7. Close Word and then close Internet Explorer.

Drilling Down

Determining the Internet Rules and Policies of Your School or Workplace

To avoid trouble in your job or your academic career, you should familiarize yourself with the rules regarding Internet usage, both in acquiring information and in web browsing in general. For example, your school might forbid you to visit sites containing adult content, and you might be prohibited from online shopping or playing online games at work. A school typically publishes its Internet usage policies. Check with your instructor to find out where to obtain this information at your school. At work, a good place to start might be the Human Resources office or the Information Technology department.

Lesson 14.9   Configuring a Web Browser

 3-3.1.13

You can customize how Internet Explorer looks and operates. While you will learn about some of the security- and privacy-related customization options in the next topic, this lesson focuses on how to change many of the user interface and user experience options.

Setting the Home Page

Recall that the home page is the page that opens automatically when Internet Explorer starts up. The home page default is typically a Microsoft-sponsored page, but you can set the home page to any web page you want. You can also have multiple home pages, each displaying on a different tab automatically at startup.

To change your home page, click Tools and then click *Internet options*. In the *Home page* box on the General tab in the Internet Options dialog box, enter the pages that you want to set for your home pages. If you want more than one, place each one on a separate line (see Figure 14.25).

Quick Steps

Set a Home Page

1. Click Tools.
2. Click *Internet options*.
3. Delete unwanted URL(s) in *Home page* box.
4. Type URL of desired page.
5. Press Enter and type additional URLs (optional).
6. Click OK.

Figure 14.25 Setting the Home Page at the Internet Options Dialog Box

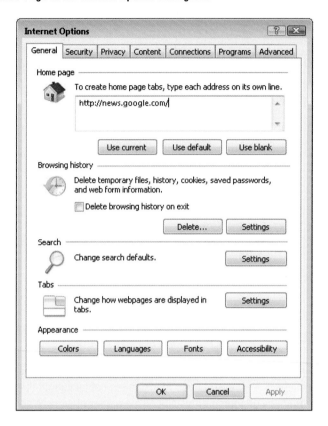

Setting Colors in Internet Explorer

Many websites are hard-coded to use specific colors. The ones that are not, however, display using Internet Explorer's choice of colors. You can change those color choices from the default Windows colors to suit your own preferences. You can specify colors for each of the following:

- Text

- Background

- Visited hyperlinks

- Unvisited hyperlinks

- Hyperlinks that change color when hovered over with the mouse (if enabled)

To change the color assignments, click Tools and then click *Internet options*. On the General tab in the Internet Options dialog box, click the Colors button to open the Colors dialog box (see Figure 14.26). From there, click the *Use Windows colors* check box to remove the check mark and then specify a color for each item on the list. To choose a color, click the colored square next to the item to see a palette of choices. If you want to enable the use of a separate hover color, click the *Use hover color* check box to insert a check mark. When you are finished, click OK.

Quick Steps

Change Windows Colors
1. Click Tools.
2. Click *Internet options*.
3. On General tab, click Colors.
4. Click *Use Windows colors* check box to remove check mark.
5. (Optional) Click *Use hover color* check box to insert check mark.
6. Click color square.
7. Click new color.
8. Click OK.
9. Repeat Steps 6–8 for other colors if desired.
10. Click OK.

The procedure you just learned changes the colors only on pages that do not specify their own colors. For some Internet users, however, it may be important that certain colors be used by default. For example, an Internet user with limited vision may have difficulty reading a page unless the page is black text on a white background. For such situations, Internet Explorer can be set up to ignore the colors specified by web pages. This is accomplished in the Accessibility dialog box. Click the Accessibility button on the General tab of the Internet Options dialog box. In the Accessibility dialog box, insert check marks in the check boxes for the formatting you want Internet Explorer to ignore (see Figure 14.27). Note that making changes to font sizes, in particular, may make some pages unattractive and difficult to read.

Figure 14.26 Colors Dialog Box

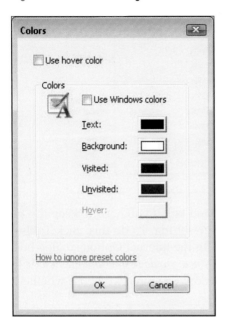

Figure 14.27 Accessibility Dialog Box

Controlling the Text Size and Zoom Level

If you are having trouble reading a page because the text is too large or too small, you can adjust it to fit your preferences. Two ways to do this are to either change the text size or to change the zoom level.

To change the text size, click View on the menu bar, point to *Text size*, and then click the size you want. The default size is Medium; you can also choose Largest, Larger, Smaller, or Smallest. This works only on pages that do not have a fixed font size. The text and graphics on the page shift as needed to accommodate the change in size; pages that are laid out to rely on a graphic falling next to a certain block of text may be distorted.

To change the zoom level, click View on the menu bar, point to *Zoom*, and then click a zoom percentage (see Figure 14.28). This does not affect the page itself; it only affects the magnification of the page onscreen. Scroll bars display in the browser window if the enlarged page does not fit in the browser window at once. This works on all pages, not just those that do not have a fixed font size.

Quick Steps

Change Text Size

1. Click View.
2. Point to *Text size*.
3. Click desired size.

Change Zoom Level

1. Click View.
2. Point to *Zoom*.
3. Click a zoom percentage.

Figure 14.28 Setting Zoom Percentage at the View Drop-down List

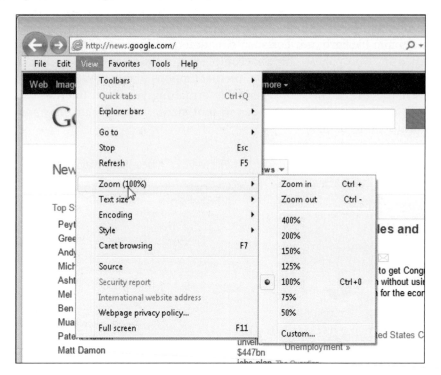

By default, the zoom is reset to 100% for each new window and tab. If you need to keep the zoom at a different level, you can take steps to prevent the zoom from resetting. To do this, click Tools on the menu bar and then click *Internet options* at the drop-down list. In the Internet Options dialog box, click the Advanced tab and then click the Res*et Zoom level to 100% for new windows and tabs* check box located in the *Accessibility* section. While you are in the *Accessibility* section, you can also choose whether or not to reset the text size to Medium for new windows and tabs.

Displaying or Hiding the Toolbars and Status Bar

By default, Internet Explorer 9 hides all toolbars and the Status bar. This creates a clean look that allows as much space as possible for viewing web pages. You can display or hide various bars by clicking View on the menu bar and then pointing to *Toolbars* to open a submenu that lists all the available bars (see Figure 14.29).

Figure 14.30 shows the following toolbars:

- **Menu bar:** The menu bar provides access to drop-down lists.

- **Favorites bar:** The Favorites bar provides a space for you to put buttons for your most-used favorites.

- **Command bar:** The Command bar provides icons to some popular activities you might want to perform, such as printing. It also has a few extra menus, such as Page, Safety, and Tools.

Each of these toolbars contains commands that can be found on other menus as well as a few unique commands.

Figure 14.29 **Displaying and Hiding Toolbars** The last three bars in this figure are third-party toolbars that other applications have added into Internet Explorer. Your own list may vary.

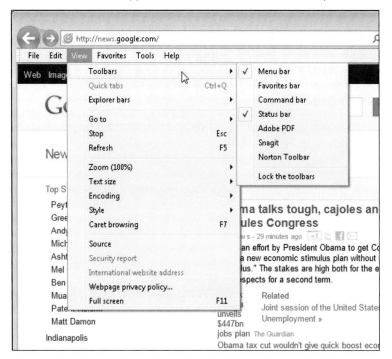

Figure 14.30 **Toolbars in Internet Explorer**

menu bar

Favorites bar

Command bar

Three separate menu systems exist in Internet Explorer—on the Command bar, on the menu bar, and in the upper right corner of the screen—and each menu contains a different combination of commands. For example, each of those three locations has a Tools menu, but they are all different. You may need to explore the menu systems on your own to become familiar with which commands are in what locations.

Quick Steps

View or Hide a Toolbar or the Status Bar
1. Click View.
2. Point to *Toolbars*.
3. Click toolbar to toggle on or off.

Exercise 14.9   Configuring Internet Explorer

1. Click Tools on the menu bar and then click *Internet options*.

2. Click the Colors button on the General tab in the Internet Options dialog box.

3. Click the *Use Windows colors* check box to remove the check mark.

4. Click the color next to *Background* to open the Color dialog box and then click the lightest yellow. Click OK and then click OK again.

   This returns you to the Internet Options dialog box.

5. Browse to several websites. Find two websites: one that now has a yellow background because of the change you made and another that does not.

6. Click Tools on the menu bar and then click *Internet options*.

7. On the General tab, click the Colors button.

8. Click the *Use Windows colors* check box to insert a check mark and then click OK.

9. Open the web page for your school or workplace.

10. Select the entire URL in the Address bar and press Ctrl + C to copy it.

11. Click Tools on the menu bar and then click *Internet options*.

12. On the General tab, click in the *Home page* box and (on a new line) press Ctrl + V to paste the school's URL.

13. Click OK to close the dialog box.

14. Close and reopen Internet Explorer to make sure that the school's web page displays as your Home page.

15. Close Internet Explorer.

Lesson 14.10 Troubleshooting Web Browsing Problems

 3-3.1.14

Problems in Internet Explorer can result from programming errors in the software, but more often they are the result of a web server being down, a web page being coded incorrectly, or a missing add-in. In this lesson you will review some common web browsing problems and how to solve them.

Dealing with Browser Error Codes

Sometimes an error code will display when you try to load a web page. The code explains why the page did not load, although sometimes the messages are not descriptive. A common error code is *HTTP 404 Not Found*. This error code displays when the referenced page does not exist or is not available. The most common cause of this error is a typing error, either when you entered the address into the Address bar or when the person who created the hyperlink entered it into the web page. Other common error codes are listed in Table 14.5.

Table 14.5 **HTTP Error Codes**

Error Code	Description
HTTP 400 The web page cannot be found	Internet Explorer can connect to the server, but the page cannot be found because of a problem with the URL.
HTTP 403 The website declined to show this web page	Internet Explorer can connect to the website, but Internet Explorer does not have permission to display the page. This might happen if the page is being generated by a shopping cart or search engine, and the folder on the server that contains the program is not correctly configured by the website administrator. This can also occur if you typed a URL without a specific page reference, and this website does not have a default page such as index.htm or default.htm.
HTTP 404 The web page cannot be found	Internet Explorer can connect to the website but not the specific page you are requesting.

continued

Error Code	Description
HTTP 405 The website cannot display the page	Internet Explorer can connect to the website, but the page content cannot be downloaded to your computer. This error is usually caused by a problem in the way the page was written.
HTTP 406 Internet Explorer cannot read this web page format	Internet Explorer is able to receive information from the website, but the information is not in a format that Internet Explorer can display.
HTTP 408 or 409 That website is too busy to show the web page	The server took too long to display the web page or there were too many people requesting the same page. Try again later.
HTTP 410 That web page no longer exists	Internet Explorer is able to connect to the website, but the web page cannot be found. Unlike a 404 message, this error is permanent and was turned on by the website administrator.
HTTP 500 The website cannot display the page	The website had a server problem that prevented the page from displaying. This can happen because of website maintenance or a programming error.
HTTP 501 Not Implemented The website is unable to display the web page	The site is not set up to display the content you are requesting. For example, the browser might be asking for a video clip but is telling the website it wants an HTML page.
HTTP 505 Version Not Supported The website is unable to display the web page	The site does not support the version of the HTTP protocol your browser uses to request the page.

When you encounter an HTTP error code, double check the URL or try again later. The problem may be temporary. If you get the same result later, the web server may be shut down permanently, or the site or page may have been deleted.

Dealing with Scripting Errors

When pages that contain programming scripts (such as Javascript) have errors in their programming, the pages sometimes display scripting errors that include an offer to debug the code. Unless you are the website creator or a programmer with the authority to fix the problem, the code will not be useful to you and you should not allow a prompt to debug.

You can turn off the prompting from scripting errors in Internet Explorer. To do this, click Tools on the menu bar and then click *Internet options*. On the Advanced tab, in the *Browsing* section, click the *Display a notification about every script error* check box to remove the check mark, and then click to insert a check mark in the *Disable script debugging (Internet Explorer)* and *Disable script debugging (Other)* check boxes.

Bypassing the Pop-Up Blocker

Internet Explorer 9 includes a pop-up blocker that prevents web pages from spawning other web pages in pop-up windows without your permission. A **pop-up** is an extra, usually small, browser window that displays automatically when you open certain web pages or click a certain button on a page. Although unrequested pop-ups are considered unprofessional, they continue to be used by some sites (even major retailers) to display

pop-up An extra, usually small, browser window that displays automatically when you open certain web pages or click a certain button on a page

advertising or special offers. A pop-up blocker works without prompting from the user. If you find that you need to allow a pop-up temporarily from a website, hold down the Shift key as you click the hyperlink that creates the pop-up. If you want to turn off the pop-up blocker altogether, click Tools on the menu bar, point to *Pop-up Blocker*, and then click *Turn off Pop-up Blocker*. You can turn it back on using the same menu. You can also configure the pop-up blocker's settings, if you do not want to turn the feature off entirely. To do this, click Tools on the menu bar, point to *Pop-up Blocker*, and then click *Pop-up Blocker settings*. From the Pop-up Blocker Settings dialog box, shown in Figure 14.31, you can allow pop-ups from specific websites. You can also set a filter level (Low, Medium, or High) and choose whether to play a sound and/or show an information bar when a pop-up is blocked.

Figure 14.31 Pop-up Blocker Settings Dialog Box

Managing Internet Explorer Add-Ons

add-on A supplemental program that works with the main program to extend the main program's capabilities

An **add-on** is a supplemental program that works with the main program to extend its capabilities. For example, Internet Explorer has no native ability to display Shockwave Flash content; an add-on is required to enable this content. Add-ons are available for various types of content, including Java, Adobe PDF, and QuickTime. Without the appropriate add-on, of the correct version, the extra content will not load, and an error message will appear.

Most of the time add-ons (also known as plug-ins) work without prompting from the user. Occasionally, however, an add-on may cause a problem, even to the point where Internet Explorer will not work properly. When this happens, you may need to get an updated version of the add-on, or remove it entirely. Internet Explorer 9 enables you to examine and manage the add-ons using the Manage Add-ons dialog box.

To see what add-ons are currently in use, click Tools on the menu bar and then click *Manage add-ons* to open the Manage Add-ons dialog box. The add-ons are separated into categories, with the categories displayed at the left of the dialog box. In Figure 14.32, all the enabled third-party toolbars and extensions are shown. When you select one, an Enable or Disable button displays for that item.

Figure 14.32 **Manage Add-ons Dialog Box**

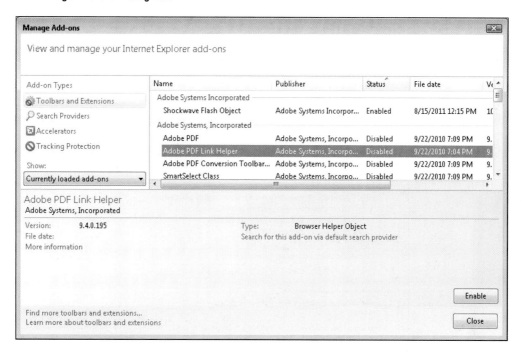

You can enable any add-ons that have been previously disabled. To do this, look in the *Status* column for the ones that are marked *Disabled*. Select the add-on you want to re-enable and then click its Enable button.

If your web browser requires an add-on, the web browsing program will usually prompt you to download it and will direct you to a website where you can do so. Simply follow the prompts as they appear. Note that some forms of malware try to download things to your computer using the browser, and security measures are in place to prevent those downloads from happening. When you are downloading an add-on, you might be asked whether you want to temporarily bypass some security measures to allow the download; be sure that you have requested a download before allowing it. If you are prompted to accept a download but you have not requested anything to be downloaded, do not allow it, because it may be malware. If you are not prompted for the add-on you need, reopen the Manage Add-ons dialog box, and then click the <u>Find more toolbars and extensions</u> hyperlink.

Quick Steps

Disable an Add-on

1. Click Tools.
2. Click *Manage add-ons.*
3. Verify *Toolbars and Extensions* is selected.
4. Click add-on.
5. Click Disable.
6. Click Close.

Enable a Disabled Add-on

1. Click Tools.
2. Click *Manage add-ons.*
3. Verify *Toolbars and Extensions* is selected.
4. Click add-on.
5. Click Enable.
6. Click OK.

Working with Advanced Internet Options

Sometimes to get a particular page or type of content to load, you must change Internet Explorer's advanced settings. In most cases, you should only make such changes under the direction of a technical support expert. The advanced settings are located on the Advanced tab in the Internet Options dialog box. Familiarize yourself with their existence (see Figure 14.33), but do not experiment with these settings on your own.

Figure 14.33 Advanced Options in Internet Explorer

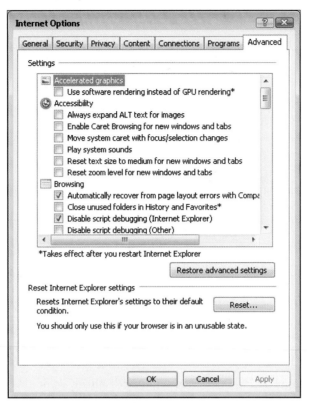

Exercise 14.10   Correcting Common Problems with Internet Explorer

1. In Internet Explorer, go to http://ic3.emcp.net/error. A 404 error will display.

   Notice that the error is a custom 404 message, not one generated by your browser. Some websites do this as a courtesy to you.

2. Go to http://ic3.emcp.net/pagenotfound. A 404 message will display.

   This site does not have a custom message; the 404 message you see here is generated by your browser.

3. Turn off the pop-up blocker in Internet Explorer by clicking Tools on the menu bar, clicking *Pop-up Blocker*, and then clicking *Turn off Pop-up Blocker*.

4. Go to http://ic3.emcp.net/popup and run one of the tests there.

   Multiple pop-ups should display to show you that you properly turned off your pop-up blocker.

5. Close the pop-ups.

6. Turn the pop-up blocker back on by clicking Tools on the menu bar, clicking *Pop-up Blocker*, and then clicking *Turn on Pop-up Blocker*.

7. Repeat the test in Step 4 to see how many of the pop-ups Internet Explorer catches.

   Internet Explorer will probably not catch them all. No pop-up blocker is 100% perfect.

8. Close Internet Explorer.

3-2.3.3, 3-3.1.4, 3-4.2.10

Staying Informed about Changes and Advances in Technology

The IC³ exam objectives require that you know how to stay informed about changes and advances in technology. Some of the ways you can stay informed include reading technology-related books and magazines, reading news articles in the Technology section of news sources, visiting computer stores to look at the latest products available, and joining computer and technology-related clubs in your area.

Many websites exist that you can use to stay informed about computer technology and other technologies that may affect your workplace and personal life. You can also search by keyword for the technology that interests you. Here are some useful sites for staying up to date on technology:

- **Tech News World:** http://ic3.emcp.net/TechNews
- **Yahoo Technology News:** http://ic3.emcp.net/YahooTechNews
- **CNET News:** http://ic3.emcp.net/CNET
- **CNN.com Technology:** http://ic3.emcp.net/CNN
- **MSNBC Technology and Science:** http://ic3.emcp.net/MSNBC

Exploring Mapping and Geographical Imaging Websites

Mapping and geographical imaging programs are one of the many applications on the web that go far beyond HTML. They enable you to input a text address and view a map, or even a photograph, of that location. You can zoom in and out on the maps and images too. You can even get turn-by-turn directions from one location to another. To explore this concept, try using one of these sites to find your home address: www.mapquest.com or http://maps.google.com.

Troubleshooting Internet Connectivity

It is not uncommon to lose a connection over the internet when you are directly connected with someone (such as in a web video conference). Failure of mail software to send and receive messages or the inability of your computer to download emailed attachments may also cause problems when you communicate electronically. Many of these problems can be resolved by determining if your Internet connection is working. Pinging a website, as you learned in Lesson 13.5, is a good way to check for Internet connectivity. If you can successfully ping a popular website, you know that your Internet connection is working. You can also use ping to check your connection to the router on your local network, by pinging its IP address. If your Internet connection appears to be lost, it may be a problem with that one computer's networking. Try restarting that computer to see if the problem is resolved, and try accessing the Internet from a different computer in your network if you have one.

If the loss of connection is happening on all the computers in your network, check to see whether they can communicate with each other locally (that is, share each other's shared drives). If not, reset the router or access point by powering it off and back on again. If so, reset the modem or terminal adapter.

If you still do not have Internet access, wait an hour or so. Sometimes service providers have temporary outages. After an hour, if service has not been restored, contact your ISP by phone.

TOPIC SUMMARY

- To browse the Web, you need web browsing software such as Internet Explorer.
- To go to a specific website, type a URL in the browser's Address bar and press Enter.
- The Back button takes you to the previously viewed page; after using Back, the Forward button becomes available to return you to the page you were on before you clicked the Back button.
- Click the Refresh button to reload a page and click the Stop button to stop a page from loading.
- The Home button reloads the default page.
- Internet Explorer enables you to open multiple tabs, with a different page displayed on each tab.
- Display the menu bar in Internet Explorer by pressing the Alt key.
- To find information on a web page, click Edit on the menu bar and then click *Find on this page*.
- Click the Favorites button to open the Favorites Center, which consists of three tabbed sections: History, Feeds, and Favorites.
- The History tab contains links to pages you have previously viewed. The Favorites tab contains links to pages you bookmarked yourself.
- To clear the History list, click Tools on the menu bar and then click *Delete browsing history*.
- To add the current page to the Favorites list, click the Favorites button and then click the Add to favorites button.
- To add the current page to the Favorites bar, click the Add to Favorites bar button.
- You can make a web page available offline by saving it to your hard disk in Web Archive format.
- You can copy text from a website with the Clipboard.
- Save an image from a website by right-clicking the graphic and then clicking *Save Picture As*.
- Print a web page using options at the Print dialog box, which you can display by clicking File on the menu bar and then clicking *Print* at the drop-down list..
- A search engine gathers information about websites using automated computer programs; a web directory relies on humans to create and update its listings.
- Web search results are ranked using algorithms that determine a page's relevance and according to advertiser fees paid to the search site companies.
- Search engine optimization is the process of coding a web page so that it displays higher in search engine rankings.
- Boolean operators can be used in web searches to combine or exclude keywords (see Table 14.3).
- You can type search keywords directly into the Address bar in Internet Explorer. Choose which search engine to use from the Address bar's drop-down list.
- When evaluating search results, consider the objectivity, authority, consensus, and age of information.
- Assume that information presented online is copyrighted, unless it clearly states that you may reuse it. Adequately cite quoted sources to avoid plagiarism.
- Change the default Home Page and default colors in Internet Explorer with options available at the Internet Options dialog box. Display this dialog box by clicking Tools on the menu bar and then clicking *Internet options* at the drop-down list.
- Click View on the menu bar to access options that allow you to change text sizes, zoom levels, and hide or display various toolbars.
- To bypass the pop-up blocker, hold down the Shift key when you click a link that will open a pop-up.
- To manage Internet Explorer add-ons, click Tools on the menu bar and then click *Manage add-ons*.

Key Terms

add-on, p. 670

Boolean operators, p. 655

copyright, p. 648

crawler, p. 653

favorite, p. 642

Favorites Center, p 635

home page, p. 635

metatag, p. 654

plagiarism, p. 662

pop-up, p. 669

search engine, p. 653

search engine optimization, p. 654

web directory, p. 654

Features Summary

Feature	Menu Method	Button, Option	Keyboard Shortcut
Add page to Favorites list	Favorites, *Add to favorites*	☆, Add to favorites	Ctrl + D
Delete browsing history	Tools, *Delete browsing history*		
Display menu bar permanently	View, *Toolbars, Menu Bar*		Alt + V, T, M
Display menu bar temporarily			Alt
Find (on web page)	Edit, *Find on this page*		Ctrl + F
Open saved offline page	File, *Open*		Ctrl + O
Print web page	File, *Print*		Ctrl + P
Save web page for offline use	File, *Save as*		Ctrl + S
Set home page	Tools, *Internet options, Home page box*		
View History list		☆, History tab	Ctrl + H

KEY POINTS REVIEW

Completion

In the space provided at the left, indicate the correct term, command, or option.

1. _____ This bar is where you type a destination URL in Internet Explorer.

2. _____ This displays when you click the star button in the Internet Explorer window.

3. _____ This page loads automatically when Internet Explorer starts up.

4. _____ Press this key to display the menu bar in Internet Explorer if it does not display.

5. _____ What are bookmarked URLs called in Internet Explorer?

6. _____ Drag what part of a window to move it?

7. _____ Which type of search engine gathers data by sending out robot-type programs on the Web to read, classify, and index pages?

8. _____ Suppose you want to find pages that contain the phrase "*static memory*" but not the word *BIOS*. What search string would do this? (Use a Boolean operator.)

9. _____ Name two considerations when evaluating the usefulness of information you find on the Web.

10. _____ What type of protection legally prevents others from copying a book, audio recording, or website and republishing it as if it were their own?

11. _____ What term is used to describe the act of copying text from a book or online source without giving credit to the original author?

12. _____ In Internet Explorer, what setting controls the magnification at which a web page displays?

13. _____ In Internet Explorer, what toolbar provides a place for you to create shortcut buttons for websites you visit frequently?

14. _____ The most common type of browser error, which occurs when Internet Explorer can connect to the website but not the specific page you are asking for, is known as what HTTP error code?

Multiple Choice

For each of the following items, choose the option that best completes the sentence or answers the question.

1. This is the default web browser in Windows.
   A. Firefox
   B. Mozilla
   C. Internet Explorer
   D. Opera

2. When you double-click a shortcut to a(n) _____, a browser window opens.
   A. website
   B. application
   C. email message
   D. attachment

3. In Internet Explorer, type the URL of the site you want to visit into the _____.
   A. *Favorites* text box
   B. Address bar
   C. toolbar
   D. *Forward* text box

4. This is the page that displays when the browser opens.
   A. home page
   B. URL document
   C. hyperlink page
   D. IP locator

5. Which of these means "web address"?
   A. email
   B. URL
   C. HTML
   D. FTP

6. To save a picture from a website to your hard disk, _____ it and click *Save picture as.*
   A. click
   B. double-click
   C. triple-click
   D. right-click

7. What button should you click to access the History list in Internet Explorer?
   A. Favorites
   B. Options
   C. News
   D. Page

8. In some browsers, favorites are known as _____.
   A. bytes
   B. Boolean operators
   C. bookmarks
   D. search engines

9. To adjust the margins on a printout from Internet Explorer, click File and then click this.
   A. *Print*
   B. *Layout*
   C. *Margins*
   D. *Page setup*

10. Which of the following is a popular search engine?
    A. Twitter
    B. Facebook
    C. Bing
    D. MySpace

Matching

Match each of the following definitions with the correct term, command, or option.

1. _____ A program that visits websites and returns information about the websites to a search site

2. _____ A search site that relies on humans to create and update its listings

3. _____ A method of coding a web page so that it displays higher in search engine rankings

4. _____ A set of logical operators that enable advanced keyword searches

5. _____ A popular search provider

6. _____ One of the criteria for determining whether the results from a website or search engine are reliable

7. _____ Using someone else's content without citation

8. _____ An error that indicates a certain web page cannot be found

9. _____ An error that indicates a server problem prevented a web page from displaying

10. _____ A program that enables a web browser to display additional types of content

A. Crawler
B. HTTP 404
C. Authority
D. Yahoo
E. Add-on
F. Optimization
G. HTTP 500
H. Boolean
I. Plagiarism
J. Directory

SKILLS REVIEW

Review 14.1 **Browsing and Searching the Web**

1. Start a new file in Notepad and then save the file as **U3T14-R1-Browse**.
2. Start Internet Explorer.
3. Go to www.msnbc.com.
4. Click a link to a news story. Click another hyperlink from that story.
5. In Notepad, type **Step 5:** and then copy and paste the URL from the Address bar in Internet Explorer into the Notepad file after the text you just typed.
6. Return to the original www.msnbc.com page using the Back button.
7. Perform a keyword search using the Address bar to find out when the next Winter Olympics will be held and in what city.
8. In Notepad, type **Step 8:** and then type the information you learned in Step 7.
9. Use Google.com to search for population information about the town where you currently live.
10. In Notepad, type **Step 10:** and then type your town name and its population as found in Step 9.
11. Save, print, and then close **U3T14-R1-Browse.txt**.

Review 14.2 **Reviewing Browsing History and Printing Web Pages**

1. Start a new file in Notepad and save the file as **U3T14-R2-History**.
2. In Notepad, type **Recently Visited Sites** and press Enter.
3. In Internet Explorer, view the browsing history for today. Revisit one of the sites.
4. Copy and paste the URL from Internet Explorer's Address bar into Notepad, below the text you typed in Step 2.
5. Repeat Steps 3 and 4 to copy another recently visited site's URL into Notepad.
6. In Internet Explorer, print one copy of the web page on your default printer.
7. Clear the browser history.
8. In Notepad, save, print, and then close **U3T14-R2-History.txt**.

Review 14.3 **Creating and Using Favorites**

1. Start a new file in Notepad and save the file as **U3T14-R3-Favorites**.
2. In Notepad, type **A Few Favorites** and press Enter.
3. View the Favorites list in Internet Explorer and visit one of the pages.
4. Copy and paste the URL of the page into Notepad under the text you typed in Step 2.
5. Repeat Steps 3–4 to copy and paste another URL of a favorite place.
6. Save, print, and then close **U3T14-R3-Favorites.txt**.
7. Go to www.yahoo.com.
8. Add Yahoo.com to the Favorites list. Name the shortcut **Yahoo Main Page**.
9. Create a new Favorites folder, name it **Search Engines**, and move the *Yahoo Main Page* shortcut into that folder.

Review 14.4 **Saving Web Content for Offline Use**

1. In Internet Explorer, go to http://news.google.com and find a news story that contains a picture.
2. Save the picture as **U3T14-R4-Picture**.
3. Save the entire web page as a single file (.mht format) and name the file **U3T14-R4-Story**.
4. Print **U3T14-R4-Picture** and **U3T14-R4-Story**.

SKILLS ASSESSMENT

Assessment 14.1 **Finding Data on the Web and Bookmarking Pages**

Using one or more of the search services from Table 14.6, find the following information, and create a favorite for each page on which you find an answer. Save your answers in a Notepad or Wordpad file and name it **U3T14-A1-Search**. Print **U3T14-A1-Search**.

Table 14.6 **Research Questions**

Question	Answer	URL
1. Who was the oldest man to win an Academy Award (Oscar) for best actor in a leading role?		
2. How many calories in a large Jamocha shake at Arby's?		
3. In what year was the first Rose Bowl football game and who won?		
4. What is the chemical formula for common gasoline?		
5. What are the operating hours for the Moweaqua Coal Mine Museum in June?		
6. What is the cash price per ride on the subway in Boston?		

Assessment 14.2 Saving Offline Web Content

1. Open Internet Explorer and go to www.mapquest.com or maps.google.com.
2. Display a map of your home town and then click the Print button to display a page that is ready to print. Print the map.
3. Save the page as a single-file HTML document and name it **U3T14-A2-Map**.
4. Go to images.google.com and search for a photo of your home town.
5. Save the picture as **U3T14-A2-Town**.
6. Visit the page from which the picture originated and find out who owns the photo.
7. Open a Notepad file and type the copyright information for the photo.
8. Save the Notepad file as **U3T14-A2-Copyright**.
9. Print and then close **U3T14-A2-Copyright.txt**.

Assessment 14.3 Creating and Managing Favorites

1. Create a new subfolder on the Favorites list and name it **Assessments**.
2. Move all the favorites that you created in Assessment 14.1 into this folder. Or, if you did not complete Assessment 14.1, create at least three new favorites from sites you enjoy and place them in the Assessments folder.
3. In Windows, browse to your Favorites folder.
4. Right-click the Assessments folder, click *Send to*, and then click *Compressed (zipped folder)*. Type **U3T14-A3-Zip** as the folder name.
5. Submit **U3T14-A3-Zip.zip** to your instructor for grading.

Assessment 14.4 Finding Information in the Help Feature

1. Open Internet Explorer Help.
2. Find a list of Internet Explorer keyboard shortcuts and fill in the following table. Submit your answers to your instructor in a Notepad or Wordpad file named **U3T14-A4-Help**.

Action	Keyboard shortcut
Switch between tabs	
Zoom to 100%	
Select the text in the Address bar	
Open the Favorites Center and display your history	
Select all items on the current web page	

Assessment 14.5 Researching Alternatives to Internet Explorer

1. Do a web search to research some of the most popular web browsers other than Internet Explorer.
2. Download and install one of these alternative browsers. For example, you might choose Firefox or Chrome.
3. Open several websites in both Internet Explorer and this alternative browser, side by side.
4. In a Notepad or Wordpad file, write notes about the differences you observe between the two browsers and the way certain pages display.
5. Save the file with Save as and name it **U3T14-A5-Browsers**.
6. Print and then close **U3T14-A5-Browsers**.

Assessment 14.6 Researching Search Engine Optimization

Imagine you are an IT consultant advising a small business that is planning to create a website. Research the topic of search engine optimization on the Web and gather reliable information about some of the most effective and up-to-date methods of improving search engine placement today. Compile your research and create an informative analysis for your client that explains current search engine optimization options. Cite your sources to avoid plagiarism. Save your work in a Microsoft Word document and name it **U3T14-A6-SEO**. Discuss your findings with your classmates.

CRITICAL THINKING

Making IT Decisions

Imagine that you are the IT manager of a local business. Do you believe that everyone in your company should be using the same web browsing software? What would be the advantages of requiring everyone to use a single browser, and what would be the disadvantages? Explain your position in a Microsoft Word document and support your views with logical reasoning. Save the document as **U3T14-CT-Browser**, print the document, and then close Word.

TEAM PROJECT

Creating Your Own Online Scavenger Hunt

1. In teams and using web searches, find 10 interesting and obscure facts to create a set of trivia questions.
   - Choose facts that are objective and have only one possible answer.
   - Choose facts that do not change over time.
   - Choose facts that are free from adult content or controversial political or religious positions.
   - Avoid unreliable online resources.
2. Record the facts and your sources in a Word document and name it **U3T14-TeamFacts**.
3. Following the formatting in Assessment 14.1, create a set of questions based on the facts you recorded. Save these questions in a new Word document and name it **U3T14-TeamTrivia**.
4. Print **U3T14-TeamTrivia** and trade the document with another team.
5. Answer the trivia questions provided to you and record the URLs you used to locate the answers.
6. Compare the other team's results with your own. Note any discrepancies and discuss them as a group.

Discussion Questions

1. Did you find any questions for which not all sources agreed on the correct answer? If so, how did you determine which answer was right?
2. As you were looking for facts to create your scavenger hunt, how often did you find sites that contained unreliable or incorrect information? What were the key characteristics of the unreliable sites?

Topic 15

Using Email

Performance Objectives

Upon successful completion of Topic 15, you will be able to:

- Understand email technology and the parts of an email message
- Send and receive email with Windows Live Mail
- Manage stored contacts
- Send file attachments with email messages
- Manage and organize email
- Minimize junk mail
- Troubleshoot common email problems

STUDENT RESOURCES

Before beginning this topic, copy to your storage medium the **Unit3Topic15** subfolder from the *Computer and Internet Essentials: Preparing for IC³* Internet Resource Center. Make this the active folder.

Although this topic does not contain any data files needed to complete topic work, the Internet Resource Center does contain model answers in PDF format for each of the applicable exercises in this topic. Use these files to check your work. The preface of your textbook provides instructions for accessing these files.

Topic Overview

Electronic mail, or email, enables you to send private electronic correspondence to anyone who has an email address. When you compose and send an email message, it becomes available to the recipient in a matter of seconds—whether the recipient is located across the room, across the country, or across the globe. In this topic, you will learn how email works and how to set up and use Windows Live Mail to manage your email communications. You will also learn best practices for managing and organizing email, and discover how to filter junk mail from your Inbox.

Lesson 15.1 Understanding Email Technology

IC³ 3-2.1.3, 3-2.2.1

As you learned in Topic 13, email enables you to send and receive private messages with anyone who has an email address and Internet access. Email is not an instant communications medium, because it sometimes takes minutes (or longer) for a message to be delivered. However, what email lacks in immediacy, it makes up for in record-keeping. You can save sent and received emails indefinitely in your email application, and refer back to them at any time. You can also use email to send file attachments, including pictures, video clips, Office documents, and even applications. Email is also useful for communicating with people who are not available at the same time that you are available.

Email messages go through **mail servers**, which are computers dedicated to handling mail. When you want to collect your email, you run a mail application such as Windows Live Mail or Microsoft Outlook. This is like going to the post office to pick up your mail. The mail server then transfers the mail from its holding area to your computer's email program and deletes the mail from the server; this is called a **store-and-forward email system**.

Your employer or school probably maintains its own mail server, and your work or school email address reflects the name of that server. For example, if your company's website is www.emcp.net, your email address might be johnsmith@emcp.net. When you send email to one of your friends or colleagues who is on the same mail server, the email travels on your company's or school's own private network.

Identifying Email Access Methods

As you learned in Topic 13, protocols are the languages, or sets of communication rules, that various network services use to exchange data. Depending on which type of email account you have, different protocols are in effect. Knowing which protocols your email server uses is important because that information will help you set up the account correctly in your email application. The following are the main protocols used by email servers today.

POP3 and SMTP **Post Office Protocol (POP)** is used for receiving email in a store-and-forward email system. The number 3 indicates that POP3 is the third version of the protocol. POP3 accounts work well for people who typically access their email from the same PC because all the received email is saved in the email application and can be accessed at any time.

Although you may sometimes hear an email system referred to as a POP3 system, POP3 is actually only one of the protocols that such a system uses. The other one is **Simple Mail Transfer Protocol**, or **SMTP**. Whereas POP3 is used to receive messages, SMTP is used to send messages. Together they form a complete email system.

One of the drawbacks of POP3/SMTP email systems in the past was that they required an email application to be stored on a single PC. This meant that users could not check their email on public computers. Today, most POP3 email providers offer a Web interface alternative that allows POP3 account users to access their email from any computer with an Internet connection.

Internet Mail Access Protocol (IMAP) **Internet Mail Access Protocol (IMAP)** is an alternative to POP3 for people who use several different computers to access their email, or for email accounts that need to be accessed by several people, such as an email account that is shared by several people in a department. The email is managed from, and remains stored on, the server, rather than on the local PC. This means the email is available no matter the location from which you access it. You can access an IMAP account using email programs like Windows Live Mail or Outlook, but the messages are not stored in these programs; they are accessed each time you connect.

HTTP (Web Mail) As you learned in Topic 13, HTTP stands for Hypertext Transfer Protocol. HTTP is the protocol used on the Web. An HTTP-based email account stores all the messages on the server, like IMAP, but the primary access to the HTTP-based email account is through a website rather than an email program. Although it is possible to set up a Web email account so that you can access it through an email program like Windows Live Mail or Outlook, this is not the way they are meant to be used. Web mail is good for people who access the Internet from a variety of public computers, because no trace of the user's email remains on the local hard disk. Examples of HTTP-based email systems include Yahoo! Mail, Gmail, and Hotmail.

When you sign up for an email account, the service provider may tell you which type of email server you have—that is, what protocols the server expects you to use to communicate with it. If you already have the email account set up in your email application and need to determine its type, you may be able to open an account configuration page or dialog box in which the server type is listed. The following are some additional ways to determine the type of protocol your email server uses:

- If you access your email account through an email client such as Outlook or Windows Live Mail, your email account is likely a POP3 or IMAP.

- If you access your email account only through a website, your account is probably HTTP. (That is not a reliable indicator, though, because some POP3 and IMAP accounts also can be accessed using the Web.)

- If you can browse messages you have previously received even when you are not connected to the Internet, your email account is likely a POP3.

- If your email account's domain is Hotmail.com, Gmail.com, or Yahoo.com, it is probably HTTP.

Understanding Email Addresses

To communicate with someone through email, you need to know his or her email address. To send and receive email yourself, you need your own email address. You can set up an email address or have one assigned to you through your ISP, school, or workplace.

An email address consists of the following parts (see also Figure 15.1):

- **User name:** This text appears before the "at" sign (@) in the email address and uniquely identifies the user on that domain.

- **@ sign:** This separator character appears between the user name and the domain name.

- **Domain name:** This text appears after the @ sign and identifies the domain name associated with the email server. Like a web address, it has at least one period in it and ends in one of the valid top-level domains, such as *.com*, *.edu*, or *.net*.

Figure 15.1 **Key Parts of an Email Address**

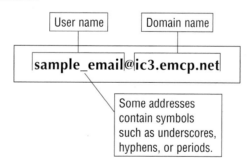

Exercise 15.1 Exploring Existing Email Accounts

1. Make a list of all your email accounts. If you do not have any email accounts, skip this exercise now and come back to it after you have set up an email account in Lesson 15.2.

   Include any school, work, or personal email accounts.

2. For each email account, find out what email technology it uses: POP3, IMAP, or HTTP.

3. Compare your list with those of your classmates and discuss how you determined which email technology each account uses.

Drilling Down

Determining When Email Communication Is Appropriate

Email is a convenient way to correspond and allows people from distant locations to communicate quickly and easily. Email is not always the ideal communication method, however, so care should be taken when determining how to use it. Email is appropriate when:

- You need to convey information without interrupting or bothering the recipient.
- You want to pass on written details or share documents.
- You want to keep in touch with friends who are far away.
- You need to keep a record of an ongoing discussion/conversation.

Some messages are better suited to other communication methods (such as in person, on the phone, or by instant messenger). Email is not ideal when:

- You need to provide sensitive personal or financial information (because most email is not secure).
- You need to have a difficult conversation in which your tone of voice will make a difference
- You need to convey bad news that may be upsetting to the recipient. (Delivering bad news through email can be considered thoughtless and unprofessional.)
- You want to get information quickly for a time-sensitive project or for a decision to be made. (A phone call or instant message chat will likely bring quicker results.)

Lesson 15.2 Configuring Windows Live Mail

In this lesson, you will start Windows Live Mail and configure it for your email account. If you are working in a school classroom, the program may have already been set up for you. This lesson is primarily for those studying independently or needing to set up their own PCs at home or work. Your instructor will advise you as to whether you can skip this lesson.

Windows Live Mail is a free email program from Microsoft. Although it does not come with Windows, it can be downloaded for free as part of the Windows Live Essentials suite. Windows Live Mail is similar to its predecessors that were associated with earlier versions of Windows: Outlook Express (Windows XP) and Windows Mail (Windows Vista).

Quick Steps

Start Windows Live Mail

1. Click Start.
2. Click *All Programs*.
3. Click *Windows Live Mail*.

To start Windows Live Mail, click *All Programs* in the Start menu, and then click *Windows Live Mail*. Depending on your system, other methods may be available for starting Windows Live Mail, such as a shortcut at the top of the Start menu or on your desktop. If Windows Live Mail is not installed on your system, download the program from http://ic3.emcp.net/windowslive.

Configuring an Email Account in Windows Live Mail

Before you can use Windows Live Mail, you must enter the server and login information for the email account. This information comes from your Internet Service Provider (ISP) or from your IT department at your school or workplace. You will need the following information:

- **Email address:** This is an address that has an @ sign in the middle and a domain name on the end, such as joestudent@emcp.net.

- **Password:** This can be any string of characters that has been assigned to you or that you have chosen.

- **Incoming mail server address:** This is an address with three parts separated by periods, such as pop.emcp.net. If you do not know this address, you can sometimes guess it. It likely uses either *mail* or *pop* for the first part, and whatever follows the @ sign in your email address for the second and third parts.

- **Outgoing mail server address:** This is also an address with three parts separated by periods, and the first part is usually either *mail* or *smtp*; for example, smtp.emcp.net.

- **Type of account:** You will need to know whether your account is a POP3, IMAP, or HTTP account. Refer to Lesson 15.1 for details.

- **Security settings:** Some email accounts require special security modes, such as an encrypted connection, for sending and receiving email. If your email account requires some special configuration settings in an email application, that information will likely be provided to you by your ISP or IT department.

Exercise 15.2   Set Up an Email Account in Windows Live Mail

1. Open Windows Live Mail and then click the File tab.

   In Windows Live Mail, the File tab does not contain the word *File*, but you will be able to recognize it as the blue tab at the far left end of the ribbon. If you hover over this tab, the ScreenTip reads *Windows Live Mail*; however, it serves the same purpose as the File tab in Office applications, so this topic refers to it as the File tab.

2. Point to *Options*.

3. Click *Email accounts* at the side menu.

4. Click the Add button in the Accounts dialog box.

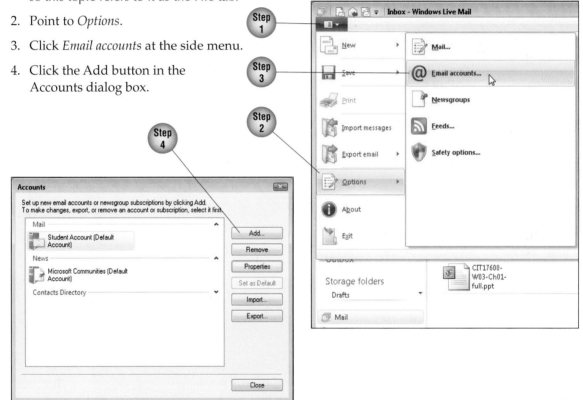

5. Click *Email Account* in the Select Account Type window.

6. Click Next.

   This opens the Add your email accounts dialog box.

7. Type the email address and password in the text boxes provided.

8. Type the display name you want to use in the *Display name for your sent messages* text box and then click Next.

   The display name is the name that will appear in the *From* text box when people receive email messages from you.

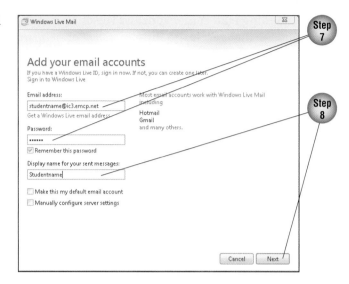

9. If you entered an email address for an HTTP based system, like Gmail or Hotmail, a box displays in the dialog box explaining any special setup you need to do for that email service.

   At this point, the Configure Server Settings window might display, or you might see a message that your account has been successfully configured, depending on your ISP. If you see a message that your account has been configured, skip to Step 16. Otherwise continue with Step 10.

10. Open the *Server Type* drop-down list in the Configure Server Settings window and select the account type: POP, IMAP, or Windows Live Hotmail.

11. Enter the incoming and outgoing mail servers in the text boxes provided.

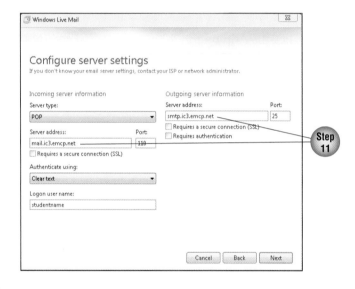

12. If your email account requires a secure server connection (SSL), click the *Requires a secure connection (SSL)* check box to insert a check mark.

   Separate check boxes exist under the boxes where you indicated the incoming and outgoing servers; mark one or both, based on the information you were provided.

13. If your outgoing mail server requires authentication, click the *Requires authentication* check box in the *Outgoing Server Information* section to insert a check mark.

14. Click Next.

15. If additional prompts display (for the check boxes marked in Step 12), enter the information requested and then click Next.

   These additional prompts do not display if you did not mark any check boxes in Step 12.

16. Click Finish.

   This action displays an Accounts dialog box.

17. Click Close.

18. Click the Send/Receive button in the Tools group on the Home tab.

This downloads to your PC any messages the account has received. You are now ready to read your incoming email and send new email.

 Lesson 15.3 **Sending Email**

IC³ 3-2.2.2, 3-2.2.4

Emails composed in Windows Live Mail can be sent to one or more recipients. The message can include text and other electronic content and there is no limit to the number of messages that can be sent.

Compose a message in Windows Live Mail using the New Message window (shown in Figure 15.2). To open the New Message window, click the Email message button in the New group on the Home tab. The New Message window contains its own Quick Access toolbar and ribbon with tabs containing commands and buttons for creating and sending a message. The New Message window includes text boxes where you can add the recipient's address and specify a subject. These text boxes are collectively known as the **message header**. The New Message window also contains a large text box called the *message body area*. This is where you enter the message itself, or the **message body**.

message header The sender, recipient, and subject information for an email

message body The main message text within an email

Figure 15.2 **Parts of the New Message Window**

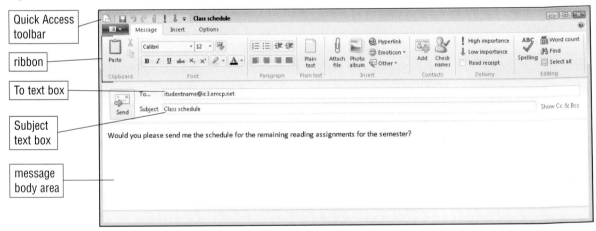

Specifying Recipients and Subject

Within the message header of an email are the following parts:

- **From:** The *From* option displays only if you have multiple email accounts set up in Windows Live Mail. Click the down-pointing arrow to open a drop-down list and then click the account from which the message should be sent.

- **To:** Enter the email addresses of the recipients in the *To* text box. Separate them with semicolons or commas.

- **Subject:** Type the subject of the email in the *Subject* text box. This information will display in the recipient's Inbox, along with your name and the date and time the message was received.

carbon copy (Cc) A copy of an email sent to someone who is not a primary recipient; also known as a *courtesy copy*

blind carbon copy (Bcc) A copy of an email sent to someone who is not a primary recipient; no other recipients can see who receives a blind carbon copy; also known as a *blind courtesy copy*

Quick Steps

Compose and Send an Email in Windows Live Mail

1. Click Home tab.
2. Click Email message button.
3. Enter recipient(s) in *To* text box.
4. Type subject in *Subject* box.
5. Type message in message body area.
6. Click Send button.

Rich Text Format (RTF) A generic document formatting standard that most word processing and email applications can understand

Rich Text (HTML) A hybrid of the RTF and HTML formatting standards; used in Windows Live Mail and some other email applications

You also have the option to send carbon copies and blind carbon copies of your email message. You would send a **carbon copy (Cc)**, also called a *courtesy copy*, to recipients who may find the message useful, but who are not the primary recipient(s). When you enter an address in the *Cc* text box, it is visible to all recipients of the email. The term *carbon copy* originates from the days of typewriters. Typists would stack several sheets of paper with sheets of carbon paper between them in a typewriter; typing on the top copy would leave an impression of each keystroke on the carbon copy page underneath it. Over time, *carbon copy* has come to mean an exact copy of something, regardless of how the copy was produced.

A **blind carbon copy (Bcc)**, or *blind courtesy copy*, is similar to a carbon copy except that the main recipients of the email cannot see the recipients of blind carbon copies. Blind carbon copies are useful when you want to keep someone informed without the knowledge of other recipients. To include Cc and/or Bcc recipients, click the To button in the message header; this action opens a dialog box from which you can select stored contacts and specify which recipients should receive To, Cc, or Bcc copies.

In most email programs, including Windows Live Mail, an AutoComplete function displays suggestions as you type an email address into the *To* text box. The suggestions come from previously typed email addresses and addresses that are stored in the Contacts list in your email application. You can accept a suggested address by clicking it in that list or by pressing the down arrow until the name is highlighted and then pressing Enter.

Type a title for your message in the *Subject* text box. Although you can type anything you like, be as descriptive as possible so that the recipient can quickly understand the purpose of your message. For example, if you need help with a school project, you might type *Help Needed on Project* as the subject. If you use a more generic subject like *Hi* or *How's It Going*, the recipient might assume it is a casual message and wait to read the contents. The *Subject* text box may also be left blank. Note, however, that messages without a subject are more likely to be caught in a junk email filter and not delivered to the recipient, so including a subject is in your best interest.

Formatting Message Text

When email was first created, all messages contained plain, unformatted text, because that was the only type of text that email servers and software supported. This limitation actually provided an advantage during the days when network and Internet transfer capacities were smaller than they are now. Plain text messages are smaller in file size and therefore would not exceed network capacity during transfer.

Today, many servers and email programs support **Rich Text Format (RTF)** and/or HTML formatted messages, which can include background images, different fonts and formatting, and even automatic bulleted and numbered lists.

Rich Text and HTML are two different formatting methods in many applications, but Windows Live Mail combines them into a single formatting type called **Rich Text (HTML)**. Rich Text Format (RTF) is a general text formatting standard used for sharing documents between word processing systems; HTML is a markup language used to apply formatting and layout to web pages. Some email programs, such as Outlook, enable you to choose one or the other when formatting a message.

When you create an email message in Rich Text (HTML) format, you can apply a variety of formatting features to your message text (see Figure 15.3). Most of these features are similar to the ones you might find in a word processing program such as Microsoft Word.

Windows Live Mail, by default, uses Rich Text (HTML) for new messages. To change an email message to plain text, click the Plain text button on the Message tab in the New Message window. Click OK at the dialog box warning you that you will lose message formatting. This action makes the formatting tools on the Message tab unavailable.

Figure 15.3 **Formatting Options on the Message Tab**

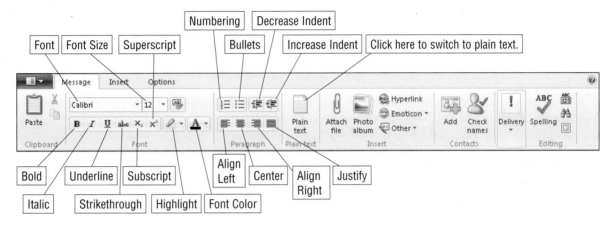

Exercise 15.3 Sending a Formatted Email

1. Start Windows Live Mail.

2. Click the Email message button in the New group on the Home tab.

3. Type your own email address in the *To* text box.

4. Type **This is a test** in the *Subject* text box**.**

5. Type **I am testing Windows Live Mail's capability for sending email messages.** in the message body.

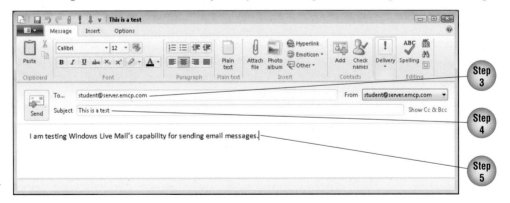

6. Use the formatting buttons on the Message tab to apply bold formatting to the words *Windows Live Mail's*. Change the font color of *Windows Live Mail's* to red and then center the paragraph.

7. Click the Send button.

Drilling Down

Problems with Formatted Messages and Embedded Graphics

Email was originally designed to send text only (no formatting). Different types of formatting like RTF and HTML have been successfully incorporated into most email systems, but occasionally a formatted message or a message with a graphic or animated effect applied may become garbled in transit, resulting in an unreadable or poorly formatted message. Formatting can also be lost, and graphics stripped out, when communicating with email clients that do not support formatting (such as some cell phones). To avoid these problems, some people choose to send email messages in plain-text format and choose not to include any graphics or animations when communicating using email.

Lesson 15.4   Managing Addresses

 3-2.2.8

Most people who use email have dozens or even hundreds of people with whom they correspond for school, work, or personal conversation. Each of the addresses is unique and needs to be typed perfectly for the message to be delivered. Fortunately, email addresses can be stored in Windows Live Mail's Contacts list and then chosen from the stored list whenever you are addressing a message. The Contacts list is a collection of contact information stored in the *Contacts* section of Windows Live Mail. It integrates seamlessly with the email section of the program, so you can select recipients from the Contacts list as you compose emails. You can also look up contact information separately when you are not actively composing email. This lesson will explain how to use and manage your Contacts list.

Adding Recipients to the Contacts List

Quick Steps

Add a Contact to *Contacts* List

1. Click *Contacts* in lower left corner.
2. Click Home tab.
3. Click Contact button.
4. Fill in information.
5. Click Add contact button.

The Contacts list stores information including names, addresses, telephone numbers, and email addresses. Adding contact information allows you to access the information whenever you are logged in to your email account and makes it easy to select the necessary addresses when composing an email message. A separate section of the Windows Live Mail application is available specifically for managing your contacts; you can get to it by clicking *Contacts* in the lower left corner of the Windows Live Mail application window. You can also work with contacts, to a limited extent, from within the *Mail* section. Add addresses to your Contacts list using any of the following methods:

- Right-click a message in your Inbox and, on the shortcut menu that displays, click *Add sender to contacts*. Click Add contact in the dialog box that displays.

- With the Contacts list displayed, click the Contact button in the New group on the Home tab. From there, type information in the text boxes that display to create a new contact. You can enter basic information on the Quick add page (see Figure 15.4), or you can click one of the other categories along the left side of the dialog box to add more detailed information.

- From any of the sections of the program *except* Contacts, click the Items button on the Home tab and then click *Contact* at the drop-down list. Fill out the form that displays (see Figure 15.4) to create a new contact.

To access your stored addresses when composing an email message, click the To or Cc button in the message header. The Click on a contact to select it dialog box displays (see Figure 15.5). Click the desired address and then click the To, Cc, or Bcc button to move that name to the corresponding text box. When you have added all the addresses you need, click OK to return to the New Message window and continue composing the email message.

Figure 15.4 Quick Add Page of the Add a Contact Dialog Box

Figure 15.5 Click on a Contact to Select it Dialog Box

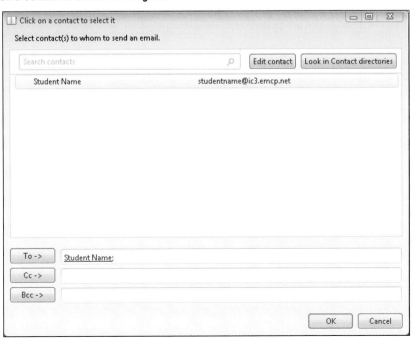

Managing the Contacts List

To view or make changes to your Contacts list, click *Contacts* in the lower left corner of the Windows Live Mail application window. This action opens the *Contacts* section of the application. There you will find a list of all your existing contacts, similar to the one shown in Figure 15.6.

Figure 15.6 Contacts List

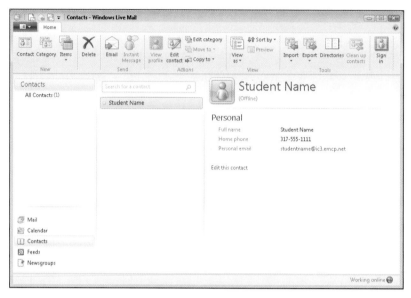

From the *Contacts* section of the application you can:

- Delete a contact by selecting the contact and either clicking the Delete on the Home tab or pressing the Delete key.

- Edit a contact by double-clicking the contact to open it, or by clicking the contact and clicking the Edit contact button in the Actions group on the Home tab.

- Create a new contact by clicking the Contact button on the Home tab.

When you open a contact, the uneditable *Summary* category displays by default. You must click *Contact* or one of the other categories at the left to get to the editable areas.

Exercise 15.4   Adding Contacts

1. With Windows Live Mail open, click the Items button in the New group on the Home tab.

2. Click *Contact* at the drop-down list.

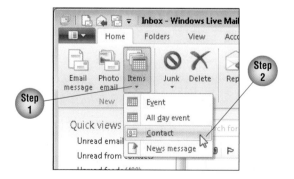

3. Type **Microsoft** in the *First name* text box within the Add a Contact dialog box.

4. Type **Support** in the *Last name* text box.

5. Type **support@microsoft.com** in the *Personal email* text box.

6. Click the Add contact button.

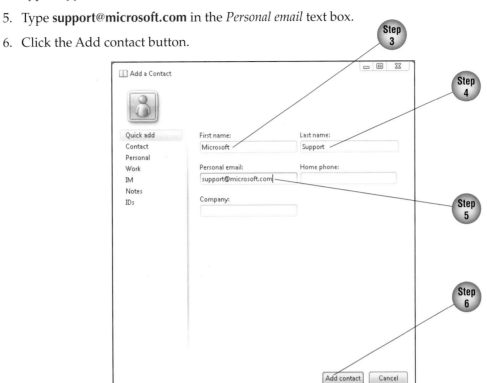

7. Click *Contacts* in the lower left corner of the application window.

8. Double-click *Microsoft Support* in the *Contacts* list box.

   This action opens the contact in the Edit Contact dialog box.

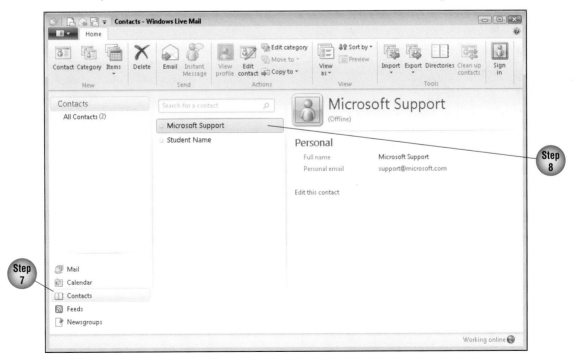

9. Click *Work* in the left pane of the dialog box.

10. Type **Microsoft** in the *Company* text box.

11. Click the Save button.

12. Click *Mail* in the lower left corner of the application window.

13. Click the Email message button on the Home tab.

14. Click the To button.

15. In the Click on a contact to select it dialog box, click *Microsoft Support*.

16. Click the Bcc button to add Microsoft Support's email address to the *Bcc* text box.

17. Click Cancel to close the dialog box.

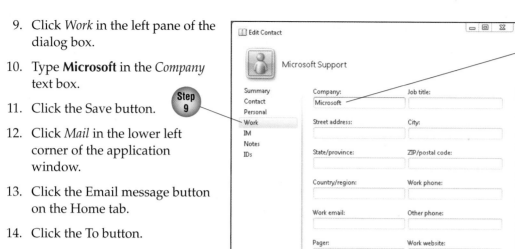

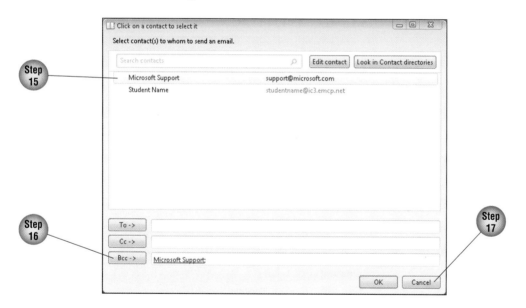

18. Close the New Message window without sending the message.

19. Click *Contacts* in the lower left corner of the application window.

20. Click *Microsoft Support* and press the Delete key on your keyboard.

21. Click OK to confirm.

22. Click *Mail* to return to the Inbox.

Receiving and Replying to Messages

IC³ 3-2.2.4

Sending email is only half the communication process. In this lesson, you will explore how to retrieve your received email from the mail server, how to view the messages, reply to the sender, and forward messages to other recipients.

By default, Windows Live Mail connects with your mail server to send and receive email automatically every 10 minutes. That means a message you send can potentially sit in the Outbox folder in Windows Live Mail for up to 10 minutes after you click the Send button. If you want a message sent immediately, click the Send/Receive button in the Windows Live Mail window. This action initiates a connection to the server right away. During this operation, Windows Live Mail connects with both the incoming and outgoing mail servers. Any incoming email is transferred to your PC and deleted from the mail server; any outgoing email is transferred to the outgoing mail server and then moved from the Outbox folder to the Sent items folder.

Quick Steps

Send and Receive Mail

1. Click Home tab.
2. Click Send/Receive button.

Viewing a Received Message

Received messages display in the Inbox folder. The Inbox shows a list of messages in the top section (see Figure 15.7). Below or to the right of the message list is a Reading pane that displays a preview of whatever message is selected in the top section. The Reading pane allows you to quickly preview the content of a message without having to open it in its own separate window. You can move the Reading pane in relation to the message list by clicking the View tab, clicking the Reading pane button, and then clicking the desired location at the drop-down list. Figure 15.7 shows the Reading pane below the message list. To open a message in its own window, double-click the message.

Messages that display in bold are unread; when you display a message in the Reading pane or open it in its own window, the message's header information loses the bold formatting in the Inbox to indicate that the message has been read.

Quick Steps

View a Message in the Reading Pane

1. Click message.
2. View message in Reading pane.

View a Message in Its Own Window

1. Double-click message.
2. Read message.
3. Close message window when finished.

Figure 15.7 Inbox and Reading Pane

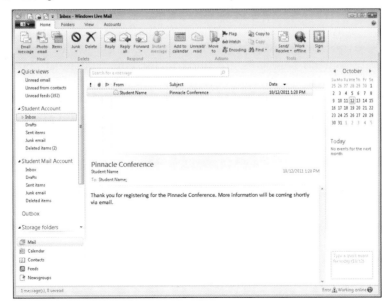

Replying to a Message

Quick Steps

Reply to a Message

1. Click message.
2. Click Reply button or Reply all button.
3. Type reply in message body.
4. Click Send button.

To reply to a received message, click the Reply button (to reply to the original sender) or the Reply all button (to reply to all of the message recipients). When you reply to a message, Windows Live Mail opens a new message with the recipient's name automatically filled in. Clicking the Reply button fills in only the original sender's email address in the *To* text box. Clicking the Reply all button fills in the addresses of the original sender and all other original recipients (except those who received Bcc copies). In both cases, the original message appears at the bottom of the message body area (see Figure 15.8).

Figure 15.8 Replying to a Message

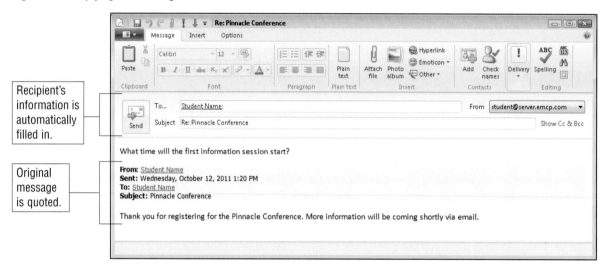

Recipient's information is automatically filled in.

Original message is quoted.

Depending on the situation, you may or may not want to quote all or part of the original message. Quoting the original message may help add context to your remarks in your reply and can provide a "history" of the discussion for tracking purposes. However, it can also significantly increase the size of the email and give the recipient more text to wade through. If you do not want to quote the original message, simply delete it from the message body.

Forwarding a Message

forward To send a copy of a received email message to another person

To **forward** a message means to send a copy of a received message to another person. Forwarding is like replying in that the original message is quoted, but no recipients are filled in for you. You must choose the recipient(s) yourself, just as you would with a new message. To forward a message, click the message and then click the Forward button. You may want to include your own introductory message text above the forwarded message text. This is especially helpful when the new recipient is not expecting the message, because it saves the recipient from having to read through the information to determine why you chose to forward the message.

Quick Steps

Forward a Message

1. Click message.
2. Click Forward button.
3. Type or select recipients in *To* text box.
4. Click Send button.

Exercise 15.5   Receiving and Replying to Email

1. Click the Send/Receive button in the Tools group on the Home tab in Windows Live Mail to send and receive all pending mail.

2. Click the message you sent to yourself in Exercise 15.3.

3. Click the Reply button.

4. In the body of the message that displays in the new window, type **Thank you for the information**.

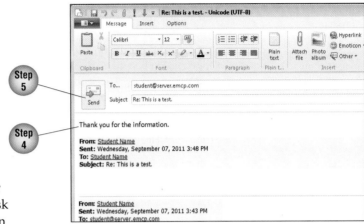

5. Click the Send button.

6. Click the Send/Receive button again to transfer the message to the server.

7. For more practice, forward your email message to a classmate, ask your classmate to reply, and then reply to the message you receive from him or her.

Drilling Down

Changing the Automatic Send/Receive Interval

You can change the interval at which Windows Live Mail connects to the server. Click the File tab, point to *Options*, and then click *Mail* at the side menu. At the Options dialog box, adjust the value in the *Check for new messages every ____ minutes* box on the General tab and then click OK. You might increase the frequency to get your messages more quickly after the sender sends them, or you might decrease the frequency to reduce the network bandwidth consumed by checking for new mail.

Controlling Quotes When Replying

Some people prefer not to quote the original message when replying because it makes the email larger and longer, which requires more bandwidth to send and receive. If you never want to quote the original message when replying, click the File tab, point to *Options*, and then click *Mail* at the side menu. At the Options dialog box, click the Send tab and then click the *Include message in reply* check box to remove the check mark. This action automatically removes the original message from your future replies.

Choosing Appropriate Email Recipients

Before you send out a message using Forward or Reply All, think carefully about whether the information is important to send to all the recipients you have specified. Some people consider receiving forwarded jokes and trivia to be a waste of their time. Similarly, when a conversation among a group of people has evolved into a private discussion between two of the participants, it is considered polite to reply only to the person you are addressing, rather than continuing to use Reply to All.

Sending Attachments

IC³ 3-2.2.5, 3-2.2.6

Quick Steps

Attach a File to a Message

1. At New Message window, click Attach file button.
2. Select file to attach.
3. Click Open button.

Almost any file can be attached to an email message. For example, you can attach a document you have created in an Office application, a picture you took with your digital camera, or a video clip you found online. In this lesson, you will learn about sending and receiving file attachments.

To attach a file to a message you are composing, click the Attach file button in the Insert group on the Message tab in the New Message window. In the Open dialog box that displays, select the file you want to attach and then click the Open button. The file displays in an Attach box in the message header, as shown in Figure 15.9.

Figure 15.9 Email Message with an Attached File

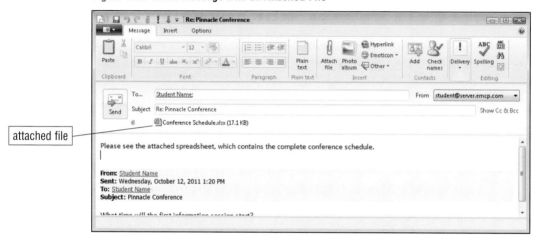

If you are not sure that your recipient has an appropriate program to open the attached file, you can include the attachment's data in the body of the email. For example, if you are sending an email to someone who may not have Microsoft Excel, copy and paste the cells from the spreadsheet into your email message rather than attaching the Excel file. This will give the recipient access to the information without having to use the program. You can also copy and paste data from websites into email messages. To copy and paste into email messages, use the standard copy-and-paste techniques: Ctrl + C to copy and Ctrl + V to paste.

Quick Steps

Open an Attachment

1. Double-click message.
2. Double-click attachment.

Save an Attachment to Your Hard Disk

1. Select message.
2. Click File tab.
3. Point to *Save*.
4. Click *Save attachments*.
5. Change save location as desired.
6. Click Save.

Working with Received Attachments

When you receive a message that contains an attachment, a paperclip symbol displays next to that line in the Inbox. You can then open the attachment in whatever program on your system is associated with its file type and save the attachment to your hard disk. If you do not have an application that is associated with that file type, an error message will appear to let you know that no application is available.

- **To open an attachment:** Double-click the message to open it in its own window and then double-click the attachment to open the file in the appropriate program. From there, you can use the Save As command in the program to save the file to your hard disk.

- **To save an attachment:** Click the message and then click the File tab, point to *Save*, and then click *Save attachments* at the side menu. When you use the Save attachments option, a Save Attachments dialog box opens. From there you can choose a save location in the *Save To* box (see Figure 15.10). You can click the Browse button to browse for the location if you do not know the exact path to type.

- **To delete an attachment before it is sent:** Select the attachment icon in the message window and press Delete.

- **To delete an attachment from a received message:** Delete the entire received message; you cannot remove an attachment from a received message and retain the message itself.

Figure 15.10 Save Attachments Dialog Box

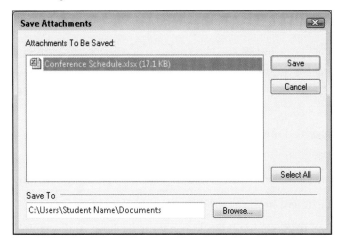

Exercise 15.6   Sending and Receiving Email Attachments

1. In Windows Live Mail, start a new email message and address the message to yourself.

2. Click the Attach file button in the Insert group on the Message tab.

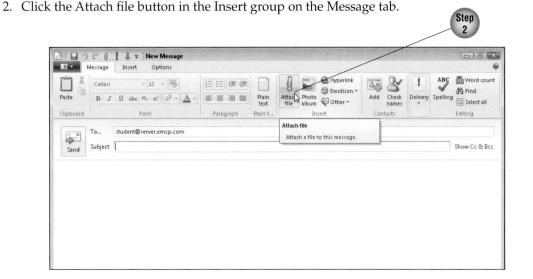

3. Select any file from your Documents folder and then click Open.

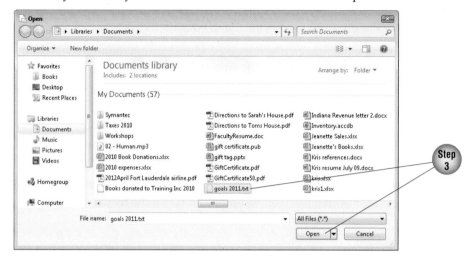

4. Type **Attachment** in the *Subject* text box of your message.

5. Click the Send button.

6. Click the Send/Receive button to send the message.

   Wait 30 seconds. If you have not received your message, click the Send/Receive button again to receive the sent message.

7. Double-click the received message.

   This opens the message in its own window.

8. Double-click the attached file to open it, and then close the message window in Windows Live Mail.

9. Right-click the attachment in the email message and then click *Save as*.

10. In the Save Attachment As dialog box, choose your desktop as the save location, and then click the Save button to save a copy of the file to your desktop.

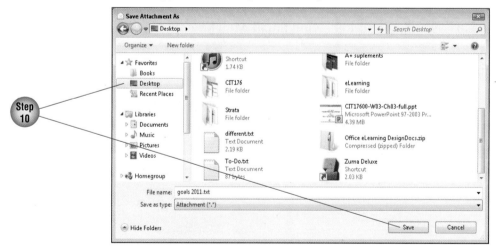

11. Minimize the Windows Live Mail window so that the desktop is visible.

12. Drag the copy of the file from the desktop to the Recycle Bin.

Drilling Down

Sending Executable Attachments

Windows Live Mail has a built-in security feature that prevents you from receiving executable attachments (program files, Visual Basic scripts, and so on) because those types of files often carry viruses and other malware. This does not prevent you from sending those types of files, but your recipients may not receive them if the recipients also use Windows Live Mail (or another mail program that blocks executable attachments). If you need to receive such files, click the File tab, point to *Options*, and then click *Safety options*. On the Security tab, click the *Do not allow attachments to be saved or opened that could potentially be a virus* check box to remove the check mark. After you have received the file(s) you are expecting, you may wish to re-enable this safety feature.

Lesson 15.7   Using Email Options

 3-2.2.3, 3-2.2.9

Depending on the email application you are using, various special options may be available when composing and sending an email. In Windows Live Mail, you can set a priority level for the email, so that a special symbol denoting high or low priority displays in the recipient's Inbox. You can also request a read receipt, which notifies you when the recipient has opened your message.

By default, each email goes out with an importance of Normal, which means it has no particular priority. In an email program, **priority** (also known as *importance*) refers to the level of urgency assigned to a message. To mark a message you are composing as high or low priority, click the desired importance level button on the Quick Access toolbar or click the appropriate a button in the Delivery group on the Message tab (see Figure 15.11). If the message window is narrower than the image shown in Figure 15.11, the Delivery group may be collapsed into a single button and you will need to click the Delivery button to open a drop-down list of message priority options.

priority The level of urgency assigned to an email message; also called *importance*

Figure 15.11 Set Message Priority

If the recipient's email program supports the Priority (or Importance) feature, your message will display in the recipient's Inbox with a special icon indicating the message's importance. If the recipient sorts his or her Inbox by importance/priority, he or she will see a message set to a high priority at the top of the message list. Different applications call this feature by different names; Windows Live Mail and Outlook both call it Importance; other programs call it Priority.

One of the drawbacks of communicating electronically is that there is no guarantee that your message will be delivered. This problem can be partially solved when communicating with email by requesting a read receipt. A **read receipt** is a return email you get letting you know when the recipient has opened your message. You can request a read receipt on any email you send; however, it is up to the recipient to return the read receipt. Typically when a read receipt has been requested, a message alerts the recipient of the request and the recipient has the option to either send the read receipt or ignore the request. To request a read receipt, mark the *Read receipt* check box in the Delivery group on the Message tab in the New Message window (see Figure 15.11).

Exercise 15.7 Setting Message Priority and Requesting a Read Receipt

1. In Windows Live Mail, start a new email message and address it to yourself.

2. Type **Priority test** in the *Subject* text box.

3. Click the High importance button in the Delivery group on the Message tab.

   If you do not see a High importance button, click the Delivery button and then click *High importance* at the drop-down list.

4. Click the *Read receipt* check box in the Delivery group on the Message tab to insert a check mark.

   If you do not see a *Read receipt* check box, click the Delivery button and click *Read receipt* at the drop-down list.

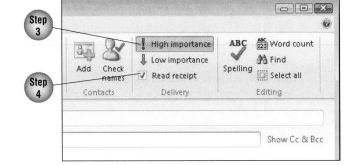

5. Click the Send button.

6. Click the Send/Receive button to send the message.

   If you do not receive your message, wait 30 seconds and then click Send/Receive again to receive the sent message.

7. Double-click the received message.

8. At the dialog box asking whether you wish to send a read receipt to the sender, click Yes.

9. Click the Send/Receive button again to send the receipt.

10. Wait 30 seconds and then click Send/Receive again to receive the message receipt.

Lesson 15.8 Managing and Organizing Email

 3-2.2.7

Over time, you will most likely find that you need some system of organization for email messages that you want to save. Windows Live Mail enables you to organize messages by allowing you to create folders and to move messages freely between them. One way to organize your email is to create a folder in your Inbox for each category of email you receive. For example, you could have a Work folder, a School folder, and a Personal folder. Other alternatives would be to create folders based on the sender or topic of the email, or based on general categories (like Teams, Classmates, Family, and so on.)

Creating New Mail Folders

Just like when you put the papers inside a filing cabinet or a desk drawer into folders to save them, creating new folders in Windows Live Mail helps you create an orderly filing system for your saved messages. Messages can be categorized by topic, by sender, or in any other way that allows you to remain organized and productive. To create a folder, start by opening the Create Folder dialog box, shown in Figure 15.12. To do this, right-click the existing folder in the Folder pane (such as the Inbox) into which you want to place the new folder, and then click *New folder* at the shortcut menu. Or, with the folder into which you want to place the new folder displayed, click the Folders tab and then click the New folder button.

Quick Steps

Create a New Email Folder

1. Click Folders tab.
2. Click New folder button.
3. Type new folder name.
4. Click folder to which it should be subordinate.
5. Click OK.

Figure 15.12 Create Folder Dialog Box

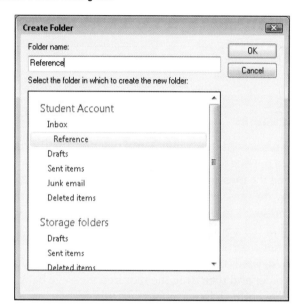

In the Create Folder dialog box, type a name for the new folder and select the folder to which it should be subordinate. Subordinate means "within" or "a part of." The most common way to organize your email folders is to place all of them subordinate to the Inbox. A folder that is subordinate to the Inbox displays beneath the Inbox in a folder tree. The subfolder appears slightly indented to show that the Inbox is its parent folder.

Moving Messages between Folders

To move a message from the Inbox into the folders you create, drag the message from the message list and drop it onto the desired folder in the Folder pane (see Figure 15.13). If you want to copy the message, rather than move it, hold down the Ctrl key as you drag. You can also use the Move to or Copy to button in the Messages group on the Folders tab. In addition, you can move email between folders automatically by applying message-handling rules (see Lesson 15.9).

Quick Steps

Move a Message with Drag-and-drop

Drag message onto folder.

Copy a Message with Drag-and-drop

1. Hold down Ctrl key.
2. Drag message onto folder.

Move a Message with Move To

1. Select message.
2. Click Folders tab.
3. Click Move to button.
4. Select destination folder.
5. Click OK.

Figure 15.13 **Moving a Message with Drag-and-drop**

Drag a message from the list...

...to a folder.

Deleting Messages

Quick Steps

Delete a Message

Drag message to Deleted items folder.

OR

1. Right-click message.
2. Click *Delete*.

OR

1. Select message.
2. Press Delete key, click Delete button on Home tab, or press Ctrl + D.

Maintaining an organized Inbox may mean deleting emails that you no longer need. To delete a message, select the message and press the Delete key on your keyboard or drag the message to the Deleted items folder. Deleting a message does not destroy the message; the message is still retrievable from the Deleted items folder. Items stay in the Deleted items folder until you manually empty the folder, unless the application is configured to automatically dispose of deleted items after a certain amount of time.

To rescue a deleted message from the Deleted items folder, open the Deleted items folder and then drag the required message back into the desired folder. To permanently delete a message without placing it in the Deleted items folder, hold down the Shift key as you press the Delete key.

Exercise 15.8   Managing Email

1. With Windows Live Mail open, click the Folders tab.

2. Click the New folder button.

Step 1

Step 2

3. At the Create Folder dialog box, type **Reference** in the *Folder name* text box.

4. Click *Inbox* in the *Select the folder in which to create the new folder* list box.

5. Click OK.

6. Hold down the Shift key and drag one of the messages you received in a previous exercise into the Reference folder.

   This moves the selected message into that folder.

7. Click the Reference folder to display the contents of the folder.

8. Delete the message from the Reference folder.

   Use any method you like for the deletion.

9. Click the Deleted items folder to display the newly deleted message.

10. Drag the deleted message back to the Inbox folder.

11. Click the Inbox folder to display its contents.

12. Select the message you just recovered.

13. Hold down the Shift key and then press the Delete key to permanently delete the message.

14. Click Yes to confirm.

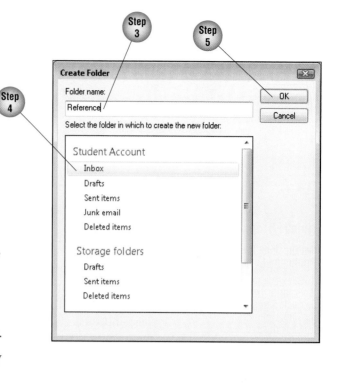

Managing Junk Mail and Solving Email Problems

IC³ 3-2.2.9, 3-2.3.3, 3-2.3.6, 3-2.3.7

Nearly everyone with an email address has received **junk mail** (also known as *spam*), which includes unwanted email messages such as advertisements and other unwanted solicitations. Junk mail can make organizing your Inbox more time-consuming, and some junk mail can carry viruses and other malware to your PC if you open their attachments. (See Topic 16 for more information on viruses.) In this lesson, you will learn how to use features in Windows Live Mail to cut down on the amount of junk mail you receive. You will also learn about several common email problems and how to solve them.

Windows Live Mail includes a junk mail filter. When a received message is identified as junk mail, the message is moved to the Junk email folder. You should check your Junk email folder occasionally to make sure that legitimate emails were not mistakenly filtered out of your Inbox. You can move a legitimate message from the Junk email folder to the Inbox by selecting it and then clicking the Not junk button in the Delete group on the Home tab or by dragging the message to the Inbox (see Figure 15.14). The Junk Mail folder in most email applications, including Windows Live Mail, is set to block any attachments or hyperlinks in messages in that folder, to minimize the chance of receiving malware through a junk mail message.

junk mail Unwanted email messages; also called *spam*

Quick Steps

Move a Message from the Junk Email Folder to the Inbox

1. View Junk email folder.
2. Select message.
3. Click Not junk button on Home tab.

Figure 15.14 Junk Email Folder

Quick Steps

Set the Junk Email Protection Level

1. Click File tab.
2. Point to *Options*.
3. Click *Safety options*.
4. Click Options tab.
5. Click desired level.
6. Click OK.

---

safe senders list A list of email addresses you have approved to send you email

---

Quick Steps

Set Junk Email Protection to Safe List Only

1. Click File tab.
2. Point to *Options*.
3. Click *Safety options*.
4. Click Options tab.
5. Click *Safe List Only*.
6. Click Safe Senders tab.
7. Click Add button.
8. Type a safe email address and then click OK.
9. Repeat Steps 7–8 to add more safe senders.
10. Click OK.

Block a Sender

1. Right-click the message.
2. Point to *Junk email*.
3. Click *Add sender to blocked senders list*.

Unblock a Sender

1. Click File.
2. Point to *Options*.
3. Click *Safety options*.
4. Click Blocked Senders tab.
5. Click address to unblock.
6. Click Remove button.
7. Click OK.

Changing the Level of Junk Email Protection You can customize the junk mail filter so that it is more or less aggressive about identifying and filtering potential junk mail. At a higher level of filtering, less junk mail gets through, but legitimate email may be incorrectly identified as junk. At a lower level of filtering, legitimate messages are rarely misidentified, but more junk mail reaches the Inbox. To change the filtering level, click the File tab, point to *Options*, and then click *Safety options* to open the Safety Options dialog box. Set the level of filtering on the Options tab, as shown in Figure 15.15. If you choose a high level, it is very important that you monitor the content of the Junk email folder frequently for any messages that you may want to open.

Receiving Email Only from Safe Senders The highest level of junk email protection is *Safe List Only* (see Figure 15.15). If you choose this option, you will not receive email from anyone except those addresses on your safe senders list and people who are on your Contacts list. A **safe senders list** is a list of email addresses you have approved to send you email. You can create a safe senders list on the Safe Senders tab of the Safety Options dialog box. This option is not recommended, though, because you might miss a legitimate message from an unplanned source, such as an old friend who just got online or a new employee working for your company.

Blocking or Unblocking a Sender You may find it necessary to block certain addresses from sending you messages. Regardless of what level you select for junk mail filtering, messages from blocked senders always go to the Junk email folder. Identify email addresses to be blocked on the Blocked Senders tab of the Safety Options dialog box. You can also block a sender after receiving a message from that sender. To do this, right-click the message you have received, point to *Junk email*, and then click *Add sender to blocked senders list*. If you find you have blocked someone in error, you can unblock the address at the Blocked Senders tab. Click the address you wish to unblock from the list of blocked senders. Click the Remove button and then click OK. This action will allow messages from the previously blocked sender to be delivered to your email account.

Figure 15.15 Safety Options Dialog Box

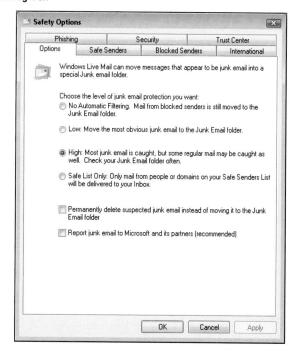

Exercise 15.9   Working with Junk Mail and Safe Senders

1. In Windows Live Mail, identify a message from someone you want to add to your safe senders list.

2. Right-click the message, point to *Junk email,* and then click *Add sender to safe sender list* at the shortcut menu. If a confirmation box displays, click OK.

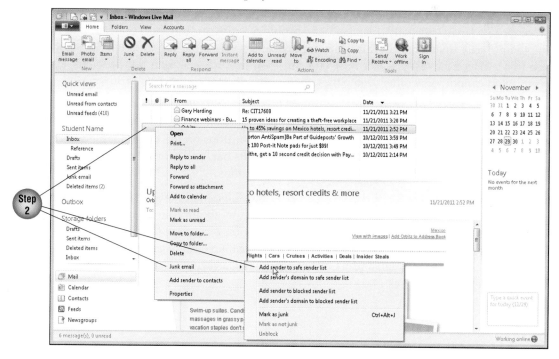

3. Identify a message that is unsolicited junk mail.

   If you do not have such a message, pretend that one of the non-junk mail messages in your Inbox is junk mail.

4. Right-click the message, point to *Junk email*, and then click *Add sender to blocked sender list*. If a confirmation box displays, click OK.

5. Drag the message to the Junk email folder.

6. Click the File tab, point to *Options*, and then click *Safety options*.

7. At the Safety Options dialog box, click the Blocked Senders tab. If the person you blocked in Step 4 was not someone you want to block, click the address and then click the Remove button.

8. Click OK.

9. Display the Junk email folder.

10. If the message you moved there in Step 5 is not junk, select the message and then click the Not junk button on the Home tab.

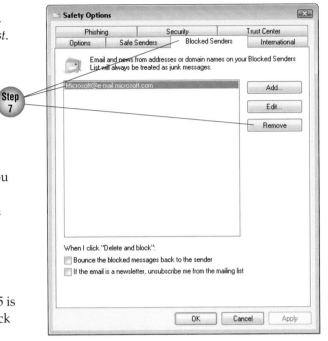

Troubleshooting Common Email Problems

Besides dealing with junk mail, you may occasionally encounter other difficulties with email. Knowing how to troubleshoot common problems is essential to being an efficient email communicator. The following are some common email problems and their solutions:

An error message displays when you send or receive email. An error message that displays when you send or receive email is usually due to either a problem with your Internet connection or the mail server being temporarily unavailable. Wait a few minutes and try again. If the problem does not resolve itself, check to see if you have Web access. If you can view web pages, then the problem is with the mail server; if you cannot view other web pages, then your Internet connection is down.

Parts of the Windows Live Mail application window are not visible. If you do not see certain elements of Windows Live Mail onscreen as they appear in the figures in Topic 15, check to see if these elements have been turned off. Click the View tab and then click buttons on the tab to toggle various portions of the screen on or off, such as the Calendar pane, the Status bar, and Storage folders. You should be able to access all parts of Windows Live Mail using these options.

Pictures do not display in emails you receive. Windows Live Mail may block pictures or other external content to prevent other users from obtaining information about your computer. An information bar should display to inform you of this. Click the information bar to see the pictures. If you want to turn this protection off, click the File tab, point to *Options*, and then click *Safety options*. At the Safety Options dialog box, click the Security tab and then click the *Block images and other external content in HTML email* check box to remove the check mark.

Outgoing messages are not immediately sent. By default, Windows Live Mail will send/receive mail every 10 minutes, but you can tell the program to send outgoing mail immediately (without waiting for the interval to pass between automatic send operations or for you to click the Send/Receive button). To do this, click the File tab, point to *Options*, and then click *Mail*. At the Options dialog box, click the Send tab and then click the *Send messages immediately* check box to insert a check mark.

Another email program opens when you click an email link on a website. If another email program opens when you click an email link on a website, that means Windows Live Mail is probably not set as your default email program. To make Windows Live Mail your default email program, open Windows Live Mail, click the File tab, point to *Options*, and then click *Mail*. At the Options dialog box, click the General tab and then, in the *Default Messaging Programs* section, click the Make Default button for the default Mail handler.

The message reading pane displays to the right of the Inbox list. While this is technically not a problem with the Windows Live Mail program, you may prefer your screen to appear more like the ones in the figures in Topic 15. To change the layout of your screen, click the View tab, click the Reading pane button in the Layout group, and then click *Bottom of the message list* at the drop-down list.

Email application fails to send or receive messages. Check to make sure you have Internet connectivity by opening your web browser and displaying a web page. If web access is working, the problem is likely that your ISP's mail server is temporarily down. Wait a few minutes and try again. If the problem persists after an hour, contact your ISP for help.

Attachments will not download. Some email programs block the receipt of certain email attachment types for security reasons. See the Drilling Down note about sending executable attachments at the end of Lesson 15.6.

Drilling Down

Understanding the Origins of Spam

Spam, or junk mail, proliferates all over the Internet because it is a cheap (nearly free) way of soliciting millions of people at once. If even one-tenth of 1 percent of the people who receive an advertisement buy the product, the ads are worth the cost. Marketing companies harvest email addresses from websites (often using automatic page-reading applications that troll the Internet, reading thousands of pages an hour). They then sell those lists of email addresses to companies that want to buy them to send out spam. Some legitimate businesses also sell their customer information databases to outside marketers to boost their company's revenue. When you fill out a registration card or buy a product online, your email address can end up in a spammer's database. Some websites have opt-out provisions in their privacy policies, but they are often buried in fine print and are difficult to locate.

Some spam is sent out by dishonest individuals and companies who want to steal your credit card information, sell you a worthless or illegal product, install malware on your PC, or drive traffic to an adult-oriented website that might install malware on your PC. You should *never* reply to spam, or click a link in it, or buy anything advertised in this fashion. Doing so only encourages companies to continue sending out spam.

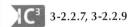 3-2.2.7, 3-2.2.9

Exploring Advanced Mail Options

The IC³ exam requires that you understand the purposes of several frequently used mail configuration options that are not available in Windows Live Mail or that are configured at the email server level rather than in an individual PC's email software. The following are key email configuration options to know.

Creating Automatic Signatures

In some email applications you can create a saved signature block, containing information you always want to include at the bottom of every email. This information might include your name, title, company, mailing address, and phone number for your work email; or your name and a favorite quote for your personal email. When you send out an email message, the application attaches the specified signature block to the bottom of the message. Signature blocks are convenient and save you the trouble of retyping frequently used information; however, care should be given to prevent the wrong signature being sent to a recipient (such as a personal signature being sent to an instructor or boss). You can set up signature blocks in Microsoft Outlook but not in Windows Live Mail.

Using the Out of Office Assistance

Some email providers enable you to create an out-of-office message that is delivered automatically to anyone who emails you while you are away from your computer for a period of time. This message will alert the sender that you are currently not able to access your email. This feature is configured at the server level by changing your email settings there, rather than in an application. Exceptions to that general rule exist, though; for example, if your company or school uses a Microsoft Exchange mail system, you may be able to configure out-of-office autoreplies using Microsoft Outlook.

Setting Up Mail Forwarding

You can set up your email account to automatically forward any messages it receives to another address. Many possible uses for mail forwarding exist. For example, you can use this capability to share messages among multiple people with a single POP3 email account, or you can temporarily forward copies of your email from an account you do not check over the summer to one that you access year round. You would usually set up email forwarding at the server level but, depending on the mail system you are using, you may be able to configure it through your email application, too.

Supplementing Mail Messages

Besides attaching files to messages, you can also embed additional content within a message. For example, you can place hyperlinks into the message body in most email applications by simply typing them in; the program converts them to live hyperlinks automatically. There may also be a command to insert a hyperlink. In Windows Live Mail, while composing a message you can click the Hyperlink button on the Message tab to insert a hyperlink.

You can also embed graphics and content from other applications into a message body by copying and pasting from the Clipboard. For example, you can select some cells in Excel, copy them, and then paste them directly into the message body as you are composing a message.

continued

Searching for a Message

You can search your Inbox for a particular message by typing a keyword in the Search for a message box above the message list. The list will be filtered to show only the matching messages. This keyword can be anything you remember about the message, such as the sender, the subject line, or a word in the message body. To remove the search filter, click the Close (X) button at the right end of the search box.

Archiving Messages

Most mail programs have an archive or backup feature that you can use to transfer old messages out of your main email storage file and into a backup file that you can access later if needed. Doing this keeps the size of your main email storage file small, so that the mail program opens and closes quickly.

In Windows Live Mail, you can archive messages by exporting them. First create a new folder into which you will archive messages. Then select File, click Export Email, and then click Email messages command to export messages to that storage location. In Microsoft Outlook 2010, click File, click Info, click Cleanup Tools, and then click Archive command.

Synchronizing Messages

If you have the right software, you may be able to synchronize your smartphone or other handheld device with your email application so that you can read your messages on-the-go. To set this up, you need to acquire special software designed to make that connection with your specific device and your specific email program. These software connectors (also called conduits) are available for many popular phones and email programs.

- Mail servers are servers dedicated to handling email. When you want to collect your email, you run a mail application that transfers your email from the server to your computer.
- Email is a store-and-forward communication system that uses mail servers to transfer email from one computer to another.
- Three main types of mail servers exist: POP3/SMTP, IMAP, and HTTP.
- In an email address, the part before the @ sign is the user ID, and the part after the @ sign is the domain name.
- To configure an email account, you need to know the email address, password, incoming and outgoing server addresses, type of account, and security settings.
- A message header contains the recipient address(es) and subject. The message body is the main part of the email, where the message is typed.
- You can format email using formatting controls within your email application. They are similar to the formatting controls in Word or WordPad.
- Most email applications enable you to store contact information, including email addresses, telephone numbers, and work addresses.
- To send and receive email in Windows Live Mail, click the Send/Receive button in the Tools group on the Home tab.
- To read a received message, click the message and view it in the Reading pane, or double-click the message to open it in its own window.
- To attach a file to an email, click the Attach file button in the Insert group on the Message tab in the New Message window.
- To open a received attachment, double-click the attachment. To save the attachment to your hard disk, click the File tab, click *Save*, and then click *Save attachments*.
- A read receipt is a return email you receive when the recipient opens your original message. To request a read receipt, click the *Read receipt* check box in the Delivery group on the Message tab in the New Message window to insert a check mark.
- When composing a message, you can flag a message as high priority or low priority with buttons on the Quick Access toolbar of the New Message window or with buttons in the Delivery group on the Message tab.
- To create a new mail folder, click the New folder button on the Folders tab in Windows Live Mail. To move messages between folders, drag-and-drop them there, or use the Move to button in the Message group on the Folders tab.
- To delete a message, click the message and press the Delete key. The message goes to the Deleted items folder, but the message is not deleted immediately.
- To control the junk mail filtering in Windows Live Mail, click the File tab, point to *Options*, click *Safety options*, and then click the desired level on the Options tab.

Key Terms

blind carbon copy (Bcc), p. 690

carbon copy (Cc), p. 690

forward, p. 698

Internet Mail Access Protocol (IMAP), p. 684

junk mail, p. 707

mail server, p. 684

message body, p. 689

message header, p. 689

Post Office Protocol (POP) , p. 684

priority, p. 703

read receipt, p. 704

Rich Text (HTML), p. 690

Rich Text Format (RTF), p. 690

safe senders list, p. 708

Simple Mail Transfer Protocol, (SMTP), p. 684

store-and-forward email system, p. 684

Features Summary

Feature	Ribbon Tab, Group	Button	Keyboard Shortcut
Add address to Contacts list	Home, New	Contact	Ctrl + N (in Contacts window)
Delete message	Home, Delete	Delete	Ctrl + D
Forward message	Home, Respond	Forward	Ctrl + F
New Message window	Home, New	Email message	Ctrl + N
Reply to message	Home, Respond	Reply	Ctrl + R
Send and receive mail	Home, Tools	Send/ Receive	F5

KEY POINTS REVIEW

Completion

In the space provided at the left, indicate the correct term, command, or option.

1. _____ This is a type of email server in which mail is accessed using an email program but remains stored on the server.

2. _____ This is the free email program that Microsoft provides for use in Windows 7.

3. _____ What type of mail server (incoming or outgoing) would have the address *pop.myschool.edu*?

4. _____ What kind of sending option sends a copy of an email to a recipient without the other recipient(s)' knowledge?

5. _____ What type of formatting is used when formatting email messages in Windows Live Mail?

6. _____ What list contains the stored email addresses in Windows Live Mail?

7. _____ This pane displays adjacent to the list of Inbox messages and allows you to preview the currently selected message.

continued

8. _____ What is it called when an email program automatically attaches certain text to the end of all outgoing messages?

9. _____ Request this when you want to know when someone reads your email.

10. _____ This is another name for junk email.

Multiple Choice

For each of the following items, choose the option that best completes the sentence or answers the question.

1. When you access email through a website like Gmail.com, you are using which protocol?
   A. HTTP
   B. HTML
   C. IMAP
   D. POP3

2. What symbol separates the user name from the domain name in an email address?
   A. #
   B. @
   C. &
   D. %

3. Which of these programs can be used as an email client application?
   A. Word
   B. Excel
   C. Outlook
   D. PowerPoint

4. Which of these is most likely to be an outgoing mail server?
   A. pop.myschool.edu
   B. smtp.myschol.edu
   C. student@myschool.edu
   D. http://secure.myschool.edu

5. When you _____ a message, you send the original message, along with an optional comment, to someone who did not receive the original.
   A. forward
   B. archive
   C. reply to
   D. request a read receipt for

6. Some mail programs do not allow you to send or receive _____ files as attachments for security reasons.
   A. video
   B. text
   C. audio
   D. executable

7. If you want to copy a message to another folder, rather than move it, hold down the _____ button as you drag the message.
   A. Alt
   B. Shift
   C. Ctrl
   D. F10

8. To move a message to the Deleted items folder, select the message and press the _____ key on the keyboard.
   A. Remove
   B. Insert
   C. Move
   D. Delete

9. You can block all email except that from senders on the _____ list in Windows Live Mail.
   A. blackout
   B. safe senders
   C. blocked
   D. junk

10. A(n) _____ is a return email you get letting you know when the recipient opens your message.
    A. read receipt
    B. postage notification
    C. marker
    D. importance flag

Matching

Match each of the following definitions with the correct term, command, or option.

1. _____ The protocol used for email that is accessed using an email client and transferred to the local PC for reading and management

2. _____ The protocol used for Web-based email

3. _____ Copy of a message that is sent without the other recipients knowing about it

4. _____ Unwanted commercial email

5. _____ Copy of a message that is sent with the knowledge of the other recipients

6. _____ The protocol used for email that is managed from a server but accessed using an email client application

7. _____ Information about a recipient, including email address

8. _____ The protocol used for sending messages in a POP3 mail system

9. _____ The part of an email message that contains the recipient addresses and subject

10. _____ The text that appears after the @ sign in an email address

A. Bcc
B. Cc
C. Contact
D. Domain name
E. HTTP
F. IMAP
G. Message header
H. POP
I. SMTP
J. Spam

SKILLS REVIEW

Review 15.1 **Sending Email**

1. Open Windows Live Mail. If it is not already configured to send and receive email from your email address, configure it to do this.
2. Compose a message to your instructor with the following text:
   Subject: **Review 15.1**
   Message body: **I am completing the reviews at the end of the chapter, and am working with text formatting.**
3. Apply bold and italic formatting to the word *text*.
4. Change the font size of the word *reviews* to 14.
5. Make all the text in the message body green.
6. Send the message.

Review 15.2 **Sending a Courtesy Copy and Forwarding a Message**

1. In Windows Live Mail, compose a message to yourself with the following text:
   Subject: **Review 15.2**
   Message body: **I am sending this to myself, but copying my instructor.**
2. Enter the instructor's email address in the *Cc* text box.
3. Send the message.
4. Do a Send/Receive operation to send the message. Wait a minute, and then do another Send/Receive to receive the message you sent.
5. Compose a forward of the message you just received to your instructor. Change the Subject to **Forward: Review 15.2**.
6. Add the following text at the top of the message:
   Here is a forward of the message I received.
7. Send the message.

Review 15.3 **Sending Email Attachments and Setting Priority**

1. In Notepad, create a new document that contains your name and your email address. Save the file as **U3T15-R3-Info**.
2. With Windows Live Mail open, compose a message to your instructor with the following text:
   Subject: **Review 15.3**
   Message body: **I am practicing sending attachments. Attached is a Notepad file.**
3. Attach the **U3T15-R3-Info.txt** file to the message.
4. Set the message to be sent with high priority.
5. Send the message.

SKILLS ASSESSMENT

Assessment 15.1 **Copying Data into an Email**

1. Open a web browser and navigate to www.wikipedia.org.
2. Display the page for the state that you live in and copy its URL from the Address bar to the Clipboard.
3. Start a new email message, and address it to your instructor.
4. In the *Subject* text box, type **U3T15-A1-Wiki**.
5. Click in the message body. Type **From:** and then paste the URL from the Clipboard. Press Enter to start a new paragraph.
6. Switch back to the Wikipedia article and copy the first paragraph to the Clipboard.
7. Switch back to the email message and paste the contents of the Clipboard into the message body.
8. Send the message.

Assessment 15.2 **Comparing Email Clients and Web Mail**

1. If you do not already have a Web-based email account, create a free Web-based email account on one of the following services:
   mail.yahoo.com
   www.gmail.com
   www.hotmail.com
2. Exchange a few emails with classmates, friends, or family using the web-based interface.
3. Start a new file in Notepad and name the file **U3T15-A2-Web**.
4. In Notepad, describe the differences in using the web-based email versus using Windows Live Mail, including the interface itself, the capabilities, the handling of formatted messages, and the handling of attachments.
5. Save, print, and then close **U3T15-A2-Web.txt**.
6. Compose an email to your instructor. In the subject line, type **Assessment 15.2**. Attach the file **U3T15-A2-Web.txt**.
7. Send the message.

Assessment 15.3 **Formatting Email**

1. Start a new email message and type the following text in the body:
   Dear Mr. Smith:

   Thank you for your interest in the DR-3432 Treadmill. Here are some specifications that you may find useful in comparing this model to others:
   Incline of 0 to 15 degrees
   Speed of up to 15 MPH

Hardwood base
Heavy-duty, durable rubber and cloth running surface
Rated for users of up to 400 pounds
15 customizable programs including 3 interval training plans
Pulse monitoring system that can be used with hand rails or clip-on heart monitor
Please do not hesitate to call me if I can be of further assistance.
Best wishes,
Norman Wiseman, Senior Sales Representative
Wiseman Fitness Products

2. Add bullets to the paragraphs that describe the specifications of the product.
3. Make the last two lines bold (the person's name and title, and the company name).
4. Apply a font that looks like script or handwriting to the name *Norman Wiseman*.
5. Increase the font for the text *Wiseman Fitness Products* by 2 points.
6. Address the email to your instructor.
7. In the *Subject* text box, type **Assessment 15.3**.
8. Send the message.

Assessment 15.4 Sending Pictures in Email

1. Find instructions in the Windows Help and Support application for sending pictures in email.
2. Following those instructions, open the Pictures library, choose one of the pictures, and email it to your instructor as an attachment. If prompted for a picture size, use the smallest picture size available. In the *Subject* text box, type **Assessment 15.4**.

Assessment 15.5 Researching How to Set Up Yahoo! Mail in Windows Live Mail

Suppose you have a Yahoo! Mail account, and you want to use Windows Live Mail to access it.
1. Start a new Notepad, WordPad, or Word document, and save the file as **U3T15-A5-Yahoo**.
2. Use Internet research to answer the following questions. Record your research in the **U3T15-A5-Yahoo** file.
   - Do you need a special type of Yahoo! Mail account for the account to be able to send and receive email in Windows Live Mail, or will the regular free type of account work?
   - Should you set up Yahoo! Mail accounts in Windows Live Mail as POP3 or IMAP?
   - What are the incoming and outgoing mail server addresses to use?
   - Are there any special security or authentication settings needed?
3. Save, print, and then close **U3T15-A5-Yahoo**.
4. Compose a new email message to your teacher (using any email account). In the Subject line, type **Assessment 15.5**.
5. Attach the **U3T15-A5-Yahoo** file to the message and send it.

Assessment 15.6 Uses for Specific Email Features and Options

Different email options may be appropriate in different situations. For each of the following email options, describe a hypothetical situation where it would be useful. Write your answers in a Word or WordPad file and save the file as **U3T15-A6-Options**.
1. Read receipts
2. Low priority
3. High priority
4. Automatic signature block

Transferring Large Files Online

Some email applications and mail servers limit the size of the attachments you can send and receive to avoid using too much bandwidth and slowing down service for other users. If you have a large file to send, or a series of large files, you might consider finding another way of delivering them to the recipient.

Analyze the following questions and use your prior knowledge and computer literacy to determine the answers. Record your views in a Notepad, Word, or WordPad document and save the file as **U3T15-CT-Attachments**.

1. Why might it be considered rude to send large email attachments?
2. What other ways could you transfer files to someone over the Internet?
3. If the Internet were not available, what ways could you transfer large files to someone?

Save the completed file and send it to your instructor as an email attachment. Type **Topic 15 Critical Thinking** in the *Subject* text box of the email message.

Researching Junk Mail Filtering Programs

The junk mail filters built into email applications like Outlook and Windows Live Mail do not usually work perfectly because they are just one feature in a larger program. For better junk mail filtering, many people prefer to buy (or acquire a free) add-on program specifically for junk mail handling.

As a team, research and evaluate several junk email filtering programs, including at least one free program, one shareware program, and one retail program. Create a PowerPoint presentation that compares and contrasts the programs and then recommends one of the programs. Base your recommendations on factors such as positive reviews, cost-effectiveness, features, and compatibility with a wide range of email applications. Include your judging criteria in your presentation. Explain the technology behind each application. Save the presentation as **U3T15-TeamPresentation**. Your teacher may ask each team to present their presentations to the entire class.

Discussion Questions

1. Discuss whether a program that is able to learn from its filtering mistakes is preferable to one that works according to preset rules.
2. How important is it to find a program that offers frequent, free online updates?
3. Compare your recommendation with those of your class and identify whether any recommendations changed after this discussion.

Topic 16

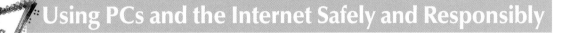

Using PCs and the Internet Safely and Responsibly

Performance Objectives

Upon successful completion of Topic 16, you will be able to:

- Understand the types of Internet threats
- Understand how to avoid malware infection
- Identify techniques to safeguard your privacy and identity online
- Protect minors from adult content
- Identify how to make computers more accessible

- Understand legal and ethical issues in computing
- Demonstrate online etiquette
- Identify health and safety hazards associated with computer use

STUDENT RESOURCES

Before beginning this topic, copy to your storage medium the **Unit3Topic16** subfolder from the *Computer and Internet Essentials: Preparing for IC³* Internet Resource Center. Make this the active folder.

In addition to containing the data files needed to complete topic work, the Internet Resource Center contains model answers in PDF format for each of the applicable exercises in this topic. Use these files to check your work. The preface of your textbook provides instructions for accessing these files.

Necessary Data Files

To complete the exercises and assessments, you will need the following data files:

Exercise 16.1–16.5	N/A
Exercise 16.6	Research.docx
Exercise 16.7–16.8	N/A
Reviews 16.1–16.3	N/A
Assessments 16.1–16.7	N/A

Visual Preview

USB 3.0 and Thunderbolt

In November of 2008, the USB Promoter group announced the completion of the USB 3.0 standard. This group consisted of representatives from many prominent hardware companies, including HP, Intel, Texas Instruments, NEC Corporation, Microsoft and ST-NXP Wireless.

The most notable advancement in USB 3.0 is the increase in raw throughput from a theoretical 480 Mbps of USB 2.0 to 5 Gbps in USB 3.0. Even after protocol overhead, the expected maximum throughput will still be over 3.2 Gbps (SATA-IO). Because the new rate is faster than that of a serial ATA hard drive, USB 3.0 devices can now be considered viable competitors to traditional hard disk drives. Popular consumer devices such as MP3 players and camcorders in particular will also benefit as it becomes considerably faster to transfer multiple gigabytes of data on and off the devices. In addition to far greater throughput, USB3.0 supports considerably more power through the connector, enabling it to power more devices and charge older ones more rapidly.

However the format is not without its flaws. Market penetration of USB 3.0, and thus the proliferation of 3.0 devices, has been slow because of Intel's decision to not support the device in its complete range of desktop PC solutions until 2011. Cable length is also an issue. In order to receive maximum throughput, the maximum recommended cable length has decreased to three meters from USB 2.0's five meter specification.

The current competing technology to USB 3.0 is Intel's Thunderbolt platform. Thunderbolt, originally codenamed Light Peak, was previewed by Intel in 2009, and was officially released as a consumer product when Apple refreshed its Macbook Pro line in February of 2011. Thunderbolt has a theoretical throughput speed of approximately 20Gbps, which is over four times the throughput of USB 3.0. Thunderbolt is currently used almost exclusively on Apple products, but is expected to be widely adopted in fields where raw throughput is important, such as in video editing.

Thunderbolt boasts incredible throughput performance, but it is not without its own faults. It requires a controller to be present in both the host computer and the connected device, so the cost of peripheral devices that operate on Thunderbolt is higher than those that operate on USB 3.0.

Works Cited

SATA-IO. Benefits of Using SATA. 2010. 30 08 2011 <http://www.sata-io.org/technology/why_sata.asp>.

Exercise 16.6 **U3T16-Research.docx**

Topic Overview

Computers and the Internet have changed society and improved people's lives in many important ways, but they have also introduced a variety of new threats and potential problems that affect people at work, at school, and at home. For example, computer viruses can infect personal computers, children can get access to age-inappropriate web content, and misunderstandings can occur because of differing expectations about proper Internet communication etiquette.

In this topic, we will look at a variety of Internet safety, privacy, legal, and ethical issues. You will learn what the rules and standards are for Internet communications, and you will learn how to protect yourself and others from online risks.

Lesson 16.1 **Understanding Secure Data Access**

 3-1.1.3, 3-1.1.7, 3-4.2.1, 3-4.2.5, 3-4.2.6, 3-4.2.9

Intranet A type of internal, secure network used by organizations and business, accessible only by members, employees, or other authorized users

Extranet A secured portion of a network that is open to users within the organization and specific users outside the organization

Companies and individuals may choose to limit online access to data. For example, some data is appropriate to share only with employees of the company, or with paid members of a club or organization. That type of secure network is called an **intranet**. (Intra means within.) Other data may be appropriate to share with certain outsiders, but not with the public in general. For example, businesses may restrict the amount of product information that they provide online to avoid giving competing companies an advantage; they may require users to register with their contact information to receive product information. A secured portion of a network that is open to certain invited outsiders is known as an **extranet**; extranets are commonly used for business-to-business communications and sharing.

Understanding Data Ownership

It is important to know who owns data being presented online, because only the owner can decide how the data is shared or restricted. Many businesses have a rule, which employees agree to when they sign their employment paperwork, that states that any products or information the employee creates while at work belongs to the company. The purpose of such a rule is to prevent employees from selling or sharing information that they discovered or created on company time. However, this rule extends to personal communications, even those that are not related to work. For example, if you use an employer-provided email address, your employer is legally entitled to read your messages and even to take action based on their content. Similarly, if an employer provides an employee with a computer, the employer continues to own the computer and all the information stored on the computer.

The same ownership rules apply to many educational institutions (high schools, colleges, universities). The schools own the computers, even though the students, teachers, and staff use them. A computer assigned to an individual still belongs to the institution and is subject to search at any time. Any emails or other personal communications that pass through the school's server are also owned by the school. Each school has its own policy; ask you instructor or school administrators for information on your school's policy on data ownership, or refer to your student handbook.

Securing Online Data

Many Internet resources employ user names and passwords to authenticate the identity of users. To access secured online data you must enter a valid user name and password.

One way that criminals steal data online is by using special applications called packet sniffers. A **packet sniffer** is an application that can intercept data packets as they are being sent or received. Recall that a packet is a container file for sending data over a network and contains the data itself plus a header and footer. Packet sniffer software that intercepts a communication between a bank and a bank member could gain access to the member's account number, balance, or other data. The criminal could then use that information to access the account and transfer the bank member's money.

packet sniffer An application that can intercept data packets as they are being sent or received

To prevent this type of theft, many websites that offer log-in access also provide encryption, which scrambles the data before it is transmitted. If encrypted data is intercepted, the person intercepting the data will not be able to decode the information. Encrypted data is unscrambled once it reaches its destination. A **secure site** is a website that employs some type of encryption technology to ensure that the data being transmitted is not intercepted by an unauthorized person. Websites that handle financial matters, such as banking and online shopping sites, protect users by providing a secure site. A secure site's URL typically begins with *https://* rather than *http://*, and depending on the browser there may be other indicators as well, such as a lock icon in the Address bar or a different-colored background in the Address bar (see Figure 16.1). **Secure Sockets Layer (SSL)** is a technology used for generating secure site connections. In a secure transmission, each packet is encrypted and can be decoded only by the authorized recipient (that is, the computer with which you are communicating).

secure site A website that employs some type of encryption technology to ensure that the data being transmitted is not intercepted by an unauthorized person

Secure Sockets Layer (SSL) A technology used for generating a secure site connection

The term *hacker* is a generic term used to describe a person who tries to gain access to other computers and networks. The damage done to networks that are attacked may include files being stolen or deleted, spyware being secretly installed, or fake user accounts being set up. Networks prevent unauthorized access by using firewalls and by keeping the operating system patched. Lesson 16.2 provides more information on operating system vulnerabilities and exploits.

Figure 16.1 Secure URL A secure web address in Internet Explorer with a pop-up that identifies the certificate issuer

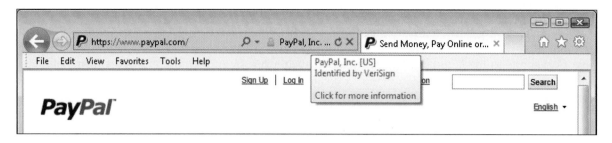

security certificate A unique code that provides an assurance that the site you are communicating with is legitimate

issuing authority A company that provides and authenticates security certificates

Data criminals sometimes set up web sites that simulate a trusted secure site to trick users into logging in and sharing private information (also known as *spoofing*). To minimize this risk, sites employ security certificates (or digital certificates) to verify that the connection is secure. A **security certificate** is a unique code that provides assurance that the site you are communicating with is legitimate. This code includes a serial number, the identity of the person or organization that issued the certificate, and the dates the certificate is valid. A certificate is issued by an **issuing authority**, a company that maintains a server that can tell your browser whether or not the certificate that a secure web page is presenting is valid. In Figure 16.1, a pop-up states that the certificate issuer is Verisign. When you visit a website that presents your browser with a certificate, your browser software automatically checks the database of the issuing authority. An authentic certificate's codes will match the codes within the issuing authority's database. Based on that cross-check, the browser software determines whether the site you are visiting is the same site that the issuing authority certified. A warning message will display if the certificate is not valid.

Exercise 16.1 Viewing a Secure Website and Examining Security Certificates

1. Open your web browser and go to www.paypal.com.

2. Look at the address in the Address bar. Notice that it begins with *https://*. Depending on your browser version, you may also observe that the address bar's background is green, or that a lock symbol displays on the address bar.

3. Click the lock symbol on the address bar if one is present.
   This action displays information about the certificate authority.

4. Click Tools on the menu bar and then click *Internet options* at the drop-down list.

5. At the Internet Options dialog box, click the Content tab and then click the Certificates button.
   This action displays a list of the security certificates. Multiple tabs exist in the dialog box for different certificate publishers and authorities.

6. At the Certificates dialog box, click the Trusted Root Certification Authorities tab and then browse the list.

   The listed companies issue and verify certificates.

7. Double-click one of the certificates to review its information and then click OK to close its box.

8. Click Close to close the Certificates dialog box.

9. Click OK to close the Internet Options dialog box.

10. Close the web browser window.

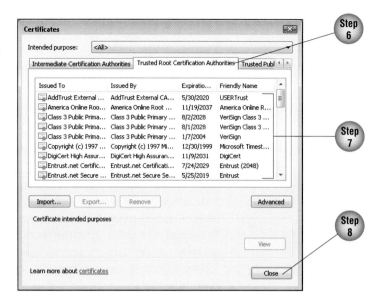

Drilling Down

Avoiding Data Loss

Network and Internet security breaches may compromise privacy, but data loss is usually the result of hardware or software failure and not security. As you are making plans to keep your systems safe and your data secure, do not forget these simple precautions:

- Save your work in progress frequently when using any application, so if a system problem occurs and the software crashes you will have a partial copy of your work to restore from. Microsoft Office applications will automatically save your work in progress every 10 minutes.
- Back up your important data regularly. Employ backup systems like Microsoft Backup or an online backup service, and schedule the backup to run automatically so you do not forget to back up.
- Store backups in a different location, or at least on a different computer, to guard against data loss from hardware failure.

Lesson 16.2   Avoiding Malware Infection

 3-3.1.13, 3-4.2.4

Recall that malware is a broad term used to describe many possible attacks on computer systems. Short for malicious software, the term malware describes any application or data file that has been installed on anyone's computer without their consent and is intended to cause harm. People who create malware usually do so to profit criminally from the data they gather; however, some malware exists only to cause trouble and provides no benefit to its creator. This lesson identifies several types of malware and discusses how antivirus and antispyware applications help combat them.

Guarding against Operating System and Application Exploits

All operating systems and applications have potential vulnerabilities that criminals can exploit. A **vulnerability** exists when a there is flaw in the programming, an attacker who is aware of the programming flaw, and a tool or technique that the attacker can use to exploit that flaw for malicious

vulnerability Exists when there is a flaw in programming that creates potential for misuse, an attacker who is aware of it, and a tool or technique the attacker can use to exploit it

exploit An attack in which a criminal uses a vulnerability to target and harm a system

purposes. When criminals actually use a vulnerability to attack a system, the attack is called an **exploit**. To guard against exploits, Windows, Linux, and Mac operating systems have mechanisms to automatically update and patch their operating system as programmers become aware of vulnerabilities. For this reason, it is important to promptly install all available updates and service packs for your operating system.

Applications can also be exploited, although it happens less frequently because an application is a smaller and less appealing target to a criminal. Widely used applications such as Microsoft Office are most often the targets of application exploit attempts. As an application or operating system ages, more and more security patches become available. Providing the individual patches eventually becomes too difficult, so the operating system or application manufacturer may release a service pack. A **service pack** is a collection of critical updates (and sometimes minor enhancements) that are released as a group. A service pack is like a regular update except it takes longer to install and you typically cannot remove the service pack after it has been installed.

service pack A collection of updates that are released as a group

Understanding Viruses, Trojan Horses, and Worms

By now you know that a virus can harm your computer. Recall that a virus is a computer code that inserts itself into an executable file. When the infected file is run, the virus's code executes along with the application's code. The virus can hide itself inside a host file, so it may not be obvious that the virus is there. A virus's code can cause all manner of issues, from annoying-but-harmless message displays, to destructive actions like deleting all files of a certain type or causing your operating system to stop working. Most viruses have a self-replicating component that allows them to spread from one executable file to another. When the infected file executes, the virus code is copied into RAM, and from there it can attach itself to other executable files.

Other types of malware are loosely grouped under the banner of "virus" and can be detected and removed by antivirus software, but many are not actually viruses because they do not hide themselves in executable files. These types of malware include worms and Trojan horses.

key logger A program that records all keystrokes and sends the information to a remote location

In Topic 3 you learned that Trojan horses are rogue applications that appear to do something useful (and may actually perform that function), but secretly harm your computer by damaging your system or installing a privacy-compromising application. One type of Trojan horse is a program that claims to scan your system for malware but instead creates system problems that it then asserts it can resolve (for a fee). Other Trojan horses may install their own malware such as a key logger. A **key logger** records all keystrokes in a file and sends the information to a remote location. The key logger creator or user can then access this file and use the keystrokes to determine user names and passwords.

Another difference between Trojan horses and viruses is that Trojan horses do not replicate themselves. The most common way that Trojan horse programs spread is through worms. Recall that worms are self-transporting applications that carry a harmful program such as a Trojan horse or a virus. Worms can be either active or passive: active worms self-transport without human assistance, whereas passive worms rely on the user's actions to move from one location to another, usually by tricking users into opening attachments or forwarding the worm to others. Active worms use email, vulnerabilities in your operating system, the Web, and DNS servers to move their content around a network infrastructure without any user interaction. Most antivirus programs can detect and remove both Trojan horses and worms.

Understanding Adware and Spyware

As noted in Topic 3, adware is a category of application that displays unsolicited advertisements on your computer. Adware creators make money when users click on the ads they display. The most common type of adware comes in the form of an add-on toolbar for your web browser that supposedly provides "advanced" or "helpful" search services, but also causes pop-up ads to display whenever you use your web browser.

Strictly speaking, not all adware is illegal, and not all adware-makers are involved in criminal activity. If you happen to download a web toolbar or application that contains too many ads or does not perform in the manner you desired, you can typically remove the application from your computer. The uninstall option for the toolbar may or may not display in the Control Panel in Windows, so you might need to connect to a website or go through extra steps to complete the removal.

Some adware has no pretense of being anything else, and such programs are typically difficult to remove, much like a virus infection. Your antivirus software may be of some help, but you also might need to do a web search on the adware's removal to find removal instructions.

Recall that spyware is software that records your computer usage without your consent or knowledge. Key loggers are a form of spyware; so are programs that track which websites you visit and what ads you click on and send that information back to their owners. Spyware makers are paid for collecting consumer marketing data, either specifically about you or about all users in general. Most spyware is illegal, works without your knowledge, and can be difficult to remove from your computer. Some antivirus software detects and removes spyware. Applications are also designed specifically to remove spyware and adware from your system, such as Windows Defender.

Spyware is not self-replicating, so to spread, it has to deceive computer users into installing it voluntarily by misleading them about its purpose. The most common way to get infected with spyware is to install a free application from a questionable website, such as one that offers illegal content for download (like copyright-protected music, movies, or games). Another way to get spyware is to run an ActiveX or Java component on a website that you visit. Many unscrupulous site owners provide "free" content to exploit site visitors by infecting them with spyware or adware.

Defending against Malware

Two main classes of applications that protect your system against malware are antivirus and anti-spyware applications. Recall that antivirus programs defend against viruses, worms, and Trojan horses; **anti-spyware software** defends against adware and spyware. Some overlap typically exists between the types of threats each application guards against; for example, an antivirus program might also target some types of nonvirus malware. Suites that combine multiple security functions are also available; for example, Norton Security Suite includes antivirus and anti-malware features, along with spam-fighting tools, identity protection tools, a firewall, a backup tool, and a PC tune-up tool.

anti-spyware software Software that defends against adware and spyware

Antivirus Software Viruses embed themselves inside an application, redirecting the application's commands and code around themselves while running as a separate task. Antivirus programs can detect a virus by opening the file and scanning the code, looking for this type of redirection. Antivirus programs also scan the code of each executable file to locate virus definitions. A **virus definition** is an identifying snippet of a virus's code, sometimes called a virus signature. An antivirus program maintains a database of known virus definitions. When it finds a match between its database and code within a file, the software signals a warning that a virus may be present. As new viruses and other threats are discovered, the antivirus software companies update the virus definition files and make the update available for users to download. Having the most up-to-date definitions. is critical for effective virus protection.

virus definition A uniquely identifying snippet of a virus's code, also called a *virus signature*

Many antivirus programs create an MD5 for each application that is installed on the computer. MD5 stands for Message Digest Version 5, a math calculation that results in a unique value representing the data being checked. Each time you run a program, the antivirus program compares the application's current MD5 value to the original one. If the MD5 value has changed, the antivirus program notifies the user that a virus may have infected the file.

When your antivirus program finds something suspicious, a message displays giving you a choice of deleting or quarantining the infected file(s). Deleting a file removes it from your system. Quarantining the file places it in an off-limits area, so it cannot be run, but can still be reviewed by an IT professional or anyone who is tracking viruses on your network.

resident Continuously running in the background of the operating system environment

Antivirus applications are typically **resident**, meaning that they are continuously running in the background analyzing your system and any programs or files when they are opened or closed. Some antivirus programs also check incoming and outgoing email and visited web pages. The user can run a complete scan of all files at any time and also review reports on the scanned files (see Figure 16.2). Popular antivirus programs include Norton Antivirus and McAfee VirusScan. Microsoft also has a free antivirus application called Microsoft Security Essentials available for download from http://ic3.emcp.net/security.

Figure 16.2 Antivirus Program's Scan History

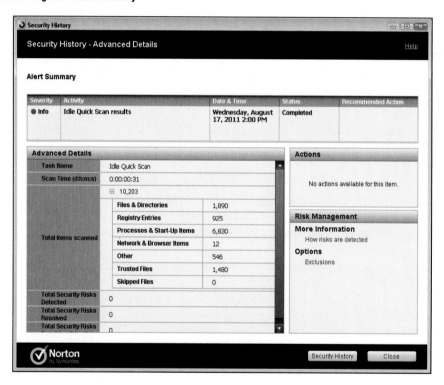

Anti-spyware Software Anti-spyware applications look for known spyware and adware programs, and offer to disable or remove them from your system. Like antivirus applications, anti-spyware programs look for signatures that identify a spyware or adware component. Most anti-spyware applications can remove lesser security and privacy threats, such as tracking cookies. Recall that cookies are text files containing your personal information that web pages place on your hard disk and then access later when you re-visit that same web page. Most cookies are harmless, but some of them can be used to compromise your privacy online. Many antivirus applications include anti-spyware protection, so you may not have to obtain a separate anti-spyware application. Some anti-spyware applications run continuously in the background, like an antivirus application. Others run only when you specifically open them up and initiate a scan.

Windows Defender is a free anti-spyware tool that comes with Windows. Other free and commercial anti-spyware programs are available, such as Spybot Search & Destroy (http://ic3.emcp.net/spybot) and Ad-Aware (http://ic3.emcp.net/adaware). As with antivirus applications, anti-spyware applications are most effective when their definitions are up-to-date.

Exercise 16.2   Checking for Antivirus and Anti-Spyware Software

1. Click Start, click *Control Panel*, click *System and Security*, and then click *Action Center*.

2. Click the down arrow to the right of the Security heading to expand that category.

3. Note whether *On* or *Off* displays next to *Virus protection* and note what application is being used.

4. Click the <u>Show me the antivirus programs on this computer</u> hyperlink.

   This opens a dialog box showing each antivirus program and its status.

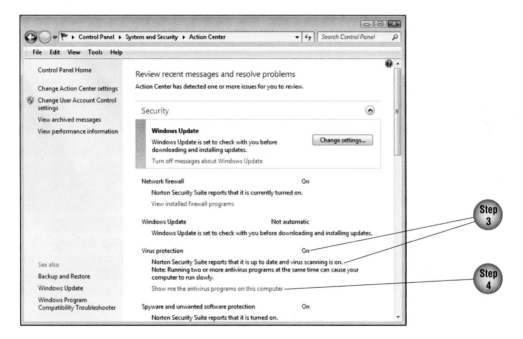

5. Click Close to close the dialog box.

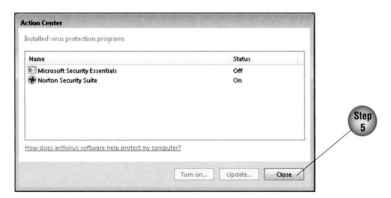

6. Note whether *On* or *Off* displays next to *Spyware and unwanted software protection* and note what application is being used.

7. Click *View installed antispyware programs*.

   This opens a dialog box showing each anti-spyware program and its status.

8. Click Close to close the dialog box.

9. Close the Control Panel window.

Diagnosing and Fixing Malware Infection

Occasionally a virus or other malware may get around the anivirus application, especially if the threat is new or if your program's definitions are out of date. When a system is infected, you may experience some of the following symptoms:

- You are prevented from installing new antivirus software or from running your current antivirus software. This is a common result of virus infection.

- Your system runs slower. Many malware infections bog down a system or cripple it.

- CPU and memory usage are unusually high. This would happen if the malware program is using your system for its own computing purposes.

- A warning or message box repeatedly displays on the screen, especially one that suggests that you buy a certain product to fix the problem.

- Your email contacts receive emails from your account that you did not send.

- You encounter more pop-up ads than normal when you use your web browser.

If you start experiencing these symptoms, check your antivirus program. If your antivirus program is running, do a full virus scan immediately. If you cannot use your local antivirus program, then access an online virus checker. TrendMicro offers a good free virus checker at http://ic3.emcp.net/housecall. Scan your system with the online checker and then follow the advice the scanner recommends. If the infected system will not open a web browser, you might need to consult an IT professional. After the infection has been removed, you may need to repair or reinstall your antivirus software and download updates.

Configuring Web Browser Settings to Avoid Malware Infection

Quick Steps

Set the Security Level for the Internet Zone

1. In Internet Explorer, click Tools.
2. Click *Internet options*.
3. Click Security tab.
4. Click Internet icon.
5. Click *Default Level* if a slider is not visible.
6. Drag slider to desired setting.
7. Click OK.

When the security settings on your browser are set too low, your computer is vulnerable to a variety of security risks. Fortunately, in most browsers the default settings provide adequate security against malware. In the Internet Options dialog box of Internet Explorer, you can drag a slider bar to choose between Medium, Medium-High, and High security presets. In most cases, Medium-High is the best balance between functionality and security (see Figure 16.3). Note that there are different zones in the Internet Explorer security settings and that each zone has a different security setting. Zones enable you to classify websites into categories and act on each category in a different way. The default zone, Internet, is the zone used for most web pages. The other zones are Local intranet (your LAN), Trusted sites, and Restricted sites. For each of these zones, you can click its name and then click the Sites button to enter specific sites to be included in that zone.

Figure 16.3 Security Tab of Internet Options Dialog Box The Medium-high setting for the Internet zone is selected.

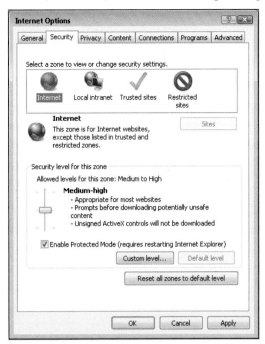

 Lesson 16.3 **Safeguarding Your Privacy and Identity Online**

IC³ 3-4.2.5, 3-4.2.7, 3-4.2.8

Once you have established an Internet connection, a new set of security and privacy concerns become relevant. Security threats can come from many directions, including pop-ups, cookies, phishing, and identity theft. In this lesson you will learn how to identify and avoid potential scams and identity threats.

Understanding Identity Fraud and Social Engineering

Impersonating someone online is relatively easy. All you need is enough personal information to convince a website or service provider that you are that person. This is how millions of consumers each year become victims of identity theft. Someone who uses your identity could make purchases or open credit accounts in your name, change your contact information in online databases (to prevent the bills for purchases from reaching you), or change your passwords (to prevent you from logging in online to check an account's status).

The most important thing you can do to prevent someone from stealing your online identity is to use strong passwords and change them frequently. (Recall that a strong password is one that is difficult for someone to guess.) Gaining access to someone's user name and password for a site is one of the most common ways that criminals operate. If you keep your passwords written down somewhere, guard that information diligently.

Unfortunately, many thieves can trick people into sharing the very information that allows identify fraud to persist. Tricking individuals into letting their guard down or sharing personal information to exploit them is called **social engineering**. Although this topic discusses social engineering as it applies to online threats, this type of social manipulation has always existed in society.

social engineering The practice of tricking individuals into letting their guard down and sharing personal information that can be used to commit fraud or other criminal activity

Social engineering online includes emails, instant messages, or pop-up messages that promise an incentive but require you to send personal information. Offline, social engineering includes calling someone on the telephone and pretending to be a representative of a bank or credit card company, or posing as a census worker to gather information in person. You should suspect a social engineering scheme when an offer comes to you unexpectedly, seems too good to be true, requires you to fill out a form with personal information to win something or get a discount, or asks for information that a legitimate company would not need to know. For example, your bank already knows your account number, so any message that appears to be from your bank but asks for your account number is probably fraudulent. Knowing if someone is honest or dishonest is difficult to determine, so be cautious when dealing with anyone who asks questions about the following information:

- Your age or date of birth

- Where you were born

- Your mother's maiden name

- The school(s) you attend

- Your current address

- Your favorite sports team

- Your favorite type of music

- The names of your pets (because people often use these as passwords)

Many of these questions could give the solicitor enough information to work out the answers to "forgotten password" security questions which could lead to identity fraud.

Understanding Phishing

phishing Creating a site that masquerades as a legitimate secure site but actually steals login information from people who visit it

Creating a site that masquerades as a legitimate secure site but actually steals your login information is called **phishing** (or *spoofing*). Phishing employs many tactics, which are evolving all the time. For example, you might get an email that looks to be from your bank, asking you to follow a link to their site to update your details. The email looks authentic and when you follow the link, the site looks much like the site of the bank, except the page is probably not secure, and some links on the page may not be operational.

Most browsers have some form of built-in phishing protection. Internet Explorer uses a different color background within the address bar to identify the legitimacy of websites. For example, if the address bar's background is green, the phishing filter has determined the site is legitimate. A yellow background indicates caution because there is a problem with the verification, while a red background indicates that this site is probably not legitimate and should be avoided.

SmartScreen filter The phishing filter in Internet Explorer

The phishing filter in Internet Explorer is called the **SmartScreen filter** and it can be enabled or disabled. Typically you would want to leave it enabled, because it provides information to you and does not prevent you from doing anything. A minor drawback to leaving it enabled is that it causes your browser to check every page you visit, which may result in slightly slower browser speed. If you seldom visit secure sites and you want to check only specific sites, you might turn the SmartScreen filter off and use the *Check this website* command to manually check a page. To do this, click Tools, point to *Smartscreen Filter*, and then click *Check this website*.

Other web browsers have their own versions of phishing filters. For example, in Google Chrome, you can turn the phishing filter on and off by clicking the wrench icon, clicking *Options*, and then in the *Under the Hood* section, clicking the *Enable phishing and malware protection* check box to insert or remove a check mark.

The following are ways to identify a phishing email message:

- The message contains misspelled words or bad grammar. Phishing emails often originate from non-English-speaking countries.

- You are asked to supply information or to log in to your existing account. Legitimate emails from financial institutions provide you with information; they are not typically used to collect information from you.

- The message is urgent or contains warnings or threats. Phishing emails often contain an urgent warning or threat that you must click on a link and act immediately to avoid a problem.

- The URL that displays when you hover over a hyperlink within the email does not match the address in the hyperlink.

- The message addresses you in a generic fashion. Phishing emails are less likely to show your name and more likely to say something generic like "Dear Customer" or "Hello!" Be aware, however, that some more sophisticated phishing schemes may have the ability to include your name in the email.

- The message was sent to numerous recipients. If a message was sent to a large list of recipients, or if the other recipients are hidden, it is more likely to be a phishing email.

- The message claims to be from a United States government agency. Government agencies like the IRS do not conduct important business through email; they use postal mail.

- The message requests that you submit a CVV code (the three digit number on the back of a credit card) to process a refund or deposit to your account. The CVV number is not required for deposits to be made on credit card accounts; it is only required for withdrawals.

- You are asked to complete a form on an unsecure site (that is, sites where the URL begins with *http* instead of *https*). Email forms on unsecure sites are never used by legitimate businesses to collect financial information such as credit card numbers.

- The message requests basic information that you would have already supplied to the business or agency. Legitimate businesses and government agencies that already have you in their record-keeping systems do not need to know your name, Social Security number, phone number, or any other personal information. Requests like these should be considered illegitimate.

Quick Steps

Turn SmartScreen Filter Off or On

1. In Internet Explorer, click Tools.
2. Point to *SmartScreen Filter*.
3. Click *Turn off SmartScreen Filter* or *Turn on SmartScreen Filter*.
4. Click OK.

Use SmartScreen Filter Manually (when automatic use is turned off)

1. In Internet Explorer, click Tools.
2. Point to *SmartScreen Filter*.
3. Click *Check this website*.
4. Click OK.

Controlling Cookies

A cookie can tell an advertiser that you have previously viewed a certain ad, or can keep track of the items in your shopping cart at a business site. Cookies are harmless 99.99% of the time and may perform useful functions that you want, such as remembering the items that you have placed in a shopping cart or on a wish list. However, two risks are involved with allowing cookies on your computer. One is a privacy threat, since a cookie can deliver personal information to a website; the other risk is a security threat, since a virus or Trojan horse infection might copy a stored password from a cookie and deliver it to someone else.

Cookies can be categorized according to how they were created. A **first-party cookie** is one that is placed on your computer by a website you visit. For example, when you go to www.amazon.com, a cookie provides your name so that the site can welcome you by name. A **third-party cookie** is one that is placed on your computer by an advertisement on a website you have visited, where the ad's parent company is not related to the owner of the website. For example, as you browse on Facebook, a third-party cookie might record which ads you have clicked on, indicating your interest in certain products.

first-party cookie A cookie that is placed on the computer by a website you visit

third-party cookie A cookie that is placed on the computer by an ad on a website

Cookies can also be categorized according to how long they remain. A **session cookie** is one that lasts only as long as the web browser is open. When you finish your web browsing session, session cookies are deleted. For example, on some websites, shopping carts are set with session cookies, so if you do not place the order in the current browsing session, the next time you visit that site the shopping cart is empty. Other websites with shopping carts use persistent cookies, so that you can return to the site after you end the session and the items you placed in the shopping cart will still be there. A **persistent cookie** is one that stays on the hard disk after the browser closes, either indefinitely or for a certain number of days.

All browsers can be configured to control how your system stores each type of cookie. You can create rules for handling cookies, identify sites from which to allow or deny cookies, and delete existing cookies. In Internet Explorer, you adjust the settings at the Privacy tab of the Internet Options dialog box by dragging the slider bar in the *Settings* area (see Figure 16.4).

Figure 16.4 Privacy Tab of Internet Options Dialog Box

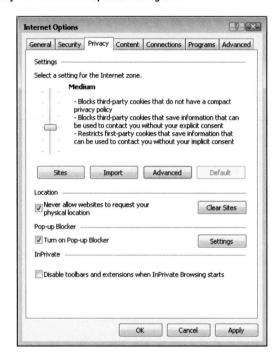

Quick Steps

Adjust Cookie Acceptance Policy

1. In Internet Explorer, click Tools.
2. Click *Internet options*.
3. Click Privacy tab.
4. Click Default if slider does not display.
5. Drag slider to desired setting.
6. Click OK.

Allow or Block Cookies from a Website

1. In Internet Explorer, click Tools.
2. Click *Internet options*.
3. Click Privacy tab.
4. Click Sites.
5. Type site in the *Address of website* box.
6. Click *Allow* or *Block*.
7. Click OK.

Specify Advanced Cookie Handling Settings

1. In Internet Explorer, click Tools.
2. Click *Internet options*.
3. Click Privacy tab.
4. Click Advanced.
5. Click desired setting under *First-party Cookies* and *Third party Cookies*.
6. Click *Always allow session cookies* check box to remove or add check mark.
7. Click OK.
8. Click OK.

You can allow or block cookies from a particular website by clicking the Sites button on the Privacy tab. From there, type a site and click Allow or Block to specify a setting for that site. To set up policies for certain types of cookies, click the Advanced button on the Privacy tab, click the desired setting for first party and third party cookies, and then choose to allow or block session cookies.

You can delete cookies that may already be stored on the hard disk using your web browser. To do this, in the Internet Options dialog box (see Figure 16.4), click the General tab and then click the Delete button in the *Browsing history* section. This displays the Delete Browsing History dialog box. From there you can choose to delete a variety of personal information from Internet Explorer, including cookies (see Figure 16.5).

Quick Steps
Clear Existing Cookies
1. In Internet Explorer, click Tools.
2. Click *Internet options*.
3. Click General tab.
4. Click Delete.
5. Verify that *Cookies* check box contains a check mark.
6. Click Delete.
7. Click OK.

Figure 16.5 Delete Browsing History Dialog Box Allows the user to delete personal information from Internet Explorer, including cookies

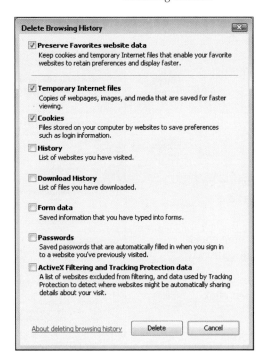

Exercise 16.3   Managing Cookies

1. Open Internet Explorer, click Tools on the menu bar, and then click *Internet options* at the drop-down list.

2. At the Internet Options dialog box, click the Privacy tab, drag the slider bar to *Medium* if it is not already there. Examine the information that displays describing the Medium setting.

3. Click the Sites button.

   This opens the Per Site Privacy Actions dialog box.

4. In the *Address of website* box, type **www.emcp.com** and then click the Allow button.

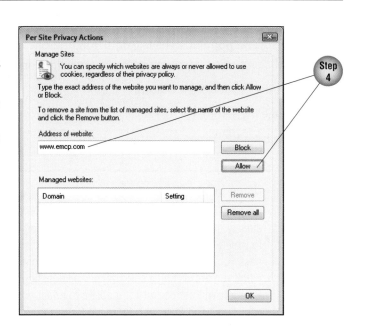

5. Click OK.

6. At the Internet Options dialog box, click the Advanced button.

   This opens the Advanced Privacy Settings dialog box.

7. Click the *Override automatic cookie handling* check box to insert a check mark.

8. Click *Prompt* under Third-party Cookies.

9. Click the *Always allow session cookies* check box to insert a check mark.

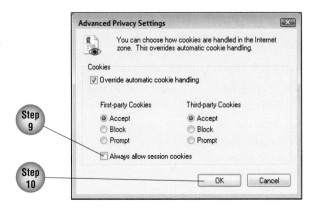

10. Click OK.

11. Click the *Never allow websites to request your physical location* check box.

12. Click the Clear Sites button.

13. Click the General tab.

14. Click the Delete button.

15. At the Delete Browsing History dialog box, click the *Cookies* check box to insert a check mark if it is not already marked.

16. Click the *Preserve Favorites website data* check box to insert a check mark if it is not already marked.

17. Clear all other check boxes and then click the Delete button.

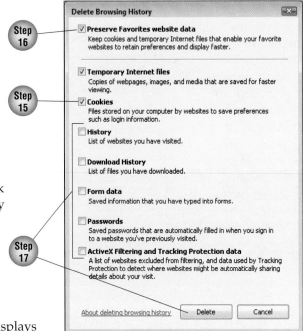

18. Click OK to close the Internet Options dialog box.

19. Click on the X on the status message that displays at the bottom of the browser window, telling you that the web browser has finished deleting the selected history.

20. Visit several popular websites, until you find one that triggers a Privacy Alert dialog box.

    The dialog box will prompt you and ask whether or not to save a certain cookie.

21. Click the Block Cookie button.

22. Change the setting back to *Allow for third-party cookies*, as you did in Steps 6 through 8.

23. Close Internet Explorer.

Drilling Down

Using InPrivate Browsing

Internet Explorer versions 8 and higher include a highly secure InPrivate Browsing mode that closely guards your privacy. When you start an InPrivate session, a new browser window opens in which none of the history is stored (regardless of your browser's normal history settings). No passwords, login information, cookies, or cached temporary files are stored. This mode is useful when you are visiting a site that may be questionable as to its safety, because in this mode Internet Explorer will not permit the website to affect your computer. To turn on InPrivate browsing, first click Tools and then click *InPrivate Browsing*. To exit InPrivate mode, close the browser window.

Lesson 16.4 Protecting Minors Online

)C³ 3-4.2.5

The Internet is designed primarily for adults, and a significant amount of content on the Internet is unsuitable for children, such as sexual content, violent images, and profanity. Those responsible for the care of a minor must be aware that a child can easily access inappropriate content on the Internet. Strict content monitoring policies and applications, however, can make it more difficult for the adults that use the computer. It is important to find a reasonable balance between protecting children and helping them avoid illegal or harmful activities and allowing the adult users of the computer reasonable freedom in using the Internet.

One way to ensure that a minor is kept away from age-inappropriate content is to monitor his or her Internet usage. Many websites are created just for children and do not contain adult content, so be ready to redirect a minor to appropriate sites as needed.

Some parents and guardians choose to use parental controls to assist in monitoring or limiting access to certain sites and content online. **Parental controls** are software features that restrict certain activities or prevent the display of certain web content. Some operating systems have parental controls built into them, but third-party parental control software can also be used. In Windows 7, parental controls are set from the Control Panel, in the *User Accounts and Family Safety* section. Click the <u>Set up parental controls for any user</u> hyperlink, choose the user for which to set controls, click *On, enforce current settings*, and then click the links for each control type to configure it.

In Windows 7, parental controls allow parents and guardians to:

* Control when users are allowed to log on to the computer by setting time limits for each user. This allows the parent or guardian to determine when children can and cannot log on. Different logon hours can be set for every day of the week. This ensures that if minors are logged on when their allotted time ends, they automatically will be logged off.

* Control access to games by determining the allowed age-rating level. Parents or guardians can determine the types of content they want to block and decide whether to allow or block unrated or specific online games.

* Allow or block specific programs. Parents or guardians can prevent children from running specific programs. For example, a parent might block a DVD player application to prevent the child from watching movies on the PC.

parental controls Software features that restrict certain activities or prevent the display of certain web content

Quick Steps

Set Parental Controls
1. Click Start.
2. Click *Control Panel.*
3. Click <u>Set up parental controls for any user</u>.
4. Click user.
5. Set desired parental controls under Windows Settings.
6. Click *On, enforce current settings.*
7. Click OK.

Exercise 16.4A Setting Parental Controls

1. Click Start and then click *Control Panel.*

2. Click <u>Set up parental controls for any user</u> under *User Accounts and Family Safety.*

3. Click the user (either your own account or an account that your instructor specifies). This action displays the settings for that user.

4. Click *On, enforce current settings.*

5. Click *Time limits.*

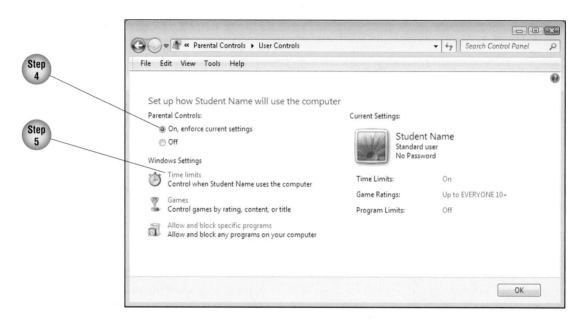

6. Drag across blocks to change their color.

   Blue blocks represent times that are not allowed and white blocks represent times that are allowed.

7. Click OK.

8. Click *Games.*

9. Click *Set game ratings.*

10. Click *EVERYONE 10+.*

11. Click OK.

12. Click OK.

    This action returns you to the user controls.

13. Click OK to accept the changes for this user.

14. Close the Control Panel.

Quick Steps

Open Content Advisor

1. In Internet Explorer, click Tools.
2. Click *Internet options.*
3. Click Content tab.
4. Click Settings *button* under *Content Advisor.*
5. Enter password if prompted.
6. Click OK.

In Internet Explorer, you can also turn on the Content Advisor feature, which is a feature that limits the websites that can be displayed. The Content Advisor feature works in different versions of Windows and also Mac OS X, as long as they are running Internet Explorer. Other browsers may have their own user-specific content restriction settings.

To configure the Content Advisor, click Tools and then click *Internet options.* Click the Content tab and then click the Settings button under *Content Advisor.* If a Supervisor Password Required message box displays (for example, if you previously have set a password), then type the password and click OK. Adjust the Content Advisor settings as needed, click OK, and then click the Enable button. Reenter the supervisor password if you are prompted and then click OK at the confirmation box.

Within Content Advisor, you can select a rating that describes the type of web content that each user is allowed to view. For example, allowing a teenager to view sites that contain content that an elementary school student should not view may be appropriate. To set the rating for each type of content, click the Ratings tab in the Content Advisor dialog box, and then click one of the categories. Drag the slider bar to set its rating. A different slider bar, with different options, is available for each content type.

You can also use Content Advisor to allow a site regardless of its rating. To allow a site, in the Content Advisor dialog box click the Approved Sites tab. Type the URL of the site in the *Allow this website* text box, click Always, and then click OK.

Many sites have no rating. You can specify whether unrated sites should be allowed or not. On the General tab in the Content Advisor dialog box, insert or remove a check mark in the *Users can see websites that have no rating* check box.

Content Advisor is password-protected. You can change its password from the General tab by clicking the Change password button and then entering the old and new passwords to confirm. You may also want to add a hint to help you remember the password. Content Advisor may be effective in preventing access to objectionable websites, but it also can impede normal browsing. If you decide not to use Content Advisor, open the Internet Options dialog box (click Tools and then click *Internet options*), click the Content tab, and then click Disable. You will be prompted to type the Content Advisor password to confirm your decision.

Quick Steps

Select Content Advisor Ratings

1. Click Ratings tab from Content Advisor dialog box.
2. Click a category, and drag the slider to set its rating.
3. Repeat Step 2 for each category.

Allow a Site in Content Advisor

1. Click Approved Sites tab from Content Advisor dialog box.
2. Type the URL of site in *Allow this website* box.
3. Click Always.
4. Click OK.

Turn Off Content Advisor

1. In Internet Explorer, click Tools.
2. Click *Internet options*.
3. Click Content tab.
4. Click Disable.
5. Type password in the *Password* box.
6. Click OK three times.
7. Close and reopen web browser.

Exercise 16.4B   Using Content Advisor

1. In Internet Explorer, click Tools on the menu bar and then click *Internet options* at the drop-down menu.

2. Click the Content tab.

3. Click the Settings button in the *Content Advisor* section.

4. If prompted, type the password in the *Password* box and then click OK.

5. Click the first category on the Ratings tab.

6. Drag the slider bar to *Limited*.

7. Repeat Steps 5 and 6 for each category, setting each one to *Limited*.

8. Click the Approved Sites tab.

9. In the *Allow this website* box, type **www.emcp.com**.

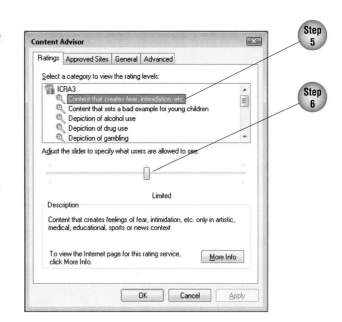

10. Click Always.

11. Click OK.

12. Click Enable (enter or create new password if required).

13. If a confirmation box displays, click OK.

14. Click OK to close the Internet Options dialog box.

15. Go to www.disney.com.

    A Content Advisor warning displays because this page does not have a rating.

16. Click *Always allow this website to be viewed*.

17. Type the password in the *Password* box.

18. Click OK.

    This action opens the site.

19. Click Tools on the menu bar and then click *Internet options*.

20. Click the Content tab, click Disable, type the password, and then click OK.

21. Click OK and then click OK to close the Internet Options dialog box.

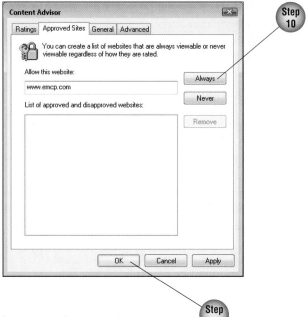

Step 10

Step 11

Drilling Down

Teaching Minors about Online Privacy

To help protect children from online predators and identity thieves, make sure the children under your supervision know the following:

- Never give out your password to anyone.
- Do not disclose your real name online. Use aliases when communicating in public forums rather than your real name
- Do not arrange to meet anyone in person that has contacted you online
- Involve your parents if you have any doubts about whether an online activity is safe

---

Lesson 16.5   **Making Computing More Accessible**

 3-4.1.4

People with physical disabilities and challenges such as blindness, deafness, or limited motor skills or mobility may find it difficult to use a computer or access the Internet using common methods. Fortunately, many devices and technologies are available that make computers more accessible. In this lesson, you will learn about some of the ways computers can be adapted to serve people with physical challenges.

Understanding Assistive Hardware and Software

People who have limited mobility or motor skills may not be able to use a regular keyboard or mouse as easily as other users. Assistive hardware is available that can help in some cases. For example:

- **Alternative keyboards:** Alternative keyboards have larger-than-normal or smaller-than-normal keys; alternative keyboard layouts are also available, as are keyboard layouts that can be used with one hand.

- **Electronic pointing devices:** Electronic pointing devices enable the user to control the mouse arrow pointer on the screen. These devices operate using ultrasound or infrared beams and can enable users to move the mouse arrow pointer with head or eye movements, inhaling and exhaling, nerve signals, and even brain waves.

- **Wands and sticks:** Pointing wands and sticks are worn on the head, held in the mouth, or strapped on the chin and are used to press keys on a keyboard.

- **Sip-and-puff:** Sip-and-puff devices enable users with substantial mobility limitations to control computers with their mouths by breathing in and out (see Figure 16.6).

- **Joysticks:** A joystick can be manipulated with a hand, foot, chin, or any other mobile body part, and used to control the mouse arrow pointer on-screen.

- **Touchscreens:** Touch-sensitive screens make it easier for people with limited mobility to select an option because it allows direct selection rather than indirect selection through the mouse or keyboard.

- **Refreshable Braille displays:** Refreshable Braille displays provide tactile information output, so blind users can read the text that displays on the screen in Braille. In Braille, each character is represented by a unique arrangement of raised dots. A refreshable Braille display mechanically lifts small rounded plastic or metal pins as needed to form the Braille characters. The user reads a line of text with his or her fingers and then can refresh the display to read the next line.

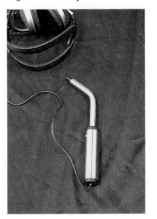

Figure 16.6 Sip-and-Puff Device

In addition to assistive hardware, many software aids exist for people with disabilities. For example, software typing aids such as word prediction utilities and add-on spell checkers can reduce the required number of keystrokes, making typing less laborious for users with limited mobility. Keyboard filters also enable users to quickly access the keys they need and avoid accidentally pressing keys they do not want. For people who can use a keyboard but not a mouse, or vice-versa, software is available that allows a keyboard to move the mouse arrow pointer, or that allows a mouse arrow pointer to access an on-screen keyboard.

For those who have difficulty seeing the monitor, special display modes are available in most operating systems. For example, most operating systems include a number of high-contrast, large-text modes. And for those who cannot see the monitor at all, screen-reading applications, also called text-to-speech synthesizers, are available that read the contents of each dialog box and window aloud, and voice recognition programs enable users to give commands and enter data using their voices rather than a mouse or keyboard.

Using the Ease of Access Center

Windows 7 includes an Ease of Access Center (see Figure 16.7) in the Control Panel that enables users to set up a computer to accommodate any combination of physical challenges. To access it, open the Control Panel, click *Ease of Access*, and then click *Ease of Access Center*. Set up the features as needed for the abilities of the person who will be using the computer. Some of the tools include the following:

- **Narrator:** The Narrator tool reads screen content aloud.

- **Audio Description:** Audio description turns on closed-captioning of videos (when available).

Quick Steps

Set Accessibility Options in Windows 7

1. Click Start, click *Control Panel*, and then click *Ease of Access*.
2. Click *Ease of Access Center*.
3. Set up features needed.
4. Close Control Panel.

- **Magnifier:** The magnifier enlarges a selected portion of the display for easier reading.

- **High Contrast:** This display mode sets the Windows display to a high-contrast, easy-to-read mode.

- **On-Screen Keyboard:** The On-Screen Keyboard provides a clickable keyboard that users can access with a mouse.

- **Mouse Pointers:** Special mouse pointers that are large and easy to see make using a mouse easier for people with limited vision.

- **Mouse Keys:** The Mouse Key feature enables the numeric keyboard to move the mouse around on the screen.

- **Sticky Keys:** The Sticky Keys feature enables key combinations, such as Ctrl + Alt + Delete, to be pressed one key at a time.

- **Toggle Keys:** The Toggle Keys feature plays a tone to alert the user when the Caps Lock, Num Lock, or Scroll Lock keys have been pressed.

- **Filter Keys:** The Filter Keys feature ignores or slows down brief or repeated keystrokes, and adjusts keyboard repeat rates.

- **Sound Sentry:** The Sound Sentry feature uses a visual cue (such as a flashing active window) instead of playing a sound when a system sound alert plays.

Most of these features can be configured in the Ease of Access Center in the Control Panel; many of them are also available as stand-alone utilities in the Start menu. Click Start, click *All Programs*, click *Accessories*, and then click *Ease of Access*.

Figure 16.7 **Ease of Access Center**

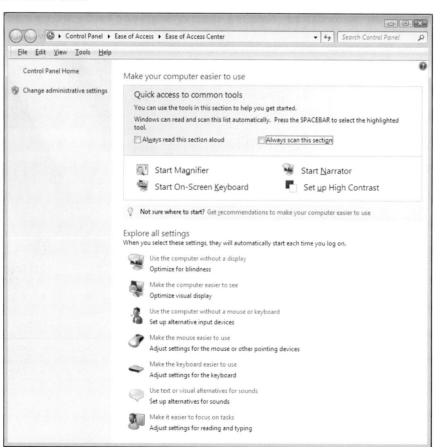

Exercise 16.5A Using the Narrator

1. Verify that your computer's sound is not muted and is audible.

2. Click Start, click *All Programs*, click *Accessories*, click *Ease of Access*, and then click *Narrator*.

   This opens the Microsoft Narrator dialog box, which immediately starts reading all your actions and typing aloud.

3. Open and close several windows, and notice what the Narrator tool reads.

4. Click Exit in the Narrator window.

5. Click Yes to confirm.

Step 4

Exercise 16.5B Using the On-Screen Keyboard Tool

1. Click Start, click *All Programs*, click *Accessories*, click *Ease of Access*, and then click *On-Screen Keyboard*.

2. Open a Notepad window and then type your name by clicking the keys on the On-Screen Keyboard.

3. Exit Notepad without saving your changes.

4. Close the On-Screen Keyboard window.

Exercise 16.5C Using High-Contrast Display Modes

1. Click Start, click *Control Panel*, click *Ease of Access*, and then click *Ease of Access Center*.

2. Click *Set up High Contrast*.

   Note the shortcut keys listed under High Contrast: Alt + Left SHIFT + PRINT SCREEN.

3. Press Alt + Left Shift + Print Screen.

   This opens the High Contrast dialog box.

4. Click Yes.

   This action causes the screen to change to the high-contrast colors.

5. Click the <u>Choose a High Contrast theme</u> hyperlink under the *High Contrast* heading.

6. Click *High Contrast White*. Note how the display changes.

7. Click *High Contrast #2*. Note how the display changes.

8. Click *High Contrast Black*. Note how the display changes.

9. Press Alt + Left Shift + Print Screen again.

   This turns off the high-contrast mode.

10. Close the Control Panel.

Drilling Down

Designing Web Pages with Accessibility in Mind

Most web pages are created with the assumption that the person viewing them has normal eyesight and is able to use both a mouse and a keyboard. For anyone that has a disability, certain websites can be difficult or even impossible to view and navigate.

To make using the Web easier for people with disabilities, the World Wide Web Consortium (W3C), an international standards organization, created a document called the Web Content Accessibility Guidelines. The Web Content Accessibility Guidelines document outlines strategies and goals for making web content more accessible. You can read more about these guidelines at http://ic3.emcp.net/accessguidelines. They are based on four principles of accessibility:

- **Perceivable:** Information and user interface components must be presented to users in ways they can perceive, meaning the content on a web page can be read with screen reading applications if required.
- **Operable:** The user interface navigation components must be operable. This means that users must be able to operate the interface, and the interface cannot require interaction that the user cannot perform. For example, each navigation link and button on a site should be accessible not only with the mouse but also with the keyboard.
- **Understandable:** The information and the operation of the user interface must be understandable and work in predictable ways. This means that users must be able to understand the information as well as the operation of the user interface. For example, any content presented in graphical format should include an alternate text-based description so that screen-reading programs can be used if necessary.
- **Robust:** Content must be robust enough that it can be interpreted reliably by a wide variety of user agents, including assistive technologies. This means that as technologies evolve, the content should remain accessible and compatible.

Individual guidelines that explain how to achieve these goals are available, and you can find many websites that recommend best-practices for accessible web design. For an extensive list of practical ways you can make a website more accessible, see http://ic3.emcp.net/techniques. For training in basic accessible web design, see http://ic3.emcp.net/accessit.

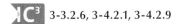

Lesson 16.6 | **Identifying Legal and Ethical Personal Computer and Internet Use**

IC³ 3-3.2.6, 3-4.2.1, 3-4.2.9

Earlier in this topic, you learned about various types of security and privacy threats that online users may encounter. Some online activities are illegal, such as stealing people's login information for shopping sites and buying things with their credit cards. **Cybercrime** is any crime that involves a computer and a network. Some common cybercrimes include:

> **cybercrime** A crime that involves a computer and a network

- Creating and spreading computer viruses or malware

- Using the Internet to commit fraud or identity theft

- Creating and using phishing sites to trick people into sharing private information

- Communicating online to set up offline crimes such as illegal sales of drugs or weapons

- Targeting a particular computer or website for harassment and attack

- Harming an enemy or competitor (individual, business, or government) by attempting to shut down their computer communications

- Creating websites that enable others to illegally download music or videos

Other online activities are not illegal, but are widely considered unethical because they profit at the expense of the greater good. Unethical activities are considered selfish, dishonest, or unkind, and include sending out unrequested advertising emails (spam); bullying or harassing other users, including posting unkind messages or comments directed at a user or users; using electronic communication tools to cheat on exams, and creating fake or embellished profiles on social networking sites for the purpose of deceiving others. For example, it is considered unethical for a person to upload a picture of someone else on a dating website, or lie about height, weight, age, or income. Although legal actions may not be taken against unethical online activity, a user who violates online ethical standards may be heavily criticized by the online community and may be banned from using certain sites or servers.

Understanding Copyright and Trademark Laws

Businesses and individuals can be sued if they received financial gain from the unauthorized use of copyrighted or trademarked material. United States law represents several types of content ownership, including the following:

> **trademark** Identifies ownership of a word, phrase, symbol, or design that identifies or distinguishes one brand from another

- **Trademark:** A **trademark** proves ownership of a word, phrase, symbol, or design, or a combination of these, that identifies and distinguishes one brand or item from another. A trademark can be created simply by common usage; it does not have to be registered. You cannot use trademarked material in a way that suggests it belongs to you and not its actual owner.

> **registered trademark** A trademark that has been established by registering the work with the United States Patent and Trademark Office

- **Registered trademark:** A **registered trademark** has been established by registering the work with the United States Patent and Trademark Office.

- **Service mark:** A **service mark** is the same as a trademark except it is for a service rather than a product. It can be registered or unregistered.

> **service mark** A trademark that is for a service rather than a product; it can be registered or unregistered

- **Patent:** A **patent** establishes the ownership of an invention. Patents are also registered with the United States Patent and Trademark Office. You can patent a process, machine, manufactured item, improvement, design of a manufactured item, or form of plant life. You cannot reproduce a patented item without the permission of the patent holder.

> **patent** Identifies ownership of an invention

- **Copyright:** A copyright identifies the ownership of an original artistic or literary work. You cannot copyright a fact, idea, system, or method of operation. Copyrights in the United States are registered by the U. S. Copyright Office, but your work is copyrighted at the moment you create it, even if you choose not to register it. If your copyright is not registered, you cannot bring a lawsuit if someone tries to steal your work. You cannot reproduce copyrighted work without the permission of the copyright holder. Some legal exceptions exist; for example, parody or satire based on a copyrighted work is legally acceptable in some cases.

Avoiding Plagiarism with Citation and Bibliography Tools

Plagiarism is a variant of copyright violation; it refers to using someone else's creative work as if it is your own without citing the actual source. Quoting directly from a source or paraphrasing the source is acceptable, but you must appropriately cite the source using a footnote, endnote, or some other citation method, so it is clear that you are not trying to pass off the work as your own. Several well-established citation methods are available, such as APA (American Psychological Association) and MLA (Modern Language Association). These citation styles have guidelines that explain exactly how each source should be cited. When you are assigned a research paper, your instructor may tell you which citation method to use or may teach you a citation method.

Microsoft Word's References tab contains Citations & Bibliography tools you can use to implement whatever citation method is appropriate for your work. Once you have filled out an information form about the source material, Word will automatically format footnotes or a bibliography page, as needed. To do this, first create citations in Word on the References tab, using the Insert Citation command. Then position the insertion point at the end of the document and use the Bibliography command (also on the References tab) to create a bibliography that lists all your sources. You can use the *Style* drop-down list in the Citations & Bibliography group to choose which citation format you want.

Responsible Online Content Creation

When you create online content, especially in places where the content will remain for a long time (such as a web page or wiki), you have a responsibility to your readers to make it as accurate and clear as possible. Keep these guidelines in mind when you create and publish content online:

- When publishing factual content, make sure you cite your sources to avoid plagiarism.

- Make sure the content you publish is valid, reliable, and relevant.

- If you have a bias or prejudice, state it upfront.

- If something is your opinion, label it clearly as such and present it in a respectful manner.

- Make sure the tone and content are appropriate for your intended audience.

Exercise 16.6   Citing Sources in Word

1. Open Microsoft Word and then open **Research.docx**. Save the document with Save As and name it **U3T16-Research**.

2. Click to position the insertion point at the end of the second sentence in the second body paragraph, immediately before the period.

3. Click the References tab, click the down-pointing arrow at the right side of the *Style* option box, and then click *APA Fifth Edition* at the drop-down list (if it is not already selected).

4. Click the Insert Citation button and then click *Add New Source* at the drop-down list.

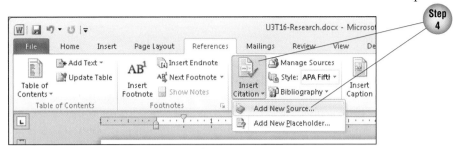

Step 4

5. In the Create Source dialog box, click the down-pointing arrow at the right side of the *Type of Source* option box and then click *Web site* at the drop-down list. Fill in the information as shown below and then click OK.

The citation is inserted in the document.

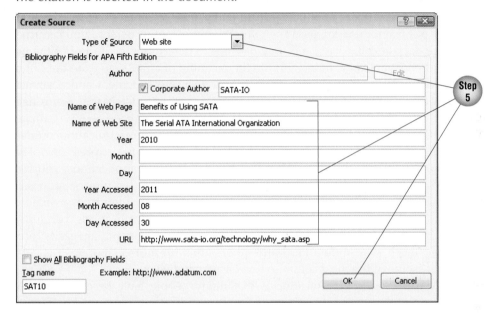

Step 5

6. Click the down-pointing arrow at the right side of the *Style* option box and then click *MLA Sixth Edition* at the drop-down list.

Notice how the citation in the paragraph changes its format; it no longer shows the date.

7. Click the Manage Sources button and then click the Edit button to edit the citation.

8. In the Edit Source dialog box, change the *Year Accessed, Month Accessed,* and *Day Accessed* to today's date and then click OK.

9. Move the insertion point to the end of the document.

10. Click the Bibliography button and then click the *Works Cited* sample at the drop-down list.

This action inserts a *Works Cited* section at the insertion point.

Step 10

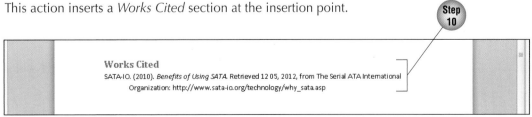

11. Save, print, and then close **U3T16-Research.docx**.

Being a Polite and Professional Online Citizen

IC³ 3-2.3.4, 3-2.3.5, 3-2.3.7, 3-3.2.6

netiquette Etiquette for online communication and behavior

In addition to rules and requirements for legal and ethical online behavior, many etiquette rules and customs exist that make the online world more pleasant and useful. Etiquette rules for online communication and behavior is sometimes called **netiquette**. If you do not know about these rules and customs, you may unknowingly anger and annoy other users and appear rude or unprofessional. In this lesson, you will learn important netiquette rules that can help you create a positive online image.

Exploring Challenges of Electronic Communication

Electronic communication (including texting, IMs, email, forum posts, and so on) is convenient and allows people to easily connect with one another. Unfortunately, this lack of face-to-face communication can result in a number of misunderstandings. When you communicate in person, you can interpret a person's body language, facial expressions, and tone of voice to determine the nature of the message. When you talk on the phone, you can gain insight into the meaning of a message from the caller's tone of voice. Tone helps you understand the difference between a sincere statement and a sarcastic one. Electronic communications lack these forms of assistance, making it more likely that a message might be misinterpreted.

emoticon A combination of symbols that represents a facial expression, such as :-); sometimes called a *smiley*

To express emotions and meaning when communicating online, some people use symbols or icons that represent facial expressions. These are sometimes called **emoticons** or *smileys*. In some applications, you can select actual icons from a list or menu that represent happiness, sadness, anger, or many other emotions. Figure 16.8 shows some emoticons available in the Yahoo! Instant Messenger application. In other applications, you must create your own by using letters and symbols. Some emoticons are easily recognized (such as a smiling face) and others are a bit more elaborate. Table 16.1 lists some of the most common text-based emoticons.

Another challenge of electronic communication is that many people have become accustomed to nearly instant responses, and they may take offense if a message is not returned quickly. For example, one person might think waiting several days before replying to a text or email message is acceptable, and another might think that a message should be returned within a few minutes. There is no "right" answer about the proper pacing of online conversations, but it is important that the participants have a common set of expectations, so that a person who waits longer than he or she thinks is customary does not feel ignored.

Figure 16.8 Emoticons in Instant Messaging

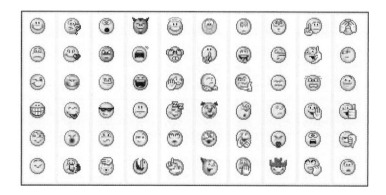

Table 16.1 Common Text-Based Emoticons

Emoticon	Meaning	Emoticon	Meaning
:) or :-)	Smile	;) or ;-)	Winking smile
>:-)	Evil grin	O.o or %-(	Confused
:(or :-(	Frown / sad	:-S	Awkward or ambivalent
:P	Sticking tongue out	:-&	Tongue tied
(((H)))	Hugs	|-O	Yawn
:-X	Kiss	:-D	Laughing
@@	Rolling your eyes	<3	Heart / love

Identifying General Etiquette Guidelines

Different communication mediums may have specific etiquette guidelines, but the following are some general guidelines that apply to all communication types:

- Choose the appropriate communication medium for the audience and the situation.

- Respond to questions and inquiries as promptly as is feasible (but not while driving), however, do not make hasty responses (a common problem of electronic communication). Think about what you want to say and review your response before sending it. If you do not know the answer to a question being asked, take the time to find the answer before replying.

- Be concise. Do not send a long message when a shorter message will suffice.

- Use an appropriate level of formality. This level may vary depending on the medium and the recipient. For example, when sending a text message to a friend, you might be more casual than when sending an email to your instructor.

- Check your spelling and grammar before sending a professional communication. Messages containing grammar and spelling errors are unprofessional and sloppy.

- Make sure that the recipient understands the tone of the message, especially if your message contains irony or sarcasm.

- Praise in public, and criticize in private. In other words, if you have something nice to say, it is okay to say it in a public forum, such as a social networking site, but if you need to complain about something, do so in a private message to only the person or group involved.

- Do not send or post any electronic communication that you would not want others to read, including your parents, instructors, and friends. Messages can be forwarded to unintended recipients.

- Do not type in all caps. In online communications, typing in all caps is the equivalent of shouting and is considered rude. Typing in all lowercase without any capital letters is also inconsiderate (although less so), because it makes your writing more difficult to read.

- Do not make libelous statements. Libel is a crime in which someone publishes or broadcasts a false statement that is damaging to someone else.

- Respect privacy. Accept when someone has chosen not to share information with you and do not try to get access to the information using other methods.

- Treat the opinions of others with respect. If you disagree, do so respectfully, criticizing the idea and not the person.

- Avoid online harassment or bullying. If encountered, notify an instructor, forum moderator, or other appropriate persons.

Understanding Text and Instant Messaging Etiquette

When sending text messages, keep in mind that many people pay for text messaging on a per-message basis. If you send several one-word or one-line messages in a row, the recipient may be charged a separate fee for each message. (You cannot assume that they are allowed unlimited text messages.) Combining multiple short messages into a single text, when possible, is a considerate step.

Abbreviations are often used in communications where you have a limited number of characters per message, such as with text messages. There's nothing wrong with using an abbreviation as long as the recipient of the message will understand it. Abbreviations should rarely (if ever) be used in formal communications. For example, you might close an IM session with a friend with *TTYL* (talk to you later), but you probably would not use that closing for an email sent to your instructor. Table 16.2 contains common abbreviations used in online communications; you may be able to think of some others as well.

Timing is also an issue when sending text messages and IMs. You should not send text messages to individuals at a time when they are likely to be sleeping, because the message notifications might wake them up.

Table 16.2 **Common Abbreviations in Electronic Communications**

Abbreviation	Meaning	Abbreviation	Meaning
AFAIK	As far as I know	JK	Just kidding
AFK	Away from keyboard	KOTC	Kiss on the cheek
B4N or BFN	Bye for now	LOL	Laughing out loud
BBIAB	Be back in a bit	OTOH	On the other hand
BRB	Be right back	ROFL	Rolling on the floor laughing
F2F	Face to face	TBD	To be determined
GMTA	Great minds think alike	TMI	Too much information
HTH	Hope this helps, or Happy to help	TTYL	Talk to you later
IDK	I do not know	THX	Thanks
IMHO	In my humble opinion	TY	Thank you
IMO	In my opinion	WB	Welcome back

Understanding Web Forum Etiquette

forum A web-based application that holds discussions and content that members upload and generate

flaming Posting a message that contains inflammatory or abusive statements

trolling Posting a message that is intentionally designed to offend others or stir up heated arguments

Many websites build online communities through forums where people can post messages that discuss topics that interest them. A **forum** is a web-based application that holds the discussions and content that members upload and generate. Some forums have their own special rules, and you can find those on the website on which the forum is hosted. Standard etiquette rules for forums include:

- Stay on topic; do not change the subject or introduce new questions in replies.

- Keep your question or comment as concise as possible.

- Do not post messages that contain inflammatory statements or personal insults (also known as **flaming**).

- Do not post messages designed to offend others or stir up heated arguments (also known as **trolling**).

- Criticize ideas, not people.

- Use proper grammar, punctuation, spelling, and capitalization.

- Do not use profanity or type in all-caps.

- Do not post the same message more than once in the same forum, or in multiple similar forums.

- Before posting a question or asking for help, search to make sure it has not already been addressed.

Most forums have moderators who police the forums to make sure everyone is following the forum rules. Any messages that violate the rules may be deleted, and users who repeatedly violate the rules may be banned from the forum.

Exercise 16.7A   Identifying Etiquette Mishaps

1. Open a web browser and find an online forum.

2. Find two or more examples of forum posts that violate different forum guidelines presented in this lesson.

3. Copy and paste the postings into a new Notepad document.

4. Under the pasted posts in Notepad, write a paragraph explaining why each post is an example of bad forum etiquette.

5. Save the document as **U3T16-Etiquette**.

6. Print and then close **U3T16-Etiquette.txt**.

7. Exit Notepad.

Exploring Email Etiquette

Even though text and instant messaging are common communication methods, the majority of online communication for businesses and schools still takes place using email. When you are sending or replying to email for school or work, you can present yourself as a considerate and professional correspondent by doing the following:

- **Keep messages concise and to the point.** Do not waste time by asking unnecessary questions or wandering off topic.

- **Avoid large attachments.** People with slow Internet connections may have to wait for a message with a large attachment to be downloaded to their PCs. Do not send large attachments unless absolutely necessary and reduce the size of the attachment whenever possible.

- **Do not forward chain letters, hoax warnings, and jokes.** Although some friends and family may want to receive forwarded messages, they are not appropriate for business and school contacts.

- **Avoid bad formatting.** Ensure good readability by using proper grammar and spelling; formatting the message using plain, easy-to-read fonts with no background color or image; including a meaningful subject line; and not writing in capital letters.

- **Put your message in context.** If there was a previous message exchange, quote it or include it at the bottom of the message if it will help the recipient remember what has been said already. However, if there was a lengthy previous exchange, limit the previous messages to the last few or only to a few pertinent sentences. Format the quoted text differently from the new text so that there is no confusion over what is new information.

- **Answer promptly.** Do not make a business or school recipient wait longer than necessary for an answer to a question or request. If there is a delay that is beyond your control, reply with a brief statement explaining the delay and letting the recipient know when to expect your full reply.

- **Reply only to those who need to see your response.** If you received a message that includes other repients, use Reply to respond only to the sender, rather than Reply to All. This avoids generating a lot of extra email traffic that the other recipients may not need.

- **Do not request delivery or read receipts.** Some email programs allow you to request a read receipt. However, this feature is viewed by many as an intrusive feature, so it should only be used when absolutely necessary.

- **Do not forward or copy private email text without permission.** If you receive an email from one person, do not assume that it is okay to forward it to other people. The correspondence was meant only for you; if you want to share it with someone else, you should get the permission of the original author first.

- **Do not use email to discuss confidential information.** You should not use email for private discussions since your message could be forwarded without your permission.

- **Do not overuse the High Priority option.** Some email programs allow you to designate an outgoing email as High Priority, and some recipients have their email programs set up so that the high priority mail displays first on the list of messages. Using High Priority is okay if your message is urgent, but using it for all messages is inconsiderate.

Exercise 16.7B Practicing Good and Bad Email Etiquette

Compose two different versions of an email to your instructor asking for a one-week extension on an assignment. In the first version, intentionally violate several email etiquette rules and list the rules you violated at the end of the email. Rewrite and resend the email to your instructor following the etiquette rules outlined in this lesson. The subject lines of the two emails should be **U3T16-Email1** and **U3T16-Email2**.

Drilling Down

Social Networking Etiquette

Social networking sites make it easy to express your opinions online, but many people make the mistake of thinking that what they post is private or does not matter. Then they are embarrassed when their words are distributed more widely than they anticipated, or when what they posted hurts someone's feelings or violates someone's trust. To avoid embarrassment—and even legal prosecution in some cases—before you post something online, ask yourself the following questions:

- Am I sure what I am saying is true, and not just a rumor or hearsay?
- Would it be unkind or hurt someone's feelings to post this?
- Is this information mine to share?
- Is it appropriate to share this information with everyone, or should I restrict it to a smaller group?
- Who else might see this, besides the people it is intended for, and what might the consequences be?
- Could someone use this posting against me or against those I represent (like my family, school, team, or organization)?
- Could this information embarrass me if I were applying for a scholarship or job in the future?

Understanding Health and Safety Issues in Computer Use

IC³ 3-4.2.1, 3-4.2.2

Compared to other activities, using a computer is not a particularly dangerous activity. However, it is possible to hurt yourself using a computer, either in the moment or through long-term usage. In this lesson, you will learn about some of the safety and health hazards related to personal computing and how you can minimize these risks.

Safety Hazards

Computers are not particularly dangerous to use, but there are several issues to be cognizant of to keep yourself and others safe. When using and maintaining a computer, be aware of the following potential hazards:

Trip-and-fall Hazards Watch out for cords that run between computers and peripherals (like monitors, printers, and routers, for example). It is easy to trip over a cord that is strung across a walkway. Re-route cords if possible so that they do not cross a path where people walk. If it is not possible, secure the cords to the floor with duct tape or cover them with a mat.

Sharp Metal Edges The metal cases of desktop PCs are bulky and have sharp corners. Position cases so that nobody is likely to bump into them or kick them. In addition, if you open up a desktop case (for example, to blow out the dust inside), be aware that the inside metal edges are sharp and some of the internal surfaces of a metal case might not be well-finished; the edges might be sharp, or there might be burrs on the metal.

Electric Shock The power supply in a desktop PC is the metal box inside the case that has colored wires coming from it. Power supplies and the wires and connectors that come out of them are safe to handle as long as you do not try to open the power supply box. You can receive a strong electric shock if you touch the capacitors inside the power supply box, so if a power supply is malfunctioning or one of its fans isn't spinning, it is best to just replace the entire power supply.

CRT monitors contain large electrical capacitors that hold charges for weeks and even months after the monitors are disconnected from power, so you should never open a CRT monitor's case. If you drop something in the vent of a CRT monitor and need to retrieve it, take it to a repair shop and have a professional disassemble the monitor. LCD monitors are generally safe to handle and even disassemble (although it is not recommended because you could easily damage an LCD monitor by disassembling it).

Heat Some parts of computers and peripherals get hot as they operate, hot enough to burn you. For example, some notebook computers get so hot that they can burn your legs if you rest the computer on your lap for a long time. In addition, laser printers have heating elements inside that melt the toner so it fuses to the paper; if you open up a laser printer (for example, to remove a paper jam), stay well away from the fuser. (See the printer's manual to determine the fuser's location.)

Back Strain Desktop computers, CRT monitors, and laser printers are all heavy, so take care when you lift them. Always lift with your knees so that you do not strain your back. If you need to transport a desktop computer, monitor, or printer to another room or location, use a cart or vehicle to transport these materials.

Exploring Ergonomics

A person using a keyboard for many hours a day can develop inflammation in the wrists from poor wrist positioning, and a person sitting at a desk all day can develop back aches, especially if the desk is not the optimal height. To minimize the health problems people experience from using computers and working in offices, business and industrial health experts rely on a science called ergonomics. **Ergonomics** is the study of designing and positioning equipment and devices to optimize their usefulness and safety to human bodies. Designing a computer work area with ergonomics in mind can make it much safer and more pleasant for users (see Figure 16.9). For more information about ergonomics, see the Occupational Safety & Health Administration website (www.osha.gov).

ergonomics The study of designing and positioning equipment and devices to optimize their usefulness and safety to human bodies

Figure 16.9 **Proper Ergonomic Positioning**

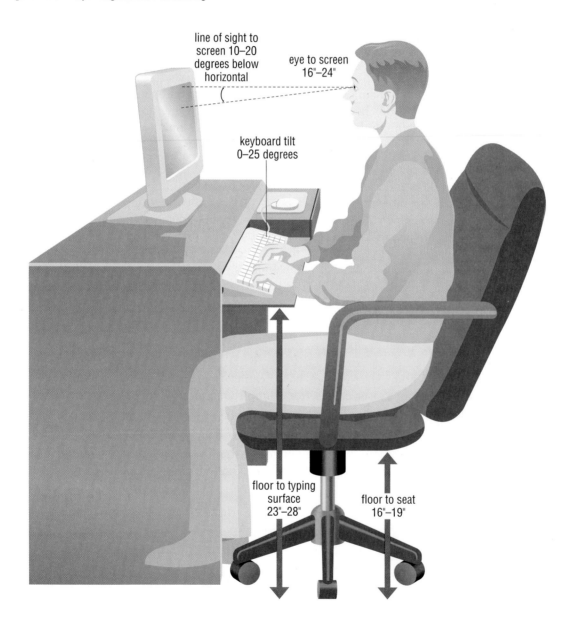

line of sight to screen 10–20 degrees below horizontal

eye to screen 16"–24"

keyboard tilt 0–25 degrees

floor to typing surface 23"–28"

floor to seat 16"–19"

The following are some basic rules for ergonomic computing:

Monitor Positioning To avoid eyestrain, the monitor should be between 16 and 24 inches from your face, and the top of the monitor should be in a straight line with your eyes when you are looking straight ahead.

Chair Positioning To avoid back strain, your chair height should be adjusted so that your thighs are parallel to the floor when your calves are perpendicular to the floor. The chair should support your lower back and, when you are sitting in it, your back should be perpendicular to the floor. If multiple people use the same workstation, the chair height should be adjustable, multiple chairs should be available, or the chair should be selected for the tallest person who uses the workstation and a footrest should be available for shorter users.

Desk Positioning To avoid back strain, your keyboard should be at a height where your upper arms are perpendicular to the floor and your forearms are parallel to the floor as you are typing.

Wrist Positioning When typing, the person's hands should extend straight out from the wrists, without the wrists bending to the left or right. This is easier to achieve on larger keyboards, or ergonomic keyboards in which the keys are split so that half point to the left and half to the right, as in Figure 16.10, so the user can type without wrist tilting. A rigid wrist brace can help you keep your wrist straight while typing. Long-term typing with improper wrist position can lead to carpal tunnel syndrome, an inflammation of the nerve canal in the wrists that can cause tingling and numbness in the hands and in some cases can require surgery.

Figure 16.10 Ergonomic Keyboard

Photo courtesy of Microsoft Corporation

Exercise 16.8   Evaluating a Workstation for Ergonomics

1. Open a new document in Word, WordPad, or Notepad and save the file as **U3T16-Ergo**.

2. Select a computer workstation to evaluate. It should be a workstation that contains a desktop PC (with a keyboard separate from the PC itself), a table, and a chair.

3. Using yourself as the current user, readjust your workspace using the concepts of ergonomics (regarding the position of the monitor, the height of your chair seat and desktop, and your keyboard).

4. Record your findings in **U3T16-Ergo** and note how much adjusting your workspace required.

5. Save, print, and then close the document and the program.

Lesson 16.9   **Understanding Environmentally Responsible Computing**

)C³ 3-4.2.11

Being a responsible computer user includes being aware of the environmental impact of your computer use and doing what you can to minimize this impact. In this lesson, you will learn several techniques for making your computer usage more environmentally friendly. These techniques include saving energy, conserving printer ink and paper, and recycling your computer and peripherals when you no longer need them.

Saving Energy

Most computers and printers have built-in power management features that enable the user to save energy by shutting down the device or by placing it in a low-power mode after a specified period of inactivity. The operating system in a computer typically controls power management, but some systems also have power management features available through the computer's BIOS setup. (Recall that BIOS stands for Basic Input Output System, and it contains the startup and low-level operation instructions for the PC's hardware.)

Different operating systems call the various low-power modes by different names, but the basic modes include sleep and hibernate. You can instruct the operating system to put the PC into one of these modes automatically after a certain period of inactivity or you can put the PC into one of these modes immediately by issuing a command.

Sleep mode A low-power mode that shuts down most of the computer components but leaves the RAM powered; also known as Suspend to RAM

Sleep In **Sleep mode**, all components of the PC except RAM are powered down so that the computer uses only the small amount of power required to keep the RAM's content running. When you resume, all the devices are powered on again. Because the content of RAM remains running, waking up from this mode is nearly instantaneous. In Windows and Mac OS, this is called *Sleep mode*; in Linux it is called *Suspend to RAM*.

Hibernate mode A low-power mode that copies the contents of RAM to the hard disk and then shuts down all components, including RAM; also known as Suspend to Disk

Hibernate In **Hibernate mode**, the content of RAM is copied to a special holding area on the hard disk and then the system is powered off completely, including the RAM. When you resume, the previous RAM content is copied back into RAM and all the devices are powered on again. Waking from this mode takes longer, but less time than it would take to start up the computer completely if it has been turned off. In Windows, this feature is called *Hibernate mode*, while on Linux this mode is called *Suspend to Disk*. When the Sleep feature is used on a Mac, the Safe Sleep mode copies the contents of RAM to the hard disk before sleeping. Then if the battery runs out and the computer loses power, hibernation automatically is in effect.

power plan Settings in the operating system that tell the computer to shut down or go into a power-saving mode after a specified period of inactivity

Some businesses and schools have energy-saving policies that dictate that everyone must place their computers in a low-power mode or turn them off completely at the end of the day. Even if an official policy does not apply to you, you may want to use a low-power mode on your own. Do this in your operating system by setting up a power plan. A **power plan** tells the computer to shut down or go into a power-saving mode after a specified period of inactivity. If it is a notebook computer, you can choose separate settings for when it is on battery power versus when it is plugged in.

Limiting energy use is good for the environment because most electricity is generated by expending natural resources. In addition, some methods of generating electricity, like burning coal, produce air pollution. Saving energy also saves you money in electrical costs. The U.S. Environmental Protection Agency's (EPA) **Energy Star** rating system for computer technology indicates devices and components that meet certain energy-efficiency standards. Look for the Energy Star logo, shown in Figure 16.11, when shopping for computer equipment. For example, an Energy Star monitor puts itself into standby (a low-power mode) when it does not detect a signal from the PC, and Energy Star laptops are able to go into Sleep or Hibernate mode when the lid is shut. Energy Star also applies to motherboards, power supplies, and BIOS that are able to manage power consumption.

Energy Star A rating from the EPA that designates a device that meets certain energy-efficiency standards

Figure 16.11 **Energy Star Logo**

Exercise 16.9A   Customizing the Windows Power Plan

1. Click Start and then click *Control Panel*.

2. Click *Hardware and Sound* and then click *Power Options*.

3. Click the *Balanced* power plan if it is not already selected.

4. Click the <u>Change plan settings</u> hyperlink for the Balanced power plan.

   Additional options will display. Note that if you are using a notebook PC, you have separate options for On battery and Plugged in. Otherwise you have only one option for each line.

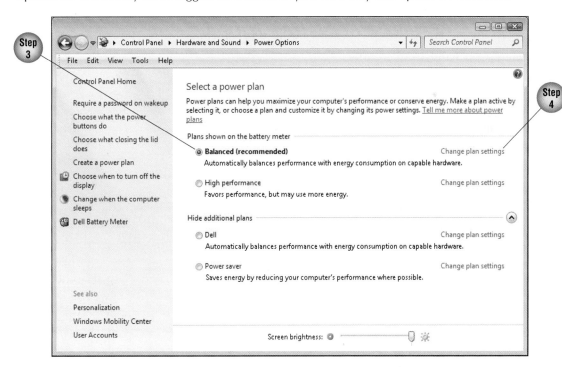

5. Open the *Turn off the display* drop-down list (for Plugged in, if you have a choice) and then click *20 minutes* at the drop-down list.

6. Click the Change advanced power settings hyperlink.

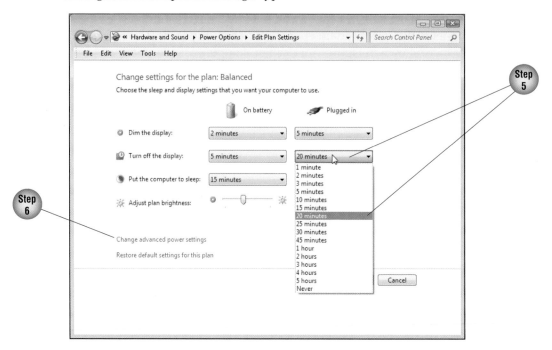

7. In the Power Options dialog box, click the plus sign next to *Hard disk* to expand the category.

8. Under *Hard disk*, click the plus sign next to *Turn off hard disk after* to expand that category.

9. Change the value to 30 minutes. (If you are working on a notebook PC, make sure to change the *Plugged in* value.)

10. Click the plus sign next to *Power buttons and lid* to expand that category.

11. Click the plus sign next to *Power button action* to expand that category.

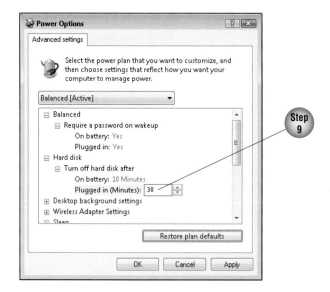

12. Change the setting to *Hibernate*. (If you are working on a notebook PC, make sure to change both settings to *Hibernate*.)

13. Click OK to close the Power Options dialog box.

14. Click the Save changes button.

15. Under the Select a power plan heading, click the *Balanced* option again and then click *Change plan settings*.

16. Click *Restore default settings for this plan*.

17. Click Yes to confirm.

18. Close the Control Panel window.

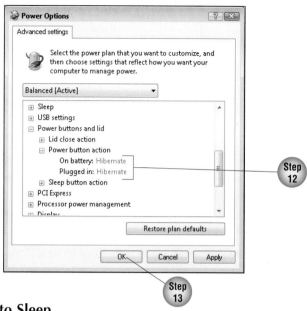

Exercise 16.9B Putting Your Computer to Sleep

1. Click Start and then click the Shut down button arrow.

2. Click *Sleep* on the menu that displays.

3. Wait for the computer to put itself to sleep.

4. Wake the computer up by pressing the power button.

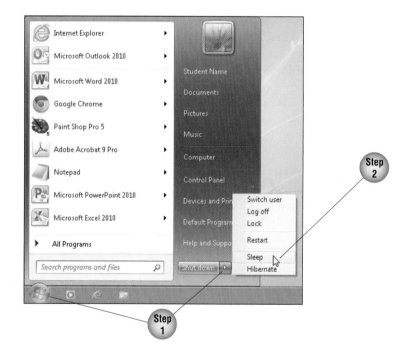

Conserving and Recycling Ink and Paper

Printing is not an environmentally friendly activity. The printer itself uses power (with laser printers using more power than inkjets), and the printer consumes paper, which takes both energy and natural resources (such as trees) to manufacture. In addition, the powdered toner in a laser printer can be carcinogenic (cancer-causing), and the plastic cartridges containing toner or liquid ink can end up in landfills. For these reasons, you should print only when necessary. It is better for the environment to share files and documents electronically, such as through email or text, whenever you can. If you must print, here are some things you can do to minimize the environmental impact:

duplexing The act of printing on both sides of a sheet of paper

- **Print on both sides of the paper.** Printing on both sides of the paper is called **duplexing.** Some printers can be set up to duplex automatically; others require you to re-insert the printed sheet upside-down for printing on the second side.

- **Recycle ink and toner cartridges.** You can send used ink and toner cartridges back to the manufacturer, or drop them off at recycling centers or your local office supply store. Most stores that sell ink and toner also accept used cartridges for recycling.

- **Buy refilled ink and toner cartridges.** Buying refilled ink and toner cartridges supports the cartridge recycling industry, which in turn prevents more cartridges from being discarded in landfills. Note, however, that a poorly refilled ink or toner cartridge can damage your printer, and some printer manufacturers will void your warranty if you use refilled cartridges. However, if you use high-quality refilled cartridges, you should have no problems.

- **Set the printer to sleep when not in use.** Printers draw power whenever they are on, even if they are not used for hours or even days at a time. If your printer has a Sleep mode, enable it, so that it will use less power when it is not actively printing.

Recycling Computers and Peripherals

Certain computer components can pollute the environment if you dispose of them along with your regular trash. For example, all batteries contain toxic substances that can contaminate the environment. Many computers have small batteries on the motherboard to keep the system date and time current when the computer is turned off, and notebook PCs have large batteries that substitute for AC power when away from an outlet. These batteries contain metals such as mercury, lead, cadmium, and nickel, all of which can contaminate water and soil and can release toxic chemicals into the air when burned. Most regions have laws requiring retailers that sell certain types of batteries to also collect them for recycling. The exact rules depend on the battery type and the region, but most office supply and computer stores will take your used batteries. You can also take them to recycling and hazardous materials disposal facilities in your area.

Monitors may also require special handling when you dispose of them. CRT monitors (the large, boxy type of monitors) contain a number of components that are hazardous. They should be taken to recycling or hazardous waste disposal facilities rather than thrown out with the regular trash. CRTs also contain phosphorous coating on the inside of the monitor glass. Phosphorous is volatile, and it can explode or start a fire when it combines with the oxygen molecules in water. CRTs also contain a small amount of lead, which is toxic, and their large size takes up a lot of space in a landfill. Computers themselves should also be recycled or taken to a hazardous waste disposal facility because their circuit boards contain lead and because their plastic cases will take up landfill space.

If your computer equipment still works, you might consider donating it to a school or charity organization rather than disposing of it. Many schools welcome the donation of used computers and equipment. If you do donate a computer that contains a working hard disk, back up and then erase the data on the hard disk to prevent the computer's new owner from viewing your personal data.

Exercise 16.9C   Researching Recycling Options

1. Research and identify three recycling or hazardous waste disposal centers in your local area.

2. Open Microsoft Word and then write an informative paragraph for each location that lists the following:

   - Type of facility, location, and hours of operation

- Types of materials collected
- Required information or payment for drop-offs

3. Save your research as **U3T16-Recycling**.

4. Print and close the document and exit Word.

More Information for IC³

 Delving Deeper

 3-4.2.9, 3-4.2.10

Keeping Up with Advances in Technology

Technology is constantly advancing, and the latest thing in computer technology today will be old, or even obsolete, a decade from now. When you work in the computer industry, it will be important for you to stay updated on the latest computer applications and capabilities. A number of ways to stay informed are available, including:

- Reading technology news articles and websites such as www.cnet.com, http://ic3.emcp.net/technology, and the Technology section of http://news.google.com
- Reading computer magazines; *PC Magazine* is one of the oldest and most respected
- Going online or visiting computer stores and browsing the specifications of the latest computer systems

Finding Information about Computer Usage Rules

Each country has laws about computer usage. Some states have their own laws as well. See http://ic3.emcp.net/cybercrime for information about the cybercrime laws around the world. For the laws in the United States, see http://ic3.emcp.net/UScyberlaw. Besides the official laws of your region, your school or workplace probably has well-defined guidelines and policies for complying with laws and conforming to ethical standards of conduct online. Check with your teacher or supervisor to find out what those policies are and how they are enforced. There are also websites, books, magazines, and other media dedicated to issues regarding the safe and legal usage of computers, as well as websites run by product manufacturers and third-party reviewers.

Understanding Firewalls and Proxy Servers

One of the ways that criminals gain access to a computer system is by looking for unprotected channels in network communications. For example, email applications typically use one channel (port 110) for incoming mail and another (port 25) for outgoing mail. Firewall programs help protect systems by closing off access to unused communication channels. Another way that some networks protect computers is by using a proxy server. A proxy server is an intermediary server that evaluates network traffic requests and then processes them according to its internal rules. Going through a proxy server can not only make network communications more difficult to spy on, but can also speed up certain operations by relying on caches that hold recently or frequently accessed data.

Sharing Your Knowledge

Another way to be a responsible computer user is to help others learn the computer skills and information that you already know. Take the knowledge you have acquired from this textbook and share it with others at home, at your school, at your place of employment, and in the community. For example, you could volunteer to help with computer literacy classes for elementary school children or senior citizens, and you could teach your parents or grandparents how to do an Internet search for information they would like to have.

TOPIC SUMMARY

- Content stored on a school- or business-owned computer or network is owned by the school or business, not the individual.

- Many websites restrict online data availability and may limit access to the data with password protection.

- Criminals use packet sniffers to access unsecured data communications. A secure site encrypts the web communications so criminals cannot easily decipher the data sent and received.

- Security certificates are used to prove the authenticity of a website. Certificates are verified by issuing authorities.

- Malware refers to malicious software, including exploits, viruses, spyware, Trojan horses, and worms.

- Installing all available Windows updates will minimize the chance of an operating system vulnerability allowing an exploit to compromise your system.

- Adware is an application that displays unsolicited ads on your computer. Spyware is an application that records your computer usage.

- Antivirus software defends against viruses, worms, and Trojan horses; anti-spyware software defends against adware and spyware. Antivirus and anti-spyware software look for virus signatures in executable files to identify malware.

- Web browser security settings can be configured to make it more difficult for malware to infect your system.

- Social engineering is the practice of tricking someone into sharing personal information.

- Parental controls, such as Content Advisor, enable adults to monitor and limit the Internet and computer usage of minors.

- Assistive hardware helps people who have limited mobility, motor skills, or sight to use a computer. Assistive hardware includes alternative keyboards and mice, wands and sticks, pointing devices, joysticks, and sip-and-puff devices.

- Windows' Ease of Access Center helps manage software tools used by people with mobility, vision, or hearing limitations.

- Copyright, trademark, and patent laws protect people's intellectual property.

- Good netiquette includes using the correct level of formality, not wasting people's time, making your communications as clear and concise as possible, and making sure your intentions are correctly perceived.

- Ergonomics is the study of designing and positioning equipment and devices to optimize their usefulness and safety to human bodies. Proper ergonomic posture should be used to prevent back, eye, and wrist strain.

- To save energy, use low-power modes (Sleep and Hibernate) on computers and peripherals that are not actively being used.

- Recycle old computers, especially old CRT monitors; do not throw them in the regular trash.

Key Terms

anti-spyware software, p. 727

cybercrime, p. 745

duplexing, p. 760

emoticon, p. 748

Energy Star, p. 757

ergonomics, p. 754

exploit, p. 725

extranet, p. 722

first-party cookie, p. 733

flaming, p. 780

forum, p. 780

Hibernate mode, p. 756

issuing authority, p. 724

intranet, p. 722

key logger, p. 726

netiquette, p. 748

packet sniffer, p. 723

parental controls, p. 737

patent, p. 745

persistent cookie, p. 734

phishing, p. 732

power plan, p. 756

registered trademark, p. 745

resident, p. 728

secure site, p. 723

Secure Sockets Layer (SSL), p. 723

security certificate, p. 724

service mark, p. 745

service pack, p. 726

session cookie, p. 734

Sleep mode, p. 756

SmartScreen filter, p. 732

social engineering, p. 731

third-party cookie, p. 733

trademark, p. 745

trolling, p. 750

virus definition, p. 727

vulnerability, p. 725

KEY POINTS REVIEW

Completion

In the space provided at the left, indicate the correct term, command, or option.

1. _____ What kind of organization issues a security certificate?

2. _____ What is it called when a criminal uses a vulnerability in the operating system to attack a system?

3. _____ This type of malware records keystrokes and sends the information to a remote location.

4. _____ A uniquely identifying snippet of a virus's code

5. _____ What is it called when someone tricks a person into sharing their password or bank account number?

6. _____ What does the SmartScreen filter guard against in Internet Explorer?

7. _____ What type of cookie is automatically deleted when you close your browser?

8. _____ In what application does the Content Advisor restrict Internet content?

9. _____ What does a registered trademark prove ownership of?

10. _____ What is the name for the study of designing and positioning equipment and devices to optimize their usefulness and safety to humans?

Multiple Choice

For each of the following items, choose the option that best completes the sentence or answers the question.

1. SSL is a technology for creating secure transmissions for
   A. receiving email
   B. sending email
   C. websites
   D. both sending and receiving email

2. A _____ is a self-replicating computer code that inserts itself into an executable file.
   A. virus
   B. Trojan horse
   C. worm
   D. key logger

3. A _____ is a self-transporting application that can carry a harmful program through a network.
   A. virus
   B. Trojan horse
   C. worm
   D. key logger

4. What type of threat would an antivirus program be likely to find and remove?
   A. pop-up
   B. worm
   C. phish
   D. cookie

5. Security certificates are issued and authenticated by
   A. an issuing authority such as Verisign
   B. the operating system's maker, such as Microsoft
   C. ICANN
   D. Internic

6. What Windows feature helps you set up accessibility tools?
   A. Network and Sharing Center
   B. Input Center
   C. Ease of Access Center
   D. Desktop Options

7. The Narrator feature in Windows would be useful for someone with a _____ impairment.
   A. hearing
   B. mobility
   C. dexterity
   D. vision

8. Which of the following is a cybercrime?
   A. creating a phishing site
   B. stealing a car stereo
   C. stealing a computer out of a car
   D. impersonating a government agent on the phone

9. Which of these protects an author's writing from being reproduced without permission?
   A. patent
   B. copyright
   C. registered trademark
   D. trademark

10. When a desk is the right height for a computer user, the person's forearms are _____ as he or she types.
    A. perpendicular to the floor
    B. at a 45 degree angle, pointing up
    C. parallel to the floor
    D. at a 45 degree angle, pointing down

Matching

Match each of the following definitions with the correct term, command, or option.

1. _____ Malware that appears to do something useful
2. _____ The feature in Internet Explorer that restricts which websites can be displayed
3. _____ An application that runs all the time in the background in Windows
4. _____ Software that displays advertising pop-ups
5. _____ A tracking file placed on your computer by a website
6. _____ Identifies ownership of a word, phrase, symbol, or design
7. _____ Identifies ownership of an invention
8. _____ Printing on both sides of a sheet of paper
9. _____ A low-power mode in Windows
10. _____ Symbols that represent emotions in electronic communications

A. Adware
B. Cookie
C. Duplexing
D. Emoticons
E. Trademark
F. Sleep
G. Content Advisor
H. Resident
I. Trojan horse
J. Patent

SKILLS REVIEW

Review 16.1 **Testing Your Knowledge of Phishing Practices**

1. In your web browser, go to http://ic3.emcp.net/phishing.
2. Click the Start The Test button and then take the test.
3. At the test results screen, press the Print Screen key to capture an image of the results.
4. Open Paint and then press Ctrl + V to paste the screen capture into Paint.
5. Save the file as **U3T16-R1-Results**.
6. Print the file and then exit Paint.

Review 16.2 **Using Email Etiquette**

1. Open your email application or web-based email.
2. Compose an email message to your instructor letting him or her know that you will be attending an out-of-town wedding next Tuesday and asking if you can have the assignments in advance. Use appropriate language, tone, greeting, closing, and formatting.
3. In the subject line, type **U3T16-R2-Etiquette**.
4. Send the message to your instructor.

Review 16.3 **Setting Up Accessibility Options**

1. Using the Ease of Access Center in Windows, turn on the High Contrast display mode, and then turn on Narrator and Magnifier.
2. Press the Print Screen key on your keyboard to capture an image of the screen.
3. Turn off Narrator by closing its dialog box.
4. Turn off Magnifier by right-clicking its button on the taskbar and then clicking *Close window*.
5. Press Alt + Left Shift + Print Screen to exit from the High Contrast display mode.
6. Open Paint and then press Ctrl + V to paste the screen image.
7. Save the file as **U3T16-R3-Ease**.
8. Print the file and then exit Paint.

SKILLS ASSESSMENT

Assessment 16.1 **Duplexing Print Jobs**

1. Determine whether your printer has automatic duplexing capabilities. Do this by finding a manual for the printer online or by checking the printer's properties dialog box in Windows.
2. Determine how to insert paper for manual duplexing on your printer. You need to know whether the already-printed side goes up or down, and whether the printed image goes in top first or bottom first.
3. Start a new document in Word and then write the instructions for creating a manually duplexed multi-page print job using your printer. If your printer automatically duplexes, also include instructions for automatically duplexing a print job.
4. Save the Word document as **U3T16-R3-Printing**.
5. Print the document and then exit Word.

Assessment 16.2 **Updating Virus Definitions**

1. Determine what antivirus software is installed on your PC.
2. Open the antivirus program's configuration window. The steps for doing this vary depending on which program you have. Ask your instructor for help if needed.
3. Find the option that checks for virus definition updates, and determine when the definitions were last updated.
4. With your instructor's permission, update the definitions.
5. In your antivirus program, display a screen that shows the date of the last update, and then press the Print Screen key to capture an image of the display.
6. Open Paint and then press Ctrl + V to paste the screen image.
7. Save the file as **U3T16-A2-Antivirus**.
8. Print the file and then exit Paint.

Assessment 16.3 **Using the Microsoft Safety Scanner**

1. Click Start and then click *Help and Support*.
2. Using Search, locate an article called *How do I remove a computer virus?*
3. In the article, find the procedure *To run the Microsoft Safety Scanner*.
4. Click the <u>Microsoft Safety Scanner</u> web page hyperlink to open a website where you can download that utility.
5. Download and run the utility. As the utility is running, press the Print Screen key to capture an image of it.
6. Open Paint and then press Ctrl + V to paste the screen image.
7. Save the file as **U3T16-A3-Scanner**, print the file, and then exit Paint.
8. Wait for the scanner to finish running. If you encounter any infections, alert your instructor.

Assessment 16.4 **Researching SSL Certificates**

1. Open a web browser and then go to www.verisign.com or to some other certificate issuing authority that your instructor specifies.
2. Research the available options for SSL certificates and their prices and benefits for a single server and a one-year period. For example, certificate options might vary in the number of encryption bits.
3. Open a new Excel worksheet and then create a worksheet that summarizes and compares the features and prices of each of the available SSL certificate types available.
4. Save the Excel file as **U3T16-A4-Certificates**.
5. Print the file and then exit Excel.

Assessment 16.5 **Investigating Cybercrimes**

Use Google News (http://news.google.com) to search for news stories about cybercrimes. *Hint: You will probably need to browse the Technology section of the news; the word* **cybercrime** *will not appear in most stories.* Find a story about someone who committed a cybercrime, and answer the questions listed below.

- What did the criminal hope to achieve?

- What type of illegal activity did the criminal engage in?

- How did authorities catch the criminal?

Cite your source and save your responses in a Word document and name the document **U3T16-A5-Cybercrime**. Print the document and then exit Word.

Assessment 16.6 **Using a Web-Based Virus Checker**

Open a web browser and then go to http://ic3.emcp.net/virusscan. This site provides access to a free, online virus scan. Download the appropriate version for your computer (32-bit or 64-bit) and run it. Note the results, including whether any problems were found and whether they were fixed. Write a report detailing the results in a Microsoft Word document. Save the document as **U3T16-A6-Housecall**. Print the document and then exit Word.

Assessment 16.7 **Warning Others of Online Dangers**

1. Open PowerPoint.
2. Based on your own experience and what you learned in this topic, create an informative presentation on what you consider to be the most dangerous threats to inexperienced computer users. Use the skills you learned in earlier topics to create a dynamic and visually appealing presentation. Use one slide for each type of threat, making sure to describe the danger and how it can be avoided.
3. Save the presentation as **U3T16-A7-Threats**.
4. Print the presentation and then exit PowerPoint.

CRITICAL THINKING

Researching and Choosing Antivirus Software

Suppose you are choosing antivirus software for a small office consisting of 10 Windows-based personal computers. Open a web browser and then go to http://ic3.emcp.net/avcompare. This site offers a comprehensive comparison and review of current antivirus applications. Take some time to look through this site and analyze your options. Create a proposal in a Word document that describes which application you believe would be best for this particular office and includes your reasoning. Save the document as **U3T16-CT-Antivirus**. Print the document and then exit Word.

Evaluating Ergonomics

1. Locate a camera; a camera on a cell phone will work.
2. Each member of the team should take turns sitting at their computer workstation and pretending to type on the keyboard. Another member of the team should take his or her picture in profile (from the side), so the angles of the forearms, upper arms, thighs, and calves are visible.
3. Transfer the photos to a computer (sending it from a cell phone camera to someone's email account is one method; transferring with a data cable that connects to a USB port is another).
4. Open the photos in Paint or some other photo editing program and analyze the ergonomic angles of each student. Compare them to the angles shown in Figure 16.9.
5. Open Word.
6. Type each team member's name at the top of the document.
7. Paste the pictures into the document using the Clipboard and number each image.
8. Write a paragraph under the pictures that evaluates whether each image represents good or poor ergonomic posture and what could be done to make each one better.
9. Save the Word document as **U3T16-ErgonomicsTeam#**.
10. Print the document and then exit Word.

Discussion Questions

1. If the legs are not in the proper position, what should be adjusted?
2. If the arms are not in the proper position, what should be adjusted?
3. What kind of physical strain might you experience if your chair is too high or too low?
4. Discuss any limitations or challenges you might encounter in adjusting your work station.

IC³ Objectives and Correlation

Module 1: Computing Fundamentals

IC³ Global Standard 3	Objectives & Abbreviated Skill Sets	Topic Number, Lesson Number
DOMAIN 1.0	COMPUTER HARDWARE, PERIPHERIALS AND TROUBLESHOOTING	
Objective 1.1	**Identify types of computers, how they process information, and the purpose and function of different hardware components**	
IC³-1 1.1.1	Identify different types of computer devices	U1-T1-L1.1, L1.2
IC³-1 1.1.2	Identify the role of the central processing unit (CPU) including how the speed of a microprocessor is measured	U1-T1-L1.3
IC³-1 1.1.3	Identify concepts related to computer memory (measurement of memory, RAM, ROM)	U1-T1-L1.3, L1.4
IC³-1 1.1.4	Identify the features and benefits (storage capacity, shelf-life, etc.) of different storage media	U1-T1-L1.4
IC³-1 1.1.5	Identify the types and purposes of standard input and output devices on desktop or laptop computers	U1-T1-L1.1, L1.5, L1.6, U1-T2-L2.9
IC³-1 1.1.6	Identify the types and purposes of specialized input devices (e.g. cameras, scanners, game controllers, etc.)	U1-T1-L1.5
IC³-1 1.1.7	Identify the types and purposes of specialized output devices (e.g. printers, projectors, etc.)	U1-T1-L1.6
IC³-1 1.1.8	Identify how hardware devices are connected to and installed on a computer system	U1-T1-L1.1, L1.5, L1.8, L1.11
IC³-1 1.1.9	Identify factors that affect computer performance	U1-T1-L1.6, L1.7
Objective 1.2	**Identify how to maintain computer equipment and solve common problems relating to computer hardware**	
IC³-1 1.2.1	Identify the importance of protecting computer hardware from theft or damage	U1-T1-L1.9
IC³-1 1.2.2	Identify factors that can cause damage to computer hardware or media (e.g. environmental factors, magnetic fields, etc.)	U1-T1-L1.9
IC³-1 1.2.3	Identify how to protect computer hardware from fluctuations in the power supply, power outages and other electrical issues (such as use of computers on different electrical systems)	U1-T1-L1.9
IC³-1 1.2.4	Identify common problems associated with computer hardware	U1-T1-L1.11
IC³-1 1.2.5	Identify problems that can occur if hardware is not maintained properly	U1-T1-L1.10
IC³-1 1.2.6	Identify maintenance that can be performed routinely by users	U1-T1-L1.10, L1.11
IC³-1 1.2.7	Identify maintenance that should ONLY be performed by experienced professionals, including replacing or upgrading internal hardware (especially electrical) components (such as processors or drives) that are not designed to be user accessible	U1-T1-L1.10; U1-T1-Delving Deeper
IC³-1 1.2.8	Identify the steps required to solve computer-related problems	U1-T1-L1.11
IC³-1 1.2.9	Identify consumer issues related to buying, maintaining and repairing a computer including: • Factors that go into an individual or organizational decision on how to purchase computer equipment • Factors relating to maintenance and repair responsibilities	U1-T1-L1.2, L1.7, L1.10, L1.11

IC³ Global Standard 3	Objectives & Abbreviated Skill Sets	Topic Number, Lesson Number
DOMAIN 2.0	**COMPUTER SOFTWARE**	
Objective 2.1	**Identify how software and hardware work together to perform computing tasks and how software is developed and upgraded**	
IC³-1 2.1.1	Identify how hardware and software interact	U1-T2-L2.1
IC³-1 2.1.2	Identify the difference between an operating system and application software	U1-T2-L2.1
IC³-1 2.1.3	Identify issues relating to software distribution (e.g. licenses, upgrades)	U1-T3-L3.1
Objective 2.2	**Identify different types of application software and general concepts relating to application software categories**	
IC³-1 2.2.1	Identify fundamental concepts relating to word processing and common uses for word-processing applications (e.g. reviewing, editing, formatting, etc.)	U1-T3-L3.4
IC³-1 2.2.2	Identify fundamental concepts relating to spreadsheets and common uses for spreadsheet applications (e.g. worksheets, data sorting, formulas, and functions, etc.)	U1-T3-L3.5; U2-T9-Delving Deeper
IC³-1 2.2.3	Identify fundamental concepts relating to presentation software and common uses for presentation applications (e.g. slides, speaker notes, graphics, etc.)	U1-T3-L3.6
IC³-1 2.2.4	Identify fundamental concepts relating to databases and common uses for database applications (e.g. fields, tables, queries, reports, etc.)	U1-T3-L3.7
IC³-1 2.2.5	Identify fundamental concepts relating to graphic and multimedia programs and common uses for graphic or multimedia software (e.g. drawing, painting, animation tools, etc.)	U1-T3-L3.8; U1-T3-Delving Deeper
IC³-1 2.2.6	Identify fundamental concepts relating to education and entertainment programs (e.g. computer based training (CBT), video, audio, etc.)	U1-T3-L3.10
IC³-1 2.2.7	Identify the types and purposes of different utility programs (e.g. virus, adware and spyware detection programs, etc.)	U1-T3-L3.9, L3.10
IC³-1 2.2.8	Identify other types of software (e.g. chat, messaging, web conferencing, accounting software, etc.)	U1-T3-L3.10
IC³-1 2.2.9	Identify how to select the appropriate application(s) for a particular purpose, and problems that can arise if the wrong software product is used for a particular purpose	U1-T3-L3.3
IC³-1 2.2.10	Identify how applications interact and share data	U1-T3-L3.11, U3-T13-L13.3
DOMAIN 3.0	**USING AN OPERATING SYSTEM**	
Objective 3.1	**Identify what an operating system is and how it works, and solve common problems related to operating systems**	
IC³-1 3.1.1	Identify the purpose of an operating system and the difference between operating system and application software	U1-T2-L2.1
IC³-1 3.1.2	Identify different operating systems (e.g. Windows, Macintosh OS, Linux, etc.)	U1-T2-L2.1
IC³-1 3.1.3	Identify that a computer user may interact with multiple operating systems while performing everyday tasks	U1-T2-L2.1
IC³-1 3.1.4	Identify the capabilities and limitations imposed by the operating system including levels of user rights (administrative rights, etc.) which determine what a user can and cannot do (install software, download files, change system settings, etc.)	U1-T2-L2.1
IC³-1 3.1.5	Identify and solve common problems related to operating systems	U1-T2-L2.10
Objective 3.2	**Use an operating system to manipulate a computer's desktop, files and disks**	
IC³-1 3.2.1	Shut down, restart, log on and log off the computer	U1-T2-L2.3
IC³-1 3.2.2	Identify elements of the operating system desktop	U1-T2-L2.2
IC³-1 3.2.3	Manipulate windows (e.g. minimize, maximize, resize)	U1-T2-L2.2
IC³-1 3.2.4	Start and run programs	U1-T2-L2.2, L2.4
IC³-1 3.2.5	Manipulate desktop folders and icons/shortcuts	U1-T2-L2.5, L2.6
IC³-1 3.2.6	Manage files (e.g. identifying files, folders, directories, moving and retrieving files, display file properties, etc.)	U1-T2-L2.6, U1-T2-Delving Deeper

IC³ Global Standard 3	Objectives & Abbreviated Skill Sets	Topic Number, Lesson Number
IC³-1 3.2.7	Identify precautions one should take when manipulating files including using standardized naming conventions	U1-T2-L2.6
IC³-1 3.2.8	Solve common problems associated with working with files (e.g. incompatibility of application programs, corruption of files, denied access, etc.)	U1-T2-L2.6, L2.4, U1-T2-Delving Deeper
Objective 3.3	**Identify how to change system settings, install and remove software**	
IC³-1 3.3.1	Display control panels/system preferences	U1-T2-L2.8
IC³-1 3.3.2	Identify different control panel/system preference settings	U1-T2-L2.8
IC³-1 3.3.3	Change simple settings (e.g. date and time, audio, security, etc.)	U1-T2-L2.8
IC³-1 3.3.4	Display and update a list of installed printers	U1-T2-L2.9
IC³-1 3.3.5	Identify precautions regarding changing system settings	U1-T2-L2.8
IC³-1 3.3.6	Install and uninstall software including installing updates from online sources	U1-T3-L3.1
IC³-1 3.3.7	Identify and troubleshoot common problems associated with installing and running applications	U1-T3-L3.1, U1-T2-L2.10

Module 2: Key Applications

IC³ Global Standard 3	Objectives & Abbreviated Skill Sets	Topic Number, Lesson Number
DOMAIN 1.0	**COMMON PROGRAM FUNCTIONS**	
Objective 1.1	**Be able to start and exit an application, identify and modify interface elements and utilize sources of online help**	
IC³-2 1.1.1	Start and start a Windows application	U2-T4-L4.1
IC³-2 1.1.2	Identify on-screen elements common to applications (e.g. menu bar, scroll bar, application window, etc.)	U2-T4-L4.1, U2-T5-L5.1
IC³-2 1.1.3	Navigate around open files	U2-T4-L4.1, U2-T5-L5.1
IC³-2 1.1.4	Use, change and change location of onscreen command buttons (toolbar/ribbon)	U2-T4-L4.2
IC³-2 1.1.5	Change views (draft/normal, print-layout/page-layout, etc.)	U2-T5-L5.6
IC³-2 1.1.6	Change magnification level (zoom)	U2-T5-L5.6
IC³-2 1.1.7	Display options for changing application defaults (where files are stored, custom display, print and auto save options, etc.)	U2-T4-L4.10
IC³-2 1.1.8	Identify and prioritize help resources (e.g. online resources, help desk, peers, etc.)	U2-T4-L4.11
IC³-2 1.1.9	Use automated help (e.g. F1 key, appropriate online resources, etc.)	U2-T4-L4.11
Objective 1.2	**Perform common file-management functions**	
IC³-2 1.2.1	Create files	U2-T4-L4.3
IC³-2 1.2.2	Open files	U2-T4-L4.4
IC³-2 1.2.3	Switch between open documents	U2-T4-L4.1
IC³-2 1.2.4	Save files in specified locations/formats (e.g. "Save" vs. "Save As", saving to directories, saving in a different file format, etc.)	U2-T4-L4.3, L4.4, L4.8, L4.9
IC³-2 1.2.5	Close files	U2-T4-L4.7
IC³-2 1.2.6	Identify and solve common problems relating to working with files (e.g. unsupported file formats, file corruption, etc.)	U2-T4-Delving Deeper
Objective 1.3	**Perform common editing and formatting functions**	
IC³-2 1.3.1	Insert text and numbers into a file	U2-T5-L5.2, U2-T6-L6.7
IC³-2 1.3.2	Perform simple editing (e.g. cut, copy, move information)	U2-T5-L5.4, L5.2, U2-T9-L9.12
IC³-2 1.3.3	Use the Undo, Redo and Repeat commands	U2-T5-L5.3
IC³-2 1.3.4	Find and/or Find and Replace information	U2-T5-L5.5

IC³ Global Standard 3	Objectives & Abbreviated Skill Sets	Topic Number, Lesson Number
IC³-2 1.3.5	Check spelling	U2-T5-L5.9
IC³-2 1.3.6	Perform simple text formatting (e.g. bold, text effects, etc.)	U2-T6-L6.1, L6.3
IC³-2 1.3.7	Insert pictures and other objects into a file (e.g. clip art, graphic files, text art, etc.)	U2-T8-L8.7, L8.8, L8.9, L8.10, U2-T12-L12.1, L12.2, L12.3
Objective 1.4	**Perform common printing/outputting functions**	
IC³-2 1.4.1	Format a document for printing (e.g. margins, paper size, etc.)	U2-T8-L8.1
IC³-2 1.4.2	Preview a file before printing	U2-T5-L5.7
IC³-2 1.4.3	Print files, specifying common print options	U2-T5-L5.7, U2-T4-L4.5
IC³-2 1.4.4	Manage printing and print jobs	U2-T4-L4.6
IC³-2 1.4.5	Identify and solve common problems associated with printing (e.g. printer issues, connection issues, etc.)	U2-T4-L4.6
IC³-2 1.4.6	Output documents in electronic format (e.g. PDF, fax, email, etc.)	U2-T8-Delving Deeper
IC³-2 1.4.7	Identify issues related to outputting files in electronic format	U2-T8-Delving Deeper
DOMAIN 2.0	**WORD PROCESSING FUNCTIONS**	
Objective 2.1	**Be able to format text and documents including the ability to use automatic formatting tools**	
IC³-2 2.1.1	Change spacing options	U2-T6-L6.5, L6.6
IC³-2 2.1.2	Indent text	U2-T6-L6.8
IC³-2 2.1.3	Display the ruler	U2-T6-L6.8
IC³-2 2.1.4	Use tabs	U2-T6-L6.11, L6.12
IC³-2 2.1.5	Insert and delete a page break or section break	U2-T8-L8.5
IC³-2 2.1.6	Display non-printing characters and identify on-screen formatting information	U2-T6-L6.2, L6.5-Drilling Down, L6.6-Drilling Down
IC³-2 2.1.7	Create and modify bulleted and numbered lists (single-level and multi-level)	U2-T6-L6.7
IC³-2 2.1.8	Insert symbols/special characters	U2-T8-L8.3
IC³-2 2.1.9	Insert, modify and format page numbers	U2-T8-L8.4
IC³-2 2.1.10	Create, modify and format headers and footers	U2-T8-L8.4
IC³-2 2.1.11	Create, modify and apply styles	U2-T6-L6.10, U2-T8-L8.2
IC³-2 2.1.12	Create and modify columns	U2-T8-L8.6
IC³-2 2.1.13	Working with tables	U2-T7 (all), U2-T7-Delving Deeper
IC³-2 2.1.14	Modify table structure (cells, rows, and columns)	U2-T7-L7.4, L7.3, L7.5
IC³-2 2.1.15	Format tables (e.g. sorting data within a table, align table cell content, etc.)	U2-T7-L7.6, L7.3, L7.7, L7.8, L7.12
IC³-2 2.1.16	Identify common uses for word processing (such as creating short documents like letters and memos, long documents like reports and books, and specialized documents such as Web pages and blog entries) and identify elements of a well-organized document	U2-T5-Topic Overview, U2-T5-Delving Deeper, U2-T6-Delving Deeper, U2-T4-L4.8
Objective 2.2	**Be able to use word-processing tools to automate processes such as document review, security and collaboration**	
IC³-2 2.2.1	Use language tools (e.g. grammar tools, Thesaurus, etc.)	U2-T5-L5.8, L5.9
IC³-2 2.2.2	Insert and modify data elements into a document	U2-T8-L8.10, L8.11, L8.12, L8.14
IC³-2 2.2.3	Use tools that support collaborative creation and editing of documents	U2-T8-L8.11, L8.12
IC³-2 2.2.4	Protect a document from unauthorized viewing or modification	U2-T8-L8.13

IC³ Global Standard 3	Objectives & Abbreviated Skill Sets	Topic Number, Lesson Number
DOMAIN 3.0	**SPREADSHEET FEATURES**	
Objective 3.1	**Be able to modify worksheet data and structure and format data in a worksheet**	
IC³-2 3.1.1	Identify how a table of data is organized in a spreadsheet	U2-T9-L9.11, U2-T10-Delving Deeper
IC³-2 3.1.2	Identify the structure of a well-organized, useful worksheet	U2-T10-Delving Deeper
IC³-2 3.1.3	Insert and modify data	U2-T9-L9.1, L9.2, L9.3
IC³-2 3.1.4	Modify table structure (e.g. insert, delete, adjust cells and rows, etc.)	U2-T9-L9.11, L9.12, U2-T10-L10.1, L10.2
IC³-2 3.1.5	Identify and change number formats, including currency, date and time and percentage formats	U2-T10-L10.6
IC³-2 3.1.6	Apply borders and shading to cells	U2-T10-L10.3
IC³-2 3.1.7	Specify cell alignment (e.g. wrapping text within a cell)	U2-T10-L10.3
IC³-2 3.1.8	Apply table AutoFormats	U2-T9-L9.6 U2-T10-L10.4
IC³-2 3.1.9	Specify worksheet/workbook-specific print options	U2-T9-L9.2, U2-T10-L10.7, L10.8
IC³-2 3.1.10	Identify common uses of spreadsheets (such as creating budgets, managing expense reports, or tracking student grades) as well as elements of a well-organized, well-formatted spreadsheet	U2-T9-Topic Overview, U2-T10-Delving Deeper
Objective 3.2	**Be able to sort data, manipulate data using formulas and functions and create simple charts**	
IC³-2 3.2.1	Sort worksheet data	U2-T9-L9.5
IC³-2 3.2.2	Filter data	U2-T9-L9.5
IC³-2 3.2.3	Demonstrate an understanding of absolute vs. relative cell addresses	U2-T9-L9.10
IC³-2 3.2.4	Insert arithmetic formulas that include +, -, * and / into worksheet cells, including formulas that reference other cells in the worksheet	U2-T9-L9.7
IC³-2 3.2.5	Demonstrate how to use common worksheet functions (e.g. SUM, MIN, MAX, etc.)	U2-T9-L9.8, U2-T9-Delving Deeper
IC³-2 3.2.6	Use AutoSum	U2-T9-L9.4
IC³-2 3.2.7	Insert and modify formulas and functions	U2-T9-L9.8, L9.9
IC³-2 3.2.8	Identify common errors people make when using formulas and functions (e.g. circular references, mathematical errors, etc.)	U2-T9-Delving Deeper
IC³-2 3.2.9	Insert and modify simple charts in a worksheet (e.g. modify chart data, background, chart type, etc.)	U2-T10-L10.9, L10.10, L10.11, L10.12
IC³-2 3.2.10	Draw conclusions based on tabular data or charts in a worksheet	U2-T9-L9.5, U2-T10-Delving Deeper
DOMAIN 4.0	**COMMUNICATING WITH PRESENTATION SOFTWARE**	
Objective 4.1	**Be able to create and format simple presentations**	
IC³-2 4.1.1	Manage slides (e.g. create, delete, and duplicate slides, etc.)	U2-T11-L11.8, L11.3, L11.7, L11.9, L11.10, L11.1, U2-T12-L12.6
IC³-2 4.1.2	Add information to a slide (text, graphics, data, multimedia, designs)	U2-T11-L11.2, L.11.11 U2-T12-L12.1, L12.2, L12.5, L12.7, L12.8, L12.12
IC³-2 4.1.3	Change view	U2-T11-L11.1, L11.4-Drilling Down, L11.5, L11.8
IC³-2 4.1.4	Change slide layout	U2-T11-L11.2
IC³-2 4.1.5	Modify a slide background	U2-T11-L11.2

IC³ Global Standard 3	Objectives & Abbreviated Skill Sets	Topic Number, Lesson Number
IC³-2 4.1.6	Assign transitions to slides	U2-T11-L11.6
IC³-2 4.1.7	Change the order of slides in a presentation	U2-T11-L11.8
IC³-2 4.1.8	Identify different ways presentations are distributed (printed, projected to an audience, distributed over networks or the Internet, etc.)	U2-T11-L11.4, U2-T11-Delving Deeper
IC³-2 4.1.9	Create different output elements (speaker's notes, handouts, etc.)	U2-T11-L11.4
IC³-2 4.1.10	Preview the slide show presentation	U2-T11-L11.4
IC³-2 4.1.11	Navigate an on-screen slide show	U2-T11-L11.1, L11.5, U2-T12-L12.4
IC³-2 4.1.12	Identify common uses of presentation software (such as facilitating meetings or classroom learning or creating and distributing content that includes a wide variety of media) as well as effective design principles for simple presentations	U2-T11-Topic Overview, U2-T12-L12.1, U2-T12-Delving Deeper

Module 3: Living Online

IC³ Global Standard 3	Objectives & Abbreviated Skill Sets	Topic Number, Lesson Number
DOMAIN 1.0	COMMUNICATION NETWORKS AND THE INTERNET	
Objective 1.1	Identify network fundamentals and the benefits and risks of network computing	
IC³-3 1.1.1	Identify that networks (including computer networks and other networks such as the telephone network) transmit different types of data	U3-T13-L13.1
IC³-3 1.1.2	Identify benefits of networked computing	U3-T13-L13.1
IC³-3 1.1.3	Identify the risks of networked computing	U3-T13-L13.4, U3-T16-L16.1
IC³-3 1.1.4	Identify the roles of clients and servers in a network	U3-T13-L13.2
IC³-3 1.1.5	Identify networks by size and type	U3-T13-L13.2
IC³-3 1.1.6	Identify concepts related to network communication (e.g. high speed, broadband, wireless (wifi), etc.)	U3-T13-L13.2
IC³-3 1.1.7	Identify fundamental principles of security on a network including authorization, authentication, and wireless security issues,	U3-T13-L13.4, U3-T16-L16.1
DOMAIN 2.0	ELECTRONIC COMMUNICATION AND COLLABORATION	
Objective 2.1	Identify different types of electronic communication/collaboration and how they work	
IC³-3 2.1.1	Identify the different methods of electronic communication/collaboration and the advantages and disadvantages of each (e.g. email, instant messaging, blogging, social networking, etc.)	U3-T13-L13.7, L13.3
IC³-3 2.1.2	Identify how unique users are identified with communication services such as instant mail, text messaging, online conferencing, and social network sites	U3-T13-L13.7, L13.3
IC³-3 2.1.3	Identify how communication tools such as electronic mail or instant messaging are accessed and used	U3-T13-L13.7, L13.3, U3-T15-L15.1
Objective 2.2	Identify how to use an electronic mail application	
IC³-3 2.2.1	Identify how electronic mail identifies a unique e-mail user by e-mail address	U3-T15-L15.1
IC³-3 2.2.2	Identify the components of an electronic mail message or instant message	U3-T15-L15.3
IC³-3 2.2.3	Identify when to use different electronic mail options	U3-T15-L15.7
IC³-3 2.2.4	Read and send electronic mail messages	U3-T15-L15.3, L15.5
IC³-3 2.2.5	Identify ways to supplement a mail message with additional information	U3-T15-L15.6
IC³-3 2.2.6	Manage attachments	U3-T15-L15.6

IC³ Global Standard 3	Objectives & Abbreviated Skill Sets	Topic Number, Lesson Number
IC³-3 2.2.7	Manage mail	U3-T15-L15.8, U3-T15-Delving Deeper
IC³-3 2.2.8	Manage addresses	U3-T15-L15.4
IC³-3 2.2.9	Identify the purpose of frequently used mail-configuration options (e.g. automatic signatures, out-of-office assistance, blocking messages, etc.)	U3-T15-L15.7, L15.9, U3-T15-Delving Deeper
Objective 2.3	**Identify the appropriate use of different types of communication/collaboration tools and the "rules of the road" regarding online communication ("netiquette")**	
IC³-3 2.3.1	Identify appropriate uses for different communication methods (e.g. email, instant messaging, teleconference, and syndication)	U3-T13-L13.7
IC³-3 2.3.2	Identify the advantages of electronic communication	U3-T13-L13.7
IC³-3 2.3.3	Identify common problems associated with electronic communication (e.g. delivery failure, junk mail, fraud hoaxes, viruses, etc.)	U3-T13-L13.7, U3-T15-L15.9
IC³-3 2.3.4	Identify the elements of professional and effective electronic communications (e.g. timely responses, correct spelling and grammar, appropriate level of formality, etc.)	U3-T16-L16.7
IC³-3 2.3.5	Identify appropriate use of e-mail attachments and other supplementary information (e.g. large attachments, embedding a URL, security issues, etc.)	U3-T16-L16.7
IC³-3 2.3.6	Identify issues regarding unsolicited e-mail ("spam") and how to minimize or control unsolicited mail	U3-T15-L15.9
IC³-3 2.3.7	Identify effective procedures for ensuring the safe and effective use of electronic communication including "netiquette", understanding school or company policies, and following guidelines.	U3-T15-L15.9, U3-T16-L16.7
DOMAIN 3.0	**USING THE INTERNET AND THE WORLDWIDE WEB**	
Objective 3.1	**Identity information about the Internet, the World Wide Web and Web sites and be able to use a Web browsing application**	
IC³-3 3.1.1	Understand the difference between the Internet (a worldwide network of computers) and the World Wide Web (a set of linked pages containing information and applications that uses the Internet to facilitate online communications)	U3-T13-L13.6
IC³-3 3.1.2	Identify terminology related to the Internet and the World Wide Web (e.g. domain, home page, HTML, URL, Wiki, etc.)	U3-T13-L13.6, L13.7, U3-T13-Delving Deeper
IC³-3 3.1.3	Identify different items on a Web page (e.g. text, graphic objects, hyperlinked text, etc.)	U3-T13-L13.6, U3-T14-L14.1
IC³-3 3.1.4	Identify different types of Web sites and the purposes of different types of sites (e.g. government sites, secure vs. unsecure sites, search sites, etc.)	U3-T13-L13.5
IC³-3 3.1.5	Navigate the Web using a browser (e.g. opening a new browser or tab, going to a website's home page, etc.)	U3-T14-L14.1
IC³-3 3.1.6	Reload/Refresh the view of a Web page	U3-T14-L14.1
IC³-3 3.1.7	Show a history of recently visited Web sites, navigate to a previously visited site and delete history of visited sites	U3-T14-L14.2
IC³-3 3.1.8	Find specific information on a Web site	U3-T14-L14.5, L14.6
IC³-3 3.1.9	Manage Bookmarked sites/Favorite sites	U3-T14-L14.3
IC³-3 3.1.10	Copy appropriate elements from a Web site to another application (such as copying text or media to a word processing document or presentation or copying data to a spreadsheet)	U3-T14-L14.4
IC³-3 3.1.11	Download a file from a Web site to a specified location	U3-T14-L14.4
IC³-3 3.1.12	Print information from a Web site or Web page	U3-T14-L14.4
IC³-3 3.1.13	Identify settings that can be modified in a Web browser application	U3-T14-L14.9, U3-T16-L16.2, L16.3, L16.4
IC³-3 3.1.14	Identify problems associated with using the Web (e.g. "Page Not Found" errors, pop-up ads, etc.)	U3-T14-L14.10

IC³ Global Standard 3	Objectives & Abbreviated Skill Sets	Topic Number, Lesson Number
Objective 3.2	**Understand how content is created, located and evaluated on the World Wide Web**	
IC³-3 3.2.1	Identify ways content is created on the Internet (e.g. blogs, wikis, podcasts, social networking sites, etc.)	U3-T13-L13.6, L13.7
IC³-3 3.2.2	Identify ways of searching for information	U3-T14-L14.5, L14.6
IC³-3 3.2.3	Use a search engine to search for information (e.g. using effective key words, using advanced search tools, etc.)	U3-T14-L14.5, L14.6
IC³-3 3.2.4	Identify issues regarding the quality of information found on the Internet including relevance, reliability, and validity.	U3-T14-L14.7
IC³-3 3.2.5	Identify how to evaluate the quality of information found on the Web	U3-T14-L14.7
IC³-3 3.2.6	Identify responsible and ethical behaviors when creating or using online content (e.g. Copyright, Trademark, avoiding plagiarism, etc.)	U3-T14-L14.8, U3-T16-L16.6
DOMAIN 4.0	**THE IMPACT OF COMPUTING AND THE INTERNET ON SOCIETY**	
Objective 4.1	**Identify how computers are used in different areas of work, school and home**	
IC³-3 4.1.1	Identify how information technology and the Internet are used at work, home or school to collect, analyze, evaluate, create communities, etc.	U3-T13-L13.5
IC³-3 4.1.2	Identify that traditional desktop and laptop computers represent only a fraction of the computer technology people interact with on a regular basis (e.g. ATM, embedded computer devises in household appliances, GPS, etc.)	U3-T13-L13.1
IC³-3 4.1.3	Identify how computers and the Internet have transformed traditional processes (e.g. e-commerce, telecommuting, online learning, etc.)	U3-T13-L13.1
IC³-3 4.1.4	Identify technologies that support or provide opportunities to the physically challenged and disadvantaged (e.g. voice recognized software, electronic government, etc.)	U3-T16-L16.5
Objective 4.2	**Identify the risks of using computer hardware and software and how to use computers and the Internet safely, ethically and legally**	
IC³-3 4.2.1	Identify how to maintain a safe working environment that complies with legal, health and safety rules	U3-T16-L16.1, L16.6, L16.8; U3-T16-Delving Deeper
IC³-3 4.2.2	Identify injuries that can result from the use of computers for long periods of time (e.g. back strain, eye strain, etc.)	U3-T16-L16.8
IC³-3 4.2.3	Identify risks to personal and organizational data (e.g. theft, data loss, etc.)	U3-T13-L13.4
IC³-3 4.2.4	Identify software threats, including viruses and WORMS	U3-T16-L16.2
IC³-3 4.2.5	Identify reasons for restricting access to files, storage devices, computers, networks, the Internet or certain Internet sites including protection of data and restricting sites to children with adult content.	U3-T16-L16.1, L16.3, L16.4
IC³-3 4.2.6	Identify the principles regarding when information can or cannot be considered personal, including the difference between computer systems owned by schools or businesses that may have rules and guidelines as to who owns data stored on the system, and computers owned by individuals where the owner of the computer has control over his or her own data	U3-T16-L16.1
IC³-3 4.2.7	Identify how to avoid hazards regarding electronic commerce (e.g. sharing credit card information on non-secure sites, checking the legitimacy of online offers, etc.)	U3-T16-L16.3
IC³-3 4.2.8	Identify how to protect privacy and personal security online (to avoid fraud, identity theft and other hazards)	U3-T16-L16.3
IC³-3 4.2.9	Identify how to find information about rules regarding the use of computers and the Internet	U3-T16-L16.1, L16.6; U3-T16-Delving Deeper
IC³-3 4.2.10	Identify how to stay informed about changes and advancements in technology	U3-T14-Delving Deeper, U3-T16-Delving Deeper
IC³-3 4.2.11	Identify how to be a responsible user of computers (e.g. recycling products like printer cartridges, safely disposing of hardware, etc.)	U3-T16-L16.9

Glossary

1000BaseT A wired Ethernet standard that transfers data at up to 1 Gbps

10GBaseT A wired Ethernet standard that transfers data at up to 10 Gbps

4G A standard for cellular wireless communications that transfers data at up to 1 Gbps

A

absolute cell reference Refers to a cell in a specific location; will not change within a formula if it is relatively copied

access control The technologies and techniques used to control who or what has access to a computer system

action button A drawn object on a slide that has a routine attached to it; the routine is activated when the object is clicked during a presentation

active cell The cell that is currently selected; identified by a dark border

Active Directory A user management service that runs on a Windows server and manages the user logins for all PCs in the network

add-on A supplemental program that works with the main program to extend the main program's capabilities

adware Applications that display unwanted advertisements on your computer

alignment The positioning of the lines of text in a document

alternating current (AC) Electrical current whose flow reverses (alternates)

analog A type of data that is continuously variable and has no precise numeric equivalent

animation effect An entrance, exit, or motion effect applied to an element in a slide

annualized failure rate (AFR) The likelihood that a device will fail in a certain year

anti-spyware software Software that defends against adware and spyware

antivirus program A program that defends against viruses, worms, and Trojan horses by analyzing and identifying suspicious files; also known as *antivirus software*

application Software that enables the user to perform a useful task such as creating a document or playing a game

B

Backstage view In Office 2010 applications, the view that appears when you click the File tab; the location from which you can save, close, open, and print files

bandwidth The maximum theoretical rate of data transmission for a communication medium

binary A numbering system based on two digits: 0 and 1

binary processing Computer data processing based on binary data and instructions

biometric reader A security scanner that identifies users by scanning for one or more physical traits

bit A single binary digit

blind carbon copy (Bcc) A copy of an email sent to someone who is not a primary recipient; no other recipients can see who receives a blind carbon copy; also known as a *blind courtesy copy*

blog An ongoing journal that displays on a publicly accessible website

Bluetooth A short-range wireless technology used to directly connect devices with peripherals, such as cell phones with wireless headsets

Boolean operators Words that represent logical yes/no statements, such as AND, OR, and NOT

border A frame that surrounds an item in a document, such as a paragraph or an entire page

build A type of animation that displays paragraphs in a slide one paragraph at a time

burn To write files to a CD or DVD

byte A string of eight binary digits (bits)

C

cable Internet A technology for delivering broadband Internet through cable TV lines

cache A temporary storage area for data that the CPU has recently needed or may need soon

carbon copy (Cc) A copy of an email sent to someone who is not a primary recipient; also known as a *courtesy copy*

card reader A drive that reads and writes from one or more types of flash RAM cards

Category 5e (Cat5e) cable A type of UTP cable that can carry data at up to 1Gbps

Category 6 (Cat6) cable A type of UTP cable that can carry data at up to 10Gbps

cathode ray tube (CRT) A large, boxy type of monitor that uses electron guns to light up phosphors on glass and create an image

cell The intersection of a row and a column in a spreadsheet

cell address The unique name for each cell, consisting of the column letter and row number in which the cell is located

cell orientation The rotation of text in a cell

cell pointer The mouse pointer that displays when positioned in a cell in a worksheet

cell pointer The white plus sign that displays when the mouse pointer is located on a cell

cell selection bar The left edge of each cell, between the left column border and the end-of-cell marker or first character in the cell; clicking here selects the cell

central processing unit (CPU) The part of a computer that performs the mathematical calculations that are the basis of all computing

charge-coupled device (CCD) The photosensitive part of a scanner or digital camera that records the amount of light bouncing off an image and converts that value to an electrical charge

chart A visual representation of numeric data; sometimes referred to as a graph

client A PC that an end-user employs

client/server A type of network that includes client PCs and at least one server

clip art A predesigned image, usually created by hand or using computer-aided graphics program

Clipboard A temporary area of memory that holds text while it is being moved or copied to a new location in the document or to a different document

command prompt A user interface based on typing text commands

concurrent license A software license that limits the number of simultaneous users but not the number of users who may install the application

conditional function A function that performs logical tests on values and formulas

continuous section break A break that separates a document into sections but does not insert a page break

cookie A plain text file that a Web page stores on your hard disk for tracking purposes

copy To place a copy of selected text on the Clipboard

copyright Ownership of an original artistic or literary work

cover page A predesigned page containing placeholders that is inserted at the beginning of a document

crawler A program that visits websites and catalogs their content; it then sends the information back to its owner

cut To remove selected text from the document and place it on the Clipboard

cybercrime A crime that involves a computer and a network

D

data throughput The actual rate of data transmission, or speed, of a communication medium

database A collection of data records

decimal A numbering system based on 10 digits; can also refer to a period that separates digits, as in *1.2*

dedicated server A server that is devoted to a single website, company, or activity

default printer The printer that is set to be used automatically if another printer is not specified

delete To remove text or objects from a document

desktop The work area of the graphical interface in Windows

desktop computer A nonportable computer with a separate monitor, keyboard, and mouse

destination program The program into which the data is pasted, linked, or embedded

dial-up network A network in which users connect using modems

dialog box launcher A button that displays the dialog box of options associated with the group

digital A type of data that is precisely defined using numeric digits

digital camera An input device that captures a picture, digitizes it, and saves it until it can be transferred to a computer

digital projector A projector that accepts video input from a computer and uses a projection system to display an enlarged version of that image on a projection screen

Digital Subscriber Line (DSL) A technology for delivering broadband Internet service through telephone lines

Digital Video Interface (DVI) A digital connection for a monitor that uses a rectangular block connector

direct current (DC) Electrical current that does not change direction; electronics usually require DC power

Domain Name Service (DNS) server A server that translates between IP addresses and domain names on the Internet

domain name A text-based name that uniquely identifies a company or server on the Internet

dots per inch (dpi) A measure of the resolution of printer output; higher DPI means a sharper image on the printout

duplexing The act of printing on both sides of a sheet of paper

dynamic memory Memory that requires constant electrical stimulation to retain its data

dynamic RAM (DRAM) RAM that requires constant electrical refreshing to hold its content

E

e-commerce Short for electronic commerce; the practice of using a computer network to buy and sell

electromagnetic interference (EMI) Data corruption that occurs because of the magnetic fields in two adjacent cables carrying data; also called crosstalk

electrostatic discharge (ESD) A shock that occurs when two objects of unequal electrical potential meet; also called static electricity

email A system that enables people to send and receive messages electronically

embed To insert a data object into a data file so that the object retains its memory of its original source application and can be edited in that application

emoticon A combination of symbols that represents a facial expression, such as :-); sometimes called a smiley

enclosed object An object drawn with any option in the Shapes button drop-down list except the options in the Lines section

endnote An explanatory note or reference printed at the end of the document

Energy Star A rating from the EPA that designates a device that meets certain energy-efficiency standards

ergonomics The study of designing and positioning equipment and devices to optimize their usefulness and safety to human bodies

Ethernet A popular networking standard that forms the basis for nearly all home and business networks

executable file A file that runs a program or performs an activity when double-clicked

expansion board A circuit board that is inserted in a slot in the motherboard to add additional capabilities to a computer

exploit An attack in which a criminal uses a vulnerability to target and harm a system

Extensible Markup Language (XML) A versatile markup language that allows users to create custom tags

extension A code at the end of a file name that tells the operating system what kind of file it is

Extranet A secured portion of a network that is open to users within the organization and specific users outside the organization

F

favorite A shortcut to a URL found in a web browser, also called a *bookmark*

Favorites Center A pane containing a list of recently viewed and bookmarked web pages, organized into three tabs: Favorites, Feeds, and History

feed reader An application that enables users to read RSS feeds

feed All the information that a certain user or organization posts

field A single column in a database table, listing one type of information

file properties Information about a file, such as its size, and type

File Transfer Protocol (FTP) A protocol used for efficiently transferring files to and from Internet servers

fill handle A small square in the bottom right corner of the active cell used to copy data to adjacent cells

filter A restriction placed on data to temporarily isolate specific data

first-party cookie A cookie that is placed on the computer by a website you visit

flaming Posting a message that contains inflammatory or abusive statements

flash drive A thumb-sized USB device that stores data on nonvolatile memory chips

flash memory card A small plastic wafer that encloses flash RAM, and that is written and read using a card reader device

flash RAM Static RAM that can be written and erased by a strong pulse of electricity

flat file database A single two-dimensional table containing database records

font The complete set of characters in a particular typeface

footer The text that appears at the bottom of every page

footnote An explanatory note or reference printed at the bottom of the page where it is referenced

form A formatted data entry template that helps to simplify data entry

format The appearance of a document in the document screen and how it looks when printed

Formula bar The area above the worksheet that displays information about the active cell; used to enter and edit formulas

formula A mathematical instruction that can be applied to a cell and that can reference the values of other cells

forum A web-based application that holds discussions and content that members upload and generate

forward To send a copy of a received email message to another person

frame The header and footer that accompany the data when it is sent in a packet over a network

freeware Software that is completely free to use

friend To request a connection from your online profile to someone else's on a social networking service

function A predesigned formula that performs calculations

G

game controller An input device designed to be used with one or more types of games on a computer

gaming console A computer designed for playing games; usually uses a television as a monitor

gigabyte (GB) One billion bytes; a measurement of storage capacity

gigahertz (GHz) One billion hertz

grammar checker A proofing tool that checks text for grammatical errors

graphical user interface (GUI) An operating system interface that relies on pictures and a pointing device for user interaction

gridlines The horizontal and vertical lines defining cells in a worksheet

H

hanging indent Paragraph formatting where every line except the first one is indented

hard copy A printed copy of a file

hard disk drive A metal box containing metal platters on which data is written in patterns of magnetic polarity

hard page break A page break that you manually insert

header The text that appears at the top of every page

hertz (Hz) A measurement of CPU speed; the amount of time it takes for a CPU's internal clock to complete a full cycle

hexadecimal A numbering system based on sixteen digits, 0 through 9 plus A through F

Hibernate mode A low-power mode that copies the contents of RAM to the hard disk and then shuts down all components, including RAM; also known as Suspend to Disk

home page The page that displays automatically when you open your web browser

homegroup A Windows 7 home or small office network

hyperlink A clickable link to a web page or some other content

Hypertext Markup Language (HTML) The programming language used to create web pages

Hypertext Transfer Protocol (HTTP) The networking protocol used to distribute web content

I

I-beam pointer The mouse pointer when it is placed over a text entry area

icon A small clickable picture representing an application, folder, document, or other file or location

indent A type of formatting that sets lines of text away from the margins

infrared technology An older wireless technology; moves data between devices using infrared light

inkjet printer A printer that creates an image on a page by squirting liquid ink onto the paper

input Data coming into a computer

input device A device designed to help enter data or commands into a computer

insert To add text or objects to a document

Insert mode A typing mode where text to the right of the insertion point is moved over to make room for new text

insertion point The flashing vertical cursor indicating where text will appear when you type

instant messaging (IM) A type of real-time, person-to-person communication on the Internet; also called chatting

Internet A global wide area network (WAN) comprised of many smaller networks linked together under a common set of protocols

Internet Mail Access Protocol (IMAP) An alternative to POP3 in which email is accessed using an email program but remains stored on the server

Internet Service Provider (ISP) A company that provides access to the Internet for a fee

Intranet A type of internal, secure network used by organizations and businesses, accessible only by members, employees, or other authorized users

IP address Short for Internet Protocol address; a numeric address that uniquely identifies a computer on a network

IP version 4 (IPv4) A version of Internet protocol in which each computer is uniquely identified by four numbers, each between 0 and 255, separated by periods

IP version 6 (IPv6) A version of Internet protocol in which each computer is uniquely identified by eight 4-digit hexadecimal numbers, separated by colons

issuing authority A company that provides and authenticates security certificates

J

junk mail Unwanted email messages; also called *spam*

K

K-slot A slot on a notebook computer for a security lock

key logger A program that records all keystrokes and sends the information to a remote location

L

land An area of greater reflectivity on an optical disc

laser printer A printer that creates an image by writing with a laser on a metal drum, transferring toner to the drum, and then transferring the toner to paper

latency Delays in data transmission on a network

leaders Visual elements, such as periods or hyphens, designed to direct a reader's eyes across the page

line drawing A shape drawn with an option in the Lines section of the Shapes button drop-down list

line spacing The vertical spacing between lines of text

link To insert a shortcut to external content into a data file so that the copy updates when the source changes

liquid crystal display (LCD) A thin, flat panel monitor that passes electricity through liquid crystals to create an image

Live Preview A feature that provides the user with an opportunity to see how a portion of text or an entire document will appear once certain formatting is applied

logical test A question that can be answered with true or false

M

mail server A computer that processes the sending and receiving of email

malware Programs that seek to harm your computer and its data; short for *malicious software*

mean time between failures (MTBF) The predicted amount of time between the expected failures of a device

mechanical device A device with moving parts

megabyte (MB) One million bytes; a measurement of storage capacity

megahertz (MHz) One million hertz

memory Data storage that uses on/off states on a chip to record patterns of binary data

menu bar A bar across the top of a window containing the names of drop-down lists; clicking a menu name opens that drop-down list

message body The main message text within an email

message header The sender, recipient, and subject information for an email

metatag An HTML code that provides data about the data (metadata)

millions of instructions per second (MIPS) A measurement of the amount of data a CPU can process

Mini toolbar A semitransparent toolbar that displays when you select text and contains buttons for formatting

mixed cell reference A reference where either the column remains absolute and the row is relative or the column is relative and the row is absolute

modem A device that converts between digital and analog data to transmit it over analog telephone lines

monitor An output device that displays text and/or images to the computer on a display screen

monospaced A style of typeface in which each character is allotted the same amount of horizontal space

motherboard The large, central circuit board inside a computer

mouse A device that you can roll across a flat surface to move an on-screen pointer

multicore A CPU that contains multiple processors that can all operate simultaneously

N

Navigation pane When turned on, displays at the left side of the screen and contains options for navigating in a document and searching for specific text

netbook computer A small notebook computer

netiquette Etiquette for online communication and behavior

network A group of connected devices that share data or resources

network adapter A device that translates instructions from the operating system into data that can be sent over the network

network address translation (NAT) A function of a router that enables the router to change the addressing on network packets to allow multiple computers to share a single Internet connection

notebook computer A portable computer with built-in monitor, keyboard, and pointing device

O

Object Linking and Embedding (OLE) A technology for including outside content in a data file so that the content retains its original source application or data file information

online learning Education courses available through the Internet that allow students access to instruction without physically attending a school; also called *e-learning*

open source Software that is free, and for which the source code is made available to the public so anyone may modify it

operating system (OS) Software that performs housekeeping tasks that keep the computer running; provides an interface between the user and the hardware

optical device A device that works by shining a light and measuring the amount of light that bounces back

optical disc A disc that stores data by using patterns of more or less reflectivity on the disc surface

orientation The layout position of a page for printing

output Data going out of a computer

output device A device designed to display or share data output from a computer

Overtype mode A typing mode where text to the right of the insertion point is replaced by new text

P

packet A container file for sending data over a network; contains the data itself plus a header and footer

packet sniffer An application that can intercept data packets as they are being sent or received

parental controls Software features that restrict certain activities or prevent the display of certain web content

paste To insert cut or copied text in the document

patent Identifies ownership of an invention

path The full address of a file, including the drive and folder

peer-to-peer (P2P) network A type of network that does not include a server; also called a workgroup

peripherals Computer-related devices that are not part of the computer system itself; examples include printers and scanners

persistent cookie A cookie that stays on the hard disk after the browser closes, either indefinitely or for a certain number of days

personal computer (PC) A computer designed for use by one individual

phishing Creating a site that masquerades as a legitimate secure site but actually steals login information from people who visit it

pit An area of less reflectivity on an optical disc

pixel An individual colored dot in an electronic image

placeholder A box that holds title or body text or an object such as a picture, chart, or table

plagiarism Using content that is not your own original work without citing the source, either implying or stating that the material is your own creation

pointing device A device designed to move an on-screen arrow pointer; contains buttons you click to issue commands

pop-up An extra, usually small, browser window that displays automatically when you open certain web pages or click a certain button on a page

port A socket into which you can connect a cable or device

Post Office Protocol (POP) A protocol used for receiving email in a store-and-forward email system

power plan Settings in the operating system that tell the computer to shut down or go into a power-saving mode after a specified period of inactivity

power sag A brief period of lower-than-normal AC voltage; also called a *brownout*

power supply The component that converts the incoming electrical power to a form the device can use

power surge A brief period of higher than normal AC voltage; also called a power spike

print queue A list of all active print jobs and the status of the print jobs for a particular printer

printer An output device that produces hard-copy printouts of the work you create on the computer

priority The level of urgency assigned to an email message; also called *importance*

proportional A style of typeface in which characters are allotted varying amounts of space

protocol A format or language for transmitting data between devices

PS/2 (mini-DIN) A small round connector used to connect keyboards and mice on some older computer systems

Q

query A set of saved sort-and-filter criteria that can be used to access a selected group of records

Quick Access toolbar A customizable toolbar containing commonly used commands

Quick Styles Predesigned paragraph and character formats that work together to help you create professional-looking documents

R

random access memory (RAM) Memory that can be written and changed by the device in which it is used

range A group of one or more cells

raster image a picture consisting of a grid of colored pixels; also called a *bitmap image*

read receipt A return email that lets you know when a recipient has opened your message

read-only memory (ROM) Memory that cannot be erased or changed by the device in which it is used

Really Simple Syndication (RSS) A means of subscribing to a frequently updated web page so that if the page's content changes, the new information is delivered to you automatically; also known as *RDF Site Summary*

record A single row in a database table, listing the information for one instance

registered trademark A trademark that has been established by registering the work with the United States Patent and Trademark Office

Registry A database of Windows settings that tells Windows what is installed and how to operate

relational database A database consisting of multiple related tables

relative cell reference A cell reference that adjusts when copied

report A formatted layout of a table or query that is optimized for printing

resident Continuously running in the background of the operating system environment

resolve To translate a domain name to an IP address

revolutions per minute (RPM) A measurement of the rotational speed of the platters in a hard disk drive

ribbon A tabbed toolbar interface that replaces the menu bar and toolbar in some applications

Rich Text (HTML) A hybrid of the RTF and HTML formatting standards; used in Windows Live Mail and some other email applications

Rich Text Format (RTF) A generic document formatting standard that most word processing and email applications can understand

rip To copy files from a CD or DVD to a computer hard drive

RJ-45 connector A connector type that is typically used for wired Ethernet UTP cables; looks like a telephone connector but slightly wider

router An advanced switch that not only physically connects and routes local network traffic, but also is able to manage incoming and outgoing traffic from an outside network such as the Internet

row selection bar The space immediately left of the left edge of each row; clicking here selects the row

S

safe senders list A list of email addresses you have approved to send you email

sans serif A term used to describe a typeface whose characters do not contain serifs

scanner An input device that converts a hard-copy picture to a digital image by measuring the amount of light that bounces back to a sensor as the light hits different parts of the original material

ScreenTip A small window that displays descriptive text when the mouse pointer is positioned on a button or command

scroll box A box on the vertical scroll bar that indicates the location of the text on the document screen in relation to the remainder of the document

search engine A utility that displays lists of relevant websites from a computer-compiled database in response to a keyword search

search engine optimization The process of coding a web page so that it displays higher in search engine rankings

secure site A website that employs some type of encryption technology to ensure that the data being transmitted is not intercepted by an unauthorized person

Secure Sockets Layer (SSL) A technology used for generating a secure site connection

security certificate A unique code that provides an assurance that the site you are communicating with is legitimate

selection bar The space located toward the left side of the document screen between the left edge of the page and the text

serif The small line that finishes off the top and bottom of a character; to describe a typeface as *serif* means that its characters contain these lines

server A computer that manages and runs network services

service mark A trademark that is for a service rather than a product; it can be registered or unregistered

service pack A collection of updates that are released as a group

session cookie A cookie that lasts only as long as the web browser is open

shading A formatting technique that applies color behind text and objects

shareware Software that you can try before you buy; if you decide to keep the program you must send payment to the owner

shell A user interface for an operating system

shortcut A path that leads to a file, folder, or drive

Simple Mail Transfer Protocol (SMTP) A protocol used for sending email in a store-and-forward email system

site license A software license that permits an organization to install an application on an agreed-upon number of PCs

sizing handles Small circles or squares that appear on the border of a selected image and are used to size the image

Sleep mode A low-power mode that shuts down most of the computer components but leaves the RAM powered; also known as Suspend to RAM

slide A single "page" of a presentation, designed to be displayed on a projector, computer monitor, or as a printout

smart card A card containing a microchip that a card reader can scan to verify or exchange information

SmartArt A visual representation of information, such as an organizational chart or diagram

smartphone A mobile phone that can also be used to access the Internet

SmartScreen filter The phishing filter in Internet Explorer

social engineering The practice of tricking individuals into letting their guard down and sharing personal information that can be used to commit fraud or other criminal activity

social networks Websites or other online services that exist to help people keep in touch with one another

soft copy An electronic copy of a file

soft page break A page break that Word automatically inserts

solid state An electronic device that operates only through circuit boards and other non-moving components

source program The program containing the data to be copied, linked, or embedded

spelling checker A proofing tool that identifies misspelled words in a document by comparing them against the words in a dictionary

spyware Software that records your computer usage

Start button The button that opens the Start menu

Start menu The main navigation menu in Windows, from which you can start up applications and browse file locations

static memory Memory that holds its data without being powered; also called nonvolatile memory

static RAM (SRAM) RAM that holds its content until it is erased or changed; does not require electricity

status flag An on/off switch for a particular property

status update A brief message that a user posts publicly using a social networking service

store-and-forward email system A system in which the server stores messages until the user logs in with an email application; it then forwards the stored messages to that program and deletes them from the server

subscribe To sign up to receive a certain feed

surge suppressor A power strip that is able to absorb excess voltage so that devices plugged into it will be protected during a power surge

switch A network connection box to which the cables for all the computers in the network connect

System Restore A utility for restoring system settings to the way they were at an earlier time

T

table move handle An icon that displays in the upper left corner of a table when you position the mouse arrow pointer in the table; can be used to move a table in a document

table resize handle A small, white square that displays in the lower right corner of a table; can be used to change the size and proportions of the table

tablet PC A small computer with a touch-sensitive screen; types of tablets include slates and convertibles

tag An HTML markup code enclosed in angle brackets, for example, *<p>*

Task Manager An interface for viewing running tasks and shutting down any that malfunction

Taskbar The bar at the bottom of the Windows desktop where currently running applications and open windows appear

telecommute To work from home while staying connected to the company through a computer or telephone network

texting Instant message delivery using a cell phone

theme A set of formatting choices that includes a color theme, a font theme, and an effects theme

Thesaurus A feature that finds synonyms, antonyms, and related terms for a particular word

third-party cookie A cookie that is placed on the computer by an ad on a website

title bar The bar across the top of the window where the window's name appears

toolbar A bar across the top of a window that contains icons for commonly used features

top-level domain The domain represented by the characters following the final decimal point in a domain name, such as .com or .edu

Total Cost of Ownership (TCO) The amount of money you spend over the lifetime of a device you own

touchpad A touch-sensitive pad, usually found on a notebook computer; you move your finger across the pad to move an on-screen pointer

trackball A stationary device with a ball on top; you roll the ball to move an on-screen pointer

trademark Identifies ownership of a word, phrase, symbol, or design that identifies or distinguishes one brand from another

transformer A block built into a device's power cord that converts the power from the wall outlet into a form the device can use

transistor An electrical gate that either blocks power or allows it to pass, depending on the transistor's current state

transition The way in which one slide is removed from the screen and the next slide displays when running a presentation

Transmission Control Protocol/Internet Protocol (TCP/IP) A suite of protocols that govern network transmission on the Internet and on most Windows networks

Trojan horse An application that appears to do something useful but also performs malicious actions within a computer

trolling Posting a message that is intentionally designed to offend others or stir up heated arguments

type size A measurement of type height in points

typeface A set of characters with a common design and shape

typestyle The variations within a typeface, such as bold or italic

U

Uniform Resource Locator (URL) The address of an Internet resource; begins with a communications protocol such as *http://*

uninterruptible power supply (UPS) A battery backup unit for a computer; contains a large battery that is charged from the AC outlet and is used to power its extension outlets when AC power becomes unavailable or inadequate

universal serial bus (USB) An interface used to connect many types of external devices to a computer

Unshielded Twisted Pair (UTP) A type of cable that carries data on pairs of copper wires that are twisted around each other to minimize the interference between the wires

updates Additional or replacement files for an application that fix or slightly enhance the application; they are usually free of charge

upgrade A new version of an application with significant new features; usually costs money

user authentication The technologies and techniques used to verify a person's identity

V

varistor A variable resistor; the component inside a surge suppressor that absorbs excess voltage

vector image A picture consisting of one or more drawn lines or shapes created by math formulas

vertical scroll bar The bar located at the right side of the screen; used for scrolling in a document

Video Graphics Array (VGA) An analog connection for a monitor that uses a 15-pin D-shaped connector

virtual private network (VPN) A secure network that operates through a larger unsecure network such as the Internet

virus Computer code that inserts itself into an executable file and executes along with the file to cause harm to a computer or its data

virus definition A uniquely identifying snippet of a virus's code, also called a *virus signature*

Voice over IP (VoIP) A system that uses a computer network such as the Internet to deliver telephone services

vulnerability Exists when there is a flaw in programming that creates potential for misuse, an attacker who is aware of it, and a tool or technique the attacker can use to exploit it

W

web conferencing software Multiuser chat software that enables full-featured audio, video, and text conferencing, as well as file sharing and application collaboration

web directory A directory listing of web content maintained by human editors

web hosting company A business that owns and maintains web servers and rents space on the servers to others

web page A single document, usually in HTML format, that contains web content

web server A server that is connected to the Internet and that has the appropriate software to be able to process requests for web content

website A group of related, interconnected web pages

Wi-Fi Short for Wireless Fidelity; a wireless version of Ethernet

Wi-Fi 802.11n The current standard for wireless Ethernet, transferring data at up to 160 Mbps

Wi-Fi Protected Access (WPA) A method of wireless network encryption that improves upon the older WEP technology and offers encryption capabilities for large networks using an authentication server

Wi-Fi Protected Access 2 (WPA2) A newer version of WPA, with stronger security capabilities than WPA

Windows Explorer The file management interface in Microsoft Windows

window A rectangular frame in which a file listing, program, message, or utility displays

wired device A device that connects to a computer with a cord or cable

Wired Equivalent Privacy (WEP) An older but still commonly used method of network encryption, controlled by entering a 128-bit or 256-bit key

wired network A network that uses physical cables and connector boxes to join the computers and devices

wireless access point (WAP) A wireless version of a switch

wireless device A device that connects to a computer using a wireless signal

wireless network A network that uses radio frequency (RF) signals to transmit data, with each device having its own radio transmitter and antenna

word wrap The automatic process of wrapping text from one line to the next

WordArt A feature used to distort or modify text to conform to a variety of shapes

workbook An Excel data file that contains one or more worksheets

worksheet area The area in an Excel worksheet that contains the gridlines

worksheet A single page of a workbook

worm A self-transporting application that carries a harmful program with it

Index

A

About dialog box, 121
absolute cell reference, 416–417
Access, relational database in, 141
access control methods, 603–605
accessibility, computers and, 740–744
accounting and personal finance software, 151–152
Accounting formatting, 447–450
Accounting Number Format button, 448
Action button, 539–542
active cell, 131–132, 175, 394
Active Directory, 603
Active Server Pages (.asp), 624
add-on, 670
Add Printer Wizard, 97
Address Bar, 75–76, 635
   adding additional search engines to, 656–657
   clearing history, 640, 642
   reviewing web browsing history with, 640
Add to Favorite dialog box, 642–643
Adobe Dreamweaver, 617
Adobe Illustrator, 143
Adobe Photoshop, 144
Advanced Encryption Standard (AES), 606
Advanced Micro Devices (AMD), 14
Advanced Research Project Agency Network (ARPANET), 608
adware, 150, 726–727
alignment, 265–268
   centering worksheet, 447–455, 451–449
   changing cell alignment in tables, 311–312
   changing table alignment, 314–315
   data in cells, 440–442
   shapes, 355
   tab alignment buttons, 283–284
   text in paragraphs, 265–268
   text in PowerPoint slides, 506
All Programs menu, 63, 69, 114
alternating current (AC), 8
analog data, 4
animation creation programs, 147
animation effect, 549–550
annualized failure rate (AFR), 22
anti-spyware software, 727, 728–729
antivirus software, 150–151, 727–729
antonyms, 237–238

AOL Instant Messenger, 152
Appearance and Personalization, 90, 93
Applications, 58, 123–124
   accounting and personal finance software, 151–152
   anti-spyware, 727, 728–729
   assistive, 741
   database software, 140–143
   educational software, 151
   entertainment software, 151
   exiting, 191
   exploits of, 726
   finding, 72
   graphics software, 143–147
   imaging programs, 673
   industry-specific software, 153
   installing, 113–120
   license types for, 117–118
   menu bar and toolbar for, 70–71
   multimedia software, 147–148
   operating system compared to, 61
   pinning to Taskbar, 177
   presentation software, 136–140
   registering, 118
   running, in Microsoft Windows 7, 68–72
   setting up compatibility mode, 72
   sharing data between, 154–158
   spreadsheet applications, 130–135
   starting, 69
   subscription, 117
   suites, 153
   uninstalling, 98, 118–120
   updating, 120–123
   upgrading to new version, 122
   utility programs, 148–151
   web authoring software, 153
   web browsing software, 152–153
   word processing applications, 124–130
Area chart, 457
Arrow option, 494, 496
ASCII (American Standard Code for Information Interchange), 23
ATMs, 586
@ sign, in email address, 685
attachments, email
   executable attachments, 703
   opening, 700
   receiving, 700–702
   saving, 701
   sending, 700–702

Audio Description, 741
audio files, inserting in presentation, 553–555
AutoArrange, turning off, 73
AutoComplete feature, 414
AutoCorrect feature, 180, 221, 273
Auto Fill Options button, 402
automatic signatures, email, 712
AutoRecover
   changing time for, 198
   customizing, 198–200
Autorun, 116, 158
AutoSum button, 402–404
AVERAGE function, 402, 410

B

Back button (Internet Explorer), 635
Backstage view, 125
   customizing Recent tab, 198–200
   exiting, 182–183
   Help tab, 200–202, 200–203
   New tab, 192
   pinning document to, 185
   Print Preview, 443–445, 459
   Print tab, 185–187, 234–235, 398, 490–491
   Save & Send tab, 195–197
Backup utility, 149
balloons
   inserting comments, 365–368
   tracking changes with, 363–365
bandwidth, 593
Bar chart, 457
   bar code reader, 28
bash, 58, 60
binary numbering system, 5
binary processing, 13
Bing, 656
biometric reader, 604–605
bit, 5
bitmap images, 144
bitmapped, 144
blind carbon copy (Bcc), 690
blind courtesy copy, 690
Blog Post, saving document as, 375
blogs, 622
Bluetooth, 590, 594
Blu-Ray disc
   memory capacity of, 21
   as optical disc, 21
   storage capacity limit, 18
bookmarks, 642

Boolean operators, 655
Border and Shading dialog box, 276–278
borders
    drawing, 308
    tables in word, 306–308
    text in Word, 276–278
broadband Internet service, 610–611
brownout, 40
Browse Help button, 88
browsing. *See* web browsers
Bubble chart, 457
build, animation, 549–550
bullets
    inserting, 272–273
    in PowerPoint slides, 506
    SmartArt graphics with bulleted
        text, 539
    turning off, 273
burn, 148
business letter
    format for, 242–243
    template to create, 193–194
business report, 287
byte, 5, 17

C
cable Internet, 610
cache, 15, 642
    hard disk and, 19
    size and levels of, 15
Calculator, 68, 71–72, 113
carbon copy (Cc), 690
card reader, 20
Category 5e (Cat5e), 590
Category 6 (Cat6), 590
cathode ray tube monitor, 29–30
CD
    burning applications, 148
    memory capacity of, 21
    as optical disc, 21
    storage capacity limit, 18
cell address, 395
Cell Options dialog box, 312–314
cell orientation, 440
cell pointer, 134, 175–176, 395, 396
cells, 130–131
    entering and editing data in cells, 134
    in Excel
        cell orientation, 440
        cell styles, 407–408
        clear data in, 438
        column width and row height
            changes, 435–437
        commands to make active,
            395–396
        cutting, copying, and pasting
            cells, 419–420
        editing data in, 398–400
        fill handle to enter data, 400–402
        formulas with absolute and
            mixed cell references, 416–417
        formulas with AutoSum, 402–405

formulas with functions, 410–414
formulas with IF logical function,
    414–415
formulas with mathematical
    operations, 409–410
inserting and deleting, 437–440
mouse to activate, 396
number formatting, 447–450
relative cell reference, 403
selecting data within cell, 405
selecting with keyboard, 403
selecting with mouse, 403
    in table. *See* tables
cell selection bar, 303
Cell Styles button, 407–408
central processing unit (CPU) , 8, 13–15
    buying a computer and, 34
    evaluating computer's, 16
    multicore, 14
    processing power of, 14
    speed of, 14
Change Chart Type dialog box, 460
charge-coupled device (CCD), 26
charts, in Excel, 457
    changing layout, 463–464
    chart type and style changes, 460–462
    creating, 457–459
    customizing layout, 465–466
    deleting, 462
    inserting shapes, 464
    label changes, 463–464
    location changes, 461
    pie chart, 465–466
    previewing, 459
    sizing and moving with mouse, 458
Chart Tools Design tab, 460, 463
Chart Tools Format tab, 465
chatting, 621
Check Disk utility, 47, 149
Check for Updates option, 121
Citation & Bibliography, 746–747
citation style, 746–747
Clear button, 438
client, 592
client/server network, 592
clip art
    downloading, 534
    in Excel, 445–447
    in PowerPoint, 530–534
    in Word, 351–354
Clip Art task pane, 445–446
Clipboard
    copying or moving with, 80
    cutting, copying and pasting with,
        224–228
    moving and copying data between
        applications with, 154
    screen capture and, 73
    Windows, 80
Clipboard Task pane, 224
Clock, Language, and Region, 90
collated page, 237

colors
    adjusting images, 351
    Picture Tools Format tab, 351
    Theme Colors, 339–340, 485
Column chart, 457
column header, 395
columns
    in Excel
        changing width, 435–437
        inserting and deleting, 437–440
    text in PowerPoint slides, 506
    in Word
        breaks in, 351
        creating, 349–350
        formatting, 350–351
        in table
            automatically adjusting, 311
            changing width of, 310–311
            managing, 308–309
Columns dialog box, 350
Column Width dialog box, 437
Command Bar, 75–76
    displaying/hiding in Internet
        Explorer, 666–667
command-line interface, 58–59
command prompt, 58
Comma Style button, 448
comments, 365–369
CompactFlash (CF), 20
Compatibility tab, 72
Computer list, 75–76
Computer Mode with Cipher Block
    Chaining Message Authentication
    Code Protocol (CCMP), 606
computer networks. *See* networks
computers, 4–13
    accessibility, 740–744
    accident protection, 39–41
    assistive hardware and software for,
        740–744
    cleaning, 42–44
    components of, 7–8
    CPUs and memory, 13–17
    data storage space, 17–23
    device, other, 61
    energy saving, 756–759
    ergonomics, 753–755
    input devices, 23–28
    operating system, 34–35
    output devices, 29–32
    power for, 36–37
    safety hazards, 753
    saving energy and recycling, 756–761
    selecting a, 12–13, 33–35
    setting up, 35–38
    System Information, 38
    theft protection for, 38–39
    turning on, 37
concurrent license, 118
conditional function, 414
Content Advisor feature, 737–738
content icons, 138

content placeholder, 137–138
Control Panel
    accessing, 91
    categories of, 89–90
    changing settings with, 92–94
    to determine installed applications, 115–116
    Ease of Access Center, 741–744
    power plan, 757–759
Convert Text to Table dialog box, 317–318
cookies, 150, 733–734
    managing, 734–736
Copy Command, 80
copying
    with clipboard, 80
    data between applications, 154
    with drag-and-drop, 80
    files, 79–80
    folders, 79–80
    text using Clipboard Task Pane, 224–228
copyright, 648, 662, 746
corrupted files, 204
COUNT function, 411
courtesy copy, 690
cover page, 344–347
crawler, 653
Create Folder dialog box, 705
crosstalk, 40–41
CRT (cathode ray tube), 29–30
Currency formatting, 447–450
Customize Quick Access Toolbar, 178–180
Custom number formatting, 450
Custom Sort, 407
cut, 79
    text using Clipboard Task Pane, 224–228
Cut Command, 80
cybercrime, 745
cycle diagram, 362

D

data, 4–5
    encrypted, 723
    moving and copying between applications, 154
    ownership of, 723
    securing data online, 723–725
database, 140–141
    queries, forms, reports, 141
database normalization, 143
database software, 140–143
    flat file database, 140
    relational database, 141
    terms and concepts, 140–141
data loss, 602
data storage, 17–23
    evaluating storage devices, 22–23
    flash drives and cards, 19–20
    hard drives, 18–19
    measurements of, 17–18

network drive, 23
optical discs, 20–21
reliability of, 21–22
remote storage, 23
summary of capacity limits for, 18
data throughput, 593
date, changing, 91
Date and Time, inserting, 341–343
Date formatting, 449
decimal number system, 5
decimal tab, 285
Decrease Decimal button, 448
dedicated server, 614
default printer, 94
default settings
    cell format in Excel, 407
    customizing default AutoRecover settings, 198–200
    font, 180, 262, 265
    page layout position, 337
    page margins, 336
    page numbering, 344
    page size in Excel, 455
    printer, 187
    worksheet margins, 451
Delete dialog box, 437–438
desktop for Microsoft Windows, 7, 62, 73
desktop computers, 9–10
desktop publishing software, 123
destination program, 557
Details Pane, 75–76
device driver, 100
Device Manager, 45
Devices and Printers window, 94–95
    setting default printer, 187
dialog box launcher, 178
dial-up network, 593, 594
digital cameras, 27, 28
digital data, 5
digital projector, 30
Digital Video Interface (DVI), 36
DIMM, 16
direct current (DC), 8
Disk Cleanup utility, 48, 149
Disk Defragmenter utility, 47, 149
DNS (Domain Name Service) servers, 610, 614
document protection, 369–371
document statistics, 238–239
domain name, 610
    in email address, 685
    identifying top-level, 620
    registering, for business, 619
donating computers, 760
dots per inch (dpi), 32–33
Doughnut chart, 457
download, installing an application by, 116–117
Draft view, 232–233
Drag-and-Drop
    copy a file with, 80–81
    move a file with, 80–81

moving and copying data between applications with, 154
Draw Borders group, 320
drawing, 143
    in Microsoft Paint, 146–147
    objects, 354–356
    in PowerPoint, 144–146
    shapes, 354–356
    table, 318–320
drawing software, 123
Drawing Tools Format tab, 354–355, 539
drop-down lists, 70
DSL (Digital Subscriber Line), 594, 610
Dual Inline Memory Module (DIMM), 16
duplexing, 760
Duration option, 496–498
DVD
    burning applications, 148
    memory capacity of, 21
    as optical disc, 21
    storage capacity limit, 18
DVI, 36
dynamic memory, 15
dynamic RAM (DRAM), 16

E

Ease of Access Center, 90, 741–744
e-commerce, 586
editing
    documents in Word
        changing document views, 232–234
        cutting, copying and pasting text using Clipboard Task Pane, 224–228
        displaying document statistics, 238–239
        finding and replacing text, 228–231
        grammar check, 239–241
        inserting and deleting text, 220–221
        insertion point movement, 217–218
        navigation in, 217–220
        previewing and printing, 234–237
        restricting editing and formatting, 369–371
        scrolling, 217–220
        selecting text, 221–223
        spelling check, 239–241
        Thesaurus feature, 237–239
        undo and redo, 222–223
    in Excel, data in cells, 398–400
Editing restrictions, 369–371
educational networks, 586
educational software, 151
Effect Options button, 496–498
e-learning, 586
electromagnetic interference (EMI), 41
electronic communication
    blogs, 622

challenges of, 748–749
common abbreviations used in, 750
email, 620
emoticons, 748–749
etiquette guidelines for, 749–752
instant messaging, 620
message board, 623
newsgroup, 623
podcast, 622
RSS feeds, 624
social networking, 622–623
VoIP, 621
web conferencing, 621
electronic pointing devices, 740
electrostatic discharge (ESD), 40, 42
email, 620, 683–712. *See also* Windows
   Live Mail
  access protocol for, 684–685
    HTTP (Web mail), 684
    IMAP, 684
    POP3 and SMTP, 684
  advanced mail options, 712–713
   archiving messages, 713
   automatic signatures, 712
   mail forwarding, 712
   out-of-office message, 712
   searching for a message, 713
   supplementing messages, 712
   synchronizing message, 713
  attachments
   executable attachments, 703
   opening, 700
   receiving, 700–702
   saving, 701
   sending, 700–702
  contact list
   adding recipients to, 692–696
   view, edit, or delete, 694
  employers and data ownership, 723
  etiquette for, 686, 699, 750–752
  junk mail, 707–710
  messages
   auto send/receive interval, 699
   controlling quotes when reply-
    ing, 699
   forwarding, 698
   read receipt, 704
   replying to, 698–699
   setting message priority, 703–704
   viewing, 697, 699
  organizing, 704–707
   creating new folder, 705
   deleting messages, 706
   moving messages between fold-
    ers, 705–706
  parts of email address, 685
  phishing emails, 733
  sending document using, 373
  as store-and-forward system, 620, 684
  troubleshooting common problems,
   710–711
  Windows Live Mail
   configuring, 686–689

setting up account in, 687–689
writing email message
  carbon and blind copies, 690
  formatting message, 690–692
  message header, 689–690
  specifying recipient and subject,
   689–690
  starting new message, 689
email address components, 685
embedding, 155
  display embedded object as icon, 563
  Word table in PowerPoint slide,
   561–563
emoticons, 748–749
enclosed object, 539
encryption
  securing online data with, 723
  wireless, 606
Encrypt with Password option, 370–371
endnote, 372–373
Energy Star, 757
entertainment software, 151
Eraser option, 494
ergonomics, 753–755
Ethernet, 589
  bandwidth for, 594
  networking with HomePlug, 596
  popularity of, 590
  speeds of, 590
Excel
  data analysis with
   closing workbook, 398–400
   creating and saving workbook,
    394–397
   to draw conclusions, 467–468
   editing data in, 398–400
   entering data in worksheet,
    396–397
   errors in, 421
   fill handle to enter data, 400–402
   formatting cell and table styles,
    407–409
   formulas copied relatively,
    403–405
   formulas with absolute and
    mixed cell references, 416–417
   formulas with AutoSum, 402–405
   formulas with functions, 410–414
   formulas with IF logical function,
    414–415
   formulas with mathematical
    operations, 409–410
   printing, 398–400
   selecting cells, 402–405
   sorting and filtering data, 405–407
  general techniques and tips for
   activating cell, 395–396
   blank worksheet screen in, 175,
    394–395
   closing files and exiting, 191, 399
   concepts and terminology for,
    130–132
   creating and naming files, 180–181

   creating files using templates,
    192–194
   creating single-table database,
    142–143
   customizing and moving ribbon
    commands, 178–180
   entering and editing data in cells,
    134
   flat-file database in, 140
   formulas, 131–132
   help resources, 200–202, 200–203
   interface of, 132–133
   managing worksheets, 417–419
   navigating in, 133
   opening program, 174–175
   other capabilities of, 134
   printing files, 185–190, 398
   rows and cells, 130–131
   saving in different format,
    195–197
   screen features, 175–177
   selecting ranges, 134
   shortcuts in, 133
   workbook and worksheets, 132,
    394–396
  linking chart with Word document
   and PowerPoint presentation,
   557–559
  worksheet formatting. *See* formatting
executable file, 116
expansion board, 8
exploit, 725–726
Extensible Markup Language (XML), 615
extension, 84, 85

F

Facebook, 622, 623
facial recognition software, 605
Favorite button (Internet Explorer), 635
Favorites bar, 646, 666–667
favorites/Favorites list, 75–76, 642
  creating folders for favorites, 644
  deleting, 645
  Favorites bar, 646
  History list, 640
  moving favorite, 645
  opening web address from Favorite
   list, 643
  organizing, 644–645
  renaming favorite, 645
  saving URL to, 642–643
Fedora, 60
feed, 623
feed reader, 623
fiber optic dedicated line, 594
fields, in database, 141
file extensions, 195
file properties, 86
files
  attachments, email, 700–702
   executable attachments, 703
   sending, 700–702
  burn, 148

closing and exiting applications, 191
common problems with opening, 204
corrupted, 204
creating with templates, 192–194
deleting unwanted, 48
downloading from website, 651
extension, 84
file properties, 86
incompatible, 204
inserting text from file, 342
in Microsoft Windows 7
    copying, 79–82
    deleting and restoring files from
        Recycle Bin, 82–84
    file properties, 86
    moving, 79–82
    selecting multiple, 78–79
    setting file management options,
        85–86
    troubleshooting common file
        management problems, 87
naming and renaming, 84, 182
opening, 126, 182–185
path, 75
printing, 185–190
recovering unsaved files, 200
rip, 148
saving, 180–182
    in different format, 195–197
    with Save As, 182–185
File tab, 125, 175–176, 394, 482
File Transfer Protocol (FTP), 619
fill handle, 400–402
filtering data in Excel, 405–407
Filter Keys, 742
financial functions, 421–422
Find and Replace dialog box, 229–231
finding
    find and replace, 228–231
    text with Navigation Pane, 228–229
fingerprint scanners, 604
firewall, 149, 761
first-party cookie, 733
flaming, 750
Flash (.swf), 624
flash drive, 18, 19
flash memory card, 20
flash RAM, 15–16, 19, 22
flat file database, 140
floppy disks, 18
folders
    creating for favorites, 644
    in Microsoft Windows 7
        browsing folder listings, 77–78
        copying, 79–82
        creating and renaming, 81
        moving, 79–82
        selecting multiple, 78–79
    for organizing email, 704–706
    sharing with homegroup, 598
    sharing without homegroup, 598–599
Font dialog box, 261–264, 442, 503

Font group buttons, 257–260, 502–505
fonts, 258
    changing default, 262, 265
    default, 180
    formatting
        in Excel, 440–442
        with Font group, 257–260
        with Mini toolbar and Font dialog
            box, 261–264
        in PowerPoint presentation,
            502–505
    previewing, 258
    Theme Fonts, 339–340, 485
    typeface, 258
    types size, 259
    typestyle, 259
footers
    in Excel, 455–456
    in PowerPoint, 509–511
    in Word, 344–347
footnote, 372–373
form, 141
Format Cells dialog box, 442
    number formatting, 447–449
Format Painter, 264–265, 506–508
formatting
    document styles
        business letter, 243
        business report, 287
        memo, 244
        personal business letter, 242
    email in Windows Live Mail,
        690–691
    in Excel
        cell and table styles, 407–408
        cells, rows, columns insertion and
            deletion, 437–440
        centering worksheet, 447–455,
            451–449
        chart creation, 457–459
        chart design changes, 460–463
        chart layout and chart formatting
            changes, 463–466
        clip art and image insertion,
            sizing and moving, 445–447
        column width and row height
            changes, 435–437
        design considerations, 469
        font and alignment formatting,
            440–442
        headers and footers, 455–456
        margin changes, 447–455, 451–449
        numbers, 447–451
        page size changes, 469
        previewing, 443–445
        scaling data, 455
        themes, 443–445
        worksheet margin changes,
            447–455
    in PowerPoint
        action button, drawing and cus-
            tomizing, 539–542

animation effect, 549–550
drawing in, 144–146
embedding Word table in, 561–563
fonts and font effects, 502–505
hiding or displaying mouse arrow
    during presentation, 496
header and footer insertion,
    509–511
inserting link to video file at web-
    site, 555
inserting slide content, 137–138,
    486–488
paragraph formatting, 506–509
picture or clip art image, insert-
    ing, sizing, moving, 530–534
shapes, drawing and customizing
    in, 539–542
slide master, formatting with,
    547–548
SmartArt graphics, inserting and
    formatting, 534–539
spelling check for, 499–500
tables, creating in, 543–546
templates for, 490
text, 502–505
themes, choosing, 484–488
transition and transition sounds
    for, 496–498
in Word, 255–287, 336–374
    aligning text in paragraphs,
        265–268
    borders and shading, 276–278
    comments, inserting, 365–369
    comparing, 271
    cover page, 344–347
    with Font group, 257–261
    with Format Painter, 264–265
    headers and footers, 344–347
    image inserting, sizing and
        moving, 351–354
    indenting text, 274–275
    line spacing changes, 268–269
    with Mini toolbar and Font dialog
        box, 261–264
    numbering and bullets, 272–273
    objects, drawing and formatting,
        354–356
    organizational charts, 359–362
    page and section breaks, 347–349
    page margins, orientation and
        size changes, 336–339
    page numbering, 344–347
    paragraph spacing changes,
        270–271
    protecting document, 369–371
    restricting, 369–371
    Reveal Formatting task pane,
        268–269
    setting tabs, 283–287
    SmartArt graphics, 359–363
    styles, 279–282

symbols and special characters insertion, 341–343
tabs, 283–287
text in columns, 349–351
themes and, 339–340
tracking changes made to document, 363–365
WordArt Text, 357–358
Formatting restrictions, 369–371
Formula bar, 131–132, 175, 394, 395, 410
Formula dialog box, 321–322
formulas, 131–132
with absolute and mixed cell references, 416–417
with AutoSum button, 402–404
changing order of operations, 410
common errors in, 421
display formulas, 411
editing, 415
with functions, 410–414
with IF logical function, 414–415
with mathematical operations, 409–410
writing by pointing, 410
forums, 623, 750–751
Forward button (Internet Explorer), 635
forwarding email message, 698
4G, 590
Fraction formatting, 450
frame, 588
freeware, 117
friend (social networking), 623
From Beginning button, 494–495
From Current Slide button, 494–495
Full Screen Reading view, 232–233
Function dialog box, 410–411
Function Library group, 410
functions, 132
AutoComplete feature, 414
categories of, 414
common errors in, 421
conditional function, 414
financial functions, 421–422
IF logical function, 414–415
inserting formulas with, 410–414
FV, 422

G

gadget, 153
game controllers, 26
gaming consoles, 12
General number formatting, 447
gigabytes (GB), 16, 17
gigahertz (GHz), 14
global positioning system (GPS) device, 585
Google Chrome, 152
Go To option, 217, 400
grammar checker, 239–241
graphical user interface (GUI), 59
graphic hyperlinks, 636
graphics/graphic software, 143–147

bitmap images, 144
drawing in Microsoft Paint, 146–147
drawing in PowerPoint, 144–146
SmartArt graphics, 359–363, 534–539
vector images, 143
gridlines, 395
displaying to position images and shapes, 542
viewing, 312
Group button, 355
grouping objects, 355

H

handouts, for presentation, 509–510
hanging indent, 274–275
hard copy, 185
hard disk, 18
hard disk drive, 8, 18
buying a computer and, 34
cache size, 19
capacity of, 19
interior of, 18
internal *vs.* external, 19
mechanical reliability of, 22
revolutions per minute (RPM), 19
solid state, 18, 20
storage capacity limit, 18
as storage device, 18–19
virtual memory and, 17
hard drive, 18
hard page break, 347
hardware
assistive, 740–741
for networking, 589–590
Hardware and Sound, 90, 92
Header & Footer button, 455–456, 509
headers
in Excel, 455–456
in PowerPoint, 509–511
in Word, 344–347
health and safety issues
ergonomics, 753–755
identifying legal and ethical computer use, 745–747, 749
making computer more accessible, 740–744
netiquette, 748–752
protecting minors online, 737–740
safety hazards and computer use, 753–755
saving energy and recycling, 756–761
Help and Support window, 87–89
Help resources
Microsoft Office, 200–202, 200–203
Microsoft Windows 7, 87–89
Help tab Backstage view, 200–202, 200–203
hertz (Hz), 14
hexadecimal numbering system, 5
Hibernate mode, 756
Hidden text, 261
High Contrast, 741, 743–744

Highlighter option, 494
History list, 640–641
Home button (Internet Explorer), 635
Homegroup, 75–76, 597–602
home page, 663–664
HomePlug, 596
Horizontal Line dialog box, 278
horizontal ruler, 175–176
displaying, 303
horizontal scroll bar, 394, 483
HTML (Hypertext Markup Language), 614, 615, 624
creating web page in Notepad, 616
email formatted messages, 690
tags, 615
HTTP (Hypertext Transfer Protocol), 614, 684
HTTP error codes, 668–669
HTTPS, 723, 733
hyperlink, 614
graphic hyperlinks, 636
inserting and navigating with, 543–544
text hyperlinks, 636
Hypertext Markup Language (HTML). *See* HTML (Hypertext Markup Language)
Hypertext Transfer Protocol (HTTP), 614, 684

I

I-beam pointer, 125, 175–176, 483
ICANN (Internet Corporation for Assigned Names and Numbers), 609
icon, 62
Auto Arrange and, 73
display embedded object as, 563
identity fraud, 731–732
identity theft, 602
IF logical function, 414–415
images
bitmap images, 144
in Excel, inserting, sizing, moving, 445–447
Picture Tools Format tab, 351–352, 445–447
saving from website, 649–650
vector image, 143
in Word, inserting, sizing, moving, 351–354
IMAP, 684
IMing, 621
Increase Decimal button, 448
indenting
hanging indent, 274
outdent, 275
text, 274–275
Indent marker, 274–275
information theft, 602
infrared technology, 591
Ink Color option, 494
inkjet printer, 31

InPrivate Browsing, 736
input, 6
input devices, 23–28
    connecting, 35
    digital cameras, 27–28
    game controllers, 26
    keyboards, 23–24
    pointing devices, 24–25
    scanners, 26–27
Insert dialog box, 440
Insert Function button, 410
insertion point, 125, 175–176, 483
    Go To option, 217
    keyboard commands, 217–218
    navigation buttons, 217
    placeholder insertion movement
        commands, 485
Insert mode, 126
Insert Object command, 155
Insert Object dialog box, 156
Insert tab, 341–343
installation, of software, 113–120
    from CD or DVD, 116
    determining what has been installed,
        114–115
    downloading, 116–117
instant messaging, 621
    etiquette guidelines for, 750
Intel processor, 14
Internet, 608–613
    copyright restrictions and plagiarism,
        661–663
    general concepts of
        creation of, 608
        electronic communication,
            620–624
        IP address, 609–610, 612–613
        path redundancy, 608
        types of connections to, 610–612
        World Wide Web, 614–619
    health and safety issues, making
        computer more accessible,
        740–744
    professionalism
        legal and ethical computer use,
            745–747
        polite and professional communi-
            cation, 748–752
    security issues
        cookies, 733–736
        identity fraud and social engi-
            neering, 731–732
        malware, 725–730
        networks and protecting data,
            602–607
        phishing, 732–733
        protecting minors online, 737–740
        secure data access, 722–724
    web browsers, 634–635
        clearing history list, 640–642
        conducting searches, 655–659
        configuring, 663–668
        display menu bar, 637

        evaluating search results, 659–661
        favorites, using and managing,
            642–646
        finding information on web page,
            637–639
        following hyperlinks, 636
        Internet Explorer interface,
            634–636
        opening, 634
        reviewing web browser history,
            639–640
        RSS, save and organize book-
            marks to, 639
        saving content for offline use,
            648–652
        search engine basics, 653–655
        troubleshooting, 668–673
        using online information prop-
            erly, 661–663
Internet Explorer, 68, 152, 634–635
    add-ons, 669–670
    address bar, 635
    advanced setting, 671–672
    Back and Forward buttons, 635
    clearing history list, 640–642
    Content Advisor feature, 737–738
    controlling text size and zoom level,
        665–666
    as default browser, 639
    displaying/hiding toolbars and
        status bar, 666–667
    Favorite button, 635
    favorites, using and managing,
        642–646
    finding information on web page,
        637–639
    Home button, 635
    managing search providers in,
        656–659
    menu bar, displaying, 637
    opening, 634
    Refresh button, 635
    refresh rate (or speed), 30
    reviewing web browser history,
        639–640
    RSS, save and organize bookmarks
        to, 639
    saving content for offline use, 648–652
    setting colors in, 664–665
    setting home page, 663–664
    Status bar, 636
    Stop button, 635
    Tabs, 636
    Tools button, 636
    troubleshooting problems, 668–673
Internet Mail Access Protocol (IMAP),
    684
Internet Service Provider (ISPs), 610
iPad, 11
IP address, 609–610
    domain name, 610
    resolve, 610
    top-level domain, 610

    understanding, 613
IP version 4 (IPv4), 609
IP version 6 (IPv6), 610
issuing authority, 724
iTunes, 148

J
Java Server Pages (.jsp), 624
joysticks, 741
junk mail, 707–711
    blocking or unblocking a sender, 708
    changing level of protection, 708
    origin of, 711
    receiving email only from safe send-
        ers, 708
justifying text, 268

K
Keyboards, 23–24
    alternative, 740
    to change slides, 489–490
    cleaning, 43, 44
    ergonomic, 755
    to modify image, 530
    navigating slide show, 494
    QWERTY layout, 28
    selecting cells with, 403
    selecting table with, 304
    to select text in cell, 306
keyboard shortcuts. *See* shortcuts
key logger, 726, 727
keywords, searches and, 655–656
kilobyte (KB), 17
korn, 60
K-slot, 39

L
lands, 21
landscape orientation, 337, 451
laptop, 10
laser printers, 32
latency, 593
Layout button, 485
LCD (liquid crystal display) monitor, 29
leaders, setting tabs with, 285–286
letters
    business, 243
    personal business, 242
    template to create business letter,
        193–194
Libraries List, 75–76
licensing, software, 117–118
Line chart, 457
line drawing, 539
lines
    borders, 276–278
    horizontal lines, 278
    in PowerPoint, 539–542
    spacing, 268–269
linking, 155
    content in Word, 156–157
    data or object within program, 559
    destination program, 557

editing linked object, 559–561
Excel chart with Word document and
PowerPoint presentation, 557–559
PowerPoint data to Word, 557
source program, 557
Linux, 60, 61, 117
liquid crystal display monitor, 29
lists
applying numbering and bullets,
272–273
inserting multilevel lists, 273
Live Preview, 225, 258, 443, 484
Local Area Network (LAN), 591
locations, browsing, 76–77
Lock option, 67, 68
logical test, 414
Log off, 67, 68
LoJack, 41

M

Mac OS X, 34–35, 59, 60, 61
Magnifier, 741
mail forwarding, 712
mail servers, 684
malware, 150, 725, 726–731
mapping and geographical imaging
programs, 673
margins
in Excel, 447–455, 451–449
in Word, 336–339
Margins button, 451
mathematical operations, formulas
with, 409–410
MAX function, 411
maximize, window, 64, 66, 176
McAfee VirusScan, 728
MD5 (Message Digest Version 5), 727–728
mean time between failures (MTBF), 22
mechanical device, 24–25
media players, 124, 148
megabytes (MB), 16, 17
megahertz (MHz), 14
memo, formatting, 244
memory, 15
dynamic, 15
measuring, 16
random access memory (RAM), 15–16
read-only memory (ROM), 15
static, 15
virtual, 17
Memory Stick, 20
Menu Bar, 70, 75–76
displaying, 71, 637
displaying/hiding in Internet
Explorer, 666–667
Merge & Center button, 440
Message Digest Version 5 (MD5),
727–728
messages. See email
metatag, 654
Metropolitan Area Network (MAN), 591
Microsoft Excel. See Excel
Microsoft Expression Web, 617

Microsoft Office
closing files and exiting applications,
191
creating and naming files, 180–182
creating files using templates,
192–194
customizing and moving ribbon
commands, 178–180
customizing default settings, 198–200
help resources, 200–203, 200–204
opening and saving files with save
as, 182–187
opening programs, 174–175
printing, 187–190
saving files in different format,
195–197
screen features, 175–177
Microsoft Paint, 146–147
Microsoft PowerPoint. See PowerPoint
Microsoft Security Essentials, 728
Microsoft Visio, 143
Microsoft Windows 7, 34–35, 60, 61–66
creating shortcuts, 73–74
customizing settings, 89–93
desktop for, 62, 73
files and folders management, 75–87
as graphical user interface system, 59
Help System, 87–89
locking, 67, 68
logging off, 68
minimizing, maximizing and restoring a window, 64, 66, 176
moving and copying data between
applications, 154
moving and resizing window, 64
parental controls, 737–738
password case sensitivity, 68
performing slow, and System
Restore, 97
running applications, 68–72
shutting down, 67–68
starting in Safe mode, 99–100
starting up, 67
Start menu, 62–63
switching between windows, 64–65
Task Manager to repair, 97–98
troubleshooting operating system
problems, 97–100
Windows Explorer, 75–87
Microsoft Windows Server, 60, 61
Microsoft Word. See Word
millions of instructions per second
(MIPS), 14
MIN function, 411
mini-DIN connector, 35–36
minimize, window, 64, 66, 176
Mini toolbar
activating, 222
formatting using, 261–264, 504
turning off display of, 264
mixed cell reference, 416–417
mobile networking, 588
modem, 593, 594

broadband, 611
to connect to Internet, 610
monitors, 29–31, 34
cleaning, 43
connecting, 36
CRT
LCD, 29
troubleshooting, 46
monospaced typeface, 258
motherboard, 8
Motorola Xoom, 11
mouse, 24, 25
to activate cell in Excel, 396
to change slides, 489–490
changing column width and row
height, 435–436
cleaning, 43
hiding or displaying during presentation, 496
to modify image, 530
move image, 530
moving and copying text with, 228
moving insertion point with, 217
properties settings for, 25
scrolling through text, 217
selecting cells with, 403
selecting table with, 303–304
selecting text with, 221–222
sizing charts, 458
troubleshooting for erratic pointer, 46
Mouse Keys, 742
Mouse Pointers, 742
Move Chart dialog box, 461
moving
with clipboard, 80, 224–228
data between applications, 154
with drag-and-drop, 80
files, 79–80
folders, 79–80
with mouse, 228
tables, 314–316
Mozilla Firefox, 152
MS-DOS, 60, 61
multicore, 14
Multilevel List button, 273
MultiMedia Card (MMC), 20
multimedia software, 147–148
multiuser license, 117
MySpace, 622

N

Name box, 175, 394, 395
Narrator, 741, 743
Navigation Pane, 75–76, 218, 220,
228–229
netbook computer, 10
netiquette, 748–752
network adapter, 589
network address translation (NAT), 612
Network and Internet category on
Control Panel, 90
Network feature, 75–76
networks, 585–588

concepts of
    bandwidth, 593–594
    client/server network, 592
    hardware for, 589–590
    with HomePlug, 596
    identifying non-ethernet networks, 590–591
    models for, 592
    network types based on physical location, 591
    peer-to-peer network, 592–593
    private *vs.* public networks, 591
    wired *vs.* wireless, 589
homegroup
    accessing shared folder, 599
    browsing for network resources, 601–602
    connecting to printer, 600–601
    create Windows 7 homegroup, 597
    sharing a printer, 600
    sharing folders with, 598
    sharing folder without, 598–599
Internet overview, 608–613
security issues, 602–607
    access control methods, 603–605
    wireless encryption types, 606
    wireless network security, 605
    wireless security on PC, 606–607
    wireless security on wireless router, 607
Windows network, creating Windows 7 homegroup, 597
World Wide Web, 614–620
New Comment button, 365–368
New Message window, 689
New Sheet option, 461
New Slide button, 485, 487
New tab, 192
Next button, 217, 367
Next Page button, 234, 491
Next Screen button, 232
Next Slide button, 489–490
Normal view, in PowerPoint, 136, 493, 500
Norton Antivirus, 728
notebook computer, 10
Notepad
    creating web page in, 616
    flat-file database in, 140
Notes and Handouts tab, 509–510
Notes Page view, 493
Notes pane, 136, 176, 483, 486
Nper, 422
Number Format button, 448
numbering
    inserting, 272–273
    in PowerPoint slides, 506
    turning off, 273
numbering systems, 5–6
    converting between, using Windows calculator, 6
    converting between manually, 9

numbers
    Accounting formatting, 447–450
    Currency formatting, 447–450
    formatting in Excel, 447–450
    General number formatting, 447
    Percentage formatting, 447–450

O

objects
    displaying embedded object as icon, 563
    drawing, 354–356
    drawing and customizing in PowerPoint, 539–542
    editing linked, 559–561
    embedding Word table in PowerPoint slide, 561–563
    enclosed object, 539
    grouping, 355
    linking Excel chart with Word document and PowerPoint presentation, 557–559
Office. *See* Microsoft Office
OLE (Object Linking and Embedding), 155
1000BaseT, 590
online learning, 586
On-Screen Keyboard, 741, 743
Open Dialog Box, 183
OpenOffice.org, 117
open source, 117
Opera, 152
operating system, 6–7, 14, 57, 58–61
    applications compared to, 61
    choosing, 34–35
    number of tasks, 60
    number of users and, 60
    troubleshooting common problems, 97–100
optical device, 25
optical discs, 20–21
    capacity of, 21
    reliability and, 22
    ROM, R, RW, 21
optical drive, 11, 34–35
order of operation, changing, 410
organizational chart, 359–363
    moving or sizing, 363
Organize Favorites dialog box, 644
orientation
    changing, 337–338
    landscape, 337
    portrait, 337
Orientation button, 440
outdent, 275
out-of-office message, 712
output, 6–7
output device
    monitors, 29–31
    printers, 31–32
output devices, 29–32
Overtype mode, 126, 221

P

packet, 588
packet sniffer, 723
page breaks, 347–349
Page Layout tab, 336–339
Page Layout view, inserting headers and footers in, 457
page margins, 336–339
Page Number button, 344
page numbering, 344–347
page orientation, 336–339
Page Setup dialog box, 451, 455
page size, 336–339
    worksheet, 455
Paint, 68, 113, 144
Paint Shop Pro, 144
paper, conserving and recycling, 760
paper size, 337, 339
paper trail, 624
Paragraph dialog box, 266–267, 508
paragraphs. *See also* formatting
    aligning text in, 265–268
    default spacing for, 270
Parental controls, 737–740
passwords, 603
    case-sensitivity of, 68
    protecting document with, 370–371
    strong vs. weak, 603
paste, 79
Paste Command, 80
Paste Options button, 225
Paste Special dialog box, 156
patent, 745
path, 75
path redundancy, 608
PDF file, saving in, 197
Peachtree Accounting, 151
peer-to-peer (P2P) network, 592–593
Pen Color button, 544
Pen option, 494
Percentage formatting, 447–450
Percent Style button, 448
peripherals, 33
persistent cookie, 734
Personal Area Network (PAN), 591
personal folders, shortcuts to, 63
petabyte (PB), 17
phishing, 732–733
photo-editing and paint software, 123
pictures
    in PowerPoint, 530–534
    in Word, 351–354
Picture Styles group, 530
Picture Tools Format tab, 351–352, 445–447, 530–531
Pie chart, 457
    creating and formatting, 465–466
pinned shortcuts, 63
    creating, 69
pinning, document to Recent tab Backstage view, 185
Pin to Taskbar, 177

pits, 21
pixel, 144
placeholder, 137–138, 485
   increasing or decreasing size of, 486
   inserting text in, 485
   resizing and moving header or footer
      placeholder, 511
plagiarism, 662–663, 746
PlayStation, 12
plug and play, 38
PMT function, 422
pointing devices, 24–25
   point of sales systems, 28
   probes, 28
podcast,622
POP3, 684
pop-up blocker, 669–670
port, 7
portrait orientation, 337, 451
Position button, 352
Post Office Protocol (POP), 684
power plan, 756–759
PowerPoint, 479–511. *See also* formatting
   exporting presentation to Word,
      555–557
   general techniques and tips for
      audio and video files insertion,
         553–555
      changing view options, 491–493
      closing files and exiting, 191
      content icons, 138
      copying slides within presenta-
         tion, 502
      creating and naming files, 180–181
      creating files using templates,
         192–194
      creating presentation in, 139–140,
         476–478, 482–484
      customizing and moving ribbon
         commands, 178–180
      customizing AutoRecover,
         198–200
      displaying slide show, 138
      inserting hyperlinks, 543–544
      inserting slide content, 137–138
      mouse or keyboard to change,
         489–490
      navigating presentation, 489–490,
         543
      opening program, 174–175
      printing, 490–493
      running presentation, 494–496
      saving in different format,
         195–197
      screen features, 175–177, 482–483
      Slide Sorter view, 136–137, 493
      working with views, 136–137
   linking Excel chart and Word docu-
      ment with, 557–559
   Normal view, 136, 493
   Notes Page view, 493
   Notes pane, 136

presentation preparation
   designing presentation, 563
   planning presentation tips, 511
   presentation cycle, 482–484
   Zoom display, 491–492
slides, 136
   creating new, 137, 485–490
   duplicating, 500
   placeholder, 137–138, 485
   rearranging and deleting, 500–502
power sag, 40
power supply, 8
power surge or spike, 40
presentation software, 136–140. *See also*
   PowerPoint
Presentation Views, 493
previewing
   Excel charts, 459
   Excel worksheets, 443–445
   Word documents, 234–237
Previous button, 217, 367
Previous Page button, 234, 491
Previous Screen button, 232
Previous Slide button, 489–490
Print command, 95
printers, 31, 32, 94–97
   cleaning print heads of, 44
   connecting, 38
   dots per inch (dpi), 32–33
   plotters, 33
   setting for Word document, 235
   sharing in network, 600
   specialty printers, 33
   Total Cost of Ownership (TCO), 32
printing
   collated and uncollated pages, 237
   conserving and recycling ink and
      paper, 760
   files, 185–190
   managing print jobs, 187–190
   PowerPoint presentation, 490–493
   print queue, 187–189
   Print tab Backstage view, 185–186
   Quick Print button, 187
   setting default printer, 187
   troubleshooting print problems, 190
   web page, 650
   Word documents, 234–237
   WordPad options, 128
   word processing documents, 128
   workbooks, 398–400
Print Layout view, 232–234
Print Preview, 443–445, 459
print queue, 187–189, 190
Print Screen button, 73
Print tab Backstage view, 185–187,
   490–491
priority, 703
privacy invasion, 602
Programs category on Control Panel, 90
Properties Dialog Box, 47, 72
proportional typeface, 258

protection, for documents, 369–371
protocol, 589
proxy, 761
PS/2 connector, 35–36
PV, 422

Q
query, 141
Quick Access Toolbar, 125, 175–176, 394,
   482
   customizing, 178–180
   Quick Print button, 187
QuickBooks, 151
Quick print, 128
Quick Print button, 187
Quick Styles, 279
Quick Table, 316
QWERTY layout, 28

R
Radar chart, 457
random access memory (RAM), 15
   buying a computer and, 34
   dynamic, 16
   evaluating computer's, 16
   static, 15–16
range, selecting, in spreadsheet application, 134
raster image, 144
rate, financial function, 421
RDF Site Summary, 623
Reading view, 493
read-only documents, 371
read-only memory (ROM), 15, 21
read receipt, 704
RealPlayer, 148
recently used shortcuts, 63
Recent tab Backstage view, 185, 200
   customizing default settings, 198–200
record, in database, 141
Recover Unsaved files, 200
Recycle Bin, 62
   deleting and restoring files from,
      82–84
recycling, 760–761
Red Hat, 60
Redo button, 222–223
Refreshable Braille displays, 741
Refresh button (Internet Explorer), 635
registered trademark, 745
registration, software, 118
Registry, 113
relational database, 141
relative cell reference, 403, 416
Repeat command, 440
replace
   Find and Replace dialog box, 229–231
   text in Word, 228–231
report, 141
Research task pane, 237–239
Reset to Match Style button, 465
resident, 728

residential networking, 588
resolve (IP address), 610
restore
    files from recycle bin, 82–84
    window, 64, 66, 176
Restrict Editing button, 369
Restrict Formatting and Editing task
    pane, 369–370
retina scanners, 604
Reveal Formatting task pane, 268–269,
    271
Reviewing Pane button, 365, 366–367
revolutions per minute (RPM), 19
ribbon, 71, 125, 175–176, 394, 482
    customize with Quick Access
        Toolbar, 178–180
    minimize/maximize, 178
    using and moving, 178–180
Rich Text (HTML), 690–691
Rich Text Format (RTF), 690
rip, 148
RJ-45 connector, 590
router, 589
    network address translation, 612
    security on wireless router, 605, 607
    wireless encryption, 606
row header, 395
Row Height dialog box, 437
rows, 130–131. *See also* tables *and* cells
    in table
        changing height of, 310–311
        designation, 301
row selection bar, 303
RSS (Really Simple Syndication), 624
    save and organize bookmarks to, 639
rulers, 125
    displaying horizontal ruler in table,
        303
    displaying to position images and
        shapes, 542
    indenting text, 274–275
    setting tabs, 283–284
Run option, 650
RW, 21

S
Safe mode, starting in, to view startup
    programs, 99–100
safe senders list, 708
safety issues. *See* health and safety
    issues
Safety Options dialog box, 707–711
sans serif typeface, 258
Save As dialogue box, 126–127, 180–181
Save button, 126, 181–182
Save command, 126
Save & Send tab Backstage view, 195–197
Save Webpage dialog box, 648–649
saving
    as Blog Post, 375
    customizing AutoRecover, 198–200
    as electronic format, 373

files in different format, 195–197
files with Save As, 182–185
files with Save button, 181–182
in PDF format, 197
read-only documents, 371
to SharePoint, 375
to SkyDrive, 374
in word processing application,
    126–127
in XPS format, 197
Scale to Fit group, 455
scanners, 26–27
Scatter chart, 458
Scientific number formatting, 450
screen capture, 73
screen resolution, 91
ScreenTips, 178, 484
scroll bars, 394
scroll box, 217
scrolling
    in Excel, 396
    in Word, 217–220
Search box, 63, 75–76
search engine, 653–654
    adding additional to Address bar,
        656–657
    crawler-based, 653
    human-powered web directories, 654
search engine optimization, 654
searches, 655–659
    Boolean searches, 655–656
    crawler and human-powered
        searches, 653–654
    evaluating search results, 659–661
    ranking of results of, 653–654
    special keywords, 656
Search Help box, 88
section breaks
    continuous, 347
    even-page or odd-page, 349
    inserting, 347–349
Secure Digital (SD), 20
secure site, 723
Secure Sockets Layer (SSL), 723–725
security certificate, 724–725
security issues
    adware and spyware, 726–727
    anti-spyware software, 727, 728–729
    cookies, 733–736
    identity fraud and social engineering,
        731–732
    malware, 725–730
    networks and protecting data,
        602–607
    packet sniffer, 723
    Parental controls, 737–740
    phishing, 732–733
    protecting minors online, 737–740
    secure data access, 722–724
    secure website and security certifi-
        cates, 723–725
    viruses, Trojan horses and worms, 726

vulnerability and exploit, 725–726
Select All button, 395
Select Browse Object button, 217
selection bar, 221
Send Using E-mail option, 372
    sensors (biomedical/environmental),
        28
serif typeface, 258
servers, 60, 592
    DNS (Domain Name Service)
        servers, 610, 614
    upload website to, 619
    web server, 614
service mark, 745
service pack, 726
session cookie, 734
Setup program, 116
shading
    tables in Word, 306–307
    text in Word, 276–278
Shape Height box, 351–352
shapes
    aligning, 355
    drawing, 354–356
    editing, 356
    grouping, 355
    inserting in Excel chart, 464
    in PowerPoint, 539–542
    WordArt text inside, 357–358
Shape Width box, 351–352
SharePoint, 375
shareware, 117
sheet tabs, 175, 394
shell, 58
shortcuts
    close file, 191
    close files and exit application, 191
    copy text, 225
    creating shortcuts, 69, 73–74
    cut text, 224
    on desktop, 69–70
    display Font dialog box, 503
    display formulas, 411
    display menu bar, 637
    in Excel, 133
    exit application, 191
    Font dialog box, 261
    Font Group buttons, 258, 502–503
    Format Painter, 264, 506
    Go To, 217
    heading styles, 279
    identifying, 73
    indenting text, 274
    insert new slide, 485
    line spacing, 268
    minimize/maximize ribbon, 178
    normal style, 279
    Open Dialog Box, 184
    open find, 637
    open history list, 640
    page break insertion, 347
    paragraph alignment, 266

paste text, 224
  to personal folders, 63
  pinned shortcuts, 63, 69–70
  printing, 398
  Print Preview, 235
  Print Tab Backstage View, 235, 490
  recently used shortcuts, 63
  redo, 222
  run slide show, 494
  Save As dialog box, 184
  saving file, 181, 396
  Select Browse Object, 217
  spelling and grammar checker, 239,
    499
  on Start menu, 69–70
  SUM function, 405
  on Task bar, 69–70
  Thesaurus, 237
  track changes, 363
  undo, 222
Shut down button, 63
Simple Mail Transfer Protocol (SMTP),
  684
single user license, 117
sip-and-puff devices, 741
site license, 118
sizing handles, 352
SkyDrive, saving to, 374
Skype, 622
Sleep mode, 756, 759
Slide Master button, 547–548
Slide pane, 176, 483, 486
slides. *See* PowerPoint
Slide Show button, 494–495
Slide Show Help window, 494
Slide Show toolbar, 494–495
Slide Show view, 138, 493
Slide Sorter view, 136–137, 500–502
Slides/Outline pane, 176, 483, 486, 500
SmartArt graphics
  bulleted text formatted into, 539
  creating, 359–363
  dialog box, 359
  inserting and formatting in
    PowerPoint, 534–539
  inserting text in the Text pane, 539
  moving or sizing, 363
  organizational chart in, 359–363
smart card, 604
SmartMedia (SM), 20
smartphones, 11
SmartScreen filter, 732–733
SMTP, 684
social engineering, 731–732
social networking, 622–623
  etiquette for, 752
SO-DIMM, 16
soft copy, 185
soft page break, 347
software. *See* applications
solid state, 19
solid state drive, 18
solid state hard drive, 20

Sort dialog box, 320–321
sorting
  customizing in Excel, 407
  data in Excel, 405–407
  in table, 320–322
sound and music editors, 148
Sound Recorder, 113
Sound Sentry, 742
source program, 557
spam, 707–711
special characters, inserting, 341–344
Special number formatting, 450
Spelling and Grammar dialog box,
  239–240
spelling checker
  changing options in, 500
  in PowerPoint, 499–500
  in Word, 239–241
Spelling dialog box, 499
Split Cells button, 310
spreadsheet applications, 130–135
  cells and rows, 130–131
  concepts and terminology for,
    130–132
  entering and editing data in cells, 134
  formula, 131–132
  function, 132
  navigating in, 133
spyware, 150, 726–727
Start button, 62
Start Enforcing Protection dialog box,
  369–370
starting up Microsoft Windows 7, 67
Start menu
  to determine installed applications,
    114–115
  for Microsoft Windows 7, 62–63
  pin shortcut to, 69–70
Start Slide Show group, 494–495
static electricity, 40
static memory, 15
static RAM (SRAM), 15–16
Status bar, 175–176, 394, 483
  displaying/hiding in Internet
    Explorer, 666–667
  Internet Explorer, 636
status flag, 86
status updates, 623
sticks, 741
Sticky Keys, 742
Stock chart, 458
Stop button (Internet Explorer), 635
storage. *See* data storage
store-and-forward email system, 684
styles
  applying, creating, modifying in
    Word, 279–282
  Quick Styles, 279
  Table Styles, 306–307
Styles task pane, 282
subnotebook, 10
subscribe, 623
SUM function, 402, 405, 410, 414

Surface chart, 458
surge suppressor, 40, 42
swap file, 17
switch, 589
Symbol dialog box, 341
symbols, inserting, 341–343
synonyms, 237–238
System and Security, 90
System Information, 38, 149
System Restore, 97–100, 149
systems maintenance utilities, running,
  47–48

T
Table button, 407–408
table move handle, 315
Table Options dialog box, 312–314
Table Properties dialog box, 314–315
table resize handle, 315
tables
  in PowerPoint
    creating, 543–546
    moving and sizing, 546
  in Word, 299–322
    cell alignment changes, 311–312
    cell margin measurements
      changes, 312–314
    changing text direction in cells,
      314
    column width and height
      changes, 310–311
    converting text to table, 317–318
    creating, 299–303
    displaying horizontal ruler, 303
    drawing table, 318–320
    embedding in PowerPoint slide,
      561–563
    entering data in, 299–303
    managing rows, columns and
      cells, 308–310
    moving and resizing, 314–316
    moving rows, 305
    navigating within, 299
    performing calculations in,
      321–322
    Quick Table feature, 316–317
    selecting cells, 303–306
    shading and borders, 306–307
    sorting in, 320–322
    splitting, 310
    table alignment changes, 314–315
    Table Styles, 306–307
    viewing gridlines, 312
Table Styles, 306–307
table styles in Excel, 407–408
Table Tools Design tab, 306–307, 320, 543
Table Tools Layout Tab, 308–309
tablet PC, 11
tabs, 175–176, 394, 482, 637
  clearing, 287
  decimal tab, 285
  deleting, 285
  Internet Explorer, 636

with leaders, 285–286
moving, 285
setting, 283–284
tab alignment buttons, 283–284
Tabs dialog box, 285–287
tags, 615
Taskbar, 62, 175–176
pinning application to, 177
pin shortcut to, 69–70
Task Manager, to shut down application, 97–98
TCP/IP, 589
TCP/IP (Transmission Control Protocol/Internet Protocol), 609
technology research, 673, 761
telecommute, 587
telephone networks, 585
television networks, 585
templates
to create business letter, 193–194
creating files using, 192–194
Office.com templates, 317
for PowerPoint, 490
Sample templates button, 192
using online, 195
Temporal Key Integrity Protocol (TKIP), 606
temporary files, 642
10GBase T, 590
terabyte (TB), as measurement of storage, 17
text
controlling size of, in web browser, 665–666
inside shapes, 355
selecting in cells, with keyboard, 306
in slides, 486–488, 502–505
in Word. *See also* formatting
AutoCorrect feature, 221
converting to table, 317–318
cutting, copying and pasting text using Clipboard Task Pane, 224–228
finding and replacing, 228–231
Hidden text, 261
inserting and deleting, 220–221
inserting from a file, 342
justifying, 268
Overtype mode, 221
selecting text, 221–223
sorting, in table, 320–322
undo and redo, 222–223
WordArt text, 357–358
in word processing programs, 126
text hyperlinks, 636
texting, 621
etiquette guidelines for, 750
Text number formatting, 450
theft, protecting computer from, 38–39
themes. *See* formatting
Thesaurus feature, 237–239
third-party cookie, 733
time, changing in system settings, 91

Time formatting, 450
Title bar, 175–176, 394, 482
title bar, 64
title placeholder, 137–138
Toggle Keys, 742
toolbar, 70
Tools button (Internet Explorer), 636
top-level domain, 610
Total Cost of Ownership (TCO), 32
touchpad, 24
touchscreens, 741
trackball, 24
Track Changes feature, 363–365
trademark, 745
transformer, 37
transistors, 13
transitions, in PowerPoint, 496–498
Transition to This Slide group, 496–498
Transmission Control Protocol/Internet Protocol, 589
Trojan horse, 150, 726
trolling, 750
troubleshooting
application installation problems, 119
common hardware problems, 44–48
email problems, 710–711
file management problems, 87, 101
general process for, 45
internet connectivity, 673
print problems, 190
running system maintenance utility, 46
web browsers, 668–673
true color, 26
Twitter, 623
typeface, 258
type size, 259
typestyle, 259

U

Ubuntu, 60
uncollated pages, 237
Undo button, 222–223
Uniform Resource Locators (URLs), 615, 634
Uninstall a program option, 98, 118–119
uninterruptible power supply (UPS), 40
universal serial bus (USB), 15
UNIX, 60, 61
Unshielded Twisted Pair (UTP), 590
update, applications, 120–123
upgrade, applications, 121, 122
URL (Uniform Resource Locators), 615, 634
saving to favorite list, 642–643
USB (universal serial bus), 15
USB connector, 35–36
USB flash drive, 18, 19
useful life, 33
User Accounts and Family Safety, 90
user authentication, 603
user ID, 603
user interface, 58–59

command-line interface, 58–59
graphical user interface, 59
operating system and, 58
user name, in email address, 685
utilities, 148–151
main utilities and functions, 47–48, 149
UTP, 590

V

varistor, 40, 42
vector images, 143, 147
Vertical Reviewing Pane, 367
vertical ruler, 175–176
vertical scroll bar, 175–176, 217, 394, 483
VGA, 36
video editing applications, 148
video files
inserting in presentation, 553–555
inserting link to, at website, 555
video graphics array (VGA), 36
view area, 176, 483
Viewing buttons, 232–234
virtual memory, 17
virtual private network (VPN), 587
virtual reality, 148
virus definition, 727
viruses, 150, 726
antivirus software, 150–151, 727–729
as risk in networked computing, 602
VoIP (Voice over IP), 587, 622
Vonage, 622
vulnerability, 725–726

W

wallpaper, 89
wands, 741
Web. *See* World Wide Web
web addresses, 615
opening from Favorites list, 643
URLs, 634
Web Archive format, 648
web browsers, 634–635. *See also* websites
add-ons, 669–670
conducting searches, 655–659
configuring, 663–668
controlling text size and zoom level, 665–666
copyright restrictions and plagiarism, 661–663
display menu bar, 637
error codes, 668–669
evaluating search results, 659–661
favorites, using and managing, 642–646
finding information on web page, 637–639
following hyperlinks, 636
history list, **639–642**
Internet Explorer interface, 634–636
managing, 663–665, 668–673
RSS, save and organize bookmarks to, 639

scripting errors, 669
search engine basics, 653–655
security, 725–735
using online information properly, 661–663
web browsing software, 152–153
web conferencing, 621
Web Content Accessibility Guidelines, 744
web design software, 124
web directory, 654
web hosting company, 614, 619
Web Layout view, 234
web log, 622
Web mail, 684
web pages, 614. *See also* websites
   creating in Notepad, 616
   creating in Word, 618–619
   designing with accessibility in mind, 744
   finding information on, 637–639
   printing, 650
   save in Web Archive format, 648–649
   scripting errors, 669
   search results, 654
   single file web page format option, 616
   web page, filtered format option, 617
   web page format option, 617
web servers, 614
websites, 614
   copying text from, 649
   copyright restrictions and plagiarism, 662–663
   downloading file from, 651
   elements of web addresses, 615
   evaluation of, 659–660
   printing web page from, 650
   saving content for offline use, 648–651
   secure websites, 723–725
   steps for publishing website for business, 619
   upload to server, 619
Wide Area Network (WAN), 591
Wi-Fi, 589, 594
Wi-Fi 802.11n, 590
Wi-Fi Protected Access (WPA), 606
Wi-Fi Protected Access 2 (WPA2), 606
Wii, 12
wiki, 661
WiMAX, 594
window, 64
   close, 64, 66
   maximize, 64, 66, 176
   minimize, 64, 66, 176
   moving, 64
   open all, 101
   resizing, 64
   restore, 64, 66, 176
   switching between, 64–65
Windows 7. *See* Microsoft Windows 7

Windows Backup utility, 48
Windows Defender, 149–150, 727, 729
Windows Explorer, 75–87
   browsing locations, 76–78
   file and folder management, 78–87
   file properties, 86
Windows Firewall, 149
Windows Live Mail, 153
   advanced mail options
      automatic signatures, 712
      mail forwarding, 712
      out-of-office message, 712
   attachments, 700–702
      executable attachments, 703
   configuring, 686–689
   contact list, 692–696
   email
      junk mail, 707–710
      troubleshooting common problems, 710–711
   messages
      auto send/receive interval, 699
      controlling quotes when replying, 699
      forwarding, 698
      read receipt, 704
      replying to, 698–699
      setting message priority, 703–704
      viewing, 697, 699
   organizing, 704–707
   setting up account in, 687–689
   writing email message, 689–691
Windows Media Player, 148
wired device, 25
Wired Equivalent Privacy (WEP), 606
wired network, 589
wireframe, 148
wireless access point (WAP), 589
wireless device, 25, 45
Wireless Fidelity (Wi-Fi), 589
wireless network, 589
   security for, 605–608
Word, 124
   document styles
      business letter, 243
      memo, 244
      personal business letter, 242
   editing documents in. *See* editing
   exporting PowerPoint presentation to, 555–557
   formatting documents. See formatting
   general techniques for
      customizing and moving ribbon commands, 178–180
      customizing AutoRecover, 198–200
      file management, 180–197,
      help resources, 200–202, 200–203
      linking content in, 156–157
      opening program, 174–175
      screen features, 175–177

      templates, 192–194
   linking
      document with PowerPoint presentation and Excel chart, 557–559
      table in PowerPoint slide, 561–563
   tables. *See* tables
   web page
      creating web page in, 618–619
      web-based file format options, 616–617
WordArt, 357–358
Word Count dialog box, 238–239
Word Options dialog box, 241
WordPad, 61, 68, 113, 124–125
   opening, 72
   printing, 128
   ribbon interface for, 71
word processing applications, 124–130
   insert or overtype mode, 126
   opening saved work, 127
   other capabilities of, 129
   printing, 128
   saving, 126–127
   selecting ranges, 134
word wrap, 180
workbooks, 132
   closing, 398–400
   creating and saving, 394–397
   printing, 398–400
workgroup, 592–593
worksheet, 132, 394
   design considerations for, 467
   formatting. *See* formatting
worksheet area, 175, 395
World Wide Web, 614–620. *See also* Internet
   creating web pages, 616–619
   understanding HTML, 615
   understanding web addresses, 615
World Wide Web Consortium (W3C), 744
worms, 150, 726
Wrap Text button, 352, 440

X

Xbox, 12
xD, 20
XPS file, 197
XY (Scatter) chart, 458

Y

Yahoo! Messenger, 152

Z

Zoom In/Out button, 445
Zoom slider bar, 232–233, 234, 445, 491
Zoom to Page button, 234, 491